Essential Papers on Zionism

ESSENTIAL PAPERS ON JEWISH STUDIES
General Editor: Robert M. Seltzer

Essential Papers on Judaism and Christianity in Conflict:
From Late Antiquity to the Reformation
Edited by Jeremy Cohen

Essential Papers on Hasidism: Origins to Present
Edited by Gershon David Hundert

Essential Papers on Jewish-Christian Relations:
Imagery and Reality
Edited by Naomi W. Cohen

Essential Papers on Israel and the Ancient Near East
Edited by Frederick E. Greenspahn

Essential Papers on Jewish Culture
in Renaissance and Baroque Italy
Edited by David B. Ruderman

Essential Papers on Messianic Movements
and Personalities in Jewish History
Edited by Marc Saperstein

Essential Papers on the Talmud
Edited by Michael Chernick

Essential Papers on Kabbalah
Edited by Lawrence Fine

Essential Papers on Zionism
Edited by Jehuda Reinharz and Anita Shapira

ESSENTIAL PAPERS ON ZIONISM

Edited by Jehuda Reinharz
and Anita Shapira

NEW YORK UNIVERSITY PRESS
New York and London

NEW YORK UNIVERSITY PRESS
New York and London

Library of Congress Cataloging-in-Publication Data
Essential papers on Zionism / edited by Jehuda Reinharz and Anita
Shapira.
p.   cm. — (Essential papers on Jewish studies)
Some papers translated from Hebrew.
Includes bibliographical references and index.
ISBN 0-8147-7448-2 (cloth : alk. paper). — ISBN 0-8147-7449-0
(pbk. : alk. paper)
1. Zionism — History.   2. Jews — Palestine — History — 20th century.
3. Hebrew literature, Modern — Palestine — History and criticism.
I. Reinharz, Jehuda. II. Shapira, Anita. III. Series.
DS149.E76   1995
320.5'4'095694—dc20   95-22296
                                        CIP

Manufactured in the United States of America

10   9   8   7   6   5   4   3   2   1

Contents

IV. The Fateful Triangle: Jews, Arabs, and the British

V. Cultural Questions

Acknowledgments

Grateful acknowledgment is due Allon Gan, Mark A. Raider, and Sylvia Fuks Fried for their assistance in the preparation of this volume.

Introduction

Anita Shapira

Over the course of the past 150 years, Zionism has been at the center of the Jewish public arena, the agent of cultural and social creativity, the focus of internal political debate, the cause of wars between Jews and Arabs, and a source of controversy in the international sphere. No other social and political movement in the modern era has so completely and fundamentally altered the self-image of the Jewish people and its relations with the non-Jewish world. As the dominant expression of modern Jewish nationalism, Zionism revolutionized the very concept of Jewish peoplehood, taking upon itself the transformation of the Jewish people from a minority into a majority, and from a diaspora community into a territorial one, through a series of sweeping demographic changes involving the relocation of millions of individuals from the European continent and Middle Eastern lands to Palestine. While Zionism was variously defined, the essence of the Zionist idea remained the establishment of a viable Jewish entity, possessing its own national attributes, in the Land of Israel. The Zionist movement for the most part believed that the realization of this goal would, at the end of a process of colonization, impel the establishment of an independent Jewish state in Palestine.

The Zionist idea was realized in a remarkably short space of time, especially considering the enormity of the task. Since the movement's inception, however, debate has persisted as to the legitimacy of Jewish nationalism as well as its universalistic and particularistic implications, the Jewish context of Zionism and the extent to which Zionism is a natural outgrowth of Jewish history, and the moral imperatives inherent in the governance of a state. The intensity of these debates, which continue to define the international Jewish public agenda, has not diminished with time. Indeed, it demonstrates that the issues which gave rise

1

to Zionism and eventually led to its realization remain vital and relevant to this day.

"The sudden appearance of the Jews in 'secular' history can be considered either a historical act or an existential one."[1] Gershom Scholem's observation reflects several key facets of the ambivalence that persists regarding the nature of Jewish history in general and its Zionist chapter in particular. How can one define Jewish survival from the Bar Kokhba rebellion—or, alternately, the conquest of Palestine by the Arabs—to the nineteenth century? Is it possible to speak about a Jewish history that spans the nearly two millennia of exile? Perhaps Yudke, the protagonist in Haim Hazaz's famous story "Ha-derashah" (The Sermon), was right. He disputed the very notion of "Jewish" history, contending that throughout that era, the Jews really had never had a separate history of their own. They had been the objects of actions by others who determined their worldly fate, compelled to endure that lot, whether they wanted to or not.[2]

Yudke, a literary representation, symbolized the new Palestinian Jew who rebelled against Jewish fate in the diaspora. Even if we reject his persistent assertion, the definition of the essence of Jewish history remains problematic. No one disputes that the Jews *qua* collective lacked the usual attributes associated with polity, and if we understand history to mean the chronicling of collectives that are politically constituted, they do not qualify as candidates by this criterion. Yet if the term signifies human collectivities from an economic and social perspective, the Jewish experience can be accommodated more easily within its scope of reference. One can even accommodate the claim that the Jews had been able at times (although partially and only in certain periods) to significantly shape reality, acting rather than merely being acted upon. Notwithstanding, theirs was a mode of existence on the margin of historical events. Even in this restricted sphere, the history of the Jewish collectivity was largely the product of the policies pursued by the non-Jewish rulers. Ultimately, Jewish history remained confined to the spiritual realm, and lends itself to the definition proposed by David Vital: "A history of culture, or of a set of kindred cultures, or of one of ideas."[3]

Scholem's comment constitutes an unconscious affirmation of that "cultural" definition, since the logical conclusion to be drawn from it is that Jewish existence prior to the nineteenth century was outside the domain of secular history—i.e., its locus fell within the compass of the history of religion, a spiritual space whose link with the arena of concrete existence was peripheral at best. Such a view is supported by Benedict Anderson's notion that the Jews were an ancient religious community. When they eventually became a people, they imagined themselves to have a national past—a process familiar in the history of other peoples as well.[4] It is an established fact that in the eighteenth century, on the eve of the Enlightenment, the Jews in Central and Eastern Europe possessed a distinctive cultural identity, shared a single sacred language and a common spoken tongue; they maintained the same way of life and customs, and regarded themselves as mutually responsible each for the other. They envisaged themselves not as a part of the non-Jewish society, but as a tolerated minority at the margin of the majority society. The history of the Jews in the nineteenth century is that of a religious, cultural, and social minority attempting to cast off its "minority" outgroup distinctiveness. Ultimately, that minority adopted new patterns of identity, borrowed from the dominant society, as means for defining its special character.

What Scholem called "the sudden appearance of the Jews in 'secular' history" came about as the result of responses and counter-reactions to the Jewish encounter with modernity. The modern world confronted Jews with a totally new challenge, unprecedented in their previous history: the prospect of existing within a society that had brushed aside (at least in principle, or as an acclaimed ideal) the religious barriers which had blocked Jewish participation in earlier generations. It had created a neutral zone free of religious values, marked by the concept of equality before the law, the separation of church and state, human brotherhood, and the loyalty of the citizen to the state. Within this neutral space, the Jews were able to find a place without being constrained to convert.[5] Secular civil society shifted the question of beliefs and opinions from the public to the private sphere, creating a new historical situation. The Jews, whether enthusiastic or hesitant, were swept into the vortex of change and new prospects; messianic hopes alternated with profound disappointments. The more gentile society showed its readiness to grant the Jews equal rights and to facilitate their integration, the more Jews hastened to discard the protective armor of their distinctiveness and to search for ways to abrogate those customs and conceptions which were likely to place obstacles in the path of their absorption into the wider society. Assimilation came gradually, with varying degrees of intensity, ranging from the adoption of so-called "external knowledge" (*hokhmah hitsonit*) or, altering one's name and dress, to the abandonment of religious practice and the link to the Jewish collective, all the way to conversion to Christianity.

In his book *Golah ve-nekhar* (Exile and Foreignness), Yehezkel Kaufmann argued that the desire for assimilation in the first half of the nineteenth century bore the appearance of a messianic movement which had come to redeem the Jewish people from their alienation and provide them with a sense of belonging and a homeland.[6] In the second half of the nineteenth century, in particular its last quarter, that *affaire de coeur* soured, changing into a drama of unrequited love, injured pride, and different responses to the challenges of modern society. The emergence of modern antisemitism was interpreted as a vestige of medieval thinking, but it soon became evident, at least in the eyes of a portion of the Jewish community, that Jew-hatred was no longer aimed at the traditional Jew, oblivious to the beauties and benefits of Western civilization, but was targeted specifically at the modern Jew, who was endeavoring to accommodate to the surrounding non-Jewish society.

The search for an answer to this unexpected turn of events led to two different patterns of response. Some aspired to a world revolution, which would sweep away all contradictions based on nation and class. Proponents of this conviction argued that the situation of the Jew, the eternal pariah, would not be remedied until *all* manner of discrimination and special privilege ended and the universal reign of justice and equality was established. This idea was not alien to the Jewish tradition, which had internalized messianic hopes for "putting the world aright" in the eschatological framework of the kingdom of heaven *(tikun olam)*. These hopes were now transposed to a secular context, taking on universal significance. The second response was emigration westward. Its advocates argued that traditional European society was founded on age-old prejudice, and discrimination of Jews was deeply rooted in this heritage of hate. In a new society, in which the principle of the separation of church and state was integral to its basic beliefs, there were no age-old protected privileges and all were in effect "newcomers"—only in such a society could Jews find true security and their proper place.

The element common to these two modes of response is that they were highly critical of the established order and sought to fundamentally transform the conditions of Jewish existence. The principle of change was integral to both, a revolutionary foundation to counteract the Jewish inclination to acquiesce in one's God-given fate as a decree of the Almighty. Both revolutionism and emigration contained an element that spurned the accepted notions of society and turned to more rebellious modes of behavior. They also reflected the readiness to act outside the existing social and cultural Jewish frameworks. But as yet there was no action of the Jews by the Jews and for the Jews as a social entity bound together by a common purpose and will.

In the course of the nineteenth century, in the initial burst of enthusiasm among Jews buoyed by the prospect of being integrated into general society, the breastplate of tradition that had provided a shield for the survival of the Jewish collective in the past was eroded. Assimilation was accompanied by a process of atomization of the Jewish traditional community, which became superfluous in the wake of Jewish emancipation from the tutelage of religious tradition and authority. When modern antisemitism reared its head toward the end of the century, Jews had to confront it standing alone, on an individual rather than collective basis, and to respond to its threat without support from a Jewish community that could serve as a source of solidarity.[7]

The search for a new path by Jews who had lost the protection and safe haven of the closed world of traditional Jewish society, and had been left to their own wits and devices to face the temptations and dangers of the gentile world, took place in a host society which itself had lost its traditional moorings and was caught up in a maelstrom of constant change. From the time of the French Revolution on, the importance of ideas as guiding factors and incentives to action became ever more salient. Over the past two hundred years, the struggles between different philosophies for the allegiance of adherents and their mobilization for action have been central factors shaping Western and non-Western civilization. After faith in God had eroded and forfeited its power to engage human imagination and determine the path of action, new conceptual models played a role analogous to that of the great religions of salvation, replicating their inherent fanaticism, promise of deliverance, and the demand for individual commitment to their cause. Pragmatic democratic liberalism, which was predicated on accepting the world as it was as a practical factor, and aspired only to remedy and improve that given world gradually, was challenged by theories of social and national redemption which refused to accept existing conditions, advocating their radical transformation by means of violent revolution. Socialism, communism, nationalism, and fascism were the battle cries of the modern world.

More than all the other doctrines, nationalism demonstrated its vitality to withstand pressures of changing reality. The history of the past two hundred years testifies to the power of nationalism, by dint of its symbols, cults, and accompanying myths, to hold sway over the hearts and minds of the members of various nations and tribes—enlightened and benighted, tolerant and fanatic. Repeatedly, the best of humankind had predicted that those primordial tribal allegiances would fade away in the face of the progressive enlightment. People would conclude that there is more that unites them as human beings than what divides them into separate nations. But when the drums of battle sounded and individuals were forced to choose between their humane beliefs and their commitment to kin and country, they forgot their allegiance to universal fraternity, and rallied round the flag.[8]

Modern Jewish nationalism was born in the shadow of this powerful struggle. At the beginning of the nineteenth century, caught up in the first flush of fervor over the prospect of being delivered from alienation, Jews turned toward two parallel paths to secular salvation: on the one hand, they styled themselves as bearers of a universal mission to propagate the conceptions of pure monotheism. They confined their Jewishness to the areas of religious and intellectual mission, free of any social or political nexus. On the other hand, they embraced the nationality of the peoples in whose midst they lived. Demonstrating one's patriotism was both a precondition for emancipation and an expression of gratitude for its granting. Jews hastened to take active part in the national struggles of peoples fighting for their independence, such as the Poles. By the end of the century, their loyalty was being increasingly called into question, and they found themselves excluded from the national framework to which they had aspired to belong. The Dreyfus affair exemplified just how feeble was the belief of the majority society in the national loyalty of the Jews. In Germany, the antisemitic movement advocated the removal of the Jews from the body of the nation and the abrogation of emancipation. In multi-ethnic states, such as the Habsburg monarchy, the Jews found themselves in a predicament, caught between the hammer of the dominant nationalism and the anvil of the nascent nationalisms of various peoples in the empire struggling for national liberation. The nineteenth century had begun in France with a new definition of the obligations, rights, and loyalties which an individual accepted upon himself by identifying with a specific social community; yet in the second half of that century, the contours of the concept of nationhood altered. It then encompassed organic and biological criteria, the notion of a human collective to which a person belonged as the result of a deterministic decree, independent of any personal decision or act of human will. Individuals belonged to the nation by dint of the fact that their ancestors were present, so to speak, at the ancient and pristine event when the nation was created. This perspective, which viewed the nation as the organic product of a common origin, history, and culture, tied to a specific territory, meant that Jews were completely excluded *per definitionem* from the orbit of European nationalism.

The search for an independent national identity was the Jewish response to the ambivalence that had arisen in regard to the question of nationalism and the Jews. In a society where national identity was conceived as an integral part of the human personality, it was difficult for the Jews to avoid some mode of self-definition. The advent of Jewish nationalism was one more expression of the Jewish desire to embrace patterns that were acceptable in the modern world: just as the adoption of universal ideas and comprehensive theories of secular redemption reflected Jewish yearnings to belong to the enlightened family of nations, Jewish nationalism was the particularistic path through which to link up with those same nations. The aspiration for national uniqueness was the dominant aspiration of the age. Its embrace by Jews reflected the internalization of values of non-Jewish society.[9]

The emergence of Jewish national consciousness was a post-emancipatory phenomenon, although it also appeared in countries where Jews still had not been granted civil liberties (such as czarist Russia). It is customary to date this development to the final decades of the nineteenth century. The critical turning point was 1881, when pogroms swept across the south of Russia, a storm of violence that sparked a new existential anxiety among Jews, and cast doubt on the prevailing contention that progress was advancing inexorably, its orbit expanding from western Europe to the east, and that it would ultimately illuminate the dark corners still remaining in the Russian state. The Jewish response to the pogroms in southern Russia was marked by a spontaneous reaction of the Jewish masses, which began to flow westward to escape the yoke of the czar's evil empire, and the vacillating beginnings of *collective* response—the search for a collective way out, not just for the individual and his family, but deliverance for the community as a whole. That redemption would not be achieved by the merciful acts of rulers, intermediaries, or philanthropists, but by a communal movement. The idea of "auto-emancipation," injected by Leo Pinkser into the vacuum of Jewish public life and discourse with the publication of his agitational pamphlet of the same title (1882), introduced an activist element into the ambit of Jewish thinking. Latent in such activism was the demand for Jews to act for themselves as a collective.[10] The definition of the Jews as a nation came fourteen years later, with the publication of Theodor Herzl's *Der Judenstaat* (1896), a pamphlet which, unlike its predecessor, did not attempt an in-depth analysis of the origins of the "Jewish problem," but placed emphasis on outlining a practical solution—namely a Jewish state.

The Zionist movement was not the only manifestation of Jewish nationalism. There were other currents which proposed their own solutions for the continued existence of the Jews as a unique human collectivity, wishing to survive while preserving its special character. The territorialists, for example, were in basic agreement with the Zionist model, but argued that Palestine should not be held up as the sole possible country of destiny. The autonomists, followers of the theories of Simon Dubnow, regarded every Jewish community as a distinctive cultural-diaspora collective, connected by its umbilical cord to the surrounding non-Jewish society, yet separated from it in terms of language, culture, and education, features which it preserved within its own autonomous framework. The Bund (Algemeiner Yidisher Arbeter-Bund), the Jewish socialist party, adopted a number of ideas from Dubnow, embracing Yiddish as the vernacular of the Jewish masses. In basic terms, the manifestations of Jewish nationalism could be divided into (1) a current aimed at preserving a separate and distinctive Jewish essence *within the framework of Jewish life in the diaspora* and (2) a camp calling for a *special country* for Jews. Among these, Zionism characterized itself from the start as a movement representative of the national interest of all Jews, regardless of community or social class. Like socialist or nationalist movements of redemption, its legitimacy was not predicated on an explicit democratic agreement by the members of the people. Rather, it regarded itself as authorized to represent the *volonté generale* of the people—be it in the name of the "national destiny" or the "spirit of the people" or some other lofty abstraction current among nationalist movements. This phenomenon was accompanied by the emergence of a new leadership echelon whose power did not derive from the traditional sources of influence in Jewish public life (capital, Talmudic learning, or "good offices"), but from an ability to articulate its views, formulate the new ideology, explicate it to non-Jews, and mobilize public support among the Jews. Here then was the first modern political leadership in the history of the Jewish people.

One characteristic often observed among national movements is the tendency for any given movement to see itself as a distinctive entity, *sui generis,* while in fact there is much in common between all national movements. Notwithstanding, I believe one can argue that Zionism, the principal Jewish national movement, bore several quite unique features. Zionism appears to be the only national movement that set out upon its path to independence at a juncture when the people it aspired to represent was not physically present on the territory the movement laid claim to as national patrimony. Now it is true that the phenomenon of the existence of a national territorial core along with a massive dispersion of the national population is not unique to the Jews. But there is no other instance of the survival of such a diaspora without the concomitant existence of a territorial center, and in order to establish such a center, the Jewish national movement needed to bring about a demographic transformation, entailing the physical transfer of large numbers of people and their resettlement in another territory. Not only did the movement have to convince its adherents that the Jews were indeed a bonafide *people* (and not simply a religious community)—a controversial question that had been debated over many decades within and beyond the Jewish world. It also had to galvanize a sense of commitment such that individuals would abandon their countries of origin and familiar surroundings to risk their lives and luck in the creation of a utopian community—one that existed only in the imagination of the thinkers who had hatched its dream. It is true that there were other peoples who saw themselves as the inheritors of an ancient cultural tradition and desired to renew their nationalism in vital connection with that past. A good example was the Greek people. Yet the Greeks were located in Greece, the people was united ethnically and religiously, spoke a vernacular related to the language of ancient Greece, and found little difficulty in appropriating the historical past of the motherland—as though the link was direct. In contrast, the bond between the Jewish people and the Land of Israel was essentially spiritual, anchored in prayer and religious worship; it did not have any concrete significance except for a very few individuals. The transformation of that link from a spiritual-religious bond into a concrete nexus rooted in action was a feat virtually unparalleled in the history of modern national movements.[11]

One of the elements typical of the Romantic movement in the first half of the nineteenth century was the desire to resuscitate and renew national languages which had declined as a result of "cultural colonization" by the ruling states in the region. A characteristic example is the Czech struggle to revive their language in the face of the dominance of German and German culture. Similar efforts were made by the Welsh and the Irish. Some such endeavors were crowned with success, others ended in failure. The revitalization of Hebrew ranks among the more successful examples in the chronicle of this process: from a holy language, circumscribed to use in the sacred domain of worship, prayer, religious commentary, and edificatory literature, it underwent a massive process of secularization. Initially, it was utilized solely as a written language of high culture by writers and poets, journalists and philosophers. But as the new Jewish settlement began to take shape in Palestine, it quickly adopted this attribute characteristic of European national movements that emphasized cultural identity as a central component in their nascent national identity, embracing Hebrew as a modern spoken and written vernacular. The transformation of Hebrew into an everyday means of communication in which children chatter, tell jokes, curse, and blaspheme; students study at school and university; novels, scientific treatises, newspapers, and magazines are written—and into which "the best that has been thought and said in the world" is translated—remains an impressive testimony to the fact that a national ethos not only expresses the national culture, but can also create it, virtually *ex nihilo*. Although there were analogous phenomena among other peoples, it is difficult to find a parallel in the annals of modern nationalism in which a national movement produced a full panoply of secular culture, proceeding from a point of departure where the national language was identified only with the sacred domain, and had initially no link with the realities of everyday life of the masses.[12]

A useful distinction in the history of national movements is that between older "veteran" peoples—those whose existence as a cultural, social, and even in some cases political entity preceded the emergence of their modern national consciousness—and "new" peoples, whose national consciousness was often antecedent to the existence of a common cultural bond (not to mention a common past) or the formation of a shared society. The nation-states of Europe are characteristic examples of the first category. The emergence of French, German, or British nationalism was the last stage in a long process of crystallization of political, social, and cultural communality. The second category evolved principally in the colonial and ex-colonial context, in countries originally colonized by Europeans, or in certain emergent nations of the developing world.

Does the Zionist movement belong to the first or second category? It is indisputable that the Jews existed for hundreds of years as a distinct community both culturally and socially. Did the Zionist movement inherit that historical legacy, or did it create a new national reality in Eretz Israel, severed from the roots of the past? On the one hand, the Zionist movement fell heir to the link with the Land of Israel from the patrimony of Jewish religion, along with that traditional dictum of solidarity that "all Jews are mutually responsible each for the other" *(Kol Israel arevim ze la-ze)*. It viewed itself as the inheritor of ancient Jewish history, the matrix in which the Jewish people had forged and perpetuated a bond of unity in its ethical and religious identity. This nexus formed the basis of the Jewish historical claim to Eretz Israel. On the other hand, the Zionist movement believed it was drawing a final line under two thousand years of Jewish history of exile and making a new start in the Land of Israel. The link to a distant mythological past, obscured in the mists of time, replaced the bond to the chronological, immediate past, with which there was a ligature of direct historical continuity. The Zionist urge to create a utopian reality *ex nihilo* is reminiscent of the dreams that inspired settlers in the wilderness of North America or other lands of European colonization: they wanted to leave the old world behind them and begin anew in a virtually virgin land, in a sense "reinventing themselves." The specific complexity of the Zionist experience lay *inter alia* in the fact that this dualism was not a feature just in the formative phase of the movement. It continued to be a factor in later stages as well, since, as mentioned, the demographic and settlement processes which were essential for the realization of Zionism necessitated a long-term period of development, based on the constant maintenance of a mutual link between the "old" Jewish people and the "new" Yishuv in Palestine. A total break with the Jewish diaspora was out of the question, and thus it was impossible to create a "new" and autonomous Jewish people *ab ovo;* rather, what evolved was a strange admixture, replete with contradictions and internal tensions, an amalgam of national identity based on a historical and cultural linkage of the first category, and an identity rooted in a sense of territorial attachment, characteristic of the second.

The idea of "normalization" was one of the basic concepts that animated the Zionist movement from its beginnings. The associated understanding, either explicit or implicit, was that the Jewish people, in its present situation, suffered from anomaly at best—and at worst from a condition that was altogether pathological. The nature of this abnormality was defined in various ways, depending on the point of view of the particular writer. There were some who saw the root of the Jewish malady in the fact that the Jews constituted a minority wherever they were, and there was no country in which they were considered to be the masters of their own house: the status of guests who are not hosts, as Pinsker observed, is the root of the Jewish sickness.[13] Others pointed to the skewed socioeconomic structure of the Jewish people as the source of the disease: Herzl, who was most familiar with the Jewish situation in central Europe, stressed that the Jewish people was lopsided in social composition, made up in large measure of the intelligentsia and the middle class. In the view of Nachman Syrkin, Ber Borochov, and their socialist associates (all Eastern European Jews in origin and outlook), the Jewish people suffered from an inverted occupational pyramid: a relatively small number of manual workers and an disproportionately large segment engaged in commerce and services, along with a sizable lumpenproletariat. The purported reason for this distortion was that the Jews in the diaspora had been prevented by antisemitism from joining the ranks of the proletariat, the class of the future. These thinkers argued that once the revolution broke out, the Jews would be ground to bits in the inevitable struggle between the forces of yesterday and tomorrow. However, beyond the problem of Jewish non-proletarianization, the inverted pyramid appeared to be proof that the Jews were unable to maintain an independent national existence, since within such an economic and social structure, Jews were dependent for their very survival on the infrastructure provided by non-Jewish society.[14]

Some believed the center of the Jewish anomaly lay in the fact that Jews were not the masters of their own fate: they were not acting "subjects," but rather objects for actions by others. Other critics stressed the absence of standard national traits among the Jews, ranging from a loyalty to the national territory to a sense of national honor, courage, and a willingness for self-sacrifice. The scope of Jewish anomalousness encompassed the network of relations between the Jew and the surrounding non-Jewish society in the political and socioeconomic spheres, the relation between Jews and their geographic environment, and the network of relations between the individual and the collectivity. It ultimately extended to include attributes of mentality, namely emotional characteristics and psychological dispositions purportedly common among Jews as individuals and in Jewish society as a whole. "Normalization" was intended to make the Jews "like all other peoples": a secular nation, settled on its own territory, bearing responsibility for its own defense, economically self-supporting, developing basic social institutions, and fostering a unique culture of its own.[15] The structural tension between the religious and secular meaning of the "Jewish state" did not become an issue until after the establishment of the state. The difficulties arising in the wake of the amalgamation of religious, ethnic, and national identity; the tension between an attachment to territory and a linkage to the Jewish diaspora, whose patterns of identity were becoming ever more obscure as its religious dimensions eroded; the ambivalence inherent in a secular definition of allegiance to a "Jewish" state; and the associated difficulties in respect to the definition of citizenship in such a state—all led, over time, to a vast literature on the issue of the separation of religion and state in Israel, as an essential component in the process of normalization. Yet it did not trouble the pre-state generations of Zionist theorists and activists except at the periphery of their consciousness.[16] When *they* spoke about "normalization," what they meant primarily was what Gershom Scholem termed "the utopian return of the Jews to their history" [17]—i.e., the acceptance of responsibility for their own fate, a reentry from the sacred world to the profane plane of practical existence in Eretz Israel.

Scholem, it will be recalled, used two adjectives to define the entrance of the Jews onto the stage of "secular" history: a "historical act" or an "existential act." Those two terms articulate a long-standing debate within the Zionist camp: is Zionism the result of an immanent development among the Jews, the product of *internal* processes, or the reaction to *external* events and factors, in particular antisemitism? The expression "historical act" hints at a conception that conceives developments as flowing from the steady maturation of the Jewish community in Palestine and the Jewish people in the diaspora. Currents of productivization on the one hand, and cultural renewal on the other, within a slow and gradual process of evolvement, functioned to facilitate the renewal of reformed and "healthy" patterns of Jewish life in the Land of Israel. There Jews were destined to create a model Jewish society, which would beam its beacon onto the Jews of the diaspora and serve as a focus of national allegiance. According to the religious version, that essential nucleus would function as a magnet to countervail the pull of the culture of the majority society and would, *ex post facto,* hasten the return of those who had strayed from the flock—i.e., those Jews who had become alienated from the Jewish people as a result of secularization—back to their origin, the "rock whence they were hewn." In terms of the secular interpretation of this view associated with the name of Ahad Ha-Am, the spiritual center to be established in Eretz Israel would supplant religion, which in the modern period was no longer able to fulfill the role of preserver of national survival, a function it had exercised for generations in the past. In the society to be created, there would be a renewal of Jewish spiritual creativity, and a profound ethical awakening. In this way, that remote and peripheral corner of the Mediterranean would be transformed into a vital center of Jewish life and a torch unto the nations of the entire world.[18]

The expression "existential act" embodies a more dramatic view of the Jewish people, spurred on by instincts of survival, embarked on a heroic and desperate effort to rescue itself from physical annihilation. The return of the Jews to history—i.e., the creation of a secular Jewish community, self-sufficient, in Palestine—was not basically meant as a solution to the problem of identity. Rather, it was a response to *existential anxiety:* how can Jews survive in a world divided among various peoples, in the face of an exclusivistic nationalism that virtually expelled them from European society? The sense of danger and the fear that the time left to the Zionist enterprise was running out were to shape the character of Zionism and its primary objectives. "Catastrophic Zionism," as conceived in the writings of Herzl and Max Nordau, was intended to furnish a solution to the existential dilemma of the Jewish masses, initially in czarist Russia, and after World War I in the new nation-states erected on the ruins of the old great empires, such as Poland, Hungary, and Romania—particularly in the face of the rising wave of virulent antisemitism in the 1930s that accompanied the Nazi takeover of power in Germany and the establishment of antisemitic, nationalist regimes in Poland and elsewhere in eastern Europe.

This internal dualism—a movement of national revival or one of national redemption (symbolized by the expressions "distress of Judaism" or "distress of the Jews")—accompanied Zionism from its inception.[19] At every juncture, when questions of destiny associated with the movement's priorities arose anew, this central issue returned to occupy the concern of the movement's leaders. The first dispute which broached this question was the 1903 Uganda Plan controversy. Over against Herzl, who was agitated over the recent pogrom in Kishinev, the majority of the Zionist representatives from Russia took a stand in favor of the presumably unattainable Palestine in preference to territory in East Africa, which seemed then to be within reach.[20] In the early 1920s, after the much-desired charter for Palestine had been obtained with the Balfour Declaration and the establishment of the British Mandate, questions arose regarding the optimum pace for building the national home. Nordau proposed the immediate transfer of half a million Jews, even if the immigrants would have to live under conditions similar to a military

camp, thus deciding in one fell swoop the question of the Jewish majority in Palestine. But the Zionist leadership, headed by Chaim Weizmann,
opted for a slow and steady path forward ("one more dunam, one more
goat"), based on the assessment that the means at its disposal would not
permit a faster pace, and fearing the attempt to "force the issue" ("hasten the coming" in messianic parlance) would end in total failure. The
utopian aspirations to build a model society were congruous with political restrictions posed by the British and the modest means at the disposal
of the Zionist movement.

In the 1930s, this debate flared up anew during the controversy over
partition (1937). Those who saw Palestine as a safe haven for the Jewish
people in the face of the stormy times were prepared to give up the claim
to a part of it in order to achieve the immediate establishment of a
Jewish state, even if dwarfed in territory. In contrast, those who viewed
Palestine as a sacred patrimony, an integral part of the nation, refused
to relinquish even an inch of soil. Admittedly, this necessarily brief
description does not do adequate justice to the subtle nuances present in
the positions of the two sides to the partition issue. Yet it should be
stressed that the tension between these two currents, the path of national
revival versus that of redemption, remained an abiding feature in the
development of the movement.[21]

In the evolution of a national liberation movement, there comes a
juncture: a transition from the realm of dreams, ideals, propaganda, and
sermonizing to the arena of political action and concrete struggle against
the "alien regime." In the history of Zionism, it is impossible to determine exactly when this point of transition occurred. That difficulty
derives from the inherent complexity of the movement, which was simultaneously a movement of national liberation and one of colonization.
Internally, Zionism had all the essential marks of a utopian movement of
national redemption bent on reshaping reality: fanatic zeal, intellectual
radicalism, intolerance toward Jewish rival forces beyond the Zionist
camp, the intensity of ideological clashes of rival factions within their
own ranks, reflecting competing global theories of secular redemption
(e.g., the traditional left and right), the objection to majority rule, and a
lack of readiness to compromise. The call for individual self-sacrifice
and the subordination of the interest of the individual to that of the
nation became a formative and guiding ethos. This was a mobilized
"frontier" society, whose orientation toward the future blunted the
importance of the present, and in which the national interest imbued the

suffering of the individual with meaning and heightened value. Its discourse used rational and materialistic phraseology, but in fact it mobilized individuals by appealing to their deepest emotional urges. And although its rhetoric adopted a secular stance, the motivation and emotions aroused were inherently religious. This was a society that lived under enormous pressure, in which at times the distinction between desire and ability was blurred, and the aspiration was assumed to be within reach. In such an ambience, there was room for social experimentation, economic innovation, and organizational creativity. Life's meaning and value derived from the progress of the enterprise; every demand made on the individual was considered legitimate, and self-sacrifice was regarded as the norm.[22]

On the other hand, the complex reality of a country of colonization, in which the local population was Arab, the authorities British, and the settlers Jewish, acted as a factor that necessitated adapting the movement's messianic ardor to pragmatic and political frameworks of action. At one and the same time, the British regime was an ally in the process of demographic change so necessary for implementing Zionist colonization, and the natural target for the enmity of a national movement which found itself thwarted by the British restrictions. The characteristic formula in countries of European colonization, according to which the regime identified with the interests of the settlers, did not apply in Palestine. In the eyes of the British, the Jews were not really Europeans, and the Arabs were not authentic Asians. This lack of clarity served to bolster the tendency among the Zionists to see themselves locked in a national struggle against British imperialism. But since the critical problem was to ensure continued Zionist immigration and settlement in Palestine (i.e., Jewish colonization), they were not in a position to speak out against British rule, as did other national movements elsewhere. Rather, they were constantly constrained to search for ways to accommodate and cooperate with the Mandatory authority. This entailed a kind of balancing act on a political tightrope, and forced the movement to descend from the utopian heights and embrace ways and means of action anchored in the given political realities.[23]

As the Zionist enterprise of settlement in Palestine put on flesh and muscle, and a base of Jewish power crystallized in territorial and demographic terms, a process of pragmatization took hold: instead of visionary flights of fancy, the attempt to come to grips with the concrete reality of the Jewish people, international politics and the nitty-gritty of life on the ground in Palestine. This process did not occur simultaneously throughout the entire Zionist movement: the political leadership—which was involved in contacts with the Mandatory authorities, and was therefore exposed in a particular way to the constraints of reality—was the first to accommodate to this process. From the mid-1930s on, one can also discern a clear tendency toward more realistic positions within the broader public. Yet a substantial segment of the population—on the political margins of the far left and far right, and particularly within the ranks of Jewish youth—still adhered to the tactic of "forcing the issue," the attempt to coerce recalcitrant reality and make its patterns conform to their revolutionary aspirations. Here again there was a general manifestation of that ambivalence mentioned earlier: although the leadership had already acknowledged the limitations on the strength of the movement and was acting to achieve the best it could under the existing circumstances, it did not reform the system of propaganda and education. A national movement that wants to mobilize its adherents cannot forego enthusiasm and ideological zeal as a means to preserve rank-and-file loyalty. For that reason, the leadership spoke with two voices: the sober voice of reason, directed in the main to the outside world, and the fervent voice of emotion, which served internal needs.[24]

The central process in constructing the national home was changing the demography of Palestine. When the British conquered Palestine in 1918, there were 56,000 Jews in a total population of 640,000. By the end of the Mandate in 1948, the Jewish population in Palestine had burgeoned to 650,000, out of a total of 1,300,000 inhabitants. The geographical pattern of Jewish population dispersion made it possible to conceive setting up two separate states in the western parts of Palestine—one Jewish, the other Arab. That idea already had been broached in 1937, when the Peel Commission proposed the partition of the country between the two peoples. Thus, in less than 20 years, the Jewish Yishuv in Palestine had taken on solid contours, becoming a community with an array of political, economic, and social characteristics that the Commission members felt justified self-rule, or at least made it a realistic option. This is worth recalling, since part of the common wisdom among politicians, and even historians, is to argue that the establishment of the State of Israel was the outcome of the mass murder of European Jewry during World War II. This position exposes the problematic nature of the choice of vantage point in approaching the problem: if one looks *from the outside* at the development of the Zionist movement, assessing its achievements based on formal-political criteria, the Shoah (Holocaust) appears to be the Archimedean point: it was that calamity which led to a change in the world status of the Jewish people, a sense of collective guilt vis-à-vis the Jews and the search for some mode of historical compensation. On the other hand, if one examines the movement *from within,* exploring its formation and growth and the features of the "state-in-the-making" of the evolving Jewish Yishuv in Palestine, it is natural to underscore the immanent processes that were crucial to the establishment of the state.

It is self-evident that a traumatic event of the magnitude of the Shoah impacted on the process of mobilizing the Jewish people for the creation of the Jewish state. This fact was particularly manifest in the process of "Zionization" that occurred among Jews in the United States, who became an influential political factor after World War II. It is reasonable to assume that it was also an element influencing the thinking of several heads of state undecided about whether to support the Jewish or Arab position in the U.N. General Assembly vote on November 29, 1947, to partition the country into two states, one Jewish, one Arab—although most determined their position on the basis of political considerations. It is also possible to find indications of indirect influence in the success of the Zionist Organization after 1945 in putting the problem of Jewish displaced persons on the agenda of the global media. Indeed, all these were important components at the decisive stages in the national struggle for independence. Counterfactually, we cannot answer the question what might have happened if the Shoah had not occurred; tragically, it did. The supposition that millions of refugees would probably have been crashing the gates of Palestine can be nothing but mere conjecture, since those millions perished. Yet it is an indisputable fact that even before the war, the Zionist movement had succeeded in establishing a viable foothold in Palestine, and had gained external recognition of its capacity to serve as the nucleus of a future state. That cannot be denied, nor can another key associated fact: the establishment of the state involved both a political and a *military* struggle waged by the Yishuv. Had it failed in the latter, the decisions in the U.N. on November 29, 1947, would have been consigned to the archives. The ability demonstrated by the Yishuv to stand firm in that war, the hardest of all battles fought by the State of Israel, remains illuminating testimony to its maturity as a political entity entitled to independence.[25]

The basic structure of the Zionist movement derived from the nature of the Jewish people, a national community scattered around the globe. The Zionist movement spread quite rapidly throughout all segments of the Jewish people. The Zionist Organization, the political instrument created by Herzl, conceived as the representative body of the Jewish people vis-à-vis the world's nations, was composed of representatives of national federations, such as the United States or Poland, as well as representatives of political currents, such as the Zionist Labor movement (the socialist left), the Revisionist Party (radical right), and Mizrahi (religious). In his day, Herzl had tried to avoid a politicization of the Zionist Organization, striving to preserve its political neutrality. In so doing, he revealed a certain myopia in his perception of the nature of national movements in such an ideologized era as the twentieth century. The more the Zionist movement became an integral part of Jewish existence, the more it was swept up in the various ideological struggles on the public agenda in Europe. The structural dualism mentioned above reflected the conceptual and organizational complexity of the Zionist movement, a sign of its vitality. However, it made life harder for the leadership, constraining them to create political power bases for themselves. Despite some ideological intersection, there also were differences manifest along the fracture lines of "communal" characteristics: the organization of German Jews was different in nature and political physiognomy from that of Polish Jewry, and both in turn differed from the Zionist Organization of American Jews. The existential problems facing Jews in each of these countries shaped the Zionist movements there differentially. The importance enjoyed by the Zionist movement in a Jewish community that was comparatively secure, such as that in the United States, and its concomitant set of priorities, were quite different from those in Poland. Moreover, the Zionists in Germany at the beginning of the era differed from German Zionists after Hitler came to power. Thus, it was not only ideological disputes which generated the opposing camps in the Zionist Organization and their attitudes toward the central issues on the agenda of the movement—the changing character of the constituent national communities also played a salient role.[26]

One of the most important topics in the history of the Zionist movement is the web of relations between the expanding Jewish Yishuv in Palestine and the Zionist movement in the diaspora. As mentioned, the dualism inherent in viewing Zionism (1) as a movement geared to continuing Jewish existence in the diaspora, albeit in other ways, or (2) as an enterprise that had embarked on a genuine new beginning, left its imprint on the movement from its earliest phase. Nonetheless, the concrete network of relations between the new Jewish entity forming in Palestine and the diaspora underwent substantial changes within a very short period. The question of the attitude toward the diaspora was on the Zionist agenda from the very inception of the Zionist Organization: should the movement focus on achieving its final goals, or also devote its energies to educational and organizational activities in the diaspora designed to gear the Jewish public toward the Zionist enterprise by deepening their national consciousness? There was some basis to misgivings that such activity, termed "work in the present" (avodat ha-hoveh)—as contrasted with avodat Eretz Israel, "work for and in the Land of Israel"—might cause a shift in the center of gravity from efforts on behalf of Palestine to activity meant to strengthen Jewish survival in the diaspora. The emotional energy and public volunteer effort expended on avodat ha-hoveh was in large part at the expense of activity designed to encourage immigration to Palestine. On the other hand, since Palestine was not considered capable of absorbing millions of Jewish immigrants in the foreseeable future, the question arose as to whether the national movement had any right to turn a blind eye to the suffering of Jews in the countries of their dispersion. Wasn't it obliged to take an active role in promoting their organization and education, enhancing their sense of national pride and ability to stand up to antisemitism? As a movement that regarded the fate of the entire people as its responsibility, it could not simply ignore the needs of Jews in the diaspora. It was called upon to provide them with leadership and assistance. One aspect of avodat ha-hoveh was aimed squarely at Eretz Israel, namely youth work, especially the wide spectrum of activities in the framework of Hehalutz (The Pioneer), the umbrella organization for all youth movements associated with "Eretz Israel ha-ovedet" (Labor Palestine). This organization had served as the reservoir for pioneers for Palestine since the 1920s, and its operations gained momentum in the first half of the 1930s.[27]

At the beginning of the century, the small Jewish Yishuv in Palestine was still linked umbilically to the diaspora. The diaspora supplied the human resources to bolster its ranks and the funds to maintain its institutions (both religious and secular); it was the source of Jewish and Zionist political power. World War I provided a vivid illustration of the fact that the Yishuv was totally dependent on the Jewish diaspora: had it not been for the financial and other assistance sent by American Jewry to Palestine, it is doubtful whether the Yishuv would have been able to survive the severe deprivation and hunger, which claimed many victims in Jerusalem. In political terms as well, the Yishuv was desperately in need of support from German and American Jewry: there was a gnawing fear that the helpless Yishuv would suffer a fate similar to that of the

Armenians. The future of Palestine was not decided in the hills and fields of Judea but in the corridors of power in London, Paris, and Washington. The Balfour Declaration, which in one fell swoop had transformed the status of Zionism from one movement among many circulating in the vestibules of great-power politics into an internationally recognized movement, had been announced in London, not Jerusalem. It had not come about due to the influence of the Jewish Yishuv in Palestine, but thanks to the political power of American and Russian Jewry (or the recurring image of that power), coupled with the diplomatic activity of such British Zionists as Weizmann.[28]

The dominant position of the diaspora vis-à-vis the Yishuv was reasserted with the arrival in April 1918 of the Zionist Commission headed by Weizmann, seen as the potential basis for an autonomous administration in the Yishuv, a kind of Zionist government in Palestine. This was a delegation sent by the movement from the diaspora, and Palestinian Jews were not invited to participate. The inferior position of the Yishuv within the Zionist framework remained in palpable evidence during the decade of the 1920s: the center of the movement was located in London, and the Zionist Executive in Jerusalem exercised only limited influence on Zionist policy.

This balance of power altered in the course of the 1930s, and had shifted significantly by the eve of World War II.[29] While the Yishuv had been enjoying a period of growth and economic prosperity, world Jewry was in the throes of a profound economic crisis; antisemitism was on the rise, existential anxieties were deepening, and Jewish international influence was on the decline. There was no more powerful and pointed expression of the weakened position of world Jewry in the 1930s and 1940s than the problem of Jewish refugees in search of a safe haven, with no deliverance in sight: two international conferences, at Evian and Bermuda, that dealt with the question ended without any tangible result.[30] Since the beginning of the 1930s, the Yishuv had become a small island of refuge and security in a world increasingly adrift without compass or anchor.

The more the base of Jewish power in Palestine became a viable entity, the greater was its political value: the rise of the Labor movement to hegemony within the Zionist Organization (1933) symbolized the transition of the center of the movement's political gravity from London to Jerusalem. The gradual waning of Weizmann's influence, beginning in 1931, was already a recognized fact by 1939: at the St. James conference, where the British government forced the MacDonald White Paper on the Yishuv, a document designed to curb the continued growth of the Jewish national home, Weizmann was unable to muster the emotional energy to stand up to the British representatives. It was Ben-Gurion who now stood at the helm of the movement and appeared at that juncture as the *de facto* leader of the entire Jewish people. The moment for a changing of the guard within the movement had arrived. During World War II, the Yishuv saw its role as one of providing assistance to European Jewry in its moment of peril and a safe haven to survivors, shouldering the task of leadership of the Jewish people in its darkest hour of crisis. The circle was now complete: within the span of less than 30 years, the center of power of the Jewish people had shifted from the diaspora to Palestine. Indeed, even now the Yishuv relied on the financial and political support of diaspora Jewry, particularly the American Jews; yet the pendulum of power that had oscillated between them would not swing back to the diaspora.

The adaptation of a religious community, devoid of any specifically political tradition, to a new territory and to the acceptance of full responsibility for the administration of its own affairs entailed acquiring a variety of characteristics unfamiliar to Jews as a collective. In the sphere of politics, this meant the need to create a national consensus, i.e., a series of guiding principles accepted by one and all which would define the rules of the political game. Jewish history offered no precedents from which one might learn national discipline, the subordination of particularist interests to the general weal—not even the definition of those basic interests that underpin any independent society. The chronicle of the Jewish Yishuv in Palestine, termed the "state-in-the-making" in Zionist discourse, is the formation of that consent, those agreements achieved even before the establishment of the formal authority of the state, which gave them the seal of legality. The creation of military power is part of this process: Jewish communities had known, in time of crisis, how to organize short-term self-defense within a local framework, but had had no experience in the creation of a full-fledged military that would, when the hour demanded, be able to play a decisive role not just in the defense of life and property, but in gaining control of territory. Such an armed force developed in the Yishuv, and ultimately stood the supreme test in the War of Independence. In the economic sphere, what had to be created was a system in which Jews occupied the entire pyramid of occupations, ranging from agriculture and industry to more sophisticated professions. Jewish inexperience with manual labor in general, and agricultural work in particular, had to be remedied if the

Jewish state was to become self-sufficient. This process was bound up with that of colonization: the settlement of Jews throughout the length and breadth of Palestine could not be made a living reality without a revolution in occupational structure. It was also within the context of this specific need for "Jewish labor" *(avodah ivrit)* that the separation between the Jewish and Arab economy in Palestine occurred.[31]

In social and cultural terms, this entailed the forging of a national ethos which would strengthen the bonds between Jews and Eretz Israel, elevating love of country into a supreme value. Transforming the collective Jewish psychology was one of the most important tasks which the leadership in the Yishuv took upon itself. The need to reshape Jewish attitudes when it came to the use of force, the relation between morality and *raison d'état* and the priority of practical "earthiness" over intellectualism, was manifested in hopes pinned to the emergence of the "new Jew." Ideally, the new Jew was to be cleansed of the dross of the diaspora, the sense of inferiority vis-à-vis the "strong and beautiful" gentile, hesitations about using physical force and the entire yoke of moral inhibitions characteristic of a member of a persecuted minority. These new Jews would be planted safe and secure on the soil of the motherland and, unlike the "wandering Jew" of the uprooted past, would not lift their eyes to alien shores. The shift of the center of gravity from universal values to those closely linked to a specific territory was part of the process of adaptation to independent political life. It was expressed in formal education, the educational programs of the youth movements, and the shaping of public opinion by the media and literature, speeches, meetings, and other instruments of discursive persuasion. Within a short period, this process of remolding had managed, for better or worse, to produce a new typical "Palestinian" personality. However, over the long term, it is doubtful whether that change will have an enduring permanent impact.[32]

The emergence of the Zionist movement was followed by the evolvement of a strong sense of Jewish self-awareness. The ideological struggle with rivals both within and beyond the Jewish community necessitated the sharpening of the argumentative skills and rhetorical instruments of the movement, including a "Zionist" narrative of Jewish history. An additional consequence was the early growth of the historiography of Zionism. Reasoned discussion about the history of the Zionist movement proceeded parallel with its genesis and formation. It was engaged in by journalists, politicians, and even historians who wanted to mold the self-image of various currents or forces within the movement, or its identity as a whole. Such topics as the causes underlying the birth of Zionism, its bipolar character as a movement of national renewal versus redemption, the contribution by currents on the left and right to its development and success—all these were political themes which the various forces in the movement found important enough to fight over. In their disputes, Ahad Ha-Am, Herzl, and their followers shaped the basic contours of Zionist historiography; Ber Borochov, Vladimir (Zeev) Jabotinsky, Berl Katznelson, and Rabbi Abraham Isaac Kook—each made use of historiography for delineating the prime characteristics of the movement. Historiography became an ideological battlefield. This was how it was treated by Yehezkel Kaufmann and Ben-Zion Dinur in such books as *Golah ve-nekhar* (Exile and Foreignness), *Israel ba-golah* (Israel among the Nations) and *Israel be-artzo* (Israel in Its Own Land).[33] This phenomenon mirrored the character of Zionism as a cultural and conceptual movement bent on restructuring not only the present and future of the nation, but also the world outlook and historical consciousness of its individual members.

Until the 1960s, it is difficult to speak about Zionist historiography separate from competing political agendas or ideological movements. The sixties constituted the watershed for Zionist historiography, as a new generation of historians appeared on the scene. University-trained professionals, they strove to contextualize the chronicle of Zionism, placing it within the context of world history, Jewish history, or the history of Eretz Israel. Although not free of ideological links, they consciously aspired to adhere to the principles of the discipline of history as a science. The rise of this generation of historians coincided with the waning of the fierce ideological struggles that had marked the first half of the twentieth century in general. That fact aided them in maintaining their freedom from the social and political systems which had shaped the historical narrative in earlier generations. The growing pluralism in Israeli society and its openness toward the West were accompanied by tendencies toward democratization, simultaneous with a disencumbering from ties to Eastern European political and ideological traditions that had marked the character of Jewish society in Palestine in previous decades. These tendencies impacted on the variegated and open character of the new Zionist historiography, the fruits of which are included in the present volume.

The new Zionist historiography has made use of various and diverse methodologies: along with diplomatic history, linked to international relations, the subfield of the history of political movements and currents developed apace, nurtured by the history of ideas. Parallel with the traditional description of the network of relations between the three principal political forces in Palestine—the Jews, Arabs, and British—social and economic history entered the historiographic picture, utilizing methodologies borrowed from the social sciences. The connection between society, culture, and history is manifest in a series of studies dealing with the mutual links between these areas. Local history emerged as a new subfield, focusing on small-scale phenomena in social growth and development, along with analyses of settlement strategy. In addition, a number of critical biographies of Zionist leaders and cultural heroes were published.

This broad gamut of fields and research methodologies does not set Zionist history apart from the histories of other national movements—on the contrary, it points up their basic similarity. Yet it does highlight a fundamental difference between the historiography of the Zionist movement and that of all other Jewish communities or periods in Jewish history since the destruction of the Second Temple. Zionist history is at one and the same time the chronicle of a cultural and political movement, a movement of immigration and settlement, the history of a Jewish collectivity, and the history of a land. This *totality* of Zionist history is a reflection of the distinctive character of the Zionist experience in modern Jewish history, and points to the key difference between it and other Jewish experiences. There is no separation here between the history of the Jews and the history of the state in which they live. It is that totalizing dimension which endows Zionist historiography with its "non-Jewish" and "general" character, serving to distinguish it from other chapters in the history of the Jewish people.

In this volume we endeavor to present the researcher, the student, and the interested reader with the finest scholarship in the field of the history of Zionism and the Yishuv (pre-state Israeli society). With the exception of Jacob Katz's path-breaking classic essay on the forerunners of Zionism, originally published in Hebrew in 1950, all the articles appeared after 1969; most of them were published after 1980. While it is natural that most of the research in this volume was conducted in Israel, it should be noted that important scholarly work produced in other countries, particularly the United States, has a significant place in this collection. This phenomenon attests to the diaspora Jewish community's profound interest in Zionism and the State of Israel. Finally, this is a methodologically diverse volume, one that includes a broad range of historical perspectives: the history of ideas, political history, social and economic history, and cultural history.

The volume is organized in five sections:

1. The Zionist idea and the ideological development of the Jewish nationalist movement. This section traces the appearance and development of the Zionist idea in two historical contexts: (a) the nationalist awakening in Europe; and (b) the beginning of modernization in Palestine and Eastern Europe.

2. Zionism and the diaspora. This section examines the philosophical and ideological *problematica* of the concept "negation of exile," debates concerning Zionism as a movement of Jewish renaissance or a movement to establish a safe haven for the Jews, and key models of Zionist organization in Central Europe, Eastern Europe, Western Europe, and the United States.

3. Zionist ideology against the test of reality. This section deals with political and social forces that shaped Zionist political debate in Palestine and which continue to dominate public discourse in Israel today, i.e., the movement's left and right wings, socialism and revisionism, the movement's leadership, institutions, and activities. At the heart of the debate remains the question, what is the proper method for creating a Jewish national home in the Land of Israel?

4. Relations between Jews, Arabs, and the British in Palestine. The formative period of the Jewish national home occurred during the British Mandate in Palestine. The contours of the Israeli-Arab conflict also took shape at this time. This section examines the dilemmas of Zionist policy under the constraints of the British regime and the national confrontation in Palestine.

5. Zionism as a movement of cultural renaissance. This section investigates the revival of the Hebrew language and the appearance of an indigenous Hebrew culture that found full expression in social and ethical mores, ethical approaches to self-government, the image of the *sabra* (Israeli Jew), and a new modern Hebrew literature. These achievements endowed Zionism with rich cultural attributes that transformed the Yishuv into the "spiritual center" of the Jewish people. The articles in this section highlight the proliferation of Zionist research throughout a wide range of disciplines including cultural, linguistic, and literary studies, in conjunction with social history.

One of the difficulties in the historical evaluation of the Zionist movement lies in the fact that it is still an active and functioning political entity, the object of considerable controversy—more perhaps among gentiles than Jews, but even within the Jewish community, both in Israel and the diaspora. The historical perspective on Zionism will take on one meaning in the event that the Jewish state establishes peace with its neighbors in the near future, and is integrated into a process of development encompassing the entire Middle East. This perspective will take on quite different meaning if the state does not succeed in forging a lasting peace, and its existence continues to be dependent on the sword.

Nonetheless, let me venture a kind of provisional appraisal: I believe it is fair to contend that Zionism has managed to create a new and different type of Jewish civilization, a form unknown to earlier generations of Jews. That civilization did not lead to the full "normalization" anticipated by the fathers of the Zionist movement, except in part, and did not bring about the disappearance of antisemitism, as they had so fervently hoped. But it did transform the basic principles underlying Jewish-gentile relations, and as a result brought about a qualitative shift in the position and status of the Jewish people throughout the world. The Jewish self-image changed, as did the image of the Jew in the eyes of the surrounding society. The existence of the state, for better or worse, became an internal formative factor within the Jewish people, creating a center of national identity which now beams its light to the entire diaspora. When one considers the extreme odds and impossible starting conditions Zionism was faced with at its inception, it seems reasonable to assume that it will be remembered as one of the greater success stories among national movements in the twentieth century.

EDITORS' NOTE

The editors have introduced some modifications in orthography and transliteration of Hebrew and Yiddish throughout the volume. For the most part, however, variant spellings in common use have not been altered and are cross-referenced in the index.

NOTES

1. Gershom Scholem, "Reshimah mi-tokh ha-izavon," *Od davar*, vol. 2 (Tel Aviv, 1989), p. 123.
2. Haim Hazaz, "Ha-derashah," *Luah ha-aretz*, 1943. *Kol kitvei: Avanim rothot* (Tel Aviv, 1970), pp. 219–38.
3. David Vital, *The Origins of Zionism* (Oxford, 1975), preface.
4. Benedict Anderson, *Imagined Communities* (London and New York, 1983), p. 149.
5. The classic work on this is Jacob Katz, *Masoret u-mashber* (Jerusalem, 1958), pp. 284–97; see also the English translation *Tradition and Crisis: Jewish Society at the End of the Middle Ages* (New York, 1993).
6. Yehezkel Kaufmann, *Golah ve-nekhar*, vol. 2 (Tel Aviv, 1932), pp. 172–218.
7. A detailed description of the development of Jewish society in that period can be

found in Jacob Katz, *Out of the Ghetto: The Social Background of Jewish Emancipation, 1770–1870* (Cambridge, Mass., 1973).

8. On the ideological struggles of the nineteenth and twentieth centuries, see the trilogy by Yaakov Talmon, *The Origins of Totalitarian Democracy* (Middlesex, 1952); *Political Messianism* (London, 1960), and *The Myths of the Nation and the Vision of Revolution* (London, 1980).

9. An analysis of the first manifestations of Jewish nationalism and the underlying historical reasons can be found in the essay by Jacob Katz, "The Forerunners of Zionism," in this volume.

10. On the programs in southern Russia and their significance, see Jonathan Frankel, *Prophecy and Politics* (Cambridge, 1981), pp. 29–132.

11. On the complex web of relations between the Jews and Eretz Israel, see the essay by Shmuel Almog in this volume.

12. Different aspects of the process of formation of Hebrew culture are discussed in the four essays in part 5 in this volume.

13. Leo Pinsker, "Auto-Emancipation," in his *Road to Freedom: Writings and Addresses* (New York, 1944), pp. 74–106.

14. For a broader treatment of this topic, see Frankel, *Prophecy and Politics*, pp. 288–364.

15. For an example of an approach that calls for a thoroughgoing revision of the entire gamut of Jewish social behavior, see Yosef Haim Brenner, "Haarakhat azmenu bisheloshet ha-krakhim," *Kol kitvei*, vol. 7, (Tel Aviv, 1937), pp. 219–67.

16. See, among others, Gershon Weiler, *Teokratziyah yehudit* (Tel Aviv, 1976); Yosef Agassi, *Ben dat u-leum: Likrat zehut leumit israelit* (Tel Aviv, 1993); Boaz Evron, *Ha-heshbon ha-leumi* (Israel, 1988).

17. Gershom Scholem, "Ha-yahadut ma-hi?" *Od davar*, p. 121.

18. These topics are addressed in essays by Shmuel Ettinger, Israel Bartal, and Yosef Salmon in this volume. For additional information, see Ehud Luz, *Makbilim nifgashim* (Tel Aviv, 1985); see also English translation *Parallels Meet: Religion and Nationalism in the Early Zionist Movement, 1882–1904* (Philadelphia, 1988).

19. A modern version of this discussion appears in the essay by David Vital in this volume.

20. A detailed examination of this topic can be found in the essay by Michael Heymann in this volume.

21. For an additional treatment of this topic, see Anita Shapira, "Did the Zionist Leadership Foresee the Holocaust?" in Jehuda Reinharz, ed., *Living with Antisemitism* (Hanover, N.H., 1987), pp. 397–412.

22. For a more detailed discussion, see the essays by Yosef Gorny, Jonathan Frankel, Elkana Margalit, Ze'ev Tzahor, and Anita Shapira in this volume.

23. These topics are examined in depth by Jehuda Reinharz, Israel Kolatt, Hagit Lavsky, Bernard Wasserstein, and Joseph Heller in this volume.

24. These topics are explored in Anita Shapira, *Land and Power: The Zionist Resort to Force, 1881–1948* (New York, 1992).

25. On the Yishuv and the Shoah, see Dina Porat, *The Blue and Yellow Stars of David: The Zionist Leadership in Palestine and the Holocaust, 1939–1945* (Cambridge, Mass., 1990) and Shapira, *Land and Power*, pp. 319–43. On the Yishuv and the survivors, see Anita Shapira, "The Yishuv and the Survivors of the Holocaust," *Studies in Zionism* 7:2 (1986), pp. 277–301.

26. A detailed examination of these topics can be found in essays by Ezra Mendelsohn, Steven J. Zipperstein, Jehuda Reinharz, Evyatar Friesel, George L. Berlin, and Hagit Lavsky in this volume.

27. These topics are explored in essays by Eliezer Schweid, Matityahu Mintz, Israel Oppenheim, and David Vital in this volume.

28. See the essay in this volume by Jehuda Reinharz on the Balfour Declaration.

29. Cf. Jehuda Reinharz, *Chaim Weizmann: The Making of a Statesman,* vol. 2 (New York, 1993).

30. See Henry Feingold, *The Politics of Rescue* (New Brunswick, N.J. 1970); Bernard Wasserstein, *Britain and the Jews of Europe, 1939–1945* (Oxford, 1979).

31. On the "binational economy" in Mandatory Palestine, see the essay by Jacob Metzer in this volume.

32. On this aspect, see Anita Shapira, "Native Sons" in this volume, and idem, *Land and Power.*

33. Yehezkel Kaufmann, *Golah ve-nekhar,* 2 vols. (Tel Aviv, 1961/62); Ben-Zion Dinur, *Israel ba-golah* (Tel Aviv, 1938) and *Israel be-artzo* (Tel Aviv, 1972).

I.

THE NATIONAL MOVEMENT AND ITS IDEOLOGICAL ORIGINS

1.

The Forerunners of Zionism

Jacob Katz

A study of the history of Zionism reveals similarities to other modern movements, such as socialism and Jewish socialism. Once Zionism came of age and emerged into the full light of history, historians discovered that its acknowledged leaders were in fact the standard bearers who had brought the ideas of others to fruition. Thus concepts such as 'forerunners of Zionism' and 'fore-history' *(Vorgeschichte)* of Zionism were created by writers to describe phenomena which seemed to them to constitute the practical or theoretical prologue to the birth of the movement itself.

EARLY INTERPRETATIONS

The concept 'forerunners of Zionism' was never defined by the historians who used it, and it is only in context that we can guess its meaning. In Nahum Sokolow's book, *History of Zionism* (1919), the term is applied so broadly that its meaning becomes vague. In his introduction Sokolow writes: 'I had to go back to the beginning of this idea and extend the meaning of 'Zionism' to all aspirations and efforts tending in the same direction' (p. vii). By applying the term 'Zionist' to any Jew or gentile who had ever expressed ideas reminiscent of those of the Zionist movement, Sokolow made it practically impossible to distinguish between the later Zionists and their predecessors.

Real content is given to the concept by Adolf Böhm in his book *Die Zionistische Bewegung* (1920). Böhm distinguishes between the Zionists

Translated from the Hebrew and reprinted by permission of the author from the *Jerusalem Quarterly* 7 (spring 1978): 10–21.

and their forerunners on the one hand, and between the aspirations and movements from which Zionism inherited its consciousness of the historical link between the Jewish people and Eretz Israel on the other. He sees the essence of these movements and aspirations in their 'Eretz-Israelness Palestinismus'—a term which he applies to all those manifestations, both material (the recurrent Jewish immigrations to Eretz Israel) and spiritual (the belief in a miraculous redemption in Zion) which testified to the actual and emotional ties between the Jews of the Diaspora and the Land of Israel which existed from the destruction of the Second Temple to the modern era of assimilation. Böhm distinguishes between the protagonists of the Zionist idea from the beginning of the Hibbat Zion (Lovers of Zion) movement on, and those who anticipated them in advocating this idea at a time when among the masses of the people and their leaders the tendency to assimilation still prevailed. It is the latter group, who espoused and propagated the Zionist idea during the period of assimilation, that Böhm labels 'forerunners of Zionism'.

In his theoretical discussion, Böhm attempts to establish a well-defined terminology describing the forerunners; however, in the actual presentation of the facts he follows Sokolow's example and includes all those who had expressed their approval of the return of the Jews to their homeland. In this category he included Jews—ranging from the American Jewish journalist Mordecai Manuel Noah (1785–1851, on whom more later) to the Hebrew writer of the Enlightenment, Peretz Smolenskin (1842–1885) and non-Jews, ranging from the novelist George Eliot who had shown herself highly sympathetic to the idea of a Jewish national revival in her novel *Daniel Deronda* (1876) to the British lawyer, journalist and adventurer Laurence Oliphant (1829–1888) who had actively encouraged the return of the Jews to Eretz Israel.

Sokolow and Böhm used the historical approach typical in the current Zionist historiography—whose literature was not solely scientific in its aims, but also proselytizing. It is clear that their vagueness about the concept 'forerunners of Zionism' (and of the concept of Zionism itself) was not due only to the usual difficulties encountered by historians in defining the limits of any historical period. Proof of the early origins of Zionism gave it credence in the eyes of a generation whose political and even moral judgements were based on historical considerations—the influence of historicism, a doctrine whose impact on modern thought cannot be overestimated.

This approach was criticised by Zionists living in Eretz Israel, who claimed that Zionism no longer needed to justify its existence and called rather for its sociological analysis. In this light, Zionism was the answer to the problem of Diaspora Jewry, who were secularized and no longer thought in terms of a miraculous redemption. Thus neither the messianic movements among the Jews, nor the various programmes proposed by Christians for a return of the Jews to Zion came under the heading of Zionist history, since those projects were not usually motivated by a wish to solve the problems of the Jewish communities or to satisfy their needs.

But if motivation is what defines a 'forerunner' then those with the right motives are Zionists even if they preceded the Zionist movement, and those with the wrong motives are not Zionists even if they actually contributed to its formation. According to this criterion it was possible for the proponents of this definition to find 'Zionists' among the German Jews of the Enlightenment, and to call Mordecai Manuel Noah 'the first Zionist'. Rabbi Kalisher (1795–1874) and his followers who initiated a movement for the return of the Jews to Eretz Israel in anticipation of the coming of the Messiah on the other hand cannot be considered Zionists at all—unless the Rabbi's real motive was to find practical solutions to practical problems, couched in traditional-messianic terms in order to avoid the disfavour of his Orthodox religious peers.

A different approach is developed in Ben-Zion Dinur's (Dinaburg) book *Mevasrei ha-Zionut* [The Forerunners of Zionism], (1939), a collection of sources prefaced by the author for the period 'from the failure of the Shabbetaian movement to the beginnings of Habbat Zion'. Dinur was the first historian of Zionism to combine a professional mastery of his material with a willingness to define his terms, and the selection and analysis of the source material in this collection proceeds in strict accordance with the conceptual framework established by the author.

According to Dinur, the emergence of the forerunners period is to be determined on the basis of the relationship between secularization and the movement of national revival. He sees the decline of the Shabbetaian movement as marking the beginning of the modern period in Jewish history, and the most striking characteristic of this new period he sees as the positive attitude towards life ('the sanctification of life instead of the sanctification of God' or martyrdom). But the national movement, which Dinur regards as the supreme affirmation of life, did not appear right at the beginning of this turning point. Rather it brought the Enlightenment—which is usually regarded as the antithesis of the national movement. But Dinur's main thesis, substantiated by a wealth of newly revealed historical documentation, discerns alongside the dominant trend of Enlightenment and assimilation the first glimmer of the dawning nationalism—from the revival of the Hebrew language to a secular conception of the Jewish national entity and its political and cultural potentialities.

The question is whether Dinur's exposition and analysis (which have been accepted by Israeli historians) justify his conclusion that these early expressions of nationalism were in fact the harbingers of the Zionist movement. In order to answer this question we must first clarify the meaning of the concept 'forerunners'.

SOCIALLY UNIFYING FORCE

Zionist history deals with the process leading to the realization of the Zionist goal. In accordance with this limitation we are bound to begin the history of the 'forerunners of Zionism' at the point at which the ideas advocated by the forerunners were translated into action, and not when these ideas were in formation.

This restriction could oblige us to discard the term 'forerunners of Zionism' altogether. Zionist history is universally agreed to begin with the outset of settlement in Eretz Israel in the early 1800s; before this time both Zionism and its forerunners exist only as ideas and their proponents. Should the distinction then be based on the difference between thought and action?

Our answer to this question is based on sociological considerations. Let us disregard for a moment the goals of Zionism, and examine its potency as a social force. To what degree did Zionism unite a group of like thinkers behind a common aim? A partisan periodical unites its readers behind a belief; at the other extreme we find actual social cohesion through the commitment to a belief such as in monastic communities. Between the two lies a whole range of social behaviour with varying degrees of cohesiveness. Zionism produced the entire range of social expression, from readers' circles and political groups to the close communal life of the *kvutza*. The *kvutza*-form of settlement was an expression of the idea of a socialist utopia, which went hand in hand with Zionism, but its staying power derived strictly from its national-Zionist sense of mission.

This social strength distinguishes Zionism from other contemporary Jewish trends and movements, and encourages the study of it as a sociological phenomenon. The birth of modern Zionism coincided with a movement of emigration among the Jews of Eastern Europe. Emigra-

tion was a solution to economic problems but as a socially unifying force
it proved almost completely barren. The few societies formed for the
purpose of joint emigration—some combining the goal of emigration
with definite social programmes—soon disintegrated, and emigration
was largely based on individual initiative, with support from relatives or
immigrant aid societies. This emigration was a 'natural' movement, a
population transfer from one country to another as a result of political
and economic pressures. And the adjustment of the emigrants to their
new life depended on social and economic conditions. Emigration was
not the fulfillment of an ideal, as it was with Zionism.

The Zionist movement grew out of economic, political and social
pressures, but in the course of its development, in the definition of its
goals, and even in the choice of its means, it was guided by an idea
which was not simply the product of such pressures. The adherence to a
specific land set it apart from the immigration movement in general. To
this were added social, religious and cultural utopias,[1] images of a
society in which social or religious principles would be realized, or in
which unique cultural values would be created. A fundamentally irratio-
nal belief, whether related to adherence to a religious tradition or to
historical links in a purely secular-national sense—connected these utopian aspirations to Eretz Israel, the only possible location for their realization.

Among the emigrants to other countries, family ties usually predominated but the Zionists were bound together on the basis of shared
ideological aspirations of the various *aliyot*. The more strongly the
aliyah was influenced by an ideological trend, the more pronounced was
its supra-familial structure: the BILU pioneers of the early 1880s were
more supra-familial than the Rumanian immigration of the same period,
and the Second (1905–14) and Third (1919–23) *aliyot* than the later
waves of immigration which were motivated more by necessity than by
ideology. At certain stages the hold which Zionism had on its adherents
was almost as strong as that exerted by religious movements in their
initial stages, when they tend to disrupt accepted social forms and draw
individuals into their own frameworks.

PREMATURE SCHEMES AND EARLY 'PROJECT-MAKERS'

The Zionist idea that the Jews should return to their ancient homeland
through colonization and political activity has been expressed many
times since the 17th century by Jews and non-Jews alike. But it remained

quiescent both as a socially unifying force and in terms of realizing its goals. Ideas which emerge but only become influential at a later stage are common enough in history, and the usual sociological explanation is that their influence does not depend on the degree of their 'rightness' or 'justice' but on their coinciding with political and social conditions which lend them urgency. But this explanation does not explain how the idea actually infiltrates into a society, a process which must take place gradually, accompanied by temporary setbacks and involving a hard social struggle. Furthermore, the idea is at first important only to a limited number of individuals, who because of their special social position and/or particular personal characteristics become its disseminators when their society is largely indifferent to it. To most of their contemporaries, they appear to be eccentrics, but the historian appreciates their role as forerunners, when he can show that the personal and objective factors motivating them are similar to those which were decisive in the eventual emergence of the movement on a socially significant scale. The identification of such 'forerunners' cannot be made on the basis of analogies in the content of the idea alone. It is only in analyzing the historical process as a whole that we can decide whether we are indeed dealing with a 'forerunner' or simply with a chance similarity in thought. Such coincidental similarities are common enough, and there is no modern idea for which analogies have not been discovered, even in totally alien cultural and intellectual contexts.

This is especially true of the Zionist idea. The general conception of the return of the Jews to their homeland or the establishment of a Jewish state in some other place was 'in the air', wherever Jews constituted a separate and distinct social body. The historical link between the Jews and Eretz Israel is in the Christian and the Jewish traditions, and it did not take much imagination or original thought to propose the establishment of a Jewish state. Not surprisingly, projects and project-makers (*Projectenmachers*) drawing on these traditions abounded especially during the first two centuries of the modern period.

The intellectual calibre of these schemes can be measured in part by the type of person who produced them. Their chief similarity is their impractical and sometimes absurd detachment from reality. The material means which the 'project-makers' could mobilize for the realization of their schemes were far short of their grandiose requirements, and they were soon reduced to ridicule and oblivion.

The 'project-makers' of the 17th, 18th and 19th centuries were solitary figures isolated from the mainstream of socio-historical development. A 17th-century example is the Danish writer Holger Paulli and other Christians like him, who preached the return of the Jews to Zion from motives of Christian millennialism. In the 19th century, there is Mordecai Manuel Noah, author of the famous 'Ararat' scheme, who proclaims the foundation of the Jewish state on an island in America over which he presides, appoints unsuspecting rabbis and scholars in Europe as his representatives and decrees the abolition of laws and customs in his first proclamation. Noah includes the education of the Indians in his programme, declaring them the descendants of the Ten Lost Tribes. Having laid the foundation stone of the new state, conducting the consecration ceremony in a church for lack of an available synagogue, Noah sits back and waits for the immigrants to start streaming in from the four corners of the earth. This is a prime example of a crank, who has abandoned the world of reality, although he was previously the American consul in Tunis.

This type differs radically from the messianic visionary of earlier generations who was involved in his society and sustained by the great faith of his contemporaries. This occurred in a transitional period when the faith in a miraculous redemption was rapidly waning, while the practical possibility of a return to Eretz Israel was still nascent. In this transition period the idea of national redemption was the domain of isolated eccentrics whose efforts were sporadic and premature.

EMANCIPATION OVERSHADOWS NATIONAL REVIVAL

The 'project-makers' of the period between active messianism and the beginning of the Zionist movement proper can by no means be described as the 'forerunners of Zionism'. Even Dinur, who sees this whole interim period as the period of the 'forerunners', does so not because of these projects but because of the emergence of certain historical trends—for example, the revival of the Hebrew language and the desire to engage in productive work—which were later to become part of Zionist involvement and, secondly, because it was during this period that a type of Jew emerged who was capable of engaging in effective political activity as a result of a new approach to the secular world. A realistic view of the Jewish people is evident in the writings of such thinkers as Spinoza and Mendelssohn, and even of Christian statesmen whose involvement with Jewish questions was a real one due to their participation in the debate on the improvement of Jewish living conditions and the struggle for equal rights for the Jews. These polemicists (as Dinur has successfully shown) frequently represent the Jewish people as a living nation whose return to their historical homeland can be considered and debated as a real political possibility.

If we define forerunners in terms of the idea alone, then Dinur's approach is certainly valid. The Jewish people is perceived as a real entity, and the possibility of a national revival is suggested. But the question remains: is the idea at this stage a potential socially unifying force, which we found above to be the chief test of its vitality in all the stages of its development? The idea in this period is expressed in the opinions of individuals, which never become a rallying point for action. It is incapable of exerting any real influence on the historical process at this time.

The national idea was still overshadowed by the idea of social and political emancipation which burst into the confines of Jewish life at that time. These goals became paramount, breaking down the old structure of Jewish society. It is to this idea that subsidiary trends such as the desire to engage in productive labour, the revival of the Hebrew language (the literature of the Enlightenment), and even the new scientific approach to Judaism, now increasingly attached themselves. Most important of all, it is to this idea that the younger generation, its eyes fixed on the goal of *emancipation* which seemed within reach, attached itself. The idea of the return to Eretz Israel receded into the past, rather than heralding a future movement.

FROM EQUAL RIGHTS TO NATIONAL RIGHTS

At what point then do the forerunners appear, signalling the renewed vitality of the Zionist idea as an active force? In terms of our previous definition, the forerunners of Zionism are the first advocates of the Zionist idea who inspired any of the forms of social *cohesiveness* described above. This places the forerunners in the late 1850s–early 1860s, when the first advocates of Zion—Rabbi Kalisher, Rabbi Gutmacher, Luria and, finally, Moses Hess attracted a following, however limited and scattered, united by personal and organizational bonds in the common belief in the future of the nation in its historical homeland. The very fact that these men, so different not only in their backgrounds but also in the basis of their common belief, could come together at all— with Rabbi Kalisher, the most practical member, acting as the central axis of the group—this fact alone proves that the idea of the return of the Jews to their land had now become a socially unifying force.

It is not difficult to understand why this generation was ready to receive the ideas which previous generations had rejected or ignored. During this period, the struggle for equal rights in the West was coming to an end, and the idea of equality and emancipation was losing its impetus as an ideal to be transformed into reality. At this point a split took place in social and intellectual trends. The mainstream continued on its course from the achievement of equal rights to full absorption into gentile society. On the intellectual plane, the demand for equality led to an ideology which sought to consolidate and justify what had already been achieved. At this stage, however, an opening appeared for an apparently contradictory aspiration, one which had existed before, but had been pushed aside by the opposing trend. At the beginning of the struggle for equal rights it had seemed to Jews and non-Jews alike that national aspiration on the part of the Jews was contrary to the struggle for full citizenship, and should therefore be abandoned. Now that the movement for emancipation had attained its goal, however, the national movement could appear not as its antithesis but as its complement. In contrast to later Zionism, the forerunners did not base their ideas on the castigation of Jewish life in the Diaspora. Consequently, the forerunners did not prepare to transfer the Jews from the West, but to create a kind of model nation in Eretz Israel, both by educating the Jews already living there, and by bringing there Jews from countries which had not granted them equal rights. What would happen after this was either not discussed (by Rabbi Alkalai or Moses Hess, for example), or was left to Divine Providence (by Rabbi Kalisher, for example, for whom making Eretz Israel into a 'settled land' was merely a preparatory step towards miraculous events whose scope and nature were beyond human speculation).

In any case, the character of the message—imminent in the national aspirations which were voiced at the exact moment of time when the conflicting trend of historical development, namely emancipation, reached its full development, and an opening for a turning point presented itself—became clear by the ties which now began to be formed between individuals on a basis of a renewal of the belief in a national future in the pristine homeland. Here begins a typical dialectic process, developing according to the pattern of thesis, antithesis and synthesis. The forerunners emerge at the beginning of the transition from the antithesis—the rejection of the belief in a miraculous return of the Jews to Zion—to the synthesis, which is modern Zionism.

THE TRUE FORERUNNERS

Rabbi Kalisher

This merging of the renewal of the belief in national rebirth and the conclusion of the struggle for equal rights can also be discerned in the lives and intellectual development of the three forerunners, Rabbi Kalisher, Rabbi Alkalai and Moses Hess. Rabbi Kalisher was still thinking in terms of a genuine messianic movement in 1836, when he approached Asher Ansel Rothschild and urged him to purchase the whole of Eretz Israel from the Ottoman ruler Mohammed Ali—or at least Jerusalem or the Temple Mount, in order to provide an opening for a miraculous redemption by an 'awakening from below': the transformation of Eretz Israel into a 'settled land' or the reinstatement of sacrificial offerings—two activities which according to the interpretation of Jewish tradition by Rabbi Kalisher were prerequisites for the coming of the Messiah. At about the same time the Rabbi approached Sir Moses Montefiore with a similar request. After this, however, he abandoned all such activities and devoted himself to Talmudic study and to the practical problems which had arisen among the religious life of Western Jewry as a result of the radical changes brought about by the emancipation movement. It was only in 1860, with the founding of the Society for the Settlement of Eretz Israel, that Rabbi Kalisher—by then 65 years old—resumed his earlier activities, with the aim of making Eretz Israel a 'settled land' now taking first place and the offering up of sacrifices thrust into the background. Rabbi Kalisher's renewed vigour and successful pursuit of practical aims through messianic motivation attest to the fact that the time was now ripe for the national movement to reassert itself.

Moses Hess

A similar pattern was followed by Moses Hess. He traced his first stirrings of Jewish national aspirations to the shame and rage aroused by the blood libel against the Jews of Damascus in the year 1840. At the time, however, Hess's writings gave no indication of these national aspirations. Even in his intimate correspondence with his Jewish friend Auerbach he gives no expression to the feelings of outrage he was to recall twenty years later. Hess's own explanation for this delayed reaction was that the Jewish pain was overshadowed at the time by 'the greater pain aroused in me by the European proletariat'. The truth of the matter is that Hess's rage did not turn him to specifically Jewish aspirations, and his concern for the proletariat included a belief in the solution of the Jewish problem. It was only after the experience of the next twenty years, which did not see the solution to the problems of the proletariat but did see a measure of emancipation for the Jews that Hess's sentiments could turn to a specifically Jewish aspiration. In developing his new theory Hess drew on the material provided by the historical school of Graetz and his associates (which was also a synthesis produced by the dialectic of the times), and with its help he arrived at a definition of Judaism as an ethnic-spiritual entity which should be preserved and strengthened because it contained forces of the future. The linking of this future to Eretz Israel, where the spiritual revival was destined to be fully realized, was exclusive to Hess (among 'secularists') at the time: it was not, however, intended as a rejection of equal rights but as a complement to it and it could be accepted as such only in the 1860s when the struggle for equal rights seemed to be over.

Rabbi Alkalai

The importance of the sixties as a turning point is equally apparent in the activities of the third forerunner, Rabbi Alkalai. While his initial awakening was not connected with developments in Western Jewry (about which he knew only by hearsay) their reactions to his ideas, which he began to publish in the forties, are an indication of the mood at that time. Insofar as any attention at all was paid to the Rabbi's views at this stage, it was derisive stemming partly from a Western feeling of superiority to the Sephardi preacher and his homiletical style, and partly from a process of disillusionment with the dreams of redemption which Rabbi Alkalai was trying to revive without making any clear distinction between their messianic and realistic elements. Equally typical was the Rabbi's failure in England in 1852, where he received more support from Christians than from Jews—a fact which should not surprise us in the light of the literal belief in the biblical prophecies of the return of the Jews to Zion among English Christian fundamentalists on the one hand, and on the other—the fact that these were the years of the struggle for equal rights among British Jewry, to whom any mention of Eretz Israel as the land of their future seemed incompatible with their present aspirations. All Rabbi Alkalai's efforts were, in fact, fruitless until the sixties, when his work as a propagandist became a link in the chain of activities conducted by Rabbi Kalisher and his circle. Until this time too his publications were only intermittent: between his first and second books in Hebrew (his first two books were written in Ladino and thus only for a limited circle of readers), five years elapsed, and in the next eight years (1848–1856) he produced only three pamphlets. From then on, however, he is more prolific (in the form of books, pamphlets and newspaper articles) and the contents themselves become increasingly clearer as the gap between the homiletical background and the realistic intentions widen, and the confidence of the writer grows with his observation of events and his extraordinary receptiveness towards the first sign of national crystallization, such as the emergence of a Hebrew press, the foundation of the Alliance Israelite Universelle, etc.—a receptiveness which was unmatched even by his fellow forerunners, Rabbi Kalisher and Moses Hess. The fact that Rabbi Alkalai, like Rabbi Kalisher, was approaching his sixtieth year when his most fruitful and important period commenced is testimony in itself to the supra-personal causes of this turning point.

UNITED BY MARGINAL POSITION IN SOCIETY

Finally, we shall attempt to answer the question: what distinguished the forerunners from their contemporaries and made it possible for them to influence the future? The historian may attribute these powers to individual personality. But objective factors and social forces may have contributed to making these individuals into the bearers of ideas or players of historical roles. The factor which is common to all the forerunners is their marginal position in Western Jewry, their ambivalent feelings during the events which signalled the process of abandonment of the hopes of national redemption. This was primarily the result of their geographical origins: Rabbi Kalisher on the border between East and West, and Rabbi Alkalai on the very edge of the 'West' in the Balkans (Hungary, especially during the period of reform, followed the lead of the West). But their geographical situation also had cultural implications. Rabbi Kalisher and Rabbi Alkalai belonged to the West in so far as they were capable of reacting to its historical developments but at the same time they were independent of it, in as much as their foundations had not yet been shaken by developments in the West.

In a slightly different sense the term 'marginal' can also be applied to Moses Hess's position *vis-à-vis* Western Jewry. Hess ascribed his ability to relate to the problem of Jewish nationality to his experiences in France, then the major power in Europe. But his emigration from Germany has additional significance. Having uprooted himself from his native soil and broken off relations with his family, he abandoned his position in society and isolated himself from Jewish public life; all these factors combined to place him outside the equal rights movement. Hess was a harbinger of the future because he gave expression to trends which were only reaching maturity in his day. Hess's withdrawal from the mainstream of society—unlike Graetz, for example, who was involved in Jewish public life in Germany—drove him to the far-reaching conclusion that the future of the Jewish people lay in Eretz Israel. This points to the interesting paradox that the men closest to Hess intellectually— the members of the historical school in Germany—did not go along with his main ideas and the enthusiasm with which they greeted his book was due to its premises rather than its conclusion; whereas the men who shared Hess's aspirations, Kalisher and his circle, based these aspirations on intellectual premises which were completely different to Hess's. What unites the forerunners as a limited historical phenomenon is therefore not the similarity in their way of thinking, but their common marginal position in society and the common aspirations which this position inspired.

NOTE

1. Following Karl Mannheim and Martin Buber, I use the term 'utopia' not in the negative sense of some illusory future which can never be realized, but in the sense of a vision which guides its adherents to their desired goal.

2.

People and Land in Modern Jewish Nationalism

Shmuel Almog

In 1903, the Zionist movement was set in turmoil by the so-called Uganda Crisis. The controversy between the "Zionists for Zion" and their rivals was said to revolve around concern for the people, as opposed to devotion to the land. Pro-Ugandist Eliezer Ben Yehuda, for example, proclaimed his position to be "people-oriented" and that of his opponents to be "land-oriented." Mizrahi leader, Rabbi Reines, explained his support for the Uganda scheme by claiming: "We have noted the needs of the people, whom we hold dearer than the land." [1]

From the outset, Jewish nationalism has been marked by a distinction between a territorial and an ethnic principle, i.e., between land and people. The Jews' anomaly in comparison with other national groups accentuated the dichotomy. Although a group with typical hallmarks, the Jews lacked the conventional national attributes, such as a common language and a territory. However, they did retain a certain link to the "Holy Tongue," classical Hebrew, as well as a spiritual link to the "Holy Land." In time, both these factors would contribute to the formation of a Jewish national consciousness. But as the non-Jewish environment—and to a large extent, the Jews themselves—deemed the link a secondary, transient factor, its role had yet to be discerned.[2] Before the national idea took root among the Jews, they were portrayed as a predominantly religious community, albeit of a certain ethnic descent. This concept suited the requirements of many Central and Western European Jews. As for Eastern European Jews, even as their neighbors were grouping into national movements, the massive Yiddish-speaking

Translated from the Hebrew and reprinted by permission of the author and The Avraham Harman Institute of Contemporary Jewry from *Yahadut Zmanenu* 1 (1983): 53–67.

communities were still not deemed a national group. Once established, the Jewish national movement was immediately confronted with the gap between the traditional ideal of the Return to Zion—the territorial principle—and the actual needs of the people, later dubbed by Herzl as *Judennot* (Jewish plight).

THE ETHNIC AND TERRITORIAL PRINCIPLES

Despite the Jewish anomaly, the problem is not specifically Jewish, but finds parallels among numerous national movements. The national consciousness of other communities also took shape amid crises and soul-searching. Needless to say, identity problems plague many a nation.[3]

An intricate concept, nationalism evokes multiple ideas—of people, land, culture, origins, political framework, to name but a few. To this day, basic concepts concerning the theory and practice of nationalism are subject to controversy. Nor is the distinction between ethnic and territorial principles confined to modern nationalism alone. It can even be discerned in the formative processes of ancient societies. Moreover, traces attributed to primal Creation acts, retained in myth and legend, often served to bolster the claims of national movements. They are thus particularly pertinent to the subject at hand.

The bond between a people and its land is not a fixed, primordial condition. Quite the contrary: it is a dynamic, highly mutable process. Whether in streams or in trickles, waves of conquerors, settlers, immigrants, and exiles spread through populated lands, gradually mingling with the local population. Existing political structures may be destroyed in the process, others take their place. Clashes between ethnic elements may ensue, as well as new social stratification. Here lies the source of conflict between the territorial principles, which represents a historical continuum related to a stretch of land, and the ethnic principle based on a group of people and possibly on a culture as well. The juxtaposition of people and land poses several questions, first for those concerned, later for scholars: Who shall prevail? Will the newcomers accept the local customs, tongue, and rituals, or will they, rather, stamp their own seal on the surroundings? To what extent will the various elements intermingle and generate a single entity? It may happen that one element overcomes the other. In other cases, local blends with foreign, or else the two coexist—as different strata of the same society, as diverse ethnic and cultural groups, or even as a variegated geographic-ethnic-social pattern.

These processes do not signify a unilinear progression towards the triumph of either a territorial or an ethnic principle. Shifting circumstances may favor, at different times, one or the other. Indeed, prevailing terminologies in Europe throughout the ages serve as symbolic illustrations of recurrent changes in each principle's status. A case in point is the introduction by the Roman Empire of the *jus gentium*. Acknowledging the validity of the ethnic principle, this law complements the authority invested in the judicial tradition of the city of Rome.[4] By the same token, modern citizenship laws bear traces of *jus sanguinis,* or, conversely, *jus soli*[5]—namely, rights derived from blood relations, as opposed to those linked to one's birthplace. In the early Middle Ages, the term *regnum Francorum* was used to denote regal power over people rather than land. Later on, the feudal monarchy made use of the territorial mode, as exemplified by the term *regnum Franciae.*[6] Conversely, during the French Revolution, the title *roi de France* (King of France) became *roi des francais* (King of the French), signifying the sovereignty of the people.[7] In this context, "people" would denote "popular" rather than "ethnic," as the emphasis rests on the nation as a political entity, not on the common origins.

The two principles have evolved into two types of nationalism, sometimes named after Rousseau and Herder, respectively.[8] On the one hand, an existing political structure acquires new meaning through the rise of national consciousness. On the other, national consciousness develops among a people that still lacks the attributes of unity and independence. Political nationalism may thus be seen as the antipode of ethnic nationalism. Yet both principles bear a mainly symbolic significance. During the French Revolution, the term "nation" in its newly-acquired sense as political entity was still a lofty abstraction. Only the gradual cognizance of its ethnic components was to lend it a more concrete substance. On the other hand, national movements have had initial recourse to ethnic, historical, and cultural sources, then proceeded to the political arena in order to realize the nation's unity and independence.[9] Due to symmetrical developments, both forms of nationalism ultimately came to resemble each other. However, vestiges of earlier traditions were sustained throughout the process and informed the distinctive symbols and political discourse applied by different nations.

Some deem the genuine national movements a parallel of earlier processes, which in the days of absolute monarchy yielded the nation-state. Nationalism, then, is the outcome of a twofold process: as the *ancien régime* undergoes changes, power is transferred from a single sovereign to the emerging people; in turn, the model of the nation-state gradually makes its way across countries and continents. This notion could shed light on a phenomenon typical of incipient nationalism: simulating the state it defies, the liberation movement usually applies the territorial principle prior to the ethnic one. Thus, the sixteenth-century Netherlands Wars were fought on behalf of all provinces, disregarding differences of religion and language between future Dutch, Flemings, and Walloons.[10] The territorial principle prevailed in the American Revolution as well, while the signs of a new American nationhood were still barely perceptible.[11] The same principle also served as the rallying cry for the wars of liberation in the Balkans, guided by the notion of a Greater Greece as the common homeland of Greeks, Albanians, Armenians, Walachians, and Turks.[12] In the Austro-Hungarian Empire, national awakening called for a revival of the "Ländergeist" (the spirit of the land), rather than of the people.[13] Joining forces, revolutionary exiles of diverse origins originated a wide array of federation programs for Southern Slavs, Hungarians, Poles, Rumanians, even Italians.[14] Of special interest in this context is the Czech national movement: based on the historical heritage of the Bohemian Crown, it adhered to the territorial principle even after gaining independence following World War I.[15] Before long, however, dissent broke out among the different bearers of the liberation banner, induced by conflicting national aspirations. National movements grew increasingly popular; the ethnic principle overrode the territorial one. An overlap then could be discerned between the divergent meanings of the terms "people" and "peoplehood": nationalism simultaneously meant both ethnic and popular. The right to self-determination has become the leading slogan of modern nationalism, especially since World War I. Critics have pointed out the concept's complexity; however, it was its simplistic appeal which lent it momentum. A universal formula in structure, the right to self-determination may suit any group whatsoever, once adopted by its spokesmen. Restrained by no political, economic, or moral qualifications, it is now sanctioned as a self-evident truth. Moreover, rather than constituting a people's right to determine their own destiny, it has become synonymous with claims to sovereignty over territory. The process thus comes full circle, with political sovereignty and territorial integrity supplementing the peoples' right of self-determination.[16]

Another point should be clarified here. The emergence of the territorial principle during the formative stage of modern nationalism fulfilled a typical need of innovative movements to fall back on a glorious past and ignore a shabby present. Greek nationalists sought to restore the glory of classical Hellenism, and the Magyars, that of the Crown of St. Stephen, to cite but two examples. Adoption of the splendid past required not only leaping beyond the period of decline, but also molding a new identity. At times the choice was between several traditions, identification either with the land and its inhabitants of yore, or with later settlers. The shaping of national identity was often attended by disputes between advocates of land versus people, or between alleged descendants of different strata within the population. In England, for example, some identified with the plebeian Saxons and others, with the Norman aristocracy; France was divided between those who favored Roman Gaul and those who sided, as it were, with the Frankish nobility.[17] Other examples abound.

In the West, such assumed pedigrees have contributed even before the advent of modern nationalism to the formation of myths on the birth of the nation. In the Middle East they grew apparent in countries which were once the cradles of civilization; the local national movements thus chose to trace their ancestry to their lands' ancient sons, not to humbled forebears. Turkey's "Young Turks" shared this approach. In Iran it was especially cultivated by the last Shah of the recent Pahlevi dynasty. A similar trend exists in Egypt and North Africa and it is rather prominent among Lebanon's Maronites.[18] The parallels in Palestine's Jewish Yishuv will be discussed below. In Russia, the trend may symbolize an orientation towards Asia and its dormant forces, rather than the identification with an indigenous culture. After the Revolution, the turning towards Asia also suggested a primeval anti-Western catharsis.[19] All these phenomena indicate a multi-faceted adherence to the land motif, as opposed to that of the people. Nonetheless, it is clear that the predominant trend in modern nationalism increasingly stresses the latter concept, in both its ethnic and popular-democratic connotations.

AUTONOMISM, TERRITORIALISM, AND PALESTINE

Turning to the Jews, one is faced with the contrast between a distinct collective consciousness and the inadequate conditions for the normal development of a national group. This discrepancy is even more conspicuous in regard to the role of the land in Jewish consciousness. A landless religious-ethnic community, the Jews nonetheless had territorial bonds with their ancient homeland, nourished by historical memories and messianic hopes. Thus, although reality was ruled by the ethnic principle, collective consciousness sustained the memory of the Land of Israel. To some extent, this territorial awareness tallied with the Jews' very existence, for the loosening of that awareness usually corresponded to the centrifugal trends in Jewish life. The Jews' ties to the Land of Israel gave symbolic expression to the idea of exile, and the sense of living as strangers in strange lands. This bond was even more decisive for Jewish distinctiveness than messianic faith. The latter could also be interpreted as a universalistic method of salvation, alleviating, among other things, the Jews' sense of alienation.[20]

Since the emancipation of the Jews, following the French Revolution, the interplay between the territorial principle and the ethnic and popular ones gave rise to new patterns in Jewish life. The rights Jews enjoyed as individuals inadvertently led to their self-determination as a group. Paradoxically, even those relegating Judaism to the confines of religion alone saw themselves as spokesmen of a community (and after all, Jewish religion itself is not restricted to the realm of the individual only). The participants in Napoleon's Great Sanhedrin in 1807, or the Reform Rabbis who convened in Germany between 1844 and 1846 to transform Judaism, were, to some extent, its representatives. Though they never invoked the right to self-determination, they did embody, to some degree, the popular principle.[21] This was true of those denying Jewish nationhood and, all the more so, of its advocates. In their efforts to extend the realm of equal rights from individuals to the collective, such personages as Moses Hess and Zvi Hirsch Kalischer could designate the emancipation as the herald of Jewish national revival.[22] They also drew on the popular principle, albeit predominantly on its ethnic aspect. With the emancipation, the territorial principle resurfaced momentarily. During Napoleon's Palestine campaign, a manifesto published in his name urged the Jews to come to inherit their patrimony. The apocryphal document cites their heritage rights, denied for thousands of years. Moreover, it speaks of renewing Jewish political existence "as a nation among the nations." Present-day scholars doubt the manifesto's authenticity. However, at the time, word of it spread rapidly in public acknowledgement of the Jews' right to Palestine.[23] Two different and not always compatible aspects of the territorial principle—political sovereignty and historical rights—were brought together in the manifesto. Its novelty lay not in the recognition of the Jewish link to Palestine, but in the retrieval of that link from the sphere of eschatology and its endowment with a down-to-earth, political dimension. The might and grandeur of Napoleon, a latter-day Cyrus, appeared to emanate onto the Jews. Inadvertently, Napoleon seemed to declare them a force that must be reckoned with among the nations. It is typical of the Jews' condition at the time that the granting and realization of their rights depended on the will of others. Only gradually would they engage in the implementation of their own rights.

The foregoing presentation of the territorial principle in Jewish nationalism suggests that it only applied to Palestine. However, initiatives did crop up to implement it elsewhere, as a provisional or permanent replacement or supplement to the Holy Land. Suggestions for solving the "Jewish Question" by gathering the Jews in a single territory are known since the eighteenth century.[24] Mordecai Manuel Noah's "Ararat" of 1825 was one such territorial plan, featuring elements of Jewish statehood.[25] It should be noted that initially, exponents of the territorial principle drew no clear distinction between the Land of Israel and other lands. Indeed, the same individuals sometimes endorsed Jewish settlement both in Palestine and elsewhere. Such was the attitude of the Am Olam movement in the 1880s. Another case in point is that of Charles Netter: having founded Mikveh Israel in 1870, Netter later cautioned against immigration to Palestine, and may even have influenced Baron Maurice Hirsch, who sponsored the Jewish colonization of Argentina.[26] Conversely, the now-forgotten Simeon Berman initially favored settling Jews on the land in his native Galicia and later in the United States; in 1870, he too turned to Palestine.[27] Nor was there a sufficiently clear distinction between the territorial settlement of Jews and a political solution to their question. Shifts in goal were often necessitated by circumstances, not by conscious, clear-cut choices. The territorial principle is therefore versatile. As people-based nationalism has both ethnic and popular components, the territorial principle likewise branches out to historical rights versus political sovereignty, and to Palestine versus other lands.

Alternatives which were realistic for other national movements were not applicable to Jewish nationalism. Even in their densely-populated centers Jews could not choose between claiming national autonomy and struggling for political independence. Under such circumstances, the mere shaping of a Jewish national consciousness was achievement enough to overshadow both the hardships of reality, and the conflicting trends within that consciousness. Cultural autonomy in Eastern Europe, overseas settlement projects, a return to Palestine—in the closing years of the nineteenth century, all these ideas intermingled in Jewish public opinion, alongside such modernization trends as productivization, social progress, religious reforms, a democratization of communal organization, and the revival of Jewish culture. The varying local conditions of different Jewish communities obscured the image of an all-embracing Jewish nationalism, but overall Jewish solidarity and the lack of distinct class polarization abetted its emergence. Traditional leaders usually opposed the apparently dangerous, novel ideas (thus joining, ironically, the assimilationist objectors to a particular Jewish entity). However, in their attempt to resist disintegration and the disruption of traditional society, some rabbis and orthodox leaders joined forces with the emerging Jewish national movement. Thus, despite their differences, the various agents of Jewish nationalism had more to conjoin them than set them apart. This held true at least until the watershed year of 1881, after which each trend had to contend for public support.[28]

As organized mass activities began, particularly after the 1881–1882 pogroms, the three trends in Jewish nationalism—autonomism, territorialism, and Palestinism—gradually crystallized as distinct options. Party ideology and structure did not always reflect these distinctions clearly; many other matters required resolution—from creeds and notions, through relations with local populations and governments, and issues of daily life, to differences of character and temperament. Nonetheless, public activity centered round these three foci until World War II.

Here one must note the relevance of the popular and ethnic principles to movements endorsing, to various degrees, Jewish autonomy in the diaspora (including the numerous supporters of the Zionist *Gegenwartsarbeit* (Present-Day Work). Despite their differences, all basically agreed that a struggle for Jewish rights must be maintained, tapping the community's latent forces. Some focused on practical activities, others expounded the vision of Jewish autonomy. However, all concentrated on mobilizing the Jewish public towards meeting its requirements as an ethnic-cultural group. Although the territorial principle did not submerge altogether, it rarely played a prominent role. The Bund applied the territorial principle to the confines of tsarist Russia (as compared with all-embracing versions of Jewish nationalism).[29] Dubnow spoke in his "Letters on Old and New Judaism" (1897–1907) of the historical rights of European Jews, who, antedating as they did the majority nations, helped maintain the continuity of civilization. But it was the right to self-determination and the popular principle, rather than this ostensible argument, which served as the real basis of Dubnow's theory.[30] The Zionist *Gegenwartsarbeit* indirectly drew upon the territorial principle as a vision for the future in Palestine.[31]

One would expect those dubbing themselves "territorialists" to pursue the realization of the territorial principle as such. However, this was not the case. The Territorialist movement was founded in 1905 in the aftermath of the Uganda Crisis, addressing itself to the Ugandan option. It later lost sight of this specific territorial goal, seeking new territories as a means to alleviate the plight of the people. Obviously, an arbitrary choice of a territory entails no claim to historical rights, but, rather, an aspiration to political sovereignty. Nevertheless, it must be said that some Zionists deemed themselves mere territorialists, who happened to have chosen Palestine as their territory. Usually socialists, they disdained romantic hue and religious import attached to the Land of Israel. However, they did appreciate the people's historical bond with the land, and relied on its powerful attraction for the still-traditional Jewish masses.[32] A line must be drawn, however, between such territorialists and some reformed ex-territorialists. The former include Ber Borochov and Shlomo Kaplansky, the latter, young Berl Katznelson and Ben-Zion Dinur, who would later become arch proponents of Eretz Israel. In turn, these people must be distinguished from certain territorialists who seceded from the Zionist movement, later to return, such as Nachman Syrkin or Jacob Leszczynski. Now that this entire trend has declined into oblivion, it is hard to gauge its indirect impact on Zionism.[33] Indeed, the ties between territorialism and Zionism warrant exploration, as do those between autonomism and Zionism. For the purpose of this presentation, suffice it to say that all three attempted to resolve the *Judennot* (Jewish plight) swiftly, by means of a mass movement, i.e., by resorting to the popular principle which implied the right to self-determination.

In this context, Sejmism should be briefly mentioned as well. A hybrid between autonomism and territorialism, it hoped to establish a Jewish parliament in Eastern Europe, to determine, among other issues, the fate of the territorial solution.[34] Sejmism thus exemplifies a dynamic combination of several ostensibly contradictory principles guiding the Jewish national movement.

THE BOND WITH THE LAND OF ISRAEL

Even within Zionism, the role played by the Land of Israel underwent considerable changes. Herzl and Pinsker, for example, revised their initial stances, eventually accepting the general notion that Palestine was essential for Zionism.[35] The Land of Israel steadily moved to center stage, the territorial principle increasingly overriding the ethnic and the popular. Although the principle was not always applied in a strictly pure form, as that preached later by the group known as the Canaanites, its predominance nonetheless marked the beginning of a new phase in Zionism. Yet another distinction emerged almost simultaneously, between supporters of historical rights and of political sovereignty.

The debate over the role of Palestine harks back to the early 1880s, in the days of Hibbat Zion (The Lovers of Zion). Moses Leib Lilienblum took his first steps as a Jewish nationalist believing that Palestine should be bought from the Turks and that some sort of Jewish government be established there. He quickly realized, however, that "The crux is not the government, but historical citizenship." Invoking the Jews' historical right, he proclaimed it still valid.[36] Lilienblum thus clung to a notion of historical rights, implicitly forgoing political demands. From this point, he focused on practical work in Palestine, aiming to gain tangible hold on the land through Jewish colonization.

Herzl, by contrast, was an exponent of political sovereignty, making only fleeting reference to historical rights. In 1898, on the eve of Kaiser Wilhelm II's visit to Palestine, Herzl alluded to the role that Zionism could play as a European bridgehead to the Orient. In a speech at the Second Zionist Congress, however, he deliberately minimized Zionism's aspirations to political standing, evoking, instead, the historical rights to land: "If there be any claims to any stretch of land at all, all believers in the Bible must acknowledge the rights of the Jews".[37] In other words, historical rights are usually invoked in lieu of political sovereignty.

The same is true of Ahad Ha-Am, who addressed the issue while debating his friend Dubnow's position on Jewish national rights in the diaspora. Denying the Jews' rights in Europe, Ahad Ha-Am designated Palestine as "a land to which our historical claim is undisputed."[38] Disdaining Herzl's quest for a Charter, he cited historical rights not in order to persuade the world, but to enhance the bond between the Jews and their land.

In 1903, when Britain offered Zionists a territory for Jewish colonization in East Africa, Zionism was put to the test. The opportunity for Jewish independence outside Palestine lured the advocates of political sovereignty, as well as those who hoped to swiftly remedy thereby the plight of the Jewish masses. The extraordinary temptation also posed a challenge for the practical and spiritual Zionists, inclined though they were toward the "Nay Sayers." Ahad Ha-Am once cautioned: "A land destroyed . . . may be rebuilt; but a people destroyed, who shall redeem it?"[39] Drawing as he did on the ethnic, not the popular principle, Ahad Ha-Am could ignore the immediate needs and the will of the masses in favor of the historical link to Palestine. Lilienblum, by contrast, was compelled to choose between the popular and territorial principle. He thus designed a construct evoking the right of future generations to participate in the decision-making process. Assured as he was of Palestine's preferability in the long run, he found it in his heart to reject the popular principle.[40]

The conflicting demands for sovereignty and the bond with Palestine would not long remain foremost on Zionism's agenda. During Herzl's lifetime, the political aspect enjoyed precedence; however, it slowly gave way to practical work in Palestine and *Gegenwartsarbeit* in the diaspora. Meanwhile, the Jewish colonization of Palestine which began in the 1880s was gradually influencing the Zionist movement abroad. New attitudes came to the fore, one, regarding relations with the Arabs, another, the relations with the Jews in the diaspora. Life in Palestine naturally bred in the newly arrived Zionists a need to adjust to the local scene and the inhabitants, and in turn, a growing distancing from the lands left behind. A strenuous process, striking roots did not always inspire the immigrants with affection for the land and its people. But the protracted stay in the orient induced a change in priorities. Relations with the Arabs rose in importance. So did the Yishuv itself, increasingly perceived as the core of Zionist fulfilment, and of decisive value to the entire Jewish people. In the twentieth century, a new Hebraic identity arose in Palestine. Although it was molded with the purpose of ultimately redeeming the Jewish people as a whole, this identity found expression mainly through territorial realization.

Transformation began on a personal level, through the day-to-day adaptation to the unfamiliar environment and the hardships of an altogether new lifestyle. Nothing the immigrants encountered in Palestine bore any resemblance to what they had left behind. They changed language, occupations, at times even their names. So radical was the change, it yielded a new identity. In Palestine a person was, as it were, reborn—a feeling often described by many early immigrants.[41] Reality's strangeness was countered by conceptual or spiritual affinity to the land, which tempered the tortuous phase of settling in. The Palestine of fantasy often outshone that of daily reality, transfiguring its newborn sons and daughters, as it were, into ancient Hebrews. The renowned Israeli writer S. J. Agnon recalled this notion: Titus, he declared, had destroyed Jerusalem and the Jews were exiled. Due to this historical catastrophe, he, Agnon, was born in the diaspora. Yet he has always pictured himself as having been born in Jerusalem.[42]

A preexistent link to the land distinguished Jewish immigrants to Palestine from immigrants elsewhere. Yet from the outset, this bond was lopsided: Jews felt they belonged to the land, but it did not belong to them. With time, a sense of ownership developed, albeit in contrast to external reality. Impregnating Zionist consciousness, it influenced practical and spiritual Zionism and to a lesser degree, political Zionism as well. When did the sense of ownership begin to take root? It stands to reason that it postdated the Uganda Crisis, for at the time many in the Palestinian Yishuv joined the "Yea Sayers," who would forfeit the Land of Israel. The Uganda lesson could well have played a part in generating the new attitude. Vivid as it was in the minds of the Second Aliyah immigrants, who arrived in the aftermath of that crisis, it also fortified the advocates of colonization in Palestine among Zionists worldwide.[43] Among the people of the Second Aliyah, the feeling of ownership was entirely conscious. Thus, on the eve of World War I, Palestine Jewry witnessed the emergence of a dynamic social force, aimed at realizing the historical rights of Jews to the land. Unlike advocates of political Zionism, members of the Second Aliyah staked their claim on achievement through labor, without any preconditions. Having established—in the teeth of enormous hardships—a groundwork for a new Jewish Palestine based on labor, these people could well believe in the eventual success of their undertaking.[44]

Then came the war. In its wake, expectations arose for a postwar world which would prove far more propitious to the implementation of Zionist ideals. There were concurrent hopes that Palestine would be made a Jewish National Home, and Jews in the newly founded European states would enjoy minority rights grounded in a binding international agreement. The Zionist movement, subscribing now to a synthesis between its various strands, integrated in its program both a realization of the territorial principle in Palestine, and an implementation of the right to self-determination in the diaspora. However, Zionist leaders disagreed as to the order of priorities.[45] Chaim Weizmann, for one, engaged in hectic diplomatic efforts in London, enlisting the aid of the venerated Ahad Ha-Am. The latter meanwhile had tempered his objection to political Zionism, provided that the British give explicit expression to Jewish historical rights to Palestine.[46] Leo Motzkin, Weizmann's colleague in the Democratic Faction where both opposed Herzl's diplomacy, headed the efforts to secure Jewish minority rights in Europe. The pioneers in Palestine, by contrast, gave precedence to consolidating the power of the Yishuv. Indeed, new prospects now existed in Palestine—a more tolerant regime, an inflow of capital for development, and renewed Jewish immigration.

A distinction should be drawn at this point between the Second Aliyah pioneers and the second generation of settlers of older Jewish colonies. Both groups were marked by a heroic ethos, generated by similar grappling with the challenges of the Orient. Both at times attempted to emulate local Arab customs and bravado. Both sought Jewish hegemony in Palestine. Antagonism between the colonists and pioneers arose over the struggle instigated by the latter group to enforce the exclusiveness of Jewish labor. It was also abetted by the farmers' aristocratic mannerisms and the workers' revolutionary airs. One particular bone of contention derived from the respective attitudes towards Jewish immigration to Palestine. The pioneers charged the colonists with trying to maintain a plantation economy, thereby preempting Jewish labor, hence Jewish immigration as well.[47] Perhaps it was the feeling of superiority towards the newcomers which was to blame. Of course, the pioneers themselves were not innocent of condescension towards diaspora Jews and their "exile mentality."[48] However, the pioneers did believe in utilizing the power of Jewish immigration to actively transfigure Palestine both nationally and socially. Deeming themselves the cornerstone of a new society, Palestine's labor parties expected the newly arrived immigrants to participate in the realization of their vision. Imbued as they were with a socialist-revolutionary ideology or Russian populist notions, the pioneers were reluctant to receive Palestine, as it were, from the hands of Great Britain. Instead, they sought to recruit the Jewish people and activate spontaneous forces, thus combining both the popular and territorial principles.[49] Even so, those engaged in the building of Palestine scarcely took interest in the struggle for Jewish minority rights in Europe, headed though it was by Zionists and Zionist-socialists.

As World War I drew to a close, Zionists were still hopeful they could establish the National Home without intense Arab opposition. According to a theory prevalent at the time, the native *fellahs* were actually descendants of the ancient Hebrews, forcibly converted to Islam by Muslim conquerors.[50] Some Jewish leaders toyed with the idea that they could assimilate the Arabs, or even proselytize them. Drawing away from the diaspora and striking roots in the land, Jews in Palestine sought a new Hebraic identity. The wish to adopt the land's non-Jewish population marked yet another aspect of this quest: a powerful desire for the continuous—and retroactive—possession of Palestine throughout the ages. To this end, it was necessary to incorporate the history of the land in its entirety, including that of its non-Jewish inhabitants.

The change of values also found reflection in a changed terminology: "Eretz Israelis" or "Hebrews" were now the preferred terms, rather than "Jews."[51] These became the accepted designations of the members of the new Yishuv, which distinguished them from other Jews in Palestine or abroad. The people of the Yishuv were intent on reestablishing a Hebrew nation in Palestine, whose ancient roots ran deep; the rent between land and nation would finally be mended. Such sentiments implied in the long run a possible severance from Jewry at large, and a relinquishment of Jewish identity in favor of one dubbed "Hebrew," "Semite," and above all, "Canaanite."[52]

Thus, the territorial principle seemed to reign triumphant. But at this point the Arabs began invoking the popular principle to claim their own right of self-determination. In all international debates concerning Palestine—beginning with the King-Crane report in 1919—the Arabs are cited as demanding the right of self-determination and the Jews, as invoking the "historical connection." (Incidentally, this term first entered the language of international law upon the approval of the British Mandate on Palestine by the League of Nations in 1922.)[53]

This contraposition places the Arab demand well within the presently accepted international discourse. Zionism, by contrast, is viewed as anomalous from the perspective of modern nationalism. Paradoxically, in the days the territorial principle bore great significance in nationalism at large, Jews tended towards the popular, leaving the choice of national identity to the individual. This was the position taken by Jewish liberal circles, who feared that ethnic nationalism was discriminatory against Jews. It was also expounded by Herzl and early Zionists, who appealed to such Jews as could not or would not assimilate.[54] Conversely, in the 1937 partition debate, the Arabs cited the territorial principle, echoing, in reverse, some Jewish objections to the partition proposal.[55] On the eve of the 1948 partition, Zionism once again had recourse to the ethnic principle, albeit by way of negation: there was no longer a place for Jews in Holocaust Europe. The popular principle was also invoked, with survivors of the Holocaust insisting on Palestine as their sole destination.[56]

After the Six-Day War the issue reemerged more forcibly in the debate over the historical rights of the Jews to all parts of Palestine. The country's territorial integrity won the support of a varied coalition:

1. Parts of the Kibbutz movement, heirs to practical Zionism, who had rejected the Partition Plan in 1947 and were inclined to question the value of sovereignty or statehood.

2. Followers of political Zionism, of the pro-sovereignty schools of Herzl, Nordau, and Jabotinsky.
3. Remnants of the "Canaanites," advocates of the pure territorial principle.
4. Gush Emunim, guided by the great Rabbi Kook's mystical territorialism, rather than by the pragmatic Rabbi Reines, who had maintained during the Uganda Crisis that people outweighed land. We thus seem to have come full circle from the Uganda Crisis to the present day.

Twin concepts concerning land or people recur throughout this essay: the territorial principle, branching out to historical rights and political sovereignty, in Palestine and elsewhere, as opposed to the popular principle, based on the right of self-determination, and/or ethnic nationalism. Only rarely does one factor gain precedence within Zionism to the exclusion of others. However, the Palestine-oriented territorial principle usually predominates; historical right likewise outweighs the right of self-determination. Thus Zionism often finds itself in a unique position in comparison with the general course of modern nationalism.

NOTES

1. E. Ben Yehuda, *Maamarim shonim al dvar hazaat mizrah Africa* (Warsaw, 1905), p. 9; Michael Heymann, ed., *The Uganda Controversy*, vol. 2 (Jerusalem, 1977), p. 180.
2. W. D. Davies, *The Territorial Dimension of Judaism* (Berkeley, 1982), p. xvii.
3. Anthony D. Smith, *The Ethnic Revival* (Cambridge, 1981), p. 18; cf. Benedict Anderson, *Imagined Communities* (London, 1983); Eric J. Hobsbawm, *Nations and Nationalism Since 1780* (Cambridge, 1990).
4. T. R. Glover, *The Ancient World* (London, 1953), pp. 258–59.
5. See "Citizens" in William Bridgewater and Seymour Kurtz, eds., *The Columbia Encyclopedia* (New York and London, 1963), p. 422.
6. Karl F. Werner, *Structures politiques du monde franc* (London, 1979), pp. 294, 303.
7. Odette Voilliard *et al.*, eds., *Documents d'histoire contemporaine*, vol. 1 (Paris, 1964), pp. 57, 60.
8. John Plamenatz, "Two Types of Nationalism," in Eugene Kamenka, ed., *Nationalism: The Nature and Evolution of an Idea* (London, 1976), pp. 24ff.
9. Anthony D. Smith, *Theories of Nationalism* (London, 1983), p. 217.
10. Eugen Lemberg, *Wege und Wandlungen des Nationalbewusstseins* (Münster, 1934), p. 10; Pieter Geyl, *Debates with Historians* (London and Glasgow, 1962), p. 214.
11. Boyd C. Shafer, *Faces of Nationalism* (New York and London, 1974), pp. 57, 142; Brane Crinton, *The Anatomy of Revolution* (New York, 1965), p. 22.
12. Hans Kohn, *The Idea of Nationalism* (Toronto, 1969), p. 538.
13. Oscar Jászi, *The Dissolution of the Habsburg Monarchy* (Chicago and London, 1964), p. 89.
14. Dimitrije Djordevic and Stephen Fischer-Galati, *The Balkan Revolutionary Tradition* (New York, 1981), p. 125.

15. Robin Oackey, *Eastern Europe 1740–1980* (London, 1982), pp. 80, 160; compare this, however, to the recent breakup of post-Communist Czechoslovakia.

16. Alfred Cobban, *The Nation State and National Self-Determination* (London and Glasgow, 1969), pp. 148–49; Elie Kedourie, *Nationalism* (London, 1978), pp. 138–39; Ingrid Delupis, *International Law and the Independent State* (Epping, Essex, 1974), p. 227.

17. Perez Zagorin, *A History of Political Thought in the English Revolution* (London, 1954), pp. 50–51; Leon Poliakov, *Le Mythe aryen* (Paris, 1971), pp. 36–41.

18. Bernard Lewis, *History—Remembered, Recovered, Invented* (Princeton, 1975), pp. 36–40.

19. Hans Kohn, *Pan-Slavism, Its History and Ideology* (New York, 1960), pp. 226–27, 263.

20. Ben-Zion Dinur, *Be-mifneh ha-dorot* (Jerusalem, 1955), pp. 324–25.

21. Georges Wormser, *Français Israélites* (Paris, 1963), p. 28; Ismar Schorsch, "The Emergence of the Modern Rabbinate," in Werner E. Mosse, Arnold Paucker, and Reinhard Ruerup, eds., *Revolution and Evolution: 1848 in German-Jewish History* (Tübingen, 1981), p. 225.

22. Shmuel Ettinger, "Yihudah shel ha-tnuah ha-leumit ha-yehudit," in Ben-Zion Yehoshua and Aharon Kedar, eds., *Ideologyah u-mediniyut zionit* (Jerusalem, 1978), p. 16; Jacob Katz, *Leumiyut yehudit* (Jerusalem, 1979), p. 10.

23. Franz Kobler, *Napoleon and the Jews* (Jerusalem, 1975), pp. 55–57, 84–87; Simon Schwarzfuchs, *Napoleon, the Jews, and the Sanhedrin* (London and Boston, 1979), pp. 24–27.

24. Meir Vereté, "Hazaot polaniot le-pitron teritoryali shel 'sheelat ha-yehudim'," *Zion*, vol. 6, no. 4 (June–July, 1941), p. 203.

25. Paul R. Mendes-Flohr and Jehuda Reinharz, eds., *The Jew in the Modern World* (New York and Oxford, 1980), pp. 364–66.

26. Hasia Turtel, *"Tenuat 'Am Olam',"* *He-Avar*, no. 10 (April–May 1963), pp. 132–33; Andre Chouraqui, *L'Alliance Israélite Universelle* (Paris, 1965), p. 48; Kurt Grunwald, *Turkenhirsch* (Jerusalem, 1966), p. 77.

27. Getzl Kressel, " 'Masot Shimon': Ha-sefer u-mehabro," *Cathedra* 14 (January 1980), pp. 184–87.

28. Jonathan Frankel, *Prophecy and Politics* (Cambridge and New York, 1981), p. 5.

29. Frankel, *Prophecy and Politics*, pp. 220–21.

30. Simon Dubnow, *Nationalism and History*, ed. Koppel S. Pinson (New York, 1970), p. 106.

31. Shmuel Almog, *Zionism and History* (New York and Jerusalem, 1987), p. 236.

32. Nahum Nir-Rafalkes, *Ershte yorn* (Tel Aviv, 1960), pp. 125–27.

33. *Kitvei Berl Katznelson*, vol. 11 (Tel Aviv, 1949), pp. 84–85.

34. Abraham Greenbaum, "Mifleget ha-Sejmistim—Vozrozhdenie," *Measef Givat-Haviva*, no. 6 (1974), pp. 82–90.

35. Ben Halpern, *The Idea of the Jewish State* (Cambridge, Mass., 1969), pp. 95, 128.

36. Shlomo Breiman, ed., *Igrot M. L. Lilienblum le-J. L. Gordon* (Jerusalem, 1968), pp. 30–31.

37. Theodor Herzl, "Rede am 2ten Zionisten Congress," *Die Welt* (2.9.1898), p. 6.

38. *Kol kitvei Ahad Ha-Am* (Jerusalem and Tel Aviv, 1961), p. 153.

39. *Ibid.*, p. 30.

40. M. L. Lilienblum, *"Teshuvah la-shoel,"* in *Mivhar ktavim*, ed. Shlomo Breiman (Jerusalem, 1968), p. 209.

41. Avraham Yaari, *Zikhronot Eretz Israel*, part 1 (Jerusalem, 1947), pp. 366, 483; *Igrot Eretz Israel* (Givatayim, 1971), p. 478; Erik H. Erikson, *Dimensions of a New Identity* (New York, 1974), pp. 76–77.

42. Samuel Joseph Agnon, *Me-azmi el azmi* (Tel Aviv, 1976), p. 85.
43. Shlomo Zemach, *Shanah rishonah* (Tel Aviv, 1965), pp. 128–38.
44. Anita Shapira, *Berl*, part 1 (Tel Aviv, 1980), pp. 121–25.
45. Salo W. Baron, *Modern Nationalism and Religion* (New York and Philadelphia, 1960), p. 233.
46. Cf. Halpern, *The Idea of the Jewish State*, p. 297.
47. E.g. Avshalom Feinberg, *Ktavim u-mikhtavim*, ed. Aharon Amir (Jerusalem, 1975), pp. 170–74 (a refutation of the charge).
48. See Yehezkel Kaufmann, *Be-hevlei ha-zman* (Tel Aviv, 1936), pp. 265–66.
49. A. D. Gordon, *Ha-umah ve-ha-avodah* (Jerusalem, 1952), p. 394; Rachel Yanait, "Min he-amal el ha-avodah," in *Yalkut ha-ahdut* (Tel Aviv, 1962), p. 558.
50. E.g. David Ben-Gurion and Izhak Ben-Zvi, *Eretz Israel in the Past and in the Present*, eds. M. Eliav and Y. Ben Arieh (Jerusalem, 1979), pp. 195–202 (translated from Yiddish into Hebrew).
51. Yizhak Avineri, *Yad ha-lashon* (Tel Aviv, 1964), p. 225.
52. Baruch Kurzweil, *Sifrutenu ha-hadashah—Hemshekh o mahapekhah?*, 3rd ed. (Jerusalem and Tel Aviv, 1971), pp. 270–73.
53. Nathan Feinberg, *Studies in International Law* (Jerusalem, 1979), pp. 274–78.
54. Moritz Lazarus, *Was heisst national?* (Berlin, 1880); Theodor Herzl, *Tagebücher* (1923), p. 268.
55. *Palestine,* ESCO Foundation for Palestine, vol. 1 (New Haven, 1947), p. 860.
56. Martin Gilbert, *Exile and Return* (Tel Aviv, 1978), p. 303.

3.

The First Aliyah: Ideological Roots and Practical Accomplishments

Shmuel Ettinger and Israel Bartal

The First Aliyah (1881–1904) was unlucky. Unlike succeeding waves of immigration, it produced no eminent personalities or highly influential institutions to leave their mark on the development of the Jewish community in Palestine and on national history. Recently historians have even questioned its greatest glory, its claim to being the pioneer of Zionist immigrations. The following arguments are often made: there were precursors of Zionism who advocated the revival of the nation in its land and who preceded the First Aliyah by decades;[1] activities on behalf of the settlement of the land of Israel had a long history and included many highly active institutions.[2] It has also been claimed that the aspiration to seek 'productive' sources of livelihood, including manual labor, was also be found in the Jewish population in Palestine long before the beginning of the 1880s.[3] In what way, therefore, can it be said that the First Aliyah was distinctive, except for the idea of establishing "model settlements" that would serve as an example to masses of Jews and thus start "the revival of the people of Israel on the land of their fathers"? In fact, even that claim is denied by those who see the beginning of Jewish agricultural settlement in the establishment of Mikve Israel by the Alliance Israélite Universelle in 1870, or in the establishment of Petah Tikva in 1878.

As for the achievements of the First Aliyah, it is true that during a quarter of a century some thirty thousand immigrants were added to the Jewish population of Palestine, and that thousands of them were

Reprinted by permission of Yad Izhak Ben-Zvi from *Jerusalem Cathedra* 2 (1982): 197–227.

undoubtedly motivated by a nationalist spirit. That is a significant number in comparison with the immigration in previous periods, although it is doubtful whether this constitutes the distinctive sign of a new era in the history of the Jewish community in Palestine. Of greater significance were the efforts at agricultural settlement. During the years of the First Aliyah some twenty settlements were established with a population of about 5,000.[4] However, at the very same time several agricultural settlements were established in Argentina by Baron de Hirsch and the Jewish Colonization Association (ICA). These settlements had about twice as many people as the ones in Palestine, and many saw them as future competitors. Moreover, a large part of the agricultural work in the Jewish settlements in Palestine, especially in those of Judea, was done by Arab laborers, although even then warning cries were heard that such a situation would distort the character of the entire effort for national rebirth.[5]

At the same time, other traits which had characterized the efforts at national renewal and made it distinctive began to be blurred and lose their glory. The enthusiasm and the impetus provided by Herzl and his leadership, the hopes of receiving recognition and support from the Turkish government, and the clear definition of the political goals of Zionism—all these gave way to feelings of discouragement and impotence. Shlomo Zemah, a pioneer of the Second Aliyah, reported that he found very few real believers in the national ideal among the Jewish colonists. On the contrary, there were many supporters of the Uganda program to establish a Jewish territory in Africa, and some of them left the country during those years, moving to the United States or Australia.

Hebrew had been revived and become the language of daily speech among wide circles of the Jews living in Palestine. Educational institutions had been founded where the language of instruction was Hebrew, and the Union of Hebrew Teachers had been formed. (A similar process also began among groups of Jews in Eastern Europe.) Nevertheless, under the influence of Baron de Rothschild's bureaucracy, and because of the position of the Alliance Israélite Universelle, French was considered the language of the social élite, and some children of settlers travelled to Paris for their education. The idea of a Jewish university in Jerusalem was then a distant dream.

Most important, the hope that agricultural settlement would give rise to a new generation of emancipated Jews, who would support themselves by manual labor and provide an example for others, did not bear fruit. The success of the settlements was largely attributable to the massive support of the 'well known philanthropist' (Baron de Roth-schild) and to ICA, a philanthropic institution. Like large segments of the Ashkenazi Old Yishuv, the settlements and the settlers of the First Aliyah were dependent upon the financial support and the initiatives of people and institutions abroad.

Thus the final years of the First Aliyah were not distinguished by expressions of strength, but rather by a sense of weakness and failure, or by the complete rejection of the ideas that had infused the early settlers. That was also the observation of the first arrivals of the Second Aliyah, who were determined to save the entire settlement enterprise by their pioneering spirit and readiness for self-sacrifice. It would seem, however, that both groups lacked the proper perspective from which to examine the achievements and failures of the First Aliyah and its place in the history of Zionist Jewish settlement.

CHANGES IN THE ATTACHMENT TO THE HOLY LAND

Two ideological underpinnings central to modern Jewish history were at the basis of the First Aliyah: Jewish nationalism, a product of the nine-teenth century, and historical ties to the land of Israel, a value inherited from Jewish tradition. One certainly ought to distinguish between these two elements, although the historical literature usually treats them as identical.[6] In fact, the complex character of modern Jewish nationalism and the tangled network of ties between Jews and the land of Israel during the nineteenth century require that a distinction be made. Jewish nationalism did not necessarily grow out of the connection between the Jews and the land of Israel; in turn, expressions of the Jewish bond with that land—both spiritual and pragmatic—retained their traditional character throughout the nineteenth century and generally did not im-pinge upon the growth of modern Jewish nationalism. In fact, at the turn of the nineteenth century, consciousness of the link with the land of Israel was attenuated in many Jewish circles, and it was seen as standing in contradiction to the growing tendency to merge with the surrounding society. The roots of the Jewish national movement actually reach deeply into the European experience and the conceptual world of the Europe-ans; the land of Israel was grafted onto it, sometimes through the intermediary of sources and concepts that were largely foreign to the traditional Jewish world. It is even possible to say that the newly in-creased attachment to the land of Israel among Jews who were merging into their surrounding societies was impelled to no small extent by the increase of its importance for Europeans.[7] In contrast, the traditional link with the land of Israel which still existed in many circles and was nourished in part by hopes for redemption, was entirely devoid of any European influence.

This incongruity between the two elements of the consciousness of nineteenth-century European Jews derives principally from the dissimilar development of Jewish communities. Whereas many of the Jews of Western and Central Europe belonged to the second or third generation of French or German acculturation, the position of those who were steeped in the world of traditional society was still strong, and they guarded themselves assiduously against outside influence. In Eastern Europe, on the other hand, most Jews belonged to the traditional society. One of the distinctive traits of the First Aliyah lies in the fact that those conflicting elements were combined within it on the ideological and practical level. The modern element that tended to merge into the non-Jewish surroundings, and the traditional element that adopted modern principles while maintaining its basic beliefs, converged in a movement whose goal was to establish permanent settlements in the land of Israel.

There does not seem to be any direct connection between the events of the first half of the nineteenth century and the period of the First Aliyah. However there is a typological and ideological link between the first signs of an awakening of modern national consciousness among the Jews in the 1830s and 1840s, and the modern nationalist urge to settle Palestine in the 1880s. In both cases, the land of Israel takes on significance as a component of the Jewish national consciousness that was developing in Europe; it was the territory where the distinctive character of the Jewish group could be completely realized in its historic homeland. Moreover, the nationalist dream also afforded an opportunity to put into action the universalistic social vision based upon both the ideas of the Enlightenment and the enlightened image of the traditional society.

Nineteenth-century Palestine was no longer the 'terra sancta' of previous centuries. In European political thought, it was seen against the background of political change in the region, and of the designs of the great powers with regard to the future of the territories controlled by the Ottoman Empire. The lively political discussion of the 'Oriental question' during the conquest of Syria and Palestine by Muhammad Ali was combined with a religious reawakening whose influence was particularly visible in English society. Palestine was visited by English, German,

French, and American pilgrims and researchers who circulated varied and detailed information in Europe. That information also reached Jewish readers who were aware of what was happening in Western and Central Europe.[8] Romantic currents in literature and art as well as historical and archaeological research gave that material an exotic charm and strengthened certain images that were likely to bring out the connection between the Jewish people and its land: the glorious past that contrasts with the miserable present, and the oriental Jews who were seen as ancient tribes uncorrupted by Europeans (unlike the Jews of Poland and Germany). Trends in Protestantism, particularly the millennarists, combined with romantic elements to create a favorable attitude towards the Jewish past of Palestine and the possibility of renewed Jewish settlement there. It was not seen in its theological context alone, but rather in that optimistic spirit which characterized the period marked by the achievements of European man and by Jewish emancipation. The readiness of prominent representatives of some European nations to further the return of the Jewish people to its land would appear to be one of the achievements of Jewish nationalism during the nineteenth century.

The political situation of Palestine was also interpreted by many Jews from a European-Christian political and ideological perspective. A striking parallel exists between the millennarian claim that the land of Israel has been barren since the exile of the Jews, and the traditional Jewish claim that the land will only bear fruits for them.[9] On the other hand, both claims are compatible with the view held by European intellectuals of the period that the countries of the East can only be saved by adopting the European pattern of development and progress. The educational and philanthropic activities of English, French, and German organizations in Palestine which, beginning in the 1840s, created an infrastructure for the modernization of the urban settlements, was seen both as an example of possible assistance for Jewish settlement as well as a competitive factor.[10] Nevertheless, Jewish statements in those years about the link between the Jews and Palestine are full of optimism about the attitude of the powers of Western and Central Europe with regard to possible Jewish settlement. Protection by European powers and the aid of the foreign consulates were viewed as guaranteeing the existence of the Jewish population of European extraction and as providing strong support for the establishment of new Jewish institutions and enterprises.[11] Indeed, protection by Europe consuls provided the basis for the expansion of the Jewish population beyond the urban boundaries, and the European settlement ventures (especially the German ones) were a fine example of the possibilities latent in agriculture, to be studied and imitated. On the eve of the First Aliyah, Palestine appeared to many Jews in a double guise, inspired both by Jewish tradition and by European religious and political influences.

One must note, however, that Jewish group consciousness and its traditional connection with the national homeland crystallized during the first half of the nineteenth century against a social and cultural background different from that of the 1870s and 1880s. During the 1830s and 1840s hopes for emancipation and for merging into non-Jewish society still occupied a central place in the consciousness of growing segments of the Jewish people. Of course one must also see as a source of the trend toward particularistic national consciousness the sense of discomfort with the demand for total assimilation into the surrounding cultures, whose universalistic character had already been placed in doubt by the romantic currents and the nationalist movements of the nineteenth century. At first, Jewish nationalism displayed an essentially 'enlightened' tendency: the Jews in the land of Israel, the heart of the traditional Jewish society, must be bettered through modern education and 'productive' occupations. Emancipation provided more possibilities in that direction, and led to the demand to merge Jewish philanthropic activity in Palestine with the political action of the European powers.

In contrast, the nationalism of the 1870s and 1880s is stamped with the conspicuous seal of disbelief about any possibility of the Jews merging with their non-Jewish environment. The experience of the pogroms in southern Russia fed the feeling of despair and alienation among some East-European Jewish intellectuals who had turned toward nationalism in their public activities during the 1860s and 1870s. Nonetheless, in the utopian dream of establishing a renewed Jewish society in the land of Israel it is possible to discern, despite differences in shading, clear traces of an optimistic heritage which was typical of the generations of the enlightened believers in progress. The immigrants of the 1880s came from a background of severe crisis and disappointment with the Russian state, but at the same time they retained some of the characteristics and ways of action of the 1840s and 1860s. Acceptance of the values of European society combined with a withdrawal from the setting that produced them and rejection of many of its important characteristics were decisive factors in the fashioning of the settlements of the First Aliyah. Thus the traditional element that was primary in the social make-up of the immigrants was viewed with appreciation by the 'enlightened' groups who were influential among the leaders of the Hibbat Zion (Love of Zion) movement. In the spirit of Enlightenment, radical criticism of traditional society and its flaws was moderated and transformed into a belief in social regeneration according to Western-European concepts. The land of Israel was no longer simply the 'land of our fathers' but a place to carry out profound changes in the Jewish society, and a framework for social experimentation. The reciprocal action of conservation and innovation, traditional society and a society that had undergone acculturation, hopes for emancipation and feeling of rejection and alienation—all of these found conspicuous expression in three periods during which contacts were made between an awakening of modern national consciousness and the traditional bond with the land of Israel: the 1840s, the 1860s, and the beginning of the 1880s.

EARLY NATIONALIST TRENDS: THE 1830S AND 1840S

Palestine appears as a focus for Jewish settlement programs already at the end of the 1830s. The great millennarian awakening within several circles, especially in England, and the hopes for a significant worldwide change around 1840, were joined to the political events bound up with the 'Oriental question.'[12] Echos of the religious awakening and the events of the period were absorbed by both traditional Jewish society and those circles in Western and Central European Jewry which had already merged to a significant extent into the culture of the surrounding societies.

The increase of public interest in Palestine took place simultaneously with an event that roused Jewish public opinion in Europe: the Damascus Affair (Blood Libel). Although Jewish activity was concentrated mainly on the struggle for acceptance by the non-Jews and for legal equality, the Damascus Affair strengthened awareness of the need to organize for an effort by the Jews themselves especially for the purpose of accelerating the process of social acceptance and removing obstacles in the path of full emancipation. In an almost paradoxical manner, the Jewish organizations which began to appear after the Damascus Blood Libel had a decidedly emancipatory character: the Jewish press in European languages advocated the acceptance of the values of the surrounding society; programs were formulated for the 'improvement' of traditional Jewish society in Eastern Europe and the Near East, and for bringing them under the influence of German or French culture, etc. In the minds of many traditional Jews these were seen as manifestations of the continuity of Jewish values, as mutual aid which was an extension of the traditional concern for *klal yisrael* (the entire Jewish people). The philanthropic activities of Sir Moses Montefiore for the benefit of the Jews of Palestine were similarly interpreted as expressing traditional Jewish concepts, as were his efforts on behalf of the Jews of Russia and Morocco in later years. Montefiore's intervention in the Damascus Affair alongside other Western European Jewish dignitaries was seen by Rabbi Yehuda Alkalay as a manifestation of the growing influence of Jewish notables in the period of Emancipation.[13] Thus, the integration of the Jewish elite in the surrounding society, and its identification with the political aims of the European powers in the East, created the basis for a positive attitude toward plans of Jewish settlement in Palestine, and even for the creation of a political framework of their own for the Jews.

In the 1840s that development had already given rise to the first harbingers of renewed mutual ties among the various parts of the Jewish people, and it paved the way for a reciprocal communication of values and ways of thought. With the strengthening of the influence of Romanticism and the growth of the *Wissenschaft des Judentums,* traditional Jewish society gained importance even among some members of the Jewish intelligentsia in France and Germany. The majority of the Jewish people who were faithful to the tradition no longer appeared to them as an object of 'improvement' alone, according to the formulation of the 'enlightened' Jews of the eighteenth century, but as a group incorporating authentic values. There is a basis for the assumption that the image of the Jewish people and the land of Israel as expressed in the Romantic literature of the first half of the nineteenth century influenced, as was mentioned above, the consciousness of the enlightened European Jew, who might well have been influenced too by the power of the millennarian religious ferment.

The lively public discussion of the opinions of millennarian and evangelical missionary circles in England about the 'return of the Jews' created a spiritual ferment that was linked to political events and was absorbed by various segments of Jewish society. Whether in direct response to the settlement programs put forward by Christian circles, or as an acceptance of the European image of Palestine that combined the Jewish nationalist vision with the awakening of nationalism in Europe, from the end of the 1830s until the 1880s, some European Jews became particularly sensitive to Christian proposals regarding Palestine. In the general atmosphere of readiness to recognize the existence of the Jews as a separate national group, as opposed to traditional Christian preconceptions and those of eighteenth-century universalistic rationalism, the suggestions of mystics and millennarian statesmen for Jewish settlement in Palestine under English protection had particular significance. Suggestions of that sort were sent to Moses Montefiore, who was in contact with millennarian activists in England for years.

Traditional circles, as well, were aware of the rising nationalism among the peoples of Europe. Combined with the optimistic feeling arising from the beginnings of the process of emancipation which was seen as a sign of the approach of messianic redemption, the actual fulfillment of the bond with the land of Israel appeared possible, with the aid of the 'kingdoms of mercy.' In the words of Alkalay: "The salvation of Israel lies in addressing to the kings of the earth a general request for the welfare of our nation and our holy cities, and for our return in repentance to the house of our mother, . . . our salvation will come rapidly from the kings of the earth. . . ."[14] The optimistic approach which led Alkalay to view the Turkish Sultan and the Russian Czar as redeemers of Israel, because of their activities reforming the status of the Jews,[15] persisted in some locales until the 1880s. The founders of the Society for Working the Soil and Redeeming the Land, eventually among the first settlers of Petah Tikva, were optimistic with regard to the attitude of the European powers toward Jewish aspirations.[16]

The dialectical character of nineteenth-century developments is particularly evident in the ideological frameworks of orthodoxy of that period. This found expression in the matter of settling Palestine as well. The feeling of crisis, which was becoming stronger among religious Jews because of the spread of the Reform movement in Central Europe, gave the traditional bond between the diaspora and the land of Israel a decidedly utopian tone. In addition to the traditional role of the Holy Land from which prayers of the Jews who lived there were heard and from whence their redemption would commence, the land of Israel was now also seen as a place where the maladies of the European Jewish communities could be avoided. The Jewish settlements in the land of Israel would serve as strongholds of traditional society. The desire to remain separate from the 'evil sect' of the innovators brought about opposition to the participation of members of the Reform communities and of others favoring religious change, in the raising of money for Palestine. At the same time, the fear of damaging the particular character of the community of scholars, 'exalted saints,' in Palestine led to complete opposition to any change in the traditional way of life there, whether in education or philanthropy, and to abstention from any act that might hint at any change in the direction of modernization. Among some members of religious circles, immigration took on an additional dimension that had not existed in Jewish society previously: abandonment of the polluted lands [17] and evildoers of Europe, and removal to a holy place which the corrupting spirit of the age had not touched. The activity of the 'Pekidim and Amarkalim' organization of Amsterdam headed by Rabbi Hirsch Lehren, a major source of fundraising for the Jewish community in Palestine, was, from the 1840s onward, a clear manifestation of those trends.[18]

The return to the old order of society (as advocated, for example, by the Hatam Sofer), and the resistance to modernization within the Jewish community of Europe, gave rise to a new trend: the establishment of a Jewish society in the Holy Land which would be an alternative to the vision of merging into the non-Jewish world—an ideal, utopian society of separatism. This trend existed within the traditional society alongside the optimistic tendency that derived from the achievements of emancipation; it was one of the components of the ideology of the founders of Petah Tikva at the end of the 1870s.

Parallel proposals for agricultural settlement in Palestine were heard during the 1840s among divergent groups: those faithful to the traditional society, students with national sentiments who were influenced by the awakening of the nations of Europe,[19] and acculturated Jewish philanthropists. However, whereas the first group saw agriculture principally from an economic and functional point of view, that is to say, as providing sustenance for the urban communities, thus allowing them to continue with their holy work, the others viewed agriculture in the spirit of the standard 'enlightened' proposals, as a means of creating a 'healthy' society and improving the economic and social structure of the Jewish community.[20] The trend toward changing the occupations of the Jews, accepted as the principal means to deal with the 'Jewish question' by government officials of Central and Eastern Europe, reached Palestine with the rising interest of non-traditional circles in the material and spiritual existence of the Jewish community there. From then until the 1880s, proposals were put forward for changing the way of life of the Jewish society in the cities of Palestine by means of agricultural settlement, proposals that were essentially similar to those of the 'enlightened' Jews of Europe. Non-Jewish visitors stressed the severance from farming pursuits as one of the conspicuous signs of weakness and degeneracy among the Jews of Palestine. The historian Graetz, who visited Palestine in 1872, and the representative of English Jewry, Montague, who travelled there in 1874, both repeated that claim.[21] The establishment of Mikve Israel in 1870 belongs essentially to the sort of enlightened European activity designed to correct that situation.

Around this issue are concentrated the three principal positions current during the sixties and seventies with regard to the question of Jewish agricultural settlement in Palestine: the 'enlightened' philanthropic position, which mainly saw in agriculture the way to modernize and correct the situation of the Jewish community; the orthodox position which opposed any change in sources of livelihood, just as it opposed any educational or welfare activity that derived from a non-traditional Jewish source; and the traditionalist position with nationalist tendencies, which saw in agricultural settlement the beginning of the way towards the messianic redemption of the land. The two former positions already existed in the 1840s, and they were expressed in the polemics centering on the settlement program of Montefiore.[22]

CHANGING TRENDS IN THE 1860S

The revival of the idea of settling Palestine during the 1860s was linked with the perception of Jewish agricultural settlement as a factor in the process of messianic redemption. Thus, in dialectical manner, an additional channel was opened for the penetration of the idea of 'productivization' through agriculture into the Jewish traditional society in Europe, while a framework was suggested for the absorption of this idea by the Jewish population of Palestine. Among traditional elements proposals for agricultural settlement were legitimatized through the philosophy and public activity of Rabbi Zevi Hirsch Kalischer, and the organization of societies for settlement in the land of Israel.

During the 1860s and 1870s, such activity continued in Central and Eastern Europe as well as among the Jews in Palestine where segments of the traditional community displayed great interest in settlement projects. David Gordon, writing in the pages of *HaMaggid*, was but one link between the 1860s and the beginning of the 1880s (see below). Support for the Society for the Settlement of the Land of Israel founded by Dr. Hayim Luria,[23] plus the organizational activity connected with Kalischer,[24] allow us to postulate the existence of a network of connections and relations which, though not mainstream, was certainly not a negligible factor in the communal activities of traditional Jewry. Proposals for an agricultural settlement made by the Jews of Jerusalem in 1863,[25] manifestations of interest by Lithuanian Jews in 1867 in the American Colony of Jaffa as an example of an agricultural experiment,[26] the support of a Jewish donor in Russia for the Yishuv Eretz HaKodesh Society in 1873[27]—these and other activities indicate that the idea of settling Palestine had taken root and influenced the minds and actions of some people.

In the 1860s, the basis was created for a reciprocal relationship between advocates of the settlement of Palestine and the earliest proponents of Jewish national rights in a modern sense. The former continued to identify the activities of the non-traditional circles with the expression of the political and economic influence of Jewish notables, and they saw in this an infrastructure for practical action in providing sources of livelihood connected with agriculture; the latter viewed all of traditional society as requiring improvement and modernization. The first attempt to combine the ideological foundations of the two groups, so far apart in their background and character, was made by David Gordon in the beginning of the 1860s. In a certain sense, this conception was a form of nationalistic trend within the 'Moderate Enlightenment' of Eastern Europe which, in those years, was involved in a sharp ideological confrontation with the more radical thrust of the Enlightenment. The latter strove for complete integration into Russian society, while at the same time advocating an orthodox philosophy that was becoming more conspicuous in the traditional society of Eastern Europe. Gordon himself tended toward an optimistic approach to the achievements of emancipation, and he tried to combine modern nationalist attitudes, as formulated by Moses Hess in *Rome and Jerusalem,* with the belief in the messianic redemption of Israel in the spirit of Alkalay and Kalischer. "The idea of the unity of the nation of Israel in all the lands of its dispersion" appeared to him to be fulfilled in Jewish organizations above the community level, such as the British Board of Deputies, and especially the Alliance Israélite Universelle, which he saw as important frameworks for the achievement of the national aspirations of the Jewish people.

The image of the Alliance as a model of international Jewish organization also grew out of the optimistic appraisal of the achievements of the emancipation. Alkalay had written of the Alliance as

the fortunate gathering, the *kol yisrael haverim* [All Israel are Friends—the Hebrew name for the Alliance Israélite Universelle] Society, they are fulfilling the commandment of taking pity upon our remnant . . . Thus, worthy sirs, the heads of the people of Israel, give strength to [the will of] God! Turn your hands to God this day, and do all that you can do, and He will complete the act for you.[28]

It is no wonder that an 'enlightener' like Gordon, who attached himself to "those who endeavor to fulfull that which the new times demand of us,"[29] should pin his hopes on an organization which, in his eyes, provided a clear expression of the freedom of the Jews of Western Europe. *HaMaggid,* Gordon's periodical, was not only the main source of information for nationalist circles, but was also a factor in combining the diverse sources of Jewish nationalism in its formative stage. The heritage of the Enlightenment, in particular the criticism of the structure of Jewish society and the sources of its livelihood, merged with appeals for support of the efforts to settle Palestine and with information about what was taking place there.

Nevertheless, when all is said and done, manifestations of modern nationalism during the 1860s and the response to the idea of settling Palestine were rather limited in both scope and circulation within the traditional society. The Jewish communities of Eastern Europe, which were to give rise to the Love of Zion movement, were then primarily involved in the changes and the expectations which resulted from the reforms of Czar Alexander II. The communities of Central Europe were involved in bitter religious and organizational polemics concerning the retention of traditional values, and the consolidation of orthodox structures continued. Thus it should be emphasized that neither the modern expressions of Jewish nationalism nor the thinking of Kalischer and his circle with regard to national reawakening along the traditional lines which spoke of messianic redemption, reached more than limited circles. However, the historical events of the 1860s and 1870s laid the foundations for the convergence of the two extremes in a new nationalist program even before the pogroms took place in Russia.

SOCIAL AND NATIONALIST RADICALISM IN RUSSIA

It is generally agreed that the change in the relationship of the surrounding society towards the Jews left its mark on the 'enlightened' Jews and on the younger generation, especially in Eastern Europe.[30] It is possible to show clearly that during the 1870s hostility towards the Jew was becoming stronger in Russia, and was encompassing ever wider circles. Despite the deep contradiction between the political views of the conservative Slavophiles and the radical revolutionary Narodniks, they were united in the belief that the salvation of Russia would come from the peasant and from his rural community. In their opinion, the peasant was the one who produced the means by which all men live, while all other social groups gain their livelihood from him, and at his expense. Crafts and manufactures were secondary to agricultural labor, and commerce, trade and finance were exploitative and parasitical occupations. The more those views were directed against capitalism as a social system and against Western bourgeois democracy as a political framework, and the more Russian intellectuals wished to protect their society from undesirable Western influence, the more the Jew appeared to them as the symbol of all those negative elements combined. Both the press and literature of that decade display a growing enmity towards the Jews.[31]

By the end of the 1860s, Jewish intellectuals of Eastern Europe who advocated varying degrees of accomodation to the Russian society were already aware of the anti-Jewish attitude which had taken hold of the Russian intelligentsia and of the state bureaucracy. Their awareness lagged behind the literary and journalistic expressions of that attitude, but it came to the fore by the 1870s. Some members of the Jewish intelligentsia who had begun their public activities during the reign of Nicolas I pinned high hopes on the reforms of the early part of the reign of Alexander II, although their enthusiasm was dampened by the second half of the sixties. Only the moderates among them, such as Gottlober, remained loyally identified with the government's policy during the seventies, still believing that eighteenth-century-style enlightened despotism could serve as a model for the inclusion of the Jews in the political life of Russia. Members of the younger generation who began their literary careers during the reign of Alexander II had already absorbed ideas from the literary and political criticism of Russian public opinion during the 1860s, and they adopted one of several varieties of social radicalism.

Among the moderate intellectuals, during the transition from the 1860s to the 1870s, the feeling of being cut off from the principal developments in Jewish society in Eastern Europe grew stronger. On the one hand, they were reluctant to merge fully with the surrounding Russian society, a step that would endanger the continuation of the specifically Jewish cultural heritage in the spirit of the 'Moderate Enlightenment'; on the other hand, they were aware of the enmity directed towards them by the traditional society, which was gradually becoming militantly orthodox. Moreover, the social criticism which intellectuals such as Yehuda Leib Gordon and Smolenskin directed against contemporary traditional Jewry presented an ideal model of an 'enlightened society' that could not exist in the reality of the 1870s. Discouragement with Enlightenment ideals as a social and political solution for the Jews of Russia led to radicalization among the young intelligentsia in two opposite directions: social radicalism, emphasizing the universalistic basis of the Enlightenment; and nationalist radicalism, emphasizing Jewish particularism.

During the 1870s, Lilienblum had already arrived at a fundamental criticism of the heritage of the Enlightenment and, like many of his contemporaries, he saw himself a victim of "imaginary Enlightenment." [32] Smolenskin came to a nationalist view through uncompromising criticism of the ideas of Moses Mendelssohn and the examination of the negative influences of the Enlightenment on the Jews. The radical intellectuals came into contact with the revolutionary movement of Eastern Europe and, influenced by it, the first Jewish socialists such as Yehuda Leib Levin and A. S. Liebermann went through a process of radicalization essentially similar to that undergone by Lilienblum. However Liebermann went further, and his position that the Jewish question would be resolved "together with the whole human question," [33] marked the peak of the universalistic trend among 'enlighteners' during the 1870s. However, in a sharp shift at the turn of the decade, most of the proponents of Enlightenment, as well as its opponents, ended up together in the beginnings of the 'Love of Zion' movement.

That the nationalist-minded supporters of the Enlightenment should have turned to 'Love of Zion' is entirely understandable; their influence was stronger there, and they gave a clear nationalist direction to those who came to the movement from other backgrounds. Consciousness of Jewish particularism, and a grasp of the centrality of national, cultural creativity (the significance of the Hebrew language, and the importance of certain symbols and literary forms) were propounded in one sweep, so that at times it is difficult to distinguish between what preceded the pogroms of 1881–82 and what came afterwards. Now, criticism against the ideals of Enlightenment took center-stage and became broader: not only nationalism versus universalism, but also 'Moderate Enlightenment' as opposed to social radicalism, and separate Jewish activity in contrast to a general political struggle which ignored specific Jewish problems. Thus, for example, tales of the loss of hope in finding a place in the surrounding society were told repeatedly in the wake of the shock of the pogroms, although several of the intellectuals said that they had already undergone such an experience in the seventies. The young Jewish intelligentsia, which grew up imbued with Russian culture, had been eager to be accepted as part of Russian society and largely ignored the development of anti-Jewish tendencies. The intelligentsia still hoped that Russia would follow the path taken by the states of Western and Central Europe and grant emancipation to the Jews. Thus its members were dealt a double blow with the outbreak of the "Storms in the South," the pogroms against the Jews in the cities and towns of the Ukraine in the spring of 1881, following the assassination of Czar Alexander II by revolutionaries.

1881 AND THE DISILLUSIONMENT OF THE RUSSIAN JEWISH INTELLIGENTSIA

The main cause of this shock and confusion which overcame the Jewish intelligentsia was neither the victims and the destruction (they were used to the evil 'decrees' of the Czar's government, although not to attacks from multitudes running wild), nor the hesitancy of the authorities to defend the victims of the pogroms. It was not even the new government policy which declared explicitly that it was the Jews themselves and their 'exploitation' of the local population which caused the pogroms and that it was necessary to find ways to prevent or reduce the damage caused to the 'principal inhabitants' by the economic activities of the Jews. With all the hopes for progress in the future, the Jewish intelligentsia in Russia with its liberal or radical leanings was prepared for even worse on the part of the autocratic functionaries of the Czarist state, and from an incited rabble. But they were deeply distressed by the fact that, with the exception of a few individuals, Russian public opinion, with its dozens of publications, did not defend the victims of the pogroms. There was nearly common agreement among the Russian intelligentsia that the pogroms were "outbursts of rage" of the masses against "Jewish exploitation," so that even the greatest Russian authors, such as Turgeniev and Tolstoy, the 'conscience of the nation,' were silent.

This fact was a hard blow to the spiritual world of the Jewish intellectuals and of the radical youth, and it forced many to change their ideas. There were still some who tried to pin their hopes on the progress of mankind as a whole and to base their views on the precedent of emancipation that was granted to the Jews in Western and Central Europe, but the antisemitic "Berlin Movement" and anti-Jewish trends in Austria and France forced some of them to subject these ideas to serious reexamination.[34] If hatred for the Jews could find a place in the public life of France, the cradle of democracy and of the rights of man, and in Germany, cultural pioneer and scientific leader, in countries where cries of contempt and insults against the Jews came not from the mouths of marginal people, but from savants, journalists, and prominent clergymen; if the Jews were considered strangers in their eyes not because of their religion or their historical heritage alone, but also because of their 'race' and their physical and spiritual essence—how could a Jewish intellectual still hope to be accepted in society with equal rights and status?[35]

The shift took place not only among those whose faith in progress and in the merging of Jews into the surrounding society had led them to view themselves as 'Russians of the Mosaic faith' (similar to definitions in the West of 'Frenchmen, Germans, etc. of the Mosaic faith'), or to promulgate the slogan 'Be a man in the street but a Jew at home.' The proponents of the nationalist idea and the believers in the revival of the land of Israel were shaken as well. Those active since the 1840s had pinned their hopes on the good will and the favor of the major powers of Europe. They started from the assumption that the enlightened nations of Europe, who assisted in the renascence of Greece, in the awakening of the Balkan peoples, and in the unification of Italy, would probably also support the national revival of the Jewish people. Then came the antisemitic pogroms in Europe which destroyed that dream. Jews had no chance of liberating themselves from their foreignness, even if they were willing to sacrifice their spiritual and social uniqueness and their loyalty to their historical heritage. Thus the Jews had to return to their own land and rebuild it, but not as a result of the good will and the understanding of the nations of Europe; rather, because of their enmity, because of the long heritage of hatred that could not be cured by the Enlightenment or by wise legislation, the Jewish people had to accomplish this themselves. Thus it was not optimism but deep pessimism that served as a background for that Jewish awakening whose leaders and spokesmen were the members of the First Aliyah.

In Eastern Europe, in the midst of the pogroms, both trends of critical attitude to the Enlightenment continued, as described previously. The nationalist trend is clearly in evidence in the literary output of Smolenskin. Among socialists and the members of the revolutionary movement, that movement was criticized for ignoring the particularity of the Jewish problem. According to Pavel Axelrod, the Jewish masses were neglected by revolutionary circles, and it was only the pogroms "which finally opened the eyes of the socialist Jewish intelligentsia to see their mistake with regard to the Jewish masses, and awakened its interest and willingness to share their destiny."[36]

That change, which took place among Jewish youth with radical leanings in the early eighties, gave the 'Love of Zion' movement concepts, values, and even organizational methods that came from the Russian radical camp. In the wake of the pogroms, a movement of 'Going to the Jewish People' arose among the students of St. Petersburg, along the lines of the movement that had developed among the Russian students in the beginning of the 1870s. The obligation of the intelligentsia towards the masses, which was one of the foundations of the Narodnik outlook, was now understood as the obligation of the Jewish intelligentsia towards its people. In self-defense organizations during the pogroms,[37] in demonstrations of identification and support for the victims, in stirrings of the trend towards emigration from Russia, the intelligentsia's new self-appraisal is demonstrated again and again. It led some who had already found a place in Russian culture to return to Jewish public activity of the sort that had been common among the Jewish 'enlighteners.' In fact, the public discussion that arose in Russia immediately after the pogroms is marked by ideological and organizational elements that had characterized the activities of the intelligentsia for the reform of traditional society. At the same time, one also finds in this group new elements that were absorbed from the Russian Narodnik movement and from activist traditional circles; these latter elements were now strengthened and legitimized in the eyes of the radical and 'enlightened' groups.

The basic assumption with regard to the social and economic structure of East European Jewry did not change, nor did the proposals for reform. However, the arena for the proposals discussed was now transposed outside of the borders of Russia; 'productivization' of the society through agricultural settlement was no longer in Southern Russia or on unoccupied lands within the Pale of Settlement itself, but in the 'New World' or in Palestine. In public discussion on the direction of emigration, it is possible to discern the meeting of these radical influences and the clash between them. The groups preaching radical emancipation in part advocated emigration to the United States, for Palestine was seen as a stronghold of orthodoxy, a place where it would be impossible to put the social values of their vision of Enlightenment into action.[38] In contrast, nationalist radicalism defined Palestine in secular nationalist terms. These ideologies were discussed intensively by emigration societies, some of which originated in associations for assistance to the victims of the pogroms, while others were linked to self-defense organizations. Some of the societies arose from the encounter of Russian-educated Jewish youth who had been influenced by radical ideology, with traditional Jewry. Members of these disparate groups had come together in several societies committed to settlement in Palestine. One fact is conspicuous; a good portion of the associations that took concrete action on behalf of the settlement of Palestine were composed of members with a traditional world-view or, at most, followers of the 'Moderate Enlightenment.'

TURNING TO PALESTINE, AND OTHER OPTIONS

Although the national reawakening of the 1880s led to intense contact between various trends of thought and was strongly marked by nationalist and social radicalism, only partial echoes were heard in Palestine. Among the hundreds and thousands of immigrants who reached Palestine as refugees from the pogroms and the terror in Russia and Rumania in 1881–1882, were (1) those seized with messianic enthusiasm for "working the soil of the land of our fathers," (2) those who depended on the Alliance or on the British eccentric, Laurence Oliphant, for support, and (3) those who calculated that the cost of travelling to Palestine was lower that the price of a trip to distant America. But there were also dozens (perhaps hundreds) of conscious nationalists. Some of them came to inspect Palestine on behalf of settlement organizations and to look for land to purchase.[39] Some of them were sent in an organized manner by the 'Central Committee of the Society for the Settlement of the Holy Land by Means of Working the Soil' (of Galati, Rumania),[40] and some were members of BILU who tried to carry out their nationalist ideas as pioneers while attempting to win from the Turkish government official recognition of the Jewish settlement program.[41] This last group was unique in that its actions were intended from the start to achieve a nationalist program whose goal was to change the situation and the image of the Jewish people and to find a cure for its ills. That does not mean that all of the 'nationalists' had a well-crystallized ideology, but rather that there was an ideological and emotional framework which encompassed most of their opinions, and upon which the conceptual world of the members of the First Aliyah was based.

The members of the First Aliyah were neither the first nor the only ones to pin their hopes on the establishment of a reformed society and model settlements in a country of immigrants. For example, French socialists attempted to establish their "Icarie" overseas, and at almost the same time and place as the members of the First Aliyah, Russian radicals tried to establish their own model settlements in the United States.[42] Moreover, in the *Am Olam* (Eternal-People) movement which arose among the Jews of Russia during the years of the pogroms and which chose to turn toward America,[43] similar ideas about the establishment of model agricultural settlements were current. There were also Russian Narodniks who took part in the attempt to establish such a settlement. However there were more arguments tied to Palestine, within the frameworks of Jewish tradition and of the longing for the social utopia, than could be projected in favor of the United States, or of Argentina after Baron de Hirsch presented his bold program in the early 1890s.

In discussions of the need for a 'Jewish Homeland' which developed in Jewish public opinion in Russia after the 'Storms in the South,' quite a few people proposed the concentrated settlement of a significant number of Jews somewhere in the United States. Since sixty thousand settlers were entitled to demand recognition as the state in the United States, it was their opinion that Jewish immigrants living in agricultural settlements in one region would be able to establish a 'Jewish state' similar to the Mormon state in Utah.[44] (Those who disagreed claimed that it would be impossible to prevent internal migration within the United States, and over a period of time the Jewish character of the region could not be maintained.)[45] Baron de Hirsch himself, in formulating his programs for the rescue of the Russian Jews by means of emigration, wrote to his agent in Buenos Aires:

Where and how are we to find a land which will permit the establishment of a sort of autonomous Jewish state, and where our coreligionists will be protected once and for all against the attacks of anti-Semitism? . . . It would have to be a Jewish state in a country which they would buy more or less in its entirety.[46]

The idea of a 'Jewish country,' a 'land of our own,' a 'land destined for us,' was thus widespread among Jewish circles, especially among the Jews living in Eastern Europe or having ties there. However the ideas with regard to the United States or Argentina were soon dropped from the public agenda. The special character of the First Aliyah lies in the continued existence of a nucleus of people who, despite difficulties and obstacles, clung to the aspiration of the settlement of Palestine throughout the whole period. At the end of the period of the First Aliyah (ca. 1900) there were very few of those settlers left, but the idea continued its unbroken existence, and received new impetus with the arrival of the members of the Second Aliyah. Only an examination of the obstacles that stood in their path and of the struggles they were required to wage can provide some concept of the steadfast strength of those few who neither gave up nor retreated.

PUBLIC JEWISH REACTION TO 'LOVE OF ZION'

After the shock of the 'Storms in the South' and the reaction of Russian society, it would seem that the entire young Jewish intelligentsia immediately began to 'return to its nation.' Except for a small class of very wealthy men and their intellectual associates, there were no Jews left in Russia who were willing to tie their fate to that country. However the flood-tide of nationalist consciousness and the desire to emigrate receded quickly. The delays and obstacles encountered in the establishment of the 'Love of Zion' movement also contributed their part, so that the movement bogged down in triviality. It became the movement of a few Hebrew writers, a few rabbis, several intellectual circles including some young students, and some of the bourgeois class. Because of the legal and social conditions in Russia at that time, there was no legal way for the movement to exist, and its leaders feared the reaction of the authorities. This fear dissuaded both the activist youth and the intelligentsia who were dependent upon public employment. These groups returned to revolutionary activity within Russia and to their customary professional work within the community. Not only did 'Love of Zion' became a minority movement, but it aroused an attitude of estrangement and contempt. Its meager accomplishments depressed people, and those who had been 'Palestinians' during the flood tide of popular opinion now joined the shiploads of emigrants to the United States. Leon Pinsker, one of the founders of the movement and its recognized leader, never held high hopes for the possibility of action by the 'Love of Zion' within Russia itself, but he hoped that the Jews of the West would heed his call and establish the leadership of the movement there. He met with great disappointment, for among the Jews of Germany not even a tiny number could be found to whom he could hand over the leadership role, or even to draw into nationalist activity.[47]

If that is how the Western Jews and many of those of Eastern Europe related to Pinsker and his colleagues, well-known and highly-placed men, then the position of the members of BILU in Istanbul or those in Palestine who turned to the Jews of Russia and the West for assistance and encouragement, was immeasurably harder. When Joseph Feinberg and Rabbi Samuel Mohilever succeeded in gaining the ear of some members of the Alliance and of Edmond de Rothschild, and assistance was granted to the Jews in the new settlements out of a desire to prove to the world that Jews were also capable of becoming farmers worthy of the name, an explicit condition was attached—that the Baron's name never be mentioned in connection with the settlement of Palestine.[48] The functionaries of the Baron found the nationalistic, ideological motivations of some of the settlers distasteful, and warnings were issued that no more immigrants were to come to Palestine.[49] Thus the need to persevere and struggle against the antagonism or indifference of most of the Jewish community and its leaders, especially among ultra-religious circles, was the lot of the 'Love of Zion' in general, and in particular of those members of the First Aliyah with nationalist consciousness.

EXTERNAL AND INTERNAL CHALLENGES FACING THE FIRST ALIYAH

The struggle with the conditions and the regime which then existed in Palestine was even more difficult. Zionist literature has made the heroism of the early settlers legendary, but authentic personal documents have been preserved which give a faithful picture of their suffering and of their powers of resistance. Difficulty in adjusting to the climate, illness, lack of familiarity with the environmental conditions, lack of knowledge of appropriate agricultural methods, the authorities' opposition to Jewish immigration, the purchase of land and establishment of settlements, the untrustworthiness of the various agents and middlemen, the opposition of the local Arabs and Bedouin—all these were the lot of the settlers from the day they arrived. For those who settled in the cities, the alien nature of the environment and of the customs were also a difficult trial. Thus many failed and returned to Europe. What is remarkable, given these conditions, is that most of the settlements stood their ground and that their number constantly grew. It was on the basis of the experience of these first settlements that the pioneering of Hadera and the rational planning of the founders of Rehovot could follow.

Internal challenges were no less difficult. The members of the Old Yishuv regarded the new settlers with great suspicion. The panicked immigration of hundreds of refugees during the years of the pogroms together with the arrival of immigrants from Yemen, North Africa, and Persia, created economic strains and housing shortages, and encouraged missionary activity in Jerusalem, thus placing the leaders of the existing community in a difficult position. It is true that they did offer aid, but their main effort was directed toward helping the refugees return to their countries of origin. A proclamation entitled 'Voice from the Sanctuary' harshly attacked the colonists and the very idea of settlement.[50] While the orthodox wing of the 'Love of Zion' strongly resisted any infringement of settlement attempts, it did try to turn the movement into one of observant Jews only.[51]

With the establishment of the colonies, the problem of observing the 'commandments connected with the Land,' cropped up. The most difficult crisis came in 1889, a Sabbatical year. Rabbinical supporters of the 'Love of Zion' movement ruled that agricultural work in the colonies was permitted that year, but the rabbis of Jerusalem forbade it. When some of the settlers attempted to act in accordance with the permission, they were strongly attacked. An important element in the enmity of the Old Yishuv was the suspicion that support of the agricultural colonies would reduce the amount of money sent to them from abroad. The Sephardic rabbis, who were not concerned with this issue (the money which was distributed went mainly to those who had come from the European countries where it was raised), tended to be more lenient.

The critical pronouncements made by the rabbis of Jerusalem about the level of observance of the commandments in the colonies, influenced the orthodox members of the 'Love of Zion'; as a result, Y. M. Pines was named the 'Director of Gedera,' a BILU village, so that he could supervise religious matters there.[52] This influenced the character of the settlements and limited the groups that could join them. The harsh criticism levelled by Ahad Ha-Am against the entire settlement enterprise after his trips to Palestine also weakened the spirit of potential immigrants, who gradually lost their pioneering verve. The settlers in Palestine became increasingly dependent upon the support of philanthropists. Nevertheless, the villages remained the principal basis for the development of the New Yishuv in Palestine. They had a national consciousness and continued to view the country as the 'Promised Land' upon which the future of the Jewish people depended.

THE SEARCH FOR 'BELONGING'

A second ideological motivation of the members of 'Love of Zion', which complemented their longing for the 'Promised Land,' was to be free of a sense of alienation. Despite the apparent success of emancipation in some circles and the cultural acceptance of many Jewish intellectuals, the problem of Jewish self-identity grew more acute during the

1880s. Many non-Jews rejected the Jew completely, for they did not believe in the sincerity of his assimilation, nor even of his conversion. Even those who were willing to befriend the Jew expected him to give up his historical tradition, his group consciousness, and his social attachments. Thus, the 'return to the Jewish people' was a return to an organic Jewish society from which most of the Jewish intellectuals in Eastern Europe had not yet completely cut themselves off.

As noted above, the example of other nations, especially those of the Balkan peninsula, who fought for their independence during the 1870s aroused the self-awareness of young Jews; these were examples of reborn nations becoming masters in their own lands.[53] The problem confronting the youth was how to assure that the Jews too would 'belong' and no longer be strangers in European states, or in countries to which they might emigrate in the future.

The thinking of those who consolidated the policy of 'Love of Zion' that was accepted by the 'nationalists' among the First Aliyah, followed two tracks. On the one hand, they sought a formal guarantee—recognition by the Ottoman authorities, by the representatives of Europe, and by the local inhabitants—of the rights of Jews to the land of Israel. Thus the desperate efforts of the BILU office in Istanbul to obtain a *firman* permitting Jewish settlement in Palestine, attempts that continued even during the period when it was already obvious that the Ottoman Sultan regarded the idea with strong reservations, if not outright hostility.[54] The desire to achieve a sense of 'belonging' also produced a rumor that the local Arabs believed that Palestine belongs to the Jews.[55] Thence came the belief that European notables would be able to convince and even exert pressure on the Ottoman authorities to obtain the *firman*. These ideas led directly to the notion of a 'charter,' found in the views of Herzl and the later political Zionists.

The other route was the attempt to create a Jewish majority in Palestine that would guarantee the status of the Jews there and have the power to establish independent or autonomous institutions. This aspiration was a central motive in nationalist activities even during the years of population decline and emigration from that country. This is the line that distinguishes the members of the First Aliyah from the Alliance and from the Old Yishuv, who endeavored to return immigrants to their countries of origin for fear of the influence of the missionaries, or because of their poverty and suffering. The nationalists, who later also warned against the immigration of those without means, viewed themselves as actively preparing the land; they considered themselves pioneers breaking new ground for others to follow.

Emphasis on the pioneering role of the New Yishuv was in fact a substantial part of the propaganda of the 'Love of Zion' and of the members of the First Aliyah. To change the image of the Jew was a primary goal. Against the heroic actions and the self-sacrifice of the revolutionaries in Russia who served as an example to many young people, they held up the deeds of the founders of Gedera and of Hadera and the firm resistance of the colonists against the tyranny of the Baron's bureaucrats and the devious scheming of Arab neighbors.

The romanticism of the East took hold among the young workers who began to concentrate in the villages during the 1890s, and they tried to copy the Arabs in appearance and dress. Despite strict administrative control of the villages and the attempts of the representatives of 'Love of Zion' in Russia and their appointees to supervise the observance of the commandments, a way of life unique to the New Yishuv began to take shape in the villages and in Jaffa. It was marked by the use of Hebrew spoken according to the Sephardic pronunciation, improved educational methods, and modern cultural activity. Efforts at independent organization and the attempt to establish a recognized body to speak in the name of the New Yishuv were also products of the feeling of 'belonging' and of the change in the self-image of the members of the New Yishuv.[56] Although few in number, it was they as a group with a national mission who gave shape to the Jewish community in Palestine at the end of the period of the First Aliyah.

THREE BASIC GOALS OF THE JEWISH NATIONAL MOVEMENT

As the Jewish national movement appeared on the stage of history, it adopted three central goals which it saw as preconditions for the renascence of the nation: auto-emancipation, productivization, and some measure of self-rule. The first goal belongs to the realm of the group-consciousness of the Jews; the second belongs to their social structure and sources of livelihood; and the third, to the form of their organization.

Auto-emancipation, self-liberation, is necessary, in Pinsker's opinion, because the Jews lack "an independent national sentiment . . . For is it not our tribe's greatest misfortune that *we do not belong to a nation, that we are nothing but Jews! A flock scattered across the face of the earth are we. . . .*"[57] Thus the meaning of auto-emancipation is the conversion of the Jews from an object to a subject of history, to a living national body with independent national self-consciousness, with shared goals and programs for achieving them. The members of the First Aliyah constituted one of the first groups moving towards auto-emancipation, a modest and sometimes unsuccessful attempt, but nonetheless a first attempt at conscious national action. Although many of the members of the First Aliyah were also observant Jews, they did not move to Israel in order to carry out the will of Providence, or to bring the redemption nearer in a miraculous manner through their actions, but rather to act as pioneers for the masses of Jews who would return to their historic homeland in order to restore Jewish national life. The European peoples struggling for national liberation served as a model to no small extent.

Members of the First Aliyah also took part in the goal of productivizing the Jews, of finding new sources of livelihood, and of changing their image both in their own eyes and in those of others by taking up physical labor, especially working the soil. Theirs was not the first attempt at Jewish agricultural settlement; they were preceded by Jewish agricultural colonies in Russia and Jewish farmers in Austria; and at the very same time similar settlements were established by Jewish immigrants in the United States. There is also good reason to assume that without the continued assistance of the 'well-known benefactor,' a reference to Baron Edmond de Rothschild, many of the settlements would not have held out, and it is possible that the settlers would have been discouraged and left Palestine.

However, what makes the settlers of the First Aliyah so unique is that their enterprise was also intended to create an independent and healthy economic and national infrastructure, the basis for the renascence of the people and its ingathering in its homeland. As noted above, Ahad Ha-Am and later observers who examined the First Aliyah from an historical perspective pointed out the weakness of the enterprise of the first settlers, their dependence on outside financial assistance, and the retreat of many of them from their original nationalistic ideals. Nevertheless, their most severe critics, the members of the Second Aliyah, established their first foothold in the agricultural villages of the First Aliyah, while continuing and diversifying the enterprise of agricultural settlement. The continuity of the settlement projects in Palestine is proof that during the days of the First Aliyah an economic and social infrastructure for the renascence of the nation was in fact created.

The first signs of self-rule were the most important expressions of a national revolution. Pinsker had already proposed the convening of a Jewish congress that would speak in the name of all the Jews. While he did not succeed in carrying this out, Herzl was able to turn the Zionist Congress into an open forum giving expression to the aspirations of the

Jewish people throughout the world. All of Herzl's energies were directed towards achieving the recognition of the Jews' aspirations by the Ottoman authorities, and obtaining the support of the European powers for the right of the Jewish people to their own territory and to independent political expression. It would appear that a serious gap exists between Herzl's political conceptions and the practical aspirations of the First Aliyah. However, as noted, the BILU did try to obtain a *firman* from the Sultan, similar to the 'charter' which was the central goal in Herzl's programs.

Beyond general aspirations of that nature, the *actions* of the first settlers are important, although only partially successful. The demand that young people give several years to national service, the establishment of the principles of cooperation and mutual assistance, the creation of organizations of settlers and workers, the use of Hebrew as a common national language, and the establishment of an educational system in that language—all of those were foundation stones for the formation of the nucleus of independent Jewish life in Palestine. Herzl, whose approach was decidedly political, recoiled from such goals, because he viewed them as an uncertain path of 'infiltration,' subject to being undermined and doomed to failure. And it is true that an examination of the difficult conditions and the hostile relations of the Turkish authorities and the local Arabs from without, and of the members of the Old Yishuv, who were disheartened and bitter, from within the Jewish community, points out the magnitude of the task and the remarkable perseverance of the members of the First Aliyah.

As we have said, those years were not marked by the establishment of new social and organizational forms of self-rule. That was done during the Second Aliyah. Nevertheless, in their own self-awareness and also in historical perspective, the latter continued the work of the former. Despite the paucity of its real accomplishments, the First Aliyah expressed a turning point in the history both of the Jewish community in Palestine and of the Jewish people as a whole.

NOTES

1. N. M. Gelber, *Zur Vorgeschichte des Zionismus* (Wien, 1927): Y. Katz, "Towards Clarification of the Concept 'The Precursors of Zionism'," (Hebrew) *Shivat Zion* 1 (1950): 91–105; idem, *Jewish Nationalism, Essays and Research* (Hebrew) (Jerusalem, 1979), pp. 263–284; B. Halpern, *The Idea of the Jewish State* (Cambridge, Mass., 1969), pp. 60–71; N. Sokolow, *History of Zionism* 1 (London, 1919).

2. M. Rothschild, *Halukkah as an Expression of the Relationship of the Jews of the Diaspora to the Jewish Community in Palestine from 1810 to 1860* (Hebrew) (Jerusalem, 1969); A. Morgenstern. *The Clerks and Treasurers of Amsterdam and the Jewish Community in Palestine in the First Half of the 19th Century* (Hebrew) (Doctoral dissertation, Hebrew University, Jerusalem, 1981).

3. Sh. Avizur, "Economic Shifts and Transfers to Working Life in the Old Yishuv," (Hebrew) *Keshet* 51 (1971): 101–23; cf. I. Bartal, "The 'Settlement Program' at the time of Montefiore's Second Visit to Palestine (1839)" (Hebrew), *Shalem* 2 (Jerusalem, 1976): 231–96.

4. According to Ruppin's 1907 memorandum, there were then about twenty Jewish villages in the Galilee and in Judea, whose inhabitants numbered 5,160; cf. A. Bein, *The History of Zionist Settlement* (Hebrew) (Tel Aviv, 1954), pp. 35–36.

5. "The question of workers is a weighty one. . . . for it is not only a social issue, but even more so a national one. A question of the entire Yishuv! Experience teaches us that without Jewish workers, the settlements cannot exist. The Arab workers are only a slender reed upon which to lean . . . It is the Jewish workers who are to the Yishuv what blood is to a healthy man's body; they will give it life. They will keep it from destruction and failure." From the introduction to the by-laws of the HaArez vehaAvodah (Land and Work) Society, which was founded in 1892 on the initiative of Meir Dizengoff. Cf. M. Braslavsky, *Workers and Organizations in the First Aliyah* (Hebrew) (Tel Aviv, 1962), p. 229.

6. See above, n. 1; also Y. Katz, *Jewish Nationalism* (Hebrew) (Jerusalem, 1979), pp. 3–35; M. Eliav, *Eretz Israel and Its Settlement in the Nineteenth Century, 1777–1917* (Hebrew) (Jerusalem, 1978), pp. 278–83.

7. Cf. Halpern (above, n. 1), pp. 251–61; F. Kobler, *The Vision Was There* (London, 1956), pp. 47–75.

8. On the increase in European interest in Palestine see Y. Ben-Arieh, *Palestine in the Nineteenth Century—Its Rediscovery* (Hebrew) (Jerusalem, 1970); M. Ish-Shalom, *Christian Travellers to Palestine* (Hebrew) (Tel Aviv, 1966), pp. 408–833.

9. M. Kedem, "Concepts of the Redemption of the Jewish People and the Land of Israel in English Protestant Eschatology in the Mid-Nineteenth Century" (Hebrew), *Cathedra* 19 (1981): 64.

10. Thus, for example, the Jews of a city in Lithuania addressed the American settlers near Jaffa, asking: "Are the Americans who settled near Jaffa tent-dwellers, or have they already carried out their wish to construct houses, and of what sort, and what is the condition of their foundations, and have they already eaten of the produce of the land? . . . A small lot, enough to support about five or six souls, how much does it cost in the money of our country? Is it easy to obtain it [the land] there at all times? . . . Is it true that one must be wary of snakes and vipers and other harmful things, as many people say?" Sh. L. Zitron, *The History of 'Love of Zion'* (Hebrew) (Odessa, 1914), pp. 63–64; see also A. Carmel, *German Settlement in Palestine at the End of the Ottoman Period* (Hebrew) (Jerusalem, 1973), pp. 198–225.

11. This can be ascertained from the material concerning the Jews in the consular archives: M. Eliav. *The Jewish Community in Palestine in the Mirror of German Policy, 1842–1914* (Hebrew) (Tel Aviv, 1973); idem, "The Austrian Consulate in Jerusalem and the Jewish Community," (Hebrew) *Cathedra* 18 (1981): 73–110; A. H. Hyamson, *The British Consulate in Jerusalem in Relation to the Jews in Palestine* (London, 1939–41).

12. Kobler (above, n. 7), pp. 58–65; M. Werété, "Why Was a British Consulate Established in Jerusalem?" *English Historical Review* (1970): 342–45; idem, "The Restoration of the Jews in English Protestant Thought, 1790–1840," *Middle Eastern Studies* 8, 1 (1972): 4–50; Kedem (above, n. 9).

13. *The Writings of Rabbi Yehuda Alkalay* (Hebrew), Y. Werfel, ed., 1 (Jerusalem, 1944),

pp. 183–84 (from the introduction to the pamphlet "Minhat Yehuda," 5603 [1843]). R. Zevi Hirsch Kalischer perceived the power of Amschel Rothschild similarly in the 1830s. Cf. his letter to Amschel Rothschild dated 12 Elul 5696 (1836) in which he suggested that Rothschild head the movement of the return of the Jews to their land by exploiting the situation that had come into being: "And especially at a time like the present, when the land of Israel is not under the sovereignty of a powerful king, . . . but the whole land is ruled by the pasha [Muhammad Ali], perhaps it would seem worthy to you, if you, my lord, our exalted friend, would spend a lot of money and buy him [Muhammed Ali] another country instead of the land which is small now in size but great in quality, for it is named the glorious land." *Drishat Zion*, ed. I. Klausner (Hebrew) (Jerusalem, 1964), p. 221. Similar to that is the plea of Yissakhar ben Yizhak (Bernard) Behrend, a Hessian Jewish merchant, in December 1832, to the very same Rothschild, to purchase a piece of land in the United States for the same purpose—Gelber (above, n. 1), pp. 85–86.

14. Rabbi Yehuda Alkalay, *Raglei HaMevasser*, 5625, in the Werfel edition (above, n. 13), p. 495.

15. *Ibid.*, pp. 498–99.

16. A. Druyanow (ed.), *Writings on the History of Love of Zion* 3 (Hebrew) (Tel Aviv, 1932), no. 1109; A. R. Malachi, "On the History of Agricultural Labor in Palestine," (Hebrew) *Hameir* 6–7 (1922): 294.

17. According to the young Graetz in his journal for 1839, *The Paths of Jewish History* (Hebrew) (Jerusalem, 1969), p. 249: "During Mussaf prayers the idea dawned upon me that in Eretz Israel we could develop such an exalted life, whereas we have to travail here in a polluted land. It was such a strong sentiment that tears streamed from my eyes."

18. I. Bartal, "The 'Clerks and the Treasurers' and their Letters"—Introduction to volume 3 of *The Letters of the Clerks and Treasurers of Amsterdam* (Hebrew) (Jerusalem, 1979), pp. 14–16; the activity of Lehren increased during the rabbinical conventions held in Germany during the 1840s for the purpose of discussing religious reforms. He initiated the protests against reform of rabbis from all over Europe, and he published them in anthologies: *Torat haKana'ut* (1845), *Shlomei Emunei Israel* (1845), *Kinat Zion* (1846).

19. S. W. Baron, "Abraham Beinisch's Project for Jewish Colonization in Palestine (1842)," *Jewish Studies in Memory of George A. Kohut* (ed. A. Marx and S. W. Baron), pp. 72–87.

20. D. Weinberg, "Problems in the Investigation of the History and Economic Life of the Jews in Palestine," (Hebrew) *Zion* 3 (1938): 75; Bartal (above, n. 3), pp. 244–66.

21. Graetz (above, n. 17), pp. 278–79: "For raising the status of Jerusalem and her Inhabitants," Jerusalem, 1875 (Hebrew, reprint from *Havazzelet*, pp. 27–31).

22. Bartal, (above, n. 3), pp. 277–81.

23. G. Kressel, "The First Society for the Settlement of Palestine," (Hebrew) *Zion* 7 (1942): 197–205; Graetz (above, n. 17), p. 268; M. Eliav. *Lovers of Zion and the Men of Holland and Germany* (Hebrew) (Tel Aviv, 1971), pp. 128–33.

24. Katz (above, n. 6), pp. 274–76; The letters of Rabbi Kalischer from the 1860s and 1870s were collected by I. Klausner, *The Zionist Writings of Rabbi Zevi Kalischer* (Hebrew) (Jerusalem, 1947); Eliav (above, n. 23), *loc. cit.*

25. Z. Ilan, "The Origins of *Havazzelet* (1863), with the Discovery of the First Five Issues," (Hebrew), *Cathedra* 7 (1978): 37–41.

26. See above, n. 10. See also the article by H. Peles, "Attitudes of the Members of the Old Yishuv to Settlement in Palestine," (Hebrew) *Zion* 41 (1976): 148–62.

27. K. Z. Wisotzky, *Collection of Letters* (Hebrew), photocopied edition (Jerusalem, 1981), p. 3.

28. Alkalay (above, n. 14), p. 499.

29. G. Kressel, ed., "Selected Articles of David Gordon" (Hebrew) *Shorashim* 2 (Tel Aviv 1942): 35.

30. Sh. Ettinger, "The Unique Character of the Jewish National Movement," in *Zionist Ideology and Politics* (Jerusalem, 1978), p. 17.

31. Cf. Sh. Ettinger, *Anti-Semitism in the Modern Age* (Hebrew) (Tel Aviv, 1979), pp. 154–67, and idem, "The Discussion of Jewish Exploitation in Russian Public Opinion," *Perakim beToldot haHevra haYehudit* (Hebrew) (Jerusalem, 1980), pp. 287–307.

32. M. L. Lilienblum, *Autobiographical Writings*, 2 (Hebrew) (Jerusalem, 1970), p. 140.

33. A. S. Liebermann, "The Jewish Question" (Hebrew), *HaEmet* 1 (5 Sivan, 5636, 1876): 5.

34. That is the essence of the claim of the "herald of change," Leon Pinsker: "There is no place where a Jew is on his own ground, where he is considered a member of the household; he is a resident alien everywhere, and forever . . . The German fences himself up within his Germanness, the Slav, the Celt—none of them admits that the Jewish Semite is a human being of equal value. . . . The events of the last few years in *enlightened* Germany, in Rumania, in Hungary, and especially in Russia, have done what the bloody persecutions, which were even crueller, could not do in the Middle Ages." *Auto-emancipation*, ed. Sh. Breimann, (Hebrew) (Jerusalem, 1942), pp. 45, 51.

35. M. L. Lilienblum gives that point special emphasis: "When an educated German sees a Jewish professor, doctor, judge, or the like, he says to himself, 'If there were no Jews among us, then I would have that professorial chair, or that job,' etc. He does not think to himself that the Jews have worked hard for the good of science, and that that very Jew, who was able to obtain a professorial chair, is doubtless more capable than himself, the citizen who did not obtain the chair, and for that reason he shouts: 'Throw out the foreigners!' " *On the Renascence of Israel on the Soil of the Land of Their Fathers*, ed. Sh. Breimann, (Hebrew) (Jerusalem, 1953), p. 64, and also, idem (above, n. 32), pp. 193–98. Cf. Sh. Breimann, "The Change in the Public Thought of the Jews in the 1880s," (Hebrew) *Shivat Zion* 2 (Jerusalem, 1951–1952): 83–227; and also the letter of A. Sh. Friedberg to Yehuda Laib Levin of 15 Elul 5641 (1881), with which A. Druyanow opens his collection (above, n. 16), vol. 1, pp. 2–3: "Everywhere where their hand was lifted against us, we see that it is the ignorant who act and the enlightened who rule them; the masses go mad and the aristocrats applaud, and not only here in a land as dark as night, but also in Germany, a land of knowledge and logic, we have no existence; not in Hungary nor in Galicia will we be in peace, and we would not find comfort even in France and in Britain if our number would have been great among the people who dwell there. . . ."

36. P. B. Axelrod, "The Goals of the Jewish Socialist Intelligentsia," (Zurich, 1882) in *Research Studies on the Jewish Workers' Movement* 1 (Hebrew) (Jerusalem, 1966), p. 20.

37. See the memoirs of Ben-Ami on the pogroms in Odessa: Y. Heilperin (ed.), *The Book of Heroism* 2 (Hebrew) (Tel Aviv, 1951), pp. 64–88.

38. Yehuda Laib Levin, "Letter to the Editor," (Hebrew) *HaMaggid* 25, n. 39 (1881): 321–22: "And thus America too is fit for the restoration of the ruins of Israel, in that it is inhabited by enlightened nations and cultured, polite people, and the Jewish people will go there not as if they were returning to their own land, which obligates them to all the commandments connected with it, but will live a good life like all the nations in that country."

39. See a typical description of that trend in the introduction of the book by Z. D. Levontin, *To the Land of Our Fathers* (Hebrew) (Tel Aviv, 1924). The author had begun publishing it in Warsaw in 1885.

40. Cf. I. Klausner, *Love of Zion in Rumania* (Hebrew) (Jerusalem, 1958), pp. 89–94.

41. Cf. Sh. Laskov, *The BILU'IM* (Hebrew) (Jerusalem, 1979), pp. 84–158.

42. On those settlement attempts in 1874 in which N. Chaikovski after whom the first Narodnik organization was named took part, cf. F. Venturi, *Roots of Revolution* (New York, 1966), p. 473. The founder of the settlement was Vladimir Heins, who was called William Frey, a social radical with religious leanings. On him and his activities in the United States, see A. Tcherikover, *The History of the Jewish Workers' Movement in the United States* 2 (Yiddish) (New York, 1945), pp. 186–87 and the bibliography there.

43. On the *Am Olam* movement, see the article of A. Menes, "The 'Eternal People' Movement," (Yiddish) in Tcherikover (above, n. 42), pp. 203–38 or in English, "The 'Am Oylom' Movement," *Yivo Annual* (1949): 9–33; H. Turtel, "The *Am Olam* Movement," (Hebrew) *HeAvar* 10 (Tel Aviv, 1963), pp. 124–43; Sh. Laskov (above, n. 41), pp. 23–26.

44. On the proposal to work towards the establishment of a Jewish state in the United States, see I. Klausner, *On National Reawakening* (Hebrew) (Jerusalem 1962), pp. 112–13; (the proposal of Moshe Shrenstel from Lvov, of Sh. P. Rabinovitz in *Ha-Zefira,* and of Yehuda Laib Levin in *HaMaggid*). Also, M. Eismann, *With the Outbreak of Pogroms against Israel* (Hebrew) (Warsaw, 1881), p. 105.

45. Cf., for example, the words of Lilienblum (above, n. 35); pp. 121–22.

46. Letter of Baron de Hirsch to Levental, dated October 10, 1891, published in H. Avni, *Argentina: The 'Promised Land'* (Hebrew) (Jerusalem, 1973), p. 65.

47. Cf. Druyanow, (above, n. 16) 1, nos. 135–37, 139; Klausner, (above, n. 44), p. 451. The warning of veteran supporter of the settlement in Eretz Israel is typical. M. Gottschalk-Lewi of Berlin warned not to mention the renewal of the national spirit in the activities of the Love of Zion, or to see it as a national union of the Jews, because that would arouse the suspicion of the Turkish authorities and lead them to forbid immigration. Druyanow, *ibid.,* 1, no. 135.

48. Sh. Schama, *Two Rothschilds and the Land of Israel* (London, 1978), p. 58.

49. Cf. the letter of K. Netter to the Jewish newspapers of March 15, 1892: "And from the point of view of the Jews of Europe there might be danger entailed in this responsible attempt to settle Eretz Israel. . . . in a short time we will be eye-witnesses to a catastrophe, the example of which the Jews have not known in the past two thousand years." Druyanow, (above, n. 16), 3, pp. 359–60.

50. Cf. Druyanow, *ibid.,* 3, no. 1239. The proclamation is dated Shevat, 5645 (1885).

51. M. L. Lilienblum, *A Path for Exiles* (Hebrew) (Warsaw, 1899), p. 84. Cf. J. Salmon, "The Confrontation between God-fearing and Enlightened Jews in the Love of Zion Movement during the Eighties," (Hebrew) *HaZionut* 5 (Tel Aviv, 1978): 43–77; see also the article by Y. Kaniel on the Old Yishuv and the settlements in the same volume.

52. Sh. Laskov (above, n. 41), pp. 282–98.

53. Cf., for example, the strong impression made by the Balkan wars and the national revivals in Europe upon the young Eliezer Ben-Yehuda, *The Dream and Its Fulfillment,* ed. R. Sivan (Hebrew) (Jerusalem, 1979), pp. 64–65, 69.

54. Sh. Laskov (above, n. 41), pp. 101–4.

55. Lilienblum (above, n. 35), p. 122.

56. M. Burstein, *Self-Government of the Jews in Palestine since 1900* (Tel Aviv, 1934), pp. 65–73; Eliav, (above, n. 6), pp. 332–34.

57. Pinsker, (above, n. 34), p. 47.

4.

Tradition and Nationalism

Yosef Salmon

One of the central problems within the Jewish national movement more generally and the Zionist movement in particular was and remains its relationship with the Jewish religious tradition. Due to the special nature of Jewish tradition as manifested in the halakhah, that problem was not only of vital concern to "religious" Zionists per se, but also to those who categorized themselves as "secular."

Halakhah, according to this definition, is omni-encompassing, bound up with all domains of life of the Jew, spiritual/religious, social, commercial, economic, and political—and even extends into the most intimate spheres of personal life. There is no distinction between "religion" and the "state," between the affairs of God and those of the monarch. The entire round of Jewish everyday life is dictated by the tenets of halakhah, whether when praying to the Creator or setting off for war. Via explicit and detailed laws, halakhah circumscribes the foods one may eat and their manner of preparation; in precepts equally as exacting and specific, it determines the nature and order of deliberations in civil law and criminal justice. Moreover, halakhah also deals with ideological and ethical questions, formulating what "correct" views are fitting and proper for a Jew to espouse, and how one should relate to the surrounding world and social environment. Maimonides's compendium *Mishneh Torah*, the classic codex of halakhah, contains mundane sections treating laws on "lending and borrowing," "leasing," and "monarchs," alongside chapters on tenets governing opinion and thought, prayer, and the observance of the Sabbath.

Translated from the Hebrew and reprinted by permission of the author from *Dat vezionut: imutim rishonim*, edited by Yosef Salmon (Jerusalem, 1990), 11–25.

It is thus clear that halakhah necessarily must be of some relevance when it comes to Jewish nationalism and how autonomous Jewish social life should be ideally arranged. A "religious" Jew who accepts the authority of halakhah in this strict definition and has consciously chosen to participate in a movement whose aim is the establishment of an autonomous Jewish society cannot disregard its strictures and precepts— all the more so when that society is to be built on soil that is sanctified, in the Land of Israel.

In point of fact, the mistaken view that Jewish religion and halakhah are solely concerned with spiritual matters and only encompass acts between man and God is a product of Western modern secular culture. Only such Zionist thinkers as Theodor Herzl, who was himself divorced from the wellsprings of Jewish tradition, were able to suppose that halakhic tradition was indifferent when it came to political and social questions. Inasmuch as their own national or Zionist outlook had not been molded in the matrix of a solid grounding in traditional Judaism, they viewed Jewish tradition through a refractive Western prism. Even the fond aspiration that inspired thinkers such as J. L. Gordon (1831– 1892) and Ahad Ha-Am (1856–1927) to make a distinction between halakhic Judaism on the one hand—and ethical Judaism, the Hebrew language and its literature on the other—was social utopian in its visionary thrust. In their efforts to realize that conception, they were hardpressed to point to any legitimate precedent for such a differentiation in the annals of Jewish history, and encountered the open opposition of observant Jews who regarded themselves as the true and faithful representatives of authentic historical Judaism.[1]

In contrast, the majority of Zionists in Eastern and Central Europe had imbibed their Zionism with their mother's milk, so to speak, and did not have the slightest doubt that halakhic tradition was the indisputable and obligatory framework governing all spheres of action of the Jew. Consequently, attitudes toward halakhah played a central role in their thinking. The traditionally minded religious Jews who joined the ranks of the Zionist movement were obliged to find a way to reconcile their tradition-oriented views with the fact of their participation in a movement that included members who did not share such convictions. Religious Zionists constituted a significant force within the Zionist movement; it was they who represented the Jewish masses of Eastern and Central Europe, a population which Zionism looked to as its principal demographic reservoir. Therefore, it is clear that the relationship with Jewish tradition remained a central ideological and practical issue even for Zionists who did not share a traditional religious outlook.

Our deliberations on this problem revolve around three pairs of concepts or categories. Although clearly interconnected, each belongs to a separate sphere: religion and nationalism, religion and society, religion and the state.

The first is philosophical in its problematic: in phenomenological terms, can a distinction be predicated between religion and nationalism in Jewish history? The second involves the question of the social order in everyday life: is it possible to be a nationally minded Jew while at the same time pursuing a free (i.e., religiously non-observant) style of life? And what is the law as it applies to a Jewish settler in Eretz Israel who chooses not to order his or her life according to halakhic injunctions? That complex can be broken down into more specific sub-questions: do all components of halakhah have equal weight in this connection? Is observance of the Sabbath equal in importance to observing the laws of the Sabbatical Year (shemittah)? It is valid to distinguish between desecration of the Sabbath publicly and in the privacy of one's own home? To what extent is it permissible for the national society to interfere in the life of the individual? What authority should be invested with the powers to monitor and supervise religious observance in Jewish society?

The third binary, religion and the state, encompasses matters pertaining to the messianic future, the era when a Jewish state will be (re)established. Will that state be based on halakhah? What will be the nature of its justice system? What spiritual authority will rule over it? How will public and private life be conducted?[2] All the various currents in Zionism grappled with the variegated dimensions of these problems, and each put forward its own views and responses.

RELIGION AND NATIONALISM

Some contend that the Zionist movement was essentially divided into two groupings: those who desired to continue the covenant (or identity) of Jewish religion and its halakhic forms in linkage with national Jewish society—and others who wished to dismantle that bond. But such an either-or categorization has been shown to be a distorted picture.[3] Rather, the various Zionist currents took a dialectical view of this problem, moving between the poles of a desire to preserve that identity and the wish to remold it anew. Religious Zionism also rejected exilic diaspora Judaism—or, more precisely, the specific variety of Jewish religious and social civilization which had crystallized in the diaspora. The hope was that the Zionist movement would effect a spiritual purification of Jewish society: in the phraseology of Rabbi Isaac Jacob Reines (1839–1915), "a remedy for the soul" *(refuat ha-nefesh)*. There was a felt need for such a process of mending *(tikun)* in a broad array of areas, including Jewish education; it was to be accomplished by means of halakhic deductive reasoning, the study of Torah and the broadening of general knowledge.

When the writer Yehiel Michal Pines (1843–1913) spoke about the identity between religion and nationalism, he was not referring to Judaism as manifested in its traditional forms among Jews in Eastern Europe. Rather, Pines envisioned Judaism in a highly refined and distilled form, bursting with life and responsive to the demands of the age—a Judaism that, from a historical perspective, had existed prior to exile and the diaspora.[4] Members of the circle around Rabbi Y. L. Diskin (1817–1898) in Jerusalem claimed, with some justification, that Pines was actually calling for reform in halakhah. It is true that Pines dismissed the idea of any reforms in halakhah due to *external* pressures, but he did affirm a process of internal development in halakhah, which he believed would come to pass in the ancient historical homeland.[5] Many decades later, the religious-national ideologue Rabbi Zvi Yehuda Kook (1891–1981?), arguing in the spirit of a rejection of exilic Judaism in the name of the preservation of halakhah, stated: "The quintessential value of the entire Torah, including its commandments that are not dependent on Eretz Israel, lies in the Land of Israel."[6]

The emergence of Jewish nationalism even among traditional circles was rooted in two basic factors: dissatisfaction with Judaism in its various social configurations at the middle of the nineteenth century, and an unwillingness to revamp it along the lines of the radical religious reform movement (Reform Judaism in Germany). The solution was to turn to the ideology of the nation. Religious Zionist nationalism comprised all the features characteristic of modern nationalism more generally: patriotism, national pride, self-determination, and a national language and culture. In their political aspirations, the religious Zionists even went as far as to espouse the conception of a Jewish state, in this perhaps outstripping the ambitions of the mainstream Zionist currents in Eastern Europe at the time.[7]

As early as 1875, Pines had asserted that he disagreed with figures such as Moses Montefiore and organizations like Kol Israel Haverim

(All Israel are Brothers [Alliance Israélite Universelle]) and the Va'ad Hashlihim (Board of Deputies of British Jews) when it came to the "aim of settling the Land of Israel." In Pines's eyes, they were basically little more than philanthropic. He hankered for a full-fledged "renewal of the dignity of the nation" in Eretz Israel. He was not a proponent of a "hermit-like viewpoint," the contention that "from the day the Temple was destroyed, Judaism ascended to take a place behind the Throne of Glory, and sundered its covenant bond with the life of the state." Pines argued: "The entire thrust of their approach . . . was to turn Jerusalem into a refuge for hermits and reclusive souls who cut themselves off from ephemeral daily life for the sake of eternity." Referring to himself, Pines declared: "I am like any individual with a political outlook on the world. My heart longs to behold Jerusalem in all her splendor, as one of the honored and extolled daughters of Europe." [8]

Despite all the modern components in the teachings of religious Zionism, religious Zionists could not conceive of any component in Jewish nationalism that was not somehow firmly anchored in Jewish tradition. They called for the cultivation of national culture, composed of both "religious studies" and "secular studies," and found a scriptural legitimation for that synthesis in the verse "In all thy ways acknowledge Him" (Proverbs 3:6). This view was cogently articulated by E. M. Lipshitz (1879–1946), director of the Mizrahi Seminar in Jerusalem, in an address delivered before the Third Congress of the Mizrahi movement in Jerusalem (1928). As he explained, "Mizrahi aspires to a blending of the holy and profane, of Israel and the Land of Israel, Israel and the Lord, Blessed be His name. That aspiration is difficult to comprehend, because in the Diaspora we have become accustomed to distinguishing between holy and profane . . . From the viewpoint of Mizrahi, we desire to build the land—a land both profane and holy." The conclusion was that a neo-Orthodox approach along the lines of Rabbi Samson Raphael Hirsh (1808–1888) could never satisfy the deepest yearnings of the religious Zionist. The notion of "Torah coupled with worldly occupation, i.e., secular education *(derekh eretz)*" compartmentalizes life into two separate worlds.[9] The religious Zionist aspires to a fusion of the philosophy expressed in the tenets "In all thy ways acknowledge Him," "devotion to God in culture and science," and "the profane is holy." [10] However, the problematic of this position remains a complex topic in itself, and will not be dealt with further in the scope of this essay.

RELIGION AND SOCIETY

Since traditional Judaism postulates an essential identity between religion and nationalism, the religious Zionist sees no justification for a separation between national social life and halakhah. This perspective is generally shared by all currents within religious Zionism, and the question of how to implement that principle is essentially one of tactics. Since the issue was indeed broached during the period of the "harbingers of Zionism," Rabbi Kalischer attempted to resolve it by assuring that the Kolonisations-Verein für Palästina (Association for the Colonization of Palestine, 1860) would appoint inspectors, monitors who would bar Jews who did not observe halakhic commandments from settling in the Land of Israel, and he proposed himself as just such an "overseer" for the settlement Mikveh Israel (1870), in the process of formation at the time.

The issue resurfaced in the course of the 1880s, with the settlement of the Biluim in Gedera. Rabbis Shmuel Mohilever (1824–1898) and Naphtali Zvi Yehuda Berlin of Volozhin (1817–1893) recommended that the Biluim be expelled from Palestine, and that observant Orthodox Jews be settled in their stead. When they realized that they would be unable to implement their proposal, since administrative power in Palestine was not under their control—and due to the express opposition of their associates in the Hibbat Zion movement—the rabbis compromised by appointing a religious monitor to watch over the Biluim. Down to the end of the 1880s, the leaders of Hibbat Zion, including Leo Pinsker (1821–1891), Moses Leib Lilienblum (1843–1910) and Menachem Ussishkin (1863–1941), did not dispute the principle that settlers in the Land of Israel were obliged to fulfill the commandments. Even Baron Rothschild was in agreement on that point.

The only question was how strictly, and to what extent the movement might actively interfere in the way of life of the settlers. Rabbi Mordecai Eliashberg (1817–1889) agreed with Pinsker and Lilienblum, concurring that "strict fulfillment of the laws" *(midat hasidut)* should not be required of them. Rather, settlers were expected to live a life in accordance with halakhah as was common among ordinary Jews. Rabbi Yitzchak Elhanan Spector (1817–1896) was prepared to permit agricultural work during the Sabbatical Year based on his ruling that the settlers should be classified as needy, thus providing a halakhic justification for rescinding the prohibition on such labor. Halakhic leniency of this kind aroused the opposition of Y. M. Pines, who refused to accept that compromise.

As a militant religious Zionist, he saw the settlers as anything but impoverished Jews: rather, they constituted a vanguard of the national Jewish revival. For that reason, he demanded specifically that the Biluim should strictly adhere to the observance of the laws of *shemittah*.

Ahad Ha-Am railed against this generally shared assumption about the proper way of life of the national Jewish society. In the name of the "spirit of Judaism," he called for tolerance and pluralism in all matters pertaining to fulfillment of the commandments. In his thinking, that liberal value was paramount, overriding the halakhic way of life. He argued that lifeways based on halakhah were in essence sectarian, and the immediate special concern of only one group within the broader national movement. Here lies the underlying cause of the unavoidable and basically irresoluble clash between the heterodoxy of Ahad Ha-Am and the religious Zionists.[11] It was possible to follow the tack of Rabbi Shmuel Mohilever and to make light of the importance of Ahad Ha-Am and his group: "One of the people [*a play on the literal meaning of the name of Ahad Ha-Am, trans. note*] transgressed, but what was the sin committed by the entire people?"[12] Yet that approach provoked the ire of Ahad Ha-Am and his adherents.

It was specifically Y. M. Pines, a religious Zionist endowed with a broad outlook, an open mind and a solid general education, who took Ahad Ha-Am's teachings seriously, basing his argumentation on them when he called for the necessity to dissolve the cooperation between observant and non-observant Jews in the national movement. The parallel lines between his thinking and that of Ahad Ha-Am meant that the two viewpoints would never converge. Pines, differing with Pinkser, Lilienblum and the rabbis Mohilever and Spector, did not think that the Land of Israel was a haven for oppressed Jews and those in severe distress, or a means for escaping from the oppressive burden of antisemitism. Jews suffering from persecution could solve their problem by emigrating, for example, to Argentina. For Pines, the building of Eretz Israel was bound up with a general process of Jewish revival, and thus there was no need to be over hasty. "The matter of settlement is not a topical question for solution today, but is a question of history, in whose eyes a hundred years are like yesterday, so why should we hasten in its resolution?" The true meaning of the renewal of national life in Eretz Israel was the cleansing of Judaism from the flaws and blemishes resulting from the long exile, and the return of Jews to a life based on fulfillment of the commandments. Since that was a socio-religious utopia, it was necessary to choose among those wishing to immigrate to

Palestine: "We are obliged to be selective, and not everyone desirous of setting up *moshav* [residence] will come and do so." Because the dispute with Ahad Ha-Am was so comprehensive and fundamental, the conclusion was: "Let there be no quarrelling between us, for we are brethren. Let us part company: if you go north, I shall go south." [13] And indeed, Pines went on to establish the movement Hovevei Zion, based on strict observance of the commandments and organized in the Kolonisations-Verein für Palästina.

With the foundation of the Zionist Organization, Rabbi Mohilever made it clear that there could be no dividing line between religion and nationalism, even though it was not the intention of religious Zionism to interfere in the private life of other Zionists. His letter on this topic, read from the rostrum at the Zionist Congress, was greeted by stormy applause. A tempest erupted at the Congress when it was revealed that a number of delegates had desecrated the Sabbath in cafes around Basel. This was reason for the religious Zionists to protest, since participation in the Congress was considered to be part of the public image of Jewish national society, a fact which in their view obliged all delegates to observe behavior in strict keeping with halakhah.

As long as the Zionist movement was only engaged in circumscribed political activity, the interference of religious circles was in any case restricted to matters of kosher dietary law. But in advance of the Second Congress, the delegates from Russia convened in Warsaw, and the demand was voiced for the first time there to establish a "rabbinical commission" alongside the Zionist Actions Committee. Its function would be to monitor the public image of the movement in everything relating to tradition. That proposal was not adopted by the conference in Warsaw, and was also voted down during deliberations at the Congress itself. In light of this rejection, large numbers of observant religious Zionists resigned from the Zionist Organization. Those who opted to stay within the organization did not abandon their principles, but thought the specific idea of a rabbinical commission was not the correct response to the legitimate desire to protect the traditional public image of the movement. [14]

After pressure mounted from the Democratic Faction to include educational activity in the planks of the Zionist platform, and it became clear at the Fifth Congress that Herzl was prepared to reach a compromise with the Faction, the Mizrahi movement organized a countervailing force to those pressures, calling for preservation of the purely political character of the Zionist Organization. [15] It should not be concluded from this that the Mizrahi leadership was indifferent to the cultural and educational dimension in Zionist activism. Mizrahi leaders adopted that position in order to ensure that the Zionist Organization would not engage in *secular* educational activity,[16] cognizant of the fact that members of the Democratic Faction were for the most part continuing in the liberal heterodox tradition of the Bnei Moshe (Sons of Moses) association founded by Ahad Ha-Am.

At the Russian Zionist conference held in Minsk (1902), a compromise was reached between the two sides, when it was agreed that the various organizations in Palestine could engage in educational and cultural activities, and that sphere would be apportioned between the two currents, religious and secular. In accepting this compromise, Rabbi Reines attempted to defend the Zionist Organization from charges raised by the traditionalists that it was actively engaged in attempts to secularize Jewish society—and had to that specific end decided to transfer cultural and educational activities from the central institutions of the movement to the organizations in Palestine.[17] After the "cultural" program proposed by Nahum Sokolow to the Tenth Congress (1911) was adopted, a sizable number of the leaders of Mizrahi withdrew from the Zionist Organization and joined in the establishment of Agudat Israel (1912). After that decision, it was no longer accurate to characterize the Zionist movement as basically "neutral" in religious affairs. After all, inclusion of education among its spectrum of activities generated competition with the traditional religious community in a crucial domain where it sought to preserve exclusive rights.

Those same religious Zionists who, despite all objections and critique, had nonetheless chosen to remain organized inside the Zionist movement, did so within an ideological framework that transposed matters of religion and society from the realm of reality and the present to the stage of a distant and remote future; i.e., they viewed the exigencies of their epoch as a transitional era, to be followed by an age marked by a prodigious change of heart as the sons returned to the patrimony of their fathers.[18] This messianic optimism meant that those who joined the national movement were part of a process whose ultimate end was to return Jews to the Judaism of the Torah and its commandments.

That optimistic faith facilitated cooperation between the two currents in the movement. When it came to the present moment and the position of religion in society, the religious Zionists were content with what was to be termed much later the "status quo in matters of religion." That construction was designed to make it possible for circles of observant

Jews to fulfill halakhic commandments within the framework of the Zionist movement, the fledgling state-in-the-making and then in the State of Israel after its establishment.

Another aspect of the relations between religion and society in religious Zionism is bound up with the various socialist utopias espoused after World War I: namely the effort to fashion a society based on socialist tenets side by side with traditional Orthodox piety. This endeavor was accompanied by an impressive intellectual momentum which boasted it could creatively assimilate the principles of socialism within Jewish tradition. In the religious workers' party Ha-Poel ha-Mizrahi (1921), members spoke of "religion and labor" and "Torah and labor"—but not of "Torah with labor." There is an abundant literature on that fine but telling semantic distinction.[19]

RELIGION AND THE STATE

Religious Zionism firmly believed that the Jewish state would have to be based on the observance of halakhah. This position was rooted in the early demands that had been voiced by religious Zionists in Hibbat Zion and in the Zionist Organization right from their inception, and it suffered the same fate as the appeals that had preceded it.[20]

The practical problems inherent in running the affairs of a modern state according to halakhic precept were far more thorny and complex than those involved in administering a Jewish community on a halakhic basis while matters of government remained in the hands of non-Jews. As a rule, religious Zionism put off grappling with such questions, although some of its members proposed a Sanhedrin in order to resolve halakhic problems.[21] After the autonomous institutions of the fledgling state-in-the-making began to crystallize, the areas in which the religious authorities would have exclusive rights were expressly delineated: matters of matrimony, the observance of the Sabbath, and kosher dietary laws in public institutions. As noted earlier, even subsequent to the establishment of the state, the majority of religious Zionists reconciled themselves to this reduction of their influence on the conduct of life in the public sphere, although their acceptance was reluctant, resounding with a deafening silence. Even during the pre-state period, within the framework of the Knesset Israel, religious Zionism had made attempts to oppose the setting up of secular Jewish courts, and demanded that legal proceedings should be conducted only "in accordance with the precepts and laws of Israel."[22] However, that call was unrealistic as long as Jewish law remained unable to answer to the needs of a modern society.

The problem was exacerbated with the creation of the state; the Israeli justice system now began to encompass all aspects of a modern polity. Efforts to integrate fundamental rules from traditional Hebrew law within Israeli law, undertaken under the influence of religious Zionism, also aroused opposition within their own camp. These religious Zionists feared that that tendency would have a boomerang effect, leading to the ultimate secularization of Jewish halakhic law and adjudication. It is an arguable thesis that at the time the state was established, religious Zionism was not ready—and perhaps unwilling—to cope seriously and in practical terms with the utopia of administering a state based on halakhah.[23] However, it was able to find excuses, hiding behind the subterfuge that since religious Zionists did not actually exercise control of state power, they were not obliged to put forward a concrete solution.

BETWEEN THE CAMPS

Questions about the Jewish national movement—i.e., whether it is modern or traditional, an outgrowth of earlier social trends or a revolutionary innovation—can be succinctly paraphrased: is the Jewish national movement romantic in inclination, aspiring to reconstruct the past, or progressive, looking forward to the future in order to remedy the ills of past? Answers to this question are rendered particularly complex when one looks at religious Zionism, and the powerful regressive element in the traditional Jewish outlook: "If the ancients were the sons of angels, then we are human beings, and if they were human beings, we then are like unto donkeys" (Babylonian Talmud, Shabbat, 112b). This cast of mind is antithetical to progressive revolutionary thinking, inspired by the power of faith in the possibility of building an advanced society of unparalleled perfection. The romantic motif of "Renew our days as of old," of "restoring the crown" of the pristine splendor of ancient Israel, recurs over and over again in the writings of religious Zionists, alongside the ideal of the new Jew, whose behavior in matters of society, economics and politics is governed by rational principles, relevant to modern times. This dialectic element is an integral part of nationalist-Zionist experience and aspirations in general, but becomes particularly pronounced in the nationalist religious current, which regards the Jewish past and rabbinical literature—halakhic and midrashic, aggadic and kabbalistic—as normative for the present as well.

The process or art of reasoning correctly

Religious Zionism found itself from the start engaged in a profound ideological conflict with the *haredi* (ultra-Orthodox) and neo-Orthodox communities, which adhered to the same normative sources but interpreted them differently. As a consequence, they had a different outlook on reality. Religious Zionism, as a phenomenon of Jewish society, was a movement that separated itself from the *haredi* and neo-Orthodox ideologies, that ultimately turned anti-Zionist.

By contrast, the conflict of religious Zionism with non-traditional Zionism was largely political, a struggle for influence and power, since their points of departure were based on radically different values. During the 1880s—the period of the Hibbat Zion movement—the struggle centered on domination of the Zionist undertaking as a whole. By the last decade of the nineteenth century, however, the crucial issue was: who should have the authority to educate and shape Zionist society, to determine the nature of the fledgling Yishuv and ultimately that of the state? It is no accident that the first political party to be established in the Zionist Organization was the Mizrahi (1902), and that it played a role in the movement's leadership. When a minority group wishes to determine the life-style of the majority, though fully aware that it cannot possibly achieve a majority itself, it has no choice but to join in a coalition, for as an opposition group it stands to forfeit all its assets and potential achievements. Its fight for political survival is a life-and-death struggle, dictated by the recognition that it is duty bound to realize its specific values.

ZIONISM AND MESSIANISM

Was religious Zionism motivated primarily by messianic goals? Needless to say, Judaism is a messianic religion *par excellence,* professing a view of the future world in which the hopes and expectations of the believer will be fulfilled. However, the content of this world view and the conditions and timing of its realization have always been a matter subject to the specific imagination and visions of Jews over the ages. The messianism of Shabbetai Zevi differed from that of David Alroy and David Reuveni, and the latter could not be likened to Bar Kokhba. Each messianic phenomenon or personality is influenced by contemporary circumstances, by the dynamics of ideas and social conditions of its time.

The believer's longing for relief from pain and suffering through a messiah—personal or otherwise—is also part and parcel of the modern Jewish religious experience. At the same time, one should distinguish between latent or implicit messianic faith, which does not guide the major efforts of the individual or society, and overt or explicit faith, which openly dictates all their actions. Phrased in these terms, the question we must address is whether the messianic element in the ideology of religious Zionism was a potential factor or an actual driving force. No account of the evolving Zionist convictions of such rabbis as Judah ben Shlomo Alkalai (1798–1878), Zvi Hirsch Kalischer (1795–1874) and Natan Friedland (1808–1883) can ignore their messianic point of departure: for them, the revival of Jewish settlement in Eretz Israel in their time was tantamount to *athalta di-geulah*—the dawn of redemption— and *itaruta di-letata*—awakening from below. Kalischer was uncertain as to the proper position of the present in the grand scheme of redemption—the first stage, "dawning of the morning star," or the second, that of "fair as the moon."

At any rate, after the establishment of the Kolonisations-Verein für Palästina, these thinkers toned down the messianic elements in their respective ideologies, in keeping with the desire to attract large numbers of traditionally minded Jews to the activities of that society. The coming of the personal messiah was relegated to the distant future, no longer dependent on human initiative, though the view of the present as the "messianic era" remained in force.[24] As it happened, Kalischer's most vehement opponents belonged to the traditional camp. Denying the messianic conception of the present, they refused to regard the settlement of Eretz Israel in our time as the "dawn of redemption." This outlook was forcefully expressed by Rabbi Meier Auerbach (1815– 1878), the Ashkenazi Chief Rabbi of Jerusalem. Responding to Kalischer's call, he claimed that the idea of redemption in Jewish literature was obscure and mystical, so that the modern Jew can be guided only by what he can see, by existing conditions. "This matter depends on repentance, love of the holy Torah, written and oral, and on bending our hearts to follow the straight path marked out by our forefathers."[25]

On the other hand, the messianic element in Kalischer's writings did not deter Moses Hess, who was far from traditionally minded, from hailing Kalischer as an ally and quoting him in his book *Rome and Jerusalem* (1862). This approach was to be characteristic of secularist attitudes toward Torah-true Zionism in the generations to come. The messianic concepts of religious Zionism, which underwent numerous transformations, were no obstacle to its acceptance as a partner of non-traditional Zionism, as the latter was not concerned with the theoretical background of religious Zionism. However, religious Zionist terminology and conceptions prompted the *haredi* and neo-Orthodox communities to keep their distance, since for them it constituted a secularization of traditional Zionism, violating the three oaths that God had imposed on the Jews: not to force God's hand in the matter of the coming of the messiah, not to go en masse ("in a multitude") to Eretz Israel, and not to rebel against the nations of the world (Babylonian Talmud, Ketubbot, 111a). Guided by the ideas of Kalischer and Alkalai, the founders of Petah Tikvah, for their part, declared that settlement of the land in our time was the "first of the Four Redemptions," signifying in kabbalistic symbolism the "first rays of the incipient dawn." [26]

Only a small number of religious Zionists of the second generation made use of messianic arguments. Among these were Rabbi Gimpel Jaffe (1820–1891), the spiritual leader of the new colonies after settling in Yehud (1888), and perhaps also Rabbi Naftali Zvi Judah Berlin. Both these leaders opposed the rabbinical dispensation permitting agricultural labor during the Sabbatical Year, arguing that strict observance of *shemittah* was expressive of the general character of the return to Eretz Israel in our era, which is the "dawn of redemption." [27] However, such arguments are absent in the writings of the major spokesmen of the second generation: Yehiel Michal Pines, Mordecai Eliashberg, Shmuel Mohilever, Samuel Jacob Rabinowitz (1857–1921), and Isaac Jacob Reines. As advocates of religious perfection and the strict fulfillment of all the commandments (which is only possible in Eretz Israel), they were faced with the dilemma of joining hands with Jews who, though not observant, wished to immigrate to Eretz Israel and settle there. They had to counter the argument that "he who encourages those professing the idea of settlement is thereby encouraging sinners and aiding transgressors." [28]

It should nevertheless be emphasized that these religious Zionists, like their predecessors of the first generation, believed that non-observant Jews had no right to settle in Eretz Israel. However, they differed among themselves as to the tactics to be adopted toward the "transgressors." Should they be treated according to the strict letter of the law, or should they be tolerated, on the assumption that they would change their ways and repent in the future? Debating the proper approach to the Biluim, Mohilever and Berlin argued that they should be expelled and observant Jews settled in their stead. Yet Pines and Reines defended the Biluim, who, they reasoned, would be inspired to repent, and whose participation in Hibbat Zion had saved them from being assimilated: "For through this movement we have gained these souls and saved them from assimilation." [29] This situation was reversed in the 1890s, when Pines demanded the removal of Bnei Moshe from Eretz Israel; in contrast, Mohilever and David Solomon Slouschz (1852–1906) advocated tolerance, in the hope that the offenders would soon repent and accept the Torah.

In any event, as early as 1889, Rabbis Joseph Dov Soloveichik and Hayyim Soloveichik did not hesitate to proclaim that "Hovevei Zion are a new sect like that of Shabbetai Zevi—may the name of the wicked rot!" In reaction to such criticism, the religious Zionist thinkers began to deny that their goals were in any sense messianic. One representative of this trend was Abraham Jacob Slutski, editor of *Shivat Zion* (1891/92), an anthology of rabbinical approvals of the Hibbat Zion movement. Slutski stated that the messianic ideals had been espoused by a minority, and that in any case they varied considerably from writer to writer. Indeed, they also had an educational role to play—to awaken Jewish hearts and to fulfill the hopes for redemption. Such ideals did not imply that renewed settlement in Eretz Israel actually marked the beginning of the process of redemption.[30]

However, even those religious Zionist thinkers who did not stress the messianic element were relying on quasi-messianic ideas when they asserted that secularly motivated settlers in Eretz Israel would eventually become observant. Indeed, in the view of Mohilever, Reines, Eliashberg, and Pines, the restoration of national awareness among the Jews was but the first stage in a supernatural process, whereby the Jewish people as a whole would ultimately return to the Torah. One might say that they embraced Maimonides's denial of the supernatural aspect of the messianic era, which signifies nothing more than relief from the gentile yoke, the ingathering of the exiles in the Land of Israel, and the adoption of halakhah as the way of life of the Jewish society. It was this conception that permitted cooperation between religious and non-religious Zionism in the rebuilding of Eretz Israel. It also enabled the religious Zionists to mask their messianic aspirations and suppress the miraculous, mystical, and catastrophic elements of the messianic era as portrayed in the redemption *midrashim* and in kabbalistic literature.

This approach continued to characterize debate in the early days of the Zionist Organization. It was explicitly stated by Rabbi Samuel Jacob Rabinowitz of Aleksot (1857–1921), the greatest spokesman of religious Zionism before Reines and the establishment of the Mizrahi: "The Zionist movement in our day does not involve forcing the issue [of messianic coming] or a messianic movement, nor does it imply going up to Israel en masse or rebelling, G—d forbid, against the gentiles. Rather, it aspires to a natural goal, to what is possible under present-day living conditions, given our position among the nations."[31] In other words: religious Zionism employs rational means to realize Jewish national aspirations. It proposes a solution to the social adversities of the Jewish people in this day and age, and as such it shares the aspirations of Zionism in general.

Would it be accurate to contend that religious Zionist ideology had, as far as its national aspirations were concerned, become secularized? This was not, it would seem, the understanding of the *haredi* opponents of religious Zionism, and they had good grounds for their position. As we have pointed out, even the proponents of non-messianic religious Zionism believed that although the messianic era was not yet at hand, the modern resettlement of Eretz Israel was nevertheless a stage in the messianic process. It is not surprising, therefore, that Rabbi Hayyim Elijah Meisel (1821–1912) of Łódź, one of the greatest rabbinical figures of the time, refused to allow religious Zionism to dodge the implications of the messianic stumbling-block: "It is not they who shall bring the Messiah or build the Temple."[32]

The shift of control in the Zionist movement increasingly to non-observant Jews, and the rejection at the Second Zionist Congress (1898) of the Orthodox proposal for the establishment of a rabbinical commission alongside the Zionist Actions Committee, in order to preserve the traditional public image of the movement, only reinformed the argument that Zionism was not a return to sanctity but just the opposite—a desecration of it. There could thus be no identification of the Zionist endeavor in the Land of Israel with redemption. One of the first polemical works against Zionism in general and religious Zionism in particular stated: "Even the last embers still glowing in the hearts of our secular members brethren will be slowly dimmed by the spirit of freedom hovering over the Zionist movement."[33] In the eyes of these opponents, the Zionist program was not aimed primarily at achieving a Jewish state or at relieving the social distress of the Jews: its goal was "to expunge messianic hopes from their hearts"—in other words, it constituted an anti-traditional program.

The realization and justification of Zionist goals by religious Zionism provoked the *haredi* camp to extreme reactions. They rejected out of hand the religious Zionist conception—the idea of redemption by stages, redemption by natural means, and the obligatory nature of the precept of settlement in Eretz Israel in the present time. On the contrary: they even justified *emigration* from Eretz Israel under the circumstances which had arisen. One of the more extreme advocates of this point of view was Rabbi Shalom Dov Ber Schneerson (1866–1920), among the most important hasidic spiritual leaders of the time.[34] To his mind, redemption by natural means ran "counter to our real hope, for all our expectation and hope is that the Holy One, Blessed be He, will bring us the Messiah of Righteousness speedily in our days, Amen, and that we shall be redeemed by the Holy One, Blessed be He."[35] At the time of the harbingers of Zionism, attention was centered on exegesis of Scripture. Now, however, it was interpretation of the present that loomed upper-most.

TRADITION AND MODERNISM

Was religious Zionism a modern phenomenon? If the term "modernism" implies rational action, use of technology, recognition of the need to obtain international approval for the achievement of national goals, establishment of a democratic political regime—religious Zionism was modern to the same degree that Zionism in general is indeed a modern national movement. From its very inception, religious Zionism rejected the doctrinal postulates of traditional society, which frowned on the notion of mere mortals attempting to bring about national redemption, or as Rabbi Kalischer put it, "a natural cause emanating from human agency": "Dear reader, cast off the veil of common usage, according to which the masses believe that the Messiah of Righteousness will momentarily proclaim himself . . . This is not so, for redemption will begin with the awakening of the nobles and the readiness of kingdoms to gather in a handful of the exiles of Israel to the Holy Land."[36] The significance of human endeavor in this regard is "to raise up its ruins and love its dust, to plant vineyards and sow the fruit of righteousness, that the land be not desolate."[37] Kalischer, fully aware of modern national values, acknowledged the need for international recognition: "We shall be accorded praise and glory in the eyes of the nations."[38]

He also stressed that national goals would not be realized without daring and devotion: "Why do the people of Italy and other countries lay down their lives for their homelands . . . while we stand far off, like men bereft of strength and courage?"[39] Kalischer also touched on the aspect of economic independence: "Every scholar who reads and studies for the sake of G—d's name will eat and drink of his own provisions, enjoying the fruit of his labors and not living on charity."[40] Kalischer and Alkalai offered practical suggestions to that end: a stock company should be established and wealthy Jews be persuaded to support the endeavor. They proposed that a charter be secured for formal immigration to Eretz Israel: "The beginning of the future redemption will be sanctioned by the foreign kingdoms and some of the exiles will be ingathered."[41] In that spirit, they joined the Kolonisations-Verein für Palästina, established by Dr. Chaim Lorje (1821–1878), which called for funds to be collected from the Jewish masses and utilized for settlement in Eretz Israel.[42]

A perusal of the first regulations adopted by the founders of Petah Tikvah,[43] whose express goal was to implement the ideas of the harbingers of religious Zionism, reveals a desire for the national normalization of Jewish society ("Why should Jacob have no share together with all the families of the earth?"),[44] for economic normalization ("they desire bread from the labor of their own hands"),[45] and an awareness of the need for international recognition ("at this opportune time, when all the nations and kings of the states are at peace with us and willing to sustain us").[46]

The details of the founding society's regulations are impressive in their modern features: a democratic awareness, the clearly defined rights and obligations of members, and the society's responsibilities for its members. On the other hand, since all these goals were anchored by citation of chapter and verse from rabbinical literature—halakhic, midrashic and kabbalistic—and also placed squarely within the justifying context of the precepts specific to Eretz Israel and its redemption, the entire initiative took on a traditional complexion, involving the use of phraseology drawn from the discourses of mysticism, faith, and halakhah, rather than modern secular nationalist thought.

The religious Zionists took issue with the exile, regarding it as a factor in the development of a defective form of Judaism in the social and religious sense. In so doing, they justified the necessity for the comprehensive political and social normalization of Jewish society, which would in turn spark a halakhic and religious reconstruction of Judaism. When they appealed to the Jewish community at large to embrace their cause, they were fully aware of the need to modernize that community's lifestyle, occupations, relationships with the surrounding environment, and level of education. Eliashberg spoke in this context of restoring the "natural wisdom" of Israel. Reines added the element of social normalization: "for all good and praiseworthy qualities can exist and be maintained only among tillers of the soil, not among merchants and shopkeepers."[47] The Zionist movement is not merely an answer to the physical and political adversities of the Jew; it also mends his spirit, it is a "remedy for the soul." The return to agriculture does not represent a longing for pre-exilic Jewish society; it is founded on a mixture of mystical assumptions and analogical reasoning: "For since observance of the Torah is ingrained in Jewish nature and observance of the Torah is linked to the land and to agricultural labor, it follows that the Jew is linked to the land; by his very nature, he is capable of farming the land and the land is suitable for this labor!"[48]

There is no modern element in general Zionism that has not left its imprint on religious Zionism. If a major element in the development of the Zionist movement since the 1880s was the reaction to antisemitism, the first thinkers to analyze that phenomenon and draw practical conclusions were the religious Zionists. Before Lilienblum and Pinsker began to grapple with the problem of antisemitism, David Gordon (1831–1886), editor of *Ha-maggid,* warned his readers of the significance of the new wave of antisemitism emerging in Austria-Hungary, France, and Germany in the late 1870s and early 1880s. Gordon declared that the efforts at assimilation among Western Jews would prove abortive: "In vain do they adorn themselves, seeking to imitate the neighboring nations in all their ways, even in their spirit and national sentiments, for such men as Treitschke, Stöcker and Henrici have not yet died, nor will they perish in any future generation."[49] "An Appeal to the Diaspora," published in the journal *Havazelet* in the immediate wake of early rumors of the pogroms in Russia, stated: "How long will you entertain illusory hopes that herein lie your rest and security, saying 'peace, peace'—but there is no peace? For G—d has spoken in His holiness: 'And among these nations shalt thou have no repose'."[50] This response expresses a total and absolute rejection of the diaspora, motivated by the rise of antisemitism: "Your way is obstructed in the land of your habitations, you have no ascendancy there, and no hope."[51] It should be recalled that the Mizrahi's support for Herzlian Zionism, including the Uganda Project (1903), derived from a pessimistic appraisal of the future of Jewish society in its present milieu and habitations, and the conclusion that there was thus an immediate need for a haven, and be it only a "haven for the night."

ROMANTIC OR PROGRESSIVE ZIONISM

Was religious Zionism romantic or progressive? This dialectic feature of Zionist thought more generally—romantic inclinations alongside progressive platforms for action—is also characteristic, though to a lesser degree, of religious Zionism. Perhaps the reason for the relative insignificance of the romantic component in religious Zionism can be traced to the preoccupation of traditional society with the norms of halakhic behavior, which is by its very nature a progressive and evolving feature—due to the authority conferred on rabbis in each and every generation to enact and revise halakhic directives. In addition, one can cite the believer's persistent expectations of the messianic future. Such features leave no room for nostalgic longings for past ages and the desire to reconstruct that past.

At the same time, romantic overtones are indeed present in the writings of certain religious thinkers, particularly those who did not place emphasis on messianic motivation. Yet Kalischer betrayed no such romantic leanings. To the extent that he invokes the past, he does so more in order to underpin his halakhic argument regarding the present and future. For example, Kalischer argued that just as the leaders of the return from Babylonian exile did not await the messiah, but went about the practical task of organizing the returnees and initiated the building of the Temple after receiving a "charter" from Cyrus, so it behooves us to act today. The code of regulations drafted by the founders of the settlement Petah Tikvah speak about the mystical bond between the people of Israel and Eretz Israel: "For the soul of every Israelite longs for its root—our ancestral inheritance." [52] However, there is no romantic expression whatsoever of this bond.

By contrast, the "Appeal to the Diaspora" published in *Havazelet* contains certain romantic threads interwoven into its arguments, which are based more on an analysis of contemporary antisemitism than on messianic hopes: "Only in Jerusalem shall they be comforted, and only there lies all their hope to raise up our standard in honor, a light onto the nations and banner to all peoples, when we return to the glories of our youth, 'for out of Zion shall go forth the Law, and the word of the Lord from Jerusalem'." [53] And perhaps even more emphatically: "Let us recall our saintly forefathers, who risked their lives upon the high places of the field and spilled their blood like water for the sake of our people and the cities of our Lord. And now that the conquest of our land is at hand, not by might nor by power . . . you remain silent . . . how great is the offence, how grievous the sin." [54]

Eliashberg also makes use of romantic motifs to determine the norms of contemporary behavior. He argued that the return to Zion in our day is destined to remedy the faults that have accumulated in diaspora society. Before they were exiled, the Jews practiced a harmonious combination of "religious sanctity" and "natural wisdom." By the latter, Eliashberg meant general education, social virtues, and an ability to cope with political realities. In his day, so he claimed, the *maskilim* (proponents of the Haskalah or Jewish Enlightenment) were the bearers of "natural wisdom," the traditionalists of "religious sanctity." In order that these disparate elements be reunited, each must enjoy equal rights within the Zionist movement. The new return to Zion will "restore the crown" of the nation to its former pristine splendor; the schism in the House of Israel shall finally be healed. Here again, the past is evoked in order to advocate norms of behavior in the present; in essence, the argument is free from romantic wistfulness.

Although religious Zionism did not cultivate the romantic aspects of national experience, neither in its literature nor in the way of life it proposed, it was clearly not entirely adverse to such proclivities. As time went on and messianic hopes were divorced from Zionist reality, religious Zionism joined the broader Zionist movement in promoting romantically colored national symbols and holidays: Hanukah as the festival of the militant Maccabees, Shavuot as the agricultural festival of first fruits. A romantic element is expressed in the first manifesto of the founders of Ha-Poel ha-Mizrahi: "We aspire to return to the Hebrew way of life of ancient days, to the original Judaism of the Bible, founded on justice, integrity and ethical conduct."[55] The tension between preservation of tradition and response to the new is an integral part of the most fundamental experience of religious Zionism.

NOTES

1. Y. L. Maimon, *Hidush ha-sanhedrin be-medinateynu ha-mehudeshet* (Jerusalem, 1951), pp. 11–14.
2. Ibid.
3. At the Third Congress of Mizrahi, held in Palestine in 1928, Rabbi Ostrovsky, head of the Executive Committee of the Mizrahi Organization in Eretz Israel, argued that only in radical circles of the left and right was there any desire to make a distinction between religious matters and affairs of the community, cf. *Ha-ve'idah ha-shlishit* (Jerusalem, 1928), p. 59.
4. On this position in the religious kibbutzim, see A. Fishman, ed., *The Religious Kibbutz Movement* (Jerusalem, 1957), pp. 13–14. Regarding different approaches within religious Zionism to the modernization of Jewish society, see Y. Salmon, "Ha-zionut ha-datit ve-mitnagdeha: masoret ve-moderniyut, meshihiyut ve-romantikah," *Zemanim* 14 (1984), 66–67. Cf. also A. Fishman, "Masoret ve-hidush ba-havayat ha-zionut ha-datit," *Bi-shvilei ha-tehiyah* 1 (1983), 127–47.

5. See "Yehiel Michal Pines: Demuto ha-historit," *Milet* 1 (Tel Aviv, 1983), p. 97.

6. Z. Y. Kook, "Ha-torah ve-ha-aretz," *Yovel ha-Mizrahi* (Jerusalem, 1952), pp. 194–95.

7. On the efforts by Shmuel Mohilever to mobilize the support of Hovevei Zion in Russia for Herzl's benefit, see also I. Nissenbaum, "Ha-Mizrahi al em ha-derekh," *Ha-Mizrahi: Sefer ha-yovel* (New York, 1936), p. 30.

8. See "Yehiel Michal Pines: Demuto ha-historit," p. 97.

9. Even if S. R. Hirsch, who formulated this duality, did not regard it as desirable, in actual practice it became a reality during his own lifetime. See M. Breuer, "Shitat torah-im-derekh-eretz be-mishnato shel Rav Samson Rafael Hirsh," *Ha-maayan* 9 (1968–69), no. 1, p. 101, no. 2, p. 291.

10. *Ha-ve'idah ha-shlishit,* op. cit., pp. 77–78. See also A. Fishman, "Shnei etosim dati-'im be-hitpathut ha-raayon 'torah va-avodah'," *Bi-shvilei ha-tehiyah* 2 (Ramat Gan, 1987), p. 130, fn. 9.

11. The dispute between Ahad Ha-Am and his teachings on the one hand, and religious Zionism on the other continued on for many years even after his death, see Y. L. Ha-Cohen Fishman, "Ha-le'umiyut ha-ivrit," *Ha-Mizrahi: Sefer ha-yovel,* op. cit., pp. 11–13.

12. Y. Shapira, ed., *Iggerot ha-rabi Nissenbaum* (Jerusalem, 1956), p. 24, fn. 15; p. 25, fn. 18.

13. See "Yehiel Michal Pines: Demuto ha-historit," p. 108, fn. 37.

14. I. Nissenbaum, *Ketavim nivharim* (Jerusalem, 1948), pp. 14–17.

15. Ibid., p. 14.

16. M. Berlin, "Kibushei ha-Mizrahi," *Ha-Mizrahi: Sefer ha-yovel,* op. cit., p. 7–8; "Ha-kruz ha-rishon shel ha-Mizrahi ha-olami," ibid., p. 34.

17. Ibid., pp. 34–37.

18. *Ha-ve'idah ha-shlishit,* op. cit., p. 17; Z. Y. Kook, op. cit., p. 25; A. Fishman, "Shnei etosim," p. 124.

19. A. Fishman, ibid., pp. 133–140. Cf. also M. Rotstein, "Hitatzmut rayonit u-maasit," in: *Torah ve-avodah ba-hazon u-va-maas* (Tel Aviv, 1985), pp. 158–159; "Torah ve-avodah," *Ha-Poel ha-Mizrahi* 1 (1923), pp. 3–4.

20. Y. L. Maimon, *Le-shaah u-le-dor* (Jerusalem, 1965), pp. 394–97, 398–99.

21. Y. L. Maimon, *Hidush ha-sanhedrin,* op. cit., pp. 35, 42, 47, 53. One of the first important figures to become conscious of this problem was Rabbi Hayyim Hirschen-sohn, a learned Talmudist from a distinguished family of rabbinic scholars in Palestine and Mizrahi activist, who went to the United States to serve as a rabbi in New Jersey. He published the book *Malki ba-kodesh,* 6 parts, (St. Louis, 1919–1923), in which he attempted to deal with the questions raised by the problems of organizing a modern state along the lines of traditional halakhah. See Y. D. Eisenstein, "Toldot ha-rav Haim Hirshenzon u-sefarav," *Apiryon* 5, no. 1 (1927/28), pp. 7–11; Sh. L. Horvitz, ibid., p. 15.

22. Y. L. Maimon, *Hidush ha-sanhedrin,* op. cit., pp. 53–56. Rabbi Maimon reviewed this demand after the establishment of the state.

23. Idem, *Le-shaah u-le-dor,* op. cit., p. 406.

24. Zevi Hirsch Kalischer, *Derishat zion* (Lück, 1862), p. 91.

25. *Ha-Levanon.* 1, no. 4, p. 20, article by Rabbi Meier Auerbach.

26. *Ketavim le-toledot Hibbat Zion ve-yishuv Eretz Israel,* 3 vols., 1919–1932, no. 1109, "Agudat ha-adamah u-geulat ha-aretz,"

27. Berlin to Fuenn, *Ketavim,* no. 924; Berlin to Pinsker, ibid., no. 873; see also G. Yaffe, "Lo et lahashot," ibid., no. 1322.

28. M. Reines, *Netzah Israel* (Warsaw, 1890), p. 26.

29. Ibid., p. 28.

30. *Shivat zion*, p. 83; cf. "Sefer 'Shivat zion' ve-rekao ha-histori," *Eshel* 2, (Beer-Sheva, 1980), p. 151.
31. Sh. Y. Rabinovitz, "Hashkafah le-tovah," *Ha-melitz*, 1899, no. 156.
32. "Mahshavot retzotzot," *Ha-melitz*, 1898, no. 257. Nissenbaum quoted this as having been said by Rabbi L., whom he met while on a journey; Rabbi Meisel is the person actually meant here. See *Alei heldi* (Warsaw, 1929), pp. 145–47.
33. D. Tursh, *Bar hedya o halom Herzl* (Warsaw, 1899), p. 38.
34. Sh. D. Schneerson, *Igeret be-davar ha-mosad ha-kadosh kupat ha-rambahan* (1907), pp. 24, 31.
35. S. Z. Landa and Y. Rabinovitz, *Or la-yesharim* (Warsaw, 1900), pp. 57–58.
36. *Derishat zion*, op. cit., p. 90.
37. Ibid., p. 76.
38. Ibid., p. 79.
39. Ibid.
40. Ibid.
41. Ibid., p. 90.
42. Ibid., pp. 173–77.
43. *Ketavim*, no. 1109.
44. Ibid.
45. Ibid.
46. Ibid.
47. I. Y. Reines, "Yishuv Eretz Israel," in: *Netzah Israel*, p. 45.
48. Ibid., p. 46.
49. *Ha-maggid*, 1881, no. 8, p. 61.
50. *Ketavim*, 3, pp. 294–301.
51. Ibid.
52. *Ketavim*, no. 1109.
53. *Ketavim*, 3, pp. 294–301.
54. Ibid.
55. *Torah ve-avodah ba-hazon*, op. cit., p. 28.

II.

THE DIASPORA AND ZION

5.

The Afflictions of the Jews and the Afflictions of Zionism: The Meaning and Consequences of the "Uganda" Controversy

David Vital

Whereas much in the history of the Jews is familiar and repetitive and much—perhaps most things—fall into some sort of pattern or order, the advent of modern, especially political Zionism represents a departure. Whatever the future may hold for us in this country, it is surely evident that the condition of the Jews as a collectivity—even, to be more precise, as a *set* of collectivities—has been transformed by the enlargement and consolidation of the bridgehead established here one hundred years ago and its equipment, in due course, with the accoutrements and instruments of a full-fledged state. It is therefore in some sense ungenerous, in some ways unfeeling, to subject this extraordinary and dramatic and, indeed, triumphant change in the national condition to the sort of scrutiny to which lesser topics by far are subjected by students of history and society. And yet. . . .

Bertrand Russell once said of the younger members of his family that, having been born after 1914, they were incapable of "happiness." We may say of ourselves that after 1945 we are incapable of happiness in something like Russell's sense. Specifically, it is difficult to celebrate one hundred years of Zionism and the new *yishuv* without the nagging thought that somehow, somewhere along the line, to some extent, the Zionists failed the people for whom they claimed to speak. For after all,

Reprinted with the permission of the author and Eliezer Don-Yehiya from *Comparative Jewish Politics, vol. 2: Conflict and Consensus in Jewish Political Life*, edited by S. A. Cohen and Eliezer Don-Yehiya (Ramat Gan: Bar-Ilan University Press, 1984), 79–91.

political independence came too late for the majority of those Jews who would have been the first not only to enjoy but to *need* it.

Of course, to speak thus of "people" and of the leaders of a move-ment—any people, any movement—is to raise not only painful, but very difficult questions. What might be the precise degree of responsibil-ity the latter may be said to bear for the former? To what extent can they be said to have been free to choose and act in the face of the great forces and events which were imperfectly understood at the time, yet overpowering in their immediate psychological and material impact? Still, the fact is that most great topics in recent Jewish history are necessarily discussed under the shadow of the wartime destruction of European Jewry; and the Zionist movement, its rise, development, and recent decline, cannot be an exception.

However, the question to which I wish to address myself here and now is of a somewhat different order from those to which I have just alluded. It concerns neither the moral right of the Zionists—specifically the Zionist leadership—to speak and act for some or all of the Jewish people; nor their deeds or misdeeds, their wisdom or otherwise, the validity or failure of their tactics. I am concerned rather with the frame of mind and the fundamental perspective in which the dominant strain within the Zionist movement, from its inception, tended to perceive the world and the place of Jewry within it: not with policy directly, but with what they conceived to be the proper order of priorities which should inform them in their formulation of policy. And my thesis is a simple one. It is that the matter was settled at a very early stage in the history of the movement. The debate on the ultimate purpose of the movement—whether it was to concern itself primarily with the Jews as living *individ-uals*, men, women and children, or with the Jewish people as a *collectiv-ity* and with Judaism (whatever that might be taken to mean) as a culture—was held very early and settled firmly in favour of the latter with two crucial, interconnected, long-lasting results. Zionism as a res-cue operation was diminished in favour of Zionism as national recon-struction in a particular way and a particular place; and what under one dispensation were seen—or could be seen—as tactical purposes, took on the aspect of absolute purposes under the other.

But before going on to show how ideology and policy came to be connected in practice and with what results, let me, by way of making clear what I have in mind, cite one, not very important, but suggestive example of official Zionist thinking in practice on the interconnection between Zionist policy and the fate of European Jewry in occupied Europe during the Second World War.

On September 13, 1944, a senior, accredited representative of the Zionist movement called at the State Department in Washington to meet members of its Near Eastern Affairs staff. The official, secret "memorandum of conversation" as recorded by the Department and relayed to American diplomatic and consular representatives in Cairo, Baghdad, Beirut, Damascus, Jedda, Jerusalem and London, was headed "Zionist Attitude toward Palestine." It reported *inter alia* two references to the rescue of Jews in occupied Europe which retain some interest today—although less for any practical effect the conversation may have had on either American or Zionist policy at the time, than for the *approach* underlying them. It is with the approach, the philosophy, if you will, that I am concerned—and that I am bound to emphasize. The first reference was to a proposal, then before the Congress, that temporary emergency shelters for Jews from Hungary be established in Palestine. The Zionist representative made it clear that he did not think much of it, partly because he distrusted the motives of those who had persuaded members of the Congress to put it forward and partly because he did not think Jews could succeed in escaping from Hungary anyway. But "in any case," he went on to say, "the Zionists were opposed to any scheme which would seek to place Jews in Palestine only temporarily and on the understanding that they would be sent elsewhere after the war."

The second reference was to the argument current at the time between the Colonial Office and the Jewish Agency on the final disposition of the 15,000 immigration certificates that still remained to be allocated under the terms of the 1939 White Paper. The Jewish representative had this to say (and I quote again from the State Department record of the conversation):

The Colonial Office took the line that preference in the issuance of certificates should be given to those Jews, i.e., those in occupied Europe, who were in imminent danger of death. [However, while] the Jewish Agency could not deny the priority to which such persons were entitled ... it had argued that some provision should also be made for potential immigrants in such "safe" areas as Italy, North Africa and the Yemen.[1]

The handwritten comments in the margin of the document suggest that our representative's American audience could hardly believe their ears. But once again it is not my present purpose to discuss, or even to criticize, the political strategy and rationale that underlay such an extraordinary view of what the Jewish national interest required even so late in the war as September 1944. It is enough that it was so conceived and articulated and not in some confidential conversation at the State

Department alone. What matters is its source, by which I mean the point in its history at which the Zionist movement—unwittingly—was set upon a course that should have led to such a position being taken and articulated in the first place.

Now it is, I think, beginning to be recognized that the point in time at which, in fact, such a course came to be set was in the immediate aftermath of what the textbooks still call "the Uganda affair." For the outcome of that great quarrel was the defeat of Herzl and his followers at the hands of what may be termed the "Hibbat Zion faction" in the movement. In a general way the argument may not be new, even if it remains unpopular. In any event, I want to go well beyond the simple— and, if I may say, vulgar—proposition that a certain, small part of modern Kenya could have been an effective substitute for Eretz Israel. What really mattered in 1903–05 and what remains of interest today are the ideological and conceptual differences between the two schools of thought, such that one school was willing, however reluctantly, at least to consider the East Africa project while the other dismissed it out of hand as a matter of absolute principle.[2] For what principle or principles were really at stake here? Was the debate only about territory: Eretz Israel, for or against? I think not. I shall try to show, at least in outline, that it ran far deeper and is not quite dead even today when the specifically territorial question has long been forgotten except as a curiosity of our recent past.

It may be said of the debate on the East Africa project as it proceeded within the Zionist movement from its beginning in the summer of 1903 to its formal conclusion some two years later that it was in every sense of the term *political*. On the one hand it reflected a struggle for leadership and authority. On the other hand, when all the surface layers of the quarrel have been allowed for—the genuine differences on strategy, the play of personalities and temperament, the private hurts, grudges and jealousies, the competition for place and influence, and the friction that could not but arise between men of different culture and social experience—there was here a clash of ideologies, of conflicting principles and incompatible prescriptions for the ills of Jewry. But far from mitigating the debate on ideology, the political fight for supremacy in the movement only intensified it—no doubt because in these, the formative years of the Zionist movement, ideology was all. The movement had no *material* power; it was a voluntary association within the larger society of Jewry that was itself devoid of any but the most tenuous centres of formal and truly enforceable authority. The influence and moral authority of Zionism were therefore functions of its power to move men's minds; and the source of such power as it had turned on the force and conviction carried by its doctrines. But its doctrines were (and have remained) very imperfectly defined. The Jewish national revival was devoid of figures comparable to, say, John Locke, or the American Federalists Hamilton, Madison and Jay; it had no great doctrinaire historian like Macaulay, no social and political theoretician of the quality of, say, Pareto—let alone Marx. The Zionists, it may be said, articulated their doctrine by stages, by trial and error, by periodic debate on matters of practical policy in so far as, and provided that, these forced them to consider fundamentals. And the unspoken rule was that action taken or action proposed led to the consideration and formulation of doctrine rather than that consideration of doctrine led to the taking of action. Hence the importance of this, perhaps the greatest of the movement's debates.

No doubt, on some points there was full agreement: that the Emancipation had failed to liberate the Jews; that, accordingly, the course of Jewish history must be reversed; that the *rule* of Exile must be ended and the Diaspora—all or most of it—wound up; and that, finally, by the setting apart of a defined territory into which the Jews would gather as a majority people, they would begin to govern themselves. This much was common ground for virtually all Zionists; this was the message and the prospect which they held out to their actual and potential adherents; and to argue otherwise was simply to put oneself outside any recognizable class of Zionists at all.

But these were very general propositions and, in practice, there were different schools, each with its distinct interpretation, none capable of squaring its differences with the others or redefining the common ground so as to minimize them. They could only fight their differences out, or suppress the intramural argument in the common interest, or retire. But to fight, in such circumstances, was to fight to win; and to win support for a particular interpretation of the common programme or for a particular strategy for making that programme effective was, in effect, to win the leadership of the movement. This was what leadership of the movement *meant;* and there was no other way of winning it.

Two linked questions had always been at issue and were to the fore throughout the debate on East Africa; what was the true and desirable relationship between the Jewish people and other nations; and what was the true and desirable relationship between the Jews and their own historic past? The starting point for the Zionists' view of these matters had been the question of the *individual* Jew and on this there had indeed been loose agreement all along. Thus, all Zionists rejected assimilation—in part because it carried with it the taint of surrender and self-abnegation, but more significantly on the pragmatic grounds that the painless, lasting, and self-induced absorption of Jews in large numbers into the surrounding population was simply not feasible. But so far as what might be termed the *collective* assimilation of the Jews was concerned, namely, the absorption (or re-absorption) of the Jewish people as a whole and as such into the society of nations, the terms on which it would take place, and the problems it would raise, matters were otherwise. There was no clear or authorized doctrine here; nor had there been, except rarely, explicit recognition that there was here an issue with which the movement was properly concerned. Least of all was there anything like consensus.

Broadly, there were two schools of thought and their classic exponents were those two somewhat eccentric figures on the institutional fringes of the movement, Zangwill and Ahad Ha-ʿAm. Strikingly different in background and views, they had this in common that both were intellectuals of independent mind and independent prestige, whose thinking revolved consistently around general, relatively abstract categories, and who granted or withheld their support in the fulfilment of solemn acts of moral and social judgement. Herzl and his closest followers—Zangwill among them—had always taken it as a matter of course that Zionism would bring peace between the Jews and other peoples. The Jews would enter the ranks of the nations on a basis of equality and benefit for all. Like Pinsker before them, they had seen no reason to reject the non-Jewish world *as such*. Their criticism of non-Jewish society had been precipitated by, and then been formulated in, the particular contemporary context of the disastrous relations between it and the Jews. But the brunt of their social and cultural criticism was directed *inwards* at Jewry itself. And the particular force and originality of what Pinsker and Herzl and, later, Zangwill had to say, lay in the combination of these two logically distinct strains of criticism: for they argued for radical and linked changes both in the relations between Jewry and other societies and in the structure and nature of Jewish society itself. Indeed, their primary reference all the while was rather to society at large, as they understood it, than to Jewry or Judaism. Ahad Ha-ʿAm had good cause therefore to pounce on Herzl's fantasy *Altneuland,* and dismiss it on the grounds that there was nothing immediately recognizable as *Jewish* in it. Indeed there was not. If anything, it was Viennese. *Altneu-*

land was poor literature: crudely constructed, of wooden characterization, psychologically superficial. It was also politically and sociologically naive. It will be recalled, for example, that the immensely complex matter of the interconnection between Jewish religious orthodoxy and Zionism as the champion of a Jewish national political renewal is disposed of in four brief sentences: "The New Society was the last to favour obscurantism among its people," Herzl wrote, "even though everyone was allowed his own opinions. Questions of faith were definitely excluded from all influence in public affairs. Whether you prayed in a synagogue, a church, or a mosque, in a museum or at a philharmonic concert—it was all one to the New Society. How you sought to get in touch with the Eternal was your own affair."[3] What emerges most clearly, in any case, is that *Altneuland* is represented as a *new* society, one which had broken away from tradition, one in which the Jews are at last a people like other peoples in all significant respects, and in which the newly gained territorial concentration and political autonomy are the basis for an internal social revolution. And it is this which permits their collective assimilation into the general society of nations on terms of equality and no greater specificity than is commonly tolerated and generally understood by all its other members.

Of course, nothing could be further from this than the ancient and profoundly ingrained notion of the uniqueness of the Jews: of their being a people eternally set apart and of their being a people dedicated to the preservation of their special character and role as a matter of first principle and above all else. It is true that in Herzl himself and in those who modelled themselves after him most closely there is a certain ambivalence from time to time on this point, a lack of ease. Every so often there is a relapse, so to speak, into the set and traditional mode of thought in which particularity and specificity are celebrated as a matter of course.

In Zangwill, however, a man free of the political pressures to which Herzl was subject and more than anxious to follow his private inclinations wherever they might lead him and to set out his views in the clearest language of which he was capable, there is no ambiguity at all, and no reluctance to make a break from the traditional mode of thought. After Herzl's death, as the retreat from Herzl's positions gathered speed and force, Zangwill tried hard to block it. His starting point, as always with the Pinsker-Herzlian school, was the current scene, what he called "the vital needs of the masses of the Jewish people at the present time," the gross inadequacy of such machinery as existed for alleviating it and for dealing with the great stream of Jewish migrants from Russia, and the inappropriateness of customary attitudes to the problem. Except that the pain and gloom which infuse Pinsker's *Autoemancipation,* which the Territorialist manifesto so greatly resembles in its approach, are replaced by a note, deliberately struck, of brisk and even cheerful pragmatism. Territorialism, Zangwill proclaims, is "business-like in anticipation of the inevitable."[4] Again, unlike the more circumspect Pinsker and Herzl there is, in Zangwill, along with the pragmatism, a great undisguised impatience with the hopeless conservatism, the pathetic absurdities, the internal contradictions, the humiliations—in a word, with the failure of Jewish life, public and private. "It is eighteen hundred and thirty-five years since we lost our fatherland, and the period of mourning should be about over," Zangwill told his listeners when he launched his movement. "We have either got to reconcile ourselves to our loss or set about recovering it. But to choose clearly between one alternative or the other is a faculty the Jew has lost."[5] There followed a renewed plea for Zionism; and all Herzl's main arguments were rehearsed, except that since Eretz Israel was unobtainable and, on the other hand, "Zion without Zionism" (that is, a return to the small-scale methods and the humble purposes of Hibbat Zion) "is a hollow mockery," then "better Zionism without Zion." Better, said Zangwill, "a Provisional Palestine." "Any territory which was Jewish, (and) under a Jewish flag," he believed, "would save the Jew's body and the Jew's soul."[6]

Now it is plain that what Zangwill was after was not so much the end of the Jewish people, once and for all, even with dignity preserved, at high noon and with church bells ringing, as in Herzl's celebrated first fantasy, as the end of Jewry as a Peculiar People. If elements of the past could be preserved without too much trouble and, above all, without impeding progress towards Redemption through Normalcy, as it might be termed, well and good. On the other hand, whatever threatened to impede such progress had to be jettisoned; and this sloughing-off of ancient burdens could be done, he thought, with a good conscience, to say nothing of some unjustified relief. It is precisely this that the other school denied.

For the opposing school of thought these ancient burdens—the past itself—were, on the contrary, of the essence, central and indispensable to their national feeling. Perhaps not *all* of it was to be preserved *intact.* Here these Zionists, like all others, took their distance from the entirely wholehearted and uncompromising traditionalists of Jewish religious orthodoxy. Further, on what precisely was to be retained and what modified or discarded they were themselves divided when not merely vague. "We remain [in the movement] to defend Zionism," wrote Yizhak Gruenbaum in a typical protest against the Herzlian approach: "Not the Zionism of diplomacy and charity for the impoverished of the East, but the Zionism that is the full renaissance of the Jewish people in Eretz Israel".[7] But what was to become of the Jews of Eastern Europe meanwhile if they were not to be the subject of what he called "charity," and just what "full renaissance" was to mean he did not (and perhaps could not) say. In any event, what *united* the anti-Herzlians was that they all thought that continuity was crucial. The Jewish society at which they aimed, however vague and ill-focused their picture of it, had to contain within it the major elements of the Jewish heritage—language, culture, history and (with reservations) faith. Like the Herzlians, they wanted to reform Jewry and alter the Jewish condition; but the target that presented itself to them was the Diaspora which they distinguished in their minds from Jewry and Judaism in some proper, unencumbered, pristine state. The Herzlians compared Jews and non-Jews. The anti-Herzlians compared modern Jews with Jews in some former or some ideal condition. They were nothing if not romantics. The original Odessa Lovers of Zion, the Ahad Ha-'Amist moralists, the Ussishkinite settlement-first men and the other sub-categories of the genus, each group in its way, were all creatures of the *haskalah*. All looked forward to a reform of the Jewish condition, but at the same time backward for the elements out of which to reconstruct it. And since the return to the cultivation of land was an essential part of their prescription for the restoration of social health in the future, and the Land of Israel specifically was of course central to past Jewish history and belief, they ended by seeing Eretz Israel as the pivot on which all would turn. To do without it was to lose an indispensable source of strength, a force for renewal as powerful as it was indefinable.

Certainly there were difficulties. The true Zionists had always known, wrote Ahad Ha-'Am, that the enterprise on which they had embarked would take generations to accomplish and that they could only approach their target very slowly and gradually. All true Zionists, Ahad Ha-'Am argued, "stood on a common, rock-solid base: belief in the power of the historic bond between the people and the land to reawaken our people to *self-recognition* and to stir them to fight for strength until such time as the conditions necessary for their free development had been established."[8] And this, of course, was why they had never had any interest in plans to resettle the Jews elsewhere. However, what had happened in 1903, Ahad Ha-ʿAm argued, was that Herzl and the "politicals" had bemused the true Zionists by holding out the prospect of the end being attained with speed, with relatively little effort or preliminary preparation, but rather by a single, great and adventurous leap. The "politicals," who seemed to think that a nation-state for the Jews could be established anywhere if only the necessary land and rights were available, might indeed be proper Jews, perhaps even proper nationalists, but they could not be *Zionists*. Not, that is, in his sense of the term.

We can see, therefore, that in both schools' thinking diagnosis and prescription were inextricable. If you were prepared to "manage . . . affairs slowly" in Ahad Ha-ʿAm's Hibbat Zion manner, and give the *yishuv* in Eretz Israel all the time it needed to develop organically; and if, above all, you accepted with more or less equanimity that the immediate, material problems of the bulk of Jewry could only be alleviated by other, i.e. non-Zionist, non-territorial means and *elsewhere,* i.e. in the Diaspora itself—then the proper concerns of the Zionists did, and not unreasonably, boil down to care for a small, very superior community in Eretz Israel, whose essential role within the nation was educative and inspirational, an example, rather than an instrument; and then the East African (or any other "territorialist") project was an obvious monstrosity, a perversion of the original ideas. And therefore, in practice, the effect on this school of the dramatic renewal of the pogroms in 1903 was less to spur them to a greater effort to rescue Russo-Polish Jewry, than to induce *concern* lest the Herzlians seek at all costs to "hasten the end."

And indeed the fact was that the hard-pressed Jews of eastern Europe themselves, and the rank and file of the movement among them, were *not* disposed to wait. They did wish to "hasten the end." They did believe—at all events, and as Ahad Ha-ʿAm and most of his disciples had always recognized, they *wished* to believe—in "a speedy Salvation" *(yeshuʿah kerovah).* And they had been drawn to Herzl because he appeared to offer—and manifestly he was working for—a rapid release for them from their intolerable situation.[9] The fundamental diagnostic question, therefore, was whether their situation allowed for delay. Just how intolerable was the present condition of the great mass of east European Jewry; and how intolerable was it likely to become in any foreseeable, let alone distant future? How *urgent* was the treatment? On this the followers of Herzl and Zangwill on the one hand, and the followers of Ahad Ha-ʿAm and Ussishkin on the other, were profoundly divided. It was this part-ideological, part-diagnostic issue that lay at the heart of the great debate—along with one other.

The two schools were as deeply divided in their fundamental approach to Jewish public policy. For Herzl and Zangwill and their school the question of what could constitute correct public policy for the Jews was an open one. It was not predetermined in any fundamental way, certainly not by the past. Herzl, in this respect, was somewhat less firm than Zangwill. He was more in awe of the past, more fearful of the inestimable, revolutionary consequences of cutting the historic umbilical cord, and more sensitive to the sensibilities of others on all these scores. Zangwill, as has been suggested, was less concerned about the inner life of the Jews, less repelled or intimidated by the imperfectly understood life and culture of the gentiles and, because even more offended than Herzl by the dualities and timidities which life in the Diaspora entailed, more anxious to break free of them, once and for all, and at whatever the cost. But for both tendencies, the moderate Herzlian and the radical Zangwillian, within what might be called the ultra-revolutionary party in Zionism, a great deal turned on what might and might not be accomplished in actual practice. And it was decisive for their attitude to the tradition. The tradition had its undeniable value, but, in their view, it was not to preserve the tradition, even a modified tradition, that the Zionists had formed their movement; and therefore it could not be made the touchstone, let alone the cornerstone, of policy. For if one did so, in the manner the anti-Herzlians had made their own, one had necessarily to re-adjust—in practice diminish—one's purposes; whereas for Herzl and Zangwill it was the purposes that were the true and necessary cornerstones of policy and whatever impeded progress towards them had to be jettisoned or circumvented. To the question what would befall the Jews who could not be encompassed by his "centre" in Eretz Israel, Ahad Ha-'Am answered, essentially, with a shrug; in his view Eretz Israel could hold out no salvation for them in any event.

Ostensibly, these antitheses were still unresolved at Herzl's death, much as the question of East Africa as a formal issue remained unsettled. But the reality was that Herzl himself, just before his death, at the grand confrontation at the Greater Actions Committee in April 1904, had already conceded crucial points to the opposition and so caused the balance to shift several months before his death. It is, of course, just conceivable, that, had he lived, he would have sought to restore his authority to the full. To that end he would have had to find fresh allies, probably to throw over the old guard of Hovevei Zion altogether. He might have appealed to the silent rank and file, to such people as had cheered him in Vilna and still looked to him to release them from their misery. It would have been in character had he done so and in accord with past precedent, as when, having failed to gain the support of the millionaire notables of western Jewry, he resolved on the creation of a popular movement. But if he had lived, he would still have been an extremely tired and disappointed man and possibly too weak in body to precipitate and carry through a fresh upheaval. Besides which, he himself had become increasingly uncertain and ambivalent in his own attitude to the tradition and had already assured the opposition that in certain respects he would uphold it. He was certainly always a man of his word.

In any event, Herzl's death rendered the shift irreversible. Zionism became identified exclusively with Eretz Israel once more. And, by necessary extension, there ensued both a long retreat from true political action and a massive blocking-off of anything like that call for radical national renewal and reform which the East Africa affair had brought to the surface of public consciousness and, in a limited way and for a brief moment, into the arena of open debate. The further and grimmer consequence was the fixing of that frame of mind and that order of priorities to which I referred at the outset.

Let me try briefly to sum up. The outcome of the great debate on the East Africa project had little to do directly with East Africa. The immediate issue had been settled long before the Seventh Congress passed its final resolution on the matter. What the debate did determine—wherein its vast importance in the history of the Zionist movement—was the approach that would come to characterize most Zionists' handling most of the time of two key classes of issues: those which bore on the society at which they were aiming and those which bore on the actual, immediate fate of the Jews as individuals.

In the course of the debate most members of the Zionist leadership discovered that they had very firm views on two great public questions. They did not often articulate their views with precision, but we, in retrospect, can see clearly what they were. First, they ascribed a higher priority to the internal rehabilitation and reconstruction of Jewry than to what might be termed its external rehabilitation, namely, the reconstruction and reordering of Jewry's position in the world at large and the establishment of relations between the Jewish people and other peoples on a fresh basis. Second, they would under no circumstances countenance progress towards either of these two fundamental Zionist goals where it entailed a radical break with the past. *Continuity had to be preserved.* To what degree and in what respects could be debated.

But the principle of continuity had to be honoured as beyond debate, implicitly, if not explicitly. And Eretz Israel was its symbol.

In contrast, Herzlian Zionism had hinged on an attempt to look at the real world, all of it, as much that of the non-Jews as of the Jews themselves; and on an attempt to prescribe as best one could for those who were in greatest distress—moral, but also and particularly material. On the issue of continuity it was, as I have tried to suggest, ambivalent. It did not really require discontinuity for itself, as some charged. It did not actively seek it except in so far as continuity was judged incompatible with the primary goals of Zionism as these were understood. But it did certainly hold these primary goals to be of overriding importance and value. It did certainly want and welcome change and was neither embarrassed nor half-hearted about it. And how far and in what direction there would be change was, for the Herzlians, a pragmatic question, not one of principle. It is, of course, hard to do full justice to their outlook in such short compass as this. The matter is extraordinarily complex. Their views were not clear-cut. But it may be said, that they took the world as they saw it and understood it and thought the Jews must go far towards adjusting themselves to it for their own good and if they were to survive at all.

The effect of the demolition of Herzlian Zionism in the last months of Herzl's life and the two years immediately subsequent to his death was, in the first instance, to resuscitate Hibbat Zion; and the adherents of Hibbat Zion had always had a more limited perspective. The real world of harsh politics and cruel choices had long since revealed itself to them as one in which they could not hope—and perhaps did not wish— to function. They had long since accustomed themselves to the thought that the task of *rescue* was beyond their meagre powers and resources. And they had long since—in what one is tempted to call the classic Jewish manner—turned for preference inwards once more.

Henceforth, of course, the mind of the movement would be almost exclusively on the *yishuv* and Eretz Israel. Henceforth the Jewish national principle would have both an acknowledged champion and a plan for its safeguard far stronger and much more strictly committed than ever Herzl and Zangwill and their followers had been. On the other hand, to the question how the Jews themselves in their great majority would fare, there were now none who would address themselves as firmly and single-mindedly as that vast and terrible problem required.

NOTES

1. Department of State, Near Eastern Affairs, Memorandum of Conversation, 13 September 1944.
2. The crisis precipitated by the British East Africa proposal of 1903 and some other topics sketched in this article are discussed in detail in the present writer's *Zionism: The Formative Years* (Oxford, Clarendon Press, 1982).
3. *Altneuland,* part V, chapter 2.
4. M. Simon (ed.), *Speeches, Articles and Letters of Israel Zangwill* (London, 1937), pp. 231–33.
5. Ibid., p. 198.
6. Ibid., p. 212.
7. Yizhak Gruenbaum, *Dor be-Mivhan* (Jerusalem, 1951), p. 36.
8. 'Ha-Bokhim', *Kol Kitvei Ahad Ha-'Am* (Jerusalem, 1951), p. 337.
9. Letter to Bernfeld, 8 March 1899. *Igrot Ahad Ha-'Am* (Jerusalem, 1925), ii, p. 250.

6.

The Rejection of the Diaspora in Zionist Thought: Two Approaches

Eliezer Schweid

The rejection of Jewish life in the Diaspora—*shlilat ha-gola*—is a central assumption in all currents of Zionist ideology. First, the concept is used to justify the denial of that other solution to "the Jewish problem" in modern times—the one which opposes Zionism and takes a positive view of continued Jewish existence in the Diaspora, based on faith in the success of emancipation. Second, the concept encourages the dedication necessary for the vast national enterprise implicit in Zionism. Zionism benefited from the attractiveness of its positive vision—independent life in a national geographical setting and the renewal of Jewish national culture. It also made use of its negative attitude toward the dispersion, i.e., fostering the conviction that continued existence under conditions of dispersion, especially in modern times, would be unbearable, arguing that if the nation remained in exile for a long time, it would face both the palpable danger of discrimination and extreme persecution from without, and national decadence from within. In its most extreme formulation, the idea of *shlilat ha-gola* implies that the condition of exile will ultimately destroy the Jewish people, first of all in the moral and spiritual sense, and afterward in the physical sense as well, whether by discrimination and persecution, or by total assimilation. There were more moderate formulations of that idea, but it is a common assumption of all Zionist trends that the Jews as a people have no future in the Diaspora without an independent "spiritual center" in the Land of Israel.

Reprinted by permission of *Studies in Zionism* 5, no. 1 (spring 1984): 43–70

The foregoing is well known, and requires no further clarification. However, it does demand further analysis in order to differentiate the various strains of the idea of *shlilat ha-gola* in Zionist thought, and to determine the effects of those distinctions upon the positive vision of Zionism, and especially upon conceptions of the task of national education. I admit unashamedly that my motivation for this reevaluation of *shlilat ha-gola* is not scientific but rather derives from sensitivity to the problem encountered in present-day education. It is apparent that the idea of negation of the Diaspora was removed from the basic premises guiding national education in the State of Israel more than twenty years ago. Perhaps there was no official decision to cease transmitting that ideological message, but in fact it was "forgotten."

In any event no serious effort was made to reassess the validity of the concept with regard to today's Diaspora, existing as it does after the Holocaust and the establishment of the State of Israel. In my opinion that was a grave error which has weakened Zionist education, the purpose of which is to provide the basis for the identification of the younger generation with the State of Israel, its people, its society, and its culture. This is particularly true given that Zionism is still posited upon a justified and reasoned preference for life in Israel as opposed to life in the Diaspora. Without an understanding of why life in the Diaspora is rejected, a primary motive for the national settlement of the Land of Israel and the necessary dedication for the construction of the state is lacking.

It goes without saying that the renewal of the message of *shlilat ha-gola* in Zionist education necessitates a confrontation with the character and quality of the Diaspora today, but it is no less important to reexamine the heritage of classic Zionist thought on that topic, as one cannot renew an ideological message without studying the factors that led to its disappearance. It is quite likely that a reorientation is called for in interpreting the rejection of the Diaspora in the light of a reappraisal of the problems that have arisen and wrought significant change.

Why has the element of *shlilat ha-gola* been removed from national education in Israel? Doubtless, one contributing factor was the need which arose after the establishment of the state to become "reconciled" with the Jews of the Diaspora and also to gain the cooperation of non-Zionist Jewish organizations for the support of the State of Israel. But long before then doubts had arisen due to concern for the identification of the younger generation of Israelis with the Jewish people as a whole. Let us recall in that context the guilt feelings among many educators in

Palestine in the wake of the Holocaust,[1] on the one hand, and, on the other hand, the appearance of "Canaanite" ideology[2] and after the establishment of the state the spread of "Israeli" patterns of thought, distinguishing between Israeli identity and Jewish identity.[3] In the wake of these factors more than a few voices were raised criticizing the ideology of *shlilat ha-gola* and its place in Zionist education in our country.

A moderate summary of that line of criticism, which became a platform for an alternative programmatic view of Israeli education, was voiced by Barukh Ben-Yehudah.[4] He argued that although it was exaggerated and one-sided, the ideology of rejecting the Diaspora was justified in its day. However, with the establishment of the State of Israel, education based on that ideology had achieved its goal and was no longer necessary and, he claimed, we must now be concerned with the identification of the younger generation of Israelis with the Jewish people at large, and not with rejection of the Diaspora, which has already been destroyed. For that purpose one must show the bright and positive side of the Diaspora too. We should point out that those ideas were expressed by the Director General of the Ministry of Education as background for the presentation of an educational program in "Jewish identity." While Ben-Yehudah's program was not adopted, the tendency to neutralize the rejection of the Diaspora as a central ideological message has had its effect. The result has been to undermine the persuasiveness of Zionism and weaken the Zionist orientation among youth.

Zionist education is based on two suppositions: (1) rejection of the Diaspora; and (2) a positive attitude toward the continuous heritage of Jewish history. Both the weakening of the positive relationship toward the Jewish heritage through *shlilat ha-gola* and the weakening of the latter because of a positive attitude toward the historical heritage of the nation have ultimately weakened that strain of Zionism which seeks to effect an overall revolution in the life of the Jewish people, but which draws its strength and motivation from its identification with the Jewish people, its history, and its heritage. Are these suppositions contradictory? Might they not cancel each other out? The vital necessity of addressing this question in order to reconstitute the ideology of Zionist education is what has motivated me to reexamine the idea of rejection of the Diaspora in all its varieties, with emphasis on the last word.

Today most educators view *shlilat ha-gola* as a single ideological formulation of rather simple and general ideas. That is why they take a simplistic and general view of it. We wish to demonstrate something which, for scholars of Zionism, is both elementary and obvious: that the idea of *shlilat ha-gola* is complex, and that there were various approaches to it, even contradictory ones. One approach invalidated any positive view of the continuous historical heritage of the Jews, especially if that positive view was unambivalent and uncritical. In fact this approach to *shlilat ha-gola* was originally dominant in the educational ideology of the Zionist movement in Palestine, leading to a basic confrontation between those who held it and those who were concerned about the identification of the younger generation with the national heritage.[5] However, other versions of the idea of the rejection of the Diaspora were also current, and they, while favoring well-founded criticism of the Jewish people's historical heritage and the desire to renew it under other conditions and within a different scope, did not wish to detach themselves from the historical continuity of the Jewish people and its heritage. On the contrary, criticism of the Diaspora and its heritage also drew sustenance from a positive though selective approach to the historical Jewish heritage.

Our task is to point out the origins of the difference between those two basic attitudes toward the Jewish heritage in Zionist ideology, and to show that there is an alternative both to the ideology condemning a positive attitude toward the Jewish heritage in the name of *shlilat ha-gola* and also to the ideology which abandons the rejection of the Diaspora in order to take a positive view of the Jewish heritage.

The most extreme version of *shlilat ha-gola* is that which dominated the ideology of secular Zionist education in Palestine, especially in the institutions belonging to the "Labor movement," before the establishment of the state, and it is represented in the literary works and journalism of Micha Josef Berdyczewski and Yosef Haim Brenner. Since the pioneering elite of the Yishuv (Jewish community in Palestine) was concentrated in the Labor movement, it exerted a great deal of influence on the Palestinian Jewish ethos at that time.

In the following remarks we shall concentrate on the views of Brenner, a figure who influenced the education of the "Labor movement" in Palestine not only on the ideational and theoretical-literary level but also personally. It should be emphasized that Brenner was not an "ideologue" in the conventional sense. It might even be said that he was an "anti-ideologue." His mission, as he perceived it, was to reveal existential truth, and he abhorred any preestablished, systematic framework of ideas by means of which ideologues attempt to interpret reality. In his view, an organized "doctrine" is nothing but a stratagem for avoiding reality, and he demanded of his readers that they confront reality directly. Accordingly, we do not find a definition of concepts or systematic analyses in his works but rather a somber depiction of the facts. He was extremely sensitive to the dark side of life, and his stories and articles tend toward gloom and despair. Brenner himself was apparently aware of the distortion implicit in that tendency to exaggerate, but he saw in it the fulfillment of his personal mission. The only source of hope, in his opinion, lay in the strength to face the bitter truth, to despair, and to act out of the inexplicable power that is born of desperation.

The picture of the reality of exile painted by Brenner in his stories and notes is a surrealistic extension of the realism of Mendele Mokher Seforim.[6] He was drawn to descriptions of extreme poverty and the moral and spiritual degradation bound up with it, as well as to the depiction of violent persecution, the cruelty of the pogroms, on the one hand, and the fear and self-contempt in the victims' response, on the other. It is of course possible to derive a kind of "sociological cross-section" of the Diaspora from Brenner's descriptions, especially that of the Pale of Settlement during the period before the Russian Revolution, but he himself did not mean to provide such a cross-section. His goal was not sociological. He intended essentially to describe the figure of the Jew, born in the Pale of Settlement, his contemporary. In his view the condition of exile was symbolized by the mental, moral, and spiritual disfigurement of the Jew under the conditions that obtained in the Pale of Settlement: degrading poverty, severance from basic sources of livelihood; pogroms and humiliation visited upon them by the non-Jewish surroundings and by the authorities; disintegration of communal organization and institutions, and the weakening of the foundations of the traditional order of life.

Brenner depicts the psychological effects of these influences in his stories and notes, the most brutal being the undermining of the mental stability of the Jew in the Pale of Settlement. That Jew is a panicky and fearful man, one with no resources—that is, a man who has no clear orientation in life.[7] The Jew in the Pale of Settlement feels that he can no longer exist in his given personal and social situation. He must change both that situation and himself. But he has no feasible way of escaping. First of all, he generally lacks a realistic view of the world, because of his ignorance and the narrowness of his horizons, the source of which lies in the Jewish education of the Heder and the Yeshiva, but also because of the constant threat that oppresses him. In his panic he tends to interpret everything that happens about him in an extremely subjective manner, whether out of a feeling that every word and act of the Gentiles is directed against him, or in his yearning to see his dreams come true. In either case there is a tragi-comic gap between reality and the interpretation that guides the Diaspora Jew's reactions to that reality. He seems to be alienated, unrealistic, depressed, despised, and, at the same time, subject to a kind of feverish vision with extreme shifts in mood: feelings of inferiority, submission, and self-abnegation before the wealthy, the powerful, the rulers, and their ilk; and feelings of superiority, of being part of the Chosen People—gloomy despair and burning hope. One result of all the foregoing, which pains Brenner in all his descriptions, is the plethora of activity together with dearth of action, a constant scurrying about that bears no fruit. That is the famous Jewish *batlones* (dissipated energy), the second conspicuous character trait in Brenner's portrait of the Jew in exile.

The above serves to explain Brenner's anti-ideological approach. The propensity for ideological argument appeared to him to be a manifestation of the disfigurement caused by the Diaspora: talk divorced from reality, a false orientation which, rather than being directed at action, is a rationale for exilic idleness. Thence derived Brenner's fidelity to the role he set for himself as a writer: the revelation of the bitter truth. If the malaise of the Diaspora is lack of contact with reality, then the necessary therapy is to forcefully open the eyes of the Diaspora Jew. It was forbidden to have mercy on the miserable Jewish reader, since it was forbidden to allow him to feel sorry for himself; self-pity would merely prolong his disease. The Jew had to confront reality and react to it realistically, as it actually was.

Now we can understand the great value placed upon despair in Brenner's writings. Despair is perhaps the last hope, since it permits true confrontation with reality, resulting in action that relates to reality as it actually is. He who despairs has already torn the veil of illusion from his eyes. He knows that he must *act,* work, not dissipate his energies, not talk, not dream. If that be the case, then despair is hope, even when he who despairs knows that he has almost no chance of changing the state of exile by means of his labors. Or especially when he knows this.[8]

The inner core of Brenner's rejection of the Diaspora is found in the foregoing remarks. But its detailed description holds many implications for every aspect of life. In the realm of ethics Brenner stressed the Jews' cowardice and faint-heartedness, their lack of self-respect and their unwillingness to defend themselves against violence,[9] their lack of faith in humanity and pettiness, especially in everything related to making a living. In the realm of aesthetics Brenner emphasized the neglect and slovenliness in dress, in and around the home, in the synagogue, and in the house of study—disorder, lack of taste, and atrophy of the sense of beauty. The Jew does not respect his environment and does not respect himself within it. That is one of the prominent dimensions of the anomie which typifies the Diaspora.

In the spiritual realm, Brenner brings out the narrowness of the Jews' horizons, the fact that the institutions of Jewish education, the Heder and the Yeshiva, were closed to the outside world. It was an education that offered no knowledge of the surroundings and the cultural environment. A feeling of being "chosen" was sustained by ignorance of the culture of European society, which was far richer than that of the Jews. Moreover, Jewish education was anachronistic. The young Jew learned things that, at best, were relevant to the world of the past, which no longer existed except in Jewish imagination. A more serious problem was that Jewish education, especially Talmudic pilpul, developed a barren sharpness of wit, finding imaginary connections, producing conclusions with no basis in fact, and fostering distorted thinking that ignores reality.[10]

Which preceded which: the Jew's lack of orientation within his environment, or Talmudic pilpul? In any event, Brenner conceived of pilpul as a palpable symbol of Diaspora-mindedness: anomie, idleness, and lack of a sense of reality in the intellectual form. His opinions on this subject are of great significance. They explain several of the most pronounced features of secular, pioneering education with regard to its relation to Jewish sources, especially to the Halacha. The Halacha in its strict normativeness and irrelevance, and in the casuistic methods of reasoning that characterize its educational content, was, in Brenner's eyes and in those of his disciples and admirers, the very symbol of the mentality of the exile. Thus it is not at all surprising that they viewed the return to the Land of Israel as an occasion for the removal of that exilic burden, for grappling with the reality of life on the soil, the life of labor, and the reality of a popular culture sustained by contact with the land and the working of it, productive and providing a livelihood.

In conclusion, Brenner's criticisms, which are tainted by a certain degree of self-hatred, reject the Diaspora not only as a complex of existential conditions that do not allow for a well-regulated national life and consign the nation to discrimination, persecution, and the danger of destruction, but also as a negative form of existence. The Diaspora Jew is a deformed human being, a tissue of life without honor or beauty, and warped intellectually. He is stamped with everything the nation does and creates in the Diaspora. To be redeemed from the Diaspora means to be redeemed from the sufferings of its heritage—emotional, social, and intellectual. We must repeat that Brenner was aware that he was painting an extreme picture and ignoring the patches of light. He knew that the spiritual heritage which he criticized so severely had nourished his own personality and his own literary production. He was aware that the power to criticize the Diaspora, the criteria for that criticism, and the linguistic and ideological tools which he used, had all taken shape within the heritage of the Diaspora, and that ultimately it had sustained him through his youth and placed its stamp upon him for the rest of his life. But it was those very facts which, as it were, justified the harshness of his criticism. For he was not only severe with others, but also, and primarily, with himself. In fact the rejection of the Diaspora, according to Brenner, only became a grave educational and moral problem when it passed from the hands of those who criticized themselves to those who criticized a life experience almost completely unknown to them.[11]

Alongside Brenner's version of *shlilat ha-gola,* it is important to present a view based on scientific, systematic, and objective observation. We could have singled out any one of several of the classical Zionist thinkers, such as S. Y. Horowitz, Jacob Klatzkin, Nachman Syrkin, or others, but we thought that the most important scientific and theoretical contribution from the point of view of its breadth and profundity was that of Yehezkel Kaufmann, especially in his great work, *Exile and Alienism.*[12]

The task which Kaufmann assigned himself in the comprehensive historical research that went into his work was to solve the riddle of the existence of the Jewish people in the Diaspora, the analysis of Jewish life as it took shape in the Diaspora, and the analysis of the changes which have taken place in Jewish life during modern times. He starts by presenting his methodology and defining the basic concepts of his study: people, nation, and religion. He proposes a sociological "law" applying to all peoples: a nation which is entirely removed from its land, is dispersed, and loses its independence will not continue to exist as a nation conscious of its national unity for more than a generation or two. It *necessarily* assimilates because the economic and sociopolitical interests of individuals are stronger than any love for a cultural heritage and any fidelity to a historical memory, and those interests require full integration into the surrounding host culture. Against that background, the fact of the continued existence of the Jewish people for hundreds of years as a nation in exile is exceptional, a surprising riddle for the scientific investigator. Kaufmann sought the scientific explanation for that exceptional fact. We must, however, emphasize that he was not motivated merely by scientific curiosity. He wanted to capsule a Jewish and Zionist world view. Kaufmann sought a *secular* explanation for a peculiar phenomenon which had commonly received a religious one, and the secular explanation was the Jewish people's need for normalization, i.e., that people's need to return, in every sense, to the natural "common denominator" shared by the other peoples.

The first step in the application of the laws of science to an understanding of the history of the Jewish people was to point out that they did in fact begin to assimilate in the lands of their dispersion, like every other people, and in several respects even faster. In other words, the Jewish people did not attempt to halt the process of assimilation. As immigrants, largely voluntary, the Jews sought to integrate rapidly within their new environment. They learned its language and began to make a place for themselves in economic and political life. Ultimately, that was their purpose in leaving their own country for the Diaspora. However, the process of integration by which the Jews of the Diaspora rapidly became typical assimilationists was halted at a certain point. From that point onwards the Jews manifested stubborn resistance to assimilation and shut themselves off from their environment. They set themselves apart and naturally provoked a reaction of opposition and hostility against them in the surrounding, alien environment.

At what point did that occur? Kaufmann sharply rejects all economic and political explanations for the halting of assimilation. The single empirical factor to which historical research points, in his opinion, was the Jewish *religion*. We must once again emphasize that despite this conclusion Kaufmann does not accept the religious explanation of the phenomenon of the Diaspora, but he singles out religion as a sociological factor that blocked the process of assimilation. Religion and it alone among all the institutions of culture can withstand the constraints of the economy, the society, and the state, because religion alone offers absolutely obligatory norms to its believers. Of course that holds true only so long as the believers have faith in the divine authority of its institutions and ordinances.

The Jewish religion is the revealed religion of a single deity who created the world. It commands and guides man and obligates its believers to remain faithful to its principles in opposition to those of the pagan surroundings, and to its particular ways of life in the secular-social sphere. More exactly: Kaufmann does not describe the Jewish religion as a national religion in its essence. On the contrary, in his opinion it was originally a universal religion proclaiming a general truth to all mankind. Actually that was why it particularized the Jewish people within its pagan environment and founded its distinctive way of life upon an absolute authority which brooks no other authority. We therefore find that the Jewish religion, or the Torah, did not oppose assimilation at the outset by prescrib'ng any necessary bonds with the Land of Israel or with a separate nationality. However, because it halted the process of assimilation at the border of the religious way of life which exists within the distinct community, it turns out retroactively to have preserved a certain, limited degree of national life.

In any event, a unique situation in human history was thus produced: a nation emerged which was half assimilated into its Diaspora surroundings and half separate from and opposed to those surroundings. It even retained consciousness of its unity with astonishing tenacity—a people that assimilated from the national and territorial point of view, but maintained its ethnic-national particularism in its religious outlook.

In the present context we need not present a detailed account of the historical description proposed by Kaufmann, in which he follows the development of the Diaspora from ancient times to the present. It is sufficient for us to state that the Diaspora came to be a situation of evident alienation with regard to the environment only after the Jewish people came under Christian and Islamic rule, and that was actually because those religions were derived from Judaism and saw themselves as its heirs. A pagan society is essentially pluralistic from the religious point of view, and it is quite able to tolerate Judaism as one of many legitimate religions. That is not true of fanatical monotheistic religions which aspire to universal rule. The Jews could not accept the claim that the doctrines of those faiths had superseded the Torah, and, for their part, those religions could not forgive the people from whose Torah they had learned for refusing to acknowledge their truths.

The tension between the Jews' tendency toward assimilation and that toward separatism thus reached its peak and was greeted with extreme ambivalence by the surroundings into which they were being absorbed. On the one hand, Realpolitik dictated the exploitation of the Jews by their hosts, and, on the other hand, the latter felt religious enmity toward the former. In the vacillation between the waxing of the tendency toward integration and that of self-segregation, and between repulsion by and attraction to the surroundings, the lifestyle of the ghetto was produced, a typical Diaspora lifestyle.

The social and cultural life of the ghetto is, according to Kaufmann, a strange intermediary product, both wonderful and repulsive, a combination of assimilation and particularism. Its most prominent symbol was the creation of Jewish languages. The Jews spoke a different language in every one of their Diaspora homelands, but each one was peculiar to the Jews, and they all had a common morphological trait: they were jargons, mixtures of the original national language of the Jews, Hebrew, and the spoken language of the host country. This is a typical case of bilingual existence. Hebrew as a national language was preserved. Kaufmann does not accept the claim that Hebrew was a dead language until the early period of the Haskala and the emergence of the Hibbat Zion (Love of Zion) movement. If Hebrew had really died, it would have been impossible to revive it.

The Jews also used the Hebrew language in the Diaspora for their own purely national purposes, which were, as we have said, identical with their religious needs: the study of Torah, prayer, and religious literature—all those were carried out in Hebrew. That was not the case with the language of daily life. For that the Jews used the "secular" language, their jargon, which absorbed, on the one hand, the influences of the sphere of religious activity in daily life (mostly Hebrew words from the sources) and, on the other hand, the influences of the sphere of socioeconomic activity, which expressed the degree of assimilation.

According to Kaufmann, the jargon, a mixture of two languages, bore witness to a flawed and misshapen social and cultural life. It was not a complete language, and not only because of the mechanical mixture of two languages completely foreign to each other from the lexical and morphological point of view, but also because of the necessary poverty of those two languages. The Hebrew which was used in the religious sphere tended to be too conservative and did not develop, remaining unsuitable for the expression of extensive areas of cultural activity, both physical and mental; whereas the linguistic material absorbed from the surrounding culture was generally taken from the lowest classes. It did not transmit creativity from many broad cultural realms which were closed to the Jews.

Poverty, restrictedness, incompleteness, and lack of integrity were features of the jargon which represent the alienated character of cultural and national life in the ghetto. The ghetto was, therefore, an intermediate situation from its very foundation, necessarily detracting from the integrity and fullness of the national culture. Here we have a nation which neither wished nor was able to create a full national culture. It made use of the full culture of the host country and was dependent on it for its very existence. But at the same time it did not wish, nor was it permitted—as long as it preserved its particularism—to be integrated in all the creative areas of the host culture. It therefore absorbed certain fragments of that culture and became partially assimilated, but remained faithful to its own culture which could not develop. The resulting poverty, incompleteness, and lack of integrity applied not only with regard to the language but to the full range of cultural creativity, as well as in the Jewish personality, in which several creative and social functions found no expression.

The word "alienism" expresses, according to Kaufmann, that situation in relation both to the inner state of the Jewish people and to the outer world. The ghetto Jew does not give shape to his environment in the way that every other nation fashions its dwelling place according to its values and style. He therefore remains alien, homeless in the national sense, and since he cannot develop his independent culture in the narrow confines under his control, he is also alienated from his own culture. Only his most immediate environment, his home and the street, were shaped by him, and that was done in an unintegrated style that reflects the tension between assimilation and self-segregation. Thence derive the temporariness, the constriction, and the lack of taste which characterized the culture of the ghetto.

Kaufmann provided an extremely negative description of the period when the ghetto was taking shape and proving to the persecutor that it had the power to survive and preserve a certain nucleus of particularist national culture. The picture is all the more negative when he describes the situation which has arisen in modern times. His rejection of the Diaspora here reaches a peak, precisely because the walls of the ghetto have been broken down and the process of assimilation is accelerated. Once again a paradoxical situation is created. The Jews seek to assimilate completely from a national point of view. The non-Jewish surroundings are responsive now, apparently even demanding assimilation. At any rate they remove the juridical and political basis for the ghetto as a separate Jewish communal organization. Moreover, it was now possible for the Jews to remain loyal to their religion from the ideological and cultic point of view, without that loyalty entailing national segregation, since the secular liberal outlook abolished the dominance of the Christian church over social and political life.

Religion is no longer the factor which defines social and cultural activity, and from the point of view of the principle of secularization, the Jews are entitled to retain their faith without detriment to their civil rights. This means, therefore, that the natural desire for assimilation in the Diaspora *had* to be totally consummated. The Jewish people *had* to disappear as a nation within a generation or two, and only the Jewish religion would have continued to exist alongside Christianity in a parallel established form. The surprising fact was that none of that actually occurred! The Jews continued to exist as a nation in exile, and the situation in the Diaspora became harsher and more humiliating than ever. The process of emancipation began, but it faltered along the way.

Kaufmann states categorically: the process of emancipation was an absolute failure. It was championed by the non-Jewish advocates of a secular, modern political and cultural outlook as the corollary of their principles, and it was also greeted enthusiastically by the majority of the Jews. But it failed. It became evident that there was a contradiction between the political ideals of European secularism and the social behavior of the peoples of Europe. European society resisted the absorption of the Jews within it, and this resistance gave rise to an organized anti-Jewish movement—racial anti-Semitism. The explanation proposed by Kaufmann for that phenomenon was also bound up with religion. The Jews who turned to emancipation were willing to relinquish their national culture completely, but a considerable portion of them were not prepared to give up the basic tenets of their faith, and the decisive majority were not prepared to accept Christianity, while European society remained faithful to the Christian ethos despite the process of secularization.

The Jew therefore remained alien in his surroundings, and as such his desire for emancipation was viewed as dangerous competition by certain segments of the non-Jewish society. The same paradox was again manifested: the non-national religion of the Jews preserved them as a separate nation. But this time such "preservation" had bitter results within the Jewish community. The community organization disintegrated and it was impossible to convert it to the modern framework of "autonomy," since the Jews did not constitute a majority in any province of any country. The national culture, even that maintained by religion, disappeared. Most of the Jews adopted the culture of the surrounding peoples and became alien to their own historical culture. The poor Jewish home which had existed, in the form of the ghetto, was therefore destroyed, without hope of being rebuilt, and the European home did not accept the Jews. This was a state of complete alienation both from the fullness of a Jewish culture and from the outside world. It was accompanied by humiliations, social discrimination, and even manifestations of violent hatred that endangered their very existence.

According to Kaufmann, such a situation is intolerable, and any Jew who had tasted political independence could not reconcile himself to it. Thence derived the necessity of the Zionist solution in Herzl's political understanding of the term. The Jewish people had to reorganize as a sovereign political nation in its own territory, a modern nation like the other nations.

Now let us turn to the essential difference between this description of the Diaspora and that of Brenner. Kaufmann had a positive, even enthusiastic, attitude toward Judaism as a message of universal truth. The monotheistic idea of the Bible was, in his opinion, one of the most exalted discoveries of the human spirit, and he devoted his lifework to the study of its origins and historical development. Moreover, he believed that the Jewish religion as a faith and a world view would withstand the processes of secularization. Religion expresses a necessary dimension of human experience and culture; it will not disappear, and secularization does not dictate its disappearance.

That view was indeed an important concomitant of Kaufmann's Zionist national outlook, and of his attitude to national education. In his opinion, upon regaining territorial sovereignty the Jewish people would develop a national culture like the European national cultures. That culture would be based on the people's natural bonds with their land, with its language—Hebrew, and with its native literature and history—like any European nation. Furthermore, as with any European nation, religion (in this case Judaism) would also be an influential factor in shaping the national ethos and symbols.

Beyond this fundamental difference in his attitude toward the Jewish religion in its most general ideological sense, Kaufmann's rejection of the Diaspora is no less extreme than that of Brenner. The Diaspora creates a flawed social and cultural existence, partial and deformed. The Diaspora is an insufferable situation not only from the point of view of living conditions but also from an ethical point of view: it is a form of humiliation that violates human dignity. Whoever reconciles himself to its existence, whoever is prepared to pay the price in the name of assimilation, is not even worthy of pity. He is worthy of contempt and ignominy. Moral contempt for existence in the Diaspora and the moral revulsion it inspired were common to Kaufmann and Brenner.

We shall permit ourselves to add one comment here: whereas Brenner directed his bitter criticism of the Diaspora primarily against Jewish life in the Russian Pale of Settlement, Kaufmann was primarily critical of Jewish life in the West. His assumption was that existence bound up with the processes of secularization would ultimately affect the entire

Jewish people, and that Zionism would have to grapple with the Diaspora in its modern sense and with those movements among the Jewish people which had been lured by the illusion of emancipation. The Jewish people had to become aware that it was confronted by a radical choice between "normalization" in its own land and a condition of moral and physical suffering and national decadence in the Diaspora.

In contrast to Brenner's and Kaufmann's rejection of the Diaspora, we have the versions of Ahad Ha'am, Hayyim Nachman Bialik, and Aharon David Gordon. First of all, we should point out that those three great thinkers all held consistently, even extremely negative views of the Diaspora, and that also holds true of Ahad Ha'am, despite his well-known ideology of the "spiritual center." For Ahad Ha'am that ideology was a necessary compromise with reality and not a vision to be hoped for from the start. On the basis of many practical considerations, he came to the conclusion that there was no possibility of gathering the majority of the Jewish people in its land. The Jewish people would necessarily remain a nation living mainly in exile. Therefore a way had to be found to change the present character of Diaspora existence, and to assure that the Jewish people could withstand the processes of national, social, and spiritual decadence that were devouring it. The "spiritual center" in Palestine was meant to help change the physiognomy of the Diaspora. Let us say that Ahad Ha'am hoped to remove a certain exilic dimension from the Diaspora by transforming it into a "dispersion," which would have a direct link with a vital national homeland. He believed that such a homeland would bestow some sense of possessing a homeland upon the Jews who lived on alien soil as well.[13]

Was there any basis for such a hope? This is a question in its own right, but we shall not discuss it here. For our purposes it is clear that Ahad Ha'am regarded the Diaspora, viewed as the lack of a homeland, as a negative condition, and that held true both for the Jews of the Pale of Settlement and for those living in the liberal countries of the West, as well as the growing Jewish community in the United States. Ahad Ha'am's view of the Jews in the Pale of Settlement was hardly different from that of Brenner. Examination of his outlook reveals that this was the very reason why he did not believe, with Herzl, that Zionism could offer a solution to what he defined as the "Jewish Problem." The establishment of a Jewish homeland in Palestine was, in the opinion of Ahad Ha'am, an historical task that would take several generations, whereas the "problem of the Jew" in the Pale of Settlement, which found expression in degrading, abject poverty, in extreme discrimination, and in pogroms, demanded an immediate solution, because the Jews could not survive in those conditions.[14]

Moreover, Ahad Ha'am was certain that the poor economic, social, and moral condition of the Jews would not permit them to assume such a weighty task as the construction of a homeland in their own country. The influence of exilic existence was so profound as to degrade the instinctive feeling of national identity. Every single individual fought only for himself to guarantee his own material existence. It would be an illusion for Zionism to attempt to rely upon the misery of the Jewish masses, since the minimal conditions for ending their afflictions did not as yet exist in Palestine. Those who came to Palestine in the hope of finding a solution to their material distress would soon be discouraged, and whatever they constructed would lie in ruins.

For Palestine idealists were necessary, and there were not yet enough of them. They must be educated.[15] That is to say, precisely because of the external and internal misery of the Diaspora in the Jewish Pale of Settlement a solution must be found in the Diaspora itself. The solution for economic distress and pogroms lay in mass emigration to America, while the long-range solution to the "Jewish Problem" which had come into being in the Diaspora had to be prepared by means of a large-scale educational effort within the Diaspora.

To complete the description of Ahad Ha'am's view of the Diaspora, one must examine his conception of the "Problem of Judaism." It too, in his opinion, is a consequence of the negative character of exilic existence, especially against the background of the conditions in modern times. The spread of the scientific and secular enlightenment and its enormous appeal gave the younger generation of Jews a strong sense of inferiority. It was drawn to the general enlightenment, exhibiting self-abnegation in response to the social and cultural expressions of the non-Jewish surroundings, despising its own national culture, from which it was alienated. Thus the process of assimilation began.[16]

Let us immediately stress that in the view of Ahad Ha'am assimilation is not only a phenomenon which endangers the particular existence of the Jewish people. It also represented the destruction of personality, for which the feeling of organic belonging to a people and the feeling of biographical and historical continuity are significant. Assimilation is a personal malady and a moral failing because it undermines the basis for the primary moral responsibility of the individual to his family and people. On the other hand, the younger generation's alienation from its heritage caused the older generation to close itself off in an extreme manner. It curled up like a hedgehog against the danger and clung to the fossilized routines of Orthodoxy, which not only held certain eternal truths sacred, but also social, ethical, and cultural patterns whose time has passed.[17]

The Jewish people is therefore being destroyed between the younger generation's leap toward a future cut off from the past and the tenacious adherence of the older generation to a past which is cut off from the future. Only a synthesis between past and future, between an independent heritage and the general culture, will rescue the people from decadence, and Ahad Ha'am assigned this national-cultural task to Zionism. In any event, he describes the insufferable external living conditions of the Diaspora in the Pale of Settlement and its internal social and cultural disintegration. The Jewish people is portrayed as being in an advanced state of material, spiritual, and moral degradation.

Against that background how does Ahad Ha'am perceive the Diaspora in the countries of the West, which had advanced toward emancipation? He expressed his opinions fully in the well-known essay, "Slavery in the Midst of Freedom." To understand his views we must once again point out that assimilation appeared to him as a phenomenon which deforms any individual's original personality. He posited that belonging to a people was founded upon the organic continuity of bonds which had persisted for generations, that an individual's consciousness of self was anchored in his people's consciousness of self, that the individual was born within the nation and was destined to further its existence. Therefore it is only in the midst of one's nation that one can give full and free expression to one's human potentials.

The assimilated Jew, who feels obligated to prove how much he has internalized the surrounding host culture, and how much he has divested himself of everything differing from that culture, has, therefore, deformed his original self, denying it and reducing it to naught for the tempting reward of civil rights. This is a manifestation of a new form of "marrano existence" which Ahad Ha'am, as well as many of the writers and thinkers among Eastern European Jewry, saw as oppressive, humiliating, and morally opprobrious. However, under the conditions prevailing in the West, there was no way to gain emancipation without paying the price of self-abnegation and self-depreciation toward the outside world, especially when the Jew who seeks emancipation has no national "center for emulation" of his own. Ahad Ha'am did not pay separate attention to the future status of Jewry in the great land of immigration,

America. However, we will not be straying from the truth if we claim
that he posited that without a spiritual center in Palestine, the status of
the Jews in America would be similar to that of those in the liberal
countries of Europe, i.e., "Servitude in the Midst of Freedom."

Condemnation of the Diaspora in the thought of Bialik is even more
extreme in some respects than that of Berdyczewski and Brenner. The
sentiments and views expressed in some of his poems (let us mention
here particularly poems such as "My Song," "A Distant Planet," "The
Dead of the Wilderness," "In the City of Slaughter," "The Scroll of
Fire," and the other poems of "wrath") raise the sense of Diaspora as a
negative form of existence to the mythic level. The first level of expression still describes the Diaspora with traditional imagery: distance from
the fields, from nature, and from manual labor, the prevailing poverty,
barrenness, hopelessness, the sense of being imprisoned both in terms of
physical conditions and in terms of lacking room for spiritual creativity.
In a poem such as "Hamatmid" (The Talmud Student), the feeling is
conveyed that the path of Torah and the Commandments symbolizes
both the distance from natural life and the sterile estrangement from the
world as characterized by the Diaspora. That way of life deprives the
Jewish boy of his childhood and youth, of the pleasures of the senses
and love, and of imagination and the free expression of feeling.[18]

However, in his more mature poetry Bialik endows the Diaspora with
mythic dimensions, bearing ominous existential and religious meaning.
The Diaspora is a desolate land. It is described as an all-encompassing
desert: barrenness which lets nothing green grow, the blaze of heat that
stifles all life, with beasts of prey who represent the imaginary, negative
side of existence—a life of barren negation that destroys itself and its
environment. The Diaspora is an accursed land, a defiled land. Life in it
entails not only distance from the holy—the true goal of the Jewish
person—but also the opposite of the holy: it is the realm of pollution.
From a thematic point of view Bialik intertwined his myth with that of
the destruction of the Temple, which originated in rabbinic allegories
and was crystallized in the Kaballah of the "Ari" (Isaac Luria), that of
the catastrophic "fall" from holiness to the contamination of the
"shells." Now even the "House of Study," the last remnant of holiness,
is destroyed, and exile becomes an immediate personal reality. The
individual is thrown "into the realm of the night and its darkening."

The significance of that myth is brought out in Bialik's poetry of
childhood, which expresses the feeling that the situation of exile denies
the spontaneous flow from the source of his own personality. The "I" is

cut off from its anchorage in the infinity of general existence, and the adult personality becomes alienated from the original "self." Bialik's poetry describes childhood as an earthly sphere with the metaphysical characteristics of the "absolute." Exile damages the primordial ability of the Jewish human being to live out his essential self and express it in the universe, and he remains a spiritual cripple all his life. Bialik's vision of the return to Zion is therefore more than the vision of return to a homeland. It is the vision of a "redemption" in the kabbalistic sense, if only with respect to life on this earth.[19]

The profound teachings of A. D. Gordon can be viewed as a theological interpretation of the myth embodied in Bialik's poetry, both on the personal and the national level. The primary detachment from nature—the source of life and the source of its sanctity and significance—and the creation of an alienated sphere of existence, in which the individual distorts the meaning of his life and falsifies the organic structures of his social being, ultimately transform everything into emptiness and destruction. These matters are conceived on the basis of observation of the course of the general development of mankind, and of the fate of the Jewish people and of the individual Jew against that general background.

In the thought of Gordon nature is conceived as an infinite supply of creative power, flowing from a hidden and unified source and creating stage after stage of beings and organic essences, more and more highly developed and complete. When nature is viewed thus, not as the sum of what has already been created—minerals, plants, and human beings—but rather as a dynamic expression of infinite creative potential, it becomes the "hidden intelligence," or the divinity which gives life to everything and unifies it all.

In that way nature is perceived as an organic unity.[20] Every individual detail in its very uniqueness is anchored within the all-encompassing environment, and it is also one of the cells which compose it. Its individuality has an absolute value, but that value only exists through its inclusion within the infinite unity surrounding it. In that situation the individual lives out both his unique essence and the significance accorded to individual existence by the totality which nourishes it and of which it is constructed. Man too is an inseparable part of the organic unity of nature, and the meaning of his life derives from this. But in man development has reached a higher stage, which is, at the same time, a dangerous turning point. By means of a higher and more perfect form of social life, man develops the power of consciousness and the power of will which permit him to change his status in nature, to distinguish his own realm from the rest of the creatures of nature, and to subjugate them at least partially for his own egotistical ends.

This is a very fateful turning point. It marks the beginning of human civilization with its marvelous achievements, but it is also the start of the process of man's alienation not only from nature, which sustains him physically and spiritually, but also from natural experience. Control over the forces of nature gradually becomes man's control over himself. Civilization becomes more and more like a prison, in which man is in servitude to his own projects, alienated from his original existence, and decadent both morally and spiritually, until in the end he destroys himself utterly.

In the teachings of Gordon, civilized human existence, especially in its modern sense, is seen as a form of exile. This finds expression in the breakdown of the organic constituents of society—family, community, and nation—and in their usurpation by "mechanical" structures which are incomplete and functional—state, party, class. The consumer-exploitative approach overcomes the creative, openhanded approach; human relations rest upon domineering competition, and international relations are predicated upon war; the suggestivity of the anonymous and alienated masses takes over the lives of individuals who have lost their place within organic frameworks. The integrity of personal life is shattered, and direct nourishment from the deep existential wellsprings of nature is disrupted. This development necessarily cuts man off from the experience of sanctity and from the existential bond with the infinite, and he sees himself as a tiny, unimportant fragment, cast into the chaos of chance and blind fate.

Against the background of this general development, the exile of the Jewish people is a microcosm of man's state of existential exile, especially in modern, urban-industrial society. The Jewish people has been sundered from the natural sphere in which it grew up on its own land, and it has been severed from direct contact with nature in the countries of the Diaspora. It has been pushed away from the primary creative processes, and since it lives under constant pressures and the influence of foreign cultures, it soon loses the distinctive external signs of its identity: its social structure, language, and lifestyle. The Jew who views himself the way others see him finds it difficult to grasp how he differs from them, despite the fact that they feel, no less than himself (and sometimes more so), that he has some particular substance. That substance does not receive clear expression; it is felt as an oppressive lack of identity, as a tendency to efface oneself before the surroundings, which do have a clear identity, for they still have a direct link with the natural environment of their homeland and with vital creative processes. This is the dual alienation of individual Jews and of the Jewish people from their primordial "self," and consequently from their peculiar relation to the universe. This is man's concealment from himself and the eclipse of his religious sense of belonging to the infinite.

The return to the Land of Israel is therefore meant to be a full redemption from exile in those deep levels of personal life: the return to nature in the homeland and to a natural way of life, the return to an organic society and a palpable and direct relationship with the infinite, the source of holiness. Gordon's utopian vision strives for redemption in the spiritual-religious sense, the restoration of unity within the life of both the individual and the nation in their natural environment.

We therefore see that, in the thought of Ahad Ha'am, Bialik, and Gordon, the Diaspora is conceived as a negative existence, no less alienated than that portrayed by Berdyczewski, Brenner, and Kaufmann. Nevertheless, there is an essential difference between them in respect to their relation to the entire heritage of Jewish culture, including that part of it which was created and transmitted in the Diaspora. That difference is given positive and clear expression in the ideological platform they proposed for national Hebrew education.

What is the root of the difference between them? It is possible, of course, to ascribe it to emotional, personal, and biographical elements. In that we are speaking of a group of thinkers whose Jewish background was almost uniform, it is permissible to attribute these differences to their emotional and intellectual reactions to that very background, to their diverse ways of internalizing it, which are an expression both of their personal makeup and of individual destinies. However, if we take an ideological view, the basic difference between two ways of understanding the concept of belonging to a nation is quite evident.

In the thought of those who adopted a completely negative attitude toward the creativity of the people in the Diaspora, the people is grasped as a group held together by bonds forged over the generations, or, in the words of Kaufmann: "Consciousness of unity on the basis of common origins." [21] However, the emphasis is on a social and political establishment which unites individuals organizationally. We therefore see that the personal existence of each individual is influenced and shaped, for good or for evil, by the national setting, but it is not determined by that setting. The roots from which it draws sustenance are individual.

In contrast, those who take a positive attitude toward the creativity of the people over the generations, despite their condemnation of the Diaspora, perceive the people as an organic unity to which all the individuals belong, like the cells or limbs of a living body. To be part of a nation is not, therefore, only to be situated in a unifying institutional setting and be shaped by that setting. It is being rooted, drawing sustenance, the development of the entire personality from within. With regard to the first-mentioned group of thinkers, national affiliation is the result of personal and historical fate. For the second group, belonging to a nation is, from the very start, the flow of the stream of life, originating and proceeding from a particular source in organic nature. Therefore it is clear that, for the first group, national affiliation is not of primary importance; they do not predicate upon it the whole complex of factors which mold the individual's world view and way of life. However, the second group regards national affiliation as being of primary and generalized importance, and it precedes every other factor in influencing and molding world views and ways of life.

It is especially important, from our point of view, to bring out the corresponding differences in understanding the relations between nationality and religion. For Brenner and Kaufmann, those are separate issues which are totally independent of each other, although they may affect each other, and can each influence the way the other is institutionalized.[22] In the view of Ahad Ha'am, Bialik, and Gordon, religion is one of the expressions—and for the Jewish people at least, the central expression—of national life. Gordon gives radical expression to that identity: through his nation the individual relates to the universe organically, and according to him one's relation to the infinite cosmos is religious. That is to say: the individual's affiliation with his nation determines not only the group in which it was "decreed" that he would exist, and for which he is obligated to be responsible, but also his basic attitudes, which determine his emotional, ideological, and behavioral development. Ethos and religion are inner expressions of the unified national existence in which a person is born and which he carries forward in his own life and in the life of his children.

The organic conception of the bond between the individual and his people holds, first of all, that this bond, even if it is possible to obscure it, to distort it, or to attempt to attenuate it, cannot be completely eradicated. Moreover, any such bid to obscure, distort, or attenuate the national bond does direct harm to the individual. Estrangement from the nation into which the individual is born is estrangement from the individual's self, and conversely, only a positive relationship to the message of heredity and inheritance which the individual receives from his people assures his full development and the realization of his physical and spiritual abilities. In other words, a positive attitude to the national heritage is in principle the foundation of a full personal life.[23] A balanced personality, integrated and full, is a personality that maintains continuity in its development, and that continuity in personal life depends on continuity of the relationship between it and the previous generations in the family and the nation.

The view that continuity is fundamental for existence is characteristic of the thought of Ahad Ha'am, Bialik, and Gordon. One might say that continuity as a value in itself is a central motif in their works. In the face of the feeling of extreme threat, which, for them, was a threat to their existence as individuals and to the existence of their people, they struggle with all their might against the breaking of continuity between the generations. For them it is the prime imperative of life. In this context we should recall the well-known article by Ahad Ha'am, "Past and Future": just as the private individual exists through continued consciousness of himself from the past through the future, that is to say, through the unification of the mental functions of memory and anticipation of the future, so the national self exists by means of the same kind of unity. Memory of the national past, and, similarly, adaptation to the present through anticipation of the national future, are an imperative of the will to live.

Ahad Ha'am's literary works are entirely devoted to the search for connecting paths between the past and the future in order to maintain the continuity of self-consciousness in the individual Jew within the history of his people. This is also the most vital motif in the poetry of Bialik and the thought of Gordon. The idea of "canonization" suggested by Bialik[24] posits as its basis the assumption that there can be no great personal creativity without constant sustenance from the nation's creativity, which extends continuously from generation to generation. In his articles Gordon reiterates the importance of loyalty to one's particular national "selfhood," and he bases that concept of "selfhood" on the continuity of life processes from the inanimate to mankind, from the individual through his family to the nation, and from generation to generation within the nation.

The conclusion which would follow from Gordon's approach with regard to national education is first of all a conception of education as a process of inculcating a heritage, and secondly the call for passing on the full scope of Jewish culture in all its dynamic variety to the younger generation. The curriculum of Hebrew schools in Israel, which was influenced, as we have said, by the views of Berdyczewski and Brenner, has fastened upon the Bible as an expression of the creativity of the nation in its own land, and upon modern Hebrew literature as an expression of the desire for national rebirth. That which lies between the ancient past and the present is barely hinted at, as if the continuity of Jewish history had been completely shattered and began anew with a "leap" over a barren period which lasted several hundred years.

Ahad Ha'am, who was already aware of that tendency in the curriculum of the Hebrew school in Jaffa, proposed a different curriculum.[25] He argued that the school should provide a representative selection of Jewish literature in its various forms and standpoints and in its full continuity: the Bible in all its parts, the oral law, the prayerbook, the ethical and philosophical works of the Middle Ages, the liturgic poetry, etc. The same idea was expressed in Bialik's well-known proposal to undertake a project of canonization similar to the canonization of the books of the Bible, the Mishna, and the two Talmuds. By extending the canonization of Jewish literature of the past, he proposed the creation of a new book, representing the nation's finest achievements from the Bible to modern Hebrew literature, with which the people could educate themselves. A similar proposal is also included in one of Gordon's letters.[26]

Of course we are speaking here of a choice to be made from a full and overflowing bookshelf. It is impossible, indeed it is not even desirable, to transmit everything. The flourishing of new creativity depends on release from superfluous burdens no less than on continued sustenance. Therefore Bialik proposed a *"geniza"* (an archive for storing disused books) along with the canonization. And beyond that, he propounded a process of editing and interpretation which would adapt the literature of the past to the ways of thinking and studying of the modern generation. But it is clear that in his conception both the process of selection and that of adaptation reflect the principle of organic continuity in the flourishing of a national culture. One should skip no period in the life of the nation, including the period of exile. The positive contents which nourished and sustained the people throughout the ages must flow through the "channels" of cultural transmission from generation to generation without interruptions or disappearances.

Is there, then, a contradiction between the element of *shlilat ha-gola* in the thought of Ahad Ha'am, Bialik, and Gordon and their positive attitude toward the cultural treasures created by the Jewish people in its exile?

If truth be told, some of the most radical of Bialik's poems do contradict the positive attitude toward the "House of Study" and its bookshelf, which was expressed in other poems and articles of his. In fact in his relation to the national heritage there is polar ambivalence, even a "divided heart." If we examine his fully elaborated world view, beyond strong emotional reactions to certain personal and communal situations, that ambivalent relationship, demanding both radical renewal and also continuity, comprises an outlook which is sufficiently unitary and consistent. The element of synthesis is expressed very clearly at the end of his poem "Hamatmid," which is permeated with elements of *shlilat ha-gola:*

> And I remember too, how strong, how sturdy
> The seed must be that withers in those fields
> How rich would be the blessing if one beam
> Of living sunlight could break through to you;
> How great the harvest to be reaped in joy,
> If once the wind of life should pass through you,
> And blow clear through to the *Yeshiva* doors. . . .

"Those fields" are the Diaspora, and they are, of course, tiny. In the three closing lines which follow that passage, the poet says of it in bitterness and pain:

> And my heart weeps for my unhappy people . . .
> How burned, how blasted must our portion be,
> If seed like this is withered in its soil. . . .

Nevertheless that "seed," that deep, devoted, thoughtful, and creative soul, lives and breathes within the people. It represents extraordinary creative national forces. The Diaspora did not, of course, allow it to discover the great potential within itself, and it deformed what was revealed. But despite the Diaspora, that "seed" remained alive and still retains its full potentiality. If only the circumstances changed, a plentiful harvest would be brought forth by the Jews of the Diaspora.

The assumption underlying the organic imagery of Bialik's poetry is, therefore, that the Jewish people has preserved a vital, strong cultural heritage despite the conditions of exile. Or, in other words, the Jewish people did not immediately "adapt" to the Diaspora and did not turn the entire content of their lives into a function of life in exile. They struggled against exile, and a considerable part of their creativity in the Diaspora expresses that struggle to maintain a positive national existence. Even if those positive creations, the fruit of struggle against the

Diaspora, are incomplete and flawed, they have permanent value, and the younger generation growing up within the nation needs them if it wishes to carry out the great revolution entailed by Zionism. For ultimately it is that exiled nation, whose existence fell apart and disintegrated in the Diaspora, which must remove itself, under its own power, from exile.

Whence will it draw that power if one must truly view everything created during the period of exile as a function of an exilic existence and if not a single spark of that vitality remains which struggled against the Diaspora and even vanquished it? In fact, in his bitter controversy with Brenner, Gordon wrote similarly, expressing his personal identification with the apparently contemptible figure of "Benjamin the Third" in the work of Mendele Mokher Seforim.[27] Gordon's consistent rejection and condemnation of the Diaspora did not keep him from realizing that he too had received something from the culture of the oppressed *shtetl*, not only being cut off from his natural environment, and not only the humped back of exile, but also a powerful personal essence, an undeniable, stubborn, and vital self which furnished the strength not only to deny the Diaspora but also to bring forth essential new national creativity.

Gordon sought to draw not only upon the exilic nature of the Diaspora, but also upon the vital creativity which was produced there despite the exile. In contrast to the words of Bialik on the barrenness of the fields in which "seed like this is withered in its soil," he argued that the essential nature of the people which withstood such a difficult trial and succeeded in creating that which the Jewish people had created *despite* the Diaspora, is astonishing and worthy of love.

The ideology of *shlilat ha-gola* in the precise meaning of the term is based on a clear and faithful analysis of the Jewish people's situation in the Diaspora, especially during the modern period. It does not in itself necessitate a negative attitude to that part of the people living in the Diaspora or to all that it has created. The correct perception that a positive relationship to the people and its tradition must provide the basis for national education does not, therefore, necessarily lead to the rejection of the ideology of *shlilat ha-gola*. If there is truth in it, then by virtue of that truth it stands by itself without contradicting the other truth of respect for the continuous tradition of the people.

An interesting historical question in itself is why the educational influence of Berdyczewski and Brenner was greater in Palestine than that of Ahad Ha'am, Bialik, and Gordon, despite the central position accorded to those three figures in the Zionist movement in the Yishuv. It is quite likely that a movement of self-realization tends, because of its political dynamics, to be one-sided and simplistic, and that it advances through extreme vacillations from one form of one-sidedness to another, while rejecting complex evaluations that relate simultaneously to both of the opposing sides. Moreover, it is possible that the political aspect of nationalism gained the upper hand over the organic conception of national life.

Today, however, we can clearly discern the error implicit both in a form of *shlilat ha-gola* which is alienated from the continuity of the nation's self-consciousness throughout the generations, and also in the desire to identify with that continuity while ignoring criticism which presses for vital change. We must now once more reorientate the educational ideology of the Zionist movement. In the face of phenomena such as emigration from Israel and alienation from Zionism both in Israel and abroad, the Zionist movement must sharpen its criticism of the Diaspora experience and bring it up to date, in order to make the people face the cruel truth of disintegration and decadence in Jewish life abroad. But this time it is incumbent upon us to beware of one-sidedness in our criticism, as in the versions of Brenner and Berdyczewski. We must develop a combined approach that remains faithful both to the organic view, which is essential in the self-consciousness of the Jewish people, and to the positive traits by which the Jewish people maintained its creative vitality even under conditions of exile, for those traits can also give support to the aspiration to renew independent Jewish life in the State of Israel.

NOTES

1. See the remarks of the educator M. Avigal, "In the Days of the Holocaust" (Hebrew), *Writings*, Tel Aviv, 1945.
2. See especially the remarks of B. Kurzweil on this topic, in his book, *Our Modern Literature—Continuity or Revolution* (Hebrew), Jerusalem, 1965.
3. See S. Herman, *Israelis and Jews*, New York, 1970.
4. See the booklet by Dr. Barukh Ben-Yehudah, *Toward the Essence of Jewish Consciousness* (Hebrew), Tel Aviv, 1966.
5. The words of Avraham Kariv are typical in this respect; see *I Shall Speak and Feel Easy* (Hebrew), Tel Aviv, 1951.
6. See the long article by Y. H. Brenner, "Self-Evaluation in Three Volumes" (Hebrew), *The Complete Works of Y. H. Brenner*, vol. 7, Tel Aviv, 1928.

7. The most lucid description of a panicked personality against the background of the Diaspora situation is in Brenner's excellent story, "Nerves" (Hebrew), *Complete Works*, vol. 1, Tel Aviv, 1956.

8. See the excellent article on that topic by Yosef Gorny, "There Is No Messiah in Israel; to Work!" (Hebrew), *Notebooks for the Study of the Works of Y. H. Brenner*, vol. 2, Tel Aviv, 1977.

9. See Brenner's sketch, "He Told Her" (Hebrew), *Complete Works*, vol. 2, Tel Aviv, 1961.

10. This is in fact the radical criticism of rabbinic Judaism voiced by the Haskalah, to which Brenner gave most extreme expression.

11. I heard very interesting information about Brenner from Yehudah Sharett. Brenner was extremely angry when his students filled up their notebooks with words they had heard from his own mouth against the Diaspora Jew. They, who had not seen the Diaspora in the flesh, and who had not felt its pain, were not entitled to say what he permitted himself to say on the basis of his own suffering.

12. *Exile and Alienism* (Hebrew), vols. 1 and 2, Tel Aviv, 1929–1930.

13. See Ahad Ha'am's article, "Dr. Pinsker and His Essay" (Hebrew), *At the Crossroads*, part 1, Jerusalem, 1961.

14. See his article, "The Jewish State and the Troubles of the Jews" (Hebrew), *At the Crossroads*, part 2, Jerusalem, 1961.

15. This is a major motif in the writings of Ahad Ha'am, and it appears in his very first article, "That Is Not the Way!" (Hebrew), *At the Crossroads*, part 1.

16. See especially "Freedom in the Midst of Slavery" (Hebrew), *At the Crossroads*, part 1.

17. See especially "The Torah in the Heart" (Hebrew), ibid.

18. This is a central motif in the story "Aftergrowth" (Hebrew), and the poem "The Talmud Student" (Hebrew).

19. See especially the tension between the opening and closing verses of the poem "The Blessing of the People" (Hebrew).

20. Gordon frequently repeats those ideas. A very condensed discussion of our issue is to be found in his article, "To Clarify Our Idea from Its Foundation" (Hebrew), *Writings of A. D. Gordon*, vol. "Man and Nature," Jerusalem, 1951.

21. *Exile and Alienism*, ch. 2: "Nation and Language" (Hebrew), Tel Aviv, 1929–1930.

22. This distinction is very clear in the systematic thought of Kaufmann, but it also is given lucid expression in several remarks of Brenner, who did not shrink from radical severance from the sources, including the Bible.

23. These remarks are very explicitly based on the thought of Gordon; again see his article cited in note 20.

24. See "The Hebrew Book" (Hebrew), *The Complete Works of Hayyim Nachman Bialik*, Tel Aviv, 1954, pp. 194–201.

25. See "The Hebrew Gymnasium in Jaffe" (Hebrew), *At The Crossroads*, part 4.

26. See the writings of Gordon in the edition of Hassifriya Hatzionit, vol. "Letters and Notes" (Hebrew), p. 111.

27. See his letter to Y. Fichmann, ibid., p. 118.

7.

Work for the Land of Israel and "Work in the Present": A Concept of Unity, a Reality of Contradictiom

Matityahu Mintz

In theory, Zionism came into being to deliver the Jewish people from the plight and terror of exile and bring it to a haven of safe refuge in the Land of Israel. The history of Zionism down to World War I, and even thereafter, is nothing but a persistent, often heroic struggle to keep that entire message intact. Such persistence did not come easily to the Zionist movement; moreover, its results were modest. From the start, the Zionist movement found itself deep in the thicket of reality, tossing on waves of despair, recoiling and rebounding in the face of ever-mounting obstacles.

Unlike matters of organization and propaganda, the concrete realization of Zionism—or in the discourse of its early period of development, *avodat Eretz Israel*—confronted the movement and its various branches and institutions with a seemingly endless array of obstacles and hurdles. Initial impediments lay in the oversights stemming from a faulty perception of the problems of adapting to Palestine, particularly those of economic relevance. The Zionist institutions had no effective conception or correct prognosis as to the proper mix of components and motivations necessary to facilitate the enterprise of settlement in Palestine at an optimum pace—one that could assure a massive immigration, transforming it into a dominant force in turning the Jewish people ideologically toward the Land of Israel. Having stated this however, I do not mean to suggest in retrospect that there was ever any real possibility for

Translated from the Hebrew and reprinted by permission of the author from *Hazionut* 9 (1987): 147–55.

a viable alternative approach to planning the system of settlement in Palestine—or, more generally, that it might have been reasonable to expect a greater degree of progress on the practical front in the period before the establishment of the state.

The Zionist movement did not succeed in bridging the wide gap in interests between the national and political needs of the Jewish people, as embodied in the Zionist political agenda on the one hand, and the *raison d'état* of the Ottoman empire on the other. In objective terms, perhaps it was not even able to accomplish such a feat. All efforts by the Zionist side to come to an accommodation with their tough and unyielding Turkish counterpart—whether by diplomatic talks or by the notion of Ottomanization, including the scheme to transform the Jews in Palestine into an integral component of the ex-territorial pan-Ottoman Jewish people under Ottoman rule—were eventually suspended; they came to naught without ever having taken on any serious concrete shape.[1]

The growing capacity of the United States to absorb immigrants in massive numbers seriously undermined the credibility of the Zionist prognosis connected with the Land of Israel. The mounting pressures of the increasingly aggravated problem of Jewish existence in Russia, Galicia, and Romania was provided with a transatlantic safety valve, vented in the great tide of immigrants to America. The fond prediction that the xenophobia beginning to eat away at American society would ultimately disrupt the flow of immigration, necessarily redirecting it to the shores of Palestine, did not appear to be a realistic assessment of the situation— at least until World War I. Even later on, it was certainly not any outcropping of xenophobia in the United States that led to a more important role for Palestine as a destination for Jewish refugees.

The intensification of the Arab problem was a source of growing concern for the Zionist venture both politically and morally. Efforts, conscious or unaware, to brush it aside or sweep it under the carpet proved myopic. The phenomenon of Palestinian nationalism gained new strength in direct proportion to the advances achieved by the Zionist enterprise in Palestine (despite its shrunken dimensions), underscoring the Jewish-Palestinian contradiction. Even later on, those who preferred to view the conflict basically in socioeconomic terms, ignoring its national aspects, were ensnared in a complex of problems arising from the programmed exclusiveness of the Jewish economy and "Hebrew labor" in the Yishuv. The implementation of such exclusivity provided the national confrontation with an alternative channel—although one no less significant or dangerous.

These observations are intended to point up the array of impediments encountered by the Zionist movement in trying to press forward with its cause. Realistically, any single one of these diverse factors should have been sufficient to shatter the movement—*a fortiori* when they acted in conjunction (and this was a view shared by Zionism's opponents). Some scholars believe that the reason for Zionism's ultimate success lay in the fact that the other popular theories with a solution to Jewish adversity in the diaspora (Dubnowian autonomism, Bundism, Sejmism, and Yevsektsia illusions) widespread among the Jews were weaker competitors: they were even less effective as practical and practicable alternatives.

However, if such an assessment were indeed historically accurate, we would be obliged to conclude that due to its characteristic practical weaknesses, the Zionist movement was destined to eke out a marginal, hollow, and shrivelled existence. Yet that was patently not the case. Indeed, when examined in the light of the record of Jewish public life in the last century, such a view appears absurd, a gross distortion of historical fact. Despite all its shortcomings in realizing the programmatic aim of *avodat Eretz Israel,* and the crying gap between Zionist ambitions and achievements in the pre-state period, the Zionist movement nonetheless proved highly instrumental in one crucial domain: crystallizing a sense of Jewish national unity and practical political consciousness.

The horrors of the Kishinev pogrom (1903), the controversy over the Uganda Plan (1903–1905) and the sharp clash between Zionist hopes on the one hand, and socialist-democratic conceptions and programs for achieving Jewish autonomy on the other, galvanized all currents of the Zionist movement into an awareness of a key practical necessity: the need to play a genuine role in the political struggle being waged by the Jews in the diaspora for their civil and national rights. In the Helsingfors (Helsinki) Program, formulated in 1906, Zionism gave equal priority to *avodat Eretz Israel* and work in the present, *avodat ha-hoveh,* in the broadest sense of the term.[2] It managed to present its objectives as part and parcel of a historical process, a pattern of stages in which prior developments and later phases were interlocked, mutually conditioning each other. Over the course of time, it became evident that Zionism was, as an organizing ideology, more effective and purposive than the ideologies of autonomism which had extolled the principle of work in the present. Abraham Idelsohn, Yitzchak Grinboim, Ze'ev Jabotinsky, and the group Razsvet (Dawn) were deft enough to grasp this pattern and its revolutionary implications.[3]

The significance of tactical and strategic decisions was crystal-clear: the Zionist Organization must cease to be one more public association alongside other similar bodies whose main concern centered on a limited sector of Jewish life, such as furthering Jewish settlement in Palestine. Now, the Zionist Organization should transform itself into a full-fledged party and endeavor to "venture forth under its own banner, proudly and courageously, into the political arena in Russia."[4] Or as an editorial published by Razsvet on the Helsinki Congress put it: "It succeeded in immediately adopting the proper and decisive perspective: namely that Zionism is a process of struggle, of active independent action by the Jewish masses in the diaspora and in Palestine. Zionism is a broad social movement, realized in the context of its everyday activities. There cannot be any Jewish struggle or Jewish interests outside the orbit of the interests of Zionism."[5]

A key factor that contributed to the passionate adoption of this new conception was the high level of readiness on the part of the organized public, and particularly its leading intellectual echelons, to espouse monistic, evolutionary, and Marxist ideologies. From this point, Zionism could be conceptualized as an objective process, the essential product of the necessary dynamism latent in modern Jewish history. Zionism now was no longer conceived to be a partial circumscribed sphere within the more comprehensive framework of Jewish life. On the contrary: it was the very embodiment of comprehensiveness, necessarily encompassing all Jewish political and community action both in Palestine and the diaspora. Zionism was all-embracing.

The more Zionism succeeded in establishing itself as a total, all-inclusive ideology, and the more it strove to absorb and integrate the entire gamut of contemporary Jewish life and to organize this within a system of priorities, the more its new image crystallized: namely as a phenomenon embodying the *continuity of Jewish life* in the diaspora. The more Zionism accommodated to the demands of work in the present, *avodat ha-hoveh*, the more tolerant it became toward the inertia of diaspora life, reconciling itself to the mentality within which it had to function. By dint of its becoming a mass political movement and creed, Zionism was transformed into an effective instrumentality for the *preservation* of patterns of Jewish life and culture in the diaspora. And the more it managed to modify these patterns in keeping with its own vision, the more subservient it became to them. In other words: it was the Jewish community that conquered Zionism rather than *vice versa*. Zionism was absorbed by the community, acclimated to it, and lowered its sights: now a stunted version of its former self in regard to final goals, it was nonetheless able to enhance significantly its actual strength. So, despite the presence of unmistakable secular components, it became evident that certain patterns of Zionist thought were in fact rooted in Jewish religious tradition. Moreover, Zionism continued to adhere quite strictly to the notion of a synthesis between (1) the call to preserve frameworks of Jewish life in the diaspora as an instrument for awakening and mobilizing the Jewish public there and (2) an unbounded espousal of the idea of national political renewal in Palestine. Unlike the Orthodox religious camp, whose view of Jewish history projected a dim and veiled future, subject to God's grace and mercy, the Zionists embraced the vision of a process unfolding by historical necessity: religious eschatology, the end of days as a miraculous occurrence, was replaced by the secular vision of a Zionist historical millennium.

This conception was manifested in a practical way in what was termed the "minimum" and "maximum" program. The maximum program was pared down whenever difficulties arose in *avodat Eretz Israel* which exacerbated the problems of immigrant absorption and matters of politics and security. In contrast, the minimum program, focused on *avodat ha-hoveh*, developed apace and took on bolder contours, becoming more attractive and operational. It served as a focus for all manner of practical activities, fueling the pragmatic approach. The minimum program galvanized Jewish life into action by its controversies and horse-trading approach to getting things done, affording a practical opportunity to anyone wishing to take part in Jewish public affairs. The longer-term goal—the maximum program—faded away, becoming more indistinct in the consciousness of the masses. It was reduced, curtailed, replaced by the *intermediary path* to the final objective: i.e., the spectrum of activities revolving around organizing, propaganda, education, fund-raising drives, various campaigns, political struggles, and all types of auxiliary action accompanying them. And numerous Zionists, consciously or unawares, began to resemble Brand, Ibsen's renowned hero, a daring climber up a steep cliff, fully expectant that the strenuous climb would never cease, and that the peak of the mountain he was scaling would never emerge into view.

As a result of these changes, Zionism ultimately developed an ability to play a decisive part in the modern-day unification of the Jewish people, and all the Orthodox religious and non-Zionist groups and currents were forced, willy-nilly, to adapt themselves to its dominant role. On the other hand, these changes effaced the soul and radical character of the movement. Thus it was that in addition to the numerous dilemmas it had struggled with, Zionism was now torn by a wrenching internal polarity: the dichotomy between Zionists wishing to fulfill the commandment of living in Eretz Israel concretely, here and now—and those who opted to postpone that positive commandment, holding it in abeyance until a propitious hour far in the shadowy future, when Jewish life would be convulsed by the fateful catastrophe conjured up by Zionism in its prophecies of doom.

The evolutionary process I have described was an integral part of the dialectical swirl of different and contradictory principles which led to confusion and dissatisfaction, bitterness and misgivings in various segments of the movement. All these kindled a constant ferment in the movement, leading to the exodus of various associations, engendering a confrontation differentially termed over the course of the years. Some hid behind the dispute between the "Palestinians" (today we would say Israelis) and the Zionists. Others dubbed the dispute one of "Palestino-centrism," or a confrontation revealed in the various groupings under the emblem of "pioneering exclusivism."

The latter, which I believe is the most embracing term ideologically, deserves further commentary. Initially, it is useful to distinguish between two versions of pioneerism: the one presented to the Helsinki Congress (1906) and that version which crystallized at the beginning of the Third Aliyah (1919–1923) and was nourished by its experience. It is obvious that this distinction cannot hope to resolve the problem, but it can serve to point up a certain link between it and the matters under consideration here.

Pioneering before Helsinki had focused on a critique of what had been achieved in settlement in the period of the First Aliyah (1881–1904). Since it did not pin its hopes on a charter, pioneerism concluded that there was an urgent need to take a reserved view toward the certainty then widespread in the Zionist camp that it would be possible to solve the problems of absorption of Jewish immigrants in Palestine by giving a free hand to the economic pressures of the free market—i.e., capitalist enterprise (in Marxist parlance). They did not reject private economic interests, but were disappointed regarding past achievements and dubious about anticipated positive results and prospects for immigrant absorption.

Since predictions had proven false regarding spontaneous capitalist development and a spontaneous massive immigration, a dispute arose over the basic premise that Zionism could, *ab ovo*, be a people's movement. Ber Borochov expressed this cogently in his essay "On the Question of Zion and Territory." [6] Borochov arguably is the most profound defensive proponent of the method of pioneering settlement. He stressed that given the existing circumstances within the Jewish people and on the ground in Palestine, Zionism necessarily had to be an "enterprise of a group of idealists." Accordingly, he categorized the initial stage of the realization of Zionism as a "therapeutic phase," styling the movement of idealists likewise as therapeutic. In other words, from the Borochovian perspective, there was no solution to the problem of Jewish existence generally within the existing framework of evolution; for that reason, it was imperative to intervene, jumbling the structure of the existing order (and, if you will, the curse of Jewish existence). Only Jewish idealists could succeed at this task; by dint of their high degree of adaptive ability, such idealistically minded activists could integrate within the requisite corrective project aimed at remedying the defects of evolution—or the creation of an unavoidable mutation which would redirect evolution in the desired direction.[7]

This conception of pioneering embraced a portion of the guidelines adopted by the Biluim movement (and even wished to adopt the name "New Bilu"). It aspired to establish a sound foundation for the Zionist enterprise based on carefully planned methods and to pave the way, by conscious and determined efforts, to transform Zionism: transmuting it from a project of pioneers into an enterprise for an entire people. Nonetheless, even though critical of past practice this trend did not break with the Zionist establishment. On the contrary: pioneering Zionism was supported by broad segments of the Zionist establishment and extolled as a useful method designed to lead to a turning-point in *avodat Eretz Israel*.[8]

The post-Balfour pioneering movement likewise did not ignore the difficulties inherent in settling Palestine. It also harbored certain doubts about an imminent massive immigration wave, but blamed the questionable credibility of the Zionist Organization for the reduction in numbers of immigrants, castigating its excessive concern for *avodat ha-hoveh*. In the view of pioneers of the Third Aliyah, this preoccupation on the part of the Zionist Organization had led to missed and bungled opportunities in Palestine. The pioneers did not reject action centered on the present in the spirit of *avodat ha-hoveh*, but stressed the need for giving greater emphasis to the basic message. Thus, pioneerism articulated its disappointment over reticence about immigration that was afflicting the established Zionist camp. For that reason, pioneers of the Third Aliyah and their successors found themselves locked in a struggle pitched first and foremost against the complacency of the Zionist parties. The latter had grown overbearing as a result of their political and communal achievements in the diaspora.

This sounded the death knell for General Zionism as the bearer of the message of practical Zionist realization. It was not in vain that the pioneering movement and its youth wing in the diaspora gladly subjected themselves to the centers of command in Palestine and their mentorship, weakening as much as possible their ties to local Zionist organizations and institutions (including Poalei Zion)—to the point that all that remained was a formal bond. Thus, by dint of their very foundations, the movements now became foci for outbreaks of rebellion. That revolt was not directed against their Orthodox observant grandfathers but against their secular Zionist fathers, who guarded the image of Jerusalem in the little blue K.K.L. collection box mounted on the wall.

Parallel with this and due to a mounting ground swell of acute opposition to their mother parties in the diaspora, the activist forces in Palestine were also compelled to close ranks and unite. Thus, those who identified with this stance now sought direct links with Palestine and the political organizations there, maintaining their distance from the Zionist parties in their country of residence. For example, Ahdut Haavodah was constrained to promote its interests in the diaspora by using various branches set up under its control over the head of Poalei Zion parties, and accompanied by constant friction with them (1920–1930). The same applied in the case of Hapoel Hatzair.

Hitler's takeover of power in Germany and the deterioration in the Jewish problem there scrambled the routines of Zionist activity, but did not eliminate it. In this instance as well, the traditional Zionist parties proved unable to spur themselves and their membership on to maximum efforts to rescue Jews and to mobilize all available resources, exploiting existing circumstances so as to further the cause of absorption in Palestine. It is of course possible to cite numerous remarks by Zionist leaders at that time about the imminent danger of the Shoah; yet their outcry had a rote, mechanical ring to it, unconvinced and unconvincing.

Rather than functioning to reflect a genuine vision, prophecies of doom served as didactic tools meant to persuade the listener of the correctness of a basic world view, and were not accompanied by operative assumptions for possible action—since the Zionist parties had by now ceased being political organizations committed to immigration.

After the establishment of the state, the character of the Zionist movement as an organizing framework for the Jewish people in the diaspora and an ideological pattern for Jewish communal life was not abandoned. On the contrary, it emerged as a dominant feature. However, as the pathos of immigration evaporated, the situation became more confusing. Those wishing to protest against the masquerade and hypocrisy were compelled (and still are today) to organize themselves separately, rebelling whenever the Zionist Organization sought to impose its tutelage on them via formal financial claims for dues. The new Jewish generation—secular, reformist, and conservative—was conscious of the unsettling contradiction inherent in a Zionism seemingly devoid of any ethos of immigration. And those who did not aspire to a fundamental change in the situation cast about for new formulas designed to provide an abstract legitimation for intensive efforts to preserve the life of the Jewish community in the diaspora that were not under the protective aegis of Zionist ideology. These new justificational constructions are largely based on the theories of autonomism of Simon Dubnow; however, it is evident that they could not fill the existential bill in practical terms, and have won over few if any adherents outside the ambit of small intellectual circles.

For the Jewish masses, the fascination of Zionism in the sense of an integral unity between Jewish existence in the diaspora and the myth of sovereignty in Palestine retains its vitality. In this sense, Zionism once again serves to embody Jewish national identity; and, paradoxically, at the same time nourishes efforts to preserve patterns of Jewish life in the diaspora. Thus, after generations of Zionist pioneering and the establishment of a Jewish state, Zionism, *qua* organization and ideology, has been transmuted into its dialectical antipode—a framework in which traditional tendencies of reserve toward immigration and settlement in Palestine, the life-breath of original Zionism, can channel themselves. Even those Zionists from earlier generations, who viewed the Jewish state as a factor which would indirectly help catalyze the assimilation of those Jews in the diaspora opting not to immigrate to the Land of Israel, never dreamed that this process would someday take place under the very banner of Zionism.

It is high time to reject the view of Zionism as a unitary entity, a single and unbroken identity. The nature of Zionism before World War I differs from that during the interwar years, from Zionism during the Shoah, and in the early postwar pre-state period. *A fortiori*, it also is different from the more recent brand of Zionism that has thrived throughout the Jewish world since the 1950s. The human mind has a natural tendency to gravitate toward economy and monism in expression: the desire to seize upon a single concept and to interpret it based on the continuum of a lengthy historical period answers to this need, and bolsters the romantic proclivity to view history essentially as a continuous and unruptured chain. However, acceptance of the perspective of continuity in history should not dictate the employment of one and the same term to designate its varying entities, since they can blur our view of the changes which necessarily occur. Faithful and rigid adherence to this concept leads unintentionally to distortions in perspective, to a subjection of our vision to what is desirable rather than the truth, to a rupture between ideology and the social reality it seeks to be applied to, and to a subjugation to fixed ideas and the enticements of political adventurism. Hasn't the time come to admit that Zionism is a richly polysemous concept open to multiple significations—and for that reason a term which acts to diminish and obscure our understanding of the ideological changes which have actually occurred over the course of a hundred years in the Jewish national movement?

NOTES

1. There is a functional link between the idea of integrating the Jewish Yishuv in Palestine within the general Jewish community in the Ottoman empire on the one hand, and demands for Ottomanization on the other. See the decisions taken at the Sixth Congress of the Social-Democratic Hebrew Workers' Party in Palestine, April 1910; Ben-Zvi, *Poalei Zion ba-aliyah ha-shniyah* (Jerusalem, 1950), pp. 219–21; D. Ben-Gurion, *Ha-hanhagah ha-atzmit ba-Vellaiot* (Jerusalem, 1914; D. Ben-Gurion and V. Ben-Zvi, *Eretz Israel be-avar u-ba-hoveh* (Jerusalem, 1980), pp. 105–12; D. Ben-Gurion, "Di rekhtlikhe lage fun di yidn in der Terkai," in *In kamf far yidishe rekht*, ed. B. Borochov (New York, 1916), pp. 53–72; Sh. Teveth, *Kinat David* vol. 1 (Tel Aviv, 1977), p. 177 ff.
2. A report on the Helsinki Congress in A. Rafaeli (Tzentzifer), "Ve'idot artziyot shel zionei Rusyah," in *Kovetz le-korot ha-tenuah ha-zionit be-Rusyah*, vol. 1 (Tel Aviv, 1964), pp. 76–104; see also Y. Slutsky, *Ha-itonut ha-yehudit-rusit be-reshit ha-meah ha-esrim* (Tel Aviv, 1978), pp. 222–24; Y. Meor, *Ha-tenuah ha-zionit be-Rusyah* (Jerusalem, 1973), pp. 315–19; Z. Jabotinsky, "Al arikhatah shel tokhnit Helsingfors," in *Sefer Idelson* (Tel Aviv, 1946), pp. 83–88.
3. On the group Razsvet in general and its position regarding the dispute under consideration, see Y. Slutsky, *Ha-itonut ha-yehudit-rusit*, op. cit., pp. 224–35; Sh. Gefstein, "Abraham Idelson: Hayav ve-kavei dmuto," in *Sefer Idelson*, op. cit., pp. 11–46.
4. *Ivreiski Narod* (1906), no. 7, p. 4.
5. Ibid., no. 8, editorial.
6. B. Borochov, *Ketavim*, vol. 1 (Tel Aviv, 1955), 18–154. See the discussion there of the therapeutic movement, p. 48 ff.
7. Ibid., 94. Borochov bases his remarks on distinctions made by A. Bogdanov, *Poznaniye iz istoricheskoi tochki zrenia* (St. Petersburg, 1901), pp. 47–63.
8. Cf. my study *Ber Borochov: Ha-ma'agal ha-rishon, 1900–1906* (Tel Aviv, 1976), p. 143 ff.

8.

Zionist Success and Zionist Failure: The Case of East Central Europe between the Wars

Ezra Mendelsohn

The question of the success or failure of Zionism in the lands of the Diaspora raises at least two major issues. One has to do with the ability of the movement to take root and flourish in a given community; the second deals with the extent to which Zionism itself succeeds in implementing its policies and reaching its proclaimed objectives. Let me begin with the first issue and ask in a general way whether we can determine with any degree of precision what factors govern Zionism's ability to mobilize substantial Jewish support. This question is rendered particularly complex by the difficulty encountered in defining the very term Zionism.[1] But however we define it, it is clear that Zionism has fared much better in some regions than in others. Two exemplary recent studies by Israeli historians serve to bring home this fact. Gideon Shimoni has described how Zionism became the dominant force in the South African Jewish community, while Stuart Cohen has analyzed the failure of Zionism to make anything like the same impact on English Jewry.[2] How are such disparities to be explained? Can we isolate the ingredients necessary to make modern Jewish nationalism in general, and Zionism in particular, a powerful force within a given Diaspora community?

Any attempt to do so must examine both the general environment in which the Jewish community under discussion is found and the actual

Reprinted by permission of the author and Herzl Press from *Vision Confronts Reality: Historical Perspectives on the Contemporary Jewish Agenda,* edited by R. Kozodoy, D. Sidorsky, and K. Sulatnik, Herzl Yearbook Series, no. 9 (Rutherford, NJ: Fairleigh Dickinson University Press, 1989): 190–209.

nature of the Jewish community. As for the former, I would suggest that the following characteristics encourage the propagation of Zionism as well as of other forms of modern Jewish nationalism: a binational or multinational society rather than a nation-state, since the latter applies assimilatory pressures of a degree difficult to resist; a society in which there has been a recent shift in political domination from one nationality to another, thereby creating a discontinuity in the ruling culture that may encourage minorities to "return" to their own culture rather than to continue their previous pattern of acculturation; a society in a somewhat backward state of development, since such backwardness tends to retard the integration of minority groups; a society dominated by strong nationalist sentiments, since such sentiments produce parallel ones among the minorities; a society in which there exists enough anti-Semitism to discourage or render impossible thoughts of Jewish integration; and, finally, a society democratic or pluralistic enough to allow minorities to organize and to play a role in the political arena.

Such a list may be somewhat misleading. Each "ingredient" taken separately is clearly not sufficient to produce a strong Zionist movement, and Zionist strength is by no means dependent upon the existence of all of them. But taken together they present a model of an environment in which Jewish nationalism should do well.

Turning to the Jewish community itself: Jewish nationalism, including Zionism, may be expected to flourish in long-standing Jewish communities rather than in recently established immigrant communities. Recent immigrants, after all, are not very likely to embrace a movement calling for their removal to yet another country, especially if they feel that their adopted land offers them good chances for upward social mobility.[3] For Zionism to thrive, the Jewish community in question should not be entirely Orthodox (either in the German or in the Eastern European sense), nor should it be thoroughly integrated into the host society. Ideal is a situation in which the old autonomous Jewish culture is still very much alive, but in which large numbers of mostly lower-middle-class and working-class Jews are moving away from the Orthodox world, while not integrating and not identifying in a national sense with the dominant nationality. These are the conditions in which the conception of the Jewish people as a modern nationality can take hold—and that conception is vital to the success of most forms of Zionism. The movement away from the old Jewish world, often the result of economic crisis and the growing temptations of secularism, led many Jews to embrace Jewish nationalism because the movement offered both a strong Jewish identity and a secure place in the modern world.[4]

If these criteria, both external and internal, are correct, then we should expect Zionism to have done well in Eastern Europe, or at least in parts of Eastern Europe, and in particular during the period between the wars. This was in fact the case, and certain countries of the region became centers of unprecedented Zionist activity. Numbers had something to do with this. The three largest Jewish communities in Europe, those of Soviet Russia, Poland, and Romania, were in Eastern Europe. But numbers are not the main factor. In some of the states of the region there existed that special combination of democracy (to a degree), a multinational context, and the abrupt replacement of one ruling nationality by another as a result of the postwar settlement. We also find a general state of economic backwardness, fierce nationalism, and strong anti-Semitic tendencies on the part both of the state and of society. Eastern Europe was also the great reservoir of Jewish Orthodoxy and autonomous, traditional Jewish culture, but during the interwar years large numbers of Jews were abandoning this culture, although not assimilating into Gentile society, a process that, as we have already said, was often conducive to the adoption of a Jewish national stance. Moreover, in the interwar years the great wave of Jewish emigration to the new world was cut off by new anti-immigration laws in the United States and elsewhere. This too was a factor important for the rise of Zionism in the 1920s and 1930s.

Let me now define a bit more closely those regions of Eastern Europe where one would expect Zionism to fall on particularly fertile soil. The Soviet Union, with its nearly three million Jewish citizens, is obviously not relevant to this study, since the regime strictly proscribed nearly all Zionist activities from the early 1920s onward. This was a calamity for world Zionism. In its prewar czarist form, Russia had been the backbone of the Zionist movement, the birthplace of religious Zionism and socialist Zionism, the source of most of the new Zionist settlers going to Palestine. The history of Zionism and of the yishuv would certainly have been very different had not the Bolsheviks, with their totalitarianism and hatred for Jewish nationalism of all kinds, gained control.[5]

There were other areas of Eastern Europe as well where Zionist prospects were not very bright. In extremely Orthodox, and especially in Hasidic regions, such as Subcarpathian Rus (Czechoslovakia) or Maramures (Romania), Zionism was obviously not very popular. There were also regions where Jewish prewar acculturation and integration had gone very far indeed, accompanied sometimes by the attainment of middle-class status, by the spread of varieties of Reform Judaism, and by the tendency to identify strongly with the dominant nationality. This was the case in certain parts of Hungary, where both Neolog and Orthodox Jews tended to regard themselves as Magyars of the Jewish persuasion, and this was the case, too, in the western regions of Czecho-slovakia (Bohemia and Moravia) and in the Romanian Regat, especially in Wallachia.[6]

Elsewhere, however, conditions for Zionism were ideal. The new state of Poland, with its more than three million Jews, was an excellent environment for the growth of Zionism—particularly in the eastern borderlands (the so-called kresy), but also in Galicia and in "Congress Poland" (the central region). The Baltic republics of Lithuania and Latvia, where new nationalities had replaced the Russians as the local rulers, were well-suited for Zionist expansion, as were the provinces of Bukovina and Bessarabia, formerly Austrian and Russian, now both Romanian. These were almost all multinational, economically backward, highly nationalistic, and anti-Semitic areas, whose Jewish communities were rooted in autonomous Jewish culture and religion but also involved in the modernization process. To be sure, one could find in all these regions many Orthodox Jews hostile to Zionism's message and many highly acculturated Jews no less hostile to the notion that the Jews constitute a nationality (there were, for example, many such Jews in interwar Poland).[7] But the "Jewish masses," as Jewish politicians liked to call them, were mostly Yiddish speaking and to some degree "national." Indeed, many of the Jews here regarded themselves, and were regarded by others, as constituting a national minority, like the Ukrainians, Belorussians, Germans, and so forth.[8] They were therefore the ideal material from which to forge the Zionist revolution. What Zionist leaders hoped to achieve was their transformation from a national minority in Eastern Europe into a national majority in Palestine.

This task was clearly facilitated by certain events occurring at the time of and immediately following the Great War. The war itself, and the heightened national struggle within the collapsing multinational empires, had a considerable impact on the Jews' national consciousness.[9] The Balfour Declaration of November, 1917 naturally enhanced the prestige of Zionism, as did the decision at San Remo in 1920 to recognize Great Britain's mandate over Palestine. And the apparent recognition of East European Jewry as a national minority at the Versailles peace conference in 1919 also made a considerable impression, despite the fact that the Jewish demands for national minority rights were only partially approved by the victorious powers.[10] Above all, the fact that hitherto unknown or virtually unknown nationalities had risen to the dizzying heights of statehood, undreamed of before the war, suggested that the Jews, too, could achieve a state of their own. If the Estonians and Latvians had succeeded, why not the Jews? If Poland, almost miraculously, had been regenerated, why not Judea? True, the Jews faced a more difficult task than the Poles or the Latvians. But in the immediate postwar atmosphere, in the wake of the great triumph of the national principle, everything seemed possible. This was Zionism's great moment.

The question that I now turn to is: Given these ideal conditions in interwar Eastern Europe, to what extent did Zionism succeed in achieving its goals? In order to answer this question I will first ask yet another one, namely: What were the goals of Zionism? One reason why this question is difficult to answer is that the Zionist movement was remarkably fragmented. Nevertheless, there were certain goals that were shared by most, if not all, Zionist parties and organizations in Eastern Europe.

First of all, Zionism aimed at the political "conquest" of the Jewish community, which meant the establishment of organizations under Zionist control that would speak in the name of the entire Jewish population and also meant the creation of Zionist-dominated Jewish parliamentary clubs in the various parliaments of Eastern Europe. Thus the Polish Zionist Federation adopted a platform that proclaimed that Zionism's task was to take over the leadership of the Polish Jewish community, to fight its battles, and to represent it to the gentile authorities.[11] This implied a major commitment to what was called in the Zionist lexicon *Gegenwartsarbeit* (in Hebrew *Avodat ha-hoveh*)—to work in the Diaspora, as opposed to a total concentration on work for Palestine. It meant a Zionist commitment to the struggle for Jewish national rights in Poland, and, in general, adherence to the notion that "nothing Jewish is alien to us." Not all Zionist groups agreed with this point of view (for example, the pioneering movement did not); but the mainstream East European Zionists had espoused it ever since the days of the first Russian revolution, and they adhered to it with great enthusiasm during most of the interwar period. The main task, as they saw it, was to bring about Zionist ascendancy by replacing the old anti-Zionist or non-Zionist leadership with a new Zionist leadership whose legitimacy would be based on the democratic will of the Jewish masses, as expressed in elections to both Jewish and non-Jewish institutions.

Closely linked to the aspirations for political domination in the lands of the Eastern European Diaspora was the aspiration to dominate the Jewish community culturally. This meant, most importantly, creating a

Zionist-inspired school system that would produce a new generation of Zionist-minded youths weaned away from both the assimilationist state school and the anti-Zionist, Orthodox heder. It also meant the effort to "Hebraize" the Diaspora through schools, newspapers, evening courses, and the like, thus striking a blow against Yiddish—the main language of East European Jewry but disapproved of by most Zionists—and against the inroads being made by the dominant gentile language.

A third aim was to bring the Jewish youth of Eastern Europe under Zionist leadership through their mobilization in youth movements. These movements were to combine scouting techniques, borrowed from foreign models, with Zionist indoctrination. The Zionist youth movement, along with the Zionist school, was designed to insure the Zionist conquest of the young generation, whose task was to build Palestine.

This leads me to the last major aim of Zionism, and the most obvious of all, namely, aliya. This was the acid test of Zionist achievement, especially in Eastern Europe, where—in distinction to the West—Zionism was always aliya-oriented. Most East European Zionists believed that the ultimate aim of Zionism was to create a Jewish majority in Palestine, and this could be achieved only through large-scale aliya from the great reservoir of national Jewry in Poland and neighboring lands. To many, aliya was the true purpose of Zionism, especially in the 1930s when the condition of the Eastern European Jewish masses deteriorated sharply under the twin blows of economic depression and rising anti-Semitism.

We have, then, four far-reaching goals, in a way summed up by the Polish Zionist leader Yitshak Grünbaum, who said in 1919 that Zionism aims "to create a new authority to replace the religious one which we have lost." [12] We may now proceed to answer my original question about the degree of Zionist success or failure.

With the new order in Eastern Europe came various Jewish efforts to establish representative bodies on a national, or at least on a regional scale. Jewish "national councils" sprang up, sometimes elected, sometimes the result of arrangements among the various Jewish political parties and leaders of the local autonomous organizations (kehiles, in Hebrew kehilot). These councils were dominated by Zionists.

Early in 1918 in socialist Russia, democratic elections were held for an all-Russian Jewish conference. Participation in these elections was not very impressive, and the conference itself was never held, but the majority of Jews voted for Zionist lists. In kehileh elections held in Russia during the brief period of freedom enjoyed in 1917 the Zionists

also proved to be the strongest single force, and they won a signal
victory in the elections to the Constituent Assembly held late in that
year.[13]

After the demise of Russian democracy the center of Jewish politics in
Eastern Europe shifted to independent Poland, where Zionists made
strenuous efforts to assume the political leadership of the Jewish population. In late 1918 various Jewish parties began meeting in an effort to
convene a Jewish Congress. These efforts came to nothing in central
Poland, where Jewish politics was characterized by extreme fragmentation and ideological polarization. In December of that year the Zionists
and various "nonparty" Jewish leaders participated in a "pre-confer-
ence" of Polish Jewry, which led to the establishment of the Temporary
Jewish National Council. This body, boycotted by Jewish socialists and
some Orthodox elements, was by default Zionist-dominated, but it
clearly represented and spoke for large numbers of Polish Jews.[14] This is
demonstrated by the elections to the constituent Sejm in Poland, held in
1919, in which about one-half of the votes for Jewish lists in central
Poland went to the Zionists.[15] Elsewhere in the Polish lands the Zionist
domination of Jewish politics was more striking. In Galicia, where both
Jewish socialism and organized Jewish Orthodoxy were relatively weak,
Zionists established national councils and in the 1919 elections won a
near monopoly on Jewish votes.[16]

Russian-Polish Jewry was the backbone of Zionism, and it was natural that Zionist politicians dominated the scene in Bessarabia and, to a
lesser degree, in the new Baltic states.[17] They also did well in Prague,
where a Zionist-run national council was established in 1918.[18] The
leaders of East European Zionism—men like Yitshak Grünbaum of
Warsaw, Ozjasz Thon of Cracow, Leon Reich of Lwów, Yaakov Vygod-
ski of Wilno, Max Soloveitshik of Kaunas, and Meir Ebner of Czerno-
witz (Cernâuți)—could justly claim to be the representatives of the
Jewish masses, or at least of large numbers of them. An observer of
the Jewish scene in Eastern Europe around 1920 would certainly have
concluded that Zionism was by far the strongest political force on the
"Jewish street."

The Zionist successes during the brief but important period of Jewish
national councils were, among other things, a function of the Zionist
commitment to the idea of *klal yisrael*, or the unity of the Jewish people.
As they themselves never wearied of pointing out, the Zionists (that is,
the Zionist federations, the Mizrachi, and the moderate Zionist left)
were the only strong political force that stood squarely behind the

principle of Jewish unity based on the conception of the Jews as a separate nationality. The Bundists, and for that matter the Poale Zion-Left, were rabid Marxists, usually unwilling to participate in joint ventures with the class enemy within Jewry; they were far happier allying themselves with Russian or Polish socialists than with the Russian or Polish Jewish "bourgeoisie." [19] The anti-Zionist Orthodox forces, usually under the political leadership of Agudes Yisroel (*Agudat Yisrael* in Hebrew), were similarly unwilling to cooperate with nonreligious Jewish organizations, since they denied that any legitimacy might be attached to secular Jewish nationalism.[20] The Folkists (members of the *Folkspartey,* or People's party), a smaller group but not an insignificant one in the early years of the interwar period, were committed to a rather narrow Yiddishist view of the future of the Jewish people and its culture, a view that made it difficult for them to cooperate with Zionists.[21] Thus ventures into the field of Jewish congresses and national councils were ideally suited to the Zionist point of view, all the more so since along with their Palestinianism the Zionists in Eastern Europe placed great emphasis on the struggle for national and civil rights in the Diaspora.[22] They alone could encompass nearly all the varieties of Jewish politics and cultural expression—Orthodoxy and secularism, Yiddish and Hebrew, socialism and antisocialism.

But despite these natural advantages, exploited to the full in the years immediately following the war, one must not paint too rosy a picture of Zionist success. The Zionist-led national councils failed to endure, owing both to government hostility and to Jewish divisiveness. In certain areas, such as Hungary, national councils on the Polish model were not even convened.[23] In Poland itself, Zionist political success was impressive but by no means as conclusive as had been expected. As we already know, the Temporary Jewish National Council could not claim to represent all Polish Jewry, and it remained, during most of the interwar period, a shadowy organization with little authority. Efforts to revive it in the 1930s were unsuccessful. In the parliamentary arena the Zionists were able to dominate Jewish representation in the Sejm during the 1920s. The main struggle for Jewish leadership in this body was waged not between Zionists and anti-Zionists, but rather between Galician Zionists and Zionists from the former Russian regions of the state. After Pilsudski's coup d'etat in 1926, however, the Polish parliament entered a period of decline, which accelerated in the 1930s, and the decline of Polish democracy naturally had an adverse effect on the Zionists' efforts to act on behalf of Polish Jewry. Indeed, in 1935 most of the Zionist parties of former Russian Poland boycotted the Sejm elections, thus putting an end to their dreams of utilizing the Polish parliament in order to take over the political leadership of Polish Jewry.[24]

The decline of the Sejm can hardly be blamed on the Zionists, but it should be noted that their tactics and strategies within that body were hardly crowned with success. In 1922 the Zionists of Congress Poland, led by Yitshak Grünbaum, joined in a minorities' bloc in order to establish a strong parliamentary opposition to the regime's alleged insensitivity to the national demands of Germans, Ukrainians, Belorussians, and Jews. This step, much debated at the time, led to an impressive electoral triumph but failed to change the policies of the Polish government. Indeed, it can be argued (and was argued at the time) that the minorities' bloc succeeded only in convincing the Polish majority that the Jews were an anti-Polish, antistate element.[25] In 1925 the Galician Zionists, who had opposed the minorities' bloc, negotiated an "agreement" (Ugoda) with the regime, in which Jewish protestations of loyalty were coupled with government promises to alleviate Jewish suffering. This strategy, too, failed to bring about a breakthrough in Polish-Jewish relations.[26] These failures, accompanied as they were by bitter recriminations among Zionist leaders and disillusionment within the Polish Jewish community, severely damaged the prestige of Zionism in Poland.

Zionist strength in the Sejm was not always paralleled in other elective bodies. In the kehiles, for example, the Aguda tended to perform much better than in Sejm elections (it received a certain degree of government support in this regard, since it was regarded as a loyal, progovernment organization).[27] It appears that many Polish Jews voted for Zionists in national elections but voted quite differently in kehileh (and municipal) elections.[28] As for the situation outside Poland, Zionist political successes were similar to those achieved in Poland in the former Russian regions of Lithuania and Latvia, but less impressive in the successor states of the Austro-Hungarian monarchy. Zionist-led Jewish national parties in Czechoslovakia and Romania had their electoral triumphs, but they were far from dominating the Jewish political scene. In Romania, for example, many Jews remained loyal to the non-Zionist, non-national Union of Romanian Jews (UER), whose leader, Wilhelm Filderman, was one of the most influential Jewish figures in the country.[29] In Hungary, as I have already remarked, Zionism as a political force within the community was virtually nonexistent.

Particularly instructive is the decline of Zionism's political clout in Poland in the late 1930s, at a time when one would have expected it to be on the rise. This was a period of rising anti-Semitism emanating both from the state and from society, and of increased demand for emigration to Palestine on the part of the Jewish population. Never had the basic Zionist attitude toward the Diaspora seemed so manifestly correct. And yet during these very years the fiercely anti-Zionist Jewish left, personified by the Bund, won unprecedented support, did remarkably well in elections to kehiles and municipalities, and came to the fore as an organizer of strikes and demonstrations against Polish anti-Semitism and Polish fascism.[30]

The strength of the Bund in Poland on the eve of World War II was to a great extent the result of a widespread feeling that the Zionist movement had failed to deliver. Its leaders in the Sejm, for all their talk of defending the Polish Jews, had little to show for their efforts. Crucially, emigration to Palestine, the cornerstone of the Zionist program, had turned out not to be an option for the Polish Jewish masses, as I will discuss below. Thus the shift to the Bund, whose links with the Polish left seemed to many more promising than Zionism's rhetoric about the return to the historic homeland, and whose roots in the Jewish lower middle class and working class proved stronger and longer-lasting than anyone had anticipated (the Zionists spoke of Bundist successes in elections to the Warsaw kehileh in 1936 as a "miracle").[31] At the same time a small but significant number of Jews made their way into the Polish Communist camp, a development that Zionists viewed with considerable alarm.[32] In sum, it is safe to say that Zionism in Poland was stronger at the beginning of the interwar period, when hopes ran high and talk of mass aliya and the imminent establishment of a Jewish state was common, than at its end, when many impoverished and demoralized Jews turned away from Zionism to its historic enemies.

The success of Zionism in mobilizing support was reflected not only in elections but in other ways as well. Particularly useful, although not above suspicion, are figures on the number of *shoklim* (people who purchased the shekel, thereby announcing their support of the world Zionism movement and their desire to participate in elections to the Zionist congress). Here are the figures for Poland in the last decade of the interwar period:[33]

Year	Shoklim
1931	157,142
1933	366,951
1935	405,756
1937	264,735
1939	275,632

These are impressive numbers, but one must note the sharp decline from 1935 to 1937 (due in part, no doubt, to the defection of the Revisionists in 1935). The number of shoklim in 1937 represented only about 8 percent of the total Jewish population (of course only adults could purchase the shekel). The situation in the second largest Jewish community in east central Europe, Romania, was not very different:

Year	Shoklim
1931	23,136
1933	35,157
1935	53,350
1937	49,816
1939	60,013

Here too a relatively small percentage of Romanian Jews (about seven percent in 1939) were willing to declare themselves adherents of the Zionist movement. And the situation in Hungary, as one might expect, was much worse:

Year	Shoklim
1931	1,500
1933	3,450
1935	5,763
1937	6,044
1939	21,562

In this case the impact of the anti-Jewish laws of 1938–39, and the annexation of new territories, which added numerous "Eastern-type Jews" to Hungary's Jewish population, led to a rise in Zionist fortunes on the eve of World War II. In 1937, however, only about 1 percent of the Jewish population purchased the shekel. In Czechoslovakia, in the same year, the figure was about 6 percent.

The most impressive performance, not surprisingly, was turned in by the small but highly nationalist Jewish community of Lithuania, where, in 1935, 47,088 people purchased the shekel out of a total Jewish population of about 150,000. This is one of many indications that Lithuanian Jewry was the most Zionist-oriented community in Europe, a community where identification with the majority nationality was negligible, where Hasidism was relatively weak, and where a Jewish national identification was embraced by virtually all Jews.[34]

The figures I have presented on shekel distribution indicate that Zionism was a strong movement, but by no means a movement which had achieved hegemony on the "Jewish street." Let us turn now to the question of Zionism's impact on the cultural life of the East European Jewish communities. To what extent did it succeed in "Hebraizing" the Eastern European Diaspora and in establishing educational institutions with a mass following? This question is somewhat easier to answer than the previous question regarding Zionism's political successes.

In general it may be said that Hebrew culture in the Eastern European Diaspora declined in the interwar period, rather than the reverse. Palestine became the center of modern Hebrew literature, press, and theater, while Yiddish and non-Jewish languages came to dominate Jewish cultural life outside Palestine. In Poland, for example, the Zionist federations could not even manage to sustain a Hebrew-language press—their main publications were in Yiddish (especially in Congress Poland) and Polish (especially in Galicia). Everywhere in the Eastern European Diaspora linguistic acculturation, particularly strong among the youth, necessitated the publication of journals and newspapers in the language of the land.[35] Zionists paid lip service to Hebrew but conducted their conferences in Yiddish or in the dominant gentile language. Only the Zionist youth movements and the pioneers made real efforts at Hebraization, and these were not always crowned with success.[36]

As for the vital question of education, Zionists set up various types of school systems, not all of which promoted Hebrew education. Of the Hebrew-language schools the most ambitious were those belonging to the Tarbut network, sponsored by General Zionists and by the moderate Zionist left. These schools adhered to the principle of Hebrew as the language of instruction for all subjects (save those that the government insisted must be taught in the language of the land). They were, by general agreement, remarkably successful educational institutions, innovative, highly responsive to student needs, and blessed with a highly motivated and dedicated corps of teachers.

The proliferation of these schools, which suffered from the obvious disadvantage of teaching in a language not native to the student body, and which were obliged to charge tuition since they were usually not funded by the state, was very much a function of regional peculiarities. In certain regions of Poland and Romania—the Polish eastern borderlands, and Bessarabia—they were quite successful, while they were extremely unsuccessful in attracting support in Congress Poland, in Galicia, and in the Regat.[37] In both Galicia and in Congress Poland linguistic acculturation among the Jews was much more advanced than in the east, and in Galicia Jews had become accustomed, during the prewar Austrian period, to sending their children to state schools. The Jews of Bucharest were not interested in Hebrew schools of this type, while in Bessarabia, where the old Russian orientation was in decline and where Jews were not interested in learning Romanian, Hebrew (and Yiddish) schools could flourish.

The great majority of Jewish children in Poland, Romania, and (it goes without saying) Hungary and Czechoslovakia, did not attend modern Hebrew schools where Hebrew was taught as a spoken language and where pupils were encouraged to speak Hebrew among themselves, in accordance with Zionist doctrine. The only country in Eastern Europe where Tarbut schools really dominated the scene was, once again, Lithuania, where conditions were ideal for Zionism. This was especially the case in the cultural arena, and for reasons already discussed: the decline of the old dominant language, lack of familiarity with and of attraction to the new dominant culture. Similar conditions led to Tarbut success in Latvia as well.[38]

All in all, however, the program of Hebraization was a failure. One may speak with certain reservations of the political conquests of Zionism, but hardly of its cultural conquests. This fact was openly admitted by many Zionist leaders; in fact some had opposed and disparaged cultural work from the very outset of the interwar period, arguing that there was no way in which Hebrew could stand against the wave of the future, linguistic acculturation, or the traditional Jewish language, Yiddish.[39] Everything we know about the period indicates that their prognosis was right, although it cannot be denied that the thousands of young Jews who did study in Tarbut schools made a great contribution to Zionism and, after their aliya, to the yishuv.

What about the organization of the young generation into Zionist youth movements? The interwar period was the golden age of the Eastern European Jewish youth movement; indeed, the institution was more or less invented during this time, beginning with the emergence of Hashomer ha-tsair in wartime Galicia and continuing with the establishment of such diverse groups as Betar, Gordonia, Frayheyt, He-haluts ha-tsair, Akiva, Ha-noar ha-tsioni, and so forth. There can be no doubt that members of these groups played a tremendous role in the development of the Jewish community in Palestine, to which they came as members of the Haluts (Pioneer), the organization that trained them in Eastern Europe prior to their aliya. But again, I am speaking of relatively small

numbers: young people who enlisted in often avowedly elite organizations that demanded of their members considerable sacrifice.

Let us look at some statistics. Ha-shomer ha-tsair was the oldest and
best established of all East European Zionist youth movements. Its
membership rose in the early 1930s, when Zionist fortunes were at a
peak, but the numbers turn out not to be very impressive. In 1934,
for example, the Polish movement boasted 24,246 members (excluding
Galicia) out of a total Jewish population of over two million.[40] The most
powerful ideological enemy of Ha-shomer ha-tsair, Betar, did not fare
much better. Here are some random figures from the movement's census
taken in 1930:[41]

City	Number of Betarists	Jewish Population
Cracow	103	56,515
Lomza	78	8,912
Lodz	51	202,497
Bialystok	268	39,165
Pinsk	192	20,220
Czortkow	77	3,314

Membership figures for this and other youth movements were highly
volatile, and there is no doubt that for tens of thousands of Jewish
youths these organizations were extremely attractive. Indeed, a study of
the numerous memoirs produced by Jews growing up in interwar Eastern Europe, and particularly in Poland, cannot fail to impress upon the
reader the realization that for a large number of young people the
Zionist youth movement was the only ray of light in a world of economic collapse and rising anti-Semitism.[42] And yet, despite the high
degree of political mobilization among youth of the Eastern European
Jewish communities in such countries as Poland and the Baltic States,
individual youth movements remained fairly small (of course, the combined membership figures for all the Zionist youth movements would
surely produce more impressive figures). The same can be said of the
Pioneer organization, most of whose members were "graduates" of the
youth movements. It seems that the highest percentage of organized
pioneers in Europe was in little Lithuania, where in 1934 there were
5,016 registered members, or 3.5 percent of the total Jewish population.
This was a higher percentage than that in Poland, the backbone of
the world Pioneer movement, where in 1933 there were about 58,800
organized pioneers[43]—a large number in terms of its potential signifi-

cance for Jewish Palestine, but of rather small weight within Polish Jewry.

Finally, let us briefly consider the question of aliya. Most Zionists assumed that the Eastern European Diaspora would send great numbers of Jews to Palestine. This region was regarded as the Jewish hinterland of Zion, the place where the combination of Palestine's appeal and the political-economic crisis would produce the ideal environment for aliya—made all the more attractive by virtue of American immigration restrictions. The American Jews, it was thought, would fund the reconstruction of Palestine; and the Jews of East Central Europe would people it. An open Palestine would absorb large numbers of Jewish immigrants. In this way the Jewish problem in Eastern Europe (excluding the Soviet Union) would be solved.

As we know, this is not what happened. During the years 1919–42 approximately 140,000 Jews went from Poland to Palestine. (Of these some returned, disillusioned and bitter, to the Diaspora.)[44] Once again we must state the obvious: this was a significant number of Jews for the yishuv, but an insignificant one for Polish Jewry. Here, it would seem, was proof that the many anti-Zionists were right in claiming Palestine to be little more than a chimera, a utopian scheme, incapable of solving the Jewish question. Outside of Poland the situation was worse. In 1935, a year of large-scale aliya, only 3,616 Jews went from Romania to Palestine. The tiny Jewish community of Lithuania sent proportionately more Jews to Palestine than did Poland, but in 1935 it was able to send on aliya less than two thousand people.[45] Here was the greatest of all Zionist failures.

What were the causes of this failure, which ultimately meant that the Jewish masses were trapped by the Nazi invasion? At the very beginning of our period the Zionist authorities themselves were not enthusiastic about mass aliya, fearing that large numbers of penniless Jews descending upon the shores of Palestine would bring disaster to the Zionist endeavor.[46] Later on many Zionists adopted the policy of selective aliya, meaning that they wanted only certain types of Jews to settle in Palestine: "productive" youngsters, highly trained and highly motivated to carry out a revolution in Jewish life. Thus, during the so-called Fourth Aliya, left-wing Polish Zionists actively discouraged what was then disparagingly called "bourgeois" aliya, fearing that these so-called bourgeois elements would bring with them to the Holy Land the most undesireable characteristics of the Polish ghetto.[47]

The decisive factor limiting aliya, however, was not the attitude of the Zionist establishment, but rather the policy of the British administration in Palestine. It sharply curtailed aliya and even brought immigration to a virtual halt during certain of the most crucial periods, among them the years 1937–39. In fact, despite the hesitations just mentioned, there was during this entire period considerable pressure from below to go to Palestine, at least in Poland; but efforts to change British policy remained unsuccessful.

It must also be remembered that in 1939 no one knew what would happen. Most East European Zionists thought that they had time before them, and that even under the existing aliya quotas established by the British a Jewish Palestine, with a Jewish majority, would eventually come into existence. In the late 1930s—when it dawned on some of the leaders (such as Jabotinsky and, to take a very different political figure, Moshe Kleinbaum) that time was running out—they were not able, by any of the strategies they devised, to overcome British intransigence.[48]

It is true that there were many Jews who voted for Zionist candidates, attended Zionist schools, and purchased the Zionist shekel, yet did not seriously consider going to Palestine. This phenomenon was more common in the West than in Eastern Europe, but it can be found in Poland just as it can be found in America. Yitshak Grünbaum settled in Jerusalem in the 1930s, but Emil Sommerstein, a Zionist leader from Galicia, remained in Poland, survived the war, and later went to America.

Nonetheless, had the gates of Palestine been opened in the 1930s, there is no doubt that substantial numbers of Polish, Lithuanian, Latvian, and Romanian Jews would have seized that opportunity. Instead of 140,000 Polish olim during the entire period, there would perhaps have been half a million who went to Palestine. (To be sure, even that figure would not have solved the Jewish question in Poland.)

So in the matter of aliya, too, we can speak of failure. But here, of course, the Zionists were dealing with factors beyond their control. Indeed, this was the Achilles' heel of the movement and was so perceived very early on by its political enemies. Zionism aimed at transporting large numbers of Jews to a land whose destiny was controlled not by Jews but by a foreign power, whose interests were by no means identical with Jewish interests. In this sense Zionism, for all its appeal, was operating under a particularly grave handicap.

Even in the best of circumstances, Zionist hopes of solving the Jewish crisis in Eastern Europe through aliya had been exaggerated and unrealistic; but given a more benevolent British policy, and the postponement of World War II for another generation, the results would have been quite different. The tragedy was that precisely at a time when the Zionist prognosis regarding the collapse of the Jewish Diaspora was obviously proving to be correct, external factors forced a decline in the aliya movement. As we have seen, this decline plunged Zionism into serious crisis and stimulated the rise of anti-Zionist forces within the Jewish community.

To sum up, then, there can be no doubt that in certain Jewish communities in interwar Eastern Europe—Poland, parts of Romania, the Baltic States—Zionism was the strongest of all organized Jewish movements. By the end of this period it could boast of many achievements: the establishment of Jewish representative bodies, the domination of Jewish representation in parliament, the creation of modern school networks, and so forth. Without Eastern European aliya, without the East European pioneering movement, the history of the yishuv would have been very different. When, in 1937, the British announced their intention to establish a Jewish state in part of Western Palestine, the Eastern European Zionists noted with pride that their efforts had made this program possible (although they were far from pleased with the proposed frontiers).[49]

On the other hand, even the most sympathetic observer cannot but conclude that there was a great gap between Zionist rhetoric and Zionist performance. The Zionists did not win national rights for Eastern European Jews, and they failed to arrest the economic decline of East European Jewry. Their Hebraic ideals foundered when confronted with such apparently irreversible sociological tendencies as acculturation. They spoke of emigration to Palestine as the solution to Jewish poverty and Jewish insecurity in Eastern Europe, but by the end of our period there were more Jews in Poland than there had been immediately after World War I.

Zionism offered hope, especially to young Jews whose prospects in the new states of Eastern Europe were very bleak. From a psychological point of view this in itself was something—hope for a better future in Palestine, pride in the activities of such national leaders as Grünbaum and Zabotinsky, the chance to foster one's own nationalism at a time when the other peoples of the region were celebrating the triumph of their own national movements. In this sense, Zionism enabled Jews to regard themselves as the equal of other groups, with their own national ideals and aspirations.[50] But when Zionism proved incapable of realizing its aspirations, disillusionment set in, and with it, often, despair.

This despair was not the result of Zionist failures alone. Other Jewish organizations were no more successful than the Zionists and in most ways were much less so. In general, the problems encountered by Jews in the East European Diaspora were far too overwhelming for the various Jewish political parties to solve. The Zionist failure was part and parcel of the greater failure of Jewish political activity. In the face of economic decline, political extremism, and highly limited emigration possibilities, no Jewish solution could prevail. It may well be, as we have noted, that the Zionist prognosis was more accurate than that of its adversaries, whether Bundists, assimilationists, or members of Agudes Yisroel. But this realization is small comfort indeed.

NOTES

1. To give just one example, Poale Zion-Left in Poland did not participate in Zionist congresses, championed Yiddish over Hebrew, and even, upon occasion, opposed aliya. It also cooperated with anti-Zionist forces such as the Bund. Was it a Zionist party? This is not an easy question to answer.

2. Gideon Shimoni, *Jews and Zionism: The South African Experience, 1910–1967* (Cape Town, 1980); Stuart A. Cohen, *English Zionists and British Jews* (Princeton, 1982).

3. Lest this be seen as contradicting Shimoni's emphasis on the Zionist character of the South African community, I should make clear that I am using the word *Zionism* here in its Palestino-centric sense; very few South African Jews went to Palestine in the interwar period. See Shimoni, *Jews and Zionism*, pp. 32–33.

4. See my book *Zionism in Poland: The Formative Years, 1915–1926* (New Haven, 1981), pp. 1–2.

5. On the heroic but ultimately unsuccessful efforts on the part of Zionist movements to maintain their existence in postrevolutionary Russia see, for example, Avraham Itay, *Korot "ha-shomer ha-tsair" be-s.s.s.r.* (Jerusalem, 1981).

6. See the analysis in my book *The Jews of East Central Europe between the World Wars* (Bloomington, 1983), pp. 1–8.

7. They have been studied by Celia Heller, *On the Edge of Destruction: Jews of Poland between the Two World Wars* (New York, 1977), pp. 183–209. See also my article "A Note on Jewish Assimilation in the Polish Lands," in *Jewish Assimilation in Modern Times*, ed. Bela Vago (Boulder, 1981), pp. 141–49.

8. This is demonstrated by census data. Most Jews in these countries, when asked to what nationality they belonged, responded that they belonged to the "Jewish nationality."

9. See, for example, Mendelsohn, *Zionism in Poland*, p. 45.

10. Ibid., pp. 106–7.

11. Ibid., pp. 61–63.

12. *Ha-tsfira*, 18 August 1919, p. 27.

13. Mordecai Altshuler, "Ha-nisayon leargen kinus klal-yehudi be-rusiya ahar ha-mahapekha," *He-avar* 12 (1965):75–89; Zvi Gitelman, *Jewish Nationality and Soviet Politics* (Princeton, 1972), pp. 77–82.

14. On this episode see Shlomo Netser, *Maavak yehude polin al zekhuiyotehem ha-*

ezrahiyot ve-ha-leumiyot (1918–1922) (Tel Aviv, 1980), pp. 47–72; Mendelsohn, *Zionism in Poland,* pp. 91–94.

15. Mendelsohn, *Zionism in Poland,* p. 108; Netser, *Maavak yehude polin,* pp. 81–84.
16. Mendelsohn, *Zionism in Poland,* pp. 95–101. In 1919 elections were held only in West Galicia, not in eastern parts of the former Austrian province.
17. Mendelsohn, *The Jews of East Central Europe,* pp. 192, 227–31, 247–48. On Lithuania see also the article by Zvia Balshan, "Maavakam shel yehude lita al zekhuiyotehem ha-leumiyot, 1917–1918," *Shvut* 10 (1984):62–82.
18. Mendelsohn, *The Jews of East Central Europe,* pp. 153–54.
19. On the Polish Bund see Bernard Johnpoll, *The Politics of Futility: The General Jewish Workers Bund of Poland, 1917–1943* (Ithaca, 1967).
20. On the Aguda see Gershon Bacon, "Agudath Israel in Poland, 1916–39: An Orthodox Jewish Response to the Challenge of Modernity," (Ph.D. diss., Columbia University, 1979). Part of this dissertation is to be published in the forthcoming second volume of *Studies in Contemporary Jewry* (Bloomington). See also my article "The Politics of Agudes Yisroel in Inter-War Poland," *Soviet Jewish Affairs* 2 (1972):47–60.
21. Mark Kiel, "The Ideology of the Folks-Partey," *Soviet Jewish Affairs* 5 (1975):75–89.
22. Nor did they abandon this position later on, when the struggle in the Diaspora seemed to be hopeless. See, for example, Moshe Kleinbaum (Sneh) in *Opinja,* 25 August 1935, p. 3.
23. Mendelsohn, *Jews of East Central Europe,* pp. 107–9.
24. Emanuel Meltser, *Maavak medini be-malkodet: Yehude polin 1935–1939* (Tel Aviv, 1982), pp. 47–49.
25. Mendelsohn, *Zionism in Poland,* pp. 213–22; Joseph Marcus, *Social and Political History of the Jews in Poland 1919–1939* (Berlin, New York, Amsterdam, 1983), pp. 302–4.
26. Mendelsohn, *Zionism in Poland,* pp. 300–309. See also Joseph Rothschild, "Ethnic Peripheries Versus Ethnic Cores: Jewish Political Strategies in Interwar Poland," *Political Science Quarterly* 96, no. 4 (Winter 1981–82):591–606, and my article "The Dilemma of Jewish Politics in Poland: Four Responses," in *Jews and Non-Jews in Eastern Europe,* ed. Bela Vago and George Mosse (New York and London, 1974), pp. 203–19.
27. Only men were allowed to vote in kehileh elections, and the Polish law governing elections to these institutions prevented "antireligious" elements from taking part.
28. In the Warsaw kehileh, for example, Aguda was the dominant force up to 1936. See David Flinker, "Kehilat varsha," *Entsiklopediya shel galuiyot, Varsha* 1 (Jerusalem and Tel Aviv, 1953):277–96.
29. Mendelsohn, *The Jews of East Central Europe,* pp. 154–57, 189–99.
30. Meltser, *Maavak medini be-malkodet,* pp. 86–87, 118–27.
31. Hartglas in *Haynt,* 10 September 1936, p. 3.
32. See Kleinbaum's remarks in *Haynt,* 15 November 1936, p. 6. It might be added that the Zionists' failure to achieve unity even within the "bourgeois" camp, not to mention the constant tension between right and left factions, was an additional factor in their decline. During the entire interwar period Galician General Zionists and "Polish" General Zionists hurled accusations at each other and denounced each other as "opportunists" or as "radicals," thus providing much comfort to anti-Zionist factions. Divisiveness, the curse of Diaspora Jewish politics, was much more evident among the Zionists than among either the Bundists or the Orthodox.
33. The figures are taken from the official protocols of the Zionist congresses of the 1930s. It should be kept in mind that the Revisionist Zionists quit the World Zionist Organization in 1935, and their supporters were not among the shoklim during the last three Zionist congresses.

34. Mendelsohn, *The Jews of East Central Europe*, pp. 231–32.

35. For the extent of Polonization within the Zionist movement see A. Druyanov, *Tsiyonut be-polaniya* (Tel Aviv, 1933), pp. 11–12.

36. In 1934 Moshe Kleinbaum declared that the only way to reach the Jewish youth in Poland was to publish Zionist journals in Polish (*Opinja*, 23 September 1934).

37. Mendelsohn, *Zionism in Poland*, 188–97; *The Jews of East Central Europe*, 199–200.

38. Mendelsohn, *The Jews of East Central Europe*, pp. 233–34.

39. Those active in the Tarbut organization were constantly bemoaning the fact that they received precious little support from the Zionist organization. See Mendelsohn, *Zionism in Poland*, p. 196, and Y. Eiges' attack on the anti-Hebrew attitude of the Zionist left in *Tarbut, Yediot ha-vaad ha-merkazi shel histadrut 'tarbut' bepolin* 11 (1 January 1933): 6, and M. Gordon's speech at the third conference of the Polish Tarbut organization in *Ha-tsfira*, 27 December 1927, p. 1.

40. *Histadrut ha-shomer ha-tsair be-polaniya: Din ve-heshbon al ha-matsav ba-tnua u-feulat ha-hanhaga ha-rashit la-veida ha-artsit ha-tshiit* (Warsaw, 1936), p. 10.

41. The census is found in the archives of the Revisionist movement and Betar, the Jabotinsky Institute, Tel Aviv.

42. The best evidence for this is the collection of autobiographies of Polish Jewish youth found in the Yivo Archives, New York.

43. Sara Neshamit, *Hayu halutsim be-lita: Sipura shel tnua, 1916–1941* (Tel Aviv, 1983), p. 122; Yisrael Otiker, *Tnuat he-haluts be-polin, 1932–1935* (Tel Aviv, 1972), pp. 30–35; Levi Arye Sarid, *He-haluts u-tnuot ha-noar be-polin, 1917–1939,* (Tel Aviv, 1979), p. 46; Leib Shpeyzman, *Khalutsim in poyln* (New York, 1959), 1:652.

44. David Gurevich and Aharon Gerts, *Ha-aliya, ha-yishuv ve-ha-tnua ha-tivit shel ha-ukhlusiya be-erets yisrael* (Jerusalem, 1944), p. 59.

45. See the table in ibid., pp. 10–11. Figures refer to legal aliyah.

46. Mendelsohn, *Zionism in Poland*, pp. 110–18.

47. Ibid., pp. 261–69.

48. For Kleinbaum's feeling that the Zionists had only a few years left to bring the masses to Palestine see *Opinja*, 14 July 1935, p. 1. For a discussion of Grünbaum's and Jabotinsky's views that large numbers of Polish Jews must go immediately to Palestine, see Meltser, *Maavak medini be-malkodet*, pp. 145–57.

49. See, for example, Grünbaum in *Haynt*, 18 July 1937, p. 4, and 2 August 1937.

50. See the comments in my article "A Note on Jewish Assimilation," p. 148 n. 12.

9.

Representations of Leadership (and Failure) in Russian Zionism: Picturing Leon Pinsker

Steven J. Zipperstein

The Hovevei Zion was remembered mostly for what it lacked: proper funding, legal standing (until 1890, and rather tentatively after that), and good leadership—a commendable precursor to the Herzlian movement but without its achievements or the charisma and imagination of its great leader. Mordecai Ben Hillel Ha-Cohen recalled an Odessa meeting of the Zerubabel branch of Hovevei Zion he attended around the time of the Kattowicz conference in 1884:

Middle-class merchants, all more-or-less rich, came and they read a letter or two from Palestine, heard reports from various places near Odessa. . . . There was no real order to the meeting, and bits and pieces of all sorts of information were mentioned.[1]

Russian Jews with little contact with the Hovevei Zion in its early stages, before the Herzlian movement cast it into shadows, recalled the past in much the same way, and this tended to justify—as Yosef Goldstein has argued in his work on Russian Zionism—their support for Theodor Herzl, who despite his lack of Jewish moorings promised them a visibility unattainable by a Russian-based movement. It was the record of the Hovevei Zion, pale, meandering, and, in their minds, fundamentally Russian Jewish that provided an empirical underpinning to the belief that it was Western, not Eastern European leaders who were capable of real achievement. The Eastern model consigned nationalists to the margins, to the arena of small deeds and political isolation.[2]

It was the poor leadership of the Hovevei Zion that most decisively

Published by permission of the author.

distinguished it from Herzlian Zionism in a milieu that placed a high premium on the quality of its leaders. The movement's chief should, much like the charismatic emblems of traditional Judaism with whom he still had to compete for authority in Russian Jewry, personify its attributes—its wisdom, prescience, and élan. From the outset, and despite the intrusion of mass politics onto the Jewish street, leaders were rather unrealistically expected to turn the tide for a beleaguered Eastern European Jewry, including such foreign Jews as Moses Montefiore, and even the English mystic Lawrence Oliphant. Such grandees were the objects of wild hopes, and—when these proved misplaced, as they nearly always did—intense disappointment. The belief in the power of a great man capable of redeeming the Jews of Russia was the backdrop to Herzl's tumultuous welcome in 1903 to Vilna, where hundreds lined the streets as his carriage passed in the middle of the night bound for the train station. A huge crowd met him there; a Bundist toasted him as the next king of Israel. The ecstatic statement, Herzl wrote in his diary, "produced a striking effect in the dark Russian night." [3]

Given these expectations, the choice of Leon Pinsker as a leader of the Hovevei Zion came to be seen as something more than a stroke of bad luck; it was the clearest explanation for the movement's failings. Here was a man of integrity and insight but without the skill, energy, or appetite for power essential for successful political life. Pinsker's career was especially susceptible to signposting: his conversion from an integrationist to a nationalist stance was well known and (so the story went) sudden; his 1882 nationalist tract *Autoemancipation* was praised as an (albeit neglected) ideological classic; and his failure as a politician was consistent with national type and one that he, and others close to him, had predicted when he was first tipped for the role. [4]

His life, then, was nicely poised for transformation into the symbolic, an example of what a generation of Russian Jews could, and couldn't, do. During the years of Herzl's leadership, Pinsker's career was used also as an illustration of why Russian Jews must never succumb and abandon Herzl despite mounting dissatisfaction in many quarters of Russian Zionism. Pinsker served as Herzl's foil—a reminder of what could occur if Western Jewish leaders, including those less able than Herzl, were repudiated. The alternative was a regime of obscurity and political chaos.

The term most frequently used to describe Pinsker—who was also, not surprisingly, praised by his movement though, as we shall see, with far more ambivalence than otherwise might have been expected—was "teacher" rather than "leader." This distinction surfaced rather early in the movement's history, between those believed to embody the characteristics of leadership (the best example being, of course, Herzl) and others, like Pinsker, whose impact was instructive, not inspiring. The first were, on the whole, Russian Jews: maskilic, good-hearted, utopians; the second were practical, European, men of the world. As Pinsker himself commented in a 1883 letter, in order to put into motion the goals of *Autoemancipation,* someone abroad must be located to take charge: "In the decades of my life in Russia, I've met among my coreligionists truly sympathetic people, extremely ethical [individuals], but those whom I could describe as leaders—such people I've not met." Perhaps a Jew with real political experience might be drawn in, he speculated. A new "Moses," he writes, may not be on the horizon but a steady, practical Western hand may well be all that is required.[5]

In Pinsker's case, such assumptions about leadership minimized his contribution to Palestinophile politics in Russia, which it seems to me was greater than his contemporaries acknowledged. Still, this essay does not seek primarily to review Pinsker's historical record. What interests me is his role as leader of Hovevei Zion as seen by the generation of Russian Jewish nationalists who came to prominence in the 1880s and 1890s. It is the view of his career as one of little value or achievement after the writing of *Autoemancipation* that interests me; I examine how Pinsker was perceived by Russian Jews in the ideological orbit of the Hovevei Zion. These recollections, in the form of eulogies, commemorative articles, biographical sketches, etc., reveal how they remembered the past, the ability of Russian Jews to run their own movement, and the shortcomings of a generation of Russian Jewish leaders.

Of course, eventually under Chaim Weizmann, Menachem Mendel Ussishkin, Abraham Idelson, Vladimir Jabotinsky, and others, Russian Zionists would challenge the supremacy of Western leaders; for models, though, they rarely harkened back to the Hovevei Zion. It is surprising for a movement so preoccupied with continuity, how decisively Russian Zionists cast aside leaders of the Hovevei Zion generation who—more starkly, as I will argue, than was justified—came to represent unsuccessful politics and bad leadership. Russian leaders of the Hovevei Zion period were thought to lack the political will, stamina, and imagination crucial for the direction of a successful nationalist enterprise and the clearest example was Leon Pinsker, that unsuccessful, uninspiring, tragic figure.

At the time of his death on December 9, 1891, Pinsker—rather suddenly and after being for some eight years the peacemaker in a contentious Jewish national movement—was an object of controversy. Much of this was muted in the days of mourning. Some surfaced even then in (sometimes rather jaundiced) reports on his funeral, the reading of his will, the way in which he had backtracked (according to some accounts) at the end of his life on his Palestinophile commitments. Almost consistently, his role as Hovevei Zion leader was minimized in these appraisals. It is ironic that for a man so adept at avoiding conflict and imposing calm on explosive situations—indeed, to the extent to which any feature of his tenure as head of the Hovevei Zion was held up for praise it was his ability to quiet battles between the movement's religious and non-religious followers—there was such turmoil after his death about his political legacy.

There were several reasons for this. First, lingering doubts about his curious decision in 1889 regarding the legalization of the Hovevei Zion. At that time, the filing of a petition before the Odessa municipal government with names of local dignitaries was required, but Pinsker (who stepped down a year earlier as chair of the Hovevei Zion) surprisingly refused to sign. This was especially odd since the group's legalization was the Hovevei Zion's main goal from the time it was first launched in 1884 under Pinsker's leadership. Without Pinsker's name, and signed by local lawyers and doctors mostly outside the movement, it was submitted and approved. Only then did Pinsker agree, rather grudgingly, to take on the chairmanship of the Odessa-based organization.[6]

True, his reluctance to affix his name to the petition was not known beyond the leadership of the Hovevei Zion. News of the contents of his will, however, was widely discussed. He allocated in it some 100,000 roubles, with a mere 2,000 roubles to the Hovevei Zion, no more than he gave to the local Jewish artisanry school "Trud" or to the Odessa Jewish hospital. Non-Jewish charities received larger sums. The Hovevei Zion bequest seemed perfunctory, a pale reflection of the devotion of a well-heeled chairman toward an organization so long under his control.[7]

This, in turn, fed speculation about Pinsker's backsliding on Palestinophilism: his embrace of a "spiritual" Zionism of the sort associated with Ahad Ha'am, or rumors that he had slid still further in a "territorialist" direction similar to the sort he had aired in *Autoemancipation* before he was drawn into Palestinian-Jewish politics. The writer Yonah Spivak, using the pen name Ish Yisraeli, proposed in *Ha-tsefirah,* at the time critical of the Hovevei Zion, that Pinsker (that misplaced "European" who found himself emeshed in the narrow, xenophobic milieu of

Jewish nationalism) repented late in life and even declared to Baron Maurice de Hirsch, head of the emigrationist Jewish Colonization Association, that Argentina, not Palestine, was the best destination for the poorest Jews. We have, he is reported to have told Hirsch, two talmuds, two liturgical traditions—why not two centers for our people? Pinsker repeated these sentiments on his deathbed, said Ish Yisraeli, along with an affirmation of a "spiritual center" as the goal of Palestinophilism. He insisted that this represented his testament (*tsavaah*) and it was transcribed by Hovevei Zion followers who, says Ish Yisraeli, suppressed the information upon Pinsker's death.[8]

Pinsker was a man who never successfully answered for himself: "Where is your home?" It is inconceivable, writes Ish Yisraeli, that he felt more comfortable with Jewish nationalists—with their separatist affirmations—than in the larger world in which he lived with such success?[9]

Ish Yisraeli, and others, made clear that even the timing of his funeral was the cause of controversy: Pinsker had requested that his body lie in state for three days, which was at variance with traditional Jewish laws demanding immediate burial. Newspapers close to the Hovevei Zion overlooked the episode; others with jaundiced view of the movement reported it with indignation.[10]

Surprisingly, ambivalence about Pinsker's role as Hovevei Zion's leader surfaced at the funeral itself. Most speakers were dignitaries from the local medical establishment who talked at length about Pinsker's research (he published one well-regarded monograph in study of pathology, his specialty field), and his warmly regarded work as a doctor.[11] When it was Menashe Morgulis's turn to address Pinsker's Jewish activities—Morgulis was a well-known Jewish communal activist and intellectual with close ties to the Hovevei Zion—he gave much more attention to Pinsker's devotion to Jewish charities and educational institutions than to his leadership of the Hovevei Zion.

In a striking passage, Morgulis insists that it is too early to provide a proper appraisal of Pinsker's work on behalf of the Hovevei Zion. His transformation into a nationalist occurred late and was comparable, he says, to how his father the scholar Simcha Pinsker—who spent the bulk of his life as an Odessa schoolteacher—emerged as a figure of stature late in life and consolidated his reputation with the posthumous publication of his major philological work. Only when Simcha Pinsker died, was his greatness recognized and, Morgulis says, "The situation is similar to that of his son."[12]

Morgulis, perhaps, was suggesting that Leon Pinsker's reputation eventually would be enhanced by the Russian publication of *Autoemancipation,* since hithertofore its translation from German and publication as a separate pamphlet either in Russian or Hebrew had been blocked by censorship authorities who thought it too nationalist. (A Yiddish translation appeared in 1884.) The most readily available version of *Autoemancipation* at the time was a rather tepid Hebrew summary that did little to enhance Pinsker's standing as a thinker.[13]

Still, it was odd to propose that the fate of Leon Pinsker, head of a political movement with international aspirations, was comparable to that of an obscure Jewish teacher. Morgulis ends the oration on this equivocal note: not Pinsker's contemporaries, but rather the wages of history, will pass judgment on his achievements. Pinsker was a man who did, Morgulis insists, what was "good and right"; it is history that will fill out the picture in ways that his contemporaries cannot. In his eulogy, Morgulis relegates Pinsker's Palestinophilism to the margins in a lengthy review of his work on behalf of the Society for the Promotion of the Enlightenment of the Jews of Russia, his editing in the early 1860s of the Russian-Jewish periodical *Sion,* and other communal activities outside the nationalist fold. His political leadership of the Hovevei Zion is barely mentioned.[14]

Much the same stance can be found in the reactions of others close to Pinsker in the Hovevei Zion, whose responses to his death—varied as they were in other respects—were similarly dubious toward his role as a political leader. In a eulogy in the Russian-language Palestinophile *Sion*—the issue was dedicated in memory of Pinsker—Vasili Berman acknowledged that the work of the Hovevei Zion was "dear" to Pinsker, who devoted himself to it with characteristic seriousness; still, Berman noted that Pinsker's writing of *Autoemancipation* was "the most important act in his life." Nothing else came close to it in importance. Similarly, Ben Ami's eulogy in *Nedel'naia khronika voskhoda,* moved from a warm appreciation of the contents of *Autoemancipation* to a quick, dreary account of Pinsker's last years at the helm of the Hovevei Zion. This already represented, it seems, the standard for accounts of his public career.[15]

Even Lilienblum's well-known assessment of the man ("Dr. Pinsker is No Longer with Us")—written, he tells, immediately upon receiving news by telegram of Pinsker's death—reveals little about his public activity which Lilienblum, as his closest associate in the Hovevei Zion office, could have said much about. It is, rather, Pinsker's uncanny, laudatory patience and his intense love for his people (which, writes Lilienblum, inundated all "the limbs of his body") that dominate the essay. Both, no doubt, are worthy traits; neither implies the capability to inspire nor lead.[16]

Lilienblum met Pinsker when the former was still a teacher of small boys and when the gap between him and the distinguished physician seemed unbridgeable. By the time he came to know Pinsker in the Hovevei Zion, however, he learned that it was Pinsker's excessive readiness to involve himself in all aspects of organizational affairs that undercut his success as a leader: Lilienblum tells of his surprise when, on the Jewish New Year in the fall of 1883, Pinsker appeared at the door of his "poor dwelling" inviting him to take part in a meeting that evening at Pinsker's home where support for Jewish colonies in Palestine would be discussed. It was at this meeting that the Odessa branch of the Hovevei Zion—which Pinsker eventually came to chair—was established. Thinking about the event some ten years later, Lilienblum was still surprised: "Dr. Pinsker, a man honored throughout the entire city, himself coming to invite the participants." This was, on one level, impressive; on another, though, it implied something disturbing about Pinsker's ability to take charge of a movement with more than a modest agenda.[17]

Throughout the piece, Lilienblum expresses admiration for the decent, self-effacing doctor but also hints that the same qualities were expressions of his weaknesses. Nothing of relevance to the fate of Jewish Palestine, however small, was too insignificant to preoccupy him. He hadn't the ability to inspire, to pit himself against the majority in a political dispute, to garner pleasure from scoring political points. Pinsker emerges from this account as a good doctor ministering to his people's terrible pains—this is the message Lilienblum seeks to get across and repeatedly he stresses the connection between his medical calling and his activity as a nationalist leader—a decent man endeavoring to maintain peace and goodwill. Still, he is someone with neither the imagination nor the passion he displayed in *Autoemancipation*.[18]

Much more explicit was Zalman Epstein, a deeply perceptive Hebrew writer who worked with Lilienblum and Pinsker in the office of Odessa's Hovevei Zion. In an essay written a year after Pinsker's death, Epstein asks directly—and without the equivocations he says that intruded on discussions of Pinsker immediately after his death (and that may have influenced Lilienblum's article)—what was it that singled out Pinsker for prominence? He was, says Epstein too, a thoroughly decent man but

someone who was rather "average." It is in this context, as an exploration of the soul of the "benoni" that Epstein frames his article. This sort
of man is usually rather small-minded, someone who finds comfort in
cloistered, closed off places. How did a man of this sort emerge as a
figure of substance and standing? [19]

Such men, writes Epstein, are almost always narcissists, little interested in much beyond themselves, hungry for petty honors, and obsessed
by jealousy. On rare occasions, however, they are transformed by
events—never by books or ideas, only by events in the larger world—
and at these moments their predictable, uneventful lives are capable
of being altogether transformed. Then "this sort of middling man,
this steadfast type of man with steady habits that remain otherwise
constant in times and places" is provided with an opportunity to be
made over, to reveal in the best of circumstances a greatness hidden
deep inside.[20]

This is the key to Pinsker's standing, says Epstein. His belated emergence as "one of the spiritual heroes of his people" couldn't have been
predicted. It was the pogroms of the 1880s and Pinsker's heroic, pre-
scient reaction to them that guaranteed him a place. He emerged as a
"tsaddik," a man of consummate self-effacement in the model of holy
men of the past. Epstein recalled sitting in Pinsker's home soon after the
1891 Jewish expulsions from Moscow when suddenly, as if from the
depths of his soul, Pinsker exclaimed: "And we are so poor, so weak!"
Imprinted on Epstein's memory was the misery on his face, his pain, his
dark eyes.[21]

This exemplary man—this "aristocrat of the spirit" accustomed to a
well-ordered life—found himself in the impossible position, as Epstein
describes it, of running the Hovevei Zion with its terrible inefficiency,
"swimming in a sea of petty interests," confusion, and vacuous debates.
Epstein says nothing more about his achievements in this regard. His
leadership of the Hovevei Zion was, as Epstein captures it, little more
than a burden, a relentless, terrible chore, a bad fate for a good man. It
darkened his last years, probably shortened his life, but also contributed
in its way toward making him immortal.[22]

There was consensus on this issue, insofar as Pinsker's achievements
were not deemed political, but were assumed to lie elsewhere in other
less concrete spheres. Perhaps the most vivid, and ironic, example is how
Ahad Ha'am appropriated Pinsker for his own ideological purposes with
surprisingly few objections from others in the nationalist camp. Indeed,
Ahad Ha'am (pen name for Asher Ginzberg) rather shrewdly adopted

Pinsker as an emblem of leadership whose characteristics were essentially the opposite from those that defined leadership for others. It was precisely those traits that others found lacking in Pinsker—his lack of assertiveness, his equivocations, his excessive honesty, his transparency—that Ahad Ha'am claimed to be the characteristics of the true leader who is repudiated because the failings of the world in which he finds himself.[23]

In his first essay on Pinsker, Ahad Ha'am, the chief internal critic of the Hovevei Zion during Pinsker's chairmanship, justified his expropriation of Pinsker. In this essay, written soon after Pinsker's death, Ahad Ha'am reported that on his deathbed—and in what Ahad Ha'am calls the dying man's "tsavaah leumit" (much the same term used by Ish Yisraeli)—Pinsker declared himself in favor of a "spiritual" nationalism of the sort championed by Ahad Ha'am as the only credible course for Palestinophilism. "What was left for him to do," asks Ahad Ha'am, "when experience taught him that it was extremely difficult to put his ideas into practice in [Palestine] and that members of the Hovevei Zion were [not yet prepared for nationalist tasks]?"[24]

The essay was written as part of Ahad Ha'am's bid to tip the movement in his ideological direction and perhaps to assume leadership of it in Pinsker's place. He used the term "spiritual center"—which would soon occupy a central place in his ideology—in this appreciation of Pinsker where he attempted to link it to the Hovevei Zion's first leader. In this piece called "Even le-matsevah" (Tombstone), Ahad Ha'am attributed the insight to Pinsker, lending it, despite its stark departure from the colonialist agenda of the Hovevei Zion, authority and continuity.[25]

Ahad Ha'am's preoccupation with Pinsker proved to be longstanding. He had deep respect for the man (a rare, cultivated European amidst self-educated Jewish "half-intelligenty"), as well as for his pamphlet (it was "scattered" and read like a "loud, bitter, heart-felt cry" but its theory of politics was immeasurably superior to Herzl's). It was in 1901 that he consolidated his hold on Pinsker's legacy once Herzl—a keen, dangerous manipulator of the masses, as Ahad Ha'am saw him—was in control of the Zionist movement. In an essay written on the tenth anniversary of his death, in what was one of Ahad Ha'am's most compelling reflections on leadership, he acknowledged Pinsker's shortcomings but argued that precisely these traits constituted the foundations for his success. This was a clever, politically dexterous essay designed to resurrect Pinsker—by now, mostly forgotten, claims Ahad Ha'am—and, more important, to put forward what was an essentially Ahad

Ha'amist mode of leadership with Pinsker as its emblem in opposition to the Herzlian one. To be sure, this alternate was rarified and unsuccessful when forced to engage in the manipulation of the masses. But it was, as Ahad Ha'am saw it, much closer to the authentic models of the Jewish past.[26]

Ahad Ha'am argues that Pinsker—and by implication also himself—would have been unlikely to compete for power with such masters of populist politics as Herzl. The masses are too fickle, the tricks used by populist demagogues too variegated, the charms of such men as Pinsker too subtle to exert much direct impact beyond a small circle.[27]

It was, Ahad Ha'am contended, at least the ideological canon of a movement, its collective memory, that men like Pinsker must dictate. Further, Pinsker's message of national selflessness and devotion must be promoted as a counterweight to the current crop of nationalist youth and the vapid teachings of official Zionism. Here Pinsker—and those inspired by his politics—are meant to be seen as an alternative to Herzl. True, Pinsker, Ahad Ha'am writes, was "a pure theorist . . . [and] like all theorists . . . of little use when it came to practical work. Men of this type, simple souls are pure-minded, know nothing except the naked truth, and such men cannot find their way to popular favor. Their words are too sincere, their actions are too straightforward." This exercise, written some three years before Ahad Ha'am's essay "Moses," resembles his portrait of the uncompromising, fiercely truthful biblical exemplar who was, as he saw it, the ideal of Jewish leadership.[28]

Had Pinsker remained at the helm of the Zionist movement through the 1890s, claims Ahad Ha'am, he would have been unable because of his honesty to carry off what Herzl did: he would have been frank with those around him that the movement's finances were in disarray, which, in turn, would have jeopardized negotiations with the Turks. He would not have excited the mob, could not have whetted the appetite of the press, and would have conducted Jewish nationalist affairs with none of the deftness, let alone the theater, of his Central European successor.[29]

But Ahad Ha'am's assertion that Pinsker was a failure is not meant to be taken at face value: in Ahad Ha'am's version it is, quite simply, the grandeur of Pinsker's soul that represents the true litmus test of his greatness and indispensability as a political leader. Pinsker's inability to impose order onto the Hovevei Zion, much like Ahad Ha'am's failure to wrest control of the movement from Herzl, must be traced, as Ahad Ha'am saw it, to the failings of the modern age: its corruptions, its dependence on mass appeal, its deafness to the need to reshape a secular

Jewish authority as inspired by the leaders of the past. Ahad Ha'am accepts the regnant gloss on Pinsker—as rarified, thoroughly decent, and unable to leave his mark on contemporary political life—but puts his distinctive signature on it and its implications. These implications are precisely the opposite of what others had assumed: the same traits of Pinsker's that others repudiated are those held up by Ahad Ha'am for acclaim.

There was surprisingly little response to Ahad Ha'am's article in the Russian Zionist press. Some took issue, claiming that its portrait of Pinsker was "incomplete" and that Pinsker was closer politically to Herzl than Ahad Ha'am admitted.[30] On the whole, though, there was silence. Ahad Ha'am had successfully claimed him, it seems, for his camp; or, to be more precise, others didn't care to claim him as more than an ideological pioneer. Russian Jewish nationalists closer to Herzl (to be sure, many Russian Jews sympathetic to the movement straddled the Ahad Ha'amist and Herzlian camps) saw Pinsker as a transitory figure who—and this is how Ahad Ha'am characterized their viewpoint—opened the door for his more prominent, fruitful successor. There seemed little more to say about him as a leader.

When prompted to comment on Pinsker's life—usually at an anniversary of his birth or death or the publication of *Autoemancipation*—members of the Hovevei Zion camp would increasingly deny his leadership ability outright, asserting that his Palestinophile career was tragic; this term was now used with some frequency to capture the tenor of his career after the writing of *Autoemancipation*. The tone was mild, disappointed rather than angry. Pinsker's political acumen tended to be measured against Herzl's, with memories of the Odessa leader meshing with more general recollections of a pre-Herzlian political past where Jewish nationalism engaged in little more than spinning wheels in the margins, gestures rather than politics.

Even a friendly comment on Pinsker—the memoir by Ben Ami of his first encounter with him (published in 1912)—said warm things about his pamphlet and, of course, the man (he was, insists Ben Ami, surprisingly accessible for someone of his stature) but it is his "honesty, holy and pure" that set him apart "not his practical work." His chairmanship of the Hovevei Zion is not mentioned in the piece though Ben Ami was a loyal, longstanding devotee of the group.[31]

Far more explicit was Yehiel Tchlenow, the leader of Moscow's Zionists, in a talk at a commemorative meeting in honor of Pinsker in December 1916. "His entire life until [the writing of *Automancipa-*

tion]," Tchlenow stated, "was a big, awful mistake." The period afterwards was not much better: he would have preferred, and assumed that he would be able, to issue his nationalist call and leave its implementation to others better suited for the task. He could not and here, insists Tchlenow, "begins Pinsker's tragedy." It is, similarly, as "Tragedy and Victory" that Moshe Glickson, in an article written the same year, sums up Pinsker's political life, the tragedy being—much as Tchlenow saw it—his misguided, involuntary entry into politics which was made over eventually into something worthwhile only because of the good work of Herzl. The Moscow Zionist Jacob Mazeh, rabbi of the Moscow Jewish community, said much the same: Pinsker was a prophet who found himself compelled, after he had fulfilled his prophetic task, to do things—practical, mundane, political—unsuitable to his temperament. This meant his Hovevei Zion years were marked by little achievement and terrible frustration. Mazeh did not in this context contrast Pinsker's career with Herzl's; by now, though, it had come to be typical to do this.[32]

No one did this quite so baldly as Russian Zionist leader Menachem Mendel Ussishkin in his "The Teacher and the Leader." Published first in 1916 by Ussishkin, a past chairman of Hovevei Zion, he evoked in this appreciation of Pinsker images of both Pinsker and Herzl: their appearances, their style of work, their strengths and weaknesses. To think of Pinsker almost inevitably meant to think also about Herzl, or so Ussishkin implied.[33]

Ussishkin writes: "The two of them appear before me as if they were alive. The first [Pinsker] of average height, his body compact, his movements heavy. A large head, round, situated on broad shoulders, thick hair, smooth, aged, his beard aged, slightly trimmed, his forehead large, prominent." He describes his eyes, his hardened lips, the general impression of his face: a man of "weighty thoughts, deep, steady emotions." [34] In contrast, Herzl is described as "proud," "splendid looking," a man of "tremendous will-power, hard as iron." At first, Ussishkin appears torn in his sympathies: deeply impressed with the human qualities of Pinsker, aware of the splendid leadership characteristics of Herzl.[35]

Whatever ambivalence Ussishkin feels about the pair is dissipated once he imagines the two of them at work: in contrast to Herzl, whom he sees in public, surrounded by crowds, speaking to them, inspiring them, Pinsker sits alone in a room where he sits and thinks aloud: he speaks here in "stray sentences, fragments," he does little more than "sigh"—and, yet, with his sigh "he cuts deep into your soul and mind."

If you dare try to reply it is obvious, almost immediately, that you've wasted your time since he can't hear you: "He is with you only in the form of his body; his spirit, his thoughts, his feelings are very far from you, far from life in the present, soaring over vast distances thousands of years into the past and hundreds of years into the future. . . ."[36]

Rarely could Pinsker be found "among the masses of people, in meetings, in congresses, in the assemblies of the people." He stays far away from them and if forced to attend a meeting he feels "afflicted." He is, quite literally, overwhelmed by his hatred of sectarian politics, the pressures of individuals or interest groups—all these mundane manifestations of political life are hateful, alien to his temperament.[37]

Where Ussishkin speaks with an unequivocal respect for Pinsker is in his evaluation of *Autoemancipation*. True, it is a small pamphlet read only by "the elect." All who have seen it, though, admit that they are unable to return as comfortably as before to their everyday affairs. It intrudes on their sleep, readers are made over into apostles spreading its lesson far and wide. Perhaps Pinsker gave his name to no particular school of Zionism. But had "the teacher [Pinsker] not established a circle of followers, the man who succeeded him [Herzl] would never have been able to come forward as a leader."[38]

The contrast between the two—and what was, as Ussishkin claimed, a symbiotic relationship crucial to the viability of Zionism—could not be more starkly delineated. Herzl is dazzling, seductive, a spellbinder (the rather stolid, unimaginative Ussishkin betrays here more than a little of his ambivalence toward the Zionist leader); Pinsker, on the other hand, is so inarticulate and tongue-tied, more than shy, in fact cut off from human contact of any meaningful sort, that the notion he could serve as a leader is laughable.

That consensus existed in terms of what Pinsker represented in Jewish nationalism was, or so it seemed, quite simply because there could be little dispute about a man whose reclusive temperament was so familiar to Lilienblum, Epstein, Ahad Ha'am, Ussishkin, and others in the Hovevei Zion. What else could possibly have been said about Pinsker's leadership ability whose shortcomings were obvious for all to see? Still, the consensus itself is surprising. Not simply because the facts are in dispute—as we shall see, these too can bear greater scrutiny—but because the frankness with which Pinsker's failings were aired, and within moments of his death, were out of character for the Jewish nationalist movement.

On the whole, this milieu was unforthcoming about itself, its failings, and especially the shortcomings of its leading figures; its treatment of its first chairman, who remained a figure of high regard despite his much-touted inadequacy as a politician, was unusual. Its characteristic reticence was an outgrowth of more than a predictable institutional defensiveness. Rather, Jewish nationalists felt themselves especially vulnerable in view of the distance between their aspirations and their rather modest achievements in Palestine and elsewhere. In Russian Jewry, Zionism was patronized by much of the Jewish intelligentsia, distrusted by most traditional Jews, and (within a few years of Herzl's death, to an extent even earlier) seen as politically suspect by the Russian government.

Its public assessments of itself were, as a result, mostly flat, self-congratulatory, and defensive. The literature it produced on its leading figures—at least, the pieces the movement itself wrote about its own luminaries—tended to overlook failings, especially the ones most likely to disturb the leaders themselves: e.g., Ahad Ha'am's fierce political appetite. In a community confronted with new, conflicting models of leadership (secular, nationalist, postliberal, socialist, orthodox) the Hovevei Zion was keenly aware that its depiction of its leaders told much about itself, its vulnerability, its potential as the flagship of modern Jewry.[39]

Why the depiction of Pinsker? This problem is all the more apparent when one looks at Pinsker's correspondence as head of the Hovevei Zion where, despite terrible, at times unrelenting problems he shows a presence of mind, charm, and often fierce resolve. Take, for example, his letters written in 1885 after the successful Kattowicz conference, when within the span of a few months, he is confronted with the following dilemmas: Moses Montefiore dies and, though Pinsker's organization has been named in his honor, he leaves nothing to it, with only a small sum left to Palestine, which Pinsker tries to siphen off to his group. The Bialystok branch rebels, and refuses to send its requisite funding to the Hovevei Zion, when it hears that non-religious settlers, in particular the politically dubious Biluim are receiving support from the organization; it, in turn, accuses leading members by name in Warsaw and elsewhere of financial improprieties. Official recognition by the government of his group seems imminent (late in the year Pinsker writes that this likely will be granted in three or four months); it proves elusive and (until 1890) unsuccessful negotiations occupy much of his time. The distinguished German Jewish historian Heinrich Graetz, perhaps the best known of the group's supporters, resigns upon learning that the group is nationalist, not merely philanthropic, which (or so he says) at first he assumed.

Any mention of nationalism, Pinsker warns Nathan Birnbaum, editor of the Vienna-based *Selbstemanzipation,* is dangerous to the organization which can speak of itself only in terms of economic support for poor Jews in Palestine: the grandeur, the unrestrained passion of Pinsker's own pamphlet which inspired Birnbaum's periodical must, he insists, be checked.[40]

In his correspondence with Birnbaum and elsewhere, Pinsker is firm and decisive; at times he threatens reprisals if his words are not heeded. He guarantees the Bialystok Hovevei Zion, for instance, that its fear that secularist members of the organization's executive might penalize such a colony as Petah Tikvah for its religiosity is misplaced: "I will honor my promise that, for as long as I remain head of the executive, no colony will ever be unfairly treated and if a member of the executive acts from personal prejudice to create problems for particular colonists, I will put a stop to his efforts with a strong hand and would even go so far as to discipline the entire executive."[41]

In the best-known sketch produced outside the Hibbat Zion—by the writer Mendele Mocher Seforim, who knew Pinsker well (he translated Pinsker's *Autoemancipation* into Yiddish and had deep respect for him despite his reservations about Palestinophilism)—much the same side of Pinsker is revealed. Here Pinsker is seen as someone with a strong, direct style of leadership. True, Mendele's sketch is a fiction, part of his short story "Be-yemei ha-raash." But its description of Pinsker, called the "Karlini" or the Karliner (the town of Karlin is adjacent to Pinsk) is, most critics agree, a realistic account of a conversation with Pinsker, who appears here as someone of authority and presence.[42]

The story's protagonist, a beggar seeking help for (what he says will be) his move to Palestine, comments, as he passes from a crowded waiting room filled with people seeking his assistance, that he is overwhelmed when he first spots the Karliner: "There are those people whom you see only once and who leave an imprint on your heart that remains forever. . . ." Recollections of people of this stature, similiar, says Mendele, to the recollections that a pupil has of his rabbi, can illuminate one's way in life.[43]

The Karliner's appearance—his medium height, his curious, intriguing smile, the wisdom exuding from the man (the narrator assumed at first it was more severe than wise), his slow speech, the distinction with which he carried himself—these casual impressions were substantiated by the exchange between the narrator and the impressive man sitting behind his writing desk. In the conversation, the Karliner, who quickly realized he could do nothing for the beggar, was decisive and firm.[44] No hint on his part of the equivocation, let alone the incoherence, of the Hovevei Zion accounts.

Precisely because it is the clear-headed, inspiring presence of the Karliner that is so pronounced in the story, the insistence in literature produced within the Hovevei Zion of Pinsker's lack of leadership qualities is all the more puzzling. Mendele's sketch suggests a more impressive Pinsker than his movement chose to recall. If so, why?

Not only did Pinsker emerge in the collective memory of Russian Zionism as the best example of the Hovevei Zion's failings as a group; even Shmuel Tsitron, the first historian of Pinsker's group, ends a deeply sympathetic book saying that the Hovevei Zion's chief achievement was "setting the foundations for that great and grand movement of the people that started from the appearance of Theodor Herzl."[45] In Pinsker's case recollections of him were flattened, in some quarters of the Hovevei Zion all but vilified, and soon after his death, precisely because it was not mere efficiency or soundness of mind that was expected of him. It was greatness which he had, in fact, shown, or so it was believed, in the writing of *Autoemancipation*. For Herzl—a foreign-born, Western Jew seen, if at all, by Russian Zionists at the well-orchestrated movement congresses—it was far easier to sustain the sort of adoration that Pinsker, an all-too-familiar figure on the streets of Odessa, never could. Pinsker's direct, untheatrical simplicity was, according to Ahad Ha'am, a trademark of his greatness, but Ahad Ha'am—one of Hebrew literature's masters of irony—knew well that his measure of Pinsker was completely out-of-kilter with that of others, which was precisely why he made the case.

As head of the Hovevei Zion, the strident, clear-headed, passionate statements that gained Pinsker visibility in nationalist circles had to be muted, as he understood it, because of the suspicions of the Russian government, the wealthy, anti-nationalistic Jews of the West, and those of his own restive, religious constituency. "If it is not your desire to cause harm to the growth of our movement," he writes Nathan Birnbaum in March 1885, "it is necessary for you to restrain yourself from advertising the 'nationalist' character of our movement and always to select instead, if possible, only its economic goals."[46] Such self-restraint became his trademark as Hovevei Zion chief. In the end, it was interpreted less as a reflection of the times—which it clearly was—than a product of his own inadequacy as a leader.

Disappointment in Pinsker was sharpened by rumors of his renouncing, or substantially modifying, on his deathbed a commitment to the colonization of Jewish Palestine (never all that firm to begin with, as many knew). Hence, the Hovevei Zion movement permitted itself to speak of him with rare candor, insisting even on seeing his remarkable talent at reaching consensus as a sign of excessive lack of firmness. As the Hovevei Zion saw it—and there was a rare unanimity on this score—Pinsker had presented himself in *Autoemancipation* as a figure embodying the passion of the prophet with the sophistication and breadth of a man of the world. His appearance was godsent, or so it seemed, and instead Hovevei Zion found itself saddled with a rather mundane leader whose moment of inspiration had passed. Pinsker had flirted with greatness and then settled down to the routine of a conscientious administrator. The Hovevei Zion never forgave him.

NOTES

This article was completed in Jerusalem during my stay as a fellow of the Institute for Advanced Studies at the Hebrew University. I am grateful for the Institute's splendid research facilities. Rachel Budd and Semion Gordin, both graduate students at the Hebrew University, assisted me in locating material. I thank Jonathan Frankel and Eli Lederhendler for comments on an early draft.

1. Mordecai Ben Hillel Ha-Cohen, *Olami,* vol. 2 (Jerusalem, 1927), pp. 99–100.
2. Yosef Goldstein, "Herzl and the Russian Zionists: The Unavoidable Crisis," *Studies in Contemporary Jewry,* vol. 2 (1986), pp. 208–32.
3. Raphael Patai, ed., *The Complete Diaries of Theodor Herzl,* vol. 4 (New York, 1960), p. 1544.
4. The fullest biography of Leon Pinsker remains Alter Druyanow, *Pinsker u-zemano* (Jerusalem, 1953) and it, alas, is incomplete and was published posthumously. A reliable summary of Pinsker's life may be found in Yosef Klausner's essay in *Sefer Pinsker* (Jerusalem, 1921), pp. 5–50. For an index to Hebrew-language periodical literature on Pinsker, compiled by A. Cohen, see the Central Zionist Archives (CZA), A9/175. Other material on Pinsker (in Russian, German, etc.) and an annotated list of editions of *Autoemancipation* may be found in *Kiryat sefer,* vol. 11 (Jerusalem, 1935), pp. 117–30. For Russian reviews of *Autoemancipation,* see *Sistematicheskii ukazatel' literatury o evreiakh na russkom iazyke so vremeni vvedeniia grazhdanskago shrifta do dekabria 1889* (St. Petersburg, 1892), p. 333. An important source on Pinsker's public life is Shulamit Laskov, ed., *Ketavim le-toledot Hibbat Zion ve-yishuv Eretz Israel,* 6 vols. (Tel Aviv, 1982–1990). On the background to Pinsker's conversion to Palestinophilism, which may well have been more protracted than the standard Zionist sources assume, see M. Kulisher, "K 25-letiiu so dnia smerti I. G. Orshanskago," *Voskhod,* November 23, 1900.

5. For further discussion, see my *Elusive Prophet: Ahad Ha'am and the Origins of Zionism* (Berkeley, 1993), esp. pp. 258–68. Ussishkin elaborates on the distinction between Pinsker as a "teacher" and as a "leader" in *Ha-aretz*, January 1, 1922. See CZA, A9/175. Pinsker's letter to Lev Levanda is published in Laskov, *Ketavim*, vol. 2., see esp. p. 226.

6. Shmuel Tsitron, *Toledot Hibbat Zion*, vol. 1 (Odessa, 1914), p. 376.

7. *Nedel'naia khronika voskhoda*, no. 24 (December 22, 1891), p. 695.

8. See *Ha-tsefirah*, nos. 1 (January 1, 1892), pp. 2–3; 2 (January 2), p. 7; 8 (January 9), p. 31; 12 (January 14), pp. 47–48; 14 (January 16), pp. 54–55.

9. Ibid., no. 2 (January 2), p. 7.

10. Ibid., no. 1 (January 1), pp. 2–3.

11. *Ha-melitz*, nos. 281 (December 17, 1891), pp. 1–2; 283 (December 19), pp. 1–2; 285 (December 22), pp. 1–3. Also see Jacob Mazeh's appreciation of Pinsker, in *Ha-melitz*, no. 26 (January 31, 1892), pp. 2–3.

12. *Nedel'naia khronika voskhoda*, no. 24 (December 22, 1891), p. 695.

13. See Shmuel Tsitron, *Anashim ve-soferim* (Vilna, n.d.), pp. 56–61, for a discussion of the history of several (abortive) translations of *Autoemancipation* into Hebrew.

14. See *Ha-melitz*, no. 285 (December 22, 1891), pp. 1–3.

15. *Sion: Evreiskii palestinskii sbornik* (St. Petersburg, 1892), pp. 297–300; *Nedel'naia khronika voskhoda*, no. 24 (December 22, 1891), pp. 692–95.

16. See *Kol kitvei Moshe Leib Lilienblum*, vol. 4 (Odessa, 1910), p. 181. The article was published originally in *Ha-melitz*, no. 287, in 1891.

17. Ibid., pp. 182–83. Also see Lilienblum's comments on Pinsker in *Nedel'naia khronika voskhoda*, no. 6 (1902).

18. *Kol kitvei Lilienblum*, vol. 4, pp. 183–84.

19. *Ha-melitz*, no. 278 (December 15, 1892), p. 2.

20. Ibid.

21. Ibid., p. 4.

22. Ibid.

23. An example of how effectively Ahad Ha'am usurped Pinsker's legacy is the content of *Sefer Pinsker:* a thin volume, it includes little more than the two Ahad Ha'am essays on Pinsker, Ahad Ha'am's translation of *Autoemancipation,* and the biographical essay on Pinsker by Ahad Ha'amist, Yosef Klausner.

24. *Kol kitvei Ahad Ha'am* (Jerusalem, 1956), p. 46.

25. Ibid., pp. 46–48.

26. Ibid., pp. 164–72.

27. Ibid., p. 172.

28. Ibid.

29. Ibid.

30. See, for example, *Ha-tsefirah*, no. 70 (March 24, 1902), p. 279.

31. *Ha-olam*, no. 49–50 (January 12, 1912), pp. 7–9.

32. Both articles, by Glickson and Mazeh, appeared in a special issue of the Moscow newspaper, *Ha-olam*, devoted to Pinsker: no. 4 (December 9, 1916). With a similiar perspective on Pinsker, see A. I. [Abraham Idelson], *Razsvet*, no. 52 (December 23, 1911), cols. 4–7.

33. See *Sefer Pinsker*, pp. 126–28. Ussislhkein's article first appeared in *Ha-olam*, no. 4 (December 9, 1916).

34. *Sefer Pinsker*, p. 126.

35. Ibid.

36. Ibid., pp. 126–27.

37. Ibid., p. 127.

38. Ibid., p. 128.

39. See, for example, my discussion in *Elusive Prophet,* pp. 21–42.
40. Laskov, *Ketavim,* vol. 3, pp. 225, 365–67, 432–33, 479–80, 538–41, 606–7.
41. Ibid., p. 367.
42. *Kol kitvei Mendele Mocher Seforim,* vol. 3 (Odessa, 1912), pp. 73–104.
43. Ibid., p. 82.
44. Ibid., p. 83.
45. Tsitron, *Toledot,* p. 383. Note also the treatment of Pinsker in Iluii Safir's *Sionizm* (Vilna, 1903), the first attempt to write a full-length book for the general public on all aspects of Zionism in Russian and which won a prize sponsored by the Zionist movement. Here, *Autoemancipation* receives ample space in a chapter of ten pages, where it is described as calling for a solution similar to Herzl's. Pinsker's standing as head of the Russian movement is noted with no discussion of his achievements. This treatment contrasts elsewhere in Safir's book to detailed expositions of the contributions of rather marginal figures, e.g. Lawrence Oliphant, to the building of Jewish Palestine. In a list of the practical achievements of the Hovevei Zion, no mention is made of Pinsker although the work of local leaders, in Warsaw and elsewhere, is praised lavishly. Remarkably, Safir has Pinsker die not retire from the Hovevei Zion in 1889 and then—on the next page—reappoints him the following year as head of the movement!
46. Laskov, *Ketavim,* vol. 5, p. 225. The original German letter is published in A[lter] Druyanow, *Ketavim le-toledot Hibbat Zion ve-yishuv Eretz Israel,* vol. 1 (Odessa, 1919), cols. 459–60.

10.

The State of the Zionist Movement on the Eve of the Sixth Congress

Michael Heymann

At its Sixth Congress (23–28 August 1903), the Zionist movement entered a period of turmoil, the first and stormiest part of which lasted until the meeting of the Greater Actions Committee (G.A.C.) in Vienna in April 1904. For some time dissatisfaction with Theodor Herzl's leadership, or rather with its meagre results, had been growing; unswerving loyalty, where it had existed, was giving way to a mood of questioning and doubt; and above all the unresolved conflicts between Herzl and the heads of Russian Zionism, which had been largely smoothed over since the First Congress in 1897, could no longer be kept under control by tacit agreements to differ. Even the Zionists of Germany, traditionally Herzl's faithful supporters, were growing restive and were making strong demands for some kind of practical work in Palestine, such as the purchase of land. Pressing for a change in the way the movement was led, some of the younger German Zionists put forward the suggestion that Herzl should accept a salary from the Zionist Organization and—if possible—move to London. This would end his irksome dependence on the *Neue Freie Presse,* as literary editor of which he earned his living, and enable him to devote himself exclusively to Zionism.[1]

Herzl himself, plagued by the premonitory symptoms of the illness which was to cause his early death, was by the summer of 1903 showing an occasional irritability and high-handedness which gave much unnec-

Reprinted by permission of the author and the Institute for Research in the History of Zionism, Tel Aviv University from *The Minutes of the Zionist Council: The Uganda Controversy,* vol. 1, edited by Michael Heymann (Jerusalem: Israel Universities Press, 1970), 14–39.

essary offence. Large sections of the movement were worried by what appeared to them the feverishness of his activities, whose purpose they could not pretend to understand and whose efficacy they were no longer prepared to take for granted. The simmering crisis finally erupted when Herzl sprang a surprise upon the Congress and disclosed to the unsuspecting delegates the British offer for the establishment of a Jewish settlement, enjoying some measure of "municipal autonomy", in what is now Kenya.[2]

When, in the summer of 1902, Herzl realized that his attempts to obtain a "Charter" for Palestine from the Turks had failed, at least for the time being, he directed his efforts towards acquiring a region outside the Sultan's realm for Jewish settlement. Joseph Chamberlain and Lord Lansdowne, the British Colonial and Foreign Secretary respectively, perhaps not unmindful of their own problem of alien immigration, were sympathetic. The prospect of settlement in an area under British control, the Egyptian Sinai Peninsula—not quite, but almost, Palestine, and therefore acceptable to any true "Lover of Zion"—awoke high hopes, which turned to keen disappointment when the British backed down and pronounced this so-called El-Arish scheme impracticable. By this time, May 1903, the Kishinev pogrom had just taken place. Overcome by a sense of urgency and fearing another wave of unorganized mass migration to the no longer uniformly hospitable Western countries, Herzl did not feel himself able to reject out of hand Chamberlain's offer for a settlement in East Africa. Thus was born the East Africa—or as it was then commonly called, the Uganda—project.[3]

After initial doubts and hesitations, the leading figures among the Russian "Lovers of Zion" [Hovevei-Zion] or Zionists, as they had begun to be called in the mid-1890's, had, with the notable exception of Ahad ha-Am, acknowledged Herzl's leadership at the First or, at the latest, the Second Zionist Congress.[4] There may have been little that was new or exciting in the ideas put forward by Herzl; Pinsker had said it all years ago.[5] But in him they encountered for the first time the ability to translate their own aspirations into political action. Such clarity of vision they had never met. As Ussischkin wrote to Ahad ha-Am on the eve of the First Congress: "They . . . [Herzl and his friends in Vienna] hope, but they also offer a plan of action; we hope but do not know what to do".[6] To this was added, on closer acquaintance, the effect of Herzl's towering personality, which even those who—often regretfully—opposed him, found irresistible.[7] They themselves, after fifteen years of work, had little to show in the way of political or other achievements. There was there-

fore every reason to give the new man and his method a chance, the
more so as the rank and file did not wait for the veteran leaders to make
up their minds, but accorded the message of Der Judenstaat a reception
of unreserved enthusiasm.[8]

Nevertheless the official leaders of Russian Zionism (and for our
purpose these were, after 1898, the Russian members of the G.A.C.)
were never fully converted to Herzl's way of thinking. They refused to
accept his thesis that any settlement activities in Palestine before the
grant of a "Charter" by the Turks would be harmful and should therefore be discontinued. His concepts of rapid mass migration[9] and the
creation of what a recent author has called "a social state through
modern technology"[10] remained beyond their ken. They could only
deplore Herzl's lack of interest in cultural questions. Also, one may
surmise, they continued to harbour a suspicion that, despite the Basle
Programme, Herzl remained at heart a Judenstaatler, whose attachment
to Zion did not equal their own.

Whatever their misgivings, the Russian members of the G.A.C. had
until the Sixth Congress refrained from collectively voicing overt criticism of Herzl, leaving this ticklish business mainly to private individuals
or—since 1901—to an unofficial group, the Demokratische Fraktion.[11]
When, in the summer of that year, one of the Russian members of the
G.A.C., Dr. Jacob Bernstein-Kohan of Kishinev, who had a reputation
for outspokenness, gave vent to his ill-humour in a circular to the
Zionist societies of his district,[12] using some rather offensive terms,[13] he
was soon disavowed by his colleagues;[14] and the "correspondence office", a kind of organization centre of Russian Zionism, which he had
headed since 1898, was dissolved shortly afterwards.[15] However, even
Bernstein-Kohan's strictures, taken so badly in Vienna,[16] were not directed against Herzl's leadership or his basic tenets; Bernstein-Kohan
himself was, by Russian standards at least, a political rather than an old-
fashioned practical Zionist. They were concerned with marginal issues:
the faulty organization of the Fourth Congress in London in 1900 and,
more important, the secretiveness of the Executive Actions Committee
(E.A.C.) in Vienna and of the Board of Directors of the Jewish Colonial
Trust in London.

This last matter—the reluctance of the executive bodies of the movement to report frequently and fully on their activities to the members of
the G.A.C., or, in other words, Herzl's refusal to submit himself to any
effective "parliamentary" supervision—had been the subject of confidential complaints by the Russian members of the G.A.C. since the early

days of the Zionist Organization. On the eve of the Second Congress (August 1898), the conference of Russian Zionists convened in Warsaw decided to ask the Congress to elect a kind of "vigilance committee" to which Herzl would be required to report regularly on his "diplomatic" activities.[17] Two months later, on 17 and 18 October 1898, the newly-elected Russian members of the G.A.C. met at Kiev. As Herzl's freedom of action had not been restricted by the Congress, the Kiev meeting adopted and forwarded to Vienna a set of detailed resolutions bearing on the relations between the members of the A.C. living in the Austrian capital (i.e. members of the E.A.C., at that time still called the *Vienna Centre*) and those living elsewhere (i.e. the members of the G.A.C.). The principal request was that, except on matters which brooked no delay, the E.A.C. should act in accordance with majority views of the members of the G.A.C., such to be ascertained in writing. The E.A.C. would inform the members of the G.A.C. of any decision reached in this way. In addition it was suggested by the Kiev meeting that: a) any proposal made by a member of the G.A.C. to the E.A.C. in Vienna should be circulated to all members of the G.A.C. and a vote should be taken on each proposal in accordance with the procedure outlined above; b) decisions taken by the E.A.C. on urgent matters should be brought to the knowledge of the members of the G.A.C.; c) the E.A.C. should distribute the minutes of its meetings to the members of the G.A.C. in order to enable the latter to maintain close contact with the Vienna Centre; and d) each Zionist Federation *(Landes-Organisation)* should send a detailed semi-annual report on its activities to Vienna, and the E.A.C. should report likewise to the G.A.C. on its own work and on that of the Federations.[18] These suggestions or requests do not seem to have caused much concern to the leadership in Vienna; the G.A.C. continued to be confronted with *faits accomplis,* and the supply of information between meetings remained irregular and incomplete.

As the years went by, the Russian members of the G.A.C. became less and less inclined to put up with such inconsiderate treatment. When the *Jewish Colonial Trust* was established as the financial instrument of the movement (1899–1901), a weighty reason was added to the Russians' insistence on receiving full and punctual information, the more so since most of its shares had been subscribed in Russia. Although the paid-up share capital of the *Trust*—approximately £250,000—was a paltry sum measured against the resources of the big London finance houses, control of its use was a matter of major importance to those who considered themselves the representatives of a poor people. At a meeting in Odessa in February 1901, the Russian members of the G.A.C. formulated another set of demands, this time designed to give them a real hold on the management of the *Trust,* and backed up these demands with the threat of resignation. They also voiced their disappointment at the ineffectiveness of the Fourth Congress in London and made some suggestions for the reform of the movement's organizational machinery.[19] This "ultimatum" did produce some improvement in the flow of information, but it did not last long. Thus, when they met again in Kiev in April 1903, a few days after the Kishinev pogrom, the Russian members of the G.A.C. were compelled to repeat their earlier complaints and renew their request for punctual information on the position of the *Trust.*[20] The participants in the Kiev meeting[21] also aired their exasperation at being kept in the dark about the El-Arish scheme. Their knowledge of Herzl's latest diplomatic effort was derived from the press, a state of affairs which, they argued with understandable irritation, undermined their authority as members of the G.A.C. It seems that an appropriate letter of protest on this subject, too, was mailed to Vienna.[22] Yet the first, and only, official notification from the E.A.C. concerning El-Arish was not sent to members of the G.A.C. until June. It contained, in addition to a plaintive statement on the premature disclosure of secret information on previous occasions, a brief announcement that the El-Arish scheme had fallen through.[23]

The communication from Kiev to Vienna, firm and uncompromising though it was, actually obscured the real conflict, for it was not concerned with the opposing stands taken by Herzl and the Russian leaders on central issues of Zionist policy and work, and therefore did not reveal the extent to which the two sides had drawn apart since the preceding autumn. At the beginning of September 1902, a conference of Russian Zionists had taken place at Minsk—the only one of its kind held with the permission of the Czarist authorities—which, in view of its size and the publicity surrounding it, had assumed many of the characteristics of a regular Congress. While problems of education and culture had been among the chief topics of debate, resolutions had been passed urging the immediate purchase of land by the Jewish National Fund, even before any sizable sum of money had been accumulated, and recommending, in a slightly oblique manner, the continuation of settlement work in Palestine in cooperation with the "Odessa Committee", that very embodiment of *Kleinkolonisation* so heartily despised by "political" Zionists.[24] All this assumed a special significance because it was no more than a month since Herzl's prestige had suffered a heavy blow through the announcement that his recent negotiations with the Sultan had come to nothing.[25] The impression consequently arose that Russian Zionists would no longer automatically submit to the domination of their Western brethren and might indeed try in future to pull their full numerical weight and impose their views on the Congresses of the whole movement.[26] There had been no open revolt against the "official line", though the invitation to Ahad ha-Am to address the conference, and the central role he was allowed to play there, showed a complete disregard for Herzl's susceptibilities. Worse had in fact happened: Herzl and his concepts had been by-passed, because they no longer seemed relevant to the immediate needs of Russian Zionism as conceived by the local leadership.

A more detailed report on his failure in Constantinople, containing the frank admission that he did not expect the prospects of a satisfactory agreement with the Turks to improve, was delivered by Herzl to the G.A.C. and to the Annual Conference which met in Vienna during the last days of October 1902.[27] This further weakened Herzl's authority and encouraged the independent tendencies displayed at Minsk. Indeed, less than one month after the meetings in Vienna, four of the most influential Russian members of the G.A.C., Ussischkin, Tschlenow, Temkin and J. L. Goldberg, took the lead in setting up *Ge'ulah*, a company for the purchase of land in Palestine on behalf of private buyers.[28] The resolutions of the Minsk conference and the establishment of *Ge'ulah*— which was followed by a considerable propaganda effort to popularize the new venture among Russian Zionists as the first practical step in the *gradual* process of creating a Jewish centre in Palestine on sound economic foundations—struck at the very roots of one of Herzl's main theses: the abstention from work in Palestine pending political guarantees which would render possible the *speedy* occupation of the country. These developments could have served to warn Herzl of the Russian leadership's increasing disillusion with "diplomacy" which produced no tangible results; but immersed as he was towards the end of 1902 in the early stages of the El-Arish negotiations, he seems to have paid little, if any, attention to the internal affairs of the movement.

Mention must be made, lastly, of a quasi-literary controversy which took place early in 1903 and generated much bitterness and mutual distrust among Zionists: the debate about Herzl's novel *Altneuland*. This was published in German in the autumn of 1902, and a little later in a Hebrew translation by Nahum Sokolow, who renamed it *Tel-Aviv*

(Hill of Spring). It will suffice to recall merely those aspects of this unseemly feud which bear directly on our subject. As a utopian and, broadly speaking, "programme" novel, *Altneuland* should have been judged by the rules applicable to this peculiar literary genre. Ahad ha-Am, however, notwithstanding that the Hebrew translation was published under the auspices of the Russian Zionist Organization, held it— and by implication its author—up to ridicule in the issue of *Ha-Shilo'ah* for December 1902.[29] The pettiness displayed by Ahad ha-Am, his wallowing in the obvious flaws and absurdities of Herzl's novel, might well have produced a reaction in the latter's favour. Shmarya Levin's public disavowal of Ahad ha-Am—"Herzl builds and you are destroying"— points to such a possibility.[30] This chance was lost when Herzl, deeply hurt by what he considered a calculated political attack on his leadership masked as literary criticism, asked his friend Max Nordau to take up the cudgels on his behalf. Nordau's counter-attack, published in *Die Welt* of 13 March 1903, could hardly be surpassed as a piece of coarse invective. No doubt wishing to emphasize Herzl's modernity as against Ahad ha-Am's old-fashioned provincialism, Nordau, by his ill-chosen words, succeeded in creating the impression that he, the *"Westjude"*, was bent on humiliating and ruining the literary reputation of the *"Ostjude"* Ahad ha-Am. The real weakness of Ahad ha-Am's critique, which was his utter lack of understanding of the feats of social reconstruction envisaged by Herzl, was completely obscured when Nordau played up Herzl's *"westliche Kultur"* and contrasted it with the *"kulturfeindlichen, wilden Asiatentum"* allegedly represented by his adversary. By his supercilious manner, Nordau achieved the very opposite of what he had set out to do. Instead of closing the ranks behind Herzl, he touched off a wave of sympathy for the wronged Ahad ha-Am, not only in eastern Europe but, more significantly, among Zionist academic youth in and from Austria and Germany.[31] Unintentionally Nordau had dragged into the open what was then one of the most difficult problems of Jewry: the relationship between its eastern and western (or central) European components. Where Zionism had sedulously endeavoured to build bridges, where the utmost tact in speech and writing was required, Nordau let himself go with a crudity astonishing in such a skilled writer. Probably embarrassed by his friend's intemperance, Herzl tried to justify Nordau's effusion as no more than "a rude reply to a vicious attack",[32] and considered the incident closed. But suspicions were more easily roused than allayed, and the offence given by Nordau continued to rankle.[33] Herzl certainly did not emerge any stronger from this affair, and the antagonism between "East" and "West" became henceforth a favourite subject of domestic Zionist polemics.[34]

It was presumably with a view to neutralizing the numerous manifestations of discontent, both overt and covert, that Herzl agreed in May 1903 to support the projects for land purchase propounded by *Ge'ulah*. The prime mover of these projects was Ussischkin, who was at this time asserting that the Kishinev pogrom had fully confirmed the correctness of his views that the centre of Zionist activity ought to be Palestine and not the diaspora; that the "preparation of the country" must precede the "preparation of the people"; and that the purchase of land by the National Fund and by *Ge'ulah,* the economic development of the country by the *Anglo-Palestine Company* (A.P.C.), and self-government in the existing settlements were the elements which would bring Zionism closer to its goal.[35] In order to carry out this ambitious programme, Ussischkin decided to pay an extended visit to Palestine; but before setting out on his journey he invited himself to Vienna, not only—it would appear—to receive Herzl's blessing, but also to obtain a binding commitment that the Zionist banks, the *Jewish Colonial Trust* and its offshoot the *Anglo-Palestine Company,* would grant large credits to *Ge'ulah,* which in the spring of 1903 did not yet possess sizable funds of its own. Ussischkin arrived in Vienna on 19 May, at the very time when Herzl was first seriously turning his mind to the "East Africa" project,[36] and he obtained among other things a promise of a credit of the order of 100,000 roubles (£10,000).[37] He thereupon returned to Russia and soon afterwards, accompanied by other emissaries of the "Odessa Committee" and of *Ge'ulah,* proceeded to Palestine, arriving there at the end of June. On his way, Ussischkin stopped for some days in Constantinople, where he made enquiries about the legal problems connected with the purchase of land and its registration in the name of non-Turkish individuals and corporations.[38] His subsequent activities during his stay in Palestine, which lasted until the middle of September and which incidentally led to his absence from the Sixth Congress, were to have a disastrous effect on his relationship with Herzl.

Herzl on his part had no reason to expect in May 1903 that he was running a serious risk in lending some, actually quite tepid, encouragement to Ussischkin's projects, since he assumed the impecunious *Ge'ulah* to be entirely dependent on its creditors, the Zionist banks.[39] Preparations for the *Anglo-Palestine Company* to commence activities in Palestine were, by the spring of 1903, in an advanced stage. Its manager, Zalman David Levontin, having received instructions from Herzl in

Vienna less than three weeks after Ussischkin's visit, arrived at Jaffa on 30 June. There he immediately opened the first branch of what was to develop into the largest banking firm in the State of Israel, the *Bank Leumi le-Israel*.[40]

The *Anglo-Palestine Company* was the first institution created by the Zionist Organization to operate in Palestine. Its establishment there did not signify any weakening of Herzl's conviction that without legal and political guarantees, embodied in a "Charter", large-scale immigration and settlement were impossible. What he hoped was that the A.P.C. would be able to take effective, though necessarily modest, action to alleviate the economic position of the existing Jewish population, while at the same time establishing good relations with the local Turkish authorities in preparation for greater things to come. He may also have conceived the despatch of Levontin to Palestine as another small, but timely, concession to the Russian clamour for practical work; though even this was later interpreted by Herzl's opponents as a clever strategem to remove Levontin, the Russians' watchdog, from the headquarters of the *Jewish Colonial Trust* in London.[41]

On the other hand, Herzl remained adamant in his refusal to accept a suggestion, pressed upon him by Victor Jacobson, that the forthcoming Congress should be addressed on the subject of settlement in Palestine by an inhabitant of the country, Dr. Hillel Joffe, who had also taken part in the recent expedition to El-Arish. Herzl insisted that since there was no prospect of settlement in Palestine, an address on settlement problems in general, without reference to any particular country, would suffice. He chose Dr. Franz Oppenheimer, whose schemes for cooperative forms of settlement were arousing much interest at the time, to deliver it.[42]

While the simmering crisis between Herzl and the Russian Zionists was slowly approaching a climax, the attitude of the Czarist authorities towards Zionism took a serious turn for the worse. At the time of the Minsk Conference—which, it will be recalled, was permitted to meet legally, owing to the contacts of some Minsk Zionists with local members of the Zubatov group[43]—hopes were being entertained that Russian Zionism, which had hitherto been barely tolerated, would soon enjoy the benefits of full legality.[44] The line advocated by Herzl, to avoid giving offence to the authorities,[45] which had provoked the scorn of *Bundists* and other revolutionaries, seemed to have been vindicated. Less than a month after the Conference these hopes vanished. On 2 October 1902 the Official Gazette of the Russian Ministry of Finance published a decision, taken some time previously by the Minister in conjunction with the Minister for Foreign Affairs, prohibiting the importation of share certificates of the *Jewish Colonial Trust* (J.C.T.) into Russia.[46] The decision was dated 25 [12] August and thus preceded the Minsk Conference. Russian Zionists therefore consoled themselves for a time by arguing that the prohibition was prompted solely by fiscal considerations.[47] But attempts to have it rescinded[48] failed, and during the months that followed the Police Department of the Ministry of the Interior commissioned a report on the Zionist Movement which was printed in St. Petersburg for official use early in 1903. This voluminous report, the existence of which was known to Chaim Weizmann in May 1903, came to the conclusion that Zionism must be considered seditious because of its alleged links with socialism.[49] No less, and probably more, important in shaping the view of the authorities was their growing conviction, for which the tenor of the Minsk Conference seemed to provide evidence, that Zionism no longer limited itself to promoting the emigration of Jews from Russia. It had become a popular movement, organizing Russian Jewry as a separate nationality and fostering Hebrew culture. Far from neutralizing the revolutionary tendencies in Jewry, the argument ran, Zionism was turning the formerly docile Jewish masses into a cohesive opposition to the established order.[50]

Towards the end of June leading Russian Zionists, and through them Herzl, were alarmed by information that the Government was on the point of taking severe measures to check the growth of the Zionist movement. For the moment it appeared doubtful whether delegates from Russia would be able to attend the forthcoming Congress.[51] These measures were set out in a "very secret" circular of 7 July[52] from the Minister of the Interior, Plehve, and the director of his Police Department, Lupochin, to the provincial authorities.[53] The prohibition on the importation of J.C.T. share certificates was reaffirmed and was also applied to collections for the Jewish National Fund. Public meetings and conferences of a Zionist nature were no longer to be held. The establishment by Zionists of schools, libraries and reading-rooms was to be brought under strict control. If these and other measures enumerated in the circular had been consistently implemented for any length of time, Zionism in Russia would indeed have been seriously imperilled.[54] Fortunately, though it was never formally withdrawn, the circular was in fact suspended after some months.[55] Its indirect effects were nevertheless considerable. Besides causing Zionism in Russia to face the possibility of having, like the revolutionary parties, to exist illegally, it brought about

Herzl's final—and this time successful—attempt to establish personal relations with the Russian rulers in order to convince them that their interest in the emigration of Jews would be best served by support of Zionist aspirations in Palestine.[56]

Once news of the dangers threatening Zionism in Russia began to circulate, events moved rapidly. A week before the issue of the notorious circular, from 29 [16] June to 1 July [18 June], some leading Russian Zionists—Belkowsky (St. Petersburg), Tschlenow (Moscow), Jasinowski (Warsaw), Temkin (Elisabetgrad), J. L. Goldberg (Vilna) and S. Rosenbaum (Minsk)—met in St. Petersburg to discuss the ominous situation.[57] As an immediate outcome of this meeting Jasinowski—who was closer to Herzl than any other Russian member of the G.A.C. except Mandelstamm—travelled to Alt-Aussee, a mountain resort in Styria, where Herzl was taking a holiday with his family. According to the account given by Jasinowski at the meeting of the G.A.C. in April 1904 (by which time Herzl's journey to Russia and the preparations preceding it had become a subject of bitter controversy), he had understood his colleagues as having delegated him to induce Herzl to find a means of reversing Plehve's repressive policy. He had first suggested to Herzl that he draft a memorandum—presumably to be presented to Plehve. When, however, Herzl read him letters concerning the political situation in Russia, he (Jasinowski) had come to the conclusion that a memorandum would have no effect. He had advised Herzl instead that he ought once more to seek an audience with the Czar and talk personally with the Minister of the Interior. This, he had told Herzl, was the appropriate moment to undertake a journey to St. Petersburg. Herzl, according to Jasinowski's account, had replied that it was a difficult task, but he considered it his duty to make the sacrifice.

Whether Herzl's reluctance to go to Russia at this juncture was quite as genuine as Jasinowski and he himself ("ein grosses Gesundheitsopfer. Ich habe Aussee notwendig gebraucht") tried to make out, may well be doubted. For years he had tried in vain to obtain an audience with Nicholas II and his ministers. After the Kishinev pogrom, and the resultant despair of Russian Jewry, such a meeting seemed to him more urgent than ever.[58] The fact that Plehve was held by many Jews, as well as by many non-Jews, to be personally responsible for the outbreak of this pogrom[59] did not make Herzl regard such a meeting as ignominious. What to others became, after the event, a repugnant action which ought to have been avoided, was to Herzl a distasteful political necessity, but a necessity nonetheless.

Some weeks before Jasinowski's visit to Alt-Aussee, in the second half of May, Herzl had himself written to Plehve and to Pobjedonoszev, the chief Procurator of the Holy Synod and once one of the most powerful men in Russia, asking them to support his request for an audience with the Czar. A similar request was submitted direct to Nicholas II by Bertha von Suttner, the famous pacifist. By the beginning of July no reply had been received from either Plehve or Pobjedonoszev, but Mme. von Suttner was informed by Count Lamsdorff, the Russian Foreign Minister, that an audience was out of the question.[60] Now, in view of the news brought by Jasinowski, Herzl decided to make another attempt at least to meet Plehve. As intermediary he turned to a somewhat exuberant Polish lady with literary pretensions, Paulina Corwin Piotrowska. An acquaintance of Jasinowski and Belkowsky, she had direct access to Plehve, a close friend, and had once before—in August 1902—been asked by Herzl to enlist the Minister's help in obtaining an audience with the Czar.[61] That project had come to naught, but this time she did not disappoint his hopes. On 8 July, after he had heard the negative reply received by von Suttner, and probably while Jasinowski was still staying at Aussee, Herzl wrote to Mme. Corwin requesting her to enquire whether Plehve was prepared to see him.[62] Jasinowski also communicated with her, and on the 18th she informed him that Plehve would be ready to receive Herzl in the middle of August. Herzl's reference to "Emigration ohne Rückkehr" seems to have been a successful bait.[63] Herzl heard the news on the 23rd, and his additional request to advance the date of the meeting by one week was also granted.[64] In the meantime Jasinowski asked Belkowsky to obtain an entrance visa for Herzl from the authorities in St. Petersburg.[65] It is therefore easy to understand Herzl's irritation when, on Tuesday the 28th, he received a telegram from Belkowsky—whose services he wished to use in St. Petersburg—announcing that he was leaving the Russian capital and expected to arrive in Vienna on Friday the 31st. If he could not prevent Belkowsky's journey, Herzl hoped that he would at least wait in Vienna until he (Herzl) returned from Alt-Aussee. But as Belkowsky insisted on seeing Herzl without delay—he took great umbrage at being kept waiting—a meeting was arranged for Saturday 1 August at Bad Ischl, a nearby watering place.[66]

It will be convenient to pause at this point and examine some of the questions which figured prominently in the subsequent controversy. What—if any—decisions concerning direct intercession by Herzl with the Russian Government were taken by the leaders of Russian Zionism when they assembled at St. Petersburg at the end of June 1903? What were the instructions given to Jasinowski and Belkowsky by the St. Petersburg meeting? And finally, what passed between Herzl and Belkowsky at Ischl on 1 August?

Jasinowski's own account has already been referred to,[67] and it is enough to add that he may well have attuned the tenor of the message he delivered to Herzl to the latter's mood. In any case, Jasinowski was hardly the man to dispute the wisdom of Herzl's conduct. We can therefore turn at once to Herzl's own version and to that of his opponents.

A clear-cut reply to the last of the above questions was given by Belkowsky in a chapter of reminiscences published—and probably also written—more than thirty years after the events themselves took place. In these reminiscences Belkowsky claimed that he had brought Herzl "material" proving that Plehve had organized the Kishinev pogrom and that [Jewish] opinion in St. Petersburg was strongly opposed to Herzl's intended journey to Russia. Herzl, according to this source, had retorted that his journey was a settled matter; he had shown no interest in the "material" submitted by Belkowsky and the "problems of the day" had not been discussed between them. As a result Belkowsky had decided not to return to Russia before the Congress, so as not to be present in St. Petersburg while Herzl was there.[68]

While it is easy enough to believe that Herzl disregarded the advice which Belkowsky tried to offer, this version is nevertheless too simple to contain the whole truth. It is hardly credible that Belkowsky would have trusted his own ability to dissuade Herzl, at the last moment, from going to St. Petersburg; the material on Plehve's involvement in the Kishinev affair in all probability included little which was new to Herzl and could not therefore have affected his decision. Nor does Belkowsky's ostensible surprise at Herzl's statement that his decision to go to St. Petersburg was irrevocable make much sense in view of the information he had already received from Jasinowski and Mme. Corwin and the request addressed to him concerning Herzl's entrance visa.

Turning to earlier sources, we first encounter some disclosures in the Hebrew press during January–February 1904.[69] These, like most reports on internal Jewish affairs issued under the eyes of the Russian police, are neither full nor frank and do not help us much in our effort to reconstruct the course of events. What they do yield are contradictory declarations by Herzl and Belkowsky. Herzl denied the allegation that he had gone to St. Petersburg without informing the Russian members of the

G.A.C., and particularly Belkowsky, in advance, though he did not claim that he had actually consulted them before deciding on his journey. He also asserted that it was only for "private reasons" that Belkowsky and Tschlenow had been absent from St. Petersburg at the time of his visit. This drew the resentful reply from Belkowsky that Herzl had not communicated with him directly but only through Jasinowski, and that his absence from St. Petersburg during Herzl's visit had not been accidental at all. He had left the Russian capital, he said, in pursuance of a decision taken by the Russian members of the G.A.C. that he should go to meet Herzl—a decision of which Herzl had been informed by Jasinowski.

More rewarding, though still not exhaustive, are the statements made at the meeting of the G.A.C. in April 1904. At this meeting Herzl maintained that the Russian members of the G.A.C. had sent Jasinowski to him to ask for his intervention in St. Petersburg and that he had complied with their request. Only after the publication of Plehve's celebrated letter at the time of the Sixth Congress [70] had he discovered that his activities were not welcome to "the gentlemen from Russia", who at that stage began to regard these activities as an interference in their domestic affairs. At a later stage of the discussions Herzl added ironically that he could not have been expected to realize that Jasinowski had been sent to him merely to announce Belkowsky's forthcoming visit.

Belkowsky's own pronouncement was circumspect rather than detailed. He went so far as to admit that the St. Petersburg meeting at the end of June 1903 had considered the possibility of asking for Herzl's participation in steps to improve the situation in Russia. Jasinowski had been despatched to Alt-Aussee to report to Herzl on the state of affairs and to inform him that Belkowsky would arrive at the end of July to deliver a more comprehensive report. Pressed by Herzl, Belkowsky conceded further that Jasinowski had also been empowered to discuss with him whether a journey (to St. Petersburg) was necessary. Belkowsky denied, however, that the Russian Zionist leaders had authorized Herzl—via Jasinowski—to rely solely on his own discretion in this matter. Simon Rosenbaum, who by the spring of 1904 had acquired notoriety as Herzl's most impudent adversary, added some illuminating touches to Belkowsky's exposition. According to Rosenbaum, the St. Petersburg meeting had originally intended to send only Belkowsky to see Herzl, but Jasinowski had offered to make an earlier journey to Austria and it was thus that two visits, with an interval of less than one month, had come about. The meeting had, Rosenbaum claimed, decided that Herzl should draft a memorandum based on factual material to be supplied by the Russian members of the G.A.C. It was untrue, he declared, that Herzl had been requested to go to see Plehve. Rosenbaum's accusations multiplied: by visiting the Minister without thorough prior consultation with the Zionist leaders in Russia, he said, Herzl had acted improperly. These leaders had, in fact, been opposed to his seeking an audience with Plehve. Had he kept in touch with them, Herzl would have known that Plehve's real motive in receiving him was to extract information which he had failed to obtain from other Zionist personalities. Rosenbaum refused to elucidate this statement, but it is likely that what he had in mind was Plehve's attempt to enlist Zionist help in silencing the discussion on Kishinev in the West in return for some conciliatory gesture to the Russian Jewish community.[71]

To sum up: while on the eve of the journey to St. Petersburg even Herzl's faithful friend Mandelstamm doubted the usefulness of an audience with Plehve,[72] it was only Rosenbaum who claimed explicitly, when the matter was debated in April 1904, that he and his friends had from the first objected to seeking such an audience. In view of what Belkowsky told the G.A.C.—and his account was not contradicted by Rosenbaum—one is justified in concluding that the St. Petersburg meeting at the end of June 1903 was not, on principle, opposed to Herzl's coming to Russia to intercede with members of the Government. The objections to his projected journey may well have crystallized in July, that is between the St. Petersburg meeting and Belkowsky's departure from the capital.

Whatever the truth of the matter, the Russian members of the G.A.C. had no right, in view of their own actions, to make a "moral" issue out of Herzl's talk with Plehve. One of them, Bernstein-Kohan, had gone to the Minister even before Herzl, as a member of a delegation from Kishinev shortly after the pogrom.[73] Nor was it for want of trying that a delegation of the newly-formed National Committee (*Landes-Comité*) of the Russian Zionist Organization, which was composed of Belkowsky's close political friends, failed to obtain an audience with Plehve some time after the Sixth Congress in the autumn of 1903. In the last resort, the objections to Herzl's journey boiled down to protests against his autocratic method of transacting business of great importance and delicacy, and therefore did not differ materially from earlier complaints. The demand of the Russian Zionist leaders for a decisive voice in all that concerned relations with their Government was much more reasonable than Herzl was prepared to admit. That his journey was inadvisable and possibly even a blunder is an arguable proposition; but the charge that by seeking a meeting with Plehve he had somehow acted disgracefully seems to the writer to be utterly groundless.[74]

Returning to the beginning of August 1903; Belkowsky's unexpected departure from St. Petersburg did not interfere with the final arrangements for Herzl's journey thither. Even before Herzl knew about Belkowsky's negative attitude, his friend and eventual successor David Wolffsohn[75] invited another prominent Russian Zionist, Dr. Nissan Katzenelsohn, to come to Alt-Aussee for consultations.[76] Katzenelsohn, who was not a member of the G.A.C., did not actually belong to the front rank of the Russian Zionist leadership. He was head of a reputable trading firm in the Baltic port of Libau and had been elected a director of the *Jewish Colonial Trust* some years previously; he had also won Herzl's confidence and even friendship, and apparently had useful financial and political connections in the Russian capital. Although he fully shared the loathing felt by Russian Jewry for Plehve, Katzenelsohn agreed to accompany Herzl to St. Petersburg, partly because of Belkowsky's refusal to do so and probably also in compliance with Mrs. Herzl's wish.[77] The visa difficulties having been cleared away,[78] Herzl and his companion set out from Vienna—Herzl had returned there from Alt-Aussee the day before—on Wednesday, 5 August. Very early the next morning, Thursday the 6th, they broke their journey at Warsaw, where they were met by Jasinowski and by Nahum Sokolow, who, it will be recalled, had translated *Altneuland* into Hebrew the year before. During their very short stay—it lasted only two-and-a-half hours—Herzl and Katzenelsohn were shown some of the sights of the town.[79] From Warsaw they proceeded to Vilna, which they reached in the late afternoon. The train stopped for a few minutes and Herzl was presented with a bouquet of flowers by some local Zionists who had come to greet him. J. L. Goldberg, the G.A.C. member living in Vilna and, like Katzenelsohn, a wealthy merchant, had boarded the train earlier at a small railway station in order to join Herzl and Katzenelsohn for the last part of the journey to St. Petersburg. The three men arrived there on Friday, 7 August.[80] On the following day, Herzl had his first meeting with Plehve.

As Herzl's own diaries contain a detailed account of his talks with Plehve, Witte (the Minister of Finance) and other Russian dignitaries,[81] it is enough to record here some assessments of their results. Herzl himself considered them, at least for some time, as one of the major achievements of his career.[82] His assertion that Jewish distress could be turned to advantage, that Russia's desire to get rid of her Jews would provide the lever for gaining the "Charter" from the Sultan,[83] seemed at long last to have become practical politics. For the first (and only) time a great Power, in a document designed for publication—Plehve's letter to Herzl of 12 August 1903 [84]—committed itself to assisting the Zionist representatives in their dealings with the Turkish Government. Moreover, among the Zionist aims which the Russian Government might favour was, according to Plehve, the creation of an independent state in Palestine (something Herzl had not asked for!). Nevertheless, however flushed with success he may momentarily have been, Herzl realized that Plehve had also used their meeting to convey the threat that Zionism in Russia would be suppressed unless its adherents improved their behaviour.[85] That Herzl had been manoeuvered into a position where on the one hand promises of diplomatic support were dangled before his eyes while on the other he was served with a brutal ultimatum, was no doubt exactly the kind of situation foreseen by those who had viewed his journey to St. Petersburg with such misgiving. His readiness to oblige Plehve by trying to induce a less hostile attitude towards Russia in the Western press [86] would also no doubt have offended a large section of Zionist opinion, had it become public. The explanation that Herzl acted as he did in order to prove to Plehve that he was facing not just another suppliant, but a person of influence with whom mutually advantageous bargains could be struck, would hardly have mollified his critics.

When Herzl delivered his report on the negotiations in St. Petersburg to the G.A.C. in Basle on 21 August, almost all the Russian members were sceptical about Plehve's promises; indeed, they seem to have stated that they considered these promises worthless.[87] Despite his disappointment at receiving not thanks but reproaches for his work,[88] Herzl nevertheless outlined the results of the Russian journey in his opening speech to the Sixth Congress, and was rewarded by tumultous applause.[89] Against the opposition of the Russian members of the G.A.C., he insisted on Plehve's letter being published, and it was released on the third day of the Congress.[90] He either would not or could not admit that his opponents were motivated not by personal ingratitude, but by their absolute lack of trust in Plehve,[91] of whom, even according to such a friendly witness as Bertha von Suttner, he took too lenient a view.[92] Not only did they feel uneasy about his making a deal with Plehve: they soon refined their argument and contended that the Russian statesman had outwitted Herzl. Russia's support for Zionism, it was stated in Plehve's letter, was contingent on a decrease in the number of Jews in the country. Yet owing to their natural increase, and despite the large-scale emigration since the early 1880's, the Jewish population continued to grow. The notion that migration to Palestine could in the foreseeable future achieve what migration to America had failed to do, i.e. reduce the size of Russian Jewry, was not taken seriously by most Russian Zionists. They seem to have considered it a dangerous illusion which would arouse hopes that were bound to be disappointed.[93] Hence it followed that Plehve's condition—a sort of escape clause—could not be fulfilled and the redemption of his promises could accordingly never be asked for.

In the event, and after some more prodding on Herzl's part,[94] the Russian Ambassador in Constantinople, Zinoviev, was finally instructed in December 1903 to make a *démarche* in favour of Zionism.[95] The instructions he received cannot, however, have borne any indication of particular urgency, and, claiming that it would not be easy to carry them out, he did nothing.[96] Soon afterwards, the outbreak of the Russo-Japanese war in February 1904 and the ensuing Russian defeats deprived the Czarist Government of the ability to exert pressure on Constantinople. The chance of Russian intervention in furtherance of Zionist aims in Palestine was therefore lost. The chief object of Herzl's journey to St. Petersburg was certainly not attained: real success had again eluded him. If his dealings with Plehve produced any positive result at all, it lay in the more tolerant attitude shown by the Russian authorities towards Zionist activities from December 1903 onwards, which amounted to a return to the state of affairs that had prevailed before the Plehve circular.[97] The fear of imminent persecution felt by the Russian leaders on the eve of and immediately after the Sixth Congress had in any case disappeared by the beginning of 1904.

Finally, brief mention should be made of Herzl's meetings with Jews during his Russian journey. The "unforgettable day of Vilna",[98] Sunday 16 August, has been dealt with in detail by his biographers. This, his only encounter with the oppressed Jewish "masses", was a highly emotional event for all concerned. It had, Jacob de Haas tells us, "burned into his brain demanding action",[99] and proved again that unlike any other Jew of his generation Herzl was a "hero" to his people.[100] No doubt his confidence that the people would follow wherever he led them was greatly strengthened by the manifestations of enthusiasm and veneration in the streets of Vilna. Indeed, the simple trust of the people in Vilna contrasted sharply with the festive but strained atmosphere at the banquet given a few days earlier in his honour by the St. Petersburg Zionists, where he had met communal leaders and Jewish journalists.[101] His solemn warning on this occasion that Zionists should confine their

efforts to the realization of the Basle Programme and drop side issues
such as Socialism or Ahad ha-Am *Kultur* profoundly impressed the
audience, as did his deprecation of Jewish involvement in revolutionary
activities. All the guests must have been aware of the connection between
Herzl's speech and his talk with the Minister of the Interior. But despite
the gravity of the admonition, it did not pass unchallenged. Herzl's
assertion that one could not be both a Zionist and a follower of Ahad
ha-Am was condemned by at least some of those present as unnecessary
and inopportune. More serious was his misjudgment of the rebellious
mood of a large number of organized Zionists when he touched on
political matters. A year earlier, Herzl's call to abstain from what to him
were extraneous activities would probably not have been contradicted in
public. Now, after Kishinev, intellectuals who were affected by developments in gentile society, and even normally cautious bourgeois elements,
could no longer stand apart from the general anti-Government movement. Nor could Zionists, it was widely held, afford to ignore completely the urgent domestic needs of Russian Jewry, especially in view of
the success of the socialist *Bund* among the poorest sections of the
Jewish population. Representative of these attitudes was the argument,
voiced by Dr. Julius Brutzkus after he had listened to Herzl's exhortation
not to flavour "pure" Zionism with alien "spices", that a Zionist could
not turn a blind eye to the pressing day-to-day problems of his people:
these problems also demanded great efforts. He himself, Brutzkus stated
defiantly, was engaged in *Gegenwartsarbeit,* but he was a Zionist nonetheless. Herzl's reply must have disconcerted the audience. The only
"present day" work of a Zionist, he said, was the propagation of Zionism: anything designed to improve the situation in the diaspora was
useless. However sincerely held, this extreme formulation of a known
view was hardly conducive to smooth cooperation between Herzl and
many of Russia's Zionists. The altercation with Brutzkus may be said to
have provided a foretaste of the by now unavoidable clash which was to
take place at the Congress in Basle a fortnight later.

Leaving Vilna during the night of 16–17 August, Herzl travelled back
via Berlin and Munich to Alt-Aussee, where he arrived on Tuesday, 18
August. During that day he received a telegram from Leopold Greenberg
reporting that his negotiations with the British Government concerning
East Africa had achieved satisfactory results, including an "authorized
statement" for Herzl.[102] The latter remained with his family for only
one day. On Wednesday the 19th he left again for Basle, which he
reached on the following day. "Preliminary conferences" *(Vorkonferen-*

zen) connected with the Congress had been meeting there for some days and a great many of the 592 delegates[103]—more than had ever before attended a Zionist Congress—had already arrived. On Friday, 21 August, presumably after first having talked with Greenberg,[104] Herzl delivered his report to the first pre-Congress meeting of the G.A.C. It contained, in addition to a short statement on his talk with Plehve, the startling news of the British offer on East Africa. After many false starts and disappointments, Zionism had finally gained recognition as a "state-building power".[105] The Congress and the G.A.C. found themselves face to face with a novel and unexpected turn of affairs for which previous experience provided no guidance.

NOTES

1. See: Document 1. Friedemann to Herzl, 11.7.1903; Document 2. Herzl to Friedemann, 14.7.1903; Document 3. Friedemann to Klee, 7.7.1903; Document 4. Draft of Resolution by some German delegates to the Sixth Congress, 25.8.1903; and cf. Document 5. Soskin to Herzl, 16.8.1903. These and other numbered documents referred to herein appear in *The Minutes of the Zionist Council: The Uganda Controversy*, vol. 1, ed. Michael Heymann (Jerusalem: Israel Universities Press, 1970), pp. 41-98.

2. Herzl told the G.A.C. of the British offer on 21 August 1903, two days before the opening of the Congress. The *Jewish Chronicle* (London) of the same date published a report from a "special correspondent" (dated Basle, 18 August 1903) containing a broad hint of an offer of assistance from one of the great Powers, the acceptance of which might cause difficulties within the Zionist camp. It is unlikely that by 23 August, many delegates had read the *Jewish Chronicle* of the 21st. The identity of the "special correspondent" is not known, but there can be little doubt that he received his information from Leopold Greenberg, who represented Herzl in the negotiations with the British Government. Jacob de Haas appears to have heard something about these negotiations when he met Max Nordau and Alexander Marmorek in Paris, one week before the opening of the Congress. See: *The Maccabaean* (New York), vol. V, no. 4 (October 1903), p. 259.

3. See: *Die Welt* (Berlin), 3.7.1914. Draft of letter by Herzl on his feelings after Kishinev. The area which the British authorities had in mind when they made their offer lay within the boundaries of the British "East Africa Protectorate", the present-day Kenya. In Zionist parlance it was commonly referred to as "Uganda". The formal British offer did not mention either the location of the area proposed for Jewish settlement or its size. Joseph Chamberlain had previously talked to Leopold Greenberg of "the part" which "lies between Nairobi and the Mau Escarpment". See: R. G. Weisbord, *African Zion; the Attempt to Establish a Jewish Colony in the East Africa Protectorate 1903–1905* (Philadelphia, 1968), pp. 1–33, 59–80; *Stenographisches Protokoll der Verhandlungen des VI Zionisten-Kongresses in Basel, 23, 24, 25, 26, 27 und 28 August 1903* (Vienna, 1903) (hereafter *Protokoll, VI*), pp. 214–16.

4. See e.g.: [Y. Tschlenow], *Yehi'el Tschlenow; Pirkei Hayyav u-Fe'ulato; Zikhronot; Ketavim; Ne'umim; Mikhtavim* (Tel-Aviv, 1937), pp. 22–23. M. Ben Hillel ha-Kohen, *Olami*, vol. III (Jerusalem, c. 1927), pp. 69–70, 72.

5. See: [Ch. Weizmann], *Trial and Error; the Autobiography of Chaim Weizmann* (New York, 1949), p. 43; S. Kling, *The Mighty Warrior; the Life Story of Menahem Ussischkin* (New York, 1965), p. 25.

6. See: S. Schwartz, *Ussischkin be-Iggrotav* (Jerusalem, 1949), p. 62.

7. See: J. Klausner, *Darki Likrat ha-Tehiyah ve-ha-Ge'ulah* (Tel-Aviv and Jerusalem, 1946), p. 54; and cf. M. Buber, *Begegnungen; Autobiographische Fragmente* (Stuttgart, 1960), pp. 23–27.

8. See: S. Levin, *The Arena* (London, 1932), pp. 130–133.

9. See e.g.: *Stenographisches Protokoll der Verhandlungen des III Zionisten-Kongresses, Basel, 15 bis 18 August 1899* (Vienna, 1899) (hereafter *Protokoll, III*), p. 69 for Motzkin's disbelief in the idea of rapid migration.

10. See: W. Kampmann, *Deutsche und Juden* (Heidelberg, 1963), p. 367.

11. For this group see: I. Klausner, *Opozitziyah le-Herzl*. Jerusalem, c. 1960; [A. L. Motzkin], *Sefer Motzkin; Ketavim u-Ne'umim Nivharim; Biyografia ve-Divrei Ha'arakha*. Ed. A. Bein. Jerusalem, c. 1939.

12. On the Zionist districts or *Rayons* in Russia, see *Minutes of the Zionist Council*, p. 11.

13. See: Document 6. Circular No. 18 by Bernstein-Kohan, 7.8.1901.

14. See: Document 7. Ussischkin to Kremenezky, 20.9.1901; Document 8. Mandelstamm to Herzl, 27.8.1901.

15. See: A. Zenzipper (Raphaeli), *Pa'ameri ha-Ge'ulah* (Tel-Aviv, 1951), p. 108.

16. See: Document 9. E.A.C. to Russian members of the G.A.C., 23.8.1901.

17. See: A. Zenzipper (Raphaeli), 'Ve'idot Artziyot shel Tzionei Russia'. In: *Katzir. Kovetz le-Korot ha-Tenu'ah ha-Tziyonit be-Russia* (Tel-Aviv, 1964), pp. 46–57.

18. See: Document 10. Mandelstamm to [E.] A.C. (Vienna), 18.10.1898; and cf. *Protokoll*, III, p. 64.

19. See: Document 11. Bernstein-Kohan to "Fünferausschuss", n.d. [End of February or beginning of March 1901]; Document 12. Bernstein-Kohan to [E.] A.C. (Vienna), n.d. [End of February or beginning of March 1901]; Document 13. [E.] A.C. (Vienna) to Russian members of G.A.C., 12.3.1901; Document 14. Bernstein-Kohan to [E.] A.C. (Vienna), 17.3.1901.

20. See: Document 15. Russian members of the G.A.C. to "Fünferausschuss", 24.4.1903.

21. The letter mentioned in the previous note was signed by Belkowsky (St. Petersburg), Bruck (Homel), Jacobson (Simferopol), Jasinowski (Warsaw), Mandelstamm (Kiev), Rabbinowitz (Sopotzkin) and Tschlenow (Moscow). According to the short minutes of the Kiev meeting (in file Z 1/380 of the Central Zionist Archives), J. L. Goldberg (Vilna) also attended the meeting. Thus eight out of thirteen Russian members of the G.A.C., elected by the 5th Congress in December 1901, participated in the Kiev meeting. See also: Document 16. Tschlenow to Kokesch, 30.4.1903.

22. The letter of complaint concerning El-Arish could not be located. That such a letter was written can be inferred from the short minutes of the Kiev meeting referred to in the previous note and from note 4 to the resolutions of the Kharkov conference as published by the Russian members of the G.A.C. after their meeting in St. Petersburg in the middle of January 1904. And see also: Document 17. Tschlenow to [presumably] Kokesch, 17.4.1903; Document 18. Tschlenow to E.A.C. and "Fünferausschus", 4.6.1903 (which mentions two letters sent by the Kiev meeting to Vienna). For the reference to El-Arish in note 4 to the resolutions of the Kharkov conference, see: *Ha-Tzefirah* (Warsaw), no. 16, 1.2.1904; *Voskhod* (St. Petersburg), vol. 24, no. 2, 16.1. o.s. [= 29.1.n.s.] 1904, cols. 16–17.

Jacobson asked the E.A.C. for information on El-Arish in a letter dated 19.5.1903 (in file Z 1/247 of the Central Zionist Archives).

Herzl had privately informed Mandelstamm of his journey to Egypt in connection with the El-Arish scheme, but had asked him, if possible, to keep the matter secret.

See: Document 19. Herzl to Mandelstamm, 20.3.1903; Document 20. Mandelstamm to Herzl, 29.3.1903.

23. See: Document 21. Circular letter from E.A.C. (signed by Herzl and Kokesch) to members of G.A.C., 12.6.1903; and cf. Document 22. Herzl to Jacobson, 4.7.1903.

24. For the Minsk Conference see: M. Nurock, *Ve'idat Tziyonei Russia be-Minsk*. Jerusalem. c. 1963; and see also: *Die Welt* (Vienna), 19.9 and 2.10.1902.

25. See: *Die Welt* (Vienna), 8.8.1902.

26. See: Ben David, 'Der Minsker Kongress', *Palaestina* (Berlin), vol. I, nos. 3–4 (1902), pp. 165–68.

27. The G.A.C. met on 29.10.1902, the Annual Conference on 29 & 30.10.1902. The minutes of these meetings are preserved in the Central Zionist Archives.

28. See: J. Pogribinsky (ed.), *Sefer Ge'ulah* (Tel-Aviv, c. 1956), pp. 11–12; *"Geulah": Ihre Entstehung und Bedeutung* (Basle, 1905), pp. 5–6.

29. The author of 'By the Way Notes' in the *Jewish World* (London) of 24.7.1903 wrote: "*Altneuland* is not to be judged by the ordinary canons of novel criticism, for it is really a newspaper leader—with a strong bias—masquerading in an imaginative work for over 300 pages". While this view comes close to the truth, it was expressed only rarely in 1903. For Ahad ha-Am's attack see: *Ha-Shilo'ah*, vol. X, no. 60 (December 1902), pp. 566–78. Ahad ha-Am's article was later included in his collection of essays *Al Parashat Derakhim*, pt. III.

30. See: S. Levin, *Bi-Yemei ha-Ma'avar* (New York, 1919), pp. 207–12, where an open letter from Levin to Ahad ha-Am is reprinted. This open letter was originally published in *Ha-Zeman* (St. Petersburg) no. 12 of 2.3.1903, i.e. eleven days before Nordau's verbal assault on Ahad ha-Am in *Die Welt*.

31. See: *Ha-Shilo'ah*, vol. XI, no. 66 (July 1903), pp. 581–84 (Report on Conference of Austrian Zionists); [S. Levin], *Iggrot Shemaryahu Levin* (Tel-Aviv, 1966), p. 25. Levin to Joseph Lurie, 7.3. o.s. [= 20.3. n.s.] 1903; 'Die Juden von Gestern; eine Erwiderung', *Ost und West* (Berlin), vol. III, no. 4 (April 1903), pp. 216–26; *Theodor Herzl Jahrbuch* (Wien, 1937), pp. 158–64 ('Briefwechsel zwischen Theodor Herzl und Martin Buber'); S. Levin, *Bi-Yemei ha-Ma'avar* (New York, 1919), pp. 215–30; Document 23. B. Feiwel to S. Werner, 19.3.1903.

32. See: *Theodor Herzl Jahrbuch* (Wien, 1937), p. 160. Herzl to Buber, 23.5.1903.

33. See e.g.: Document 24. Leo Winz to Adolf Friedemann, 15.8.1903. For an attempt by an "Easterner" to put an end to the controversy see: Document 17. Tschlenow to [presumably Kokesch], 17.4.1903.

34. The polemical literature which grew out of this controversy fills many columns in the contemporary Jewish press, especially in Russia. Herzl's own attempt to explain his attitude towards Ahad ha-Am during his visit to St. Petersburg in August 1903 was not well received; see: Document 61. Report in *Ha-Zeman* (St. Petersburg), no. 58, 13.8.1903.

A. Bein in his *Theodor Herzl* (Tel-Aviv, c. 1961), pp. 327–34, has put the whole matter into proper perspective; Leon Simon in his *Ahad Ha-Am; Asher Ginzberg* (Philadelphia, 1960) appears to have misunderstood Herzl.

For a contemporary view of the problem *Westjuden* v. *Ostjuden* with reference to *Altneuland*, see: A. Ruppin, *Die Juden der Gegenwart; eine sozialwissenschaftliche Studie* (Berlin, 1904), pp. 287–90.

35. See: S. Schwartz, *Ussischkin be-Iggrotav* (Jerusalem, 1949), p. 76 (Circular concerning Ge'ulah, c. May 1903); Document 25. Herzl to Ge'ulah, 4.5.1903.

36. Ussischkin's visit to Vienna is not mentioned in Herzl's diary, which during May 1903 has entries on various settlement projects outside Palestine. Seven months later, Ussischkin stated that during his visit Herzl had asked him: "And what if I should propose a new country to the Congress?" See: *Ha-Tzofeh* (Warsaw), no. 312,

26.1.1904; J. Klausner, *Menahem Ussischkin; his Life and Work* (New York, 1942), p. 57; Document 26. Ussischkin (Ekaterinoslav) to Central Zionist Office (Vienna), [date of delivery] 5.5.1903; Document 27. Ussischkin to Herzl, 6.5.1903; Document 28. Ussischkin to Herzl, [date of delivery] 10.5.1903; Document 29. Ussischkin to unknown addressee, 11.5.1903; Document 30. "Comité Guéoulah" to Herzl, 13 or 14.5.1903.

37. See: Document 31. Kremenezky to Ussischkin 26.5.1903; Document 32. Draft of Resolution of Board of Directors of Anglo-Palestine Company concerning *Ge'ulah*, n.d.; Document 33. E.A.C. to Manager of *Jewish Colonial Trust*, 13.7.1903.

38. See: Z. Gluskin, *Zikhronot* ([Tel-Aviv], 1946), pp. 78–79; Document 34. Levontin (Constantinople) to Herzl, 18.6.1903.

39. At Ussischkin's request, Herzl asked Sir Francis Montefiore whether he would permit *Ge'ulah* to register land in his (Montefiore's) name. Montefiore refused and Herzl showed no regret. See: Document 35. Herzl to Ussischkin, 4.6.1903; Document 36. Herzl to Levontin, 22.6.1903; Document 37. Levontin to Herzl, 16.7.1903; Document 38. Herzl to Levontin, 29.7.1903.

40. See: A. Bein, *Im Herzl u-be-Ikvotav* (Tel-Aviv, c. 1954), pp. 78–80; Z. D. Levontin, *Le-Eretz Avoteinu*, vol. II ([Tel-Aviv], c. 1924), pp. 43–45; Document 39. Levontin to Herzl, 1.7.1903.

41. Simon Rosenbaum (Minsk) put this interpretation on Levontin's despatch to Jaffa at a "closed" meeting of leading Berlin Zionists at the end of December 1903. He repeated it to Herzl's face at the meeting of the E.A.C. on 6 January 1904 in which he and Belkowsky, sent to Vienna as a delegation of the Russian members of the G.A.C., participated; he then saw to it that the press took up the matter. That Rosenbaum leaked information to the press was admitted by him in a letter dated 18.[= 31. n.s.] 1.1904 to Chaim Weizmann and Zvi Aberson, which is preserved in the Weizmann Archives at Rehovot. See also: *Ha-Melitz* (St. Petersburg), no. 4, 19.1.1904 [Interview given by Herzl to V. A. Lubetzky]; *Voskhod* (St. Petersburg), vol. 24, no. 1, 9.1. o.s. [= 22.1. n.s.] 1904, cols. 35 and 37.

42. For Jacobson's suggestion, which was also supported by at least one other member of the G.A.C., see: Document 22. Herzl to Jacobson, 4.7.1903; Document 40. Jacobson to Central Zionist Office, Vienna, 21.7.1903; Document 41. Rabbinowitz to [E.]A.C. 10.7.1903. For the invitation of Oppenheimer see: F. Oppenheimer, *Erlebtes, Erstrebtes, Erreichtes; Lebenserinnerungen* (Düsseldorf, 1964), pp. 212–14; A. Bein, 'Franz Oppenheimer als Mensch und Zionist', *Bulletin des Leo Baeck Instituts* (Tel-Aviv), vol. VII, no. 25 (1964), pp. 1–20; 'Briefwechsel zwischen Theodor Herzl und Franz Oppenheimer', *Ibid.* pp. 21–55 (especially p. 45. Herzl to Oppenheimer, 14.7.1903). Herzl's original intention was to let the Congress hear, in addition to Oppenheimer's address, another address on 'Emigration and Settlement" by Nordau. Nordau, however, refused, as he did not consider himself qualified to deal with the subject and because of the attacks to which he had recently been exposed in connection with the *Altneuland* affair. See: Document 42. Nordau to [E.] A. C. (Vienna), 21.6.1903.

43. See: M. Nurock, *Ve'idat Tziyonei Russia be-Minsk* (Jerusalem, c. 1963), pp. 4–6; E. Mendelsohn, "Worker Opposition in the Russian-Jewish Socialist Movement from 1890's to 1903', *International Review of Social History* (Amsterdam), vol. X, pt. 2 (1965), pp. 268–82.

44. See: Y. Eppel, *Be-Tokh Reshit ha-Tehiyah* (Tel-Aviv, c. 1936), pp. 138–9; [Ch. Weizmann], *Trial and Error; the Autobiography of Chaim Weizmann* (New York, 1949), pp. 75–7; Y. Gruenbaum, *Ha-Tenu'ah ha-Tziyonit be-Hitpathutah*, vol. II (Jerusalem, c. 1953), p. 49; *Die Welt* (Vienna), 2.10.1902, pp. 6–9; and cf. B. Z. Katz, 'Yahadut Russia lifnei Hamishim Shana', *He-Avar* (Tel-Aviv), vol. I (1952), pp. 7–8.

45. Ussischkin also supported this policy; see: S. Schwartz, *Ussischkin be-Iggrotav* (Jerusalem, 1949), p. 69; and cf. J. Frumkin et al. (eds.), *Russian Jewry (1860–1917)* (New York and London, 1966), p. 154.

46. See: Document 43. Belkowsky to [E.]A.C., 4.10.1902; Document 44. N. Katzenelsohn to Herzl, 6.10.1902.

47. See: Document 45. H. Urysohn to "Fünferausschuss", 13.10.1902; Document 46. Z. D. Levontin to D. Wolffsohn, 9.10.1902.

48. See e.g.: Document 47. Belkowsky to [E.]A.C., 15.12.1902.

49. See: A. Zenzipper (Raphaeli), 'Ha-Tziyonut be-Einei ha-Boleshet ha-Russit', *Shivat Zion*, vol. I (Jerusalem, 1950), pp. 225–31.

50. This argument is expressed in Plehve's circular of 7.7 [= 24.6. o.s.] 1903, about which see below, note 53, and see also: B. Dinaburg, 'Ha-Nes shel Tekumat Yisrael vi-Yesodotav ha-Historiyim', *Shivat Zion*, vol. I (Jerusalem, 1950), p. 31.

51. See: Document 48. Tschlenow to E.A.C., 25.6.1903; Document 49. Herzl to N. Katzenelsohn, 30.6.1903; Document 50. S. Rosenbaum to Herzl, 21.6.1903. See also: Y. Morenu, *Der Zekster Tsionisten Kongres; a Berikht* (Vilna, 1904), pp. 4–5.

    M. Medzini, in his *Ha-Mediniyut ha-Tziyonit me-Reshitah ve-ad Moto shel Herzl* (Jerusalem, 1934), p. 249, considers it possible that Weizmann's long letter to Herzl of 5.5.1903 convinced Herzl of the necessity of approaching the Russian rulers, in view of the deteriorating situation in Russia.

52. Usually it is referred to as the circular of 24 June, the old style date it bore.

53. The existence of the circular was reported in the Western press shortly after the Sixth Congress, see: *Die Welt* (Vienna), 18.9.1903; *The Annual Register for 1903* (London, 1904), p. 309.

    The full text was first published in 1915 in *Yevreiskaya Starina* (St. Petersburg), vol. VIII, pp. 412–14. A Hebrew translation was published in *He-Avar* (Tel-Aviv), vol. VI (1958), pp. 54–55.

    The circular was known to Russian Zionists soon after its issue. Mandelstamm refers to it in his letter to Herzl of 2.8.1903; see: Document 51.

54. See: Document 51. Mandelstamm to Herzl, 2.8.1903

55. See: A. Zenzipper (Raphaeli), *Pa'amei ha-Ge'ulah* (Tel-Aviv, 1951), pp. 214–15. From the out-letter book of J. L. Goldberg in his capacity as member of the G.A.C. and head of the Vilna district, which is preserved in the Central Zionist Archives, it is apparent that by February 1904, Zionist work in this district was again being conducted without interference from the police, only public meetings still being prohibited. Jasinowski told the G.A.C. in April 1904 that while on the eve of the Sixth Congress the police in Poland had confiscated *Jewish Colonial Trust* share certificates, now (early in 1904) the police in many places were telling Zionists: "Do your work, we won't interfere."

56. See: Document 49. Herzl to Katzenelsohn, 30.6.1903; *Theodor Herzls Tagebücher*, vol. III (Berlin, 1925) (hereafter *Tagebücher* vol. III), pp. 460, 467–69, 481–82; M. Medzini, *Ha-Mediniyut ha-Tziyonit me-Reshitah ve-ad Moto shel Herzl* (Jerusalem, 1934), pp. 249–50.

57. At the meeting of the G.A.C. in Vienna in April 1904, Belkowsky stated that it was he who had convened the St. Petersburg meeting. He had acted in accordance with a decision of the Russian G.A.C. members, taken at the time of the "Annual Conference" of October 1902, that he should head a small St. Petersburg committee charged with ascertaining what was going on in "Government circles" regarding Zionism, so that counter-measures could be taken. Belkowsky said that he had also been authorised to consult (or co-opt to his committee) additional Russian members of the G.A.C. The St. Petersburg meeting is referred to in a circular-letter by Jacobson of 9.7 [= 26.6. o.s.] 1903, a copy of which is in the Central Zionist Archives.

58. See e.g.: Document 49. Herzl to Katzenelsohn, 30.6.1903.

59. For a discussion of Plehve's responsibility—or lack of it—for the Kishinev pogrom, see: B. Z. Katz, 'Yahadut Russia lifnei Hamishim Shana', *He-Avar*, vol. I (1952); I. Berman, 'Ma'azan shel Yovel', *He-Avar*, vol. II. (1954); Y. Maor, 'Yehudei Russia bi-Tekufat Plehve', *He-Avar*, vol. VI (1958).

60. See: *Tagebücher*, vol. III, pp. 431–36; T. Nussenblatt, *Ein Volk unterwegs zum Frieden* (Wien, 1933), pp. 129–32, 141–42.

61. See: *Tagebücher*, vol. III, pp. 287–88.

62. See: *Tagebücher*, vol. III, pp. 448–49.

63. See: Document 52. Corwin to Jasinowski, 18.7.1903.

64. See: *Tagebücher*, vol. III, p. 454; Document 53. Jasinowski to Herzl, 20.7.1903; Document 54. Herzl to Jasinowski, 24.7.1903. On 26 July Herzl received a telegram from Corwin: "Ankommen sie wie sie es bitten."

65. See: Document 53. Jasinowski to Herzl. 20.7.1903. On 24 July Herzl received a telegram from Jasinowski: "drahtete eben bielkowski passierschein gleich besorgen jasinowski".

66. On 21 July, Belkowsky had sent a telegram, the text of which reached Herzl mutilated. From this telegram Herzl could have inferred that Belkowsky intended to come to see him, but he presumably assumed that Belkowsky would give up his plan to come to Vienna as soon as he realized that Herzl's journey to St. Petersburg was imminent. And see: Document 55. Herzl to Jasinowski, 28.7.1903; Document 56. Herzl to Jasinowski, 2.8.1903; Document 57. Nissan Katzenelsohn to Herzl, n.d. (probably 31.7.1903); Document 51. Mandelstamm (Munich) to Herzl, 2.8.1903; *Ha-Melitz* (St. Petersburg), no. 13, 3.2 [= 21.1. o.s.] 1904 (letter to the editor from Belkowsky, dated 30. [= 17. o.s.] 1.1904).

67. See pp. 220–21.

68. See: Z. Belkowsky, 'Daf le-Toldot ha-Tziyonut', *Ha-Tziyoni ha-Kelali* (Tel-Aviv), vol. III, no. 16 (101), 17.1.1935.

69. See: *Ha-Tzofeh* (Warsaw), no. 296, p. 1289, 7.1.1904 ('The Truth about the Kharkov Resolutions', by a special correspondent); *Ha-Melitz* (St. Petersburg), no. 4, 19.1.1904 (Interview given by Herzl to V. A. Lubetzky); *Ha-Melitz* (St. Petersburg), no. 13, 3.2.[= 21.1. o.s.] 1904 (letter to the editor from Belkowsky, dated 30.[= 17. o.s.] 1.1904).

70. See pp. 225–26.

71. Nissan Katzenelsohn, who accompanied Herzl to St. Petersburg, told Adolf Friedemann in April 1914 (almost eleven years after these events took place) that Plehve had asked Herzl to prevent "too much" discussion on Kishinev at the forthcoming Congress ("Herzl solle zu viel Debatte über Kischinew auf dem Congress hindern."). The memorandum on Katzenelsohn's talk with Friedemann—who was at that time collecting material for his biography of Herzl—is in the Friedemann archives in the Central Zionist Archives. And see also: *Tagebücher*, vol. III, pp. 464–65, 480; M. Ben Hillel ha-Kohen, *Olami*, vol. III (Jerusalem, c. 1927), p. 154.

   That Herzl's journey to St. Petersburg was connected with Russian atempts to put an end to discussions on the Kishinev pogrom was believed not only in Jewish circles. The German Consul-General in Warsaw, von Haxthausen, reported on 18 August 1903 to the Chancellor, Count Bülow, as follows: "Vor Kurzem sind, wie ich höre, zwei Warschauer Führer des Zionismus von dem Minister von Plehve in St. Petersburg empfangen worden, der an sie das Verlangen stellte, dahin zu wirken, dass auf dem Baseler Kongress die Vorgänge in Kischinew nicht erörtert werden. Da beide erklärten, ein solches Versprechen wohl für die russischen, nicht aber für die Delegierten anderer Länder abgeben zu können, so hat sich, wie es heisst, auf Wunsch des Ministers der bekannte Führer der Zionisten, Dr. Herzl, dessen Durchreise durch Warschau hiesige Blätter kürzlich meldeten, nach St. Petersburg zu einer Besprechung mit Herrn von

Plehve begeben." The report of von Haxthausen to Count Bülow is filed in "Acten betreffend die Alliance Israélite Universelle und Judenpresse, Bd. l. (Europa Generalia 84)" of the German Foreign Ministry of which a photocopy is available in Jerusalem.

72. See: Document 51. Mandelstamm to Herzl, 2.8.1903.

73. [J. Bernstein-Kohan], *Sefer Bernstein-Kohan; Divrei Ha'arakha; Zikhronot; Iggrot* (Tel-Aviv, c. 1946), p. 131. On the Jewish delegation from Kishinev which was received by Plehve in May 1903 and Plehve's threatening utterances, see also: *The Annual Register for 1903* (London, 1904), p. 308.

74. Cf.: S. Levin, *The Arena*, (London, 1932), pp. 253–54.

75. Wolffsohn, a timber merchant living in Cologne, who served also as chairman of the board of directors of the *Jewish Colonial Trust*, stayed with Herzl at Alt-Aussee for two or three days (apparently from 25 to 27 or 28 July) while on a business trip to Slavonia.

76. It seems that Katzenelsohn stayed at Alt-Aussee for a day or two only and from there went to Baden bei Wien via Vienna, where he met Belkowsky before the latter's meeting with Herzl, i.e. on 31 July or very early in the morning of 1 August. He returned to Vienna on 4 or 5 August.

   We learn about Katzenelsohn's invitation to Alt-Aussee (from Bad Kissingen where he was taking one of his lengthy holidays) from a telegram sent by him to Herzl dated 28 July 1903 and from the memorandum on Katzenelsohn's talk with Adolf Friedemann referred to in note 71.

77. See: N. Katzenelsohn, 'Aus meinen Erlebnissen mit Herzl/Herzls Reise nach Russland', *Die Welt* (Cologne), 20.5.1910. Additional information in the memorandum referred to in the preceding note and in note 71.

78. Johann Kremenezky, a member of the E.A.C. in Vienna, appears to have arranged for the Russian Consulate-General in Vienna to grant Herzl a visa there, instead of giving it to him only when he arrived at the frontier. Herzl had objected to the latter procedure. And see: Document 56. Herzl to Jasinowski, 2.8.1903; Document 58. Herzl to Kremenezky, 2.8.1903.

79. On Herzl's stop at Warsaw, see: *Der Fraind* (St. Petersburg), no. 166, 10.8.1903; *Ha-Zeman* (St. Petersburg), no. 57, 11.8.1903; *Ha-Tzefirah* (Warsaw), no. 172, 7.8.1903; *Die Welt* (Vienna), 21.8.1903. Katzenelsohn informed Sokolow of the time of Herzl's arrival in Warsaw by telegram.

80. On the short stop at Vilna and on Goldberg joining Herzl and Katzenelsohn, see (in addition to the sources referred to in the preceding note): J. Broydes, *Wilna ha-Tziyonit we-Askaneiha* (Tel-Aviv, 1939), p. 160; and *Tagebücher*, vol. III, p. 459. Broydes quotes a telegram sent by Katzenelsohn to J. L. Goldberg announcing that Herzl would pass through Vilna on Thursday (6 August).

81. See: *Tagebücher*, vol. III, pp. 459–87; and for an additional Jewish-Russian source, M. Medzini, *Ha-Mediniyut ha-Tziyonit me-Reshitah ve-ad Moto shel Herzl* (Jerusalem, 1934), p. 253, n. 1.

82. See: A. Friedemann, *Das Leben Theodor Herzl* (Berlin, 1919), p. 72; and cf. A. Bein, *Theodor Herzl* [Hebrew] (Tel-Aviv, c. 1961), p. 362; W. Kampmann, *Deutsche und Juden* (Heidelberg, 1963), pp. 411, 413; M. Medzini, *Ha-Mediniyut ha-Tziyonit me-Reshitah ve-ad Moto shel Herzl* (Jerusalem, 1934), p. 256.

83. See e.g.: Document 49. Herzl to Katzenelsohn, 30.6.1903.

84. Plehve's letter was published in the French original and in a German translation in *Die Welt*, Separat Ausgabe, Basle, no. 2, 25.8.1903. The original letter in Plehve's own handwriting is preserved in the Central Zionist Archives. The Jewish press in other countries published the letter a few days later, e.g. the *Jewish World* and the *Jewish Chronicle* of London on 28 August 1903. Very strange, but characteristic of the situation in that country, was the manner of publication by the Jewish papers in

Russia: they printed it without mentioning its date, the place of issue or the name of the writer, so that on the face of it the letter made no sense at all. See e.g.: *Ha-Zeman*, (St. Petersburg) no. 63, 1.9.1903; *Der Fraind* (St. Petersburg), no. 183, 30.8.1903. For the text of Plehve's letter see illustration facing p. 56.

85. See: *Tagebücher*, vol. III, p. 483.

86. See: *Tagebücher*, vol. III, pp. 480–81, 536. And cf. *Theodor Herzl Jahrbuch* (Wien, 1937), p. 155. Herzl to Max Wirth, 27.12.1903.

87. For the minutes of the meeting of the G.A.C. in Basle on 21 August 1903, see below pp. 101–6.

88. See: *Tagebücher*, vol. III, p. 492 (entry of 22.8.1903).

89. See: *Protokoll*, VI, pp. 3–10.

90. See: Note 84 and also *Tagebücher*, vol. III, p. 495 (entry of 1.9.1903); *Protokoll*, VI, pp. 120–21, 123–24.

91. See: S. Levin, *The Arena* (London, 1932), p. 254, Levin mentions "cynical lying" as one of Plehve's "virtues."

92. See: T. Nussenblatt, *Ein Volk unterwegs zum Frieden* (Wien, 1933), p. 142 (entry by Bertha von Suttner in her diary on 1.12.1903).

93. See: *Ha-Zeman* (St. Petersburg), no. 63. 1.9.1903; and cf. J. Klausner, 'Sheker Muskam', *Ahi'asaf* [for the year 5664], vol. IX (Warsaw, 1903), pp. 68–70.
Victor Jacobson also mentioned *en passant* during the meeting of the G.A.C. in April 1904 that despite the large-scale emigration of Jews during the preceding twenty years, the Jewish population of Russia had continued to grow.
Another objection was raised against Herzl's dealings with Russia by students in Switzerland. In the opinion of these critics any attempt to enlist the support of a Power with longstanding territorial designs in the Near East was self-defeating, as it would frighten the Porte and stiffen resistance to Zionist plans. A charter, they suggested, would only be obtained with the help of a so-called "disinterested" Power. See: L. Wohlmann, 'Eine Zionistische Episode aus der Schweiz', *Theodor Herzl Jahrbuch* (Wien, 1937), pp. 173–76.

94. See: *Tagebücher*, vol. III, pp. 518–20. Herzl to Plehve, 28.10.1903 (drafted on 24.10.1903).

95. See: Document 59. Plehve to Herzl, 6.12.1903; *Tagebücher*, vol. III, pp. 523–24. Herzl to Plehve, 11.12.1903.

96. On 26 December 1903 Herzl wrote to Zinoviev asking him, among other things, whether he had made a *démarche* at the Porte. This letter was handed to the Ambassador by Dr. David F. Markus, the rabbi of the Ashkenazi community in Constantinople. Dr. Wellisch, Herzl's unofficial representative in the Turkish capital, informed him on 30 December 1903 of Zinoviev's discouraging reaction. Thereupon Herzl again wrote to Plehve repeating what he had already stated earlier, that an ordinary *démarche* by the Ambassador would not be sufficient to influence the Turks in the desired direction. See: *Tagebücher*, vol. III, pp. 532–34. Herzl to Zinoviev, 26.12.1903; *Tagebücher*, vol. III, pp. 538–39. Herzl to Plehve, 4.1.1904; *Tagebücher*, vol. III, p. 539. Herzl to Mme. Corwin, 4.1.1904; Document 60. Wellisch to Herzl, 30.12.1903.

97. See pp. 219–20.

98. See: *Tagebücher*, vol. III, p. 487; J. de Haas, *Theodor Herzl*, vol. II (Chicago & New York, 1927), p. 180.

99. See: *Ibid.* p. 181.

100. This aspect of Herzl's Russian visit was stressed while he was still in St. Petersburg by the only Yiddish daily published in the Russian capital; see: *Der Fraind*, no. 170, 14.8.1903.

101. For the fullest account of the banquet, which, it seems, took place on the evening of

Wednesday, 12 August (and not as commonly reported on 11 August), see: Document 61. Report in *Ha-Zeman* (St. Petersburg), no. 58, 13.8.1903; And see also: *Der Fraind* (St. Petersburg), no. 170, 14.8.1903; *Ha-Tzofeh* (Warsaw), no. 180, 17.8.1903; *Ha-Melitz* (St. Petersburg), no. 173, 14.8.1903; *Ha-Tzefirah* (Warsaw), no. 180, 17.8.1903; *Die Welt* (Vienna), 21.8.1903 and the sources given in Th. Herzl, *Bifnei Am ve-Olam* (Tel-Aviv, c. 1961), vol. II, p. 215.

Herzl met the Jewish press of St. Petersburg for a second time on Saturday, 15 August, some hours before his departure. He repeated his warning against mixing Zionism with other doctrines and chivalrously advised Zionist journalists not to attack the opponents of Zionism (he presumably had the Bundists in mind), as these were not always able to answer back. For this meeting see: *Ha-Zeman* (St. Petersburg), no. 59, 18.8.1903, and Ben-Zion Katz's reminiscences in *Ha-Am* (Moscow), no. 69, 6.12.1917.

102. See: Document 62. Greenberg to Herzl, [date of delivery] 18.8.1903. On 9 August Greenberg had written Herzl a letter in which he reported on the progress of his negotiations with Chamberlain and with the Foreign Office, which at that time had jurisdiction over East Africa. In his report Greenberg expressed the hope "of getting something through satisfactorily in time for Basle", but warned of the slow pace at which the Foreign Office moved. The formal British offer, in the shape of a letter to Greenberg signed by Sir Clement Hill, Superintendent of African Protectorates at the Foreign Office, was dated 14 August. This letter was brought by Greenberg to Basle and read out to the Congress on 26 August. See: *Protokoll*, VI, pp. 215–16; *Die Welt*, Separat Ausgabe, Basel, no. 4, 27.8.1903; *Die Welt*, Separat Ausgabe, Basel, no. 6, 29.8.1903.

103. See: *Protokoll*, VI, p. 122.

104. If Greenberg arrived at Basel "early" on Friday (21.8.1903), as was his intention, he would naturally have talked to Herzl before the meeting of the G.A.C., which took place at noon or during the early afternoon. Jacob de Haas, on the other hand, maintains that Greenberg was still travelling at the time of the G.A.C. meeting. De Haas says that Herzl read out to the G.A.C. a letter he had received from Greenberg while in Russia; this can only have been the letter dated 9.8.1903 which is mentioned in note 102 above. See: Document 62. Greenberg to Herzl, [date of delivery] 18.8.1903; J. de Haas, *Theodor Herzl*, vol. II (Chicago and New York), p. 161.

105. On 19 July Herzl had written to Max Nordau regarding the negotiations with the British Government: "Wir haben vor Allem seitens dieses gewaltigen Faktors die Anerkennung als *staatbildende* Macht (Vgl. im Völkerrecht die Qualität als 'kriegführende Macht')". A copy of this letter by Herzl to Nordau is in the Central Zionist Archives.

11.

Hehalutz in Poland between the Two World Wars

Israel Oppenheim

The present discussion will be concerned with the principal ideological characteristics that distinguished the Hehalutz movement in Eastern Europe. Alongside the common elements, emphasis will be given also to what was unique. The discussion will focus primarily on the organization of Hehalutz in Poland, where most of the membership of the worldwide Hehalutz movement was concentrated.[1] But the importance of the movement in Poland does not derive merely from the size of its following. Rather, and perhaps chiefly, the position its membership held depended on the fact that it was there that the ideological doctrine of the movement was shaped. It was there that both the methods of training for pioneer settlement and the characteristic modes of activity were developed. These served the Hehalutz organizations in other countries as a model to be adopted and initiated, even if their connections with Hehalutz in Poland initially had been only tenuous. The chronological setting of the present discussion is confined to the period between the two World Wars. Although it is true that efforts to realize the ideals of Zionism had accompanied the Zionist enterprise from the very outset, these attempts had on the whole been sporadic and short-lived, and were undertaken on a modest scale.[2] Only in the period following the First World War were countrywide organizations set up which had as their objective the realization of Zionism within the framework of the Labor movement in Eretz Israel.

Translated and adapted from the Hebrew and reprinted by permission of the author and Haifa University from *Uma velashon: sefer zikaron leprofesor Aryeh Tartakower*, edited by Menahem Zahari, et al. (Jerusalem, 1985), 51–94.

Along with the distinctive character of Hehalutz in each country, there emerged features which were also common to the movement as a whole. We shall consider these first, before going on to deal with each national organization individually.

1. Until the establishment of Hehalutz, the idea of *hagshamah azmit*, personal commitment, was something which was honored more in the breach than in the observance. Apart from small groups, from the time of Hibbat Zion onward, Zionists at large tended not to take the principle seriously. It was Hehalutz, in its diverse guises which, when the opportunity arose, had salvaged the idea from those who preached and advocated its virtues in public, and had turned it into a major instrument to bring about a revolutionary change in the Jewish experience in both the diaspora and Eretz Israel. The existence of Hehalutz served, among its other functions, as both a challenge and a test for the seriousness and authenticity of Zionist ideology. Once Hehalutz had become a public force to be reckoned with, it was no longer possible to treat the concept of *hagshamah* with the same lack of personal commitment as had been done in the past.

2. Disgust with pointless debate and the pervading atmosphere of "meetings" gave rise to political trends among various circles within the Zionist pioneer movement, first in Russia and then elsewhere. These were sometimes expressed by anti-intellectualism on the one hand, and admiration for crudity on the other.[3] Although these tendencies were a transitory and chance development, we should regard them as having represented a form of protest against the inaction of Zionist leadership, and as deriving from the desire to give precedence to practice over theory in a situation in which no efforts were being made to carry out the latter.

3. These trends should also be seen as deriving from the conviction that no achievement in either the political sphere or in the domain of public persuasion would last, and that mere political accomplishments would be void of any content whatever, unless they were also accompanied by action toward the personal commitment to Zionism. Hehalutz did not regard its aim as consisting of abstract intellectual innovation. All it sought was to transform the various ideological doctrines with which it identified into an implement by which the process of changing reality might be set in motion.

4. The centrality of the Zionist principle of *hagshamah* had the effect of causing Hehalutz to aspire to encompass the whole human being, to mold a new image of man through the internalization of the principles of the movement. This contrasted with the purposes of political parties,

which were content with obtaining only partial identification from their constituencies. This was often confined to a mere declaration of support. Thus the goal of Hehalutz was to impress its mark upon every aspect of existence, both of the individual and of the group as a whole. Its aim was to create a synthesis between, on the one hand, the realization of broad and overall national and social goals, and on the other hand, the aspiration of finding a solution to the distress of young Jews living in an alien society which had rejected them. Indeed we can observe in the Russian Hehalutz, during the initial period of its existence, an ascetic attitude of mind which sought to give the organization the character of a vanguard and of an elite order whose members were prepared to sacrifice themselves upon the altar of the redemption of the Jewish people and its homeland. This was a passing phase, however, and it left no permanent mark on the character of the movement.[4]

5. Spontaneity is another general feature worthy of mention which characterized all of Hehalutz during its formative period. The movement arose almost everywhere not as a consequence of initiative taken from above or externally, but following a spontaneous awakening, sometimes obscure, of young people in various places. Small groups arose simultaneously which set themselves the aim of settling in Eretz Israel and working the land. It was only at a later stage that the pattern of countrywide and European organizations was to emerge. It seems to us that the formation of these organizations should be regarded as representing a response on the part of young Jews to the challenges of the times, whether embodied in revolutionary events in Russia and the concurrent breakdown of Jewish communal life, or in events elsewhere in Eastern Europe, such as the national awakening taking place among peoples ruled by the various empires and accompanied by evident manifestations of aggressively xenophobic nationalism. As regards internal Jewish matters in this connection, we should mention the enthusiasm that was aroused by the Balfour Declaration.

6. As noted earlier, the reception of the ideas of Hehalutz did not follow the same pattern everywhere. Not all of the local organizations arose in consequence of connections with the Labor movement in Eretz Israel, or out of ideological or organizational identification with it;[5] all of them, however, found themselves to be in sympathy with the Labor movement. Membership in the society of workers was a matter of principle among them, and had the status of an obligation upon all members. At a later stage all the local organizations of the movement educated their memberships toward the goal of life in the *kibbutz*. Each of these

organizations was connected with a particular current in the *kibbutz* movement, so that unity gave way to particularism.

7. The principle of *hagshamah,* as an obligation to which the entire membership was committed, leadership as well as rank and file, turned Hehalutz into an organization of unique character, and with a continually changing leadership. In this way bureaucratization was avoided and a distinction between leaders and followers was prevented. A strong sense of equality pervaded the ranks of Hehalutz, especially in the decade of the 1920s, before it had become a mass movement. The developments that altered the character of the movement were often the result of local initiative, and were not always welcomed by the leadership. One of the most obvious examples of this was the process of development of the *hakhsharah* (training) *kibbutz* in Poland.[6] On the other hand, the continuous turnover among the leadership team resulted in a growing dependency on "imported" leadership, in other words, on emissaries from Eretz Israel. The situation ultimately led to the suppression of the movement's original spontaneity. In time this was not only to cause a gap between the leadership of the movement and its ordinary members, but would also result in a loss of ideological vitality. This applies particularly to the 1930s, when Hehalutz had become a movement with scores of thousands of members throughout the various countries in Europe.

8. The exclusive devotion to Eretz Israel that was characteristic of Hehalutz came about as a result of pessimism regarding the future of Jews in the diaspora. This pessimism was often conjoined with a contempt for the Jewish diaspora experience. This attitude gave rise to skepticism concerning the practical relevance of the struggle to obtain civic and national rights in the diaspora in which an important section of Zionist leadership was then taking part, and to which it was also devoting a considerable portion of its energies, frequently at the expense of activity on behalf of Eretz Israel. However, although Hehalutz conducted itself as a radical opposition to these trends, it did not enjoin its own membership from political activity within the local setting, so long as this did not supplant the major object of this concern, which was *hagshamah.*

9. Repudiation of the future of Jews in the diaspora gave rise to a preoccupation with quasi-eschatological themes among Hehalutz membership, and on occasion they had indeed defined themselves along such lines. However theirs was a messianism which represented a longing for action, and which had its origins in the fear of failing to act before it was too late. They did not intend single heroic actions, but rather an

ongoing and coherent enterprise with the goal of achieving a transformation of the present state of things. This was to be no matter of leaping in
a single bound from the realities of the current situation into a redemptive age. It was in this that Hehalutz was distinguished from other Jewish
messianic movements, to which Hehalutz had occasion to refer more
than once in negative terms, notwithstanding the fact that the apocalyptic outlook of such movements also involved a rejection of the diaspora.
For this reason, Hehalutz also managed to avoid the pitfalls of disappointment and despair that accompanied messianic manifestations
among the Jewish people in the past.

10. The desire for unity was another feature which was shared
throughout Hehalutz. There was a strong conviction widely held in
Hehalutz that the very enterprise of reshaping reality in a new pattern
had itself the capacity also of overcoming differences in the abstractions
of ideology and principle, which had the natural effect of deepening
contradictions and dividing forces which were otherwise close to one
another. It was the belief of Hehalutz that a unification of forces would
make it possible for the movement to carry the burden of the great task
with which it had been charged, and that such unity had the power of
healing the chronic sickness of the people as a whole.

The yearning for unity had profound roots in the Labor movement as
a whole, as well as in the Jewish Labor movement in particular. But
there were few movements in which the myth of unity was responsible
for as much factionalism as it had been in the case of the Socialist
movement. Hehalutz was no exception in this.

Moreover, the desire to achieve an overall unity based on broadly
shared ideological grounds, which of necessity were of a more or less
amorphous nature,[7] came into conflict with another tendency, namely,
the ambition to arrive at a comprehensive and perfect ideological doctrine whose values and constituent elements would be adequate to the
task of acting as a cohesive force for the great mass of young Jews that
would join the ranks of the movement. It was as a consequence of this
dichotomy that differences of opinion ultimately led not only to the
well-known schism in the Russian Hehalutz, but also in Hehalutz organizations in other countries. So, for example, in Poland the division in
Hehalutz lasted for a considerable time, and during the 1930s almost led
to a split in the movement there as well.

Like its counterpart in Russia, Hehalutz in Poland aspired during
the years of its existence to serve as a general framework that would
accommodate all pioneer youth movements. But to achieve this end, it

found itself constrained to forego important elements of its ideology and organizational conception. The first such concession took place when Hashomer Hatzair and Gordonia succeeded in obtaining the privilege of broad autonomy in exchange for joining Hehalutz. The majority in Hehalutz were prepared, at least in theory, to make further concessions to General Zionist organizations, among them Akiva and Hanoar Hazioni, so that these might join the ranks of the movement.[8] The upshot was that to the degree that the goal of achieving general unity was being realized, the common ground upon which it was based grew increasingly more general and amorphous. Homogeneity was thus weakened and centrifugal tendencies became more powerful, until Hehalutz in Poland had by the 1930s ceased to be a cohesive movement in respect to ideology, and had become instead a federation devoted to arranging matters of training for *hakhsharah* and immigration to Eretz Israel.

It would seem to us, therefore, that Hehalutz relinquished ideological homogeneity in the interests of expansion on the one hand, because of its conviction in the overriding power of unity, and on the other, in consequence of a pragmatic and even operative calculation that had to do with the desire to augment its role in the matter of the allotment of immigration certificates and other resources. What we witness is thus a paradoxical phenomenon: the wish to put an end to internal divisions had motivated the majority in Hehalutz to grant the privilege of broad autonomy to the groups that had recently joined them, but these very groups also weakened the ideological preference which favored overall unity. The majority, which had aspired as well for Hehalutz to assume the character of a movement possessing a comprehensive ideological and educational doctrine, while at the same time drawing into its ranks the greatest possible number of Zionist trends, was itself to become a factor in the preservation of particularized interests, namely its own, after it had joined one of the established *kibbutz* movements, Hakibbutz Hameuhad.

The time under review can be subdivided into two major periods: (1) The period of the 1920s, when Hehalutz was still a marginal force among the Jewish public, except for the brief span of growth during 1924–1925, during the peak of the Fourth Aliyah;[9] and (2) The years 1930–1935, when Hehalutz was at its height and could boast a membership comprising 100,000 adherents.[10] This quantitative growth was accompanied by qualitative changes which will be considered further on in our discussion.

HEHALUTZ IN POLAND IN THE 1920S

When Russian Jewry ceased being a leading force among the Jewish people, the position of precedence passed over to the Jews of Poland.[11] This was the case in regard to Hehalutz as well. Any consideration of Poland in the period following the First World War must take into account that the country's reunification and renewed independence, after centuries under foreign rule, did not eradicate regional differences at a single stroke. These differences had evolved in the course of the country's being ruled by three powers, Russia, Prussia, and Austria. Moreover, what was true of Polish society in this regard also held for the Jewish community of that country. It would therefore be advisable in dealing with Hehalutz in Poland to distinguish between the parts of the country that were ruled by Russia, where approximately two-thirds of Polish Jews resided, and the two regions of East and West Galicia, which had been under Austrian rule and in which about a third of the Jews of Poland had made their homes.[12] There are other regional differences of some importance as well, but the present discussion is not the appropriate context in which to consider them.

With the establishment of Hehalutz beyond the frontiers of Russia, where it had first been created, there developed two models of organization of the movement.[13] One of these took root in what had formerly been Russian Poland (hereafter "Poland"). In this region, youth movements of the type represented by Hashomer Hatzair and Gordonia had not been openly active in the formative period of the establishment of Hehalutz. The model that emerged here, which we shall call the "unity model," was dominated by the concept of an open mass movement which accommodated a membership with a variety of social points of view, and which ranged in its make-up from those who had been brought up within the youth movement to those who were referred to at the time as *stam halutzim,* or persons who had not been educated in any youth movement whatever and may have belonged to non-Zionist or even anti-Zionist movements prior to joining Hehalutz.

Chronologically the formation of *halutz* groups in Poland corresponded with the process which took place in Russia. It began in 1916, after the seizure by the Germans of the parts of Poland under Russian control, and occurred simultaneously with the renewal of public activity in the Jewish community, this having come to a standstill when war broke out, in consequence of the severe restrictions that Russian authorities had imposed on Jews.[14]

The aim of these groups, which like their counterparts in Russia had arisen spontaneously and at about the same time, was settlement in Eretz Israel at the earliest possible opportunity. Until such time, their membership engaged in cultural and educational activities, which also consisted of seasonal training in agriculture and gardening in areas located in the neighborhood of their home towns.[15]

The spontaneous formation of such groups in Poland was accompanied by an amorphousness of ideology, especially as regards the social domain. The pervading atmosphere within which the Polish Hehalutz operated was altogether opposite to that in Russia. The general mood in Poland was one of ascendant nationalism in association with dreams of imperial grandeur. This state of mind drew its inspiration from the romantic and heroic traditions of the nation's past. Among the Polish public there was a sense that the aspiration of past generations was about to be fulfilled. To hasten the realization of these national ambitions, two military legionnaire units were formed in the two camps of fighting men. These were conceived of as having the function of lending greater force to the national aspirations in the international sphere. Concurrently there was a rise in antisemitism among broad sections of the Polish populace which was the result of the growing influence of nationalist circles in the country. The wave of anti-Jewish feeling was already in evidence in the years preceding the First World War, and had resulted in the economic ostracism of Jews. As the war progressed, manifestations of antisemitism became even more severe.[16] There were also other factors that aroused young Jews to form Hehalutz groups in Poland; among these was the news of the Jewish Legion which had fought on the Allied side during the war, the Balfour Declaration, and the disappointment that was beginning to be felt in regard to universalist ideas.

An analysis of the ideological motives of the founders of Hehalutz in Poland demonstrates in our view that while they did not deviate from the general concepts of Zionism, the social aspects of their ideology lacked definition and were of secondary significance. In this respect Hehalutz in Poland differed from its counterpart in Russia, where from its very beginnings the organization's identification with the Labor movement in Eretz Israel was an integral and organic part of the movement's character. The process of identifying with the Labor movement and the adoption of a coherent doctrine unfolded slowly and only by degrees in the Polish Hehalutz.[17]

An important role which gave impetus to the formation of a fully articulated social doctrine, and to the emergence of an identification in Hehalutz with the Labor movement in Eretz Israel, was performed by *halutzim* from Russia and the Ukraine during their stay in Poland while on their way to Palestine. Some of this group remained in Poland for a considerable time and became active in the Hehalutz movement in that country. Prominent among this group were the members of a group named Dror. They served as a catalyst for the emergence in the Hehalutz of socialist tendencies that had already become widespread within their own ranks. Later, these same Russian and Ukrainian *halutzim* would also play a part in assisting the Polish Hehalutz to achieve its rapport with the Hakibbutz Hameuhad.[18]

The movement in Poland had not adopted a position of extreme selectivity; nor did it ever assume an obvious elitist character. During the period of crisis of the Third Aliyah, the Polish Hehalutz evolved a fully developed conception of the movement as one which was receptive to all young Jews, irrespective of their social origin, education, prior affiliations, or political outlook, so long as they sympathized with the movement's principles.[19]

RELATIONS BETWEEN HEHALUTZ AND THE ZIONIST ORGANIZATION

Hehalutz in Poland was formed within the national Zionist Organization; its founders accepted the authority of the leadership from the very outset, and the latter, for their part, supported the movement unreservedly, at least during the early phase of its existence. However the early harmony between the two was not to last. Very soon it became clear, and somewhat to their mutual astonishment, that despite their agreement in regard to the ultimate objective of Zionism, they differed significantly on the question of the manner in which this Zionist goal ought to be accomplished. Or, to state the case another way, as the movement's concrete Palestine-oriented activity and its work in behalf of pioneer training and *aliyah* came to occupy the principal place in the existence of Hehalutz, while at the same time the "exigencies of the present" increasingly thrust aside such activities in the preoccupations of the Zionist leadership, the tension and alienation between the two bodies increased. To their elders, *halutz* maximalism bore all the earmarks of precipitousness, whereas the young regarded the caution of the former as vacillation that was likely to result in missing a unique historic opportunity which might never recur, and which had been created by both the Balfour Declaration and the national awakening then taking place among broad sections of the Jewish public.[20]

The general effect of all this was that the growing consciousness of uniqueness among the rank and file of Hehalutz fueled and deepened criticism of Zionist leadership within the movement. As this criticism became manifest, it aroused a sharp response from Zionist leaders against the movement. This gave added impetus to the process of deepening self-consciousness in the young, and reinforced the tendency among them to detach themselves both ideologically and organizationally from General Zionism on the one hand, and to identify more closely with the Labor movement on the other. In 1921, during consultations by Hehalutz representatives from various regions in Poland, a decision was reached that the movement would from then on be organizationally autonomous and affiliate itself ideologically with the General Federation of Labor (Histadrut Klalit) in Eretz Israel.[21] Thenceforth, its criticism of Zionist leadership grew in intensity, being leveled now from the perspective of belonging to a rival camp.[22] Hehalutz thus was transformed from an essentially broad movement with a vague and indefinite ideology to one that was self-aware, and for which *hakhsharah* (training), in all of its variety of forms, assumed the status of a primary instrument for instilling collectivist and socialist values among its adherents.

The Fourth Aliyah represented the first test in the period in which the idea of a mass movement was preeminent, since previously Hehalutz in Poland had been, notwithstanding its significance, a relatively marginal force in Jewish public life. At the time of the Second World Congress in 1923, the membership of the movement numbered only 1,700 persons.[23]

With the start of the Fourth Aliyah, the situation underwent a total change. Within just a year-and-a-half the number of the movement's adherents increased eight times, to as many as 13,000 members.[24] The expansion resulted in a change in the social makeup of Hehalutz. The middle-class students, who had formerly made up the majority of its membership, were now joined by young unemployed workers, among whom were also members of socialist parties which were non-Zionist and even anti-Zionist. A great many of these latter regarded immigration to Eretz Israel as offering a solution to their economical, social, and personal difficulties. Their motives were thus not always entirely ideological. This massive expansion was random and unorganized. Yet despite dissatisfaction on this point in many circles within the movement, the majority regarded the new development very favorably because they perceived it to be a realization of the hope that Hehalutz had nourished from its very beginnings. The massive expansion was seen by this majority as confirming the guiding principle that every Jewish young person is capable of being a *halutz*. There were even those who went further, asserting that, in the wake of the expansion of the scope of *hakhsharah* (training), "we have become the principal element in the enterprise of productivization. . . . Our entire position among the Jewish public has changed." [25] The fact that workers were joining was a particular source of satisfaction. Some interpreted it as a sign that the traditional hostility of Jewish workers to the Zionist enterprise had passed out of existence permanently.

But as we know, this rising tide was not to last. The effects of the economic crisis in Eretz Israel which followed shortly thereafter began to be felt among the ranks of Hehalutz throughout Eastern Europe. Branches of the movement dissolved, *hakhsharah kibbutzim* were closed down, and its membership dwindled. In Poland, Hehalutz lost over two-thirds of its members. [26] Nevertheless, unlike other Zionist organizations, some of which had nearly disintegrated altogether, Hehalutz managed to retain a stable core of members who resisted being drawn into the pervasive mood of despair and powerlessness which had overwhelmed the Zionist movement. In these difficult years, when the organization existed in a state of isolation and had to contend with hostility from all quarters, it was able to create a new form of *hakhsharah* which was in time to become a model for imitation by Hehalutz in other countries. This was the permanent *hakhsharah-kibbutz*, which became an instrument for the absorption of tens of thousands of young people who joined Hehalutz in the 1930s. The principal position in this regard was occupied, during a period which is rightly regarded as the heroic age of Hehalutz, by two *kibbutzim*: the first was the Klosowa *kibbutz*; and the second, and perhaps somewhat less prominent, was Shahariyah. Both *kibbutzim* were situated on the eastern frontier of Poland.

As in other instances in the history of Hehalutz during the 1920s, the permanent *hakhsharah-kibbutz* owed its existence to the spontaneous local initiative of rank and file members rather than being the consequence of the actions of the leadership. The latter were not infrequently taken aback by the courage and daring of those who initiated permanent *hashsharah-kibbutzim*, and even sought to restrain their radicalism.

There is a geographical aspect, as well, to the change in the form of *hakhsharah*. Hehalutz began as a movement in the heavily populated Jewish centers of Poland. However during the low point of the Fourth Aliyah, the movement had all but ceased to exist in these areas. Its principal activities were now transferred to the regions on the country's eastern frontier, which were also the most backward economically. The several scores of members (later to number a few hundred) were largely employed in the lumber industry, which was for the most part Jewish owned. The one exception was a Klosowa, where the members worked at the quarry.

The choice of these isolated districts, remote from the centers of Jewish population, was in part the result of conscious decision, and partly the outcome of objective factors. It was seen as a protest against the bankruptcy of bourgeois Zionism, as revulsion against the "decayed" mode of existence in the Jewish shtetl, and as a rejection of its intellectual and cultural values. In 1931, in anticipation of the return to the city following the "Great Wandering," [27] the abandonment of Jewish society was explained as deriving from the wish to be separated "from the corrupt environment and repulsive manner of life." [28] The departure also had a positive side to it, namely, the desire to realize the entire complex of goals which permanent *hakhsharah* had set for itself, and to do so in a consistent and uncompromising fashion. This was not to be preparation for merely physical work alone; but rather the creation of a new human type, one that was imbued with collective social values, and of a new Eretz Israel ambience in the diaspora which was as nearly perfect as could be achieved.

The major group which had taken on itself the task of fulfilling the principles of equality and partnership, with a consistency which verged on fanaticism, was the *kibbutz* at Klosowa. There was a daily struggle to separate the individual from his parental home and from his past, and to adopt the cooperative way of life as a goal to be realized in the immediate present. This struggle was undertaken by way of rigorous severity toward oneself, which was to become a value in its own right. The effort was undertaken in the circumstances of exhausting labor in the quarry and in sawmills, at low wages, and in exceedingly difficult living conditions in a hostile environment. The story of Klosowa has been recounted at length, and has served as an educational inspiration to generations of the movement's members. This is not the appropriate place to consider the story in detail.[29] We can summarize, however, by observing that at Klosowa, and to a lesser degree at Shahariyah, a mode of existence took shape that was marked by utopian characteristics with an admixture of anarchistic and ascetic elements, these being attended by tendencies to turn away from the Jewish world, preoccupied with its own manners, customs, and cultural "hypocrisies." The sense of freedom that characterized this mode of life was regarded by young people as being, on the one hand, an expression of liberation from the hated petit-bourgeois heritage, and on the other, a revelation of a new proletarianism. The external tokens of these were carelessness of dress, roughness of speech, indifference to both private and public property, and chiefly a maximalist radicalism which was not to be compromised even in the smallest degree. The Klosowa group conceived of itself as representing an ideal pattern for a popular mass movement open to all young Jews, without distinction as regards their affiliation with other movements, or their social origins and class. Nevertheless, it appears to us that the success of the founding group in fact derived from its consisting of a small circle of elite vanguard. The conception that underlay the Klosowa group was submitted to the test when it was supposed to serve as a model for a mass movement in the 1930s.

The *hakhsharah-kibbutzim* did in fact succeed in absorbing thousands of young people, and prevented a repetition of the crisis experienced by the Fourth Aliyah. But it seems to us that they failed to instill their values with the same consistency as had been done in Klosowa.[30] Even so, it can be said that the principle of permanent *hakhsharah* had entirely supplanted the provisional forms of *hakhsharah* practiced earlier. Permanent *hakhsharah* was an authentic and productive response to the crisis that had overtaken Zionism in the mid-1920s.

HEHALUTZ AND THE YOUTH MOVEMENTS

During the period under review, the structure of Hehalutz remained homogeneous. Notwithstanding the new notions that had arisen in regard to the various issues, a feeling had emerged of uniqueness and of the legitimation of autonomous existence. However, the general desire for unity impelled Hehalutz to seek ways in which to merge with the other Jewish pioneer youth movements, among them the veteran Hashomer Hatzair as well as Gordonia and other similar groups. Most of these groups, after following different paths, had adopted a Zionist Socialist outlook and the principle of personal realization of the Zionist ideal.[31] There thus seemed to be no apparent obstacle to their merging with Hehalutz, were it not for the fact that all of them had evolved a consciousness of their own uniqueness separate from that of Hehalutz, a consciousness which they were also zealously anxious to preserve.

Negotiations between the sides began in 1925[32] and lasted until the end of 1928, ending in a signed agreement which was the result of compromise. It was decided that Hashomer Hatzair and Gordonia would join Hehalutz, although preserving their autonomy on the branch level and as regards *hakhsharah* and *aliyah*.[33]

It would be difficult to say that the union was received with particular enthusiasm in either camp. As opposed to the demand made by Hashomer Hatzair and Gordonia, Hehalutz made no concessions regarding either the special status of its own youth movement, Hehalutz Hatzair,[34] or its connections with Hakibbutz Hameuhad. On the other hand Hehalutz was constrained to give up, albeit temporarily from its own point of view, the idea of achieving a general unity—actually turning Hehalutz into a federative organization of autonomous movements. Hashomer Hatzair and Gordonia continued to preserve their independence and sought to expand the federative base of Hehalutz. The majority, on the other hand, regarded the agreement as furnishing only a point of departure for effecting a complete and general unification in Hehalutz and the *kibbutz* movement in Eretz Israel. The upshot was that from the very moment of unification the seeds were already sown for the tensions which were to grow more intense in the 1930s. Centrifugal tendencies thus began to overwhelm the centripetal tendencies.

THE "GREAT WANDERING"

Just as the crisis of the Fourth Aliyah produced an escapist tendency, so too was the return to the heavily populated regions of Poland the result of objective pressures whose origin was the worldwide economic crisis. Its effect on a weak and backward Poland was especially severe. For example, the lumber industry, most of whose production was devoted to export, was among the most seriously affected sectors of the industrial economy.[35] The winter of 1931–1932 was particularly hard on the nearly 1,000 members of *haskhsharah-kibbutzim,* the majority of whom were employed in that industry. The standard of living, which was depressed in any case, had fallen to an unprecedented low. The average wage, which had previously stood at one *zloty,*[36] was now only thirty *groszy;* moreover this was paid out not in money but in commodities— that is, if any work at all was to be had. Famine and disease spread among *kibbutz* members. Conditions in Eretz Israel were bad as well, both politically and economically. Politically the situation worsened following the Shaw Commission and Hope Simpson reports, which put into doubt Zionist chances for success. Economically, the Zionist movement's lack of funds resulted in a cessation of investments. *Aliyah* stopped altogether. In Hehalutz an atmosphere of pessimism began to assert itself. It appeared that *hakhsharah* was now in danger of being eliminated. Only two choices remained. One was to send the members home and await better times; in other words, to put an end to all the achievements which had been obtained by dint of extraordinary efforts since 1925. The other possibility was to begin searching for alternative places of work. It was the second option which was chosen. This was when the hakhsharah-*kibbutzim* of both the majority in Hehalutz (calling themselves the "Gush Klali"), and Hashomer Hatzair set out on their "Great Wandering." Initially they made their way to districts that bordered on the neighborhoods in which they had earlier established themselves. Subsequently they moved progressively further away, into former Russian Poland, and eventually some wandered as far as to parts of Galicia. The following account conveys the prevailing atmosphere at the time:

Anyone passing through Volhynia in the preceding months would have obtained some idea ... of the exertions of pioneering and the unending wanderings. Along the railway running from Rowno via Sarni, which continues onward to Baranowicz and Lida. .. , members of the *kibbutz* wander and everywhere throughout ... the district in search of work. .. , and at road junctions many stories are told about travelling from place to place and of encounters, about assistance from branch offices and estrangement, and about demand for work in the Jewish communities.[37]

The first to set out was Kibbutz Shahariyah, followed by Klosowa, Tel Hai, and the *kibbutzim* of Hashomer Hatzair. These wanderings were chaotic. At times representatives of the various *kibbutzim* encountered one another at the same place and found themselves in confrontation, so that the Hehalutz center was required to intervene and decide who would stay. In the course of these travels, small places were sometimes selected which were unable to provide for the arrivals, and these would soon be abandoned. However, in the course of the wanderings pioneering *hakhsharah* was brought to many localities which it had never before reached. When the journeying came to an end in 1934, five territorial blocs had been established, belonging to the Gush Klali, which was associated with Hakibbutz Hameuhad:

1. The Klosowa bloc in Volhynia, which consisted of thirty-two detachments distributed over an area that included some places in eastern Galicia.
2. The Shahariyah bloc, also in Volhynia, which extended over an area

of hundreds of kilometers and extended as far as Vilna in the north. This bloc contained thirty detachments.

3. The Tel-Hai bloc, in the region of Bialystok-Grodno, which contained a total of fifteen divisions.

4. Kibbutz Borochov, which had spread through the industrial centers of Congress Poland, and comprised twenty-nine detachments.

5. The Grochow bloc, centered at the first agricultural farm established by Hehalutz in Poland. It was located near Warsaw and had branches in the city and its immediate neighborhood. This bloc had fifteen units in all.

These blocs were centrally organized, with the principal body consisting of a chief *kibbutz*, from which its detachments and branches radiated. The latter were subordinate to the bloc secretariats, which looked after such matters as regulation of manpower, educational and cultural activities, and certificates of immigration to Eretz Israel.

As we noted earlier, the *kibbutzim* of Hashomer Hatzair and the Gordonia groups also took part in these wanderings. The degree of autonomy of each unit among the youth movements was far greater than that of the groups in the Gush Klali.[38]

Although these wanderings had resulted in the scattering of *hakhsharah* detachments throughout Poland, thereby creating an infrastructure for mass absorption, this fact of itself is insufficient to explain the growth of Hehalutz. Other factors were at work as well. Among these were the worsening conditions of Jews as a result of the economic crisis, the increasingly antisemitic policy of the government, the closure of countries to which immigration traditionally tended, and Eretz Israel becoming the principal target of immigration by the Jews of Poland.[39] It was a combination of all these factors that was responsible for the expansion of Hehalutz and its becoming an important element in Jewish public life.[40]

HEHALUTZ IN POLAND IN THE 1930S

The majority of members of Hehalutz in the 1920s, particularly in the low period of the Fourth Aliyah, were from the middle or lower-middle class. They came from the small towns and cities of eastern Poland. A great many had been educated in the Tarbut Hebrew schools, knew Hebrew, and were familiar with Hebrew culture. As we have seen, the theme of rebellion against the surrounding Jewish society was one of the factors which shaped their ideas and actions. We should emphasize, however, that this rebellion was relatively restrained. It never went beyond the bounds of the national movement. In our view this situation derived from the fact that the attitude of the older generation toward Hehalutz and its activities, although not always friendly, never became radically hostile. It would appear that this situation was a consequence of the social character of the Jewish populace in the regions under consideration. This part of Poland consisted primarily of little towns and small cities in which the traditional social bonds had not yet been entirely destroyed, so that the rift between the younger and older generations had not gone as far as it did in the large urban centers. These circumstances left their mark on the character of Hehalutz and the movement's relationship with its environment.

The collective character of the young generation that joined Hehalutz in the 1930s was rather different. A portion came from central and western Poland, regions in which the processes of social disintegration among the Jewish population was particularly evident. These were industrialized areas in which a new heterogeneous population was concentrated, originating in cities and towns and having no organic ties to bind them to one another. The result was alienation not only between groups coming from different parts of the country, but between the generations as well. Moreover, in the social domain we find influences being exerted by radical non-Zionist and anti-Zionist movements on the one hand, and by the hasidic orthodoxy on the other. The consequence was strong hostility toward Zionism in general and Hehalutz Zionism in particular that was widespread among various strata in the Jewish population.

On the whole, the young generation that joined Hehalutz in the 1930s may be characterized as having had either a Polish elementary school education or having gone to a *heder,* and sometimes having no formal education at all; both their general and their Jewish cultural level tended to be low.[41] Nor was the political and social culture from which these young people came especially distinguished—being sometimes shallow and crude, and drawing principally on the popular press. Their brief stay at a Hehalutz branch, before moving on for a short period of *hakhsharah,* did not particularly strengthen their motivation to identify with the national and social aims of the movement. Hehalutz was in danger of becoming nothing more than an immigration movement. The leadership was aware of this, but did nothing to arrest the development. To the contrary, the movement's massive increase of membership tended rather to legitimize the concept of a mass movement, and lent support to the belief that the pioneering idea could attract a mass following of young people from a variety of social strata. Hehalutz leaders persisted in believing that the Hehalutz idea was powerful enough to turn this heterogenous mass into a single, unified, group, sharing a consciousness of purpose and ready to take an active part, within the framework of the *kibbutz* movement, in building Eretz Israel.

However, it soon became clear that the integrating force of symbols and ideas and of the cooperative framework was insufficient to accomplish this end. Most of the young members hastened to leave their *kibbutzim* upon arrival to Palestine, thus demonstrating their skin-deep convictions and shallow preparedness.[42]

To mend the situation even in part, administrative measures were taken such as making a certificate of immigration dependent on a candidate's knowledge of Hebrew and an assessment of the chances of the person joining a *kibbutz* on arrival in the country. Members of Hehalutz called these measures *gzeirot* (i.e., "oppressive edicts"). Given the circumstances, these may have been justified, but their effect was the opposite of what was intended for they only augmented alienation between rank-and-file members and the movement's leadership and local representatives. The movement's values began to symbolize artificial barriers which an alien and hostile leadership was putting in the way of members to prevent them from realizing their principal aspiration, this being to leave Poland and to begin a new life, not necessarily of a collective nature, in Eretz Israel.

Manifestations of hypocrisy, insincerity, and surrender to the rule of the organizational apparatus became more frequent, all of this in order to obtain certificates of immigration. The negative consequences of this state of affairs were not long in coming. Entire groups did not even wait to arrive in Eretz Israel, and already declared their withdrawal from the movement while still on board ship.

In the meantime, the *aliyah* had come to a stop, and in the years that preceded the war, Hehalutz entered a new period. There was a drop in membership, the numbers of *stam halutzim* in the movement being reduced. The place of the latter was increasingly taken by members of the youth movements, and *hakhsharah* in Hehalutz increasingly came to resemble that of the youth movements and took on a more homogeneous character.

Generally speaking, the process of absorbing many thousands of young people was attended by difficulties and failures. But there were no few successes as well; these must moreover be credited to the creation of the permanent *hakhsharah-kibbutz,* as a result of which Hehalutz was rescued from failures of the kind that the movement experienced during the low period of the Fourth Aliyah. Despite falling membership from 1935 onward, no doubt was cast on the right of Hehalutz to continue to exist, as had been the case in the decade of the 1920s. When war broke out Hehalutz was ready to undertake new tasks which the troubled times had imposed on it.

INTERNAL RELATIONS IN HEHALUTZ DURING THE 1930S

As already mentioned, the years 1932–1935 were a period of massive growth. At this time attention was focused on the social and organizational problems which attended the absorption of thousands of new members at local branches and *hakhsharah-kibbutzim.* The various levels of the movement were preoccupied with such complex social issues as the question of preserving internal democracy and of equality in rapidly changing circumstances. In a word, this was a decade of crystallization and institutionalization.[43]

The departure from economically backward regions on the borders of Poland to the industrial districts of the country had raised hopes in *hakhsharah-kibbutzim* that they might obtain access to permanent areas of work which offered higher wages, thereby raising their standard of living.[44] On the other hand, living in the cities produced dialectic tensions in *hakhsharah-kibbutzim* which continued throughout the 1930s. Under the pressures of reality, close relationships were established between these *kibbutzim* and the local Jewish population, the very same population from which they had sought to escape in the 1920s. What this meant was that isolation was no longer possible for the *hakhsharah* enterprise as a defense against external temptations, either real or imagined.

Although the majority in Hehalutz had not changed their views concerning the rejection of the diaspora, they were constrained to acknowledge the relative importance of the national struggle of Jews in the places where they actually lived. Thus its members were allowed to take part in that struggle so long as this activity did not supplant the principal goal, which was to realize the Zionist enterprise.[45]

With the establishment of *hakhsharah* in the cities, it was hoped in Hehalutz that a change would be brought about in the movement's social make-up, and that the participation of workers and the children of workers would increase as a result.[46] However, most of the new members came from the petty and middle bourgeoisie. Only a small number were young workers from the big city. University students made up an insignificant part of the new membership,[47] since this group was mostly under the influence of ideologies of the radical left and right.[48]

It is against the general and schematic background set out in the preceding that the relationships among the various factions of Hehalutz must be examined.[49]

UNITY AND FEDERATION

We have already had occasion to discuss the function of the myth of unity in the worker's movement and Hehalutz. The idea was given impetus with the establishment of the Mifleget Poalei Eretz Israel, or the Eretz Israel Workers' Party (Mapai). The minority continually complained about the strong pressure exerted by the majority, at times attended by administrative measures, and about discrimination in *hakh-sharah* and *aliyah*, all this in order to compel it to give up its rights. It was argued by the minority that Hakibbutz Hameuhad was trying to force Gordonia and Hashomer Hatzair to join the Gush Klali, and to separate Hever Hakvutzot and Hakibbutz Haartzi from their human reserve in order to bring about a unification of *kibbutzim* in Eretz Israel.[50] The Gush Klali dismissed these claims and explained that its struggle was directed against efforts to deprive Hehalutz of its significance, and to convert it into an empty vessel entirely void of ideological content.[51]

Undoubtedly there was a solid basis for the claims concerning the double loyalties of the youth movement. The question of autonomy was regarded among the youth movements and their associated *kibbutz* movements as a fateful issue bound up with their very existence.[52]

In addition to the defense of real and practical interests however, profound differences came to the fore in these disputes. These differences had their origin in the different social and cultural histories of the two sides, and in their differing perceptions concerning their tasks and aims.

The youth movements came into being against a background of adult Philistinism,[53] and were created in the hope of establishing an alternative culture which was free and spontaneous. Elitist attitudes naturally arose within such movements, and these gave rise to a consciousness of representing a vanguard in Hashomer Hatzair and, to a lesser extent, in Gordonia. An accepted principle among all youth movements was that the molding of a young person could be achieved only by long-term processes which began at an early age. The focus of this molding was the individual and his place in society.

Hakibbutz Hameuhad, with which the majority in Hehalutz were associated, drew on a number of very different historical and cultural sources, among which was the populist tradition of the Narodniki. It developed an activist mass outlook. The focus was not on the individual and his aspirations, but on the masses and on aims that were national and social.

The Gush Klali was convinced that the rising importance of Eretz Israel in the consciousness of the nation, at a time when the foundations of Jewish life in the diaspora were crumbling, would necessarily lead to an objective process of mass identification of young Jews with both Zionism as a whole and Hehalutz in particular. It was for this reason that the idea of a vanguard was rejected, in which the capacity of a person to live a *kibbutz* life was contingent on a long-term and profound process of education. Such a notion was regarded as anachronistic and paternalistic, and as deriving from a lack of belief in the positive potentialities latent in the people. Contempt for the ordinary person, it was argued, had lead to alienation from the masses and indifference to its suffering and hopes.[54]

The continuing growth of Hehalutz seemed to justify the position of the Gush Klali. It seemed as if the movement's expansion would never end, and that very soon a closely knit network of Hehalutz branches and *hakhsharah-kibbutzim* would cover all of Poland.[55]

The Gush Klali's basic position was reinforced by its victory in the elections for the Sixth National Congress of Hehalutz in Poland, when it won 65.5 percent of the vote (Hashomer Hatzair receiving 23.1 percent, Gordonia 8.1 percent, and the remainder 3.3 percent).[56] This victory was interpreted as an expression of democratic historical processes taking place among the Jewish people. On the other hand, the youth movements did not abandon their view that the idea of a mass movement would lead to a blurring of values, a turning away from the individual, bureaucratic rule, and the sort of vulgarity and pretentious ignorance that often assumed the guise of anti-intellectualism.[57] The crisis that overtook Hehalutz from the beginning of 1935 was regarded among the youth movements as a demonstration of the correctness of their position.

In consequence of its concept of the character of Hehalutz, the Gush Klali proposed the establishment of a mixed *hakhsharah* for both *stam halutzim* and persons coming from the youth movements. In these *hak-sharah-kibbutzim*, members would be trained for all types of cooperative settlement, with each member being allowed to choose freely which framework he preferred to join on arriving in Eretz Israel. The Gush proposed that its plan should be put up for discussion throughout the movement, in anticipation of a decisive consideration of its merits at the congress of Hehalutz.[58] Although the proposal did not formally cancel the rights of the youth movements to autonomy, it was interpreted as a gross violation of the agreement of affiliation, and was regarded as undermining their existence and justifying a dissolution of the movement. The minority were willing to remain in Hehalutz only if their rights were honored, and they proclaimed that if the majority persisted in imposing mixed *hakhsharah*, they would be constrained to leave Hehalutz.[59]

As elections to the Halutz Congress drew near, relations within the movement grew increasingly strained. The congress was supposed to convene in May 1934. The Histadrut, however, intervened, and in response to the demand of the youth movements, the date of the meeting was postponed. Another effort to convene the congress in May 1935 failed as well. In the meantime *aliyah* was dwindling, and Hehalutz reached a low point in its history. The situation of Jews in Eastern Europe was growing increasingly worse, and the problems that the congress was supposed to address ceased being relevant. The whole subject of convening the congress was dropped, although neither side retreated from its position with regard to the principles involved.

EMISSARIES FROM ERETZ ISRAEL

Almost from its beginning Hehalutz worked to establish ties with Eretz Israel and the Labor movement in the country. These contacts were initially random and sporadic. The emissaries from Eretz Israel took on the character of an established institution only at the time of the Fourth Aliyah, when the *kibbutz* movement began its search for new sources of pioneering manpower, after Jewish emigration from Russia was cut off. The other East European countries, and particularly Poland, now became the principal reservoir of pioneering immigration. Gdud Haavodah was the first group to establish regular contacts with the diaspora. However internal difficulties prevented Gdud Haavodah from extending and strengthening these ties.[60] Kibbutz Ein-Harod had also made similar approaches at the time. Members of Ein-Harod formed part of the delegation of the Histadrut which was sent abroad, and it was their activity which created sympathy for Hakibbutz Hameuhad among the

majority of Hehalutz members in Poland, Lithuania, and Czechoslovakia, a sympathy which eventually assumed the status of identification.

As noted, Hehalutz too was interested in establishing such ties; moreover it was in greater need of emissaries from Eretz Israel than any other
Zionist movement. The reason for this was that the overriding principle
of personal commitment *(hagshamah)* had resulted in a continuous turnover of those at the head of the movement, thereby preventing the
emergence of an established local leadership. Continuity required the
presence of people who were both experienced and connected with
Hehalutz. Both requirements were met by members of the movement
who had already settled in Eretz Israel, and who were therefore familiar
with conditions in both that country and the regions from which they
had emigrated.

In the early 1920s, the balance was still preserved between local
Hehalutz leadership and representatives from Eretz Israel. One of the
consequences was that the various national organizations could determine their own policies on the basis not only of the requirements imposed by conditions in Eretz Israel but also of the long-term needs of the
movement in the diaspora, even when these were at odds with current
demands in Eretz Israel.

The situation changed completely in the 1930s, and dependence on
emissaries from Eretz Israel increased considerably. This had to do with
internal developments in Hehalutz that led each of its factions to identify
itself with a specific *kibbutz* movement. It was through the emissaries
from Eretz Israel that the *kibbutz* movements continued to exert their
influence on the different factions in ways which were both ideological
and organizational. The Eretz Israel leadership were the final arbiters in
all matters great and small. This dependency was reinforced further by
the growing authority of Eretz Israel and concurrent decline of the
authority of the diaspora among the Jewish public, especially after the
doors to the traditional countries of immigration were closed and Eretz
Israel had become the chief target of immigration of Eastern and Central
European Jews, whose conditions were growing continually worse in
their countries of origin.

Dependency on emissaries from Eretz Israel exacted a heavy price.
Creativity, spontaneity, and originality came to an end as regards the
orientation and development of Hehalutz. The emissaries from Eretz
Israel became the force which now guided the activities of pioneer youth
movements in all spheres. Local initiative was reduced to nil. Every

change in Hehalutz was determined by the Eretz Israel leadership, and sometimes imposed by them when local activists resisted.

The insistence of the factions in Hehalutz on protecting their own interests, and the many urgent practical needs that had to be met led to increased intervention by the emissaries. In the process, one of the fundamental goals of the movement was neglected, namely, that of educating toward a democratic and egalitarian mode of existence based on the principle of independent self-rule.

These circumstances did not escape the notice of contemporaries, and there were those who warned against the situation. Berl Katznelson, for example, during his visits to *haksharah-kibbutzim,* was clearly aware of the dangers inherent in the enormous power wielded by Eretz Israel emissaries.[61] Pinhas Labon, too, pointed this out when he observed: "The youth movement of the diaspora has ceased existing as an independent educational factor. The center which dictates all authority is the enterprise in Eretz Israel; it does the thinking, it looks after things, it decides, it determines."[62] The situation was also a matter of concern in Hakibbutz Hameuhad. As early as 1930, Hershl Pinsky, one of the representatives of Hakibbutz Hameuhad to Hehalutz in Poland, described the state of affairs in the following terms:

The movement has not brought forth people in recent years, and there is no one to manage operations. The Hehalutz Center is almost entirely made up of members from Eretz Israel. Members of *kibbutzim* for the most part only come and count the days they must . . . remain here. Understandable I too impatiently bide my time here, waiting to finish my exile.[63]

The warnings of Berl Katznelson and others could not change either the situation or the conditions that had given rise to it. Moreover, those who had sent the emissaries saw neither the necessity nor possibility of change, since things as they were served their ends and they believed there was no better alternative.[64] We are thus confronted by the paradox of a movement which began as an expression of the independent aspirations of young people, and which advocated the principles of full democracy and of equality between its leaders and followers, losing its distinctive character and becoming an instrument which was entirely dependent on outside forces. This happened by virtue of the movement having scrupulously adhered to the goal of being true to its original principles. The situation was a mixed blessing. But whatever our view of the position of the Eretz Israel emissaries in Hehalutz in Eastern Europe, there can be no doubt that they did perform a vital function in the movement.

HEHALUTZ IN THE PERIOD 1936–1939

When political and economic conditions in Eretz Israel changed for the worse, a perceptible decline in Hehalutz membership was immediately felt. This happened in the late 1930s. Initially the change was gradual, but in time it took on momentum. Unfortunately we have no confirmed date concerning the rate of departure of Hehalutz members from the movement for the period as a whole. However even the partial figures available reveal that there was a loss of membership in *hakhsharah* groups, and more drastically in the movement's branches, most of which ceased functioning altogether. Thus in the period 1935–1936 membership in *hakhsharah* fell by 25 percent. The trend was to continue in the years that followed.[65]

The "selective vanguard" view was therefore characteristic of Hehalutz at this time. The place of *stam halutzim,* who constituted an element that had virtually disappeared from the movement as immigration to Eretz Israel declined,[66] was now taken by youth movement pioneers.[67] Optimism about the chances of early immigration to Eretz Israel now gave way to feelings of despair and disappointment among the Jewish public and Hehalutz membership. The time had passed when parents would bring their children to the movement and to pioneer training in the expectation that settlement of their sons and daughters in Eretz Israel would pave the way for their own immigration.[68] Contemporary evidence reveals that cynicism, nihilism, and opportunism were rampant among young Jews at the time, and these attitudes were also shared by the members of Hehalutz.

For the autonomous youth movements, the situation of Hehalutz during these years of crisis served to confirm them in their conception of an elite pioneering vanguard. As they saw it, the situation had proved once again that it was the youth movements alone that could be counted on in times of crisis to furnish a reliable basis for Hehalutz; it was they, rather than the unaffiliated *stam halutzim,* who were the backbone of the movement as a whole.[69] This, however, was not the view of the adherents of the Gush Klali, who regarded the crisis as representing a passing phase and as the consequence of outside factors which in no way undermined the validity of the idea of Hehalutz being a receptive mass movement. Moreover, they considered that the seriousness of the current situation, particularly as regards the branches, was in part the fault of the youth movements, which had isolated themselves from *stam halutzim,* whom they treated as being beneath them.[70] By early 1939 there were signs of increasing membership. Contemporary reports speak of hundreds of new members joining *hakhsharah-kibbutzim* to replace those who were now beginning to leave for Eretz Israel in the "illegal" *aliyah*.[71] Illegal immigration had opened up new vistas before Hehalutz, until the outbreak of the war brought a halt to everything. With the Second World War, a new chapter began in the history of Hehalutz and the pioneering youth movements.

NOTES

1. Russian membership at the beginning of the twentieth century, and later Polish membership after the closure of Russia, accounted for 80–90 percent of the total membership in the movement internationally. See Israel Oppenheim, *Tnuat Hehalutz be-Polin, 1917–1929* (Jerusalem, 1982), chaps. 1 and 5. Regarding the 1930s, see *Heatid*, 74–75, August 1929; ibid., 103, September 1930; Leyb Shpizman, *Halutzim in Poyln* (New York, 1959), pp. 652, 656–58; Memorandum of the World Hehalutz Center to the Fourteenth Zionist Congress, Lucerne 1935, *Unzere yediyes*, no. 12, August 15, 1935. For a detailed account of the trends in Hehalutz in Poland, see Israel Otiker, *Tnuat Hehalutz be-Polin, 1932–1935* (Tel Aviv, 1972).

2. See Yehuda Slutzky, "Haraayon Hehalutz utnuot halutziot shonot lifnei milhemet haolam Harishonah," *Asufot*, 12 (Tel Aviv, July 1968), pp. 7 ff.

3. Concerning these attitudes in the Russian Hehalutz, see Dan Pines, *Hehalutz bekur hamahapekhah* (Tel Aviv, 1930); Oppenheim, *Tnuat Hehalutz be-Polin, 1917–1929*, chaps. 1 and 9.

4. See Eliahu Munchik, "Im hastadia hashlishit," quoted in Moshe Basok, ed., *Sefer Hehalutz* (Jerusalem, 1940), pp. 15–17. See also Israel Oppenheim, "Hehalutz be-Rusyah bashanim 1918–1922," in *Measef* (Writings on the Study of the Jewish Workers' Movement), 1, May 1971, 53–55.

5. Such was the case with Hehalutz in Poland. See Oppenheim, *Tnuat Hehalutz be-Polin, 1917–1929*, chap. 2.

6. See discussion below.

7. On the efforts of Trumpeldor and his associates to give Russian Hehalutz the character of an open mass movement founded on broad common foundations, see Binyamin Vest, ed., *Naftulei dor: Toldot Zeir-Zion vehitahdut be-Rusyah hasovietit*, part 2 (Tel Aviv, 1941); Pines, *Hehalutz*.

8. See below for an account of the conditions for Hashomer Hatzair and Gordonia to join the movement.

9. For the figures on the brief period of growth and subsequent sharp decline, see Shpizman, *Halutzim in Poyln*, pp. 652–53.

10. As opposed to a total of 8,000 during the low point of the Fourth Aliyah in all of the countries in which the movement was active; also there were 16,000 members in *hakhsharah*, as opposed to 4,000 in the 1920s. Regarding the distribution for the different countries, see Shpizman, *Halutzim in Poyln*, pp. 652, 656–58.

11. The prominence given in this article to the development of Hehalutz in Poland (formerly the Russian Hehalutz) is justified on two principal grounds: (1) the development of Hehalutz in Poland can be traced over a continuous period of fully two decades, and (2) the position of Hehalutz in Poland led even in numerical terms, as compared to the Jewish national movement as a whole. See, for example, Shpizman,

Halutzim in Poyln, pp. 279, 325–26, 652. Moreover, this leadership was evident in the ideological and social spheres; see below.

12. The number of Jews living under Prussian rule was exceedingly small, and accounted for no more than 1.5–2 percent of the total population. Their influence was insignificant.

13. There were also intermediary types; see below.

14. See *Die Juden in Kriege: Denkschrift des juedischen sozialistischen Arbeiterverbandes Poalei-Zion an das Internationale Sozialistische Bureau* (The Hague, 1917).

15. See, for example, *Dos yidishe folk*, 5, March 15, 1917; also 7, April 12, 1917, and 10, May 10, 1917; also *Hazfirah*, 14, May 13, 1917, and 18, May 2, 1918, etc.

16. On the nature and content of Polish nationalism, see, for example, H. Kohn, *Pan Slavism: Its History and Ideology* (Notre Dame, 1953); H. Roos, *A History of Modern Poland* (London, 1966). Concerning the nationalism of right-wing Democratic Nationalists, see Israel Oppenheim, "Mekomah shel hasheelah hayehudit baiton *Glos*, 1894–1896: Likdam-historiyah shel yahas hayamin hapolani lasheelah hayehudit," in Sh. Almog et al., eds., *Kovetz maamarim: Shai li-Shmuel Ettinger* (Jerusalem, 1988), pp. 129–56; Israel Oppenheim, "Yahas shel 'Hademokratiah Haleumit' lasheelah hayehudit beshalhei hameah ha-19 vereshit hameah ha-20," *Galed*, 10, 1987, pp. 87–119.

17. See for example *Hazfirah*, 40, October 3, 1918; or Dr. Hayyim Horowitz, "Hehalutz un di arbeter artelen in Erets Yisroel," *Bafrayung* (Organ of Zeirei-Zion), 18, September 11, 1919.

18. Concerning *halutzim* of Russia and the Ukraine, see Decisions of the Second National Congress of the Hehalutz Organization in Poland, 21–24 Tammuz, 1921, *Hazfirah* 169, October 19, 1921; A. Sh., "Aharei veidat Hehalutz," *Hazfirah*, 163, August 2, 1921; Yehuda Reznichenko (Erez), "Histadrut hahalutzim yotzei Rusyah ve-Ukrainah be-Polin," *Measef litnuat Hehalutz*, pp. 175–80; idem., "Halutzim hayinu," pp. 227–92. For a detailed description and bibliography, see Oppenheim, *Tnuat Hehalutz be-Polin, 1917–1929*, pp. 121–38.

19. See Aharon Berdichevski, "Shtei veidot," *Hehalutz*, May 2–3, 1923.

20. See Meetings of Fourth National Congress of the Zionist Congress in Poland, *Hazfirah*, 34, August 18, 1919, and 36–37, September 4, 1919.

21. See *Hazfirah*, 65, March 21, 1921.

22. See for example Feibush Bendori, "Hareformah hahistadrutit batnuah hazionit," *Dror*, August 1, 1922; Yisrael Merminski, "Kamtzanut o binyan leumi," *Hazfirah*, 7, January 7, 1921; Y. L., "Mitokh mikhtavim pratiim," *Hapoel Hatzair*, 14–15, February 10, 1922. On the debates concerning immigration to Eretz Israel, see for example *Bafrayung*, 1, December 31, 1918, and 4, February 20, 1920; Ben-Hava, "Shtrikhn," *Hehalutz* (Yiddish), 11, February 19, 1920; Oppenheim, *Tnuat Hehalutz be-Polin*, pp. 237 ff. Regarding the attitude of Hehalutz toward *avodat hahoveh* as opposed to that of the Zionist Organization, see for example *Hehalutz* (Yiddish), 3, May 4, 1919; also, 5, May 28, 1919; and a detailed account in Israel Oppenheim, "Yahasav shel 'Hehalutz' be-Polin laavodat hahoveh," part 1, *Measef*, 15, 1985, pp. 119–31; also part 2, 16, pp. 89–95. About the clash over the importance of *hakhsharah*, see for example discussions at the Fourth National Congress of the Zionist Organization in Poland in *Hazfirah*, 36–37, September 4, 1919; *Hehalutz* (Yiddish), 9, December 11, 1919.

23. Eliyahu Dobkin, *Veidatenu hashniah* (Berlin, 1923), pp. 12–18; *Heatid*, 35, April 30, 1926; *Hahlatot vetaarikhim* (Warsaw, 1936), pp. 99–100.

24. *Heatid*, 74–75, August 15, 1929, and *ibid.*,103, September 30, 1930.

25. Yitzhak Tabenkin, from a lecture to the World Congress of Hehalutz, 1926, *Measef litnuat Hehalutz*, pp. 266–67.

26. By 1927 a mere 4,200 members of a total of 13,000 had remained in Hehalutz in Poland. The number of *hakhsharah* members reached 820 at the beginning of the Fifth Aliyah. See *Hahlatot vetaarikhim* (Warsaw, 1935); Otiker, pp. 26, 106–8.

27. See discussion below.

28. See Hayim Fish (Dan), "Din-vaheshbon hamazkirut bemoetzet Kibbutz Klosowa, Dombrowicza, 26–28 Bedetzember 1931," *Yediyes fun merkaz Hehalutz*, 2, Warsaw, January 28, 1932; "Going to the *kibbutz*, too, was a withdrawal from existing society. A Jewish public among gentiles, a public which was closed off [. . . and] isolated. Here it was possible, was necessary to begin everything anew." Also Moshe Braslavsky "Lehearat darkei Hehalutz, *Heatid*, 125, October 15, 1931.

29. See Hayim Dan, compiler and ed., *Sefer Klosowa* (The Ghetto Fighters' House, 1978).

30. I deal with this question in the second volume of *Tnuat Hehalutz be-Polin, 1929–1939* (Ben-Gurion University of the Negev Press, 1993).

31. See *Sefer hashomrim* (Warsaw, 1934); Elkana Margalit, *Tnuat hanoar "Gordonia": Raayon veorah hayim* (Tel Aviv, 1986).

32. See Yaakov Amit, Daniel Ben Nahum, and Levi Dror, eds., *Mireshit ad aharit: Hashomer Hatzair be-Lita* (Givat Haviva, 1985), pp. 94–96.

33. See wording of the agreement in *Heatid*, 6, December 31, 1928. The agreement served as a model in negotiations with other youth movements, such as Hanoar Hazioni and Akiva.

34. Hehalutz Hatzair was established in the initial period of the crisis of the Fourth Aliyah, as a result of the initiative of young people from various regions, particularly that of eastern Poland. See Rivka Perlis, "Hehalutz Hatzair be-Polin berishito: Tnuat noar bezmihatah" *Galed*, 4–5, 1978, pp. 197–229.

35. See Z. Landau and J. Tomaszewski, *Zarys Historii Gospodarczej Polski* (Warsaw, 1981), chap. 5; S. Segal, *The New Poland and the Jews* (New York, 1936), p. 36; J. Marcus, *Social and Political History of the Jews in Poland 1919–1936* (Berlin, New York, and Amsterdam, 1983), parts 2 and 3.

36. About 15–17 cents, at the exchange rate current at the time.

37. Moshe Braslavsky, "Badrakhim," *Heatid*, 123–24, 133–37, 1931–1933.

38. I discuss this period in detail in *Tnuat Hehalutz be-Polin, 1929–1939*.

39. In 1929, Eretz Israel absorbed merely 10 percent of Jewish emigration from Poland. This figure increased to 39.9 percent in 1932, and 80.6 percent in 1935. As a result of limits set on immigration to Eretz Israel, the rate subsequently dropped to 37.6 percent in 1937. See Apolinary Hartglas, "Milhemet yehudei Polin al zkhuyoteihem haleumiyot vehaezrahiyot," in Israel Halperin, ed., *Bet Israel be-Polin*, 2 (Jerusalem, 1948), pp. 128–51, esp. pp. 146–51.

40. In 1928, *hakhsharah* in Poland had 879 members; in 1935 membership rose to as high as 8,500. More impressive was the growth in general membership in Hehalutz. While at the beginning of 1929 there were 4,000 members in the movement, the census for 1935 reveals a total membership of 30,000 in that year. See *Hahlatot vetaarikhim*, p. 100; Shpizman, *Halutzim in Poyln*, pp. 327–28; *Sefer Hehalutz*, p. 417.

41. The figures for December 1935 reveal that 78 percent of the total membership of *hakhsharah* had gone to elementary school, 12 percent had been educated at home, 8.7 percent had received a high school education, and 0.1 percent had received a higher education. The distribution among *hakhsharah* members in Hashomer Hatzair and Gordonia was somewhat different. In Hashomer Hatzair, 82 percent had gone to elementary school, 1.8 percent were educated at home, 15 percent (!) had attended high school, and 0.3 percent had received a higher education. The comparable figures for Gordonia are: 80.7 percent had an elementary school education, 8.2 percent were educated at home, and 11 percent had gone to high school. In the Gush Klali on the other hand, 76.5 percent had gone to elementary school, 16.5 percent (!) were edu-

cated at home, 6.9 percent had gone to high school, and 0.1 percent had received a higher education. See Otiker, p. 165. According to Otiker, not all who reported having a primary or secondary school education had officially completed their studies, so that the educational level was even lower. Moreover, some of those who had reported having been educated had in fact never been educated and were nearly illiterate. See *ibid.*, pp. 166–70.

42. Approximately 70 percent and perhaps more, of the membership that had settled in Eretz Israel left the movement. See the heated discussion in the Secretariat of Hakibbutz Hameuhad at Kibbutz Ramat Hakovesh in 1933. One of the participants was Berl Katznelson, who was highly critical regarding the situation of *hakhsharah* in Poland and Eastern Europe following his inspection tour abroad. He went so far as even to propose that *hakhsharah* should be disbanded. However this was opposed by the delegates from Hakibbutz Hameuhad. Excerpts from the discussion are published in Sarah Segal and Arieh Phialkov, eds., *Shahariyah* (The Ghetto Fighters' House, 1983), pp. 401–12.

43. The various newspapers of Hehalutz and the youth movements offer a thorough account of the problems which preoccupied both the movement as a whole and its sections and affiliated groups. See for example *Heatid*, 1931–1935; *Unzere yediyes*, Yiddish language organ of the Hehalutz Center intended for rank and file members unable to read Hebrew; *Hashomer Hatzair* (adult newspaper); *Gordonia*. Another important source consists of the massive correspondence between the various sections of Hehalutz, between the movement and its membership in Eretz Israel, and between the Hehalutz Center and the Executive Committee of the Histadrut. This material is preserved at The Ghetto Fighters' House, Efal, Givat Haviva, and in Kibbutz Hulda. Significant material is contained as well in the minutes of meetings of the Histadrut Executive Committee, the Mapai Center, the Secretariat of Hakibbutz Hameuhad, the Executive Committee of Hakibbutz Haartzi, and elsewhere.

44. Concerning the extent to which these were reasonable expectations, see Oppenheim, "Mifal hahakhsharah hahalutzit be-Polin ben shtei milhamot haolam," in Menahem Zahari, ed., *Uma velashon: Sefer zikaron le-Aryeh Tartakower* (Jerusalem, 1985), pp. 53–94.

45. See *Measef litnuat Hehalutz*, pp. 315–16; *Heatid*, 134, October 1, 1931; *Unzere yediyes*, 78–79, December 1937. Also see Israel Oppenheim, "Yahaso shel Hehalutz be-Polin leavodat hahoveh," *Measef*, 15, 16.

46. *Heatid*, 135, July 30, 1932.

47. See note 58.

48. On the growing Communist influence among Jewish university students, see H. L. Fish (Dan), Letter to Hehalutz Center, January 26, 1933, Histadrut Executive Committee Archive, Serial No. 868 (old marking); concerning the influence of Betar among the young, see Israel Oppenheim, "Hahakhsharah hakibbutzit shel Betar be-Polin bishnot ha-30 (1936–1940)," *Divrei hacongres haolami hashlishi lemadaei hayahadut*, 2, (Jerusalem, 1976), pp. 295–305.

49. Israel Sheinboim, "Mifal hahakhsharah shelanu," *Heatid*, 11, February 15, 1935.

50. See, for example, *Sefer hashomrim*, pp. 129 ff.

51. Moshe Basok, "Legoralenu hameshutaf," *Heatid*, 130, November 30, 1932. See also discussions at the Plenum of the Hehalutz Center, October 1932, *Beshaah zo* (Warsaw, 1932).

52. See Joint Memorandum of Gordonia and Hashomer Hatzair to the Executive Committee of the Histadrut, *Hashomer Hatzair*, November 14–15, 1933. Also see the many articles appearing on the same topic in the press of the youth movement of the period 1931–1935.

53. On this key concept of social criticism in the youth movement, see Chaim Schatzker,

Tnuat hanoar hayehudit be-Germanyah 1900–1933, a doctoral dissertation (Jerusalem: Hebrew University, 1969); Walter Laqueur, *Young Germany* (London, 1962). On differences and similarities between the youth movements and Hehalutz, see Oppenheim, *Tnuat Hehalutz be-Polin, 1917–1929*, pp. 14–16.

54. See for example Nahum Benari, "Al hinukh kibbutzi," *Heatid*, 152, April 30, 1934. We learn that these accusations were not without foundation from Meir Yaari's article, "Darkenu bagolah." Yaari admits that such tendencies did exist in Hashomer Hatzair, but regards them as marginal and incapable of invalidating the avant-garde conception. He suggests moreover that the same faults could be found among other factions of Hehalutz. See *Sefer hashomrim*, pp. 529–32.

55. The same hope was also shared by persons in the leadership of the Histadrut. Berl Katznelson, reporting on his visit to Poland at the meeting of the Mapai Center on November 24, 1935, was optimistic about the possibility that Hehalutz would eventually expand its membership to include hundreds of thousands of young people. See minutes of the meeting of the Mapai Center, in the Archives of the Histadrut, File 1933.

56. *Dos vort*, 141, December 1933.

57. Regarding the views of the majority, see Moshe Basok, "Lemaan goral meshutaf," *Heatid*, 138, November 30, 1932.

58. See decisions of plenum of the Hehalutz Center, October 1932, *Beshaah zo*, pp. 35–36.

59. Yehuda Gothelf, "Haorganiut hakibbutzit," *Hashomer Hatzair*, 2, February 1, 1933; Feivel Gavze, "Hakhsharah meurevet veotonomit," also, 14–15, November 15, 1933.

60. This question was dealt with at length in the Gdud Haavodah. See *Mehayenu*, organ of Gdud Haavodah, issue of the Arkhion Haavodah, Bibliographical Center of Hakibbutz Hameuhad and Bet Yosef Trumpeldor, Tel Yosef, vol. 1–3, 1971–1973.

61. See *Shahariyah*, pp. 404 ff.

62. See Pinhas Lubianiker (Labon), "Hamashber banoar hayehudi bemizrah Eropah," in Gershon Hanokh, ed, *Darkei hanoar* (Jerusalem, 1937). The article is quoted in Labon's book, *Binetivei iyun umaavak* (Tel Aviv, 1968), pp. 220 ff. See also Eliezer Liebenstein (Livneh), "Gorala shel tnuat hanoar haivrit: Darkei hinukh," pp. 50–60.

63. Hershl Pinsky to the Executive Committee of the Histadrut, June 1, 1930. The letter was published posthumously in *Hapoel Hatzair*, 16–17, January 28, 1935.

64. For their reasons, see *Shahariyah*, pp. 410–11, 414.

65. See H. Shinar, "Halutsim in der kibutsisher hakhshore loyt a tseylung fun oktober 1936," *Yidishe Ekonomik* (Warsaw, 1937), pp. 204–6. The decline was felt in all countries in which the Hehalutz organization was active—apart from when the movement did finally decline in Germany, the effect was more moderate than elsewhere. The sharpest decline relative to the total Jewish population was in Romania, followed by Czechoslovakia and Poland. See also circular letter of the World Center of Hehalutz, February 4, 1935, File 018.

66. The total number emigrating from Europe to Eretz Israel in 1935 was 61,854; in 1936 the figure was 24,727; in 1937 it was 10,536; and in 1938 it was 12,866. See Shpizman, *Halutzim in Poyln*, p. 277.

67. *Unzere yediyes*, 1, April 18, 1938.

68. *Hashomer Hatzair*, 3, February 1, 1938.

69. Zeev Blokh. "Mitn ponim tsu der yugnt," *Unzere yediyes*, anniversary issue, March 1938. See also various articles written in the same spirit in *Hashomer Hatzair*, 1938–1939.

70. Avraham Tarshish, "Im hatmurot," *Heatid*, anniversary issue, March 1938; *Sefer Hehalutz*, pp. 516–17.

71. *Unzere yediyes*, 87, March 1938; also, 88, April 1939.

12.

Ideology and Structure in German Zionism, 1882–1933

Jehuda Reinharz

Until World War I the Zionistische Vereinigung für Deutschland (hereafter called ZVfD)[1] was the most influential branch of the World Zionist Organization (hereafter called WZO). The strength of the German Zionists lay in the personal qualities of some of their leaders and in the fact that the offices of the WZO were in Cologne (1905–1911) and Berlin (1911–1920). German influence was greater than the actual membership figures of the ZVfD would suggest, in comparison with other national Zionist organizations. Before 1914, the highest estimate of Zionist members in Germany was 10,000, yet the ZVfD was more vital and active than many larger branches in other countries. To a great extent the leadership of the German and WZO was identical. This ever-present support of the WZO gave the ZVfD the stamina to withstand attacks by the large German Jewish organizations such as the Central-Verein deutscher Staatsbürger jüdischen Glaubens (hereafter called C.-V.) whose individual membership reached close to 40,000 in the pre-1914 period, and as many as 70,000 in the Weimar period.

At the central offices of the WZO, the members of the ZVfD constituted most of the staff and heads of departments. While the central office of the WZO was located in Cologne, David Wolffsohn and Otto Warburg were members of the Engeres Aktions-Comité (hereafter called E.A.C.) of the WZO. During the years in which the central office was located in Berlin, Otto Warburg and Arthur Hantke were members of the E.A.C. From 1905 to 1911, David Wolffsohn, one of the ZVfD cofounders, was president of the WZO, and Otto Warburg was chair-

Reprinted by permission of *Jewish Social Studies* 42 (spring 1980): 119–46.

man of the E.A.C. from 1911 until Chaim Weizmann took office in 1920 with the transfer of the central office to London. Before 1920, therefore, the leadership of the WZO and that of the ZVfD often over-lapped; the most striking example is Arthur Hantke, who from 1911 until 1920 served simultaneously as chairman *(Vorsitzender)* of the ZVfD and as a member of the E.A.C.

Many of the men who led the ZVfD in the 1920s acquired their initial training and experience in the offices of the WZO in Berlin; among them were Kurt Blumenfeld, Richard Lichtheim and Martin Rosenblüth. All the important publications and offices of the WZO were located in Germany and to a considerable extent were staffed by German Zionists. Full cooperation between the ZVfD and the WZO was symbolized by the fact that both organizations were located in the same building in Berlin, at Sächsische Strasse 8. Meetings of the E.A.C. were often held in Berlin, and thus many leaders of Eastern European Zionism came into direct contact and were influenced by ideas and ideologies current in the German movement, which in turn influenced their counterparts.

The influence of the ZVfD within the WZO declined during World War I owing to the need to keep the World Organization as neutral as possible. After the war, when the official headquarters of the WZO were transferred to London, its influence within the general movement waned even further. Nevertheless, the ZVfD, which now numbered some 20,000 members, continued to play an important role in the intellectual life of World Zionism. Many of its members were active in the E.A.C. and Grosses Aktions-Comité (hereafter called G.A.C.) and other interna-tional Zionist institutions.

The task of writing the history of the Zionistische Vereinigung für Deutschland is not easy. The archives of the ZVfD have been lost and, to date, their location, if indeed they are still extant, has not been determined. Historians are thus dependent on those letters, memoranda and other correspondence sent by the ZVfD to the WZO headquarters in London or on the personal files of active Zionists such as Salman Schocken, Max Bodenheimer, Alfred Klee and others. Based on these documents the attempt will be made to delineate here four main stages in the development of German Zionism: the period of scattered national organizations which developed prior to the formal constitution of Ger-man Zionists into the ZVfD; the period of organizational and ideologi-cal crystallization between 1897 and 1914; the special situation created by World War I; and the transformation and development of German Zionism during the Weimar Republic.

One can start the writing of the history of German Zionism in 1882, although many question marks and problems in the choice of this date exist. There are a number of "Lovers of Zion" groups (Zionsfreunde, later known as Hoveve Zion), and individual thinkers in Germany throughout the nineteenth century with whom one could conceivably commence this history. In a somewhat arbitrary fashion one can start with the beginning of organized and sustained activity on German soil which seems to have had a lasting and wide impact in the years to come. Thus this history begins with the B'nai B'rith of Kattowitz. For most of the nineteenth century, religious motivations were the primary factors in the activities of German Jews on behalf of Palestine. From the early 1880s on, a new chapter opens when, beside the religious factors, there are also practical, moral, and philanthropic elements coupled with national motivations as well. These changes in ideology within the German borders are intimately tied to the events in Eastern Europe as well as to the rise of political and racial antisemitism in the West.

Following the murder of Tsar Alexander II on 13 March 1881 a reactionary government under Alexander III came to power in Russia. Shortly after the new tsar's accession to the throne, a wave of pogroms spread throughout southern Russia during the summer months destroying more than a hundred Jewish communities. The official reactionary policy of the new regime condoned the pogroms and instituted the May Laws of 1882 limiting Russian Jews to the Pale of Settlement. The persecution of the Jews continued into the 1890s. Under the reign of Nikolai II (term 1894–1917), ruthless pogroms and expulsions persisted with governmental approval.[2]

The pogroms of 1881 were a turning point in Jewish history. They shattered forever any hope of real emancipation in Eastern Europe. The largest emigration and population transfer in Jewish history followed, whereby most of the emigrés went to the United States. This large-scale movement also affected Germany and German Jewry. From the turn of the century until World War I, Germany shared a border with Russia. Owing to its geographical proximity and access to the sea, Germany became the transit country for Eastern European Jews traveling to the United States. Not all of them who passed through Germany reached their overseas destination; under some circumstances, or for a variety of personal reasons, many chose to settle in Germany. During these years, therefore, the number of Eastern European Jews in Germany increased dramatically. The philanthropic organizations of Western Jewry, and foremost among them the German Jewish organizations, undertook to help these Eastern European Jews but above all to organize and direct the emigration to America and other countries.[3]

In general, the pogroms had great impact on some segments of German Jewry and helped shape their attitudes toward settlement in Palestine. Throughout the nineteenth century efforts to rebuild and settle Palestine or to help its Jewish inhabitants came from Orthodox circles whose motivations were religious and philanthropic. Following the pogroms, and the reawakening of national feelings among East European Jewry, an increasing number of German Jews began to talk about the settlement of Palestine within a Jewish national context. Plans for rebuilding Palestine became more concrete now and those who joined associations which promoted such ideas were no longer solely of an Orthodox background. The main problem of these new associations was to find financial support for the execution of their ideas.[4]

The first such association to be founded in Germany in May 1882 was the B'nai B'rith of Kattowitz founded by Selig Freuthal and Moritz Moses. The association, which had some fifty members, was also in touch with similar associations in Russia, Rumania and Austria. It published an information bulletin *(Monatsbericht)* and, toward the end of 1882, it began the publication of *Der Colonist,* which became a weekly in 1883. This was the first organ of German Jewry wholly devoted to matters concerning Palestine.[5]

At the initiative of the B'nai B'rith association, a conference was convened in Kattowitz in November 1884 of all the Hoveve Zion associations throughout Europe concerned with the settlement of Palestine. These associations elected a central committee headed by Leon Pinsker. In Hamburg, the founding of Ahavass Zijon in May 1885 was a direct result of this conference.[6] Pinsker had a staunch supporter in Germany in the person of Rabbi Isaak Rülf of Memel who for some twenty years already had been a member of the Israelitischer Verein zur Kolonisation von Palästina. Under the impact of Pinsker's *Autoemancipation* (1882), Rülf published his *Aruchas Bas-Ammi,* which demanded a return to Palestine.[7]

Prior to the Kattowitz Conference, in early 1884, two more associations were established; one in Heidelberg, called Zion, was founded by Hermann Schapira whose main aims were "the spread of knowledge of Hebrew history, language and literature among Jews . . . the colonization of Palestine by Jews."[8] Response to this association was meager and it did not accomplish much. In January 1884 a group of young men founded the Verein Esra, Sammelbüchse für Palästina in Berlin for the purpose of encouraging settlement in Palestine. The national element in this effort was not overt, yet it must be counted as one of the first manifestations of Jewish nationalism in Germany.[9] An important step forward in the reawakening of the Jewish national spirit in Germany was the founding by the leading members of "Esra" of the monthly *Serubabel* in September 1886 which replaced the defunct *Selbst-Emancipation*.[10] For the next two years it became the main spokesman for the various Hoveve Zion groups in Germany. It closed publication in July 1888 for lack of funds. Shortly before the demise of *Serubabel*, another association, Lema'an Zion, was founded in May 1888 at the initiative of Rabbi Esriel Hildesheimer.[11] Its character, aims and organizational framework differed from those of the "Esra." The board of this association consisted of Jews opposed to the *Halukah* system—the organized collection of funds in the diaspora for distribution among needy Jews in Palestine—hitherto prevalent. It encouraged self-sufficiency among Palestinian Jewry, fought against missionary activities, and tried to settle Jews in Arab villages and towns.

The first consciously nationalist group in Germany was the Russischer jüdischer wissenschaftlicher Verein founded in December 1888. Its charter members were twelve Russian Jewish students joined by Heinrich Loewe of Wanzleben who sought to alleviate the plight of those Jewish refugees who passed through Germany.[12] A counterpart to the Russian association was established by Heinrich Loewe in May 1892 in Berlin. It was called Jung Israel and it sought to attract German Jews into its ranks. As the Hoveve Zion movement in Germany gained momentum, it was decided to move the center of Zionist activity from Vienna to Berlin and, after the *Selbst-Emancipation* folded once more because of financial difficulties in 1893, it was transferred to Berlin under the name *Jüdische Volkszeitung, früher Selbst-Emancipation*. Thus this organ and the Jung Israel became the new focal point for Jewish national activity in Germany.[13]

Despite its efforts, the ability of Jung Israel to attract German-born Jews to its ranks were unsuccessful. Apparently its twenty-odd members were still too "radical" to attract the sons of the well-to-do Jewish middle class. The indefatigable Heinrich Loewe, Max Bodenheimer and Max Oppenheimer, therefore, founded the Jüdische Humanitätsgesellschaft in 1893, whose program was as vague as its name. Perhaps because of this haziness, which merely demanded the fostering of Jewish self-awareness, it was more successful in attracting academic youth to its ranks.[14] On 4 July 1895 Jung Israel and the Jüdische Humanitätsgesellschaft merged to form the Vereinigung Jüdischer Studierender (hereafter called V.J.St.), which changed its name around 1900 to Verein Jüdischer Studenten an der Universität Berlin (hereafter called V.J.St. Berlin).[15] This group was in sympathy with the emerging Zionist movement and can therefore be recognized as the forerunner of the Kartell Jüdischer Verbindungen (hereafter called K.J.V.).[16]

The outlines of the K.J.V. history are well-known. On 16 January 1901 the V.J.St. Berlin and like-minded fraternities in Leipzig, Breslau and Munich founded the Bund Jüdischer Corporationen (hereafter called B.J.C.). Almost concurrently, the Freie Verbindung Hasmonäa was founded in 1902 at the University of Berlin. Its founder was Egon Rosenberg, who had belonged to the Zionist fraternity Veritas in Brünn. The Hasmonäa was explicitly founded to further the Zionist idea. In 1905 a similar fraternity in Munich joined the Hasmonäa and on 11 January 1906 they formed the Kartell Zionistischer Verbindungen (hereafter called K.Z.V.). Over the next decade the B.J.C. also became more explicitly Zionist and the two student federations (B.J.C. and K.Z.V.) merged on 19 July 1914 to form the K.J.V.[17]

After 1918 there were reforms in the K.J.V. which allowed for much greater flexibility in ideology. About 130–150 members disagreed with these reforms and, in 1919, established their own organization, the Bund Zionistischer Korporationen (hereafter called B.Z.K.). In Berlin they were called the Kadimah. The spirit behind the B.Z.K. was Isaak Zwirn. They were for the most part more conservative. This Bund lasted as a separate academic organization until 1929 when it rejoined the K.J.V.

Early in 1891, a young lawyer from Cologne, Max Bodenheimer, published a pamphlet called *Wohin mit den russischen Juden? Syrien ein Zufluchtsort der russischen Juden* in which he advocated the settlement of the Eastern European Jews in Syria and Palestine, both to protect them and to rehabilitate them socially in occupations such as farming and crafts. (In the same year the less well-known brochure by Paul Demidow—pseudonym for Isaak Turoff—*Wo hinaus? Mahnruf an die Westeuropäischen Juden* also appeared). Bodenheimer's brochure appeared in many copies. It proved useful in making contact with other Hoveve Zion groups in Germany and abroad. In July 1891 an initiative came from circles close to Nathan Birnbaum; it was suggested that a conference be convened in Paris of all leaders of the Hoveve Zion associations. Birnbaum informed Bodenheimer of this plan whereupon the latter published in the Hamburg *Menorah*, "Zionists of All Lands Unite!"[18]

In February 1896 Theodor Herzl's *Der Judenstaat* appeared. His political plans for the attainment of Palestine were immediately accepted by most Hoveve Zion groups in Germany. His pamphlet proved divisive; some of them joined his movement and some, such as Willy Bambus and Hirsch Hildesheimer, preferred practical settlement over political solutions. German Zionists, such as Bodenheimer, who supported Herzl's basic position, became political Zionists but with certain modifications. Bodenheimer took care not to disrupt the civil and political status of German Zionists and the community in general. In 1896 he founded with Wolffsohn and others the National-jüdische Vereinigung in Köln. The statutes confirmed the ethnic bonds of the German Zionists to the Jewish people, but they also emphasized patriotism toward Germany.[19]

Soon after, Herzl issued the call for the first Zionist congress in Munich, whereupon a chorus of protest arose from the Munich Jewish Community. Rabbis Sigmund Maybaum (Berlin) and Heinemann Vogelstein (Stettin)—dubbed by Herzl as the "Protestrabbiner"—denounced Herzl's plan on religious, political and practical grounds. They were fearful lest the Zionist movement taint their loyalty to the fatherland.[20] The effect of these reactions became apparent at the first *Delegiertentag* (hereafter called Convention) of German Zionists which took place in Bingen on 11 July 1897. The first order of the day was the formulation of a response to the rabbis. Paragraph two of the Zionist declaration, however, reaffirmed loyalty to Germany. The delegates *(Delegierten)* also agreed that it was the duty of Jews to help their suffering brethren as long as this did not compromise their civic duties *(Staatsbürgerpflichten)*. Phrases like "building a state" or "Jewish state" were avoided.

At Bingen the National-jüdische Vereinigung Köln changed its name to National-jüdische Vereinigung für Deutschland.[21] The organizational procedures were completed during two later meetings which took place the same year in Basel on 28 August and in Frankfurt am Main on 31 October where, in order not to offend the sensibilities of the majority of German Jewry, it was decided unanimously to adopt as the name of the organization Zionistische Vereinigung für Deutschland (ZVfD). This change in name was caused by the insistence of Professor Hermann Schapira who felt that the name Zionistische Vereinigung would be less offensive or threatening to German Jews, than the name National-jüdische Vereinigung, since it would be less likely to be open to interpretation as adherence to a nation other than Germany.[22]

Despite repeated reassurance by the Zionists of their loyalty to Germany,[23] there were vociferous anti-Zionist voices heard from liberal as well as Orthodox circles, from rabbis and their congregations *(Gemeinden)*, as well as from individuals. As of 1897 the ZVfD became a fermenting element in German Jewry and the Zionists were perceived as a threat by many to a continuation of the process of assimilation and integration. The Zionists were not too concerned with statements by anti-Zionists that Jewish nationalism was contrary to the Jewish religion since, for the most part, such attacks did not have political consequences. They responded to such attacks sporadically. The Zionists were all the more sensitive to accusations that their Jewish nationalism detracted from their German patriotism. This was one charge that could not stand unchallenged. Until the demise of the ZVfD in the 1930s, the Zionists repeated in innumerable articles, pamphlets, and speeches, that there was no conflict between one's nationality and one's citizenship *(Staatsbürgertum)*.[24] In addition, during the presidency of Max Bodenheimer from 1897–1910, the ZVfD tended to present a non-doctrinaire ideology which carefully toned down the national character of Jewry. This policy tended to downgrade the attacks against Zionism. The Jewish organizations preferred to conduct a policy of silence on Zionist matters *(Totschweigen)*, which was founded on the assumption that to deny publicity to the Zionists would undermine their organization and purpose.

The newly founded group needed an open forum. In 1896, therefore, the German Zionists used the *Israelitische Rundschau* as their official organ. In 1901 the ZVfD purchased the paper.[25] Heinrich Loewe became its editor under the condition that its name be changed to *Jüdische Rundschau*, the title it retained until 1938. In 1919, Robert Weltsch, a former member of the Bar Kochba group of Prague, became the editor of this publication, a position he held until 1938. It is estimated that the number of Zionist periodicals in Germany between 1897 and 1938 was thirty-nine.[26] This profusion of literature and propaganda is an indication of the prolific and energetic Zionist activity in Germany. The official publishing house of the WZO, the Jüdischer Verlag in Berlin, was founded in 1902.[27] Outstanding intellectuals within the movement contributed to its publications, and it became the cultural center for the German Zionists and the WZO.

The Zionist publications in Germany rarely reported contemporary political events and developments unless they were of direct interest to the Zionist cause. Until the last years of the Weimar Republic the

Jüdische Rundschau dealt with the problem of antisemitism when the editor and the leadership of the ZVfD perceived the need to do so in the wake of particular political, social or economic events. The subject, however, did not preoccupy the Zionist press. The Zionists believed that efforts at defense on the model of the Central-Verein were doomed to failure because the Jewish problem was a condition of life in the diaspora. This problem could not be solved through the courts or other legal means. Thus concern with antisemitism was often relegated to secondary importance in German Zionist ideology, but during certain emergencies the Zionists did modify their positions. In 1930, for example, the Zionists worked closely with the Central-Verein deutscher Staatsbürger jüdischen Glaubens during the Reichstag elections, which were accompanied by particularly violent outbreaks against Jews. Even during their few weeks of cooperation, however, the Zionists disassociated themselves from the ideology of the C.-V. and other organizations.[28]

The Zionists declared that antisemitism could not be eradicated either by enlightenment or by Jewish assimilation. To counteract assimilation, the Zionists sought to educate Jews in self-reliance and national pride. As a base and target for these activities, some Zionists chose the Jewish communities, and promoted their ideas there. Since most Jewish communities were opposed to the Zionist aims, the Zionists entered a few community elections as early as 1901 and thus tried to gain influence.[29]

One of the most active and effective instruments in this struggle was the Jüdische Volkspartei (hereafter called JVP), led for many years by Max Kollenscher and Alfred Klee. Their aim was to transform the communities, which had become religious and philanthropic bureaucracies, into institutions that would serve all the needs of their residents. The leadership of the ZVfD initially opposed these demands. Until the mid-1920s the ZVfD considered that the efforts of the JVP contributed very little to Zionist goals. In the twenties, however, it began to devote some of its energies to the politics of the Jewish communities and created a Gemeinde-Kommission.[30] Despite the reluctant cooperation of the ZVfD, the JVP managed to make considerable progress within the German Jewish community, and from 1926 to 1930, even managed to dominate the board of the Berlin Jewish community.

It is clear that the adherents to the JVP were in the minority. The theories of political, autonomous, practical and cultural Zionism influenced German Zionism at various times and to varying degrees, but in the period from 1897 to 1910 it was largely Herzl's influence that shaped the ideology of the first generation of German Zionists. Bodenheimer, and others who had been early members of Hoveve Zion groups that supported settlement in Palestine, rallied around Herzl's strict opposition to "infiltration" although they did not agree with all his policies. His leadership was sought, because he was regarded as the only man capable of unifying the scattered and ineffective Hoveve Zion groups. In general, the ZVfD maintained a tradition of loyalty to the leadership of the WZO, a factor which was clearly manifested in their support of Herzl's Uganda proposal.[31]

Despite their adherence to Herzl's political ideology, the early German Zionists differed with his conception of the Jews' position in the diaspora. They insisted on their status as German citizens, and unlike Herzl, took seriously their problem of dual loyalty as Germans and Zionists. They urged their followers to participate in their country's cultural, economic and political life in order to hasten the acquisition of Palestine as an end in itself. They agreed with Herzl's view that it was futile to establish separate Jewish political parties, but they refused to accept his appraisal of Zionists' life in the diaspora as meaningless.

Unlike Herzl, the first generation of German Zionists did not reject Jewish life in the diaspora. This group continued to live in Germany and considered themselves worthy Germans by virtue of their sociocultural values and their unquestioned loyalty to the fatherland. Nevertheless, they advocated a conscious fostering of Jewish ethnic and national traits as instruments to inform Jewish youth of its heritage. They considered emancipation a humanitarian and charitable act but also a piece of legislation which was built on the illusion that political emancipation would solve the "Jewish Problem." Contrary to the position of the majority of German Jewry as characterized by the liberal/assimilationist Central-Verein, the German Zionists rejected the equations of citizenship with acceptance into German nationality or the German Volk. Instead they claimed that whereas Jews could never become fully integrated into the German nation, they had the right to preserve their own ethnicity within the framework of remaining loyal Germans.[32]

Although the ZVfD mainstream did not observe religious ritual, but like the Central-Verein was religiously liberal, the Zionists considered themselves the true representatives of Jewish culture. In contrast to the liberals, however, the Zionists felt a common bond of Volk and nationality with Jews throughout the world. This feeling was intensified during World War I when they actually encountered Eastern European Jews (Ostjuden). Their sense of common responsibility derived from their perception of the Jews as a scattered, but autonomous, people.[33]

The ZVfD had grown up in the cultural and political milieu of late nineteenth century Wilhelminian Germany. Despite their official adherence to Zionist ideology by virtue of their common background, age, and upbringing, this first generation of German Zionists, possessed a Weltanschauung similar to that of the C.-V. members. Both groups had had the same formative generational experience: they were "men of honor" who had founded Jewish organizations in defiance of antisemitic insults and threats encountered during their student years. Both sets of leadership came from the middle class and the same socioeconomic background and entered professions that gained them a place in the middle and upper-middle classes. Most German Zionists were as completely estranged from the Jewish religion as were most German Jews. Their children received the same education as that of other middle-class liberal Jews, an education that in no way emphasized Jewish or Hebrew culture.

Dissimilar to members of the C.-V., however, the first generation of German Zionists gave at least equal weight in their Weltanschauung to Jewishness *(Judentum)* and German values *(Deutschtum)*. Nevertheless, their concern for things Jewish, such as Jewish folklore, Hasidism, and the Jewish colonies in Palestine, often remained an individual matter or the subject of interesting articles in the *Jüdische Rundschau*. They did not attempt to devise even a limited cultural program in the diaspora. Since they did not make any personal or practical application of their theory of Jewish nationalism, they were tolerated by the other Jewish liberal organizations as members of just another philanthropic group. For the founding members of the ZVfD it was always clear that their personal destinies were in Germany. Their Zionist ideology provided them with a systematic world-view that anchored them in Germany and enabled them to see their Jewish identity as compatible with German culture. In essence, the program of the first generation of German Zionists was almost solely directed to the suffering Jews of the East. It was not designed to change the lives of its adherents in Germany.[34]

This point of view persisted until 1910–1912. Shortly thereafter radical revisions in the ideology of German Zionists were made in response to changes in the WZO and to the new experiences encountered by the second generation of young German Zionists. On the one hand, these younger men were influenced by the general trend within the World Organization toward practical and cultural work in Palestine and the diaspora and by the ideas of Ahad Ha'am and to some degree by Martin Buber. Their ideological orientation become a composite whose main features were influenced by Herzl's negation of the diaspora and Buber's admonition to search for their roots in Judaism.

On the other hand, Zionist youth of pre-World War I Germany was influenced by the ideas that permeated Western European middle-class youth: a rejection of the mechanization and self-satisfaction of bourgeois ideology. These young men turned instead to nature, simplicity, and comradeship. The activities and ideology of German youth were highly regarded by the young Zionists. Soon Jewish scout groups *(Wanderbünde)* developed which initially imitated the German Wandervogel and were later transformed into groups directed primarily toward Jewish fulfillment (Blau-Weiss).[35]

The young Zionists understood the "Jewish Question" in a manner completely different from that of the "confession-oriented" Jews of the older generation. They criticized both the older Zionists and the members of the C.-V. as assimilationists of the worst kind. These "radicals" felt that assimilation into the German Volk was undesirable and unattainable. Unlike the members of the older generation, these young Zionists intended to act on their theories. Although they had borrowed some of their ideals from the same intellectual sources which shaped the Wandervogel, they stressed their dissimilarity from the rest of the German population in custom, habit, and innermost being. These men were no longer satisfied with clichés and conventional ideas. Like many members of the European youth of the period, they, too, searched for roots and a new, wholesome identity. In turn this search led to endless discussions about *Deutschtum-Judentum-Zionismus;* debates with anti-Zionists and others forced new definitions and redefinitions of concepts and ideas and a constantly evolving reevaluation of themselves and their Zionist ideology.[36]

The young generation within the ZVfD formulated its Weltanschauung into a program between 1910 and 1912. In 1909 the ZVfD appointed Kurt Blumenfeld, a man of brilliant ideas and an excellent orator, as party secretary and official propagandist. Insofar as historical change can be attributed to a single personality, one can attribute Blumenfeld with altering the ideological course of the ZVfD between 1910 and 1914. Challenging the political-philanthropic orientation of their elders, the young second-generation German Zionists recognized in Blumenfeld their most capable spokesman and interpreter of Zionism within the context of German cultural and political conditions. He was immediately successful in winning over to his ideology the contemporary Zionist student and youth movements.[37]

Blumenfeld's conflict with the liberal Jewish middle class began with a rebellion against the ideology of the older generation of German Zionists. The young Zionists very often came from the same assimilated background as their elders but their differences of Weltanschauung stemmed from differences in their generational experiences with antisemitism, from dissatisfaction with what the other generation had failed to accomplish, and from ideological, practical, and political transformations that had taken place within the ZVfD and WZO. Buber's exhortations, coupled with lessons they extracted for their Jewish purposes from German sources, made the young Zionists reject all that interfered with their Zionist convictions. Whereas the first generation of German Zionists had been content to wait in Germany for a charter for the Eastern European Jews, the young Zionists declared, in fact, that all who did not incorporate Palestine into their life's program were not true Zionists.

Thus the radical Zionists could not accept compromise, either with early Zionism or with the liberal establishment. They tried to achieve a modicum of consistency by seeking to put their theories into practice. Their achievements before 1914 were threefold: the formulation of a theory to express their existential needs; the break with the ideology of the liberal establishment and first-generation Zionists; and the systematic ideological indoctrination of their members to the end that they should maintain a "distance" between themselves and German nationalism.

As a tiny minority within a hostile Jewish community, the young Zionists could succeed only through the process of radicalization.[38] An important catalyst in this process and in heightened Jewish nationalism was the Posen Resolution of May 1912, which adopted the concept of Palestine-orientation *(Palästinozentrismus)* as a cornerstone of the ideology of the ZVfD. With this resolution the Zionists declared that Palestine was part of their personal goal.[39] It was at best a vague resolution, but in the eyes of the older generation of German Zionists and especially the non-Zionist and anti-Zionist majority of the German Jewish community, the resolution was interpreted as a radical statement which was fought and denounced on many occasions.[40] The older generation of German Zionists, which had espoused a political-philanthropic version of Zionism, could not ignore the changes that occurred within the ZVfD between 1912 and 1914. Just as the rest of the German Jewish community, they saw their very existence, their most basic ideological principles, threatened by the radical statements of members of the younger generation. When, despite their vehement protests, the Leipzig

Convention of 1914 confirmed the ideology of Blumenfeld and his followers most of them resigned from all active positions within the ZVfD.[41]

By 1 August 1914 the Zionist position in Germany had become well-defined. World War I showed, however, that the radicalization of the Zionists had not yet struck deep enough roots. When called upon, the Zionists, like the rest of the German Jewish community, felt committed to aid the fatherland.[42] There were only few exceptions among the many Zionists who felt that Germany's war was not their cause and who counseled the Jewish youth to fight instead for the Zionist cause.[43] The war also affected relations within the German Jewish community. In view of the Zionists' patriotism and self-sacrifice, the Central-Verein and other anti-Zionist organizations halted their attacks against them and acknowledged their contribution to the war effort. For nearly four years all bitterness and strife between Zionists and anti-Zionists was kept to a minimum.

World War I presented the German Zionists with new challenges. Like all German Jews, the Zionists also believed that a German victory was Russian Jewry's only chance of liberation from tsarist persecution. At the same time they could present the Jews of Eastern Europe as potentially valuable allies of the Central Powers. Some Zionists believed that no time should be lost in aiding the Eastern European Jews. Millions of Jews were caught between the battling armies. Masses of refugees fled before the advancing Russian forces. Hundreds of thousands of Jews were forcibly evacuated from the front lines by the Russians.

On 6 December 1914 the Germans captured Lodz. Between May and September 1915, they took many towns and cities with large Jewish communities, including Libau, Kovno and Warsaw. By September 1915, almost half the Jews of Russia were living in Polish, Lithuanian and White Russian sectors under German occupation.[44] There were about 100,000 Jews under arms in Germany of which at least 78 per cent saw front line action.[45] Among the Jewish soldiers were many Zionists who encountered their Yiddish-speaking brethren for the first time. They were deeply impressed by the solidarity and the inward Jewish piety which they observed, and by the feeling of comradeship and hospitality with which they were met.

A concrete attempt to aid Eastern European Jewry was made soon after the outbreak of the War. On 4 August 1914, Max Bodenheimer, at the time chairman of the Jewish National Fund, submitted a memorandum to the German Ministry of Foreign Affairs showing how the support of Eastern European Jewry could be enlisted in furthering Germany's aim to destroy the tsarist Russian Empire.[46] As a result of the memorandum and of subsequent discussions with German officials, it was decided to form the Komitee für den Osten. Some of the more prominent members of the older generation of German Zionists headed the "Komitee" with the tacit approval of the WZO. The main aims of the "Komitee" were the protection of the rights of Eastern European Jewry and the hopes of furthering Zionist goals through the support of German war efforts. Much to the disappointment of Bodenheimer and his associates, the German government showed increasing coolness toward the work of the "Komitee." Similarly, after an initial approval, the official leadership of both the E.A.C. and the ZVfD dissociated themselves from the "Komitee" for fear that its policies endangered the larger Zionist cause through too close an identification with the German war aims. By 1916 the "Komitee" was confining its work to philanthropic activities.[47]

Another area of concern for the German Zionists was the fate of Palestinian Jewry. When the First World War began, the *Yishuv*, the Jewish settlement in Palestine, was placed in a precarious position. Blockaded by the Allied fleet, denied access to Western markets, the country faced economic paralysis. Even the flow of the *Halukah* money was stopped. Meanwhile, Djemal Pasha, the Turkish governor of Palestine, subjected the *Yishuv* to a continuous barrage of harassments and persecutions. The political fate of the *Yishuv* was unclear. Turkey had been counted as an historic British ally, but at the very beginning of the war, it joined the Central Powers. The German Zionists, as well as Zionists throughout the world, tried to prevent the persecution of the *Yishuv* by appealing to the Sublime Port directly.[48] At the same time, they also tried to obtain the support of the German Foreign Office, which, as a rule, intervened in response to such requests, being conscious of the fact that Zionism might indeed be a helpful ally in its future Middle East politics.[49] On the other hand, Germany's foreign policy regarding the fate of Jews in Palestine and Eastern Europe was not matched by its internal policy toward its own Jewish citizens. The directive by the War Ministry *(Kriegsministerium)* of 11 October 1916 to count the number of Jewish soldiers in the German army shocked and dismayed the Zionists no less than other segments of German Jewry.[50] The German Kaiser's words at the inception of the war: "I don't recognize any parties, I know only Germans," apparently did not apply to Jews.

While it became clear that even the war had not succeeded in accomplishing a genuine peace between Germans and Jews, Kurt Blumenfeld suggested a closing of ranks or at least an alliance within the German Jewish community itself. In an article titled "Innere Politik" in the newly established *Der Jude* of February 1917, he contrasted Zionism with the assimilated segments of Jewry. Having stated that a full understanding between these two camps was not possible, he nevertheless suggested a so-called *Bündnispolitik:* limited cooperation between Zionists and non-Zionists for specific purposes and for limited goals. In the midst of the war this suggestion by Blumenfeld did not find a response, but his ideas for cooperation with non-Zionists finally materialized in the 1920s in two institutions: the Keren Hayesod and the Jewish Agency. True to his ideology, however, even when Blumenfeld cooperated with non-Zionists on practical issues, he nevertheless waged a sharp ideological fight against them.

In the minds of some Zionists the war did not spark ideas for constructive Zionist work *in Germany,* with or without non-Zionists. They were concerned by the compromises with their Zionist ideology which were necessarily components of life in Germany. As in the period prior to 1914 these young men called their friends to take the logical step of immigrating to Palestine immediately after the war before they had a chance to strike deeper economic and professional roots in Germany.[51] Although the signers of this appeal met with some vehement objections, their proclamation received an unexpected political boost with the Balfour Declaration issued on 2 November 1917.[52] Shortly thereafter the German government, too, endorsed the Zionist goals in Palestine in a special declaration on 5 January 1918.[53]

The German government also supported in the spring of 1918 the establishment of the Deutsches Komitee Pro Palästina whose aims were "To alert German public opinion to the political significance of Jewish striving for settlement in Palestine as it is crystallized in Zionism." The activities of this committee ceased naturally in 1919.[54] In November 1926, following Germany's admission to the League of Nations, the Pro Palästina Komitee was reorganized. Its aim was to gain support in private and government circles for the Zionist endeavor in Palestine. Again the German Foreign Office showed some interest in the "Komitee" which it viewed as an instrument through which economic ties with Palestine could be developed. In addition, it meant to use the "Komitee" to further its relations with the Zionist leadership.[55]

In short, then, the period just prior to and following the end of World

War I seemed to the ZVfD and Zionists everywhere as an era of promise, and of constructive Zionist work both in the diaspora and in Palestine. From a narrower perspective, the ZVfD now lost its prominent role within the WZO. Germany's defeat was coupled with a transfer of the WZO headquarters from Berlin to London. The center of power was in England and, to an increasing degree, Polish and American Jewry gained in prominence. The ZVfD lost its central role in shaping Zionist policy, though it still retained an important part in shaping its ideology. At the same time, within the German Jewish community, the ZVfD now occupied a more respected and respectable position than it did prior to 1914. This, of course, was caused by the international recognition of Zionism as a political force with which to be reckoned. The immediate result of this new position was the general toning down of anti-Zionist propaganda within Germany. For a while, the ZVfD was seen by the rest of the German Jewish community as an equal, but this newly-found influence did not last for more than a few years.

In the turmoil that accompanied the German defeat and the revolutionary occurrences of November 1918, only the Zionists were ready to step forward with a program for immediate action. Their main aim was to create a *Kongress* movement in Germany similar to the one created in the United States, Russia, Austria and the Austrian successor states. This congress, which would constitute a component part of the Jewish World Congress Movement, would express the disposition and the demands of Jewry as a whole before the Peace Conference. The ZVfD also regarded the congress movement in Germany as a fitting instrument for establishing an autonomous representation of the Jews in Germany. The Zionist plan found a remarkable echo among German Jewry and almost succeeded but, mainly owing to the opposition of the Central-Verein, it failed by the end of 1919.[56]

The experiences of World War I—the encounter with Eastern European Jewry, the heightened degree of antisemitism in the army and elsewhere in the German population and the Balfour Declaration among others—greatly affected German Zionism. The realities of the post-World War I period presented new challenges to the Zionist youth in Germany. The founding of the Keren Hayesod, the British Mandate, the struggle of the *Yishuv* to expand its economic and political base, the cooperation with non-Zionists culminating in the founding of the Jewish Agency and the tremendous increase in antisemitism in Germany between 1918–1923, all demanded new, far-reaching commitments from each Zionist and a revised assessment of his identity as a Jewish nationalist living in Germany.[57]

New trends appeared among the young Zionists with regard to the issues of personal fulfillment and immigration to Palestine, which were not unique to the German context. They took place throughout Central and Eastern Europe. Their concrete realization was in the founding of pioneer youth movements. In Germany they found expression in the creation of the Jungjüdischer Wanderbund and the Hechaluz movement and among the religiously oriented Zionists, the founding of Zeire Misrachi and Brith Chaluzim Datiim. Immigration to Palestine was included in their platform and all groups prepared themselves for it. From 1919 every Convention of the ZVfD devoted considerable time and energy to discussions concerning Palestine and the role of the German Zionists in the upbuilding of the country. These Conventions often included representatives from Palestine who lectured on the political, economic and cultural advancements of the *Yishuv* and exhorted German Zionists to join personally in the effort. No other Zionist organization was as insistent as the ZVfD that its members pay a tithe *(Ma'aser)* for the Zionist cause.[58]

Who were the members of the third generation of German Zionism and what was their ideological stance? In their own words they had the right to call themselves the "third generation" of German Zionism because they had become Zionists after World War I, when Palestine was already a reality shaping their ideology.[59] There were a number of major tenets that stamped the character of this generation:

1. Their attachment to the Palestinian labor movement;
2. Their attempt to implement pioneer Zionism in their own lifetime and a belief that this was the way to redeem Zion;
3. Their commitment to a regeneration of Jewish life—especially in the social sphere—in Palestine, and their strong desire to emulate and adopt this new model in their own personal lives; and
4. Their attempt to form a synthesis between Zionism and socialism; even though well aware of the anti-Zionist tendencies in European socialism, they were nevertheless eager to find formulae that would bridge the gap between these two ideologies.

The ideal of the Jewish worker in Erets Yisrael building the Jewish land and forging a new free and constructive community greatly excited the imagination of the German Jewish youth.[60] The Balfour Declaration and England's take-over of the Mandate for Palestine with a promise of new and large immigration, propelled the Zionist movement into a fresh stage which was paralleled in Germany and elsewhere by a surge of selfless devotion and dedication. The Hechaluz movement began in Russia and soon was organized in other countries as well.[61] The Hechaluz wanted, in a systematic manner, to train its members professionally for immigration to Palestine. The organization founded farms and instruction sites and attempted to create a ready cadre of workers for Palestine. Immediately after the war an appeal for vocational retraining was sounded also among the largest Zionist youth organization, the Blau-Weiss, which was founded in 1912. Many young Zionists left their schools and universities in order to train themselves as farmers or skilled workers and thus participate constructively in the upbuilding of Palestine. A new ideal was created: the *Haluts* became a new type of a Jew unlike the orthodox segment of Jewry concerned mainly with its own internal Jewish affairs or the assimilating majority of German Jewry.[62]

The German Zionist youth and student movements were of course influenced by the ideologies current within the World Zionist movement but they were influenced to no lesser degree by the European youth movement. These two forces determined the course of the German Zionist youth, though, at times, they conflicted with one another. The goal remained Palestine, but at times the influence of the Wandervogel which preached individualism, a "program of aimlessness," and so forth, had greater impact on the Zionist youth.

The meshing and conflict between Zionist and European ideas was probably most pronounced in the Wanderbund Blau-Weiss. In its early phase, prior to World War I, the Blau-Weiss was largely influenced by the Wandervogel from whom it borrowed the hike, bonfires, song, the tone, dress and attitude. With time, the ideals of the Jewish liberation movement gained prominence. The symbols and forms borrowed from the Wandervogel were given a new, Jewish and Zionist meaning. After the war, when the possibility of settling in Palestine seemed a reality, the Blau-Weiss declared vocational retraining and immigration to Palestine as its educational goals. The Pioneer, the *Haluts,* was the ideal, and the working of the land of Palestine was the most important goal. "Bourgeois" professions were shunned as contradictory to the ideals of the youth. Thus, hundreds of Blau-Weissen followed the call of their leaders to settle Palestine. Their enthusiasm, however, was shattered by the harsh reality of conditions existing in Palestine in the early 1920s. The work colony *(Handwerkersiedlung)* and the Blau-Weiss workshops *(Werkstätten)* failed. The Blau-Weiss Bund in Germany itself dissolved,[63] and only a small number banded together in the Praktikantenschaft Blau-Weiss, which prepared its members for farm life in Palestine. Even in its heyday the Blau-Weiss never achieved a position of central importance within the ZVfD. This owed in large measure to its systematic insistence on a separation between itself and the world of adult politics. On the other hand, it is perhaps this strong sense of independence which was a source of the Blau-Weiss attraction for Jewish youths who were rebelling partly against assimilation but mostly against the bourgeois liberalism of their parents.

The Wanderbund Blau-Weiss was replaced by the Kadimah—Ring jüdischer Wander—und Pfadfinderbünde. In parallel development to the German youth movement, it was not influenced by the classic ideals of the Wandervogel. It made the same transformation as the general youth movement from romantic hikes to scouting. In addition, the Kadimah reacted to certain ideologies and tendencies and the failure of the Blau-Weiss—especially the overemphasis of the Blau-Weiss on Zionist ideology—by deemphasizing the political aspects of Zionism, claiming that the boys in its charge were not yet mature enough for such teachings. Only in the late 1920s and early 1930s did it move again toward Zionism until in 1933 it united with Brit Haolim to found the Habonim.

The most important group of those who set their goal on Halutsiut was centered around the Brit Haolim which was founded on 1 January 1923.[64] This group was strengthened by its union in 1925 with the Jung-Jüdischer Wanderbund (hereafter called the J.J.W.B.). Their combined membership included some 2,000 people and this united group was thus the largest young generation of the Palestinian labor movement. Regardless of earlier reservations in their individual historical development, the J.J.W.B. clearly expressed the goal of its members: "We firmly believe . . . that in Palestine the cornerstone for a new society is being laid. . . . We cannot do a thing here except to prepare ourselves to become worthy helpers of the Palestinian workers and to teach the German Jewish youth the ideal of a new dignified life in Erets Yisrael."[65]

As can be seen, each generation of German Zionists defined its Zionist ideology in ways which were consonant with its cultural milieu, upbringing and generational experience, the political, social, and economic realities within Germany and those within the WZO. In brief, the first generation can be characterized by its adherence to philanthropic-political Zionism. The second generation was concerned with its "personal Jewish Question" and its ideology stemmed from the cultural crisis of the German Reich. The third generation was committed to socialism, Halutsiut, the Palestinian labor movement and pioneer Zionism.

On the surface, when one examines German Zionist ideology from Posen to the program of the Brit Haolim, these ideologies appear to represent a progression toward an intensified personal commitment by German Zionists to immigrate to Palestine and to sustain a personal physical stake in the development of the country. It is a fact, however, that very few German Zionists immigrated to Palestine before May 1933. No more than thirty German Zionists moved to Palestine before World War I, and the total number who immigrated between 1919 and 1933 may have reached 2,000.[66] These figures show that despite the increasing of their ideological intensity in negation of the Galut, the majority of German Zionists were comfortable in Germany. Nevertheless, Zionism was a meaningful ideology for the German Jews of all three generations, whether it eventuated in immigration to Palestine or served as a catalyst for a personal return to Jewishness.[67]

Despite the many factions and variety of ideologies within the ZVfD ranging from Poale Zion and Ha-Po'el ha-Tsa'ir on the left to the Mizrachi and the Revisionists on the right, it was a source of great pride to the German Zionists that their organization was a unified/undivided organization *(Einheitsorganisation)* and not merely a "roof" organization *(Dachorganisation)*. The ZVfD alone among national Zionist organizations was able to maintain a sort of truce among its constituent members. In fact, the multiplicity of parties was one of the ZVfD's criticisms against the WZO. While representation at the Conventions was apportioned to some extent according to the relative support won by various lists of candidates whose parties were aligned with the World Zionist factions, the significant phenomenon was that all of these delegates sat in a single national convention.[68] Even the German Mizrachi which was tied to the World Mizrachi movement—the first party within the WZO to form a faction on an international scale (1902)—remained loyal to the ZVfD. The German Mizrachi was often critical of the ZVfD leadership, but, interestingly, it did not break ranks in Germany. Yet, for non-ideological reasons, in 1931, it chose to sever its ties with the Mizrachi World Organization.[69]

There were some attempts at the Conventions of Breslau in 1928 and Jena in 1929 to disrupt the concept of unity, but these attempts were unsuccessful. The most important challenge to this unity, however, occurred in the early 1920s. If one compares German Zionism until World War I with that of the postwar period, one may say that the early stage was a period of ideological controversies. The period after the war was marked by a will to concretize and fulfill the Zionist dream. One of the early vehicles of this realization and pragmatic work was the Keren Hayesod which at its inception raised a controversy between Chaim

Weizmann and Louis Brandeis, disagreements which were to have far-reaching implications for the future Zionist work throughout the world.

At the Annual Conference of July 1920 held in London, Weizmann and Brandeis had fundamental divergences of opinion concerning the future Zionist tasks. Brandeis saw the work of the WZO to be mainly in the economic field. He believed that non-Zionists, too, should aid in the upbuilding of Palestine through the Zionist movement. Weizmann and his associates, on the other hand, were convinced that the political work of Zionism was far from completed. They stressed the need for continued Zionist propaganda efforts and advocated contacts with important non-Zionist Jewish groups with a view to having them share in the growth of Palestine through a Jewish Council (which later assumed the form of an expanded Jewish Agency). The proposals of the Brandeis group regarding the functions and character of the WZO were not accepted, a development which led to a cleavage between the disciples of Brandeis and those of Weizmann.

Another controversial problem at the conference was that of the budget. An immigration and colonization fund was created, to be known as the Keren Hayesod, of which at least 20 per cent of the monies collected were to be turned over to the Jewish National Fund. Of the remaining funds acquired, not more than one third was to be allocated to current expenditures for education, social welfare, immigration and kindred purposes in Palestine, while at least two thirds were to be invested in permanent national institutions or economic undertakings. Brandeis and his associates were firmly opposed to such investments by the Keren Hayesod, insisting that the financing of commercial endeavors should be handled separately on a business basis. This view was not accepted, and the Karlsbad Congress of 1921 confirmed Weizmann's position.

The controversies at the Annual Conference in London and at the Karlsbad Congress were reflected within the German Zionist ranks. They resulted in the creation of Binjan Haarez, one of the few serious challenges to the unity of the ZVfD. The members of this group were for the most part older Zionists, members of the first generation who had opposed Blumenfeld and his intense, nationalistic ideology since the Leipzig Convention and were often also associated with the Jüdische Volkspartei. Their long-standing opposition to the Blumenfeld faction, which supported Weizmann, was coupled with support for Brandeis and an avowed goal to support private capital investments in Palestine and reject socialist experiments.[70] The attempt by Binjan Haarez, however, to constitute itself as an independent faction was beaten back by a coalition of the major groupings within the ZVfD. Blumenfeld and his associates were able to convince the ZVfD membership that it would be detrimental for Zionism to gloss over real ideological differences between themselves and non-Zionists. The only constructive way to cooperate without ideological compromise was through a true *Bündnispolitik* as enunciated by Blumenfeld in 1917. At the beginning of January 1922 the Keren Hayesod turned to the public to join its ranks,[71] and in the 1920s, Germany was consistently among the three to five largest contributors to that fund next to the United States, Canada, South Africa and England.

In 1924 Kurt Blumenfeld was elected chairman of the ZVfD, a position held from 1920 to 1924 for short periods by Felix Rosenblüth, Alfred Klee and Alfred Landsberg. Blumenfeld retained this post until his immigration to Palestine in 1933. Under his administration the ZVfD continued to support the leadership of the WZO which was led by Chaim Weizmann until 1931. As was noted, the German Zionists were always "loyalists" in their attitude toward the official leadership since the days of Herzl. Yet, an even tighter bond was now forged because of the ideological closeness German Zionists felt toward the policies of Weizmann. The trust was mutual and the president of the World Organization greatly valued the support of German Zionists. As a result, the 1920s saw the ZVfD, despite its small numbers, move closer to the inner seat of power. Men like Kurt Blumenfeld and Robert Weltsch had the ready ear of Weizmann and, therefore, a direct and indirect influence over Zionist policies. In all the issues that arose in the 1920s—the problems created by the attitude of Britain toward Zionism, the efforts to create an enlarged Jewish Agency, the procurement of funds for the Palestinian *Yishuv,* and the attempt to deal with the emerging Arab nationalist movement in Palestine—the German Zionists gave their full and unreserved support to Weizmann. Their position within the World Zionist movement, which was leaning toward a socialist-idealist political course, called the Left Center, was curiously not represented in the congresses by workers, but by intellectuals who united with the left-of-center parties in Erets Yisrael.

One of the central issues in the 1920s was the expansion of the Jewish Agency to include non-Zionists. Article 4 of the Mandate for Palestine, confirmed by the League of Nations in 1922, provided for the recognition of an appropriate "Jewish Agency as a public body for the purpose of advising and cooperating with the Administration of Palestine. . . ."

The mandate itself recognized the WZO as such a Jewish Agency. Soon thereafter, negotiations were initiated by Chaim Weizmann with prominent, non-Zionist Jews which had the purpose of uniting them into an enlarged Jewish Agency. The plan was opposed by several leading Zionists who feared that a mixed Zionist and non-Zionist body would retard, rather than advance, the implementation of the Zionist program and endanger its political character. They remained in the minority, however, and after six years of negotiations the XVI Zionist Congress (Zürich, 1929) approved Weizmann's plan. As in the case of the Keren Hayesod here, too, the ZVfD supported Weizmann's position.[72]

The year in which the Jewish Agency was founded saw momentous events take place which had decisive implications for the WZO, and in Germany resulted in a heated controversy at the Jena Convention. Deliberations in Jena were the result of debates among German Zionists regarding the Arab Question. In general, Zionists always believed that an accommodation with the Arabs in Palestine could be reached. The representative German Zionist position advocated a large measure of moderation and self-restraint in advancing Zionist interests in Palestine. The most articulate and strongest advocate of this policy was the aforementioned Robert Weltsch, editor of the *Jüdische Rundschau*. Weltsch warned against excessive nationalism and supported a binational federation backed by national guarantees.[73] He and his close associates encouraged and supported the work of the Brith Shalom, a small group founded in Palestine in 1925 which fostered a binationalist accord with the Arabs. They founded a German branch which adopted the name Arbeitsgemeinschaft für zionistische Realpolitik.[74]

These ideas were for the most part left unchallenged, as long as peace prevailed between Arab and Jewish settlers. In fact, a period of relative quiet followed the Arab riots of May 1921. This uneasy truce, however, was shattered in August 1929. The pretext for the conflict which had been brewing for about a year, was over the conflicting rights of the Jews and Arabs at the Western Wall. A series of incidents in 1929 culminated on 23 August, and the following days, in wide-spread Arab riots in Jerusalem and other cities which resulted in the death and wounding of hundreds of Jews.

The news of the riots in Palestine were accompanied by heated debates within the ZVfD ranks which were triggered by a series of articles written by Weltsch and published in the *Jüdische Rundschau*. After demanding the restoration of order and the protection of life and property, and after accusing the British government of criminal negligence,

Weltsch reiterated his demands for a policy of accommodation with the Arabs. He accused the Zionist leadership of having missed the opportunity to find a modus vivendi and a path of conciliation with the Arabs, merely having given perfunctory declarations and resolutions to this effect. Since the Zionists were required to live peacefully with their neighbors in and around Palestine they were forced to find realistic and serious plans for mutual coexistence which could best be realized in a binational state. Weltsch strongly counseled against any use of force in solving the conflict.[75] These views were reiterated in a memorandum (Denkschrift) sent to the Zionist executive on 16 September 1929 and bore beside Weltsch's signature that of eight other prominent German Zionists, among them Kurt Blumenfeld.[76]

Weltsch's views drew strong criticism from a number of quarters, including German Zionists who had already immigrated to Palestine.[77] Under these circumstances the question of whether Weltsch's position enjoyed the support of the ZVfD membership became particularly urgent and figured as the principal issue at the Convention held in Jena at the end of December 1929. This was the so-called "decisive battle" of Jena which was to determine the attitude of the ZVfD toward the Arab question. Weizmann, who spoke at the Convention was evasive and noncommittal, but Blumenfeld, despite some hesitations expressed in private, fully supported Weltsch in public. The Convention confirmed both Weltsch and Blumenfeld's positions. A vote of no confidence against the Jüdische Rundschau was defeated, and Blumenfeld was reelected as the chairman (Vorsitzender) of the ZVfD.[78]

Less than a year after the Convention in Jena, the National Socialists won 107 seats in the Reichstag. The Zionists, for the first time, cooperated with the Central-Verein during the election campaign of 1930 and were as horrified as the rest of the German Jewish community by the implications of the Nazi challenge and increased might.[79] The antisemitic forces in the Reich became even more aggressive, and whereas the Zionist debate with communists remained ideological and theoretical,[80] the Nazis confronted Jews to an increasing degree with direct acts of physical violence. The official response of the ZVfD to the Nazi challenge was expressed at the Convention in Frankfurt which took place in September 1932. This Convention was the last to take place during the Weimar period. It was marked by a penetrating and analytic speech by Blumenfeld and ended with a resolution which declared that Zionism condemns a nationalism whose foundations include the conviction of the inferiority of other national groups and that Zionism struggles for the equal legal status of the Jews in Germany. The resolution demanded the protection of these rights.[81]

The Zionists' optimism, that a state of national pluralism and freedom to develop their own ideals under Nazi rule might be created, was shattered soon after the establishment of the Nazi regime in January 1933. This date marks the close of an epoch in modern German Jewish history that had begun some two hundred years earlier. With the Nuremberg Laws of 1935 Jewish Emancipation was definitely rescinded. Formally the ZVfD—now under the leadership of Seigfried Moses—like all other German Jewish organizations, remained in existence for the next five years but similar to them, it was deprived of any meaningful freedom for action and thought and was forced to adapt to changing external conditions.[82] This was reflected in the *Jüdische Rundschau* and every other official organ and correspondence of the ZVfD. They were all subject to a state of terror and, if they wished continued existence, had to pass over many violent political events silently. It took extreme courage for these official publications to print a note of protest from time to time. By the end of 1938 even these limited freedoms were taken away and the ZVfD ended its forty-one year history.

NOTES

1. A scholarly history of German Zionism between 1882 and 1938 has yet to be written. Richard Lichtheim's *Die Geschichte des deutschen Zionismus* (Jerusalem, 1954), contains much important information, but is sketchy and replete with mistakes. There have been a number of studies which deal with various periods in the history of the ZVfD, such as Jehuda Reinharz, *Fatherland or Promised Land, The Dilemma of the German Jew 1893–1914* (Ann Arbor, Mich., 1975) and Jehuda Reinharz, ed., *Dokumente zur Geschichte des deutschen Zionismus* (Tübingen, 1980); see also Stephen M. Poppel, *Zionism in Germany 1897–1933* (Philadelphia, Pa., 1977). There are, of course, quite a few dissertations, articles and essays written on aspects of the history of German Zionism which cannot be listed here. The following article is intended as an outline of the historical development of German Zionism: its internal conflicts as well as its major ideological currents and organizational groups. (Ed. note: In view of the established practice of German-Jewish organizations, it was decided to leave the spelling of their Hebraic names unchanged from their accepted German transliterations except in cases where their American counterparts are well known here).

2. See Simon Dubnow, *History of the Jews in Russia and Poland* (Philadelphia, Pa., 1918), II, 243 ff.

3. See Shalom Adler-Rudel, *Ostjuden in Deutschland 1880–1940. Zugleich eine Geschichte der Organisationen, die sie betreuten* (Tübingen, 1959), p. 6.

4. Mordechai Eliav, *Ahavat Tsion ve-Anshe HOD* [Love of Zion and Men of HOD:

German Jewry and the Settlement of Erets Yisrael in the Nineteenth Century] (Tel Aviv, 1970), pp. 355–56.

5. See the first public proclamation of the B'nai B'rith in the Central Archives for the History of the Jewish People (hereafter called CAHJP), located in Jerusalem, GA Beuthen, S97/20. See also, Israel Klausner, "The Association B'nai B'rith in Kattowitz" (Hebrew), *Jubilee Volume in Honor of N. M. Gelber,* ed. Israel Klausner, Raphael Mahler and Dov Sadan (Tel Aviv, 1962); Jacob Toury, "The First Issue of the Earliest German Hoveve Zion Periodical" (Hebrew), *Zionism,* 3 (1973), 490–501.

6. See the first public proclamation of Ahavass Zijon, May 1885, in Jerusalem's Central Zionist Archives (hereafter called CZA), 147/23/2.

7. Mordechai Eliav, "Zur Vorgeschichte der jüdischen Nationalbewegung in Deutschland," *Bulletin des Leo Baeck Instituts,* 48 (1969), 289. See also, Julius H. Shoeps, "Autoemanzipation und Selbsthilfe: Die Anfänge der nationaljüdischen Bewegung in Deutschland, 1882–1897," *Zeitschrift für Religions-und Geistesgeschichte,* 31, no. 4 (1979), 345–65.

8. Alter Druyanov, *Ktavim le-Toldot Hibbat Tsion ve-Yishuv Erets Yisrael* [Documents on the History of the Love of Zion and the Settlement of the Land of Israel] (Tel Aviv, 1925), I, 206–11; CZA, A13/18.

9. See *Festschrift zum fünfundzwanzigjährigen Jubiläum des Esra* (Berlin, 1909); *Die jüdische Presse,* nos. 15–16, 9 April 1884, p. 160. See also, Jehuda Reinharz, "The Esra Verein and Jewish Colonization in Palestine," *Leo Baeck Institute Yearbook,* 24 (1979), 261–89.

10. The first issue of *Serubabel* appeared on 29 September 1886. The periodical was founded by Albert Katz and Willy Bambus. The *Selbst-Emancipation* was the first Zionist-national periodical before Herzl began his activities. Its first issue appeared in 1885 in Vienna under the editorship of Nathan Birnbaum. It ceased publication in mid-1886. The *Serubabel* replaced the *Selbst-Emancipation* until it also folded in July 1888 owing to financial difficulties. On 1 April 1890 the *Selbst-Emancipation* commenced publication once more and appeared until 1893 under that name. In 1894 the periodical's name was changed to *Jüdische Volkszeitung* and it appeared in Berlin until 1895.

11. *Die jüdische Presse,* no. 19, 10 May 1888.

12. See the statutes of the association in CZA, A126/12/1.

13. See Jehuda Louis Weinberg, *Aus der Frühzeit des Zionismus, Heinrich Loewe* (Jerusalem, 1946).

14. *Jüdische Volkszeitung,* no. 2, 9 January 1894.

15. See "Jüdische Kommilitonen!" [4 July 1895], CZA, A231/4/2.

16. See Paul Graetz, "Organisatorische Daten zur Geschichte der Zionistischen Studentenbewegung in Deutschland," CZA, A231—Aktenverzeichnis.

17. Jehuda Reinharz, "The Origin and Development of the Bund Jüdischer Corporationen," *The Wiener Library Bulletin,* 30, n.s. nos. 43/44 (1977), pp. 2–7.

18. *Die Menorah,* 4 September 1891 in CZA, A15/I/4. Similarly, on 14 July 1893 the association, Jung Israel, turned to other Hoveve Zion groups with a call to form a congress which would decide on final aims and strategies of all Jewish national groups. See Mordechai Ehrenpreis, "Vor Herzl und mit Herzl," *Theodor Herzl Jahrbuch,* founded and published by T. Nussenblatt (Brünn, 1929). See also Alex Bein, "Von der Zionssehnsucht zum politischen Zionismus, zur Geschichte des Wortes und Begriffes Zionismus," *Robert Weltsch zum 70. Geburtstag,* Hans Tramer and Kurt Loewenstein, eds. (Tel Aviv, 1961).

19. CZA, A147/23/3 and CZA, A1/VI/2/20. See also the correspondence between Hermann Schapira and Max Bodenheimer in *Toldot Tokhnit Basel* [The Evolution of the Basel Program], Henriette Hannah Bodenheimer, ed. (Jerusalem, 1947). Members of

the first generation of German Zionists such as Max Bodenheimer and Adolf Friede-mann always claimed that they were Herzl's true and loyal disciples, while in reality they did not accept his views on Jewish life in the diaspora. In his *The Jewish State,* Herzl states that those Jews who would not or could not move to the new Jewish state, would assimilate into other peoples'. On the other hand, it seems that following the first Zionist congress Herzl did not discuss this issue again with his supporters.

20. *Allgemeine Zeitung des Judentums,* no. 29, 16 July 1897, p. 338.
21. CZA, A15/II/13; and CZA, A1/2/2/6, Collection of Printed Mss.
22. *Ibid.*
23. See the circulars of the ZVfD *(Flugblätter)* in CZA, W/147/1 and CZA, Z1/433.
24. See "Der Nationaljude als Staatsbürger," CZA [July/August], 1897. Also, CZA, W147/1.
25. See *Israelitische Rundschau,* no. 20, 24 May 1901.
26. Reiner Bernstein, "Zwischen Emanzipation und Antisemitismus—Die Publizistik der deutschen Juden am Beispiel der 'C.-V. Zeitung' Organ des Central-Vereins deutscher Staatsbürger jüdischen Glaubens, 1924–1933," Diss. Freie Universität (Berlin, 1969).
27. See Buber Archive, Jerusalem, Ms. Var, 350/38.
28. See "Protokoll der Sitzung des Landesvorstandes vom 18. Mai 1930 in Berlin," Leo Baeck Institute, Jerusalem.
29. CZA, 2/7/10/2, Collection of Printed Mss. See also, "Unsere Stellung zur Gemeinde-politik" [May 1908], CZA, A142/47/5.
30. "Protokoll der V. Sitzung des Landesvorstandes vom 20. Mai 1925," Schocken Ar-chive, Jerusalem, File 53/32.
31. See, e.g., Draft of Resolution by some German Zionist delegates to the Sixth Zionist Congress 25 August 1903: CZA, A142/36/1. See also, CZA, A19/2.
32. For an analysis of the Central-Verein and the ZVfD and their relationship, see Jehuda Reinharz, *Fatherland or Promised Land.* Among the published literature there are some other works which deal with the Central-Verein in the period prior to 1914. They include: Ismar Schorsch, *Jewish Reactions to German Anti-Semitism, 1870–1914* (New York and Philadelphia, Pa., 1972); Arnold Paucker, "Zur Problematic einer jüdischen Abwehrstrategie in der deutschen Gesellschaft," in *Juden im Wilhel-minischen Deutschland 1890–1914,* ed. Werner E. Mosse with the assistance of Arnold Paucker (Tübingen, 1976); and Marjorie Lamberti, *Jewish Activism in Impe-rial Germany; The Struggle for Civil Equality* (New Haven, Conn., 1978). See also, Arnold Paucker, *Der jüdische Abwehrkampf* [2nd enlarged edition] (Hamburg, 1969), which deals with the C.-V. during the latter years of the Weimar Republic.
33. See ZVfD "Aufruf" [January 1910], CZA, A15/VII/22.
34. See, e.g., Franz Oppenheimer, "Stammesbewusstsein und Volksbewusstsein," *Die Welt,* no. 7, 18 February 1910, pp. 139–43.
35. See, e.g., Kurt Blumenfeld, "Deutscher Zionismus," *Jüdische Rundschau* (hereafter called *J.R.*), no. 35, 2 September 1910, pp. 414–15, and "Der XII Delegiertentag," *J.R.,* no. 38, 23 September 1910.
36. "Zur Apologetik des Zionismus," CZA, Z2/409 and Moses Calvary, "Die Erzieher-ische Aufgabe des Deutschen Zionismus," *Die Welt,* no. 1, 6 January 1910.
37. *J.R.,* 12 August 1910, p. 377.
38. This process was manifested in various controversies such as the *Kunstwart* and Sombart debates, the language debate in Palestine, the conflict with the Central-Verein and the Antizionistisches Komitee. For details and an analysis, see Reinharz, *Fatherland or Promised Land,* Chap. 5.
39. See "Persönliches Interesse in Palästina," *J.R.,* no. 24, 14 June 1912, p. 222.
40. See the C.-V.'s reaction on 30 March 1913 and the ZVfD's response on 1 May 1913 in CZA, A102/H9, Collection of Printed Mss.

41. *J.R.*, no. 25, 19 June 1914, p. 271. See also, Adolf Friedemann to Max Bodenheimer, 25 February 1914, CZA, A15/VII/27.

42. *J.R.*, no. 32, 7 August 1914, and "An die Blau-Weissen," *Sonderausgabe der Blau-Weiss-Blaetter*, August 1914.

43. Gershom Scholem, "Laienpredigt" and "Palaestina," *Die Blauweisse Brille*, no. 2 [September 1915].

44. Zosa Szajkowski, "The Komitee fuer den Osten and Zionism," *Herzl Year Book* (New York, 1971), VII, 202–203.

45. Abraham Duker, "Jews in the World War," *Contemporary Jewish Record*, 2, no. 5 (Sept.–Oct. 1939), 6–29.

46. "Richtlinien des Deutschen Komitees zur Befreiung der russischen Juden," CZA, A15/VIII/7, as well as CZA, A15/VIII (files 11–16) and CZA, A8/37.

47. See Egmont Zechlin, *Die deutsche Politik und die Juden im Ersten Weltkrieg*, (Göttingen, 1969).

48. See, e.g., Bodenheimer to the Turkish Ambassador Mahmud Mukhtar Pasha, 27 August 1914, CZA, A142/95; ZVfD circular of 2 April 1915, CZA, A15/VII/28 and ZVfD: "An das Auswärtige Amt" 4 October 1916, CZA, A142/47/2.

49. Kurt Blumenfeld, "Der Zionismus," *Preussische Jahrbücher*, 161 (no. 1), July 1915. See also Isaiah Friedman, *Germany, Turkey, and Zionism 1897–1918* (Oxford, 1977).

50. "Judenzählung," *J.R.*, no. 43, 27 October 1916. See also, "Bericht über die PlenarSitzung des Zentralkomitees vom 12. November 1916," CZA, A15/III/28.

51. Berthold Cohn and Walter Preuss, "Nach Palästina," *Der Jüdische Student*, 26 January 1916.

52. "An die Ortsgruppen und Vertrauensmänner!," 22 November 1917, CZA, A102/12/9.

53. *J.R.*, no. 2, 11 January 1918.

54. "Denkschrift betreffend Gründung eines Deutschen Comités pro Palästina," Bundesarchiv (Koblenz) R431/2192. See also, *Mitteilungen des Pro Palästina Komitees*, CZA, 1401.

55. See Schocken Archive, 531/67. See also, Joseph Walk, "Das Deutsche Komitee Pro Palästina 1926–1933," *Bulletin des Leo Baeck Instituts*, 52 (1976), 162–93, and Francis R. J. Nicosia, "Weimar Germany and the Palestine Question," *Leo Baeck Institute Yearbook*, 24 (1979), 321–45.

56. See "Protokoll der Plenar-Sitzung des Zentralkomitees vom 23. Dezember 1917," CZA, A15/IV/12; "Protokoll der Sitzung des Central-Komitees am Sonntag den 24. November 1918," CZA, A15/VII/29; "Zur Kongressbewegung," CZA, F4/13. See also Jacob Toury, "Organizational Problems of German Jewry—Steps toward the Establishment of a Central Organization (1893–1920)," *Leo Baeck Institute Yearbook*, 13 (1968), 57–90.

57. See letter from Nahum Goldmann to Gustav Landauer, 14 March 1919, Buber Archive, Ms. Var, 432/167. There is no doubt that the tremendous increase in antisemitism in the period between 1918–1923 also had strong impact on the "third generation" of German Zionism. The degree to which it shaped this generation's ideology during the Weimar Republic is not easy to determine and warrants a separate study.

58. *J.R.*, no. 80, 12 November 1920.

59. "Unsere Lage," *Der Junge Jude*, no. 1, November 1927. The "third generation" includes such members of the J.J.W.B. as Fritz Noack and George Lubinski as well as members of the Blau-Weiss and perhaps even Gershom Scholem, although the latter's Zionist identity was to a large extent formed already just prior and during World War I. See Gershom Scholem, *Von Berlin nach Jerusalem* (Frankfurt am Main, 1977).

60. See "Zionistische Arbeit in Deutschland," at the XVII Convention, *J.R.*, nos. 39/40, 17 May 1921.

61. See "Resolutionen angenommen von der Konferenz des deutschen Hechaluz am 14.15. und 16.12.1922," Archives of the Jewish Labor Movement, Tel Aviv (43), 38 III.

62. Siegfried Kanowitz, "Die Zionistische Jugendbewegung," *Die neue Jugend, Forschungen zur Völkerpsychologie und Soziologie*, IV, ed. Dr. Richard Thurnwald (Leipzig, 1927).

63. Geschäftsführender Ausschuss des Blau Weiss, "An die Mitglieder," 23.2.1927, CZA, A66/13/2.

64. See *Die Arbeit*, nos. 4/5, December/January 1923.

65. Circular of the J.J.W.B., no. 25/17, 18 March 1925. Archive of the Ghetto Fighters' House, Kibbutz Lohamei Hagetaot, 2501.

66. See Jewish Agency, Department of Immigration and Works, *Ha-Aliyah [Immigration]*, I, 32 (1935); Richard Lichtheim, *Die Geschichte des deutschen Zionismus* (Jerusalem, 1954), pp. 234–35. These figures do not reflect Eastern European Jews who immigrated to Palestine through Germany and were therefore registered as Germans, nor do they indicate the number of those who returned to Germany.

67. See Jehuda Reinharz, "Three Generations of German Zionism," *The Jerusalem Quarterly*, 9 (October 1978), 95–110.

68. *J.R.*, no. 3, 9 January 1925, p. 3.

69. See "Resolution des Delegiertentages der Landesorganisation des Misrachi für Deutschland vom 28. September 1930," The Archives of Religious Zionism, Jerusalem, File 235/A. See also *Zion*, 8/9 (October 1931).

70. See "Was Will Binjan Haarez?", *Mitteilungsblatt des Binjan Haarez*, 1 (June 1921). See also *Stenographisches Protokoll der Verhandlungen des XII. Zionisten-Kongresses in Karlsbad vom 1, bis 14. September 1921* (Berlin, 1922).

71. *J.R.*, no. 4, 13 January 1922.

72. See circular signed by Kurt Blumenfeld on 14 February 1929, CZA, Z4/3366.

73. See, e.g., report on the XXI Convention of the ZVfD, *J.R.*, nos. 66–67, 27 August 1926.

74. See "Resumee einer Sitzung im Hause von Herrn Berger, 16.9.29," Leo Baeck Institute, Jerusalem.

75. See, e.g., *J.R.*, no. 68, 30 August 1929.

76. "Denkschrift an die Zionistische Executive in London," 16.9.1929, CZA Z4/3567/IV.

77. See, e.g., Aron Barth to the executive committee of the ZVfD, 10 September 1929, CZA, Z4/3567/IV; *J.R.*, no. 86, 1 November 1929, and "Protokoll der erweiterten Sitzung des Landesvorstandes am 10. November 1929," CZA, Z4/3567/V.

78. See *J.R.*, no. 1, 3 January 1930.

79. See "Protokoll der 6. Sitzung des Geschäftsführenden Ausschusses vom 19.2.1930," CZA, Z4/3567/VI; "Protokoll der Sitzung des Landesvorstandes vom 18. Mai 1930," Leo Baeck Institute, Jerusalem; and "Protokoll der Sitzung des Landesvorstandes vom 12. Oktober 1930," CZA, Z4/3567/VI.

80. Fritz Loewenstein, "Zur Auseinandersetzung mit Kommunisten," *J.R.*, no. 7, 26 January 1932.

81. Kurt Blumenfeld, "Die Zionistische Aufgabe im heutigen Deutschland," *J.R.*, nos. 73/74, 16 September 1932.

82. See Siegfried Moses' speech on Zionist Politics in Germany, "Sitzung des Landesvorstandes vom 9.1.1933," CZA, Z4/3567/VIII and circular from Landauer to members of the executive committee of the ZVfD, 22 March 1933, Leo Baeck Institute, Jerusalem.

13.

Criteria and Conception in the Historiography of German and American Zionism

Evyatar Friesel

The history of Zionism in both Germany and the United States has recently become a subject of interest among scholars. New insights and several significant innovations can be observed in the approach of scholars in the field, among them an interest in the position of the Zionists within the Jewish community, the so-called "function" of Zionism in each country, and its relative "success."

Till recently, the predominant trend in Zionist historiography was, more or less, "Palestinocentric." Scholars dealt with the movement as a whole, in its orientation towards its ultimate goals in Palestine. They stressed ideological expression, policy, and organizational developments on the leadership level. Only a limited interest was shown in Zionism as a local phenomenon, or its meaning in the context of the specific Jewish community.[1]

The new research on Zionism is "locally" oriented. It attempts to analyze each movement within the context of the Jewish community whose characteristics it bore and upon which, in turn, it had an influence, even when—as in the case of German Zionism—it sharply criticized the situation of German Jewry. This type of study is so readily integrated into research of local Jewish history that it is sometimes difficult (and perhaps unnecessary) to distinguish between the historian of German or American Jewry, and the historian of German or American Zionism.[2]

The function of Zionism—whether considered the role of the movement in each Jewish community or the life of the Zionists in their Jewish

Reprinted by permission of the author and *Studies in Zionism* 2 (Autumn 1980): 285–302.

and non-Jewish environments—is one of the leading questions of this locally-oriented research. Though not adopted by all historians of American or German Zionism, the functional approach is rather common. Indeed, researchers of American-Jewish history have for quite some time called attention to what they consider the psychological and sociological functions of American Zionism. As far back as the fifties O. Handlin and W. Herberg stressed the importance of Zionism in America as an outlet for the perplexities of second-generation Jews.[3] In more recent years, Yonathan Shapiro, an exponent of the functional approach, has stated: "Our inquiry starts with the assumption that the American version of Zionism served the function of providing an ideology of survival for the Jewish community of the United States."[4] One of the characteristics of Jewish life in America, according to Shapiro, was the gap between the assimilation of the Jews and their acculturation. Zionism was one of the many ideologies brought by the Jews from Europe. At the time when Louis D. Brandeis was the outstanding leader of American Zionism (types of leadership are a major theme in Shapiro's research), Zionist ideology in the United States underwent an inner development that transformed it into "Palestinianism." Palestinianism renounced the definition of American Jewry as a separate political and cultural entity and concentrated on work for the upbuilding of the Jewish National Home in Palestine. The new position represented an important component of the Jewish acculturation process in the United States, was part of the emergence of an American Jewish culture, and contributed to Jewish survival as a specific group under American conditions.[5]

Other researchers of American Zionism have concentrated more on different facets of the Americanization of the movement and its ideology.[6] However interpreted, it is generally accepted that American Zionism fulfilled important functions in American Jewish life.

As for German Zionism, the development of the functional approach has been more recent, and the functions suggested different from those of American Zionism. One articulate representative of this position is Stephen S. Poppel who stresses what he considers the discrepancy between the ideology of the German Zionist movement and the actual behavior of its members and leaders. Starting from the premise that the mainstay of Zionist thought was the idea of "the negation of the Galuth," and, consequently, *aliya* ("emigration to Eretz Israel"), it is clear, in Poppel's view, that German Zionism before 1933 failed: Zionists did not leave Germany. On the contrary, the contradiction between the idea and its non-realization created a situation in Germany where Zionism actually made continuing to live there spiritually easier. The subtitle of Poppel's book, *Zionism in Germany—The Shaping of a Jewish Identity*—that is, a *German*-Jewish identity, sums up this line of interpretation. Seen in terms of Zionist "success," the German movement remained numerically small and, considered in the light of its original intentions, ineffective. Any radical formulation of classical Zionist aims "seems to have been limited to rhetoric." But German Zionism succeeded in a different sense: "The real personal significance of Zionism" was not "fund raising, charitable work for the *Ostjuden,* or the promotion of *aliya,* but as a source of . . . a viable and supportive identity." This type of Jewish identity proved to be particularly suited to the situation of German Zionists: "This ideology of national distinctiveness and even separation paradoxically provided the Zionists with a rationalization of their lives in Germany." Considered from this point of view, German Zionism went from one extreme of Zionist ideology to the opposite: starting from the classical "negation of the Galuth," it ended, actually, by "affirming the Galuth." [7]

The research in question suggested new perspectives for understanding Zionist history, but at the same time arouses serious methodological questions, among them those of Zionist "success" and "function" attributed to Zionism in Germany and in the United States.

1. ZIONIST "SUCCESS" AND "FAILURE"

The criteria mentioned for the evaluation of Zionism—the size of the organization, the extent of *aliya,* and ideological consistency—raise a number of problems.

With regard to size, its relevancy is doubtful: small elitist groups or movements have brought about some of the most fateful revolutions in modern history. As for *aliya,* the Zionist movement as a whole was never successful. The 475,000 Jews that lived in Palestine in 1939 represented less than 3 percent of the Jewish population of the world. During the last quarter of the nineteenth century, Jews emigrated from Europe in ever-growing numbers. Millions settled in various parts of the world while only a trickle went to Palestine. Of about 3,700,000 Jewish emigrants that left Europe between 1881–1939, less than 12 percent went to Palestine, and many eventually left the country. [8]

Furthermore, the use of *aliya* as a central criterion for measuring Zionist "success" before 1948, is anachronistic. Only *after* the creation of the Jewish state was the obligation of *aliya* established as *the* major expression of Zionist commitment. During the Mandate years, neither the political situation in Palestine nor the financial resources of the Zionist movement permitted a resolute appeal by the World Zionist Organization to Zionists to settle massively in Palestine. The debacle of the Fourth Aliya, during the twenties, caused the Zionist leadership to exercise even greater caution. Prior to 1948 there were only one or two sectors of the movement or of the Jewish people that adopted *aliya* as an immediate step. The *halutz* ("pioneer") movements were one, but they were revolutionary in several senses. Yemenite Jewry was another. They were strongly *aliya*-oriented and nearly half of Yemenite Jewry was already living in Palestine by 1948. But even if the Yemenites came for reasons that were "Zionist" in the pure sense, their motivations were at opposite poles from the social and political premises underlying European Zionism. Still, the matter of *aliya* as a measure of Zionist success will be considered again further on.

The third criterion, mentioned more with regard to German Zionism but applying equally to the American movement, has to do with ideological consistency. Undoubtedly, non-Zionist Jews have always been more "consistent" in their way of life. But this is the unavoidable difference between the conservative (or the liberal-conservative, as was the case with many non-Zionists), who adheres to the concepts and rules of behavior of an existing social and ideological order, and the revolutionary or the radical, whose ideological inclinations belong to a different order, still to be created, but whose existential basis is rooted in the very reality he is trying to change. This situation was especially complex for the Zionists, whose radicalism implied national, cultural, geographical and even social change. German Zionists were very "German" in many ways, as American Zionists were American—or, for that matter, Russian Zionists Russian. Since their national hopes lay elsewhere—in a country yet to be built, a language yet to be learnt, and a culture yet to be created—ambiguity, confusion and inconsistency were unavoidable, and they took many forms and found a variety of expressions.

In light of the above reservations expressed regarding the three criteria for measuring the success of Zionism, it could be suggested that the new research on Zionism in Germany and in the United States has not solved some of the more fundamental problems concerning the complex relationship between Zionism as a local phenomenon and as a general Jewish movement. In the following pages a different view will be presented.

2. ZIONISM IN THE GERMAN-JEWISH MILIEU

The Weimar period in German history represents a convenient point for evaluating the situation of German Jewry and its organizations, the Zionist movement among them: the twenties were the most advanced stage of development for German Jewry, preceding the internal changes that followed in the wake of Hitler.

It is the opinion of some that there was a perceptible awakening of Jewish consciousness in Germany during the transition years between the end of World War I and the beginning of the Weimar Republic.[9] A sober analysis of Jewish life in Germany, however, would appear to produce little corroboration for this thesis.

Demographically, German Jewry was on the decline after World War I. There were 564,380 Jews in 1925, only 499,680 in 1933.[10] Additional data show the classical components of a negative demographic situation: a high percentage of mixed marriages, small families, unfavorable age composition. A closer look at the numbers adds further negative elements. About 20 percent of all Jews living in Germany during the Weimar years were foreigners, almost all from Eastern Europe—the so-called *Ostjuden*. Since the disruptive demographic trends just mentioned were not characteristic of the *Ostjuden*, one must conclude that the demographical situation of the older German Jewish society was even more critical than shown by the general statistics.

The community life of German Jewry during the twenties indicates problems of a rather subtle character. German Jewry was highly organized ideologically, religiously and around civic and communal enterprises. But the level of communication and the amount of collaboration between the various kinds of organization was surprisingly low. The two most articulate groups were the integration-oriented "Centralverein" and the Zionist Federation, the "Zionistische Vereinigung für Deutschland." During the twenties there was little understanding and almost no collaboration between them, or between them and the other ideologically defined groups in German Jewry: the right (such as Naumann's "Verein Nationaldeutscher Juden"), or the neo-orthodox. None made much headway on its own, either in terms of organizational development, or in matters that were ideologically important. German Zionism, for example, never became the central factor in German Jewish life that it aspired to; the Centralverein was unsuccessful in the fight against anti-Semitism; neo-orthodoxy did not expand beyond its walled bastions; and so on. German-Jewish intellectuals were not oblivious to the

Jewish situation. The terms "Untergang" and "Krisis," concepts much in vogue in Germany during the Weimar years, recurred with significant regularity among those analyzing the German-Jewish scene.[11]

Other West-European Jewish communities were, apparently, no better off. But nowhere else had the problems and alternatives of modern or modernizing Jewry been defined as clearly as in Germany. It was in Germany (though not always by German Jews) that the main ideas of the Jewish Enlightenment, the "Science of Judaism," and Jewish religious reform had been formulated and translated into active programs. The same was true for Zionism. Some of the most important ideological expressions of classical Zionism (or its forerunners) had originated in Germany or in German, from Hess's *Rom und Jerusalem* in 1862, through Herzl's *Judenstaat* in 1896, to the different versions of Klatzkin's *Probleme des Modernen Judentums* after World War I. It was in Germany or in the German "Kulturkreis"—in Basel, Vienna, Cologne, Berlin—that organized Zionism had been established. The high level of ideological lucidity—which need not be taken as an indication of Jewish vitality—was maintained during the Weimar period. Nowhere in Western Europe were the spiritual alternatives of modern Judaism and the ideological options of Zionism and anti-Zionism as thoroughly analyzed and understood—but not necessarily acted upon—as among Jews in Weimar Germany.

It is surprising, therefore, that one of the conclusions reached in the "function"-oriented research on German Zionism is that there was little difference between the Zionists and the integration-oriented members of the Centralverein, since the leaders of both sides had a similar Jewish and German background, an enhanced Jewish consciousness, and a program for continued Jewish existence in Germany. Their differences, it has been stated, were mainly rhetorical, and it was a matter of chance that a Jew became a Zionist rather than an active Centralverein member.[12]

Actually, the differences between Zionists and non-Zionists in Germany, besides being fundamental, were expressed on the ideological level and in the realm of Jewish public activity. The Centralverein (as well as other Jewish groups in Germany) clung to a vision of Jewish life built on the conceptions of eighteenth century Enlightenment and nineteenth-century Liberalism. The integration of German Jewry was built around "emancipation," that strange concept loaded with so many meanings and implications. They envisaged a world where rational principles would direct mankind's progress, where social organization was based on belief in the fundamental rights of all men, and where Jews, citizens as all other citizens, would have the right and the duty to contribute to the progress of the state and society. The German Zionists, on the other hand, adopted a vision of Jewish life based on the principles of European nationalism of the nineteenth and twentieth century. The Zionists proclaimed the failure of Jewish emancipation and believed that in the social and political conditions of modern Europe only political self-definition in the frame of a separate Jewish state would provide a necessary condition—albeit not a sufficient one—for the continued existence of the Jewish people.

It is true that by the twenties some of the sharper edges of the ideological divergences between the camps had become blurred. Integration-oriented German Jewry had not remained oblivious to the historical meaning of its Jewish roots, and could not ignore the many setbacks to its emancipation-inspired hopes. German Zionists, on the other hand, born and educated in German culture, were unable and even unwilling to erase their deep attachment to German life. Both sides were equally affected by feelings of Jewish "togetherness" and mutual responsibility, an expression of the age-old principle of "Klal-Israel" reverberating quite strongly in the air, although not translatable into the concepts of modern European ideologies.[13] But when both Zionists and non-Zionists were forced to examine their principles in terms of their ultimate consequences—as was the case during the debate between the Zionists and the Centralverein in 1912–1914—the contradictory implications of the two conceptions were stated in unmistakable terms.[14] For the Zionists, emancipation meant compromising the national future of the Jewish people. For the German Jews of the Centralverein type, emancipation represented the mainstay of their conception of themselves as Jews and as Germans. To adopt the Zionist prognosis of Jewish life in Germany would have meant the destruction of the ideological foundations of Jewish existence in Germany.

These differences were *not* restricted to rhetoric, but had serious practical consequences, some of them even tragic, seen from a later perspective. The Centralverein steadily refused—for ideological reasons—to participate in any of the pro-Palestinian initiatives of the Zionists, including those of a purely practical character which were also sponsored by non-Zionist Jews, like the Keren Hayesod or the enlarged Jewish Agency.[15] As for the Zionists, it would have been plausible for them to have directed some effort to Jewish communal work, as was the case in other countries, in order to strengthen their influence in the

Jewish communities. But this happened only in a limited way. Compared with Zionism in Poland, in the United States, or anywhere else, Zionism in Germany demonstrated a relative *lack* of interest in local affairs. For reasons that belong to a different frame of considerations—but that were surely not an indication of the internal strength of German Zionism—the movement there never developed the East-European Zionist position of *Gegenwartsarbeit*, participation in Jewish communal work. The Zionists were active in social work and their cultural presence was strongly felt in German Jewry, but this never added up to a Zionist program of activity in the Diaspora. It is true that the Zionists dominated one of the major parties in German Jewish communal life, the Jüdische Volkspartei, one of the most influential factors in the Jewish community of Berlin. Some of the leading figures of this party, like A. Klee, A. Sandler, S. Moses, and others, were respected veterans of the German Zionist movement. Nevertheless, there were no formal organizational ties between the Jüdische Volkspartei and the Zionist Federation, no clear formulation of common purposes, and consequently, little influence of the latter on the former.

But the main political problem facing German Jewry during the twenties was the growing menace of political anti-Semitism. The brunt of the increasingly difficult fight against it was borne by the Centralverein. The Zionists' position regarding this vital matter was decidedly passive, partly because of their opposition to the Centralverein, but mainly for ideological reasons.[16] Their position on Jewish life in Germany "disconnected" them, not from consciousness of modern anti-Semitism, but certainly from the will to struggle against it in Germany. Since Jewish emancipation was an illusion and true equality was denied to Jews in the political climate of Weimar Germany, it seemed to the Zionists that their prognosis of the German-Jewish situation was all too true. As late as 1930, when a Jewish election commission was formed for the September elections which included the Centralverein, the Zionists, the German Bnai-Brith Order and the Berlin Jewish Community, Zionist collaboration was only lukewarm.[17] In 1932 so representative a German Zionist as Gustav Krojanker was still able to ponder the rise of the Nazi movement in rather complacent terms.[18] It was only after the Nazis attained power in 1933 that the political behavior of German Zionists changed radically. During the thirties the main groups in German Jewry found their way to political cooperation (the "Reichsvertretung der Juden in Deutschland"), but even then their collaboration was far from simple.[19]

Historically, German Zionism remains difficult to understand if our attention is directed only to the local German-Jewish scene. The German movement drew much of its inspiration and even its sense of existence from participation in the World Zionist movement in general—from Congresses, world-wide activities, from efforts in Palestine.

Indeed, the German Federation was one of the most disciplined sections of the world movement. It loyally supported most of the initiatives and positions of the central Zionist leadership (the Zionist Executive), from the internal reorganization in 1919–1920, through the Brandeis-Weizmann controversy in 1921, the establishment of the Keren Hayesod, up to the formation of the enlarged Jewish Agency in 1929. During the twenties, when Chaim Weizmann was fighting his difficult, protracted, and finally, losing battle as head of the World Zionist Organization, he could always count on the full support of the German Federation. It is true that some representative German Zionists became interested in Brit Shalom and developed their own ideas regarding the Arab question, but this was never translated into an official or even widely supported position of the German movement.

The identification of the German movement with the Zionist Executive was, in part, a matter of tradition. Up to 1919 the central Zionist leadership had been based in Germany. During the years 1911–1919 the Central Zionist Office and the office of the German movement had worked out of the same building in Berlin and strong personal ties had developed between the leaders and activists of both bodies. The German leadership had been very close to the work of the Zionist Executive, and in a sense had been educated to a close understanding of world-wide Zionist considerations. Over the years these ties assumed an element of importance that was more perceptible with regard to the German movement than to other Zionist federations; it was as if German Zionism drew its sense of existence more from its participation in the general movement than the others.

All in all, the German Zionist movement had only a limited influence on organized Jewish life in Germany and hardly responded to the major problem facing German Jewry in general, the fight against anti-Semitism. Its cooperation in the up-building of the Jewish National Home was limited: there was some success in raising money, but otherwise the contribution of German Zionism in this field remained very modest. Although the conventions of the Zionistische Vereinigung für Deutschland provided a stage for almost ritual, self-congratulatory speeches, in their more sober moments—and they apparently were many—the leaders of German Zionism knew better: the movement was small, it attracted few new members, the number of active members was decreasing and the older leadership was tired.[20]

In conclusion, it is difficult to understand the function attributed to German Zionism in the shaping of a German-Jewish identity. The *Ostjuden* that composed the rank and file of the German movement did not become better German Jews because of Zionism, nor did Zionism add new meaning to their existence in Germany. The personal situation of the small group of older German Jews in the leadership of the German Federation was far more complex than that of the corresponding level of Centralverein leaders. Culturally integrated into Germany but politically disengaging; deeply attached to the country, but dreaming about a Jewish National Home; living with the knowledge that the "radical" obligations assumed back in 1912 had not been realized—there was nothing easy in being a conscientious German Zionist. Right or wrong in historical retrospect, the alternatives open to the Centralverein Jew were, up to 1932, simpler, based on traditional principles, and supported by a significant segment of non-Jewish German society.

3. ZIONISM IN THE AMERICAN-JEWISH MILIEU

The first quarter of the twentieth century was one of the most dynamic periods in the history of American Jewry. Its main characteristics were entirely different from those of German Jewry. This was the peak time for Jewish mass immigration, the era of the creation and development of most of the institutions of American Jewry, the years when the social character of the new community was being established. There were about one million Jews in the United States at the beginning of the century, more or less three million by 1915, and about four and a half million in 1925, after the Johnson Act put an end to free Jewish immigration.[21]

The rapid growth of the community, its vitality, and the general atmosphere of optimism, strongly influenced the character of its organizational life. American Jewry during those years lacked the measure of ideological stability found in German Jewry, the well established relations (or absence of relations) between different ideological trends and bodies. In America, organizational confusion reigned supreme. Jews had brought with them from the Old World a rich communal tradition, which in the changed conditions of the American environment flowered in a chaotic mixture of under- and over-organization. In 1917/18 the Jewish Communal Register of New York City mentioned 3,600 Jewish organizations, for a population of 1,500,000.[22] And still the feeling was that not enough was being done.

Spiritual positions or ideological consistency turned out to be meaningless in this "confusion worse confounded," where everything was developing into something else. When Solomon Schechter started his work at the Jewish Theological Seminary at the beginning of the century, his intention was to create an institution orthodox in religious belief and practice, but adapted to the English language and to English and American culture.[23] It did not take long before the movement that grew up around the Seminary moved in a direction of its own, and Conservative Judaism emerged. On another side of the ideological spectrum, that of the Jewish socialists, Nathan Glazer observed that "it was not uncommon for a Jewish worker to read an anti-religious Yiddish newspaper, vote Socialist, join a Socialist union, and yet attend the synagogue weekly, or even daily, and observe most of the Jewish law."[24] Contradictory trends were to be found among the integration-oriented "German"-Jewish leadership, represented by Jacob H. Schiff, Louis Marshall and their associates. Again differently from what happened in Germany, they initiated a long and complex dialogue with the new segment of American Jewry—Yiddish-speaking, orthodox, Zionist—and gradually created patterns of collaboration. It was expressed by the participation of "German"-Jewish notables in the reorganization of the Jewish Theological Seminary in 1901/02, the creation of the Kehillah of New York in 1909, and discussions concerning the establishment of the American Jewish Congress during the years 1915–1918. Though difficult and sometimes tempestuous, an ongoing dialogue between the different segments of American Jewry evolved.[25]

Zionism too underwent a process of transformation and adaptation to the conditions of the New World. Indeed, most of the premises that had created Zionism in Europe did not quite apply to the realities of the American and the Jewish-American scene, and sooner or later they underwent a re-evaluation. Relations between Jews and non-Jews, the experience of anti-Semitism, and expectations about the future of Jews and Judaism in the United States led to conclusions and attitudes different from those of the European Jewish experience. American Zionism never produced a meaningful current which proclaimed the hopelessness of the Diaspora—which meant the *American* Diaspora. As early as the first decade of the century (incidentally, before Brandeis appeared on the Zionist scene) the movement in the United States elaborated what may aptly be called the American Zionist approach. A very important exponent of it was Israel Friedlaender, who later coined the phrase "Zionism plus Diaspora, Palestine plus America."[26] Friedlaender and, like him, Judah L. Magnes, Solomon Schechter, Harry Friedenwald and others aimed at a Jewish-Zionist position that combined the interests of Eretz Israel with the continued Jewish existence in the United States. The "negation of the Galuth" may apply to the East-European Jewish communities, they said, but not to America, where a new Jewish center and a new Jewish culture were developing, rich in hope, heavy in promise.[27] Later on, Brandeis and his associates added their own ideas to this approach,[28] and over the years this conception underwent further formulations that emphasized diverse sides of the same idea. The platform of American Zionism formulated as late as 1958 (with the leading participation of Mordecai M. Kaplan) was built on the conceptual foundations laid half a century earlier.[29]

One reason that made this development possible was the fact that American Zionism never took a critical stance against the ideology of Jewish integration the way German Zionism had done—an element characteristic of European Zionism in general. Sometimes the impression may have been different: there was the young Lipsky throwing the barbs of his considerable wit against the Reform Jewish establishment, or Bernard G. Richards scornful of those former Zionists that had "deserted our movement as soon as they became prosperous, and have settled into the blissful state of being called Bal Habatim."[30] But these opinions were patently not representative: American Zionism was looking for the "Balabatim," the pillars of Jewish society; it was bent on respectability rather than national or national-social transformation.[31] The only real Zionist critique of the "Jewish way of life" in the United States came from the American Socialist-Zionists, the Poalei Zion. But whoever listened to them? The eloquent tirades of men like Syrkin, Waldstein, Zuckermann and others reverberated futilely on the pages of the "Yiddisher Kaempfer."

The position adopted by American Zionism also implied a major change in their Zionist ideology. As Ben Halpern has so forcefully argued, the whole question of "emancipation," that bone of contention between Zionists and non-Zionists in Germany, was totally foreign to the Jewish experience in America.[32] The main historical polemic between American Zionists and the older segment of American Reform Jewry gravitated around the desired image of the community. This discussion went on on several levels for the decade prior to 1914. It represented one of the most important ideological developments in the history of American Zionism, and its outcome paved the way for the understanding and later collaboration between the American brand of "cultural" Zionism and the Reform Jewish leadership, represented by men like Jacob H. Schiff and Louis Marshall.[33]

During this protracted debate the Zionists gradually introduced into the discussion a distinction between the social and spiritual aspects of Jewish life in America, a distinction unknown to European Zionism. The Zionists compromised on the social issue, adopting an optimistic view of the future of American Jewry. But they held on to their broader concept of the nature of American Jewry, which transcended the narrow religious definition of Reform Judaism. Jews were a nationality, at least in the cultural sense. Cultural nationalism did not infringe on true Americanism.[34] Jews were a people, American Jews had the characteristics of "peoplehood."

Once the Zionists and non-Zionists came to an understanding over the nature of American Jewry, a wide range of possibilities opened before American Zionism. Historical analysis shows that during the first two decades of the century American Zionism developed a very ambitious ideological program. They hoped to "Zionize" the whole of the American Jewish community—although this Zionism was already of the American brand. Slowly, the Zionists brought round the leadership of the older Jewish establishment—and over the years a majority of all American Jews—to their ideological vision of American Judaism.

This development was not restricted to questions of ideology, but had clear practical consequences. Leading Zionists took a leading part in most of the organizational initiatives of American Jewry during the first quarter of the century like the Kehillah of New York, the American Jewish Congress and the development of the Conservative Synagogue. Indeed, one of the most debated questions among Zionist activists before 1914 (and, for that matter, after 1921) was the discrepancy between the possibilities and the realities of Zionism in America—between the fact that there was so much Zionist "sentiment" among American Jews, and so little Zionist "organization."[35] Zionists seemed more successful in American-Jewish enterprises than in building a *Zionist* organization. But this contradiction between "Jewish success" and "Zionist failure" was not accidental. It conformed to the clear conceptual aims enunciated by the American Zionists. When Judah L. Magnes resigned in 1908 from the secretaryship of the Federation of American Zionists in order to dedicate his considerable skills to the creation of the New York Kehillah, he explained this step at the annual convention of the Federation: "I feel that I shall be able to do more for our Federation and our movement if I am relieved of the duties which have been mine during the last three years. Our Zionism must mean for us Judaism in all its phases; Zionism is a complete and harmonized Judaism." [36] Even more explicitly, Louis D. Brandeis saw the American Jewish Congress (dominated by Zionists, according to his plan) as the instrument for the "organization" of the whole of American Jewry: "The Congress is not an end in itself. It is an incident of the organization of the Jewish people, an instrument through which their will may be ascertained, and when ascertained, may be carried out"—he proclaimed in January 1916.[37] Louis Lipsky too was conscious of the community-directed trend in American Zionism—the difference being that he was very much against it, and stressed the importance and necessity of concentrating on exclusively Zionist work.[38] But Lipsky, here too, was alone.

It seems apparent that the ideological "compromise" made by American Zionism—the fact that it curbed the more extreme Palestine-oriented tendencies in its midst and encouraged instead significant participation in American Jewish life—was not at all defensive. There was nothing in the position of its leaders or leading groups, or in their motives, that could be historically understood as impelled by a sense "of providing an ideology of survival for the Jewish community in the United States." [39] The leading role American Zionism played in shaping the inner structure of American Jewry represented one of the most positive programs of action elaborated in modern Jewry: it was ambitious and oriented to the future.

How far these ambitions were realized has become a question of interest to historians during the last decade. One thing, however, seems clear: the adaptation of Zionism to the conditions and the possibilities of America demanded a heavy price as far as the Palestine-directed component of the Zionist program was concerned. The concept of "Palestinianism" introduced by Y. Shapiro poorly defines the American Zionist position regarding the upbuilding of the Jewish National Home. The re-definition of Zionism in American terms *reduced* the involvement of the American Movement both in the world movement *and* in Palestine. American Zionist participation in Palestine always had a quality of conditionality about it that affected its effectiveness and the depth of its influence. The limits of American Zionist involvement were clearly drawn during the times of the movement's strength, like the Brandeis period in 1914–1921. Almost no one of the magnificent human team around Brandeis, the "Brandeis Group," was a full-time Zionist.[40] Brandeis himself found that he was unable to accept the full and open leadership of the world Zionist movement, when it was suggested to him in 1920.[41] The Mack-Brandeis administration ended in 1921 struggling for less involvement in the affairs of the World Zionist movement (and, implicitly, also in Palestine) and for more autonomy for local Zionist federations—which meant, more autonomy for the *American* federation.[42] Brandeis was here voicing more than his own disappointments with the European movement and its leadership. He was expressing the deep incompatibility that had developed between the direction of the World Zionist Organization and that adopted by the American movement long before the Brandeis period. The American organization continued as part of the world movement—indeed, a very important part of it. But the trend of mind and of activity developed by American Zionism, the fact that so many of its interests and ambitions were local American, may explain the limits of American Zionist participation in the shaping of the political, social and religious institutions of the Jewish National Home, and later, of the Jewish state.

4. CONCLUSIONS

The conclusions arrived at in this article diverge from those of other historians mentioned as a result of a difference in the historiosophical conception of Zionism as well as in methodology.

If Zionism is defined in clear-cut terms as a political movement leading to the realization of clear-cut political goals—the creation of a Jewish state and the concentration of all Jews there—then one set of evaluative criteria is called for. These are the criteria used by many of the historians mentioned in their analysis of German Zionism and of certain periods of American Zionism: ideological consistency, extent of *aliya,* and the size and quality of organization. If, on the other hand, Zionism is also considered as an expression of Jewish life in the Diaspora, then these well-defined goals are inadequate. If Zionism is not only directed towards a historical goal, but is a continuing process, it requires new evaluative criteria. It has then to be considered as part of the redefinition of modern Jewry, in all places and at all levels. The spiritual and social definition of modern Jewish life, the relationship between Zionists and other segments of Jewish society, the participation in local Jewish affairs and other questions all become relevant to considerations of Zionism.

The difficulty implicit in any historical understanding of Zionism is the fact that both trends, each one different in its internal meaning, are integral components of Zionism, as an idea and as a movement. One possesses a quasi-Messianic dimension which has anti-historical characteristics in its logic, revolts against the Jewish past, is directed towards "realization," towards an "end." The other is historical and evolutionary in its inner sense, directed towards "continuation." In Zionist history, as illustrated by the German and the American case—or, for that matter, by any other case—these two elements combined differently in each movement. But they were both essentially inseparable, necessarily related to one another. Finally, the inner composition of forces in Zionism should be considered a repetition of similar patterns present in modern Jewish history in general. As a matter of fact, it is this similarity that makes Zionism an integral part of the ongoing process of Jewish history.[43]

Zionist historiography which is unfamiliar with this complex mosaic of influences and relationships can hardly arrive at a convincing historical picture. To do so, it must offer an interpretation of the idea and the movement showing in each case how the inner combination of trends relate in each case to the general conditions of the Jews in each country, as well as to the Zionist movement as a whole.

It is apparent that new locally oriented research on Zionism has stumbled on historiosophical questions that it was unaware of. No distinctions were made between inner trends in Zionist history. Criteria of "realization" were applied to Zionist situations which aimed at "continuation." On the other hand, Zionism as Jewish "continuation," both in Germany and in the United States, was analyzed with disregard for the fact that local Zionism anywhere drew its raison d'être from being part and parcel of the Zionist movement as a whole—a movement with quite lucid historical aims and, in spite of everything, still cohesive enough to keep its different branches together, actively directed towards the realization of its major goals.

The introduction of the functional approach only adds methodological confusion to historical complexity. "Function" belongs to the realm of sociological or psychological categorization. This is certainly worthwhile and interesting in itself, but it introduces here non-historical aspects of the Jewish and Zionist situation in Germany and in the United States and transforms them into central points of reference. Historically seen, they were rather irrelevant. Considered as points of historical reference to promote the "shaping of a Jewish identity" in Germany or to provide "an ideology of survival for the Jewish community of the

United States," tells us very little. After all, *every* idea or movement in modern Jewish life, religious or non-religious, nationalist or anti-nationalist, of the left or of the right, aimed at fulfilling these same functions, i.e., guaranteeing Jewish survival (however defined), and creating for its adherents a basis for Jewish group identity. But that does not grant us an understanding of the historical meaning of these ideas or movements, nor throw light upon their complex internal relations or developments. They belong to a different set of considerations, and a rigorous methodological approach, whether sociological or historical, should refrain from mixing the two.

As it is, the lack of clear historiosophical conceptions and methodological categories has led to interpretations of German and American Zionism that do not square with historical fact and do not contribute to historical understanding. As regards the German case, Zionism made the life of its followers neither more rewarding nor more secure, either in Jewish or in German-Jewish terms, and can hardly have contributed by itself to the formation of a positive German-Jewish identity. German Zionism was basically "disintegrational" in its attitude towards Jewish existence in Germany. It never developed a significant *Gegenwartsarbeit* program, and the ties it established with German Jewry and its influence upon it were, up to 1933, rather ineffective. There is reason to believe that this was less the result of an explicit program of action (or non-action), on the part of the German movement, than a reflex of the lower tenor of vitality that characterized German-Jewish life during those years, and affected German Zionism as well.

As for American Zionism, its vision of the Jewish future in America was obviously too self-serving to be classified as a "function," and too vital and positive to be linked with the idea of "survival." American Zionism was basically "integrational" in its attitude towards Jewish existence in the United States. It concentrated on the far-reaching task of molding the spiritual structure of growing American Jewry according to the ideological brand of Zionism it had elaborated. Its ideological originality was applied to American matters, the "Palestinian" component being the weaker element in its position. It seems that up to a point American Zionism succeeded in its endeavors. But the lack of equilibrium between its local intentions and its general Zionist aspirations severely limited American Zionist involvement in Palestine and its influence in the formation of the Jewish National Home and its institutions.

NOTES

I would like to thank my friend Abraham Margaliot for the penetrating observations made on a first draft of this essay.

1. For a classical example see Adolph Boehm, *Die Zionistische Bewegung*, Berlin, 1922 (expanded version, Tel Aviv, 1935–1937). Among more recent works written in a similar vein: Walter Laqueur, *A History of Zionism*, London, 1972, David Vital, *The Origins of Zionism*, Oxford, 1975, and Mordehai Eliav, *David Wolffsohn, the Man and his Times—The Zionist Movement 1905–1914* (Hebrew), Jerusalem, 1977.

2. On German Zionism see Ismar Schorsch, *Jewish Reactions to German Anti-Semitism, 1870–1914*, New York, 1972; Jehuda Reinharz, *Fatherland or Promised Land*, Ann Arbor, 1975; Abraham Margaliot, *The Political Reaction of German Jewish Organizations and Institutions to the Anti-Jewish Policy of the National Socialists, 1932–1935* (Hebrew), Jerusalem, 1971, Ph.D. thesis; Stephen M. Poppel, *Zionism in Germany 1897–1933*, Philadelphia, 1977 and Arnold Paucker, *Der jüdische Abwehrkampf*, Hamburg, 1969, are not far from this new trend though Poppel concentrates more on the Zionists. On American Zionism, see Yonathan Shapiro, *Leadership of the American Zionist Organization, 1897–1930*, Urbana, Ill., 1971; Melvin I. Urofsky, *American Zionism from Herzl to the Holocaust*, Garden City, N.Y., 1976; Evyatar Friesel, *The Zionist Movement in the United States 1897–1914* (Hebrew), Tel Aviv, 1970; Naomi W. Cohen, *American Jews and the Zionist Idea*, New York, 1975.

3. O. Handlin, *Adventure in Freedom*, New York, 1954, p. 217; W. Herberg, *Protestant, Catholic, Jew*, Garden City, N.Y., 1960, p. 185.

4. Shapiro, *Leadership*, p. 5.

5. Shapiro, *Leadership*, pp. 5–6, and in detail, chap. IX ("From Zionism to Palestinianism"), pp. 248–261; also Cohen, *Zionist Idea*, p. XVI, pp. 142–49.

6. On the Americanization of Zionism, see M. I. Urofsky, lecture, H. L. Feingold and H. M. Sachar, comments, "Zionism: An American Experience," *American Jewish Historical Quarterly*, vol. 62, 1973, pp. 215–43.

7. Poppel, *Zionism in Germany*, pp. 92, 164–65, 96. In a more moderate vein, see also J. Reinharz, "Three Generations of German Zionists," *Jerusalem Quarterly*, no. 9, 1978, pp. 95–110, especially p. 109.

8. U. O. Schmeltz, "Migrations," *Encyclopaedia Judaica*, 16: 1519–1524; D. Gurevich et al., *The Jewish Population of Palestine*, Jerusalem, 1944. The 12 percent that went to Palestine include about 61,000 Jews that came from Germany between 1933–1939, but can hardly be considered coming for ideological reasons alone.

9. E. G. Reichmann, "Der Bewusstseinwandel der deutschen Juden," *Deutsches Judentum in Krieg und Revolution, 1916–1923*, ed., W. E. Mosse, A. Paucker, Tübingen, 1971, pp. 511–612.

10. E. Bennathan, "Die Demographische und Wirtschaftliche Struktur der Juden," *Entscheidungsjahr 1932*, ed., W. E. Mosse, A. Paucker, Tübingen, 1966, pp. 87–131.

11. See, e.g., A. Marcus, *Die Wirtschaftliche Krise der Deutschen Juden*, Berlin, 1931; F. Teilhaber, *Der Untergang der Deutschen Juden*, Berlin, 1921; J. Klatzkin, *Krisis und Entscheidung*, Berlin, 1921.

12. See Poppel, *Zionism in Germany*, pp. 99–100.

13. Max Naumann, the leader and ideologist of the "Verein Nationaldeutscher Juden," sharply opposed the concept of "Klal-Israel" but was nevertheless very aware of its existence and did not lose any opportunity to castigate the Centralverein on this score. See his *Ganz-Deutsche oder Halb-Deutsche*, Berlin, 1921.

14. See J. Reinharz, *Fatherland*, chaps. 4, 5. See also L. Holländer's speech "Zur Klarstel-

lung" at the C.V. convention March 29–30, 1913, *Im Deutschen Reich,* May 1913, nos. 5–6, pp. 194–200, and on pp. 245–47.

15. See resolutions of C.V. Council meeting, February 11–13, 1928, *C. V. Zeitung,* Feb. 12, 1928, no. 7, p. 103; meeting of March 23–24, 1929, *ibid.,* March 29, 1929, no. 13, p. 160. For former resolutions, see *Centralverein: Deutschtum, Judentum, Zionismus und Palestina-Arbeit,* 1926 (?).

16. A. Paucker, *Abwehrkampf,* pp. 40–43. Regarding the efforts of the Centralverein, *ibid.,* pp. 45–61.

17. F. Brodnitz, *Leistung und Kritik,* Berlin, 1931, pp. 11–12; Pauker, *Abwehrkampf,* pp. 42–43.

18. G. Krojanker, *Zum Problem des Neuen Deutschen Nationalismus,* Berlin, 1932, pp. 30–33.

19. A. Margaliot, "The Dispute over the Leadership of German Jewry (1933–1938)," *Yad Vashem Studies,* vol. 10, 1974, pp. 129–48.

20. Correspondence K. Blumenfeld—R. A. Jacobson from about April 1928, in *ZVfD: Beitraege zur Frage unserer Propaganda,* Berlin, 1928, letters 3 and 4.

21. On development of American Jewry, see L. P. Gartner, "Immigration and the Formation of American Jewry, 1840–1925," *Jewish Society Through the Ages,* ed., B. H. Ben Sasson, S. Ettinger, New York, 1971, pp. 297–312.

22. Kehillah of New York City: *The Jewish Communal Register of New York City 1917–1918,* New York, 1918, p. 101.

23. See S. Schechter, "The Charter of the Seminary," (1902), *Seminary Addresses,* New York, 1959, pp. 9–33.

24. *American Judaism,* Chicago, 1972, p. 67.

25. For the trends underlying this development, see E. Friesel, "The Age of Optimism in American Jewry," *A Bicentenial Festschrift for Jacob Rader Marcus,* New York, 1976, pp. 131–55.

26. I. Friedlaender, *Past and Present,* New York, 1961, p. XXIII.

27. The best statement of this opinion is to be found in Friedlaender's essay from 1907, "The Problem of Judaism in America," *Past and Present,* pp. 159–84.

28. Brandeis, "The Jewish Problem—How to Solve It" (1915), J. de Haas, ed., *Louis D. Brandeis,* New York, 1929, pp. 170–90; J. W. Mack, *Zionism and Americanism,* New York, 1918; M. M. Kaplan, *A New Zionism,* New York, 1959.

29. Kaplan, *A New Zionism,* pp. 187–89.

30. L. Lipsky, "The Duty of American Jews," *Maccabaean,* Feb. 1909, pp. 41–46; B. G. Richards, "The Faults of Our Organization," *Maccabaean,* June 1911, p. 179; see also in *Dos Yiddishe Folk,* May 12, 1911, no. 10, p. 2.

31. Friedlaender's observations on problems of American Zionism, *Dos Yiddishe Folk,* May 26, 1911, no. 12, p. 2; for H. Conheim on Zionist situation in New York City (April 1910), in M. Davis, "Israel Friedlaender's Minute Book of the Ahava Club (1909–1912)," *M. M. Kaplan Jubilee Volume,* New York, 1953, p. 183.

32. B. Halpern, "America Is Different," *The American Jew,* New York, 1956, pp. 34–69.

33. M. Rischin, "The Early Attitude of the American Jewish Committee to Zionism," *Publications of the American Jewish Historical Society,* 49 (1959/60), pp. 188–201; H. Parzen, "The Purge of the Dissents: Hebrew Union College and Zionism, 1903–1907," *Jewish Social Studies,* vol. 37, 1975, pp. 291–322; Friesel, *Zionist Movement in U.S.,* pp. 90–108, 160–68.

34. J. L. Magnes, "A Republic of Nationalities" (Feb. 1909), *The Emanuel Pulpit,* vol. 2, 1909, no. 6; "What Zionism Has Given the Jews," *American Hebrew,* Aug. 11, 1911, pp. 412–12; Brandeis, "The Jewish Problem—How to Solve It," in de Haas, *Brandeis,* pp. 170–90.

35. See, e.g., *Report of the Administrative Committee of the F.A.Z. Convention,* June

1913 (Cincinnati), p. 12; interview with B.A. Rosenblatt, Nov. 1963, Oral History Project, Dept. of Contemporary Jewry, Hebrew University, Jerusalem; Shmaryahu Levin, letter to the Inner Actions Committee, July 3, 1914, Central Zionist Archives, Jerusalem, Z3/395.

36. *Maccabaean*, August 1908, pp. 68–69; also Magnes's speech, Davis, "Israel Friedlaender's Minute Book," p. 183.

37. S. Goldman, ed., *Brandeis on Zionism*, 1942, p. 105.

38. L. Lipsky, "What Is Wrong with the Zionist Organization in America?" *Maccabaean*, May 1914, p. 140; [L. Lipsky], "The Results of the Tannersville Convention," *Maccabaean*, July 1911, pp. 16–17.

39. Shapiro, *Leadership*, p. 5.

40. Jacob de Haas was the exception to this rule. But then de Haas was the most untypical member of the Group in other senses as well.

41. See presentation by Lipsky, and Brandeis's answer, at caucus of the American delegation to the London Zionist Conference, July 14, 1920, Brandeis Zionist Papers.

42. See "Summary of the Position of the Zionist Organization of America in Conference with Dr. Weizmann and Associates" (March 1921), reproduced in: *Statement to the Delegates of the 12th Zionist Congress on Behalf of the Former Administration of the Zionist Organization of America*, 1921.

43. See the author's "The Jewish State and Jewish History: Contradiction or Continuation?" *Judaism*, 27, 1978, pp. 421–30.

14.

The Americanization of Zionism, 1880–1930
Ben Halpern

The late Judd L. Teller once published in *Commentary* a striking analysis which anticipated many of the clichés of current discussions of American Zionism.[1] America, he said, had two distinct Zionist traditions, of which one was foreign—specifically, East European—and the other was "native," and uniquely American. The style of native American Zionism was Romantic (or to use his term, "Messianic"), in contrast to the Social Realism of the Europeans; it was not based, like theirs, on a real need to achieve political enfranchisement, since American Jews were long since emancipated; and it was a Jewish reflection of the contemporary Social Gospel among liberal Christians. The pedigree of native American Zionism was long and distinguished, going back to Mordecai Manuel Noah and Emma Lazarus; but it was fully defined only in the course of Louis D. Brandeis' historic quarrel with Chaim Weizmann in 1920–21; and in the 1950's it became the consensus opinion of American Zionists in opposition to David Ben-Gurion's Israeli Zionism.

Recent versions of Teller's thesis, especially since the 1967 Six-Day War, hold that Zionism has now attained the status of a consensus shared by the whole of American Jewry, whether enrolled in Zionist organizations or not. As Norman Podhoretz put it, "We are all Zionists."[2] If so, according to Melvin Urofsky, this is because ours is a "Brandeisian Zionism" which owes very little to Eastern Europe and sharply opposes the Israeli version. He explains the rise and fall of Zionist fortunes and Zionist numbers in America as directly dependent on the acceptance or rejection of the Brandeis approach, which pur-

Reprinted by permission of the American Jewish Historical Society from *American Jewish History* 69, no. 1 (September 1979): 15–33.

portedly solved the problem of "dual loyalties" that Zionism posed for American Jews.[3]

To test this thesis fully would require covering a longer period and wider area than this brief chapter can consider. It is clear that at any rate in the half century of American Jewish life from 1880 to 1930, the allegedly unique "native" Zionist tradition of Teller's hypothesis had not yet overwhelmed the European tradition of the immigrants. Indeed, Brandeis (like Herzl before him) was decisively repudiated by the movement in 1921. In Teller's words:

A strange and sad Zionist pattern repeated itself; the East European Zionists had once before renounced a messiah who had come to them from outside the Pale.[4]

Like other messiahs, Brandeis had his devoted followers who remained loyal to him after the fall; and in 1930 his supporters came back to power, in a way, in American Zionism. However, even according to the currently conventional version of the events, the issue of the conflict between the two purported Zionist traditions certainly remained in doubt throughout the period covered in our survey. In order to describe the period *wie es eigentlich gewesen,* we shall try to deal with the conventional thesis in a realistic, or at least sober, rather than romantic manner. Our focus will be upon the specific functions Zionism performed for the various types of Zionists who flourished, or languished, from 1880 to 1930.

As everyone knows, early American Zionists (like their contemporaries in West European countries) were mainly new immigrants from Eastern Europe.[5] Their Zionist attitudes and activities were, in the main, directly imported from the Old Country. They sent funds to support new settlements and Zionist institutions in Palestine which they raised from the dues and contributions of their fluctuating membership, and from other sympathizers, collecting donations in the synagogue, from charity boxes deposited in homes, and by other traditional Jewish methods. Some Zionist societies, going under the name of *Shave Zion* ("Returning to Zion") pooled small regular savings for investment in land purchase and other prospective costs of their own intended settlement in the Holy Land.[6] Their leader and organizer, Adam Rosenberg (Philadelphia-born; raised in a German Orthodox home in Hamburg; became a lawyer who practiced in New York), was prominently active from 1891–97 in efforts to unite pre-Herzlian Zionists in England and America with major philanthropists, the Barons Maurice de Hirsch and Edmond de Rothschild, in order to purchase and colonize lands in

Palestine, east as well as west of the Jordan.[7] When many of the unstable societies in Europe, responding to Herzl's call for a Zionist Congress in 1897, regrouped and joined the new World Zionist Organization (WZO), their American counterparts were quickened into new life in the same way. So too when, in the opening years of the twentieth century, the religious Zionist Mizrachi and socialist Zionist Poalei-Zion arose in Russia and Poland, emigrants from those countries simultaneously organized feeble branches of those movements in America.

The immigrant Zionist factions, sharing vicariously the experiences of European Zionism, were not of course fully engaged in the European quarrels. The issues between religious and secular Zionists, as well as between the splinter groups of Russian, Polish, and Austrian socialist Zionists, were muted and neutralized in America. Even the most doctrinaire among them, the socialists, recognized that imported ideologies only partly applied in America.[8] Also, in England as well as in America, Zionism performed certain specific functions in the adjustment of new immigrants, functions that were not relevant in the Old Country.[9] They provided the comfort of a familiar, Old Country milieu for small groups of strangers in the New World. Zionist societies often took the form of lodges and fraternal orders or of landsmanshaften composed of fellow-townsmen from abroad. They adopted measures of mutual aid in sickness and need and for burial; organized picnics, balls, and lectures; and in adopting this common pattern of behavior, they became an integral part of a broader institutional network that promoted the first adjustment of the Jewish immigrant ghetto at large. In this way Zionist societies, landsmanshaften, and lodges, like other similarly organized immigrant groupings, even while recreating copies of the Old Country overseas, served no less than trade unions and the ghetto settlement houses did to advance the Americanization of the immigrants as a cohesive community.

It appears, therefore, that early American Zionism was very largely an import brought in by East European immigrants, exactly as was the case of Zionism in Western Europe. While it served—or as sociologists say, had a "latent function"—to advance the Americanization of the immigrants, and while they understood at once that their old doctrines could not be applied totally and unchanged in the New World, a major attraction of early American Zionism for the bulk of its membership was that it provided an Old Country milieu for them. But one might perhaps still argue that this feature, by attracting some, repelled a potentially larger group of adherents, since everyone agrees that early Zionism was hardly a mass movement in America.

Jewish immigrants in nineteenth-century America were generally considered (for example, by union organizers) to be notoriously resistant to the demands of discipline and organizational solidarity.[10] Not until a later generation, in the twentieth century, did the Jewish trade unions achieve impressive size and notable success. The Zionist clubs and lodges were small like all other Jewish immigrant societies in the 1880's and 1890's and had a constantly fluctuating membership. But the Zionist presence was felt well beyond its organized framework. The Zionist causes with which some identified themselves fully were also occasional concerns of other, similar societies or family circles.

The new Hebrew and Yiddish press that arose to serve the immigrant ghetto reported items of Zionist interest together with the other news of Old Country happenings, celebrations, wars and calamities that were its major features.[11] The printers and writers who manned the press included many, like the Mintz brothers, who came to America from Palestine, the polemicist and bibliophile Ephraim Deinard, and the lodge organizer Leon Zolotkoff, who had been Zionists abroad and continued their activity in New York, Philadelphia, and Chicago. Later, in the twentieth century, the socialist newspaper, the *Forward,* rose under the editorship of Abraham Cahan to a dominant position in the American-Yiddish reading world, and it adopted a generally anti-Zionist tone; but in the Yiddish press at large writers of strong religious or secular Zionist leanings were even then a major, if not predominant, element. The Yiddish press remained into the middle of the twentieth century the most reliable means for rallying the Jewish public for mass action and demonstrations. Men like Louis Marshall who wished to exert influence on Jewish popular opinion, whether to restrain or arouse it, found it necessary to control or at least be significantly represented in the Yiddish press.[12]

If the mass of early Zionists were new immigrants, the main source of their leadership, as of the leadership of American Jewry at large, were older, settled American Jews. The established community was acutely aware of the immigrants as a problem from the beginning, in the 1880's, and by the end of the century it had learned to consider them a potential force of significant strength in communal affairs. The immigrant Zionists were an element that various factions in the older Jewish community responded to differentially, not only in terms of their basic attitudes to the doctrine of Zionism but because of its bearing on other issues that divided them.

The Jewish religious Reform movement, which came to dominate the organized American Jewish community from the 1870's to the end of the century—that is, during the first decades of mass Jewish immigration from Eastern Europe—was inherently anti-Zionist, since its commitment to an absolute separation between religion and politics was opposed in principle to the aspiration—inherent in Zionism—to restore the Jews as an independent nation-state.[13] But there was another side of Reform that could, on occasion, see Zionism in a more positive light.

The Reform movement was a strenuous effort to retain the uncertain loyalty of succeeding generations of young Jews, exposed to the seductions of secularism and assimilation, and it pursued this aim by refashioning traditional Judaism in a more modern, decorous style, like that of contemporary liberal Christianity. But some Reform leaders, especially after witnessing the inroads made on their congregations by the vogue of Felix Adler's new Ethical Culture, feared the side-effects of their own liberalism and were inclined to preserve whatever they could of older ritual and ethnic-cultural traditions.[14] Zionism, it seemed to them, was one way to combine loyalty to Jewish folkways and traditional sentiments with the impulse to modernity; and it seemed particularly apt to stem the erosion of religious belief and communal attachment among the radicalized young East European immigrants, who were increasingly becoming a problem for the established leadership, whether Reform or conservative in its tendency. The settled American community, especially its Orthodox and conservatively Reformed congregations, had long supported the Jews resident in the Holy Land, in the same way that Jews everywhere did, seeing in this an obligation of religious sentiment and brotherly charity.[15] In the same spirit, some now extended their support to the new Zionist settlements founded in Palestine after 1880. A few men like the Reform Rabbis Gustave Gottheil, Bernard Felsenthal, Benjamin Szold, and the young Stephen S. Wise joined Orthodox leaders and the newly arrived immigrant Zionists in their Zionist activities, especially after the 1897 Zionist Congress added a Western aspect and new éclat to the struggling, mainly East European, pre-Herzlian movement.

The combination of motives that made Zionists out of such American Jews who were not part of the immigrant ghetto also affected others like them who, however, did not become Zionists. They too nurtured a tradition of charitable support for the Jewish community in the Holy Land, and they too appreciated the value of any influence which, like Zionism, might counteract the assimilationist radicalism that estranged young immigrants, as well as young native American Jews, from their religious community.

Such concerns were particularly active among a new group of old-line American Jewish leaders who arose in the coastal cities where the mass of immigrants congregated.[16] For it was the peculiar fate of the Reform leadership concentrated in Cincinnati that no sooner had it consolidated its position of dominant authority in the religious life of American Jewry, controlling the national union of congregations and the central rabbinical seminary which served the preponderant majority of old American synagogues, than the mass immigration of East Europeans, concentrating in Eastern metropolitan centers, removed the center of gravity of American Jewry from their orbit and increasingly rendered them, their doctrines, and their authority, all irrelevant to its current concerns. Cincinnati, the capital of the Reform German Jews meant nothing, or less than nothing, to the Orthodox or irreligious Russian and Rumanian Jewish immigrants in New York and Philadelphia. Other old-line leaders, however, the Sulzbergers and Adlers of Philadelphia and the Schiffs, Strauses, and Marshalls of New York, became closely involved with the care and Americanization of the newcomers, and it was they who now succeeded to the authority once claimed by Cincinnati. These new leaders carried out their task in a spirit of closer understanding of their wards than the "classical Reform" doctrine of Cincinnati could provide, and with greater flexibility and willingness to adjust their preconceptions to the developing new situation. In 1906, after having led a major relief campaign of American Jewry following the 1903 Kishinev pogrom, these men consolidated their leadership by founding the American Jewish Committee. One of the effects of their rise was the close, if ambivalent and often problematic, relationship they developed with Zionists, among the other exotic varieties that came in and flourished, more or less vigorously, in the immigrant ghetto.

The East coast old-line leaders undertook to support in addition to the Hebrew Union College, Cincinnati's Reform rabbinical school, another more conservative institution in New York, the Jewish Theological Seminary.[17] They hoped to be able to attract young Eastern Europeans better than Cincinnati had done by offering them a more traditional, yet modern, scholarly curriculum. In 1902 they brought in to head the Seminary the famous Reader in Rabbinics at Cambridge University, Dr. Solomon Schechter, and he brought with him from Europe an outstanding faculty of young scholars, including Louis Ginzberg, Alexander Marx, and above all Israel Friedlaender from the University of Stuttgart, already known as the translator and popularizer of both Ahad Ha-am and Simon Dubnow. All these men shared in the Ahad Ha-amist cultural

Zionism and the Dubnowian Diaspora nationalism that was current among some Russian Jewish students and also among some Orthodox German Jewish students in West European universities, and it soon transpired that such views, interpreted in a conservative religious vein by these men, were shared by Schechter. The close ties that this group retained with the American Jewish Committee, in spite of some irritations that their public adherence to Zionism caused, were fortified when the young rabbi Judah L. Magnes, upon returning from his studies in Germany, became their close associate and developed especially strong relations with the immigrant Zionists on New York's East Side. Magnes had even closer ties with uptown Jewry, as the brother-in-law of the leading light of the American Jewish Committee, Louis Marshall, and for a while as rabbi at Temple Emanu-El, the synagogue attended by nearly all the New York leaders of the Committee. He, together with the Zionist group of Seminary scholars, provided the effective leadership of the Federation of American Zionists from 1904 to 1911 under the nominal Presidency of an eminent Baltimore ophthalmologist, Dr. Harry Friedenwald.[18]

Thus, the period from Herzl's death to the accession of Brandeis saw a far more decisive Americanization of Zionism than the earlier years. By its close ties with the Jewish Theological Seminary and indirectly—not to say, more often than not, antagonistically—with the American Jewish Committee, the Herzlian Federation of American Zionists became involved in a complex relationship with the central power installation of American Jewry. The writer Louis Lipsky, who led American Zionism in opposition to Brandeis through the decade of the 1920's, was for much of this time simultaneously an editor of the leading non-Zionist journal, *The American Hebrew,* and of the official Zionist journal, *The Maccabaean.* Judah Magnes, who more or less ran the Zionist administration until 1911, thereafter organized a united New York Jewish community, the Kehillah, for the American Jewish Committee. But if the influence and prestige of American Zionism grew during those years, its enrolled membership and organized efficiency, after a sharp rise in response to the 1903 Kishinev pogrom and the crisis that followed the 1905 revolution in Russia, fell off in a disheartening way. After 1911, "prominence deserted" the American Zionist movement, as Lipsky put it, when Magnes and Friedlaender concentrated their efforts on building the Kehillah, and the Zionist federation was left to the devices of second-rank East Side leaders and of young Lipsky himself. Thus the heightened influence that came with the greater Americanization of Zionism was not reflected in greater or more effective strength of the Zionist organization.[19]

One further feature of the Americanization of Zionism immediately preceding the advent of Brandeis should be noted. What raised the prestige and influence of Zionism in those years was a process of rapprochement between the established American Jewish leadership and the immigrant community, in which the old Americans moved closer to European Jewish patterns and values as much as, or more than, the immigrants adopted conventional Americanism. The main instruments of the rapprochement, the Jewish Theological Seminary group, were East Europeans themselves or, in the case of their associate, Dr. Magnes, had become profoundly identified with the ideas and attitudes of East European Jewish fellow-students in Germany. As for other leaders, new immigrants who arrived at that time—including men like Chaim Zhitlovsky, Nachman Syrkin and those poets and playwrights who raised the Yiddish press and culture of the East Side to unprecedented new heights—they brought to the New World a principled radicalism that made their Zionist followers strongly inclined to challenge, rather than passively submit to, demands of unilateral Americanization. Their pressure, exerted not only through the tiny socialist Zionist party but more generally through the Yiddish press and in other Zionist circles, tended to pose exigent demands regarding general social and specific Jewish issues upon the American and the Jewish community.[20]

Restless spirits like these, not to speak of older immigrant leaders displaced by the Seminary group, could not be satisfied with the state of American Zionism, especially after "prominence" turned its attention away to concentrate on other projects. Another type of American Zionist, usually native-born or thoroughly Americanized, also took issue with the 1904–1911 leaders, and with the strongly rabbinical variant of cultural Zionism and Diaspora nationalism that they promoted. From the beginning of American Zionism—again, precisely as in the case of West European Zionism—there were men and women, strongly conscious of their Jewish identity and yet without firm religious belief, who were attracted to the movement. They appeared at all stages of American Zionist history, beginning with Emma Lazarus' article on "The Jewish Problem," in which a typical young Russian Jewish nationalist intellectual among the immigrants of the 1880's is praised for being "fully emancipated from the yoke of dogma."[21]

The appearance of Herzl attracted young Zionists of agnostic or extreme liberal religious views like Stephen S. Wise, Louis Lipsky or

Horace M. Kallen, then at Harvard. For some of them, the implicit opposition to Herzl which they saw and resented in the cultural Zionism of a Magnes was a primary reason to seek a radical change. Brandeis, himself an agnostic secularist Jew, was inducted into the Zionist movement under the auspices of precisely such people; in particular by Herzl's personal emissary to America, the British Jewish journalist, Jacob de Haas, editor of the Boston *Jewish Advocate*.[22]

Brandeis' accession was the crowning achievement of a concerted effort by the Federation since 1911 to recapture "prominence" for American Zionism.[23] The East Side leaders tried to reach new sources of support, more affluent and better situated to influence native Americans, by offering such persons special conditions of membership. For men, "Zion Associations" were established which dispensed with the routine of regular meetings and petty fund collections characteristic of other Zionist societies in return for contributions on a larger scale, in funds, counsel, or personal influence. Women were offered a similar form of association with still more modest demands. They were not even expected, like their male counterparts, to purchase the shekel, the certificate which identified one for participation in Zionist elections. However, the women who in 1912, under the decisive leadership of Henrietta Szold, organized the truly unique American Women's Zionist Organization, Hadassah, as a form of Zion Association, insisted on full Zionist rights, duties, and credentials within the general organization, together with autonomy in carrying out their own special social welfare project with the aid of both full and associate members, the latter to be gradually raised to full Zionist consciousness and commitment.[24] Brandeis himself entered Zionist ranks through the Boston Zion Association, but from the beginning he was considered a prospect for top Zionist leadership. He was expected in any case to preside over American efforts to advance the industrial development of Palestine. Then, upon the outbreak of the First World War, he agreed to take over the leadership of the entire American movement, which many thought at the time would also serve as the leadership, from a neutral base, of the whole war-disrupted international Zionist movement.

The Zionist organization expanded under Brandeis' leadership at an explosive rate not to be equalled until the emergency of the Second World War produced a parallel rapid inflation of its ranks. Urofsky's insistent suggestion that Brandeis' defense of Zionism against charges of "dual loyalties" was the sufficient cause of this growth—a thesis for which he offers no documented evidence—cannot be sustained. Other

American Zionists before Brandeis, and Zionist leaders in all Western countries, dealt with the same problem and offered similar rebuttals without producing a similar expansion of membership. It was unquestionably the emergency of the war years, 1914–1918, which was the operative factor in Zionist growth, for no sooner was it over than American Zionist membership began its precipitous drop, years before the defeat of the Brandeis group in 1921. Brandeis' personal prestige, his constant surveillance of a previously slipshod administration, his unending demands for "Men! Money! Discipline!" made it certain that the challenge of the times would be fully and efficiently responded to.[25]

Brandeis' *persona,* if not his Zionist formulas, had a more direct impact on certain kinds of Zionists who now joined, partly because he himself recruited them. Irma Lindheim recalls in her memoirs that aspiring young lawyers saw in the reinvigorated Zionist movement, now headed by a man so close to the Wilson administration, a promising field for pursuing professional and political ambitions. Brandeis conducted a vigorous search of his own for "college men," particularly young graduates of Harvard Law School, whom he co-opted to leadership or special assignments for the regular and emergency Zionist organizations he controlled. Among those recruited were men like Felix Frankfurter, Judge Julian Mack, Walter Lippmann, Bernard Flexner, Benjamin Cohen, and others who achieved national and international eminence. Upon Brandeis' acceptance of Zionist leadership, "college men" and professionals among already enrolled Zionists enthusiastically offered him support. The Harvard Menorah Society group, which Horace Kallen hoped to expand into a nationwide elite order (the "Parushim"), undertook to supply him with young and able volunteers for any and all special duties. Older Zionists like Richard Gottheil, Stephen Wise, and above all Jacob de Haas, who had stood somewhat apart from Zionist affairs for a decade, now saw in Brandeis an inspiring leader through whom they hoped to restore a new Herzlian regime in Zionism.[26]

The old Zionists, apart from those who were close to the American Jewish Committee, pressed Brandeis from the start to adopt a militant attitude in American Jewish affairs and challenge the non-Zionists for the leadership of the whole community. Kallen, then teaching in Wisconsin and active in the Middle West, wanted an open confrontation with the Reform establishment in its Cincinnati headquarters. De Haas and Wise, together with Lipsky and his East Side friends, urged Brandeis to do battle with the American Jewish Committee on behalf of the project of an American Jewish Congress launched by "downtown" Zionists.

Brandeis was not prepared to begin his work in this new field by getting involved in internal quarrels over unfamiliar issues, but sought, as was his custom, to lead by general consent.[27]

His first major effort was to mobilize and organize his Zionist forces for participation in the major relief campaigns initiated in response to war needs. Zionists under his lead cooperated with the American Jewish Committee in forming, first, the American Jewish Relief Committee (AJRC) and later, the American Jewish Joint Distribution Committee (JDC). The latter was a roof-organization set up to coordinate the campaigns and allocate the receipts of the AJRC and two other organizations, the Central Relief Committee (CRC) established by Orthodox (including Zionist) immigrant circles and the People's Relief Committee (PRC) established by socialist workers (including Zionists) downtown. The cooperation between these bodies, while remarkably effective, was not always harmonious, and gradually Brandeis was drawn into the general competition for power in the Jewish community as the leader of his ardent Zionist partisans. In spite of the remarkable achievements of his Zionist fund raising campaign and the demonstrated value of his Washington contacts for the efficient distribution of aid in Palestine, he had to concede controlling power in this field to the non-Zionist JDC leaders. However, he took up the fight against them on the issue of the American Jewish Congress, and led his cohorts to a victory which, more than any other factor, convinced government circles abroad that the Zionists, under Brandeis, represented the true leadership of American Jewry. It was this, above all, that made possible the major contribution of American Zionism to the issuance of the Balfour Declaration.[28]

By entering the fight for a democratic, popularly elected American Jewish Congress, Brandeis committed himself to a cause whose ideology had been framed, and was being forcefully articulated, by immigrant intellectuals, many of whom had actively fought out this very issue over the past decade in Eastern and Central Europe.[29] Nachman Syrkin, Chaim Zhitlovsky, Abraham Shomer, and other stalwarts of East European Jewish nationalism saw the democratic organization of world Jewry, starting with America, as an objective of primary and permanent importance, expecting all else to flow from the political activation of the Jewish masses. Their disciples and counterparts in Europe had organized Jewish political parties active in Russian, Austrian and even, briefly, in German politics, and they had promulgated the Helsingfors Program, a plan prefiguring the most ambitious "national minority rights" projects to emerge from the First World War.

Brandeis' immediate aides who were most committed to this cause, men like Lipsky, de Haas, Wise, and Bernard G. Richards, did not share the uncompromising ideological commitment of these downtown allies, and certainly Brandeis himself was far more cautious and reserved on the issues of principle.[30] The doctrine of cultural pluralism which these Americans defended, and which was most explicitly argued by Horace Kallen, was pale and bloodless in comparison to the full-blooded Diaspora nationalism of the Europeans. (It did not take on a more forceful political complexion even in Mordecai M. Kaplan's version in later years; only Black nationalists and Hispano-Americans in our own times produced a close, albeit more violent, American equivalent.) Brandeis' adoption of cultural pluralism, a striking departure from his previous condemnation of "hyphenated Americanism," was based on very narrow grounds, and reflected no more than the mature afterthoughts of liberal American social workers like Robert Woods or Jane Addams upon realizing the disastrous effects of "100-percent" Americanization programs. Accordingly, while Brandeis and his aides employed the rhetoric of a clash between "democracy" and "plutocracy" with vigor and conviction, they fought for the American Jewish Congress less for ideological reasons than because of the advantage they hoped to gain for the specific objectives of the Zionist organization.

Brandeis had won major victories in this campaign by mid-1916, when he was appointed Associate Justice of the Supreme Court, but he still faced the determined opposition of the American Jewish Committee. Judah Magnes, in what Brandeis considered a plot planned by the Committee leaders and the *New York Times* in concert, attacked Brandeis publicly in July, 1916 for allegedly abusing his new judicial position by involving himself in communal quarrels.[31] Brandeis at once withdrew from all his Jewish offices, and thenceforth continued his active involvement in private, through agents like de Haas who acted on his behalf in various official capacities.

He also sought a compromise by which the conflict with the American Jewish Committee over the Congress issue could be resolved. What emerged was an agreement for a one-time Congress session after the war ended, an arrangement strongly resented by some downtown Zionists, particularly the socialists and Mizrachi, but acceptable to associates like Lipsky, Bernard Richards, Wise, and above all to Julian Mack, who retained strong ties to the American Jewish Committee. It was equally acceptable to the Committee leader, Louis Marshall. The mutual understanding was consolidated when the Congress finally met in January,

1918, two months after the Balfour Declaration was issued, and adopted a resolution in favor of a Jewish Commonwealth in Palestine, and another in favor of "group rights" for Jews in such countries as would grant similar rights after the war to their other national minorities. Marshall then went with the Congress delegation headed by Julian Mack to the Paris Peace Conference and manfully and loyally worked for the formula adopted by the popularly elected, Zionist-dominated Congress.[32]

The Balfour Declaration of November 2, 1917, enthusiastically received by the mass of Jews and gracefully accepted by Marshall, Schiff, and the American Jewish Committee as a body, offered Brandeis an opportunity to further the general understanding he aimed at in the Jewish community, and thereby to ensure that his own role could be successfully carried out within the bounds of judicial propriety. He adopted an idea proposed earlier by Magnes whereby the Zionist organization would confine itself to the work in Palestine, which implied leaving the Diaspora responsibilities chiefly to the American Jewish Committee (after the one-time session of the American Jewish Congress) and to the Joint Distribution Committee. He assumed that, once the Balfour Declaration was embodied in an internationally recognized Mandate for Palestine and the Mandate assigned to Great Britain, the political tasks of the Zionist movement would be ended, and it would then reorganize for the pressing practical work of building up the Jewish National Home. He envisioned that project as primarily an economic and technical endeavor, with some preliminary labors (especially sanitation) to be financed by voluntary donations in the traditional Zionist way and the remaining, decisive work to be financed by bank credits and private investment. The several Zionist organizations, each committing itself to a specific, philanthropically organized project—on the lines of Hadassah, or of the American Red Cross—would encourage but not control the agencies set up for investment on commercial and industrial lines. Given this set-up, he hoped to be able to enroll men like Jacob Schiff as Zionists, and enlist their resources and talents in the financial and development projects that were anticipated. Such an arrangement would enable him, within the discretion expected of a Supreme Court Justice, to direct the entire American and world Zionist undertaking through expert officers in whom he had full confidence and on the basis of a general consensus subscribed to by virtually the whole Jewish community.[33]

The Brandeis organization scheme, rather utopian in its conception,

broke down because other Zionist leaders, including above all Weizmann (whose special role seemed more vital for the future of the movement than that of Brandeis), favored a somewhat different strategy and
required rather different arrangements in order to make their own work
possible. Weizmann, who was Britain's chosen instrument for cooperating with Jews and Zionists, needed to gain the acceptance of his leadership by the East European and Palestinian sections of the movement,
and they viewed the Zionist organization still, until succeeded by a
Jewish state, as something like a government-in-exile rather than a set of
philanthropic societies and investment trusts. From his point of view,
Brandeis insisted on earmarked funds to be used according to the desires
of the donors or the investment strategies of trust managers. From their
point of view, the Europeans and Palestinians viewed Zionist funds as
tax receipts to be budgeted out of a common treasury for all needs,
according to the political preferences of the dominant party combination
at the Zionist Congress. Weizmann had to maneuver his way between
the pressures of both points of view. The position he adopted at the
crucial London Zionist Conference of June, 1920 leaned far more to the
side of Brandeis than, for example, of Menahem Mendel Ussishkin, the
Russian Zionist leader; but Weizmann's method of securing his own
position, which made Brandeis' position virtually untenable, outraged
the American leader, who thereafter self-righteously considered his former ally a treacherous, morally unclean fellow.[34]

The actual differences between Weizmann's and Brandeis' proposals
for Zionist reorganization were, from the perspective of history, fairly
minor and technical. In addition to the differences over the proper
administration of funds, which only came into clear focus later, they
differed in 1919 and 1920 over whether non-Zionists should be recruited individually to the National Home project, and become members
of an apolitical Zionist organization as Brandeis planned, or, according
to Weizmann's notion, the Zionist organization should be preserved
intact and non-Zionist organizations should become corporate partners
of the Zionists in the proposed Jewish Agency.[35] (In the event, neither
conception was fully carried out in the 1929 "expansion" which brought
non-Zionists into the Jewish Agency as partners.) Both sides, however,
regarded their quarrel as stemming from more basic differences which
they saw as dividing American and East European Zionists. Brandeis
explained to the German Zionist leader, Kurt Blumenfeld, that Americans would not agree to a centralized World Zionist Organization, since
they viewed this as implying the "Diaspora nationalist" view that Jews

everywhere were in fact, and should be effectively organized as, a coherent political entity. At the meetings in 1919, he replied in similar terms to a challenge by Weizmann, softening his line to the extent of conceding the possibility that at some remote future time American Jews might come to share the European position. Weizmann, for his part, was deeply convinced that the differences between him and Brandeis on details of organization—about which, indeed, he was inclined to show great flexibility—really stemmed from far more fundamental differences in conception and attitude, and that such Americans as Brandeis, Mack and Frankfurter were not Jewish nationalists at all.

The conflict came to its climax when Weizmann, with Einstein in train, came to America in 1921 to set up the all-purpose general Palestine fund, the Keren Hayesod, and joining his forces to the anti-Brandeisian local Zionist opposition, deposed his rivals from the leadership of the American organization.[36] In the following years, it was shown with increasing clarity that the differences were far less significant than the similarities between the two. During the 1920's, while Weizmann worked with Louis Marshall—another rival of Brandeis—to build a Zionist partnership with non-Zionists in the Jewish Agency, both the official Zionist organization and a Brandeis-organized group of "Palestine development" associations labored on parallel lines in Palestine, devoting themselves to practical tasks of philanthropic aid and special project investments. The group of Brandeis supporters suffered steady attrition during this time as their work proved disappointingly slow, and Abba Hillel Silver, Stephen Wise and finally even Julian Mack drifted back into regular Zionist work. On the other hand, the American Zionist organization, together with the world organization, suffered its own severe setbacks, all the more damaging for being far more public than those of the Brandeisists. In the end both of them had to bear the humiliation of turning to the non-Zionist leaders, not only to rescue them from their defeats, but—a crowning blow—to act as arbiter between them and help resolve their internal quarrel. Thus Weizmann's compact with Marshall to expand the Jewish Agency was followed in the next year by the deposition of Lipsky and the election of the Brandeisist Robert Szold as head of the American organization—and it was Felix Warburg, successor to the late Louis Marshall as head of the non-Zionists, who helped bring this about.[37]

When Warburg succeeded to leadership upon Marshall's death, he immediately sought the advice of Brandeis. Was this then a seal of completion upon the process of Americanization which, throughout the

1920's, had increasingly turned American Zionism into a philanthropic, fund raising apparatus that so little differed from the attitude of non-Zionists in relation to Palestine that they could finally join together? Did the Brandeis conception from then on indeed become the essential consensus of all American Jews?

If this is so, it is only true in the most shallow sense. Fundamental differences still divided the American Zionists, not to speak of American Jews. Brandeis differed from Lipsky, and both of them from Magnes, and certainly from Felix Warburg. The full equivalent of East European Zionism, including a sense of "exile" that could see only Zion as a Jew's true home, may have survived in America solely among those— primarily in the Socialist and Orthodox wings of the movement—who felt severely estranged in America. This was nevertheless a permanent element in American Zionism, sometimes latent, but perpetually awakened and activated among sensitive Jews when crises of Depression, political anti-Semitism, McCarthyism, or the upheavals of the 1960's disenchanted many Americans, in one or another way, with conventional Americanism.

The least-common-denominator model of Zionism implied by the thesis that Brandeis supplied a consensus philosophy, upon which not only American Zionists but American Jews as a body could unite, veils important differences dividing Brandeis from other Jews and other Zionists. If Brandeis failed in the end to enroll Jacob Schiff and other non-Zionists in a reorganized, apolitical, Zionist organization, it is not simply because Weizmann and Lipsky pulled the rug from under his feet. The approach to Schiff failed in 1917 because the old magnate insisted, and Brandeis could not agree, on publishing his own definition of a form of Zionism based on a religious commitment to Judaism.[38] This was a rock on which not only Schiff but Zionists like Schechter, Magnes, and Mordecai Kaplan among others—including, in its own way, the Orthodox Mizrachi—at times split, or threatened to split, from their fellow Zionists.

As a secular Jew at odds with all forms of positive Judaism, Brandeis (or Horace Kallen, who felt impelled to proclaim that "secularism is the will of God") differed more sharply from such very American Zionists than did that other secular Jew, Chaim Weizmann. Given the conditions of Jewish life in Western countries, irreligion combined with a positive self-identification as a Jew made it necessary—for Brandeis as for Weizmann, for Kallen as for Lipsky—to be a Zionist and impossible to be a non-Zionist or anti-Zionist. Only a strong religious commitment, or self-denial as a Jew, could motivate for some the other choice. What divided Weizmann and Lipsky from Brandeis and Kallen was not the substantive nature, but the intensity of their Jewish commitment. Zionism for Weizmann or Lipsky was central to their lives, and they devoted themselves to it wholly. For Brandeis and Kallen, Zionism was important; it provided answers to dilemmas that, without Zionism, would continue to plague them—but it was not central, and they did not devote themselves to it wholly.

It is a familiar idea to American historians that American conditions fostered ethnic nationalism among immigrant groups in the early decades of the twentieth century, and, we may add, such nationalism served in various ways to Americanize them. We have sketched the parallel development among American Jews in brief, noting the Americanizing function of Zionism for various types of Zionists. The question may now be asked, which of these groups produced the most thoroughly American variant of Zionism, and which succeeded most fully in impressing its stamp upon American Jewry at large?

There can be little doubt that those who would carry off the palm in such a contest would be the group of rabbinical Zionists around the Jewish Theological Seminary, beginning with their ally Judah Magnes and culminating in the fully developed theories of Mordecai Kaplan. Their religious revision of the ideas of Ahad Ha-am and Dubnow fitted well into the place allotted to the Jews as a religious community in the American scheme of things, and it was well-suited to command the support first of Schiff and Marshall and ultimately of the general American Jewish consensus.

If there is an irreligious, Brandeisian, consensus Zionism broadly shared by American Jews, it exists only to the degree that Jewishness, and not only Zionism, becomes peripheral in their lives. But American life is also capable of making the Jewishness of Jews salient, or even central, in their lives, and in such cases American Zionism expresses itself in forms sharply deviating from the norm of the semi-involved consensus. That is still the case today, as it was more clearly the case in the first half-century of American Zionist history.

NOTES

1. Judd L. Teller, "America's Two Zionist Traditions," *Commentary*, XX, 4 (October, 1955), 343–52.

2. *New York Times Magazine*, Feb. 3, 1974, 6ff.

3. Melvin I. Urofsky, *American Zionism from Herzl to the Holocaust* (New York: Doubleday, 1975), pp. 127–33, 144–50; *cf.* pp. 90f., 271, 305f.

4. Teller, *loc. cit.*, p. 350.

5. Urofsky, *op. cit.*, pp. 149, 455; Evyatar Friesel, *Ha-Tenuah ha-Tsiyonit be-Artzot ha-Brit* (Tel-Aviv: Hotza'at Ha-Kibbutz Ha-Meuhad, 1970), *passim*.

6. Friesel, *op. cit.*, pp. 39–41; Julius Haber, *Odyssey of an American Zionist* (New York: Twayne, 1956), pp. 63–73.

7. Israel Klausner, "Adam Rosenberg: One of the Earliest American Zionists," *Herzl Year Book*, I (1958), 232–387.

8. Leib Shpizman, "Etapn in der Geshikhte . . . ," in *Geshikhte fun der Tsionistisher Arbeter Bavegung in Tsofn Amerike* (New York: Idisher Kemfer Farlag, 1955) vol. I, pp. 139f.

9. Elhanan Orren, *Hibbat-Tsiyon bi-Vritannia, 1878–1898* (Tel-Aviv: Hotza'at Ha-Kibbutz ha-Meuhad, 1974), pp. 54ff., 76ff., 81–86; Lloyd P. Gartner, *The Jewish Immigrant in England, 1870–1914* (Detroit: Wayne State University Press, 1960), pp. 262–69.

10. Irving Howe and Emanual Libo, *World of Our Fathers* (New York: Harcourt Brace Jovanovich, 1976), pp. 109ff., 295ff.

11. See J. Chaikin, *Idishe Bleter in Amerike* (New York: 1946); Jacob Kabakoff, *Halutsei ha-Sifrut ha-Ivrit ba-Amerika* (Tel-Aviv: Yavne, 1966).

12. Lucy S. Dawidowicz, "Louis Marshall's Yiddish Newspaper, *The Jewish World*: A Study in Contrast," *Jewish Social Studies*, XXV, 2 (April, 1963) 102–32.

13. W. Gunther Plaut, *The Growth of Reform Judaism* (New York: World Union for Progressive Judaism, 1965), pp. 18–43, 145ff.

14. Herschel Levin, "The Other Side of the Coin," *Herzl Year Book* V (1963), 33–56.

15. Salo W. and Jeannette M. Baron, "Palestinian Messengers in America, 1849–79," in *Steeled by Adversity* (Philadelphia: The Jewish Publication Society of America, 1971), pp. 158–266.

16. Naomi W. Cohen, *Not Free to Desist* (Philadelphia: The Jewish Publication Society of America, 1972), pp. 3–16.

17. Moshe Davis, *The Emergence of Conservative Judaism* (Philadelphia: The Jewish Publication Society of America, 1963) pp. 233–74, 311–26; Cyrus Adler, *Jacob H. Schiff: His Life and Letters* (New York: Doubleday Doran, 1929) vol. II, pp. 50–54.

18. Friesel, *op. cit.*, pp. 77–89.

19. *Ibid.*, pp. 109–24, 143ff.; Yonathan Shapiro, *Leadership of the American Zionist Organization, 1897–1930* (Urbana: University of Illinois Press, 1971), pp. 37–52.

20. Boruch Zuckerman, "Dos Idishe Lebn in Amerike in Ershtn Fertl fun Tsvantsikstn Yorhundert," in *Geshikhte fun der Tsionistisher Arbeter Bavegung*, vol. I, pp. 10–26; Arthur A. Goren, *New York Jews and the Quest for Community* (New York: Columbia University Press, 1970), pp. 4f., 10–42.

21. *The Century* (February, 1883), 611.

22. Ruth L. Deech, "Jacob De Haas: A Biography," *Herzl Year Book*, VII (1971), 331ff.

23. Friesel, *op. cit.*, pp. 171–74; Shapiro, *op. cit.*, pp. 50–59.

24. Donald H. Miller, "A History of Hadassah, 1912–1935" (Ph.D. dissertation, New York University, 1969), pp. 42–46, 56–65; Carol B. Kutscher, "The Role of Hadassah in the American Zionist Movement, 1912–1922" (Ph.D. dissertation, Brandeis University, 1975), pp. 1–40.

25. Urofsky, *op. cit.*, pp. 114–18, 133–50, 156ff., 242; *cf.* Shapiro, *op. cit.*, p. 128f.

26. Irma Lindheim, *Parallel Quest* (New York: Thomas Yoseloff, 1962), p. 83; Sarah L. Schmidt, "Horace M. Kallen and the Americanization of Zionism" (Ph.D. dissertation, University of Maryland, 1973), pp. 90–96, 141–83.

27. Urofsky, *op. cit.*, pp. 165–67, 175–78; "Zionism" files in the Brandeis Archive, University of Louisville Law Library; Zuckerman, *loc. cit.*, p. 48.

28. Shapiro, *op. cit.*, pp. 77–80, 86–90; Herbert Parzen, "Brandeis and the Balfour Declaration," *Herzl Year Book*, V (1963), 309–50.

29. Oscar I. Janowsky, *The Jews and Minority Rights, 1898–1919* (New York: AMS Press, 1966), pp. 51–85.

30. Shapiro, *op. cit.*, pp. 109–13.

31. *Ibid.*, pp. 94–96.

32. Janowsky, *op. cit.*, pp. 178–90, 263–68, 271f., 282–319.

33. Shapiro, *op. cit.*, pp. 96, 99–104, 108f., 114–19.

34. Evyatar Friesel, *Ha-Mediniyut ha-Tsiyonit le-ahar Hatsharat Balfour* (Tel-Aviv: Hotza'at ha-Kibbutz ha-Me'uhad, 1977), pp. 135–51.

35. *Ibid.*, pp. 90–96.

36. Urofsky, *op. cit.*, pp. 246–98; *cf.*, Shapiro, *op. cit.*, pp. 135–79.

37. Urofsky, *op. cit.*, pp. 299–371; *cf.*, Shapiro, *op. cit.*, pp. 180–247.

38. *Ibid.*, pp. 114–17.

15.

The Brandeis-Weizmann Dispute

George L. Berlin

INTRODUCTION

The first post-World War I meeting of world Zionist leaders took place
in London in July, 1920. The war years and the peace settlement had
witnessed momentous events for the Zionist movement. The Balfour
Declaration, expressing British support for "the establishment in Palestine of a national home for the Jewish people," and the San Remo
conference, at which the Supreme Council of European Powers declared
Palestine a mandated territory and granted the mandate to Great Britain
on condition that she administer her trust under the terms of the Balfour
Declaration, seemed to insure that the Jewish national home had become
a formal part of the postwar world. These gains presented the Zionist
movement with both unprecedented opportunity and severe challenge,
for while Great Britain was to administer the mandate, the task of
building the national home fell to the Jews.

Whether the Zionists could successfully meet the challenge was a
matter of considerable doubt in 1920. The war years had sorely taxed
the major Zionist sources of strength. The bulwark of the movement,
the Jewries of Eastern Europe, was greatly weakened. Wartime losses
complemented by postwar economic boycotts affected Polish Jewry.
Antisemitism was on the rise in Germany and Austria. Increasing hostility on the part of the Bolshevik authorities threatened the movement in
the Soviet Union.

The situation of the *Yishuv*, upon whose success lay all Zionist hopes,
was no less critical. The flow of *Halukah*,[1] the sole means of support for

Reprinted by permission of the American Jewish Historical Society from *American Jewish
Historical Quarterly* 60 (1970): 37–68.

the settlers of the Old *Yishuv* stopped with the outbreak of war in Europe. A reduction in exports, resulting in economic decline, and political persecution of the Zionists by the Ottoman regime combined to impoverish the *Yishuv* and reduce effective Zionist activity.

Meanwhile, across the Atlantic, a new source of Zionist strength had arisen. Hitherto insignificant in general Zionist affairs, the American Zionist movement became a primary factor due to its impressive growth in numbers and resources during the second decade of this century under the leadership of Louis D. Brandeis. American Zionism filled the vacuum in Zionist leadership that the war had caused. The outbreak of war had disrupted the administrative apparatus of the World Zionist Organization (W.Z.O.). With its membership scattered among all of the belligerents, the W.Z.O. had to adopt a policy of neutrality. Accordingly, the central office moved from Berlin to Copenhagen, and the headquarters of the Jewish National Fund from Cologne to The Hague. This scattering of the Zionist administration made effective conduct of W.Z.O. daily business nearly impossible. To meet this emergency, an extraordinary conference of American Zionists convened in New York on August 14, 1914. All factions of American Zionism were present as was Dr. Schmarya Levin representing the W.Z.O. The conference resulted in the selection of a Provisional Executive Committee for General Zionist Affairs which was empowered "to deal with all Zionist matters, until better times come."[2] Brandeis was named chairman, and thus, for the first time an American Zionist became an active leader in the world movement. This was a development of supreme importance, for not only would the growing influence and wealth of the American Jewish community be an invaluable aid to Zionism, but the peculiar Zionist theories of the American leadership under Brandeis would bring the movement to a crisis of grave proportions.

The source of Brandeis' Zionism lay in his conception of Americanism. For Brandeis, the basic ideals of America were "the development of the individual for his own and the common good; the development of the individual through liberty, and the attainment of the common good through democracy and social justice."[3] Shared by all religious, racial and ethnic groups in America, these ideals were the tie which bound all of them together. Furthermore, Brandeis believed that "the individual is dependent for his development in large part upon the development of the group of which he forms a part."[4] Hence, it was fundamental to Brandeis' concept of Americanism that the various ethnic and national groups be allowed to retain their identity. "Jews collectively should likewise enjoy the same right to live and develop as do other groups."[5] Indeed, it was only through the preservation of their own identity that the various ethnic groups could preserve and transmit to America the best in their respective traditions.

Brandeis saw an identity of spirit uniting Judaism and Americanism. He declared that "the Jewish spirit . . . is essentially modern and essentially American," and that "not since the destruction of the Temple have the Jews in spirit and in ideals been so fully in harmony with the noblest aspirations of the country in which they lived."[6] Therefore, in order to become a better American, the Jew must first become a better Jew, and this required becoming a Zionist. For Brandeis, "loyalty to America demands . . . that each American Jew become a Zionist," for "only through the ennobling effect of its strivings can we develop the best that is in us, and give to this country the full benefit of our great inheritance."[7] The "ennobling effect" on American Jewry was a result of the example set by Palestinian Jewry. Zionism had produced no criminals in Palestine. Instead, it had created "a spiritual and social development . . . a development in education, in health, and in social order, and in the character and habits of the people." The Zionist movement had brought forth in Palestine people who, both in their personal dedication and in their accomplishments were proving to be an inspiration and a source of pride to Jews everywhere.[8]

Unlike European Zionism, Brandeis' Zionism was not born of an emotional reaction against antisemitism nor was it a rejection of emancipation as a solution to the Jewish Problem. American Jewry had undergone a fundamentally different experience than had European Jewry, for American Jews were emancipated, to all intents and purposes, from the very beginning. Moreover, unlike Europe, the American way of life, symbolized by its stress on individual merit and by its fluidity, did not demand conformity on the part of any group or individual to any preexisting standard of Americanism defined along racial or ethnic lines.[9]

The historical experience of American Jewry caused American Zionism, as represented by Brandeis, to differ from European Zionism in several important aspects. Brandeis rejected the European theory that the Jews were everywhere a group of homeless aliens, and Zionism, therefore, "was not a movement to remove all the Jews of the world . . . to Palestine." Settlement in Palestine was the solution to the Jewish Problem for those Jews who were persecuted in the lands where they lived. Since this was not true of American Jews, they need not go to Palestine, and Brandeis never considered migrating there himself. Zionism would do no more than give to American Jews the "same right now exercised by practically every other people in the world: to live at their option either in the land of their fathers or in some other country." [10]

The solution to the Jewish Problem, according to Brandeis, was tied to the eventual victory of liberalism. Countries now "grant to the individual equality before the law; but they fail to recognize the equality of whole peoples or nationalities." [11] This was liberalism's great failure. However, America was different in that it did grant this equality to nationalities, and Brandeis saw the solution to the Jewish Problem in the spreading of American ideals.

Brandeis' Zionism met head on with European Zionism in 1920, and the result was a major convulsion that shook the world Zionist movement. Indeed, the differences between the two groups seemed so fundamental and irreconcilable that, on one occasion, Weizmann told the Americans, "I do not agree with the philosophy of your Zionism. . . . We are different, absolutely different. There is no bridge between Washington and Pinsk." [12] The first major skirmish in the battle took place at London.

THE LONDON CONFERENCE

Controversy marked the conference from the outset. Brandeis was disturbed by the long and rambling general debate which, in line with Zionist tradition, opened Zionist Congresses and conferences. [13] The fact that he had agreed to serve as presiding officer of the conference only after he had received Weizmann's assurance that there would be no lengthy debate, only served to fuel Brandeis' displeasure. To make matters even worse, the debate was carried on in a babel of tongues, and in a manner which, from the American point of view, lacked customary parliamentary procedure. [14] The evident lack of preparation for the conference was another factor that disturbed the Americans. The physical accommodations were poor. More serious, no reports on various contemplated projects had been prepared. Hence, the conference committees appointed to deal with such projects as Nordau's proposal to bring 500,000 Jewish immigrants into Palestine during the coming year, Weizmann's plan for Palestinian hydro-electrical development, and a plan for the rapid development of industrialized agriculture in Palestine, could not submit proposals or recommendations due to the lack of material. Finally, no formal agenda had been drawn up for the London meeting, delegates were late in arriving, and the conference was marked by interruptions lasting several days. [15]

The American displeasure over the general conduct of the Conference was merely a forerunner of far more important conflicts soon to arise. The Americans sought to introduce important administrative and financial changes in the W.Z.O., and in this they aroused the determined opposition of the Europeans. The first of these reforms called for the dissolution of the Zionist Commission.[16]

On July 11, the American members of the Palestine Committee of the W.Z.O. recommended the abolition of the Zionist Commission and its replacement by a Jewish Advisory Council consisting of seven members chosen by the present conference. The Zionists were to seek British permission for the Council to act in concert with the Lord High Commissioner in matters pertaining to immigration, colonization, and Hebrew education in Palestine. Unlike the Zionist Commission, the Council's work would be clearly delimited and its actions dependent upon British approval. The conference rejected this proposal.[17]

Brandeis, whose distaste for the Zionist Commission went back to his 1919 visit to Palestine, opposed the continuation of that body because he believed it no longer useful to Zionism. In fact, its continued existence would actually serve to hinder the development of the national home. For Brandeis, "the work of the great Herzl was completed at San Remo."[18] The political goal of the Basel Program had been achieved with public recognition and international support for the establishment of a Jewish national home in Palestine. Now, a "new era" had dawned for Zionism, and the "qualifications of success and the conditions of success in the future are something entirely new."[19] In the new era, all Zionist energies should be expended on the only task left for Zionism— the creation of a Jewish national home in Palestine under the tutelage of the mandatory power. Under these circumstances, the Zionist Commission was superfluous. The Commission's political activities in Palestine would be carried out by direct dealings between the local Jewish authorities and the newly appointed civil administration headed by Herbert Samuel, a Jew and a Zionist sympathizer in whom Brandeis expressed confidence. According to Brandeis, the continued existence of the Commission would hinder the work in Palestine because its members were too busy squabbling among themselves and perpetuating the "super political life" of Palestinian Jewry.[20]

In his analysis of the causes leading to the London quarrel, Weizmann placed great stress on the American proposal to abolish the Commission.[21] For Weizmann, it was most unrealistic because it rested on the assumption that the political work of the W.Z.O. had ended. Weizmann had been in Palestine with the Commission several times during the preceding few months, and there had witnessed the deterioration in Arab-Jewish relations. Arab nationalist extremists were becoming more vocal in their opposition to Jewish immigration into Palestine. Moreover, British-Jewish relations in Palestine were worsening. Many of the British officers were blatantly antisemitic. It was at this time, reported Weizmann, that he had his first encounter with the notorious "Protocols of the Elders of Zion." When the civil administration assumed power in 1920, many of the antisemitic officeholders of the military administration were retained in the new government. Weizmann concluded that "for those whose facile optimism had led them to believe that all political problems were safely out of the way, and that all we had to do was to get on with the practical work," the deteriorating conditions in Palestine "should have been the writing on the wall."[22] Weizmann professed amazement that Brandeis, recently returned from Palestine, had obviously failed to notice the writing.

According to Weizmann, Brandeis' disavowal of "political" Zionism was attributable largely to the influence of the English Zionist Jacob De Haas.[23] De Haas had been a close confidant of Herzl, the father of political Zionism. Journeying through the United States in order to gain support for Zionism, De Haas met Brandeis in 1910, and soon thereafter converted him to the Zionist cause.[24] Weizmann, who had never gotten along very well with De Haas, claimed that De Haas, the "political" Zionist, resented the political achievement of Weizmann, the "practical" Zionist, in gaining the Balfour Declaration.[25]

This resentment on the part of De Haas may very well be true. Although a dedicated and selfless worker for Zionism, De Haas did not possess the most winning of personalities. In fact, he was disliked by many Zionists, American as well as European. Furthermore, it is quite true that as Brandeis' mentor in Zionism, De Haas exercised a certain degree of influence over the American leader. Brandeis valued De Haas' advice and trusted him implicitly. However, Brandeis' opposition to political Zionism at London really cannot be attributed to the influence of De Haas' vindictiveness. Rather, it was part of Brandeis' total conception of the nature of Zionism and Zionist activity.

Despite Weizmann's defense of political Zionism against what he considered to be the wholly practical Zionism of Brandeis, there seems to be a close affinity between the positions of the two men. Weizmann was an admirer of Ahad Ha'am, the great antagonist of political Zionism. Also, during the years immediately after the 1920 dispute, Weizmann stressed practical work in Palestine. "Our political progress will only be made in the fields and in the orchards, in the vineyards and in the towns, in Nahalal, Nuris, and Petach Tikvah."[26] Furthermore, it was Weizmann's refusal to embark upon any "political offensive" in the 1920's that led to the founding of the Revisionist movement under Vladimir Jabotinsky in 1925.[27] Finally, and perhaps most startling was the fact that at the London conference, Weizmann, in addressing the American delegation at its first meeting with him, had remarked that "our political work is over."[28]

While all of this seems to mark Weizmann as a practical Zionist, it must not be forgotten that he worked to give the Zionist movement its most important political victories. He was in every sense a diplomat. He had negotiated hard and long with British officials for the promulgation of the Balfour Declaration.[29] Throughout the next three decades, he was engaged in the political task of trying to persuade Britain to fulfill her mandate responsibilities. On the whole, therefore, one can say that Weizmann was neither a dogmatic political nor a dogmatic practical Zionist.

Brandeis also can be characterized as neither a wholly political nor a wholly practical Zionist. He had collaborated closely with Weizmann in the struggle to gain the Balfour Declaration. He received many written and oral reports concerning the deteriorating situation in Palestine, and it was, in fact, after a talk with Brandeis on August 4, 1919, that Lord Balfour sent a message to the British military commander in Jerusalem impressing upon him the fact that the development of the Jewish national home was basic to British policy, and commanding him to discourage Arab opposition to that policy. On the other hand, Brandeis predicated his entire program at the London conference on the assumption that the W.Z.O. must now use all of its energies exclusively for practical work in Palestine.

We must therefore consider the practical versus political aspect of the fight as merely a symptom of a deeper cleavage between the Americans and the Europeans.

After the rejection of the proposal for a Jewish Advisory Council, Brandeis submitted a sweeping reorganization plan to the American delegation.[30] If adopted, the Brandeis reforms would have markedly changed the entire administrative apparatus of the W.Z.O. The supreme policy-determining body of the W.Z.O. was its biennial Congress, where the democratically elected representatives of world Zionism would meet to formulate plans and policies. Between Congresses, executive power lay in the Greater Actions Committee, later called the General Council.

This group met between Congresses, and formulated policies within the general framework of Congress resolutions. In addition, there was an Executive Committee, originally called the Inner Actions Committee, which had the task of overseeing the continuous direction of Zionist affairs between Congresses. The American reorganization plan proposed to change both the makeup and the tasks of the Executive and the Greater Actions Committee by setting up entirely new qualifying standards for membership on these bodies, and by defining specifically the nature of their work.

Brandeis proposed to reduce the influence and power of the London office of the Zionist administration. Since Zionist work was now to be centered in Palestine, Brandeis wanted the headquarters for the new Executive to be in Jerusalem, while limiting the London office to the "development of financial arrangements . . . and to such other work of coordination as will be required by the new Executive."[31] Seeking greater coordination, Brandeis suggested that the new Executive be so composed that "all forces working in Palestine shall be combined in the Executive committee." Therefore, it should include representatives of the Jewish Colonial Trust, Jewish National Fund, Palestine Development Company, and two representatives elected by Palestinian Jewry.[32] The members of the Executive with the exception of the Palestinian representatives, were to be appointed by the London conference, and they were to serve until their successors could be chosen at the next scheduled Zionist Congress.

The Executive Committee would be "the sole executive and administrative agency of the World Zionist Organization," and would devote itself to such activities as were "in accordance with the resolutions adopted by the conference or by the Zionist Congresses, and should develop in Palestine the Jewish national home."[33] The plan specified just how the executive was to go about its task. It would establish in Palestine bureaus "charged with the performance of defined obligations in departments of government service."[34] There would be, for instance, departments of education, colonization, agriculture, industry and labor, each department to conduct its business independently of the others, and the heads of the departments responsible to the Executive as a whole for the work of their respective departments. The representatives of Palestinian Jewry were also to receive "definite departmental responsibilities" from the Executive. In addition, the Jews of Palestine were to create an Advisory Council to cooperate with the Executive "in coordinating the relations between their constituencies and the Executive."[35]

The American plan also called for a new Greater Actions Committee. Composed of representatives of the "responsible national federations that are supplying the necessary financial support for all of the work in Palestine," it would exercise control over the Executive by annually passing judgment on its proposed budget. However, the Committee was to have no power to override the decisions of the London conference or of any future or past Zionist Congress. The plan also called for a "Jewish Congress" in which "all parties shall have full representation according to the proportional basis of the different (national) federations." Meeting every two years this Congress would deal "not with the question of the budget, but with the question of general policy" of the Greater Actions Committee.[36]

A major controversy developed over who was to serve on the new Executive and the bureaus under its supervision. According to Brandeis, the sole criterion for office-holding was efficient service. Many of the old-time Zionists who held positions in Palestine for which they were unqualified would be retired on a "pension fund just as governments and public bodies do."[37] The Americans proposed that all of the present office-holders resign from their posts.[38] Furthermore, they called for a reduction in the number of office-holders in Palestine, "using that term as applying to anybody who is paid by the Zionist Commission directly or indirectly or to whom the Zionist Organization in any way makes a financial contribution."[39]

Just as in his quest for experts to head the bureaus in Palestine, Brandeis wanted the Executive to be "composed of members possessing those qualities which especially fit them for specific tasks in Palestine."[40] Their only qualifications need be sound business ability and a sincere desire to help in the development of Palestine. Old-time Zionists who lacked the former qualification would have to go, their loyal service in the past notwithstanding. "Recognition of service performed may not be given by appointment to office of the unfit."[41] The Americans felt that such veteran Zionists as Schmarya Levin and Vladimir Jabotinsky did not meet their standards and that the reappointment of Menahem Ussischkin to the Executive would result in the "absolute demoralization" of the administration in Palestine.[42] Instead, they recommended the appointment of less colorful figures such as Julius Simon and Lord Rothschild. The administration needed men like Nehemiah De Lieme who possessed "an exactness and a care in expenditure which rises even to closeness."[43] The only present office-holders that met Brandeis' requirements were Weizmann and Nahum Sokolow. These two men he considered worthy of service "not on account of our gratitude to them" for past services, but because they possessed the requisite ability to serve, and they enjoyed the confidence of the greater part of world Jewry. In addition, the British government looked especially to Weizmann "to carry out what he and they have represented would be done by the Jews."[44]

With this utilitarian rather than sentimental criteria for service, Brandeis went further and stated that he had no objection to the inclusion of non-Zionists both on the new Executive and as heads of the Palestine bureaus.[45] Later, Brandeis reported that before the opening of the London conference, Weizmann had agreed that "good propagandists were not as a rule efficient business administrators" and that only experts should be used for the practical work in Palestine.[46] Weizmann also allegedly agreed that men who had not been connected with the W.Z.O. might be named officials of that body. At the urging of Weizmann and Sokolow, Brandeis then presented his plans to the conference. However, after seeing the opposition aroused by the proposed use of non-Zionists, Weizmann, to the consternation and shock of Brandeis, came out against Brandeis' proposals. Brandeis himself admitted, however, that "the extent of agreement, that is whether it covered an analysis of difficulties as well as a plan for meeting them" was a legitimate point of dispute.

The issue of non-Zionists also appeared in another context at London. Meeting privately with Brandeis, Weizmann had given his assent to Brandeis' proposal to solicit through Lord Reading the support of a group of English Jews who could "assume the responsibility and obtain the necessary aid for the economic upbuilding of Palestine."[47] Lord Reading, along with Sir Alfred Mond and James de Rothschild were to organize the English group which would be granted power for a period of three years. Weizmann had expressed his gratitude to Brandeis for this plan by "impulsively kissing Brandeis' hand." However, after a conference with Mond and Rothschild, Weizmann apparently changed his mind and without notifying Brandeis, he submitted a different plan to Mond and Rothschild. They rejected Weizmann's plan and withdrew from the whole project. Brandeis considered this a betrayal on the part of Weizmann, and the trust between the two men was broken, never to be restored.

Weizmann, for his part, was not opposed to the participation of non-Zionists in building the national home. On the contrary, he struggled for many years to overcome Zionist antagonism to this.[48] Weizmann finally prevailed, and the expanded Jewish Agency called for in Article 4 of the

Mandate, included non-Zionists as well as Zionists. However, the Jewish Agency was an organization separate from the W.Z.O. It did not replace the W.Z.O., but merely assumed some of its responsibilities. Writing later, Weizmann explained his opposition to the inclusion of non-Zionists in the W.Z.O. on the ground that it was necessary to form a separate organization wherein Zionists and non-Zionists might cooperate in the purely practical and political problems of upbuilding Palestine.[49] The W.Z.O., on the other hand, served other functions in which only committed Zionists could participate.

Brandeis' reorganization proposals included one further suggestion that irked the Europeans. He wanted to shift the bulk of the Zionist work to the various national Zionist federations composing the W.Z.O. First and foremost the federations would raise money for land reclamation in Palestine and for training the inhabitants of Palestine, "to build the men who are going to use that land." Secondly, by an "immense development of the work in the several countries of the Diaspora," the Zionists had "to raise men with the money, men who will administer the money that we send there." Accordingly, Brandeis told the American delegates that the strengthening of the organization in America was their "first proposition," and insisted that "all other countries, beginning with Great Britain and the Dominions," develop their possibilities to the utmost of their abilities.[50] Brandeis also wanted each individual federation to make its own unique contribution to the development of Palestine. Part of America's unique contribution was the American Medical Unit established in Palestine during the war for the purpose of aiding the relief work there.

The European Zionists vigorously opposed the American reorganization plan and its emphasis on national federations. Weizmann considered it an attempt on the part of the Americans to reduce the authority of the W.Z.O. to the status of a "technical bureau with doubtful authority, and the Zionist Congress . . . would become a conference of experts." The Americans, in his view, were proposing that "the old unity which had been the background of the authority of the Congress should be replaced merely by co-ordination."[51]

All of these issues—political Zionism versus practical Zionism, reorganization, use of non-Zionists, stress on national federations—were actually manifestations of a basic difference between the Americans and Europeans over the nature and tasks of the W.Z.O.

The Europeans conceived of the W.Z.O. as the deliberative and legislative forum of the Jewish people. It was an assembly which represented the sovereignty, as it were, of the united Jewish people. The Zionist movement, whose heart was its Congress, was "to us who had grown up since childhood in the movement . . . in a sense Jewishness itself set in motion for the recreation of a Jewish homeland." From this point of view, it was inconceivable to include in the W.Z.O. men who denied the organic national unity of the Jewish people, and the right of the W.Z.O. to exercise sovereignty for that people. A separate organization had to be formed for those Jews who did not subscribe to the Zionist view of the role of the W.Z.O. but, who out of humanitarian and religious feelings desired to aid the national home. Furthermore, veteran Zionists, regardless of qualification, should not, and, indeed, could not be discarded since they were the "spiritual leaders" of the Jewish people, and any attempt to weaken the heart of the W.Z.O.—its Congress—was obviously unacceptable.

The Americans did not agree with the European view of the nature of the W.Z.O. For them, the rebuilding of Palestine was the sole purpose of the W.Z.O. Political work had been a necessary evil until 1920. Now, however, it was unnecessary, and hence the Zionist Commission was superfluous. The Europeans attacked the American conception of the nature of the W.Z.O. They charged the Americans with making Zionism into "a sociological plan . . . instead of the folk renaissance that it actually was." Worst of all, the Americans were denying Jewish nationalism.[52]

The truth was that the American Zionists were Jewish nationalists, although of a different sort than the Europeans. This was illustrated by their support of the American Jewish Congress movement. Interestingly, in Brandeis' view, the American Jewish Congress would serve for American Jewry some of the same national functions that the Europeans invested in the W.Z.O. for world Jewry. In a speech delivered to a mass meeting held in Carnegie Hall on January 24, 1916,[53] Brandeis declared that the American Jewish Congress was to be a democratic body, the "effective instrument of organized Jewry in America." Brandeis went even further and made a claim for the proposed American Jewish Congress which struck directly at the European conception of the authority of the W.Z.O. by stating that "the Congress, by creating spokesmen for American Israel who are representative, will provide a body through which the Jews of America . . . may not only authoritatively address other governments, but may be so addressed by other governments desirous of dealing with representatives of the whole Jewish people."[54]

Despite the fact that Brandeis had wanted the American Jewish Congress and not the W.Z.O. or the Z.O.A. to serve as the legitimate spokesman for American Jewry, he did not think it desirable that the American Jewish Congress replace or absorb these other bodies. In a letter to Louis Marshall, Brandeis suggested several reasons for the necessity of the W.Z.O. The good-will that it had fostered, and the confidence which Great Britain and other nations had placed in it "could not be transferred to a new body," and besides "the difficulties and expenses in time, etc., of creating any new body could not be faced." Most important of all, Brandeis wanted the W.Z.O. to continue exclusively as an instrument for carrying on the practical work in Palestine.[55]

There was, however, a significant difference between the type of nationalism that Brandeis attached to the American Jewish Congress and that which the Europeans attached to the W.Z.O. American Zionists believed in the peoplehood of all Israel. However, no political ties united the Jewish people. Only a Jewish government in a Jewish state in Palestine could exercise sovereignty for the Jewish people, and this sovereignty would be limited to the Jews of Palestine. The W.Z.O. could not exercise it for the whole Jewish people, who were citizens of the various countries in which they resided. As for the American Jews, they considered themselves American citizens wholly and completely, and no body such as the W.Z.O. could possibly claim to represent or act for them in any political sense.[56]

The American view conflicted also with the European Diaspora nationalists. While supporting the idea of a small settlement in Palestine, the Diaspora nationalists stressed the securing for the Jews in their respective Diaspora countries, the same rights of national autonomy granted to other minority nationalities.

The Americans supported the aspirations of the Diaspora nationalists. In fact, the call to establish the American Jewish Congress proclaimed this as one of its main tasks. But while the European Diaspora nationalists considered the attainment of national minority rights for the Jews as the solution to the Jewish Problem everywhere, the Americans rejected that solution for the United States. They would support the Europeans in their struggle to gain these rights, but since American Jews lived in freedom, they neither needed nor wanted national autonomy. From a European Zionist point of view, the nationalism of the Americans lacked the depth and all-embracing nature of their own. From an American point of view, the European Zionists held mistaken and even dangerous ideas, and the Diaspora nationalists were proposing something which had no relevance or meaning for American Jewry.

These disagreements between the Europeans and the Americans were aggravated by the American position on the proposed use of W.Z.O. funds for propaganda and educational work in the Diaspora. On July 22, a meeting of the American delegation protested a resolution submitted to the conference proposing a budget for educational work in the Diaspora. Rabbi Stephen S. Wise, a close associate of Brandeis, told the meeting that although the Americans supported "all necessary institutions for the propagation and advancement of our national cultural program in the Diaspora," they were "unconditionally opposed to the appropriation of Zionist funds for any purposes other than purely administrative and Palestinian." The American delegation refused to assume any financial obligations or responsibilities in the matter of the Diaspora work budget.[57]

In point of fact the Americans did not oppose cultural work for the Diaspora. They believed, however, that the various national federations and not the W.Z.O. should direct this work. The Europeans, on the other hand, considered this educational and cultural work an integral part of the national renaissance, and its furtherance one of the primary tasks of the W.Z.O. This clash of views, apparent in the administrative proposals of the Americans, became even more obvious in the financial controversies that arose at London.

Brandeis believed that the budget proposed by Weizmann for the expenses of the W.Z.O. in the coming year was far too extravagant. Too much money was being wasted in Palestine, and this was having a harmful effect on the Palestinian population. Brandeis wanted Palestine "to escape from schnorrerdom."[58] He believed that Zionist financial policy was leading Palestine into a new *Halukah* which had none of the justifications of the old one. The W.Z.O. should provide work and not money for the settlers in Palestine. Moreover, complained Brandeis, America was contributing too large a proportion of the money, and other countries should donate more. Brandeis was disturbed by what he considered wasteful and unwise expenditures. Whereas the American delegation had designated a special fund of $10,000 to cover travelling expenses to and from the conference, the London office had paid £8,000 toward the travelling expenses of the East European delegates. And, according to the Americans, some £50,000 of unauthorized money taken from various accounts and institutions had been spent in Palestine from the Fall of 1919 until the London conference.[59]

The friction caused by all of these controversies came to a head in the dispute over the Keren Hayesod. The Keren, proposed as a fund to finance the development of Palestine, called for the collection of a sum of £25,000,000 from the whole Jewish people over a period of five years. Reminiscent of the Biblical tithe, every Jew would tax himself ten percent of his income and assets for a period of five years. This money would pay for all projects needed to rebuild Palestine. The American delegation opposed this proposal. Here again, the American emphasis was on practicality and efficiency while the Europeans stressed the national effort. Specifically, the Americans objected to the Keren because it represented a "commingling of donations and investments." Instead, the Americans wanted to establish the Keren in America as a fund exclusively for donations to be used for such things as the American Medical Unit, afforestation, some educational needs, and other similar non-profit projects. The rest of the money for Palestine would come in the form of investments, from which an eventual, if not an immediate, return might be expected.[60]

The Europeans denounced the American version. According to Weizmann, it represented a "premature emphasis on private enterprise and profits," and reflected the American's lack of enthusiasm for the idealistic cooperative system which prevailed in *Yishuv* agriculture.[61] While agreeing with the Americans on the need for industrial and urban development, Weizmann maintained that "the backbone of our work is and must always be agricultural colonization," and that the agricultural village was "the soul of the people."[62]

In reality, the American position was very close to that of the Europeans on the question of the economic development of Palestine. The official statement of American Zionism on Palestinian economic affairs favored "the ownership and control by the whole people of the land, of all natural resources, and of all public utilities." It went on to state that "the cooperative principle should be applied as far as feasible in the organization of all agricultural, industrial, commercial, and financial undertakings." This statement, penned by Brandeis, was never repudiated, and always remained a basic point of American Zionism under Brandeis.[63] The difference between the Europeans and the Americans was rather one of emphasis. Both advocated a cooperative *Yishuv* agriculture. The Europeans, many of whom were Labor Zionists, were committed to this ideologically while the Americans generally favored it because it seemed most practical.

A more telling European objection against the American position on the Keren was that the Americans were flouting the authority of the W.Z.O. and had become, in effect, secessionists.[64] This was all the more serious because the Keren would fail without American support. The Europeans sought to substantiate their charge of secession by citing the fact that Brandeis refused to serve in the new administration chosen in London, and that he forbade any American to serve on the Executive.

Meeting on July 14, the American delegation expressed support for Brandeis' proposed reforms, and urged that he serve the W.Z.O. in some important capacity in the reorganized administration. "We have been presented with a great opportunity, and the man to lead us through the wilderness is here. We know him, and we want him—will he serve?"[65] Brandeis emphatically refused. It was more important for him, he believed, to stay and work in the United States because, as a Supreme Court Justice, he wielded considerable influence in the American government which, in turn, influenced Britain. Moreover, he felt that were he to become an officer and devote his full time to Zionism, it would be an implicit concession to anti-Zionist charges that a Jew could not be a good American and a Zionist at the same time. This, in turn, would deprive Zionism of much of the financial support that it was receiving from non-Zionist sources in America. Brandeis, however, did offer to serve as honorary president, and declared that he would give "more than occasional advice in the conduct of our affairs" during his annual four month summer vacation.[66]

However, after Weizmann's about-face on the use of non-Zionists, Brandeis became most reluctant to serve even in this limited capacity. Nevertheless, upon the urging of the Roumanian delegation, Brandeis agreed to serve as honorary president on condition that the conference agree to his serving, the incoming Executive assure him that the future administration in Palestine be "capable and effective," there be no separate political entity (like the Zionist Commission) in Palestine, and the conference adopt no budget.[67] The conference was obviously not going to agree to these conditions. Nevertheless, some of the American delegates made other attempts to induce Brandeis to accept an official post.

On July 19, the Americans proposed that the conference elect Brandeis honorary president and name Weizmann and Sokolow to the Executive empowering them to select the remaining members of the Executive. Brandeis refused because he wanted the full Executive elected before he consented to serve. In response to another compromise proposal, Brandeis not only refused to serve, but forbade any American to serve on the Executive. The Americans, stated Brandeis flatly, "were needed at their posts in their own country."[68]

A final proposal was submitted to Brandeis on July 20, calling for the election of a presidium with Brandeis as honorary president, Weizmann as president, Sokolow as chairman of the Executive, and Bernard Flexner or Rothschild as treasurer. Together with the Greater Actions Committee, the presidium would be responsible for appointing all of the important officers of the W.Z.O. Brandeis refused this offer too on the grounds that were he to accept, it would result in "misrepresentation," for he would "not be able to carry out our views as to how things should be done."[69]

The Europeans took the American reluctance to serve on the Executive and the refusal to endorse the Keren as something tantamount to secession. To the Europeans, the Keren was the "fulfillment of an historic mission; it is the writing of Jewish history."[70] The great and decisive moment had come when "the great Jewish venture in Eretz Israel will either be carried through triumphantly to the eternal glory of Israel, or God forbid, may show that we have not proved worthy of the great gift that is ours if only we will have it."[71] Those who hindered the Keren were, therefore, traitors. To the Americans, the struggle against the proposed Keren was part of the larger fight to bring more efficiency and practicality into the work of the W.Z.O., itself a moral cause. From a "moral standpoint," stated Brandeis, any "departure from it (efficiency) is in a sense real treason to our cause." This high pitch of emotional moralism pervaded all of the issues dividing the Americans and the Europeans at London and proved to be the chief obstacle to compromise, and the main cause of the failure of the London conference.

POST-CONFERENCE CONFLICTS

The American delegates returned from London in a mood of anger and disappointment, reflected in the proceedings of the annual Z.O.A. convention held in Buffalo during the last week of November, 1920. Stephen S. Wise succinctly reiterated the basic American position.[72] He declared that the Jews of the world had three main tasks: the rebuilding of the Jewish homeland in Palestine; the abolition of all political, civil, and religious disabilities imposed upon their brethren anywhere; and the promotion of cultural and educational work in the Diaspora. Zionism, however, should concern itself only with the first of these tasks.

The tone of the Wise address echoed through the entire convention. His speech was followed immediately by the passage of a resolution in which the delegates acclaimed Brandeis' leadership with "rejoicing and pride," and pledged to him "our loyalty and support." At the same time, however, the convention did nothing to dissociate itself from the world Zionist movement. In fact it voted to send a message to the Executive Committee of the W.Z.O. containing "our assurance of loyal support, realizing that only the efforts of a disciplined World Zionist Organization [with] the united cooperation of world Jewry, can make possible the upbuilding of Palestine as the Jewish national homeland."[73]

The Buffalo convention formalized certain reforms and structural changes in the Z.O.A. along Brandeisian lines. As far back as September, the Americans had been contemplating reducing their staff "so that the total [administrative] expenses are covered by membership dues and specific contributions for that purpose."[74] In addition, the Americans decided not to commit themselves to give any definite sum of money towards the expenses of the W.Z.O. for the coming year. On September 30, the National Executive Committee of the Z.O.A. proposed that the Americans send $25,000 to the W.Z.O. for each month from October to December, the money to be sent "with instructions that it be used for the budget expenditures in Palestine only."[75] Previously, the Z.O.A. had contributed $75,000 every month to the W.Z.O. Now, however, the Americans claimed that they just did not have this money to give any more. Even if the Americans had had the money, it is unlikely that they would have given more because they believed that their large contributions in the past had been partially responsible for the "demoralization of the Palestine and London administrations." There had been "no constructive industrial or agricultural development in Palestine as a result of the [American] funds during the past year."[76] The National Executive Committee of the Z.O.A. was also instructed to form a general committee composed of representatives of all of American Jewry to "further Palestinian development." Members need not be Zionists, nor did they have to join the Z.O.A. in the future. On the local level, Zionist district organizations were allowed to solicit "the affiliation of [any] local Jewish organizations interested in the Palestinian activities of the Zionist Organization of America," and these affiliated organizations would be entitled to "representation on the district committee of the Zionist Organization of America."[77]

On November 27, Julian Mack reaffirmed the American position regarding the separate national federations.[78] In addition to the Medical Unit the Americans now proposed to add another contribution to the Palestinian work in the form of a Palestine Development Committee, whose main task would be "to further quicken constructive industrial and agricultural development in Palestine."[79] Composed of "men with business ability, who would have at their disposal experts in the various technical projects which they would be called upon to consider," the Committee would circulate information about, and sell stock in projects or prospective projects in Palestine. Committee members might be men who "have not been hitherto recognized as Zionists, men of wealth and ability." To insure efficiency, the Committee would be headed by a salaried manager skilled in the "selling of stocks, and [be] able to deal with engineers and bankers of high calibre." The committee's work would become the "vital, primarily important function of the Americans for the coming year" with all other efforts "incidental and for the purpose of aiding this work."

The Americans also reorganized the administrative structure of the Z.O.A. Reflecting Brandeis' attitude towards Zionist cultural and educational work in the Diaspora, this change left the Z.O.A. with only two departments—the Organization department to deal with membership and lecturing, and lend whatever aid possible to the Palestine Development Committee, and the Executive department to concern itself with political problems such as the relations between the Z.O.A. and the American government. This reorganization resulted in the "abolition of the Education department, the abolition of Hebrew teaching and cultural work, and all the indirect work which is done." The publicity and printing departments were abolished, and the budgets for the Hebrew Bureau and Zionist publications were reduced from $56,000 in 1920 to $6,000 in 1921, and general Jewish educational work in America from $88,000 to $38,000.[80] These drastic reductions did not mean the total abandonment of all cultural and educational activity, since the convention adopted a plan proposed by Emanuel Neumann whereby the Z.O.A. would sponsor but not assume financial responsibility for a special institution for the promotion of such efforts. Some of Brandeis' closest associates, however, felt that Neumann's plan did not go far enough and opposed having the Z.O.A. act even as sponsor for such an agency.[81]

The Europeans were also disappointed and angry after the London conference. They realized that American aid was essential if anything were to be accomplished in Palestine. Consequently, in an attempt to satisfy the Americans, the W.Z.O. initiated certain reforms. In a letter to De Haas, Julius Simon and Nehemiah De Lieme noted that the W.Z.O. was cutting expenses by reducing the personnel of the London office from 118 to 70. Furthermore, the administration of the W.Z.O. would be centered in Palestine, by transferring there the departments of Immigration, Trade and Industry, and Education. In addition, they promised that the Executive of the W.Z.O. "is determined to inaugurate a well-organized and rigidly controlled financial administration."[82] An American Zionist observer in Palestine, Ben V. Cohen, wrote that the Zionist Commission was cutting expenses in Palestine, although reluctantly.[83] The budgets for the Hebrew Language Committee, and Zionist sponsored Arabic language newspapers in Jaffa and Jerusalem had been markedly reduced, and the Statistics and Information Department had been abolished. On November 8, Cohen advised[84] that the Publicity department was to be eliminated, the Hebrew newspaper of the W.Z.O. *Haolam* was to suspend publication and indications pointed to a further reduction in the staff of the London office so that it would number no more than 30 people by the spring of 1921. Cohen concluded that "an honest attempt at reform under difficulties which have been, perhaps, even greater than you imagine" had been undertaken. These reforms, however, were made grudgingly, and were due largely to the efforts of Simon and De Lieme. Bernard Flexner informed Brandeis that although "an effort had been made to cut down operating expenses in London," it did not amount to much, and since Simon had suffered a physical breakdown, and De Lieme was away from London on other business, prospects for further progress were not good.[85]

The limited reforms introduced by the W.Z.O. in Palestine were the result of the work of the Reorganization Commission, sent to Palestine by the W.Z.O. The Americans had consented to appoint one representative, Robert Szold, to this commission. Szold accepted this position, on condition that the commission be given full power to carry out needed reforms in Palestine "irregardless of objections or circumstances."[86] Although this condition was met, some of Brandeis' close advisers opposed sending Szold to Palestine. De Haas told Brandeis that "no one can straighten the situation out in Palestine in four weeks, the length of time Bob is going to allow himself." Moreover, warned De Haas, "all that we are going to get is a sort of paper reform."[87]

De Haas' analysis proved to be essentially correct. Even before the commission could begin its work in Palestine, Simon and De Lieme had resigned, and the commission never really did get off the ground. The Americans, incensed over the resignations and the resulting crippling of the commission, believed that Simon and De Lieme had resigned because the work of the commission had been sabotaged even before it could begin by a secret agreement between Weizmann and Jabotinsky. Jabotinsky, who was the head of the Press and Propaganda department of the

Keren, was not elected to the Actions Committee at London. According to the alleged agreement, Weizmann was to help get Jabotinsky elected to the Executive, (with the understanding that he would support Weizmann in his fight against Brandeis) and Weizmann would agree to Jabotinsky's demands concerning the rights of the Board of Directors of the Keren. Jabotinsky wanted wide powers for this Board, powers that would preclude any reforming attempt by a body such as the Reorganization Commission. Actually, there is no proof to verify the American assertion that any secret agreement had been made by Weizmann and Jabotinsky. Ben Cohen wrote to Mack that "the yarn about the limitation of the powers of the Reorganization Commission is unfounded," and reported his doubts that Weizmann had made any definite commitments to Jabotinsky.[88]

The agreement that was finally concluded between the W.Z.O. and the Keren Board was a cause of great consternation to the Americans. This agreement provided that: 1) the Zionist Executive name a governor to head the Keren Board who would control 51 percent of the votes on the Board; 2) the Board have sole power to decide the use made of its money; 3) the internal administrative matters of the Keren and the organization of its propaganda be handled by the Central Office of the Keren; 4) the Zionist Executive provide the Central Office of the Keren with all of the data concerning their plans for propaganda work, and with information concerning all of the Palestinian affairs of the W.Z.O.; and 5) the Board of the Keren decide on all Keren expenditures in Palestine, the budget for the Keren, and have a voice in all "questions of fundamental importance."[89]

Before the promulgation of this agreement, the American attitude towards the Keren had been one of cautious waiting. On September 29, the National Executive Committee of the Z.O.A. had appointed a special Committee on Palestinian Activities, with the purpose of determining what activities on behalf of the Keren should be promoted by the Z.O.A. This committee objected to the Keren on the same grounds as Brandeis at London, i.e. it did not separate donations from investments.[90] This policy of cautious waiting changed to one of opposition after the promulgation of the W.Z.O.-Keren agreement. Despite the power of the governor of the Keren Board, it was felt that "in practice, the Board directs the work, and feels itself at least the co-partner of the Executive, and not its loyal servant." This Board, which was "neither particularly representative nor particularly able" was to "exert an undue influence on important questions of policy."[91]

After the main features of the Keren and its organization had become clear, the Americans devised their own system for investment funds outlined in a plan presented by De Haas to the National Executive Committee on October 31. Under this plan, the Z.O.A. would take the initiative in developing a Palestine Investment Corporation in every Jewish center in America. Each city was to develop one such corporation, and the money raised would be invested in enterprises "as the directors may from time to time determine." The Z.O.A. would assume no responsibility for private enterprises, and would not share in their management or control. Nor were these corporations to be directly connected with the local district organizations of the Z.O.A. The Z.O.A., however, was to help coordinate some of the operations so that the various enterprises might benefit from a "synchronization of effort," and it would employ one or two men in Palestine who would give the benefit of their knowledge and experience to the corporations. This plan was formally accepted by the Z.O.A. at Buffalo.

This alternate plan along with the American opposition to the Keren brought the charge of secession against the Americans to a new high pitch of intensity. The Americans countered by claiming that the W.Z.O.'s agreement with the Keren Board undermined the authority of the W.Z.O., and this, they maintained, was the real act of secession. By now, however, a new complicating factor had come into the picture, the growth of a group of American Zionists who opposed Brandeis.

Before 1914, American Zionists had been a small, rather inefficiently managed, loosely organized group lacking any appreciable degree of influence. However, after Brandeis had assumed leadership in 1914, this changed radically as the American organization grew in numbers, financial resources, and influence. This remarkable growth was due in large part to the sympathy which the wartime plight of European and Palestinian Jewries aroused in the hearts of American Jews. However, Brandeis, his influence, and the changes that he instituted in the management of American Zionist affairs also aided this growth. Brandeis introduced a system which in the words of De Haas, brought to an end the "slippered ease" with which American Zionists had conducted their affairs. He introduced a "habitual punctuality" into American Zionist work and conducted affairs in a manner which "called for an orderliness and a systematization, a compactness and a precision which often irked volunteers as well as the paid staff." Brandeis was decisive; he was endowed with an intensity and a single-mindedness which knew nothing of "doubtful assent or hesitating dissent." Perhaps most abrasive of all, he expected his coworkers to match these high standards.[92]

Many of the American Zionists, however, could not meet these standards, nor did they approve of them. Opposition was especially noticeable among those who were immigrants of East European origin.[93] They thought Brandeis too autocratic for such an open and democratic movement as Zionism. He seemed distant and aloof. Many resented the fact that they could seldom see Brandeis personally, and were told to take their problems and suggestions to lesser officials. Moreover, for some of these people, "too little time was devoted to theoretical review and academic formulations of policy." The Brandeis method was "too practical . . . too much concerned with practical plans."[94] In addition, there were some native American Zionists who felt more attached emotionally, intellectually, or religiously to the East European Zionists than they did to Brandeis. Having lain dormant for the most part during the war years, this opposition to Brandeis rose to the surface after the London conference.

At the September 29 meeting of the National Executive Committee, Horace M. Kallen presented a resolution expressing support for Brandeis' conduct at London. The ensuing discussion included some sharp criticism of the Brandeis administration. Louis Lipsky, who had recently attacked the Brandeis policies at a meeting of New York Zionists, criticised Brandeis' refusal to allow any American to serve on the Zionist Executive, declaring that he had supported Brandeis at London, at times against his own better judgment.

As a result of this criticism, Kallen's resolution was sidetracked. Instead, the Executive Committee adopted an alternative proposal submitted by Wise which called for the establishment of a committee to draft resolutions to deal with the problems before the Z.O.A., and "to try to allay doubt and unrest now existing in Zionist circles."[95] Some weeks later, the opposition made its presence felt at the Buffalo convention, although it was still rather insignificant. Nevertheless, on November 30, De Haas wrote to Brandeis that "a new and unwholesome spirit has come into our organization—a small but very determined group who have developed the idea that every personal interest or every personal prestige is superior to all other considerations."[96]

Brandeis did not respond directly to the charges made against him at the September 29 meeting for several weeks. Instead, his chief lieutenants De Haas, Felix Frankfurter and Bernard Flexner carried the burden of defending the cause. Brandeis finally did reply to his critics in an interview with Rabbi Abba Hillel Silver on October 12.[97] Denying that he had ever intended to break away from the international movement, Brandeis defended the reduced American financial contribution to the

W.Z.O., and claimed that the American delegation at London had unanimously agreed to leave the decision as to American contributions to the National Executive Committee of the Z.O.A. He added that "Mr. Lipsky was emphatic in urging the delegates not to bind themselves to any specific agreements for the future." Brandeis claimed that his opposition to American representation on the Zionist Executive was based on the fundamental difference between himself and the Europeans as to the "moral justification of the use of certain means to accomplish ends which all desired," and as to the binding effect of agreements made. In answer to the charge that he had not discussed his reorganization plan with the American delegation at London, Brandeis stated that he had done so on July 14. Criticizing the American delegates for quietly watching him take the blame for things that were not his fault, Brandeis complained that the delegation did not even consult him before voting to oppose the spending of Zionist funds for educational and cultural work in the Diaspora. Yet, he alone was blamed for this.[98]

The battle continued to rage during the winter months of 1920–1921. The high degree of suspicion and distrust resulted in American refusal to attend a winter meeting of the Actions Committee of the W.Z.O. The Americans feared that the attendant publicity had led the public to believe that the meeting had been called by Weizmann for the purpose of effecting a rapprochement with Brandeis. A memorandum on the subject presented to Brandeis stated that the Americans "have been asked to meet Dr. Weizmann and the Keren Hayesod group on the bridge, but he and his colleagues have already made sure that if we accept the offer, we shall be walking the plank." [99] The memorandum recommended that the Americans should attempt to outsmart Weizmann by asking for a postponement of the Actions Committee meeting, and calling instead for a Zionist Congress to be held during the summer. The proposed Congress would be more appealing to the public than a mere Actions Committee meeting, and Weizmann would have to agree to it. Following the suggestion of the memorandum, the Americans refused to attend the Actions Committee meeting without, however, calling for a Congress meeting.

Weizmann came to the United States in April, 1921. In his autobiography Weizmann wrote that the idea of his coming to America first arose at the London conference. There, Brandeis had objected to the budget submitted by Weizmann for the coming year. Weizmann, in turn, had protested against Brandeis' proposed reductions, and told him that "if this was all he could find in America, I shall have to come over and try for myself." [100] Apparently Weizmann made arrangements with the entire American delegation to come to America and this plan was approved by Brandeis. According to the agreement Weizmann would come at an opportune time for the sole purpose of "raising funds for the development of the crown land in Palestine." No agreement was reached concerning collecting money for the general budget. [101]

Later, Weizmann expressed a desire to come to America in time to attend the Buffalo convention. At a meeting of the National Executive Committee on October 17, the Brandeis followers objected to this proposed visit because Weizmann had not as yet secured any concessions from the British concerning the crown lands. Moreover, he would be coming at a time of strife in America, and the Brandeis people did not want to give their American opponents an opportunity to rally around the figure of Weizmann. Therefore, the meeting defeated a resolution introduced by Lipsky welcoming Weizmann to the convention. It drafted instead a substitute resolution stating that it was "very inopportune for him to come at present." [102] As a result, Weizmann postponed his visit until late in April. Even then, however, the Brandeis followers considered him persona non grata. According to Weizmann, the purpose of his April visit was two-fold: to set up the Keren in America, and "to awaken American interest in the Hebrew University." [103] The Brandeis followers, however, believed that his real purpose was to rally the American opposition in order to challenge directly the authority of the Brandeis leadership.

Weizmann's arrival witnessed the beginning of a period marked by attempts to compromise and bridge the gap between the positions of the two groups on the Keren. Soon after he landed, Weizmann received a memorandum from Mack, the terms of which were to serve as a basis for agreement. [104] Calling for the immediate establishment of the Keren in America by the Z.O.A., the memo proposed limiting the American effort to donation funds, allowing non-Zionist representation on the Keren Board, and the deposit of funds collected in America in American banks. Mack's memo further stipulated that the Medical Unit be the first charge on the American fund, and finally, that the Zionist Executive control American Keren funds designated for the Palestine budget. Without definitely accepting these conditions, Weizmann insisted that the "congress shall have the right to direct that funds be turned over to such an agency as it might designate for expenditures in Palestine." This was an obvious reference to the Keren Board. There was considerable discussion in American circles as to whether or not to accept this condition. Mack was ready to accept it. De Haas, however, opposed it. Frankfurter also opposed acceptance, and stated that the Americans must show "uncompromisingness whatever the consequences" on the Mack memorandum.[105] The discussion came to an abrupt end when Weizmann suddenly rejected the entire memorandum.

Weizmann's motivation in turning down this plan is not too clear. The Americans did not blame Weizmann directly for disregarding the Mack proposals, believing that he had been forced into doing this. Mack wrote to Brandeis that there were "those about Weizmann both Europeans and Americans who had prevented, and would prevent any agreement." [106] The Americans singled out Shmarya Levin and Ussishkin as the two leading European opponents of compromise. De Haas wrote Brandeis that Levin's conception of "united Israel is excluding all those who are not Russian Jews," [107] and Mack is quoted as having told Weizmann that "I sincerely believe that if it were not for Mr. Ussishkin, we could get together very easily." [108] It was also charged that Neumann and Lipsky had threatened "to break" Weizmann in America if he agreed to the Mack proposals.[109] There is no other proof to verify these charges, and it is possible that the Brandeis followers may have been carried away by the heat of the battle. Nevertheless, the suddenness with which Weizmann dropped the Mack proposals after apparently having given them serious consideration, lends some credibility to the statements.[110]

With the failure of compromise, Weizmann declared the Keren as projected by the W.Z.O. to be established in America. Shortly thereafter Mack stated that the Z.O.A. was going to set up a Palestine Donation Fund, the American version of the Keren. Thereupon, Lipsky resigned from his post in the Z.O.A. and called for the convening of an extraordinary conference of American Zionists to take place on May 1, in order to discuss the rapidly deteriorating situation.[111] Meanwhile, the Brandeis administration issued a call for a convention of American Zionists to obtain a vote of confidence in its leadership.

Both sides now began campaigns to gain member support. The *New Palestine*, official organ of the Z.O.A., presented the Brandeis point of view. This journal, normally published weekly in English, now appeared twice a week, and on one occasion added a long Yiddish supplement to reach the large non-English-reading Jewish community. Practically the entire Yiddish press in America, however, supported Weizmann. On May 1, the opponents of Brandeis established the *New Maccabean* to publicize their position, and Weizmann himself carried the fight throughout the country by addressing mass meetings in many large cities during April and May.

On May 24, the Brandeis cause suffered a major blow when the Z.O.A. received a disappointing letter from Julius Simon. Ben Cohen had urged Simon to send a message supporting Brandeis in the approaching convention. Simon wrote instead that although he did not approve of Weizmann's tactics, he believed it best for the movement if "the American federation supports as well as it can the European leaders and that the Organization as a whole develop through painful and bitter experience to healthier conditions throughout." [112]

Both sides reiterated their stands with great passion at the convention which convened on June 5 in Cleveland. Wise and Mack, in the absence of Brandeis, bore the brunt of the battle for the American administration while Weizmann, Ussishkin and Lipsky were the main spokesmen for the Europeans and the American opposition. The convention, weighted heavily with opposition forces, failed to give the Brandeis administration the requested vote of confidence. Immediately thereafter, Brandeis and his lieutenants resigned their posts to become in Brandeis' words "humble soldiers in the ranks where we may hope to hasten the . . . coming of the day when the policies in which we believe will be recognized as the only ones through which our great ends may be achieved." [113]

After the Cleveland convention, Brandeis and his supporters, while remaining members of the Z.O.A., followed an independent course. Brandeis proposed to his followers the establishment of a "co-operative wholesale organization with a view to enabling the people of Palestine to procure the necessities of life at the lowest possible cost." [114] This resulted in the creation of the Palestine Co-operative Company and Palestine Development Leagues to sponsor specific projects in Palestine. A Palestine Development Council was formed to coordinate the work of these various groups.

As time passed, the Brandeis dissidents assumed a more active role in Z.O.A. affairs. At the 1922 convention of the Z.O.A., a conciliation committee was established to heal the breach, and by the late 1920's the Brandeis group joined a coalition administration with the Lipsky group. By the mid-1930's when grave new problems confronted Zionism and world Jewry, the controversies of 1920 had receded into the background, and the breach in American Zionism was healed.

For Brandeis, however, the gap was never closed. He never again played an official role in American Zionism. Continuing to espouse the Zionist cause, he brought to bear all of his influence to aid the movement. Though retired from a position of leadership, Brandeis continued to retain his sublime faith "in the ultimate achievement of Zion restored and Israel redeemed." [115]

NOTES

1. *Halukah* was the name given to the system under which funds collected in the Diaspora were distributed among the various Jewish religious communities in Palestine. These religious communities collectively composed the Old *Yishuv*. The New *Yishuv* came into existence with the settlement of Zionist groups in Palestine in the early 1880's.
2. Jacob De Haas, *Louis D. Brandeis* (New York: 1929), p. 59 and Chaim Weizmann, *Trial and Error* (Philadelphia: 1949), v. I, p. 165.
3. Felix Frankfurter, ed., *Brandeis on Zionism: A Collection of Addresses and Statements by Louis D. Brandeis* (Washington: 1942), p. 5.
4. *Ibid.*, p. 13.
5. *Ibid.*
6. *Ibid.*, p. 29.
7. *Ibid.*
8. *Ibid.*, pp. 27 and 30–31.
9. A definition of Americanism along racial lines, however, began to take form in the two or three decades before the Brandeis leadership, and such a definition actually was in vogue during the era of Brandeis' leadership of American Zionism. See Oscar Handlin, *Race and Nationality in American Life* (Garden City: 1957), pp. 57–73.
10. Frankfurter, *Brandeis on Zionism*, p. 24.
11. *Ibid.*, p. 17.
12. "Dr. Weizmann's Reply to His Critics," *New Palestine*, June 17, 1921, p. 7.
13. Louis Lipsky, *A Gallery of Zionist Profiles* (New York: 1956), p. 162.
14. Proceedings of the National Executive Committee of the Zionist Organization of America, August 29, 1920. University of Louisville, *Correspondence from the Collection of the Late Justice Brandeis Pertaining to Zionism and Palestine, 1913–1938*, Roll *12*, film number 614.
15. Minutes, Meeting of the American Delegation to the International Zionist Conference, June 30, 1920. *Correspondence*, Roll *12*, 547. Despite all of this, Weizmann, in a speech to the American delegation on July 5, urged close cooperation between the English-speaking delegates, and on July 6, the American delegation passed a resolution to that effect. *Ibid.*, Roll *12*, 551–52.
16. The Zionist Commission was created by Great Britain in April, 1918 to advise the British military administration in Palestine "in all matters relating to Jews, or which may effect the establishment of a national home for the Jewish people." Representatives of British, French and Italian Jewries were included in the Commission headed originally by Weizmann. The Americans had no representation on the Commission since, at the time of its inception, the United States was not at war with the Ottoman Empire, and it was felt that the Ottomans would have considered American participation an unfriendly act. Until September, 1921, when it was succeeded by the Executive chosen by the first postwar Zionist Congress, the Commission operated as the agency of the W.Z.O. in Palestine.
17. For the proposal, see Minutes, Meeting American Delegation, Sunday, July 11, 1920, *Correspondence*, Roll *12*, 560.

18. From Brandeis' speech to the first formal meeting of the conference on July 7. De Haas, *Brandeis*, p. 233.
19. Minutes, Meeting American Delegation, July 14, 1920. *Correspondence, Roll 12*, 565.
20. Minutes, Meeting American Delegation, July 16, 1920. *Ibid., Roll 12*, 569.
21. Weizmann, *Trial and Error*, v. I, pp. 261–62.
22. *Ibid.*, p. 256.
23. *Ibid.*, p. 248.
24. De Haas, *Brandeis*, pp. 51–53. Brandeis, however, did not become an active Zionist until March, 1913. Yonathan Shapiro, "American Jews in Politics: The Case of Louis D. Brandeis," *American Jewish Historical Quarterly*, LV, 200–201.
25. "Political" Zionists were those who believed that the primary task of the W.Z.O. was to gain a political commitment from the leading world powers in support of the Jewish national home. "Practical" Zionists were those who stressed the gradual building up of Palestine through constant immigration and settlement of the land. Once the Jews gained a large enough foothold in Palestine, the world powers would then have no choice but to grant a commitment in favor of the Jewish national home.
26. Oskar K. Rabinowicz, *Fifty Years of Zionism* (London: 1950), p. 40.
27. *Ibid.*, p. 40. The Revisionists, headed by Vladimir Jabotinsky, felt that the W.Z.O. did not take a strong enough stand towards the mandatory power. They believed that it was not up to the Jews to build the national home while Britain merely kept the peace in Palestine. Rather, it was Britain's responsibility to establish a national home for the Jews. Accordingly, the Revisionists wished to extract from the British an explicit statement promising a Jewish state in Palestine. All Zionist activities should be aimed at achieving these two "political" goals. Furthermore, the Revisionists wanted Transjordan to be included in the Jewish state.
28. Minutes, Meeting American Delegation, July 5, 1920. *Correspondence, Roll 12*, 550.
29. Paul L. Hanna, *British Policy in Palestine* (Washington: 1942), pp. 30–38.
30. The Brandeis reorganization plan was presented to the American delegation on July 14, 1920. *Correspondence, Roll 12*, 559–63. The plan is quoted in a somewhat abridged form in De Haas, *Brandeis*, pp. 235–59.
31. Minutes, Meeting American Delegation, July 10. *Correspondence, Roll 12*, 554.
32. The Jewish Colonial Trust was the Bank or "Jewish Company" envisaged by Herzl. It was to finance Zionist enterprises. The Jewish National Fund was established by the W.Z.O. in 1901 for the purpose of purchasing land in Palestine.
33. Minutes, Meeting American Delegation, July 12. *Correspondence, Roll 12*, 557.
34. De Haas, *Brandeis*, p. 248.
35. Minutes, Meeting American Delegation, July 12. *Correspondence, Roll 12*, 557.
36. Minutes, Meeting American Delegation, July 10. *Ibid., Roll 12*, 554.
37. De Haas, *Brandeis*, p. 249.
38. Minutes, Meeting American Delegation, July 10. *Correspondence, Roll 12*, 554.
39. Minutes, Meeting American Delegation, July 16. *Ibid., Roll 12*, 569.
40. Minutes, Meeting American Delegation, July 12. *Ibid., Roll 12*, 557.
41. De Haas, *Brandeis*, p. 255.
42. Minutes, Meeting American Delegation, July 19. *Ibid., Roll 12*, 573.
43. Minutes, Meeting American Delegation, July 16. *Ibid., Roll 12*, 572.
44. De Haas, *Brandeis*, pp. 255–56.
45. *Ibid.*, p. 257.
46. For this and the following, see Brandeis' report to the National Executive Committee of the Z.O.A., August 29, 1920. *Correspondence, Roll 12*, 614.
47. De Haas, *Brandeis*, p. 133.
48. See Ben Halpern, *The Idea of the Jewish State* (Cambridge: 1961), pp. 188–94.
49. Weizmann, *Trial and Error*, v. I, p. 261.

50. De Haas, *Brandeis*, pp. 243–45.
51. Weizmann, *Trial and Error*, v. II, pp. 269–70.
52. *Ibid.*, p. 268. See also "Zionism and Assimilation," *Zionist Review*, IV, November, 1920, 119–20.
53. De Haas, *Brandeis*, pp. 218–31.
54. *Ibid.*, pp. 226–28.
55. Letter from Brandeis to Louis Marshall, October 24, 1919. *Correspondence, Roll 12*, 436.
56. Address of Julian W. Mack delivered at the Cleveland convention of the Z.O.A. on June 5, 1921. *Report of the Proceedings of the Twenty-Fourth Annual Convention of the Zionist Organization of America* (New York: 1921), p. 10.
57. Minutes, Meeting American Delegation, July 22. *Correspondence, Roll 12*, 577.
58. Minutes, Meeting American Delegation, July 19. *Ibid., Roll 12*, 570.
59. Proceedings of the Meeting of the National Executive Committee of the Zionist Organization of America, August 29, 1920. *Ibid., Roll 12*, 615.
60. See the Zeeland Memorandum, written by Brandeis on his return trip from London aboard the U.S.S. Zeeland. De Haas, *Brandeis*, pp. 269–70.
61. Weizmann, *Trial and Error*, v. II, p. 273.
62. *Ibid.*, p. 278.
63. See the Pittsburgh Program adopted by the 1918 convention of the Z.O.A. De Haas, *Brandeis*, pp. 96–97.
64. Weizmann, *Trial and Error*, v. II, pp. 269–70.
65. Minutes, Meeting American Delegation, July 14. *Correspondence, Roll 12*, 564.
66. *Ibid., Roll 12*, 565–66.
67. Minutes, Meeting American Delegation, July 19. *Ibid., Roll 12*, 573.
68. *Ibid.*
69. Minutes, Meeting American Delegation, July 20. *Ibid., Roll 12*, 574–75. This final proposal was drafted by a joint sub-committee composed of Europeans and Americans which had been appointed to formulate a compromise whereby Brandeis could be induced to serve.
70. Berthold Feiwal, "Our Task," *Zionist Review*, IV, February, 1921, 184.
71. "Keren Hayesod." *Ibid.*, November, 1920, 118.
72. For the complete text of the Wise address, *Roll 12*, 581–85.
73. Resolutions Offered by the Resolutions Committee Adopted at the Twenty-Third Annual Convention of the Zionist Organization of America. *Ibid., Roll 12*, 586.
74. Memorandum as Basis for Discussion on Plan to be Submitted to the Executive Committee Meeting, September 29, 1920. *Ibid., Roll 12*, 600.
75. Minutes of the Meeting of the National Executive Committee Held on September 29 and 30. *Ibid., Roll 12*, 622.
76. Memorandum for September 29, *Op. cit.*, 601–2.
77. Report of the Organization Committee as Adopted at the Twenty-Third Annual Convention of the Zionist Organization of America. *Ibid., Roll 12*, 588.
78. For the full text of Mack's address to the Buffalo Convention. *Ibid., Roll 12*, 978.
79. Memorandum as Basis for Discussion on Plans to be Submitted to the Executive Committee Meeting, September 29, 1920. *Ibid., Roll 12*, 603.
80. *Ibid., Roll 12*, 604–5.
81. Telegram from De Haas to Brandeis, November 28, 1920. *Ibid., Roll 12*, 984.
82. Letter from Simon and De Lieme to De Haas, September 19, 1920. *Ibid., Roll 12*, 824–26.
83. Letter from Ben V. Cohen to Mack, September 21, 1920. *Ibid., Roll 12*, 837.
84. Letter from Cohen to Mack, November 8, 1920. *Ibid., Roll 12*, 951.
85. Letter from Bernard Flexner to Brandeis, September 24, 1920. *Ibid., Roll 12*, 860.

86. Minutes, Meeting of the National Executive Held on October 17, 1920. *Ibid., Roll 12*, 649.

87. Letter from De Haas to Brandeis, October 7, 1920. *Ibid., Roll 12*, 878.

88. Letter from Cohen to Mack, November 12, 1920. *Correspondence, Roll 12*, 963.

89. Agreement Between the Executive of the Zionist Organization and Messrs. Naiditch, Zlatopolsky, and Dr. Feiwal as Representatives of the Keren Hayesod concerning the Organization of the Keren Hayesod, October 22, 1920. *Correspondence, Roll 12*, 898.

90. Appendix I to the Minutes of the National Executive Held on October 31, 1920. This document was entitled "Majority Report of the Committee on Palestine Activities." *Ibid., Roll 12*, 632.

91. Letter from Cohen to Mack, October 28, 1920. *Ibid., Roll 12*, 897.

92. De Haas, *Brandeis*, pp. 62–64.

93. Judd Teller, "America's Two Zionist Traditions," *Commentary*, XX, October, 1955, 349.

94. De Haas, *op. cit.*, p. 68.

95. Minutes, Meeting of the National Executive Committee Held on September 29 and 30. *Correspondence, Roll 12*, 621.

96. Letter from De Haas to Brandeis, November 30, 1920. *Ibid., Roll 12*, 989.

97. Memorandum of a Conversation With Justice Brandeis at Washington on Tuesday Morning, October 12, 1920. *Ibid., Roll 12*, 912.

98. Some Brandeis supporters opposed publication of this interview, fearing that it would merely serve to keep the flames of dissension burning. Others, like Flexner and Mack, urged publication. Letter from Flexner to Brandeis, November 24, 1920. *Ibid., Roll 12*, 974, and Telegram from Mack to Brandeis, November 25, 1920. *Ibid., Roll 12*, 976.

99. Memorandum on Policy, January 14, 1921. *Ibid.*, 993–94.

100. Weizmann, *Trial and Error*, v. II, p. 262.

101. Minutes, Meeting American Delegation, July 22, 1920. *Correspondence, Roll 12*, 578.

102. Minutes, Meeting National Executive Committee Held on October 17, 1920. *Ibid., Roll 12*, 649.

103. Weizmann, *Trial and Error*, v. II, p. 265.

104. The memo submitted by Mack to Weizmann and Weizmann's reaction are found in a long telegram sent by Alexander Sachs to Brandeis on April 15, 1921. *Ibid., Roll 12*, 1076.

105. Letter from Frankfurter to Mack, April 15, 1921. *Ibid., Roll 12*, 1077.

106. Letter from Mack to Brandeis, May 24, 1921. *Ibid., Roll 12*, 1101.

107. Letter from De Haas to Brandeis, April 28, 1921. *Ibid., Roll 12*, 1084.

108. Julius Haber, *Odyssey of an American Zionist* (New York: 1956), p. 180.

109. "Why Did Weizmann Break With the Zionist Organization of America." *Correspondence, Roll 12*, 1079.

110. Other attempts at compromise were made, but these too failed. Walter Lippmann tried unsuccessfully to set up a meeting between Weizmann and Brandeis. Telegram from Frankfurter to Brandeis, April 25, 1921. *Ibid., Roll 12*, 1082. Louis Marshall, who regarded the Zionist rupture as "most unfortunate," failed in his attempt to set up a new meeting between Mack and Weizmann. Letter from Louis Marshall to James H. Becker, March 19, 1923. Charles Reznikoff, *Louis Marshall—Champion of Liberty* (Philadelphia: 1957), v. II, p. 732. Finally, on May 19, a meeting was held between Weizmann and Ussischkin representing the Europeans, Neuman and Lipsky representing the American opposition, and Mack, Szold, Frankfurter and Cohen representing the Brandeis group. The meeting produced no agreement. Cohen in-

formed Brandeis that Weizmann had been "extremely impatient and intolerant," and that Frankfurter had added fuel to the fire by accusing Weizmann of acting like a dictator. Letter from Cohen to Brandeis, May 20, 1921. *Correspondence, Roll 12*, 1099.

111. See the "Call for Extraordinary Conference" issued by Lipsky and addressed "to all Zionist districts loyal to the World Zionist Organization, and who care for the Keren Hayesod." *Ibid., Roll 12*, 1085.

112. Letter from Simon to Cohen, May 24, 1921. *Ibid., Roll 12*, 1102.

113. De Haas, *Brandeis*, p. 145.

114. *Correspondence, Roll 12*, 275. The suggestion was made in a speech delivered by Brandeis to a group of his followers on June 10, immediately after the close of the Cleveland convention. De Haas, *Brandeis*, 273–78.

115. De Haas, *Brandeis*, p. 150.

III.

ZIONIST TRENDS IN ERETZ ISRAEL— IDEOLOGY AND REALITY

16.

Changes in the Social and Political Structure of the Second Aliya between 1904 and 1940

Yosef Gorny

I behold those few in the vanguard who are the first to participate in the public gatherings that determine the fate of the nation; I behold those few who accept the duty to remain, even when others do not follow or join them.
—A. D. Gordon

This research is based on a population survey of members of the Second Aliya conducted by the Labour Archives in the mid-thirties and early forties.

The survey studied 937 persons—644 men and 293 women. It was concerned primarily with those of the Second Aliya who worked on the land after their arrival in Palestine. Thus, the organizers of the survey chose a value-standard, concentrating on those immigrants who had fulfilled one of the central ideals of the Second Aliya and who had joined the labour movement. But the surveyors were not consistent in adhering to this value-standard and included city workers who had not engaged in agriculture. Since most of them were affiliated with the labour movement, we did not consider it proper to exclude them. Thus, our investigations will deal with both city and farm workers who immigrated to Palestine during the period of the Second Aliya.

The aim of this investigation was threefold:

a) To examine the social and political structure of the immigrants before their immigration, and to discover whether the Second Aliya had a social distinctiveness in addition to its ideological distinctiveness. The

Reprinted by permission of the author and Daniel Carpi from *Zionism: Studies in the History of the Zionist Movement and the Jewish Community of Palestine,* edited by Daniel Carpi and Gedalia Yogev (Tel Aviv University, 1975), 49–101.

social structure of this group was compared with that of—1) East European Jewry, from which most of these immigrants came; 2) Jewish immigration to the United States during the same period; and to the extent that available data permitted; 3) the general immigration to Palestine during this period.

b) To trace the changes in occupations and political affiliations among members of the Second Aliya over three periods: before immigrating to Palestine; during the Second Aliya, i.e. between 1904 and 1914; and during the mid-thirties and early forties, when the survey was made. This was complemented by a further question: Can the members of the Second Aliya be said to have become a political elite during this last period?

c) To try to ascertain whether a causal connection existed between objective social factors—such as social grouping, educational level, place or area of residence, etc.—on the one hand, and political affiliation, before and after immigration, on the other.

Finally, for the sake of accuracy and to avoid misunderstandings, it must be pointed out that the statistical data in this investigation and the conclusions drawn from them, pertain *only to European-born rural and urban labourers, who remained in the country.* The farm workers, who are the overwhelming majority of those surveyed, numbered altogether 1,000–1,300 men and women.[1] This group cannot serve as a sample for all the immigrants of the relevant period, whose estimated number was between 35,000 and 40,000.[2] Most of the immigrants left the country or were deported at the outbreak of World War I. It should therefore be borne in mind that we are concerned only with those who remained in the country.[3]

Despite its small size, we have come to call this group the Second Aliya. The term is not intended to describe a sociological phenomenon or a trend within the general Jewish immigration, but rather a revolutionary political value-concept, whose influence endured long afterwards. It was this group of farm workers who achieved the self-fulfillment of their ideals and who moulded the basic social and political thought-patterns of most of the Jewish community in Palestine during its struggle to achieve socio-economic strength and political independence.

It is not intended to negate or belittle the important contribution to the Jewish settlement of Palestine by workers from Yemen or immigrants from Europe who did not join the labour movement. We merely confined ourselves to the group whose members were the active proponents of the specific ideals of the Second Aliya.

A. DISTRIBUTION OF THE SECOND ALIYA ACCORDING TO YEARS, COUNTRIES AND AREAS OF ORIGIN

In this section we shall try to describe the social structure of members of the Second Aliya in their countries of origin and make a threefold comparison: with the social structure of East European Jewry, with the Jewish immigration to the United States and with the data on the total immigration to Palestine between 1905 and 1909.[4]

To begin with, let us compare the flow of immigration to the United States with aliya to Palestine between 1904 and 1914, by years (Tables 1 and 2).

The data on aliya are only partial, and mainly represent the flow of immigrants who passed through the port of Odessa and were registered in the offices of the Zionist Organization there. Many immigrants embarked at other ports—Constanza, Trieste, etc. and there were also some who did not register. An estimate of the total number of immigrants to Palestine during that period should include those from Yemen, estimated at 6000.[7] However, since the immigrants to both Palestine and the United States came primarily from Eastern Europe, it is meaningful to compare the two streams from this area, as they appear in the two tables.

Table 1   Table 2
Distribution of Immigration to the U.S. and Palestine (1904–1914)

	Immigrants to the U.S.[5]		From Russia by Way of Odessa	From Other Countries		
Year	Number	%*			Total	%
1904	106,236	9.0	—	—	—	—
1905	129,910	11.0	1230	—	1230	5
1906	153,748	13.0	3459	—	3459	13
1907	149,182	12.5	1750	—	1750	7
1908	103,387	8.5	2097	—	2097	8
1909	57,551	5.0	2459	—	2459	9
1910	84,260	7.0	1879	—	1879	7
1911	91,223	7.5	—	2376	2376	9
1912	80,595	6.5	1182	2282	3464	13
1913	101,330	8.5	1600	300	1900	7
1914	138,051	11.5	—	—	6000	22
Total	1,195,423	100.0				100

(header spanning) Immigrants to Palestine[6]

* The percentages in the tables are approximate.

A first glance at Tables 1 and 2 shows that immigration to both countries increased as a result of the persecutions of the years 1903 to 1906, or under the impact of anticipated dangers from international political events on the eve of World War I. At the same time, it should be pointed out that the extent of the aliya was not determined exclusively by these events. Thus, for example, the aliya in the "quiet" year of 1912 is identical with that of the post-pogrom year of 1906. Furthermore, in the pogrom year of 1905, it was the lowest of all.

This assumption is strengthened by the distribution, according to year of immigration, of 2,519 members of the Second Aliya who were included in a census by the Histadrut in 1922 (Table 3).

These data on immigrants who remained in Palestine show that 36% immigrated during or immediately after the pogrom years between 1904 and 1907, as well as on the eve of World War I; whereas 64% arrived during the five relatively "quiet" years of 1908–1913.

Table 4 shows the distribution of these immigrants according to their countries of origin.

According to this table, those originating from the area of the Russian Empire constitute 94.3% of the Second Aliya. This ratio is higher than that of the Jews in this area to the Jews in Europe as a whole (59.5%).[9] It is also higher than the ratio of Jews from this area to the total Jewish immigration to the United States between 1900 and 1914 (72%).

A study of the distribution of immigration from Czarist Russia by

Table 3
Distribution of the Second Aliya by
Year of Immigration according to
Census of 1922 [8]

Year	Number	% (rounded)
1904	108	4
1905	133	5
1906	170	7
1907	174	7
1908	174	7
1909	193	8
1910	251	10
1911	159	6
1912	456	18
1913	380	15
1914	321	13

Table 4
Distribution of Immigrants in the Second Aliya Survey according
to Countries of Origin

Country of Origin	Number	%	Combined %
1. Russia	582	62.11	
2. Lithuania	61	6.51	94.3
3. Poland	186	19.85	
4. Bessarabia	55	5.86	
5. Galicia	25	2.66	
6. Austria	7	0.74	
7. Rumania	9	0.96	
8. Bulgaria	3	0.32	
9. Turkey	2	0.21	
10. England	1	0.10	
11. Germany	6	0.64	
Total	937		

areas, in comparison with the Jewish population of those areas (Table 5) shows that the Second Aliya was markedly regional, South-West Russia being the most important area of origin.

Under the category "Russia" we included the immigrants who came from outside the Pale of Settlement and those who did not precisely specify their place of origin, noting only that it was "Russia." Some of the latter presumably came from the Ukraine, Lithuania or White Russia. Places in Poland and Bessarabia were easier to identify. The data on Russian Jewry as a whole are taken from Leschinsky.[10]

If the 17.8% whose area of residence is unspecified are distributed proportionally among the other areas, about 8% will be added to the

Table 5
Distribution of Immigrants to Palestine from Czarist Russia as
Compared to Its Total Distribution of Jews—According to Areas

Area	Immigrants to Palestine	% of Total Immigration	Combined %	% in that Area of All Russian Jews
Russia	155	17.8	17.8	
Ukraine	368	41.6	47.8	42.5
Bessarabia	55	6.2		
White Russia	59	6.7	13.7	28.0
Lithuania	61	7.0		
Poland	186	20.7	20.7	25.6
Total	884	100	100	

47.8 of the South-West, bringing the proportion of those originating from there to 55.8% of the total.

It should be noted that the distribution of immigrants passing through Odessa between 1905 and 1909 [11] more closely approximates the distribution of all Russian Jews than that of our sample. According to these data, 17% immigrated from Poland, 26% from Lithuania and 40% from South-West Russia, further reinforcing the assumption of a marked regional character for the Second Aliya.

This fact cannot be explained by political or economic pressures which were hypothetically stronger in the South-West than in Lithuania, White Russia and Poland. If this had been so, it would have been noticeable also in the distribution of all immigrants in the turbulent 1905–1909 period.

We sought an explanation in the greater intensity of political activity in this region as compared to the others. We assumed that since the strongholds of the anti-Zionist Bund [12] were located mainly in the northern part of the Pale, the high proportion of political affiliation to Zionist parties or organizations might have been a stimulus for aliya. However, an examination of the distribution of members of Zionist parties or organizations in the various areas of Czarist Russia did not confirm this assumption. In fact, the highest proportion of political affiliation— 69.3%—was in Lithuania and White Russia; it was 60% in Poland and 56.6% in the South-West. The extent of political affiliation is, therefore, in almost inverse ratio to the general distribution of Jews among the areas.

Another possibility was that the place of residence—city, small town or village—might have had a determining effect on the aliya. It was reasonable to assume that the political ferment in cities such as Odessa, Warsaw, Minsk, Poltava, etc., was more intensive than in the small towns and villages. However, the assumption is incorrect on both counts. First, the proportion of Jews who emigrated to Palestine from large and medium-sized towns is identical to the proportion of all Jews who lived in such towns in Russia, and is not very different from that in Poland (Table 6). Secondly, the proportion of political affiliation among immigrants from large towns was only slightly higher than of those coming from small towns: 60% as against 58.5%.

It appears, therefore, that while the Second Aliya was markedly regional—about half the immigrants came from the South-West—it was not distinctive as to place of residence abroad. They were not preponderantly city dwellers. This conclusion does not necessarily contradict our

Table 6

Distribution of Second Aliya Survey according to Place of Residence in Europe

Place of Residence	Number	%	Proportion of All Jews in Russia and Poland	
			Russia	Poland
Large and Medium-sized towns	271	28.92	28.2	25.6
Small towns	631	67.34		
Villages	34	3.62		
Unknown	1	0.10		
Total	937			

previous assumption about the overall effect of political ferment, particularly in the large cities, on the decision to emigrate to Palestine. As will be shown below, there is a correlation between the political fabric and aliya. It may also be assumed that some of the immigrants had lived for a time in the large cities, or had moved there in order to work or study—and so were influenced by the political ferment. But, there are no relevant data.

It is possible to arrive at a different conclusion from the data—that precisely in the smaller towns there were stronger incentives toward aliya than in the large cities. There was a dialectic development: the desire to create an alternative to the traditional-exilic Jewish environment was much stronger in the small towns. The economic anomaly of the Jews was more pronounced there and the power of traditional-religious authorities more pervasive than in the city, which offered more opportunities for acquiring a general education and for participation in Jewish and general political activity. Life in the cities had fascination and novelty as compared to life in the small town and was liable to dampen the ardour for aliya. On the whole it would seem that life in the city did not constitute a particular incentive to aliya, though it was not a deterrent.

The Demographic Structure

Let us now analyze the demographic structure of the immigration to Palestine in comparison with Jewish immigration to the United States. An examination of the distribution by sex shows that the proportion of

Table 7
Distribution of Second Aliya
Survey according to Sex

Sex	Number	%
Male	644	68.7
Female	293	31.3
Total	937	100

Table 8
Distribution of Jewish Immigrants
to the U.S. according to Sex (in
percentages)

Year	Male	Female
1900–03	57.5	42.5
1904–07	57.1	42.9
1908–12	54.2	46.0
1913–14	53.6	44.8

men among immigrants to Palestine was some 15% to 20% higher than among Jewish immigrants to the United States (Tables 7 and 8).[13]

On the other hand, the statistics on sex distribution of all immigrants to Palestine in the 1905–1909 period show an almost absolute correlation with those for Jewish immigrants to the United States—58% men and 42% women.[14]

A comparison of the proportion of children among immigrants to Palestine and the United States yields similar results (Tables 9 and 10).

The proportion of children among the immigrants to the United States was 5% to 7% higher than in our sample, while the proportion of

Table 9
Distribution of Second Aliya Survey
according to Age at Aliya (1903–1914)

Age Group	Number	%
1–14	151	16.11
15–20	359	38.31
21–25	212	22.62
26–30	87	9.28
30 and over	87	9.28
Age unknown	41	4.37
Total	937	

Table 10
Distribution of Jewish Immigrants to the U.S. according
to Age (in percentages)

Years	Children up to 14	Adults 14–44	Over 45 Years Old
1900–03	24.6	69.7	5.7
1904–07	24.7	70.3	5.0
1908–12	25.2	68.5	6.3
1913–14	21.9	71.2	6.9

children among all the immigrants to Palestine amounted to 25% —
identical with the proportion of children among immigrants to the
United States.

The immigrants were divided acording to social groupings as follows
(Table 11):

Table 11
Distribution of Second Aliya Survey according to Social Groupings

Aliya Groupings	Number	%	Combined %
Individuals	526	56.13 ⎱	65.3
Organized Group	86	9.17 ⎰	
With Parents	155	16.54 ⎫	
With Other Relatives	37	3.94 ⎬	34.7
Married	53	5.65 ⎥	
Married with Children	80	8.53 ⎭	
Total	937		

The proportion of immigrants to Palestine who were either alone or
organized into groups came to 65.3%. The highest proportion of single
immigrants was in the 21–25 age group—67% of the group, and the
lowest was in the 31-and-over age group. On the other hand, this age
group had the highest proportion of married couples—69%, while the
21–25 age group had the lowest—14.3%.

Taking into consideration only the adult population, a considerable
difference between the immigrants to Palestine and the United States is
revealed when comparing the percentage of unmarried people among
the two (Table 12).

There were more unmarried people among Second Aliya immigrants
to Palestine than among those to the United States—22% more single
men, and 10% more single women.

Table 12
Distribution according to Family Status

Second Aliya Survey Group			Immigrants to the U.S., 1910–14	
Type	Number	%	Type	%
Single men (14–40)	487	86.3	Single men (14–44)	64.1
Married men (14–40)	65	13.7		
Total	552			
Single women (14–40)	166	71.0	Single women (14–44)	61.5
Married momen (14–40)	68	29.0		
Total	234			

Aside from demographic differences according to sex, age and family status, there was a particularly striking difference in the type of initial reception accorded them (Tables 13 and 14).[15]

About 93% of the immigrants to the United States joined their relatives whereas only 15.5% of the immigrants to Palestine had relatives there. Even if we assume that in order to expedite immigration to the United States some of the declarations stating a family relationship were false, the supposed "relatives" must at least have been good friends of the immigrants.[16] Thus, the immigrants arriving in the United States usually had some personal ties in the new country.

On the other hand, 53% of the immigrants to Palestine had no one to meet them on their arrival. The fact that the proportion of those received

Table 13
Initial Reception of Second Aliya Survey Group

Received by	Number	%
Relatives	145	15.47
Friends	217	23.15
Official Institutions	65	6.93
Political Parties	16	1.70
None of the above	494	52.72
Total	937	

Table 14
Initial Reception of Immigrants to the U.S.

Years	By Relatives	By Friends	By No One
1908–1914	92.6%	5.2%	2.2%

by friends is higher than those received by relatives indicates that ties of friendship largely replaced family ties. The loneliness of the immigrant to Palestine, cut off from his family circle, strengthened the ties of friendship and laid the foundation for communal living of one kind or another.

Education

Let us now analyze the level of education and knowledge of Hebrew among the immigrants to Palestine. We have divided education into various levels and according to type—traditional-Jewish and general (Tables 15 and 16).

The two tables show an almost absolute absence of illiteracy among immigrants to Palestine, while among those to the United States, the proportion of illiteracy was as high as 26%.[17] The latter high rate of illiteracy is ascribed primarily to the number of women among them. There were presumably some illiterates among the immigrants to Palestine who declared that they had been taught at home. This assumption

Table 15
Distribution of Second Aliya Survey according to Their Traditional-Jewish Education

Level of Education	Number	%
Heder (elementary)	293	31.27
Yeshiva (advanced)	148	15.79
Educated at home	105	11.20
No information	391	41.72
Total	937	

Table 16
Distribution of Second Aliya Survey according to General Education

Level of Education	Number	%
Elementary	214	22.83
Secondary	215	22.94
Teacher's Seminary	27	2.88
University	76	8.11
Extra-mural study	38	4.05
No information	368	39.16
Total	937	

is strengthened by the fact that 33% of the latter were women. By no means, however, should all those included in this category be considered illiterate, since quite a few children were educated by private tutors in the parental home.

Another noteworthy particular is the relatively high proportion—about 23%—of those who attended secondary school as compared to the low proportion of those who obtained a university education. (Actually, it may be said that 31% attended secondary school, since those who reached the university certainly completed secondary school.) This was an outcome of Czarist policy which created a bottleneck between secondary school and university by means of the *numerus clausus* in education.

It would be a mistake, however, to assume that the Czarist government enabled more than 30% of those who eventually emigrated to Palestine to attend secondary schools. An analysis of the degree of secondary school and higher education according to the age of the immigrants on arrival shows that the youngest age group had the highest proportion of people with secondary school education (Table 17). As the age level rises, the proportion with secondary education is lower. A reverse tendency is apparent in higher education. The explanation for this phenomenon lies in the fact that some of those who arrived as adolescents received their secondary education in Gymnasia Herzliya in Tel Aviv.

On the other hand, for a number of reasons—the absence of institutions of higher learning, the general economic situation and the necessity of earning their living after finishing secondary school, and the outbreak of World War I—they could not continue their studies. If we examine the proportion of workers having some degree of higher education, we must consider those older than 20, and here it is 13%–14%. This figure

Table 17

Proportion with Secondary and Higher Education
according to Age Group (at time of aliya)

Age Group	Secondary School %	Higher Education %
1–15	30.0	2.0
15–20	27.2	5.0
21–25	16.0	12.7
26–30	11.5	12.6
30 and over	3.0	13.7

should be treated with caution as regards the pre-war period. Some of the immigrants doubtless acquired their higher education after the war and it is difficult to determine how many of them went abroad in the twenties in order to continue their studies.

It should be pointed out that the proportion of extramural students was extremely low—4%. This means that those who obtained a general education received it primarily in official institutions of learning. To some extent this indicates the economic level of those immigrants' parents who could afford to send their children to secondary school and university. This often involved engaging private tutors to help prepare for examinations, bribing, or buying a place to circumvent the *numerus clausus*. Expenses were especially high when parents sent a boy to study at Gymnasia Herzliya. This is further proof of the middle-class or lower middle-class origins of the Second Aliya.

An analysis of the general education of the immigrants to Palestine according to sex offers surprising results (Table 18).

The proportion of women who attended elementary school, secondary school or seminary was higher than the equivalent proportion for men, although in the traditional Jewish community the girl was more limited in her educational possibilities. The inclination to emigrate to Palestine was more pronounced among women who had acquired some general education. For them, aliya was a continuation and ultimate expression of rebellion against traditional society.

The fact that 47% of the immigrants had attended a heder or yeshiva (especially that 16% had attended a yeshiva) clearly testifies that members of the Second Aliya had strong Jewish cultural roots and a considerable knowledge of the Hebrew language.

The proportion of those who knew Hebrew in varying degrees was high (Table 19).

Even if we question the claim of 45% of the immigrants that they had a full command of Hebrew upon arrival in Palestine, certainly for most of the immigrants the change of language was fairly easy. This facilitated their absorption into the new cultural environment.

Table 18
Level of General Education of Second Aliya Survey according to Sex

	Elementary	%	Secondary	%	Teacher Seminary	%	Extramural	%	University	%	No General Education	%	Total	%
Men	126	19.56	147	22.82	17	2.63	35	5.43	63	9.77	254	39.44	644	100
Women	88	30.00	68	23.12	10	3.40	3	1.20	13	4.40	110	37.50	293	100

Table 19
Distribution according to Knowledge of Hebrew

Knowledge of Hebrew	Number	%
Complete	423	45.14
Partial	122	13.02
No knowledge	392	41.83
Total	937	

Table 20
Ignorance of Hebrew according to Sex

Sex	Number	%	Total
Men	194	30.1	644
Women	198	60.1	293

Furthermore, a knowledge of Hebrew before their aliya is evidence of the familiarity of the immigrants with traditional and renascent Hebrew culture which, in turn, intensified their attachment to the Jewish homeland. Contrariwise, we know that the absence of Hebraic and Jewish cultural roots was one of the causes of emigration from Palestine. An example is the group from the Crimea who wanted to make Russian the spoken language in the new land.

The fact that there was a total ignorance of Hebrew among only 30% of the men as compared to 60% of the women (Table 20) also alleviated the pangs of cultural adjustment; for a transition crisis especially affects men, who are more active outside the home than women.

The wide gap between men and women in their knowledge of Hebrew is explained by the fact that only 9.5% of the women studied in a girls' "heder"; 30% reported that they had received home tutoring, and 60.5% did not report attendance at any traditional institution. This proportion is identical with that of women who did not know Hebrew at all.

The same holds true for the men: 33% did not report attending a traditional institution and 30% reported no knowledge of Hebrew—proving the correlation between knowledge of Hebrew and study in traditional institutions which emphasize devotion to Hebraic-Jewish culture.

B. CHANGES IN THE SOCIAL STRATIFICATION

Before Aliya

The analysis of the social stratification of the immigrants was conducted from two points of departure: according to the occupation of the parents of those included in the survey, and of their own occupation. We also compared the data from the survey with the vocational structure of East European Jewry as a whole, and the composition of all immigration to Palestine (1905–1909) with the Jewish immigration to the United States during the same period (Tables 21 and 22).[18]

Table 21
Distribution of Second Aliya Survey according to Occupation of Parents

Occupation of Parents Abroad	Number	%	Combined %
1. Merchants	517	55.17	
2. Manufacturers	36	3.84 ⎫	
3. Craftsmen	125	13.34 ⎬	19.3
4. Labourers	18	1.92 ⎭	
5. Farmers	36	3.84	
6. Clerks	51	5.44	
7. Medical personnel	21	2.23 ⎫	
8. Teachers	62	6.61 ⎬	12.7
9. Rabbis	26	2.77 ⎭	
10. Religious functionaries	31	3.30	
11. Liberal professions	6	0.64	
12. Artists	5	0.53	
13. Without definite occupation	3	0.32	
Total	937		

Table 22
Occupational Distribution of East European Jewry (1897–1900) (in percentages)

Country	Farmers	Industry and Crafts	Commerce and Credit	Transport	Clerks and Liberal Professions	Others	Total
Russian							
Poland	2.0	39.1	29.3	3.1	4.2	22.3	100
Galicia	17.6	18.7	36.4	1.9	5.4	20.0	100
Russia	2.8	36.8	33.6	3.2	5.2	18.4	100

A comparison of the two tables in regard to Russia and Poland, from which more than 90% of the immigrants to Palestine came, shows a relatively small ratio of children of manufacturers and craftsmen— 19.3% as against 39.1% in Poland and 36.8% in Russia—out of all the Jews in those countries. However, the most significant finding is the high proportion of children of merchants—55.17% as against 29.3% and 33.6% respectively for all the Jews in Poland and Russia.

Another noteworthy figure is the proportion of religio-traditional intellectuals—12.7% were teachers, rabbis or religious functionaries. This is only slightly lower than the percentage of children of craftsmen— 13.3%. Within the former group the children of teachers constitute a preponderant section—6.6% of the total or 50% of the group.

This comparison proves paradoxically that the parent generation of the Second Aliya represented to the extreme the anomalous occupational pattern of Diaspora Jewry. Their occupational structure more closely resembled that of East European Jewry at the beginning of the nineteenth century than the one prevalent at its end.[19]

This may, to a certain extent, explain the dialectic and revolutionary change in the outlook of members of the Second Aliya. The fanatic pursuit of the ideal of physical labour, and especially of agricultural work had, for the children of merchants and intellectuals, not only national but also personal value significance. Their rebellion was not only an objective opposition to the anomaly of the Diaspora, but also a subjective revolt against the occupations of their own parents.

A comparison between the occupational structure of the parents and that of their children shows a substantial difference in only two categories—merchants and those without a definite occupation. Only 2.34% of the children were engaged in commerce as against 55.2% of the parents; 62% of the children were classified as being without an occupation as against less than 1% among the parents (Table 23). The lack of a definite profession or occupation may be ascribed to the youth of the immigrants, as will be seen below.

The large number without a definite occupation distinguishes the Second Aliya not only from their parents but also from the Jewish immigration to the United States (Table 24).

The "unskilled" category in both tables includes mostly women and children, but this does not explain the higher proportion among the immigrants to Palestine, since the number of women and children among the immigrants to the United States was definitely higher, as has been shown in the previous section. A calculation of the "unskilled" in both

Table 23
Distribution of Second Aliya Survey according to
Occupation in their Countries of Origin

Occupation	Number	%	
1. Merchants	22	2.34	
2. Craftsmen	136	14.51	
3. Labourers	31	3.30	
4. Farmers	5	0.53	
5. Clerks	45	4.80	
6. Medical personnel	32	3.41	
7. Teachers	70	7.47	
8. Physicians	5	0.53	
9. Engineers	2	0.21	9.06%
10. Journalists	2	0.21	
11. Artists	6	0.64	
12. No occupation	581	62.00	
Total	937		

tables in relation to the adult population, aged 14 years and over, shows that the proportion among immigrants to Palestine reached 55.4% while among the immigrants to the United States it was only 24.8%.[20] Furthermore, the proportion of unskilled among all adult immigrants to Palestine between 1905 and 1909 was 8% less—47.3%[21] as against our 55.4%.

In comparison to immigration to the United States, aliya to Palestine as a whole and especially the labouring class was notable for its large non-productive element.[22] As regards the total aliya, this may be explained by the fact that, between 1905 and 1909, 50% were children up to the age of 16 or adults over the age of 50.[23] On the other hand, the high proportion of non-productive workers may be explained on

Table 24
Occupational Structure of Jewish Immigrants to the U.S.
1900–1925

Occupation	Number	%
Liberal professions	19,620	1.1
Definite vocation or occupation	638,142	35.2
Other occupations	334,568	18.5
No skill or	818,442	45.2
definite occupation		
Total	1,810,752	100.0

ideological grounds. More than 50% of the immigrants (499 out of 937) came to Palestine with the clear intention of being farm workers. Agriculture at the time required no special skill, and readiness to engage in farm work relieved the immigrant of the need for acquiring vocational training to ease the difficulties of absorption in the new land.

Was there a causal connection between the social stratification of the parents and the occupations, level of education and political affiliation of the children? First, let us discern to what degree the children tended to continue in the professions and occupations of their parents (Table 25).

According to this table it appears that the children of craftsmen showed the greatest tendency to continue in their parents' occupation, with 37.6% of them engaging in a craft. In contrast, the smallest inclination was shown by the children of merchants (3.3%). Children of craftsmen, of course, are able to learn their parents' trade at an early age whereas the children of merchants were mostly too young to engage in commerce before leaving for Palestine. Second to craftsmen's children, the children of teachers showed the strongest tendency to follow in their parents' footsteps.

The proportion of the unskilled or those without a definite occupation was lowest among the children of craftsmen: 52% as against an average of over 60% among children of parents with other occupations. The conclusion is that only a partial and marginal overlapping existed between the professions of parents and those of their children. On the other hand, there was a correlation between the social origin of the parents and the level of general education of the children (Table 26).

This correlation is particularly pronounced in secondary and higher education, which involved considerable expenditure. The highest proportion studying in secondary schools and universities was among the children of manufacturers, clerks and teachers. It should be noted, parenthetically, that more than a quarter of the children of rabbis attended secondary schools.

Table 25

Occupations Abroad of Second Aliya Survey Compared with Occupations of Their Parents (in percentages)

	Number	Merchant	Clerk	Teacher	Crafts-men	Unskilled
Merchant's children	517	3.28	5.41	7.35	10.44	63.05
Clerks' children	51	—	9.80	9.80	9.80	64.70
Teachers' children	62	3.30	1.60	11.29	16.12	66.12
Craftsmen's children	125	—	3.20	3.20	37.60	52.00

Table 26

Level of General Education of Immigrants according to Social
Stratification of Their Parents (in percentages)

Parents	Number	Elementary	Secondary	Teachers' Seminary	Extra-mural	University
Merchants	517	24.60	24.40	2.30	3.20	7.70
Manufacturers	36	19.10	39.00	2.80	2.80	22.20
Clerks	51	13.70	37.20	3.90	7.80	11.70
Teachers	62	19.30	22.50	4.80	1.60	9.70
Liberal professions	6	16.60	16.60	16.60	33.20	33.20
Rabbis	26	—	27.00	11.50	19.20	11.50
Religious functionaries	31	96.00	4.20	2.10	4.20	2.10
Craftsmen	125	25.00	14.00	0.80	3.20	4.00
Labourers	18	39.00	16.00	—	5.50	11.00
Farmers	36	33.30	14.50	—	2.80	5.60

One last problem remains to be examined—was there a correlation between the social standing of the parents and the political affiliation of the children?

We have ascertained that a positive correlation exists for the level of general education, but here it is not so pronounced. It is true that 26.4% of the children of craftsmen joined the proletarian Poalei-Zion Party,[24] but so did 30.5% of the children of manufacturers and 20% of the children of merchants. Furthermore, the proportion of the children of merchants, manufacturers, clerks and teachers in Poalei-Zion is higher than in the other parties or political groups. This applies especially to the General Zionist[25] group where the proportion of children from non-proletarian strata, though high, was lower than in Poalei-Zion.

After Arrival in Palestine

We shall now trace the dynamic process of social change which the immigrants underwent as a result of the transition to socio-economic and political patterns different from those in the countries of their origin. First, let us investigate their occupational distribution in Palestine as compared with what it had been abroad (Table 27).

First and foremost, it should be noted that 60.2% of the immigrants became farm workers, while the category of 'no occupation' disappeared entirely. The almost absolute correlation between the proportion with no occupation abroad (62%) and the proportion of farm workers in

Table 27

Distribution of Second Aliya Survey according to Occupations
before and after Aliya

Occupation in Palestine	Number	%	Occupation before Aliya in %
Farm workers	564	60.19	62.00 *
City workers	39	4.16	3.10
Artists	12	1.28	0.64
Craftsmen	87	9.28	14.51
Medical personnel	35	3.73	3.41
Public functionaries	7	0.75	—
Teachers	60	6.40	7.47
Clerks	31	3.30	4.80
Students	84	8.96	—
Journalists	4	0.42	0.64
Engineers	4	0.42	0.21
Physicians	6	0.64	0.53
Farmers (farm owners)	4	0.42	0.53
Total	937		

* No occupation

Palestine (60.2%) indicates that most of the former became farm workers. This assumption is strengthened by the fact that most craftsmen
remained in their trade—9.3% compared with 14.5% abroad—while
the proportion of medical workers, teachers and clerks rose. Those
appearing in the category of students were children or young people
enrolled in Tel Aviv's Gymnasia Herzliya or the Hebrew Teachers Seminary in Jerusalem. They were included in the category of those without
a profession or occupation prior to aliya.

An analysis of the occupational structure of the Second Aliya as
compared with that in their countries of origin confirms our previous
assumptions. The category of those without a definite occupation (except for children of farmers, who were so few as to be insignificant)
displayed the greatest inclination to transfer to farming—62%. On the
other hand, medical workers (69%), teachers (67.6%) and craftsmen
(53.3%) showed the greatest inclination to continue in their professions
(Table 28).

It is clear that persons in these occupations showed the least tendency
to shift to farming (medical workers 19%, teachers 26%, craftsmen
39.5%). It follows that for most people with professions, aliya did not
involve a radical change in their occupation.

Table 28
Vocational Distribution of Second Aliya Survey according to Occupations Abroad (in percentages)

Occupation Abroad	Number	Farm Worker	City Worker	Craftsman	Medical Worker	Public Functionary	Teacher	Clerk	Artist	Student	Journalist	Engineer	Physician	Farmer
Merchant	22	59.5	—	4.5	—	—	4.5	13.50	—	4.5	—	2	—	4.50
Clerk	45	43.0	6.6	—	—	2.20	4.4	31.00	—	—	—	—	—	2.20
Teacher	70	26.0	—	1.4	1.4	—	67.6	3.20	1.40	—	—	—	—	—
Craftsman	136	39.5	2.9	53.3	1.4	—	—	0.73	0.73	—	—	—	—	1.50
Labourer	31	54.6	35.4	3.2	3.2	—	3.2	—	—	—	—	—	—	—
Medical worker	32	18.7	—	—	68.8	12.50	—	—	—	—	—	—	—	—
Physician	5	—	—	—	—	—	—	—	—	—	—	—	—	—
Journalist	2	—	—	—	—	—	—	50.00	—	—	50.0	—	—	—
Artist	6	16.6	—	—	—	—	—	16.60	66.80	—	—	—	—	—
Engineer	2	—	—	—	—	—	—	—	—	—	—	100	—	—
Farmer	5	100.0	—	—	—	—	—	—	—	—	—	—	—	—
No occupation	581	62.0	3.6	1.9	1.4	0.34	1.7	1.40	0.85	14.0	0.5	—	—	0.34
Total	937													

Table 29
Distribution of Second Aliya Survey according to
Place of Employment

Place of Employment	Number	%
City	285	30.41
Moshava [26]	431	46.00
Kvutza [27]	164	17.50
City + Moshava	20	2.13
Moshava + Kvutza	20	2.13
City + Moshava + Kvutza	1	0.10
City + Kvutza	6	0.64
Not indicated	10	1.06
Total	937	

Table 30
Distribution of Aliya according to Destination between 1905–1909

Safed-Tiberias		Moshava (colony)		Beirut		Haifa		Jaffa		Jerusalem-Hebron	
No.	%	No.	%	No.	%	No.	%	No.	%	No.	%
248	2.5	1150	10.5	184	1.5	174	1.5	3958	36	5272	48

The radical change which did occur in the overall vocational distribution of members of the Second Aliya—the transition of the majority of those who had no previous occupation to agriculture—obviously determined the distribution according to places of employment and residence (Table 29).

This distribution is different from that of the entire aliya in the period 1905–1909 (Table 30).[28]

Even if we assume that some of the immigrants who first went to the towns later moved to a moshava, or that the proportion going there between 1909–1914 was higher (24% went to a moshava in 1910),[29] still we may figure that the distribution between city and moshava of the entire 1905–1909 aliya was the inverse of that in our sample (Table 29); that is, two-thirds went to the city and one-third to the moshava.

During the Mid-Thirties and Early Forties

When the survey of members of the Second Aliya was made in the mid-thirties, the economic and social structure of the country was substantially different from what it had been during the 1904–1914 period. As a result of a number of factors—the rapid growth of the Jewish population in Palestine at the time of the Fifth Aliya; increased investment, particularly in industry; the progress of urban settlement; the increased employment in industry, commerce and services; the emergence of a stratum of professionals—a normal society began to take shape.

To what extent was the socio-political structure of the Second Aliya affected by these changes?

The vocational distribution of members of the Second Aliya during the thirties, as compared with the beginning of the century, indicates that substantial changes had taken place (Table 31).

The most striking change is the sharp drop of 29% in the number of agricultural labourers. Only 51.7% of those who worked the land during the period of the Second Aliya remained in agriculture. On the other hand, there was an increase in those engaged in urban occupations— workers and craftsmen, as well as white collar workers in services, commerce and the liberal professions. The proportion of functionaries in political parties or institutions increased threefold.

One should not conclude from this, however, that all those who left farming transferred to the professions or occupations enumerated above.

Table 31

Distribution of Second Aliya Survey according to Occupations (in percentages)

Occupation	Number	During the Thirties	During Second Aliya	Before Aliya
Farm workers	292	31.16	60.19	—
Urban labourers	81	8.64	4.16	3.10
Craftsmen	87	9.28	9.28	14.50
Clerks	114	12.16	3.30	4.80
Teachers	85	9.07	6.40	7.47
Medical personnel	35	3.75	3.73	3.41
Physicians	3	0.30	0.60	0.53
Public functionaries	24	2.56	0.75	—
Journalists	14	1.45	0.42	0.64
Engineers	15	1.60	0.42	0.21
Lawyers	8	0.85	—	—
Artists	13	1.38	1.28	0.64
Merchants	41	4.37	—	—
Citrus growers and Farmers	5	0.53	0.42	0.53
No occupation	120	12.80	8.96	62.10
Total	937			

Nearly 13% of the people in the survey had retired—80% of these were women, most of whom became housewives, and the rest, elderly or infirm men. Therefore, the number of those who switched from farming to other occupations was actually smaller than 29%.

Nonetheless, a trend towards the abandonment of manual labour is clearly evident. Manual labourers, who had constituted 73.6% of the Second Aliya, made up only 49% of the group later. But a comparison of the vocational distribution of breadwinners within the total Jewish community in Palestine in the thirties, shows that the proportion of manual labourers in the Second Aliya survey is still 3% higher than in the total Jewish population—56% to 53%,[30] and the proportion of agricultural workers amounted to 35.3%, while for the totality of bread-winners it was 18.4% in 1931 and 19.3% in 1939, a difference of 16%–17%. At the same time, the proportion of urban blue collars among them was 10%–12% less than the general ratio, and the proportion of urban white collars in services, commerce and the liberal professions was smaller by 50%.

In short—although there was an occupational shift within the Second Aliya group, farming continued to engage a greater percentage than in the Jewish population as a whole. The high proportion of teachers (9%) is also noteworthy.

In spite of changes in the vocational structure and advancing age, members of the Second Aliya did not tend to revert to the occupation of their parents. Only 5% of the children of merchants returned to commerce whereas 33.6% stuck to agriculture. In other occupations there was a greater, though no overwhelming, tendency to follow parents. For example, whereas 7.8% of the children of clerks did office work upon their arrival, 23.3% of them now engaged in such work. Among the children of teachers, the proportion rose from 11% to 13%; among the children of craftsmen it dropped from 31% to 28%. The strongest tendency to continue was among the children of farmers—50% of them remained in agriculture.

These changes were related to the process of urbanization (Table 32).

Here the change is radical, showing a reversed city-village ratio as compared to the time of the Second Aliya. Whereas a generation earlier two-thirds of this group had lived in either a moshava or kvutza, this was now the proportion of town-dwellers, while only one-third had remained in agricultural settlements and villages. Nevertheless, the proportion of members of the Second Aliya living in collective agricultural settlements is still strikingly higher than in the community as a whole;

Table 32
Distribution of Second Aliya Survey according to Residence at
Time of Survey

Place of Residence	Number	%	Total Jewish Settlement in %
Towns	616	65.74	74.6
Moshava	123	13.12	12.0
Moshav Ovidim[31]	113	12.06	2.9
Kibbutz[32]	84	8.96	4.7
Uncertain	1	0.10	—
Total	937		

21% to 7.6%.[33] In both farming as such and as members of collective
farm settlements, the Second Aliya continued to display a relatively high
degree of dedication to the ideals of their formative period.

C. CHANGES IN THE POLITICAL STRUCTURE

The characteristic factor in the political structure of members of the
Second Aliya before their immigration, was the high rate of affiliation
with a wide range of political parties or groups (Table 33).

Fifty-eight percent were politically affiliated, while of the 42% who

Table 33
Political Distribution of Second Aliya Survey
according to Parties in the Diaspora

Political Party	Number	%
Poalei-Zion	188	20.06
Tseirei-Zion[34]	121	12.91
Socialist-Zionists[35]	21	2.24
Sejmists[36]	2	0.21
General Zionist	149	15.90
Hatehiya[37]	16	1.70
Bund	16	1.70
Social Democrat	15	1.60
Social Revolutionaries	12	1.28
Non-affiliated	395	42.15
Independent[38]	1	0.10
Tolstoyans[39]	1	0.10
Total	937	

declared themselves as unaffiliated, almost a third were children under 14. So, the proportion of adults over the age of 14 who belonged to some political group was actually much higher, about 67%. Close to 75% of the adult men were affiliated, but only 59% of the women. Evidently, there was a causal correlation between political activism and inclination toward aliya, for, surely, such a high rate of political affiliation cannot have been generally characteristic of East European Jewry or even of its youth.

Poalei-Zion constituted the largest political group among the immigrants (20%), which contradicts the notion that Poalei-Zion members abroad played only a minor role in the pioneering aliya, because of their party's sceptical attitude toward this ideal. The party's reservations concerning the haphazard character of the aliya and its fear that the failure of pioneering aliya might adversely affect all future aliya—did not deter members of the Poalei-Zion from immigrating to Palestine. The pioneering element within the Poalei-Zion was evidently stronger than in other parties or groups.

The proportion of those belonging to socialist parties (Poalei Zion, Socialist-Zionist, Social Democrats, the Bund, Social Revolutionaries) did not exceed 30%: less than a third of the immigrants had a social-revolutionary outlook.

It should also be pointed out that only 4.6% of those included in the survey were members of Socialist parties opposed to Zionism. This may possibly indicate that the political and social activities of these Russian parties prevented their young Jewish members from losing their belief in them and from adhering to the Zionist pioneering ideal. With the same note of caution, we may assume that the proportion of immigrants who had belonged to these parties was originally much higher, but that in the difficult trial of adjustment they proved weaker than their comrades who had received a Zionist political training and that many of them left the country. Be that as it may, the ratio between members of Zionist Socialist parties and members of anti-Zionist parties certainly demonstrates a correlation between ideology and the actual decisions of individuals.

The degree of political activity among the immigrants abroad was high, even though it fell short of the percentage of party affiliation: 47% of the adult population over the age of 14. On the other hand, membership in self-defence groups was low—7.5%—and only 16% declared that they had participated in the 1905 Revolution in Russia. Of all the adult immigrants, about 5% had been imprisoned for revolutionary activity and 9% had been arrested for Zionist activity. Clearly, most

Table 34
Political Affiliation of Second Aliya Survey
(1904–1914)

Political Party	Number	%
Poalei-Zion	201	20.45
Hapoel Hatsair	228	24.33
Non-affiliated	482	51.44
General Zionist	22	2.35
Mizrahi[41]	4	0.42
Total	937	

members of the Second Aliya had not been active in Jewish self-defense nor in Russian revolutionary circles.

Changes in the Political Structure during the Second Aliya

Two basic changes took place in the political alignment. First of all, the number of parties or political groups was smaller than in Russia. In Palestine the immigrants split into three main groups: two were clearly defined politically and ideologically—Poalei-Zion and Hapoel Hatsair;[40] while the largest group remained uncommitted and unaffiliated (Table 34).

The second change was the rise in the number of the politically uncommitted. The ratio of non-affiliated among the adult population rose by 18%—from 33% in the Diaspora to 51% in Palestine. A more significant decline took place in the amount of political activism (Table 35). A process of de-politization is apparent and it was to gain momentum during the thirties and forties. During the earlier period this was not, apparently, a manifestation of political apathy, but would seem to have resulted partly from the reduction in the number of political parties, which left some people without a group whose ideology they could whole-heartedly endorse.

Table 35
Political Activism in the Second Aliya

Extent of Activism	Number	%	Extent of Activism Abroad in %
Active	136	14.51	47
Passive	801	85.49	53
Total	937		

But essentially, this change must be related to the emergence of surrogates for traditional political activities. Firstly, there was the controversy over the use of Jewish labour in the Jewish settlements and the physical and spiritual effort required of each individual worker who had to inure himself to agricultural work. Secondly, there was the burden of guard duties. This affected not only members of the Hashomer[42] organization, but also workers who intermittently took a hand in guarding the settlements. These new challenges produced an affinity between the routine preoccupations of the individual immigrant and the ideological and political outlook. The daily concerns occupied the individual completely, both physically and spiritually, and party politics became ancillary to them. Evidence of this can be found in contemporary articles decrying the decrease in political activity among party members and the consequent neglect by the party (the reference is to Poalei-Zion) of traditional Socialist activity. These surrogates, which had a marked ideological and national significance, and the natural physical fatigue caused by hard work, were among the main causes for the decline in the membership of political parties and in political activity.

While preoccupation with conventional politics diminished, there was an increase in security activity. In the Diaspora, only 4.5% of the adult population (mostly men) had participated in self-defence, whereas in Palestine 26% of all the immigrants, or 37% of the men, did guard duty in the settlements. This development is attributable not only to the insecure conditions then prevalent in Palestine, but also to the transformation of values among the immigrants after their aliya. The willingness to stand guard and the desire to openly bear arms were a romantic expression of the political aspiration to create a free and independent nation.

For some members of the Second Aliya, especially the Poalei-Zion, the bearing of arms became a sacred duty. Those young people held a rifle for the first time with a kind of tremulous reverence. The emotion was an obvious counter-reaction to the exilic sense of ethnic and personal humiliation. Furthermore, the increased tension between Jews and Arabs fostered a growing awareness that just as there was no future for Jewish settlement without Jewish labour, there was no hope for its survival without an independent self-defence force. They were also convinced that peace and co-operation between the two peoples could develop only on the basis of strength and equality; only when the Jews were an economic and military power in the country, would they constitute a political factor to be reckoned with by the Arabs, who would then be compelled to reach an agreement on peaceful co-existence.[43]

Table 36
Attitide to the Jewish Legion

Attitude	Number	%
Positive	454	48.4
Negative	103	10.9
Undefined	380	40.7
Total	937	

It should be noted here, that although Hashomer was a selective organization, it recruited local workers during the grape harvest or at times of unrest at the settlements which it guarded.

The yearning for political and military power was expressed in their attitude toward the Jewish Legion[44] during World War I and in the numbers which joined it (Tables 36 and 37).

There was an intense public debate over the question of volunteering for the Legion, and the opponents presented important national and political considerations, especially affecting the labour movement. Nevertheless, 48.5% indicated a positive attitude toward volunteering, while only 11% rejected it. The proportion of volunteers came to 11.7% of those surveyed or 16.7% of the men (women were not inducted into the Legion). In view of the fact that no compulsion was exercised, this represents a high rate of participation.

Let us now analyze the internal configuration of the three main political groupings: Poalei-Zion, Hapoel Hatsair and the non-affiliated. The interesting question is whether these groups had any specific attributes in addition to their respective ideologies.

An examination of the groups according to sex shows that the ratio of women in them is in inverse proportion to their political extremism (Table 38) whereas for the men the opposite is true. Women comprise only 15% of the total membership of Poalei-Zion, 24% of Hapoel Hatsair, and 42% of the non-affiliated; while the men comprise 84.5% of Poalei-Zion, 75.8% of Hapoel Hatsair and 57.8% of the non-affiliated.

Table 37
Participation in the Jewish Legion

Participation	Number	%
Joined	110	11.7
Did not join	826	88.2
Unknown	1	0.1
Total	937	

Table 38
Political Distribution of Second Aliya Survey according to Sex

	Men	% of Total	% of Party Membership	Women	% of Total	% of Party Membership	Total
Poalei-Zion	170	26.3	84.57	31	10.60	15.43	201
Hapoel Hatsair	173	26.6	75.87	55	18.70	24.13	228
Non-affiliated	279	43.3	57.88	203	69.20	42.12	482
General Zionists	18	2.8	18.81	4	1.36	18.18	22
Mizrahi	4	0.6	100.00	—	—	—	4
Total	644			293			

Sixty-nine percent of all the women and 43% of the men were unaf-filiated. A comparison with the figures concerning political affiliation in the Diaspora reveals that women showed a greater tendency than men to forsake organized politics—12% as against 9%.

An examination of the political alignment according to age shows little difference in the average age of members of Poalei-Zion and Hapoel Hatsair (Table 39).

On the other hand, there was a considerable difference between these two parties and the non-affiliated group. The highest rate of non-affilia-tion was in the youngest and the oldest age groups. This can partly be explained by the absence of a tradition of political affiliation and activity prior to immigration. The younger age group were still children at the time of their aliya and the older group were mostly religious people and heads of families not concerned with political activity.

Their youth or the lack of an appealing political programme is not, however, the only explanation for the young people's apathy towards political parties. Most of this group matured between 1904 and 1914— 96% of them reached working age and had to find employment as labourers. Immaturity was therefore not the only cause of their political

Table 39
Political Distribution according to Age (in percentages)

	Number	1–14	15–20	21–25	25–30	31–40	Age not given
Poalei-Zion	201	11.44	44.27	26.86	8.45	1.49	5.97
Hapoel Hatsair	228	6.57	46.49	25.00	9.63	3.49	5.26
Non-affiliated	482	15.35	33.40	19.91	9.12	12.65	3.52
General Zionist	22	—	9.09	22.72	18.18	50.00	—
Mizrahi	4	—	25.00	—	—	75.00	—

apathy, they evidently felt little interest in the ideological controversies between Poalei-Zion and Hapoel Hatsair.

Let us now analyze the occupational structure of these groups. There is no difference among the three, except for the large concentration of teachers in Hapoel Hatsair (Table 40).

Paradoxically, the proportion of agricultural workers in Poalei-Zion was slightly higher (by 4%) than in Hapoel Hatsair, despite the fact that Hapoel Hatsair considered work on the land not merely an occupation, but a national task, and emphasized its intrinsic personal worth more than did Poalei-Zion.

An examination of the occupational composition of the parties according to the social origins of the immigrants or according to their occupations abroad also reveals no significant differences among them (Table 41).

There was obviously no causal relation between the ideological-political differences among the parties and their social composition. The social status or occupation of the immigrant did not influence his political affiliation or non-affiliation, nor did it determine his choice between the two major parties.

The same holds true for geographic backgrounds. No group seems to have had any special regional base. The dominant group in all groups were the Ukrainian immigrants, followed by those from Poland (Table 42).

Was there a relation between political affiliation and level of education? Table 43 shows that there were only slight differences.

The proportion of members with secondary and higher education was highest among Poalei-Zion and lowest among Hapoel Hatsair, but, as noted, the differences are so slight that no claim to intellectual distinctiveness can be based on them.

On the other hand, Hapoel Hatsair had the highest percentage of members who had had a traditional Jewish education, with a relatively large concentration of ex-yeshiva students (Table 44).

That the proportion of persons with a traditional education was lowest among the non-affiliated may be explained by the large number of women and children in this group. The proportion of those having a traditional education correlates with those knowing Hebrew—64.5% in Hapoel Hatsair, 43.3% in Poalei-Zion and 36.3 in the non-affiliated group.

It may be concluded that familiarity with Jewish and Hebrew culture was more pronounced among Hapoel Hatsair members than among the

Table 40
Political Distribution according to Occupations (in percentages)

	Number	Farm Worker	City Worker	Artist	Craftsman	Medical Worker	Public Functionary	Teacher	Clerk	Student	Journalist	Engineer
Poalei-Zion	201	66.6	5.0	1.50	10.0	2.0	1.00	6.0	1.5	4.5	1.50	—
Hapoel Hatsair	228	62.3	2.6	0.86	6.9	1.3	0.43	10.4	4.7	8.2	0.43	0.86
Non-affiliated	482	58.0	4.7	1.50	9.3	5.6	0.80	4.5	2.8	10.8	—	0.20
General Zionist	22	27.2	4.5	—	22.8	4.5	—	12.5	0.9	0.9	—	4.50
Mizrahi	4	50.0	—	—	25.0	—	—	—	25.0	—	—	—
Total	937											

Table 41
Political Distribution according to Occupations Abroad

	Number	Merchant	Clerk	Teacher	Craftsman	Labourer	Medical Worker	No Occupation	Journalist	Artist	Engineer	Farmer
Poalei-Zion	201	0.99	5.47	5.97	17.41	4.97	3.48	60.69	0.49	0.49	—	—
Hapoel Hatsair	228	0.43	7.45	11.84	10.52	6.14	1.75	61.84	—	0.49	—	0.43
Non-affiliated	482	2.90	3.11	5.80	14.52	2.07	4.14	64.52	—	0.82	1.03	10.30
General Zionist	22	18.18	9.09	13.63	27.27	—	4.54	27.27	—	—	—	—
Mizrahi	4	25.00	—	—	25.00	—	—	25.00	25.00	—	—	—

Table 42

Political Distribution according to Country of Origin (in percentages)

	Number	Russia	Ukraine	White Russia	Lithuania	Poland	Bessarabia	Galicia	Austria	Roumania	Bulgaria	Turkey	England	Germany
Poalei-Zion	201	18.40	38.50	4.00	6.00	22.00	6.00	3.50	0.50	0.50	—	—	—	—
Hapoel Hatsair	228	14.14	39.56	8.17	4.73	16.34	8.60	2.58	0.86	1.24	0.43	—	—	—
Non-affiliated	482	16.70	38.68	6.62	7.45	20.70	4.55	2.48	0.82	1.03	0.41	0.41	0.20	0.82
General Zionist	22	13.62	54.80	—	—	27.24	4.54	—	—	—	—	—	—	—
Mizrahi	4	—	75.00	—	—	25.00	—	—	—	—	—	—	—	—

Table 43
Political Distribution according to General Education (in percentages)

	Number	Elementary	Secondary	Teacher Seminary	University	Extra-mural	Other
Poalei-Zion	201	23.00	28.00	1.00	1.50	10.80	36.00
Hapoel Hatsair	228	16.34	22.36	6.02	8.60	6.00	38.70
Non-affiliated	482	26.67	22.26	2.31	2.94	7.36	38.85
General Zionist	22	9.00	4.50	—	4.50	18.00	67.50
Mizrahi	4	25.00	—	—	—	—	75.00

Table 44
Political Distribution according to Traditional Education

	Heder	%	Yeshiva	%	Home Tutoring	%	None of These	%	Total
Poalei-Zion	65	32.50	32	16.00	10	5.00	94	47.00	201
Hapoel Hatsair	88	37.84	52	22.36	18	7.74	70	30.10	228
Non-affiliated	126	26.46	59	12.39	76	15.96	221	46.41	482
General Zionist	12	54.48	4	18.16	2	9.08	4	18.16	22
Mizrahi	2	50.00	2	50.00	—	—	—	—	4

Poalei-Zion. This may to some degree explain the differences between the nationalistic concepts of the two groups. Whereas Hapoel Hatsair sought an authentic Judaic-Hebraic path to national redemption, Poalei-Zion endeavoured to attain a synthesis between the unique aspects of the Jewish problem and the universality of the Socialist idea. This conclusion is further reinforced by the fact that the proportion of immigrants from cities was highest in Poalei-Zion and lowest in Hapoel Hatsair, with the reverse regarding towns and villages (Table 45).

All this holds true if we accept the previous assumption that the traditional social structure was much more cohesive in the small towns than in the cities.

Table 45
Political Distribution according to Residence Abroad

	City	%	Town	%	Village	%	Total
Poalei-Zion	70	34.82	126	62.68	5	2.50	201
Hapoel Hatsair	51	22.36	164	71.49	13	6.15	228
Non-affiliated	145	30.08	322	66.80	15	3.12	482
General Zionist	18	18.81	4	18.19	—	—	22
Mizrahi	1	25.00	2	50.00	1	25.00	4

Table 46

Political Distribution of the Second Aliya Survey according to Place of
Employment between 1904 and 1914 (in percentages)

	Number	City	Moshava	Kvutza	City + Moshava	Moshava + Kvutza	City + Moshava + Kvutza	Kvutza + City	Un-known
Poalei-Zion	201	25.37	53.73	15.92	0.99	2.48	—	—	1.49
Hapoel Hatsair	228	29.82	41.22	24.21	2.19	0.87	—	0.87	0.87
Non-affiliated	482	31.95	55.81	15.56	2.48	2.69	0.2	0.82	1.45
General Zionist	22	50.00	45.45	—	4.55	—	—	—	—
Mizrahi	4	25.00	75.00	—	—	—	—	—	—

Let us now consider two aspects in which ideology may be said to have constituted a determining cause rather than effect. First, was there a relation between the ideology of the party and the place of employment chosen when its members were faced with the three alternatives: city, moshava or kvutza? Hapoel Hatsair is known to have placed emphasis on the "conquest of labour" in the villages, whereas Poalei-Zion gave equal weight to the "conquest of labour" and to the organization of Jewish workers in both towns and villages.

A glance at Table 46 proves that there was no correlation between ideology and the choice of place of employment. The proportion of town dwellers was higher among Hapoel Hatsair members than among the Poalei-Zion and the reverse is true of the villages.

The above may be explained by the greater tendency of farm workers, members of Hapoel Hatsair, to join a kvutza. This, despite the fact that Poalei-Zion were the first to support the establishment of cooperative agricultural groups, while Hapoel Hatsair opposed them, fearing that they would induce Jewish workers to abandon the moshavot and thus undermine the struggle for the employment of Jewish labour.

The second aspect concerns the correlation between political affiliation in the Diaspora and affiliation or non-affiliation to political parties in Palestine (Table 47).

First, we note that only 61% of the members of Poalei-Zion had been members of the party abroad. Out of 188 persons who had belonged to Poalei-Zion abroad, 65 (34.5%) left the party after arriving in Palestine: 11% went over to Hapoel Hatsair and 23.4% remained unaffiliated. This tendency to leave the party can be interpreted in two ways. It can be viewed as an expression of doubts about the validity of the party's tenets in the new environment and circumstances—many of those who left apparently did not have the patience to wait for ideological changes

Table 47

Political Distribution of Second Aliya Survey according to Affiliation in Political Parties Abroad (in percentages)

	Number	Poalei-Zion	Tseirei-Zion	Socialist Zionist	Sejmists	General Zionist	Tehiya	The Bund	Social Democrats	Social Revolutionary	Non-affiliated	Independent	Tolstoyan
Poalei-Zion	201	61.15	4.00	1.00	0.5	8.00	0.50	0.50	2.50	4.00	18.00	—	—
Hapoel Hatsair	228	9.65	35.08	0.43	—	19.35	3.44	0.43	1.30	0.43	22.24	—	—
Non-affiliated	482	8.69	6.21	3.72	0.2	15.31	1.44	2.89	1.44	0.62	58.70	0.2	0.2
General Zionist	22	9.08	13.62	—	—	54.48	—	—	—	—	22.70	—	—
Mizrahi	4	—	—	—	—	50.00	—	—	—	—	50.00	—	—

to take place in the party. Nevertheless, in spite of the vast differences between conditions in the Diaspora and in Palestine, and in spite of the widespread ideological perplexity, 65% of the members remained loyal to the party. This testifies not only to the loyalty or political conservatism of the members of Poalei-Zion, but also to the political flexibility of the party and to its ability to adjust to new and different circumstances.

During the Second Aliya the Poalei-Zion made far-reaching ideological changes in its theoretical and practical approach to the new realities of Palestine. It replaced the dogmatic belief that the country would be developed by the middle class as a stage in the class struggle, with a realistic and flexible approach; the new theory of "Constructionist Socialism" held that the working class would undertake the pioneering tasks which were of decisive importance for the rebuilding of the country. At the same time, the party did not relinquish the dogma of the class struggle which became an integral part of Constructionist Socialism.

This theoretical change was the basis for the party's approach to the various social problems posed by agricultural settlement. Instead of opposing cooperative settlement, Poalei-Zionists became its prime supporters. Hesitancy toward advocating aliya and pioneering was replaced by enthusiastic appeals for the immigration of pioneer workers. The naïve belief in cooperation with the Arab workers gave way to a realistic political awareness that the Jewish position in the country must be strengthened before such cooperation can be achieved.

That 39% of its members in Palestine were new joiners who previously had spanned the entire political spectrum, shows the flexibility of the Poalei-Zion party.

This political mobility was not true of Poalei-Zion alone. It was evident in Tseirei-Zion, a group ideologically close to Hapoel Hatsair. Of this group, 66.2% joined Hapoel Hatsair, and 24.8% were unaffiliated; whereas in Poalei-Zion, 65% stayed with the party and 22% were unaffiliated.

This shows that, apart from ideology, there were personal motivations making for political mobility. It seems, for instance, that Poalei-Zion, finding that its revolutionary ideology could not be implemented in terms of class struggle under conditions then prevailing in Palestine, sought a new way by setting itself tasks in the spheres of self-defence and nation building. This tendency attracted elements with more activist inclinations than did Hapoel Hatsair. This hypothesis is supported by the figures in Table 48.

The proportion of Poalei-Zion members who participated in self-

Table 48

Participation in Self-Defence Activities before and after Aliya according to Party (in percentages)

	Number	Self-Defence Abroad		Guard Duty in Palestine		Jewish Legion		Attitude towards the Legion		
		Yes	No	Yes	No	Yes	No	Positive	Negative	Indifferent
Poalei-Zion	201	12.43	87.57	39.30	60.70	18.41	81.59	55.72	11.44	32.83
Hapoel Hatsair	228	6.15	93.85	30.00	69.73	10.09	89.91	39.47	24.56	35.96
Non-affiliated	482	4.00	96.00	20.33	79.66	10.38	89.62	29.04	6.43	64.32
General Zionist	22	9.10	90.60	16.19	81.81	—	100.00	50.00	9.10	40.90
Mizrahi	4	—	100.00	—	100.00	—	100.00	100.00	—	—

defence abroad or in guard duty in Palestine, who volunteered for the Jewish Legion, or who favoured the idea of volunteering—was higher than that in Hapoel Hatsair and the non-affiliated. The significant comparison is between Poalei-Zion and Hapoel Hatsair, because of the higher proportion of women and children in the unaffiliated group.

Changes in the Political Structure during the Thirties and Forties

At the beginning of the thirties, a significant change took place in the political structure of the Palestine Jewish community, especially in the labour movement.

In 1930, two labour parties, Ahdut Ha'avoda[45] and Hapoel Hatsair, merged into one party—Mapai. Mapai quickly became the main political power in the Jewish community. This was the era of intensified political struggle, both internal and external, and the growing tension between the Jews and the Arabs created a sense of emergency. The political struggle heightened the differences between Jewish moderates and maximalists in Palestine and created tensions within the labour parties themselves.

Did the new situation affect the political affiliation of members of the Second Aliya? Did their public or party activity increase as a result of the tension? It would seem that members of the Second Aliya did not tend to switch political loyalties (Table 49).

There is an indication of political conservatism in the lack of any tendency to join a new political grouping; but this does not mean that they were always loyal to the traditional political parties with which they had been familiar. This is shown by the greater proportion of unaffiliated in comparison with the earlier period—58.9% as against

Table 49

Political Distribution of Second Aliya Survey in Thirties and Forties

Party	Number	%	Party at Time of Aliya	Inclusive Number	%
Mapai	329	34.04	Poalei-Zion + Hapoel Hatsair	429	44.78
Left Poalei-Zion[16]	7	0.74	General Zionist	22	2.39
General Zionist	53	6.29	Mizrahi	4	0.42
Mizrahi	6	0.63	Non-affiliated	482	51.44
Non-affiliated	542	58.91			
Totals	937			937	

51.4%. The labour parties, now combined in Mapai,[47] were hardest hit by this de-politicization. Whereas, during the Second Aliya period the affiliation to Hapoel Hatsair and Poalei-Zion reached 44.8%, in the thirties only 34% of them belonged to Mapai. It must be borne in mind that this also included the unaffiliated from the days of the Second Aliya. Table 50 shows that 45.7% of the members of Poalei-Zion, 49.5% of the members of Hapoel Hatsair and 25.7% of the unaffiliated joined Mapai.

The process of de-politicization which had already begun during the Second Aliya and had now reached its peak, can also be seen in the sharp decrease in the number of people active in communal or party functions. Their percentage decreased from 14.5% to 7.4%.

This de-politicization, especially within the labour parties, was paradoxical, for the period was marked by increased political tension, of the kind which normally encourages political activity, while the growing political power of Mapai could have been expected to attract new members. Nevertheless, the reaction of members of the Second Aliya did not conform to the general pattern.

In order to explain this, a thorough analysis is necessary. Let us first see if there was any correlation in sex (Table 51) or age (Table 52).

It would seem that there is some correlation here, but not in the expected direction. The prior assumption of a stronger tendency among women not to affiliate is not confirmed. To the contrary, the proportion of unaffiliated women decreased slightly compared with the period of the Second Aliya—by 4.1%, from 69.2% to 65.1%. As against this, the number of unaffiliated men rose from 43% to 56%. This unexpected discovery makes it even more difficult to find an answer to the question which we have posed.

Shall we assume that there was a tendency to abandon politics as people got older? Does the proportion of non-affiliation rise as the age of the immigrants increases?

A comparison between the age distribution of the non-affiliated groups during the Second Aliya period and the thirties proves that there is no basis for this assumption (Table 52).

The greatest increase of non-affiliation, 9%, was in the intermediate group, 15–25 years of age (that is, those who were 40–55 years old in the period now under discussion). On the other hand, among the older people the increase was 7%. It is true that in the youngest age group there was a 6% decrease in non-affiliation, but this group still has the highest proportion of non-affiliated of all age groups except the oldest.

Table 50
Political Distribution in Thirties and Forties according to Political Affiliation during Second Aliya

Political Party in Thirties and Forties	Poalei Zion	%	Hapoel Hatsair	%	Non-affiliated	%	General Zionist	%	Mizrahi	%	Total
Left Poalei-Zion	7	3.48	—	—	—	—	—	—	—	—	7
Mapai	92	45.77	113	49.56	124	25.72	—	—	—	—	329
Non-affiliated	99	49.25	96	42.10	343	71.16	4	0.7	—	—	542
General Zionist	3	1.49	17	7.45	15	3.11	18	33.9	—	—	53
Mizrahi	—	—	2	0.87	—	—	—	—	4	100	6
Total	201		228		482		22		4		937

Table 51
Party Affiliation in Thirties and Forties according to Sex

	Left Poalei-Zion	%	Mapai	%	Non-affiliated	%	General Zionist	%	Mizrahi	%	Total	%
Men	5	0.7	238	38	351	54.5	44	0.7	6	0.8	644	100
Women	2	0.7	91	31	191	65.1	9	3.2	—	—	293	100

Table 52
Non-affiliated Groups according to Age

Age at Time of Aliya	During Second Aliya Period		In the Thirties		Total by Age Groups	%
	Number	%	Number	%		
1–14	103	68.2	94	62.2	151	100
15–20	161	45.1	194	54.0	359	100
21–25	96	45.2	120	56.6	212	100
26–30	44	50.0	45	51.6	87	100
31–40	61	70.0	67	77.0	87	100
Age unknown	17	41.4	22	53.4	41	100

Thus, the strongest tendency towards de-politicization was in the two extreme age groups—the youngest and the oldest.

We may now ask whether it is possible to establish a correlation between vocational and political distribution: did the change in occupational structure affect the tendency to de-politicization?—and, secondly, to what extent was the political distribution related to class?

Table 53 shows that the answer to the first question is positive and to the second—negative.

The overall proportion of non-affiliated people was 59% of the total,

Table 53
Political Distribution according to Occupation of Immigrants (in percentages)

	Number	Poalei-Zion	Mapai	Non-affiliated	General Zionist	Mizrahi
Farm worker	292	0.34	51.0	45.2	3.1	—
Urban worker	81	2.50	33.2	64.0	—	—
Craftsman	87	—	24.0	64.0	10.8	1.2
Medical personnel	38	—	21.0	73.7	5.3	—
Public functionary	24	—	54.9	41.0	4.1	—
Teacher	85	1.2	32.4	56.4	10.8	1.2
Clerk	114	0.9	36.6	56.4	5.2	0.9
Merchant	41	—	12.5	70.0	15.0	2.5
Lawyer	8	—	62.5	25.0	12.5	—
Journalist	15	6.6	46.2	39.6	—	6.6
Engineer	14	7.0	36.0	43.0	14.0	—
Artist	13	—	—	82.3	7.7	—
No definite occupation	125	—	16.8	77.6	5.6	—

whereas their proportion among the farm workers was 45%. Among other occupations, the proportion of unaffiliated was higher than—or equal to—the average.

In regard to the second and largest group, Mapai, the position is reversed. The proportion of farm workers affiliated to this party was as high as 51%. Among the liberal professions, clerks and political functionaries, the proportion of Mapai members was also above average. With the exception of political functionaries and lawyers, the greatest tendency to belong to a political party was among the farm workers. Among the rest, there was a greater tendency to non-affiliation.

This finding is true, not only for the thirties, but also for the period of the Second Aliya itself. In the thirties, the agricultural workers constituted 45% of the total Mapai membership, and 24.5% of the unaffiliated. During the period of the Second Aliya, agricultural workers constituted 64.3% of the Poalei-Zion and Hapoel Hatsair combined, while among the non-affiliated they were 58%. Thus, during the period under discussion the correlation between agricultural occupations and membership in a labour party is especially high, more so than during the period of the Second Aliya.

The internal distribution of farm workers shows that 34% of them were former Hapoel Hatsair members, 32% were unaffiliated, and 24% were Poalei-Zionists. It follows that members of Hapoel Hatsair persisted more than others in their devotion to the ideal of the land.[48]

The correlation between occupation and political affiliation influenced the distribution of members of the Second Aliya according to place of residence (Table 54).

The proportion of Mapai members in the cities and the moshavot was 7% to 10% less than their proportion among those surveyed. On the other hand, it was double that proportion in the collective agricultural

Table 54
Political Distribution according to Place of Residence

Party	City	%	Moshava	%	Moshav	%	Kvutza or Kibbutz	%
Left Poalei-Zion	5	0.9	1	0.81	1	0.88	—	—
Mapai	165	26.7	30	24.30	70	61.60	64	76.1
Non-affiliated	401	64.8	81	65.60	40	35.20	20	23.9
General Zionist	41	6.8	10	8.80	2	1.76	—	—
Mizrahi	4	0.8	1	0.80	—	—	—	—
Total	616		123		113		84	

settlements, that is, in the moshavim and the kibbutzim. The largest proportion of non-affiliated is in the cities and in the moshavot. The distribution between urban and village settlements was equal among the members of Mapai—50% lived in the cities and 50% in the rural settlements. On the other hand, among the non-affiliated, the urban group predominated—74% as against 26%.

It is worth noting that despite the distinct political character of the collective agricultural settlements, 35% of those on a moshava and 24% on a kibbutz were unaffiliated.

Is there a correlation between political distribution and social class? We found above that there was none. Sixty-four percent of the urban hired labour was unaffiliated and only 33.2% of them belonged to Mapai. In this respect, the unaffiliated group was more proletarian than Mapai—the Socialist party! The merchants, too, showed no inclination to belong to a party identified with their class: 70% of them were unaffiliated; 12.5% were members of Mapai; and only 15% belonged to the General Zionists.

The above findings still have not provided a satisfactory explanations for the widespread de-politicization of members of the Second Aliya during the thirties and forties. After finding no correlation between this process and age or sex, we established that there was a certain correlation between a person's occupation or place of residence and his inclination to join a political party in general, and a labour party in particular. But here, too, only a partial explanation was obtained since a third of the people in the collective agricultural settlements were unaffiliated, despite the marked political character of this type of settlement. It is also difficult to give a satisfactory objective explanation for the inclination of the town dwellers to affiliate with a party.

The explanation given for a similar trend during the Second Aliya period cannot apply here. During the mid-thirties, the earlier surrogates for traditional party activity—the "conquest of labour" and self-defence—were no longer valid for this group.

We thus have no choice but to try to relate this phenomenon to subjective and ideological factors. The subjective personal factors which led people to leave their parties are unknown, but were certainly numerous and varied. It may be assumed that some members of the Second Aliya were among those who objected to the union of Ahdut Ha'avoda and Hapoel Hatsair in 1930.[49] However, a statistical analysis of the matter is not yet possible.

We have now reached the last question which we had already posed at the beginning of this investigation—can the Second Aliya be considered to have become a political elite in the thirties?

If a political elite is a group of people with a defined common set of values and style of life, struggling for political power, it is difficult to apply this definition to the members of the Second Aliya in the thirties. In this sense, organized labour possessed some characteristics of a political elite during the Second Aliya period, for it constituted a cohesive group, organized in the labour parties and unions on the basis of common values and a distinct way of life. In spite of differences in ideology and on the tactics of political-social conflict, there was an agreement on basic issues—Jewish labour, social justice, the aspiration for national independence and social activism. This set of values gave rise to a special life-style which had two facets; puritanism, hard work, simplicity and minimal needs combined with a rejection of private property, *wanderlust* and a bohemian-romantic pride in poverty.

The Second Aliya could continue as a social group upholding a defined political and ethical system only so long as the majority of its members and the focal point of its activities were in agrarian society, where they shared a common basis in work, values and style of life.

The process of urbanization, the abandonment of farm labour, the occupational diversification and the reduced inclination to political activity and affiliation in general and in the labour parties in particular— all these destroyed the common basis of the Second Aliya and invalidated it as a group with a common social distinctiveness and vocation. Only 21% of the members of the Second Aliya, those who belonged to the cooperative agricultural settlements, continued to maintain the original ideals as a group and not as individuals.

The Second Aliya cannot be considered to have constituted either a social or a political elite in the thirties. Only 7.4% were active in political or public life; only a third belonged to Mapai—the largest party in the country, and the main source of political power, while over half were unaffiliated.

The fact that most members of the higher echelons of Mapai were from the Second Aliya does not contradict our conclusion; (16 of the 20 members of the Mapai Central Committee in 1930 had arrived in the country during the Second Aliya.) They attained leading positions in their party and in the Jewish community of Palestine by force of their own personalities, their ability and their political leadership. They did not attain power as representatives of a specific social group, with distinctive political aims and values.

Paradoxically, at the very time when its ideas concerning Jewish labour, an independent national defence force and the absorption of mass immigration were at last being realized, the Second Aliya itself ceased to exist as a socio-political entity.

Did the Second Aliya then cease to influence the development of the Jewish Community in Palestine? It would seem that it did not. It was in the mid-thirties and forties that the legend of the Second Aliya was created as an educational and nationalistic theme.[50]

Over the course of the years, as the era of the Second Aliya receded into the past and the Second Aliya, as a group, ceased to be a bone of contention in political life, the national legend took root and flourished. This gave rise to the last of the paradoxes of this aliya—the more its political power diminished, the more its national-educational value grew. Neither in its existence nor in its disappearance as a concrete political force, did the Second Aliya cease to affect the Jewish National Movement. And who knows, what shape the movement would have taken without the values cherished and handed down by the Second Aliya.

Notes

1. More precisely, towards the end of World War I, there were 400 male and female Ashkenazi workers in the agricultural colonies of Judea out of a total of 762 from all ethnic groups. In Samaria and Galilee, there were 355 Ashkenazi workers (male and female) out of 517. To these should be added the city workers, especially in Jaffa and Jerusalem. See, Census of the Jews of Palestine, published by the Palestine Office of the Zionist Organization, Part A., p. 50; Part B, p. 100.
2. See D. Gurevich, A. Gertz and R. Bachi, *The Jewish Population of Palestine; Immigration, Demographic Structure and Natural Growth,* Jerusalem, 1944, p. 21.
3. According to a calculation made on the basis of the census of Palestine Jews held in 1918 in the cities and colonies of Judea, Galilee and Samaria—including refugees from Jaffa and Hebron but excluding Jerusalem—there were 5965 Jews who had immigrated to Palestine between 1904 and 1914. Of these, 70% lived in the colonies and 30% in the cities. This was undoubtedly a result of war conditions, which caused an exodus from the cities to the colonies where it was easier to obtain food. If the same ratio between towns and colonies held good for Jerusalem, approximately 2000 people who had immigrated during the Second Aliya period must have been living there at the time. This means that altogether 40,000–45,000 Jews remained in Palestine. See, Census of the Jews of Palestine, Part A., pp. 109–110; Part B, p. 110.
4. Curt Nawratzki, *Die Jüdische Kolonisation Palästinas,* Munich, 1914, p. 441 ff.
5. See Jacob Leschinsky, *Di Idishe Vanderung far di Letste 25 Yor*—Jewish Wandering during the Past 25 Years, Berlin, 1927, Table 2, p. 8.
6. See note 2 above.
7. See Nawratzki, *op. cit.,* p. 441.

8. See *Pinkas,* publication of the Jewish Labour Federation in Palestine, Supplement 8, Table 3.
9. See Jacob Leschinsky, *Di Entviklung fun Idishen Folk far di Letste 100 Yor*—The Development of the Jewish People during the Past 100 Years, *Shriften far Ekonomik un Statistik,* Vol. 1, Berlin, 1928, p. 21.
10. See Leschinsky, *Di Idishe Vanderung,* p. 61.
11. See Leschinsky, *Di Entviklung,* p. 21.
12. The Bund (Algemeiner Idisher Arbeter Bund in Lite, Rusland un Poilen) was a Jewish Socialist workers' party, founded in 1897.
13. See Leschinsky, *Di Entviklung,* p. 43. Table 19.
14. See Nawratzki, *op. cit.,* p. 441 ff.
15. See Leschinsky, *Di Idishe Vanderung,* p. 79.
16. A detailed examination of the ways in which the passage of Jewish immigrants to the United States was financed, might give us a more accurate picture of their family ties in the new country. Between 1908 and 1925, 61.4% of them received passage money from relatives already there. Only 32.5% of non-Jewish immigrants received such aid from relatives. See Leschinsky, *Di Entviklung,* p. 70.
17. S. Yoseph, "Haherkev Hamishpati Vehamiktsoi shel Hamehagrim Hayehudim Le'artsot Habrit Vedargat Haskalatam"—The Family and Occupational Composition of Jewish Immigrants to the United States and their Level of Education, *Klal Yisrael, Perakim Basotsiologia Shel Ha'am Hayehudi*—Chapters in the Sociology of the Jewish People, Jerusalem, 1954, p. 182.
18. See Leschinsky, *Di Entviklung,* p. 43, Table 19.
19. See R. Mahler, *Divrei Yemei Yisrael, Dorot Aharonim*—History of the Jewish People in Modern Times, Merhavia, 1955, Vol. 3, p. 141.
20. See Leschinsky, *Di Idishe Vanderung,* p. 29. Table 13.
21. This calculation was made on the basis of the tables given by Nawratzki, *op. cit.,* p. 442.
22. Even if we assume that some of the immigrants to the United States falsely declared they were artisans in order to facilitate their immigration, the difference between the immigration to Palestine and to the United States in this respect, is still striking.
23. See Nawratzki, *op. cit.,* p. 442.
24. Poalei-Zion was a Jewish Socialist Zionist party, established in Russia in 1906. It held that the Jewish homeland was the only place where Jewish workers could hope to win the class war.
25. The General Zionists adhered exclusively to the Basle Programme adopted at the First Zionist Congress in 1897, and did not incline toward any particular political party or ideological trend in Zionism.
26. A *moshava* was the form of agricultural settlement first adopted in modern Palestine; it was a village consisting of individual farms.
27. *Kvutza*—a small communal agricultural settlement; the number of members was deliberately restricted on the theory that the community would thus be more homogeneous and harmonious.
28. See Nawratzki, *op. cit.,* p. 441.
29. *Ibid.*
30. All data on the occupational structure of the Jewish community in the thirties are taken from D. Gurevich, A. Gertz and R. Bachi, *Ha'aliya, Hayishuv, Vehatnua Hativ'it shel Ha'ukhlusia Be'erets Yisrael*—Immigration, the Jewish Community, and Natural Population Movement in Palestine, Jerusalem, 1945, p. 89, Table 45.
   The calculation of the proportion of manual labourers in the Second Aliya does not take into account retired people.
31. *Moshav Ovdim*—an agricultural settlement with various cooperative institutions.

32. A *kibbutz* is a communal agricultural settlement which, unlike the kvutza, never had ideological restrictions on the number of members.

33. In seeking an explanation for the urbanization trend, over and above the factor of vocational change, we sought a correlation between the place of residence abroad and that in Palestine during the relevant period. No important correlation exists. Immigrants from cities abroad displayed only a slightly greater tendency to settle in cities in Palestine than people from small towns—69% as against 65%.

34. Tseirei-Zion, founded in 1903, was a moderate Zionist-Socialist movement. Its membership was mainly in Russia and it was later active in Hechalutz.

35. The Socialist-Zionists (S.S.) were a Jewish Socialist party which joined the Jewish Territorialist Organization and sought to establish a Jewish homeland elsewhere than in Palestine.

36. Sejmists was one of the names applied to the Idishe Sotsialistishe Arbeter Partei, which demanded a Jewish parliament (*sejm* in Polish) as the basis for Jewish self-government and autonomy within Russia. In 1917 it joined with the S.S. to form the Fareinikte (United) Sotsialistishe Partei.

37. Hatehiya was a Zionist youth group, founded in Warsaw in 1903, which was ideologically close to Tseirei-Zion. It advocated practical work in Palestine, pioneering and the study of Hebrew.

38. The Independents were a non-Socialist Jewish labour party founded in 1901 at the instigation of the Tsarist secret police in order to draw off support from the Bund and the Social Democrats. It was disbanded in 1903 under police pressure, because its founders could no longer control it.

39. Tolstoyans, or Tolstoyists, followed the teachings of Tolstoy, advocated the simple life, and rejected Marxism. To the extent that they affiliated politically, it was with the Social Revolutionaries.

40. Hapoel Hatsair—a Jewish workers' party in Palestine, founded in 1905. It opposed class struggle and rejected affiliation with the international workers' movement. It merged with Ahdut Ha'avoda (see note 45) to form Mapai (see note 47) in 1930.

41. Mizrahi—a religious Zionist party founded in 1902.

42. Hashomer—The Watchman—was the self-defence organization established in 1909 in Palestine, to provide Jewish guards for the settlements. Candidates for membership had to qualify as to courage, horsemanship and discipline. Although inactive after 1920, most of its members were Poalei Zionists, and it is regarded as a forerunner of the Hagana.

43. See Yosef Gorni, "Hayessod Haromanti Ba'ideologia shel Ha'aliya Hashnia"—Romanticism in the Ideology of the Second Aliya, *Asufot*, Tel Aviv, January 1966.

44. This name was applied to three Jewish battalions of the British army, recruited mainly from Britain, Palestine and the United States. Two battalions participated in the Palestine campaign of 1918, and all three served in the occupation army. Despite the absence of formal relations between the three, liaison was maintained by the Palestinian battalion, whose members took part in preparations for the establishment of the Ahdut Ha'avoda party and the Histadrut.

45. Ahdut Ha'avoda was a Socialist party founded in 1919. See also note 47.

46. The Left Poalei-Zion seceded from Poalei-Zion in 1920 over the issue of joining the Third International. It advocated the use of Yiddish and did not participate in Zionist Congresses until 1939.

47. Mapai (acronym of Mifleget Poalei Erets Yisrael—Palestine Workers' Party) was a Socialist Zionist party formed in 1930 through the merger of Ahdut Ha'avoda and Hapoel Hatsair.

48. The following table shows the proportion of agricultural workers in every group during the Second Aliya period and during the thirties respectively:

Party	During the Second Aliya	During the Thirties
Poalei-Zion	67%	24%
Hapoel Hatsair	62%	34%
Non-affiliated	85%	32%

49. See M. Braslavski, *Tnuat Hapoalim Ha'erets Yisra'elit*—The Palestine Labour Movement, Tel Aviv, 1956, Vol. 2, p. 134. In a referendum carried out among members of the two parties, Hapoel Hatsair voted 85% for unification, 10% against, with 5% abstaining. Ahdut Ha'avoda voted 81.6% for, 16.6% against, with 1.8% abstaining. The percentage of those opposed and abstaining was greater in the cities and moshavot than in the communal and cooperative settlements.

50. *Sefer Ha'aliya Hashnia*—The Second Aliya Anthology, was published in 1947. *Kovets Hashomer*—The Hashomer Anthology, appeared ten years earlier. These two collections established the legend of the Second Aliya.

17.

The "Yizkor" Book of 1911—A Note on National Myths in the Second Aliya

Jonathan Frankel

How nationalistic did the labor movement founded by the young Jewish immigrants to Palestine (the Second Aliya, as it is often called) become during its first decade, 1904–1914? This is a question of great importance in the history of Zionism.

After all, the small remnant of the Second Aliya which was still in Palestine in the early 1920s succeeded to a remarkable extent in stamping its mark on the fast-growing Jewish population, organizationally (through the Histadrut, the Hagana, the kibbutzim, the moshavim); ideologically (with its concept of labor hegemony); and culturally (with its strongly secular but also strongly national ethos). Veterans of the Second Aliya attained positions of political dominance both in Palestinian Jewry (the *Yishuv*) and in the World Zionist Organization from the 1930s. At critical moments—in 1937 (at the time of the Peel Commission), in 1947–49 (when the Jewish State was created amidst turmoil and battle) and in 1967 (following the June War)—a crucial role was played by leaders who had arrived as very young men even before 1914. Some, Berl Katznelson and Levi Eshkol, for example, were at the center of affairs during only one of these crises; but others (most notably, Yitzhak Tabenkin and David Ben Gurion) were, astonishingly, on the public stage during all three.

However, it is enough to mention these few names in order to recall that among them they held totally conflicting views on such fundamental

Reprinted by permission of the author, The Historical Society of Israel, and The Zalman Shazar Center for Jewish History, from *Religion, Ideology, and Nationalism in Europe and America: Essays Presented in Honor of Yehoshua Arieli* (Jerusalem, 1986): 355–84.

issues as the partition of the Land of Israel, or, for example, military retaliation against Arab violence (the correct balance to be struck between *havlaga*, restraint, and "activism"). And to a large extent, these divisions can be traced back to the period before the World War I.

As a safe generalization, it can be said that, in great part, those members of the Second Aliya who were still in Palestine in 1914 were imbued with a strong and palpable spirit of nationalism. But when it comes to describing the nature of that nationalism, the historian finds himself face to face with patterns kaleidoscopic in their complexity and elusiveness. The fast-changing and inchoate development of the Second Aliya during its first decade made not only for disagreements between various groups and between various individuals, but, frequently, also for a lack of consistency on the part of one and the same person.

True, at one level, the politics of the Second Aliya can be seen as unfolding along lines familiar from Russia during the years of the revolutionary upheaval and the pogroms, 1903–7. There were the two Zionist labor parties, both established in Palestine late in 1905 by veterans of party organization in the Pale of Settlement, one socialist (the Jewish Social Democratic Labor Party in Palestine—Poale Zion); the other radical (Ha-Poel Ha-Tsair). They had their party programs, annual conferences, and resolutions; their conflicts and debates, often highly acrimonious. In theory, it was their task to formulate the ideologies which had to extrapolate long-term political strategy and day-to-day tactics from an over-arching world-view.[1]

But in reality, the bold experiments, which eventually proved to be of decisive importance in the development of the labor movement, were initiated for the most part without help from the parties or, even, in contradiction to their avowed principles. This was true of the first tentative move towards cooperative farming by the workers (Ein Ganim); of the first steps towards collective settlement (the Sejera *kolektif* and Um Juni); and of the Farm Labor Unions. It was also true of the paramilitary organizations, Bar Giora, founded in 1907, and the Ha-Shomer, founded in 1909. The parties had not been responsible for bringing the young immigrants to Palestine; could do little to help them once they had come; and lacked the financial and organizational means to impose their leadership. As often as not, they had to adapt their ideological formulations to accommodate the new policies developed by groups over which they had, at most, only nominal control.[2]

Again, while each party founded its own journal, neither forced its contributors to follow its own line of thought. On the contrary, *Ha-*

ahdut, and still more, *Ha-poel ha-tsair,* reflected in their pages the highly individualistic, disorganized and even anarchic nature of the Second Aliya.

The limited role played by the parties meant that the actual attitudes and behavior of the young immigrants can hardly be described or explained in ideological terms alone. The ways in which they acted and thought were often more the result of deep emotions aroused by their experiences in revolutionary Russia and in the Palestinian colonies than of logical deductions from theoretical premises.[3]

And here, too, the party ideologists found themselves talking ever more frequently not in the language of cool analysis and socio-political strategy but rather in that of national and religious traditions (albeit reworked to meet current needs). National legends and myths, with their appeal to the group psyche, the collective subconscious, were conjured up to inspire the faith and tenacity which the imported ideologies had been able to sustain only in part and only by dint of frequent (and hence costly) adaptation.

The importance of the *Yizkor* (or memorial) book published in 1911 lies in the fact that nowhere else, perhaps, is it possible to observe in so concentrated a manner, the process by which members of the Second Aliya were developing ways of thought and speech suffused with mythological motifs. The decision to publish an entire volume on the death of men, very few in number but all killed in combat by Arabs, almost all in their first youth, provided an ideal forum for those who felt driven at that time to create a pantheon of heroes, or perhaps a martyrology, for the movement. Inevitably, the enterprise aroused the strongest possible emotions and called forth a broad range of reactions, both ideological and personal, involving different views of the past, the present and the future of the Jewish people.

It was Yehoshua Radler-Feldman (better known by his *nom de plume* Rabi Binyamin) who first conceived the idea of the memorial volume. He had been abroad, in Galicia, when three young men, Dov, or Berele, Shveiger, Shimon Melamed, and Yisrael Korngold were killed in the spring of 1909 as the result of attacks by Arab villagers in Lower Galilee. But he had known Shveiger for some years before that, even before the latter had become a full-time guard, and he greatly admired him. He had personally witnessed how Shveiger, although still a youngster not out of his teens, had been put in command of Mesha (Kfar Tabor) in 1908 when it was in threat of a major assault from the surrounding population, and how he had handled this assignment with a calm confidence.[4]

Shveiger had died of wounds in the Scottish hospital in Tiberias and had been given little more than a pauper's burial by the local Jewish community. And on his return to Palestine, Radler-Feldman undertook to produce a commemorative book in order, as he put it, to compensate for the absence of a suitable memorial stone.[5]

There was no reason when the *Yizkor* book was first planned to have expected it to produce any controversy within the labor movement. It was conceived as a personal tribute more than a political statement. If Radler-Feldman had any political message in mind then it was directed against the passivity and ultra-conservatism of the so-called Old *Yishuv* (pre- and mainly anti-Zionist) as represented by the Jews of Tiberias.

When Shveiger and his comrades were killed early in 1909, almost no questions had yet been raised in the labor movement about what was, or was not, the correct role to be filled by those workers who chose to earn their living as paid guards in the Jewish colonies. That work in the colonies (whether farm labor or guarding) should be undertaken increasingly not by Arabs (or Circassians) but by Jews had come to be regarded by the Second Aliya as essential and beyond dispute. As a result, when the watchmen established their own organization, Ha-Shomer, in the spring of 1909, it at first attracted almost nothing except admiration not only from Poale Zion (from which its members were mainly drawn) but even from Ha-Poel Ha-Tsair.[6] That a memorial volume should have been built around Dov Shveiger (termed the "first Jewish guard" in the colonies of Galilee) was natural enough.

The task of editing the volume was taken upon themselves by two of the best-known writers and intellectual figures associated with the Second Aliya, Alexander Ziskind Rabinovich and Yosef Haim Brenner. As the former had ties to Poale Zion and its new journal, *Ha-ahdut,* and as the latter then published articles regularly in *Ha-poel ha-tsair,* their joint editorship served to emphasize the non-partisan nature of the enterprise.

They made no attempt to limit the kind of contributions which could be offered, and opened up the volume to Hebrew writers both in the country and abroad as well as to the "young people here in Eretz Yisrael who for the most part were the comrades of our holy fallen [*harugenu ha-kdoshim*]." The volume *Yizkor,* was to be dedicated not only to Shveiger, Korngold and Melamed but, in general, to "the workers and guards who have been killed guarding the Jewish colonies in our country."[7] In March 1911 an advertisement was published in the press calling for contributions and this was followed up by another, more urgent one, in May.[8] In that same month, we find Rabinovich and Brenner jointly writing to Micha Yosef Berdichevsky in Germany, thanking him for the short tales which he had sent for the volume.[9]

However, the book which had been conceived in a spirit of consensus in 1909 did not see the light of day until the very end of 1911 when, in fact, it served to highlight deep disagreements within the Second Aliya about both the rhetoric and the substance of Jewish nationalism and of Jewish-Arab relations. Even before the book was published, Brenner had resigned as co-editor. What is more, he chose to withdraw his contribution to *Yizkor* and to publish it as an article in *Ha-poel ha-tsair*, adding a note in which he explained his action quite specifically as the result of "disagreements between me and Mr. A. Z. Rabinovich."[10] And no sooner had the book appeared than Zerubavel (Yaakov Vitkin) brought out a major article in *Ha-ahdut* attacking a number of contributions, and indeed the whole structure of the book (to which he himself had contributed) in bitter terms. In turn, Rabinovich and Radler-Feldman defended the volume (and themselves) publicly, the former in reply to Brenner, the latter in answer to Zerubavel.

Of course, much of the material which went into the making of *Yizkor* was politically uncontroversial. Many of the Hebrew authors sent in pieces of work which they had, from all appearances, been in the process of writing (or had earlier completed) anyway. Here, for example, Agnon first published his tale drawn from the folk life of Galician Jewry, "The Wood Cutter." A. Reuveni (Aharon Shimshelevich) and Shlomo Tsemakh both contributed stories, permeated by a strong note of pastoralism, about the day-to-day and peaceful life of the farm workers, young immigrants from Russia, in the Jewish colonies of Judah and the Galilee. Berdichevsky sent a few of his renderings of medieval legends which described the rise and fall of warrior messiahs.

The book was dedicated to eight men who had been killed in clashes with Arabs between the years 1890 and 1911. And a number of the contributions took the form of obituary notices written in a strictly cut-and-dried form. This was true for the most part of A. Z. Rabinovich writing on Yaakov Plotkin whom he had known for many years in Poltava (both men belonged to an older generation, perhaps twice as old as the average member of the Second Aliya). On Zvi Bartanovsky, who was killed when the book was already in press, only a few lines were published: "He was a guard at Sejera and on Saturday, 13 July 1911, at dawn, he saw two Arabs descending the hill. When he asked them who they were, they did not reply but fired at him. Two hours later he died."[11] (The book also contained a photograph of Bartanovsky.)

The differences of emphasis which can clearly be perceived in the book—and which immediately became the cause of open dispute—involved essentially three separate, albeit interrelated, issues. What was the correct approach to Jewish-Arab relations in Palestine, to the history and religious traditions of the Jewish people, and to the memorialization of comrades who had lost their lives so soon after arriving in Palestine?

In the short introduction to *Yizkor,* signed by the anonymous "editorial committee," a relatively large amount of space was devoted to discussing the relationship between the Jewish and Arab peoples. It was much easier from the psychological point of view, so the argument there went, to accept the many deaths suffered from malaria, an impersonal force, than to reconcile oneself to those resulting from violence

at the hands of human beings, at the hands of brothers, members of a nation *[am]* which is close to us from the racial point of view—deaths caused without point, without real reason, without conscious thought.

We have returned to our country, to our homeland, with strong feelings of affection *[ahava]* for the nation living here. We have had more than enough of the domineering arrogance of the Aryan peoples and we know that the one God, the God of Israel and of the world, calls upon us and upon the Arabs to unite in the common cause—to restore our country which lies waste to prosperity; to spread knowledge together; to share the benefits of human culture.

Now, too, we remain convinced that at long last the Arabs will recognize the fact that *their* progress depends today on truly and fully cooperating with us—just as in the Spanish period, which was so enlightened, the Jews *['ivrim]*[12] and Arabs worked shoulder to shoulder, making remarkable contributions to every sphere of knowledge.[13]

But, of course, this could only be one side of the coin and there followed the assurance that "until those fortunate days arrive we shall not desert our flag, the flag of labor and of life."

It emerged in the subsequent public exchanges that this editorial note had been written, in whole or in part, by Radler-Feldman (Rabi Binyamin)[14] although it must have been approved by A. Z. Rabinovich (and presumably by the other committee members, Yaakov Rabinovich, Yosef Shprintsak and M. Titelman).[15] And in another, a signed, contribution to *Yizkor,* Rabi Binyamin returned to the theme of Arab-Jewish relations. In his recollections about his friend, he put great emphasis on the fact that Berele Shveiger had chosen to go to Galilee and become a guard not simply because he loathed dull routine and longed for adventure but also because he envied *the life of the Arabs*. That life for him was a symbol, an aspiration, the highest and the finest. What liberty! What space! As high as the mountain! What strength! What a sense of honor! What self respect!

During that same walk [from Petah Tikva to Jaffa] we came across a galloping horse; Berele at one go jumped on to its back and put on for me a demonstration *[fantasia]*, Arab-style.

He developed a real yearning for the life of the Arabs.[16]

Shveiger was by no means alone in his admiration for the bolder aspects of the Arab (or perhaps more exactly, the Beduin) way of life. To a very great extent, members of the Ha-Shomer organization tended not only to ride their horses hard and fast in local style but also to wear Arab clothing and head-dress. They also made an effort to learn Arabic, and entertained Arabs in accordance with the etiquette of the country.[17] In 1912, Yosef Aharonovich, the leading ideologist of Ha-Poel Ha-Tsair, would complain that the net result of all this was that the guards tended to speak only Yiddish and almost no Hebrew. ("The moral state of the organization," he then concluded, "is totally unsatisfactory.")[18]

However, Radler-Feldman clearly saw this motif in Shveiger's short career as legitimate and even admirable. In general, both he and Yaakov Rabinovich[19] in their recollections about the men whom they had known personally (Shveiger and Korngold) made a determined effort to bring out their individuality, their eccentricities, weaknesses as well as strengths: two young men, the one from the Moldovanka district of Odessa, the other from some unspecified place in the Pale of Settlement, who had begun to become part of the Galilee landscape before death struck them down.

Representing a totally different position, another pole even, was Zerubavel's contribution to *Yizkor*. His prose poem, "Lines" *(Kavim)* made no direct reference to the Arabs in Palestine, but there was the clear, albeit implicit, assumption that Jewish settlement in Palestine would not be able to advance without coming up against and defeating persistent, violent resistance. The work was divided into four parts: "On the sea" (a symbolic reference to the Exile); "The soil" (the motherland); "Graves," and "Creating."

In the third section, the narrator contrasts the "here" (Eretz Yisrael) with the "there" (the Exile):

Graves there and graves here ... Which blood is dearer to [one's spirit]? ... More people fell there; and here there is only a beginning and only few ...

But here they fell in a *different way* ... Here they labored in the sweat of their brow and here their blood was spilt ... And the blood fell on the soil which they had ploughed and the soil soaked it up. And new life, stormy and many-coloured, springs up around those graves . . .

I fell on the earth, soaked in blood, and gave it my oath that I would not leave, that I would keep faith with my comrades, that their memories might be perpetuated for ever.

Where there is life there is battle. And where there is battle, the grave cannot be escaped.

I am still young, and the urge to be is strong within me . . . I have land . . . I shall go to do battle . . . there will be new graves . . . blood which is new and fresh . . . And the earth, the soil of the motherland, will renew its days; . . . new life will break forth. . . .[20]

This theme of blood and soil recurs elsewhere in the volume. K. L. Silman, in another prose poem, "Personal Thoughts" (Me-hirhurei liba), described in encapsulated form a number of savage attacks on young Jews, workers and guards. But he, too, suggested that death in such circumstances should be seen as a guarantee of collective renewal:

Blood, blood. Its color is beautiful and the soil in which it sinks becomes dear to us, is cherished. For, as the body has need of blood, so does an entire nation and so does the earth . . . Take away the memories of our blood and one removes much from the great past of the world and of ourselves. If we had not irrigated the land with our blood we would not be standing on it today. . . .

We shed our blood and we live here. Our life is the continuation of the past and so too is the spilt blood. A nation does not build its life except on the foundations of its past and blood is joined to blood.

Silman concluded in these words:

And you should know that one song of long ago brought us, the young generation, here to their country:
"Neither the fire nor the sun but our blood
Will turn your mountains red, O Zion!"[21]

In his essay, "Self-Sacrifice" (Mesirut nefesh), Dr. Joshua Thon gave expression to the identical theme. "National aspirations," he wrote,

cannot be realized unless for their sake people lay down their lives. Without the sign of blood [hotem ha-dam] no national hope in history was ever fulfilled. Our hopes have already received the stamp of blood, warm blood, young blood. Now we can rest assured that their time will come. The nation will live for ever and the memory of the young men who shed their blood guarantees that our hope, eternal [life], will never be erased from our history.[22]

The theme of self-sacrifice was presented in very different form by Yisrael Giladi in his short obituary notice on Yehezkel Nisanov, but the moral was very similar. Unflinching bravery had to become the norm in the confrontation between the Jewish guard and the Arab marauder.

Nisanov was killed in 1911 when he refused to surrender the mules pulling his cart on the way from Merhavia to Yavniel.

Of course, he preferred to be killed rather than to give up his mules to the Arabs. When they stole the animals from some farmer Nisanov would reproach him bitterly: "How is it that you are still alive and your animals are gone? Shame on you!" And now he has shown that he was as good as his word. "I have shown," Nisanov would say, "that a Jewish worker will not permit himself to be put to shame, even if it costs him his life, for on this depends the honor and future of his nation [amo]."[23]

That such a wide gap separated the message of Rabi Binyamin (Radler-Feldman) from that of Zerubavel (and the others writing along the same lines) was by no means surprising. Disagreements about Jewish-Arab relations can be traced back to the very first years of the Second Aliya and were becoming more acute with the passage of time.

In 1907, Radler-Feldman had published a short article on the subject in the Hebrew journal, Ha-meorer, edited by Brenner in London. Although written in quasi-Biblical verse, and oddly entitled "An Arabian Prophecy" (Masa'arav), it presented a clear enough conception of how the Zionist movement should seek to order the relationship between the Yishuv and the Arabs.

Yosef Gorny, in a pioneer and important essay on the thought of the Second Aliya,[24] has argued that this article by Rabi Binyamin can be seen as belonging to the same category as Yitshak Epstein's (by now famous) article of the same year, "An Unasked Question" (Sheelah neelama). And it is certainly true that both these writers advocated policies of the utmost caution and tact in all that concerned the highly sensitive issues of land purchase and agrarian settlement by the Jews. There was, however, also a significant difference between them. Epstein insisted that a bitter conflict between the two nations in Palestine was inevitable unless Jewish settlement was strictly confined to areas which were marginal agriculturally (mountain or swampland) and therefore unworked by the Arabs.[25] That such a strategy was bound to put tight limits on the potential size of the Yishuv was not of primary concern to Epstein who, like Ahad Ha-Am, thought of Zionism (or Hibat Zion) more in terms of quality, a national center, than of quantity, a refuge for the Jewish people as a whole.

While Epstein was thus very much the pessimist, Rabi Binyamin developed a highly optimistic prognosis. True, he too warned against the enormous dangers which were bound to result from any idea that the Jews had the right or the possibility to treat the country simply as their own and to take it over at the expense of the Arab inhabitants. ("And do not think in thine heart any evil thought of driving them out of the land of thy fathers, for it is not wise. And such a thing can never come to pass . . . [for] thou might stir up against thee the sons of Shem who are thine own kith and kin. And they shall become enemies unto thee and thou shall be scorned in thine own land and among the nations. And thou shall be beset by enemies at home and abroad.") [26]

But, for his part, Rabi Binyamin argued that there was no insurmountable obstacle to the Arab population's accepting Jewish settlement on a massive scale. Rapid development of the country, the introduction of modern education open to Arabs and Jews alike, and strict adherence to full equality between the two peoples, would eradicate the potential causes of conflict. Given modernization, Palestine could absorb five million Jews without infringing on the rights or standing of the half-million Arabs already living there. Given the common racial origins of the two nations, they could well merge eventually to form a single people. [27]

It is clear that Rabi Binyamin remained true to this vision throughout the entire period of the Second Aliya. Following the publication of *Yizkor*, he wrote at least two more articles where he developed the points he had first made in 1907. In one of them, he argued against Ahad Ha-Am that full scale economic advance would make possible a solution both to the "Jewish question" abroad, through mass immigration to Palestine, and also to the national question in Palestine. ("The Jew and the Arab are not two opposing forces.") [28] In the other, he called for the establishment of a Shrine of Peace in Jerusalem which would contain a major library of books on the theme of peace and also, for its deterrent effect, a photograph and picture exhibition of those killed and wounded in war. Of the Yishuv he wrote: "We are for peace; our eyes are turned to peace." [29]

On these issues, Rabi Binyamin was by no means speaking for Ha-Poel Ha-Tsair as a whole. In 1908–9, leading spokesmen for the party had sharply refuted the idea that the Jews set aside part of their own funds to further Arab economic and cultural development. The extremely limited financial resources of the Zionist movement, wrote Moshe Smilansky, for example, had to be devoted exclusively to the overriding goal of attaining "the majority here in our own country." [30] For his part, Aharonovich noted that the "constant hatred and national conflict" did, at least, act as a powerful incentive for the farmers to employ Jewish rather than Arab workers. [31] And A. D. Gordon, while granting that "one cannot say that the Arabs have no part," no rights, to the country, still concluded that it "will belong more to that side which is the more able, willing, to suffer and work for it." [32]

Nonetheless, it was by no means unusual to find statements in *Ha-poel ha-tsair* expressing disgust at the way in which many of the colonists treated their Arab workers. ("How is it," asked Smilansky, "that a wise and intelligent people ... threatened by its neighbors who are native to the country ... acts with arrogance and, at times, with terrible contempt towards them ... [It seems that] we are not wise nor intelligent, not in part, not at all.") [33] This fact goes a long way to explaining why Radler-Feldman, although outside the mainstream of party thought, could still be invited to take part in writing the introduction to *Yizkor*—the editorial board was made up primarily of men associated with Ha-Poel Ha-Tsair.

In marked contrast, Zerubavel belonged to the leadership group of Poale Zion and was one of the editors (together with Ben Gurion and Ben Zvi) of its organ, *Ha-ahdut*. While the high-pitched tone which characterized his contribution to, and his articles about, *Yizkor* was to a great extent a matter of personal choice and taste, the views there advanced were typical enough of opinion at the higher level of the party.

There was, of course, much of the paradoxical in the fact that somebody of Zerubavel's background should have emerged not only as an advocate of nationalist militancy but also as a writer ready to employ a mythological and mystical mode of political expression. After all, like Ben Zvi, he, too, had been an active member of the Poale Zion party in Poltava. Ber Borochov, another native of the town, had totally dominated the party there, and Ben Zvi and Zerubavel saw themselves—and were generally so perceived—as among his most loyal and most important disciples, dedicated *Borokhovtsy*.

The basic doctrine of the party, as formulated by Borochov in *Our Platform* of 1906, was strictly Marxist. The triumph of Zionism, he there postulated, was guaranteed by the unfolding of long-term socio-economic processes (the flow of international capital, industrialization, the marginalization of the Jewish middle and working classes, migration). Determinism was the key note and the terminology entirely "scientific." There was no room for voluntarism, still less for romanticism in any shape or form. The primary and essential task of the party was to conduct the class struggle of the proletariat. Borochov argued that as capitalism transformed the economic basis of the society in Palestine, so the Arab population, caught up by the forces of modernization, would eventually and inevitably adopt the Jewish culture and be assimilated into the Jewish people, soon to become the great majority. The Jewish proletariat could thus dedicate itself to class rather than national conflict.[34]

Variations on this theme frequently made themselves heard in the immediate post-revolutionary period. Thus Efraim Blumenfeld, a leading member of Russian Poale Zion, could write in 1908 that it was the task of the party in Palestine to explain to the Arab workers

the common interests which they share with the world proletariat in general, and with the Jewish proletariat in particular, and take them into our trade-union organizations. We must in no way exclude the Arab working-class from Jewish production (we ourselves have been too often and too long excluded). On the contrary, we must render the Arab worker more capable of fighting against Jewish exploitation.[35]

Similarly, Ben Zvi, writing from Palestine in 1908, could insist that the Jewish working-class would grow not as the result of the manifestos of Ha-Poel Ha-Tsair but rather in response to the economic laws of supply and demand. Skilled or experienced workers would be drawn naturally to appropriate jobs. "It is stupid, utopian," he wrote,

to say that the approximately six thousand Arabs [working in the colonies] . . . are going to be replaced by Jewish *eksterny,* clerks, accountants . . . It is . . . actually treasonable to create the illusion . . . that one must have "young Zionists" to drive out the Arabs.[36]

However, Marxism, as formulated by Borochov in 1906, was by no means the only major influence at work in the early years of the Poale Zion party in Palestine. The party members who founded Bar Giora in 1907 had almost all arrived in the country in the years 1904–5 and had brought with them far more romantic and voluntaristic conceptions of Zionism. Yisrael Shohat, the leader of Bar Giora and Ha-Shomer, found inspiration more in the Russian Socialist Revolutionary movement (with its traditions of political terrorism) than in Social Democracy.[37] Another key figure in these para-military organizations, Alexander Zaid, has testified to the enormous influence exerted on Poale Zion circles in Russia before 1905 by Michael Halperin, a pioneer and adventurer who had founded a secret society in the early 1890s to plan an armed uprising against Ottoman rule and who advocated the formation of Jewish groups in Sinai which would live like Beduin and eventually join the British in conquering Palestine.

Bar Giora itself followed the most conspiratorial rules.[38] Their members were initiated in a mysterious nocturnal ceremony, and sworn to silence and absolute loyalty ("whoever enters the society cannot leave it alive").[39] When the group was in Sejera in 1907–8, it kept its activities secret even from long-time members of Poale Zion working at the settlement, among them David Ben Gurion (Grin). Ha-Shomer, ostensibly a trade-union organization representing the Jewish watchmen, was in reality controlled by the inner nucleus belonging to Bar Giora.[40] Both these para-military organizations shared the same motto (taken from a poem by the well-known Hebrew poet, Yaakov Cohen): "In blood and fire Judeah did fall; in blood and fire shall Judeah arise." [41]

Yitshak Ben Zvi, who arrived in Palestine in 1907 and from the first became the leading ideologist of the Poale Zion party, was among the founding members of Bar Giora. Why precisely a man committed, publicly at least, to the idea of a Social Democratic party based on a mass proletarian membership should have involved himself on arrival in a tiny, clandestine and adventurist group is not entirely clear. But there is no doubt that the pogroms during the Russian revolution (particularly during the month of October 1905) had produced a deeply traumatic effect particularly on those who, like the Poale Zion, were fully involved in the desperate attempts at self-defense. (Ben Zvi opened his reminiscences of Yaakov Plotkin in *Yizkor* with a description of the fear which pervaded a meeting held at night in a Bet-Midrash in Poltava as the Cossack cavalry roamed the streets outside, "a period of mighty events, in the days of the revolution, the pogroms and the self-defense *[ha-hagana]*.") [42] The urge to arm, to prepare for any contingency, to defend the honor of a people which had just suffered (for so it was felt) the profoundest humiliations, was for many of the young immigrants the overriding emotion.

Until the revolution of the Young Turks and the establishment of constitutional government in Istanbul, it had been possible to explain the para-military activities of Bar Giora and other groups nominally attached to Poale Zion as part of the build-up towards the coming anti-feudal, anti-autocratic, revolution in the Ottoman Empire. When, in 1908, Turkish troops (in response to a violent clash between party members and Arab youths in Jaffa) attacked the Hotel Spektor, shooting wildly and wounding over a dozen of the young Jewish workers there, Ben Zvi explained what had happened as the result not of Arab nationalism but as "a pogrom instigated by the lower echelons of the Turkish administration."

We have always anticipated as inevitable a conflict between the incoming Jews
. . . and the Turkish regime. We have never fooled ourselves into thinking that
the Jewish forces in Palestine could always grow through a process that is always
calm and slow. . . . [It] is bound to involve those long-term revolutionary factors
that solve the problems of the people not by paper rights but by blood and
iron.[43]

(In contrast, Moshe Smilansky was highly critical of the young radicals
who "spoke openly in Jaffa of barricades and bombs . . . ; [who] could
hardly grasp that the time was not ripe to order our relationship with
the Arabs on the basis of strict reciprocity . . . , [who] in their fantasies
saw themselves as already rulers of the country; . . . [and argue] . . . that
the Arab only respects the strong.")[44]

However, under the new constitutional order of things, it could no
longer be maintained that the *raison d'être* of Jewish para-military organization was, in essence, revolutionary and anti-imperialist. There could
be no denying that Ha-Shomer was quickly becoming a key factor in
Arab-Jewish relations nor that those relations were marked by increasing
tension. On the one hand, opposition to Zionism among the Arabs of
Palestine became much more vocal, finding expression in the local press
(most notably in the Haifa paper, *al-Karmil*) and in the central Turkish
parliament, the Mejlis.[45] The more frequent armed attacks on the Jewish
settlements in Galilee were now widely seen as a symptom of an emergent and militant Arab nationalism. On the other hand, in Ha-Shomer,
the Jewish labor movement had an armed force of its own, albeit num-
bering only several dozens, which, unlike Bar Giora, was a matter of
public knowledge and acted openly.

And it became increasingly evident that for Ha-Shomer to avoid
involvement in recurring cycles of violence was almost impossible. When
it supplied the guards to a given colony, it made direct enemies of the
group (neighboring Arabs or Cherkassy) which it had replaced. In the
ensuing clashes, the Jewish guards had to demonstrate their determination not to give ground while at the same time seeking to avoid at all
costs any loss of life. Once a local Arab had been killed, a blood feud
of fearsome proportions could only be avoided, if at all, by endless
negotiations, court hearings, and huge monetary payments. To expect
that all the very young men involved would be able to combine absolute
courage with complete self-discipline was to ask the impossible.[46] More
Jews than Arabs ended up being killed and still the colonies and settlement organizations found themselves struggling to fend off the nightmare of the vendetta.

It was against this background that Zerubavel became involved in 1911 (well before the publication of *Yizkor*) in a polemical defense of the Jewish guards. As Ha-Shomer grew in size, power and the scope of its activities, so, however gradually, it came to be seen as a legitimate object of public criticism. The articles which provoked Zerubavel to come to an impassioned defense of the guards were both published in June 1911, the one by the famous Hebrew writer, David Frishman, who had come to Palestine on a visit in order to write a series of personal reports for the Warsaw papers *Haynt* and *Ha-tsfira*, the other by Yaakov Rabinovich writing in *Ha-poel ha-tsair*.

The latter chose his words with extreme care and made manifest throughout his support for the principle that the colonies should be guarded by Jews alone. But, he asked, was not too high a price being paid for the sheer bravado of the guards? "One of the most difficult questions which we face," he wrote,

is how to treat the matter of guarding and yet this question is being handled with a certain frivolity . . . In Galilee, it seems . . . there are some things not right in the [existing] system. The frequent loss of life incurred year after year raises the suspicion that the methods of guarding employed do not take local conditions sufficiently into account. . . . To hold the sword in one hand while working with the other has in it much of the poetic; it lifts the spirit; but do we have so many forces at our disposal that we are entitled to sacrifice Jewish lives for the sake of a sheaf of corn or a foal?[47]

Reacting to the recent clashes around the new settlement of Merhavia, Frishman was much more outspoken. He dismissed as absurd reports in the Polish Jewish press which described the events there as a "pogrom." The level of violence in Palestine, he declared, was non-existent when compared with what the Jews had experienced in the Russian Empire. "At the most somebody, perhaps accompanied by two or three others, attacks somebody else, and it can even end in bloodletting and death." But as for a pogrom, "the country has simply not yet reached that level of culture."

What had struck him as an outside observer was how confident, even arrogant and contemptuous, the Jewish colonists often were in their behavior towards the Arab population. And he also came away with the clear impression that for their part, the young guards seemed to regard intimidation as the best form of defense:

These youngsters, forever on horseback, forever full of fire, are always ready (like the Beduin in the desert) to demonstrate every variety of show and acrobatics on their horses—a *fantasia*, as they call it. What these guards do is not so much to defend themselves as to provoke others. As far as they are concerned, the main thing is that everybody else should see that the [Jewish] people here are harsh and of quick temper and so, out of fear, refrain from theft.

Summing up his impressions of colonists and guards alike, Frishman wondered whether "just as there is that wonderful phenomenon in the world, antisemitism, shall not we, when we only have the ability to do so, create 'anti-goyism'? Are we witnessing a permanent trait in human nature which leads the persecuted, given the chance, to become the persecutor?" [48]

In his response, entitled "Tolerance" [Savlanut], and published in Ha-ahdut, Zerubavel argued that the Yishuv had simply no right to be easy-going in its relationship with the Arabs. To advocate relaxation, concessions, was to follow the ways of the Exile,

to adapt . . . to bend, to bow one's back, to swallow politely every insult and choke down every protest— . . . There is no room here [in this Galut outlook] for unadulterated emotion: the main thing, in its eyes, is *calculation*. Is it worthwhile? Will it not produce a greater evil? . . . Here rationality and mea-surement take the place of feeling and create the Galut mentality even in the modern Jew.

Those fired with "the yearning for Redemption [Geula]" had to refute this entire approach. Yehezkel Nisanov had been absolutely right not to surrender his horses, even though by so doing he risked and lost his life. If, as was the case, the Jewish guards had lost seven men over recent years while only two Arabs had been killed, how could the former be accused of seeking to intimidate? "The root of our problem lies not in a lack of tolerance but in the fact that tolerance has rooted itself too deeply in many of us." [49]

This theme recurred in a number of articles published by Zerubavel during the year of 1911,[50] and it can therefore have come as no surprise that he reacted furiously to Yizkor when it was finally published. His response was so long that it had to be divided up and brought out in two successive issues of Ha-ahdut. As shall be discussed below, he had his own very clear-cut concept of the place of the Second Aliya in Jewish history and this concept was simply not shared by all the contributors, nor indeed by the editor. He was also highly critical of the fact that a book dedicated in its entirety to men who had fallen in combat did not present a strong political message, was lacking in singleminded didac-ticism.

But, above all, he was repelled by the unsigned editorial note (which he must surely have known was written primarily by Rabi Binyamin).

Zerubavel found the introduction so pusillanimous in both content and tone, that, as he put it, it must have been written not from sincere conviction but simply to silence potential critics outside the *Yishuv*. He did not clarify whether he had in mind Zionist or other Jewish liberals and socialists in Europe, the Turkish authorities, or the Arab publicists, who by then were avidly seeking material for use against the *Yishuv*, although he was probably referring to the last of these groups.

He quoted at length from the introduction in order to demonstrate how ridiculous it was. For example, he picked out the passages on "[our] feelings of affection *[ahava]* for the nation living here"; on the Arabs as "close to us from the racial point of view" ("Incredible!" was his interjection here); and on the idea that progress by the Arabs was dependent "on truly and fully cooperating *with us.*" (The italics were added by Zerubavel who also wrote, ironically, "So you, Arabs, now know what you have to do for your own good!")[51]

This insistence on self-abnegation, he argued, was clearly a survival from the Exile: "The Galut Jew *[yehudi]* takes it upon himself to prove that his life is of use, of use to others; that his development is essential . . . essential to others." Or, as he summed it up elsewhere in the article:

Even when here and there a rebel cry breaks forth from the heart, nonetheless the eyes, full of fear, dart around to make sure some outsider does not catch what is being said. . . .

The editorial introduction to *Yizkor* speaks in a weak voice, frightened and false. It is as though these fresh graves are here because of mere accident— [deaths] "caused without point, without real reason, without conscious thought." Thus, all that is wrong is that the Arabs have not reached the level of consciousness and do not know what they do. They do not understand us and we have to enlighten them . . . The Jew *[ha-yehudi]*, the light unto the nations, has opened his mouth and he is *apologizing*. The entire introduction addresses itself not to us, but to others, to those outside.[52]

Radler-Feldman replied at once to Zerubavel's attack, publishing a short response, "On *Yizkor*," in the *Ha-poel ha-tsair* of 24 January 1912. He dismissed as absurd the charge that the introduction was written in a spirit of hypocrisy to mislead the outside world and pointed out that he had published the same ideas in his "Arabian Prophecy" when he was still living in Bukovina. But the main point was different. To do everything within reason, to avoid unnecessary conflict, was not a mark of the Jew as coward.

Whoever knows anything at all about international affairs knows to what an extent nations are ready to apologize—that is, avoid pointless provocations against their neighbors ... We do not have a government of our own [to negotiate] with the nation living next door to us. But is it a cause for shame if, wanting to live on the best of terms and in peace, we say so in print ... ? Our settlement work has to be carried through together with *the Arabs*. And I really do believe that there is something which unites these two nations, the Hebrew *[ha-ivri]* and the Arab. The fact that there are cases of temporary conflict does not mean much. Lovers also quarrel, but such quarrels perhaps mark the most beautiful moments in their relationship.[53]

These sentiments, frequently expressed by Radler-Feldman in this period, were to provoke an irritated rejoinder from Yosef Haim Brenner in 1913. As Brenner saw it, there was nothing random in the emergent conflict between Arabs and Jews. It was inevitable that the Arab population should feel itself ever more threatened as Jewish immigration and agricultural settlement gathered momentum. However underdeveloped in the cultural sense, the six hundred thousand Arabs in the country were,

for practical purposes, the masters of this country and we are pushing into their midst. .... There is now, there is bound to be, hatred between us, and it will exist in the future, too. They are stronger than us in every sense ... but we Jews have long since become accustomed to living as the weak among the strong ... But those gentle souls who talk of love—let them be damned! The last thing we need is sentimentality and idealization.

To gloss over harsh realities, to indulge in self-deception, was absurd and ultimately dangerous. "In this idealized view of the world, in these childish and beautiful dreams, which lack all basis in the profoundest instincts of man, there is, as I see it, something simply immoral."[54] (Given this clear-cut disassociation from Rabi Binyamin, it is not beyond the realms of possibility that Brenner resigned in 1911 as co-editor of *Yizkor* in opposition to the introductory note. However, as Brenner's article on Arab-Jewish relations came out years later and made no reference to *Yizkor*, such an explanation is improbable. There are much stronger clues, as shall be described below, to suggest that his resignation was caused by his revulsion from idealization, myth-making, of a different kind.)

In his reply to Zerubavel, Rabi Binyamin did not confine himself to the issue of co-existence between the two nations living in Palestine. He also refuted another fundamental principle in the Zionist ideology as it was understood by Zerubavel, and, indeed, by a large body of opinion in the Second Aliya.

As Zerubavel saw it, the life of labor to which the young immigrants had pledged themselves represented a total break with two thousand years of Jewish history. To work the soil in the ancient homeland, to settle the country, to defend the settlements, meant to pick up the thread where it had been dropped by the Jewish people with their final defeat by the Romans. He constantly stressed the basic dichotomy between the new life, the new men, with their determination to create an independent nation, and the old life, static, other-worldly, wrapped up in prayers, passive politically and physically. The forces of the *Geula* (Redemption) stood in opposition to those of the *Galut,* the Exile.

A major complaint which he had against *Yizkor* was that commitment to this stark dichotomy, this total break, by no means dominated the book. He himself registered his protest against this fact by dedicating the first section of his two-part article in *Ha-ahdut* entirely to the contrast between passivity and action. Since losing their independence, he argued, Jews had chosen to perpetuate the memory of famous rabbis because of their learning or piety—and in many cases because they had died as martyrs rather than accept apostasy. The prayer book recorded for ever the names and sufferings of the great rabbis *(harugei malkhut)* tortured to death by the Romans. Every year, in the Holy Land, large crowds of traditional Jews flocked to the burial place of Shimon Bar Yohai in Meron as well as to the graves of many other great sages. But a people who for ever awaited salvation from the Heavens was not capable of remembering its forefathers who had fought for its freedom nor of recalling those who had led it into battle. With the final military defeat had begun the "tragedy of our passivity"; and there followed

the Inquisition and the stake, the expulsions the tortures, the pogroms . . . and the martyrs *[meunim].* What other people is so rich in martyrs . . . in tragedies which have their source in the passivity of our faith . . . ? What can this people, so unproductive, so dependent on hand-outs, so twisted in its feeling, have in common with Modiin? with Gush Halav? with Masada?[55]

However, the new way of life lived by the pioneers was producing a new form of historical consciousness.

As of now thousands stream to Meron and a few dozen to Modiin . . . but only the youth and the workers go to Modiin . . . And now there is *Sejera,* too, an entirely new name . . . The Galilee knows no peace . . . ; the smell of blood is in the air . . . There are fresh graves and this is a sign that new life is forming in the country. . . . Martyrs are remembered in the hours of helplessness; heroes are taken for an example in times of courage and action . . . The Sicarii *[biryonim]* and the warriors of Bar Kochba were the last to fight for political freedom and for the chance to work freely in Eretz Yisrael; their grandsons, the Hebrew workers, are the first to fight for a free Jewish life. . . .[56]

Measured against this yardstick of Modiin as opposed to Meron, Zerubavel concluded, the editors of *Yizkor* had failed. "The Exile *[Galut],* he wrote, "has entrenched itself deep in the Jewish soul and this book which was meant to be a call to Redemption *[kriat ha-geula]* demonstrates this fact too."[57]

And, indeed, both Alexander Ziskind Rabinovich and Rabi Binyamin made it clear in *Yizkor* and in their subsequent comments that, as they saw it, the Second Aliya neither could nor should make so radical a break with Jewish history, tradition as it had developed in the Exile. In their conception, even the book itself was designed to encourage a free interweaving of continuities and discontinuities.

Thus, Rabinovich could add a footnote to the article of Joshua Thon in order to dissent from the latter's view that the guards had given their lives not because of the past but for the sake of the future alone, not for "the land of the fathers" *(eretz avot)* but for that of "the sons" *(eretz ha-banim).* It was neither necessary nor possible, Rabinovich responded, to separate these two concepts. "On the contrary, because it is the land of the fathers, the sons are returning to work it. And in the past there were many who sacrificed their lives simply because it was the land of the fathers. Yehuda Ha-Levi was not alone in this respect."[58]

Again, his decision to include a long article in the book on Safed, on the kabbalists and their customs (including the pilgrimages to Meron), could be seen as another way of making the same point.[59] In the summer of 1912 (when responding to criticism by Brenner), he made it clear that, as far as he was concerned, the young guards who had been killed had won the right to a special memorial because according to Jewish tradition they could be considered to have died a holy death, to be *kdoshim*. To die violently *(mita meshuna)* was sufficient to enter this category and there could certainly be no doubt with regard to those youngsters who had "endangered their lives in order to work our holy land."[60]

Rabi Binyamin made very much the same kind of point, although with a different emphasis. Zerubavel, he admitted, was right to notice that *Yizkor* carried the mark of Exile, but it could not be otherwise:

The history of two thousand or more years cannot be simply wiped out by a mere phrase or by mere will . . . The soul does not change just because one moves from one place to another. We owe a debt of gratitude to the editors of the book for not having tried to put on a disguise, for not having tried to hide themselves behind cheap phrases in order to play a part in the Redemption [Geula].⁶¹

Thus in the historiographical, as in the political, sphere, the gap dividing Radler-Feldman (here speaking for the editorial committee) and Zerubavel had its origins in two highly disparate visions of the Zionist enterprise. In the last resort, though, what lent Zerubavel's critique of *Yizkor* its special energy was his belief that the editors had missed a unique opportunity to infuse the volume as a whole with the spirit of a purposeful and single-minded didacticism. What should have been done, in his view, was to ensure that the disparate contributions all meshed together to produce a single and inspiring picture of the life lived by those who had been killed and by those still at work in the fields or on guard. The individual portraits (of Shveiger, Korngold, Plotkin) written by Rabi Binyamin, Yaakov Rabinovich and, above all, Yitshak Ben Zvi were, he granted, admirable in themselves, but they did not bring out the typical. Far more effective was the short note of Yisrael Giladi on his comrade, Nisanov, one *shomer* describing another. ("The character of Yehezkel Nisanov emerges so much more sharply, so much clearer, from the ordinary remark he made, as reported by his comrade: 'How is it that you are still alive and your animals are gone? Shame on you!' ") Here, wrote Zerubavel, "is revealed the image of the guard *[ha-shomer]* in his glory *[be-hadaro]*—his own image and that of the other workers, his comrades, the fallen." ⁶²

Nothing could have been more effective, he granted, than to open the book, as the editors did, with the first word of the prayer possessing the greatest popular resonance in the Jewish liturgy and then to follow it up by a new phrase which totally revolutionized the original meaning. In place of the words handed down from time immemorial, "Let God remember" came, "Let the People of Israel remember." *("Yizkor . . . yizkor na 'am yisrael)*. "This," he wrote,

is a new *yizkor* directed not to Heaven but to the Jewish people, not a prayer, not a supplication but a demand. Let the Jewish people remember and know how a few among its sons lived a life worthy of the name—and fell in battle . . . Let the memory of the heroes reach into every Jewish home where the spirit of the Galut is felt.

However, he concluded, the work itself had not lived up to this expectation: "The people who brought out this book did not remember. They forgot. They did not remember how those who were killed lived nor how they fell." ⁶³

No real attempt was made by the editors to respond to this particular line of attack, although Radler-Feldman did point out that repeated and largely futile efforts had been made to coax articles about the dead men out of their friends and comrades. In order to gain an understanding of an approach essentially opposed here to that of Zerubavel, it is necessary to turn to Yosef Haim Brenner. All the circumstantial evidence suggests that Brenner resigned as co-editor of *Yizkor* out of a growing sense of revulsion against the readiness of A. Z. Rabinovich to include (and indeed to write) material which he felt smacked either of hagiography or of mythologizing.

One of the most intriguing features of Brenner's role in the *Yizkor* episode was that long before he accepted his appointment as co-editor of the volume, he had found an opportunity to dissociate himself from any attempt to read world-historical significance into the tragic death of the young guards in Galilee or to transmogrify them into instant martyrs or heroes.

In the novel which he published in Warsaw in 1910, *Between the Waters (Ben mayim le-mayim)*, Brenner had described in thinly veiled terms one of the public meetings called by the young workers to mourn the death of Berele Shveiger in Galilee in the spring of that year.[64] He drew a picture of the hushed and depressed atmosphere in the hall of the Bet Ha-Am (People's Club) in Jerusalem, of the woman crying in the corner ("She was neurotic and was always talking about how essential it was to win over the Oriental Jews in general and especially the Kurds and Moroccans whom she loved in particular"), and he then went on to describe what was said there. "These speeches," he wrote,

in no way concentrated on the sadness of it all, on the fact that somebody had gone never to return, on the life brought to an end like this without any sense or meaning, on the forlorn existence of one particular man who had been alive (an existence lost and gone without reward), on the final riddle and all-embracing tragedy . . . Rather, they spoke words of consolation . . . The chairman, an old Zionist organizer, did not say: "He's dead and soon I'll be following him" . . . but linked the event to the idea of the Rebirth *[ha-tehiya]* and consoled . . . everybody with high-flown phrases about the fact that the young hero had not been killed in the blood-soaked country we had left behind [Russia], but rather had fallen on the fields of Israel—the fields walked throughout the ages by our Prophets and heroes.

Somebody else . . . spoke about how we should learn from this and set our course accordingly—that is to say, a militia, . . . armaments (. . . ah-ah!).

There was even somebody who tried to enter into the psychology of the Arabs and without actually justifying them from our point of view, nonetheless, suggested that they too are right.

One felt that the truth, the truth of reality, was floating away somewhere overhead hidden behind that special assumption of "chosen-ness" [ha-atah-behartanu] which you find in this country. . . .[65]

If, despite all this, Brenner nonetheless decided to take on the editorship of *Yizkor*, it must surely have been in order to ensure that whoever wanted to record his personal reminiscences about friends or comrades now dead would have the chance to do so in his own way. The article which Brenner wrote for, and then withdrew from, *Yizkor*, certainly was highly individual in character.

It opened with a short summary of the ideological reevaluations which had marked the history of the Russian Jews over the previous hundred years. The Haskala with its slogan of "Be a Jew at home and a man outside" had given way to Hibat Zion with its call to be "a Jew at home and a Jew outside." Now the pioneers in Palestine had pledged their lives to the idea of living as "a man at home and a man abroad [and ready to do battle *(likrat ha-oyev)*]." True, "these few, simple Hebrews are a mere handful, but they are there. They are new, a new type among the Jews [bne yisrael]." [66]

Brenner then proceeded to write in detail about two such individuals. One had been a guard and was killed; but the other (a certain Shmueli) had been a worker and had died of exhaustion and illness.[67] In making this choice, Brenner was clearly arguing against the idea (defended implicitly by A. Z. Rabinovich) that to be killed in combat places the victim in some special state of grace. When *Yizkor* was finally published, it was Rabinovich's conception which prevailed (violent death at Arab hands was the criterion for inclusion in the book).

Of the *shomrim*, Brenner wrote, he had known only one, "but of the workers who have died as the result of their labor it has been my privilege to know a number and to know them better." Brenner described a speech made by Shmueli at a conference of Ha-Poel Ha-Tsair in 1910 where he had called on those assembled there not to abandon the idea of Jews becoming agricultural laborers. He spoke

with pauses, stuttering, as if to himself, diffidently (something along the lines of "I shall make thy tongue cleave to the roof of thy mouth" from Ezekiel), but he talked consistently, clearly and with an extreme obstinacy, a sort of Amos ("I was a herdsman and a dresser of sycamore trees . . .") He spoke out: "If I find five . . . if I find one righteous man . . . I shall save the entire place . . . Thus it was said unto Abraham . . . Let everybody do his work! . . . It is not in our hands to save the nation . . . Perhaps the Almighty One [ha-meyuhas] no longer wants the Redemption . . . Perhaps He wants it but does not have the strength for it . . . Let each one of us save himself . . . The labor of each one of us redeems ourselves . . . creates soil under our feet . . ."

He spoke of one righteous man *[tsadik]*, but, of course, that was his gloss . . . Genesis talks of ten . . . He was that one man, one of the Jews *[ha-yehudim]*, a man of everyday reality.[68]

Almost a year later, in June 1912 (again in *Ha-poel ha-tsair)*, Brenner returned to the subject of *Yizkor,* this time making his reservations explicit. True, he spoke more in sorrow than in anger and (employing the genre of the dialogue) put most of his criticism into the mouth of a putative friend. He had, after all, great respect for, and was on close terms with, Alexander Ziskind Rabinovich.[69] In all probability, though, he had decided that following what was by then a decent interval, the time had come to explain why he had resigned from the co-editorship.

A major problem about life in the *Yishuv,* he wrote, was the tendency to observe the present not as existing in itself, but only as an aspect of the distant past and the promised future. As a result, for "every grain of actual work or reality there are nine times as many declarations, nerve-shattering statements and endless talk." The *Yishuv* was not perceived for what it was—a few thousand Jews living their lives much as the twelve million Jews did elsewhere—but rather, "without any justifica-tion," as "the elite, the saviors of the nation." Was it surprising, he asked, if "people who see themselves as always standing before the judgement of History and of the Future become highly nervous?" As for *Yizkor,*

this small book shows *how over hasty we are to make history,* how we rush to sanctify things which can be sanctified only over the space of generations. . . . Granted that we, the writers and intelligentsia in this country, are nothing compared with the hundreds of people who are living as workers in the hills of Judeah and Galilee and are guarding our colonies against enemies seeking ven-geance . . . Yet nonetheless, they are few, very few in number, and among them not all live up to their ideals. After all, we ourselves actually knew the four or five who fell . . . Can *we* turn their lives into a legend *[agada],* a legend of saints *[kdoshim]* and martyrs *[meunim]?* Can we do that without blanching?

Among the dead recalled in the book; among those not recalled there; and, still more, among those still alive there are individuals in whom even nations, more profound than we are, could take pride. But do we not do them an injustice if we make too much of them in public?[70]

He closed this article with a plea for a different tone in public dis-course: "If only a few real steps could be taken away from prying eyes. What a blessing that would be. If only the waters could flow hidden, truly hidden."[71]

Some years after the publication of *Yizkor,* Zerubavel found himself in a position to bring out a memorial volume constructed very much along the lines envisaged in his fierce critique of 1912. Forced by war-time exigencies to move temporarily to the United States, he was able to put his stamp on a new version of *Yizkor,* published in New York in 1916.[72] Like the earlier book, it was dedicated essentially to members of the Second Aliya, killed by Arabs, but this time it was in Yiddish. The other two editors, Yitshak Ben Zvi and Alexander Khashin (Zvi Averbuch), had likewise crossed the Atlantic as temporary exiles from Palestine.

Unlike the Hebrew original, the Yiddish variation did not have a non-party character. It was published by the Poale Zion Palestine Committee in the USA; the proceeds were to go to the Palestine Labor Fund (run by the party); and the three editors were all party activists. Nothing remained of the literary section which had made up the bulk of the original. The editorial note of 1911 had been replaced by a longer (unsigned) introductory essay which, on examination, turns out to be a translation, slightly altered, of Zerubavel's article in *Ha-ahdut* which opposed Modiin to Meron, the active heroism of the *geula* to the passive martyrdom of the *Galut.* (On the cover was depicted a guard in Arab headdress, mounted on a stallion with a rifle slung across the horse's neck. The 1911 edition had been in plain black.)

For the most part the book was now made up of biographical articles and notes on the dead ("guards" *[vekhter]* as well as "workers" were now specifically mentioned on the title page). The list of those killed had more than doubled since 1911, and, taken altogether, the various accounts and reminiscences did, perhaps, add up to something like the collective portrait which Zerubavel had found so lacking in the Hebrew volume. A long piece by Ben Gurion, "From Petah Tikva to Sejera," which interwove autobiography with selected themes from Second Aliya history, added to the sense of a much greater inner unity.

Nevertheless, even though the new *Yisker* was a Poale Zion publication inspired by a strong spirit of didacticism, it had certainly not become a narrow work of organizational partisanship. The reminiscences of Yaakov Rabinovich and Rabi Binyamin were retained from the 1911 edition. And the article by Brenner which he himself had withdrawn from the Hebrew version was now included. Clearly, the Poale Zion group was not seeking to "mark itself off" in Bolshevik style; but, rather, in catholic spirit, was laying claim to the entire heritage and achievement of the Second Aliya. (The emphasis on individual *shomrim* and workers made it easy to pass with hardly a word over the role of organizations such as Ha-Poel Ha-Tsair and Ha-Shomer which represented an actual or potential threat.)

Within a few weeks of its publication, *Yisker* in Yiddish had sold out. (The first printing was in 3500 copies.)[73] And no time was lost in the production of a second edition. This time, though, Ben Gurion was the chief editor (Zerubavel and Ben Zvi were absent from New York when the new editorial board was chosen), and he made some basic changes. Most notably, Zerubavel's (unsigned) introduction was removed and replaced by a shorter preface. And Ben Gurion's article was brought from the back to the front of the new edition. Ben Gurion was absolutely adamant in insisting on the total excision of Zerubavel's article which he described as "self-inflated and would-be-poetic journalism" and which Khashin called "barbaric—it infuriates everybody with the slightest taste or sense."[74]

However, even though the new preface was shorter than Zerubavel's and written in more disciplined prose, it was not as free of high flown, even mystical, language, as might have been expected from these comments. True, more emphasis was placed on the defensive spirit of the guards ("For all their profound hatred of violence and force, they were compelled to take up the sword in order to defend the property, honor and worth of their people").[75] At the same time, though, Ben Gurion and Khashin pronounced that "to act as guard in Eretz Yisrael is the boldest and freest deed *[tat]* of Zionism."[76]

The sweat of those working the fields and the blood of those killed on guard mix together in the stream of new Jewish life. It is this blood which awakens our past, inspires our present and, above all, invigorates our *future*. . . .

The fallen are near and dear to the people *[folk]* because they are bone of its bone, flesh of its flesh . . . They are not heroes who happen to be Jewish, but *Jewish* heroes . . . In the midst of this grey, ordinary, every-day Jewish world, their deaths are a cause for hope *[yontevdike meysim]*.[77]

The second Yiddish edition sold extraordinarily well (over 14,000 copies in a period of months). In 1918, two *Yizkor* books were published in Europe: a Yiddish edition in Lodz; and a German edition in Berlin.[78] Both these publications followed the content of the New York editions closely, but the introductions were new (and pitched at a lower key), the one written by Shmarya Levin, the other by Martin Buber.

The powerful myths which took shape during the Second Aliya acted as only one among a number of important factors in the later development of Jewish nationalism in the *Yishuv*. True, the images of blood and soil, of sheer heroism[79] as the negation of *Galut* (Exile) and guarantee of *Geulah* (Redemption); of the new man as direct heir to the warriors of ancient times (Judas Maccabeus, Bar Kochba) had established a firm grip on the collective psyche by 1914. It would be hard to exaggerate the power and the resonance of these symbolic codes. Their importance was rendered still greater because they had taken hold particularly in the Poale Zion party which was to produce so many of the dominant leaders of the labor movement and the *Yishuv*.

Nonetheless, there is no doubt that there was profound resistance within the Second Aliya itself to this particular set of myths. In some cases, opposition expressed itself in symbolisms of a contrary type (Rabi Binyamin's Semitic fraternity; Alexander Ziskind Rabinovich's fidelity to the traditional image of the "martyr" or "saint"). For his part, Brenner (and he spoke for an important strand of opinion) expressed a dogged scepticism when faced by a politics translated into hagiography or mythology.

No less important is the fact that mythologies do not work their influence in a vacuum. Their power depends on a combination of ideological, organizational, historical, socio-political, and contextual factors. It is ironic to note that of the editors of the Poale Zion *Yisker* books, with their clearly nationalist thrust, Khashin soon became a Communist, while Zerubavel emerged after the World War I as a leader of the pro-Communist Left Poale Zion in Poland, once again an orthodox Borochovist. And Ha-Shomer Ha-Tsair, which no doubt took its name (partly, at least) under the impact of the *Yisker* books, published and republished between 1916 and 1920, developed as a bulwark against nationalist maximalism.

The mythology recorded by Zerubavel during the *Yizkor* controversy of 1912 represented an important part of the political legacy passed on by the Second Aliya. It made the emergence of the most extreme forms of nationalism within the labor movement a possibility. Potentialities are not necessities, but they are none the less important for that.

NOTES

In preparing this essay I benefited very much from conversations on the subject with colleagues and friends at the Hebrew University: Menachem Brinker, Hannan Hever and Shmuel Werses. I would like to take this opportunity to thank them for their generous advice (though, of course, responsibility for the contents and for any possible errors is entirely my own).

1. For semi-official histories of the labor parties during the Second Aliya see, *e.g.* Y. Ben Zvi, *Poale tsiyon ba-aliya ha-shniya* (Tel Aviv, 1950); Y. Shapira, *Ha-poel ha-tsair: ha-rayon ve-hamaase* (Tel Aviv, 1968).

2. On ideological adaptation during the Second Aliya, *e.g.* Y. Kolatt, "Ideologya u-metsiut bi-tnuat ha-avoda be-erets yisrael," Ph.D. thesis (The Hebrew University, Jerusalem, 1964); Anita Shapira, *Berl Katsnelson* I (Tel Aviv, 1981), pp. 45–95. (*Cf.* J. Frankel, *Prophecy and Politics: Socialism, Nationalism and the Russian Jews 1862– 1917*, Cambridge, 1981, pp. 366–452).

3. For a rare insight into the extreme psychological strain to which the pioneers were often subject, see Aliza Zhidlovsky, "Hevle klita," in B. Habas, ed., *Ha-aliya ha-shniya* (Tel Aviv, 1947), pp. 554–58.

4. On the crisis at Mesha: M. T. "Khronika: mi-mesha," *Ha-poel ha-tsair*, nos. 10–11 (Tamuz–Av 5668/July–August 1908), p. 26. (Rabi Binyamin was employed in the administration of the Kinneret training farm at the time and was among those who went to join the defense of Mesha. He added a note to M.T.'s article calling on the workers in Judea to find jobs in Galilee, thus reinforcing the small and beleaguered Jewish labor camp there.)

5. R. Binyamin, "Al-odot 'yizkor'," *Ha-poel ha-tsair*, no. 8 (24 January 1912), p. 12.

6. *E.g.* Yosef Aharonovich wrote in 1910 with clear reference to the *shomrim:* "Only the worker who says (to use the words spoken by a Jewish worker in Galilee)—'If my rifle were taken from me in an attack, proving me incapable of guarding our property here in Eretz Yisrael, I would commit suicide'—is capable of guarding our property and the honor of the nation." "Le-inyanei ha-shaa," *Ha-poel ha-tsair*, no. 19 (27 July 1910), p. 4. A report from Hadera in *Ha-poel ha-tsair* described enthusiastically the arrival of Ha-Shomer in the colony and a typical member as "covered from head to foot with ammunition—and there is pride on his face: the pride of the man whose work as guard is honorable and is executed faithfully." Ben-Yona, "Mikhtav me-hadera," *ibid.*, no. 22, 4 September 1910, p. 14.

But an early sign of doubt at this time can be seen in the refusal by Yitshak Vilkansky, the manager of the Bet Arif farm (but also associated with Ha-Poel Ha-Tsair) to permit the workers to take on the armed guard of the crops, reportedly declaring: "This is not Galilee! You don't need weapons here. This is none of your business." "Mikhtavim la-maarekhet," *ibid.*, p. 16.

7. *Ibid.*, no. 11 (13 March 1911), p. 16.

8. "Al-odot 'yizkor'," *ibid.*, no. 16 (26 May 1911), p. 19.

9. 12 May 1911, in the Brenner papers, Archive and Museum of the Jewish Labour Movement (Tel Aviv) (henceforth AMJLM) IV/104/74.

10. Y. H. Brenner, "Tsiyunim," *Ha-poel ha-tsair*, no. 22 (28 August 1911), p. 7, note.

11. "Tsvi Bartanovsky, zikhrono li-vrakha," "*Yizkor: matsevet zikaron le-halele ha-poa-lim ha-ivriyim be-erets yisrael*, ad, A. Z. Rabinovich (Jaffa, 1911), p. 16 b.

12. The use of the term '*ivrim* (Hebrews) rather than *yehudim* was frequent in Second Aliya writing. This distinction often served a clear ideological purpose, usually to emphasize the existence of, or need for, a new type of Jew. Here, the author probably chose the term in order to underline the close racial and historical links of the Jews ('*ivrim*) and the Arabs ('*aravim*).

13. Maarekhet Yizkor, "Hakdama," *Yizkor*, pp. iv–v.

14. *I.e.:* "I have no doubt that if the two peoples understood their present role in history, they would realize the necessity of sharing the one and same position. It was out of this awareness that I wrote what I did in the introduction to *Yizkor*." R. Binyamin, "Al-odot 'yizkor'," *Ha-poel ha-tsair*, no. 8 (24 January 1912), p. 12.

15. For the composition of the board: "Mikhtavim le-maarekhet," *ibid.*, no. 11 (13 March 1911), p. 16.

16. R. Binyamin. "Shlosha she-metu ke-ehad," *Yizkor*, p. 2. This article was first published in *Ha-poel ha-tsair*, but the following passage in the original version was not reproduced in *Yizkor*: "He [Shveiger] was becoming—or, at least, wished to become—Arabized; to be like the best among the Arabs. In seeking to be totally Hebrew, he wanted to be like them. He wanted the Hebrew in him to be like the Arab in them. That writer who expressed fear in *Ha-shiloah* regarding the influence of the Arabs on the young generation in our country could have selected B. [Shveiger] as a perfect example. But so could all those who, from Benjamin Disraeli to the author of these lines, believe that the entire Semitic race really does have a great deal in common." *Ha-poel ha-tsair*, no. 12 (12 April 1910), p. 7. The writer referred to here was Yosef Klausner; see Ish Ivri [Klausner], "Hashash," *Ha-shiloah*, vol. 17 (July–December 1907), pp. 575–77.

17. See, *e.g.* Manya Shohat-Vilbushevich, "Ha-shmira ba-arets," *Kovets ha-shomer* (Tel Aviv, 1936), pp. 51–52; and Yisrael Shohat, "Shlihut va-derekh," *Sefer ha-shomer* (Tel Aviv, 1957), p. 26.

18. Y. Aharonovich, "Klape pnim," *Ha-poel ha-tsair*, no. 5–6 (1 November 1912), p. 4.

19. Y. Rabinovich, "Zikhronot ve-hirhurim," *Yizkor*, pp. 4–8. (In this article, Rabinovich, *inter alia,* described the following qualities as characteristic of the Russian-Jewish youth at the time of the Second Aliya: "taut nerves; the negation of the existent; ceaseless yearning; and a gallows-humor." [p. 5])

20. Zerubavel, "Kavim," *Yizkor*, pp. 76–77.

21. K. L. Silman, "Me-hirhure liba," *ibid.*, pp. 50–51. The poem/song quoted here is by Sara Shapira, "Al tal ve-al matar," republished, *e.g.* in Y. S. Segal (ed.) *Ha'meshorer ha'ivri: kovets shie tsiyon* (Cracow, 1905), pp. 42–43.

22. J. Thon, "Mesirut nefesh," *Yizkor*, p. 20.

23. Y. Giladi, "Zikhronot," *ibid.*, p. 16 b.

24. Y. Gorny, 'Shorasheha shel todaat ha-imut ha-leumi ha-yehudi-aravi ve-hishtakfuta be-itonut ha-ivrit ba-shanim 1900–1918," *Ha-tsiyonut*, vol. 4 (1975), pp. 72–113.

25. Y. Epstein, "Sheela neelama," *Ha-shiloah*, vol. 17 (July–December 1907), pp. 193–205.

26. R. Binyamin, "Masa-arav," *Ha-meorer*, no. 7 (July 1907), p. 272.

27. *Ibid.*, p. 273.

28. R. Binyamin, "Be-reshit," *Benatayim: kovets sifrut* (Jerusalem, 1913), p. 98.

29. R. Binyamin, "Hekhal ha-shalom," *Ha-toren*, no. 1 (New York, 1913), pp. 37–39.

30. Heruti [M. Smilansky], "Me-inyane ha-yishuv," *Ha-poel ha-tsair* (Shvat-Adar 5668/ January February 1908), p. 9. (*Cf.* his view there: "If Palestine belongs, in the national sense, to the Arabs who have settled here . . . then we have no place in it. . . . And if it belongs to us, then the national interests of our people come before everything else. There is no room for compromise here." *Ibid.*, p. 5.)

31. Y. Aharonovich, "Kibush ha-avoda o kibush ha-karka," *Ha-poel ha-tsair*, no. 12 (Elul 5668/August–September 1908), p. 3.

32. A. D. Gordon, "Pitaron lo ratsyonali," *ibid.*, no. 17 (1 July 1909), p. 5.

33. Heruti [M. Smilansky], "Me-inyane ha-yishuv," *ibid.* (Tevet 5668/December 1907– January 1908), p. 6.

34. On Borokhov, *e.g.* M. Mintz, *Ber Borokhov: ha-maagal ha-rishon (1900–1906)* (Tel Aviv, 1976). *Cf.* B. Borokhov, *Ktavim*, ed. L. Levite *et al.*, vol. I (Tel Aviv, 1955).

35. E. Blumenfeld [David Bloch], "Tsu der frage vegn der realizirung fun der teritoryal-polit. oytonomye in palestine," *Der yidisher arbeter* (Galicia), no. 18 (28 May 1908), p. 2.

36. Avner [Ben Zvi], "Undzer arbet in palestine," *ibid.*, no. 19 (4 June 1908), p. 2.

37. Y. Shohat, "Shlihut va-derekh," *Sefer ha-shomer*, p. 7. On this general theme: Y. Gorni, "Ha-yesod ha-romanti ba-ideologya shel ha-aliya ha-shniya," *Asupot*, no. 10 (1966), pp. 55–74.

38. A. Zaid, *Haye rishonim: mi-yomane Aleksander Zayd*, ed. E. Smoli (Tel Aviv, 1942), pp. 24–30.

39. Ester Beker, "Me-haye mishpahot shomer," *Sefer ha-aliya ha-shniya*, ed. B. Habas (Tel Aviv, 1947), p. 511.

40. See *e.g.*, *Sefer le-toldot ha-hagana*, ed. S. Avigur *et al.*, vol. 1 (Tel Aviv, 1954), pp. 213–15.

41. Y. Cohen, "Biryonim mi-[ye]me ha-pulmusim shel Titus ve-Shimon Ben-Kokhav," *Ha-shiloah*, vol. 12 (July–December 1903), p. 565.

42. Y.-n. Zvi [Ben Zvi], "Zikhronot," *Yizkor*, p. 12.

43. Avner [Ben Zvi], "Di yafo'er lektsyon," *Der yidisher arbeter*, no. 12–13 (14 April 1908), p. 3 (On this armed clash, he wrote there: "The Land of Canaan, after an interval of hundreds of years, has again reached out to taste the warm blood of its children.")

44. Ha-mashkif [M. Smilansky], "Hashkafa ivrit," *Ha-shiloah*, vol. 18 (January–June 1908), p. 381.

45. See *e.g.*, N. J. Mandel, *The Arabs and Zionism Before World War I* (Berkeley, 1976); and Y. Ro'i, "Yahase rehovot im shkeneha ha-aravim," *Ha-tsiyonut*, vol. 1 (1970), pp. 150–204. *Cf.* Y. Ro'i, "The Zionist Attitude to the Arabs 1908–1914," *Middle Eastern Studies*, vol. 4 (1967–68), pp. 198–242.

46. There were recurring demands in Ha-Shomer, when members were killed, that it permit retaliation in accord with the local usage of the blood feud. *E.g.* Y. Shohat, "Shlihut va-derekh," *Sefer ha-shomer*, pp. 26, 37; D. Zelbich, "Reshito shel ha-roe," *ibid.*, p. 119.

47. Y. Rabinovich, "Ba-arim u-vamoshavot," *Ha-poel ha-tsair*, no. 18 (27 June 1911), p. 4.

48. D. Frishman, "Ha-yadata et ha-arets? Reshimot mi-masaai be-erets yisrael," *Ha-tsfira*, no. 126 (3–16 June 1911). The same thought was expressed by Ahad Ha-Am in a letter to Moshe Smilansky two years later: "If things are like this now, I cannot but wonder what our attitude to others will be if one day we were to become the dominant force in Eretz Yisrael! If this is the Messiah, I prefer not to be here when he comes [yete ve-lo ahimine]." Ahad Ha-Am, *Igrot*, vol. 5 (Tel Aviv, 1959), pp. 201–2.

49. Zerubavel, "Savlanut," *Ha-ahdut*, no. 35 (11 Tamuz 5671/7 July 1911), p. 14.

50. *E.g.* Zerubavel, "Shte shitot," *ibid.*, no 36 (18 Tamuz 5671/14 July 1911), pp. 4–5, where he wrote that unless the Jews took upon themselves both to work and to guard their land, education in the new values would be impossible; "The spirit of the Redemption must permeate the entire enterprise."

In Zerubavel's view, the *shomrim* were duty-bound to insist on the employment of Jewish workers in the colonies. Otherwise, he insisted, the role of the guards would lose its historic centrality. Thus he could write later in 1911: "When we separate guarding from all the other branches of labor, it loses its significance in every way. Is it really such an ideal to sacrifice one's life in defending the property of some plantation-owner in Petah Tikva? Why is he privileged more than some money-lender or timber merchant in Kiev or Moscow to be defended by the best of the Jewish people? Is it really enough that the one makes his money out of the sands of Eretz Yisrael and the other out of the wood of the Russian forests? . . . What is so marvellous for us if we have a few dozen youth who in, and for, their job have learned to ride well and to shoot straight and fearlessly? Do we not have such elements in Exile too?" Zerubavel, "Shmira ve-avoda," *ibid.*, no. 5 (26 Heshvan 5672/17 November 1911), p. 4.

The tension endemic in the relationship between Ha-Shomer and its mother-party,

Poale Zion, which is evident in these lines, would lead to open confrontation during and after World War I. The Hagana was set up essentially to replace Ha-Shomer.

51. Zerubavel, "Yizkor (shivre raayonot)," *Ha-ahdut*, no. 13 (19 Tevet 5672/9 January 1912), pp. 17–18.

52. *Ibid.*, p. 17.

53. R. Binyamin, "Al-odot 'yizkor'," *Ha-poel ha-tsair*, no. 8 (24 January, 1912), p. 12.

54. Y. H. B. [Brenner], "Mi-tokh pinkasi," *Revivim*, no. 3–4 (Jerusalem, 1913), p. 165.

55. Zerubavel, " 'Yizkor' (shivre raayonot)," *Ha-ahdut*, no. 11–12 (12 Tevet 5672/2 January 1912), pp. 30–31. On the traditional Jewish attitude to history and historiography see *e.g.* Y. H. Yerushalmi, *Zakhor: Jewish History and Jewish Memory* (Seattle, 1982).

56. *Ha-ahdut*, no. 11–12 (12 Tevet 5672/2 January 1912), pp. 33–34.

57. *Ibid.*, no. 13, p. 17.

58. *Yizkor*, p. 20, note. In 1912, Chaim Tchernowitz (Rav Tsair), following a visit to Palestine, noted the fact that the rejection of the Galut had become a key factor in modern education there as nationalism replaced religion as the central didactic motif. "Only one thing," he wrote, "is clear to them [the teachers]: the old values have to be put aside and replaced by new values which are entirely national. But what are national values? A love for the past, perhaps? But the past is the Exile *[galut]* . . . [So some try] to create a Jewish type based on the period of the First Temple, on a Jefthah, . . . or a Samson, who lives by his sword and his bravery . . . This method is enthusiastically adopted by most of the teachers . . . who arrange rambles, olympic-type meets . . . and jousts in order to bring them [the children] up like Gideon, Jefthah and Samson, and they even try to teach the Bible from this point of view." Chaim Tchernowitz, "Rishme erets-yisrael: matsav ha-hinukh," *Ha-olam*, no. 11 (19 June/2 July 1912), pp. 3–4.

59. Asher Ben-Yisrael, "Mishkan ha-kabala (matsevet zikaron le-hayim atikim be-erets avot)," *Yizkor*, pp. 85–98.

60. A. Z. Rabinovich, "Al ha-neenakhim," *Ha-poel ha-tsair*, no. 19–20 (12 July 1912), p. 9. *Cf.* Yisrael Halperin, who notes that: "Every Jew who was killed as a Jew in the Middle Ages was considered holy *[nitkadesh]*." *Sefer ha-gvura*, ed. Y. Halperin, vol. 1 (Tel Aviv, 1941), p. xv. On Jewish martyrology, see Shimon Bernfeld, *Sefer ha-dmaot*, 2 vols. (Berlin, 1924).

61. R. Binyamin, "Al-odot 'yizkor'," *Ha-poel ha-tsair*, no. 8 (24 January 1912), p. 12.

62. Zerubavel, "Yizkor (shivre raayonot)," *Ha-ahdut*, no. 13 (19 Tevet 5672/9 January 1912), p. 19.

63. *Ibid.*, p. 17.

64. For contemporatry reactions to the death of Shveiger, Korngold and Melamed in the spring of 1909, see *e.g.* the mourning notice put out by Poale Zion and headed: "Comrades and Brothers." Among other things, it declared: "The best among us are falling victim to the barbaric attacks *[hets ha-pera]* of the Arabs. We have to ask: Where are you, the heirs to the Maccabees, the decendants of Bar Giora and Bar Kochba? Come to take the place of the fallen heroes." The Ben Zvi papers. AMJLM, IV/104/52. *Cf.* "Al kvarim hadashim," *Ha-poel ha-tsair*, no. 12 (23 April 1909), p. 16; and Sh.R., "Yafo: yediot meyuhadot," *Ha-tsvi*, no. 154 (2 Iyar 5669/22 April 1909) which describes the speeches given at a memorial meeting called by the workers in Jaffa.

65. Y. H. Brenner, *Ben mayim le-mayim* (Warsaw, 1910), pp. 54–56.

66. Y. H. Brenner, "Tsiyunim," *Ha-poel ha-tsair*, no. 22 (28 August 1911), pp. 7–8.

67. Shmueli sent reports and correspondence for *Ha-poel ha-tsair* from the colonies where he worked. His *nom de plume* was Mamashi; his original name, Menahem Mendel Shmuelevich.

68. Y. H. Brenner, "Tsiyunim," *Ha-poel ha-tsair*, no. 22 (28 August 1911), p. 8. The Biblical references here are to Ezekiel 3: 26; Amos 7: 16; and Genesis 18: 32.

69. See *e.g.* A. Z. Rabinovich, "Dvarim le-ahar heratsho," in M. Kushnir (Shnir), *Yosef Haim Brenner: mivhar divre zikhronot* (Tel Aviv, 1971), p. 300.

70. Bar Yohai [Brenner], "Gam ele anahot sofer," *Ha-poel ha-tsair*, no. 18 (21 June 1912), p. 11. For Brenner's view in this period of the role of martyrs and martyrology in Jewish history, see "Miluim," *Revivim*, vol. 5 (Jerusalem, 1912), pp. 112–16.

71. *Ibid.*, p. 12.

72. *Yisker: tsum ondenken fun di gefalene vekhter un arbeter in erets-yisroel,* ed. Zeruba-vel, Y. Ben Zvi, A. Khashin (New York, 1916).

73. For a detailed, and most interesting, description of the publication process of *Yisker* in New York, see Shabtai Tevet, *Kinat David: Ben Gurion ha-tsair* (Tel Aviv, 1976), pp. 339–357. The success of the Yiddish edition can be gauged by the fact that the *Forverts* devoted a full-scale and highly critical article to it. Olgin, "Di yidishe kolo-nyes in palestine zaynen geboyt oyf umglik fun di araber—un di araber firen a bitere milkhome gegen di yiden. Gedanken vegen tsiyonistishe bukh, 'yisker')," *Forverts* (3 June 1916).

74. S. Tevet, *Kinat David*, pp. 345, 350.

75. *Yisker: tsvayte fargreserte oyflage,* ed. A. Khashin and D. Ben Gurion (New York, 1916), p. 10. It should be noted, though, that Khashin and Ben Gurion were at pains to depict the Arab attacks as the result of robbery rather than of national conflict. Galilee was described as a "half-deserted region where the Beduin roam and where the Arab masses who live there have respect only for the hand which can defend itself." It is probable that attacks, such as Olgin's, from the "internationalist" wing of the socialist movement had brought home the problems involved in stressing the skirmishes in Palestine as the result of a basic conflict between two nations. (Ben Gurion had written a reply to Olgin which was so sharp that Leon Khazanovich, the editor of the Poale Zion journal, *Der yidishe kemfer,* refused to publish it.)

76. *Yisker: tsvayte fargreserte oyflage,* p. 9.

77. *Ibid.*, p. 10.

78. *"Yisker": a denkmal de gefalene shomrim un arbeter in erets-yisroel* (Lodz, 1918); *Jiskor: ein Buch des Gedenkens an gefallene Wächter und Arbeiter in Lande Israel, Mit einem Gedenkwort von Martin Buber* (Berlin, 1918). A second edition was published in 1920, trans. Gershom Scholem.

79. A full-scale analysis of national myths in the Second Aliya would require an extensive examination of the contemporary background: nationalism in Europe in the period prior to the World War I. See *e.g.* George Kennan, who notes "the survival into those decades of the romantic chivalric concept of military conflict: the notion that whether you won or lost depended only on your bravery, your determination, your sense of righteousness, and your skill. In this view, warfare became a test of young manhood, a demonstration of courage and virility, a proving-ground for virtue, for love of country, for national quality." *The Decline of Bismarck's European Order: Franco-Russian Relations 1875–1890* (Princeton, 1980), pp. 423–24. *Cf.* George L. Mosse, "National Cemeteries and National Revival: The Cult of the Fallen Soldiers in Germany," *Journal of Contemporary History* 14 (1979), 1–20.

18.

Social and Intellectual Origins of the Hashomer Hatzair Youth Movement, 1913–1920

Elkana Margalit

The Hashomer Hatzair youth movement was born in the Polish province of Galicia, then part of the Habsburg Empire, on the eve of the First World War. At the time Galicia was still agrarian and rather backward, inhabited chiefly by Polish and Ukrainian speaking peasants and a large Jewish urban minority, and it already enjoyed a certain measure of cultural and administrative autonomy. The great majority of those who founded the first Hashomer Hatzair kibbutz and shaped their group objectives came from this part of the world. During the war the movement spread into Congress Poland (under Russian rule), and at a later stage those members who came from there played an equally important part in it.

Most of the Hashomer Hatzair youngsters (known as Shomrim) who arrived in Palestine in or immediately after 1920 were between 18 and 20 years old. A few were in their early twenties, a difference which in youth movements is usually of considerable importance. What matters is that the group had matured during the war and while independent Poland after the war was struggling to fix its boundaries. This experience was decisive in shaping their attitude. Most of them had studied at secondary schools where the language of instruction was Polish, while a minority had attended German-speaking institutions. Those who had not attended high school—shop assistants, manual workers, and youth

Reprinted by permission of the author and The Institute of Contemporary History from the *Journal of Contemporary History* 4, no. 2 (April 1969): 25–46.

from religious circles—were a minority. The majority came from reasonably well-to-do Jewish families; their fathers were merchants, business agents, members of the liberal professions. A few had grown up on farms owned and administered by Jews, while a handful were children of highly skilled and well-to-do craftsmen. During the war, no doubt, they shared in the general impoverishment, but they still belonged to the upper middle classes in local Jewish society.

Many of them belonged to circles that were assimilationist in language and culture. The vernacular used in branches of the movement was Polish, particularly in the larger towns. The literature of the movement as late as 1920 was very largely Polish, and even today statements by those who were then its members display the influence of Polish literature and Polish cultural nationalism, particularly of the literary circle known as Young Poland. However, an influential part of the movement originated in homes that were imbued with Jewish learning and the Jewish national tradition, and where Hebrew was the language of cultural intercourse and literary expression. Others came from homes where Yiddish was the vernacular and where the full range of traditional Jewish orthodoxy was practised, even though the children could and did speak Polish and attended Polish schools. But there were some who came from homes where the parents regarded themselves as Poles of the Mosaic persuasion; they were young intellectuals on the verge of assimilation.

Yet by the eighties and nineties of the nineteenth century, Galician Jewry as a whole had realized that there were no prospects for assimilation, and that there could be no genuine symbiosis with the majority surrounding them. Polish society simply rejected them, economically, socially, professionally, and culturally. It regarded them as a foreign body even (and possibly all the more) when they spoke and thought in Polish and identified themselves emotionally with Polish national aspirations. It was only natural that Jewish intellectuals and students, who were the first to try to leave the Jewish quarters both physically and spiritually and expected to acquire status and role in non-Jewish society, were also the first to find themselves facing a barrier that set a term to their expectations. They found themselves being *returned* to Jewish society in spite of their attempts at linguistic, cultural, and emotional assimilation. They found themselves rejected, uprooted, filled with a sense of frustration and social and national deprivation. People in this situation have been classified by social psychologists as marginal men, that is, persons falling between various cultures, torn between their desire for the society to which they aspire and the society to which they have been restored.

Yet it was not only the rejection by Polish society which affected them; the Jews of Galicia were still subject to unifying national urges, the small towns in which they lived still preserved their traditional way of life, the rich Yiddish vernacular, the traditional costume, faith, and educational system. Life was still effectively influenced by the late-eighteenth-century Hassidic (quasi-revivalist)[1] and Haskala (enlightenment) movements, while Zionism and its predecessors were making considerable headway. But the power of tradition, that is, the capacity of organized Jewish society to ensure continuity, to inculcate its spiritual, cultural, and religious values among the younger generation, was gradually being eroded following the economic impoverishment which accompanied their economic and social extrusion from and rejection by Polish society. The chief signs of this erosion were the movement from small country towns to larger urban centres, overseas emigration, and the inroads of secularization. Possibilities of going to the Land of Israel, which might have served as a cohesive factor, were still very uncertain in those years before and during the war. Traditional Jewish society was simply unable to accommodate these young men and women who were being returned to the Jewish fold.

The inevitable reaction took shape in the emergence of a Jewish cultural nationalism. These potential assimilants were moved by the desire to find an alternative identification, a social and spiritual fellowship that would dispel the sense of uprootedness; as an immediate answer to their own problems, Zionism was not yet a practical choice. Therefore the student and secondary school societies of a Zionist character before the war stressed the struggle against assimilation and for the most part engaged in sports, hiking, and scouting activities. There were few political attachments. Indeed there was a detachment from political activity. In general, intellectuals who are alienated from the surrounding society tend in certain conditions to be apolitical, to concentrate on individual inner experiences, to refrain from assuming any real responsibility towards society at large. Karl Mannheim described the German romantic intellectuals as 'alien to the world . . . socially unattached'.

It was from this cultural and social milieu that the two main organizations of what was later to be known as Hashomer Hatzair came into being.[2] First there were the scouting and athletic societies which in 1913 adopted the name Hashomer organization. These societies, to be sure, followed the pattern of the Polish Scout organization with its disciplinary and even para-military character. But scouting played an important part in the spiritual balance and physical education of young Jews at that time. Scouting and communion with nature instilled habits of order and cleanliness, a sense of duty and discipline, while reducing the tensions and anxieties which beset marginal men. Scouting hardened the physique and will of the young Jew, and fortified him against the difficulties of his life. It made him more 'natural', more 'elemental', and compensated for the intellectual and emotional hypertrophy from which he suffered. At the same time the Scout groups implanted a certain measure of national consciousness.

The second component of Hashomer Hatzair consisted of student and secondary school societies which called themselves Tseirei Zion (Youth of Zion). These study groups, first established in 1903, aimed to improve their knowledge of Jewish matters and were characterized by a Jewish national spirit; their devotion to learning combined variegated elements, carrying on the traditions both of the Haskala and of the casuistic system of reasoning in the Talmudic tradition. These qualities also became part of the heritage of the Shomer Hatzair type, counterbalancing the 'pagan' or non-Jewish elements that might be held to derive from the Scout movement. The two organizations united in 1913 under the name Hashomer; the name Hashomer Hatzair seems to have been adopted only in 1919.

In the first world war the whole of Galicia became a war front. At the opening of hostilities the Russians invaded eastern Galicia and penetrated as far as Cracow, finally withdrawing from the entire territory in July 1917. Almost half of the Jews of Galicia, some 400,000, fled in fear of the Russian invader; some went to Hungary, Moravia, and Bohemia, but more to Vienna, where about 175,000 Galician Jewish refugees were concentrated in conditions of great want and suffering. Families were broken up and were left without means of support. Fathers and older brothers were conscripted, the younger children found such work as they could. Those who remained behind under the Russian occupation suffered from want and pogroms, and large numbers were expelled, particularly in the districts near the front. Even when the Austrians returned to these areas the possibilities of reconstruction were restricted because of the shortage of food supplies and raw materials. Jewish social and political life was virtually paralysed. The press was strictly censored, while political leaders were either in the army or in Vienna.

The establishment of an independent Poland at the end of the war also proved to be a bitter disappointment to the Jews both politically and nationally, and involved physical and economic ruination. A wave of anti-Jewish excesses spread over Galicia and the whole of Poland during the wars between Poles and Ukrainians in Galicia in 1918 and 1919, and the war between the Poles and the Bolsheviks which ended only at the close of 1920. The most serious pogrom, in Lwow, coincided with the Armistice of November 1918.

The Judophobia of liberated and independent Poland was also felt in the schools. Jewish pupils and students were expelled, Polish pupils maltreated them, and there were anti-Semitic outbreaks on such charges as Jewish assistance to the Bolsheviks or evasion of military service. The Poles also consistently opposed the Jewish demand for national autonomy within the sovereign Polish state, and for safeguarding of the status of minorities.

During this general collapse of Jewish society, and in the absence of any assured future that marked the years 1914–20, the generation of the founders of Hashomer Hatzair, mostly born round 1900, grew to maturity. All their written and verbal statements show that the dominant experiences of their adolescence were refugee life in Vienna, and anti-Jewish excesses in Galicia and Congress Poland during and after the war. In brief, the tragedy of Polish and Galician Jewry during that period, and their exclusion from Polish society.

Hence it is not surprising that they were a grave, thoughtful, and introspective group, yet equally enthusiastic and full of faith, radical, thirsting for life, gay, and poetic. They longed for roots and community identification because they were tense, perplexed, rootless, isolated, lacking security and without the least confidence in the maintenance of the contemporary social patterns and their own future social and professional status. As inner compensation they developed a sense of purpose, a belief in a communal mission requiring their personal dedication, fulfilment of their ideals in their own lives; fervent in their zeal and their desire to reassess all values, they were also anxious, tense, and restless, to a degree that was almost neurotic. They thirstily accepted all kinds of influences and contradictory ideas, no matter how superficial, and equally swiftly rejected them. They displayed considerable initiative and vitality, which found expression in the establishment of institutions, funds, journals, and organizations, and in the emergence of a leadership. This was achieved with their own meagre resources, with virtually no assistance from adult society.

The Vienna period during which the Hashomer Hatzair youth were refugees, lasted roughly from 1915 to 1918 and had an important effect on their organization. (It might be more correct to describe this as the Vienna-Galicia period, since contact with Galicia did not cease even during those years. Indeed, Jewish refugees began to return as early as 1915, with the partial withdrawal of the Russian occupying forces.) The Vienna branch dominated the movement; it had about 1000 members when the refugee influx was at its height. Most of them continued to attend Polish high schools, spoke Polish, and conducted their group activities in that language. Young Austrian Jews did not as a rule meet the refugees, nor was there much contact between the latter and non-Jewish youth movements. Even during the war Galicia continued to be the spiritual homeland of the movement, and when the war came to an end Galicia regained its prominence, particularly the Lwow branch. Nevertheless, Vienna had exerted on them a western influence, both Jewish and non-Jewish. There they met other young people belonging to the western Jewish 'Blau-Weiss' movement, whom they admired for their freedom, calmness, and naturalness (in their relations with the other sex, for instance), although they had reservations about their Jewish and Zionist inadequacies.

In Vienna they met Z. Bernfeld and the group connected with the journal *Jerubaal,* including members of the Jewish youth movement from Germany. They attended the Jewish youth rallies held in 1917 and 1918 on the initiative and under the inspiration of Bernfeld, who also helped to introduce the ideas of Gustav Wyneken, one of the main figures of the German Free youth movement. They also met Martin Buber. Considerable influence was likewise exerted by the circle of refugee Jewish intellectuals from their own country who had rallied round the journal *Moriah,* to which Hashomer members gave their support. So it is not surprising that in 1917 the first general Hashomer Hatzair publication appeared in Vienna and served to define their essential identity. This was *The Guide to Hashomer Leaders* (referred to hereafter as *The Guide*). Vienna also saw the beginnings of a press that spoke for the united movement (the Scouts and the Tseirei Zion as mentioned) in a journal called *Hashomer,* issued in Polish.

However, what was most important in this period was the emergence of leaders who gave expression to the longings of their generation and helped to educate them. They were a group of intellectuals, some of them slightly older than most of those who in due course would set up Hashomer Hatzair in Palestine. Some of them studied at the Vienna Rabbinical Seminary. They came from well-to-do homes (study at the Seminary required an appreciable outlay and secured exemption from the army) and families which claimed descent from outstanding Jewish scholars and learned rabbis. They had a thorough knowledge of Judaism and were equally familiar with Haskala, Hassidic, and Jewish national literature. They were serious, enthusiastic, and full of faith, with a marked talent for analysis and exposition. The destruction of Jewish society as it had existed before the war turned them into leaders of, preachers to, and spokesmen for the younger generation, formulating what they described as a 'world outlook' for youth. Without material resources and with rare self-dedication, they journeyed from town to town and village to village, preaching, educating, singing, and walking with their younger members, and shaping a group identity for the younger generation. The arts of mass manipulation and control, tools of the professional revolutionary, were alien to them. Class and political movements, the view of society as a 'mass', made little appeal to them, even after the experiences of war and revolution. By origins and education, their concern and activity lay almost entirely within the educational and moral spheres. They remained introvert intellectuals. More experienced and more resolute than their younger companions, whose distress often bordered on neurosis, they could both express in pictures and symbols (admittedly macabre and morbid on occasion), the psychosocial conflicts and difficulties of the others, and speak to them in the lively and comforting idiom of east European Jewry, with its own special brand of humour, the friendly wit and shrewdness of the small Jewish town. At the same time they set out guiding lines and demanded action and responsibility. No doubt some among them were aware of political opportunities, but their main influence was felt during the period described imaginatively as that of the father at home, or of the Hassidic rabbi. Many of them had been at the 'courts' of Hassidic rabbis, and were familiar with the Hassidic modes of expression, dance, and song, and had imbibed the fervour and devotion that mark the Hassidic spirit.

Just as the leadership emerged spontaneously, so the youth movement as a whole grew rather than organized itself. It is hard to estimate their numbers. In May 1918 one of the leaders in Galicia estimated the membership of the movement, including the Vienna branch, at about 3000 in roughly 40 centres. In April 1919 the total number for the whole of Poland was given as 7,736 members in 110 branches. Compared with the total number of Jewish high school pupils, this was by no means negligible; but it was only a small proportion of Jewish youth as a whole.

During the war Vienna served as a centre of communication and

information about developments in the Jewish world. Despite censorship, the Viennese press reported the issue of the Balfour Declaration
early in November 1917; and news of the establishment of the Jewish
Battalions, also known as the Jewish Legion, reached them as well. By
1919 Vienna was the centre through which persons expelled from Palestine by the Turks in the early part of the war were already returning
home, and it was there that the Hashomer Hatzair met the elderly labour
ideologist Aaron David Gordon and other leaders of Hapoel Hatzair,
the Labour Party which had originated in the Land of Israel itself. This
meeting was to have a very considerable influence.

Although its cultural sources were many and varied, Hashomer Hatzair as a phenomenon was characteristic of east European Jewry in
general, and more particularly of Galician Jewry, and it was the first and
only 'free' youth movement within that community. A primary leitmotif
during the Galicia-Vienna period as expressed in *The Guide* was the
Hebraic-Judaic one, not the theme of Jewish economic and physical
distress, but the theme of 'Jewishness' itself, that is, the spiritual problem
of being a Jew among the Gentiles, and the sense of frustration of the
intellectual young marginal Jew who continued to view himself and
Jewish society with Gentile eyes, that is, in terms of the rejection by the
dominant group whose language and norms he had adopted. In some
the consciousness of their position reached the point of self-hatred, an
almost pathological sense of deficiency. 'We are neither full and healthy
men nor full and healthy Jews . . . There is no harmony in these elements
within our character', *The Guide* insisted as it listed the defects and
shortcomings of the Jew. Young Jews lacked resolution, energy, and *joie
de vivre;* they were consumed with despair and *Weltschmerz,* suffered
from excessive spirituality, immersed themselves in the study of faded
writings of an out-of-date and irrelevant culture. The reason for this
split in their character was the failure of the attempt to assimilate and
the contradiction between the norms and standards inculcated in Jewish
homes and the realities of Polish schools and streets. As a result, these
youngsters said, young Jews were incapable of spiritual identification
and emotional unity. They could not dedicate themselves to or love
anything with all their might. And since neither the Jewish nor the
surrounding society could provide solutions, this uprooted youth sought
salvation and redemption from within, in almost eschatological terms
and out of sheer despair. What was required was personal improvement
from within, and the improvement of character and mores within the
community of youth which should create its own independent values.

The Guide demanded that they should once again be 'whole and healthy men, and whole and healthy Jews'.

This meant a return to the life not of the diaspora Jew, but of the historical 'Hebrew'. They were to be 'young Hebrews' in the likeness of the 'ancient Hebrews', in the spirit of the prophets. The Bible was a source of inspiration to all who seek the divine and the beautiful. Without being religious, they were to be imbued with a religious spirit, in the sense of a moral revivalism and inner faith. In the camps held in 1918 the Shomer leaders praised the early revivalist movement which had revolted against religious petrifaction and external ceremonials such as those of the Essenes and Hassidism. They studied the Prophets, the New Testament, and the writings of Buber. They studied Nietzsche and Weininger, and discussed the teachings of Schopenhauer as an example of the heroic approach to life. This emphasis on the prophetic religious ideal, on moral perfection, possibly involved a considerable withdrawal from reality, but was necessary as an inner compensation and balance for marginal man—the 'compensatory phantasy' of eschatological movements, to use Norman Cohn's term. Hence their devotion to the Jewish past, and to the Hebrew language (*not* Yiddish), and to education in Judaism. Hence also their eager desire for an all-embracing and redeeming outlook on the world.

Yet it is impossible to conceive of any Jewish group of intellectuals in the struggling mass of east European Jewry that could remain absolutely alienated and separate. *The Guide* in 1917 already spoke of the objective of Aliya (immigration) and productive labour on the soil of Israel, although not as something obligatory, and in the same year a group of Halutz (pioneer) Shomrim had been formed in Vienna with the aim of going to Palestine as ordinary workers and settling on the land. *The Guide* also stressed the community of fate of the youth and the Jewish masses. It rebuked Jewish intellectuals for the Chinese wall they had erected between themselves and the masses, and praised the 'incomparable Russian youth who go to the people'. (This was written before the 1917 Revolution and refers to the populists.) It called on the Shomrim to bring the message of national revival to the masses, for although the 'ancient Hebrews' and the morals of the Prophets were foci of self-identification for the youth of Hashomer Hatzair, they kept in view from the start the image of the pre-war Hashomer, the watchmen, and what was described in 1919 as 'heroic and zealous Zionism'. In the early years of the war this was almost the sole link between them and the labour movement in Palestine.

During the Galicia–Vienna period they found in Martin Buber the principal spokesman of their ideas on the return to Judaism and of their psycho-social situation in general. In his *Drei Reden über das Judentum,* Buber, too, referred to the 'deep cleft in our being' for which his proposed remedy was the self-affirmation of Jews as Jews and the passionate effort to achieve wholeness. His ideals were 'all-embracing justice and all-embracing love'; he too looked back to the Jews of the patriarchal age, and made a distinction between the ancient Jews and diaspora Jews. The goal must be to create a world under Divine rule. He called on Jewish youth to become men, but in a Jewish fashion, and this phrase became a password and slogan for Hashomer Hatzair. He called for a return to the Jewish people, not as it was then but as it could become in accordance with its moral and messianic mission. Conscious identification with the *Volkstum* and the community would overcome the division in the consciousness of the young.[3]

Today these statements no doubt appear confused and misty, but for the young of those days they corresponded to a deep spiritual need. Throughout Europe there was a sense of decline and collapse, widespread fear and a feeling that things were coming to an end. The Viennese intellectuals in general, many of whom were Jewish, had this feeling even before the war, and it found expression in the Young Vienna Circle, which included Schnitzler and Karl Kraus. Friedrich Heer[4] wrote that the three major intellectual currents in Vienna before 1914 were depth psychology, represented by Freud and Adler; the religious-philosophic approach, particularly existentialism, among whose founders he includes Buber; and the literary efflorescence. Heer looked on all three as a search for certainty and faith in the face of the impending collapse of the Habsburg Empire. More recently Lefebvre described the intellectual currents in Vienna round about 1910 as a reflection of the collapse of society, state, and family, and of the undermining of all intellectual certainties.[5] The leading representatives of these movements served Hashomer Hatzair as the exponents of their own psycho-social situation.

It was characteristic of this situation that of all the various tendencies then operating in the German youth movement, Hashomer Hatzair found itself closest to that of Wyneken, with its demand for uncompromising morality as a basis for a specific youth culture with ethical socialist, humanist, and pacifist aims, rejecting the philistine, materialist culture of the bourgeoisie and the anti-Semitism which was already permeating German youth movements.

The Hashomer Hatzair followers of Wyneken formulated his ideas as follows: Youth is an uncompromising aspiration towards ideals, towards an ethical absolute. It is an eternal cultural value bearing its own moral ideals, and being eternal must not be regarded merely as a stage in development, a stage when the individual was an incomplete and immature human being. Youth is therefore called upon to establish its own culture within its own free community and without any compulsion or imposition of opinions on the part of adults. To this Wyneken's Hashomer Hatzair followers added the ingredient of traditional Jewish culture.

Historians in general are agreed that German Wilhelmine society could not satisfactorily accommodate its youth. It was authoritarian, given to malaise and cultural despair, and marked by the flight from reality of many of the young into the bosom of nature and the historical past. This was their protest against and rejection of the family with its authoritarian structure, the German school with its oppressive discipline, the Church, and in general the conventions of a society which they regarded as false, hypocritical, and philistine.[6]

Not so Hashomer Hatzair. Its members did use similar expressions, and it did bear a certain resemblance to the Wandervogel, but they were not in flight from a powerful, secure, and entrenched Jewish society like the prosperous German middle class of those days, nor from an oppressive and tyrannous Jewish school and family system. On the contrary, its literature often expressed esteem for the patriarchal-style Jewish family and the fear that it was on the verge of collapse, a fear that grew following the outbreak of war. It called on young Jews to honour family practices, including the religious *mores,* to exert themselves at school, to respect their teachers. The young Jewish mother was urged to teach her children the principles of Jewish nationalism and Zionism in order to counteract assimilation. Even the belief in God and adherence to the Jewish faith are referred to in the early Hashomer Hatzair documents. The revolt against the parents, in connection with pioneer training away from home and emigration to Palestine, came later. These young Jewish intellectuals from Lwow and Prszemsyl did not belong to the company of Karl Fischer and the Wandervogel; they were as far from them as from Wilhelmine society.

If the Wyneken terminology nevertheless found a place in their vocabulary, it was largely because it expressed the ideas of independence, self-identity, and 'freedom' of youth. Their own frustrations on their return to a collapsing Jewish society, their need for complete revaluations, made them open to such ideas, but for specifically Jewish reasons. The idea that the young had a lofty moral and radical cultural mission appealed to their own sense of mission. Flight to the culture of the past also suited parallel tendencies in Hashomer Hatzair, with its inclination towards religious and Hassidic revivalism. These aims were rephrased in terms of the 'objective spirit' and 'moral absolute' formulated by Wyneken. Buber's 'all-embracing love' was equated with the 'Eros' of the German movement, with Freud and Blüher.

A similarity of language is to be found again in the denunciation of what they termed 'philistinism'. The term was never defined, but was understood to comprehend the characteristics of the bourgeois way of life, denounced for moral and aesthetic reasons. Hashomer Hatzair members used the term to express disapprobation of those elements which they rejected in the adult Jewish environment: materialism, the pursuit of 'concrete' results, the mockery of youthful idealism and of its belief in change and improvement. Contempt for bourgeois values was widespread in European intellectual society, and was not confined to the young. The writings of Ibsen and Nietzsche were well known in Hashomer Hatzair circles, and their popularity is easy enough to understand if one considers their rejection of the domestic Jewish environment. The mood of cultural despair, of disappointment with European civilization, and the theme of the 'decline of the West', originating before the war, was even more marked after its conclusion.

Hashomer Hatzair was also influenced by another intellectual trend in Europe, namely Romanticism, particularly the varieties that emerged in Germany and Poland. In a sense the structure of Galician society and the position of its intellectuals were not entirely dissimilar from the social conditions which favoured the Romantic movement in late-eighteenth- and early-nineteenth-century Germany, and the style and ideals of German Romanticism found a possibly unconscious echo within Hashomer Hatzair. It reached the movement through the German youth movement, the cultural influences of Vienna, Martin Buber, and above all, Polish literature, as can be seen from even a superficial acquaintance with Hashomer Hatzair publications between 1917 and 1920 and during the early years in Palestine. They clearly reveal the resemblance, in forms of expression, concepts and character types, to those generally classified as 'Romantic'. The ideas of organicism and idealism, as against the mechanistic and materialistic outlook; of self-perfectibility and the significance of the individual; the force of ethical radicalism and the mood of religiosity.

The Romantic style and the Romantic individual were marked by lyricism, enthusiasm, emotionalism, and imagination, by the tendency to poeticize life, by a delicacy of feeling in particular towards Woman. They were also inclined towards meditation and self-analysis. All these characteristics were to be found to a greater or lesser degree in the youth movement. Many of them were also to be found in Polish Romanticism: the gravity and pathos, the romantic ecstasy, the enthusiasm, the heroism, the sense of martyrdom, abstraction, symbolism and allegory, devotion to the legendary past and religious feeling. The Polish homeland did not then exist as such; it was something in which the Pole had to believe. The major Romantic Polish writers were exiles, counting on revolutions that had either failed or not yet come about. Mickiewicz, Slowacki, Krasinski, evinced a dualism, a helplessness, a withdrawal from reality which arose from the absence of any practical connection with political and social realities; the Polish nobility, more particularly those in exile, concentrated on the past because they had nothing except the past and their high hopes. Nationalism, national suffering, and national history were the central and decisive themes of this literature. Theirs was, however, a frustrated, spiritual, mystical, and eschatological nationalism. The Poles were the holy people, the martyr people suffering for the whole of humanity, the crucified nation; and the soil of Poland was the Holy Land.[7] Schultz and Wellek account for German Romanticism by the country's backwardness, the slowness of industrialization and the delayed emergence of the middle classes, the absence of any unifying political or social organization, the *Kleinstaaterei* resulting from having been a collection of petty dukedoms. Some at least of these characteristics were undoubtedly to be found in Galicia as well.

Given these psychological and social influences, Hashomer Hatzair developed a special form of societal relationship—the youth community or educational group representing an intimate emotional association of companions. Its literature describes the small educational group as a community, consisting of eight to ten members with a leader of about their own age, held together by ties of love and brotherhood. It was intended to serve as a kind of family, and to enable them to live a full and varied life. This was no ordinary study, sports, or rambling group, but a cell to which they were fully committed, and concerned for the moral improvement of the members. Within the group, the sense of identification was established by conversation, by joint confession, and by shared silence, from which emerged the style characteristic of the first Hashomer Hatzair members in Palestine: a style made up of despair, declamation, outpourings of the soul and confession. One of the early members described it in the terminology of the German youth movement as *Personen und Ideengemeinschaft*—community of individuals and ideas. This concept of community is stressed in Romantic thought as well as in Buber. It is defined as a category of 'organic' or 'natural' societal relationships, unconscious and non-purposeful, based on 'sympathetic sentiments', in contrast to society, which is based on pragmatic and rational ties. The concept has also been enlarged and diversified, and defined as one that stresses 'emotional decisions and voluntary submission to a principle of salvation that makes men friends and brothers'. In its Jewish manifestation, the youth movement contained all these elements.

With the approach of peace and the return of the Galician refugees to their homes, Hashomer Hatzair members were beginning to ask whether their organization would continue to be restricted to its own community and to passive meditation 'outside the world', or whether they ought to join in some public and social activity 'within the world'. At a large meeting of Shomrim in Galicia, the adherents of Wynekenism came under fire. The critics rejected Wyneken's meditative, experiential, and passive aims as being totally unrelated to the problems of society. It was not surprising that his ideas had attracted German youth, for the affluent German society lacked ideals, disregarded the life of the mind and inner experience, and so they had been carried away by Wyneken's exaggerated romanticism and peculiar morality and taken refuge in experiential individualism and fantasy, in 'living life to the full' and in self-expression, self-declaration, when alone in their own youth community. The sufferings of Jewish youth had different origins. They required youthful energy, discipline, and education in Zionism, not sentimental self-contemplation. They should prepare themselves for a life of labour in the land of their fathers. This plea was made in particular by Eliezer Rieger. Even before this meeting, some Hashomer Hatzair leaders had been calling for training in physical work within the Pioneer movement which also emerged in eastern Europe during the war years, in preparation for emigration to Palestine and a year of service there.

Opinions were divided. Shlomo Horowitz, an intellectual and idealistic young leader, thought the essence of Hashomer consisted in the primacy of spirit over matter, belief in socialism not in its materialistic aspects, but as a system placing the interests of the whole society before the interests of the individual, and in activism, which meant the *personal* realization and implementation of principles. All these features connected it with Prophetic Judaism. Other speakers rejected every political programme and party activity; for them the Jewish question was a subjective one, and the goal of Hashomer Hatzair was only to educate a fine and healthy Jewish type. In general political and broad social questions received little attention. The meeting adopted no resolutions about training for and emigration to Palestine, or about adherence to any political party.

For many of those attending the meeting, born about the turn of the century, the time had come to leave the youth movement and to choose a profession, to think about making a living. If Jewish society had been capable of absorbing them, or if non-Jewish society had been prepared to receive them, it is possible that the impact of the experiences they had gone through would have faded as they adapted themselves to social realities, as happened in other 'free' youth movements. But the years 1918–19 were years of anti-Jewish excesses. Impoverishment and pogroms reinforced their Zionist education in the movement, and now that the war was over, the chance to train for and emigrate to Palestine seemed far greater than it had been until then. Towards the end of 1918 the Central Committee had called on the Shomrim to join the Jewish Legion in the British army. Some of the Polish members were on their way to Palestine in November 1918, but emigration on a large scale developed only in 1920.

From Hashomer Hatzair literature and reports of the time, it is clear that the members had no common opinion about party affiliation. Some suggested joining the General Zionists, which was a non-socialist movement, while others proposed joining the Zionist left-wing Marxist party, Poale Zion, provided certain conditions were met. The suggestion had been made earlier that they should join Hapoel Hatzair, a group in Palestine which, while emphasizing the value of physical work, was non-Marxist and rejected socialism and the class war. A further proposal was that the proper thing to do was to set up an independent Hashomer party in the spirit of the youth movement, consisting of the small individually-linked groups which had emerged from the movement.

As against all these, there were those who rejected the very idea of a political party. In 1920 Meir Yaari, who in due course was to become the leader and principal spiritual mentor of the movement suggested that only when they reached Palestine should the members decide on the party they wished to join; he himself felt drawn (albeit with various reservations) to Ahdut Haavoda, a socialist party embracing the principle of class war, which had been established in Palestine on the close of hostilities.

Nor was there any unity among the members before they emigrated regarding socialism as a practical policy. For some the ideal was a moral and educational socialism based on Jewish tradition and rejecting historical materialism. Both Meir Yaari and David Horowitz[8] believed that the aim of socialism should be to create economic conditions which would permit the full development and liberty of the individual within the cooperative community. Hence Yaari rejected official communism because it enslaved the individual to 'the metaphysical concept of the state', although he did not completely reject the possibility of class war in Palestine, along the lines represented by Ahdut Haavoda.

Horowitz drew his inspiration from the German party known as *Die Geistigen,* inspired by Wyneken and Kurt Hiller. Hiller belonged to Gustav Landauer's circle and wrote for the journal *Aufbruch,* pacifist and socialist in tendency. Horowitz rejected the doctrine of historical materialism, demanded a full share in the economy for every person 'through the equal distribution of work and bread', and the creation of a classless nation; but he did not elucidate the means by which these objectives were to be achieved.

The idea of collective settlement in Palestine, referred to as the Shomer Colony, attracted those who were graduating from the movement and already planning their move to Palestine. Horowitz, the first advocate of this kind of settlement, claimed that there was the place where the revolt of the youth against materialist society, against urban life and poverty, against the street, the home, and the school, could be carried forward, and the ideals of the Prophets, of Jesus, Spinoza, and Marx, could be made a reality. The new society, the Shomer Colony, would be based on common property.

If Hashomer Hatzair members had no common political concepts, what gave them the remarkable cohesive force which held them together in the diaspora and sustained them when they came to Palestine, while other bodies crumbled away or were absorbed? The organization went through many crises, and was open to the penetration of political and party influences. What sustained it was that it was first and foremost a 'free' educational youth movement; culturally, emotionally, and socially it embodied a special mentality and communion, a special way of experiencing things and the surrounding world.[9] The idea of the community as an independent and voluntary association based on partnership, with common belongings and equality in economic satisfaction, which also served as the locus for the education of the individual and his moral improvement, was what made Hashomer Hatzair hostile to any form of mechanical, compulsory, and disciplinary organization. It was the mainspring behind the approach to the kibbutz, which they called the 'organic' kibbutz.

Believing in the primacy and liberty of the creative individual within the community, in the responsibility of the individual and his capacity to decide about his own deeds, Hashomer Hatzair warned against the subjugation of the individual to any centralized apparatus, including the state. In the Shomer Colony there would indeed be common property and economic equality, but no 'communism of life', since each and every person had to be an individual. Man had to make demands on himself. Life should be noble and beautiful. Throughout Hashomer literature we repeatedly find phrases like 'the aspiration to the beautiful life', 'the ideal and great life'. Nationalism and Zionism had to be heroic, and socialism had to be morally 'aristocratic' and idealist. Hashomer was presented as an inner truth; the Kingdom of Heaven need not be sought outside the human personality. The characteristic Hashomer style is exemplified in such phrases as 'human revolution from within', 'the revolt of youth', 'the aspiration towards truth and beauty', all charged with an enthusiastic emotionalism which has something religious about it and a good deal that is neurotic. The language was in part adopted from Dostoevsky and Nietzsche, Freud and Blüher, Jesus and the Prophets, A. D. Gordon and Gustav Landauer; the words 'suffering', 'weltschmerz', 'Eros', and 'salvation' recur again and again. So do large generalizations intended to comprehend and solve all the problems of the world. These more solemn preoccupations were supplemented by guidance on personal behaviour, such as how to behave in society, how to sing and dance and when to be quiet, relations between one man and another, and above all those between man and woman.

The consciousness of independence and identity, largely derived from the conditions within Jewish society during the war, in addition to the attitudes referred to above, generated in Hashomer Hatzair the sense of being an elite, a spiritual and moral vanguard. It was highly selective in its choice of members, among whom there developed a strongly marked 'We' consciousness. They displayed many of the characteristics that investigators have observed in religious sects (as against churches); enthusiasm and moral radicalism among the youth, the search for self-adjustment, and the preference for the spiritual as against the material, the introspective withdrawal into the community, the consciousness of exclusivity, faith in the inner truth that has been revealed to them. Yet there is a difference between a religious sect and a common age-group in respect of the capacity of each for continuity. Moreover, the youth movement lacked the supernatural element, the factor of the sacred which appears to ensure the stability and continuity of a sect. Religiosity is not in itself religion. Nor did the Hashomer Hatzair youngster ever reach that extreme point of alienation from society which alone makes the emergence of a sect possible. But in their scheme of redemption and salvation, and their awareness of being an elect, it is possible to find eschatological features, the 'chiliasm of despair' which marks radical messianic movements. But the parallel should not be pushed too far; Hashomer Hatzair was after all a youth movement which set itself rationalist, cultural, educational, social, and political goals, although it was (and remains) salvationist insofar as it was a protest and perfectionist movement, aspiring to the establishment of lofty personal and social moral standards. These may be criticized as impractical, as falling outside reality; yet few would argue that the totality of man is exhausted by the utilitarian and the rational.

It was this peculiar character of the movement which largely explains the independent course it has taken since. During the early twenties, the two kibbutzim established in Palestine by Hashomer Hatzair members differed from other kibbutzim by stressing their 'organic' character, the ties holding the members together. In 1926–7, when a severe economic crisis hit the country and the Zionist movement, Hashomer Hatzair grafted on to the youth movement and its kibbutzim a revolutionary Marxist ideology, embracing historical materialism, class war, and social revolution. But it was still a specific Zionist-Pioneer Marxism, differing from other varieties, Jewish and non-Jewish alike, in its voluntarism, its emphasis on the freedom and education of the individual, and above all in deferring the realization of the social revolution until after Zionist aims had been achieved.

Later, in the thirties, its members described themselves as independent Marxist revolutionaries. They rejected both the Socialist and the Communist International, severely criticizing the latter for its opposition to Zionism and also on democratic grounds; they tried to establish ties with like-minded independent socialist groups such as the ILP in Britain. At the same time they became an important factor in the Zionist organization, with which they were always willing to co-operate, as they were after the State of Israel was established with liberal and non-socialist parties. At the same time they have always sought ways to achieve co-operation between the Jewish and Arab workers of the country; they advocated a binational constitutional regime as a method of achieving peaceful relations between the two peoples.

Hashomer Hatzair was and remains a complex structure, combining an educational youth movement with the kibbutz style of life and a Zionist-Marxist political party of the 'third force' variety. These three elements do not always dwell at ease together. If it has overcome contradictions and dangerous deviations this is largely due to its heritage from the youth movement, embodied in a consciousness of group identity of a very special type, in the pioneering Zionist spirit, and in dedication to the kibbutz way of life.

NOTES

1. Hassidism was, and in a somewhat different form still is, a mass religious Jewish movement, containing mystical, enthusiast, and revivalist messianic elements, which began to spread in the second half of the eighteenth century. In this movement a central part was played by the charismatic figure of the Tsadik (Saint, righteous man) or Rebbe (teacher), the spiritual and real leader of the Hassidic community, who delivers and is concerned for his followers and is a Man of God graced with special powers enabling him to influence God's will and dispensation.
2. Hashomer was an organization of Jewish watchmen or guards, founded in Palestine in 1909. Its first members belonged largely to the Poale Zion Socialist Party. It aimed to defend the lives and property of the young Jewish settlements, and to establish guard villages which would combine agriculture with regional watch and ward activities. It also had certain political aspirations and in general symbolized the pioneering spirit for the younger generation of Jewish nationalists, in eastern Europe and elsewhere.
3. M. Buber, *Drei Reden über das Judentum;* 'Zion und die Jugend', *Der Jude,* 1918–19, 'Jüdish leben', *Jerubaal,* 1918–19.
4. F. Heer, *Land im Strom der Zeit; Osterreich gestern, heute, morgen* (Vienna, 1959); H. Kohn, *Karl Kraus, Arthur Schnitzler, Otto Weininger (aus dem Jüdischen Wien der Jahrhundertwende)* (Tübingen, 1962).
5. H. Lefebvre, *Le langage et la société* (Paris, 1966), 25–26.
6. See G. Masur, *Prophets of Yesterday* (London, 1963); G. L. Mosse, *The Crisis of German Ideology* (New York, 1964): W. Laqueur, *Young Germany* (London, 1962); H. Blüher, *Wandervogel: Geschichte einer Jugendbewegung* (Berlin, 1912); G. Wyneken, *Der Kampf für die Jugend* (Jena, 1920), *Schule und Jugendkultur* (Jena, 1919), *Die Neue Jugend* (Munich, 1914).
7. Cf. G. Brandes, *Poland—A Study of the Land, People and Literature* (London, 1904).
8. David Horowitz was one of the most brilliant ideologists of Hashomer Hatzair while still in Galicia, and during his early years in Palestine. Later he became Governor of the Bank of Israel and has written many books on economic and social problems.
9. Of the Hashomer Hatzair literature on which this essay is based, the following may be mentioned: *Poradknik dla Kierowników Szomrowych* (Vienna, 1917); *Haszomer,* periodical (Vienna, Lwow, Warsaw); *Nowa Mlodziez,* periodical (Lwow); *Hazak We'emac,* periodical (Warsaw).

19.

The Histadrut: From Marginal Organization to "State-in-the-Making"

Ze'ev Tzahor

Chaim Weizmann arrived in Palestine in April 1918. The shore of Jaffa, where he disembarked from his ship, was only four short kilometers from the front lines between the great powers, then locked in battle in the closing weeks of World War I. Weizmann had hurried to Palestine, which had not yet been completely conquered by the British, in order to take judicious advantage of the momentum created by the Balfour Declaration and lay the groundwork for the "Jewish National Home" that had been promised. For that purpose, he was accompanied by the Zionist Commission, a distinguished group of renowned Jews from Britain, France, Italy, and elsewhere. The objective of that body was to unify the Yishuv within a single framework and take over the reins of leadership.

At the outset, Weizmann was received as a statesman by personages of the Yishuv, and the Zionist Commission he headed was seen as the potential basis for an autonomous administration in the Yishuv.[1] But it soon became evident that the powerful tradition of fragmentation was older than the Yishuv, greater than any aspirations for organizational unification. Moreover, the new British government, preoccupied with the problems attendant on the military conquest of Palestine, did not rush to extend its support to an autonomous Jewish government. Indeed, there were no less than seven different chairmen of the Zionist Commission over its first three years of activity; its prestige plummeted, and in 1921 it was disbanded.

Published by permission of the author.

In the formative period between the British conquest of Palestine in 1918 and the establishment of the British Mandatory government in 1922, there were several bids to unite the Yishuv within an agreed organizational framework. During that same time span, a number of different bodies were set up: the Temporary Committee for the Jews of Palestine, the Founding Assembly, the Palestine Council, the Assembly of Delegates *(Asefat Hanivharim)*, and later the Zionist Executive and the National Council. The very fact that there were so many different trial runs to generate new structures in such a brief period points to the myriad difficulties involved. Hopes to reach a solid full-scale agreement that would constitute the basis for a broad-based joint organization, encompassing both ultra-Orthodox Jews in Jerusalem and socialists who wanted to settle the Jezreel Valley, proved illusory, and repeatedly came to naught.[2]

The thrust to forge a comprehensive unity founded on internal consensus was ahead of its time. Yet efforts aimed at unification yielded partial fruits, principally among secondary groupings that formerly had been active on a local basis and now, after conquest by the British, had expanded to become in effect organizations on a national level in the Yishuv. The middle class in the towns and in the agricultural settlements set up the associations B'nei Binjamin and Ha-Ezrah. The ultra-Orthodox community created the United Rabbinical Council, and religious Zionists gathered around the Chief Rabbinate. Voluntary associations of Jews with a common origin that had been active at a local level became Yishuv-wide associations, such as the Organization of Sephardi Jews and the Association of Yemenite Jews. The Women's League was founded, and the official green light was given for political parties to engage in a range of activities.

In retrospect, it is evident that all this intense activity by an array of organizations was confined to the limited arena of special interest groups. At that juncture, there was only one voluntary body set up that rapidly expanded to become a significant national force, namely the organization of Jewish workers, known officially as the Histadrut, the General Federation of Hebrew Workers in Palestine. The present chapter intends to examine the process by which the Histadrut was transformed into the central organization of the Yishuv.

ESTABLISHMENT OF THE HISTADRUT

In December 1920, eighty-eight delegates, the elected representatives of 4,433 workers, gathered in the still unfinished workshop of the Technion in Haifa for the founding convention of the Histadrut. Those delegates, chosen by small workers' parties, did not have a clear conception of the organization they wished to set up. Initial ideas had been fuzzy and inchoate. Behind all the rhetorical pathos, one can discern the general will to create a socialist workers' organization aspiring to build Palestine on a new social basis. The spectrum of conceptions on whose foundation the founding fathers wanted to erect the edifice of the Histadrut was variegated, paralleling the number of diverse socialist currents then active in Europe. The delegates to the founding convention brought with them vivid memories of the constant rivalry and squabbling that had plagued and fragmented the workers' movement during the period of the Second Aliyah (1904–1914), in particular the split between the two main labor parties, Hapoel Hatzair and Ahdut Haavodah. The founding convention was stormy, its deliberations rocked by contention. The leaders of the two parties, all from the ranks of the Second Aliyah, recalled the many previous attempts to forge unity that had failed, foundering on the rocks of internal rivalry and mutual distrust. They had felt compelled to launch this renewed bid in light of the fact that each party was now eagerly wooing the mounting waves of immigrants beginning to flow into Palestine, the first tide of the Third Aliyah (1919–1923).

The virtual ultimatum from immigrants who had arrived a few months earlier, arguing that it was now imperative to set up a unified organization for all workers, paved the road to the establishment of the Histadrut.[3] Thus, the founding convention had been convened under escalating pressure from new immigrants, but it was conducted under the seasoned hand of veteran leaders from the Second Aliyah. They had a legacy of long and trying experience, during which they had watched many of their associates who had immigrated together with them to Palestine leave the country, seared by the flames of ideological dispute. As a result, these veterans were specifically concerned about the ideological ardor of the new immigrants. The majority of this new wave came from Russia, and a number had either actively participated in the Bolshevik revolution or had watched from close-up as a small group of zealots, well-organized and totally committed, had altered the course of history. This brief brush with destiny and revolutionary experience became their guiding banner. Soon after arrival in Palestine, even before the establishment of the Histadrut, they had set up the "Labor Legion" (Gdud Haavodah), which conceived of itself as a vanguard that would steer the workers' movement toward the bright dawn of social and national revolution. Members of the Second Aliyah feared that the revolutionary model the young immigrants had brought with them in their ideological and experiential baggage might shift the focus of activity from "pioneering constructivism," in tune with the special requirements of the situation in Palestine, to dangerous shortcuts inspired by Soviet Bolshevik praxis. Those same veteran workers, who later demonstrated their special gifts as leaders, understood in the course of deliberations at the convention that the pressures of the day allowed them precious little leeway: they had no choice but to agree to the establishment of the Histadrut. Even in their first year of immigration, this new wave of immigrants already far outnumbered the entire membership of all the old parties taken together. They were firm in their resolve to create this organization, with or without the blessing—or if need be even the participation—of the Second Aliyah workers. Although the latter acceded to their call for a joint organization, they were careful to ensure it would be under their complete control. Thus, although the founding convention was convened under pressure from members of the Third Aliyah—and against the express wishes of veteran Second Aliyah activists—the organization that was finally launched was firmly in the hands of the latter.

Following its establishment, the Histadrut announced that it was taking over responsibility for all spheres of constructive activity in the workers' movement: settlement, defense, trade unions, education, housing construction, health, banking, cooperative ventures, welfare, and even culture.[4] The problem was how to transform such an ambitious all-embracing program into concrete practical results on the ground.

Despite the fact that the founding convention proclaimed an appropriation of areas of activity of the parties and various other organizations established by the Second Aliyah, the leaders of the Histadrut ran up against difficulties in attempting to gain control over the new domains that the organization had staked out. They discovered that their old party associates remained faithful to the earlier arrangements and structures. In point of fact, they themselves were also torn between the two frameworks. In the initial period, this dilemma had a paralytic effect, hindering them from shifting their office base—which was in principle their focus of party identification, and where they were personally familiar with each and every worker—to the still amorphous Histadrut.

The interests of the parties, in particular the dominant party, Ahdut Haavodah, were not always isomorphic with those of the Histadrut, which had invaded its former territory. The latter was reluctant to transfer its periodicals, funds for mutual aid, subcontracting firms, and shares in various cooperative schemes. It is true that those assets were comparatively small, and the accounts of most of these ventures were in the red, yet each was imbued with its own unique set of feelings and values; above all else, these had been the instruments that had enabled the party to survive.[5]

It soon became clear that apart from the internal difficulties, the Histadrut found it necessary to struggle to consolidate its status and position externally as a brand-new organization in the Yishuv. Outside the ranks of the Labor movement, its creation had been accorded very little attention and was generally ignored; in other instances, it met with open opposition.[6] The new British government, the Zionist movement, and various groups and persons in Britain and the United States who had agreed to assist in the creation of a Jewish National Home showed no interest in the fledgling Histadrut. The array of broad national tasks which the organization had staked out as its responsibility made cooperation indispensable, especially in the form of financial assistance from sources outside the Labor movement. There was no certainty that those potential sources would be forthcoming with any concrete help, since they viewed the Histadrut with suspicion as a new socialist organization.

Together with their families, the initial members of the Histadrut amounted at the most to some 10 percent of the total population of the Yishuv. Even among the ranks of laborers and salaried workers, only a small fraction joined the organization. For example, nothing but a minute percentage of Sephardi wage-earners in Jerusalem decided to join, though they constituted the main core of the city's "proletariat."[7] Its feeble beginnings were acutely manifest in the fact that even from among its "natural constituency," supporters of the parties that had founded the Histadrut, participation sorely lagged. Thus, almost 8,000 votes were cast for the parties Ahdut Haavodah and Hapoel Hatzair in the elections to the Assembly of Delegates held in April 1920, but only half of this number chose to become Histadrut members.[8]

The Histadrut was not alone: there was an array of analogous organizations active in Palestine at the time it was founded. The Mizrahi Organization, for example, operated an educational system, employment offices, soup-kitchens, and a periodical. It had considerable public potential, and this not only by dint of the fact that a substantial proportion of the Yishuv was aligned with the religious establishment.[9] There was even reason to think that the communist party in the Yishuv, the Socialist Workers' Party (Mifleget Poalim Sozialistim, Mapas), would prove successful in setting up a competing local organization of its own.[10]

Gnawing doubts about the practical underpinning for the ambitious plans proclaimed by the founding convention were manifested the very day after its creation. The announcement that the new organization would now serve as the main address for new immigrants, a source for employment and a bank for financial assistance, led to a situation where on the first day it opened its offices, there was already a throng of workers, largely unemployed, waiting at the door and expecting to be helped. The initial structures that had been set up in relative haste were not prepared to meet the expectations which the infant organization itself had spawned, and they cracked under the pressure after a few short days—though not before the first office of the Histadrut in Tel Aviv had been ransacked during the first week of operation by disappointed and disgruntled jobless workers.[11] The initial picture that emerges is one of a fledgling and feeble organization, devoid of genuine support, lacking in financial means, leadership, or direction.

FIRST FLEDGLING STEPS

In the first half of the 1920s, some 100,000 immigrants poured into Palestine, joining a Yishuv that numbered some 60,000 at the beginning of the decade. The gap between the burgeoning wave of immigration and the relatively weak absorptive capacity in Palestine generated substantial unemployment and an acute economic crisis. Yet sweet are the uses of adversity: that very crisis was harnessed for the Histadrut's benefit, and transformed into a positive impetus.

The acute unemployment buffeting the economy of the Yishuv immediately after the setting up of the British civil administration was the first breach through which the Histadrut was able to penetrate into new social strata. It did not have the requisite instruments ready to deal with the crisis, and the majority of those who sought assistance went away empty-handed, but an important new precedent had been established: the Histadrut was now the identified institution for workers to turn to, and its operating arrangements began to take on palpable contours.

A kind of waiting list of unemployed workers was set up. The Histadrut had taken over the economic firms operated by the parties, which operated by subcontracting, and now accepted all manner of work from any government center—on occasion even certain jobs which it itself initiated, although there was no specific organization or individual that had placed the order. Naturally, the managers of the Histadrut economic companies wanted the highest possible remuneration in return for their subcontracting services, but profitability was not the bottom line. The main idea was quantity: to amass as many jobs as possible, and almost at any cost. In this way, the acute economic crisis at the time of the organization's establishment was harnessed as an engine for change, transformed into an instrument of expansion into new sectors. Already during its first few months of existence, the Histadrut had managed to become the largest single employer in the Yishuv. Some 1,800 persons were working in the subcontracted jobs it handled, approximately one third of its entire membership.[12] These numbers were supplemented by workers in the cooperative agricultural settlements (hahityashvut haovedet), and those on the payroll in other institutions of the Histadrut.

Histadrut historiography tends to stress the national mission of the organization and its role in the various domains of pioneering constructivism, while its somewhat less heroic task as a trade union defending workers and their rights is underplayed. However, the initial important achievements of the Histadrut were precisely in that field. During its formative period, the overwhelming majority of wage-earners in Palestine were recent immigrants, without any support structures to fall back on in the public domain, lacking a profession and source of economic assistance. They were hired under difficult working conditions at low pay, without any workers' rights firmly anchored in law or in the traditions of labor relations.[13] In those spheres, the Histadrut was able to inject a new ethos into public consciousness, including the sector of private employers—an ethos that prior to its creation had been quite rare in labor relations in Palestine. Although there had been workers' committees for decades in the Yishuv, the fundamental right of workers to organize was recognized only after the Histadrut's establishment. The incentive for work was transformed: instead of the image of a brutal "supervisor" standing over workers with a whip in his hand, now there was a place to turn to if a worker had a complaint about physical abuse by an employer. Now, for the first time, the right to strike was recognized, and in the event of dismissal, it was the obligation of the employer to explain the reason. The Histadrut devoted substantial attention to the problems of the individual worker on the job, to complaints about swindling and trickery in the workplace, tardy payment of wages, etc. The Office of Information that had been operated by the political parties during the period of the Second Aliyah was expanded into a well-organized Labor Exchange, creating a network of information on available jobs throughout Palestine. In this way, the Histadrut became a source for job placement in the private sector as well.[14] Institutions such as "workers' courts," aid funds, and programs for recreation and education became an integral component of the everyday Histadrut activities from an early period, and in these areas it could boast evident success.

Upon closer examination, it is clear that there was a manifest link between the economic and social crisis in the Yishuv and new phases in the Histadrut's development. This is not meant to invoke a thesis that conceptualizes the history of the Histadrut as dialectical stages of crisis and upswing. Its ability to answer to the needs of the immigrants and workers was not the product of any deterministic processes. Rather, it was the result of a correct reading of the concrete, given situation by the activists who rose to the top echelons of leadership during the trying circumstances of the period of the Second Aliyah. They had amassed a fund of intensive practical experience based on trial-and-error, learning to distinguish between theory and reality. While attaching high value to utopian ideals, they had also learned to make necessary compromises between ideological fundamentalism and practical possibilities, and to implement those compromises immediately. The adversities they faced during the Second Aliyah gave birth to institutional means such as communes, the Kupat Holim sick fund, and funds for mutual aid—all of which enabled them to survive in the harsh social and economic environment in Palestine. These various instrumentals were part of the survival kit of vital experience they brought with them to their new functions in the Histadrut; with their aid, they had been able to cope with and adjust to the swirl of changing conditions in the past.

The British administration, the leadership of the Yishuv and the local councils were not in a position to provide social services to the mounting wave of immigrants flooding into Palestine. In the wake of the British victory, the Zionist movement published a dramatically phrased announcement: "Do not force the issue!" Appropriated from the arsenal of traditional messianic discourse, this was tantamount to a suggestion not to migrate to Palestine at that juncture.[15] Even though the Zionist Executive also wished at a later point to restrict immigration, its leaders did not attempt to stop the Histadrut from promoting itself as a national tool for immigrant absorption.

The Zionist Executive may have had various motives. Perhaps they did not see the Histadrut, which had no internal resources of its own to fall back on, as a serious threat to their own position. They may also have been pleased there was an organization to which new immigrants could turn directly, a body ready to help absorb the pressures of rising immigration. It is possible there was another consideration as well: there may have been some Zionist leaders who welcomed the advent of a radical organization, expecting it would be prepared to push ahead with controversial bold steps which no responsible political movement could permit itself except at great risk.[16] In any event, the expansion of the Histadrut into the very center of public activity was both rapid and multiform.

During the first year of its existence, a central leadership and organizational structure had not yet crystallized; as a result, initiative was shifted downward to various localities and to the level of local leaders. This approach, based on conditions prevailing in the field and the readiness of the members at the grass roots to volunteer their services, was remarkably well-suited to the orientation of veteran immigrants of the Second Aliyah, their ethos and personal experience. Within a short number of weeks, local committees, called "workers' councils," were set up across the length and breadth of the Yishuv, from Metulla in the far north to Beersheba in the south. In general, these were small committees that brought together only several dozen workers.

In each locality, the activities took on a local complexion in keeping with the specific problems of the branch. Thus, for example, the Kupat Holim opened by the workers' council in Tiberias was supported financially by the women's organization Hadassah in the United States, while the branch in Rehovot recruited a doctor using its own funds. The fee for medical assistance in the two localities also differed, as did the method employed to collect it. The workers' council in Zikhron Ya'akov was formed by merging the party branches there; in Petah Tikvah, by contrast, the parties had refused to transfer their assets, and the workers' council was forced to rent new premises. In Hadera, the local Histadrut council took it upon itself to cut down the trees in town at its own expense, while the workers' council in Rishon le-Zion erected storerooms for the British Army in Sarfand as a subcontract arranged (as circumstances would have it) by an Arab contractor. The local leadership also developed along different lines from place to place. In the majority of cases, it was drawn from party activists, mainly Ahdut Haavodah members, yet there were places, particularly in towns such as Haifa and Tel Aviv, where the old-timer activists preferred to continue to serve the party, while the Histadrut workers' council was made up of Third Aliyah newcomers.[17]

This phase in the shaping of the Histadrut ran parallel to the formative stage of the Yishuv under the new conditions ushered in by the British Mandate. The ability of the Histadrut to adapt flexibly to the shifting situation was a significant factor during its first year of existence. This was a necessary—albeit not sufficient—condition for institutional survival. The very advantages which enabled the Histadrut to take the initiative and expand into every conceivable arena also proved to be serious drawbacks. It soon became evident that there was a gap between promise and reality: the ambition of the organization as a place to turn to for beleaguered Jews in financial distress, or in the spheres of health and unemployment, and its ability to fulfill worker expectations. The fuzzily defined borders between its own domains and the parties which had set it up generated mounting friction. The pressure from such bodies as agricultural settlements and cooperatives to receive preference, special privileges based on a common party past, or the historical right to work as a pioneer *(halutz)* generated internal tensions and led to bitter altercations.

The principal obstacle was the lack of a financial mainstay, a reliable source to fund activities. The great latitude given to initiatives and the encouragement of a broad spectrum of diverse programs was not based on a solid budgetary framework. Even the source expected to cover the salaries of Histadrut activists on the organization's payroll was not spelled out from the start. The basic deficit was created in the sector of subcontracting arrangements initiated by the Histadrut, which was done without proper accounting or careful review. There were localities in which loans had to be taken out, in others salaries were not paid, and in the majority of places the deficit simply piled up until the point was reached where all activities had to be discontinued.[18] This situation compelled the Histadrut to halt its uncontrolled expansion, take a hard look at what it was doing, and search for other ways to put its house and activities in order.

From its inception, its outreach was ambitious; the Histadrut did not limit itself to dealing only with the immediate needs of its 4,500 members. The spread of its activities, the tasks it overburdened itself with, and the facilities it managed to set up within a short span of several months were numerous and diverse. Seen from this perspective, it rapidly gained a broad foothold in a number of critically needed areas, particularly associated with the massive influx of immigrants and their absorption. However, this headlong expansion far exceeded the Histadrut's organizational capacities and meager finances. Consequently, it was evident that the Histadrut's amalgam of stubborn resolve, brazen energy, and uncritically exuberant growth also harbored a potential threat: it could undermine and destroy the very edifice being built.

The May 1921 riots, some six months after its establishment, constituted a key juncture where a kind of mirror was held up in which the Histadrut could ponder its own reflection. Beginning on May 1, Arabs attacked Jewish settlements in the center of the country. In concrete terms, these disturbances represented the first manifestation of Arab rebellion against the Jewish presence, extending beyond the confines of a mere local incident. Havoc was widespread: forty-seven Jews lost their lives in the riots, and some 150 were injured.

The direct link between this tragic violence and the Histadrut existed in several domains. First, according to the findings of the Haycraft Commission of Inquiry appointed by the British High Commissioner Herbert Samuel after the disturbances, the riots had exploded in response to a demonstration organized by Jewish workers to mark international May Day. The Arab violence was explained by the argument that Jewish immigrants were introducing Bolshevik ideas to Palestine, and this was the consequence.[19] Second, disturbances centered on Immigrants' House in Jaffa, in which several dozen new Jewish immigrants were living at the time. They had joined the Histadrut immediately after arriving in Palestine and were to be absorbed in the Yishuv with the help of the organization. The bloodbath perpetrated against these isolated, abandoned, and helpless immigrants was interpreted as being a serious failing on the part of the Histadrut. Third, there was the brutal murder near Jaffa of the writer Yosef Chaim Brenner (1881–1921), the angry prophet of the Histadrut. Brenner had taken an active role in its establishment, and during one of the moments of crisis at the founding convention had demanded the "right to shout" in the name of the workers who wanted to set up the Histadrut, in opposition to the view of their leaders. At the time of his death, he was regarded as the greatest literary voice of the working class in the Yishuv. Fourth, the Haganah, the military organization for self-defense and security which the Histadrut had set up in 1920, failed to protect the Yishuv—or at least the workers and facilities of the Histadrut.

On this occasion as well, the acute crisis harbored a constructive element, advancing the Histadrut to a further stage in concerted efforts to consolidate its position in the Yishuv. The gap between intentions and ability to perform and deliver, so painfully obvious during the turmoil of the Arab riots, forced the Histadrut leadership to engage in self-criticism. The basic conclusion drawn was that it needed to change its modus of operation. The organization would have to develop a committed and energetic central leadership, to gain control of various internal initiatives, to hammer out a method of action that was unified and unambiguous, to deal seriously with the setting up of a military defense force, and most importantly—to accept national responsibility in the political sphere as well.[20]

As a direct consequence of the disturbances, individuals in the private sector in the Yishuv, in particular the owners of orchards in the agricultural settlements, agreed to replace Arab workers by Jews, relying on the Histadrut to supply Jewish workers organized in their locality.[21] Now for the first time, the Histadrut was granted direct financial aid from the national institutions, although this move was described as a one-time loan allocated for the well-defined purpose of paying the bill for security. But here was a narrow breach, an opening that would quickly widen.[22]

In retrospect, the most important consequence of the tremor in the wake of the riots was felt in the arena of leadership. As mentioned earlier, the Histadrut had been founded without any prior preparatory administrative steps; its day-to-day operations were handled by the leadership of the parties as a by-product of their party activity, without any coordination and or clear policy guidelines. Given the Histadrut's operational problems, it was decided to find someone who would dedicate himself to managing its daily affairs and the strengthening of its position. The man chosen for that task was David Ben-Gurion.

BEN-GURION

Like most of his associates from the Second Aliyah, Ben-Gurion had not been overly enthusiastic about the creation of the Histadrut. He did not attend the founding convention, since he was away on assignment in Europe at the time as a party representative, but when he learned that a decision had been made to go ahead with the organization, he gave it his formal blessing.[23] When he returned to Palestine in the summer of 1921, he carried out a comprehensive review of the overall situation in the Yishuv. Ben-Gurion came to the conclusion that it was necessary to radically alter the forms of organization in order to adapt them to the challenge of the great opportunity confronting the Zionist movement.

He was convinced that the spearhead of Zionism was the Labor movement, but that it was not properly organized. The method for the proposed new organization was revolutionary: he worked out a plan centered on the idea of a "general commune, held together by military discipline, of all workers in the Yishuv. It would be given control of all agricultural settlements and urban cooperatives, the job of supply and maintenance of the entire working population in the Yishuv and the ordering and management of all public work projects in Palestine."[24] In terms of his plan, the workers' movement was to be the "sole contractor for all public and private work in Palestine." All wages of all workers would be deposited in a common community chest, and that fund would in turn take care of the entire range of material and non-material needs of all Jewish workers in the land.

Yet the apparent revolutionary radicalism of a man who had voiced sympathies for the Bolshevik party[25] is deceptive. Ben-Gurion's aim was not the radical reform of man and society. In spelling out the specifics of his plan, he stated explicitly that the purpose of his scheme was not "revolutionary pronouncements on the matter of international class antagonism, war against imperialism and the like." His proposal was designed to place powerful organizational tools in the hands of the workers' movement in the Yishuv—for the express objective of advancing their specific aims. A careful examination of what Ben-Gurion termed the "messianic vision" indicates that his first and foremost goal was the realization of Zionism.[26] Ben-Gurion's proposal was debated in the institutions of his party Ahdut Haavodah and turned down. His comrades believed it was unrealistic. In all likelihood, they viewed him as a man whose primary talents lay in managing an organization—he was not an idea man, a theorist and thinker who could point the path forward.[27] It is probable this is the reason they suggested to him that he become centrally involved in Histadrut operations.[28]

In the historiography of the Histadrut, Ben-Gurion is customarily mentioned as its first General Secretary—this despite the fact that during the first few months after its establishment, he was not in Palestine, nor was he in any way active in the organization. Moreover, when he was elected as a Histadrut official, he was not appointed General Secretary, but rather to a post as one member in a troika making up its secretariat. However, this formal distinction is actually of secondary importance. After all, in the final analysis, everyone, including those who preceded him in the Histadrut, agreed: only now, one year after its creation, had the Histadrut become an independent organization capable of implementing its own activities, and this achievement was directly attributable to Ben-Gurion's personality and authority as a leader.[29]

His special talents that would make him one of the outstanding leaders of the Jewish people in the modern era became evident immediately after he took up his post in the Histadrut, which was then small and faced with a welter of practical hurdles in efforts to consolidate its position. The first such special attribute was his faith in his mission and his capacity to realize that task. He believed in his ability to transform the Histadrut into a national instrument for the realization of Zionism. He was endowed with an extraordinary capacity for work, and his dedication was limitless. Ben-Gurion had little truck for useless idle talk, and the work atmosphere that he introduced in the leading institutions of the Histadrut differed radically from the inefficient approach that had typified operations at the party offices. He was painstakingly thorough, a perfectionist, and anything he looked into was examined from A to Z, down to its most minute specifics. His diaries were replete with surprisingly detailed individual impressions based on his extensive reading of books and reports. While not disregarding such details, he also developed a special ability to focus on the central issue. He later characterized himself as a "man devoted to a single task"—depending on the major task demanded of him at the given moment.[30] "Infatuated with the possible," he knew the secret of the alchemy between obstinacy and the readiness to compromise, between fundamentalist ardor and operational pragmatism, between "vision" and policy, between concentration of authority in his hand and the decentralization of responsibilities among his aides.

By dint of these abilities, and not some delegated authority—after all, he was only one of three members of the secretariat of the Executive Council—Ben-Gurion succeeded over the short span of a few months in virtually transforming the Histadrut. As a first step, he immediately called a halt to the local initiatives that had characterized the operations of the Histadrut right from its beginning. He set about classifying the various experiments, distinguishing those that had retained vitality from initiatives that had misfired. He built up a well-defined hierarchy, reduced the competencies of the local workers' councils, and occasionally replaced the activists in the districts without consulting anyone else.[31] The leadership of the Histadrut, the Executive Council, was set up on the basis of a binding code of regulations. Following Ben-Gurion's proposal, nine members were elected to the Executive, three of them full-time secretaries, plus six additional persons drawn from the ranks of the heads of important institutions, such as the Agricultural Center, the Department of Immigration, and the Office of Public Works and Building. This executive body, composed of leaders of the principal operative arms of the Histadrut, strengthened the tendency toward concentration and central control. The way the Histadrut was managed was drastically revised. Initially, the source of initiatives and basis for authority had been concentrated in local branches; now, a centralized top-down structure of administration was instituted.

Ben-Gurion knew each and every member of the Executive personally before his election, and was well-positioned to evaluate their specific skills and past achievements. It is true that Executive members were elected to their jobs by the parties, four of them by the opposition party Hapoel Hatzair. Nonetheless, the common lines of approach shared by members of the new Executive chosen along with Ben-Gurion—and especially the fact that they all were primarily concerned with practical matters and not abstract intellectual or theoretical issues—point to his influence in their election. It is a fact that those elected to the new Executive were not the prominent party figures from the Second Aliyah. Shlomo Kaplansky and Efraim Bloch-Blumenfeld, leaders of Poalei Zion, Berl Katznelson, the most outstanding among the "non-affiliated," and Eliezer Shohet and Eliezer Yafe, leader of Hapoel Hatzair, along with high-profile intellectuals such as Aharon David Gordon, were not on the Council. Their non-participation did not express any act of rejection. Each had their personal reason for not taking part in the active executive echelon of the Histadrut. Yet it appears that Ben-Gurion did not particularly regret their absence.

Significantly, there was not a single leader from the ranks of the Third Aliyah in the Histadrut Executive, despite the fact that they constituted a decisive proportion of those who had originally set up the organization. Ben-Gurion had strong suspicions about their revolutionary ardor, imported from Eastern Europe. Years later he spoke about "alien, unholy fire," [32] alluding to the fact that the active segment of people from the Third Aliyah had come from "back over there," the ambience of the Russian Revolution. It is true that the majority had not necessarily participated on the Bolshevik side, but their excitement about that stupendous event which had changed the face of history implanted its mark on them, a lasting imprint from which they would never break free. In contrast with the revolution in Soviet Russia, the Histadrut was a minor and insignificant organization, limited and local in outlook. They longed for something much more bold. Ben-Gurion also dreamed of a large and daring organization; he himself, only a short time previously, had proposed a general commune of all workers in the Yishuv, and, as mentioned, he displayed certain sympathies for the Bolsheviks' methods.

But there was a salient difference between Ben-Gurion and the radicals. In his view, a powerful organization that wished to control and harness the life of the individual was not a design for realizing universal conceptions—rather, its sole purpose was to further the cause of national redemption. He had misgivings about any kind of dogmatic teaching and all-embracing "scientific" ideology. Ben-Gurion had learned from hard experience during the Second Aliyah that the special conditions in Palestine militated against transferring the complex of revolutionary ideas that had conquered hearts and minds in Europe to the struggle in Eretz Israel. Thus, for example, he was quick to drop dogmatic Marxism. In this he resembled his associates from the Second Aliyah, while prominent leaders of the Third Aliyah had strong and pronounced leanings toward the Marxist conceptions then gaining new ground throughout Europe.[33]

Thus, though Ben-Gurion aspired to grand and bold designs, he was well aware of the limits of what was possible. For that reason, he tried to appoint "men of action" to leadership posts, persons who had taken upon themselves the great responsibility of steering the Histadrut's helm in a concentrated and constructive manner. Even after changes in leadership personnel, the basic structures of the Executive were retained for many years. Although the new immigrants constituted a majority when the organization was formed, and their proportion rose as the wave of immigration continued to flow in, the Executive Council of the Histadrut, consisting of nine to twelve members, elected anew on an annual basis, was composed almost exclusively of activists from the Second Aliyah. In its first decade of operation, a total of some ninety members served on the Executive Council, and more than eighty of these were experienced old-timers. The remainder occupied only marginal functions on the Executive.

With the establishment of the central leadership, a new and decisive phase was reached in the building of a financial framework for the Histadrut. The initial basis for funding was membership dues, a resolution that had been passed at the founding convention. It is true that the collection of dues had begun even before Ben-Gurion took office in the secretariat, but it was handled by the individual branches. As a result of financial problems and needs at the branch level, the funds gathered there were completely exhausted before ever reaching the central organization.

Ben-Gurion carried out a membership count, created a top-down central framework for collecting dues and prevented any possibility that a portion of the meager funds collected might be siphoned off on their way up to the organization's main office. For the first time, there was a clear stipulation that services, such as health care, were to be provided based on the payment of a fee.[34] Nonetheless, the relative importance of such fees within the overall Histadrut budget remained marginal. The several thousand members, most of whom had few resources of their own, did not have the means to finance the diverse activities of the Histadrut—which had taken upon itself the challenge of national aims far beyond the immediate needs of its members. However, the assessment of dues provided a first basis for the very survival of a system that from then on would call for budgetary support from national sources.

One of Ben Gurion's moves proved a resounding failure. He decided to transfer the seat of the Executive Council to Jerusalem. Members of the Second Aliyah, who were well-known for their Palestino-centrist proclivities and loved to travel all around the land and sing its praises, were nonetheless not particularly enamored of Jerusalem. Thus, Berl Katznelson, who often roamed about the country, did not get to Jerusalem for the first time until 1917 (as far as is known), seven years after immigrating to Palestine![35] Ben-Gurion, who often spoke about his travels in "Judea and the Galilee,"[36] recalls that his first visit to Jerusalem was some three years after his arrival in Palestine as an immigrant. Against this background, the decision to transfer the central institutions of the Histadrut to Jerusalem came as something of a surprise. The base of the public power of the Histadrut lay in Tel Aviv and the agricultural settlements in Judea, and its principal attention was concentrated on cooperative workers' settlements and communes on the periphery, stretching from Kfar Giladi in the north down to Beersheba in the Negev.

Though nearly half of the Jewish population in Palestine at the time lived in Jerusalem,[37] the number of wage-earners there who had joined the Histadrut was small. The office personnel and teachers in the city who were employed by the Mandatory government or the Zionist Executive showed no interest in socialist organizing. The remainder were largely religious ministrants from the ultra-Orthodox community—ritual slaughterers, religious teachers, and synagogue caretakers. The Sephardi Jews in Jerusalem, who comprised the majority of the wage-earners in the city, were suspicious of the Histadrut and generally avoided joining up. Sephardi leaders expressed a clear opposition to the participation of members from their various ethnic communities in the workers' movement.[38]

On this sensitive subject, it is worth recalling that the Histadrut leadership was also at fault: it failed to comprehend the nature of the Sephardi community, stating that "its social, national, and class consciousness was at an unsatisfactory level."[39] This aggressive assertion was deeply rooted in the consciousness of socialists from Eastern Europe, and would help create a growing barrier between the Histadrut and Oriental Jews that lasted many years. This issue remained covert, concealed from view. The Sephardim were in any case indifferent to the Histadrut and the ideas and initiatives it represented.

The shapers of Histadrut policy assumed that the great waves of future immigration would come from Eastern Europe, that massive Ashkenazi influx would alter the demographic makeup of the Yishuv, and the overall proportion of Sephardim in the population would decline. In the course of time, they would undergo profound cultural changes and their level of consciousness would rise in any case, so that the problem would solve itself. Many years were to pass until it became evident just how mistaken that assessment was, and the whole matter was handed over to Israeli society as an unresolved legacy of false judgment.

In any event, it is a fact that the Workers' Council of Jerusalem was an extremely weak body, and failed repeatedly in attempts to organize the workers in the city.[40] This notwithstanding, Ben-Gurion chose to transfer the Histadrut's central offices specifically to Jerusalem, a city divorced from and alien to the young Labor movement. The irony is that the Histadrut's weakness in the city was precisely one of the important factors in the decision to move there. Not that the city had been singled out as a target for agitation and conquest. On the contrary, Ben-Gurion desired to set up a clear dividing wall between ongoing regular local operations, in the hands of the local workers' council, and activity at the national level. It was imperative that the latter had to be free from the welter of problems afflicting the local level. In stormy, problem-ridden Tel Aviv, such a clear-cut division between the spheres was considered impossible. The very day after its founding, the Tel Aviv offices of the Histadrut had been a target for demonstrations and violence actions by unemployed, hungry workers, and such demonstrations soon became a daily occurrence. During the first days of its existence, no one in the Histadrut thought it was necessary to station guards at the door who would hinder crowds of the hungry and unemployed from storming the offices of the Histadrut secretariat—and thus prevent physical and mental pressure from being exerted on the members of the Executive Council.[41] One primary purpose of the transfer of offices to Jerusalem was to facilitate work in a more relaxed atmosphere far from Tel Aviv.

The second motive was political, though there appears to be nothing in the written sources on this. The decision to transfer the running of the Histadrut to Jerusalem was sudden and even hasty. The claim that it was a politically based move rests on the enormous efforts Ben-Gurion made, immediately after the transfer to Jerusalem, to participate in the life of a city where the great political decisions in the country were being made, in the office of Herbert Samuel, British High Commissioner for Palestine, and the quarters of the Zionist Executive. But his efforts to gain recognition from the policy-makers in Jerusalem proved disappointing. No direct connection was welded between the High Commissioner and the Histadrut, and even the junior officials of the Mandatory government generally tended to ignore the Histadrut. Their ties with the Yishuv and its institutions were via the agency of local mayors and heads of agricultural settlements—and, of course, the Zionist Executive. Nor did the latter maintain a direct and well-organized link with the Executive Council of the Histadrut either.

The heads of the Zionist Executive, who were far from enthusiastic about the pretensions of the small Labor movement to being the leading social and political factor in the Yishuv, preferred to maintain direct links with the relevant secondary Histadrut bodies. Thus, the link in health matters was between the Department of Health in the Zionist Executive and Kupat Holim. When it came to the formal contact in matters relating to job placement, this was handled directly between the Department of Labor in the Zionist Executive and the labor exchanges operated by the Histadrut. Likewise when it came to settlement, security, etc.

The transfer of Histadrut institutions to Jerusalem is symbolic of the gap that existed between the early idealistic ambitions of the organization and its weak base outside the Labor movement. Hopes to be integrated into the leadership echelons of the Yishuv and the Zionist Organization proved illusory. Just as the move to Jerusalem had been precipitous, the subsequent return to Tel Aviv likewise was not the product of prolonged deliberation. The process of return of Histadrut offices to Tel Aviv was handled in stages, but implemented rapidly. Already during the course of the first year after the move to Jerusalem, most of the economic institutions had been returned to Tel Aviv, and by the end of two years, everything had been shifted back there. Now that the entire operation was larger and far more ramified, it was possible to station a guard at the entrance to the Histadrut offices in Tel Aviv. The division between the role of the local workers' council and the general management of the Histadrut was now clear.

The first year of existence of the Histadrut was a stormy confused period in which activities were conducted without a method or responsible leadership. That phase ended at a critical juncture: though there had been an expansion to more ramified activity, that thrust remained without a solid base and the entire operation was at the point of crisis. This phase also lasted approximately one year, beginning with Ben-Gurion's entry into the Executive. During that period, a leadership formed, the blueprint for the Histadrut structure, hierarchy and method of financing activities was drawn up, and future tendencies began to crystallize. The organizational framework that had taken shape assumed firmer contours, and would later prove capable of weathering the numerous vicissitudes the Yishuv would face on the rocky path to statehood.

CRISIS AS AN INSTRUMENT OF EXPANSION

Despite the changes which stabilized the Histadrut, it was still the same intimate organization of several thousand immigrant pioneers from Eastern Europe two years after its foundation, molded by universal social ideas that were ideologically characteristic of a single stratum in the society. Only a few isolated members had come from the Yishuv's "working masses," i.e., Sephardi wage-earners or the various religious communities. The desire of the Histadrut to play a key role in the organizational structures of the Yishuv was still far from realization.

Ben-Gurion, who was basically a skeptic when it came to individual human nature,[42] concluded that given the voluntary conditions under which institutions of the Yishuv were operating, there was only one thing that could lead the broad masses to the ranks of the Histadrut: the building of a structure rooted in a symbiosis between the individual and the organization. That symbiosis would have to be based on economic components that would guarantee the readiness of the individual to join the Histadrut and create a dependence on the organization that would enable it to establish and maintain its authority. He persevered in this conception for the entire half-century that would remain to him as a leader. This was the reason he endeavored to build the Histadrut as a total instrument that could satisfy all human needs, ranging the gamut from birth in a Histadrut hospital, schools, employment, cultural needs, health care, and financial aid, to a retirement home in the autumn of life.

In the early stage of the building of the Histadrut, at a point when almost all its members were young immigrants, without a profession or economic basis, minimal housing or even a fixed address, the first and foremost task was employment: the creation of jobs. In that field, the Histadrut did not have to begin from scratch. The parties of the Second Aliyah had done the groundwork, and at the time it was created, an Office for Public Works already existed. That office supervised relatively large-scale projects requested by the British administration; it had been set up by the parties, and was transferred to the Histadrut. During the period of rapid expansion, it engaged in tasks that were highly ambitious in relation to its size, principally in the area of road construction in the north of Palestine. The mixture of a lack of professionalism on the part of workers and bosses, and the principle of branching out into every feasible activity without first carefully assessing the economics of the project, soon exacted the unavoidable toll of a mounting deficit.

It was typical that the preliminary reports by the management of the Office for Public Works and Building to the Executive Council of the Histadrut only contained data on the scope of the project, the number of workers and their distribution at various sites throughout Palestine. They do not give an itemization of expenses and made no mention of deficits incurred.[43] This intentional decision to ignore the economic dimension was a precondition for the very survival of the Histadrut, and enabled it to put the concept of "integration of functions" on a firm structural footing. The organization was the largest single employer in the Yishuv and simultaneously its only trade union. Inherent in this strange amalgam, which appeared to be a fundamental contradiction, is the dilemma between the interests of the contractor—in this instance, the Office for Public Works and Building—to exploit cheap labor on the one hand, and the interests of the trade union to improve the working conditions and wages of the worker on the other. The Histadrut resolved the dilemma by ignoring the economic interests of the Office for Public Works, allowing a huge deficit to pile up.

In the spring of 1924, the Office for Public Works collapsed and went into bankruptcy.[44] It was the Zionist Executive which finally bailed the organization out and covered the deficit. It was forced to do that by recognizing the deficit in the category of "expenses for immigration absorption." The Histadrut had succeeded in becoming the first body to which the immigrants turned; it absorbed a large proportion of them in its network of activities, providing them with initial assistance, medical help, and, most importantly, with employment. The Zionist movement did not have any parallel or similar instrument at its disposal. The

Zionist Executive now faced a dilemma: to deny financial aid to the contracting office was tantamount to abandoning the immigrants to hunger and a betrayal of the main task of the Zionist movement. Thus, against its will, the Zionist Executive picked up the bill, covering a sizable proportion of the debts incurred by the Office for Public Works and Building—on the condition that the Histadrut dismantle the office and operate in the future on the basis of budgetary discipline.

The Histadrut leadership was well aware of the dilemma facing the leadership of the Zionist movement. It did not consider it improper to exploit that dilemma in order to advance Histadrut interests in light of the identify between it and the objectives of the Zionist movement. It is therefore not surprising that only a few days after the collapse of the Office for Public Works and its closure, the Histadrut initiated the creation of a new company in its stead. The new firm, Solel Boneh, was nothing more than a change in name. Its managers were precisely the same staff who had directed the now defunct Office for Public Works. The work procedures were also left unaltered, as was the time-honored method of taking on any and all types of jobs without analysis of projected cost and associated expenses. Three years later, the same story was repeated: in 1927, Solel Boneh also collapsed, and for identical reasons. Once again, the wheel had come full circle, and in this instance as well, the Zionist Executive bailed the firm out, providing the necessary funds to enable it to continue operations. Similar scenarios were played out in other Histadrut economic institutions.

By and large, there were no consequences for the managers. It does not appear that any of them felt they were responsible for the deficits accumulated or the collapse of the enterprise that a particular manager headed. Within the terminology popular in the Histadrut, the expression "bankruptcy" (literally, "breaking a leg" in Hebrew parlance) was given a totally different meaning. At one of the very first meetings of the Executive Council of the Histadrut, Yosef Sprinzak, a key leader of the organization, remarked that if the Histadrut would not engage in expanded works projects for the purpose of absorbing immigration, "there is a danger that all our activity and our very cause will go the way of bankruptcy."[45] In other words, bankruptcy in this conception was not economic—on the contrary, to yield to the pressure of economic considerations was the true meaning of the term.

In January 1923, after two years of existence, the Histadrut convened for its second convention. Despite the impressive development, the membership had not grown significantly. Ben-Gurion, its acknowledged leader, now wished to anchor his objective of creating a web of dependency relations between the individual and the Histadrut in its constitution. With that objective in mind, he proposed his wide-ranging plan for a body known as Hevrat Haovdim (Society of Workers). The idea was that Hevrat Haovdim would concentrate the entire economic sector of Histadrut activity, including the subcontracting offices, Bank Hapoalim and the cooperatives within a single legal framework. Hevrat Haovdim was supposed to transform the full array of existing and future institutions of the organization into an encompassing network that would satisfy all human needs in matters of culture, health care, education, employment, housing, and supply of basic foods and commodities. Hevrat Haovdim would determine pay scales, fix prices for produced goods, and decide on areas of development for the whole spectrum of Histadrut institutions.

It appears that Ben-Gurion's initial objective was to set up a general commune of all Histadrut members via the instrument of Hevrat Haovdim.[46] That utopian idea was not given a chance to ripen to fruition. Ben-Gurion, who was highly adept at recognizing the hidden line between impracticable utopia and practicable vision, finally gave in and abandoned the commune idea. Nonetheless, the program that was adopted in the end was quite bold and far-reaching. Thus, for example, the constitution of Hevrat Haovdim included the setting up of "air terminals" and firms for air transport among its future arenas of activity—this at a time when civilian air service, even in countries much more developed than Palestine, was only in its infancy.[47]

And so, while the Histadrut was dreaming of creating something akin to an airline company, it was hard put to provide its members with assistance in essential areas. Its medical program, the Kupat Holim, was not able to offer minimal services. Once again, even in the crucial matter of health care, the Histadrut was forced to turn to outsiders for help, this time to the organization Hadassah in the United States.

Hadassah had begun to operate in Palestine in October 1918, immediately after the British victory. The philanthropic Zionist conception that underlay its mobilization of Zionist women in the United States to assist the Yishuv was what brought the delegation of doctors from the States specifically to the remote settlements of the workers' camps.[48] The bond deepened and soon became a major source of support for Kupat Holim. But the Hadassah representatives demanded there be supervision of the handling of the assistance and professional management, while the representatives of the Histadrut for their part were opposed to any interference and involvement on the part of outside organizations. These differences of opinion were exacerbated, turning into a heated dispute. The Americans were amazed at the impudence of the demands of the workers and the manner in which they presented them. In particular, they grumbled about the lack of responsibility among the negligent management, which in their view bordered on irrationality and outrageous wastefulness. In contrast, the Histadrut representatives were convinced that the Americans were strangers to their pioneering enterprise, unable to comprehend it, and wished to restrict the scope of Histadrut operations.

Yet the fact is that despite the depth of the dispute and its essential significance, a reciprocal dependence developed. On the one hand, the Americans honestly wished to assist those same *halutzim* who were so impressive in their sheer insolence; on the other hand, the leaders of the Histadrut were desperately in need of aid. Thus, albeit accompanied by friction and wrangling, the support of Hadassah was institutionalized and sealed in a signed agreement. Hadassah set up hospitals and clinics for the Histadrut members and footed a large part of the bill for health care, although that did not prevent Kupat Holim from launching a parallel program involving the establishment of hospitals funded by other sources.[49]

This cooperation between workers and the institutions of the "bourgeoisie" rested on a delicate balance between the aspiration of Jews outside Palestine to contribute to the creation of something novel and exciting in Eretz Israel and the readiness of the workers there to be the standard-bearers of that creation. Delegates to the Twelfth Zionist Congress, which decided in 1921 to grant the workers' movement the land of the Jezreel Valley, purchased by the Zionist movement (Jewish National Fund) after a substantial financial effort, were not enamored of the fact that those who had received these lands from them were young, secular-minded socialists whose way of life many of these delegates regarded as objectionable, even licentious. However, there was no other movement that could accept the challenge of settling in that arduous place. The ardor and élan of the young pioneers helped to cover over and counterbalance the element of license and anarchy in their lifestyles. For that reason, they were deemed suitable candidates for support, despite the fact that they were engaged in "dubious experiments," such as the creation of *kibbutzim*.[50] They were entitled to a doctor, medicines, and a great deal of attention.

The alienation of the Histadrut toward the donors, which at times resembled a biting of the hand that feeds you, was regarded as an added embellishing quirk of unruly youth. Chaim Weizmann, the president of the Zionist movement, believed they were his pioneer vanguard, and perhaps the only army the movement had at its disposal for the purpose of realizing the Zionist idea. He had a certain degree of patience when it came to their biting the movement's hand. It is true that he, like other senior officials in the leadership of the Jewish people, thought that the bill for their deficits occasionally reached exaggerated proportions,[51] but he had great esteem for what they were creating, in particular the agricultural settlements. And in any case, he had no other suitable alternative.[52]

What the donors saw as a gesture of good will was considered a fundamental entitlement by the recipients. At the second convention of the Histadrut, Ben-Gurion formulated that right pointedly, stating that without the direct financial support of the Zionist movement, the Histadrut would not be able to function; at the same time, if it were not for the presence of mass immigration, the world Zionist movement would not be in any position to mobilize funds. Immigration to Eretz Israel had been made feasible by the Histadrut's mobilization efforts to absorb those immigrants. Thus, the funds the Zionist movement had received were thanks to the Histadrut, where the money rightfully belonged.[53]

The representatives of the parties and Histadrut also encroached on areas of activity of the Zionist Executive. Their emissaries were active among the broader public in Palestine and abroad. Yosef Sprinzak, a member of the Executive Council of the Histadrut, was appointed in 1921 to the Zionist Executive and given responsibility for the budget of the Zionist movement in the fields of public works, health care, labor exchanges, and the hiring of workers—the very same bailiwick in which the Histadrut was active. One can well imagine what the Council did in that position of strength, and the degree to which it "exploited" this for the advantage of the movement.[54]

Well aware of the limits on their ability to make demands, cognizant of the fact that the support of the Zionist Executive for the workers' movement was a product of a delicate balance that could be easily upset and altered, the leaders of the Labor movement prepared for the possibility of a crisis with the Zionist Executive. The latter was likely to switch its support should they find another organization more amenable and closer to the ideology of the mainstream, the General Zionists.

The next crisis was not long in coming. In the years 1924–1925, a massive wave of immigration flooded into Palestine, known in Zionist historiography as the Fourth Aliyah. In the course of a short twenty-four months, as many immigrants joined the Yishuv as in the entire previous twenty years. They were spurred to immigrate by discriminatory economic restrictions placed on Jews in Poland and the new strict immigration quotas that had been imposed in the United States, severely curtailing free immigration there from Eastern Europe. In the imagery of the period, they were considered "capitalists," with "bourgeois" tendencies, strangers to the pioneering ethos and experience of the New Yishuv. Chaim Weizmann accused them of importing an "atmosphere of the ghetto." [55] That massive immigration appeared like the very antithesis of the workers' movement. Chaim Arlosoroff assumed that these "capitalists" would propose that they were a new factor in the equation, ready to bear on their shoulders the weighty task of establishing a National Home. It was a promising alternative: they were arriving in large numbers, would be relatively easy to absorb, and were not encumbered with any revolutionary leanings and ambitions. It would be easier to develop a basis of cooperation with the Zionist establishment, since this immigration wave was non-ideological, made up of ordinary Jews whose main wish was for a better life. They imported with them a set of familiar and accepted values, the desire to settle and build their lives in an urban area, in the traditional branches of economy, while preserving a Jewish way of life—and most important of all, without any divisive demands for the funding of "social experiments." [56]

Another picture soon became apparent: this image was misconstrued, the proportion of capitalists among these immigrants was in fact quite small, while the number of pioneers exceeded that in those waves of immigration commonly regarded as *"halutzi."* [57] Nevertheless, the image had a power of its own. The concentration of these immigrants in Tel Aviv, the upsurge in commerce, and their bourgeois lifestyle led to moral encouragement for the developing middle class and the call to give priority to private initiative—and to restrict assistance being handed out to the Histadrut. Jabotinsky, who wished to channel that new mood into a political force, founded the Revisionist Party in 1925, which styled itself as an alternative to the Labor movement. Arthur Ruppin, the head of the Settlement Department in the Zionist Executive, which supported the Labor movement, assumed prior to the Fourteenth Zionist Congress in 1925 that a new executive would be elected, without any representatives from the ranks of the workers, and that fresh leadership would guide the movement toward a new path in the building of Eretz Israel.[58] He was too early in his predictions; workers' representatives participated in the Zionist Executive for two more years, though now in an inferior position. Although the new Executive did not demonstrate any great sympathies for the Histadrut, it was well aware of the positive image enjoyed by the workers' settlements in the Jezreel Valley among ordinary Jews outside Palestine, and that such pioneering enterprise was much more exciting to the Jewish imagination abroad than the construction of Tel Aviv—as though that expanding city was like an upgraded, palm-lined version of Warsaw.

Nonetheless, the focus of attention was indeed shifted from settlement in the Jezreel Valley to the streets of Tel Aviv. The accelerated pace of development of the city when contrasted with the difficulties of life in the settlements and agriculture had a negative impact on the concept embodied in pioneering constructivism as an ideology. Many *halutzim* left the settlements and tried to build a new life based on the newfound "prosperity" in the city. The alternative of constructive private capital was a suitable way forward for some isolated members of the Histadrut who wished to establish a home of their own. Now it was possible to cut the umbilical cord of dependency on the Histadrut, and to build— and in turn "be built" (in the discourse of the era)—in Tel Aviv. The process of erosion in the status of the Histadrut was bidirectional: from outside, the national institutions cut the budget, carefully monitored it and reduced the position and status of the Histadrut. From within, Histadrut members voted with their feet for Tel Aviv over the Jezreel Valley. Meir Ya'ari, leader of Hashomer Hatzair, noted with sorrow that "the Fourth Aliyah undermined our deepest foundations. At the high tide . . . the social bonds between the workers were torn asunder, how many groups were disbanded then! In the city, the worker became a narrow-minded petty bourgeois." [59]

Calling into question the way the workers' movement was headed gave rise to doubts about the very concept and methods employed, specifically among the vanguard groups. In the most bold and important of them, the Labor Legion, those doubts burgeoned into criticism of the supposed symmetry between Zionism and revolutionary socialism. The assumption of Ben-Gurion that the socialist Histadrut was the instrument for national redemption now appeared to have been refuted in light of the rapid success of the "capitalists," who brought with them prosperity and the capability to be absorbed in the economy and society in large numbers, based on the principles of private enterprise. If the Zionist idea could be realized in such a simple manner, without the ethos of the "conquest of labor, swamps and malaria," the efforts of *halutzim* from the Labor Legion, who were settled in some twenty detachments across the land, from the Galilee to the Negev, were totally superfluous.

From there, it was but a short step to heretical thoughts about the nature of Zionism and new doubts regarding the true superiority of revolutionary Zionism, which was not content with simplistic nationalism, over "bourgeois" Zionism that desired to carbon-copy Warsaw to Tel Aviv. And indeed, among certain avant-garde groups in the Histadrut, such as the Labor Legion and Hashomer Hatzair, there were signs of deepening radicalization and a shift further left. These changes in consciousness led a segment of members to eventually identify with Marxism—all the way to renouncing Zionism as reactionary and leaving Palestine.[60]

While this internal process within the workers' movement was doing palpable damage to a Histadrut that was in any case in a ramshackle condition, a sudden and far more acute crisis developed in the Yishuv as a whole. The new prosperity had been based on accelerated construction, primarily in Tel Aviv. The year 1926 brought a powerful economic shockwave that pushed the building industry, at that time the major source of employment in the Yishuv, to the point of virtual collapse. Some 35 percent of all wage-earners, most of them recent immigrants, were left jobless. Unemployment gave rise to hunger and despair. Demonstrations and violent protest became common, everyday occurrences. Immigration to Palestine was halted, while emigration mounted, and with it disillusionment with Zionism.

Once again a recurrent phenomenon familiar from the history of the workers' movement reoccurred: the crisis was transformed into an instrument to spearhead a new breakthrough. Ben-Gurion, talking about himself, remarked that in the course of a single year, 1926, his famous shock of bushy hair had turned white; he linked this with that same period of crisis, when hungry unemployed workers would stand across from his office in the Executive Council in Tel Aviv, crying out for their minimum rights: "bread and work."[61]

The Histadrut leadership was able to exploit the crisis to its own political advantage, and to help redirect the bitterness and anger of the unemployed immigrants against the national institutions and the Zionist Executive. Indeed, there were those who called for channeling the demonstrations in the direction of revolutionary "class warfare."[62] Ben-Gurion chose the opposite path. He guided the Histadrut toward close cooperation with the Zionist Executive. The leadership of the Histadrut took on the task of being the executive arm of the Zionist Executive in all matters related to financial aid, which was partial and extremely meager for those in great need. The Histadrut built up a kind of "bank" of jobs and work schedules, and distributed that modest resource in a way that would at least make it possible to prevent the scourge of hunger.

Once again, a dialectic process was in play: it was specifically this relatively invisible activity of the Histadrut, assistance to wage-earners reduced to penury, which acted to bolster the organization. The efforts by the Histadrut to provide aid to all those in the Yishuv who were hungry functioned to restore the strength which the Histadrut had forfeited in the brief period of ephemeral prosperity. The network of aid to the needy brought the strata of the "broad masses" into the ranks of the Histadrut. In this way, it finally managed to push out beyond the limited framework of a power base anchored solely among those ready and able to serve in the pioneering movements. The national responsibility it had taken upon itself was held up publicly as persuasive proof of the advantage of the laborious and demanding path of the workers' movement over the "easy Zionism" of the bourgeois camp that had led straight to the crisis.

Assistance from internal sources, based on distribution of available jobs in towns, was insufficient to meet the needs, and the Zionist Executive was asked to supply additional funding so as to prevent hunger and put a halt to the rising wave of emigration from Palestine. There was a veiled hint that if such aid was not forthcoming, thousands would pour into the streets to demonstrate.[63]

The deepening symbiosis that developed between the Histadrut and the Zionist Executive was not to the liking of either side. The organized workers could not shake off the image they had of the broader Zionist movement as being bourgeois—while the majority of leaders of the Zionist movement had serious reservations about the socialist radicalism of the workers' movement. They both regarded the link between them as a temporary necessity, and looked forward to the time they could sunder the bonds. In 1927, the crisis in Palestine was still at its peak, but the alarm and anxiety that had accompanied its sudden outbreak diminished. After the network of assistance began to shape up and the first signs of stability appeared, the two sides attempted, each for its own reasons, to cut loose from the reciprocal dependency that circumstance had forced upon them.

At the Fifteenth Zionist Congress in 1927, a new Zionist Executive was elected, this time without any workers' representatives. That Executive decided to halt the broad assistance to the plants and firms of the workers' movement, to press for past loans to be reimbursed and to give preference to initiatives in the private sector. The new Zionist Executive, dubbed the "Executive of consolidation," indeed did call a halt to new settlements and narrowed the ability of the Histadrut to function. It relied on the help of a committee of international experts chosen by the Congress that included world-famous authorities. This distinguished committee, thought to have no ulterior motives whatsoever, declared the methods of action of the Histadrut and its arms and branches to be completely unacceptable. The Histadrut network, which for seven years of its existence had been maintained by the Zionist movement, now faced a difficult situation, placing its future survival once again in doubt. Yet here too, it succeeded in transforming the crisis into a breakthrough to a higher stage.

The same summer the Zionist Congress convened, which in Ben-Gurion's words had "alienated itself from our activities,"[64] the third convention of the Histadrut also met. The detailed report presented to convention delegates indicated that Ben-Gurion's plan to stitch an umbilical cord of economic dependency between the individual and the Histadrut had indeed been successful. Its membership was approaching 25,000, four times the number of members at the time of the previous convention four years earlier. The areas of activity overlapped with all the topics that Ben-Gurion had mentioned in the constitution of Hevrat Haovdim, which back then had seemed a fanciful dream. Even the airline, an idea that was considered an apocalyptic vision, was soon to be realized in the guise of the "aviation club," which was later hoped might become a commercial venture, equipped with planes. The expansion of the Histadrut's range of activities included *kibbutzim* and *moshavim*, urban cooperatives, labor exchanges, a health care network, newspapers and culture, a youth movement, schools, a bank, companies for purchasing and marketing, and a sports organization. The most significant factor now was the members' self-confidence and pride in what they had built. All this transformed the Histadrut into the most important organizational and political factor in the Yishuv.

The attempt to limit the Histadrut by closing the economic pipeline brought it to a new juncture of decision. At the end of the Fifteenth Zionist Congress, when the direction of the new Zionist Executive became clear, Berl Katznelson proclaimed: "From here, let us go forth to conquer the Zionist movement. There is no path to the realization of Zionism except via conquest by the workers' movement."[65] Ben-Gurion mapped out the operational plan for the political conquest of the Zionist movement. He saw himself as a national leader, not as the secretary general of an association of workers. He often traveled abroad, and during his visits to the world's capitals, especially in Jewish centers, took an interest in the situation and position of the Zionist movement there. Ben-Gurion's on-the-spot examination led him to conclude that the image of the Zionist movement as something bourgeois in social makeup was mistaken. In this assessment, the important component in its composition was the "national-popular"[66] element, but that popular stratum had its reservations about the revolutionary ethos of the workers' movement. In order to bring that group nearer to the movement, it was necessary to shift the emphasis of the workers' movement in Palestine from the focus of class to that of the people, the nation: *ha-am*. From now on, his slogan was "from the class to the people" as a political call to battle whose declared objective was to expand the frameworks of the workers' movement, in particular the Histadrut, into arena of the broad general public. Indeed, from 1927 on, the ideological focus of the Histadrut was shifted from class to national radicalism.

The first step in the direction of winning over the sympathies of the broad Jewish public in the Diaspora was the unification of the Zionist Labor movement. The union between the two major parties in the Histadrut, Ahdut Haavodah and Hapoel Hatzair, matured slowly by degrees, giving birth to Mapai. Mapai was set up in 1930, a full ten years after the establishment of the Histadrut. Its founding marks the end of a phase in the history of the Labor movement and the start of a new stage which shifted the focus of efforts of the leadership of the workers' movement from the building of an organizational and economic network to political activity.

One year after its creation, Mapai had become the second largest party in the Zionist movement. At the Seventeenth Zionist Congress in 1931, it emerged as the dominant force in the Zionist Executive. Two years later, at the Eighteenth Congress in 1933, it became the largest party in the Yishuv and the Zionist world, ready to lead the Zionist movement and Yishuv forward on the road to statehood, and then to hold the reins of power in the State of Israel for another twenty-nine years.

CONCLUSION

At its inception, the Histadrut was a weak macro-framework of divided workers' organizations, and its influence on the Yishuv as a whole was minuscule. In the course of the 1920s, it succeeded in transforming itself into the largest and most important organization in the Yishuv. The process which changed the Histadrut from a marginal group into the dominant force in the Yishuv was complex and tortuous. It derived from a historic conflux of several interacting factors, at a conjuncture when the British Mandatory regime took control of Palestine and two massive waves of immigration poured into the country, tripling the size of the Yishuv.

The first and foremost factor was the conviction of the founders of the Histadrut that it was their prerogative to be the standard-bearers of the national revival. Their socialist ideology, in its various refractions and hues, the collective ethos, the willingness to pay a personal price for realization of the idea and vision they espoused, were all in keeping with the spirit of the times.

Their determinism did not deform into fundamentalist notions of class conflict, a process that was afoot elsewhere at that time. It is true that the pressure to establish the Histadrut came from the recent immigrants of the Third Aliyah, many of whom had just arrived from Soviet Russia, where they had witnessed the Bolshevik revolution and wanted to emulate it in Palestine. But the founders of the Histadrut were veterans of the Second Aliyah, and their experience under Ottoman rule in Palestine had taught them the secret of the delicate balance between grand aspirations and designs and the realistic range of possibilities available for their concrete implementation. They did not abandon fundamental ideological principles, but the focus of their action lay in the operational realm, a tack dubbed "constructivism." Constructivism concentrated on what they termed "settlement, construction, and immigration."

Constructivism was realized by a process of trial-and-error. The heads of the Histadrut spearheaded the organization into all areas of the economy, at a conjuncture marked by the beginnings of an accelerated momentum of growth in Eretz Israel. Their basic and at times sole concern was development and expansion. Considerations such as economic utility, financial underpinning, and the needs of the economy were deferred in favor of the most important objective: development as rapidly as possible. Constructivism was not based on careful planning or professional expertise. It was an aim in itself. Indeed, one year after its establishment, the Histadrut had become the largest employer in the Yishuv and the central organizer for the absorption of the continuing influx of immigrants.

The position of the Histadrut as the largest employer in Palestine altered the basis of participation in its ranks. It is true that it remained a voluntary organization, based on membership by personal choice, but in its capacity as an employer, an institution for agricultural settlement, and a source of services such as health care and education, it forged a net of dependency relations between itself and a large proportion of its members. That system of relations provided its leaders with substantial power. It was the basis for upward authorization in dealing with higher levels of administration and the binding authority of leadership over the rank-and-file membership. In this way, a leadership crystallized which was able to concentrate power and decision-making in its hand—an echelon that would, by dint of this enormous power, later become the leadership of the nation.

The Histadrut leadership was embodied in one figure in particular, David Ben-Gurion. He had a profound sense of his own mission in the process of national redemption. Tapping the power of that conviction, Ben-Gurion developed a broad "national vision." But he was also a seasoned politician who knew the secret of the delicately calibrated balance necessary between vision and compromise. In addition to these qualities, he was a gifted organizer, blessed with untiring energy and a readiness to learn. Under his guiding hand, the Histadrut was built up as a broadly based structure that encompassed all the necessary organizational foundations for an autonomous national society.

Given the lack of its own funding sources, the Histadrut created a symbiotic network of relations with the Zionist Executive. It asked the Zionist Executive to foot the bill for deficits that had built up. The ability of the Histadrut to pressure the Zionist Executive into covering a deficit to which the Executive had in fact been adamantly opposed from the beginning derived from one central fact: the Histadrut was the force actually engaged in realizing the tasks which the Zionist movement aspired to, but had been unable to successfully implement itself. As a dominant factor in immigrant absorption, agricultural settlement, defense, and expansion into new professional fields and areas of production, the Histadrut became a kind of executive arm of the Zionist movement—but an arm acting on its own.

The double dependence—internal, of the Histadrut members who needed the organization for their daily survival, and external, of the Zionist movement that required the Histadrut as the instrument for the realization of its ideas—provided the Histadrut leadership with its strength as an organization. The amalgam of organizational strength and the sense of national and social mission transformed it into a "state-in-the-making."

NOTES

1. Remarks by Yosef Sprinzak, *Ba-aretz u-ba-avodah,* no. 2–3, Sivan 1918, p. 1.
2. It is typical that when Herbert Samuel, the British High Commissioner in Palestine, wished to appoint Jewish representatives to the advisory council he had set up, he was unable to locate a Jewish forum that had any formal authority. See N. Caplan, *Palestine Jewry and the Arab Question, 1917–1925* (London, 1978), pp. 160–63.
3. For a detailed treatment of this topic, see my *Ba-derekh le-hanhagat ha-yishuv* (Jerusalem, 1982) [hereafter: *Ba-derekh*].
4. On the areas of activity the Histadrut designated as objectives in the minutes of the founding convention, cf. *Asufot* 1 (14), December 1970.
5. Debate in the Council of Ahdut Haavodah on the topic of transfer of the firms to the Histadrut, Heshvan 1921, Minutes of the Ahdut Haavodah Executive Council, Labor Movement Archive [hereafter: LA], 404.
6. E. Friesel, *Ha-mediniut ha-zionit le-ahar hatzarat Balfour* (Tel Aviv, 1977), p. 119.
7. Cf., for example, the letter from the secretary of the Workers' Council of Jerusalem to the Executive Council of the Histadrut, February 1921, LA, 128/1b.
8. Histadrut leaders expressed their astonishment at the small number of participants from the ranks of the parties. See also letter from Y. Efter to Executive Council, Shvat 1922, LA, 208/2b.
9. M. Friedman, *Hevrah ve-dat* (Jerusalem, 1978), pp. 34–53; *Ha-Ivri*, no. 5 New York, February 4, 1921.
10. Discussions on the efforts by the communists to set up a rival organization in: Minutes, Executive Council, January 11, 1921 (from a copy of the records of the minutes of the Executive Council deposited in the Ben-Gurion Memorial Archive, Sde Boker; hereafter: Minutes).
11. From the minute-book of the Executive Council, *Kuntres*, no. 5, Shvat, 1921.
12. Report D. Remez, Head, Office of Public Works, meeting of the Council for Public Works, 27 Nissan, 1922, LA, 124/1b.
13. D. De-Vries, "Tenuat ha-poalim be-Haifa, 1919–1929," diss., (Tel Aviv University, 1991), pp. 62–67.
14. Ibid., pp. 249–60.
15. The manifesto was published, among other places, in *Ha-aretz*, August 14, 1919. The term *"lidhot et ha-ketz,"* to "force the issue," "hasten the coming" is used in modern Hebrew to refer to impatient demands to accelerate the coming of something fervently expected, a "shortcut" approach, and in traditional eschatological discourse, to anticipate the era of redemption and the coming of the Messiah [trans. note].
16. On this, cf. interesting testimony by Albert Hyamson, head of the Department of Immigration of the British Mandatory government, 1921–1934, in A. M. Hyamson, *Palestine under the Mandate* (London, 1958), pp. 51–65.
17. *Ba-derekh*, 156 ff.
18. The files of the Executive Council for its first year are filled with documents dealing with deficits and financial requests, see in particular the reports for 1921, LA 208/1a.
19. Report of the Haycraft Commission of Inquiry, "On the Disturbances in the Town of Jaffa and Surrounding Area, 1921" (Jerusalem, 1921).

20. Minutes, May 7, 1921.

21. Report on this in the periodical *Mikhtav,* 17 Kislev, 1922, pp. 21–24.

22. On the allocation of 16,000 Egyptian pounds, see Council of Delegates to Eretz Israel, *Din ve-heshbon le-shnat 5681* (Jerusalem, 1921), p. 3.

23. The letter of congratulations he sent from London to the founding conference expresses certain reservations, Ben-Gurion, *Igrot,* vol. 2 (Tel Aviv, 1972), pp. 41–43.

24. *Kuntres,* no. 6, Elul 1921.

25. Cf. his letter from Moscow to the Executive Council of the Histadrut, September 24, 1923, in Ben-Gurion, *Igrot,* vol. 2, pp. 156–74.

26. Z. Tzahor, "Ben-Gurion: From Socialism to Statehood," *Midstream* (January, 1986): 36–41.

27. On the discussions within the party concerning Ben-Gurion's program, see Y. Gorny, *Ahdut Haavodah,* (Tel-Aviv, 1973), pp. 191–200.

28. The decision on that came in a session of the Council of Ahdut Haavodah. Tishri 27, 1921, LA, 404/0.

29. Berl Raftor, who was a rival of Ben-Gurion all his life, also noted the change in the functioning of the Histadrut after Ben-Gurion took over his post, B. Raftor, *Lelo heref,* vol. 1 (Tel Aviv), p. 70.

30. M. Avizohar, *Ha-zionut ha-lohemet* (Sde Boker, 1985), p. 61.

31. A complaint on this comes up in an argument during a session of the Executive Council of the Histadrut, Minutes, November 23, 1921.

32. S. Sh. Yariv (Ben-Gurion), *Al ha-komunizm ve-ha-zionut shel Hashomer Hatzair* (Tel Aviv, 1953). *"Esh zara,"* literally "heathen fire," is an ancient Hebrew expression applied here to designate a dangerous or alien enthusiasm [trans. note].

33. Z. Tzahor, *Shorshei ha-politikah ha-israelit* (Tel Aviv, 1987), pp. 37–45.

34. Minutes, November 23, 1921.

35. See Anita Shapira, *Berl: The Biography of a Socialist Zionist* (Cambridge, 1984), pp. 67–68.

36. A story by this title published in *Lu'ah Ahiever,* No. 2 (New York, 1921), pp. 102–16.

37. According to the 1922 census, 34,000 of the 70,000 Jews in Palestine were resident in Jerusalem, see *Statistical Abstract of Palestine* (Jerusalem, 1930), p. 25.

38. M. Friedman, *Hevrah ve-dat,* p. 181.

39. Report on Jerusalem, *Kuntres,* no. 23, Shvat 1921, pp. 25–26.

40. Reports of the Council of Workers of Jerusalem to the Executive Council during the year 1920/21, LA, 208/1b.

41. Cf. remarks by Z. Livneh, Minutes, November 23, 1921.

42. This is one reason why he assigned the Israel Defense Forces the task of absorbing immigrants and shaping the society during the early years after the establishment of the state. See M. Lisk, "Binyan mosdot be-tfisat Ben-Gurion," in: Sh. Avineri, ed., *David Ben-Gurion: D'muto shel manhig poalim* (Tel Aviv, 1988), pp. 110–17.

43. Minutes of the Council for Public Works, 27 Nisan, 1922, LA, 124/1b.

44. Supplement to balance sheet, Office of Public Works, January 11, 1924, LA, 124.15. It is characteristic that even at the time of the dismantling, the heads of the office were still unable to determine the size of the deficit, ibid.

45. Y. Sprinzak, Minutes, January 25, 1921.

46. On this, see Y. Gorni, *Ahdut Haavodah,* p. 103.

47. Regulations of Hevrat Haovdim, Booklet no. 11, 27 Adar A, 1924, pp. 271–75.

48. *New Palestine,* no. 2, January 21, 1921, p. 2.

49. On the relations between Hadassah and the Histadrut, see Sh. Shvartz, "Hitpathut Kupat-Holim, 1911–1939," diss., Ben-Gurion University of the Negev, Beersheba 1993, p. 112 ff.

50. Thus, for example, the Twelfth Zionist Congress (1921) allocated 34 percent of the

total budget set aside for Eretz Israel to settlement funding, principally in the Jezreel Valley, cf. Minutes, Zionist Executive, May 28, 1922.

51. In its last year, the Council of Delegates allocated more than half of its total budget to workers' firms and companies, see N. Gros and H. Lavski, *Hanahat yesodot le-mediniyut finansit zionit* (Jerusalem, 1978), p. 44.

52. See R. Weltsch, "The Fabian Decade," in: M. Weisgal and J. Carmichael, eds., *Chaim Weizmann: A Biography by Several Hands* (New York, 1963), pp. 171–206.

53. From an address by Ben-Gurion at the second convention, in D. Ben-Gurion, *Ha-poel ha-ivri ve-histadruto* (Tel Aviv, 1964), pp. 106–7.

54. The Mizrahi representative on the Zionist Executive, Prof. Pik, complained that all the funds allocated for immigrant workers, including the religious workers, were being channeled to the Histadrut. See his letter dated Shvat 12, 1925, Central Zionist Archive, Sq/1761a.

55. Chaim Weizmann, *Trial and Error* (London, 1952), pp. 300–301.

56. Ch. Arlosoroff, "*Le-haarakhat ha-aliyah ha-reviit,*" *Ketavim*, vol. 3 (Tel Aviv, 1934), pp. 109–14.

57. D. Giladi, *Ha-yishuv bi-tekufat ha-aliyah ha-reviit* (Tel Aviv, 1973), pp. 161–76.

58. A. Ruppin, *Pirke hayyai*, vol. 3 (Tel Aviv, 1968), p. 103.

59. M. Ya'ari, speech at the third convention of the Histadrut, July 1927 in: D. Zayit et al., eds., *Meier Yaari: Dyokano shel manhig ke-adam tzair* (Givat Haviva, 1992), p. 218.

60. See A. Shapira, *Ha-halikhah al kav ha-ofek* (Tel Aviv, 1989), p. 118 ff.

61. Personal interviews with Ben-Gurion, January 1971.

62. There was a hint of this in deliberations in the Seventeenth Histadrut Council, March 1927. Those calling for class war were the representatives of the Left Poale Zion. Minutes of the Histadrut Council, Ha-Va'ad Ha-Poel Publishing House (Tel Aviv, 1927).

63. A detailed report on assistance and financial sources is contained in the financial statement on activities of the workers in Jaffa, *Hoveret din ve-heshbon mi-peulot poalei Yafo, 1925–27,* (Tel-Aviv, 1928), pp. 125–143.

64. Letter from Ben-Gurion to Eliyahu Golomb, October 10, 1927, Ben-Gurion Memorial Archive, Letters, 1927.

65. B. Katznelson, "Ha-kongres ve-le-aharav," *Ketavim*, vol. 3 (Tel Aviv, 1946), pp. 163–77.

66. The Hebrew term is "*amami*"; letter to Golomb, op. cit., October 10, 1927.

20.

"Black Night—White Snow": Attitudes of the Palestinian Labor Movement to the Russian Revolution, 1917–1929

Anita Shapira

In one of the first issues of the monthly, *Haadamah,* a journal of the Ahdut Ha'avodah party, edited by Yosef Haim Brenner (from 1919 to 1921), Alexander Blok's poem "The Twelve" appeared. The poem opens with the words, "Black night—white snow," and the line could serve as a fitting epigram for the contradictory attitudes of the Palestinian Jewish labor movement toward the Bolshevik Revolution during the 1920s. As in workers' movements all over the world, no other event in their generation seems to have aroused such universal hope or generated such intense disappointment. In Palestine, however, reactions were more highly compounded.

Most of the people in the Palestinian labor movement during the 1920s could trace their origins to Tsarist Russia. The Second Aliyah (1904–14), from which the founding fathers of the labor movement are generally considered to have come, was Russian in essence and not only in origin. In addition to Yiddish and Hebrew, Russian was their natural tongue. There were even some among them (Joseph Trumpeldor; the poet, Rachel; Devorah Dayan) who for a long time knew only Russian. Their knowledge of Hebrew was acquired later in life. They were all well versed in Russian literature, and the revolutionary political subculture of

Reprinted by permission of Oxford University Press from *The Jews and the European Crisis, 1914–1921,* edited by Jonathan Frankel, *Studies in Contemporary Jewry,* vol. 4 (New York: Oxford University Press, 1988): 144–71.

Imperial Russia ran in their veins. They hated the Tsarist regime for the way it subjugated the peoples of Russia, not least for the way it treated the Jews, restricting them to the Pale of Settlement and depriving them of civil rights. Their affinity to the Russian revolutionary movement and the Russian intelligentsia—or, to be more precise, to what they symbolized—was central to their entire way of thinking.

For its part, the much larger Third Aliyah (1919–23)—many thousands strong—was a product of the October Revolution. It was composed of Jewish youth who had reached maturity in the wake of World War I and the concomitant destruction and displacement of the Jewish communities of Poland and the Ukraine. Separated from home and family, the revolution became for many of them the be-all and end-all of existence. Alexander Penn was to write in 1929:

> If my world has survived and I can survive in it,
> If in the verses of song the words will live,
> There was one miracle, one that's called—October![1]

The October experience was real for them, part of their own personal history, and even if they had witnessed acts of cruelty, wanton destruction and callousness, their image of the revolution remained, to a surprising extent, untarnished.

The attitude of the Palestinian labor movement to Soviet Russia was, then, in many ways a function of direct personal connection. Their attitude to the October Revolution reflected their affinity to socialist philosophy and to the world socialist movement (of which they considered themselves an integral part) as well as their yearning for the land of their birth. It was a land that both attracted and repulsed them, tempted and threatened them. It was a land at once remote and terribly much their own.

This essay deals with the changing attitudes of the mainstream of the Palestinian labor movement toward the Soviet Union in the 1920s, primarily with reference to Ahdut Ha'avodah and its affiliates such as the Labor Brigade (Gedud Ha'avodah) and (to a lesser extent) Hapoel Hatzair. These were the movements that considered themselves responsible for the socialist-Zionist construction of Palestine. The positions of the other labor parties in Palestine, such as the Communist party or the Left Poale Zion are of less interest because their attitudes were, a priori, pro-Soviet. The two mainstream parties were more given to doubt, irresolution and ambiguity.

THE YEARS OF THE THIRD ALIYAH (1919–23) AND THE IMPACT OF WAR COMMUNISM

During the war and afterward during the revolution, the concern of the Palestinians was matched only by their insatiable curiosity about events in Russia. Because of the unstable situation, information was sparse and not always reliable; at that time very few people undertook the long journey to Russia.[2] But everyone was concerned, first of all about his family and friends and then about the course of political events. Berl Katznelson wrote to Alexander Kheshin on the eve of Passover 1919:

It would be wonderful if you sent us letters. Here everyone is dying for information, for opinions, for news on how things are going and all we have to go by are scraps. It would be wonderful if we could publish some good reliable letters from the world in convulsion.[3]

The members of the Jewish Legion (the Palestinian units in the British army), regardless of party affiliation, were fervently interested in what was happening in Russia.[4] In a letter to the editors of the weekly, *Kuntres,* an Ahdut Ha'avodah legionnaire complained about the paucity of information and asked rhetorically whether, "our movement isn't in some way a reflection of the exciting, tempestuous life there, so exhilarating and full of elan?"[5]

Soon after, reports began to appear in the papers about the massacre of Jews in the Ukraine and in Poland being perpetrated by the White and various other anti-Bolshevik armies. It was quite natural to assume that the enemies of the revolution were antisemitic murderers, whereas the Red Army soldiers were the only defenders of the Jews. As reports of the massacres increased from the spring of 1919, so did sympathy with the Bolshevik government.[6] Nachman Syrkin, who had published a series of articles in *Kuntres* favorable to the revolution, was echoing common sentiment when he wrote:

Who will help us? Jews all over the world are beginning to realize with greater force than ever that the destruction of the capitalist system carries with it their civil and national redemption. . . . Even Jewish capitalists prefer Lenin to Kolchak. Lenin may deprive them of their property but Kolchak will split their heads open.[7]

Worrisome items about the treatment of Jews in the new national states, particularly in Poland, began to appear as well.[8] At the same time it was known that the Soviet government was fighting tenaciously against all forms of antisemitism: "Anyone coming out openly against Jews is severely punished. Antisemitic actions are viewed as inimical to the revolution." [9]

In this atmosphere it was no wonder that even a relatively moderate labor newspaper like *Hapo'el hazair* considered reports of Red atrocities to be suspect.[10] The intervention of the Western countries in the Russian Civil War was sharply and universally criticized in Palestine.[11] It was described as ideological warfare against the revolution, offensive to decent people.[12] Syrkin took fierce exception to the activities of the revolutionary exiles in Paris (veteran Russian Social Democrats and Socialist Revolutionaries) who supported the Intervention through the League for the Rebirth of Russia. "This counterrevolution, which sprang from the bosom of the revolution itself, arouses wonderment and distress," he wrote. "These people have undergone an emotional catastrophe." [13] At the beginning of 1920 reports were reprinted from the European and Soviet press condemning the Intervention and describing its failure with great relish. The French socialists and intellectuals were lauded for demanding an end to their government's active part in it.[14]

At this stage the sympathy of the Palestinian labor movement rested on the revolution itself, the subsequent Civil War, the White Russian atrocities against the Jews, the Intervention and its subsequent failure— that is, on a series of actual events. A good illustration of the intuitive, spontaneous response of the movement to concrete developments was the way it mobilized support for the victims of the famine in 1921. The Workers' Council in Jaffa announced that the workers there would contribute one day's wages to help alleviate the situation of the victims of famine in Russia, and the executive of the Histadrut (the General Federation of Jewish Labor) immediately followed suit.[15] The announcements generated a public controversy. Joseph Aharonowitz, one of the leaders of Hapoel Hatzair, criticized the fact that the aid was not intended exclusively for the Jewish victims whose suffering, he wrote, was greater than that of others.[16] *Kuntres* responded with two articles to the effect that the aid was being dispensed primarily on humanitarian grounds.[17] This was a somewhat disingenuous explanation. The contribution was clearly intended to express both moral and material support for the Soviet Union.

A more direct response was made by Shlomo Zemach, a Second Aliyah veteran and himself a member of Hapoel Hatzair. Zemach took issue with the pronouncements of a certain A. Tiron (apparently a nom de plume) who had fulminated against the Soviet government, claiming that the money would not reach the hungry but would all be swallowed up by the government bureaucracy. Zemach's answer is revealing in many ways. First of all, the sins of the revolutionary government, it appears, were already common knowledge—the Cheka, the abolition of parliamentary rule, proletarian favoritism and the appropriation of private property, which severely hurt the Jews. Although admitting all this, he, nevertheless, declared that the workers of Palestine had decided not only to help the victims of the famine but also to recognize the Soviet Union as a workers' government. The aid, he continued, "does not indicate blind acceptance or joint responsibility for what goes on there or for the system as a whole." It was, rather, *"a demonstration of where we belong, what our inclinations are and what our aspirations are for the structure of life and society"* [italics mine]. Here, the attitude toward the Soviet Union had become a standard for judgment: Are you for us or against us?

Zemach took issue, likewise, with an article that had appeared in *Hashiloah* (the well-known liberal Zionist monthly). The worst thing about it, he wrote, was that the author had not bothered to "hide his great satisfaction at the fact that the [Soviet] experiment had not succeeded."[18] Zemach's essential legitimation of the revolution is sharply delineated in the article. The fact that he had never before displayed any inclination for Marxism or Communism nor was he to do so ever again is a reflection of the universal sympathy that the Soviet experiment evoked at that particular moment in history, the year 1921.

Sometime during the stormy period of the Intervention and the Civil War, blockaded by the Western powers, the besieged Soviet Union became a symbol with which to identify. Familiarity with the negative realities of Soviet life had come to coexist with a positive evaluation of the myth of revolution. The gap between reality and myth would only widen with time.

Communications between Palestine and Russia during the 1920s were direct and regular. Members of the Third Aliyah provided a reliable source of information on developments there; Soviet ships often dropped anchor in Jaffa port; mail service was regular; and there were private visits, though not in great numbers. From the mid-1920s, a small but unusual group of immigrants began arriving from the Soviet Union: people who had been imprisoned for Zionist activities, veterans of the socialist-Zionist parties, members of Hashomer Hatzair, Hehalutz and other left-wing Zionist groups. Direct contact with the Soviet Union would cease during the 1930s, and in that period it could be claimed that there was no direct or reliable source of information. News came only from the Western press, which in matters concerning the Soviet Union was suspect. But this was not the case in the 1920s. Sources of information were direct, reliable and certainly not hostile to the Soviet Union. The labor press in Palestine during this period was full of news about life in Russia as well as about the condition of Soviet Jewry. The facts of life were known. One has, therefore, to conclude that the prevailing attitude toward the Soviet Union did not result from ignorance of the facts but rather from certain needs, wishes and predispositions. It was almost as if attitudes to the Soviet Union operated at one and the same time on two separate levels, that of empirical knowledge and that of political consciousness.

Affinity to the revolution was part and parcel of the self-image of most members of the small labor movement in Palestine at the time, and this affinity had two dimensions: the moral and the revolutionary. In the struggle between workers and employers, between socialism (or Communism) and imperialism or capitalism, there was no question for them where right resided. Whether they were Communists, socialists, members of the Bund or socialist Zionists, the most active elements of the Jewish people were identified with the left. Their hope for a better world and their struggle to achieve one overlapped with their hope for the liberation of the Jews—whether as individuals or as a people—from the thralldom of generations.

At the beginning of the third decade of the twentieth century, the Soviet Union could be seen as humankind's first attempt to achieve the kingdom of heaven on earth. The Palestinian labor movement, for the most part, considered itself a partner in this historical breakthrough. As such, it needed the approval of the world movement. It was terribly important in its eyes what the world socialist movement in general and revolutionary Russia in particular thought about it. Consequently, it looked for similarities and correspondences between what it was doing in Palestine and what was happening in the Soviet Union.

Moreover, Ahdut Ha'avodah, the major labor party in the Yishuv, considered itself—as did specifically Third Aliyah groups such as the Labor Brigade—to be closer to the revolutionary than to the reformist wing of socialism. Impatience with, and disbelief in, evolutionary processes came to characterize both the leadership and the rank and file and were, to a certain extent, substitutes for any ordered body of dogma— something neither was prepared to accept. Their revolutionary impulse was expressed in their belief in "Zionism on a grand scale" (tsiyonut gedolah) and in socialism here and now. The history of Ahdut Ha'avodah could be largely described in terms of the way reality frustrated the revolutionary impulses of its leadership, although Berl Katznelson, David Ben-Gurion and Yitzhak Tabenkin each reacted differently to this experience. But these developments were still in the future. At that time, the dominant feeling was that there were emotional and psychological bonds between revolutionary Palestine and revolutionary Russia, two partners, so to speak, in the same historical process.

Yet from the earliest days, directly following the October Revolution, reservations were expressed. True to form, veterans of the Second Aliyah such as Berl Katznelson, Yosef Haim Brenner and Mordechai Kushnir were the first to raise doubts. They were people with a deep affinity to Russian culture and an intimate knowledge of the reality of Russian society; at the same time they felt no need to belong to a world movement or receive legitimation from it.

Katznelson gave natural vent to this duality, although he did so anonymously. He was spurred on by the contrast between Russian literature, "the greatest in the world," and the Russian people, "the most primitive and backward"; between the absolute moral imperatives of the best in Russian literature and the still unclear reality of the new regime. He wrote:

If I ever attain the highest level of human progress and happiness, I shall demand of historical Providence a reckoning for every lost soul, and if no answer is forthcoming, then I shall cast myself from the highest storey and smash my skull—this we heard from Vissarion Belinsky. Which road, therefore, are you treading, tortured and weary, sacred and crazed Russia? And who can understand you? Childishly pure as Raskolnikov or darkly profane as Smerdiakov? Homeland: both so distant and so close; alien yet dear.[19]

Brenner's attitude was very similar. It was highly significant that he chose to publish extracts from Maxim Gorky's diaries in his weekly, *Haadamah,* during the months of November and December 1917. These diaries contained Gorky's criticism of the revolution. His feeling that it had come too soon, that the Russian people were not yet ready for it; and that, although its influence on the future was still uncertain, its immediate effects had caused millions of people untold suffering. "The tyranny of a half-educated mob will celebrate an easy victory while the spirit of man will remain oppressed as before." It was not the revolution he had envisaged:

In these outbursts of animal passion, I cannot see the true foundations of a social revolution. This is a Russian rebellion which has nothing in common with the spirit of socialism or the psychology of socialism.

His conclusion was forthright:

In the life of Russia today, there is no place for a social revolution. You cannot make eighty-five percent of the population of our peasant country socialists by fiat or command.

On the other hand, Gorky was unable to divorce himself from the revolution:

Better to be consumed by the fire of the revolution than to rot away slowly in the sewers of the monarchy as we did until February.[20]

In the final reckoning Brenner's attitude was somewhat more positive than that of Gorky. He rejected the idea that Russian backwardness precluded the possibility of the socialist revolution. Revolutionary actions could themselves prepare the proletariat for socialism. He accepted the destruction of the old as a necessary evil, despite the fact that at heart he did not really believe that it had any constructive value. He was prepared to reconcile himself to censorship and even terror—up to a certain point.

After all, we're not going to demand from Lenin the strict moral behavior of the landlady of some boarding house. But where is the line drawn? Where is our assurance . . . that they won't become rulers for the sake of ruling?

The question for Brenner thus remained open:

What is this great vision—Soviet Russia? Does it take the form of a *political* party which, despite all the horrors imposed on it from within and without, despite the hunger and the cold, will overcome its enemies and remain in power by means of the terror and the violence it has at its disposal; or, perhaps, are these really the first steps taken toward reforming the Russian state in the spirit of real socialism, a holy search for the renaissance of humanity through common creative labor and the just distribution of the fruits of this labor?[21]

His doubts never left him. True, he knew that he was not in possession of all the facts. But his instincts, as a Russian, guided him. It seemed to him that the foremost sin of the Bolshevik regime was the bureaucratization of the revolution and the rise of a class of bureaucratic commissars. Brenner's last written words before his death in 1921 were:

Three crimes of the Bolsheviks I cannot forgive—no Marxism, no democracy and no patriotism; nay, four—they have turned the high to low and the low to high and have not done away with the god of privilege. Their many commissars are nothing but *chinovniki* [bureaucrats].[22]

One is made even more aware of the profound and personal affinity felt by B. Katznelson and Brenner for the Russian intelligentsia and culture if one compares their attitude to the revolution with that of Bertrand Russell. Russell visited the Soviet Union in the spring of 1920 (May 11–June 16) in a Labour party delegation. Following the trip he published a series of articles in the *Nation,* and they were reprinted in *Hapo'el hazair.*[23] Russell displayed a largely positive, albeit critical, attitude toward the experiment, Soviet Russia, but his observations are those of an outsider, untinged by either affection or hatred; this was their business not his. He compared the Bolsheviks under Lenin to the Puritans under Cromwell and concluded, with elegant detachment, that life under both these regimes was in some way contrary to man's natural instincts; and if the Bolsheviks, too, were to fail, it would be for this same reason. There comes a moment when people begin to prefer the comforts and pleasures of life to all other good things.[24]

Such detachment was not possible for the Ahdut Ha'avodah leaders in Palestine. "Comforts and pleasures" were not to be taken seriously, certainly not in weighing the pros and cons of the revolution. They could hardly accept Russell's notion that world revolution, with its ultracentralism, would result in the decline of civilization for a thousand years; and they would have responded, as Brenner put it, "[I]f civilization and comfort are the products of inequality, better that they should not exist."[25] As for centralism—that was precisely what Berl Katznelson and his comrades then believed in.

Russell's personal encounter with people who had absolutely no doubts about anything had intensified his own doubts, not only about Communism but about every faith imposed at the cost of widespread poverty and want.[26] But the leaders of Ahdut Ha'avodah belonged to a political culture that sanctified the zealous belief in one idea, and they were thoroughly convinced that it was justified to sacrifice comfort, well-being and even life for the cause. Russell reached the conclusion that the Bolsheviks were not, in fact, putting Communism into practice, but he added that because Russia was a backward country Bolshevik methods were more or less necessary there. For the British socialists to consider imitating their methods of enslavement, however, would be an unjustifiable step backward.[27]

Russell's nonchalant dismissal of the Bolshevik experiment as relevant only to Russia, a primitive country, was considered in Palestine the shallow approach of a typical British intellectual. No matter what doubts Katznelson and Brenner entertained about the revolution, they were constitutionally unable to look on it with detachment. They could understand and, to a great extent, share Gorky's impassioned critique;

they could not countenance Russell's distance. Thus, despite any misgivings that they might have had, the labor movement in Palestine identified totally with the appeals made by Gorky to the workers of the world and by Kropotkin to the Western Allies to desist from the Intervention and to oppose anti-Bolshevik émigrés of all colors.[28] The labor press in Palestine gave detailed accounts of these appeals, reflecting their profound belief that the revolution was *the* most significant event of the century. Even people known for their reservations came to its defense.

When Kropotkin died, Abba Ahimeir published an article about him in *Kuntres,* the journal of Ahdut Ha'avodah. He presented him as a revolutionary of the previous generation who from his youth had believed in progress and in the fundamental goodness of man. He was, in short, the symbol of the Narodnik Russian intelligentsia that, since the October Revolution, was fast being driven off the stage of history.[29] A year later Ahimeir wrote a similar eulogy for Korolenko, under the title, "Not a Hero of Our Times." Describing Korolenko as a favorite of the Hebrew reader who "still drinks profusely from the great well of Russian literature," he added, almost in passing, "We Jews, in remembering Russia, can be compared to a traveller lost in the desert for some days who suddenly, beyond the dunes, sees an oasis."[30] The publication of a number of such articles about Korolenko in the Hebrew press in the years 1917–22 clearly involved implicit criticism of Communist policies toward non-Bolshevik socialists.[31] Praise for yesteryear's revolutionary heroes expressed both the bond with the now almost nonexistent Russian humanist intelligentsia and disapproval of the present regime. Yet, at the same time, what was seen as the verdict of history was accepted by the socialists in the Yishuv—just as it had been accepted, ultimately, by Kropotkin, Korolenko and Gorky.

Moreover, it has to be stressed that, when all is said and done, Katznelson, Brenner, Kushnir and the others who had their reservations about the revolution were the exceptions in the Yishuv. Most members of Ahdut Ha'avodah during the first half of the 1920s identified with the revolution as a matter of course and considered it a model to be emulated. If Joseph Klausner, the right-wing Zionist, could speak of "Israel's traditional spirit of prophecy" incarnated in "the desire for equality and social justice which is at the basis of Bolshevism,"[32] how could anyone criticize the enthusiasm of the young socialists who wanted to duplicate both the forms and the content of the Russian Revolution in Palestine? Berl Katznelson himself was even known to borrow from Soviet terminology at times. He wrote to his brother in America that Ahdut Ha'avodah was "a kind of Palestinian Soviet of Workers and Soldiers."[33]

Ahdut Ha'avodah frequently attempted to mold its typically Palestinian ideologies in accordance with what was approved of "over there"— as did its daughter movements such as the Labor Brigade. This was the case, for example, with the idea of the historical shortcut. Soviet Russia had skipped the stage of capitalist development—a necessary historical period according to traditional Marxist theory—going directly from feudalism to socialism. And a comparable leap forward, argued many members of the Third Aliyah, was both possible and desirable in Palestine. There, of course, the old had to be destroyed before the new could be built; here, the Yishuv could be built up from scratch on cooperative, socialist or even Communist principles. The fact that Lenin in 1917 had adopted much of the agrarian program of the Socialist Revolutionary party was now used to justify the theory, developed by the Second Aliyah, that insisted on the feasibility of constructing a socialist society *de novo* in Palestine. Arguing with a delegation of Poale Zion comrades from Russia in 1920 who expressed certain doubts with regard to this theory, Tabenkin let fly, "As far as Palestine is concerned you are Mensheviks, not Bolsheviks!"[34] The idea of the shortcut, though, was even more popular among the Third Aliyah pioneers.

Given this background, one can understand Ben-Gurion's proposal of 1921 to constitute the Histadrut as a general commune. It would organize and distribute employment to all the workers of Palestine, receive their wages into a common treasury and then meet all their needs— from food and clothing to educational pursuits. All the settlements of labor Palestine would be subordinated to the commune, and all their produce would accrue to the movement as a whole. Until the planned comprehensive commune materialized, all members of Ahdut Ha'avodah were to be mobilized in a disciplined "labor army" subscribing to these principles.[35] Instead of the decentralized, diffuse labor society that had begun to take shape in the days of the Second Aliyah, Ben-Gurion was now thinking in terms of a totally centralized society. That War Communism served as the source of inspiration here is obvious.

Ben-Gurion's conception of the Histadrut was not received very well by his comrades. Katznelson did not like the idea of running the labor federation according to the "commands and edicts of a conference."[36] In the end the idea petered out and was replaced by the idea of the Workers' Society, a legally representative body but one that did not impose draconian discipline on its members and constituent organizations. Nonetheless, the organizational concepts of the Histadrut remained under the influence of the Russian model. It was a form of state socialism, however vaguely formulated.

The conflict that developed in the mid-1920s between the Labor Brigade and the Public Works Office, set up by the Histadrut to deal with the management and allocation of building work, can be seen, from one angle, as a fight between an anarchist and a Bolshevik approach. The Histadrut believed in a central body as the source of authority and discipline—and Ben-Gurion referred to this as "class rule." The Labor Brigade believed in a grass-roots and autonomous social organization and considered the Histadrut as nothing more than a flimsy coalition among a number of organizations. At the same time, though, in its own internal organization, the Labor Brigade itself reflected, according to one source, at least, the models of War Communism: the same kind of quasi-military framework, the strong discipline, the centralization and the maximalist economic goals.[37]

The fact that the socialist leadership in Palestine copied, to a large extent, the Russian organizational model, whether consciously or not, can apparently be explained by the fact that its position in some ways paralleled that of the new ruling elite in Russia. The class-conscious Bolsheviks who took power in October 1917 and the politically conscious leadership of the Second Aliyah, particularly of Ahdut Ha'avodah, were both relatively very small groups determined to inculcate the working class with their own ideas and to shape society in their own image. In both cases, the impetus for organizing and educating a broad following along specific lines came from a centralized, political-ideological nucleus.

Furthermore, like the Bolsheviks, the leaders of Ahdut Ha'avodah did not fully share the belief of the early revolutionaries such as Kropotkin and Korolenko that man was essentially good. The children of the failed Revolution of 1905 were, at heart, deeply suspicious of the masses, and their insistence on a central authority reflected this fact.

At the Fourth Conference of the Ahdut Ha'avodah at Ein Harod in 1924, Bolshevik notions were voiced by Yitzhak Tabenkin in the argument over settlement practices. Criticizing the Histadrut for not taking firm enough steps to achieve its main goal—the maximal settlement of workers—he declared that working-class control of the economy "like the dictatorship of the proletariat over the national economy, cannot be reduced to outward control, to matters of 'ownership' or even of a common budget. The entire economy must be directed to meet the needs of the workers."[38] Actually, Tabenkin's main goal was the realization of Zionism through the expansion of labor settlements. But his organizational concepts, like his terminology, came from another sphere and were, in fact, an extension of Ben-Gurion's mode of thought in the early 1920s.

Tabenkin applied the name *Communist colonization* and *Communist units* to describe the large-scale kibbutz *(hakvutsah hagedolah)* he favored. In comparing this form of collective organization with other types of communal endeavors, he said:

What is characteristic of Communism, here and all over the world, in the labor movement as a whole, is not equality between certain sections of the population . . . but the social control of the economy. For us, this means Histadrut control over the economic direction of the kibbutz.[39]

The idea that the essence of Communism was public or state control of the means of production did not prevail for long. The economy of the Yishuv developed along pluralistic lines and the labor movement began to stress the value of equality more than that of public ownership. But during the first half of the 1920s the idea of state socialism reigned supreme.

The constant use of terms like *Communist collectives, Communist settlement* and *Communist kibbutzim* in itself reflected the emotional affinity felt by the Palestine labor movement for the spirit of the October Revolution. Even *Hapo'el hazair* tried to draw analogies between "the communist agricultural collectives founded in Russia in recent years" and the various forms of labor settlement in Palestine.[40] Again, when Eliezer Liebenstein of Kibbutz Ein Harod fought for the idea of the large-scale kibbutz as the form of settlement to be given priority by Ahdut Ha'avodah, he referred to it as "communist," explaining that "our communism is attained in the way we fulfill Zionism."[41] And Ben-Gurion used words like these to justify class rule (i.e., Histadrut hegemony) over the settlements, "We have to consider the moral force inherent in communism—in the dictatorship of an idea which makes life bend to it."[42] Tabenkin explained the struggle between private and cooperative agriculture as follows:

A society based on mutual responsibility and mutual assistance, a society which maintains a non-competitive economy and a progressive culture, is both a condemnation of and a threat to capitalist society (which is one of the main reasons that capitalist Europe is trying to overthrow Russia).[43]

The kind of analogies and the terminology used here by Tabenkin, Liebenstein and Ben-Gurion were clearly imprecise and demonstrated a muddled logic, but they do show how determined these leaders were to apply Russian revolutionary language to their own problems in Palestine.

For its part, the Labor Brigade, which consisted largely of immigrants from Russia who had grown up at the time of the October Revolution, hoped to establish a "general commune" in Palestine. Their white tents, pegged into the soil of the Valley of Jezreel, were pervaded by the messianic atmosphere of impending revolution:

At the time . . . the young people of the Brigade dreamed that they were on the barricades fighting for the social revolution, and when they woke they rubbed their eyes to see if, indeed, it was approaching.[44]

The draw of the revolution could be felt in the simplicity of the lifestyle adopted by the members of the labor movement—what they wore, how they behaved to one another, the total absence of social ceremony in their lives. Their bohemianism became the symbol of their ideological identity and was sanctified in the prose and poetry of Uri Zvi Greenberg. The *rubashka* or Russian tunic sported by Berl Katznelson and Ben-Gurion was practically de rigueur in the 1920s. *Kuntres* published congratulatory messages on the birth of a child, which often read "May you raise him [or her] as a loyal son [or daughter] of the Hebrew proletariat." Presumably inspired by the introduction of the New Economic Policy (NEP) in Russia, the leader of the Palestine Communist Party (PCP), Daniel (Volf Averbukh), attacked the leaders of Ahdut Ha'avodah in 1923 for trying to impose a "communism of poverty" on the country, at the expense of the working class.[45] But the truth is that, apart from the country really being very poor at the time, they believed that simple dress, unadorned homes and honest relationships were an integral part of the revolutionary order.

Admiration for the Soviet Union was in general anchored more in the area of praxis than ideology. It was as though the October Revolution had put an end of the period of ideological disputation. The very fact that the revolutionary regime was building a country and reshaping man and society seemed sufficient.[46] It was no coincidence that Ahdut Ha'avodah adopted the organizational conceptions of the Bolsheviks rather than their ideology. They were thrilled by the upsurge of collective effort through which the Soviet leadership hoped to sweep the Russian people into the twentieth century. They were carried away by the great aims: education for all, the liberation of women, respect for the rights of children, vast industrialization. The slogan "Socialism = Soviets plus Electrification" won their enthusiasm. Those building a socialist Palestine believed that they were shouldering the same burdens as the revolutionary Russians. They, too, had to educate the working class to feel responsible for the economy; they, too, were prepared to learn from trial and error; they, too, wanted a rationally planned economy. On board the SS *Chicherin* in the Black Sea on his visit to the Soviet Union in 1923, Ben-Gurion recorded in his diary:

How similar the economic problems of new Russia are to ours in Palestine. True, there is one small difference: Russia has a state and a government and the Red Army and vast natural resources while we have only our ideals and good will.[47]

It did not take long before the Palestinians began to cultivate an image of themselves as the democratic counterpart of dictatorial Russia. When it became clear that the revolution was going to be confined to the borders of the Soviet Union ("socialism in one country"), a further analogy was made:

Russia is a large social laboratory in which we find our own relations and problems on a larger scale. . . . The socialist economy in Russia is an island in a capitalist sea. . . . The transition between the two worlds generates the same problems which face us as we attempt to build a socialist economy in the sea of capitalism.[48]

But the comparison did not mean, perforce, exact imitation, as Tabenkin pointed out, replying to charges of the PCP that the labor movement was not acting in strict accord with the tenets of socialism, "We must go our own way as the Russians go theirs. . . . The one thing we do know is that we are meeting the requirements of reality."[49] The Ahdut Ha'avodah leaders were clearly conscious of the Leninist principle that ideology could be adapted to the specific and changing circumstances if revolutionary necessity so demanded. Their attitude to the Soviet Union, accordingly, was not based on blind acceptance but rather on equality and—in certain ways—even on competition.

The Ahdut Ha'avodah leaders' stress on praxis was strongly illustrated by their attitude toward Lenin. About ten articles dealing with the Russian leader appeared in the Hebrew labor press during the 1920s. As time passed, particularly after his death, he was variously described as the father of the revolution, the captain of the ship, a political genius and a man of socialist morals—and also as gravedigger of the revolution and as an ideologically lost soul. All in all, though, Lenin became a mythical hero for Ahdut Ha'avodah and those to its left, and there was a growing tendency to dissociate him from what was happening in the Soviet Union, especially as the situation there became less and less attractive.

The first description of Lenin in the Hebrew papers after the revolution had appeared in the translation of Gorky's diaries published by Brenner in 1917—and, of course, it was less than flattering. Gorky described Lenin as a dogmatist whose knowledge of the people came from books, as a result of which he was prepared to experiment at their expense. The only compliment he gave him was also double-edged, "He is a man of many talents, gifted with the traits necessary for a 'leader.' But he also suffers from that same amorality and brutal 'aristocratic' imperiousness without which a man cannot be a leader." [50] Russell's impressions published in *Hapo'el hazair* were less emotional. In his characteristically cool and detached manner, he noted Lenin's dictatorial tendencies—he was calm, fearless, absolutely free of self-interest. Lenin was a theory in human shape.[51] However Ben-Gurion during his trip to the Soviet Union in 1923 referred to Lenin in far more favorable terms, calling him, for example, the "prophet of the Russian Revolution, its leader and teacher, ruler and spokesman, lawgiver and guide." He saw him as a man of

iron will, prepared to sacrifice human life and the innocent blood of infants for the revolution. He is an absolute tactical genius, ready to retreat from battle in order to fortify himself for a new attack, ready to negate today what he had confirmed yesterday and to confirm tomorrow what he had negated today. He won't allow a web of phraseology to becloud his thinking or allow himself to be caught up in the mesh of formulas or be tripped up by dogma. His glance never swerves from naked reality, cruel truth and the real balance of power; in all the twists and turns and complexities of the convulsion, his eye is fixed on the one unchanging goal, burning in a red flame—the goal of the great revolution, the fundamental revolution, which tears existing reality out by the roots ... down to the very foundations of the rotten and perverse society.[52]

The poet Uri Zvi Greenberg, who was shortly to publish his first book of poems, *Eimah gedolah veyareah (Great Fright and the Moon)*, with a red star on its cover, eulogized Lenin fervidly in "El 'ever moskvah" ("Facing Moscow").[53] Not long after, Greenberg was to become extremely right-wing, but at the time he wrote:

What is that?! Mystery, extraordinary reality.
Dictatorship joined by miracle, as well as splendor.
And something more: in every impossibility, which is like
a stone wall to man, there is one wonderful moment
when a porthole is opened. Lenin knew the secret

when to pass through
to the other side, enter and remain unscathed.
The most courageous man in six thousand years,
who could rule and terrify,
and whom all could love, as a father,
even the barefoot pioneers.

He ended the eulogy with the words, "The Hebrew proletariat stands on the Hebrew island/facing Moscow, in a salute to Lenin's funeral." [54]

The adulation of Lenin reached new heights a year after his death with the publication of an article by Eliezer Liebenstein. He accepted all of Ben-Gurion's superlatives, adding a few of his own. Lenin's ability to adapt his positions to the changing situation was a mark of real greatness, a refusal to buckle under to dogma, a profound understanding of dialectics. But even more, if the achievement of socialist revolution was the task of this generation—which Liebenstein was sure it was—then everything had to be subordinated to it. "Pure" ideology was the province of those who failed to understand the movement of history. Lenin, on the other hand, "always considered theory to be nothing but a useful tool for blazing a trail to deeds."

In Liebenstein's opinion, Lenin was "a democrat (if we use this word in its proper sense and not in the way it is used by all kinds of liberals and social liberals) to the depths of his soul." His democracy consisted in constantly searching for the keys to the consciousness of the masses: that is, to what motivated them. Furthermore, "Lenin was not only a man of truth. In the revolution he was the representative of proletarian morality. And again, not that morality so dear to the hearts of the bourgeoisie." Lenin's morality, according to Liebenstein, was anchored in an absolute conviction that the deeds of the insurgent proletariat "were absolutely just and a moral necessity." It followed that revolutionary terror was a moral duty that could not be shirked during revolutionary times. He praised Lenin for denying the bourgeoisie "the moral right to fight for its existence" and, at the same time, for "openly and proudly justifying the right to terror when performed by the insurgent proletariat." [55]

Ben-Gurion, Uri Zvi Greenberg and Liebenstein reflected, in this context, a common Weltanschauung: a moral relativism in which the end justifies means; the adoration of the deed, of the historical breakthrough and of the man of destiny—the activist who sees into the future, advances historical processes and understands the needs of the as-yet-immature masses.

AWKWARD REALITIES: (1) THE STRATEGY OF THE SHORTCUT IN RETREAT

The belief in the idea of the shortcut, of socialism here and now, had been, as noted above, a concept popular in Ahdut Ha'avodah in the early 1920s but was notably absent from the posthumous articles on Lenin. By 1925–26 it was apparent that a socialist Palestine was not yet in the cards. There was very little money forthcoming from the Zionist national funds for building the country. The immigrants of the Fourth Aliyah (1924–26) were no longer barefoot revolutionary idealists, but mostly Jewish storekeepers, family men and women from Poland who wanted to make ends meet. Revolution was the last thing that interested them. Whatever funds were available at the time came from private sources and were invested in private enterprise. These developments gradually persuaded the labor movement that Palestine, too, was destined to go through a period of capitalism. The revolution would have to be postponed.

A similar disenchantment with the idea of the historical leap had, of course, already taken place in Russia; War Communism had been abandoned in 1921; the revolutionary regime had been forced to take a breather, and the NEP—a compromise with a market economy and the principles of capitalism—had been initiated. Ahdut Ha'avodah did not like the NEP. The word *Nepman* was distinctly pejorative. It connotated a type of Jewish speculator in Russia and was readily used to criticize the newcomers of the Fourth Aliyah in Palestine.[56] The NEP was seen as an about-face from the great surge of building and productivization that had enthused everyone in the early stages of the revolution. Even though Lenin had been the architect of the NEP, none of the acclamatory articles about him mentioned it as one of his achievements.[57] It seems that the latter-day (apparently widespread) veneration of Lenin as visionary served as a form of compensation for the routine drudgery that had come upon socialist Zionism now that the exciting times were over. The shortcut had failed. The road ahead held only another *dunam,* another cow, another tree. Socialist Zionism required a rethinking of basic questions.

It was now that ahdut Ha'avodah adopted the theory of class struggle.[58] This was the period in which parts of the Labor Brigade and some of the labor settlements began to see themselves no longer as cells of a socialist society in the process of being built, but rather as the prototypes of a future society. But this conception was not adequate, socially and psychologically speaking, for the more militant elements. This explains the crisis that gripped parts of the Labor Brigade, some of whom retraced their steps to Russia. There they hoped to find a future for the commune that in Palestine (so they believed) was sure to degenerate into an inconsequential unit within capitalist society.[59] Others sought answers in avant-gardist activism. Their model was Lenin—not the Lenin of Marxist dogmatism or the NEP, but the uncompromising, utterly convinced, self-assured leader molding history, untrammeled by bourgeois morality, turning the future into the present. At this point, Ben-Gurion's political activism was matched up by the avant-gardist tendencies prevalent in Kibbutz Ein Harod, where Tabenkin was making his constant references to War Communism. This avant-gardism, with its clear Leninist overtones, was by no means marginal. It was central to the thinking of important elements within Ahdut Ha'avodah.

However, there was vigorous opposition in the movement as well—from the same people who had questioned the virtues of the revolution from the very beginning. Time had not mitigated their doubts. Among them, as could be expected, were Berl Katznelson and Moshe Beilinson. To delegitimize the Soviet Union as the focus of identity for Ahdut Ha'avodah, they had to do two things: put an end to the idea that the USSR was the leader of the forces of justice and progress in the world and weaken the image that Ahdut Ha'avodah had of itself as a revolutionary movement. Ahdut Ha'avodah, in their view, had to reconcile itself to the gradual achievement of Zionism and socialism.

As early as 1923, Katznelson had noted:

[A]part from its political orientation, Bolshevism brought with it a new morality, unknown to socialism. . . . There is no need to explain that this code of ethics can be of no use in building a labor society in Palestine.[60]

And now, when Beilinson struck out against the Lenin cult, it was on two counts—moral and socialist.[61] What others saw as tactical genius, Beilinson saw as simple opportunism. Lenin had eroded both democracy and socialism even though he had spoken in the name of these principles while seeking power. In the final analysis, according to Beilinson, Lenin was a victim of his own deceit. He believed that he could cheat history, but history could not be fooled. In the end he had been forced to compromise with those same forces that he had so scorned, as proved by the introduction of the NEP.[62]

Beilinson's description of Lenin was based on fact and on the reality of Russia and the international workers' movement. Lenin's admirers, on the other hand, took abstract ideas and embodied them in a human being. Both sides spoke of Lenin but meant Palestine. For his admirers Lenin symbolized the revolutionary impetus and the historical shortcut in a positive way. In the atmosphere prevalent in Ahdut Ha'avodah at that time, it was difficult for Beilinson to come out directly against the idea of the historical shortcut. He chose instead to attack Lenin.

Berl Katznelson's doubts about historical shortcuts as a system had emerged earlier, in 1922, when he began to develop heretical thoughts about the Narodnaya Volya, the movement often seen as the epitome of revolutionary idealism. He wondered if their belief in the shortcut through acts of terror, apart from satisfying "a thirst for self-sacrifice," was not simply a preference for the sensational over the routine of "simple and slow work." And he asked, "Wasn't this the reef upon which Bolshevism foundered?"[63] He considered the failure of the short-cut a reason to revert to the more moderate ideology that had character-ized the Second Aliyah as opposed to the grandiose plans characteristic of the immediate postwar years. Increasingly, both Katznelson and Bei-linson came to see the strategy of the shortcut as utterly inappropriate to the complex situation in Palestine.

Beilinson wrote a series of articles during the years 1925–26 dealing ostensibly with events in Russia and in Europe, but best understood primarily in their Palestinian context. He described the Russian Revolu-tion as an armed peasant revolt decked out as a socialist revolution. He presented both Bolshevism and Italian Fascism as employing similar political methods: the negation of democracy and the rule of a politically conscious minority.[64] But in propounding his view that the masses had to be slowly educated before the revolution could be carried out, he was attacking members of his own movement who (theoretically at least) wanted to take upon themselves the role of history's midwife.[65]

Clearly, both Katznelson and Beilinson were determined to bring their comrades down to earth from the dizzying heights of messianism by pointing up the vast differences between the vision of the revolution and its results, between Leninism and the ethical code of the Palestinian labor movement, between an avant-garde and a mass movement.

AWKWARD REALITIES: (2) SOVIET ANTI-ZIONISM AND THE LABOR MOVEMENT IN PALESTINE

There was a second, parallel drama being played out in the relationship between the Soviet Union and the Palestinian labor movement—a drama of unrequited love. It had become apparent at a very early stage that the Bolsheviks were hostile to Zionism in general and to socialist Zionism in particular. In 1920 the Hebrew press reported that the Third International had decided that, from its class viewpoint, Zionism was fraudulent. Its aim was the exploitation of the majority of Arab workers by a minority of Jewish workers.[66] There had been at the same time a split in the ranks of the socialist-Zionist movement between those who wanted to join the Third International at all costs and those who were not ready to desert the hard core of Zionism for the wide spaces of the majestic revolution.

From information that reached Palestine in 1919, it was clear that there had been large-scale defections from the Poale Zion movement, first in Russia and then in the other countries of Central and Eastern Europe. The promise of universal redemption acted as a magnet of enormous power. Members of the right-wing of Poale Zion (Ahdut Ha'avodah among them) were hurt at the ease with which their long-time comrades abandoned principles only recently declared sacrosanct. They also feared the battle that was sure to ensue for the souls of Jewish youth.[67] The feeling was, "the devil lay in wait," and this became common currency in describing the appeal that "the religious fire of world revolution" had for young Jews.[68] This factor encouraged certain sections of the Palestinian labor movement—Berl Katznelson among them—to adopt, long before others, a critical attitude to the Soviet Union.

But there were alternative ways of looking at the hostile attitude of the Third International to Zionism. Nachman Syrkin, for example, blamed it on the agitation of various Jewish groups and individuals who saw vociferous anti-Zionism as an easy way to demonstrate their new-found loyalty to Bolshevism—Social-Democratic assimilationists or traditionally anti-Zionist Bundists or simply obsequious socialist Zionists.[69] "Ridiculous and disgraceful behavior," was the way Marc Yarblum, one of the leaders of Poale Zion in France, described the behavior of the Left Poale Zion delegates to the meeting of the Third International in Moscow that adopted the historical anti-Zionist resolution. Neither revolutionary principles nor the interests of Soviet Russia had anything to do with it.[70]

Ben-Gurion enthusiastically approved of Syrkin's approach that condemned the resolution of the Third International but blamed the resolution on renegade Jewish socialists rather than on the Bolshevik leadership.[71] "In my opinion," he wrote, "there is no other International and all socialists must belong to it."[72] Therefore, he added, "We must explain to them in person the essence of real Zionism, and especially of socialist Zionism and its work in Palestine." He tried to convince Syrkin, who was in London, to go to Russia for this important purpose.[73]

In time the blame came to be focused specifically on the Evsektsiia (the Jewish section of the Communist party). The Evsektsiia, it was declared, was responsible for the suppression of Hebrew and the persecution of Zionists. It was thus possible to identify fully with the Soviet regime and at the same time to damn the Evsektsiia. An illustration of this differentiation between "pure" and "impure" can be found in Ben-Gurion's description of his visit to Moscow in 1923 (to attend an agricultural exhibition that included a display sent from Palestine). His meetings with both Jewish and non-Jewish Bolsheviks were full of mutual goodwill and understanding. Only the Evsektsiia and what he saw as the fawning behavior of the Left Poale Zion ruined the idyll. He found the Soviet authorities helpful in raising the Jewish national flag side by side with the Red flag over the Palestinian exhibition hall. He was able to explain the nature of the Histadrut to a Soviet official without any difficulty, even mentioning its ties with the International Federation of Trade Unions in Amsterdam, to which the Soviets objected. Everything was amicable.[74]

On the other hand, the central committee of the Left Poale Zion proved to be afraid of the Evsektsiia with regard to both the flag and the exhibition. "We have," wrote Ben-Gurion, "no common language with the Evsektsiia. We also don't need them. . . . That's not young Russia."[75] As he saw it, it was necessary and possible to change the attitude of the Soviet regime to the Zionist enterprise in Palestine. Its present opposition, he concluded, "is not integral to the Soviet system or to Communist theory (which, by the way, is not steering the course of the new Russia)."[76] Ben-Gurion gave a number of reasons for seeking a dialogue with the Bolsheviks: the stability of the regime, the importance of Soviet Jewry and particularly of the Jewish youth as a pioneering potential for Palestine.[77] But at the heart of the matter was his eagerness to obtain legitimation for socialist Zionism from the leaders of the revolution.

Ben-Gurion's meeting with socialist-Zionist youth in Russia was very emotional. The members of Hashomer Hatzair impressed him enormously, and he made great efforts to get them exit visas from Russia and entrance visas to Palestine.[78] But even the bitter stories that he heard from leaders of the Hehalutz and Hashomer Hatzair about the persecution, harassment, penal exile and imprisonment of the socialist Zionists did not change his basically positive approach to the Soviet Union.

Ben-Gurion's visit, made together with Meir Rotberg and the tour of the Crimean kolkhozy by Yehuda Kopellewitz (Almog), a member of the Labor Brigade, represented a concerted effort by leaders of the labor movement in Palestine to open up direct contacts with the Soviet Union. In the summer of 1924 forty-one released Zionist prisoners, whose imprisonment had been commuted to deportation, arrived in Palestine on board the SS *Novorosiisk*. Most of them were from socialist-Zionist organizations, and the outstanding group among them were members of the clandestine Socialist-Zionist party (SZP).[79] Party activists since their early youth, they quickly became integrated into the activities of Ahdut Ha'avodah, frequently lecturing on the situation in the Soviet Union.[80] From that point on more and more reports appeared in the Hebrew labor press about the persecution of the SZP in Russia and the situation of Hehalutz there.[81]

At Ben-Gurion's initiative, trade negotiations were opened between the Histadrut and the Soviet Union.[82] Two of the major Histadrut subsidiaries, the Workers' Society and Solel Boneh (a construction company), were invited to participate in a conference of the Tsentrosoyuz, the Union of Cooperatives in the Soviet Union. David Remez and Levi Shkolnik (Eshkol) were sent as representatives in an advisory capacity, and on May 16, 1925, Remez addressed the conference in Hebrew in the name of the labor cooperative movement in Palestine.[83] He emphasized the common ideological roots of the socialist experiments in Palestine and in the Soviet Union.

Remez also met with leaders of the Zionist underground in Russia,[84] and he must have discovered that the campaigns against the Hebrew language and against Zionism had been intensified. In the wake of reports about the persecution of the SZP, the council of Ahdut Ha'avodah, held at Nahlat Yehuda, adopted a resolution to extend help "to the persecuted comrades in Russia." It was decided to devote the week following May Day of 1925 to the subject.[85] A special issue of *Kuntres* appeared soon after describing the activities of the SZP in Russia, their heroism, suffering and their harassment by the GPU. On August 3, 1925, an announcement was published in *Davar* from the National Public Committee for Assistance to the Imprisoned and Exiled Zionists in Russia that was signed by Chaim Nachman Bialik and that called on the Yishuv to supply aid, both material and moral, to the victims of persecution in the USSR.

Apparently, there was some disagreement in Ahdut Ha'avodah about the wisdom of launching such frontal attacks on the Soviet Union because two days later, Beilinson, in a column, "To the Aid of Russian

Jewry," apparently felt compelled to respond to some unspecified criticism:

Even if we were completely convinced that Russia has embarked upon the total renewal of human society, and for its sake the Jewish people had to sacrifice its honor and freedom—even then we would not agree to such a price.[86]

He went on to contend that if the Russian Revolution hoped to survive, it would have to purify itself. As part of this process, it would have to grant the Jewish people in Russia the right to engage in a struggle for its own national freedom:

Every Jewish worker knows that by helping the Jews of Russia in their struggle, he is fulfilling an elementary national duty and contributing to the real victory of the Russian Revolution.[87]

In the fall of 1925 reports began to appear in the Hebrew press concerning plans to encourage Jews in Russia to settle as farmers in the Ukraine and Crimea. It was intended to create a community of one hundred thousand families from nearby areas crowded with Jews who lacked all sources of subsistence. The revolution had wiped out the middle classes to which most of Russian Jewry had belonged. Yaakov Rabinowitz came out in *Davar* in favor of the plan as a positive solution that would enable thousands of Jews "to cease being middlemen and take up a life of labor and productivity."[88] This view enraged Uri Zvi Greenberg, who replied with his usual acerbity in the pages of *Kuntres*.[89] Thus opened the great debate on Palestine versus the Crimea. At first, the discussion was almost hysterical. The Soviet Union was creating an alternative to Zionism. And when Mikhail Kalinin, the president of the USSR, was quoted in November 1926 as saying at a conference of OZET (Association for Jewish Agricultural Settlement) that a Jewish republic might be established in the Crimea, these fears grew still more.[90] Members of Ahdut Ha'avodah were astounded by the positive Jewish response, both widespread and intensive, all over the world.

During 1926 the Palestinian press reported on Israel Zangwill's support for the idea (Palestine, he said, was the size of Wales and it could never really provide an answer to the plight of the Jewish people);[91] on how the Agro-Joint (of the American Jewish Joint Distribution Committee) had mobilized assistance for Crimean settlement;[92] and—with particular pain—on the defection in New York of Reuben Brainin, who had been one of Herzl's early followers. Brainin had made a tour of Palestine and Russia in 1926. He was not disappointed with Palestine, but he returned from Russia with an enthusiasm that knew no bounds, unsullied by any word of criticism, not even of the Evsektsiia. There was no conflict, he argued, between the two countries, and they were of equal value—but, of course, in the last resort, the Soviet experiment was bound to be seen as the more significant because it was destined to solve the problem of three million Jews.[93] Here was a real slap in the face to the Zionist claim that it alone could solve the Jewish question.

At a mass rally in New York, widely covered in the Palestinian press, enthusiasm for the projected Jewish republic knew no bounds. The prevalent feeling there was unmistakable:

Kalinin's announcement heralds the fulfillment of a dream of two thousand years. In the end, one has to admit that those who claimed that the social revolution would solve all the Jewish problems were right.[94]

All the Jewish socialist organizations that were opposed (for one reason or another) to mainstream Zionism—the Bundists, the Territorialists of different hues, and the Left Poale Zion—now, of course, enjoyed a new surge of energy.

The element of competition between the two settlement programs was built in. One side saw the Palestinian enterprise as a unique national enterprise and sought to mobilize the best forces of the Jewish people on its behalf.[95] The other denied the exclusivity of the Zionist undertaking and succeeded, if only for a moment, in offering an appealing, and apparently feasible, alternative. The ideological debate on the subject revolved around questions of resources and priorities. A group of leading Yiddish writers in New York, for example, failed to respond to an appeal by Palestinian writers to support the Jewish National Fund; yet they mobilized on behalf of the settlement in the Crimea.[96] The Joint (as already noted) had also lent great support to the Russian project although it had reservations about settlement in Palestine. The Jews were clearly unable to support adequately two such movements at the same time.

Even the most fervent supporters of Zionism could not honestly object to the productivization of destitute Jews in Russia. First, of course, the idea of working on the land touched a deep chord in the socialist-Zionist ideology. Second, because the project had originated with the Soviet government, it seemed to imply a recognition of national rights for the Jewish people. At least that is how Kalinin's announcement was widely interpreted. Criticism had once again to focus on the Evsektsia.[97]

In describing the goals and problems of the Crimean enterprise, the plight of the Jews of Russia became a topic that could not be avoided. In none of the numerous articles that appeared, however, was the Soviet government blamed. The economic problems were described as the result of objective circumstances, common to the country as a whole; assimilation was explained away by the openness of Russian society; the outlawing of Hebrew and Zionism was the work of the Evsektsiia. A. Ben-Adir (Rozin) was the exception when, writing in *Davar,* he heaped derision on this approach:

The Soviet government was never responsible for any of the difficulties of the Jews in Russia, especially not for their cultural-spiritual devastation. Only the Evsektsiia—"these criminally destructive brethren"—can be blamed.[98]

The kid gloves used when describing the Soviet Union, however, did not blunt the sharp edge of the competitive element, and there was much anxiety. Potential support for the Zionist movement was being sapped. And the timing could not have been worse. The Fourth Aliyah, which had arrived in Palestine during the mid-1920s, served to emphasize the limitations of socialist construction in Palestine. The achievements of the labor movement had proved meager when measured against the dimensions of the Jewish problem. A few tens of thousands of people had been absorbed with the aid of enormous investments while in Russia there was talk of half a million Jews being settled by the government on public land. At a time when ideas were being judged in accordance with the concrete answers they provided to existential problems, Palestine was no match for the Soviet Union. Moreover, the rising sun of the country of revolution was lighting up the horizon. It appeared that the Crimea had liberated the Jewish national idea from the parochial confines of Palestine.

No wonder, then, that news of the drastic limitations imposed on the Crimean project that began to reach Palestine at the beginning of 1927 did not cause much grief. Yaakov Rabinowitz, who two years earlier had praised the idea, did write that "there is no reason for joy,"[99] and there was no gloating—just a deep sigh of relief. In the fall of 1927 Arthur Ruppin (the noted Zionist and an expert on agricultural settlement) left for a tour of the Jewish colonies in the Ukraine and Crimea. His dry factual report on what he found brought the discussion from the ideological heights down to earth. There was not much land (he wrote) available in the Ukraine or the Crimea for new Jewish colonies, and there were only about thirty thousand people scattered in various localities. With one or two exceptions, this fact precluded the possibility of administratively autonomous Jewish regions. As for a Jewish republic in the Crimea—it was out of the question. The entire enterprise had proved of value for individual families hard put to make a living elsewhere, but it was devoid of any larger national or cultural significance. Certainly, settlement in Russia was cheaper but that in Palestine had proved capable of attracting idealistic youth prepared to sacrifice personal comfort for the common good. The difference between the two enterprises was summed up by Ruppin as being philanthropic in Russia and of national importance in Palestine.[100]

Thus, Crimea ceased to pose a problem.[101] Here and there one continued to hear of some achievements, as in a report of Sholem Asch after a visit there.[102] But the threat was never renewed. Reports of the Birobidzhan plan in the late 1920s failed to excite the old fears.[103]

REACTING TO THE EMERGENT REGIME OF STALIN (1928–29)

Together with the failure of Jewish settlement in Russia came more news about the persecution of Zionists, of Hebrew and of socialist-Zionist organizations.[104] In April 1928 the last remaining legal mainstream Zionist movement, the Hehalutz, was banned and its members arrested and brought to trial. Its famous training farm in the Crimea, Tel Hai, which had garnered much praise from Western visitors, was likewise disbanded. The Left—or Communist—Poale Zion party was also forced out of existence in 1928. Only now, for the first time, did Ahdut Ha'avodah begin to place the blame for the persecution of the Zionists directly on the Soviet regime as such.[105]

On April 17, 1928, a mass meeting was held in Tel-Aviv to protest the liquidation of Hehalutz and other anti-Zionist measures. However, two of the speakers, Joseph Sprinzak and David Ben-Gurion, reflected the ambivalence still prevalent in the labor movement with regard to the phenomenon of the Bolshevik Revolution. Sprinzak, who came from the moderate Hapoel Hatzair wing of the labor movement said:

We followed the revolution with trembling hearts. We knew there were mistakes, acts of cruelty, unrealistic historical short-cuts, but after the great slaughter of the nations, we were lovingly prepared to accept all the errors: we saw here the moral uprising of mankind.

Therefore, he went on, "our position toward the Bolshevik regime was: 'Do not judge your fellow-man until you reach his place.' " Ben-Gurion spoke in the same vein, "We were constant in our love for the great revolution in Russia."

Both men became poetically effusive when they touched on the subject of their spiritual affinity to Russia. Sprinzak recalled "the intimate bond with Russia" that characterized his generation and the generation before him, "It was a country of oppression and slavery but also of great sadness; of profound agitation; of the search for God and for the salvation of man." Ben-Gurion pointed out that although they were steeped in the Jewish heritage, he and his comrades owed a great debt of gratitude to the heritage of Russia, "The Russian Revolution is the force that fructified our work during the Second Aliyah and during the Third." What was being critically examined, he went on, was "the Russia in our hearts." At one time, Ben-Gurion continued, he had explained away the terrorist methods used to impose the new regime as a necessary evil, forced on them by intervention and reaction. But

if any of us were still convinced that the accusations were not true, that they were the invention of Russia-haters, the liquidation of Hehalutz has put things in their true light.

One gets the impression that had it not been for the persecution of Hehalutz in particular and the Zionists in general, Ben-Gurion and his comrades would hardly have found it opportune to express publicly any reservations about the revolution. Even as it was, their criticism was clearly half-hearted.[106]

Beilinson was indignant, "One can be sure that Sprinzak's sympathy for the Communist Revolution would have been a good deal less conspicuous were the revolution not in distant Russia but, let's say, close by, in Palestine." And in opposition to Ben-Gurion, he declared bluntly that "one cannot say that we feel constant love for a revolution whose terrorist methods we abhor morally and ideologically." In his view it was incomprehensible that his comrades had had to wait for the liquidation of the Hehalutz to realize that the revolution had failed its disciples; and he dissociated himself from their tendency to make Delphic statements of the kind that, "We give due weight to the power of the revolution both to destroy—and to build."

Ben-Gurion and Sprinzak were not yet ready to make the final break with the revolution; in this respect they probably reflected the mood of their audience. But Beilinson insisted on making the distinction between democratic socialism and dictatorial Communism. As far as he was concerned the rift was caused not only by the issue of Zionism but also by the fact that "the labor movement in Palestine has throughout been guided by an attitude both socially conscious and humane." [107] So, whereas Ben-Gurion and Sprinzak attempted to preserve the myth of the revolution and to concentrate their criticism on one point, Beilinson rejected its validity *in toto,* considering it utterly unsuitable as a didactic symbol from both the moral and the political point of view. It was only logical, then, that Beilinson should have warned against Ben-Gurion's tendency to find a "psychological affinity" between the "millennialists" *("dohkei hakez")* in Soviet Russia and those in the Yishuv.

But when all was said and done, despite the persecution of the Zionists and the liquidation of the socialist-Zionist organizations, despite the Crimean affair, despite reports in the press of the struggle between Stalin and Trotsky, sections of the Palestine labor movement still looked on revolutionary Russia as the source of their moral and revolutionary legitimacy.

Thus, the gap, opening up ever wider between the tangible realities of life in the USSR and the revolutionary legend, in turn, produced ever-more polarized reactions in the Palestine labor movement. There were two levels of awareness: one based on events and factual reports, the other based on myth. As for the first, it appears that there was no other foreign subject that enjoyed such vast and detailed coverage. *Kuntres* published an exhaustive series of articles on the Soviet economy by Z. Kulton and one by Yitzhak Norman (a member of the SZP who had recently arrived in Palestine) on the power struggles within the Soviet regime.[108] For its part *Hapo'el hazair* carried a series by Y. Gelft on the Soviet economy and another by Y. Lederman on Soviet Jewry. *Davar* published detailed reports on Stalin's maneuvers against his various adversaries. Every visit to Russia merited coverage. In short, everything that went on in the Soviet Union was reported in detail by the Hebrew labor press. Even Lenin's testament (containing his critical evaluation of Stalin, Trotsky and the other Soviet leaders) was printed in full, taken presumably from the version published by the left-wing American journalist, Max Eastman.[109] Nothing of any public interest was denied the labor readership in the Yishuv.

At the same time the myth acquired flesh and bone. No matter how frequently disappointment followed disappointment in the area of fact— the failure of the historical shortcut and the dreary life of the people as well as the callousnous of the authorities toward the opposition at home and abroad, toward the socialist movement and toward the Jews and Jewish culture—the myth prospered. The revolution had become a sym-

bol. The "Days of Wine and Blood" (October [November] 1917) signi-
fied the hope of generations.[110] Any subsequent failures, if and when
acknowledged, were described not as the natural outcome of the revolution, but as a temporary or local deviation. Negative developments in
the Soviet Union were unable to destroy the mass yearning for liberation,
for immediate redemption, for the cataclysmic change bringing salvation
to humankind.

This emotional commitment to the idea of a great revolutionary
convulsion was, apparently, even greater within the Palestine labor
movement than one would conclude from what appeared in the press.
After all, it should be remembered that Berl Katznelson and Moshe
Beilinson were the chief editors of the Histadrut journals and that they
had been exceptional in adopting a highly guarded, sceptical attitude to
the revolution from the first. Their evaluation had been based on the
lack of symmetry between the backwardness of the Russian people and
the high level of consciousness demanded by a socialist society. Nothing
that eventually happened in Russia surprised them. They believed that
the process of self-destruction and the degeneration into tyranny, however tragic, had been predictable. They expected nothing; so they did
not become disillusioned. As admirers of the Revolution of 1905, which
had failed while (in their view) retaining its moral purity, they measured
the successful Revolution of 1917 not according to its political achievements, but according to its ethical standards. In the course of time they
became ever more convinced that from the didactic point of view, it was
essential for the Palestinian labor movement to loosen, or even sever, its
bond with the October Revolution and to put an end to the quest for,
and the expectations of, legitimation from the revolutionary Communist
camp that had in any case refused it admittance.

The values of the first revolution were therefore revived by them as
an alternative to the values to October, "Moral maximalism, the refusal
to bend to evil, the anticipation of a radical change in society, revolutionary fervor, devotion, stringent demands on the individual." [111] Katznelson and Beilinson looked back in longing at the image of *old* revolutionary Russia. It satisfied both their emotional need for affinity to
Russia—their physical and spiritual homeland—and their ideological
need to identify with a revolutionary movement. The Revolution of
1905 became their lodestone. It was a reaffirmation of the Second Aliyah
values. Of course, among those who defended the Soviet system, there
were those, like Tabenkin (also a Second Aliyah veteran) who never
denied their own affinity to the broad revolutionary camp that had

fought in 1905, even as they were captivated by the spirit of October. As a result, the contradiction, which Berl Katznelson increasingly emphasized (and perhaps exaggerated), between the value systems of 1905 and 1917 was long in emerging into full view. It was not until the 1930s or 1940s that this dispute came out into the open, but the dichotomy could be clearly perceived by the second half of the 1920s. Katznelson and Beilinson had the leading press publications of the labor movement at their disposal—first *Kuntres,* then *Davar.* It can cause no surprise, then, that what was published there was increasingly either critical or neutrally informative. It appears that the public had more sympathy for the Soviet Union than was reflected in the press. Beilinson's indefatigable campaign against the USSR was (as far as he was concerned) an educational attempt to wean the public from its excesses. But Ahdut Ha'avodah took a long time in coming around around to this view. In its broadsheet of May Day 1927, it accompanied its criticism of Soviet anti-Zionism with praise for the success of the Soviets in pulling the masses out of the lower depths, in liberating women and in strengthening the economy.[112] In the leaflet of the following year, it was noticeable that much of this praise was gone.[113]

Still, truly sharp criticism—like that of Abba Ahimeir—was not well received. Ahimeir had written that the February Revolution had been a moment of historical grace, whereas the October Revolution had plunged the country back into the Tsarist mold:

The public has once again been transformed into an irresponsible opposition and rule has reverted to a bureaucratic government, which pays no attention to public opinion. . . . In October 1917, Russia reembarked on its historical course: the repression of public freedom, the victory of administrative power over society.[114]

Moreover, even those who were critical of the Soviet Union still could not entirely escape the pull of October, the liberating revolution.[115] Thus, D.S. (presumably Dov Stock-Sadan) could publish in mid-1928 an enthusiastic view that clearly identified with John Reed's *Ten Days That Shook the World.*[116] In the final analysis the myth of the revolution proved more powerful for many than the reasoned arguments of its critics: "This myth is potent in the world at large," declared an article in *Kuntres* by Y. N. Steinberg—a veteran Left SR and a member of Lenin's government in the winter of 1917–18—now a political émigré.

Because the world today is depressed, is so aware of the failures of civilization, eyes are turned, eleven years later, upon that period in which one people proved what is *possible,* what is *necessary.*[117]

The process of dissociating Russian reality from the revolutionary myth would only be reinforced during the 1930s with the worldwide depression, the rise of Nazism and the crisis of social democracy in Europe. If in the 1920s there had still existed certain possible alternatives with which to identify—such as the Austrian Social Democratic party—by the 1930s they were mostly gone, swept into the dustbin of history. With the perceived failure of reformist socialism, the appeal of redemptive revolution again grew strong. The dispute, formulated in terms of the first Russian Revolution as opposed to the Bolshevik Revolution, was fought more bitterly than ever. It was a contest waged within the world of Russia's traditional political culture. Western ideas and criteria played only a marginal role. The key words and the standards of judgment derived from a political tradition that, at one particular point in history, had bifurcated. The battle of ideas and ideals in Mapai,[118] between the camp of October and the camp of 1905 would take on new forms in the 1930s and 1940s. But that, of course, is another subject.

NOTES

1. Alexander Penn, *Leilot bli gag* (Tel-Aviv: 1984/85 [1929]), 94.
2. See, for example, Berl Katznelson to the vegetable growers of Jerusalem, 18 July 1918, *Igerot Berl Katznelson*, vol. 3 (Tel-Aviv: 1976), 12.
3. *Ibid.*, Passover eve, 14 April 1919, 216.
4. Berl Katznelson, *'Arakhim genuzim* (Tel-Aviv: 1940), 111–12.
5. B. Katznelson, *Igerot*, vol. 3, 445.
6. See, for example, "Hashehitot beukrainah" [excerpts from the Russian press], *Hapo'el hazair* (25 November 1919).
7. Nachman Syrkin, "Mikhtavim meeiropah," *Kuntres* (7 October 1919).
8. "Mimah shehayah beukrainah," *Kuntres* (3 December 1919); "Me'al dapei hahaganah beukrainah," *Kuntres* (30 January 1920); "Kiev—migay hadamim," *Kuntres* (6 February 1920).
9. "Berusiah," *Kuntres* (24 October 1919).
10. "Mitokh hahafekhah," *Hapo'el hazair*. (13 February 1920). The editorial board dissociated itself from the contents of the article.
11. *Hapo'el hazair* (24 September 1919; 25 November 1919).
12. Syrkin, "Mikhtavim meeiropah," *Kuntres* (5 July 1919).
13. *Ibid.*
14. "Le'inyanei hahit'arvut berusiah," *Kuntres* (7 October 1919); Syrkin, "Mikhtavim meeiropah" (24 October 1919); "Hatenu'ah lehazalat rusiah," *Kuntres* (23 November 1919).
15. *Hapo'el hazair* (13 September 1921).
16. Y. Aharonowitz, " 'Ezrah lare'evim," *Hapo'el hazair* (30 September 1921).
17. Michael Assaf, "Teshuvah," *Kuntres* (10 October 1921); Mordecai, "Lema'aseh," *Kuntres* (10 October 1921).

18. S. Zemach, " 'Akalkalot," *Hapo'el hazair* (30 September 1921).

19. Y., "Merahok," *Kuntres* (4 July 1919).

20. Maxim Gorky, "Mahapekhah vetarbut," *Haadamah* (19 November 1917), 701; *ibid.* (7 December 1917), 702; *ibid.* (10 December 1917), 703–704; *ibid.* (24 December 1917), 704; *ibid.* (31 December 1917), 705.

21. Bar-Yohai [Brenner], "Mipanim umeahor," *Haadamah*, 585–94.

22. *Ibid.*, 594.

23. Bertrand Russell, *Hapo'el hazair* (10 September–12 November 1920).

24. Russell, "Reshamim merusiah habolshevikit" (translated from English) *Hapo'el hazair* (10 September 1920).

25. For the reference to Brenner's remarks, see "Mipanim umeahor." *Haadamah*, 590.

26. Russell, "Reshamim merusiah."

27. *Ibid.* (12 November 1920).

28. *Kuntres* (24 September 1919); "Mikhtav miKropotkin," *Kuntres* (7 November 1919); cf. Korolenko, "Likutim," *Haadamah*, 207–9.

29. Abba Ahimeir, "Kropotkin," *Kuntres* (1 April 1921).

30. Ahimeir, "Mi shelo hayah gibor zemanenu," *Kuntres* (19 January 1921).

31. Korolenko, "Likutim," 207–9; S. Friedman, "Shnotav haaharonot shel Korolenko," *Kuntres* (27 January 1922).

32. Lecture by Joseph Klausner, reprinted in *Kuntres* (31 December 1919).

33. B. Katznelson to Haim Katznelson, Jaffa, 6 September 1918, *Igerot*, vol. 3, 226.

34. Yitzhak Tabenkin, *Devarim* (Tel-Aviv: 1967), 32.

35. David Ben-Gurion, "Hatafkid hamishki shel hahistadrut haklalit," in his *Mima'amad le'am* (Tel-Aviv:1932/33), 123–4.

36. B. Katznelson to Eliyahu Golomb, Cherbourg, 22 October 1921, *Igerot*, vol. 4, (Tel-Aviv: 1970), 338.

37. Baruch Meir, "Gedud ha'avodah," *Kuntres* (21 October 1921).

38. Y. Tabenkin, *Have'idah harevi'it shel ahdut ha'avodah be'ein harod* [12–20 May 1924] (Tel-Aviv: 1924/26), 59.

39. *Ibid.*, 60.

40. See editorial in *Hapo'el Hazair* (15 November 1923).

41. Tabenkin, *Have'idah harevi'it shel ahdut ha'avodah*, 77.

42. *Ibid.*

43. *Ibid.*, 108.

44. A. Knaani, " 'Al ha'hasmalah' bagedud," *Mehayenu* (16 February 1927).

45. *Protokol have'idah hasheniyah shel hahistadrut haklalit shel ha'ovdim beerez yisrael*, ed. Mordechai Sever (Tel-Aviv: 1923), 41.

46. Bar-Yohai [Brenner], "Mipanim umeahor."

47. D. Ben-Gurion, *Zikhronot*, (Tel-Aviv: 1971), 25 August 1923, 225; cf. Meir, "Gedud ha'avodah."

48. "Bitnua'at hapo'alim ha'olamit," *Pinkas* (Jerusalem, 30 May 1923).

49. Tabenkin, in *Protokol have'idah hasheniyah*, 47.

50. Gorky, "Mahapekhah vetarbut," 699.

51. Russell, "Reshamim mirusiah."

52. Ben-Gurion, *zikhronot*, 268, 254–55; Yisrael Kollat, *Avot umeyasdim* (Tel-Aviv: 1975), 25–26; Michael bar-Zohar, *Ben-Gurion* (Tel-Aviv: 1975), 176–77.

53. Z. David, "Turim," *Kuntres* (28 May 1925).

54. Uri Zvi Greenberg, *Kuntres* (25 January 1924).

55. Eliezer Liebenstein, "Lenin," *Kuntres* (24 April 1925). Liebenstein quotes an article by Lenin during the Terror (*Pravda* [2 June 1918]), in which Lenin compares the revolution to birth. It tortures the mother and almost kills her, but this will not prevent people from loving and having children.

56. For Ben-Gurion's criticism of the NEP during his visit to Russia, see his *Zikhronot*, 267–68.

57. "Lenin," *Kuntres* (8 February 1924).

58. See, for example, Ben-Gurion, "Haye'ud haleumi shel ma'amad hapo'alim," in *Mima'amad le'am*, 231–34ff.

59. On the end of the theory of historical leap and the transition to the theory of class struggle, see the speech by Elkind (1 May 1925) at Tel Yosef, in *Mehayenu* (24 May 1925); Y. Richter, "Agadat hakomunizm hakonstruktivi," *Mehayenu* (31 October 1925).

60. B. Katznelson, *Kuntres* (19 January 1923).

61. Beilinson, "Lenin," *Kuntres* (1 May 1925).

62. *Ibid.* (15 May 1925).

63. Katznelson's notes for 1921/22, *Igerot*, vol. 3, 342.

64. Beilinson, "Hafashizm haitalki," *Kuntres* (30 November 1923); *idem*, "Romantizm vesozializm," *Davar* (9 July 1926); also *Ketavim*, vol. 1, 162–68.

65. Beilinson, "Lenin."

66. "Bainternazional hashlishi," *Kuntres* (22 October 1920).

67. See, for example, Katznelson to Kheshin, *Igerot Berl Katznelson*, vol. 3; also B. Katznelson to Ahdut Ha'avodah Executive (Paris, 2 September 1919), *Igerot*, vol. 4, 18–19. Katznelson to Lea Meron-Katznelson (Vienna, 5 August 1920), *Igerot*, vol. 4, 126.

68. Katznelson to the office of the World Alliance of Poale Zion (London, 31 October 1919), *Igerot*, vol. 4, 66; B. Katznelson to Ahdut Ha'avodah Executive (Vienna, 5 August 1920), *Igerot*, vol. 4, 127. See also, for example, Ben-Gurion to Zalman Rubashov (14 December 1921), "Hasitrah hasmalit," *Igerot Ben-Gurion*, vol. 2 (Tel-Aviv: 1972), 92.

69. See, for example, N. Syrkin, "Hainternazional hashlishi vehaziyonut," *Kuntres* (29 October 1920).

70. M. Yarblum, *Kuntres* (27 February 1921).

71. *Ibid.* (29 October 1920).

72. Ben-Gurion to Syrkin (London, 2 December 1920), *Igerot*, vol. 2, 47.

73. *Ibid.*

74. Ben-Gurion to the Histadrut Executive (Moscow, 24 September 1923), *Igerot*, vol. 2, 161–164; also, Ben-Gurion, "Hehaluz berusiah," *Kuntres* (22 February 1924).

75. Ben-Gurion to the Histadrut Executive (24 September 1923), *Igerot*, vol. 2, 170.

76. *Ibid.*

77. *Ibid.*, 170–72; also Ben-Gurion, "Hehalutz berusiah," *Kuntres* (7 March 1924).

78. Ben-Gurion to Zionist Executive in London (Berlin, 18 November 1924), *Igerot*, vol. 2, 260.

79. "Bein habaim merusiah," *Kuntres* (25 July 1924).

80. See, for example, list of speakers from Ahdut Ha'avodah, *Kuntres* (5 September 1924).

81. For example, "Baziyonut hasozialistit," *Kuntres* (21 November 1924); "Bahalutz unvano'ar," *Kuntres* (13 March 1925).

82. "Hahlatot mo'ezet hahistadrut," *Pinkas* (Jerusalem, 27 August 1923).

83. D. Remez, "Mishlahat hahistadrut lerusiah," *Kuntres* (24 April 1925).

84. See Zalman Aranne, *Autobiografiah* (Tel-Aviv: 1971), 177.

85. *Kuntres* (1 May 1925).

86. Beilinson, "Le'ezrat hayahadut harusit," *Davar* (5 August 1925).

87. *Ibid.*

88. Yaakov Rabinowitz, "Reshimot," *Davar* (13 September 1925).

89. Uri Zvi Greenberg, "Krim, 1924/25," *Kuntres* (24 September 1925; 2 October 1925).

90. On Kalinin's speech, *Davar* (27 December 1926); cf. the analysis by Baruch Zuckerman, "Erez yisrael verusiah," *Davar* (4 January 1927).

91. "Zangvil 'al hahityashvut berusiah," *Davar* (3 March 1926).

92. "HaOzet, HaJoint, vehaziyonut," *Davar* (18 June 1926).

93. "Reuven Brainin veDavid Shor 'al erez yisrael vekrim," *Davar* (27 August 1926); "Ko amar brainin," *Davar* (2 January 1927).

94. "Hasofrim hayehudim 'al hahityashvut berusiah," *Davar* (2 January 1927).

95. M. B. (Beilinson), "Krimizm," *Davar* (7 December 1925).

96. See n. 94.

97. See, for example, Zuckerman, "Erez yisrael verusiah," *Davar* (4 January, 21 January 1927); also Yitzhak Yatziv, "Zelalei hateritorializm," *Kuntres* (14 January 1927).

98. A. Ben-Adir, "Bolshevizm vehanekudah hayehudit," *Davar* (9 August 1926).

99. Yaakov Rabinowitz, " 'Od lehityashvut hayehudim bas.s.s.r.," *Davar* (21 March 1927).

100. "Dr. Ruppin 'al bikuro berusiah," *Davar* (3 November 1927); Ruppin, "Hityashvut yehudit berusiah uveerez yisrael," *Davar* (13,15, 16 January 1928).

101. See Ab. Cahan on the subject, *Davar* (25 November 1927).

102. Sholem Asch, *Davar* (26 June 1928); cf. Warburg's impressions of his trip to Russia, *Davar* (20 July 1927).

103. Zuckerman, "Medinat hayehudim besibir," *Davar* (16, 18 March 1928).

104. See, for example, M. Lichtman, " 'Od redifot," *Kuntres* (26 March 1926); "Lebikurei mishlahot hapo'alim mihuz laarez berusiah," *Kuntres* (19 November 1926); "Anusei s.s.s.r.," *Kuntres* (2 April 1928); "Nifsekah hademamah," *Kuntres* (5 June 1928); "Lezekher haver," *Kuntres* (9 December 1927). Cf. *Davar* (14 November 1927, 3 December 1928); Eliezer Galili, "Sifrut ziyonit bilti legalit," *Davar* (3 December 1928); Bialik's open letter in *Davar* (26 May 1929).

105. A. Ben-Naphtali (Eliyahu Golomb), "Leferuk 'hehaluz' berusiah," *Kuntres* (2 April 1928).

106. For the protest against the disbanding of Hehalutz in Russia, see *Davar* (18 April 1928); cf. Bar-Zohar, *Ben-Gurion*, 180.

107. Beilinson, "Leshem behirut ha'emdot," *Davar* (25 April 1928).

108. *Kuntres,* nos. 264–72 (11 June–6 August 1926); nos. 325–28 (20 January–10 February 1928).

109. Max Eastman, *Davar* (9 November 1926).

110. Gorky, "Mahapekhah vetarbut," 703.

111. Beilinson, "Mitokh hipusei haemet hasozialistit," *Davar* (2 February 1928); also *Ketavim,* vol. 1 (Tel-Aviv; 1940), 157.

112. *Kuntres* (29 April 1927).

113. *Ibid.* (30 April 1928).

114. Abba Ahimeir, " 'Eser shanim larevoluziah hafebruarit," *Hapo'el hazair* (17 March 1927).

115. See, for example, Yitzhak Norman, "Basevakh: lehag he'asor shel mahapekhat oktober," *Kuntres* (17 December 1927).

116. D.S. (Dov Shtock-Sadan), "Beshulei sefer," *Kuntres* (10 August 1928).

117. Y. N. Steinberg, "11 shanah aharei hamahapekhah harusit," *Kuntres* (23 November 1928). Emphasis in original.

118. In 1930 Ahdut Ha'avodah and Hapoel Hatzair merged to form Mapai (the Palestine Labor Party).

21.

Fire and Water:
Ze'ev Jabotinsky and the Revisionist Movement

Yaakov Shavit

Someone said that redemption will be brought about by blood and fire, not by water. Why not water? In order to build the Jewish State we need fire and water—everything is sacred. Let no one say, I will work with water, therefore you are forbidden to work with fire.
— Ze'ev Jabotinsky, Congress of The World Revisionist Movement, 1932.

1. THE IDEA OF THE "LEADER"

In a short article entitled "Leader," published in 1934, Ze'ev Jabotinsky was asked to clarify his ideas on the subject.[1] It was not the first time, for we know that he was preoccupied with the question of his status as leader of his movement. The clarification of this issue was important to him both for himself and in relation to others. "Is it a law," he queried, "that the more one deals with a phenomenon, the more enigmatic it becomes?" How did Herzl become a leader? Was it because he had "the character of a leader?" What is "the character of a leader?" In the same article he continues:

Nowadays there is a fashion for leaders. In almost every nation we find a romantic longing for adventurism, and when there is no suitable leader around, they fix on an unsuitable one, bestow a title upon him, and try to relate to him as a bona fide leader. We, the Jews, even at the height of our Zionist enthusiasm, are deferring to the dictates of assimilation and aping this trend. We are as taken with the search for a leader as are our neighbors, and with the same results. . . . Our children will be astounded when they read the *real* biographies of these leaders, so numerous in almost every country. They will be astounded when they discover that much of the time, many of them were no more than clay in the

Reprinted by permission of the author and *Studies in Zionism* 4 (October 1981): 215–36.

hands of chance. What is especially hard to understand is the character of those who so long for leaders.

Against the background of this phenomenon, he saw Herzl as a leader of a completely different mold. He was not a leader because of his title or his role, but because the public "simply obeyed him." He was, in the words of a Russian writer, "a conqueror of thoughts." He did not demand leadership; the people were simply carried away by him in the same way "that they are carried away by a great singer, because his singing expresses our own longings. And there is still another sign: when a man like Herzl dies, he remains our leader even thirty years after his death."

In this article, Jabotinsky was attempting not so much to evaluate Herzl as to clarify the character of his own leadership. He did not see himself as a leader who aimed to satisfy the impulse of adventurism and the longing for leadership at any price; nor a superficial leader who was actually a creation of the imagination of the masses; nor a leader by dint of official titles; he was rather a leader who conquered the minds of his contemporaries, who gave expression and direction to their experience and to their deepest emotional makeup and, by so doing, actually structured their world. There is no doubt that what he said about Herzl applies to him and to his movement even more so. The phenomenon of a leader remaining a "leader" and "conqueror of minds" (even "controller of minds"), for those who see themselves as his disciples forty years after his death, is a phenomenon worthy of note.

It is unique not only because Jabotinsky retained his status in the face of a general "idol-smashing." No other Zionist leader aroused such extreme views within the Zionist movement. His opponents saw him as a politician and leader who erred and caused others to err all the way down the line, an unrealistic, superficial mouther of empty phrases. His adherents, on the other hand, saw him as the perfect leader, unerring in his presentation of goals and in his diagnosis of problems, versatile, talented in every field of endeavor, in short—perfect. These extreme opinions underwent further polarization for as long as Jabotinsky was at the center of ideological conflict and all-encompassing political rivalry. He was a man who attracted a wealth of descriptions, characterizations, and definitions, a man whose words and personality became "canonized" in his movement. Today, forty years after his death, not only is his glory undiminished, unfaded, but there are people who still draw inspiration from his writings, who attempt to act according to them, who search them out in order to justify every important move they make. It appears that they are seeking a sense of continuity, not merely with a set of ideas or a political party, but with one man and his teachings, with Ze'ev Jabotinsky.

2. THE PERSONIFICATION OF THE MOVEMENT: INTERNAL DYNAMICS

In the remarks that follow, I do not intend to evaluate Jabotinsky, his teachings, or his historical activities, where he was right and wrong, where he was "ahead of his time," or where he was out of step with his times. Most studies of Jabotinsky and his teachings are too heavily weighted by political considerations, either for or against. In the context of this article, I will avoid taking sides. It should be seen rather as an attempt to examine the relations that existed and developed between Jabotinsky and the Revisionist movement or the "Jabotinsky national movement," as it was sometimes called.

Epithets like this give credence to the notion that this was a movement created by one man, who formed and led it, conquered the minds and emotions of its members, directed them and continued to direct them even beyond the grave. Indeed, the movement as a whole saw in Jabotinsky an undisputed leader, a guide, and even more—a way of life. He was a man who shaped the biographies of individuals and of an entire generation of followers. Without doubt, he was a man whose relationship to his movement (which was not just a small faction or limited group of zealots) can not be compared with that of any other Zionist party leader. However, the aim of this article is to point up another phenomenon hovering behind the solid image and the political myth: the phenomenon of a dual relationship and a set of mutual tensions between the movement and its leader. The personification of the movement in the image and personality of Ze'ev Jabotinsky, so emphatically expressed by both followers and adversaries, is *not* an unequivocal historical fact. Moreover, such a one-dimensional and unequivocal representation of the facts not only creates a political myth; it also blurs one of the most decisive and important factors in the inner dynamics of the history of that movement.

3. JABOTINSKY'S ATTEMPTS TO MIX "FIRE" AND "WATER" IN METHOD AND IDEOLOGY

Our interest here is not with the question "What kind of man was the 'real' Jabotinsky?" Or if there was a cleavage between his public image, as reflected in some memoirs, evaluations, and his own public appearances, and—on the other hand—his "intimate," private image as seen in other memoirs and personal letters not intended for publication. The plethora of documentation does not present a single, clear, unequivocal image. Practically every person has "his own Jabotinsky"; and beyond the common denominator there are contradictions and contrasts. The versatility of the figure, his talents and occupations, tempted many to try and clarify whether Jabotinsky had synthesized his many facets into one integrated personality or, perhaps, was well aware of his internal contradictions but could differentiate sharply among them (e.g., between Jabotinsky the esthete and man of the arts, and Jabotinsky the public, political figure).[2] Or perhaps, as one of his sharpest critics put it, he was a very spotty figure, full of numerous inclinations, which never coalesced into a unified whole.

It is the presence of these contradictions, or this integrity, which is of primary interest to the biographer. The historian is more likely to be interested in the source of sources or the diametrically opposed interpretations of Jabotinsky's political philosophy.

Was Jabotinsky different in 1905 from what he was in 1919, or 1931, or 1939, or is it possible to find a continuity, differing perhaps in shading but not in content? What is the source of the continuing discussion, not only of the "rightness" or "wrongness" of his views and ideas, but even of their actual content? Is one side interpreting his figure correctly while the other is spreading error and falsification? In order to answer these questions, it is necessary to turn to a precise examination of the development of Jabotinsky's ideas in the specific historical context in which they crystallized. Moreover, we must examine what role these ideas played and what role they were intended to play. Jabotinsky was a political figure, and we must therefore examine his ideas in relation to the audience to whom they were addressed. I shall attempt to show and prove that Jabotinsky was, to use his own metaphor, simultaneously a man of "fire" and "water," and a man of both in content and method. He tried to synthesize these two elements, but the inner dynamics of his movement resulted, first and foremost, from the continual tension between the elements of "fire" and "water" within it and within him.

4. THE DEVELOPMENT OF THE DIFFERENCES OF OPINION BETWEEN JABOTINSKY AND THE LABOR PARTIES

There is a solid line of continuity in the views of Jabotinsky, his behavioral patterns, his reactions, the means he recommended, his moods, etc. However, from the minute he decided to leave the official Zionist establishment and become the leader of an opposition movement, a certain change occurred. This change took place not in his formal positions (that is, his basic views), but in his status and position in the Zionist movement. The same Jabotinsky who wrote in a moment of respite (or inner truth) "I am by nature a tent-dweller, and it was others who always dragged me into politics,"[3] became once more the Jabotinsky who saw in statesmanship the highest form of art. There is a decisive difference between a statesman actively bearing the formal responsibility for the implementation of policy and the leader of a popular activist-radical political movement.

When Jabotinsky first began his oppositional activity, Moshe Glickson, editor of the daily, Ha'aretz, tried to explain certain changes which, in his opinion, had their origin in Jabotinsky's resignation from the Zionist Executive in 1923. Before this, Glickson wrote, Jabotinsky was a clear-eyed, far-seeing leader. He was a realist, pragmatic in his assessments and a man of the highest integrity. He was unable to head a political party because of his moderation and desire to compromise. This spiritual wholeness and moral strength, wrote Glickson, were "disastrous and sinful in a political leader." And indeed, in 1927, he found Jabotinsky excessively paradoxical, demagogic, full of destructive contradictions, and deprived of his sense of reality. He explained that Jabotinsky acclimated quickly to the "brushfire of the Revisionist clubs in Palestine."[4] It is interesting that years later, within the party itself, there were those who accused Jabotinsky, on the one hand, of adapting too much to the mood of "general Zionism" in the movement, and, on the other, of an inability to reach necessary compromises and a total lack of tactical sense.

Jabotinsky had ideas and views before he became the leader of a political party. One can find much continuity in his views, but there were certain changes in his stance on some basic issues. He had an outlook before he had a movement which followed him; he had ideas and views before that movement made him its leader. The movement had heroes (Herzl, Trumpeldor), but it had no leader. When Jabotinsky was called upon to unify the different and divided activist groups in both Eastern and Western Europe, he became the leader of groups whose image had already been established. Moreover, although he was the "crowned and uncrowned" leader, and his personality drew people to the movement, the movement was nevertheless established first and foremost because it answered the social and ideological needs of a wide stratum of Jews. As a result, Jabotinsky never had the possibility of controlling and directing the development of the movement in its broad social makeup. To a certain extent it is possible to say that Jabotinsky's fate was similar to that of Herzl. Herzl established an organizational framework on the basis of an already-existing organized popular movement which itself had deep and diverse roots and aspirations. In its new unity, the World Zionist Organization was conditioned by Herzl's conception of it and his expectations from it.

One can understand the changes which evolved in several of Jabotinsky's positions and in the role he filled, by studying the development of his relationship with the Palestine labor movement. In spite of the general coldness which existed between him and the labor parties, stemming from their differing ideologies and backgrounds, Jabotinsky showed a pragmatic appreciation for the labor movement as a movement of pioneering-elitist Zionist fulfillment. He saw it as a suitable partner for his activist policy. In spite of certain disagreement over the defence of Tel Hai and what followed, he still described the Third Aliya in sympathetic terms. His attitude at the time was much more supportive than Weizmann's, who in 1920 described the communal settlements as tending to sectarianism: "The overwhelming extent of Russian assimilation and this sectarianism leads to fanaticism," which in turn produces a "union of the bitter." [5] Only after 1924 did the labor parties become—in Jabotinsky's eyes—spoiled children, dependent on Weizmann's handouts. Only then did a total political and ideological struggle emerge in the course of which each side endeavored to destroy the ideological and moral basis of the other.

Until 1923 there were differences of opinion between Jabotinsky and the labor parties, stemming from a difference of approach and tactics and from their divergent backgrounds. But it wasn't until the political and organizational polarization occurred, and Jabotinsky became the leader of a socio-ideological movement fighting for power and the Zionist "soul," that he realized the necessity for formulating a total oppositional ideology.

As early as November 1925, Jabotinsky wrote that, without a doubt, from the point of view of caliber and ability, the central social class of Zionism was the Jewish proletariat or—what he meant in effect—the educated Jewish workers. They were the "best material in the world," intelligent youth who desired "simple reform." [6] The "trouble" with this high-caliber social class was that it had become imbued with socialist ideology and retreated into national and political minimalism. The Ahdut Ha'avoda movement had given up its political activism in deference to Weizmann, because it needed his material help to realize its practical socialist-Zionism.

5. THE IMPORTANCE OF THE MIDDLE CLASS IN THE EYES OF JABOTINSKY

If the pioneering intelligentsia could not provide the social support for Jabotinsky's political ideas, which other social class could? In the wake of the Fourth Aliya, among other things, Jabotinsky came to the conclusion that any serious revision in Zionism must be based on the middle class which had no ideology outside Zionism proper.

The choice of the middle class was problematic in many ways, not the least of them ideologically. The "common people," which Jabotinsky called the "intermediate class," were not necessarily composed of the property owners who came to Palestine, and he himself had difficulty in characterizing them precisely. "Believe me," he wrote to a close friend, "it is more in sorrow than in anger that I say that I myself know that all these other [social] elements are unstable and cannot be counted on." [7]

He felt that he was being forced to rely on unstable and indefinable social elements who were powerless to organize, lacked motivation, and were not, in his opinion, the most suitable element to begin with. It was difficult if not impossible to assign a major economic and settlement role together with an activist national outlook to a class which was—in Revisionist terms—minimalist in its Zionism. This contradiction, in my opinion, was not resolved in either theory or practice. But the attempt to do it had far-reaching results. It became apparent that in order to provide the movement with an ideology, a political viewpoint was not sufficient. One needed a full set of ideas and an all-inclusive program for every area of life. The middle class had to be given a sense of mission. The result was inevitable—new areas were opened to Revisionist-labor conflict.

Of course Jabotinsky made studious attempts to solve this inner contradiction. For example, he made a distinction between the narrow-minded "bourgeoisie"—enslaved by private property, politically conservative and passive—and the "citizen," the patriot activist endowed with political consciousness. His movement would be made up first and foremost of "middle-class youth," a young, popularly-based cadre, like the members of the Hashmonai student organization he had addressed in Riga in 1923. He claimed that his movement was classless and neutral, "monistic" because of its popular nature and because it did not represent any clearcut economic and social interest. But the contradictions were not solved by these distinctions. The movement continued to represent a certain social class. Meanwhile, another part of this class—which ostensibly lacked clear economic interests—found itself in open alignment with a specific side in the discussion of social and settlement policy, not only because of their Zionist reasoning but also from clearcut, succinctly stated ideological considerations.

This development had been clearly diagnosed by Jabotinsky himself, years before it actually surfaced in the Zionist movement. When, in 1915, he analyzed the nationalism of the middle class in Eastern Europe, he wrote:

Dyed-in-the-wool, abstract liberalism, whatever its authorization, is beyond their attainment. The middle class does not yearn for liberalism if one has the wisdom to offer them something else. Organically, the middle class cannot respond to socialist propaganda; the economic ideals of these circles must of necessity be reactionary . . . There is only one ideal which, in these circumstances, can raise the masses of the urban class, can purify and ennoble their outlook: the ideal of nationalism. If they are now attracted to the Right, it is not only because they preach "a hard hand and a mighty arm," but also because the Right have succeeded in touching their nationalist sympathies.[8]

Neither ideas of abstract liberalism nor the ideological defense of a certain economic class motivated that political, social, and ideologically cohesive movement; it was rather a deeply emotion-laden nationalism, rich in symbols, hopes, and expectations that animated Revisionism; neither economic nor political liberalism, but a combination of anti-socialism and active nationalism. In order to respond to the demands of its following, it was necessary to combine anti-socialism and even virulent anti-socialism (which did not sit well with Jabotinsky's assertion that he was not an adherent of virulent anti-Marxism), with simple, straightforward, unequivocal nationalism.

6. JABOTINSKY'S STATUS IN THE REVISIONIST MOVEMENT

It was, therefore, necessary to "find" the public to address and recruit, to define its character and quality, and to diagnose its aspirations and respond to them. This public needed a leader. As we have already seen, Jabotinsky was well aware of the deep psychological roots of this need, yet maintained an ambiguous attitude to the unquestioned leadership status so quickly accorded him by the movement. He had even tried to fight against it at first, to no avail. The second and third generations of the movement exalted the leader even more.

When he went out to "conquer the congress" (the Fourteenth Zionist

Congress, 1925) from without—not from within—he at first examined the possibility of forming a properly organized political party with means at its disposal. In August 1925 he wrote:

and as long as it has no real federation, with organized branches in every important place, with active offices and officials, and with party propaganda as well, I will not agree to any outside "activity." [There can be no "attacks" while] there is no army, no tents, and no rifles. . . . We need a network of societies and offices . . . a bureaucracy which functions like clockwork, so that we can press a button in Dan and hear a bell ring in Beersheba. For that we need propaganda and organization. . . . I can't see it any other way.[9]

The army became a reality. But it was not an army of "tents" and "rifles" or a well-oiled bureaucratic machine. The movement was, on one hand, a core of activists, a cadre and, on the other, a broad public. There were no resources, no organization, no phalanx of organized supporters, but rather diverse groups which had coalesced very quickly. The "leader" held the movement together by force of his personality and his personal authority. The Revisionist movement was not satisfied with a guiding idea: the idea had to be personified in the image of a leader. Jabotinsky was wary of the status of charismatic leader, inundated with displays of admiration and zeal. He tried to separate his informal from his formal status as head of the movement. But it soon became clear, at the cost of internal rifts and the resignations of his old friends, that he must combine his formal and informal status. He understood the reasons which obliged him to become the crowned "leader," even though he did not cherish them. He formalized the relationship between himself and his movement, and acknowledged the profound necessity of the movement to give him unquestioning admiration. In a recently-published letter to the secretary of the head office of the Revisionist Executive in London, written in 1930, he argued against the "cult of leadership" and the sense of "elitism" which prevailed in the movement.[10]

You touch on problems which worry me deeply. There are two questions: (1) we, and (2) myself. Even to my closest friends I seem ridiculous if I speak of "ourselves" as an elite. The word "race" has turned into a good joke, and it is not difficult to joke about it. The present composition of the movement is far from elitist; perhaps even the contrary is true. This is nothing new; movements of the kind which sanction inner moral purity are usually the ones which have impure elements. That is what happened to the early Christians, and the beginning of the Quaker sect. There were many who honestly wanted to improve themselves, but there were doubtless also those who saw in the new adventure a good way to seem better without actually becoming better. Perhaps, and it seems so, we have many of this type. And nonetheless I am sure I am right: the essence of the movement is the desire to help bring the world a better, nobler Jew with fewer of the defects of the ghetto and more of the virtues of Biblical times. In order to understand this, one must perhaps close one's eyes occasionally, eyes used to looking through the microscope, and turn an ear inwards to the murmuring of the soul. I am certain that the storm of Revisionism—perhaps after years during which it will reach its height—will bring a lofty generation to the Jewish people.

I am much more pessimistic with regard to the second question. I have an organic hatred for personality worship, and I am repulsed by it. Fascism has some good ideas, but I am simply physically unable to discuss them serenely and directly; I am repelled by the worship of the *Duce* as I am by any public dishonesty. When something similar happens among us, I see it as a real danger. Twice in *le murmure des âmes,* I protested the title "leader." In Basel I had my friends grant the title "president" to the late W. Tyomkin. I would have done the same in Prague as well (for Grossman), but at the time when I was forbidden entry to Palestine, this gesture was considered unfitting. I go to meetings of student groups, but I don't sing well, something I hate. [I want] no remnants of an idol's pedestal to remain, and to no avail. The need on the part of today's generation to take a person and turn him into a myth, is inevitable. Even if I were to declare that I am the man who stole Susskin's pocket watch, it would be of no avail. I am beginning to fear that in my constant concern not to play "leader" for fear of [over-] influencing the movement, I keep silent when I should speak out and even insist on my opinion, like anyone else.

As concerns this problem, I am at a loss.

There are two important assertions in this letter which is somewhat apologetic in tone: (1) the Revisionist movement was one into which divergent elements entered. (Jabotinsky said elsewhere that he couldn't vouch for the "human crop" that his propaganda reaped.) According to Jabotinsky, although the movement's ideas were correct, there was not always perfect harmony between the idea and those who carried it out. At any rate, the objective was paramount, not those implementing it. (2) He personally rejected the hero worship which surrounded him, but he saw in it the "need of the times." He had attacked this manifestation sharply when Weizmann was on the pedestal; he now found himself able to understand its roots. In order to preserve the unity of the movement, in order to satisfy demands from within it, he had to assume all the titles, as he actually did in 1933. He wrote sarcastically to his friend Yaakobi at the end of that year: "You and your whole fascist generation were right about one thing. One cannot camouflage leadership."[11] In any event, even if out of some honest aesthetic revulsion, he had attempted to reject the position forced on him. it would probably not have made much difference. An abstract idea and solid principles were not enough. It was necessary that they be epitomized in a single man.

7. THE POLITICAL PARTY AND THE YOUTH MOVEMENT

The need for a leader was in part a result of the gap which existed between the various components of the movement: between the Revisionist party and its youth movement, Betar, and later between these two and its military arm, the *Etzel* (Irgun Tzvai Leumi). Jabotinsky was aware of the differences in background and mentality between these organizations. Revisionism, he said, was one stout trunk from which several main branches sprouted. Such a situation, nonetheless, creates conflict and tension. Almost from the outset there was an obvious incompatibility between the legalism of the political party and the nationalist radicalism of the Betar youth movement. This polarization was exacerbated during the thirties as a result of political events in the Diaspora and in Palestine. The differences between Betar and the party, and their attempts to interfere with each other's development, greatly pained Jabotinsky. He tried to preserve Betar's autonomy, describing it as an educational movement which was creating a new Jew, rooted in a national ideology and psychology. As such it would be in the movement's interests not to impair this attempt at self-education and responsibility. Still in all, the different roles which they were called upon to play in the Zionist political system created deep cleavage. For example, a political party had to employ tactics which a youth movement could not accept. In July 1931, Jabotinsky wrote to the Secretary-General of the Betar Executive:

A party which participates in Zionist congresses must agree to tactical compromises whose usefulness is in doubt, while their decided educational value is in no way in doubt but, rather, completely negative, dangerous and harmful, and likely to embarrass the ranks of Betar youth . . . Trumpeldor Youth is above all an educational institution. We have the great responsibility for the souls of youth, and we must not be allowed to misdirect them in any way which suggests a dangerous compromise, a compromise which might affect the holy of holies of the Zionist idea. A youth movement must be hard line: "yes" must be "yes and "no" must be "no." [12]

At its founding meeting in 1925, the Revisionist party was able to decide upon a moderate wording of its political demands. They could assert that Zionism desired "the gradual transformation of Palestine (including Transjordan) into a Jewish community, that is, an *autonomous community* led by a Jewish majority which will have come into being." This wording was considered the only possible definition of "National Home." [13] It was followed by an enumeration of the practical steps which would be taken with regard to taxation, land laws, etc. Betar, on the other hand, could not agree to this in any form. There could be no substitute for the term "state" in its charter. "The Betar Idea" [14] opens in a totally different style by stating: "The role of Betar is simple in object, yet very difficult: to create the type of Jew which the nation needs in order to create the *Jewish state as quickly as possible* and in the best way possible." The idea of the creation of the state as a gradual process, to be completed only once certain conditions are fulfilled, is almost absent from Betar ideology.

It is my contention, therefore, that the changes in Jabotinsky's political terminology and declarations of purpose were not only a reaction to the political events which changed Jewish and Zionist perspectives. They were also a reaction to pressures from the radical maximalist factions in his movement. They could not reconcile themselves to compromise, or "moderate" wording or any substitute for the clear, unequivocal idea in which they believed and to which they were educating others.

8. THE DIALECTIC OF RELATIONS BETWEEN JABOTINSKY AND THE MOVEMENT

It is obvious that changing historical circumstances are the major cause for changes in Jabotinsky's views at different periods. In 1905, for example, in the spirit of practical Zionism, he wrote: "Don't clamor about Palestine, don't shout about achievements; and when there are achievements, don't shout about plans." [15] Later he wrote that for as long as Zionism needs diplomacy and statesmanship, Weizmann must remain the leader. One must evaluate these statements in light of their historical context and of Jabotinsky's status at the time. It is possible to interpret his articles (and one should interpret their content *and* their style), not as part of a closed ideological system, but against the background of the times, and bearing in mind the audience to which they were addressed. No one who attempts, for example, to draw specific conclusions about Jabotinsky's credo on the basis of articles he wrote in his "Russian period" can ignore the political-cultural context in which these articles were written and the special phraseology they employed.

The combined weight of changing historical circumstances and of the movement's inner conflicts and development on the real or imagined paradoxes in Jabotinsky's Zionist outlook, do not accord with the views held by both his followers and adversaries. Both sides like to describe his credo and actions as unequivocal, one-dimensional. The following subjects will serve to substantiate these assumptions:

1. The relationship between liberalism and monism.
2. Social considerations in monism.
3. Was Jabotinsky really the architect of the movement's outlook?

Liberalism and Monism. In the Betar Idea there is no sympathy for what Jabotinsky called "abstract liberalism." In it only the idea of monism comes across clearly. And if monism is the banner, then nationalism and national fulfillment cannot be linked with either socialism or liberalism. There is no mention of the middle class being the preferred class to settle Palestine. There is, rather, a setting forth of a mechanism whose objective is to create social-economic harmony out of national, "neutral" considerations. The synthesis to which the Betar Idea aspired was not a synthesis of social ideas and national outlook, but a synthesis of free will, discipline and hierarchy. This point of view inevitably troubled the party. The exclusion of social conflict from the pale of Zionist endeavor—at least during the period of the upbuilding of Palestine—contradicts to some extent the view of Jabotinsky (and his party) as upholders of a liberal social philosophy. Yet, nationalism and national fulfillment were seen in Jabotinsky's monistic view as being above all other considerations. This view is called "integral nationalism" by the more moderate of his critics. Extreme commentaries on Jabotinsky clash over this point. Liberal or anti-socialist? Democrat or authoritarian, even totalitarian? I would suggest that Jabotinsky consciously suited the content and style of his words to whichever sector of his movement he was addressing, thus giving rise to two versions of his outlook.

In a letter to David Ben-Gurion in March 1935, directed to the radicals in Mapai and perhaps, incidentally, to his own party, Jabotinsky responded to Mapai's rejection of the "London Accords." (These accords were proposed to end the hostility and violence between the Revisionists and the labor movement in Palestine.) He wrote:

How will you fight this brutality, what is your prescription? Will you try to teach them your art (that is, the art of the delicate balance between Zionism and socialism)? I doubt if this generation has the ability to understand it, or if it even has the desire to. *This generation is very "monistic."* Perhaps this is not a compliment, but it is the truth.[16]

And so, the generation of the labor movement, whom he accused of having a hodge-podge of ideas, at a stroke becomes a "monistic" generation, similar to that part of the same generation of which he is the leader. Further, this is a fact that needs to be understood, and taken into consideration, even though it is not praiseworthy.

Not only the content, but the style changes. In a certain context Jabotinsky had deep reservations about the style of the party newspaper, *Hazit Ha'am (Popular Front)*, of the early thirties. He wrote that since most readers did not understand symbolism, one should avoid using strong language, unverified accusations and historical references. Only after did he show tolerance for the style of the paper, when he discovered "the ugly group they must fight against."[17] He himself did not avoid symbolism and "strong language." The writing of publicists, he explained, has a "cadence" which differs from that of poetry or even essays. And, in fact, the cadence of Jabotinsky's poetry and literature differed completely from that he used for ideological and political battle. Further, the Jabotinsky who wrote for the Revisionists used a different cadence from that he used when he wrote for Betar.

Social Considerations in Monism. Monism was ostensibly meant to separate social considerations from those of Zionist ideology and Zionist fulfillment, at least during the interim period before the establishment of the Jewish state. The realization of national-political aims was to be the only goal during this period, and there was no need to discuss the type of society which would come into being in Palestine. Such monism, however, was impossible to maintain, not only in practice, but even in theory. Thus, Jabotinsky, who dealt with problems of settlement and society in a great many articles addressed to members of the party, was obliged to explain the importance of social questions to the members of Betar. The political dimension of the Zionist idea could not exist alone; the social dimension was also necessary. The plan which Jabotinsky set forth envisioned a bourgeois state with elements of a welfare state. But what interests us here is not the plan itself but whether or not its existence did not, at least partially, contradict the monistic character of Betar ideology. And another question presents itself: Why did he feel that the members of Betar should be aware of the importance of social problems and not merely satisfied with a knowledge of the central principles of the Betar Idea?

The answer, perhaps, is that Jabotinsky was more interested in social questions than is usually conceded; that he was aware of the fact that the process of creating a Jewish majority in Palestine—as a prerequisite for the establishment of the state—was not just a political process, but a social process as well. Moreover, Betar members in Palestine were not just proponents of the *idea* of the Jewish state. They were also a social group involved in the daily social and economic problems of Palestine. It was necessary to explain to them why they were not just "political beings," but "social beings" as well; to explain how they were involved in the crystallization of the society and economy of the Yishuv. From this followed the attempt to infuse social-economic theory into the monistic idea, whose essence was educational-national-political.

Ostensibly, the idea of a "national compromise" and the formulation of various methods for labor arbitration were supposed to blend into the monistic idea. But this was not sufficient. What really gave Jabotinsky's social ideas a monistic flavor, as he set them forth for Betar, was their Biblical garb. Party interpreters of this socio-economic credo wrote: "The well from which Jabotinsky drew his ideas was Jewish," or "In the Bible of Israel, Jabotinsky has found the general groundplan for the structure of the ideal society of the future Hebrew state." [18] The general admiration was such, that there were even those who saw in him one of the most important social thinkers of the twentieth century.

This is puzzling. Jabotinsky was deeply rooted in universal culture. His diary emphasizes the conscious adaptation of ideas of various Western philosophers. He himself admitted that his social theories were based on assumptions acquired, in one way or another, from the teachings of the major philosophers of the late eighteenth and early nineteenth centuries. Anyone familiar with these ideas can easily arrive at the sources of most of his assumptions and conclusions. He himself never aspired to be an original thinker in social matters. Why then did others endow him with the image of a social philosopher who based his teachings solely on ancient Jewish sources?

The answer seems to be that articles such as "The Idea of the Age," "Class," "The Social Philosophy of the Bible," and others, were all written for Betar youth. In view of the background of this youth, it was clearly impossible to write an article based on the ideas of Antonio Lavriola, Benedetto Croce, Josef Popper or Max Weber. These names meant nothing to most of them. They had been brought up on a monism rooted in Judaism, in a kind of national-cultural autarchy. They did not feel at home in the languages and culture of the Western world as Jabotinsky did. Their horizons were much more limited. They could best understand symbols which were familiar to them. Thus, an "original Jewish" theory was offered which could pass as monist. Here was an idea whose essence was Jewish nationalism (or, more precisely, "Hebrew" nationalism), combined with original Hebrew social ideas. Liberalism and socialism had never been part of traditional Judaism, and were therefore inimical to monism and the singularity and unity of the idea. Here again, the intended audience for the ideas, the character, education and goals of this audience, determined their content as well as their style.

Was Jabotinsky Really the Architect of the Movement's Outlook? The third subject is perhaps the most crucial in understanding the development of the movement. Did Jabotinsky really play such a dominant, even exclusive role in the shaping of the movement, its methods and its immediate goals?

In order to answer this question we must differentiate between long-term goals and immediate ones, and between declared goals of the movement and the means used to achieve them. Jabotinsky indeed determined the long-term goals and basic tenets, but there was a good deal of tension between him and the movement in relation to immediate goals and the means for achieving them. Even in those years when he was the supreme authority, perhaps especially during those years, decisive policies were resolved in which—initially—Jabotinsky had no part. It is true that he unified Betar and the Revisionist party and stood at their head; it is also true that he brought about the break with the World Zionist Organization and the creation of the New Zionist Organization. But he was not the creator of the military arm—the Etzel, nor the initiator of its actions. It was not Jabotinsky who directed the Etzel's endeavors in the Diaspora to gain influence in the Betar cells. He was not, in my opinion, the spiritual father of the "uprising" of the Etzel against the Mandatory regime in 1944.

Jabotinsky's dramatic protest at the Seventeenth Zionist Congress in 1931 did not result from the Congress's rejection of the Revisionist formula calling for the immediate establishment of a Jewish state in Palestine. It was not even suggested that it be done at once. The Revisionist resolution simply called for a public declaration to the effect that the establishment of a Jewish state in Palestine was the goal of Zionism and, specifically, that the area of the Palestine Mandate on both sides of the Jordan be transformed into a Jewish state, that is, a commonwealth with a Jewish majority. Opinion was divided mostly over tactics and timing (with, of course, a strong dash of ideology thrown in). In 1938, when war was in the offing and shortly after the partition plan of the Peel Commission had been retracted (to Jabotinsky's satisfaction),

Jabotinsky suggested a "Ten-year Plan" as an alternative to partition. It was a ten-year plan of settlement, of mass immigration (1,500,000 immigrants) and of economic development which would lay the groundwork for the state. "After ten years of such a regime, the Mandate should be abolished and Palestine given the right of autonomy." He added: "In spite of all the storms raging now, we see the future of the League of Nations as strong and steadfast, and the Mandate for Palestine as a valid contract." [19]

The basic tenet in Jabotinsky's political outlook was that the means existed for using the legal possibilities provided by the Mandate to create a Jewish majority in Palestine as a pre-condition for the establishment of a state. These possibilities could be realized if the Zionist movement would *publicly* declare its aims and then activate English public opinion on its behalf. For this reason he attempted, until 1935, to gain a majority within the World Zionist Organization. One major field of action which, he felt, would advance his political aims was based on the distress of the Jews in the Diaspora and action to arouse English public opinion to alleviate this hardship. Thus, Jabotinsky organized a mass petition signed by hundreds of thousands, addressed to England and the League of Nations. At the Fifth World Convention of the Revisionists in 1932, his description of the petition, meant to put moral pressure on Britain, was rather high-flown rhetoric:

This is not merely a verbal formulation with lots of signatures. This is a movement, a vast mass movement, whose stage is the entire world, and not just one country. This is a process which will electrify the soul of the world, and the presentation of the scroll will only be the final scene in the last act of the play. Millions of hands, all extended in one direction. [20]

When he spoke of British opposition, he did not speak of an armed uprising, but of a political offensive "which will force England to change her policies and return their rights to the people of Israel." When he spoke of real opposition in Palestine, not "verbal opposition," he spoke of all manner of civil rebellion—rebellion without revolt, active protest and not war against the Mandate. When he was under pressure from the ranks of the activists in his movement to express his stand on "the question of opposition," he answered that "we will have to think out ways of making the life of the government miserable while still being able to use the situation to our advantage," [21] and he suggested, for example, a tax strike. The idea of giving up the Mandate or perhaps forcing Britain to give in through active resistance did not come primarily from Jabotinsky. One need only compare the wording, style and reasoning of Jabotinsky's speech to the Peel Commission in 1937 with the fervid tone and contents of a book of poems, *The Book of Accusation and Belief*, by Uri Zvi Greenberg, composed at the same time. The latter had an enormous influence on that generation of the movement. To a certain extent these are two different worlds.

The first document presented to the institutions of the Revisionist movement which included a demand for the immediate establishment of an independent Jewish state in Palestine was presented in 1938 and it was not worded by Jabotinsky. It was first set forth in the pamphlet, "Our Eyes are on the Government," which was published earlier in serial form in the daily *Hayarden* as a personal opinion, by Uriel Halperin (the poet Yonathan Ratosh).

Jabotinsky did not demand the immediate establishment of a Jewish state until 1939, nor did he call for its creation through revolt against the British government and the destruction of the Mandate. His concept was gradual, not revolutionary, legal and political, not underground-military. But the radical-activist current in the ranks of the movement grew, and in 1937 the Etzel was established. From then on, Jabotinsky's movement was composed of a political party cum independent Zionist organization, a national youth movement, a national workers' organization and an underground military organization. The internal tensions among them were deep, sharp and all-embracing. All the attempts at compromise, which were tried continuously until 1939, failed. Jabotinsky's attempt to differentiate between the movement's responsibility and the "irregular" actions of individuals in the movement also fell flat. The famous petition was not even a "bridge of paper." While it was an authentic expression of Jabotinsky's political outlook and the popular character of the movement, it had no substance.

What happened ultimately was that Jabotinsky's movement revealed the weakness which lay at the root of his Zionist outlook: the great gap between the idea of the Jewish state and the education towards the realization of national goals, on the one hand, and the methods and means of arriving at this goal, on the other. To one part of his movement Jabotinsky spoke the language of gradualism and legality, while to the other he spoke a language of nationalism which brooks no delay in the complete fulfillment of Zionism. The part of the movement that was to carry the idea into action discovered that it had to detach itself from the political methods suggested by its teacher and leader, and to choose its own mode of action. The basic weakness in Jabotinsky's political system was not, as has recently been claimed,[22] that he demanded a policy of force when the system had no real strength to back it, but rather that he made political demands in the name of "morality" when moral considerations had little force. Jabotinsky once said that whoever does not believe in the world's conscience should drown himself in the Vistula. He could hardly have known how soon this "conscience" would be indicted.

It is true that Jabotinsky supported the para-military activities of the Etzel (as against the Hagana's policy of "restraint") and encouraged them after they had already begun. He advocated daring and encouraged illegal immigration; but none of these were a substitute for his basic political system, only an addition to it. In general he strayed only in moments of disappointment. This he did principally in order to weaken the foundation of the "fraudulent" Mandate, and to pressure the British government to change its policy. Even the hazy and unrealistic "Plan for Rebellion" (on the eve of the Second World War, which created the myth of continuity between Jabotinsky's activities and the Etzel uprising in February 1944), was only formulated in response to pressure from activist groups in Betar and the Etzel. And if it was a departure from his essential stance, it was a very short-lived one. Nor was the plan to land forces on the shores of Palestine at the end of 1939, which was meant more as a protest than an attempt to bring down the government, typical. Much more organic to Jabotinsky's political views, from 1917 until his death in 1940, was his attempt to create a Jewish army within the framework of the allied forces during World War I and of a Jewish Legion under British command in Palestine after the conclusion of peace.

It is possible to argue with this by saying that Jabotinsky should be evaluated on the basis of his ideas and the grand goals which he set, in their own right and in comparison with the ideas and goals of leaders of other Zionist camps. From this point of view, the changes and even the reversals in his methods were only technical or organizational, never ideological. All the methodological changes arose from the same tensions between the elements of "fire and water," in Jabotinsky himself.

From the above Jabotinsky emerges as someone who set farreaching goals and as such was "ahead of his time." But a politician is not only a person who sets and preaches goals. He does not merely make plans for a movement and give his followers a feeling of common striving. He must also fashion the tools and provide the *means* with which to realize the idea. He must work on the concrete political plane. Strategy and tactics are essentially interlocked. In August 1913, in a letter to Leopold

Greenberg, Chaim Weizmann put his finger on a core problem of the entire Zionist movement when he wrote: "Differences in method matter very considerably where the '*Endziel*' is so remote." [23] And of course this was true for the Revisionist movement as well.

One could claim that the idea itself was the determining factor since it preceded its time, and pointed the way to others. If it was not Jabotinsky's movement which carried the idea to fruition, other parties adopted several of his principle ideas and did. But Jabotinsky was not satisfied with the mere creation of a political-educational movement, nor did he desire to be a prophet. He wanted to be a statesman who moved the "pieces" on the historical chessboard. He created a political movement which was meant to realize its aims rather than bequeath them to others. From this point of view, the inner tensions, the conflicts and the dialectics between Jabotinsky and his movement are of great meaning.

9. HOW DIFFERENT IMAGES OF JABOTINSKY AROSE

What are the deep-seated reasons for the formation of diametrically opposed evaluations of Jabotinsky as a statesman and Zionist leader? Why does one image represent him as a national leader, while another represents him only as the leader of a militant opposition? These differences derive in part from Jabotinsky's place and role in the Zionist movement, that is, his role as the leader of an opposition in the World Zionist Organization which sought to present an alternative ideology to that of the official leadership, and to gain political ascendancy in the Zionist movement and in the Yishuv. As a political, social and ideological movement, the Revisionists could not be satisfied *under any circumstances* by the exclusive emphasis on political objectives in the fulfillment of Zionism. Political principles were the cornerstone, but the building itself was constructed from a variety of ideological and emotional elements. Therefore, one must evaluate the movement not only on its political objectives, but on its full ideological and experiential content.

Close friends of Jabotinsky frequently called his attention to the fact that the movement was deviating from its principles and was being dragged into discussions and conflicts which were foreign to its nature and which had no direct bearing on "the greater goals." They claimed that the movement could not fight on too many fronts at once, and that it should restrict its field of action. They further claimed that Revisionism need not isolate itself by letting itself be turned into a movement with a separate social-ideological-cultural content. But these warnings were to no avail if only because they were not realistic. Revisionism did have a political viewpoint, but its broad base was cultural-ideological. It could not possibly exist without its all-embracing ideology. As the leader of a movement which was involved in all aspects of national life, Jabotinsky had to speak out on every issue and make suggestions on every front. Not all parts of the movement were interested in the same subjects; priorities existed, and this explains the great divergency of his utterances. He took part not only in the "serious" discussions in the movement; he was involved in the "little grey" discussions as well. His image outside the movement was constituted, as a result, not only by his political views, but also by his active involvement in a variety of matters. Thus, a caustic article written about an apparently minor issue—the strike in a biscuit factory in Jerusalem—contributed to his image and to feelings toward him, especially on the part of his adversaries.

10. JABOTINSKY'S STATUS IN THE MOVEMENT

The epitomization of the movement in the person of Jabotinsky and the unequivocal descriptions of the man reduce our historical knowledge and understanding. It is unfair to the movement as a whole and to large numbers of people who helped to fashion it, its ideas and activities. Moreover, it promotes an over-simplified, one-dimensional picture which ignores the conflicts and tensions which existed in the movement itself.

That Jabotinsky maintained his authority in the movement in spite of these tensions explains his extraordinary standing. And his authority was the primary factor in keeping the movement together and preserving its organic and ideological continuity. His unique position is even more apparent in that not only those who followed him blindly, but even those who at times disagreed with him, continue to look to him for legitimization. It is as if every action draws inspiration from him and every positive deed is only a carrying out of his principles. The relationship between the ideal and the reality was determined, and continues to be determined (either sincerely or out of dogmatism), through the relationship between the teachings of the man and the partial realization of his principles—some of which may have become twisted in the course of action, some of which may not have been achieved at all. Such a position is indeed unique, so much so that it even influences the character of historical research.

It seems that no Zionist leader continues to be as relevant for his followers as does Jabotinsky, which explains their attempt to make him relevant for the entire public. The question of what elements in his credo and methods really remain relevant necessitates another discussion. It is worthy of note, however, that the one person who best described the relationship which existed between Jabotinsky and his movement was Jabotinsky himself. In *The Story of My Life,* he wrote:

In the beginning God created the will of the individual, but in old age perhaps that same individual can recognize the *echo of his desires in the hearts of the multitude.* This is not my philosophy. On the contrary, this is a philosophy which I hated all my life ... No, not my philosophy, but that of reality, sometimes to my great sorrow.[24]

NOTES

This article is based on a lecture delivered at a symposium sponsored by the Chaim Rosenberg School of Jewish Studies, Tel Aviv University and the Jabotinsky Institute, on December 4, 1980.

1. Ze'ev Jabotinsky, *Memoirs of a Contemporary* (Hebrew), Tel Aviv-Jerusalem, n.d., pp. 213–17.
2. Itzhak Oren, "Between Conflict and Harmony" (Hebrew), in: *Vladimir Jabotinsky and I,* Tel Aviv, 1980.
3. Joseph B. Schechtman, *Rebel and Statesman, The Vladimir Jabotinsky Story* (Hebrew), Tel Aviv, 1959, p. 18. (English ed., New York, 1956.)
4. Moshe Glickson, *Writings* (Hebrew), vol. 1, Tel Aviv, 1940, pp. 117–28. See also "Bad Service" (Hebrew), ibid., pp. 128–31.
5. January 7, 1920, *Minutes of the Zionist General Council, 1919–1920,* vol. 1, Tel Aviv, 1975, p. 266.
6. Letter to Oscar Gruzenberg, in: Ze'ev Jabotinsky, *Letters,* Tel Aviv-Jerusalem, n.d., pp. 72–74.
7. Schechtman, *Jabotinsky Story,* pp. 309–12.
8. "The Lesson of Schevchenko's Jubilee" (Hebrew), in: Ze'ev Jabotinsky, *Art and Literature,* Tel Aviv-Jerusalem, n.d., pp. 134–40.
9. Letter to Eliahu Ben-Horin, August 9, 1925, Jabotinsky Institute, 15/2/1/A.
10. Letter to Mrs. Miriam Lang, August 27, 1930 (German), *Ha-Umma,* vol. 3/4, (61/62) (September 1980), pp. 332–37.
11. Letter to Shlomo Yaakobi, in: Schechtman, *Jabotinsky Story,* p. 235. See also Yaakov Shavit, *From a Majority to a State* (Hebrew), Tel Aviv, 1978, pp. 98–106.
12. Letter to Arieh Dissenchik, Jabotinsky Institute, 2/21/2/1 A.
13. *Grundsaetze des Revisionismus aus den Resolutionen der I, II und III Weltkonferenzen der Revisionistischen Union,* Paris, 1929.
14. "The Betar Idea, Principles of the Betar Outlook, 1934" (Hebrew), in: Ze'ev Jabotinsky, *B'sa'ar,* Tel Aviv-Jerusalem, 1958, p. 308.
15. "What Is to Be Done? 1905" (Hebrew), in: Ze'ev Jabotinsky, *Articles,* Tel Aviv-Jerusalem, n.d., pp. 163–214.
16. Letter to David Ben-Gurion, March 30, 1935, in: Jabotinsky, *Letters,* pp. 42–45.
17. Letters to Shlomo Gabstein and Oscar Gruzenberg, December 7, 1930 and September 27, 1927, in: Jabotinsky, *Letters,* pp. 82–93.

18. Articles by Yosef Nedava and Yehuda Benari, *Ha-Umma*, vol. 3/4 (61/62) (September 1980), pp. 386–96.
19. "Pre-Conditions for the Ten Year Plan" (Hebrew), in: Jabotinsky, *B'sa'ar*, p. 241.
20. "Petition in the Diaspora, Opposition in Palestine (1932)," in: Ze'ev Jabotinsky, *Writings*, pp. 144–46.
21. Ibid.
22. Shlomo Avineri, *Varieties of Zionist Thought* (Hebrew), Tel Aviv, 1980, pp. 214.
23. Letter to Leopold Greenberg, August 3, 1913, *Weizmann Letters, 1913–1914*, Series A, vol. 6, Jerusalem, p. 126.
24. Ze'ev Jabotinsky, *The Story of My Life* (Hebrew), Jerusalem, 1958, pp. 177–78.

22.

Economic Structure and National Goals—The Jewish National Home in Interwar Palestine

Jacob Metzer

The formation of the Jewish national home in Palestine provides an opportunity to examine the economics of an unusual "nation building": the planning and making of a national existence without a state. The revival of Jewish nationality in Palestine started in the late nineteenth century with the first immigration motivated by national ideology *(Alia Rishona)* and with the establishment of the World Zionist Organization (1897), whose goal was to create a Jewish political entity and ultimately a state.[1] It was not, however, until the end of World War I that the revival achieved momentum. The Balfour Declaration (November 1917) proclaiming Britain's intention to promote the formation of a Jewish national home in Palestine and the establishment of the British mandate in Palestine after the war provided the supportive political environment for the renewal of Jewish nation building. Moreover, both the League of Nations (which officially granted Britain the mandate) and the British government recognized the Zionist Organization as the legitimate representative of world Jewry and as the leading body of the emerging Jewish community in Palestine for matters concerning the national home. This gave the Zionist Organization an international legitimacy to add to its legitimacy among Jews as a quasi-governmental institution for the purpose of re-establishing their national existence.

The Zionist organization concentrated in the late 1910s and the early 1920s on building the institutional and operational framework for the

Reprinted by permission of the author and the *Journal of Economic History* 38, no. 1 (March 1978): 101–19.

projected national entity. Economic issues were especially important, particularly defining national economic objectives, forming the sectoral structure of the economy, and determining the role of the Zionist public sector in the Jewish economy. It is these issues that are the focus of this paper.

The conceptual framework for the analysis is provided by the economics of nationalism in new post-colonial nation states, of which the Jewish experience is treated as a special case. What made it a special case in this respect was the particular conditions in interwar Palestine: the Jewish community was not yet a sovereign state; it was still in the process of establishing its population and territorial basis. As will be shown below, these conditions significantly affected Zionist national objectives in the economic sphere, the considerations in "choosing" the economic system, and the mechanism for public involvement in it.

The evidence examined here is the Zionist deliberations and resolutions in the early interwar years (1918–1921). This period has been chosen for two reasons: first, focusing on this formative stage enables me to examine directly the motivations and objectives that underlined the formation of the Jewish economic system. Second, at these early stages the majority in the Zionist organization was non-socialist and the economic resolutions (both the structural and the operational ones) of its elected bodies were dominated primarily by national considerations. By concentrating on these early interwar years it is thus possible to examine the economics of Jewish nationalism by itself, other things— particularly social considerations—being equal. It should, however, be noted in this respect that the basic sectoral structure (particularly as far as the role of the Zionist public sector is concerned) did not change appreciably during the period starting in the late 1920s of the socialist hegemony in the Zionist Organization. The major structural development in the Jewish economy that can be associated with the shift to the left was the increasing importance of the collective economic sector of the Histadrut, the General Federation of Labor. On the operational level, socialist domination led to greater emphasis by the Zionist executive on social criteria in allocating national capital resources; this was done, however, within the sectoral structure defined in the formative years of the early 1920s.

Economic nationalism is commonly identified in the literature with national objectives that are either economic themselves or that require economic means to be achieved.[2] National objectives (which clearly require the idea of the nation as a single homogeneous political and economic entity) may be divided into three major categories: maximization of the nation's material welfare in terms of national income, as conventionally defined; non-pecuniary objectives that are perfectly consistent with the maximization of material welfare (consider, for example, the advancement of the nation's political strategic position by means of economic development); and non-pecuniary national objectives that impose constraints on the maximization of national income or its rate of growth.

Viewed thus, economic nationalism may call for a variety of sectoral structures and economic policies;[3] it is most frequently used, however, to describe governmental policies that affect resource allocation by the private sector. Such policies are implemented either to raise the level of national income and stimulate economic development or to achieve non-pecuniary national objectives even at the expense of income. The attempts by governments to realize the latter set of objectives have inspired economists and economic historians to use the notion of economic nationalism as a motivational explanation for policies that seem otherwise irreconcilable with ordinarily defined rational economic behavior aimed at maximizing material welfare.

This type of economic nationalism has been treated by Albert Breton and Harry Johnson. Breton has developed a model in which the economic attributes of nationalism and their implications are analyzed. Johnson later extended and applied it to the post-colonial experience of newly created and economically underdeveloped nation states[4] (identified in the rest of the paper as new states). Since this model and its empirical implications serve as a reference point to our subsequent discussion of the Jewish experience, it seems appropriate at this point to briefly describe its essential features.

The point of departure for the model is the idea that nationalism is a public good from which nationals derive non-material income in the form of national identity and esteem. In the economic sphere this psychic income is mainly generated by the following interrelated collective modes of behavior: (1) Exclusion of non-nationals from ownership of capital assets and natural resources within the state. (2) Exclusion of non-nationals from white collar (middle class), technical and managerial jobs. (3) Emphasis on industrialization in general and on advanced and technologically sophisticated industries in particular. (4) Attempts to achieve a high degree of self-sufficiency.

These characteristics are supposed to contribute to national identity and esteem by satisfying two (often conflicting) objectives: the achievement of particularism and independence from other nations; and the attainment of a socio-economic structure comparable to the most advanced ones as a demonstration of national maturity. These objectives could be expected to be most important in new or relatively backward nation states, which presumably still need self-assurance as to their national identity. Indeed, policies of discrimination against foreign property and skilled labor, protective trade policies, and the building of modern industry for industrialization's sake have been commonly observed in the new states.[5]

Economic nationalism is obviously not a free good. Its production usually requires a different resource allocation from an income maximizing one—at least in the short run—and its cost can thus be measured by material income forgone. Its public-good nature in consumption calls for collective governmental production; specifically, the government's role is to guarantee national ownership and employment and to achieve the "nationally desired" industrial composition. Pursuing the goals of economic nationalism as typically observed in new states tends to imply a centrally controlled economy. This may explain, according to Breton, the observed alliance in many national economies between nationalists and socialists in forming a public dominated sectoral structure.

The question is what can explain investments in nationalism and substitution of its derived psychic income for material income. One simple (although somewhat tautological) answer is that there must be, by revealed preference, a strong taste for economic nationalism to make for a high enough social rate of return on the investment in it. A different ex-post "justification" has been suggested by Nash. He argues, on the basis of the Mexican experience, that the feeling of national unity and identity among nationals may be a necessary motivating attitude to facilitate economic growth.[6] To the extent that this is the case, nationalism may be regarded as a complement rather than a substitute for long-run growth prospects, and the investment in nationalism can be viewed, at least in part, as a contribution to the economy's infrastructure.

Another line of explanation has been put forward by Breton, who argues that the public-good attributes of nationalism are not sufficient to explain the investment in it. For a full explanation one has to resort, according to this argument, to the redistributional aspects (in terms of material income) of economic nationalism. The basic contention is that the nationalistic discriminatory policies and the inducement of modern industrialization tend to create gainful jobs and other economic opportunities for members of the educated middle class. They derive material as well as psychic income from these policies. These gains in material income, however, are a transfer from the rest of the nation since the net effect of nationalism on national income (at least in the short-run) is a negative one. That being the case, investment in economic nationalism may result from the dominant political position of the middle class or from its ability to convince the rest of the nation to substitute nationalism for material income.

This line of explanation may be consistent with the former one because a well motivated middle class could be an important factor in the process of economic growth. It has even been suggested by Johnson that the redistribution of material income "may perform a necessary function in the early stages of forming a nation, in the sense that the existence of a substantial middle class may be a prerequisite of a stable society and democratic government. In other words, an investment in the creation of a middle class, financed by resources extracted from the mass of the population by nationalistic policies, may be the essential preliminary to the construction of a viable nation state."[7] Viewed thus, policies of economic nationalism in a new state can be regarded as an investment in the formation of the nation state itself and not just as overhead investment to facilitate future economic growth. This general nation-building aspect best characterizes the motivation for, and the nature of, economic nationalism in the pre-state Jewish case.[8]

The major categories of investment in nationalism as a public good— namely, a nationally determined industrial structure, capital and labor market discrimination on a national basis, and independence of the national economy—were characteristic of the yet-to-be-created Jewish state. But the actual components of investment in Jewish nationality in each of these categories were quite different from the standard new-state experience.

The basis for a Jewish national home was more a plan than a reality in the early mandatory period. The Jewish community in Palestine lacked political sovereignty. Most Jews were still in the diaspora at the time. The country was populated mainly by Arabs, who also owned most of its land.[9] These initial conditions were instrumental in determining the specific forms of investment in Jewish economic nationalism.

As far as the industrial structure was concerned, the Zionist[10] objective throughout the interwar period was to promote agriculture as the key national industry in contrast to the emphasis on manufacturing in the ordinary new state. Although the possibility that agriculture could have a comparative advantage in the Jewish economy was not ruled out, the rationale for making it the preferred industry was primarily non-pecuniary. Jewish agricultural settlement (on land to be purchased from the Arabs and on public domain expected to be allocated for Jewish use) in *all parts* of the country, regardless of allocative efficiency, was viewed in Zionism as an indispensable means of making Palestine a *de facto* Jewish country and thereby reinforcing the legitimacy of the demand for a Jewish national home there.

One could obviously ask why agriculture was singled out for these purposes which, in principle, could be served by any kind of productive activity that was capable of being distributed all over the country. This question is particularly justified in view of the notion, already well established in the 1920s, that industrialization is instrumental in forming a modern national economy. Zionism provided an answer to this question on both a practical and an ideological level. As a practical matter, agricultural settlement was considered most efficient for the purpose of re-establishing a territorial basis in Palestine because it was believed to require less investment in physical and human capital and a shorter gestation period than manufacturing industry. In addition, these resource and time saving advantages were expected to make agriculture the most efficient and effective occupation in absorbing large flows of immigrants in short periods of time. Apart from these considerations, agricultural settlement played a special role in Zionist national ideology. Farming (particularly on a self-employment basis) was assumed to generate non-pecuniary returns to the farmers by making them emotionally attached to the land, over and above any material considerations. This was believed to contribute to the stability and longevity of Jewish colonization in Palestine and to make the Jewish people a "normal nation" in the sense of having an actual and not just a metaphysical link with the land.

Agriculture was thus given a role somewhat analogous to the one that modern manufacturing industry plays in the new nation states. In both cases the industry promoted was supposed to narrow the gap between the evolving nation and established states. Since the typical new state has a well defined national territory and a rural sector, the promotion of modern industry and technology is usually regarded as a natural first step in the catching up process. In Zionism in the early 1920s, however, catching up meant essentially the formation of a territorial nation. This required, as a first priority according to Zionist perception, the establishment of a viable agricultural sector.

A similar contrast can be seen in the area of occupational distribution and the nationally preferred socio-economic classes. The post-colonial new state has usually promoted white collar occupations and the establishment of a strong middle class. Zionism, on the other hand, emphasized manual work, material production, and the formation of a Jewish working class to achieve similar objectives of national maturity. Here, too, the differences can be largely attributed to the different initial conditions in the nation-building process. The new state has usually suffered from a relative shortage of skilled technical and managerial personnel, whereas Jewish Palestine was expected to absorb a labor force concentrated in the provision of services and other white collar occupations. Thus the Zionist objective of changing the occupational structure of diaspora Jews (inverting the occupational pyramid as it was called in the Zionist jargon) by reducing the share of services and by increasing the share of blue collar material production was, like the promotion of the middle classes in the new states, a means to achieve a more balanced socio-economic structure which could be a basis for a mature national economy.

The national considerations underlying the Zionist attitudes towards agriculture and manual work were also instrumental in determining the special characteristics of capital and labor market discrimination in the Jewish economy. The notion of Jewish exclusiveness in the capital market focused primarily on land ownership. Having as much of Palestine's land as possible in Jewish possession was regarded as a complement to agricultural settlement in establishing the territorial basis for the Jewish national home. This explains the Zionist emphasis on land purchase as such, particularly in large contiguous areas, even when the expected productivity of the land would not have justified the transaction or the price paid for it.

As for the labor market, Jewish national discrimination (segregation) was directed at manual labor and specifically at the exclusion of Arab unskilled laborers from Jewish agriculture; by contrast, most new states discriminated against foreign skilled labor. The focus on the agricultural labor market was a logical extension of the national roles of agriculture and Jewish land ownership. The exclusion of Arab labor from the Jewish economy was regarded as indispensable if prospective Jewish immigrants were to be absorbed in agriculture and other blue collar occupations. Given the service-oriented occupational distribution of diaspora Jewry, Arab laborers were expected to have an initial comparative advantage in material production; this created an incentive for Jewish employers to hire them and not Jewish immigrants. Such an incentive could be weakened if the Jewish and Arab labor markets were kept segregated.

Jewish land was viewed as a necessary condition for making Palestine a Jewish country, but it was considered a sufficient condition for that purpose only when combined with Jewish labor. It was firmly believed by the majority in the Zionist movement that the national character of a settlement derives from those who actually till the land rather than from those who just own it. This was essentially an argument aimed at preventing colonialist type Jewish settlement from developing. It was feared that such a structure might evolve if Arab workers were allowed to be a significant share of the agricultural labor force in the Jewish economy. Besides moral considerations, the possibility of Jewish colonialism in Palestine was objected to on national political grounds. It was believed that such a structure would be a threat to the revitalization of the ties between the Jewish people and the land of Israel as well as to the viability and the legitimacy of the Jewish national home.

It is interesting to note the inverse symmetry between the anti-colonialist attitudes in the new states and in the Zionist movement. In the former case, the objective was to free the new nation from a colonial economic state that was expected to persist (even after national independence had been achieved) if the major fixed capital assets and the key technical and managerial positions continued to be held by foreigners. In the Jewish case, as we have seen, the objective was to avoid becoming a colonialist nation by minimizing reliance on Arab indigenous unskilled and semiskilled labor.

The avoidance of a colonialist structure may be viewed as part (in many cases a dominant part) of the more general objective of economic independence. In the new states, it usually meant independence from the developed industrialized nations; this implied self-sufficiency, achieved mainly by attempting to concentrate on domestic production of industrial import substitutes. In the Jewish case, economic independence meant primarily independence from the Arab economy; the question of independence from foreign nations was of secondary importance and was limited to preventing non-Jewish foreign (especially British) capital from being invested in the economy. Moreover, since the development of the Jewish community was to be dependent on the diaspora Jews—particularly from the advanced industrialized countries—for labor and capital, it was in the Zionist interest not to jeopardize the potential economic relationships between the Jewish community in Palestine and the countries of residence of world Jewry.

In view of the considerations that led to the Zionist promotion of a large Jewish agricultural sector, the potential dependency on the Arab traditional agricultural economy was largely limited to the labor market.

Labor market discrimination, in addition to its other functions, was in Jewish economic nationalism a substitute for protective devices in the product markets as a means of realizing the national objective of economic independence.

So far in our discussion, I have dealt primarily with the psychic income attributes of Jewish economic nationalism, but it obviously also had pecuniary redistributive implications. In other new states the middle class was expected to benefit materially from the national constraints on resource allocation (at the expense of the workers), but in Zionism the prime beneficiary was to be the working class. The more effective the segregation of the Palestine labor market, the larger the benefits would be. It was the Jewish capitalist middle class which was to be the relative loser by being deprived of the use of abundant, and hence relatively cheap, unskilled Arab labor. Indeed, in Jewish Palestine it was the socialists and the general labor organization which were the most vigorous advocates of forming and maintaining a nationally segregated labor market. The arguments used by the spokesmen of the Jewish working class were similar in nature to those used by the middle class in the new states; namely, emphasizing the psychic income generated by the public-good of nationalism which was expected to benefit all socio-economic groups and to outweigh the possible pecuniary private losses.[11]

What were the implications of economic nationalism for the sectoral structure (that is, the public-private mix) of the emerging Jewish economy? There are two aspects to this question. One is the extent of Zionist institutional involvement in the economy. The other is the form that this involvement would take in the absence of a sovereign Jewish polity. The external public-good attributes and the redistributional consequences of the nationally induced industrial composition and discrimination obviously called for public incentives or control, as in the ordinary new state. Another consideration working in the same direction was that of timing. Zionists believed it was politically necessary to establish the Jewish national existence in Palestine as fast as possible after World War I in order to provide a safeguard against potential objections (particularly Arab) to this development. This consideration required public investment in various projects that, in principle, could have been undertaken by the private sector at some later date. As Louis Brandeis, the U.S. Supreme Court Justice who was the leader of the American Zionist Organization in the 1910s and early 1920s, said, "the present unremunerative character of these needed investments of capital is intensified by the present high cost of construction yet we cannot wait until prices fall. Their need is urgent. The expenditure must be made immediately like a war expenditure regardless of cost because speed in settlement is indispensable. For the same reason we cannot, as in the case of other colonial development, leave would-be-settlers to work out problems slowly and painfully through successive failure to ultimate success. We must succeed reasonably soon in effecting the settlement, partly because others will intervene; partly because our effort will be ever on general exhibition and subject to hostile criticism." [12]

These considerations, plus the emphasis in Zionism on economic development as such and on the role of the Zionist public sector in promoting it, would seem to lead to a decision for a centrally controlled, command economy. There was, however, a major element in Zionist attitudes toward the sectoral structure of the economy which worked the other way. The non-socialist majority in the Zionist organization in the early 1920s thought that, ceteris paribus, the existence of a private enterprise system in the Jewish economy was in itself a national objective. The basic contention was that although a substantial number of prospective immigrants were expected to be young Jewish socialists who would need public assistance to finance their immigration and absorption, the main reservoir of manpower and capital for the Jewish colonization was concentrated in the bourgeois, capitalist-oriented classes of diaspora Jewry. A private enterprise system was therefore regarded as a prerequisite for the attraction of the Jewish masses and their resources to the Zionist cause.

The interesting thing about the Zionist advocacy of private enterprise and free markets in the early 1920s is that, although consistent with private utilitarian and libertarian considerations, it was based primarily on national collective goals. A free enterprise system was perceived in Zionism as a means of economic nationalism; it was expected to generate high enough net social returns by inducing an influx of people and capital to warrant its institutionalization, regardless of any direct concern for private material welfare or allocative efficiency as such.

Jewish economic nationalism thus required some weighting of the goals leading to public involvement in the economy against those which called for the provision of a proper institutional framework for free private economic activity. Indeed, this kind of weighting is precisely what was done in the deliberations of the late 1910s and early 1920s. It resulted in a planned mixed economy in which a Zionist public sector—whose main purposes were (apart from the provision of public social services) to ensure the realization of national objectives in the areas of economic development, industrial composition, occupational structure, employment, and land ownership—was expected to exist alongside a private sector operating in an essentially market economy.

Given these goals, Zionists faced special problems in implementing the type of institutional involvement in the economy that they sought. Collective involvement in economic activity can, in general, be exercised by using political coercive power to regulate private economic activity *administratively* or by utilizing public property rights in key economic areas as a means of guidance and control. The option of using governmental coercive power was practically non-existent in the Jewish case. The Zionist executive could obviously use national ideology as a means of persuasion, but not being a government, it could not use legal coercion and had to resort exclusively to purely economic means. Thus the modus operandi of the Jewish public sector was perceived in Zionism in terms of economic means aimed primarily at guiding the allocation and utilization of capital and land in the economy. Reference here is to public funds (national capital in the Zionist terminology) which were expected to originate in contributions from diaspora Jewry and to be used in Palestine for direct public investments in land and other capital assets, for grants in aid to immigrants and settlers, and for the control of channels of subsidized credit particularly in agriculture. The allocation of these resources according to national objectives and the imposition of national constraints (such as adherence to the principle of Jewish labor) on their private utilization were expected to be instrumental in realizing the goals of Jewish economic nationalism in the prestatehood era.

Of all the economic means at the disposal of the Zionist executive, by far the most important one was supposed to be Zionist public ownership of Jewish land in Palestine. The idea of limiting private rights on Jewish land to tenancy was an old biblical principle vested in the basic notion that the land of Israel is divine property. It was revived in Zionism as part of the plan to establish the Jewish National Fund (JNF) as a fundraising body for purposes of public purchase of land for Jewish settlement in Palestine (the Fifth Zionist Congress, 1901). After World War I, this concept became a key component of Zionist policy.

Basically, the idea of national land was an extension of the notion that Jewish possession of land was both a prerequisite and a substitute for the still non-existent Jewish political sovereignty. Nationalizing the land would reflect the right of the Jewish people as a collective entity to Palestine, as distinguished from mere individual property rights. In addition, national land was expected to be the single most important instrument in realizing the specific objectives discussed above. First, and most obvious, public ownership would operate as a safeguard against possible sales of Jewish land to non-Jews. This consideration is similar to the nationalization of productive establishments in new states, a policy aimed at the exclusion of foreigners from actual and potential ownership of particular capital assets.

Aside from that, the Zionist Organization planned to use public land as an effective means of assisting and guiding agricultural settlements according to its national economic goals; this was to be done (1) by allocating public land for agricultural settlement according to national geopolitical considerations; (2) by providing an inducement to settle on national land in the form of subsidized rents; (3) by giving settlers on national land the highest priority for the receipt of public institutional credit; (4) by making the availability of public land for private settlement (in renting it out) conditional upon adherence to the requirements of in-residence cultivation by the tenants and on the exclusion of non-Jewish hired labor.[13]

It is interesting to note that some of the equity-oriented arguments (heavily influenced by the ideas of Henry George) for land nationalization raised in the Zionist movement were, at least partly, motivated by national considerations. For example, private land ownership was expected (because of imperfections in the capital market) to lead to a concentration of landed wealth and hence to a monopsonistic position of the land owners in the labor market. This in turn was expected to result in a lowering of the agricultural wage rate, which because of the assumed higher elasticity of the derived supply of Jewish (compared with Arab) agricultural labor,[14] would drive the Jews out of agriculture into mostly urban, service-oriented, occupations. Such an outcome would obviously run contrary to the Jewish national objectives outlined above. Similarly, it was believed in Zionism that private land ownership would inevitably result in speculative landholding. This, it was felt, would have an adverse effect on the amount of land cultivated and on the stability of Jewish agricultural settlement.[15] Considerations of nationalism and equity united in Zionism to form a broad consensus with respect to the structure of land tenure in Jewish Palestine. The nature of this consensus was quite similar to the agreements found in the new states between nationalists and socialists on questions of nationalization and public ownership of capital assets where each side supports it for entirely different reasons.

The policy on land ownership was the most effective means available to the Zionists. By owning the land, the Zionist quasi-government could have some power of compulsion over all economic activities to be undertaken on public land, including those that would be privately and independently financed. In this respect, national land was truly a substitute for the political power of a government. The effectiveness of other means, such as public financial assistance, was, for a given resource constraint, dependent upon and limited by the intensity of the private demand for them. In other words, public land ownership was by itself a sufficient condition for Zionist control of the economy, whereas institutional financial assistance was obviously not a necessary condition (in view of the alternative of public land ownership) and would only by chance be a sufficient one.

It thus follows that it was mainly the extent of public possession of Jewish land and the nature of *private* property rights on leased public land that were to determine the public-private mix and the characteristics of the sectoral structure of the Jewish economy. As to the question of private rights on national land, the resolutions of the World Zionist Conference held in London in July 1920 stated explicitly that the land owned by the JNF would be leased to settlers on a hereditary basis and that tenants would have full hereditary rights on all structures built by them on the land.[16] These provisions (together with the subsidized rent to be charged on agricultural uses of national land) were believed to make renting of national land an attractive alternative to private ownership from a pecuniary point of view. It would enable the users of public land to treat it as a private asset for all practical purposes in terms of both the expected return and of the durability of their users' rights.

Zionists of course recognized that on the one hand expected JNF resources might fall short of the amount needed for purchasing all the non-Jewish land available for sale, and that on the other hand there might be some private Jewish resources available for investment in privately owned land that could not be transferred to the JNF. In view of these possibilities, and considering the high priority on acquiring as much land in Palestine as fast as possible and on inducing prospective Jewish immigrants and capital to move to Palestine, private Jewish purchases of non-Jewish land were explicitly encouraged—as a short-run practical matter—although the principle that ultimately all Jewish land should be publicly owned was never abandoned.[17]

Since the JNF was expected to allocate its resources first to buying

land of the highest national value, a measure of division of labor between the Zionist public sector and the Jewish private sector was bound
to evolve. The former would concentrate on the purchase of land to be
used primarily for nationally motivated agricultural settlement in which
resources would be allocated subject to national constraints; the latter
would devote its resources mainly to the purchase of urban land, as well
as to other non-agricultural pursuits,[18] which would be largely free of
any such constraints.[19] This differentiation was to be the basis for the
mixed Jewish economy—a sectoral structure which, as we have seen,
was by itself a consequence of Jewish prestatehood economic nationalism.[20]

The preceding sections have examined Zionist national objectives and
their implied sectoral structure by comparing them with economic nationalism in new but *already existing* nation states. It also seems appropriate to make some comparative observations based on a somewhat
analogous non-state nation-building endeavor (although an ultimately
unsuccessful one) in which the initial conditions, the national-economic
goals, and the implied sectoral structure were similar to those of the
Jewish experience. This case is the attempt of the Mormons to establish
their Great Basin Kingdom in the nineteenth-century American West.[21]
Although they never seriously tried to secede from the United States, the
Mormons' organized settlement in the territory of Utah was definitely an
attempt to establish a territorially defined, self-managed and maintained
regional community identified by its religious homogeneity; the community was supposed to be administratively and economically separate
from the "gentiles," that is, from the rest of the United States. These
attributes of group identity and particularism, especially as viewed by
the Mormons themselves, justify the characterization of their nineteenth-
century experience as a nation-building endeavor.

The basic national communal goals in Mormonism were to people a
new territory, to make it a *de facto* Mormon territory, and to develop it
as a regional economy completely independent of the rest of the American economy. Here, too, in close resemblance to the Jewish case, the
role of publicly (that is, church) guided settlement was to be a crucial
factor in achieving the basic goals. Besides actually defining the Mormon
territory in the absence of any political or legal collective territorial
jurisdiction, the policy was aimed at achieving self-sufficiency in agriculture as well as in other material output.

In regard to the sectoral structure called for by collective economic considerations, Mormonism faced the same basic problems as did Zionism. There was, for instance, the need to find a proper pragmatic balance between church economic collectivism and a private enterprise system. The former was needed for the financial support of immigration and absorption, to guide settlements, and to substitute for the lack of a sovereign Mormon political framework (in addition to implementing the basic values of communalism which were embodied in the Mormons' religious beliefs); the latter would promote growth and provide a safeguard against the economic pull from the outside world. The result was one that is by now familiar: an undogmatic mixed economy whose major function was to guarantee the development of a viable Mormon system that could be maintained independent of the gentiles.[22]

The principal mechanism that the Mormon church planned to use for the institutionalization of a mixed economy in the Basin Kingdom was the implementation of the principles embodied in the basic Mormon postulate: the Law of Consecration and Stewardship. Under this law ultimate property rights in all productive assets within the Mormon territory (which consisted primarily of land) were to be vested in the church—the Mormon collective entity—following the consecration to it of members' private property. The members were then to receive from the church pieces of property in the form of stewardship, which they could use freely in terms of input and output mix to maximize their pecuniary returns. Part of the annual net returns, a loosely defined surplus over consumption, was also to be consecrated to the church as a form of taxation that could be imposed on members.[23]

The Law of Consecration and Stewardship was designed in early Mormonism as a device to facilitate wealth and income redistribution, to generate public (church) revenue, to maintain communal cohesiveness and identity, and to serve as an instrument of collective control in the absence of other political and legal means of exercising power. All this was supposed to function in an institutional environment that would allow for the free operation of private enterprise, constrained by the public sector's (at least nominal) possession of the land and other productive capital assets.[24]

The communal considerations (to be distinguished from pure equity) in using the mechanism of Consecration and Stewardship were particularly evident in the attempts by the church to implement this policy during the 1850s. At that time outside incentives—the expected profit from California's gold and the increasing opportunities for beneficial economic relations with the westward moving, gold-seeking gentiles—

threatened not only the independence and self-sufficiency of the regional Mormon economy but the very existence of the Mormon community. The consecration of private property to the church, and its utilization by members under the conditions of stewardship was expected (in addition to being a source of revenue for public expenditures in the areas of immigration, colonization, and public work) to counterbalance the pull of California gold by providing pecuniary incentives for members to stay within the community. These incentives were supposed to be generated by the fact that individuals who would "desert" the Kingdom would lose the expected income generated from the consecrated property. Church control over consecrated property was expected also to restore self-sufficiency by eliminating trade with the gentiles.[25]

In its general outlines, the mechanism of consecration and steward-ship was very similar to that of nationalized land in Zionism. Both were aimed at providing the public sector with economic means designed to substitute for political control and to advance the formation of a viable independent communal entity by means of collective guidance and incentives. At the same time, the actual structure of public property rights was to be such that it would allow for the private sector to use the public property relatively freely.

The major practical advantage of the Zionist scheme over the Mormon one was that its implementation depended upon contribution from an exogenous, largely unaffected group—diaspora Jewry. Indeed, the JNF was able to purchase and nationalize about 63 percent of all the land bought by Jews in Palestine between 1922 and 1945 and thereby to increase the share of public-Zionist land in total Jewish land holdings from 4 percent in 1914 to 46 percent in 1945.[26] The realization of the Mormons' consecration and stewardship program, on the other hand, depended on the willingness of individual Mormons to forgo at least part of their property rights, a sacrifice that fewer were willing to make than their leaders had expected. These obstacles prevented the program from succeeding and forced the Mormon Church to resort to much looser devices of collective economic cooperation and control in the latter part of the nineteenth century.[27]

These differences notwithstanding, there were important similarities between the Mormon and the Zionist experiences. They suggest that the national-economic goals and the basic sectoral structure implied by the conditions of a non-state territorial nation in the making may have been of a more general character than that exemplified by the special case of the Jewish national home in pre-Israel Palestine.

NOTES

1. The Zionist Organization was (and still is) a voluntary democratic institution of world Jewry. Jews become members in the organization upon payment of annual dues (shekel) which makes them eligible to elect and to be elected to the Zionist legislative body—the congress—and to the executive organs of the organization.

2. See Harry G. Johnson, ed., *Economic Nationalism in Old and New States* (Chicago, 1967), for a comprehensive source of the various treatments of economic nationalism in the literature.

3. For example, Roger Weiss has convincingly argued that both the free trade policies of Britain in the mid-nineteenth century and her trade restriction in the second half of the century were motivated by the same objective of economic nationalism; namely, the maximization of national income. Roger Weiss, "Economic Nationalism in Britain in the Nineteenth Century," in Johnson, *Economic Nationalism*, pp. 31–47.

4. Albert Breton, "The Economics of Nationalism," *Journal of Political Economy*, 72 (1964), 376–86. Harry G. Johnson, "A Theoretical Model of Nationalism in New and Developing States," in Johnson, *Economic Nationalism*, pp. 1–16.

5. What seems to be uniquely characteristic of new states is the combination of all these policies and not necessarily the implementation of one or only part of them which may be observed in other cases as well.

6. Manning Nash, "Economic Nationalism in Mexico," Johnson, *Economic Nationalism*, pp. 71–84.

7. Johnson, *Economic Nationalism*, pp. 15–16.

8. The analysis in the two following sections of Jewish economic nationalism and of the implied sectoral structure in the Jewish economy is based on the factual background contained in Jacob Metzer, "National Capital as a Basic Concept in Zionism: The Economic Philosophy in Zionist Thought, 1918–1921" (Hebrew), Falk Institute Discussion Paper No. 763, 1976 (mimeographed).

9. The Jewish population in Palestine was 69,000 in 1921 and 425,000 in 1939; this constituted 9.5 percent and 28.1 percent respectively of the total Palestine population. As far as land-holding is concerned, Jews owned about 2 percent of Palestine land in 1921 and 6 percent in 1939. See Nachum T. Gross and Jacob Metzer, "Public Finance in the Jewish Economy in Interwar Palestine," *Research in Economic History*, 3 (forthcoming), Table A-5; and D. Gurevich, A. Gertz and A. Zanker, eds., *Statistical Handbook of Jewish Palestine* (Jerusalem, 1947), p. 140.

10. The terms Zionist and Jewish are used interchangeably.

11. Zvi Sussman, "The Determination of Wages for Unskilled Labor in the Advanced Sector of the Dual Economy of Mandatory Palestine," *Economic Development and Culture Change*, 22 (1973) 95–113.

12. *Statement to the Delegates of the Twelfth Zionist Congress on Behalf of the Former Administration of the Zionist Organization of America* (New York, 1921), p. 16.

13. The resolutions of the World Zionist Conference, London, July 1920 in the *Reports of the Executive of the Zionist Organization to the XII Zionist Congress*, III, *Organization Report* (London, 1921) p. 95.

14. The implicit assumption about the elasticity differentials rested on the notion that the relatively uneducated and unskilled Arab labor force had very limited employment opportunities outside agriculture at the time, not like the educated Jewish laborers whose comparative advantage may very well have been in non-agricultural pursuits.

15. All of these contentions obviously rested on some questionable assumptions with

regard to profit-maximizing behavior, the nature of speculation, and the a priori efficiency of nationalization in preventing speculative capital gains.

16. See *Organization Report*, p. 95.

17. Ibid.

18. In actuality, the share of Zionist public funds in total capital imports of the Jewish economy during the interwar period was quite small, about 21 percent (calculated on the basis of Tables 1 and A-5 in Gross and Metzer). The rest consisted primarily of private transfers by immigrants, most of whom were of urban background and inclination. This may have contributed to the fact that although agriculture was the preferred national industry, its share in the Jewish economy declined from 15.9 percent in net domestic product and 26.5 percent in employment in 1927, to 9 percent and 20.8 percent respectively in 1939. [Robert Szereszewski, *Essays on the Structure of the Jewish Economy in Palestine and Israel* (Jerusalem, 1968), pp. 29–40.] Nevertheless, it was by and large agricultural settlement that determined the geographical extent of prestate Jewish colonization in Palestine as envisaged by the Zionist organization in the planning stages of the early 1920s.

19. For example the Zionist national (and social) principle of Jewish labor was successfully implemented only on agricultural settlements using national land. Farmers who settled on non-national land (particularly citrus growers) and non-agricultural Jewish employers (especially private contractors) did use Arab labor quite extensively during most of the interwar period. See Sussman, "The Determination of Wages."

20. It should be emphasized that a substantial part of what would be technically defined as a private sector in our context was essentially collective in its structure and objectives. Reference is here to the productive establishments belonging to, or associated with, the Histadrut (the General Federation of Jewish Labor). Their value added constituted about 20 percent of the net domestic product of the Israeli economy in 1953 [see Haim Barkai, *The Public, Histadrut, and Private Sectors in the Israeli Economy* (Jerusalem, 1968), p. 2.] and it was probably of a similar order of magnitude in the Jewish economy during at least the last interwar decade. The Histadrut used its productive establishments in coordination with the Zionist executive to achieve various national objectives in infrastructure investment, colonization, and other economic undertakings. Thus the public component of the mixed Jewish economy during the interwar period was actually larger than that revealed by the share of the economic activity and the possessions of the Zionist executive in any of the macroeconomic aggregates.

21. For comprehensive treatments of the economic aspects of the Mormon settlement see Leonard J. Arrington, *Great Basin Kingdom* (Cambridge, Mass., 1958); Leonard J. Arrington, Feranory Y. Fox, and Dean L. May, *Building the City of God* (Salt Lake City, 1976); and Jonathan Hughes, *The Vital Few* (London, 1973), pp. 67–116.

22. See Hughes, *The Vital Few*, pp. 88–105.

23. Arrington et al., *Building the City of God*, pp. 15–40.

24. Ibid., p. 15.

25. Ibid., pp. 63–78.

26. Gurevich et al., *Statistical Handbook*, p. 140.

27. Arrington et al., *Building the City of God*, passim.

IV.

THE FATEFUL TRIANGLE: JEWS, ARABS, AND THE BRITISH

23.

The Balfour Declaration in Historical Perspective

Jehuda Reinharz

It has been noted before that few sentences have elicited so much print-matter as the one which constitutes the Balfour Declaration. The number of articles and books on the subject can easily fill a few shelves. Historians and others have debated the origins of the Declaration, its significance for the British, the Zionists, and the Arabs. There has also been much debate over Chaim Weizmann's part in its attainment. This essay is a contribution toward an understanding of Weizmann's role within the broader political context of World War I.

At the end of July 1917 the Zionist movement had entered into a new and critical stage. Since the spring it was increasingly clear to Chaim Weizmann and his close associates that they would have to mobilize all their human and organizational resources for what seemed to be an imminent public declaration by Britain which would commit its support for the Zionist cause. During the months leading to the Balfour Declaration, Weizmann was not at first fully aware of the force of the anti-Zionist opposition. At a meeting of the political committee, on August 28, 1917, the discussion focused on what the Zionist "Demands" would include, once the British declaration had been issued and a sub-committee was constituted to consider drafting the appropriate memorandum.[1] Both the Zionists and their supporters in the War Cabinet and its secretariat, were so certain of the outcome of the War Cabinet meeting on September 3, 1917, that they did not adequately prepare for it. Both

Reprinted and adapted by permission of the author from the *Journal of Modern History* 64 (September 1992): 455–99.

Arthur Balfour and Lloyd George were away on vacation and thus did not take part in the meeting; the Prime Minister contracted ptomaine poisoning and did not return to London until the last week of September. Even Ronald Graham, who had constantly played such a crucial role in promoting the Zionists' interests, was on vacation and could not advocate their cause behind the scenes. In Lloyd George's absence, Andrew Bonar Law presided at the meeting. Though he was later charged by Scott and Wickham Steed as having opposed a pro-Zionist declaration,[2] the minutes do not reveal such an attitude.[3] They do show that Edwin Montagu objected vehemently when the three drafts—of Rothschild, Balfour, and Milner—were presented, to any description of Palestine as the home of the Jewish people. There was a suggestion voiced that the matter be postponed, a suggestion which was strongly opposed by Lord Robert Cecil, the Acting Secretary of State for Foreign Affairs. He pointed out that this was a question on which the Foreign Office had been very strongly pressed for a long time. Cecil drew attention to the importance of the Zionist Organization in the United States whose support would substantially assist the cause of the Allies. "To do nothing was to risk a direct breach with them."

In the end it was decided, that the views of President Wilson should be obtained on the desirability, in principle, without reference to the wording of any of the drafts, of a pro-Zionist declaration.[4] As instructed, Cecil cabled to Colonel House the following day: "We are being pressed here for a declaration of sympathy with the Zionist movement and I should be very grateful if you felt able to ascertain unofficially if the President favours such a declaration."[5] House took his time before replying. The form of the question put to him by Cecil did nothing to allay his suspicion that the British might wish to involve America in a joint defense of their position in Egypt, though he treated it as a matter in which the British were primarily concerned. House's advice to the President was that "there are many dangers lurking in it, and if I were the British, I would be chary about going too definitely into that business."[6]

In his cable to Cecil on September 11, 1917, House pointed out that the President had been staying with him at his summer home for two days, and he had delayed his reply in order to thoroughly discuss the matter with Wilson. He could now state that in the President's opinion "the time is not opportune for any definite statement further perhaps than one of sympathy provided it can be made without conveying any real commitment. Things are in such a state of flux at [the] moment that he does not consider it advisable to go further."[7] President Wilson, backed by House's own inclination, was in effect advising the British to follow his example and hold off on further postwar commitments until the war ended or some other indefinite future time. The British, Balfour among them, understood this cable as an American veto of the proposed declaration.

These events took place without prior notice to the Zionists, or to Weizmann personally, who was then embroiled in the serious differences with his own constituency. On September 8, he met with Graham's deputy, Sir George Clerk, who—perhaps on orders from Robert Cecil—failed to inform Weizmann on what had transpired at the Cabinet meeting. Thus on the following day Weizmann suggested that the British government might want to issue a declaration on the eve of the Jewish New Year a week hence.[8] Probably only on September 9 or 10, at a meeting with Leopold Amery and William Ormsby-Gore, both members of the War Cabinet secretariat, did Weizmann hear for the first time the details of what had transpired at the meeting of September 3. Alarmed, he brought the matter before the political committee on September 11; his suggestion to cable Brandeis for help was accepted.[9] In the meantime Ronald Graham returned from his vacation, and with his permission and assistance, Weizmann launched a series of urgent pleas to his American contacts, and to Brandeis in particular, for their aid in a situation in which the future prospects of Zionism were critically involved. So, too, was his own future as a Zionist leader.

Weizmann pinned his hopes on Louis Brandeis as the person most capable of influencing President Wilson. In addition to "assimilationist" objections in London, Weizmann cabled, President Wilson was said to be impeding British considerations because of his view that the time was inopportune. In his cable—held back by the Foreign Office and therefore received by Brandeis on September 19, a week after it was first composed—Weizmann also included the text of the statement proposed by Lord Rothschild in July. Though the War Cabinet had considered a somewhat toned down version, successively moderated by Balfour and Milner, this was not revealed to the Zionists at that time.[10] Brandeis then telephoned for an appointment with Colonel House and, together with Stephen Wise, visited him in New York on September 24.[11]

The only available account of their discussion, the rather short entry in Colonel House's journal, naturally concentrates on the author's own role, his impressions and conclusions, with little direct information about the other participants. One can imagine, however, that the President's reported veto of the suggested British statement must have seemed at odds with the assurances the Zionists had received from the same source, not only to an enthusiast like Wise, but to the sober Brandeis, after his May 6 interview with Wilson. They evidently compared notes with the Colonel, whose journal records that he told them that "the President was willing to go further than I thought advisable" and that he "had advised him against a more definite statement than the one . . . cabled to Cecil." On comparing that text with the text Weizmann sent to Brandeis—of which, together with the entire correspondence between the Zionists, House had been supplied copies by British intelligence— House, at least, ruled that they were "practically identical."

House then approved a series of cables which Brandeis sent to London on September 24, 1917, indicating on the basis of his previous conversations with Wilson and "from expressions of opinion given to closest advisers"—i.e. Colonel House—that the President was in entire sympathy, and Brandeis himself in hearty agreement, with the formula Weizmann had sent.[12] Thus, what had been interpreted by the Foreign Office and Weizmann as an American veto, was redefined as a positive suggestion for the form of a British statement of sympathy for Zionism.

If this was a revision of the message originally intended by House, on certain other points Brandeis's May 6 interview with the President gave him no grounds to differ with House's restricted view of the official policy. The Zionists were fully aware of the President's unwillingness— at least, for the time being—to make a public statement of his own and they accepted it once more, explicitly, in framing the cables to be sent to London. Nor could they easily oppose House's request that they bring the French, Italian, and Russian Governments as near the attitude of Great Britain and the United States as possible.[13]

On the first point, however, they were not satisfied simply to reassure Weizmann themselves and let the matter rest, as House proposed. They hoped for a direct assurance by the President to the British approving of a statement by them, without a public commitment of his own; for they realized that such support might be crucial in London—as far as they understood Weizmann's needs—in view of the opposition that had developed.[14] The matter was raised by Brandeis with House at the end of September, but apparently without an immediate response. On the second point, Brandeis was in a position to refer to Sokolow's mission to Paris and Rome; and he also supplied House with a set of news clippings indicating Russian approval of Zionist aims—a matter in which House continued to show a special interest, in light of his talks with the Russian ambassador about the new Russian doubts concerning Turkish partition.[15]

In the summer of 1917, House continued to be interested in the possibility of a separate peace with Turkey, and the American Zionists had to respect the limits which this preoccupation imposed on their ability to apply pressure to the Administration. Henry Morgenthau, whose new interest in keeping Turkey-in-Asia intact was becoming more anti-Zionist in tendency, was no longer considered a useful channel for government approaches to the Turks. His successor as Ambassador in Constantinople, Abram Elkus, who had returned from the field, was ready to take up the task instead, if House desired. Elkus, like Morgenthau, had been a leading member of Stephen Wise's Free Synagogue, and he told the Zionists that he was ready to make a public avowal of his support. Clearly, neither he nor the leading American Zionists considered his Zionist sympathy incompatible with his prospective service in the negotiation of a separate peace with Turkey. Brandeis, however, advised that House be consulted before Elkus's pro-Zionist statement were decided on. House promptly vetoed the idea, and the Zionists were obliged to accept the decision with good grace—though in the end, no Elkus mission to the Turks was ever launched.[16]

In England Weizmann watched the developing situation with growing strain. Not only did America still fall short of the support he felt he needed, but the Russian Zionists' response to his pleas was disappointing, in spite of the positive reactions he communicated to his British and American contacts. Weizmann's urgent arguments failed to move the Russian Zionist leader, Yehiel Tschlenow, to give up the fixed policy of Zionist neutrality in favor of reliance on a single power, England.[17]

On September 24, 1917, Tschlenow wrote to Weizmann and Sokolow that the Russian Zionists would not be prepared to come out, as they had been pressed to do, in favor of a Jewish Palestine under British protection in the absence of clearer and more positive pledges from the British government. Tschlenow also demanded to know, whether sufficient thought had been given to the situation which would arise if the war ended without the Turks having been expelled from Palestine. He himself believed that the Zionists could count on the support of the Russian government.[18]

A few months earlier, Weizmann (though, to a lesser degree also Sokolow), were reprimanded by the Smaller Actions Committee, which met in Copenhagen at the end of July, for their breach of Zionist neutrality. Arthur Hantke, a member of the World Zionist Organization executive, conveyed the dissatisfaction of that body:

The entire work of Weizmann and his colleagues is undertaken in too partisan an English direction . . . Weizmann's statement at the conference of the English

Zionist Federation [on May 20, 1917], fills the Jewish public with expectations which bear no relation to that which had been accomplished [in England]. Finally, Weizmann and Sokolow have operated much too independently, without consultation with the SAC or the Committee in The Hague.[19]

Thus, during the months of August and September 1917, as he looked around him to assess the measure of support he could count on, to push the declaration through, Weizmann found little of it in the Zionist world, while his own close circle had also begun to question his judgment on certain key issues.

In England, meanwhile, the Zionist drive for the declaration was encountering resistance both from the Jewish side and from the cautious and skeptical British civil service. Montagu, too, was not content to let matters rest after his partial victory at the War Cabinet meeting. In a letter to Robert Cecil, dated September 14, 1917,—and like the former document also distributed to members of the War Cabinet—Montagu claimed that the majority of British Jews were anti-Zionist; his evidence for this statement was the more or less balanced vote on the issue of Zionism at the Board of Deputies of June 17. Though not a member of the War Cabinet, Montagu was well briefed, and he also made reference to President Wilson's non-committal cable as transmitted by House. He also came back to a common anti-Zionist charge which had been made on occasion by Lucien Wolf, namely that Zionism was a movement of foreign origin, led by foreign Jews:

It was founded by Theodor Herzl, an Austrian, . . . his successor as leader of the Zionist movement was David Wolffsohn of Koeln, who was succeeded by Otto Warburg of Berlin . . . Jews of foreign birth have played a very large part in the Zionist movement in England. Among its best known leaders in England are Dr. Gaster, a native of Roumania, Dr. Hertz, a native of Austria, and Dr. Chaim Weizmann, who is, I believe, a native of Russia.

Montagu concluded by stating that a British declaration "would be felt as a cruel blow by the many English Jews who love England." He suggested a formula which would state that Jews who wished to go to Palestine would receive the aid of the British government which would also consider any suggestions made by Jewish or Zionist organizations.[20]

It is not clear whether the Zionists actually read Montagu's official documents, but they had heard enough from their various good contacts in the Foreign Office and War Cabinet secretriat—transmitted chiefly via Weizmann—to know the gist of his arguments. In a letter to Louis Brandeis, Ahad Ha'Am commented: "Unfortunately . . . we must admit that there are still too many in our midst whose hearts, like those of

Pharaoh, are hardened and whose eyes are blind to the 'signs' of the time . . . we here are faced by the shameful spectacle of Jews doing their utmost to wreck the ancient hope of Israel for a national resurrection."[21]

Weizmann's rage was channeled into much more sarcastic prose when he wrote to Philip Kerr, the Prime Minister's trusted adviser:

The 'dark forces' in English Jewry have again been at work and this time they have mobilised their great champion who although a great Hindu nationalist now, thought it his duty to combat Jewish Nationalism. It is—I confess—inconceivable to me, how British statesmen still attribute importance to the attitude of a few plutocratic Jews and allow their opinion to weigh against almost a unanimous expression of opinion of Jewish Democracy. Here we are after three years hard work, after having enlisted the sympathies practically of everyone who matters in England, faced again by opposition on the part of a handful of 'Englishmen of the Jewish persuasion.' . . . [The] declaration . . . is still hung up owing to opposition of a few Jews, whose only claim to Judaism is that they are working for its disappearance.

The fact that the British Government with all its sympathies towards national Judaism does not desire to give a definite expression to it, is doing considerable harm not only to Zionism, but also to the interests of the British Government.[22]

Lloyd George was about to return to London on September 23 and Weizmann asked Philip Kerr to arrange a meeting with the Prime Minister "for a few minutes it may help to clear it all up."[23] In the meantime, he met on September 19 with Arthur Balfour who provided some more details about the September 3 Cabinet meeting. Balfour also promised to see Lloyd George on the matter.[24] Yet, two days later Balfour received Lord Rothschild in his office, and was more discouraging. Rothschild reported to Weizmann: "Balfour began, before I could open my lips, by saying he had seen you, and that he had told you that in his and the Prime Minister's absence, the Cabinet had discussed the matter and had concluded the moment was not opportune for a declaration."

Balfour—who should have known from his staff about Weizmann's contacts with Brandeis—also urged Rothschild to get the American Zionists, Brandeis in particular, to bring pressure on President Wilson to break the impasse.[25] A few days later, Balfour minuted on a memorandum Ronald Graham had written to Lord Hardinge urging a declaration, which would be at least as strong as the Cambon letter to Sokolow: "Yes. But as this question was (in my absence) decided by the Cabinet against the Zionists, I cannot do anything until the decision is reversed."[26]

Lord Hardinge had a different view on the matter. His minute to the Graham memorandum read: "I think we might and ought to go as far as the French."[27] In a letter to Sir Reginald Wingate of September 21, Graham noted that Lloyd George, Arthur Balfour and Robert Cecil were "all in strong sympathy with Zionist ideas and aspirations," but owing to Montagu's opposition and Wilson's coolness to the idea of a declaration, "we ought not to move too fast."[28] Mark Sykes, too, gave his views in a paper setting the background for the conflict between Zionists and their opponents and pronouncing Zionism "a positive force." He suggested that either the United States or Great Britain be chosen to govern Palestine, guaranteeing equal rights to all religious groups.[29] Jan Smuts, since June 1917, a member of the War Cabinet, met with Weizmann on September 21 for one hour. He assured Weizmann of his sympathy and asked for literature on Zionism.[30] Philip Kerr, too, spoke to Lloyd George who promised to support the declaration; and on September 28, 1917—the cable from Brandeis assuring Wilson's support already in hand—C. P. Scott contrived a three-minute meeting between Weizmann and the Prime Minister, who ordered his secretary, in Weizmann's presence, to place the question of the Zionist declaration on the agenda of the next War Cabinet meeting.[31] On October 1, Weizmann managed to get an interview with George Barnes, the Labour Party representative to the War Cabinet. With the exception of Lord Curzon, he had thus managed to meet and impress most of the important members of the Cabinet.

Contributing to the perceived urgency of the subject were reports, conveyed by the Zionists and the British press, that the Germans were contemplating measures of their own, to persuade the Jews that only the victorious Central Powers would grant the Jewish people a new status in Palestine.[32] Before the Cabinet meeting, not wishing to leave anything to chance, Weizmann sent in a joint statement with Lord Rothschild, setting forth the Zionist arguments and objecting strongly to the "one-sided manner" in which the views of Jewry had been permitted to be presented, through Montagu's participation in the last Cabinet session.[33]

When the Cabinet met on October 4, 1917, Montagu was again present, but so too were Arthur Balfour and Lloyd George, who presided over the meeting. The cabinet was now presented with a revised draft, hastily drawn up by Leopold Amery—at Lord Milner's request—some thirty minutes before the deliberations commenced. Instructed to take account of the objections raised in the preceding debates, he drew on letters written by Lord Rothschild and others to the *Times* in answer to Montefiore's and Alexander's open letter, in which claims that Zionism endangered the citizenship of British Jews or the rights of Arabs were denied.[34] The draft he composed, in language drawn from these sources and Milner's earlier draft, read:

His Majesty's Government views with favour the establishment in Palestine of a national home for the Jewish race and will use its best endeavours to facilitate the achievement of this object, it being clearly understood that nothing shall be done which may prejudice the civil and religious rights of existing non-Jewish communities in Palestine, or the rights and political status enjoyed in any other country by such Jews who are fully contented with their existing nationality [and citizenship].[35]

Balfour opened the debate. In the ten days since he minuted his equivocating remark on Ronald Graham's memorandum, he had become firm in his resolve wholeheartedly to support a pro-Zionist declaration. His remarks, as recorded in the minutes, also took account of the opposition to Zionism:

This Movement, though opposed by a number of wealthy Jews in this country, had behind it the support of a majority of Jews, at all events in Russia and America. . . . He saw nothing inconsistent between the establishment of a Jewish national focus in Palestine and the complete assimilation and absorption of Jews into the nationality of other countries. Just as English emigrants to the United States became, either in the first or subsequent generations, American nationals, so, in future, should a Jewish citizenship be established in Palestine, would Jews become either Englishmen, Americans, Germans, or Palestinians. What was at the back of the Zionist movement was the intense national consciousness held by certain members of the Jewish race. They regarded themselves as one of the great historic races of the world, whose original home was Palestine, and these Jews had a passionate longing to regain once more this ancient national home.[36]

It was Montagu's turn and once again he forcefully argued his position. What was more disturbing, from the point of view of the Zionists and their supporters, was that Lord Curzon—a former Viceroy of India and now Lord President of the Council—"urged strong objections upon practical grounds." Curzon, who had visited Palestine before the war, stated that "the country was, for the most part, barren and desolate; . . . a less propitious seat for the future Jewish race could not be imagined." Moreover—and that seems to have been his more urgent worry—"How was it proposed to get rid of the existing majority of Mussulman inhabitants and to introduce the Jews in their place?" In any case, how many Jews would actually wish to come to Palestine and how will they earn their livelihood? He suggested that granting Jews already in Palestine equal civil and religious rights was quite sufficient; repatriating the Jews on a large scale was "sentimental idealism, which would never be realised and His Majesty's Government should have nothing to do with it." [37]

At one point during the proceedings, possibly after Montagu and Curzon had made their statements, it was suggested that Weizmann be called in to answer the various objections raised. He could not be found, though he was at that very moment close by, in Captain Amery's office.[38] One can only speculate whether the outcome of the meeting would have taken a different turn, had he made a presentation. In the event, the Cabinet, instead of coming to a decision on the matter, again proposed to consult President Wilson.

In view of Montagu's strenuous opposition and the promise once made to consult the Conjoint Jewish Committee, reconstituted as the Joint Foreign Committee, it was agreed to solicit instead the opinions of a representative group of Zionist and non-Zionist Jews. The list of non-Zionists to be approached for a statement was provided by Montagu and Sir Lionel Abrahams. They included Sir Stuart Samuel, the new chairman of the Board of Deputies, Leonard J. Cohen, the chairman of the Jewish Board of Guardians, Claude Montefiore, President of the Anglo-Jewish Association and Sir Philip Magnus, M. P. Weizmann suggested Dr. Joseph Hertz, the Chief Rabbi of England, Lord Rothschild, Sokolow, and himself.[39] The suggestions were accepted and the requests were solicited by the Cabinet Secretary, Maurice Hankey on October 6.[40]

Montagu had in the meantime, shortly after the Cabinet meeting of October 4, written directly to Lloyd George. Apparently referring to Weizmann, he half threatened—intimating resignation—half pleaded with the Prime Minister:

It is a matter of deep regret to me . . . that you are being . . . misled by a foreigner, a dreamer, an idealist . . . who . . . sweeps aside all practical difficulties with a view to enlisting your sympathy on behalf of his cause. . . .
I don't want to make difficulties. If I were to resign now I believe that after what has happened . . . a match would have been put to the Indian fire. . . .
It seems almost inconceivable that I should have to give it up [his office] for something wholly unconnected with India at all, and yet what am I to do? I believe firmly that if you make a statement about Palestine as the national home for Jews, every anti-Semitic organisation and newspaper will ask what right a Jewish Englishman, with the status at best of a naturalised foreigner, has to take a foremost part in the Government of the British Empire. Palestine is not now British. It belongs to our enemies. At the best it can never be part of the English Empire. The country for which I have worked ever since I left the University— England—the country for which my family have fought, tells me that my

national home, if I desire to go there, therefore my natural home, is Palestine. How can I maintain my position?[41]

Montagu did not sit back, waiting for the answer he requested from the Prime Minister. He expended much effort and time in the days prior to his departure for India, to gather as much evidence as he could as to the harmful impact a Zionist declaration would have on British interests in India, and submitted to the Cabinet the names of prominent English Jewish anti-Zionists who agreed with his views.[42]

The decision by the Cabinet to solicit more opinions brought Weizmann again into a state of alarmed indignation.[43] The Milner-Amery draft itself held some disappointments; it contained neither the reference to the historic title that Zionists claimed ("Palestine . . . *reconstituted* as the national home of the Jewish people"), nor the clause implying, if not conferring, a special status for the Zionist organization—both present at earlier drafts. It was acceptable, nevertheless, as the best then obtainable, and the Zionists were prepared to do vigorous battle to secure it. What alarmed them, and made a battle seem necessary, was the provision to poll non-Zionist as well as Zionist opinions.[44] The reference of the matter to the American President also aroused some uncertainty.

The English Zionists at once mounted a campaign of public meetings and mass resolutions which, together with the balance of opinions received by those the government consulted, as per Weizmann's suggestion, left an impression of strong support in British Jewry for the Zionist demands.[45] They also—through Weizmann—appealed at once for similar action, as well as for urgent intercession with their own government, by Brandeis and the other American Zionist leaders. Weizmann, moreover, sent letters requesting mass demonstrations and written support from Jewish leaders in Russia, Australia, France and elsewhere.[46] On October 23, he was able to send Ronald Graham a list of some two hundred and fifty representative Jewish bodies in the United Kingdom which, as a result of the campaign launched by the EZF, had passed resolutions favoring the "reconstitution of Palestine as the National Home of the Jewish People."[47]

This strong demonstration of support from official Jewish organizations, was coupled with a weakening of resolve and commitment to obtain a declaration on the part of some members of the British Palestine Committee. Some of them were discouraged by what they considered to be British indecision and insincerity. As usual, it was Harry Sacher who sounded the harshest note as he wrote to Leon Simon: "I agree that this

Declaration business is of no very great importance and I do my best with my own little circle to keep the sense of proportion. It's not hard, because they take a pretty similar view. I incline to think also that W.[eizmann] has outlived his usefulness as a Zionist leader."[48] The tensions among his closest advisers must certainly have taken their toll, but Weizmann continued to maintain the air of a man in full command of his forces.

By mid-October, Weizmann—together with Ahad Ha'Am and with Wickham Steed's stylistic assistance—[49] had composed his reply to Maurice Hankey's letter asking for his view on the draft declaration. He could not refrain from starting his letter with yet another attack on "those Jews who by education and social connections have lost touch with the real spirit animating the Jewish people." He then made three suggestions for rewording the declaration: "re-establishment" instead of "establishment," a suggestion also made by Sokolow and not accepted; "Jewish people" instead of "Jewish race," a suggestion which was accepted in the final draft; and the revision of the passage in the draft declaration which could be interpreted as saying that those Jews who will not emigrate to Palestine, would totally dissociate themselves from the Jewish national home. This was a suggestion which was also made by Dr. Hertz, and the final part of the last sentence of the Milner-Amery draft was in the end simply dropped.[50]

Even before receiving the draft declaration from the Cabinet Secretary, Weizmann sent a long letter to Brandeis in which he described Montagu's attempts to sabotage the British declaration and asked for the support of American Jewry for the Zionist position.[51] After he received a copy of the Milner-Amery draft declaration, Weizmann cabled it to Brandeis on October 9.[52] In the meantime, the British government acted expeditiously as well. On this occasion, its approach to its American ally was clearly intended, by the form it took, to elicit a positive, favorable reply. On October 6, 1917, two days after the Cabinet session, Balfour cabled Colonel House, this time including the text of the declaration under discussion.[53] A second cable, sent at the same time, called attention to reported German overtures to the Zionists which made it timely to take up the proposal for action.[54] All these communications, Weizmann's and, of course, the official British messages, reached House's desk through his regular, British intelligence contacts.

On October 13, House went to Washington to confer with President Wilson.[55] His journal entry for the day mentions, in regard to the

Ottoman area, that, "We spoke of . . . the partition or non-partition of Turkey." At that time House was still actively considering the possibility of a separate peace with Turkey and had recently spoken with Elkus about employing his services for the purpose. He also spoke with the Russian ambassador about the desirability of leaving Turkey "intact" after the war. The President's reaction, however, hardly encouraged either idea: "The President suggested the making of another speech in which to say that our people must not be deceived by Germany's apparent willingness to give up Belgium and Alsace Lorraine, for it would leave her impregnable in both Austria and Turkey." House nevertheless was able to get the President's agreement that if he made such a speech— which House carefully did not recommend—he should not confine himself to the formula he originally intended: that "Turkey should become effaced, and . . . the disposition of it should be left to the peace conference." To this House proposed to add—and the President agreed— "that Turkey must not be partitioned among the belligerents, but must become autonomous in its several parts according to racial lines."

House's journal for October 13 does not mention one matter which must nevertheless have come up in their discussion, namely, the British request for an opinion on their proposed pro-Zionist declaration. On October 16, following his return to New York, House received in the morning mail Wilson's note of October 13, evidently written after their meeting: "I find in my pocket the memorandum you gave me about the Zionist movement. I am afraid I did not say to you that I concurred in the formula suggested by the other side. I do, and would be obliged if you would let them know it." House then sent through British channels the following message: "Colonel House put formula before President, who approves of it but asks that no mention of his approval shall be made when His Majesty's Government makes formula public, as he had arranged that American Jews shall then ask him for his approval, which he will give publicly here."

In the meantime, Weizmann's cable to Brandeis with the text of the proposed declaration was received by the justice on October 14. Brandeis sent the text on to Wise and DeHaas in New York and asked them to see Colonel House immediately. They did so, and met House on October 16. By then Wilson's note had been received and acted upon. All that remained for House to do was to inform the Zionists that their wishes had been anticipated and that no publicity must be made of the President's cooperation in this matter with the Entente Governments. The President, House said, would later express his approval in response to an enquiry by "leading Jews"—which, of course, Wilson did in reply to Wise only much later, many months after the Balfour Declaration was issued.

DeHaas, in reporting the interview to Brandeis, asked what should be the response to Weizmann's request for public pressure by American Jews in support of the British Zionists in their still pending battle for the declaration. Brandeis, perhaps sharing House's view that if the Zionists had the governments on their side, they need no longer defend themselves against non-Zionists, decided that the Americans should take no further action.[56] Brandeis's cable to Weizmann of October 17, 1917, simply states that "President has sent London message of approval but believes public declaration by him would be injudicious."[57]

Some American suggestions however, were introduced into the text, and Wise regretted that Brandeis had not been consulted before the President agreed.[58] The Americans conveyed to Colonel House their objections to the section of the draft declaration that referred to the Jews as a "race" and, by its assurances to "such Jews who are fully contented with their existing nationality," seemed to base Zionist claims on a principle of discontent, not shared by these American Zionists with regard to their country.[59] House does not seem to have sent on the American observations. In any case, Weizmann, and others who were consulted by the War Cabinet, had made the same general suggestions for revisions as the Americans themselves had desired.[60] It would seem moreover, that the Americans sent their suggestions to Weizmann and Sokolow much too late to have made an impact.[61]

All seemed set for government approval of a pro-Zionist declaration. Not only the Zionists were anxious for this final step, the Foreign Office, too, was impatient. Once again Ronald Graham reminded Arthur Balfour on October 24—more than three months after Lord Rothschild had first submitted the Zionist draft—that

further delay will have a deplorable result and may jeopardize the whole Jewish situation. At the present moment uncertainty as regards the attitude of His Majesty's Government on this question is growing into suspicion, and not only are we losing the very valuable co-operation of the Zionist forces in Russia and America, but we may bring them into antagonism with us and throw the Zionists into the arms of the Germans who would only be too ready to welcome this opportunity . . .

The French have already given an assurance of sympathy to the Zionists on the same lines as is now proposed for His Majesty's Government, though in rather more definite terms. The Italian Government and the Vatican have expressed their sympathy and we know that President Wilson is sympathetic and is prepared to make a declaration at the proper moment.

Graham then went on to discuss the important role attributed to Russian Jewry in determining the political alliance of their government. Their sympathies were currently with the Germans, but an assurance by England might turn them around. He then continued with a promise Weizmann must have made countless times in the offices of government officials:

The moment this assurance is granted the Zionist Jews are prepared to start an active pro-Ally propaganda throughout the world. Dr. Weizmann, who is a most able and energetic propagandist, is prepared to proceed himself to Russia and to take charge of the campaign. Propaganda in America is also most necessary. I earnestly trust that unless there is a very good reason to the contrary the assurance from His Majesty's Government should be given at once.[62]

Balfour no longer needed to be convinced, as is clear from his minute to the Prime Minister the following day, that the Zionists "have reasonable ground for complaint."[63] Weizmann, for one, was increasingly nervous. He had heard rumors that the matter would come up before the War Cabinet on October 23; it was actually on the agenda for the 25th, but was postponed in order to give Lord Curzon time to complete a memorandum on the subject.[64] On hearing the news that day, Weizmann felt he was at the end of his tether. "I shall never in my life forget this day," he wrote to Ahad Ha'Am. "I was awaiting the decision in the morning and it ended with a postponement. I went wearily to the Laboratory and found that there had been a fire and that half of it was burnt out . . . I shall be in touch with you when I have recovered a little."[65] Wickham Steed, head of the Foreign Department of the *Times*, also became alarmed at the delay and urged in a leading article in terms similar to those used by Ronald Graham in the internal Foreign Office correspondence—for a British declaration.[66]

The same day, October 26th, on which Steed published his article in the *Times*, Lord Curzon finally distributed his memorandum to his colleagues. Like Herbert Samuel, more than two years earlier, Curzon also titled his paper "The Future of Palestine." He focused on two issues: the meaning of the phrase "a National Home for the Jewish race in Palestine," showing the many contradictions in statements made by supporters of Zionism as to whether or not a Jewish state was the final aim of the movement. The bulk of his arguments—as was the case when he stated his case at the Cabinet meeting of October 4—related to the question as to what the chances were for the successful realization of such a British policy. Curzon pointed to the poverty of Palestine, its lack of resources, and the need for prolonged and patient toil of its soil by people who had no agricultural tradition. Then one had to consider what would become of the existing half million Arab population who "will not be content either to be expropriated for Jewish immigrants, or to act merely as hewers of wood and drawers of water to the latter." How could such a country, then, absorb a large number of Jewish immigrants or be called a national home of the Jewish people?[67]

Mark Sykes, who had shepherded the Zionists ever since his meeting with them on February 7, 1917, was given another chance to rise to their defense. On October 30 [possibly after consulation with the much-admired Aaron Aaronson who had arrived in London at the beginning of that month] he submitted a long paper, relating almost exclusively to Palestine's absorptive capacity of large immigration. He did so by contradicting Curzon's assertions and pointing to the rich agricultural potential of the country. He cited many examples of the enormous strides that had been made in the cultivation of oranges, vegetables, and grapes. He argued that the population of Palestine could be doubled in seven years, provided the necessary security and infra-structure were provided.[68]

On October 31, 1917, at the War Cabinet meeting, Balfour made it quite clear that it wanted to issue a statement endorsing Zionist aims.[69] The Foreign Secretary stated that "he understood that there were considerable differences of opinion among experts regarding the possibility of the settlement of any large population in Palestine, but he was informed that if Palestine were scientifically developed, a very much larger population could be sustained than had existed during the period of Turkish misrule." In any case, as he observed in his opening remarks, everyone [including Curzon] seemed to agree that the most important underlying reasons for a declaration were of a diplomatic and political nature. As to the meaning of the words "national home. . . . It did not necessarily involve the early establishment of an independent Jewish state, which was a matter for gradual development in accordance with the ordinary laws of political evolution." He also felt that Zionism would not hinder the process of Jewish assimilation in Western countries.[70]

Edwin Montagu had sailed for India some two weeks earlier and it was left to Curzon singlehandedly to hold the banner of opposition. His was now much less forceful than at the last Cabinet meeting which discussed the declaration or even a few days earlier in his memorandum. He admitted the force of diplomatic and political considerations, and he even conceded that the majority of the Jews were Zionists. In any case, he did not approve of Montagu's attitude. His objections centered on his—as he saw it—more sober assessment of conditions in Palestine, and he feared Britain was raising unrealistic expectations. The Christian and Moslem Holy Places, moreover, had to be protected and if this were to be done effectively, how could the Jews build up their own political capital? He agreed to some declaration of sympathy, but asked that it be done in guarded language.[71] With this statement, then, all present deemed that the objections to a pro-Zionist declaration had been removed. The War Cabinet then authorized the Secretary of State for Foreign Affairs to take a suitable opportunity of making such a declaration.

On November 2, 1917, Balfour sent the declaration to Lord Rothschild which thenceforth bears his name, describing it as a "declaration of sympathy with Jewish Zionist aspirations,"—in this way satisfying at least nominally the Zionist interest in being recognized as the accredited agent representing the Jews in negotiating and carrying out the policy foreshadowed in the declaration. In its familiar final form, the Balfour Declaration read:

His Majesty's Government view with favour the establishment in Palestine of a national home for the Jewish people, and will use their best endeavours to facilitate the achievement of this object, it being clearly understood that nothing shall be done which may prejudice the civil and religious rights of existing non-Jewish communities in Palestine, or the rights and political status enjoyed by Jews in any other country.[72]

While the War Cabinet began its deliberations behind closed doors, at noon, on October 31, Weizmann was anxiously waiting a few feet away, no doubt wondering whether this time, too, he would be disappointed. Some two hours later, Sykes came out, exclaiming, as Weizmann has recorded in his autobiography: "Dr. Weizmann, it's a boy!" In the hindsight of some thirty years, Weizmann wrote that this was not quite the boy he had expected,[73] but on that momentous day and for a long time to come, he felt he had advanced the cause of Zionism a great step forward. On more than one occasion in the past few months he had frankly acknowledged that he had done most of the political work leading to the declaration, often without consultation with others.[74] He knew well that if the Zionist efforts would have failed, the blame would have been laid at his feet. He also understood well, that a successful outcome would be interpreted as his personal achievement.

Conscious of his historical role, he had insisted since the summer of 1917, that proper archives be maintained by the Zionist bureau;[75] he hoped that such an archive would make possible the writing of a well-documented history of the Zionist-British negotiations.[76] Clearly, he would have preferred Balfour's letter of November 2, 1917 to be addressed to himself, rather than to Lord Rothschild. Had he been in England on July 18—rather than in Paris on the final leg of the Morgenthau mission—he might have been the person submitting the Zionist draft declaration to Balfour, and, in turn, the person to whom Balfour would have most likely sent his famous declaration. As it was, Lord Rothschild had asked in his letter transmitting the draft declaration that "His Majesty's . . . message" be sent to him. When the Government was ready to send the final declaration to the Zionists, Lord Hardinge pointed out, "The publication will depend upon Lord Rothschild to whom the declaration of the Government will be made in a reply to his original letter."[77] Weizmann had to content himself with a private letter from Ronald Graham, his most reliable ally in the Foreign Office, who on November 1, 1917, sent Weizmann his warm congratulations to which he appended "for [Weizmann's] private information," the text of the declaration.[78] Thus, ironically, one of Weizmann's best known political achievements is associated with a member of the Rothschild family who, until he had met Weizmann, was far removed from Zionist affairs.

It was a period of great joy and expectations for the Zionist and Jewish world.[79] The Balfour Declaration, coupled as it was with the military conquests in Palestine, seemed to promise a great deal. It remained to be seen whether Lord Curzon had been right when he warned that it might raise too high expectations in the Jewish world. Upon hearing that the declaration had been approved by the War Cabinet, Weizmann went to thank Arthur Balfour. The Foreign Secretary responded: "Now we expect you to turn it into a success."[80] This would prove to be the Zionists' greatest challenge.

The Balfour Declaration had for a long time been considered Weizmann's greatest political achievements; even his political enemies had to concede that this feat had captured the imagination of most Jews and had a force and magic of its own. Though later historians—mostly those friendly to the cause of Zionism—have in hindsight questioned Weizmann's role in obtaining the Balfour Declaration, in the immediate aftermath of the Cabinet's decision there was little doubt in the minds of those who had observed the entire political process at close range as to who deserved the lion's share of the credit. On November 2, 1917, the day Balfour signed his letter to Lord Rothschild, one of Weizmann's long-term opponents, Leopold Greenberg, wrote to Weizmann:

I am sure I did not say half or even much less of what I felt in regard to your wonderful success when I had the pleasure of seeing you this evening. You have performed miracles, especially having in mind surrounding circumstances and not only have you abundant justification for being proud of your accomplishment, but the Jewish People has manifest reason for being proud of you, one of its truest and best sons. Your victory so far should be an encouragement to you to carry on further for there is much to be done and only the beginning—great and glorious as it is—has been reached.[81]

Greenberg would hardly have gone out of his way to praise a man with whom he had so often in the past had profound ideological differences. The evidence available on Weizmann's political activities must have seemed clear cut to him. The editor of the *Jewish Chronicle* maintained good contacts in government circles and was no doubt also being kept informed by James Malcolm, Sykes's friend, whom he had introduced to Weizmann early in 1917.

Yet few knew as intimately what transpired behind the scenes as the editor of the *Manchester Guardian* who a few days later wrote in response to a letter from Weizmann "heartiest congratulations on the great step forward of your movement. To you personally it will be a tremendous relief. . . . The movement owes almost everything to you."[82] Lord Rothschild, to whom Balfour's letter was addressed, saw the declaration as the joint personal achievement of Weizmann and Sokolow.[83] The American Zionists, however, who had been pressed into action by Weizmann, saw him—not his senior partner Sokolow, nor anyone else—as the Zionist most responsible for bringing about the Declaration.[84] There were, of course, dozens, if not hundreds of letters and telegrams sent to Weizmann in the months that followed, praising his political and diplomatic acumen in fulsome terms.[85]

As noted, historians have been divided on this issue. On one end of the spectrum we find a noted British historian stating that "Weizmann was the main creator of the National Home [because he secured the Balfour Declaration]. . . . It was in my opinion the greatest act of diplomatic statesmanship of the First World War."[86] Sir Charles Webster was in 1917 a staff officer in the Intelligence Directorate of the British War Office. One of his tasks was to study and appraise Zionism for the general staff, thus placing him in a position to evaluate Weizmann's statesmanship on the basis of close personal observation. In his magisterial work on the Balfour Declaration and in a subsequent lecture, Leonard Stein, who had also been privileged to watch events at close range, has confirmed, though in somewhat more subdued tones, Sir Charles's evaluation.[87] Subsequent historians of a younger generation, who have devoted full length monographs to the origins of the Balfour Declaration, have reached similar conclusions.[88]

On the other end of the spectrum one finds the Israeli scholar Mayir Vereté whose influential article on the subject has greatly discounted Weizmann's role in the attainment of the Balfour Declaration. His interpretation seems to accord Sokolow's diplomatic efforts in Paris and Rome, culminating with the Cambon letter, greater importance than Weizmann's parallel efforts in England. Herbert Samuel's role as the first person to place the Zionist agenda before the cabinet early in 1915, is similarly highlighted. Vereté's thesis is that Weizmann was simply a convenient tool in the hands of British policy makers. His detailed and sophisticated analysis of the data lead him to conclude that Weizmann's role was incidental in the process which led to the Declaration. He clearly demonstrates the long-standing British interest in Palestine[89] and the specific reasons leading them to make a public statement on behalf of the Zionists. One of these reasons was their desire to eliminate the French from Palestine, a position they were entitled to by virtue of the Sykes-Picot Agreement. Indeed, "had there been no Zionists in those days," asserts Vereté, "the British would have had to invent them."[90]

Vereté does not deny Weizmann's work in sounding out ministers and important British public figures, such as Sykes, Balfour, Lloyd George, Cecil, and Smuts and many other officials of various ranks in the Foreign Office, War Office, and Cabinet Secretariat. At the same time Vereté is unwilling to concede that Weizmann had a greater share in the work than Sokolow, nor does he think that the Balfour Declaration was the personal triumph of the Zionists, be they Weizmann or Sokolow. The British had their own reasons for granting the declaration; in Vereté's interpretation of the events they could be compared to "the lady who . . . was willing and only wanted to be seduced. Britain likewise willed Palestine, wanted the Zionists and courted them. Weizmann happened to come her way, talked to her to have the Zionists and go with them to Palestine, as only her they desired and to her they would be faithful. Britain was seduced. She was ready to be seduced by any Zionist of stature."[91] Few historians have joined Vereté's strong critique of the "Weizmann myth," until another Israeli historian, David Vital, followed his lead.[92] Though Vital declares that Weizmann "probably did more than anyone, even Sokolow, to persuade the British that the Zionists would, in the final analysis, serve their purposes,"[93] he asserts elsewhere that "Weizmann was more the epitome of the momentary alliance that was . . . in the making than its engineer,"[94] and that, "In its two essentials . . . the British decision to couple Palestine with Zionism . . . was one to which the Zionists themselves had made no direct contribution."[95]

Not many historians have agreed with these conclusions and for good reason. The factors leading to the Balfour Declaration are so complex and intertwined that a decisive, one-sided evaluation on either side of the spectrum is clearly inaccurate. In the final analysis one can perhaps be permitted to present a few observations which may lead to a more nuanced evaluation than has been provided by either Charles Webster or Mayir Vereté and those who have followed their respective analyses.

There is little doubt in the mind of all of the historians who have occupied themselves with the origins of the Balfour Declaration, that it was meant, first and foremost, to serve British aims and interests. Sir Edward Grey's proposal in March 1916, independent of Zionist pressure, clearly demonstrates the case; it shows that British policy makers of the highest rank judged Zionism to be a potentially serious force worth support and cultivation. As it turned out, Grey's timing was inauspicious.

Throughout 1915 and 1916 Weizmann had no contact with either the Prime Minister or the Foreign Secretary. He understood that the political climate in England and abroad was not yet ripe for a pro-Zionist declaration. That moment arrived after Lloyd George assumed office as Prime Minister, though not simply because "Lloyd George . . . had always wanted to acquire Palestine for Britain,"[96] nor solely because Balfour had pronounced himself a Zionist or because any number of other ministers had declared themselves in sympathy with Zionism. Their personal and deeply felt attachment to Jewish aspirations in the Holy Land would not have been sufficient to move the British Cabinet to issue the Balfour Declaration.

Until the end of October 1917, Balfour equivocated and did not press for passage. The Cabinet approved the issuance of a declaration after it was fully convinced that it was in its own best interests to do so. That moment came late in the spring of 1917 when Britain's political and military fortunes were at a low ebb and the myth of Jewish power and influence in America and Russia, and the rumors of an impending German initiative to woo the Zionists had reached new heights.

Yet, if the only, or even decisive factor, at play was Britain's own interests, one needs to ask why it took three cabinet meetings to arrive at a resolution. Nothing prevented the British from legitimizing their moral hold over Palestine by promises to Arab representatives who had been in touch with British agents in Egypt and elsewhere. If they wished control over Palestine, why then was Balfour interested in sharing such power with the United States? Why, moreover, did they not jettison the Balfour Declaration after the war, as soon as their needs had been served, and, instead, strengthened their ties to the Zionist cause by incorporating the concept of a Jewish national home into the Mandate?

The fact of the matter is that until 1917 the British were indecisive as to the best course they needed to follow in regard to Palestine and tried to keep all their diplomatic options open. Yet, if the British did not yet have a clear policy for the dismemberment of the Ottoman Empire, Weizmann had one from the very start of the war. The long duration of World War I, ironically, gave Weizmann ample time to prepare the ground for his ideas among British policy makers, much as it moved the government to seek wider support and new allies—with the help of the Zionists. The British ultimately reached the conclusion that a pro-Zionist declaration was in their own best interests, but it was Weizmann who convinced them that Zionist and British interests were not in conflict. As was noted earlier, the move from a state of readiness to act, to action, needed a catalyst. Weizmann, the congenial insider/outsider served as the ideal partner in creating the necessary fusion. Neither the Arabs nor the Armenians—the two other groups in Mark Sykes's tripartite configuration for a new Middle East—had someone with similar personal assets and qualifications to press their respective cases.

Weizmann had proposed to Ronald Graham on June 1, 1917, that a declaration supporting Zionist aspirations in Palestine be issued. Balfour was even then still skeptical whether the moment for such a declaration had arrived. In his response to Balfour of June 19 Graham cited the Cambon letter as an important precedent. Graham's letter demonstrates the weight the Foreign Office officials assigned to Sokolow's great achievement on the continent, though his role in England was more limited. Sokolow made a singular and ground-breaking contribution by securing the Cambon letter. In content and form it was a document that was much more favorable to the Zionists than the watered-down formula of the Balfour Declaration. Yet, once Balfour invited Lord Rothschild and Weizmann to present a draft declaration, Sokolow continued to play a preeminent role only as long as Weizmann was on his mission to Gibraltar. Beginning in July 1917 the Zionists actually worked out the wording of the declaration with the Foreign Office personnel under the more or less watchful eye of Balfour. It was, in fact, a mutual enterprise—not a unilateral act—as befits two partners with mutual interests, each watching out for himself while sensitive to his interlocutor's needs.

There was, of course, a readiness in England to support Zionism. Without the religious, moral, strategic, political, and even capricious sentiments animating Lloyd George,[97] Balfour, Smuts, Barnes, Milner, Sykes, and others, the process might have taken longer or might possibly have been frustrated altogether. Clearly, there were some factors working in favor of the Zionists which had not been initiated by Weizmann and his colleagues, but of which they were aware. And, of course, there were many avenues which they did pursue and ideas they did suggest to the British.

But someone had to provide the necessary background for all the British statesmen and civil servants who were unfamiliar with the history of Zionism and Jewish aspirations. Someone had to read and interpret the entire political map and fuse the various disparate human and political elements. Someone constantly had to remind those who counted of the mutuality of interests between the British Government and the Zionist movement. Someone had to overcome personal hesitations and even antisemitic arguments. Someone had to supply the correct and convincing arguments which the British were looking for and which made sense, in order to justify to themselves, on moral and humanitarian grounds, actions which they were ready to undertake on political grounds. That person was Chaim Weizmann.

Weizmann carefully addressed the entire range of concerns of British statesmen and politicians, be they of a personal, religious, imperial, colonial, or moral nature. He knew which arguments to use with whom and he was able to keep the political process on track—by appealing directly to the Prime Minister—when it threatened to be derailed. More than thirty years later Field Marshal Smuts told a London audience that "we were persuaded, but remember that it was Dr. Weizmann who persuaded us."[98] Weizmann, as we have seen, had the talent of turning incidental meetings into fateful encounters. He knew how to seize the moment, the idea, the opportunity which often does not recur. This did not make him a mere opportunist, since he truly believed that British and Zionist ambitions were intertwined to the benefit of both.

In the process of working for the British government and in negotiation with its leading representatives, Weizmann had become an Anglophile, a man totally imbued with his adopted country's values and ideals, while promoting his own movement's goals. His partners no doubt sensed this volitional identification and shared ambitions, and were therefore more ready to be persuaded by him. Weizmann's method was not that of a petitioner. Rather, he tried to provide the British with arguments buttressing their resolve to control Palestine. Weizmann supplied strategic, historical, religious, and general humanitarian reasons; often he used all arguments simultaneously. His main aim was to give substance and reality to the idea of a British protectorate while reassuring them that the Jewish People approved of the idea.

One of Weizmann's chief assets, from the British point of view, was that he freed them of responsibility for mobilizing Jewish support which was deemed so valuable by the Foreign Office. Weizmann, almost single-handedly—at least in the first two years of the war—served as a one-man ministry of propaganda, foreign affairs, and strategic planning. By the time Sokolow and Tschlenow appeared in England, Weizmann had already crystallized his ideas concerning a British Protectorate, had met with Balfour and Samuel, courted the Rothschilds, and won the confidence and invaluable support of C. P. Scott. All along he had built around him a loosely defined "think tank" of men and women whose judgment he trusted and on whom he could rely. Ideas which germinated in that group, he translated into political action. Within the context of the fragmentary and split Jewish and Zionist world, in England and elsewhere, this group filled a vacuum by its resolve and activist stance. With Ahad Ha'Am as the moral guide and with Sokolow providing official cover, Weizmann and his loyal, if sometimes more radical, group stood out by their determination.

One needs to keep in mind that Weizmann simply elected himself— with authority from no one—as a representative of the Jewish people, even before he had offered the government his scientific discoveries. What one must wonder at is the fact that the British accepted him almost from the start as such a legitimate representative, though they were well aware that he lacked official credentials. But perhaps even more remarkable was his ability to build sufficient consensus in the Zionist ranks to back up his particular point of view. This was perhaps his most difficult task. Whereas those British statesmen and officials with whom he spoke, tended to be favorably inclined toward his cause, there was no unanimity in the Jewish or Zionist world that Britain ought to be the protector of the Jews in Palestine.

Appearing cool and confident to the men of authority in England, whom he assured of world-wide Jewish support, or potential support, for Britain, Weizmann was at the same time engaged in a complicated balancing act. He had to convince his own colleagues in Russia and the United States that he had the full backing of the British Government, while trying to get their support to move their own governments to support his point of view. Moreover, his own colleagues in England did not always back him—particularly when prospects of success seemed bleak. Sokolow, Lord Rothschild, Sieff, and Tolkowsky were among the few who supported him throughout.[99] Amazingly, and solely due to his own powers of persuasion, Weizmann was able, when called upon, to mobilize the kind of support from his reluctant, or discouraged fellow Jews, both abroad and in England itself, when critical moments demanded such support.

Weizmann's relentless and singleminded determination that the only possible course for the Zionists was to have England as the patron of the Jews, won the day in—at least a segment—of the Zionist world, as his stature in the eyes of the British rose. The source of his authority within the Zionist movement was based on the esteem he acquired among the British. Thus, Weizmann's rise to power within his own movement, was not gradual and organic; it was sudden and effected from the periphery. A man as finely attuned to political nuances as Weizmann, was, of course, aware of the source of his power which, in turn, deepened his attachment to England. Similarly, he understood that if his political course were to fail, the blame would all be his.[100]

Whether Weizmann was the prime begetter of the Balfour Declaration or simply a tool in the hands of British imperialists, is a subject that will no doubt be debated for a long time to come. But it is indisputable that Weizmann had an inkling from the start of the war—in fact from October 1914 on—that the fate of Zionism was bound with that of England. He acted on this instinct and became its most eloquent promoter. In the process, he discovered that there were many British statesmen who had similar notions. If one examines the entire record, not singling any one document, one is left with the impression that both on the British side and on the Zionist side there were men who were not afraid to put the wheels of history in motion to translate their mutual desires into political facts. The British produced many such activists as Mark Sykes and Ronald Graham. In the Zionist camp Weizmann first and foremost masterminded and carried out the lion's share of the political work though other activists included Aaron Aaronsohn and Vladimir Jabotinsky. The evidence suggests that if the British "used" the Zionists for their own purposes, the Zionists also "used" Britain. They needed each other, and they benefitted from one another, at least in the short term. A long history of mutual affinities between some leading Zionists and some British statesmen who were in control at the crucial moment, made the process of securing the Balfour Declaration smoother and personally more gratifying to such men as Lloyd George, Balfour, Milner, Smuts, Carson, Barnes, and, of course, Weizmann. One observer has commented that "The Balfour Declaration had a very British begetting. It was born out of a mingling of self-interest and a moral attitude informed by powerful sentimentality." [101]

From the point of view of the British policy makers, the Balfour Declaration was a last minute bid to tip the scales of the war in their favor.[102] But as just another arrow in the secondary quiver of the Middle East, it created little interest in the corridors of Whitehall and Westminster. That task was left in the hands of a few ranking civil servants of the Foreign Office and cabinet secretariat. Even on October 31, 1917, when it came up for discussion for the third time, it was not the first item on the agenda. The Declaration came to be invested with moral and political meaning principally by the Zionists (and later by their enemies who, of course, gave it a different moral and political interpretation).[103] What makes the Balfour Declaration stand out from so many other documents that were issued by the British is the fact that the British did not renege on their promise—at least not at first—which suggests that this particular declaration was issued for reasons that went beyond political expediency. The fact that for thirty years following its issuance, the British had still not formally renounced this—by-then distasteful policy [104]—can be attributed mostly to Weizmann. This, perhaps, was his greatest political accomplishment.

NOTES

1. See Minutes of the London Zionist Political Committee meeting held on Tuesday, August 28th, 1917. Weizmann Archives, Rehovot, Israel (hereafter cited as W.A.).
2. See Scott Diaries, October 19, 1917. See also Wickham Steed to Lord Northcliffe, October 14, 1917. See Private Papers Collection, File: Papers Concerning Balfour Declaration. Middle East Centre, St. Antony's College, Oxford.
3. See Minutes of the War Cabinet, September 3, 1917. Cabinet Office Papers, Public Record Office, London (hereafter cited as CAB), 23/4.
4. *Ibid.*
5. CAB, 24/27.
6. Edward Mandell House, *The Intimate Papers of Colonel House. Into the World War*, vol. III, arranged by Charles Seymour (Boston, 1926–1928), p. 175.
7. Cable from Colonel House to Lord Robert Cecil, September 11, 1917. CAB, 24/26.

8. Weizmann to Sir George Clerk, September 9, 1917. *The Letters and Papers of Chaim Weizmann,* ed. Meyer W. Weisgal et al., English ed., ser. A, vol. VII (Jerusalem: Israel Universities Press, 1972) [hereafter cited as *WL,* followed by volume and page numbers], p. 504.

9. Shmuel Tolkowsky, *Yoman zioni medini,* London, 1915–1919, ed. Dvorah Barzilay-Yegar (Jerusalem: Hasifriyah Hazionit, 1981), p. 174.

10. See Weizmann to Louis Brandeis, September 11, 1917. *WL* VII, pp. 505–6.

11. The account concerning Brandeis's intercession with House and Wilson relies, with minor alterations, on Ben Halpern's article "Brandeis and the Origins of the Balfour Declaration," *Studies in Zionism* 7 (1983): 93–100. See also Richard Ned Lebow, "Woodrow Wilson and the Balfour Declaration," *Journal of Modern History* 40 (1968): 501–23.

12. The text of the Brandeis telegrams is reproduced in CAB, 24/27.

13. CAB, 24/27.

14. See Jacob DeHaas to Louis Brandeis, September 24, 1917. Jacob DeHaas Papers, Central Zionist Archives, Jerusalem (hereafter cited as CZA).

15. Halpern, "Brandeis and the Origins of the Balfour Declaration," pp. 94–95.

16. Halpern, "Brandeis and the Origins of the Balfour Declaration," pp. 95–96.

17. Weizmann to Yehiel Tschlenow, September 1, 1917. *WL* VII, pp. 495–98.

18. See Yehiel Tschlenow to Nahum Sokolow and Chaim Weizmann, September 24, 1917. CZA, A18/41/2/8.

19. *Protokoll der Sitzung des Engeren Actions-Komitees am 29. bis 31. Juli 1917 im Zionistischen Bureau in Kopenhagen.* CZA, L6/64I.

20. Edwin Montagu to Robert Cecil, September 14, 1917. CAB, 21/58.

21. Ahad Ha'Am to Louis Brandeis, October 3, 1917. DeHaas Papers.

22. Weizmann to Philip Kerr, September 16, 1917. *WL* VII, pp. 511–12.

23. *Ibid.*

24. Weizmann to Philip Kerr, September 19, 1917. *WL* VII, p. 516.

25. Rothschild to Weizmann, September 21, 1917. W.A.

26. See Ronald Graham to Lord Hardinge, September 24, 1917. Foreign Office Papers, Public Record Office, London (hereafter cited as F.O.) 371/3083.

27. F.O. 371/3083.

28. Ronald Graham to General Wingate, September 21, 1917. Sir Reginald Wingate Papers, Durham University, School of Oriental Studies, Durham.

29. This paper, titled "Note on Palestine" was sent to Weizmann for comments which were made in the margins. The paper is in the Weizmann Archives. Weizmann returned the paper to Sykes on September 22, 1917.

30. *Yoman zioni medini,* p. 176. See also Harry Sacher to Weizmann, September 25, 1917. W.A.

31. *Yoman zioni medini,* p. 178; Weizmann to Nahum Sokolow, September 30, 1917. *WL* VII, p. 520.

32. See, e.g., letter from Heron Goodhart to Arthur James Balfour with attached memorandum. October 2, 1917. CAB, 21/58.

33. Weizmann and Rothschild to Arthur Balfour, October 3, 1917. *WL* VII, pp. 521–22.

34. Leopold S. Amery, *My Political Life,* vol. 2 (London, 1953), p. 116.

35. See Leonard Stein, *The Balfour Declaration* (New York: Simon and Schuster, 1961), p. 664. The last two words were added at the Cabinet meeting.

36. *Ibid.* October 4, 1917. CAB, 21/58.

37. *Ibid.*

38. *Yoman zioni medini,* p. 179.

39. See William Ormsby-Gore to Hankey, October 5, 1917. CAB, 21/58.

40. See form letter from Maurice Hankey of October 6, 1917. CAB, 21/58.

41. Edwin Montagu to Lloyd George. October 4, 1917. David Lloyd George Papers, House of Lords Record Office, London, (hereafter cited as LlGP, HLRO) F/39/3/30.

42. See Edwin Montagu, "Zionism," October 9, 1917. F.O. 371/3083. This paper too was distributed to the Cabinet.

43. See, e.g., Weizmann to Philip Kerr, October 7, 1917. *WL* VII, pp. 526–28.

44. The replies of all those contacted by Maurice Hankey are contained in a document titled "The Zionist Movement" and dated October 17, 1917. F.O. 371/3083.

45. See Stein, *The Balfour Declaration,* pp. 519–20.

46. See *WL* VII, pp. 523–37.

47. Weizmann to Ronald Graham, October 23, 1917. *WL* VII, p. 539. The list is available in the W.A.

48. Harry Sacher to Leon Simon, October 7, 1917. W.A.

49. See *Yoman zioni medini,* p. 181.

50. Weizmann to Maurice Hankey, October 15, 1917. *WL* VII, pp. 533–34. Also in F.O. 371/3083.

51. Weizmann to Louis Brandeis, October 7, 1917. *WL* VII, pp. 523–26.

52. Weizmann to Louis Brandeis, October 9,. 1917. *WL* VII, pp. 530–31. In Brandeis' reply to Weizmann he states "Your cable of tenth received." See Brandeis to Weizmann [October 17, 1917]. Sir William Wiseman Papers, Yale University. Drawer 91, file 130.

53. See Balfour [through Wiseman] to Colonel House, October 6, 1917. F.O. 371/3083.

54. *Ibid.*

55. The discussion concerning the steps leading to Wilson's approval of the British draft declaration relies, with some minor deviations, on Halpern, "Brandeis and the Origins of the Balfour Declaration," pp. 96–100.

56. See report of DeHaas to Brandeis of October 16, 1917, and Brandeis's reply on that same memorandum. See also DeHaas to Brandeis, October 17, 1917. DeHaas Papers.

57. Brandeis to Weizmann October [17], 1917. Wiseman Papers, Drawer 91, file 130.

58. See Stephen Wise to Louis Brandeis, October 17, 1917. DeHaas Papers.

59. See Stephen Wise to Louis Brandeis, October 15, 1917. DeHaas Papers. See also letter by the American Zionists to Weizmann and Sokolow, October 26, 1917. DeHaas Papers.

60. Jacob DeHaas assured the members of the Provisional Executive Committee that the changes made in the third part of the draft declaration were due to suggestions made by the American Political Committee. See Jacob DeHaas to Members of the Provisional Committee, November 12, 1917. DeHaas Papers. Stephen Wise too believed, until his last days, that it was he and Brandeis who were responsible for the change in the wording of the Balfour Declaration. See the letter from Stephen Wise to Meyer W. Weisgal, October 8, 1948. W.A.

61. See Provisional Executive Committee for General Zionist Affairs to Weizmann and Sokolow, [October 29, 1917]. W.A.

62. Ronald Graham to Secretary of State [Balfour], October 25, 1917. LlGP, HLRO F/3/2/34.

63. Arthur Balfour to Lloyd George, October 25, 1917. CZA, KH/207/1. Balfour appended Graham's memorandum to his note to the Prime Minister. It seems that Ronald Graham's memorandum was written on October 24; however, it may have been retyped in the Secretary of State's office before it was forwarded to Lloyd George. With Graham's memorandum, Balfour sent along a "note" outlining the most significant dates in the evolution of the declaration, beginning with Rothschild's letter of July 18, 1917.

64. October 25, 1917. CAB, 23/4.

65. Weizmann to Ahad Ha'Am, October 25, 1917. *WL* VII, p. 540.

66. See Wickham Steed, "The Jews and Palestine," *Times,* October 26, 1917.
67. C.[urzon] of K.[edleston], "The Future of Palestine," October 26, 1917. CAB, 21/58.
68. Sykes's paper [October 30, 1917] is undated and without a heading. F.O. 371/3083.
69. See Blanche Dugdale, *The Balfour Declaration: Origins and Background* (London, 1940), p. 29.
70. October 31, 1917. CAB, 23/4.
71. *Ibid.*
72. Arthur James Balfour to Lord Rothschild, November 2, 1917. F.O. 371/3083.
73. Chaim Weizmann, *Trial and Error* (New York: Schocken Books, 1949), p. 208.
74. *Yoman zioni medini*, p. 183.
75. *Yoman zioni medini*, p. 163.
76. Weizmann to Simon Marks, [October] 8, 1917. *WL* VII, pp. 528–29.
77. Minute of Lord Hardinge, November 1, 1917. F.O. 371/3083.
78. Ronald Graham to Weizmann, November 1, 1917. W.A.
79. See, e.g., "The Reception of the Declaration," *Palestine,* vol. II, no. 16. (November 24, 1917): 145–52.
80. *Yoman zioni medini*, p. 189.
81. Leopold Greenberg to Weizmann, November 2, 1917. W.A.
82. C. P. Scott to Weizmann, November 9, 1917. W.A.
83. See Lord Rothschild to Weizmann, November 1, 1917. W.A.
84. Jacob DeHaas to Weizmann, November 20, 1917. DeHaas Papers.
85. See e.g. the letter signed by the executive council of the English Zionist Federation of November 6, 1917. W.A. The Weizmann Archives contain letters and declarations of praise for Weizmann in a number of containers.
86. Charles Kingsley Webster, *The Founder of the National Home.* The Chaim Weizmann Memorial Lecture. (Rehovot, 1955), p. 14. Even if we take into account that this statement was made in Rehovot, in a lecture honoring Weizmann, it cannot be dismissed as mere hyperbole.
87. See Stein, *The Balfour Declaration;* Leonard Stein, *Weizmann and the Balfour Declaration.* Sixth Chaim Weizmann Memorial Lecture. (Rehovot: Yad Chaim Weizmann, 1961).
88. See Isaiah Friedman, *The Question of Palestine* (London: Routledge and Kegan Paul, 1973), p. 283; in Ronald Sanders' book *The High Walls of Jerusalem* (New York, 1983), Weizmann also emerges as the central hero. See also Norman Rose, *Chaim Weizmann* (New York, 1986), p. 187. One could add to this category of historians the late Richard Crossman, who had been the official biographer of Weizmann before his untimely death. See in particular his article "Weizmann," *Encounter* XIV (1960): 50–51.
89. On this issue see also D. Z. Gillon, "The Antecedents of the Balfour Declaration," *Middle Eastern Studies* 5 (1969): 131–50.
90. Mayir Vereté, "The Balfour Declaration and its Makers," *Middle Eastern Studies* 6 (1970): 50.
91. *Ibid.,* p. 67.
92. Vital's high regard for Vereté is expressed in the annotated bibliography to his book *Zionism: The Crucial Phase* (Oxford, 1987), p. 383. He expressed similar admiration in a lecture he gave in Jerusalem at a symposium commemorating the 70th anniversary of the Balfour Declaration (November 1987). For a highly critical review of Vital's book see Evyatar Friesel, "David Vital's Work on Zionism," *Studies in Zionism* 9 (1988): 209–25. See also Isaiah Friedman's review of the book, "Zionist History Reconsidered," *Studies in Contemporary Jewry* VI (1990): 309–14.
93. Vital, *Zionism: The Crucial Phase,* p. 161.
94. *Ibid.,* p. 223.

95. *Ibid.*, p. 236.
96. See David Fromkin, *A Peace to End all Peace. Creating the Modern Middle East 1914–1922* (New York, 1989), p. 267.
97. See, e.g., Philipp Aronstein, ed. *Speeches of British Statesmen on Judaism and Zionism*, (Berlin, 1936), p. 34.
98. Quoted by Stein, *Weizmann and the Balfour Declaration*, p. 15.
99. Even an outsider, like Mark Sykes, could discern those Weizmann could trust. He cabled the Foreign Office in the spring of 1917: "Please tell Weizmann from me that it would be best to keep all negotiations strictly to himself and Sokolow. James R.[othschild] is enthusiastic and rash." Mark Sykes to Foreign Office, May 1, 1917. F.O. 371/3053/88954/84173.
100. In a letter to Weizmann of April 28, 1917, Israel Sieff pointed out to Weizmann that he would be the first to blame if Turkey, e.g., were to sign a separate peace treaty with England. W.A.
101. See Patrick O'Donovan, "The Balfour Declaration," *Rehovoth* (Winter 1967/68): 31. See Also Conor Cruise O'Brien. "Israel in Embryo," [a review of Ronald Sanders's book], *New York Review of Books* XXXI (1984): 37–38.
102. There were, of course, other pro-Zionist declarations which followed the Balfour Declaration, each given for a variety of reasons. There was a Serbian declaration on December 27, 1917; a French declaration on February 14, 1918; and an Italian declaration on May 9, 1918, to mention but a few. See Israel Klausner, "Hadeklerazyah haserbit," *Haolam*, November 4, 1937. Perhaps one of the most remarkable declarations was that issued by the Japanese Government in January 1919, in response to Weizmann's request: "The Japanese Government gladly take note of the Zionist aspirations to establish in Palestine a national home for the Jewish people and they look forward with a sympathetic interest to the realization of such desire upon the basis proposed." T. Chinda to Chaim Weizmann, January 6, 1919. CZA, Z4/2039.
103. See, e.g., the comments of Elizabeth Monroe, in a file titled "Balfour Declaration," Middle East Center, St. Antony's College, Oxford.
104. See Elizabeth Monroe, *Britain's Moment in the Middle East 1914–1956* (London, 1963).

24.

The Zionist Movement and the Arabs

Israel Kolatt

In recent years, scholars and the general public alike have taken great interest in Jewish-Arab relations. From the standpoint of Zionist history, the very change of emphasis from the various aspects of "the Jewish question" to the problem of Jewish-Arab relations is highly significant. It moves the area of discussion—and the field in which the problem is defined—from the history and distress of the Jews to the evolution of Middle-East relations. It changes the Zionist historical view from one in which the entire course of Jewish history was of the essence to one in which what was previously considered of local and relatively minor import becomes central.

Discussion of this subject puts the historian to the test—the test of his or her ability to examine the facts without distorting them or apologizing for them, and the test of dealing not only with the political, military, economic, and ideological facts, but with political systems and social structures as well. On a more abstract plane, an historical examination enables one to distinguish between a history possessing a predestined significance, on the one hand, i.e., the history of the realization of absolute values, and on the other, a history which is open to human choice and decision.

The example of other nationalist movements is likely to be of only partial aid to us in our discussion of the evolution of Jewish-Arab relations; the phenomenon at hand comprises not only a national conflict with regard to territory and population majorities, but also a reli-

Reprinted by permission of the author, The Historical Society of Israel, and The Zalman Shazar Center for Jewish History from *Zionism and the Arab Question*, edited by Shmuel Almog (Jerusalem, 1983): 1–34.

gious and cultural one. The people in conflict intermingle, and the encounter is not only a theoretical one on a national plane, but a pragmatic encounter of individuals in their day-to-day life; injury and deprivation are the lot not only of the population as a collective, but of the individual as well. Not only are Jews and Arabs embroiled in a dispute over the same territory (and this dispute is relevant not only to the destiny of the nation as a whole, but also to that of the individual); there is also the burden of the historical relationship between Islam and Judaism. In our times, there has emerged the further conflict regarding the very definition of nationality. The Arabs officially dissociate Arab nationalism from Islam, despite the admission of strong bonds between the two. On the other hand, they see in Jewish nationalism an illegitimate nationalism linked to a particular religion. This accumulation of conflicts has resulted in the non-recognition by the Arabs of the very existence of Jewish nationhood.

The Zionist position with regard to the Arabs and to Arab nationalism has undergone many transformations, engendered by both the nature of Zionism and historical reality. On the surface, these attitudes would appear to be derived from the extent to which various Zionist ideologies defined Zionism: the more maximalist the Zionism—insistence upon mass immigration, a Jewish majority in Palestine, and Jewish sovereignty—the less compromising it should be with regard to the Arabs. In fact, this is not the case.

In reality, the Zionist attitude towards the Arabs has also been influenced by other factors: the attitude towards the Orient, the attitude towards the use of violence, and the liberal or socialist elements which were added to the Zionist idea. An appreciation of the realities of Palestine also played a role in forging these attitudes. There have been maximalist Zionists dedicated to arriving at an agreement between the Jews and the Arabs, and more moderate Zionists who did not believe in the possibility of such an agreement. The evolution of these relationships will be discussed below.

Historical literature is replete with the accusation that Zionism ignored "the Arab problem"; this contention has been stated in an even broader form: that Zionism ignored the realities of Palestine and the area, and that Zionism is by nature an illusory movement. It is true that Zionism's point of departure was not in the actual realities of Palestine, but rather in the problem of the Jews and the Jewish people and in the notion of Jewish rights to and bonds with the Land of Israel. But this does not mean that the realities of Palestine were not considered at all.

Both the "old" and "new" *Yishuv* certainly considered them. Those outside Palestine also took these realities into account. But what both groups took into consideration was the reality of the nineteenth century, and we must consider that period today if our discussion is not to be anachronistic.

In the middle of the nineteenth century, Palestine belonged to the Ottoman Empire and was not a separate political unit in the administrative division of that Empire. Arab nationalism had not yet developed, and Arab nationalism in Palestine was certainly non-existent. The local population was a patchwork of local, family-oriented, and religious loyalties. The population was united to a certain degree in its opposition to the reforms of the central regime, particularly the Muslim population. Opposition to the Jews was secondary to opposition to foreigners, mainly to the Christians.

The pre-Zionists of the 1860s and 1870s, and the Zionists from 1882 until 1914, could envisage Zionism's realization within the framework of the Ottoman Empire. The Empire had been subject to an ever-increasing influence by the world powers, restrained somewhat by the pan-Islamic policy of Sultan Abdul Hamnid (1876–1909). There took place, too, the gradual formation of units of limited autonomy on a religious and ethnic basis, with the occasional guarantee of European powers (as in the case of Lebanon). The demand for greater freedom for the various national groupings within the Empire after 1908 was interpreted by the Zionists as a chance for realizing the Zionist idea.

The first confrontations of Zionism were not with the Arab nationalist movement, but with the Ottoman regime, which limited immigration and land purchase, and with the local population. The latter clashes centered around the purchase of land, soil cultivation methods, and guarding the settlements. The Jews, ignorant of the way of life of the local population, occasionally offended its customs and feelings. At the turn of the century, these issues stimulated Jewish discussions of relations with the Arabs.

Around the time of World War I, Zionist leaders (among them Arthur Ruppin, for example) recognized the mistakes that had been made in this context during the first stages of settlement. They believed that if they would put an end to the dispossession of tenant-farmers, compensating those who had already been dispossessed, and increase the number of Jews able to speak Arabic and familiar with their way of life, Jewish-Arab tensions would be eased. And indeed, the end of the Ottoman regime saw the beginning of a policy—one that continued during the Mandate as well—aimed at compensating Arab tenant-farmers, together with payments made to the land-owners. But by that time the conflict had already risen to a higher level, attaining the status of a general national conflict.

Day-to-day friction was not the only factor which forced a discussion of Jewish-Arab relations. By the end of the nineteenth century the conflict also reflected European anti-Semitism which had penetrated Arab journalism and literature. Yet, despite this, more relevant to the discussion than any Arab challenge was the fate of the Zionist enterprise itself.

By way of a broad, imprecise generalization, one might say that the foundations of social and economic relations between Jews and Arabs were laid in the wake of developments during the Ottoman period. Political relations were forged during the Mandate.

The slow development of Jewish immigration and settlement in Palestine at the end of the last century together with the economic and social weakness of the *Yishuv* at the beginning of the next raised fears in the field of Jewish-Arab relations. The flow of Jewish capital to Palestine was liable to reach the Arab sector and accelerate its development; the small number of Jewish settlers was liable to be assimilated by the larger Arab population in terms of language and life style. The economic crisis of the Jewish agricultural settlements at the beginning of the century served only to increase that danger.

These considerations, in addition to others, more essential ones, led to the erection of economic and social barriers. The Jews and the Arabs who had been religiously separate now became further separated on a national level, both by the use of the Hebrew language and the new content given to Hebrew education. The first decade of the century saw the implementation of an economic policy aimed at creating a closed Jewish economy in which accumulated capital would go to further internal expansion rather than flowing outward.

The attitude of the workers' parties, which stressed "Jewish labor," corresponded to this policy. The objective of Jewish labor and of "conquest of labor" had a double implication with regard to the Arabs: the Jewish workers struck at the Arab workers whom they meant to evict from their jobs; on the other hand, the Jewish workers intended to build a Jewish society that would not be dependent upon the labor of "outsiders." Jewish labor was intended to prevent the combination of a national conflict with a class-oriented one.

Within the workers' parties—*Poalei-Zion* and *Hapoel Hatzair*—the

idea of Jewish labor was, from the very beginning, given different interpretations. The incipient *Poalei-Zion* version prescribed the broad, all-
inclusive development of the land by Jews, which would give an advantage to educated workers (i.e., Jewish workers), but would also leave
room for Arab workers. The members of *Hapoel Hatzair* advocated the
conquest of labor as a precondition for the realization of Zionism, that
is, the exclusive employment of Jewish workers. The limited possibilities
of the Jewish economy justified the attitude of *Hapoel Hatzair,* but
economic considerations—and, eventually, considerations regarding relations with the Arabs as well—limited the applicability of the principle
of conquest of labor, and motivated many Zionists to advocate "mixed
labor" in one ratio or another. In the context of Jewish labor, the Jewish
workers became the expression of a general Zionist principle which
conceived of the development of the *Yishuv* in Palestine in a unique way.
Unlike the previous generation of settlers, they even wanted a public
discussion of Jewish-Arab relations as well as of other problems of the
Yishuv. They saw in Jewish labor not only the way to acquiring the real
right and the moral right to Palestine and eliminating the danger of
rebellion on the part of exploited Arab labor; they also claimed that the
national character of the working class would determine the nature of
Jewish society in Palestine. The existence of a sector both nationally *and*
socially inferior would create a Jewish society that did not value freedom
and human dignity, and have a negative influence on the entire character
of the Zionist enterprise.

The Jewish workers, particularly those of *Poalei-Zion,* also changed
the views on the question of guarding the settlements: instead of a
professional, practical matter it became an expression of national dignity
and national strength. In this area, the workers became the leaders of
the *Yishuv* before they became leaders in the political and social spheres.
But the farmers, as well as many influential people in the *Yishuv,* protested this leadership as well as the nature of the workers' relations with
the Arabs, in matters of settlement security and labor.

The Jewish workers in Palestine found themselves embroiled in some
very paradoxical situations with regard to these two issues. They considered the establishment of a Jewish working class in Palestine a precondition for the realization of Zionism, and at the same time believed in
international brotherhood and proletarian solidarity. *Poalei-Zion* represented a militant tradition, copied from the self-defense organizations in
Russia and the socialist struggles there, and transferred to the national
sphere.

The policies and methods employed by the Jewish workers became part of the trend towards an independent and separate Jewish economy and society, which took shape within the *Yishuv* at the beginning of the century and was later strengthened by the course of action of Arthur Ruppin, the father of Jewish settlement. The separation of the two communities in Palestine purported to prevent two distinct types of Jewish-Arab assimilation. One type was the blurring of differences between the communities and nations—which threatened the assimilation of the Jewish minority into the Arab majority. The nationally oriented *Yishuv* was against this. The second possibility was that of a ruling class of Jews employing Arab masses. Mainly, it was the Jewish workers who were against this. Nor were they alone in their objections: even before the Jewish-Arab national conflict became prominent, the Zionists were aware of the possibility of revolt on the part of an oppressed population. They realized that social oppression itself, even without nationalist overtones, would create an excuse for incitement and rebellion. They were also aware of the negative possibility that Zionism might be compared with colonial and imperialist enterprises—such as the British takeover of South Africa—and hoped to prevent such comparisons.

Both concepts—separation and assimilation—were subject to widely differing interpretations: the loss of Jewish identity, Jewish control of the Arabs, arrogant Jewish self-isolation, the autonomous development of the two societies. There was also a marginal idea which suggested the possible assimilation of the Arabs among the Jews, whose economic and cultural level was deemed to be higher.

The Revolution of the Young Turks in 1908 and the renewal of the representative institutions of the Ottoman Empire added a new dimension to Jewish-Arab relations. The Zionists at first believed that the Revolution would create a constitutional framework that would remove the limitations on the entry of Jews to Palestine and purchase of land. Freedom appeared to them as freedom for Jewish development. The *Yishuv* also looked forward to a political partnership among all sectors of the Palestinian population. Within such a framework, the Jews would work hand-in-hand with the Muslims, perhaps even obtaining some sort of representation at the Parliament in Constantinople.

In fact, however, national and political developments in the Empire aggravated Jewish-Arab relations. Parliamentary elections became more a focus of Jewish-Arab conflict than a basis for partnership. Arab nationalism, encouraged at first by Christian Arabs, served to cement relations between Muslims and Christians. The acceleration of Arab national awareness brought about an emphasis on the Arab language, a desire for autonomy, and opposition to the pattern of Jewish separation. The Jews sometimes found themselves faced with the choice between supporting the Ottoman regime or supporting the Arabs. Furthermore, the hope of sowing dissension between Christian and Muslim Arabs failed to materialize. The routine conflicts that had existed between Jews and Arabs were raised to the level of a national conflict by the Arabs. Arab opposition to the Jews was expressed by aggressive articles in the press, attacks in Parliament, refusal to sell land, and even by violence.

The Jews had to soften Arab resistance for the sake of Jewish progress: it was indirectly causing the government to enforce and even tighten restrictions on the Jews. But even beyond the need to moderate Arab resistance, the issue of the relations between two peoples with nationalist aspirations, was being raised as a matter of principle.

The Jews adopted several courses of action to deal with Arab resistance during the years 1909–1911. Willing to appease the Arabs they continued to claim that the development of Palestine was to the Arabs' advantage and tried to convince them of the positive nature of Zionism. They also tried, as mentioned above, to undo the injustices in their land-purchasing methods and in their attitude towards the tenant-farmers, injustices that were attributed to the early stages of settlement. Opponents of the "closed economy" increased, and many demanded moderation of the principle of Jewish labor. But there was very little willingness to consider the Arabs' accusations that the Jews were maintaining a segregated economy and a segregated society. The Jews were not willing to relinquish the Jewish character of their settlements, schools, and associations.

But the mainstream of Jewish reaction was not conciliatory. It was rather the acceleration of the purchase of land, increased investments, and stronger organization and education. Furthermore, the Zionists tried to strengthen their own legal and political status in the framework of the Ottoman regime.

In the wake of the Jewish-Arab confrontation, as it was even before 1914, the theoretical discussion of the subject revolved around relations between the East and West or relations between branches of the Semitic race. Zionist leaders like Ahad Ha'am and Menahem Ussishkin chose to consider the Jews a nation which dissociated itself from the West, which itself was attacking the Orient (as represented by the Ottoman Empire). They chose to consider the Jews an Oriental people which, returning to its roots, also served as a link between the two worlds.

The Sephardic Jews, on the other hand, sought linguistic, cultural, and social affinities with the Arabs, the two nations belonging to a common Semitic race. These attempts aroused the suspicion that the Sephardic Jews were trying to blunt the edge of independent Jewish identity and foster acculturation of the Jews among the Arabs.

Before World War I, the attitude of Zionism towards the Arab problem was a topic which was discussed both by the *Yishuv* and by the Zionist movement—and the connection between the two was not always constant. With the establishment of a Zionist delegation in Constantinople in 1908, the problem of relations with the Arabs became a concern of Zionist policy. Victor Jacobson and Richard Lichtheim, who represented the Zionist Organization, were in contact with the Zionist Executive in Cologne and Berlin, on the one hand, and with Arthur Ruppin in Palestine, on the other.

At the Seventh Zionist Congress in 1905, Max Nordau already expressed an opinion about the first stirrings of Arab nationalism. He suggested the existence of a conflict between the idea of Arab independence and the unity and integrity of the Ottoman Empire, and proposed a partnership between the Empire and the Zionists to ward off Arab secession and the dissolution of the Empire. Nordau was expressing for the first time a political objective that would later be expounded by Richard Lichtheim and Ze'ev Jabotinsky, particularly during World War I. They would then attempt to have the *Yishuv* viewed as an entity allied to Europe and forming a breach in continuous Arab control from the Atlantic Ocean to the Persian Gulf. Richard Lichtheim favored Germany, Jabotinsky Great Britain, but the two assigned similar roles to the Jews with regard to the Arab world.

The Zionist representative in Constantinople, Victor Jacobson, as well as many of the Russian Zionists, were opposed to this trend. They wanted Zionism to be an integral part of the emancipation—even the renaissance—of the Orient. The democratization of the Empire after 1908 was supposed to justify this goal. Jacobson tried to negotiate with the Arab delegates in Constantinople, including those from Palestine. He did not want to create the impression that these negotiations were directed against the Ottoman authorities. They were mainly intended to convince the authorities to retract their opposition to Jewish immigration and settlement.

Recognizing the upsurge of Arab nationalism, Jacobson sought to maintain a dialogue with the Arab nationalists by diverting their interests from Palestine itself. He wanted to convince them that the benefits they would reap from cooperation with the Jews far outweighed their interests in Palestine—interests which were secondary from their standpoint.

Just before the outbreak of World War I, an attempt at top-level contacts was even made between a Zionist delegation headed by Nahum Sokolow, who came to visit Palestine in 1914, and Arab leaders in Syria and Lebanon. But contacts were broken off because of reservations on both sides. The Jews feared their loyalty to the Ottoman regime might be questioned; the Arabs, for their part, voiced demands that were insupportable.

An examination of the position of both sides before the negotiations shows that there was little hope of a successful dialogue. The Arabs might have been willing to cooperate with Jews prepared to relinquish their separate national features and contribute to a general Arab nationalism. But this, of course, was in contradiction to Zionist aspirations and to the crystallization of a specific Jewish national identity. Furthermore, the Jews did not believe they possessed the means to develop significant social services—such as health and education services—in the Arab sector, and they opposed opening their Jewish institutions to the Arabs.

The changes that took place during the war put Jewish-Arab relations on a completely different plane after the war ended. A debate developed within the Zionist movement as to whether the dissolution of the Ottoman Empire, the transformation of Palestine into a separate political unit, and the special, privileged status granted the Jewish people there were indeed an unambiguous achievement for Zionism. The Brit Shalom movement contended that the Zionists' bond to the great powers, particularly Britain, and the advantage given to the Jews by the Mandate served only to aggravate Arab resistance. But at the end of the war and during the first few years thereafter, it seemed as if the Jewish people had found a regime which enabled them to work for the establishment of a Jewish state in Palestine, even though they comprised at the time only 10 percent of Palestine's population.

The pro-Zionist regime in Palestine did not seem to the Zionists in 1918 to be opposed to the Arab movement. On the contrary, Britain was considered a power extending its good offices to the establishment of both an Arab and a Jewish state. Chaim Weizmann's Zionist policy towards the Arabs at the end of the war continued, to a certain extend, the line begun by Jacobson: helping to satisfy Arab aspirations outside

Palestine in exchange for Arab support of a national homeland in Palestine. This is the fundamental idea inherent in the Weizmann-Feisal agreement as it was understood by the Zionists.

Towards the end of the war, the *Yishuv* also became politically more nationalist in contrast to its attitude during the Ottoman period. Action within the framework of the Ottoman Empire, cultivation of the Hebrew language, and autonomous organizational patterns now gave way to ideas of a Jewish state, ideas which contrasted sorely with the decentralized structure of Jewish society in Palestine. The Arabs were to be given extensive autonomy in municipal government, as well as in the areas of justice, welfare, and education.

The years 1918–1920 represent the peak of Jewish claims from the standpoint of both government and territory. The Zionist program referred to a Palestine on both sides of the Jordan, in which a state would arise containing an overwhelming Jewish majority. Until this Jewish majority was attained, an interim government would serve. Responsibility for this interim government was given in theory to an international authority, and in practice to Britain. Britain was charged with the realization of the Jewish National Home, as stated in the Balfour Declaration. Maximalist Zionism was based on the political-national consciousness which had evolved among the Jewish people during the war, as well as on the national military activity of the Jewish Legion that had fought within the framework of the British Army. On the other hand, the revolutionary events in Europe created grave distress in Eastern Europe, leading to the expectation that Zionism would provide a solution to Jewish hardship.

Despite the belief that Britain and the other world powers would support Zionism politically, and despite the urgent need for a solution to the problems of the Jews in Eastern Europe—one that could compete with Communism—Chaim Weizmann prudently avoided defining the Zionist goal in terms of a Jewish state. He feared accusations that the Jewish minority was coming to dominate the Arab majority. He believed that the process of creating a Jewish majority was a gradual one which would culminate in the emergence of a state whose character would reflect that of the national majority. The immigration rate advocated by Weizmann was slower than that of other Zionist leaders (among them Max Nordau), who called for a mass influx, leaders who were associated with the school of "political" Zionism (as opposed to "practical").

Notwithstanding differences in formulation, the maximalist principle was shared in those years by Weizmann, the "political" Zionists, Jabotinsky and the labor movement. The latter called for a "greater" Zionism that would answer the needs of the Jewish masses of Eastern Europe, and consequently demanded wide borders, including both banks of the Jordan, immigration, and (ultimately) independence. They had reservations about cooperating with Britain, but believed in Jewish-Arab understanding. In the spirit of the socialist solution to the problem of nationality, they believed national autonomy would satisfy the Arabs.

The years 1918–1920 saw only very small-scale intra-Zionist opposition to these positions, which aimed at the creation—rapid or gradual—of a Jewish majority in Palestine, a majority which would mold the character of the country. Among them were the school of Martin Buber in Central Europe and Haim Margalit-Kalvarisky in Palestine. Margalit-Kalvarisky proposed, in 1919, to the "Provisional Committee" of the *Yishuv* a plan based on a social and political binational state in Palestine and its integration within the Semitic region.

The Arab riots of 1921 brought about a new British interpretation of the Mandate and of the character of the Jewish homeland in Palestine, an interpretation expressed in the White Paper of 1922. While the future of the Palestine government was not explicitly determined, it was stated that it would not necessarily lead to a Jewish state. A pluralist state was hinted at, in which no nation would leave its exclusive mark on the country. The eastern bank of the Jordan river was implicitly excluded from the boundaries of the Jewish National Home.

The riots of 1921 also led to the polarization of Zionist attitudes, with Jabotinsky at one pole and, eventually, Brit Shalom at the other. Jabotinsky began to develop his positions during the controversy over the reestablishment of the Jewish Legion in 1921. He believed that there was no chance of a Jewish-Arab agreement while Jews were settling the country, and that Jewish settlement could take place in Palestine only under the protection of an "iron wall." This attitude was based on a realpolitik as regards relations with the Arabs and an orientation on Western culture rather than on Oriental culture. Still, Jabotinsky was a liberal insofar as relations between peoples within a single state were concerned. And he expressed this in the context of the future rights of the Arab minority in Palestine. His attitude towards the Arab independence movement outside Palestine was also an affirmative one. A different approach was that of Martin Buber, who called for Jewish-Arab partnership beyond conventional terms of national power policy.

At the Twelfth Zionist Congress in 1921, an acceptable formula was agreed upon with regard to relations with the Arabs. The formula was firm in its adherence to the Balfour Declaration and the idea of a Jewish National Home, but also defined Palestine as "common homeland" and spoke of the unimpeded national development of Jews and Arabs together. At the Thirteenth Zionist Congress in 1923, a formula was even approved which referred to the participation of the Jewish people in the "rebirth of the Orient."

The mid-twenties were marked by relative calm in Jewish-Arab relations, but it was precisely during these years (1925) that the Brit Shalom was created. Its basic assumption was that agreement between the Jews and the Arabs was a necessary condition for the realization of Zionism. Brit Shalom criticized Zionist policy that addressed itself to the world powers, rather than to the Arabs.

The members of Brit Shalom believed that eliminating the idea of sovereignty from the realization of the Jewish national idea, and working towards the establishment of a binational state in Palestine, would make Arab approval of Zionism possible. They also favored the development of a common Jewish-Arab society, and envisaged the slow growth of the Jewish national homeland in Palestine, a process that would help bring the two peoples closer together.

In the same year in which Brit Shalom was founded, the Revisionist Party was created. It developed Jabotinsky's political ideas from 1921 to 1923, and opposed Weizmann's refusal to define the goal of Zionism and the Mandate, as it took shape following the White Paper of 1922.

The conflict between those who supported a "common fatherland" for Jews and Arabs in Palestine and those who supported the "iron wall," was particularly troubling to the Labor movement. The Labor movement was faithful to maximalist Zionism: the ingathering of the exiles, a Jewish majority, and a Jewish state. But it was also faithful to democratic ideals and to the right of nations to self-determination. Its members believed that solidarity between the Jewish and Arab workers would insure rapprochement between the two nations.

Although the General Federation of Labor (the *Histadrut*) was established in 1920 exclusively as an organization of Jewish workers, the members of the labor movement in Palestine continually sought channels of cooperation with Arab workers. They believed that the socialist view could produce a political solution that would allow the realization of mass immigration and the establishment of a Jewish state, while still preserving the rights of the Arabs—not only as individuals, but also as a national entity. In the social field, they predicted changes in Arab society which would put an end to the domination of the Muslim establishment and the *effendis,* and enhance the influence of workers and intelligentsia. These latter were supposedly more apt to accept Zionism, firstly, because of its development-oriented nature, and, secondly, out of recognition of the rights of the Jewish people.

The controversies within the large workers' party itself, *Ahdut Ha'avoda,* indicated that the socialist solution was not all that unambiguous. At the Fourth Convention of *Ahdut Ha'avoda* in Ein Harod in 1924, Shlomo Kaplansky proposed that *Ahdut Ha'avoda* approve the establishment of a democratic legislative council in Palestine, which would give expression to the Arab majority in the country. Kaplansky's condition for this was that the Arabs recognize the international Mandate and guarantee the invulnerability of the Jewish National Home.

Only in the atmosphere of the twenties and in the world of socialist thinking could it be imagined that the Arabs would not use a legislative council with an Arab majority to undermine the Jewish National Home. The opponents of Kaplansky's proposal inundated him with socialist argumentation in favor of Zionism, based primarily on the socialist right to develop barren land. This gave the Jews an unlimited right to develop Palestine. The leaders of *Ahdut Ha'avoda* further elaborated their position in accordance with the realities of Palestine. They claimed that establishing representative institutions at the present stage of development of Arab society would merely strengthen the class of notables. They supported the idea of a separation between Jewish and Arab society that would allow the Arabs to preserve their identity and the Jews to shape their own society. Berl Katznelson, in particular, elaborated the idea of autonomy to include an ever-increasing separation of the national entities, which would prevent exploitation of one people by the other. Ben-Gurion envisaged the crystallization of each national entity within defined territorial bounds. He claimed that the Jewish National Home could be developed "without wronging a single Arab child." He sincerely believed that the struggle for Jewish labor and for a Jewish state in no way injured the Arabs. Differing from Brit Shalom, he continued to demand a Jewish majority and a Jewish state. But the state as he saw it would be "neither a Prussian nor Czarist state, but a socialist one." This meant local and regional self-rule, which would give the Arabs an outlet for national expression.

The workers' parties found themselves in a dilemma, not only politically, but also in the sphere of trade-unionism. Their members wanted both Jewish labor and class solidarity. In the wake of lengthy disputes which were carried on between 1923 and 1927, the *Histadrut* decided to carry out organizational work among the Arabs, but not to open the ranks of the *Histadrut* to them, as was demanded by the left-wing factions. The low wages demanded by the Arabs and the Zionist character of the *Histadrut* were the arguments used against a joint Federation of Labor. Activity among the Arabs was supposed to be carried out by an autonomous federation of Arab workers, which would cooperate with the General Federation of Labor within the framework of the Palestine Labor Alliance *(Brit Poalei Eretz Israel).*

It was typical of the twenties that striking ideological differences within the Zionist camp did not make any difference to movement policy. In London, in part of Europe, and in Palestine, Jewish-Arab contacts were carried out by people who did not support the official positions of the movement with regard to the Arab question. We know, for example, of the negotiations with leaders of the Arab nationalist movement held by Asher Sapir at the beginning of the twenties, in which he tried to obtain Arab support for the Jewish National Home in exchange for Zionist support of the Arab independence movement. The Zionists were represented as a force conducive to development and progress, neither European in character nor dominating in behavior. On the other hand, the Zionists could not jeopardize their relations with Britain and France. Zionist policy in Palestine was handled by Frederick Kisch, aided by Haim Margalit-Kalvarisky, whose position lay far afield of the accepted Zionist program. They sought highways to those Arabs who opposed the leadership of the Husseinis, namely, members of the Hashemite family, particularly Abdallah, Emir of Transjordan, and the Nashashibi "opposition" in Palestine. Kalvarisky even tried to set up "friendly" organizations among the Arabs of Palestine, which would enjoy Jewish patronage and aid. The relative moderation of the Arabs during the mid-twenties was attributed to this policy. Whatever the reasons for the moderation, it was shattered by the events of 1929.

The events of the late twenties generated changes in Jewish nationalist awareness within the Zionist movement. The crisis of the Fourth Aliya seemed to prove the impossibility of mass immigration and the transfer of the demographic center of the Jewish people from Europe to Palestine. Some of the German Zionists, and the members of Brit Shalom in Palestine, interpreted Zionism as the establishment in Palestine of a qualitative center for the Jewish people. The Revisionists, and the Labor movement on the other hand, supported mass Zionism, a Zionism that would solve the problem of the Jews in Eastern Europe and compete with Communism for the souls of Jewish youth.

These differences of approach became significant in the wake of the events of 1929, when public discussion of the attitude of the Zionist movement to the Arabs was renewed. Ideological approaches that had begun to take shape in the early twenties acquired political significance. The enmity that exploded in riots in 1929 put an end to hopes of reconciliation between Jews and Arabs as a result of modernization, economic cooperation or limited cooperation on the governmental plane (as, for example, in the municipalities).

British commissions of enquiry brought out the fundamental problems of the Mandate, and Arab complaints claimed that even from an economic standpoint, the Arabs as individuals were disadvantaged by Zionism.

Zionist reaction to these events was a test of the way the *Yishuv* evaluated its own needs, what it considered to be the value of Jewish nationalism, and, further, an exploration of the nature of the realities of Palestine. The official Zionist position was that the Jews had no intention of dominating or of being dominated in Palestine. In other words, the Jews would not impose Jewish majority rule upon an Arab minority in the future, but at the same time refused to recognize the right of the existing Arab majority to rule in the present. This was an explicit retreat from the definition of the goal of Zionism as a Jewish State, and the question posed was a proper one: Did this mean surrendering the "Jewish majority" formula, or perhaps even the majority itself? Was the realization of Zionism dependent upon mass immigration which would solve the problem of Jewish distress in Eastern Europe, or could Zionism, in fact, do without mass immigration, do without a Jewish majority to substantiate the notion of a National Home? Were conflict and violence too dear a price?

The position of the Revisionists, the *Mizrahi*, and some of the members of the General Zionists was clear: they rejected any proposal that did not accord with Jewish majority rule of Palestine. Brit Shalom, on the other hand, demanded that an agreement with the Arabs be given priority over a policy which would attempt to broaden the scope of the National Home under Britain's auspices, and involve clashes with the Arabs.

The Palestine Labor Party *(Mapai)* belonged to the camp of maximalist Zionism from the standpoint of the demand for mass immigration, liquidation of the Diaspora, and a Jewish economy and society in Palestine. Its policy stressed neither constitutional nor political formulations but rather substantial progress in the areas of immigration, land purchase, and the construction of a Jewish economy. But many of the party's leaders were prepared to establish a state in Palestine which would be common to Jews and Arabs (in distinction to a mixed society and/or a binational state), a state that would not impose majority rule of one nation upon another. Basically, the post-1929 period represents the greatest willingness on the part of the Zionist movement to open a dialogue with the Arabs at the cost of far-reaching concessions, like relinquishing the idea of Jewish majority rule. Many Brit Shalom members even believed that their conception had captured the hearts of the Zionist movement.

The immediate reason for the theoretical political debates of the thirties was the question of the legislative council which the Mandatory government was supposed to set up. Some of the leaders of *Mapai,* among them Haim Arlozoroff and David Ben-Gurion, were willing to discuss changes in the Palestine constitution through the establishment of a legislative council—on the proviso that there not be an Arab majority on the council and that the Jews' right to build a national homeland not be jeopardized. The British were considered the third factor in a proposed legislative council. Ben-Gurion even went as far as supporting the inclusion of Arabs in the executive branch of government and proposed ideas for a federal state in the future. This was a revision of the position of *Ahdut Ha'avoda* in 1924.

This was not the only position in *Mapai.* Many members of the party had reservations with regard to the chances of cooperating with the Arabs. Their position was based not only on the right of the Jews to Palestine, but also on the "underdeveloped nature" of Arab society. At most, they agreed to a reform in municipal government that would give the Arabs more autonomy. After lengthy debates, the position of Berl Katznelson was accepted, a position which assumed constitutional changes (including the establishment of a legislative council), but with parity for the two national groups. Berl Katznelson's forecasts for the future envisaged the development of Palestine into a "state of nationalities," in which autonomous national societies would exist side by side.

At the time of the controversy over the Peel Plan in 1937, and even more so in 1942, Ben-Gurion contended that the notion of parity was limited to the period of the Mandate. This claim is not substantiated by the facts. According to several formulations, the federal state—the "state of nationalities"—was to fashion the character of the permanent government. Still, one must distinguish between two different sets of ideas, that of a "state of nationalities" or parity and that of the binational state, as advocated by Brit Shalom.

The differences were crucial in a number of areas and the labor movement was conscientious in stressing them. They were careful to point out that there was no equality between the attitudes of the two peoples towards Palestine. Palestine "belonged" to the *entire* Jewish people, on the one hand, and to the *Arabs of Palestine,* on the other. The practical interpretation of this theoretical postulate was that the Jewish population was a dynamic national group which would increase through immigration, whereas the Arab population was stable. The Arabs' affinity to the country was limited to those Arabs actually living there, while Jewish affinity attached to potential immigrants as well. Another difference between parity and binationalism concerned the makeup of the society and the economy: in these domains—in contrast to the political domain—*Mapai* negated the idea of pluralism, insisting on Jewish labor, Jewish manufacture, Jewish services and Jewish schools. The party supported the separation of societies, cooperation being possible only between autonomous societies. This could be seen clearly in the fight over labor during the thirties. The left-wing factions in the *Histadrut*—*Hashomer Hatzair* and Left *Poalei-Zion*— were opposed to complete separation, particularly among workers, and supported one form or another of mixed Jewish-Arab labor. All the proposals for changes in the type of government and structure of society, however, from whatever quarter, were based on hopes for large-scale Jewish immigration which would create an overwhelming Jewish majority in Palestine—even if that majority did not attain sovereign power. In the thinking of that period, it would appear, the state was not a necessary tool for forging social policy.

From 1930 on, Zionist policy towards the Arabs operated on two levels, seeking an agreement with them and speeding up the realization of Zionism through increased Jewish strength in Palestine. Increased immigration—particularly of young people—as well as the acceleration of settlement, investment, and the building of the economy resulted in economic prosperity and a stronger defence potential. This accelerated rate of progress could have produced one of two reactions among the Arabs: a willingness to participate in the development of the country or an effort to undermine the increasing strength of the Jews as quickly as possible. It may be that the Jews themselves became less enthusiastic about the idea of Jewish-Arab parity in the administration of Palestine as their numbers rapidly increased, growing from 175,000 in 1931 to almost 400,000 in 1936.

The pressure of the Jews of Europe to immigrate, together with the total refusal of the Arabs to reach an agreement, led to a change in position in the early thirties. The hope for conciliation among the nations, as a result of economic and social progress, gave way to the stubborn struggle for independence in the region. The ascent of fascism and Nazism aggravated relations, not only because it increased Jewish pressure for immigration, but also because it challenged British influence in the region and encouraged extremist elements among the Arab nationalists.

The demand of Brit Shalom that priority be given to Jewish-Arab cooperation over Jewish-British cooperation, was not accepted by the majority of the Zionist movement during the years 1929–1935. Nonetheless, policy was shaped on the assumption that such an agreement was possible. Arlozoroff, for example, expected that the Arab extremists would find themselves isolated while Jewish-Arab cooperation was reached through the good offices of Britain. Ben-Gurion held talks with Arab leaders on the assumption that the Arab independence movement would benefit from a Jewish state incorporated in an Arab federation.

The Zionist orientation upon Jewish-Arab agreement failed during the first half of the thirties. The Arab political position and the social and political structure of Arab society led in the opposite direction. As early as 1931, Arthur Ruppin, one of the founders of Brit Shalom, who later dissociated himself from its position, defined Jewish-Arab relations as follows: "What we need we cannot get, and what we get we do not need."

Relinquishing the aim of Jewish majority rule in Palestine, offering maximum compliance with Arab demands for autonomy, and supporting the movement for Arab independence and unity were all considered by the Jews to be far-reaching concessions. But the Arabs were not satisfied. They demanded of the authorities that the Arab majority be given power. In fact, however, they would have been satisfied with the cessation of Jewish immigration and land purchase, even without the immediate establishment of representative institutions.

The Jews hoped for a change in Arab society, one which would lead to internal democratization and free it from the authority of the Supreme Muslim Council. But just as the hopes placed by the Zionists in the Nashashibi opposition had proved a disappointment in the twenties, so the Jews reaped no benefit from the changes which took place in Arab society in the thirties. The old leadership of the Arab Executive Council of the twenties did die out during the thirties, but as a result the leadership of the *Mufti*, Haj Amin al-Husseini, was strengthened. The politicization of Arab society during the thirties and the creation of the *Istiqlal* party, which protested British protectorship, openly aggravated Jewish-Arab relations. In one sector of Arab society, the idea of terrorism was beginning to ripen, not as an incidental phenomenon but as a political method. All this led to the outbreak of the riots of 1936, the so-called Arab Rebellion.

The riots of 1936 led to another change in the attitude of the Zionist movement towards the Arabs. In the wake of the 1929 riots, as we have seen, two parallel courses of action were adopted: the search for an agreement on the basis of constitutional concessions, and an accelerated pace of Jewish immigration and enterprise in Palestine. The search for agreement took place both with regard to Palestine and to the region as a whole, but reached an impasse. The ideas voiced during the early thirties advocating territorial partition or cantonal rule could not be implemented. Zionist policy was concentrated, therefore, on preventing British restrictions in the areas of immigration and land purchase, as well as on preventing the establishment of representative institutions embodying an Arab majority.

The riots of 1936 refuted once again the Zionist expectations with regard to the possible development of Arab society. Economic progress in Palestine did not produce an Arab social structure more tractable to the Zionists. In light of the broad scope of the Arab rebellion of 1936, one could no longer claim that these were freak occurrences, the product of incitement by the *Mufti* of Jerusalem and the Husseini religious establishment. It became evident that the development of Arab society was leading towards stronger nationalist awareness, with progressively more acute anti-Zionist overtones. The Zionists were confronted with the distressing fact that what they faced was not a self-interested group of *effendis* or fanatic religious leaders, but a nationalist movement. The Jews were no longer the only ones calling for national emancipation. The Arabs, too, wished to take their place in this historical course, which in the thirties was considered progressive and unequivocal. The Jews reacted with the assertion that even if Zionism were faced with a nationalist movement, it was not a liberal movement, like Mazzini's, willing to recognize the rights of others. It was a fascistic nationalist movement, of the twentieth-century variety, demanding everything for itself. Berl Katznelson was the main proponent of this concept.

Not only did attempts to reach an agreement with the Arabs of Palestine fail; attempts to open a dialogue with Arabs outside Palestine also proved fruitless. The intervention of Arabs from neighboring countries in the relations between the peoples of Palestine, beginning in 1936, did nothing to bring Jewish-Arab agreement any closer. They did succeed in bringing about a certain degree of moderation among the Arabs of Palestine, but only with respect to the British and not with respect to the Zionists.

The choice facing the Zionists was either to utilize the riots of 1936 to extend cooperation with the British and strengthen the Jewish National Home, or to seek an agreement with the Arabs based on further concessions.

The Zionist leadership chose the first option, realizing that all channels to Jewish-Arab dialogue were blocked. In effect, Zionist leadership was willing to propose parity—equal representation for Jews and Arabs—as a possible formula for reforming the administration of Palestine, but without any great hopes that this was really possible.

This time, Brit Shalom, or what remained of it, could not go on thinking its method had captured the hearts of the Zionist movement, as they had judged—mistakenly—after 1929. Nonetheless, the riots brought together a number of non-aligned public figures, impelled to seek new ways for Jewish-Arab conciliation. They did not believe that a violent confrontation was a test that Zionism had to pass, but rather a failure on the part of a policy that had not been able to avoid that confrontation. Pinhas Rutenberg, Gad Frumkin, Moshe Smilansky, Moshe Novomeysky, and Judah Magnes, known as "the Five," sought an agreement on the basis of a regional arrangement, binationalism in Palestine, and stronger Jewish-Arab cooperation. They could not ignore the pressure of Jewish immigration in 1936, but hoped to divert at least part of it to countries adjacent to Palestine, thereby assuaging Arab fears of an overwhelming Jewish majority in Palestine. Within the bounds of Palestine itself, they proposed restrictions on immigration, even including a ceiling on the number of Jews in Palestine. They proposed that for ten years the Jews not comprise more than 40 percent of the population.

Their agreement to restrictions on immigration and to a fixed ceiling on the number of Jews in Palestine became the focus of their controversy with the Zionist leadership who saw the intensification of immigration as Zionism's function—regardless of the political situation. It was immigration that would determine the status of Zionism among the Jewish people and the chances of its realization in Palestine, and every plan was measured by that supreme yardstick. "The Five" also believed in opening the Jewish economy to the Arabs to a certain extent which, together with cooperation in the fields of capital and labor, would bring the two nations closer.

The year 1936 also saw the establishment of a public society for the advancement of Jewish-Arab relations, known as *Kedma Mizraha*. It was somewhat of a continuation of Brit Shalom, though its social makeup and intellectual trends were more varied. In addition to members of Brit Shalom, it included members of the veteran Sephardic community, new immigrants from Germany, and people from the left. The central figure was Kalvarisky. *Kedma Mizraha* did not condemn the Arab nationalist movement as negative as Berl Katznelson, for example, had done. It tried to open a dialogue with Arab leaders in the region on a very general basis, incorporating references to traditional relations, the desire to become an integral part of the Orient and national amity. They were particularly active in Egypt.

The sharpest change in the approach of Zionism to the Arabs came not as the result of Zionist initiative but as the result of British initiative when, in 1937, a Royal Commission headed by Lord Peel proposed the partition of Palestine and the establishment of two states—one Jewish, one Arab. It has been noted that during the twenties and early thirties, Chaim Weizmann and his followers believed the Mandate to be the most fitting framework for the realization of the Jewish National Home. According to him there was no Zionist formula (like a "Jewish state") that had the power to bring about constitutional change favorable to the Jews. On the contrary, any such formula could only incite the Arabs, and Arab insurrection came even without the Zionists' explicitly formulating their ultimate goal. Ideas for the territorial partition of Palestine had been voiced in the Zionist camp as early as the early thirties. These ideas had included many elements which were disadvantageous from a Zionist viewpoint, and the Mandate was preferable. In 1937 the choice was either a reduced Mandate or a Jewish state in part of Palestine. Differences of opinion in the Zionist camp over the recommendations of the Royal Commission reflected only partially the attitude towards an agreement with the Arabs. From the vantage point of today, the Zionist positions of 1937 were somewhat surprising. A large number of those who supported Jewish-Arab agreement were vociferously opposed to partition, while today "territorial compromise" is considered the highroad to Jewish-Arab agreement. Territorial partition in 1937 was considered an admission of the failure to reach an agreement, and the failure to remove the element of national sovereignty from the complex of Jewish-Arab relations, thereby harmonizing Arab and Jewish nationalist aspirations. It was an admission of the failure to achieve accord between two peoples through a moral solution (Magnes), a Semitic solution (Kalvarisky, Rabbi Benjamin), or a socialist solution *(Hashomer Hatzair)*.

Those who sought Jewish-Arab agreement saw partition not only as a failure with respect to the past but as a powderkeg for the future: the establishment of two sovereign states in such a small area would engender continuous strife between Jews and Arabs.

The point of departure of the proponents of partition, on the other hand, had nothing to do with Arab-Jewish relations whatsoever. Their main argument was that the establishment of a Jewish state—even in part of Palestine—was a better way of advancing the Zionist enterprise than any of the alternatives. But they also contended that a Jewish state would bring about Jewish-Arab agreement. The order of priorities of Jewish-Arab accord changed during the debate over the partition proposal: Jewish-Arab agreement would come after the realization of Zionism, as a product of it, and not before, as a condition for it. So, although the 1937 partition plan was not implemented, it nevertheless served as a milestone in the crystallization of Zionist policy towards the Arabs.

The partition proposal was born of British despair over the possibility of Jewish-Arab cooperation within the framework of a Palestinian state. It brought about a change in Zionist thinking which placed Jewish sovereignty above Jewish-Arab agreement. Nonetheless, it also produced new attempts at negotiations for such an agreement. Herbert Samuel, for example, the first high commissioner, strongly criticized the partition plan in the House of Lords. He foresaw an endless struggle between the two states, whose territories would be interlocked. Samuel recommended that the problem of Jewish-Arab relations be settled by means of a regional solution. At the same time, a number of other proposals were suggested by various mediators, such as Albert M. Hyamson and Col. S. F. Newcomb. (Hyamson was a British Jew who had served as an official in the Mandatory; Newcomb was a Briton with pro-Arab sympathies.) The trustfulness of these mediators was dubious. Jewish Agency leaders suspected that their proposals were aimed at preventing the establishment of a Jewish state in part of Palestine, as well as at forcing prior concessions out of the Jews in order to weaken their status in any future negotiations with the government. Judah Magnes, on the other hand, saw the proposals as portals to an agreement.

The Hyamson-Newcomb proposal, which purported to represent Arab views as well, called for the establishment of a democratic Palestinian state, namely, one in which the existing majority would rule. According to them, the Arabs agreed to Jewish immigration to Palestine, even to Transjordan. Their proviso was that the Jews not comprise more than 50 percent of the population.

Even if this proposal had been at all practicable, it could only have been accepted by those whose primary interest was Jewish-Arab agreement. It provided the possibility of Jewish settlement in Palestine at a slow growth rate. But the primary interest of the overwhelming majority of the Zionist camp at that time was massive Jewish immigration which would solve the problem of European Jewry and allow the social and political realization of Jewish nationhood in Palestine. It may very well be that the proposal was intended to split the Zionist camp.

The White Paper of 1939 brought Zionist orientation on Britain to a point of crisis. It became clear that the advancement of the Jewish National Home as construed by the Zionists was no longer possible under the British aegis. Two plausible, and different, conclusions could have been drawn from this with regard to the question of relations with the Arabs. The first, which continued the Brit Shalom line, was that realization of the National Home would be possible only as an outgrowth of agreement with the Arabs. The absence of such agreement could only lead to an undermining of the partnership with Britain as well. The second, opposite, conclusion was that if a Jewish-Arab agreement was impossible even while Britain supported Zionism, it would be even more impossible once such a support was withdrawn. It could not be supposed that the Arabs would give the Zionists what the British had denied them.

The year 1939, therefore, witnessed a parting of the ways within the Zionist camp, a split which had begun in 1936 and ripened by 1942. The proponents of the first option organized themselves into the League for Jewish-Arab Rapprochement. The proponents of the second represented the official Zionist line. Their first and foremost aim was to undermine the White Paper policy through active resistance. They did not address themselves to the Jewish-Arab problem, but rather to the international scene and to world Jewry. Only after certain Zionist goals were achieved, they felt, could the ground be prepared for a Jewish-Arab agreement that would permit full Zionist realization. The conflict between these differing assessments was to become more acute in 1942.

World War II broke out in September 1939, as the Zionist movement was preparing itself to do battle against the White Paper. The Zionist leadership hoped the war would lay the foundations for renewed cooperation between the Jews and Britain. The latter's need for a faithful ally in the region, and for the sympathies of the Jews, might suspend the White Paper. The change of government in 1940 and Churchill's rise to premiership seemed to promise change. But the immediate needs of the war increased Britain's dependence upon the Arabs, a dependence which comprised one of the major contributing factors to the promulgation of the White Paper. The Arabs who supported Britain, like Nuri Said of Iraq, were not satisfied with the publication of the Land Purchase Restriction Law of February 1940, and demanded implementation of the constitutional clauses of the White Paper. Their demands were not granted.

The orientation of the Zionist leadership on improved relations with Britain because of the war differed from that of those who sought Jewish-Arab agreement. People like Judah Magnes hoped that the mobilization of Jews and some of the Arabs in support of Britain would serve as a new basis for Jewish-Arab cooperation. The Zionist leadership, on the other hand, claimed that with regard to the war itself, the interests of Jews and Arabs were different, indeed conflicting, and each camp sought a different outcome.

The war opened up new areas of action for the Zionist movement, beyond the sphere of Jewish-British relations. The problem of the administration of Palestine became a subject of international interest. The United States and the Soviet Union became active in determining the destiny of the two nations in Palestine.

Ben-Gurion began to claim that the centrality assigned to the "Arab problem" was not justified, and not at all comparable to the "Jewish problem." While the Jews had been uprooted from Europe and lacked a homeland, the Arabs ruled vast territories sufficient to house the existing Arab population, and more. The "Arab problem," in his opinion, was limited to the status of the relatively few Arabs living in Palestine, where "millions of Jews" would live.

During the first stage of the war, the objective of Zionist policy was the establishment of a Jewish army, an objective which did not materialize. For a while it seemed that the proposal would be approved, but at the end of 1941 the British government voiced its final rejection of the idea. Only in 1944 was a Jewish Brigade established.

The transfer of the decisive area of concern from Palestine and Jewish-Arab relations to the problem of the Jewish people and the world powers resulted in the formulation of a new political program. Since the failure of the Peel Commission's partition plan, the Zionist movement had been left without a program. In actuality, it demanded a return to the Mandate as originally defined, but it was clear that the Mandate was no longer practicable in light of the new political constellation. The reforms proposed to the Peel Commission by the Jewish Agency—like parity—had been rejected. For some time, the Jewish Agency had tried to advance a federal solution which would provide freedom of immigration to part of Palestine, but this proposal, too, was rejected and in its place came the White Paper of 1939. The struggle against the White Paper was a negative goal, without a positive objective. For the first time since the Peace Conference of 1919, the Zionist movement was obliged to draw up a political program.

In light of the realities of 1942, advancing a political formula had more advantages than risks. The position on Jewish-Arab relations expressed in the Biltmore Program of 1942 may be seen as the opposite of the Brit Shalom formula. A Jewish-Arab agreement was not the precondition for the realization of Zionism; rather the realization of Zionism, through the establishment of a Jewish state, would bring a Jewish-Arab agreement in its wake. The relationship between the possible establishment of an Arab federation and the establishment of a Jewish state changed. It was not a federation of Arab nations, expressing their desire for unity and independence, that would permit the establishment of a Jewish state; rather, the establishment of a Jewish state would insure the status of the Jews in case a federation was indeed set up. The creation of a *fait accompli* would, thus, insure the inclusion of the Jews as a factor in any new regional constellation.

There was no difference between David Ben-Gurion and Chaim Weizmann on this issue. The differences between them had little to do with relations with the Arabs. Weizmann, who in 1931 had tended towards minimalist formulations in order to placate the Arabs, had, since 1937, accepted the conclusion of the Peel Commission: the only solution to the problem was separation. Weizmann considered the authenticity of the Arab movement to be even less significant than did Ben-Gurion. He believed that the Arab states and their leaders were bound to an alliance with Britain and that consequently a British or British-American decision would have to be accepted by the Arabs. He placed less weight than Ben-Gurion on the efforts towards Arab unity and independence as a factor independent of Britain or as a factor embodying a positive or negative potential from the Zionist standpoint. Weizmann linked the Zionist plan to a partnership with Britain and saw Zionist realization as a gradual process rather than as the revolution foreseen by Ben-Gurion. As a result, he considered the idea of Commonwealth less as a revolutionary change and more as a new stage in Jewish-British cooperation.

The Biltmore Program aroused opposition from various quarters. Abandoning the Mandate might jeopardize immediate demands for immigration; the establishment of a sovereign Jewish state in Palestine was contrary to the policy of "non-domination" of one people over another. The Program was interpreted as a death warrant for future prospects of a Jewish-Arab agreement.

The Biltmore Program spoke of the creation of a Jewish majority in Palestine and of the establishment of Palestine as a Jewish state; but declaring for sovereignty while the Jews were still a minority in Palestine implied the idea of partition—and aroused the opposition of those who had formerly opposed partition.

The representation of the Biltmore Program as the official program of the Zionist movement brought forth alternative programs from those who sought Jewish-Arab conciliation and cooperation. In 1942, the League for Jewish-Arab Rapprochement extended its influence and was joined by *Hashomer Hatzair*. The alternatives to Biltmore were based on proposals dating from the thirties, which had distinguished between nationalism and sovereignty. The authors of these alternative plans tried to give the old proposals a topical quality in light of the political reality that had emerged during the war. The two proposals in question were the Kaplansky Plan and the Bentov Plan. The Kaplansky Plan was a summary of the work of a committee for research on Jewish-Arab relations set up by the Jewish Agency in 1940, while the Bentov Plan was a summary of the work of a committee appointed by the League for Jewish-Arab Rapprochement.

Both plans were based on different assumptions from those of the Biltmore Program. They did not demand state machinery in order to facilitate mass immigration. They insisted on an interim period under international supervision, the eventual establishment of a permanent regime incorporating elements of federalism, binationalism, representational parity for Jews and Arabs, and autonomy on both a national and territorial basis. Jewish immigration was made conditional upon the economic absorptive capacity of the country and on agreed ratios of population. The assumption was that the improvement of relations after the interim period would permit further agreement. Neither group could prove that their plan would be acceptable to the Arabs. But it was clear to them that the Biltmore Program put an end to any possibility for Jewish-Arab agreement.

The League for Jewish-Arab Rapprochement was not a homogeneous body after 1942. It included at least two clearcut groups. The members of *Hashomer Hatzair* considered themselves maximalist Zionists on questions of immigration and mass settlement. They disagreed with Ben-Gurion over the tempo of Zionist realization. Forgoing the idea of a Jewish state was, for them, not a way of reducing Zionism but of expanding it; Jewish-Arab agreement, they felt, was a prerequisite. The members of the second grouping, *Ihud,* saw in Zionism the creation of an ethical Jewish society. They did not believe that Zionism could put an end to the Jewish problem and opposed its engagement in power politics. They were willing to forgo both a Jewish state and a Jewish majority. But they, too, would not be satisfied with the status of a minority in Palestine, and could only accept numerical equality between Jews and Arabs.

The Biltmore Program settled the question of Zionist priorities: mass immigration and Jewish nationhood were given priority over agreement with the Arabs, even over a dialogue with the British. But the program said nothing about the status of the Arabs in Palestine. Even the assumption that the Zionists would achieve a national majority government in Palestine required them to define the status of the Arabs who would live there. If the Zionists expected the support of the victorious democratic powers, they would have to clarify the rights of the Arabs in the future Jewish state. From 1943 until the meeting of the Zionist Executive in 1945, various formulas were drawn up in which the Arabs were promised not only full civil rights, but also extensive autonomy. The Jewish state would pass laws and invest its resources in efforts to bring about gradual equality in the standard of living of the two populations. Equal rights, self-rule, and a rise in the standard of living were, then, to be the compensation granted the Arabs in lieu of the majority status they had lost.

The problem of the status of the Arabs uncovered one of the contradictions inherent in the Biltmore Program. One could not speak of a Jewish state in Palestine as long as the Jews comprised only a third of the population. This was a clear contradiction in terms. Equal civil rights and democratic rule could not be commensurate with a Zionist government. The proponents of Biltmore dismissed this, claiming that the process of creating a Jewish majority would be a rapid and evolutionary one.

All of this notwithstanding, the Zionists had to clarify their reasons for rejecting the possibility of a Jewish minority in a majority-rule Arab state, while supporting a proposition that would make the Arabs in

Palestine a minority. Zionists propaganda insisted that Palestine was the only place where the Jews would ever comprise a majority, while the number of Arab states was steadily growing. Furthermore, the preservation of the rights of the Arab minority in the Jewish state would be guaranteed both by the presence of the neighboring Arab countries and the vulnerability of the Jews dispersed throughout the world.

The war years witnessed the definition of the political goal of Zionism, and despite the fact that Jewish-Arab relations were relegated to a lower rung on the ladder of Zionist priorities, certain developments took place in that sphere too. There was a quest for contact with the Arabs on the regional, rather than the local, plane. The extremism of the Arabs of Palestine and the fact that some of them supported the Nazis, not to mention the deterioration of their political organization, prevented any possibility of dialogue with them. A study of Zionist policy in the region has yet to be made, but a number of fundamental lines may nevertheless be discerned. British protectorship could theoretically have served as a point of departure for a Jewish-Arab dialogue. In fact, any British policy which favored Arab unity was contrary to Zionist policy.

For some time, the British tried to strengthen Ibn Saud's position in the region. They hoped to initiate negotiations in which he would agree to a Jewish entity in the region in exchange for becoming a key figure in the Arab world. Chaim Weizmann was attracted to this idea for a while. The attempt was illusory, and was rejected by Ibn Saud.

Zionist policy then addressed itself to the Maronites of Lebanon, to the Emir Abdullah of Transjordan, and to the Syrian National Bloc. Any one of these parties could have found interest in cooperating with the Zionists: the Maronites sought an additional non-Muslim element in the region; Emir Abdullah considered the Husseinis his enemies; and the National Bloc sought independence from France and could have been aided by the Zionists.

Parallel to these efforts, the League for Jewish-Arab Rapprochement looked for Arab parties who would be receptive to Jewish-Arab agreement along the lines of the League's own plan.

The post-war period saw a sharp decline in the chances for a dialogue between the Zionists and the Arabs. The Arabs of Palestine reorganized and the influence of the Husseinis remained strong, albeit more limited. Their opposition to Zionism also remained extreme. The formation of the Arab League in March of 1945, inter alia, frustrated Zionist attempts to find more moderate voices in the Arab world. Even Lebanon, which had been considered somewhat out of the ordinary in the area, joined the Arab League. Transjordan received its independence in 1946 and sought connections in the Arab world. Syria and Lebanon were granted independence, and held elections which strengthened the tones of their opposition to Zionism.

More independence and growing unity in the Arab world did not bring the Arabs any closer to accepting a Zionist entity in Palestine; on the contrary, opposition increased. The campaign against the Zionist enterprise, which was a heavy burden on the Arabs of Palestine, was transferred to the shoulders of the Arab League. But Arab independence and unity did strengthen the Jews' demand for independence because of the ever-increasing hostility which accompanied it.

The expectations upon which the Biltmore Program was founded did not materialize at the end of the war. Britain and the United States did not join forces to effect a rapid, revolutionary solution to the population issue in Palestine by bringing hundreds of thousands of Jews from Europe. The fate of the "Arab alternative," proposed by the League for Jewish-Arab Rapprochement, was no better. Relinquishing the idea of a Jewish government in Palestine did not insure Arab willingness for an agreement.

With regard to the dispute that had existed within the Zionist camp since the end of World War I, as to whom the Zionist should address first—the world powers or the Arabs, Zionist policy continued to address the world powers. The summer of 1946 saw a breach in Zionist-British relations, and in August of 1946 the Executive of the Jewish Agency abandoned the original principles of the Biltmore Program and agreed to discuss partition. Agreement to partition, however, was not a concession to the Arabs, but to the United States—in order to obtain their backing against British anti-Zionist policy.

At the time of the dispute with Britain and the proposed partition plan, some new ideas flickered on the horizon regarding a new basis for cooperation with the Arabs. Based on common opposition to Britain and to imperialism and voiced within Lehi and even IZL circles, the ideas were not tenable. The Arab states at that time saw Britain as their chief ally. The idea of partition seemed to be an opening of a dialogue with Transjordan, and even with certain circles in Egypt. But it became apparent that such contacts could be fruitful only after partition was carried out. The first objective of partition was to establish a Jewish state as soon as possible. Such a state would provide the basis for agreement.

At the Twenty-second Zionist Congress in 1946 Ben-Gurion said: "I believe in peace with the Arabs and am entirely convinced that sooner or later we shall attain federation or permanent cooperation, but the necessary prerequisite is a Jewish state."

The value of the Palestine Arabs to Zionist policy lay in their extreme anti-Zionist position. This position frustrated even British policy, which was forced to allow some immigration and Jewish autonomy in a Palestinian state with an Arab majority. The Arab states were a bit more moderate, but they, too, would not allow concessions to the Zionists, largely because of pressure from the Arabs of Palestine.

The impasse into which the British government was forced, and the insuperable breach between Jews and Arabs, led the majority of the UN Special Commission on Palestine in 1947 to return to the idea of the Royal Commission of 1937 and to propose the partition of Palestine into two states—one Jewish, one Arab.

The State of Israel was founded in 1948 in the midst of a valiant confrontation with the Arabs of Palestine and the neighboring Arab countries. The development of relations both in Palestine and in the region did not lead to a solution, but to an overall conflagration.

From a Zionist standpoint, the ideology of maximalist Zionism— maximum immigration and maximum settlement—merged with the actual needs of the survivors of the Holocaust in Europe. The successful implementation of mass immigration necessitated a sovereign national framework, and the immediate attainment of a Jewish majority had to be accomplished by governmental institutions. The Jewish majority and Jewish government were not only an ideological tenet of Jewish nationalism, but were dictated by the need for the absorption of immigration, national development, and military defense. Those who demanded a state claimed that the act of relinquishing this demand would not advance the chances of a Jewish-Arab agreement, since the Arabs were not willing to accept even minimalist Zionist demands. Still, they hoped a decision in favor of a Jewish state would promote Jewish-Arab peace. The willingness to establish the state in part of Palestine came as the result of both the international constellation at the time and the urgent need for the state; the time factor took precedence over the question of area. The decision to accept a state in part of Palestine was not intended as a gesture to compensate the Arabs of Palestine, as they were the most extreme in their opposition to Zionism. It did, however, make a certain arrangement with Transjordan possible. The Zionist could not cite their agreement to partition as a concession to the Arabs, since the partition proposal was not theirs; had they proposed it, it might have been possible to reach an agreement on that basis.

Developments which took place after 1936 and in the wake of the Peel Commission were accelerated as a result of events during and after World War II. These events vanquished the ideas of the twenties and early thirties, which had been the fruit of a period marked by hope for liberal pacifist developments in the relations between nations. Ideas of extensive autonomy for an Arab minority, mutual enjoyment of economic development, cantons, parity, federation, and binationalism, were all relegated to the archives of unrealized possibilities.

The State of Israel was founded in a manner unforeseen in the two previous decades—not as the product of an agreement with the Arabs and under the aegis of the British, but out of a military confrontation with the Arabs and a political confrontation with Britain. The state was established not in all of Palestine but in part of it, not for the mass immigration of all the Jews of Eastern Europe, but for the remnant of their decimated communities.

The Arabs of Palestine did not enjoy the social progress which the Zionists had presumed would reconcile them with Zionism; they were stricken in battle and their political community was shattered. Hundreds of thousands became refugees and were never integrated into the Arab countries to which they fled. Gaza came under Egyptian rule and the West Bank under Jordanian.

Israel succeeded in Palestine and maintained the balance of power in the region, but it became the focus of pan-Arabic opposition of a strength and depth unknown before 1948. The Arabs of Palestine did not disappear as a group with a collective national consciousness. The constellation of relations was not resolved in the wake of the establishment of the state. Arab protests were addressed to the very existence of a separate Jewish state and its bonds with the Jewish Diaspora.

25.

German Zionists and the Emergence of Brit Shalom

Hagit Lavsky

Brit Shalom (Covenant of Peace) has gone down in Zionist historiography as a Palestine-based association initiated by several Yishuv leaders in 1925. It demanded linking the fulfillment of the Zionist dream with endeavours to reach accord with the Arabs, based on a plan for a bi-national state. By implication, Zionism was to forfeit its exclusive claim to the whole of Palestine.

Brit Shalom's only historian, Aharon Kedar[1], has noted the central role played by intellectuals of Central European, especially German, descent in the founding of the association. These include Arthur Ruppin, Shmuel Hugo Bergman, Georg Landauer, Gershom and Escha Scholem, Samuel Sambursky, and Akiva Ernst Simon. Kedar attempts to explain the leaning in this circle towards Brit Shalom. He also notes the widespread appeal the association held in Germany. Like Lichtheim[2] before him, Kedar believes the key to an answer lies mainly in the influence of Robert Weltsch. The spokesman of Brit Shalom in Germany, Weltsch was the editor of *Juedische Rundschau*, the prestigious journal of Germany's Zionists.

However, the study of German Zionism may shed more light on the ties between Brit Shalom and Germany's Zionists. This perspective provides an insight into their role in the germination, development, and materialization of the bi-national concept and of Brit Shalom within the framework of the Zionist movement. It also elucidates the authority and status the concept and its heralds have commanded among the German

Translated from the Hebrew and reprinted by permission of the author from *Yahadut Zmanenu* 4 (1988): 92–122.

Zionist movement. A study of these aspects of the history of Brit Shalom enables us to date its establishment, point out its causes, explain the prestige it was accorded within the Zionist movement despite its modest membership, and view Weizmann's Zionist policy in light of its connections with Brit Shalom. This essay will focus on the role of German Zionism in the association's emergence and first steps, and explore the essential bond between Weizmann, Germany's Zionists, and Brit Shalom.

THE ROOTS OF THE BI-NATIONAL THESIS IN THE ZIONIST MOVEMENT

The bi-national alternative was first forged as a concept and a platform for Zionist policy in the period between the riots of May 1921 in Palestine, and the convening of the Twelfth Zionist Congress in Carlsbad in September of that year. Breaking out on May Day, following a demonstration of Jewish workers in Jaffa, the riots wrought death and destruction in Jaffa and neighboring colonies. In their wake, Arab-British-Jewish relationships topped the Zionist agenda. Under consideration were the riots themselves, the British administration's reticence regarding military action, and the immediate halt of immigration ordered by the High Commissioner. (A new immigration policy was later declared, complying with the interests of the Arab population.) Foremost on the agenda was Ze'ev Jabotinsky's demand that the British government be prevailed upon to uphold its Mandate commitment to the National Home, and especially to re-establish the Jewish Legion. Jabotinsky's recent appointment to the Zionist Executive lent his words considerable clout.[3]

The re-establishment of the Jewish Legion was the major topic discussed by the Zionist Actions Committee during its Prague convention in July 1921. The riots, Jabotinsky argued there, were decisive proof that Arab resistance to the Zionist enterprise was inevitable. Zionism thus has no choice but to create a Jewish majority in Palestine—a reality the Arabs would have to accept. A protective "colonization regime" of the Mandate administration would be needed to enforce that reality. Deterrent military power, the main factor of political enforcement, would serve as the "Iron Wall" safeguarding the uninterrupted development of the National Home. The military power would be exercised by the Mandatory government, with the active participation of Jewish armed forces.[4]

A heated debate attended Jabotinsky's demands, evincing a wide array of responses and positions. However, with agitation over the May riots still running high, most members of the Actions Committee endorsed to some extent the founding of a Jewish Legion. Furthermore, only two members of the Zionist Executive openly opposed Jabotinsky: Arthur Ruppin, head of the Settlement Department of the Zionist Commission (who during the session was co-opted on to the Zionist Executive), and Menahem Ussishkin, head of the Zionist Commission. The session ended with a resolution authorizing the Zionist Executive to take any measures necessary to facilitate the re-establishment of the Jewish Legion.[5]

But the riots, Jabotinsky's demands, and the extensive accord they won in the Zionist movement, also elicited an altogether different response, centering round four eminent exponents: Martin Buber, Robert Weltsch, Hans Kohn, and Hugo Bergman. Weltsch, Kohn, and Bergman were friends and ideological comrades since their student days in Prague, when they were members of the Bar-Kochba Student Circle. The three deemed their elder Buber as their mentor.[6] After the war Weltsch settled in Berlin. In 1919 he became editor of *Juedische Rundschau*. Bergman first moved to London, to the Education and Culture Department of the Zionist Organization. In 1920 he immigrated to Palestine, to head the National Library in Jerusalem. Kohn travelled from Prague to Paris, then London, working in Keren Hayesod. In 1925 he too immigrated to Jerusalem, as director of its Propaganda Department.[7] After the war, all three, like Buber, were active members of Hapoel Hatzair (the Young Worker's Party). With him they numbered among its ideological leaders, and the founders of Hitahdut—the World Union of Hapoel Hatzair and Zeirei Zion, in 1920 in Prague.[8] Since the Bar-Kochba days, Buber, Weltsch, Kohn, and Bergman shared the ideas of national revival in the spirit of Ahad Ha-Am's "Revival of the Hearts" and practical-cultural Zionism. In the Zionist movement, the herald of these notions was the Democratic Faction. Organized at the turn of the century in opposition to Herzl's political Zionism, the Faction was headed by Weizmann, Motzkin, Buber, and Feiwel.[9] As the disciples of Ahad Ha-Am, and influenced by Buber, the former members of Bar-Kochba did not ground Zionism in the Jewish question and its political resolution, but in the yearning for a spiritual revival of the Jewish people through its historical center in the Land of Israel. To them, such revival entailed a return to those Jewish sources which could be incorporated and re-applied in modern humanist thought to promote the fulfillment of the Jewish people's vocation as "a light unto the nations," committed to universal values of justice and morality. Thus, the group believed, their Zionism transcended not only the narrow political-material framework of political Zionism, but also the isolationist nationalism which could collide with universal human justice.[10]

The establishment of a center in Palestine was considered an essential precept of Zionist realization. An independent Jewish community, subsisting on its own land, its social life founded on justice and morality, was to furnish the groundwork for the revival and renewal of Jewish culture, its light projecting upon the entire Jewish people. The Palestine center was thus to be a means rather than an end. Furthermore, the center's ability to fulfill its function in Zionist realization hinged on its construction mode and social character, on its rehabilitation methods and external relations. In order to serve as the focal junction in the revival of the Jewish people, the center had to be established and developed in keeping with universal Judaic, moral, and judicial imperatives.

These views tied the former members of Bar-Kochba and followers of the Democratic Faction to other trends in Zionism which attributed decisive value to the nature of the National Home, and to the construction process itself, demanding that it be gradual, deliberated, and selective. Such, for example, was the outlook of members of Hapoel Hatzair, disciples of A. D. Gordon. Inspired by their teacher, these deemed the personal renewal of the Jew as a creative person to be the cornerstone of Zionist realization. No wonder then that both Buber and his disciples found their Zionist home in Hapoel Hatzair.[11]

The position of these followers of Ahad Ha-Am also generated their attitude towards the Arab people, and their notion that Arab-Jewish relationships posed a key question to Zionist realization. Buber, in particular, interpreted the revival of the Jewish spirit and the destiny of the Jewish nation in terms of a universal calling. His message struck a chord, particularly among the young Jews of Central Europe grappling with their Jewishness. These eventually arrived at Zionism both as a means of returning to Judaism and of fulfilling their social-moral aspirations for world reform. Therefore, they stressed the moral, anti-coercive features of Ahad Ha-Am's legacy. In turn, they refused to set value on the amassment of material, quantitative, or political power, both in itself and for its implicit conflict with the rights and justice of others— namely, the Palestinian Arabs.[12]

The spiritual-political experience of World War I coincided with Zionism's moment of truth following the Balfour Declaration. This proved crucial to the moulding of the group's position on the Arab question. The radical aggressive nationalism evident in Central Europe at the time presented them with the challenge of distinguishing their own brand of nationalism by founding Zionism on a moral-humanistic basis. However, the Arab question was forcefully impressed on them by the May riots and by Jabotinsky's attendant demands to form a Jewish Legion. Thus they felt compelled to offer a solution which would remove the contrast between the realization of Zionism and the fulfillment of the spiritual-moral vocation of Jewish nationalism. Now they felt obligated to shape a realistic alternative to radical, violent nationalism. After all, Jewish nationalism was a protest against the oppression of other nations. Put to the political test concerning its own attitude towards the rights of another nation, it could not lose sight of the human-moral vision inherent in the very concept of national revival. By definition, if Zionist realization entailed coercion, denial of the rights of others and violent struggle, it contradicted the very essence of their own Zionism, for it meant the National Home would be constructed in total opposition to Judaism's moral calling.[13] The group thus deemed the Arab question a touchstone for the possibility of incorporating Zionism into their overall world-view.

Practical considerations joined the ideological. Palestine, the young Central European Zionists believed, could not be taken by force, nor could Arab resistance be quashed for long by threat of force. Sooner or later, they argued, that resistance would gather counter force. To its advantage, it would not be confined to Palestine and the local population, and spread throughout the Middle East. Palestine, though entirely Jewish, would be but a drop in the ocean. Thus, as an alternative to fighting Arab opposition, they proposed to win the understanding and consent of the Arabs by integrating in the region. Only by relinquishing the Jewish claim to the exclusive possession of Palestine could that goal be attained. Such relinquishment was consistent with their outlook, which never saw in the fulfillment of the Zionist vision a solution to the material-existential plight of European Jews, or a way of building up quantitative might in Palestine.

Such was the inception of the scheme for a bi-national state, years before the establishment of Brit Shalom: "Palestine cannot be a nation state, not only because this is not a step forward, but also because it is impracticable. It must be bi-national rather than Eretz Israel."[14] Morally and pragmatically, they argued, the Palestinian state was to be built upon a drawing together of Jews and Arabs and a gradual creation of political equality between them. An accord in this spirit could be reached within the conceptual-political framework of the League of Nations and under the auspices of the Mandatory power. The hope for a new order of national rights and international relations, underlying the establishment of the League of Nations, made the Zionist movement a testing-ground for the feasibility of that new order. For Zionism did not pursue a policy of power, but rather the development of an immanent, free nationalism within a broad international political entity.[15]

The concept of Zionist realization according to a bi-national formula thus emerged in the Zionist movement several years before the establishment of Brit Shalom, and outside Palestine. The tracing of the origins of this ideology and its forgers and bearers places them within an array of groups and people, including the Democratic Faction, the Bar-Kochba Circle, Hapoel Hatzair, Ahad Ha-Am, Weizmann, and Buber. All postulated a radical alternative to political Zionism, both in their definition of the future aim of Zionism and in the operative program they fashioned for the present. The groups of the radical school have defined the future goal of Zionism in a far more comprehensive and demanding manner than political Zionism. A new national entity was to be built, generated by cultural revival and a liberation from the bonds of the social and economic anomalies marring Jewish existence in the diaspora. From this perspective, the political goal was merely one component, destined to serve as a frame for the foundation of the national entity in Palestine. However, content was to outweigh form. A new society, a Hebrew culture, taking root in the land and agriculture—these would be the primary components of Zionist realization.

Diverse groups of this school called for taking more radical action in the present as well. In various emphases and nuances, they demanded to go beyond organization and diplomacy, and focus on the process of regeneration both in the diaspora and in Palestine. The directions of radicalization they postulated stressed spiritual-moral-social revival, rather than political rehabilitation; internal action in the spheres of culture, education, and land cultivation, rather than political activity oriented towards external accomplishments; economic buildup guided by the aims of national revival and social renewal, rather than the gaining of political sovereignty.

The Zionist movement's first moment of truth on its course towards realization came with the Arab problem and the challenge posed by Jabotinsky. In response, several members of the radical school, of which Chaim Weizmann was one of the leaders, produced the idea of a bi-national state. This, no doubt, is the source of the belief shared by proponents and opponents alike regarding the great affinity between Weizmann and the leaders of the future Brit Shalom association. Moreover, this will serve as the context for explaining the role of German Zionism in the implementation of the concept.

GERMAN ZIONISM AS THE FORUM FOR THE SHAPING OF THE BI-NATIONAL IDEA, 1920–1921

In the annals of the Zionist movement, postwar German Zionism has been remarkable for its political moderation and consistent loyalty to the leadership and policy of Chaim Weizmann. The socio-political roots of this moderation are grounded in the spiritual and political milieu of modern German Jewry, i.e., the liberal humanism of the enlightened Middle-European bourgeoisie. As a rule, German Jewry adopted the trends of enlightened liberalism. Its cultural, economic, and social integration in its surroundings hinged upon liberal tolerance and openness, and lead it since the days of the Second Reich to the social stratum guided by those principles.

It seems that what held true for German Jews in general was doubly true for German Zionists. At least their leadership, on both the national and local levels, emerged from the universities, arriving at Zionist activity through the Zionist student associations. Therefore, in their education, learning, and social stratification, members of mainstream German Zionism distinctly belonged to the "intellectual bourgeoisie," marked by a tendency to political skepticism, openness to new ideas and progress, social sensitivity, and a distaste for a narrow self-serving approach.

Other forces also spurred German Zionism towards political moderation. A tracing of the maturation process and education of German Zionists reveals the formation of a deep, inherent bond between them and the radical Zionist school as a whole. The process generated an inclination towards a humanistic nationalism, peace-loving and politically lenient. A similar tendency, as we have seen, prompted the former Bar-Kochba members to produce the bi-national idea as an offspring, though somewhat exceptional, of the radical school.

The German Zionist movement figured among the founding fathers of the Zionist Organization in Herzl's day, and later served as its administrative and political focus until World War I. The first generation of German Zionists generally evinced a distinct orientation towards

Herzlian political Zionism. They found it suitable, for it refrained from posing radical claims pertaining to the present or future life of the individual.[16] Not so the second generation, who ascended to the leadership of the movement in the postwar years. These experienced throughout their adolescence the rise of antisemitism, and lost faith in the chances for assimilation in German society. However, they could not revert to traditional Jewish heritage, cut off as they were by their assimilationist upbringing and adherence to the values of modern society. Thus, they turned to Zionism, bent on fulfilling a profound need for modern Jewish identity. This generation's most prominent spokesman, Kurt Blumenfeld, dubbed its Zionism a "post-assimilatory Zionism." [17] The generation's needs could therefore be met by a Zionism far more personal, comprehensive, and binding than the first generation's political-philanthropical, Herzlian version. Indeed, the young Zionists in prewar Germany readily embraced the radical Zionist doctrines. The Democratic Faction found a wide scope for action there, e.g. founding the Jewish publishing house Juedischer Verlag in Berlin upon the initiative of Martin Buber. Ahad Ha-Am's doctrine was quite popular among young German Zionists, whether mediated by Buber or by the German translations launched by the Juedischer Verlag.[18] Practical Zionism won widespread sympathy as well, stimulated by the dedicated activities of Otto Warburg and Arthur Ruppin towards the promotion of Jewish settlement in Palestine.

World War I intensified and amplified the radical trends among German Zionists. Encounters with Jewish communities in the occupied Eastern European lands increased the Jewish soldiers' longing for the full Jewish life they were denied by cultural assimilation. Moreover, German antisemitic phenomena on the front shattered the remnants of their faith in the chances for integration in German society. Both factors nurtured the expectation that Zionism would fulfill their needs for national identity on both the social and the cultural levels. On the other hand, the causes of the war and its developments confronted German Zionism with a nationalism degenerated into aggressive chauvinism, which was especially conspicuous in their country. Germany's defeat, with its political and economic consequences, exacerbated the aggressive manifestations of that nationalism. In the first postwar years, it threatened to undo the new socio-political fabric which the Weimar Republic attempted to weave. Within the general reaction prompted by this nationalism among German Jews, the country's Zionists were called upon to fashion their deepening Zionism as a moral nationalism which bore no resemblance to the German.[19] Furthermore, German Zionists were also exposed to the new socialist spirit of their day. The radical socio-political reshuffle in Europe at the end of World War I opened new horizons, offering hope for the regeneration of the continent. Many of the younger generation of German Jewry joined the revolutionary camps, envisioning the eradication of all social injustice, especially nationalism. However, the Zionists among them were affected otherwise by the new expectations. *Ab initio,* they constructed their Zionism on a fundamental despair of finding political and social solutions for the Jews within existing frameworks. To them, Zionism had long been the expression of their yearning for the creation of a new, just, and enlightened society. Naturally, they were not inclined to seek the answer to their yearnings within Marxist, cosmopolitan, class socialism. Nonetheless, the socialist awakening sweeping European youths stirred them to complete the moulding of their radical Zionism as an ideal at once national and social. Associated as this Zionism was with socialism, its ranks swelled with youths whom the experience of war had already provided with a Zionist leaning.[20]

The impact of the war on the radical young generation thus paved the way in Germany for the emergence of a socialist Zionism, moderate in its social as well as its national-political ideology.

The process resulted, among other things, in the reinforcement in Germany of Hapoel Hatzair, which originated in Palestine during the Second Aliyah. The party's appeal lay in its combination of a moderate nationalism fed by the reaction to extremist German nationalism, and a moderate socialism fed by the rejection of cosmopolitan class socialism. Humanistic and moral, its own socialism served mainly as a formula for nationalism which did not stress political conquest. Rather, the party stipulated the moral, social, and cultural regeneration of the Jewish individual and Jewish community through returning to menial labor—mainly agriculture—and to the sources of Hebrew culture. As of 1917, Hapoel Hatzair grew increasingly influential in Germany. Initially it attracted Eastern European youth in Berlin, guided by Chaim Arlosoroff and Israel Reichert. However, it soon spread across Germany, winning over many of the younger generation, student associations, and intellectuals, including such thinkers and leaders of German Zionism as Martin Buber, Kurt Blumenfeld, Robert Weltsch, and Georg Landauer. The German Hapoel Hatzair thus became the central agent in the establishment in 1920 of the Hitahdut party, and in determining its course. The leaders of the German Hapoel Hatzair launched the party's ideological journal in Europe, *Die Arbeit,* a bi-weekly published in Berlin since 1919. The journal also consolidated and enhanced the status and prestige Hapoel Hatzair had won among Germany's Zionists.[21]

The political and spiritual shaping of German Zionism up to the founding of the Weimar Republic thus touched upon and bore parallels to the emerging of the ideology inspired by Bar-Kochba in Prague. No wonder then that members of the inner circle—Buber, Weltsch, Bergman, and Kohn—who had forged the idea of a bi-national solution, found Germany a suitable scene for setting it on the public Zionist agenda. They developed and preached their ideas from the pulpits of German Zionism, not only in *Juedische Rundschau* edited by Weltsch, but also in the journal of Nahum Goldmann and Jacob Klatzkin, *Freie Zionistische Blaetter,* and particularly in *Die Arbeit.*[22] In Germany they found public support for their opposition to Jabotinsky's notion of the Jewish Legion, to which their model furnished an alternative. They also supplemented their ideological preaching with a political program based on the bi-national idea, submitting it for discussion at the Twelfth Zionist Congress in September 1921. This initiative too was forged and put into practice by the German Hapoel Hatzair.[23] Clearly, the groundwork for the bi-national idea and for political action towards its implementation in Zionist policy had already been laid in 1921 outside Palestine. In Central Europe, the meeting ground for German Zionists, disciples of Ahad Ha-Am and Buber, and the German Hapoel Hatzair, the Arab issue was posed as the key question for Zionism, and a desire expressed to reach accord with them. Moreover, a concrete program for a bi-national state was drafted as well. The heralds of the notion, both in Germany and in Palestine, would later work again together for the establishment of Brit Shalom.

THE BACKGROUND FOR THE ESTABLISHMENT OF BRIT SHALOM

The year 1925—the high-tide of the Fourth Aliyah—marked the exacerbation of the struggle over the the socio-economic buildup of Palestine. Massive immigration, a prosperous middle class, and economic achievements in Palestine, induced the circles of private enterprise in the Yishuv and in the Zionist movement to attack the existing settlement policy of the Zionist Executive, based as it was on a large public sector rather than on the promotion of private investments. The prosperity of the Fourth Aliyah also gave rise to basic political problems. The ultimate goal of the Zionist movement was questioned, as were its ways of dealing with external constraints. The debate centered around the dilemma whether the Zionist leadership should continue on its present course of concerted economic efforts, or, rather, exert active political pressure on the British Mandate to fulfill its obligation to the Jewish National Home.

Such was the background for the establishment of the Revisionist Party and the Brit Shalom association—political groups which drew upon issues far broader than the economic buildup of Palestine. The two must not be lumped together, since they differ in size and political and public gravity. Moreover, the one was a party, the other, merely an association. Nonetheless, there is a connection and a common ground for the establishment of the two. Both emerged very much in response to the same background factors of economic prosperity in Palestine, and formulated political concepts to meet the same challenge. Moreover, the founding of Brit Shalom largely must be explained as a reaction to the crystallizing of the Revisionist opposition within Zionism.[24] This reaction, as we shall see, was readily embraced and promoted by German Zionists.

When the Revisionist Party was formed in the spring of 1925, Jabotinsky's doctrine was well beyond its formative phases, and he himself had long since joined the ranks of the Zionist opposition. However, the shifting economic circumstances in Palestine in 1924–25 stirred those circles whose interests in the economy and economic policy matched his political concept. These developments facilitated the fruition of Jabotinsky's concept into a comprehensive world-view. They also contributed to the foundation of the new party by generating public support both in the Yishuv and in its wellsprings of potential interest-groups (mainly in Poland). At the founding convention of the Zionist Revisionist movement in Paris in April 1925, major speeches cited the interests of the Palestine middle class.[25] The new movement's first appearance as a faction in the World Zionist Organization also marked an attempt to organize the representatives of the General Zionist middle class of Palestine.[26]

The Revisionist opposition forged its alternative Zionist doctrine both in the face of the Fourth Aliyah, and as an additional articulation of middle-class interests. It flatly denied the role of the Zionist Organization in shouldering the burden of settlement, whether on its own or through the proposed extended Jewish Agency. That function, claimed Jabotinsky and his colleagues, rested with the Mandate government, whose duty it was to maintain the framework for the settlement enterprise and to furnish it with the required public tools. Only thus could the Zionist goal be achieved, namely, the securing of a Jewish majority in Palestine. That aim was to be reached by massive settlement of middle-class immigrants and a rapid industrialization of the economy by the numerous bourgeois Jews thronging to Palestine. The Zionist leadership, the Revisionists argued, must cease its efforts in the spheres of economic and settlement policy. In the absence of a supportive governmental framework, such efforts are futile. Furthermore, they divert attention from the main objective, namely, increasing the Jewish population, and from the primary, urgent mission to exert political pressure on the British government to fulfill its committment to the National Home.[27]

The objection voiced by Rightist bourgeois circles to the Zionist settlement policy was consistently countered by German Zionists. These figured among the leading authors of Zionist economic policy shaped by the early 1920s. Drawing on the legacy of the radical Zionist school, that policy aimed at economic-social regeneration of the Jewish people in Palestine. Thus, it assigned a central role to the public Zionist sector as a settling agent (by means of the Palestine Foundation Fund and the Jewish National Fund), and to its cooperation with the Labor movement. German Zionists thus rallied against the Right, claiming its demands reflected a tendency to turn Zionism into a mere immigration and settlement movement rather than one of national revival.[28] From this perspective, German Zionists also rejected the political position of Revisionism. To their minds, the Revisionist attacks missed the mark, whether aimed at the slackness of British government policy as regards the expansion and absorption of immigration or at Weizmann's conciliatory policy towards Britain. Ascribing the utmost importance to the gradual, intentional, and well-planned building of the National Home, they demanded to turn the efforts inwards, to national settlement, and to the administrative and financial strengthening of the Zionist Organization. They tended to ask no more of the British government than the creation of a framework enabling the Jews' own activity.[29]

As mentioned before, the reaction leading to the establishment of Brit Shalom arose when the Rightist challenge crystallized into the Revisionist party. Within the general Rightist attack on Zionist policy, Revisionism was unique in demanding to avert the main Zionist thrust from internal activity to an external political campaign. Moreover, the Revisionists demanded that the British government engage in an active, pro-

Zionist policy, entailing a favorable discrimination of Palestine's Jewish minority, and a British committment to serve as a barrier between that minority and the Arabs. Jabotinsky's outlook in the matter ("The Iron Wall") was known since 1921, when he posed the demand for a Jewish Legion. In 1925, it was part and parcel of the crystallizing Revisionist platform.

Thus a further, political response to Revisionism was required, beyond the general dispute with the bourgeois Right. Indeed, such a response did arise from the Zionist leading school of spiritual-economic-social revival which guided Weizmann's Executive and the collaboration with the Zionist Left. The response was voiced by the current's most distinctive spokesmen: Arthur Ruppin, Head of the Settlement Department and patron of cooperative agricultural settlement (hahityashvut haovedet) in Palestine, and Robert Weltsch, the interpreter and disseminator of Weizmann's policy in Europe by means of Juedische Rundschau. It is true that in their phrasing, the counter-claim bore political implications transcending the proclaimed common platform of the radical school, thus heralding the establishment of Brit Shalom. However, German Zionism at large was a bastion of radical Zionism and Weizmannian policy, and a staunch upholder of anti-Revisionism. Small wonder, then, that it served as fertile grounds for the germination of the response leading to the birth of Brit Shalom.[30]

THE BI-NATIONAL STATE SCHEME AS PART
OF THE ANTI-REVISIONIST FORMATION

In the spring and summer of 1925, as Ruppin engaged in covert efforts in Palestine to organize a discussion group on Jewish-Arab relations,[31] the anti-Revisionist opposition in Germany began to emerge as a defined political program, expounded by Weltsch and Felix Rosenblueth.[32] The latter had compiled his own list for the elections to the Fourteenth Zionist Congress. The two argued that it was precisely the massive immigration, the peacefulness in Palestine, and the realistic possibility to achieve a Jewish majority there in the near future, which called for political initiative other than that prescribed by the Revisionists. A "peace campaign" must be undertaken to dispel the Arabs' mounting fears in face of massive immigration. The idea of a Jewish nation-state must be announced as erroneous, and a bi-national policy be implemented in Palestine. Arab consent was deemed essential not only to the realization of the enterprise, but to the existence of Zionism as an ideal of liberty, equality, and justice. The economic policy of the Zionist Organization and the policy of immigration and settlement should comply not only with internal national-social considerations, but also with the needs and rights of the local population. It must prevent economic friction with the Arabs, and of course avert an economic catastrophe which would harm them as well. Economic injury would intensify Arab resistance, refuting the Zionist claim that the settlement enterprise in Palestine augurs well for its Arab inhabitants.[33]

At that stage, confrontation with the Revisionists in Germany took place mainly within the debate over expanding the Jewish Agency, on the one hand, and the flaring dispute with the Zionist bourgeoisie on the other. Discussion focused on Zionist internal policy. When Rosenblueth's list won the pre-congressional elections in Germany, one major background feature was cited to explain the victory: the broad pro-Weizmann consensus aligned against both opposition fronts—the Rightist-bourgeois, and the objectors to expanding the Jewish Agency. The Revisionists, who set themselves up on both fronts, failed to win a single mandate.[34] The steadfast rallying of German Zionism against the opposition and the widespread identification with Rosenblueth's anti-Revisionist list, coupled as it was with the Revisionist downfall, paved the way for a new counter-initiative. This state of affairs enabled Weltsch, with his full-fledged political stance, to launch a frontal attack on the Revisionists, laying bare the urgency of the political dilemma. His impression, sustained since the Legion debate in 1921, was finally confirmed: German Zionists had no taste for activist policy. Quite the contrary, they greatly sympathized with the wish to reach an understanding and match interests with the Arabs.[35]

It should be stressed that Weltsch never abandoned the ideas he and his colleagues had formulated in 1921, and continued expounding them on many occasions in various settings. But it was only at this point that he became convinced he had the appropriate backing to publicly champion the bi-national state as a clear-cut political plan, to be set before the tribunal of the Zionist public. He now issued a programmatic article, linking Weizmannian Zionist policy and its response to the Revisionist challenge with the bi-national state plan:

It would be a mistake not to recognize that the opposing trend in Zionism has gathered strength. Although those known as Revisionists are but a tiny group, their venom seeps through the healthy organs of the Zionist body as well . . . their temperament is not suited for the prolonged, laborious, prosaic work . . . they throng towards military romance.[36]

Weltsch charged the Revisionists with war psychosis, narrow-mindedness, self-delusion, and lack of political understanding. He found it necessary to refute their accusations against the Zionist Executive, based, to his mind, on faulty assessment of the political reality. Furthermore, he pointed out the danger in their very awakening:

Jabotinsky demands: a declaration of a Jewish state, including the trans-Jordan, an annulment of the White Paper of 1922, the establishment of a Jewish Legion. These demands are reprinted everywhere, especially in the Arab press ... *In view of all these, the Congress may not remain silent* [source's emphasis]. It must be clearly stated that this is not Zionist policy, neither in goal nor in strategy.

Weltsch demanded an explication and a declaration of Zionist policy, articulating the positive alternative it offered to the Revisionist challenge, beyond its basic rejection. The assumptions and conclusions of the program he presented may be summarized as follows:

1. The Balfour Declaration is the frame to be filled with content in accordance with existing conditions, namely: the Zionist movement must interpret the Balfour Declaration, reformulating the Zionist objective and the way to its realization.
2. The basic Zionist objective, pursued by Herzl as well, is to solve the Jewish Question by creating a framework for independent Jewish existence—political, judicial, and cultural. However, Herzl believed the goal was attainable through the framework of a Jewish state: "To a people without a land, a land without a people" [This saying was mistakenly ascribed to Herzl].
3. It has meanwhile become evident that Palestine was not a land without a people, and that it harbored a large Arab population emotionally bound to its homeland: "Even if in thirty or forty years we become the majority of the population, it will be, perhaps, a 51 percent majority. In other words: *Palestine shall always be populated by two peoples, Jews and Arabs* [source's emphasis]."
4. Given this situation, the country cannot develop normally if one of the two peoples becomes a ruler, the other, a subjected minority. Therefore, "Palestine's future, tranquil development and well-being can only be assured by a political framework wherein both peoples live side by side with equal rights, bound by the natural ties of transportation, economy and cultural relationships ... and so it is not a state of Jews that we seek, but a Palestinian bi-national community."
5. This framework will guarantee the realization of the Zionist objec-

tive, i.e., the creation of a complete legal basis for the buildup of an independent people with a sound socio-economic structure and national freedom. That base-structure would also be compatible with the framework outlined by the White Paper of 1922.

Here, then, was an explicit political plan with well-defined goals. It also included the stipulation that a special item of the budget of the Zionist Organization be allocated to internal and external propaganda, and to the teaching of Arabic and Arab culture. The plan for a bi-national state was thus presented not merely as a response to the Revisionist argument, but as a challenge to the Zionist-Weizmannian leadership. It predated the Fourteenth Zionist Congress as well as the presentation of any clear ideas on the subject by Ruppin and others in Palestine.

THE FOURTEENTH ZIONIST CONGRESS AND THE ESTABLISHMENT OF BRIT SHALOM

The Fourteenth Zionist Congress, convened in Vienna in August 1925, served as the final catalyst to the establishment of Brit Shalom. Several factors converged in bringing this about: the Revisionist challenge issued at the Congress, the response of Weizmann and Ruppin, and the confluence of Palestinian and German initiatives under the leadership of Ruppin and Weltsch. This juxtaposition lent the feeble efforts preceding the Congress a cohesive and ideological force which produced Brit Shalom.

Centering around the great socio-economic debate, the Congress served as the setting for the first appearance of the Revisionist party as a faction in the World Zionist Organization. As we have seen, Revisionism was not merely an integral part of the campaign of the bourgeois Right against the settlement policy of the Weizmannian leadership. Rather, the Revisionist challenge formed the very heart of the political debate at the Congress. In his speech, Jabotinsky presented the Revisionist alternative to the ruling Weizmannian policy.[37] The economic challenge, ran his major argument, requires a political response. He emphasized that the Zionist objective—even in its narrow demographic-economic definition (a Jewish majority)—cannot be attained without diplomatic efforts which would compel the British government to provide an infrastructure for economic development. Furthermore, he argued, political intervention was necessitated by more than the magnitude of the economic challenge, or by the obligation of the Mandate government to develop the Jewish National Home. It was also required by the presence of another population in Palestine, one which opposed Jewish immigration and the Balfour Declaration included in the Mandate. Hence, the power of the custodian state was also needed to enforce the Jews' prerogatives anchored in the Mandate in preference to the democratic rights of the local Arabs. Otherwise, by sheer superiority of numbers, the latter could prevent the realization of the Jewish rights.

Jabotinsky's challenge met with the response of both Weizmann and Ruppin. Both stressed the political repercussions harbored by the Arab problem. In opposition to Jabotinsky, they argued for the equal rights of the Palestinian Arabs. They differed, however, in the extent to which they drew political conclusions. Weizmann asserted: "Palestine is not Rhodesia, but home to 600,000 Arabs who in the world's sense of justice have as much the right to live in Palestine as we have to our National Home." But his conclusions were only short-termed, with no clear political implications:

In true friendship and partnership with the Arabs we must open the Near East to Jewish enterprise . . . Palestine must be built in such a way, that legitimate Arab interests are not impinged upon in the slightest . . . —we must take Palestine as it is, with its sands and stones, Arabs and Jews as they are. That is our work. Anything else would be deception . . . We shall rise or fall by our work alone.[38]

Ruppin, who had been preoccupied with the issue of Arab-Jewish relations in the months preceding the Congress,[39] was clearer in his assumptions and more decisive in his conclusions: not only were the Arabs at present a large part of the Palestine population, but "the Arabs would always be a large part of the land's population . . . Palestine is destined to become a state of two nations." Economic and political, his conclusions pertained to both the short range and the long range. In the future,

there is the possibility . . . to establish in Palestine a community where both nations, with no ruling advantage (*Vorherrschaft*) to the one, nor oppression of the other, shall work shoulder to shoulder, in full equality of rights towards the economic and cultural development of the country.

In the present, therefore, achieving peace required that "both nations, in their common lives, will bear in mind each other's national needs. We must see to our own national needs, but simultaneously we must respect those of the others."

Ruppin emphasized that all economic projects should be implemented with the anticipated bi-national framework in mind. Not only was economic damage to the Arabs to be avoided, but the Arab population should be helped to attain equality with the Jewish. Economic equality would serve as the basis for political equality and enhance harmonious relationships between the two peoples. Therefore, Ruppin demanded that a special congressional committee be founded to design a program for building that partnership, particularly the economic.[40]

It appears that the open confrontation between Jabotinsky, Weizmann and Ruppin regarding the Arab question furnished the decisive thrust towards the foundation of Brit Shalom, conveying as it did a forceful impression that the Weizmannian leadership backed the trend espousing a bi-national solution. True, Weizmann proposed no definite plan. However, he sided publicly and most emphatically with moderate, conciliatory Zionism, which, resigned to the presence of an Arab entity in Palestine, entailed Zionist realization with the coexistence of both peoples. As for Ruppin, his prior engagement with the problem had been covert, attended by no real articulation of his position. Here, for the first time, he issued a public unequivocal declaration of his stances, delineating them in a rather methodical programmatic fashion. Although he resigned at the Congress from his office as head of the Settlement Department, he too was deemed a member of the central leadership, and a representative of Weizmannian policy. The statements made by Weizmann and Ruppin won special resonance among German Zionists against the background of the ideological soul-searching published in *Juedische Rundschau* prior to the Congress. Many took their anti-Revisionist words as indication of the Zionist leadership's support of the bi-national camp.[41] The initiators of Brit Shalom attached great significance to the leadership's fundamental approval of their approach, tying Zionism with efforts to resolve the question of Arab-Jewish relations.

The Congress also served as the forum where Zionists from Palestine and abroad, their ideas at various stages of fruition, could form an action group seeking to resolve the Arab question. Thanks to the auspicious setting furnished by the Congress discussions, their meeting became a springboard for the establishment of Brit Shalom. In any case, a short conference was held during the Congress between Ruppin, Weltsch, and Hans Kohn.[42] Shortly after the Congress, Hans Kohn immigrated to Palestine. Joining the local activists there—including Hugo Bergman, common friend of Weltsch and himself, he bolstered Ruppin's earlier initiative.

On November 15 and 17, 1925, consultations were held at Ruppin's residence. A commission was established at these meetings for founding Brit Shalom as an "independent association for fostering Jewish-Arab understanding." A premise was set down for an ensuing program: the association shall aspire to realize the Jewish National Home on the grounds of full equality of rights to Jews and Arabs in Palestine as a bi-national state *(Zweinationalitaetenstaat)*.[43] The statutory assembly convened in Jerusalem on November 30, 1925. Based as it was on personal invitations, word of its convening never reached the press.[44]

FIRST STEPS

Despite the joint initiative of Zionist leaders in Palestine and in Europe, especially in Germany, Brit Shalom was founded as a Palestinian association, and all its activities took place there in clandestine closed meetings. Meanwhile, in Germany, no corresponding association was founded, nor was there group activity. However, that country became the arena of comprehensive and intensive propaganda. Since the founding of Brit Shalom, *Juedische Rundschau* devoted much space to inculcating and promoting the bi-national idea. Most articles were written by Weltsch, whether under his name or as editorials. But *Juedische Rundschau* also served the heads of Brit Shalom in Palestine as the major, almost the sole podium for disseminating their ideas in public, until the association published its first pamphlet, *Sheifotenu* (Our Aspirations) in 1927.[45] *Juedische Rundschau,* the quasi-official Zionist publication in the German language, soon became the uncontested mouthpiece of Brit Shalom. Jabotinsky even defined Berlin as the source of the bi-national position.[46]

The heads of Brit Shalom attached great significance to the support they believed the Weizmannian-Zionist leadership lent their ideas. This is witnessed by the first steps of the association in Palestine and Germany. *Juedische Rundschau* presented the bi-national solution as compatible with official Zionist policy. Elaborated in countless articles, the concept was presented as a basis for addressing political events and as an explication of Weizmann's policy.[47] Weltsch saw no contradiction between the role of the journal as an exponent of Weizmannism and its role as the mouthpiece of Brit Shalom. In his articles he repeatedly claimed that the ideas of the latter were actually the ideological platform of the former. True, explicit support of the bi-national plan had never been voiced either by Weizmann, or by other members of the Zionist Executive—except the resigning Ruppin, and newly-appointed Rosenblueth, both German Zionists. However, Weltsch interpreted this as an evasion of political declarations capable of sparking needless debates about issues of no immediate relevance, such as that of the Jewish majority in Palestine. As a responsible journalist and political commentator, Weltsch felt entitled—indeed, compelled to expose ideological tenets and general trends. To his mind, this responsibility was analogous to Weizmann's. As a statesman, Weizmann was barred by tactical considerations from giving free and explicit expression to his views. Weltsch thus believed he was voicing Weizmann's true views.[48] He was not alone in this belief. The founders of the association in Palestine, especially Ruppin, had noted from the outset the basic compliance of their own position and the central positions of the Zionist movement. Their tendency towards theoretical and muted non-political activity stemmed from a desire not to sabotage this basic compatibility but to turn it, instead, into a channel of influence. Weizmann, too, kept providing evidence of his fundamental approval. Thus, for example, he lent the association material support, albeit covertly, by means of a financial grant which facilitated the publication of the first issue of *Sheifotenu*.[49]

Most noteworthy of all is the basic bond between Brit Shalom, its notions and personages, and the broad and varied Zionist school—to which Weizmann also belonged. That school's premises regarding the moral, social, and cultural renaissance of the Jewish people were then being challenged by an ever-growing Revisionist camp which laid stress on political Zionism. It was the political crystallization of Revisionism which prompted Weizmann to display notable affinity with the bi-national position at the Fourteenth Congress. He thus bolstered the belief of the initiators of Brit Shalom, and perhaps of others as well, regarding their like-mindedness. Moreover, that common denominator, or even more so, the very belief in its existence, served as the basis for the unique role Brit Shalom was to play in German Zionism.

NOTES

1. A. Kedar, "Le-toldoteha shel Brit Shalom ba-shanim 1925–1928," in: *Pirkei mehkar be-toldot ha-zionut* (Jerusalem, 1976), pp. 224–85; A. Kedar, "Le-hashkafoteha shel Brit Shalom," in: B. Z. Yehoshua and A. Kedar, eds., *Ideologyah u-mediniut zionit* (Jerusalem, 1978), pp. 97–111.
2. R. Lichtheim, *Toldot ha-zionut be-Germanyah* (Jerusalem, 1951).
3. Interview with Jabotinsky, in *Jewish Chronicle*, May 20, 1921. Jabotinsky was also a member of the Board of Directors of Keren Hayesod (Palestine Foundation Fund).
4. Protocol of the Zionist Actions Committee (AC) Central Zionist Archives (CZA) Z4-257-2.
5. AC Protocol, *ibid.*, A. Ruppin, *Memoirs, Diaries, Letters,* ed. Alex Bein (London and Jerusalem, 1972). Note on July 17, 1921; A. Boehm, *Die Zionistische Bewegung,* II (Jerusalem, 1937), pp. 154–55.

6. H. Kohn, *Buerger vieler Welten* (Frauenfeld, 1965), pp. 72–81; H. Kohn, *Martin Buber, sein Werk und seine Zeit* (Koeln, 1963), pp. 90–91, 147, 314–15; R. Gladstein-Kestenberg, "Athalot Bar-Kochba," in: F. Weltsch, ed., *Prague vi-Yerushalayim: Sefer le-zekher Leo Herrmann* (Jerusalem, 1956), pp. 86–110; J. Reinharz, "Martin Buber's Impact on German Zionism before World War I," *Studies in Zionism*, vol. VI (1982), pp. 171–83. The close ties between Kohn, Weltsch, and Bergman are evinced by their extensive correspondence kept in the Weltsch Archive, the Leo Baeck Institute, New York [hereafter: Weltsch Archive], and at the Bergman Archive, the National and University Library, Jerusalem [hereafter: Bergman Archive].

7. Kohn, *Buerger vieler Welten; S. H. Bergman, 1883–1975,* centenary exhibition, National and University Library (Jerusalem, 1984).

8. B. Ben-Avram, "Hapoel Hatzair ha-Germani: Parashah shel kvuzat intellectualim (1917–1920)," *Hazionut* VI (1981), pp. 49–95.

9. J. Reinharz, *Chaim Weizmann—The Making of a Zionist Leader* (New York and Oxford, 1985), and note 6 above.

10. Buber's series of speeches in Prague between 1909 and 1911 was especially influential: M. Buber, *Drei Reden ueber das Judentum* (Frankfurt am Main, 1920). See Kohn, *Buerger vieler Welten* and *Martin Buber.*

11. Kohn, *Martin Buber;* R. Weltsch, "Deutscher Zionismus in der Rueckschau," in: *An der Wende des modernen Judentums* (Tuebingen, 1972); See also Weltsch's letter to the author of this essay, July 20, 1979.

12. On the impact of the legacy of Ahad Ha-Am, and its channeling through Buber, see mainly: Kohn, *Buerger vieler Welten,* pp. 74–81; Kohn, *Martin Buber,* pp. 40–50; A. E. Simon, "Martin Buber and German Jewry," in: *Leo Baeck Institute Year Book,* vol. III (1958), pp. 3–39; A. E. Simon, "Al darco ha-politit u-tefisato ha-leumit shel M. Buber," in: M. Buber, *Am ve-olam* (Jerusalem, 1964); Buber's speech at the Twelfth Zionist Congress, in: *Stenographisches Protokoll der Verhandlugen des XII. Zionisten-Kongresses in Karlsbad vom 1. bis. 24. September 1921,* Berlin, 1922, pp. 123–29 [hereafter: Protocol of the Twelfth Congress].

13. Buber's speech at the Hitahdut convention in Karlsbad, September 1921: M. Buber, "Nationalism," in: P. R. Mendes-Flohr, *A Land of Two Peoples—Martin Buber on Jews and Arabs* (New York, 1983), pp. 47–57; M. Buber, "In spaeter Stunde," *Der Jude,* 5. Jahrg, no. 1, April 1920; H. Kohn, "Legionen," *Freie Zionistische Blaetter* [FZB] 1, January 1921; H. Kohn, "Aufgaben der Stunde," FZB 2, 1921; H. Kohn, "Unser Weg," FZB 4, 1921; R. Weltsch, "Krieg oder Verstaendigung," *Die Arbeit* 3. Jg. Heft 3 (August 1921). See also same sources, note 10.

14. Hans Kohn to Weltsch, August 15, 1921, Weltsch Archive 7185/4/4 (citation translated from the German by the author of the essay); see also Kohn's letter to Weltsch, July 30, 1921, *ibid.,* 7185/14/2; Kohn, "Unser Weg"; they also found explicit support in Ahad Ha-Am's postwar discourse, see Kohn, *Martin Buber,* p. 339 and epilogue by Weltsch, *ibid.,* pp. 434, 439.

15. Weltsch, "Deutscher Zionismus"; Weltsch, "Krieg."

16. J. Reinharz, "Three Generations of German Zionism," *Jerusalem Quarterly* 9 (Fall 1978): 95–110.

17. K. Blumenfeld, "Urspruenge und Art einer zionistischen Bewegung," *Bulletin des Leo Baeck Instituts* 4 (July 1958): 129–40; J. Reinharz, "The German Zionist Challenge to the Faith in Emancipation, 1897–1914," *Spiegel Lectures in European Jewish History,* 2 (Tel Aviv University), 1982; also see Reinharz, "Three Generations of German Zionism."

18. J. Reinharz, "Achad Haam und der deutsche Zionismus," *Bulletin des Leo Baeck Instituts,* 61 (1982): 3–73.

19. "Die K.J.V.er und die Ostjuden," *Der Juedische Student* 10 (Kriegsheft), August

18, 1916; E. Simon, "Unser Kriegserlebnis," in: *Bruecken: Gesammelte Aufsaetze* (Heidelberg, 1965), pp. 17–23. Many retrospective testimonies to the singular Zionist reaction to German nationalism are found, for example, in the discussions of the national leadership of German Zionists following the 1929 pogroms, September 1929, CZA Z4/3567/IV; A. Landsberg to Ch. Weizmann, November 18, 1929, Weizmann Archive. Likewise in interviews held with R. Weltsch in Jerusalem, February 21, 1980; with A. E. Simon in Jerusalem, March 16, 1982, and March 23, 1982; with M. Flanter in Jerusalem, May 9, 1982; and with P. Jacoby in Jerusalem, January 11, 1982.

20. Ben Avram, "Hapoel Hatzair"; Simon, "Martin Buber and German Jewry."

21. Ben Avram, "Hapoel Hatzair"; Weltsch, "Deutscher Zionismus"; also according to interviews with A. E. Simon (above, note 19); and interviews with Weltsch, July 9, 1979, and S. Sambursky in Jerusalem, May 27, 1982.

22. See, for example, citations of the essays in note 13 above.

23. H. Lavsky, *Be-terem puranut: Darkam ve-yihudam shel zionei Germanyah* (Jerusalem, 1990), chap. 8.

24. See, for example, R. Weltsch's programmatic article of August 14, 1925, to be discussed below; see also: H. Kohn to R. Weltsch, May 19, 1925, Weltsch Archive 7185/14/2, with an impassioned detailed report on the military organizing of the Revisionists.

25. J. B. Schechtman and Y. Benari, *History of the Revisionist Movement, I: 1925–1930*, Tel Aviv, 1970, pp. 33–45.

26. *Protokoll der Verhandlungen des XIV. Zionisten-Kongresses von 18. bis 31. August 1925 in Wien*, London, 1926 [hereafter: Protocol of the Fourteenth Congress]; list of delegates: p. 7; the opening of Jabotinsky's speech: p. 236; the vote of confidence: pp. 469–76.

27. Jabotinsky's speech at the Fourteenth Congress, Protocol of the Fourteenth Congress, p. 236 ff; see also the discussion of this speech below; *Kol ha-revisionistim: Gilion ha-behirot shel Histadrut Hazionim Harevisionistim*, Tel Aviv, December 23, 1926. See also: Y. Shavit, *Jabotinsky and the Revisionist Movement, 1925–1948* (London, 1988), pp. 190–96.

28. Lavsky, *Beterem Puranut*, chaps. 3, 6, and 7.

29. Weltsch's article preceding the July 1925 session of the Actions Committee, *Juedische Rundschau* (JR), July 14, 1925; R. Weltsch, "Facing Two Fronts," *ibid.*, July 3, 1925; F. Rosenblueth in an election meeting of the Berlin Zionists, *ibid.*, July 31, 1925 [hereafter: Rosenblueth].

30. On the ideological and organizational formation in Palestine, see note 1 above.

31. Kedar, "Le-toldoteha shel Brit Shalom."

32. Rosenblueth (later, Pinhas Rosen), one of the leaders of German Zionism, was chairman of the Zionist Organization of Germany until 1923. Following the Fourteenth Congress, he entered the Zionist Executive as head of the Organization Department.

33. Rosenblueth; R. Weltsch, Editorial, *JR*, August 7, 1925.

34. The election results, *JR*, August 7, 1925; R. Weltsch, assessment article on the results, *JR*, August 11, 1925.

35. Weltsch, *JR*.

36. "Worum es geht," *JR*, August 14, 1925. This article has a follow-up dealing with all the other problems on the agenda of the Fourteenth Congress. Its major part, under discussion here, has been republished in the collection: H. Kohn und R. Weltsch, *Zionistische Politik* (Maehrisch-Ostrau, 1927), pp. 169–82.

37. Protocol of the Fourteenth Congress, pp. 236–50.

38. Citations from the part of the speech on pp. 328–29, Protocol of the Fourteenth Congress, translated from the German by the author.

39. Kedar, "Le-toldoteha shel Brit Shalom."

40. Protocol of the Fourteenth Congress, 438–39, at the opening of his speech in reply to the disputants in "the Palestine Debate" (citations from p. 438; translated from the German by the author).

41. See R. Weltsch's letter to S. H. Bergman on September 4, [1925], Bergmann Archive 1502/1334.3, describing various events and meetings during the Congress. See also Weltsch's articles during the Congress: "After the General Debate," *JR*, August 25, 1925; "Towards Conclusion," *JR*, August 28, 1925.

42. R. Weltsch to S. H. Bergman, above, note 41. According to his report, an intended meeting was prevented by the Viennese police, whom the antisemitic disturbances attending the Congress had prompted to act with undue severity. Also compare note 21 in Kedar, "Le-toldoteha shel Brit Shalom."

43. Protocol of the consultations at Dr. Ruppin's residence, November 15 and 17, 1925, Weltsch Archive 7185/3/1. Attendants: S. H. Bergmann, Hans Kohn, Joseph Lurie, Yehoshua Radler Feldmann, Arthur Ruppin, and Jacob Thon; H. Kohn to A. Ruppin, December 6, 1925, copy sent to Weltsch, Weltsch Archive, *ibid.*

44. H. Kohn to A. Ruppin, above note 43.

45. The following is a sample list of articles published in the *Juedsiche Rundschau*: R. Weltsch, "Idea and Delusion," September 25, 1925; "Our Nationalism," December 11, 1925; "The Report of the Mandate Commission," December 18, 1925; "Changes," January 26, 1926; "After Five Years," April 10, 1926; M. Bileski, "Our Policy of Understanding," February 2, 1926; M. Buber, "Self-Examination," April 16, 1926; H. Kohn, "On the Political Shaping of Palestine," July 25, 1926; A. Ruppin, "Brit Shalom," July 6, 1926. On activity in Palestine, mostly covert and clandestine, see: Kedar, "Le-toldoteha shel Brit Shalom." See also: Protocols of meetings and activities in Weltsch Archive, 7185/3/1, 7185/3/6. Most, e.g. the detailed program proposal and its discussion, are labeled "Secret" or urge secrecy.

46. See citation and reference to his article "On a Bi-National Palestine," published in the *Wiener Morgenzeitung, JR*, March 5, 1926.

47. See, for example, Weltsch's articles, "On the Actions Committee Meeting," *JR*, July 20, 1926; "Zionist Problems," *JR*, July 23, 1926; "Our Political Campaign," *JR*, December 10, 1926.

48. R. Weltsch, "Our Political Campaign," *ibid.* In this article he writes of the responsible publicist's obligation to interpret the meaning of the policy, on which the responsible statesman cannot speak freely. For many years to come, in his interviews in Jerusalem on July 9, 1979 and August 15, 1979, this was Weltsch's explanation of Weizmann's silence and of his own belief that Weizmann shared his views, but was not at liberty to say so. See also: R. Weltsch, "A Tragedy of Leadership: Chaim Weizmann and the Zionist Movement," *Jewish Social Studies*, vol. 13, no. 3 (July 1951): 211–26.

49. See Kedar, "Le-toldoteha shel Brit Shalom," and note 97 there; Kedar, "Le-hashkafo-teha shel Brit Shalom"; G. Landauer to Ch. Weizmann, August 4, 1927, Weizmann Archives.

26.

Patterns of Communal Conflict in Palestine

Bernard Wasserstein

The purpose of this essay is to suggest that a characteristic, recurring pattern of communal violence can be detected in Palestine in the modern period—a pattern which bears striking resemblances to that of communal disturbances in other places and periods. The focus is on the Palestine riots of the mandatory period (especially those of 1920, 1921 and 1929), with some glances back to the final decades of Ottoman rule. The discussion is divided into six parts. First, what is the *calendar* of communal rioting? Secondly, is there a characteristic *prelude* to these riots? Thirdly, what is the *geography* of communal violence? Fourthly, *who* are the rioters? Fifthly, what is the role of the *authorities* in relation to these disturbances? Sixthly and finally, what may such an examination suggest as to the *character and significance* of the riots?

1. THE CALENDAR OF COMMUNAL RIOT

The calendar of communal violence in Palestine was closely bound up with the calendar of religious festivity. Certain feast days were traditional occasions of riot. The conjunction of feast days of different communities living close together was a particularly common occasion of riot. Sometimes secular anniversaries or commemorations acquired a quasi-religious garb which was red rag to the bull of communal riot. Further, the creation or revival of competitive festivities was traditionally associated with communal disorder.[1]

On 4 April 1920 serious communal riots between Muslims and Jews

Reprinted by permission of the author from *Jewish History: Essays in Honour of Chimen Abramsky*, edited by Ada Rapaport-Albert and Steven J. Zipperstein (London: Peter Halban Publishers Ltd., 1988), 611–28.

broke out in Jerusalem. It was the (western) Christian Easter, the Jewish Passover, and the Muslim pilgrim festival of *Nebi Musa*. The latter was an annual pilgrimage to the supposed tomb of Moses in the Judaean desert between Jerusalem and Jericho, which attracted participants from all over Palestine. The pilgrimage was not fixed by the Muslim calendar, but by the Christian calendar in Easter week, so that (as the Mufti of Jerusalem put it in 1920) 'the Muslims at that time should have a feast as those of other communities'.[2] This was the traditional season of communal strife in Jerusalem. In 1847, for example, the British consul in Jerusalem, James Finn, reported:

A Greek pilgrim boy, in a retired street, had thrown a stone at a poor little Jew boy, and strange to say, the latter had the courage to retaliate by throwing one in return which unfortunately hit its mark, and a bleeding ankle was the consequence. It being the season of the year when Jerusalem is always thronged with pilgrims, a tumult soon arose, and the direst vengeance was denounced against all Jews indiscriminately, for having stabbed (as they said) an innocent Christian child with a knife, in order to get his blood, for mixing in their Passover biscuits.[3]

At the same season in 1852, Finn noticed

serious alarm lest a collision should occur between the crowds of Greek pilgrims assembled for Easter—sturdy, well-armed fellows, some of whom had been Russian soldiers, and the Moslem pilgrims to Nebi-Moosa, who poured into the city in unusual numbers from the Nabloos district. The Nabloosians are noted for their brutality and fanaticism.[4]

In 1914 an English Jewess observing the festivities in Jerusalem reports the torture and murder of a Christian by Turkish soldiers at the *Nebi Musa* pilgrimage.[5] Ronald Storrs, who was military governor of Jerusalem at the time of the 1920 riots, noted that the Easter season 'when, if only for three days, the death of strife becomes the victory of peace . . . in the Holy Land, and most of all in the Holy City, had meant for generations the sharpening of daggers and the trebling of garrisons.'[6]

On 1 May 1921 bloody communal disturbances broke out in Jaffa between Muslims and Jews. The date was the Greek Orthodox Easter. It was also the date of quasi-religious festivities by sections of the Jewish community celebrating the socialist May Day. Indeed, the fighting in Jaffa began with a clash between rival processions of socialists and communists, later developing into a communal riot. Meanwhile at nearby Ramleh 25,000 Muslim pilgrims were gathering for their annual festival at the tomb of *Nebi Saleh*. This concourse provided the occasion for the spread of the riots from Jaffa to Jewish villages inland.[7]

On 23 August 1929 Muslim–Jewish riots broke out again in Jerusalem. The riots began after the Friday morning services in the mosque of al-Aqsa. In this case too the cycle of violence began on a holy day of two religions. The previous Saturday, 17 August, the Jewish Sabbath, was also the date of the Muslim celebration of the birthday of the Prophet. An Arab–Jewish disturbance in the Bukharan quarter of Jerusalem resulted in the death of one Jew and injuries to Arabs and Jews. From this beginning tension increased until the explosion on the following Friday.[8]

Other religious or quasi-religious festivities provided similar, if less bloody, cues for communal disturbances. The celebration by the Zionists of the anniversary of the Balfour Declaration on 2 November often produced Arab protests and communal violence—for example, in 1918 and 1921. More recent communal disturbances have often followed a similar pattern. For example, the Jewish–Muslim clashes in Hebron in 1976 took place on the Jewish Day of Atonement, Yom Kippur, a date which since the outbreak of the Yom Kippur war in 1973 has acquired special political significance in the eyes of many Muslim Arabs.

2. THE PRELUDE TO COMMUNAL RIOT

The calendar of communal violence was not a secret. Police, government, communal leaders were all generally aware of the traditional seasons of danger and made appropriate dispositions. The expectation of riot was consequently often a major element in the prelude to trouble. But communal riots were rarely the consequence of self-fulfilling prophecy alone. Neil Smelser stresses among the preconditions for riot a period of intensified rumour and provocation of crowds by symbols.[9] Music, particularly loud, raucous music, as if designed with the express intention of provoking the opposing group, was a recurring element in the prelude to communal riot. Above all, processions, marches, parades past places of worship or residential districts of opposed groups tended to provide the immediate occasions of riot.

In 1856 Muslim anti-Christian riots at Nablus were preceded by the symbolic pealing of a bell in the Protestant missionary chapel in the town on the orders of the Anglican bishop in Jerusalem. The British consul in Jerusalem described this bell as 'an instrument of peril to the public peace for such a town as Nablus'.[10] Jewish riots directed against Christian missionaries in Jerusalem in the mid- and late-nineteenth century were often precipitated by symbolic outrages against graves. For example, the British consul W. T. Young reported to the Earl of Aberdeen on 31 March 1843 that a Jewish commotion against missionaries and Jewish converts to Christianity had followed the spreading of rumours that converts 'have been to the Jews' cemetery and desecrated the Tombs, by displacing some, and inscribing crosses and their names as Believers in Christianity on others, to the great annoyance of the Jewish community'.[11] Jewish anti-missionary riots, sparked off by such incidents, have been a recurring feature of communal relations in Jerusalem until the present day.

The prelude to the major Muslim–Jewish riots of the 1920s falls into the familiar pattern. The *Nebi Musa* riots of April 1920 were preceded by a period of intense, threatening rumour. On 1 January 1920 a Zionist intelligence report noted a speech said to have been delivered in a mosque at Ramleh by a Muslim sheikh who declared: 'The days of revenge are nearing ... Get rid of the Jews who want to rob your country and violate your wives.'[12] This was succeeded by a spate of similar reports which seriously alarmed the Jews. A report by a Zionist agent in Jerusalem on 16 March 1920 stated: 'There is a great movement felt for "Neby Moussa" ... The Extremists are sure that a great revolution could be brought forth on this occasion.'[13] Rumours among the Arab population of troubles in Egypt appear to have contributed to the excitement.[14] As the date of the outbreak of the riots approached, the rumours of impending violence assumed an increasingly specific character.[15] The rumours stimulated Jewish military preparations for defence of the community in the event of an outbreak.[16] As the official British commission of inquiry into the riots concluded, 'It seems to have been evident to everybody that a storm was beating up and might burst at any moment.'[17]

In the riots in Jaffa and the coastal plain of Palestine in May 1921, rumour played a major part in the spread of the violence. For example, the attack on the Jewish settlement of Haderah on 6 May appears to have been stimulated by widespread rumours that the Jews had destroyed a neighbouring Arab town, and that Jews in Haderah were holding prisoner a large number of Arab labourers.[18]

In the prelude to the riots which erupted in Jerusalem in 1929, general rumours among the Arab population that the Jews were planning to seize the Muslim holy places on the Haram al-Sharif (Temple Mount) were given wide currency by the Arabic press and played a major part in the heightening of communal tension.[19] Jewish anxieties were increased by the publication of specific threatening rumours in the Hebrew press. The issues of the Hebrew daily newspapers, *Davar* and *Ha-Aretz*, dated

22 and 23 August reported rumours that disturbances were scheduled for Friday 23 August. Village Arabs were said to be flocking into Jerusalem, angered by reports that the Jews were planning to attack the mosques on the Friday. Crowds were said to be gathering in the vicinity of the mosques armed with bludgeons.[20] After the morning prayers in the mosque of al-Aqsa on the Friday, the riots duly began. The spread of the violence beyond Jerusalem to towns such as Hebron and Safed was hastened by exaggerated rumours as to the extent and nature of the violence in Jerusalem.

Processions and provocative music were major elements in the prelude to communal riot in Palestine in the 1920s. The immediate occasion of the outbreak in Jerusalem in April 1920 was the arrival of the *Nebi Musa* procession of pilgrims at the Jaffa Gate of the old city. In accordance with Turkish custom, the British military authorities had provided gun salutes and a regimental band which marched with the pilgrims. The question of the participation of the government band was a matter of issue in 1920: on orders from London it had originally been decided to refuse permission for the band to participate; but, upon the urgent representation of the military governor of Jerusalem, Colonel Storrs, the prohibition was rescinded and the band played, to the satisfaction of the pilgrims and the chagrin of the Jews.[21] The 1921 riots seem to have been sparked off by a clash between rival Jewish socialist and communist processions celebrating May Day. The 1929 riots were preceded by rival processions and demonstrations by Zionists and Arab nationalists focused on the Western ('Wailing') Wall holy place. On 15 August 1929 a procession of Jewish youths had marched to the wall and sung the Jewish national anthem, 'Hatikvah'. The following day a large Muslim demonstration had convened at the same spot. During the months preceding the riot particular offence had been taken by Jews at the revival by the Muslims of the old and noisy custom of banging drums and cymbals during Muslim prayers; the Jews complained that these percussive accompaniments to songs and chants appeared to be deliberately timed and positioned so as to drown the words of Jewish services taking place in the wall passage immediately below the Muslim holy compound.[22]

Symbolic violence and affronts which helped to exacerbate communal feelings were also signs of impending violence, especially when magnified (perhaps on occasion invented) by rumour. For example, in 1920 it was the rumour that a Jew had spat contemptuously at one of the banners being carried by the *Nebi Musa* pilgrims that was said to have sparked off the violence.[23] In 1929 the tearing by Arabs of prayer books, and the burning of supplicatory notes left by pious Jews in the crevices between the stones of the Western Wall, were regarded by Jews as outrages. As in the case of communal riots in India, animal provocation accompanied human: in 1929 there were Jewish complaints that Muslims were driving mules through the narrow passage adjacent to the wall, and encouraging them to drop excrement near Jews performing their devotions.[24]

3. THE GEOGRAPHY OF COMMUNAL RIOT

Appropriately, the characteristic location of riots between adherents of different religions or sects was the holy place—church, mosque, synagogue or shrine, or their precincts. In particular, places whose holiness was a matter of competitive dispute between different religions or sects tended to be riot 'black spots'. If the primary focus of religious riot was often the holy place or holy city, its tendency was to spread rapidly to neighbouring areas of mixed population, and thence often further afield.

Jerusalem, with its large concentration of holy places and mixed population of three religions and a multiplicity of sects, was a natural focus of communal disturbance. But it is the greatest, not the only, holy city of Palestine. Bethlehem, and in particular the Church of the Nativity, was a traditional location of unedifying disputes, often degenerating into physical violence, between adherents of different Christian sects. For example, Storrs noted shortly after his appointment as military governor of Jerusalem in December 1917:

The Greeks and Armenians, whose respective Epiphany and Christmas fall on the same day, came to blows in the Grotto of the Nativity at Bethlehem, and had to be parted by the special guard (chosen from experts at these disgraceful brawls) that I had posted there.[25]

Hebron, holy to both Jews and Muslims, was the scene of occasional bloodshed in the nineteenth century, of a terrible massacre of Jews in 1929, and of renewed communal strife centred on rivalry over holy places from 1976 to the present.

The geography of the riots in Palestine in the 1920s provides striking examples of the contagious spread of crowd violence. In 1921 the bloodshed swept from Jaffa and the Muslim pilgrim shrine of *Nebi Saleh* near Ramleh, northwards and southwards through the Jewish townships of the coastal plain, but not to the hill country of the north and east. In 1929 the reverse was the case. From the initial outburst in Jerusalem, the disturbances spread south to Hebron and north to Safed (also a city holy to the Jews), encompassing other Jewish settlements on the way. In 1929, however, the coastal plain was relatively quiet. The 1920 riots did not spread beyond Jerusalem at all. The reason is perhaps that on that occasion the British army managed to seal off the area of rioting from the outset, inside the walls of the old city of Jerusalem; unauthorized access or egress was forbidden for four days. Lack of troop strength prevented any such hermetic enclosure in 1929. In 1921 no such attempt could have been contemplated by the authorities: neither the sprawling urban mess of Jaffa nor the open countryside around Ramleh afforded scope for such action; instead, the authorities tried to head off marauding crowds by means of aerial bombardment.[26]

4. WHO ARE THE RIOTERS?

The works of George Rudé and others on the composition of revolutionary crowds have taught us the importance of not treating the crowd merely as an anonymous lump of humanity and have warned us of the limitations of taking at face value statistical conclusions derived from inherently biased sources such as police or court records. In Palestine, as elsewhere, the repressive authorities are the main chroniclers of disorder. Rather than attempting to deduce any quantitative conclusions from these flawed data, the less ambitious approach used here is to isolate certain characteristic faces in the communal crowd.

In his pioneering study *The Crowd*, Gustave Le Bon divided crowds into two types: homogeneous and heterogeneous.[27] The former included crowds defined primarily by sect, caste or class. In the case of religious riots we are generally confronted by homogeneous crowds defined primarily by sect. This may seem an obvious conclusion: it is not. For it applies not only to those riots which occur in societies where two religious groups live together (such as anti-Jewish riots in mediaeval England, or anti-Protestant riots in sixteenth-century France), but also to riots which take place in societies where *more than two* groups live in close proximity. Third parties to religious conflict are rarely found to join in the violence.[28]

Palestine affords an excellent illustration of these general points. For here, in spite of the proximity of three major religious communities and a myriad of minor splinters, riots have traditionally been two-sided confrontations, one Christian sect versus another, Muslims versus Jews, Jews versus Christian missionaries, and so on. Occasionally in the nineteenth century there were Muslim attacks against both Jews and Christians, but such a triangular pattern is exceptional. In the case of the Arab–Jewish riots of the mandatory period, Christian involvement was slight. Indeed, we may more properly call these riots Muslim–Jewish rather than Arab–Jewish, since Christians in general remained ostentatiously neutral—to the extent of displaying large crosses on the outsides of their houses.[29] This is the more noteworthy in that the Muslims made great efforts in the 1920s to draw Christian Arabs into a joint political movement on a nationalist basis.[30]

Let us now try to identify some characteristic faces in the rioting communal crowd. In Palestine there appear to be at least three: young males, strangers from out of town, and policemen.

Children and youths seem to have been prominent particularly in the early stages of riots in Palestine. In 1918 the military governor of Jerusalem reported that a riot had narrowly been prevented when 'two or three ragamuffins of the lowest class, one a Muslim and one a Christian' (such references to Christian participation, however, are exceptional) had seized a processional banner from a Jew, and started beating it about its bearer.[31] Among those arrested by the police as a result of the riots in Jaffa in May 1921 were reported to be two children aged six and eight; both were Jews accused of Bolshevism.[32] A government report on a near-riot in Jerusalem in March 1923 stated:

The procession was headed by a crowd of small boys of the riff-raff (not the schoolboy or Boy Scout type), led by an Effendi who appeared to be giving them the time for the songs they were singing. When the vanguard had got just beyond the Governorate Gate, preceded by the Commandant of Police and some of his officers, they began to sing

> Filastin biladna
> Al-Yahud kilabna
> [Palestine is our country
> The Jews are our dogs]

Mr Quigley [Police Commandant] twice ordered them to desist, and at his second warning was struck by one of them with a large stone on the hand, while his orderly received a stone in the face. He thereupon ordered the Police to turn back the crowd. This they did . . . Truncheons were freely used.[33]

An Arab nationalist version of the same incident stated:

The Commandant of Police instructed his mounted men to attack the first line of the crowd, which consisted of a number of boys of nearly [sic] ten years of age, and began to strike at them with clubs in a rough way . . . It is regrettable to state that some of the Boy Scouts were also beaten while they were attending to the injured.[34]

The two accounts agree at least on the extreme youth of the demonstrators. However, the role of children appears in general to have been greater in the initial stages of Palestinian riots than in later serious bloodshed.

After children and young men, a characteristic face in the communal crowd is that of the stranger from out of town. In Palestine peasants from the surrounding countryside appear to have played a major role in urban communal violence, particularly in Jerusalem. This may be explained in large measure by the coincidence of riots with major pilgrim festivals. James Finn's anxieties regarding the propensity to violence of pilgrims to the *Nebi Musa* festivities have already been cited. In the riots of 1920 and 1921 pilgrims to *Nebi Musa* and *Nebi Saleh* were outstanding among the rioters. Similarly in 1929 villagers from surrounding districts were prominent in attacks on Jews in Jerusalem.

Thirdly, we find police and soldiers among the most bloodthirsty of communal rioters. In Jerusalem in 1920, Arab policemen participated in the attacks on Jews to such an extent that the entire force had to be withdrawn, disarmed and confined to barracks. The men were reported to be 'inclined to be mutinous on receipt of these orders'.[35] Meanwhile in Jaffa, although there was no serious outbreak of bloodshed, tension was running high and there were minor affrays between Jewish soldiers (members of the so-called 'Jewish Legion' in the British army) and Arab policemen and civilians.[36]

Policemen played a major role in the riots of 1921 in Jaffa and the surrounding district. In one of the most bloody incidents, the attack by a crowd of Arabs on a Zionist hostel for new immigrants in Jaffa, Arab policemen firing rifles led the attackers. A senior Arab police officer, Hanna Effendi Bordcosh, a Christian, who witnessed the incident, was severely censured by the British commission of inquiry into the riots for merely going home to lunch. Mounted Arab policemen were in the thick of the attack a few days later on the Jewish colony of Haderah. The British chief of police was reproved by the commission for having 'left Arab policemen in control of an Arab mob . . . They were being swept along with the crowd, clinging to it, but quite unable to control it.'[37] Jewish soldiers from the nearby military camp at Sarafand rushed to Jaffa to join in the defence of the Jewish quarters. They remained there under arms until ordered to disband and disarm by a senior British officer.[38]

In 1929 Arab policemen were once again leading figures among the rioters. A British police constable in Hebron during the massacre of Jews there describes one such incident:

On hearing screams in a room I went up a sort of tunnel passage and saw an Arab in the act of cutting off a child's head with a sword. He had already hit him and was having another cut, but on seeing me he tried to aim the stroke at me but missed. He was practically on the muzzle of my rifle. I shot him low in the groin. Behind him was a Jewish woman smothered in blood, with a man I recognised as a police constable named Issa Sherif from Jaffa in mufti. He was standing over the woman with a dagger in his hand. He saw me and bolted into a room close by, and tried to shut me out, shouting (in Arabic), 'Your Honour, I am a policeman.' . . . I got into the room and shot him.[39]

5. THE ROLE OF THE AUTHORITIES

The frequent presence among the rioters of low-level authority-figures such as policemen and soldiers immediately leads to a consideration of the role of the authorities in these disturbances. In communal riots in Palestine the ability of the relevant authority (whether Turkish, British or Israeli) to mobilize its forces effectively was often limited by the questionable impartiality of policemen and soldiers in riots involving their own co-religionists.

Almost as important as the actual attitude of the authorities, particularly in the early stages of riots, are popular beliefs concerning the governing power. Often the crowd seems to see itself as acting in some sense on behalf of the authorities in order to root an evil element out of society. The belief in the indulgent wink of government, whether or not based on reality, can be a stimulus to riot. On other occasions the crowd sees itself as acting in the stead of the authorities where the latter are constrained by weakness or malign forces from acting resolutely against an enemy group. Conversely, the belief on the part of the victim group in communal riots that the government has winked at or helped to engineer communal aggression, may stimulate the organization of self-defence measures by the victim group, measures which may raise communal tension further, and increase antagonism between the victim group and the authorities.[40]

In Palestine, as elsewhere, rioting communal crowds have traditionally seen themselves as acting either with the support of the government, or (in cases where the authorities are felt to have been remiss) in place of the government. In the mid-1830s there were Muslim anti-Christian and anti-Jewish riots in various parts of Palestine in the course of a general revolt against the authority of the Egyptian ruler, Ibrahim Pasha, son of Muhammad Ali. A major element in these disturbances was resentment by Muslims of the grant by the new government of rights of equal status to Christian and Jewish communities. Muslim susceptibilities were further upset by the use of mosques as barracks for Egyptian troops, the carrying of crosses by Christians in processions, the granting of permission to build or repair churches and synagogues. The primary grievances of the rebels appear to have been as much economic and social (objections to conscription, to taxes, to administrative reforms) as religious. But the riots against Jews and Christians were not merely anti-government; the rioters were also acting, in a sense, on behalf of the legitimate government of the Muslim state; the riots represented efforts by the Muslim majority to reaffirm, in place of the apparently remiss government of the Egyptian usurper, their traditional status of superiority. Ma'oz notes the complaint of Muslims: 'O my brother, the state has become a Christians' state, the Islamic state has ended.'[41]

If Muslims required the ideological encouragement derived from the idea that they were defending the traditional Muslim state in order to embark on communal riot, Jews, as a small and depressed community in Palestine in the nineteenth century, would rarely dare to engage in riot unless they were confident of tangible government backing. Moreover such Jewish riots were never directed against Muslims (for attacks on Muslims could hardly be expected to gain the support of a Muslim government), and appear to have been restricted to Jerusalem where the Jews were the largest community by the middle of the century. In 1846 there were Jewish riots in Jerusalem directed against the hospital of the London Society for Promoting Christianity Amongst the Jews. The British consul in Jerusalem reported to Lord Aberdeen:

The butcher who kills the meat for the hospital, a French subject, has been mobbed and severely beaten, and the hospital has been daily surrounded by a number of Jews sent by the Rabbies to prevent patients and even servants access to it . . . Without wishing to interfere in the least with the motives [sic] of the Rabbies for preventing Jews from frequenting the hospital, I think they are using unlawful means to prevent free access to the house of a British subject. His Excellency, the Pasha, however, answers my application for protection against these outrages by an accusation against the Protestant clergy residing at Jerusalem; accusing them from information obtained from the Rabbies of unworthy attempts to convert the Jewish Raias; an accusation entirely without foundation.[42]

In a later dispatch the consul complained that the Pasha 'has made himself a party with the Rabbies against the British residents here'.[43] But the Pasha, in a letter to the consul, rejected such criticism, insisting that it was his duty to uphold the Jews' freedom of worship, and that the activities of the missionaries were being conducted 'd'une maniere peu digne, d'après les dires de ces Rabbins, mes protégés'.[44] The final words may be seen as a sly dig at the consul, since one of the traditional functions of the British consulate in Jerusalem (based on an instruction dispatched by Palmerston in 1841) was the protection of Jews.

The Jerusalem riots of 1920 led to Jewish accusations of government complicity in what they insisted on terming the 'pogrom'. Izhak Ben-Zvi wrote:

We have lived to be eye-witnesses to an actual pogrom in Jerusalem, a pogrom the like of which we did not have during hundreds of years of Turkish rule . . . Worst of all is the attitude of the local authorities to the whole matter. All our doubts have become certainties. The English administration knew of all the preparations for the slaughter, and not only did not try to prevent it but even did everything in its power to encourage the thieves and murderers, and on the other hand used every means to impede the Jewish self-defence and arrest its members. Now it is trying to suppress any publication of the disturbances, even mention of the word 'pogrom' in a telegram.[45]

In an interview with the *Manchester Guardian*, shortly after the riots, the Zionist leader Chaim Weizmann similarly insisted that they could 'only be characterized as organized pogroms'.[46] The Jews were supported in this view by the strongly pro-Zionist chief political officer of the military government, Colonel Richard Meinertzhagen, who accused his colleagues in the administration of having directly encouraged Arab leaders to organize violent disturbances in order to impress the British government with the strength of popular feeling in Palestine against Zionism. In his diary Meinertzhagen noted: 'On the day of the rioting the following notice was displayed all over Jerusalem: "The Government is with us, Allenby is with us, kill the Jews; there is no punishment for killing Jews." '[47]

Whatever the truth of Meinertzhagen's allegations, there seems little doubt of a widespread popular belief among Arabs in Jerusalem, immediately before the riots, that the government looked favourably on the Arab cause. The Arab nationalist newspaper *Suria al-Janubiyyah*, on 26 February 1920, described an interview between the governor of Jerusalem and one of the nationalist leaders regarding a nationalist demonstration to be held two days later. The newspaper remarked:

You see, o people, that the government has not forbidden peaceful demonstrations on condition that we will be orderly in all our actions, and for this we should thank the government because it has proved that it does not want to block the path of our development, our renaissance, and our unity, and our efforts to make our words heard in the outside world. We are very hopeful that it will transmit our complaints to the higher authorities and add to our complaints what it itself sees and feels of our national feelings, and that it will add action to words in this matter, famous as it is for justice and good government.[48]

The fact that senior officials of the government were known to be sympathetic to the claim of the Emir Faisal's Damascus regime to extend its authority over Palestine seems further to have encouraged popular belief on the eve of the riots that 'the government is with us'.[49]

In the riots of 1929 the Muslims seem to have been stimulated less by the belief that they were acting with the support of the government than by the feeling that they were acting in place of the government in order to assert their rights at the holy places, rights which, as they saw it, the government openly admitted, but was too pusillanimous to vindicate. In a public proclamation (apparently designed for use as a wall poster) issued immediately before the outbreak of the violence in August 1929, the Association for the Protection of the Aqsa Mosque and the Islamic Holy Places in Jerusalem declared:

In the matter of the *Buraq* [the Western Wall] . . . the right of the Muslims is quite clear, in their possession of every part of its grounds, its walls, its skies, and its ends. The London government could not but admit this Muslim right unequivocally in its White Paper which the Colonial Secretary published about ten months ago. Unfortunately, until this day it has not been implemented.[50]

In all riots in mandatory Palestine the capacity of the government to contain communal violence was limited by the fact that the majority of the police were Muslims or Jews. The Palestine Defence Scheme in 1920 stated: 'In the case of universal internal trouble, the 3000 police must be reckoned with as a potential hostile factor.'[51] The behaviour of Arab policemen in the disturbances of the 1920s, as we have seen, certainly lent substance to this reckoning. The government was, however, anxious not to rely only on Jewish forces in communal conflicts, fearing that this might further provoke Arabs. Hence the disarming of Jewish soldiers in 1921 in Jaffa. In 1929 the government had at its disposal only 292 British policemen in the whole of Palestine.[52] The armed forces other than the police were almost non-existent. As soon as the riots broke out, therefore, the government hastily enrolled as special constables a party of fifty theology students from Oxford who happened to be on a pilgrimage to Jerusalem. A further seventy government officials were enrolled, and these included a number of English Jews in government service. The cry immediately went up that the government was arming the Jews. On government insistence, the Mufti of Jerusalem and other Muslim leaders issued a statement declaring the rumour false: nevertheless it persisted. The acting high commissioner, H. C. Luke, reluctantly decided to demobilize the Anglo-Jewish special constables, although his decision aroused considerable Jewish indignation. Luke described the decision as 'very unpleasant, distasteful' and 'one of the most painful and difficult decisions, if not the most painful and difficult, I have ever had to take in my service'.[53] Luke's uneasiness may be readily understood, since he himself was rumoured (correctly) to be of what was termed 'Hebraic blood'.[54] Such actions by the government had the perhaps inevitable effect of stimulating the creation by the Jews of their own underground military force, the Haganah, which first saw action in the riots of the 1920s.

6. CHARACTER AND SIGNIFICANCE OF THE RIOTS

Three tentative conclusions suggest themselves. First, one is struck, in the case of the crowd in Palestine as elsewhere, by its overwhelming traditionalism.[55] This was accentuated by the fact that the ostensible issue of dispute was so often conflict over rights in holy places. In such disputes, in Palestine tradition, lay the beginning and the end of the debate. It was by tradition that rights accrued in all matters relating to holy places. Hence the elaborate efforts of the Jewish Agency in 1929 to prove to the Shaw Commission that the Jews had traditionally brought screens and chairs to the Western Wall in the Ottoman period. Such proof, if accepted, would of itself have strengthened immeasurably their claim to be allowed to continue these practices under the British. Conversely the Muslim crowd was concerned, above all, to vindicate the tradition of Jerusalem as the site of the first *Qibla* (the direction in which Muslims turn to pray, now that of Mecca), and the place of Muhammad's miraculous ascent to the seventh heaven after his night-time flight from Mecca on the winged steed al-Buraq. The Jewish tradition that the *Shekhinah*, or spirit of God, hovered especially around the last few standing stones of the Temple was of no less importance. Traditionalism often magnified or distorted existing tradition in order to suit current political needs. The ascription to Jerusalem of the passage in the Koran describing Muhammad's ascent is dubious, and probably dates only from the Caliphate of 'Abd al-Malik bin Marwan (685–87), who, being engaged in conflict with a rival caliph installed at Mecca, 'avait grand besoin d'un texte sacré qui affirmât la supériorité du sanctuaire de Jérusalem', as one historian has put it.[56] Little had, in fact, been heard before the 1920s of the particular holiness to Muslims of the

Western Wall area; yet the sanctity in Islamic tradition of the 'stable of Buraq' became an article of faith when the Jews began to assert new 'traditional' rights there.

Secondly, behind this exaggerated traditionalism may be detected on the one hand attempts to redefine the balance of communal power and status, on the other reaction against such redefinition.[57] In the 1830s and 1850s, Muslim riots against Christians and Jews expressed defiance of attempts by the Egyptian and Ottoman governments of Palestine to redefine the status of these traditionally second-class citizens. In nineteenth-century Palestine the Jews were traditionally the most despised element in the population, not fit to walk on the same pavement or wear the same clothes as the Muslims. Unlike Jewish communities in other parts of the Ottoman Empire, the Jews of Palestine had no notable class to protect them. They were known to subsist primarily on charitable doles from abroad. Suddenly, in the early twentieth century their status and power were transformed. The country was conquered by a Christian power with the avowed object of establishing a Jewish National Home. Large-scale Jewish immigration and land purchase began. The Jews began to establish their own institutions of communal self-government with the recognition of the authorities. The numerical balance of the population began to change. In 1920 a Jewish high commissioner was appointed as head of the government of Palestine. Riots represented an attempt to restore the communal 'balance' of Ottoman times.

Thirdly, the concept of riot as a form of political bargaining may well be applicable here. Just as the food riot was a form of bargaining in early nineteenth-century England, perhaps the only 'means by which normally inarticulate sections of the population served notice of grievances to the authorities',[58] so it may be suggested that the communal riot in Palestine in the 1920s was a form of political bargaining designed to counter the Zionist attempt to redefine the traditional Jewish position in Palestine. That the government of Palestine tended to regard the riots much in this light is apparent from the official response to the troubles, especially in 1921 and 1929. In 1921 the civil secretary, Wyndham Deedes, hurried down from Jerusalem to the *Nebi Saleh* pilgrimage shrine shortly after the outbreak in Jaffa and secured an agreement with the leading notables among the pilgrims whereby they would prevent further outbreaks; they were given to understand that Jewish immigration would be temporarily halted; no public announcement, however, was made to this effect. The riots continued; on 14 May the town crier in Ramleh announced that immigration had been suspended; the riots stopped. In 1921 the riots did not spread to Jerusalem; in effect, this can be seen as the result of a bargain between the high commissioner and the former nationalist politician Haj Amin al-Husseini, whereby the latter was appointed Mufti of Jerusalem in return for his assurances (given to Sir Herbert Samuel on 11 April, three weeks before the riots in the rest of Palestine) 'that the influence of his family and himself would be devoted to maintaining tranquillity in Jerusalem, and he felt sure that no disturbances need be feared this year.'[59]

Seen in this perspective, communal riots may be regarded as a traditional form of political mobilization utilized for new purposes. The political enemy might be Zionism; but the immediate victims of attack in the riots of April 1920 in Jerusalem and August 1929 in Hebron were non-Zionist Orthodox Jews resident in the ancient Jewish quarters of these holy cities. The riots of the 1920s conformed to the traditional character of religious riot; they were preceded by the characteristic pattern of rumour, music and processions; they spread according to the customary geographical pattern; the participants were familiar faces in the communal crowd; the role (both perceived and actual) of the authorities was unchanged, even though the rulers were now British rather than Turks. A broad comparative survey lies beyond the scope of this discussion, but those acquainted with patterns of communal and sectarian violence between Protestants and Catholics in early modern Europe and in modern Ireland, or between Hindus and Muslims in modern India, may find that these features ring some familiar bells.[60]

NOTES

1. Cf. R. C. Cobb, *The Police and the People: French Popular Protest 1789–1820* (Oxford, 1970), p. 20: 'The calendar of violence and riot [is] almost as fixed as that of the saints. To the general eighteenth-century pattern of May to September, Sundays and Mondays, feast days, hot days, the Revolution adds the anniversaries of revolutionary *journées,* or of counter-revolutionary atrocities.'
2. Evidence of Muhammad Kamil al-Husseini, Mufti of Jerusalem, to the Commission of Inquiry into the Jerusalem riots, *Palestine Weekly,* 25 June 1920.
3. J. Finn, *Stirring Times* (London, 1878), vol. 1, p. 107.
4. *Ibid.,* p. 203.
5. H. Bentwich, *If I Forget Thee: Some Chapters of Autobiography 1912–1920* (London, 1973), p. 20.
6. R. Storrs, *Orientations* (London, 1943), p. 304.
7. *Palestine. Disturbances in May 1921. Reports of the Commission of Inquiry with Correspondence Relating Thereto* (Haycraft Commission), Cmd. 1540 (London, 1921), p. 41.

8. *Palestine. Commission on the Disturbances of August 1929: Minutes of Evidence* (Shaw Commission), Colonial no. 48 (London, 1930), 3 vols.

9. N. J. Smelser, *Theory of Collective Behaviour* (London, 1962), p. 247.

10. A. L. Tibawi, *British Interests in Palestine 1800–1901* (London, 1961), p. 116.

11. A. M. Hyamson, *The British Consulate in Jerusalem in Relation to the Jews of Palestine, 1838–1914* (London, 1939), vol. 1, p. 61.

12. Report dated 1 January 1920, no. 117, Central Zionist Archives, Jerusalem, (CZA), L4/276 III.

13. Report dated 16 March 1920, Jerusalem, CZA L4/276 Ia.

14. Zionist intelligence report, 20 March 1920, Jaffa, CZA Z4/3886 1.

15. Report to Zionist Commission by Alex Aaronsohn, 28 March 1920, CZA L4/276 IIb; Dr. IIb; Dr Sonne to L. J. Stein, Jerusalem, 30 March 1920, CZA Z4/16084/55.

16. 'Extract from a private letter from a reliable source', Jerusalem, 30 March 1920, CZA L3/27; Note by Colonel Storrs, 31 March 1920, CZA Z4/16078/66.

17. Report of Commission of Inquiry into 1920 Jerusalem riots (Palin Commission), Port Said, 1 July 1920, Public Record Office (PRO) FO 371/5121/83 & ff.

18. Haycraft Commission (note 7 above), pp. 7–11.

19. *Al-Jami'a al-Arabiyya*, 11 February and 15 August 1929; *Al-Yarmuk*, 18 January 1929.

20. *Davar* and *Ha-Aretz*, 22 and 23 August 1929.

21. Storrs (note 6 above), pp. 329–30.

22. Shaw Commission *Minutes* (note 8 above), *passim*.

23. Palin Commission (note 17 above), pp. 83ff.; Frances Newton, *Fifty Years in Palestine* (London, 1948), p. 133.

24. Shaw Commission *Minutes* (note 8 above), *passim*.

25. Storrs (note 6 above), p. 304.

26. Haycraft Commission (note 7 above), pp. 7–10.

27. G. Le Bon, *The Crowd: A Study of the Popular Mind* (London, 1947), pp. 155ff.

28. Cf. the 1915 riots in Ceylon which consisted almost entirely of affrays between Buddhists and Muslims; members of other communities, Tamils, 'Burghers' (of Portuguese origin) and Sinhalese Christians, largely stood aloof. See C. S. Backton, 'The Action Phase of the 1915 Ceylon Riots', *Journal of Asian Studies*, vol. 29 (1969–70), no. 2, pp. 235–54.

29. Shaw Commission (note 8 above), vol. 1, p. 42.

30. Y. Porath, *The Emergence of the Palestinian Arab National Movement 1918–1929* (London, 1974), esp. pp. 293–303.

31. Storrs to Occupied Enemy Territory Administration Headquarters, 4 November 1918, PRO FO 371/3385/424.

32. H. B. Samuel, 'The Palestine Government', *Fortnightly Review*, August 1921, p. 272.

33. Storrs to Chief Secretary, Government of Palestine, 16 March 1923, Israel State Archives (ISA) 2/169.

34. Omar Bittar, acting president of Executive Committee of Fifth Palestine Arab Congress, to high commissioner for Palestine, 15 March 1923, *ibid.*

35. Palin Commission (note 17 above), pp. 181ff.; Meinertzhagen to Foreign Office, 13 April 1920, PRO FO 371/5117/126.

36. Note of telephone conversation between military governor of Jaffa and G. S. R. I., 3rd Division, Ber Salem, 9 April 1920, Tolkowsky Papers, CZA A/248/1/6.

37. Haycraft Commission (note 7 above), pp. 14, 26.

38. *Ibid.*; report by Colonel Byron, 14 May 1921, PRO CO 733/13/99.

39. Report by Constable R. Cafferata on events at Hebron, 24 August 1929, Shaw Commission (note 8 above), vol. 2, p. 983.

40. In communal riots in India in 1906 one witness reported: 'Priestly mullahs went

through the country preaching the revival of Islam, and proclaiming that the British Government was on the Mohammedan side, that the law courts had been specially suspended for six months, and no penalty would be enacted for violence done to Hindus or for the loot of Hindu shops, or for the abduction of Hindu widows.' Ram Gopal, *Indian Muslims: A Political History, 1858–1947* (Bombay, 1959), pp. 93–5.

41. Moshe Ma'oz, *Ottoman Reform in Syria and Palestine, 1840–1861* (Oxford, 1968), p. 18. See also A. J. Rustum, *The Royal Archives of Egypt and the Disturbances in Palestine, 1834* (Beirut, 1938).

42. H. Newbolt to Lord Aberdeen, 5 March 1846, in Hyamson (note 11 above), vol. 1, p. 86.

43. H. Newbolt to Sir Stratford Canning, 25 March 1846; *ibid.*, p. 87.

44. Mehemed Pasha to Newbolt, 4 March 1846; *ibid.*, p. 90.

45. Article in *Kuntres*, April 1920, printed in I. Ben-Zvi, *The Hebrew Battalions* (Jerusalem, 1969), p. 242.

46. *Manchester Guardian*, 26 April 1920.

47. R. Meinertzhagen, *Middle East Diary 1917–1956* (London, 1959), p. 82, entry dated 26 April 1920.

48. *Suria al-Janubiyya*, 26 February 1920. I am grateful to Mr. Musa Budeiri for showing me a rare copy of this newspaper which is in his possession.

49. See Porath (note 30 above), p. 99.

50. 'Statement Concerning Recent Incidents at the *Buraq*', CZA S25/2948.

51. Quoted in Palin Commission (note 17 above).

52. 'Establishment of the Palestine Police, 1929', report by A. Saunders, ISA 65/01940.

53. Shaw Commission (note 8 above), vol. 1, pp. 273, 314.

54. Colonial Office minutes, PRO CO 733/60/117ff.

55. Cf. 'What *is* the distinctive feature of the "pre-industrial" crowd is, I believe, its attachment to the traditional ways (or the believed traditional ways) of the old village community or urban craft—and its violent reaction to the sort of changes promoted in the name of "progress" by governments, capitalists, corn-merchants, speculative landlords or city authorities. So we find the constant and continuous presentation of demands for the "restoration" of "lost" rights, such as the "just wage", and the "just price." ' George Rudé, 'The "Pre-Industrial" Crowd', in *Paris and London in the Eighteenth Century: Studies in Popular Protest* (London, 1970), pp. 22–3.

56. M. Gaudefroy-Demombynes, *Mahomet* (Paris, 1969), p. 93.

57. Cf. 'Violence is more likely to occur when the minority group is not content to accept the assignment of low rank from the so-called majority group, and when it attempts a redefinition of the situation which will bring about assimilation or at least equal status without assimilation. This means that a redistribution of power and of opportunities is to be effected. This struggle will bring forth the opposition of the superordinate group. H. Otto Dahlke, 'Race and Minority Riots—A Study in the Typology of Violence', *Social Forces*, vol. 30, no. 4 (1951–2), pp. 419–25.

58. J. Stevenson, Introduction to Stevenson and R. Quinault (eds.), *Popular Protest and Public Order* (London, 1974), p. 26.

59. Note by Sir Herbert Samuel, 11 April 1921, ISA 2/245.

60. See e.g. N. Zemon Davis, 'The Rites of Violence', in *Society and Culture in Early Modern France* (Stanford, 1975), pp. 152–87; S. E. Baker, 'Orange and Green Belfast, 1832–1912', in H. J. Dyos and M. Wolff, *The Victorian City: Images and Realities* (London, 1973), vol. 2, pp. 789–814; K. W. Jones, 'Communalism in the Punjab: The Arya Samaj Contribution', *Journal of Asian Studies*, vol. 28, no. 1 (1968–9), pp. 39–54.

27.

The Anglo-American Committee of Inquiry on Palestine (1945–1946): The Zionist Reaction Reconsidered

Joseph Heller

The end of the Second World War found the Zionists at a cross-roads. On the one hand, they were faced with the shattering consequences of the Holocaust which extinguished their hopes for preparing a Jewish state for the great reservoir of Eastern European Jewry. In addition to that, the Damoclean sword of the 1939 White Paper was still hanging over their heads with its ominous articles concerning limited immigration and the establishment of a Palestinian Arab state. On the other hand, the Holocaust was their best justification for Zionism, being the best proof that if anti-Semitism could reach such catastrophic proportions, the Jews could no longer rely upon the Gentiles, but must enhance their efforts to bring about a Jewish state.

A clash therefore between Britain and the Zionist movement, who only a decade before were on the best of terms (enabling the Zionists to increase their numbers in Palestine up to 554,000 by 1945), was just around the corner. No matter which government was in power in England, Labour or Conservative, the clash was bound to come, since now the Zionists were neither prepared to agree to the 1,500 monthly limit for immigrants fixed by the White Paper, nor were they ready to wait for another delay in fulfilment of their long-drawn dream of a Jewish state. Most important of all, they could now rely not only on themselves as in the past, but on the assistance of the great mass of American

By permission of the author and Frank Cass Publishers from *Zionism and Arabism in Palestine and Israel,* edited by Elie Kedourie and Sylvia G. Haim (London: Frank Cass Publishers, 1982), 137–70.

Jewry, and on the thousands of remnants of Jewish refugees which they succeeded in concentrating in the American zones of occupation in Germany, Austria and Italy.

However, if for the first time in the history of Palestine, a British government decided to call on the United States government to assist it in finding a solution to the long-festering Jewish and Palestinian issues, it was not because of Zionist pressure, least of all from the United States. Rather, it was a decision influenced by the considerably weakened position in which Britain found herself as a result of the war. Her overall weakness, especially in economic and financial matters, which endangered her political and strategic status both as an empire and as a world power, necessitated American support more than ever before in British peace-time history.

Zionists have generally seen the Anglo-American Committee of Inquiry as an intended hindrance to them. Weizmann, Shertok and Eban saw British procrastination as an attempt to get British support against them.

Indeed, the very failure to implement its recommendations, specifically the British refusal to permit the entry of 100,000 refugees, according to Eban, enabled the Zionists to keep their strongest and vital card, and Bevin became Israel's George III.[1]

Britain's motive, it was alleged, was clear, according to Yigal Allon, then Commander of the Haganah shock troops, the Palmach. Faced with the Yishuv's struggle in Palestine, supported by world Jewry, Britain was forced to look to Washington for help.[2]

Even more uncompromising, Menachem Begin, Commander of the Irgun, saw the Committee as redundant from the start. Bevin's attitude, in any case, had made him, according to the Stern Group, 'our agent meriting a statue in his memory'. Had Bevin in fact accepted the proposals of the Committee it would have dealt a greater blow against the underground than any number of arrests and executions.[3]

Was this image justified? I shall attempt to show that the Committee's record as a complete and utter failure was an exaggerated one, because Zionists overestimated the American identification with Bevin's policies, and ignored Washington's sympathy for their own ideas. They too easily assumed that Truman, by collaborating in the Joint Committee, had fallen into Bevin's trap.

Their attitude had already hardened before the public announcement of the Committee on 13 November 1945. The Zionist leadership had reason to believe that the British had made up their minds against free immigration and a Jewish state. David Ben-Gurion, Chairman of the Jewish Agency Executive, and Moshe Sneh, Head of the Haganah National Command, therefore agreed to co-operate with the Irgun and the Freedom Fighters of Israel (the Sternists), the first act of joint resistance being the blowing up of 153 bridges on 1 November 1945.[4] Thus by 13 November, the official establishment of the Committee, the Zionists were already in a militant state.

Here, by contrast, it might be worth mentioning that the Arabs, and in particular the Palestine Arabs, initially opposed the Committee because of the participation of the Americans and because of Truman's pro-Zionist statement. But they eventually gave evidence for tactical reasons rather than out of any spirit of compromise.[5]

Zionist misunderstanding can now be seen more clearly in the light of the British and American Archives, and more emphasis might now be put on Arab attitudes than was done at the time.

The central questions, then, are: Why was Britain so keen on a joint Committee, instead of a purely British one, for example, on the lines of the Peel Commission of 1937? Why did the Americans want to get involved, albeit in co-operation with a friendly power, in an area not particularly in their sphere of influence, when there was such a fundamental difference between them on the Jewish and Palestine questions?

It now seems clear that although differences could not be ignored or underestimated, the need to find some solution was urgent enough to overcome the gulf separating the two powers. Furthermore, in the aftermath of the Second World War, Britain felt too weak to deal with the Middle East by herself.

As in other issues, Truman seemed to cut through Roosevelt's ambiguity. Writing to Churchill and Attlee in July and August he was prompted by the Earl G. Harrison mission to examine the conditions of Jewish refugees in occupied Germany. Harrison's findings were influenced by Zionist officials, and he condemned the American military authorities for the appalling conditions of the recently liberated refugees and recommended their immediate transfer to Palestine.[6] Truman's motive for supporting this had doubtlessly been humanitarian rather than political, but it nonetheless associated him with the Zionists' viewpoint. Yet clearly, though Truman favoured the immediate entry of 100,000 Jews, he did not go so far as to consent to the establishment of a Jewish state. Since 1938, and with the exception of the Cabinet partition proposal of 1943–44, this had in any case been unthinkable from the British point of view; Bevin had done little but accept the foreign policy establishment consensus that Zionism, if it won the day, would set the whole Middle East and India on fire. But by establishing the Joint Committee he surprised, (even enraged), his subordinates in London and the Middle East, since they were convinced, like the Arabs, that the Americans were entirely pro-Zionist, and therefore no valuable contribution could be made by them to the solution of the Palestine problem. Bevin on the other hand was confident that the Americans, once they shared responsibility through the Committee, could come round to accept the British point of view. But a few days later he expressed the fear that Zionist propaganda in New York had destroyed what a few weeks before had looked to him as a reasonable atmosphere in which Britain could get Jews and Arabs together. In many ways the idea of the Committee for Bevin was only a prelude to an Arab-Jewish-British Conference on Palestine. In a letter to Halifax he accused the Americans of being 'thoroughly dishonest' and added: 'To play on racial feelings for the purpose of winning an election is to make a farce of their insistence on free election in other countries'.[7]

Bevin himself first brought up the idea of a Joint Committee in the Cabinet meeting of 4 October 1945. Halifax, formerly Foreign Secretary, and then Ambassador to Washington, was worried about the effect of Zionist pressure, particularly important because of the Jewish vote, manifested in widespread support in Congress, and as James F. Byrnes admitted, in view of the impending election for the Mayor of New York. Failing the immediate possibility of United Nations intervention, and of United States reluctance to take responsibility solely on herself, the best alternative was to persuade her to share it with Britain.

All this was in the background of the possible collapse of British policy. The pressure was particularly acute because of the deteriorating condition of the Jewish refugees, the eruption of hostilities in Palestine, and the uncertainty caused by the changeover from the Mandate system to a Trusteeship of an entirely new kind.

Britain, lacking confidence in herself at this crucial juncture for Palestine, turned to the United States for help. Nonetheless, Bevin had come to accept that the Joint Committee should examine the plight of Jewish refugees in Europe and indeed consider how many of them should go to Palestine, or elsewhere.[8]

The most forceful criticism of the plan came from the Colonial Office, less influenced by American considerations, but Bevin indeed had the final say.[9]

Yet, whilst Britain hoped to draw the United States through the Committee into shared responsibility, Washington's idea was merely to influence Britain in favour of Zionism. The British had seriously underestimated Truman's commitment in this direction, relying too much on the line of continuity from Roosevelt's caution, and saw the role of the Committee as correcting the 'improper' conclusions of Harrison's report.

For the Americans, Palestine had to be the focus as the main target for the rehabilitation of Jewish refugees, or there would be no Joint Committee at all. Attlee finally accepted this in his meeting with Truman, seeing it as a tactical compromise rather than a major concession, since actual participation in the Committee would force the Americans to realize that there was an Arab side as well as a Jewish one.[10]

The Zionists also misinterpreted Truman's attitude and both Silver, Wise and Weizmann in America and Ben-Gurion in Palestine took their cue from Bevin. For them the Committee could never be neutral.[11]

Belief in such neutrality could be found only amongst the moderates of Aliya Hadasha and Ichud, and the ultra-orthodox of Agudat Israel. Nonetheless, the Zionists would have to face the question of their political attitude to the Committee.

The members of the Committee, six British and six American, announced on 10 December 1945, were, with co-chairmen from both groups: Sir John Singleton, a High Court Judge, co-chairman; W. F. Crick, Adviser to the Midland Bank; R. H. S. Crossman, then an activist left-wing Labour back-bencher; Sir Frederic Leggett, previously Bevin's Deputy Under-Secretary at the Ministry of Labour during the war; R. E. Manningham-Buller, a back-bench Conservative M. P.; and Lord Morrison, a Labour peer. The American members included the co-chairman Judge Joseph C. Hutcheson of the Texas High Court; Frank Aydelotte, Professor of History at Princeton; Frank W. Buxton, editor of the *Boston Herald;* Bartley Crum, a Democratic Senator, James G. MacDonald, formerly League of Nations High Commissioner for Refugees, and the former American Ambassador to India, William Phillips.[12]

The Jewish Agency Executive could not at first agree on whether to give evidence to the Committee. Abba Hillel Silver, the prominent American Zionist leader, together with Moshe Sneh, became the most implacable opponents. Ben-Gurion suggested that bodies outside the Agency rather than the Agency itself might give evidence. Only one member of the Agency Executive, Werner D. Senator, a member of Ichud and representative of the non-Zionists, was unhesitatingly in favour of giving evidence.[13]

But, argued Nahum Goldmann, supported by Moshe Shertok, America's participation was a real factor which might prove to be crucial for Zionism. Shertok emphasized that Zionism ought not to boycott it because the Committee was to be the focus of the diplomatic campaign on Palestine and the Jewish question. Above all, he did not share the view that Zionism was strong enough to avoid the use of diplomacy. A policy of boycott and violent action without a parallel diplomatic struggle was a luxury which Zionism could ill afford, unlike the Arabs or the Indians. Zionism was still in its transitory period, in the midst of the process of the gathering-in of the exiles and the reconstruction of the Jewish people. It should therefore try and win the sympathy of the Committee. Furthermore, Zionism was facing a severe struggle in view of the new British, indeed United Nations, policy to replace the Mandate by a Trusteeship which would eliminate Zionism as a political force.[14]

Though not sharing Sneh's position of complete rejection of the Committee, Ben-Gurion believed that if the Jewish Agency was right in its assumption that Zionism would be defeated by the Committee then it was better to boycott it. His main fear was that the Committee would sanction the abolition of the Mandate with its Zionist articles. He was also worried because, whilst the Arabs were united, the Jews were divided into Zionists, non-Zionists and anti-Zionists.

However, Ben-Gurion's line was already defeated in his own party by a large majority (16:2) on 10 December. Two days later the Zionist Small Action Committee voted. Unlike the undecided vote of the Executive, the vote was clear-cut: sixteen in favour of appearance and eleven against.[15]

Little did the Zionists know that the Committee's future was in jeopardy in view of the mounting violence in Palestine. Luckily, the Cabinet subordinated its law and order measures to its attempts to win over American support for its Palestine policy through the Committee.[16] Consequently, plans for general search for arms had to be delayed until the Committee had completed its work, otherwise power would have been thrown into the hands of the extremists.

The Zionist protest against the Committee began in America, when after protest from the British members, the work of the Committee was begun. Wise and Silver, the foremost American Zionist leaders, had already condemned it on 30 October and after Bevin's announcement it was again denounced by the great majority of the American Zionist Emergency Council (AZEC).[17]

After a debate as to where its work should start from, the Committee began its hearings on 7 January 1946 in Washington. The Zionists, like their Arab opponents, were given full opportunity to present their case. Earl G. Harrison and Joseph Schwartz, the Director of the Joint Distribution Committee in Europe, gave 'excellent' reports from the Zionist viewpoint, both emphasizing the critical situation of the refugees. Reinhold Niebuhr, the famous theologian, gave the 'best' analysis of the Zionist idea. Economic experts such as Walter Lowdermilk explained how the absorptive capacity of Palestine could be increased from 100,000 acres to 750,000 at the cost of 200 million dollars. Others like Robert Nathan and Oscar Gass pointed out that Palestine could absorb another 600,000 to 1,200,000 people.[18]

On the whole the Zionists were not worried by the presentation of the Arab case or by anti-Zionist Jews. Of the pro-Arab witnesses Frank Notestein alone caused the Zionists some anxiety. Notestein, Professor of Demography at Princeton, refuted Nathan's claim that a Jewish majority in Palestine was feasible by 1950. Notestein argued that the Jews would never be able to obtain a majority and that the country would not be able to feed a large population. The 'territorialist' I. N. Steinberg argued in favour of settling the Jews in Australia instead of Palestine, and confused the Committee, as did Peter Bergson of the Committee for the Freedom of the Nation, with his idea of a Hebrew Nation as distinct from the Jewish one. Lessing Rosenwald, of the notoriously anti-Zionist American Council for Judaism, seemed ineffective.[19]

The proceedings in Washington gave encouragement to the Zionists. Of the six Americans, three, Buxton, Crum and MacDonald seemed fervently pro-Zionist, whilst amongst the British Crossman looked promising. His enthusiasm was generated by Zionists like David Horowitz, of the Agency's Political Department, who could conjure up for him the image of the resistance fighters of Europe.[20]

Such was the tide of optimism after these initial proceedings that Silver, who had just refused to appear before the Committee to leave himself room for manoeuvre, should it prove inimical to Zionism, now changed his mind. In the view of the British observers, however, it was the strength of the Arab case that had really been established.[21]

At this juncture a major shift in the Zionist position took place, originating from the Agency's representative in Washington, Eliahu Epstein (later Elath). He suggested to Shertok that partition of Western

Palestine be substituted for the Biltmore plan which had claimed the entire area. They had more chance of becoming a majority in a partitioned state, as the Jews constituted only one-third of the population and, although the Americans (and certainly the British) would not yet countenance a Jewish state, yet they might favour immigration and settlement in the area.[22]

Epstein's dramatic shift was made with regard to key changes in the attitudes and relationships of the great powers. The Zionists would have to move quickly, as hostility between the United States and the Soviet Union was growing, and Russia might now halt the flow of Jewish immigrants, making it even less likely that the Jews would achieve a majority in Palestine. The case might be argued however for a partitioned State. Britain for her part might be seduced by the new Jewish state offering her military bases as she had in Transjordan.

It is not yet clear whether Epstein was the first to suggest partition or whether it was Goldmann's or Shertok's idea. It certainly was favoured by Weizmann and even Ben-Gurion, though in secret. They envisaged the Jewish share as the area allotted to the Jews by the Peel Commission minus the Arab triangle, but with the addition of the Negev. Less than this would be tantamount to political suicide.[23] It was not however until the Black Sabbath on 29 June 1946 and the King David Hotel incident that the Jewish Agency was officially to accept the partition plan.

The London hearings of the Committee began on 25 January 1946, again with none of the Zionist witnesses appearing in the name of the Jewish Agency.

The general policy amongst the Zionists was that the hearings did not advance the Zionist cause. The only substantial witness in their favour seemed to be Leo Amery, a life-long Zionist, who had held the Secretaryship of State for India, amongst other Cabinet posts. He suggested partition with the Peel area, without the Western Galilee but with the Negev. The former Zionist and High Commissioner Viscount Samuel, and Leonard Stein, President of the Anglo-Jewish Association, both opposed a Jewish State. Bevin himself was particularly impressed by the Arab viewpoint as put forward by General Edward Spears and he dismissed Smuts' mention of the Balfour Declaration. 'It was a unilateral declaration and did not take into account the Arabs. It was really a power politics declaration.'[24]

Nor did the proceedings appear to have influenced the members of the Committee in the Zionists' favour. Even the pro-Zionist members favoured only political autonomy with Jewish control of immigration and economic union with Lebanon, Syria, and Transjordan. Crossman particularly was in a 'confused and exasperated' state. He felt the Zionists had made a 'serious tactical mistake' in pushing for a Jewish state: first with their attempt to create a Jewish rather than an Arab majority, and second because of the double loyalty problems which a Jewish state might engender for the Diaspora Jews and because of the impetus the establishment of the state would give to anti-Semitism.

The Zionists thought the Committee would be swayed by the visit to Palestine. Yet Weizmann, even if he could see the Committee recommending partition, remained pessimistic: 'HMG will say they need six Divisions to carry that through and will ask the USA to send some. USA will refuse and HMG will be delighted for excuse to do nothing, and the Yishuv will then lose patience.' This prediction, which proved almost correct, left Weizmann 'very gloomy and bitter'. A few days later he wrote: 'I really don't know what to expect of them [the Committee], the best is to expect nothing.'[25]

Before the Committee visited the Middle East, it was due to investigate the conditions of the Jewish refugees in Europe. The members eventually visited Germany, Austria, Italy, Switzerland and Greece, but the Russians only allowed them into Poland and Czechoslovakia.

Independent investigations by the United Nations Relief and Rehabilitation Administration (UNRRA) and the American army made it clear that many camp dwellers wished to emigrate to Palestine, although attempts by the Jewish Agency such as the despatch of Gideon Ruffer (later Rafael) to ensure Zionist loyalty, had the effect opposite to that intended on some of the Committee members, and indeed encouraged the British to emphasize the evidence to the contrary.

When members of the Committee did in fact see the camps, as was the case with Leggett and Crum in Germany, they were appalled, and suggested the emigration of 200,000 over the next few years. For his pains Crum was rebuked by Singleton and threatened resignation.[26]

But to the Jewish Agency too few of the camps had been seen by too few of the members of the Committee, and suspecting British intervention, they got Judge Simon Rifkind, Eisenhower's advisor for Jewish affairs, to demand immediate evacuation of the camps and the transfer of their occupants to Palestine, a demand rejected by the Committee. It would doubtless recommend a transfer of the whole problem to the United Nations, where Zionism would get a first-class burial.[27] Yet, although the Zionists thought that the full impact of the camps had not really been felt, there was support from Crossman and Leggett and Hutcheson for Crum's evacuation plan.

The crucial argument however was bound to take place in Palestine. Shertok had to defend the Agency's case before the Elected Assembly of the Yishuv on 13 February 1946. The Agency itself would still not appear before the Committee, nonetheless individuals and groups had to present some sort of evidence. It was true that the grant of independence to Transjordan at a time when the Jewish nation was treated like a beggar was a 'serious blow' but despite the Arabs the 1,500 monthly quota had been renewed, and the United States was now directly involved.[28]

Shertok was able to hint at partition, but he was not yet able to make a clear statement in favour of it, so undivided Palestine (according to the Biltmore Resolution of 1942) still had to be the basis of the united Zionist front that he insisted should be presented to the Committee. Both Aliya Hadasha and Hashomer Hatzair refused to comply.[29]

Ben-Gurion had meanwhile been making some rapid tactical adjustments in his position because of his perception of an increasingly anti-Jewish Soviet attitude. He argued that the claim for a Jewish State and the demand that the Powers proclaim it should now be dropped, and that the Executive should press the Committee for: (a) the immigration of a million Jews in the minimum of time and with the assistance of the Great Powers; (b) the granting to the Jewish Agency of control over immigration, settlement and development. These two conditions were bound to bring about a Jewish majority and a Jewish State.

Shertok could not see how they could get one million immigrants to come to Palestine within the next two years. Five to ten years was a more realistic time span, for unlike the Greeks in 1922 the Jews were not faced with the desperate dilemma of massacre or flight. In any case 200,000 rather than two million was the likely number of potential immigrants, for he doubted whether the oriental Jews would be willing to come. Playing the numbers game was unsavoury to Ben-Gurion and his group of 'idealists' (Sneh, Fishman, Schmorak, and Joseph). For them the Bible was a surer guide to the righteousness of their cause, although even Ben-Gurion had to take tactical considerations into account. He saw the first million as a political rather than a statistical concept. His real fear was that Iraq and Russia would not let the Jews out, an anxiety not lessened by the Soviet attempt to propagate the Birobidjan Jewish autonomous region.[30]

The Russian hostility to Zionism was detected by a British observer, who saw Russia posing as the great Moslem power, supporting a United Nations rather than a British solution to the Palestine question. In any case they claimed there was no Jewish problem in areas under their influence. Hence their rejection of the Committee's request to examine the condition of the Jews in Hungary, in Rumania, and in Bulgaria.[31]

Much as they might welcome the visit of the Committee to Palestine, consideration by the Committee of the views of the Jewish communities in the rest of the Arab Middle East was quite another thing from the Zionist point of view. In the Arab capitals, the Rabbis and the notables, the traditional leaders of the community, in which Zionists were generally a minority, had an awkward time choosing between government and Zionist pressures. Hence, minorities like the Maronites and the Assyrians were often more outspokenly pro-Zionist than the Jews themselves.[32]

Weizmann, the first Zionist leader to give evidence before the Committee in Jerusalem, appeared moderate in his view that the 100,000 could not arrive in such a short span as one year, but to the British authorities in Palestine he had lost much of his authority there. Yet there were others, like Ben-Gurion and Shertok, who suggested partition in camera, and indeed some members of the Committee were presented with a detailed partition map. The Committee however remained unimpressed.[33]

The hearings in Palestine turned, as they had in London and Washington, into a verbal battleground between the Zionists and the Arabs. Neither side appeared to compromise, at least in public. The Zionists claimed that Palestine had already been divided in 1921–22 by cutting off Transjordan. But the Jewish Agency knew all too well that this could not be a sufficient answer. Hence the argument that economically Western Palestine was able to absorb several million Jews without expelling even one single Arab. Furthermore, inside the future Jewish State the Arabs were promised full and equal rights as individuals, followed by an alliance of friendship with the neighbouring Arab States. The Jewish Agency did not recognise the Palestine Arabs as a separate nation. Not unlike the Pan-Arabists, they claimed that the Arabs constituted one nation, who had sufficient territories in the Middle East.

If this was the kind of policy the Zionists adopted towards the Arabs, why, one may ask, did the Jewish Agency make so much of the Arab collaboration with the Axis Powers before and during the Second World

War, or place such emphasis on the tottering and dangerous position of the Jewish minorities in the Arab world? The reply was that this was justified after the murder of more than one hundred Jews in Tripoli in November 1945 and the notorious Baghdad pogrom of 1941, coupled with the similar fate of the Assyrians, Kurds and Maronites. The idea was to impress the Committee that no minority, Jewish or otherwise, and least of all Palestine Jewry, could live under any Arab regime.[34]

Indeed, the Arab press was full of indications of uncompromising enmity to Zionism. The Arab leadership in Palestine, and outside, made it quite clear that if a Zionist solution was recommended to the Committee, they would resort to violence and, Auni Abd al-Hadi threatened, with the assistance of the other Arab States. Palestine Jews would do better to give themselves up to the Arab majority, who had no religious or racial enmity towards them. Jamal Husseini, the foremost Palestine Arab leader in the Mufti's absence, did not lag behind Auni's declaration of war. He stated to the Committee that since Britain and America had failed to solve the Palestine problem, it would be better if the British were to evacuate Palestine, to be followed by a military showdown between the Jews and the Arabs. Other Arab politicians of the neighbouring countries, from Feisal of Saudi Arabia to Bourgibah of Tunisia, were not far behind in their threats.

It was only on the surface that the Jewish Agency failed to take the Arab threats seriously. In practice increasing efforts were being made by the Haganah to improve its capability to withstand Arab attack. Although Shertok admitted that the immigration of the 100,000 could lead to bloodshed, Ben-Gurion himself told the Committee that the Jews could look after themselves if assaulted by Palestine Arabs, for conflict was only temporary. Their confidence seemed justified for a number of reasons. The military weakness of the Arab states, not to mention the Palestine Arabs, was well known. The Jewish Agency was convinced that the Arab States had no interest in getting themselves involved in the Palestine question, because this might result in confrontation with Britain and America. Furthermore, Egypt was busy demanding the evacuation of the British Army, its natural interest being in the Sudan and Libya. Iraq was preoccupied fighting the Kurds, and was completely dependent on the British army. Syria and Lebanon had no army at all. Saudi Arabia had no common frontier with Palestine, and being in conflict with Transjordan it was unreasonable to imagine that she could send troops to Palestine.

In short, the Jewish Agency envisaged only a repetition of the 1936–

39 infiltration of 'gangs' from the neighbouring countries. The Palestine Arabs would be unlikely to repeat their former revolt after learning a hard lesson both militarily and economically. The Jews could themselves take care of the small 'gangs', and there was no need for the half-million American soldiers which Truman had mentioned at Potsdam. A few air-force squadrons would be sufficient to watch the borders. Sneh claimed in his memorandum on the Jewish Resistance: 'Never has the dependence of the independent Arab states on Britain, on her favour and assistance, been greater than it is now. The pro-Soviet blackmail of the Arab states must therefore be regarded with suspicion—it is but a new and revised edition of their pro-fascist blackmail in golden age of the Rome-Berlin Axis.'[35]

Once it had proved that Arab military might was imaginary, the Jewish Agency thought it only natural to demand the establishment of a Jewish state through the initiative of the great powers. Both the Jewish question and the Palestine problem were international issues, and had nothing to do with the Arab world. Zionism had been internationally recognized by the Balfour Declaration and the ratification of the Mandate although that had now failed but the Jewish claim for Palestine had existed long before 1917. Above all, the tragic fate of the Jewish people was the most powerful argument for the Jewish state.[36]

Yet, while demonstrating a great deal of self-confidence in its public stance, the Jewish Agency felt considerably disturbed as to what could be expected from the Committee. Shertok called upon the Executive to seriously contemplate the possibility of partition emerging from the Report, whilst Ben-Gurion stressed that Biltmore must be kept as a tactical line. It would be disastrous if the Agency were to initiate a partition plan. Zionism had better prepare itself for the renewal of the Jewish Resistance, since the British government might reject the Committee's proposals.

Contrary to its public arguments, the Zionists were very concerned with Arab opposition because of the growing Arab birth-rate and Arab immigration into Palestine and the mounting difficulties in buying land because of internal Arab terror and the high prices. Ben-Gurion was frightened of sudden changes in the area, especially the possibility that the United Nations might impose a trusteeship on Palestine excluding the Zionist articles of the Mandate (4, 11, 12). This distrust of the United Nations led him to the conclusion that only a state would solve these issues not in ten years ('God forbid') but in two years.

Ben-Gurion however found it difficult to agree to partition without a *quid pro quo,* such as the annexation to the Jewish state of some unoccupied areas of Transjordan in return for the Arab Triangle. In view of the complaint made by some Zionists that the Agency's tactics were confusing, he was ready to suggest this plan as the official Zionist programme.[37] Divided as the Zionists were concerning the right tactics, all were agreed that at this stage this debate was academic, in view of the fact that all the cards were still in the hands of the Committee.

On 26 March the Committee left for Lausanne to compose its final report. At this stage three members out of twelve—Buxton, Crum and MacDonald—could be considered as convinced Zionists, whilst Crossman was still uncertain. In this situation the chances of a Zionist solution were not very great. A suspicion existed in Zionist circles that the Committee might adopt the British intention of outlawing the Jewish Agency and the Haganah as an *imperium in imperio.*[38]

In view of this deep division in the Committee, the Zionists were not agreed whether two reports would be better than one. The moderates preferred one report, believing that a minority Zionist report could have only a demonstrative value. So a special committee, headed by Shertok and Goldmann, went to Switzerland in an attempt to influence the Committee's discussions. They soon realized that the American co-chairman, Judge Hutcheson, who had hitherto doubted whether the Jews were a nation at all, now rejected the Arab solution. Significantly, his visit to Syria and Lebanon had convinced him that Jews could not live under Arab rule. Moreover, he now supported an immigration of 100,000 in 1946, and further immigration to be decided according to the potentialities of the country. He rejected partition because it would create two bi-national states in view of the mixed character of the population. Rather he preferred one bi-national state in an undivided country, probably under Magnes' and Hashomer Hatzair's influence. Legally speaking the Zionists were right and sooner or later they would win. The White Paper was unjust and the Land Laws must be abolished. The Zionists regarded this apparent change of Hutcheson's as a breakthrough in their favour.[39]

Sir John Singleton, the British co-chairman, was amazed that his American colleague had 'betrayed' him. Their relationship worsened a great deal. Singleton was obviously indignant because Hutcheson carried with him the rest of the non-committed American members (Phillips and Aydelotte). Manningham-Buller, who shared Singleton's views, argued that the Balfour Declaration had already been fulfilled and that now an

Arab State must be established in Palestine. Hutcheson replied that Jews should not be submitted to Arab rule. The majority of the British members called for the abolition of the Jewish Agency and the Haganah. Palestine, they added, should be under a United Nations Trusteeship. But now Leggett followed Crossman, and Manningham-Buller's suggestion was defeated. The turning point was so sharp and astonishing that the Zionists were afraid Hutcheson might again change his views. MacDonald telegraphed to the White House to encourage Hutcheson in his new attitude.[40]

Thus by mid-April 1946 the Committee was so divided that there was a danger of its ending up with two or even three reports. Four Americans were against either a Jewish or an Arab State, but in favour of unconditional entry of the 100,000 refugees to Palestine, with a reaffirmation of the Mandate to include further Jewish immigration. Three British members agreed that there should be neither a Jewish nor an Arab state, but that the 100,000 should enter slowly on condition that the illegal armies disband. A third group, consisting of one Englishman and two Americans, Crossman, Crum and Buxton, were in favour of partition, if no unanimity could be achieved.

At this stage, Morrison, Leggett and Crossman were convinced that it would be disastrous if no consensus were achieved. They were adamant in their belief that the entry of the 100,000 should not be made conditional on disbandment of the illegal organizations, since it might weaken Weizmann, strengthen the extremists and enrage American opinion to the extent of enlisting Truman again behind Zionism. They finally managed to gain unity by including 'a full and objective' factual statement about the illegal organizations and by drafting Recommendation No. 10, which was interpreted by Whitehall as implying that the immigration of the 100,000 was conditional on disarmament.

No less objectionable to the British dissenters was Singleton's and Manningham-Buller's claim that Hutcheson's line implied war with the Arabs, unless the United States offered military assistance. To Crossman this seemed an irrelevant factor, being based on expediency rather than on justice. The American members, claimed Crossman, were on guard lest the British try to involve the United States in a military adventure in the Middle East. 'This stress, therefore, on the need for American military assistance aroused their keenest suspicions that the whole Committee had been framed for this express point of view. They argued, not unreasonably, that the Committee's job was to establish facts and to recommend a just solution and that they were not in a position to commit the President to active intervention.' Furthermore, Crossman, writing to Hector McNeil, Parliamentary Under-Secretary for Foreign Affairs, claimed that he did not underrate the Arab point of view, since he and the rest of the Committee favoured the establishment of an Arab self-governing community on the lines of the Jewish community to replace 'the present set of charming degenerates.'

Crossman was sure that the British members made no sacrifice whatsoever of British interests. He felt that the Committee did justice by offering a compromise. Whilst rejecting the pro-Arab policy of the Foreign Office they also disposed of the Jewish claim for a state, pointing to the Jewish failure to face up to the Arab problem, and to Jewish terrorism.[41]

There were other pressures for producing one report. The Montreux-based Zionist committee advised the pro-Zionist members of the Committee to favour one report since otherwise Hutcheson might retreat to his previous position. Both the British and the American governments also recommended one report, apparently after Singleton and Harold Beeley, the British Secretary, had visited London, and Philip Noel-Baker, the Minister of State at the Foreign Office, had visited Lausanne.[42]

Arthur Lourie, a senior Zionist diplomat, could now write from Montreux that Zionism was coming true. Senior American officers responsible for Displaced Persons (D.P.s) had been called from Germany to Lausanne to testify about how long it would take to evacuate the camps. Their reply, which startled the British, was that it could be done in one month. In vain did the British attempt a last minute manoeuvre by demanding that the number of immigrants should be limited by the housing situation, the Zionist Achilles' heel.[43]

At this critical stage, the Zionists attempted a dramatic coup in order to achieve partition. For this purpose they called Weizmann from the cold to intervene with the British government, in order to point out a new opportunity to solve the Palestine question.

The coup had its origins in a sensational report from Eliahu Sasson, the Head of the Arab section in the Agency, claiming that there was little objection to partition on the part of the Arab states provided the Powers would agree. Both King Abdullah and Ali Maher, the Egyptian Prime Minister, had stated that partition was acceptable. For the first time since the appointment of the Committee, Weizmann could see 'a glimmer of light' at the end of the long tunnel. Unfortunately, there was nothing real in the proposal in view of the overwhelming opposition to Zionism in the British establishment and in the Arab states.[44]

Again, at the last minute Singleton tried to make the 100,000 immigration conditional upon the consent of the Arab states, with further
immigration to be decided by the United Nations, but this failed owing
to his complete isolation amongst the British members. Leaking the
Report to the Zionists before its publication, Buxton, Crum and Mac-
Donald told the Zionists that now they had a great opportunity and
advised asking the President for help.[45] Indeed, the great opportunity
was there, but for how long?

Although the Report of the Committee, signed on 20 April 1946 and
formally issued on 30 April, did not try to suggest a new long-term
solution to the Palestine and the Jewish questions, it was bold enough to
make some revolutionary recommendations for short-term policies. The
Committee unlike the Peel Commission of 1937, was unable to reach a
final decision on the constitutional aspect, because of the division
amongst its members. Indeed, the United Nations Special Commission
on Palestine (UNSCOP) was bound to return to the partition idea first
raised by a purely British Commission a decade earlier. The Anglo-
American consensus on Palestine and the Jewish question was too frail
to arrive at a bold decision such as partition.

Yet even the short-term recommendations constituted a major Zionist
victory. However, it is also understandable why the Zionists were basically disappointed. In the post-Holocaust period they lived in a Messianic mood, i.e. unless their solution to the Jewish question was accepted
their opportunity would be lost for ever, as they confessed more than
once. How could they then accept the Committee's Recommendation
No. 1 which said that Palestine could not possibly solve the problem of
the Jewish remnant in Europe?

The Committee had accepted nonetheless that the majority of
the Jewish refugees regarded Palestine as their home. They had then
in Recommendation No. 2 favoured the immediate immigration of
100,000 Jews from Europe, out of 391,000 Jewish refugees.[46]

Again, the Agency found further ground for objection in Recommendation No. 3 that neither a Jewish nor an Arab state should be established and that world peace would be disturbed if any independent state
or states were established. Neither could it digest Recommendation No.
4, that it was necessary to continue the existing Mandate until the end
of the present animosity and a new Trusteeship agreement. Similarly
objectionable was Recommendation No. 5 which stated that the raising
of the standard of living of the Arab community was essential for an

understanding between the two nations. The Jewish Agency believed the conflict was basically a political one. Instead the Committee should have mentioned the economic improvement amongst the Palestine Arabs resulting from Jewish settlement.[47]

Recommendation No. 6 was more acceptable. This stated that until the Palestine question was dealt with at the United Nations the Mandatory Power must ensure Jewish immigration without injuring the Arabs. Recommendation No. 7 suggested that the Land Laws of 1940 should be abrogated but new laws to defend the Arab peasant should be introduced. Was not the Committee following here the British contention that Palestine was overpopulated? As far as the Jewish Agency was concerned this was nothing but a myth, since the country was underdeveloped and a 'physiocratic approach' was unhelpful, and in any case the Jews owned only 7 percent of the country's land. Nor was the Agency very happy when, in Recommendation No. 8 the Committee, though appreciative of the Agency's development plans, stated that these plans were conditional on peace prevailing in the area. This, claimed the Agency, was an invitation to the Arabs to start trouble. How could the Committee possibly come up with such a condition, whilst the Arab states boycotted Jewish industrial production? Neither was Recommendation No. 9 to the Agency's taste, since it condemned the Jewish education system as chauvinistic. The Zionist reply was that the idea behind this proposal was to limit Jewish autonomy in education. Indeed, moderate Zionists like Weizmann and Magnes agreed with the Committee's view on this point.[48]

It is hardly surprising that Ben-Gurion disliked the Report, pressing as he was for a Jewish state. Shertok tried his best to persuade him that Zionism profited ('the wolf was satisfied and the lamb was still alive'). Harry Sacher, a prominent British Zionist and Weizmann's life-long friend, warned that Ben-Gurion's reaction was disastrous, and no better Report could have been anticipated. It would be better to accept the Report and meanwhile delay the Zionist long-term solution. Although he still feared crisis, Ben-Gurion finally admitted that his view was perhaps incorrect, and that it was incumbent upon Zionism to come to an understanding with Britain.

Sneh however, surprised by the Report, viewed it as an Arab defeat, so until the British actually accepted it, and in view of Arab pressure, it constituted a 'great danger'. But Weizmann was satisfied it aided the Zionist campaign whether fulfilled or not. Arab pressures could be countered by American Zionism. Most of the 100,000 could be brought and sheltered within one year, and within five years the Jewish state could materialize.[49]

Sneh's pessimism proved justified with the British rejection of the Report on 1 May 1946. And Britain's attitude to the illegal armies proved harder than expected. Some Zionists thought Attlee had meant only the Irgun and the Sternists, but as Hall indicated to Crossman in a stormy meeting, he regarded the Haganah too as responsible for the terror.[50]

Paradoxically, it has been claimed, the British rejection saved Zionism from the most serious crisis in its history, and 'achieved' greater unity in the Zionist movement. Weizmann, following Crossman, had stated at a meeting of the London Zionist executive before the rejection that it was the time to end the terror and finish off both the Irgun and the Sternists.

Now it was clear that there would have to be a renewal of Jewish Resistance activities with intensified diplomacy, particularly in America. Israel Eldad, the Sternist ideologue, later admitted that it was a great miracle that Bevin saved the Yishuv from civil war.[51]

Attlee's statement threw Weizmann himself into a state of shock: 'I am absolutely bewildered . . . I feel deeply distressed'. A few hours before he had experienced the greatest elation after a year of crisis. If they did not allow the 100,000 to go to Palestine, he warned Attlee, Britain would be confronted with terror.[52]

There was little to be salvaged from Britain. Churchill, now in opposition, persistently evaded the Zionists, proclaiming that the conflict between Jacob and Esau would go on for a very long time, and Tom Williams, the Minister of Agriculture and a former Zionist, justified Attlee's statement when approached. Furthermore, at the Labour Party Conference at Bournemouth on 12 June 1946, Bevin made it clear that if the Report's recommendations were implemented, another division and a further £200 million would be required.[53]

In their despair some Zionists demanded an uncompromising reply to the British questionnaire, but again it was decided it should be diplomatic (16 June 1946). More dramatic was a parallel decision to renew the Jewish Resistance on the lines of 1 November 1945. On 17 June the Palmach destroyed the bridges connecting Palestine with the neighbouring countries. As Shertok explained to his colleagues it was necessary to buttress Zionist diplomatic pressure in America and to save the Committee's Zionist recommendations. Also, the Jewish refugees were packing their bags since the publication of the Report.[54]

Yet tactics and diplomacy triumphed over the sense of anger and despair at least in the American scene, where Goldmann argued they ought to push for the 100,000, and ultimately accept partition rather than Biltmore in order to avoid the ominous Trusteeship. But in the Yishuv as before Zionist differences were reduced to a minimum. The only opponents of diplomacy-cum-resistance were, as anticipated, the minority: Hashomer Hatzair, the leftist bi-nationalists and Aliya Hadasha and Ichud. Yaacov Hazan of Hashomer Hatzair warned that the British were preparing for counter-attack. Shlomo Kaplansky, the Director of the Haifa Technical College, warned that Britain even in decline could still break Palestine Jewry.[55]

How accurate was the Zionist assessment of Britain's policy? We are now in a better position to answer this in the light of the recently opened British official archives. Generally speaking the Zionist perception of British policy was only partially correct. The Zionist assumption that Britain's 'fear' of the Arab reaction to the Report, and the need to follow an 'appeasement' policy, engendered the official rejection of the Report, was correct. But neither was it quite as Crossman presented it: 'Why should HMG make less justice with more divisions when it is possible to make more justice with less divisions?'[56] Whitehall clearly believed the opposite. Although British military intelligence greatly exaggerated the strength of the Haganah, a view recently submitted to the Committee itself by General D'Arcy, G.O.C. Palestine, this led neither D'Arcy nor the Chiefs of Staff to the conclusion that Jewish military potential needed more British divisions than the Arab military nuisance value. British strategists did not wish as yet to give up their bases in Egypt, Iraq's oil or for that matter the oil terminal to Haifa. The crux of the matter was that neither the military nor the political establishment considered Palestine as detached geopolitically from the rest of the Middle East. Given this frame of mind, deeply rooted in Britain's policy-making elite for the preceding decade, the Zionists had only little hope of playing on their own nuisance value.[57]

Moreover, the fact that the Committee did not suggest a Jewish state did not change Britain's unfavourable attitude. For Britain the Commission's support for Jewish immigration was bad enough. After all the Arabs regarded immigration (as indeed did the Zionists) as a stepping-stone for a Jewish state.

It is clear that those moderate Zionists who believed that Britain could be persuaded to change the course of its Palestine policy were entirely wrong. These moderates established their hopes on the pro-

Zionist recommendations of the Committee and on Truman's aid, which they believed would eventually convince Britain. Equally wrong however were the extremist-Zionists, who thought that the British government could be convinced by a show of strength.

In fact the British government itself was greatly surprised by the Report. The majority of the British members of the Committee, with the aid of Harold Beeley, were doing their best to bring the American members over to the British point of view. Just before leaving the country, Beeley had in Jerusalem already expressed some fear that the Committee's Report might be far removed from Britain's policy. Beeley was apprehensive lest lack of coordination between the two governments over simultaneous publication of both the Report and the statement of policy, would lead to a complete failure to achieve common policy with America over Palestine: 'It would lead to a situation in which HMG would be confronted with the alternatives of submitting to the pressures of American public opinion or deliberately confronting it: if that were to happen the Committee would have lost its *raison d'être* as a means of a better understanding of the Palestine problem'. The only way to overcome this dilemma that Beeley could see was to enlist the War Department, possibly more effective than the State Department, to accept the British view on Palestine. But future events were to prove that public opinion was a more effective factor than both War and State Departments put together.

Nevertheless, to Whitehall the situation did not look so fragile as to Beeley. The consensus amongst the Foreign, War and Colonial Offices was that it was indeed possible to enlist American agreement to steps against the Haganah and the Jewish Agency alongside a 'reasonable' scale of immigration. But nonetheless, Britain should be prepared to fulfil such recommendations even without American support.[58]

Beeley, generally quite influential in the Foreign Office, was not alone in thinking that the predominantly Zionist American public opinion could be defeated. Nevile Butler, Head of the American Department, thought that this was conceivable (a) if the oil pressure group in America could be effectively used against Zionism; (b) if Britain explained that they could not implement large scale immigration recommendations without the sanction of the United Nations, in view of the pledge which had been given to the Arabs in the 1939 White Paper. Moreover, there were no outstanding American personalities in the Committee, and therefore it was not an American 'show', hence the rejection of its recommendations would not be regarded as a national insult.[59]

Similarly, one of the most influential experts on Palestine at the Colonial Office, Sir Douglas Harris, had thought it unlikely that the Committee would repeat the 'sweeping' suggestion which Truman had made concerning the 100,000. Before the publication of the Report he saw little likelihood of any interim solution satisfying either Jews or Arabs, and he was inclined to favour a permanent solution through the United Nations, although the probability of agreement between both sides was remote. 'A difficult and dangerous operation is inevitable and the more speedily it can be accomplished the better chance will the patient have of recovery.'[60]

Once the Committee's Report became known to the public it aroused a considerable amount of emotional reaction on the already greatly agitated Arab side. As usual the Arab point of view was brought home with great zeal by the British diplomatic representatives in the Middle East. According to Grafftey-Smith, the Minister in Jedda, forever alarming the Foreign Office on forthcoming ominous Arab reactions, the Report was 'disastrous' to Anglo-Arab relations. Apart from its failure to point to an end to immigration, the recommendation to move the 100,000 was a 'bombshell' for them. Here was yet another erosion of the White Paper of 1939, the Arab 'Charter'. Similarly, he was critical of the Commission's futile attempt to solve the conflict by reviving the 'old fallacy' that economic benefit should stifle Arab national sentiment.

Terrence Shone, the Minister to Syria and Lebanon, did not lag behind in forecasting 'intense and uncompromising' opposition in the Levant states, adding a plausible prediction that the Soviets would do all they could to exploit the situation to the detriment of both Britain and America. Nor was the reaction from the Cairo and Baghdad Embassies, and from the Viceroy in India, of a different nature. The leitmotif was that the Report was offensive to the Arabs and a victory for the Zionists and for the Americans. At the time of negotiating the revised Treaties with Egypt and Iraq, the Report could only aggravate the situation.[61]

The Colonial Office took a more balanced view. Though not underrating the intense Arab dislike for the Report, they thought the initial reaction was bound to be vocal but ultimately would depend on Anglo-American unanimity and the degree of determination shown in its implementation. No less significant was the Colonial Office assessment that even if the Jewish leadership preached moderation, which they doubted, it was an open question whether they would be listened to. The local Arabs might resort to violence, but considering the fact that they were greatly dependent on the Arab states, the Colonial Office was doubtful whether the latter would back the use of force by the Palestine Arabs. Paradoxically, however, they concluded that the Report could be implemented only by Arab-Jewish cooperation, hinting at the 'considerable' influence the Report might have on moderate opinion on both sides.[62]

The first reaction in the Foreign Office was rather positive, but only on the junior level. Wikeley, who had to brief Bevin on the Report, thought it could be implemented although the Arabs would hate it. The Arab threats should not be taken too seriously since they were too frightened of Russia to turn against Britain. Jews must be disarmed, as well as the Arabs. Yet for this purpose American military assistance was needed.[63]

This view, however, as Wikeley anticipated, carried little weight. When the Cabinet Defence Committee came to deal with the Report on 24 April 1946 there was little enthusiasm for it. Bevin, though he feared Arab reactions, still felt that it would be difficult to avoid its acceptance. Its unanimity was for him an 'augury of cooperation by the United States government in solving the problems of Palestine.' Naively Bevin believed that he could gain American military support for the suppression of the Jewish illegal organizations as a condition for Britain's agreement for the immigration of the 100,000. Otherwise these immigrants might join the ranks of the illegal organizations.

Attlee took a less favourable view of the Report than Bevin. He was irritated by the fact that Palestine was alone considered as a destination for the Jewish refugees. Contrary to Bevin, he found only little ground in the Report to suggest that Britain could expect American cooperation in solving the Palestine question. Believing that the implementation of the Report would aggravate the situation in Palestine, he suggested that it 'was time that others helped to share it with us'. He correctly assessed that pressure rather than support for the British point of view was to be expected from the United States.

Following the High Commissioner's advice, Hall too did not sound optimistic. Replying to complaints by some members of the Defence Committee about the heavy burden of the Palestine Mandate, the Colonial Secretary said that only by obtaining a new Trusteeship agreement which would be taken over by another country or countries was it possible to get rid of the present responsibilities.

But this was only wishful thinking. In reality, as Field-Marshal Alanbrooke, the C.I.G.S., explained, with the concurrence of the rest of the Committee, Palestine could be the last foothold Britain might have in the region in view of the uncertainty of the position in Egypt. He further stressed the 'very great' importance of Middle Eastern oil resources which made Palestine strategically indispensable.[64]

Before the Cabinet itself came to deal with the Report, a special Ad Hoc Official Committee was established to assess its value. Headed by Sir Norman Brook, Joint Secretary to the Cabinet, it included the well-known experts from the Foreign and Colonial Offices, and representatives from the War and India Offices and the Treasury. Thus its composition assured the rejection of the Report. The Committee was horrified by the 100,000 immigration recommendation, pointing out that never before had so many immigrants been admitted to Palestine in one year (the maximum had been 64,137 in 1935). They were particularly annoyed that the Commission had ignored the absolute objection by the Arabs to Jewish immigration. Still, they envisaged the possibility of conceding on the question, although with the proviso of a fully shared responsibility with the United States.

The Ad Hoc Committee shared the views of the British Representatives in the Middle East that the Palestine Arabs were not interested in social and economic betterment, which they would regard as a bribe, but rather in retaining Palestine as an Arab country. Following the usual pattern of thought they noted that although the Committee did not make disarmament a condition for the execution of the Report, yet in Recommendation No. 10 an invitation was made to the British government to suppress terrorism, both Arab and Jewish.

They took a pessimistic view of the reaction of the Palestine Arabs, and could find little comfort in the possibility of American military support, for the Palestine Arab's martyrs would gain the support of the Arab and Moslem world.

Whilst the Committee preferred the view of the British Representatives on Arab extremism, rejecting the more hopeful view of the High Commissioner, they adopted the latter's assumption of a violent Jewish reaction, summarizing that the Report would satisfy no one and lead to aggressive reactions from both sides.

In conclusion the Ad Hoc Committee suggested that the British government consider two alternatives: either to invite the United States to participate in the implementation of the Report, or to place the Palestine question before the Security Council of the United Nations. But they did not believe that the United States would agree to active participation. Hence they decided to recommend the Cabinet to make an early reference to the United Nations for two reasons: (1) In the event of the implementation of the Report either the Arab States or Russia would refer the Palestine issue to the United Nations. It would be better if the

British government did so before committing themselves to the Committee's Recommendation. (2) The government had already undertaken, in Bevin's speech on 13 November 1945, to bring an agreed solution before the United Nations.[65]

The next day, 27 April 1946, Bevin tried to explain the British government's view to Byrnes, the American Secretary of State, whilst both of them were attending the Foreign Ministers' Conference in Paris, overlooking the fact that Palestine policy had become the domain of the White House rather than that of the Department of State. Typical of the British misunderstanding of this basic tenet of American politics was Bevin's plea to Byrnes on 28 April that the United States government should not make any statement about the Report without consulting Britain. As usual Halifax, the Ambassador, who more than once warned the Foreign Office as to the immense influence of Zionism in the United States, was unable to correct this distorted image.[66]

It was Bevin himself however who, more than his subordinates at Whitehall, understood the importance of trying to obtain direct American participation in Palestine politics. This was his view in the Defence Committee of 24 April and he repeated it to the Cabinet on 29 April, although the Ad Hoc Committee recommended the contrary. Reminding the Cabinet of his opposition to the immediate transference of the Palestine issue to the Security Council, Bevin explained that 'this would be regarded as a confession of failure and would have unfortunate effects on other aspects of our foreign policy'. Again, Bevin still refused to believe that the United States government would not eventually grasp that the fulfilment of the Zionist demands or part of them was impractical. Bevin miscalculated his ability to persuade the American government not to issue any statement of policy following the publication of the Report. Surprisingly, Bevin dissociated himself from the British Representatives in the Middle East who predicted violent Arab reactions to the Report: 'We should not be unduly alarmed by some initial clamour from the Arab States.'

Agreeing with Bevin, Hall said that only if the Americans were unwilling to help should Britain refer the issue to the United Nations. In any event, as pointed out by Alanbrooke and Hugh Dalton, the Chancellor of the Exchequer, further military and financial commitments should be taken into account. On this and on the need to suppress terrorism, there was a general agreement in the Cabinet. In addition the Cabinet backed the idea of asking for alleviation of America's immigration laws to allow more Jewish refugees into America.

Although the tendency in the Cabinet was to accept Bevin's line of

pursuing a joint policy with America, some Ministers were still preoccupied with the possibility that Russia would not tolerate its exclusion
from handling the Palestine problem. Nonetheless, it would be better to
obtain in advance a common policy with the Americans in the event of
the Palestine issue being referred to the Security Council. In conclusion,
Bevin's opinion remained predominant in the Cabinet, and a final attempt to bring the Americans to Britain's point of view was to be
made.[67]

However, Britain soon found out that it was far easier to convince
the Conservative opposition and the Dominion Prime Ministers than to
persuade the Americans. Even Smuts, despite confessing that his sympathy lay with the Zionists, admitted that the problem was insoluble and
approved Britain's policy. Speaking to the Dominion Prime Ministers
Attlee stressed the point that the Report would lead to a storm on both
sides. The Zionists committed to Biltmore could not accept it. The
Committee's recommendations that the 'legitimate national aspiration'
of both sides could be realized was rejected by Attlee as impractical, as
had been proved in India, Ireland and South Africa.[68]

As before, the British Cabinet and Bevin in particular expected too
much of the Americans. On the same day, 30 April 1946, Halifax
reported that Truman was shortly to issue a statement of policy that was
far removed from Britain's views, not mentioning the need to suppress
the illegal organizations and going so far as to announce his great
relief at the 100,000 Recommendation and that, in effect, the Report
amounted to the abrogation of the White Paper. As if that was not
enough Byrnes informed Bevin the next day that the United States could
not endorse a policy which would involve them in further military
commitments.[69] Bevin replied with a stiff letter to Byrnes in which he
condemned the unilateral American declaration. He went so far as to
hint that this was bound to encourage acts of murder by Jewish terrorists. He warned that this was a position which the British people could
tolerate no longer: 'If the United States does not accept the implications
regarding the need for disarming illegal armies before immigration, a
situation which will endanger the security of the Middle East is likely
to arise.'[70]

Following Truman's bombshell the Cabinet assembled for the second
time in forty-eight hours in an attempt to reassess the situation. Now
Attlee emphasized that they would have to issue an entirely different
statement from that previously intended. Nevertheless, a complete break
with the United States over Palestine was unthinkable.[71]

Again, Halifax was trying hard to bring home to the Foreign Office that the demand for the 100,000 had captured the American public mind. Apart from the fact the government's objection to the 100,000 was a 'slight' to America's prestige, he doubted whether the latter would agree to Britain's present policy. Halifax therefore recommended placing the issue before the United Nations General Assembly in the coming September or at a specially convened meeting. Since the Arab states or Russia were bound to sooner or later, Halifax preferred that Britain herself should come forward as 'the appellant rather than the defendant in the dock'. However, since the Foreign Office did not yet have any clear idea as to the solution to recommend to the United Nations, especially a policy which ensured Palestine as a British strategic base, Halifax's suggestion was rejected.[72]

Truman's statement had indeed wrecked Britain's Palestine policy. On 8 May 1946 however, the President offered to initiate joint consultations with both Jews and Arabs. He said that after they had received the views of both sides the British and the American Governments could determine their common attitude to the Report as a whole. They would not, however make any approaches before the 20th May in order not to prejudice the Egyptian negotiations.[73]

This time it was Attlee who reacted with unwarranted enthusiasm to Truman's new move. On 9 May he told the Cabinet that it was a 'further admission by the United States Government of some share of responsibility in the Palestine problem'. While realizing that Truman did not refer to any financial or military assistance, he hoped to raise these points later on. Probably Attlee relied on Bevin's suggestion to Byrnes on the previous day that before undertaking consultations with both sides, a study of the Report by experts should be initiated by the Governments.[74]

Indeed, on 20 May Bevin, convinced that Britain was nearing a breakthrough, confidentially told the Cabinet that the Americans 'now seemed to be willing to remove this question from the realm of propaganda and to study its implications on a business-like footing.'[75]

The new American move was a much needed fillip to Britain's policy in view of the alarming reports, especially from the Ambassador in Baghdad, that the economic and social policy initiated in the London Middle Eastern Conference of September 1945 was doomed to failure. Since then, however, strategic considerations proved to be of far more importance than economic and social ones.[76]

Thus the Morrison (Brook)-Grady Committee was established, in effect making it clear that the Anglo-American Committee of Inquiry had failed in view of the failure of the two Governments to agree on the basic principles of Palestine policy, or even on a compromise.

Was the compromise offered by the Anglo-American Committee of Inquiry a practical solution, or was it only a middle-of-the-road formula which merely reflected the need for agreement amongst a group of people who had been chosen at random to deal with a highly complicated issue of which they had little prior knowledge?

Crossman perhaps proves the exception. He was sufficiently aware to realise in advance that the British government would be lukewarm over the compromise, because of the heavy military commitment. Yet he attempted to base his case on other factors.

Primarily, the implementation of the Report would contribute towards the return to power of the moderates headed by Weizmann, who had surrendered the leadership to Ben-Gurion as a result of the White Paper policy. Hence the strength of the terrorists and the demand for a Jewish State. By nullifying the White Paper and allowing 100,000 Jews to enter Palestine, Crossman hoped that Jewish opinion around the world could be split between moderates interested only in saving European Jewry and the continued growth of the National Home, and the extremists who were 'exploiting humanitarian feelings for achieving totalitarian political ambitions'.

Crossman grossly overrated the strength of the moderate Zionists when he expected them to retain authority. Yet with the rest of the Committee's members he doubted whether the Jewish Agency would be able to absorb the 100,000 in view of the looming economic crisis. Consequently, it would have to collaborate with Britain in every possible way, including the suppression of terrorism. Here again Crossman had high hopes of the moderates headed by Weizmann and Kaplan, the Agency's treasurer.

Crossman indeed believed that the Report might defuse the Arab-Jewish conflict since it accepted the grievances of both sides, so far as the disparity in the standard of living was concerned. Hence the recommendation regarding the need for cooperation with the neighbouring Arab countries.

But what Crossman was really worried about was the long-term consequences of the Report's Recommendations. At least twenty-five years, if not fifty, were demanded for the fulfilment of these Recommendations. But neither the Mandate nor Trusteeship could continue for such a long time since both sides were in fact ready for independence.

This bleak future led Crossman to the inevitable conclusion that the only solution could be partition in a matter of five years. At the present moment Crossman felt that partition involved too big a risk since it would have to be imposed by force, but given time, the Foreign Secretary might be able to force both sides to rethink along more realistic lines.

Again, although Crossman had listened to Arab evidence he obviously underrated the uncompromising extremism presented by the various Arab witnesses. Rather, he was impressed by the Jewish readiness to agree to partition.

After the official attack on the British members of the Committee complaining that the Report was a sell-out to the Americans, Crossman was not taken aback, but remained strongly convinced that it was just. Since he was preoccupied with the Jewish rather than with the Arab case, believing that a full confrontation with the Jews would be worse than the one with Ireland after the First World War, he and Leggett thought that to make the entry of the 100,000 conditional on disarmament, might be extremely dangerous since it might leave the Jews defenseless *vis-à-vis* possible Arab attack. He told the Government that the immigration of the 100,000 would not cost them a great deal. Here was an opportunity to bring back the moderates into the saddle.[77]

The other four members of the Committee had different views from those of Crossman and Leggett, but they too failed to convince the Government. Singleton tried to convince Attlee that the Report was not necessarily a sell-out to the Americans. The Report had emphasized that Palestine was not a Jewish state, the private armies were declared illegal, and after the admission of the 100,000 immigration was to be conducted on a new basis: the well-being of the country as a whole. Singleton felt that it was essential to obtain the consent of the American Government for these three conclusions. He fully supported the view that the Jewish Agency must accept it as a whole. He also believed that the Report removed the Arab fear of Jewish economic domination. The Committee, added Singleton, favoured a bi-national State, but had left the question of a constitution for the future.

Lord Morrison, who, at Lausanne, a month earlier, had sided with Crossman in an attempt to prevent the break-up of the Committee, now sided with the British government. He castigated the Zionists for adopting only those parts of the Report which fitted into their own policy. He believed that Zionism succeeded in Palestine because it used the methods of the Hitler Youth movement, and in the United States because of its unscrupulous use of anti-British propaganda.

Crick felt joint action with America was plausible, but on anti-Zionist lines: the special status of the Jewish Agency should be abolished and the Jewish refugee question should be solved by the United Nations. Subject to strategic considerations, the Americans should simply be told that if they did not come forward actively in support of Britain's Palestine burden, she would surrender the Mandate to the United Nations.

Manningham-Buller also saw the Jewish Agency as the chief stumbling block to Arab-Jewish co-operation. Clipping its wings through disarmament would restore power to the British Administration. Unlike Crossman, Manningham-Buller regarded partition as a dangerous solution which might lead to serious trouble.

So the British government was supported by four out of the six members appointed by the government. Those four, had, in Lausanne and after, the support of two American members, Aydelotte and Phillips. On the other hand two British members, Crossman and Leggett, and the rest of the American members opposed the Government. All the British members including Crossman feared it would bring Russia in, and warned against joint Trusteeship with America.

Attlee had expressed his disappointment with the Report with regard to immigration. In particular, Singleton, much as he sympathized with the British position, apologized that the Report could not directly attack the Jewish Agency or the Haganah, since that would have split the Committee. He felt that any proposal to abolish the Agency would have led to open war in Palestine.[78]

The Anglo-American Report was indeed a compromise between its members, but, although it rejected the Zionist demand for a state, it sounded pro-Zionist to the British government. The Arabs, who had long before rejected any kind of compromise, reacted with a mixture of anger and despair to what they regarded as a major Zionist victory. They however laid the blame at the door of America rather than Britain. Meeting in Lebanon, at Bloudan on June 1946, the Council of the Arab League rejected Jamal Husseini's suggestion of establishing an Arab army to conquer Palestine and suppress the Jews. But they admitted that in the coming military confrontation they could not prevent volunteers from joining their brothers in Palestine. This indeed was a secret decision, as was the one which approved a cooling down of relations with both Britain and the United States in the event of the implementation of the Report.[79]

It is difficult, however, to say whether the Report offered a practical solution, because it was never implemented. Undoubtedly it would have demanded a heavy military commitment. But would the later Morrison (Brook)-Grady solution have required fewer divisions? In fact none of these plans was practical, as the reaction of both sides proved. What was practical was the partition plan recommended by Crossman, Crum and MacDonald; and a handful of Arab statesmen like Abdullah, and British soldiers of the magnitude of John Glubb and Brigadier Clayton, were ready to give their support. Indeed, a year later, in view of the bankruptcy of Britain's Palestine policy, the United Nations Special Committee on Palestine (UNSCOP) returned to partition as more practical than all other solutions. To be sure, even if the majority of the Anglo-American Committee had accepted the idea of partition, there is no doubt that Britain would have rejected it, probably against Truman's view.

Faced with the choice of supporting either the Zionists or the Arabs, Britain made her decision. Obviously, it was an expedient one. The Labour government accepted without murmur the deeply rooted concepts of the military and the officials of the Foreign and Colonial Offices that the Arab case was a stronger one. In these circumstances the failure of the Anglo-American Committee of Inquiry was inevitable, as was the alternative policy of the British government.

Yet Bevin was hardly George III, since the Jews had yet to deal with a far more ruthless enemy than the British, the Arabs. Guided by his advisers, Bevin never thought of winning a 'major victory' over the Jewish Agency by a compromise of 50,000 immigration, instead of 100,000 as Dalton suggested,[80] and some Zionists feared.

The Anglo-American Committee of Inquiry demonstrated the failure of Britain and the United States to give the Palestine issue a top priority on the world agenda. Rather, Palestine was treated as a nuisance, a second-rate problem, which did not warrant a top-level agreement between the two Powers. Alternatively, one can argue that such an understanding was never possible between them, and the reference to the United Nations was inevitable.

NOTES

1. C. Weizmann, *Trial and Error* (London, 1949), p. 554. M. Sharett (Shertok), *On the Threshold of Statehood* (Tel-Aviv, 1958), p. 14. (In Hebrew). A. Eban, '1939–1949: Tragedy and Triumph', in *Chaim Weizmann: A Biography by Several Hands*, eds. M. Weisgal and J. Carmichael (London, 1962), p. 311. Sir I. Berlin, *Zionist Politics in Wartime Washington: A Fragment of Personal Reminiscence* (Jerusalem, 1972), p. 65.

2. Y. Allon, *A History of the Palmach* (Tel-Aviv, 1965), p. 142. (In Hebrew).

3. M. Begin, *The Revolt* (London, 1951). I. Eldad, *Maaser Rishon* (Tel-Aviv, 1963), pp. 196–97. (In Hebrew).

4. Y. Slutsky, *The History of the Haganah*, Vol. III (Tel-Aviv, 1972), pt. 2, pp. 816 ff. (In Hebrew). N. Yalin-More, *The Fighters for the Freedom of Israel* (Jerusalem, 1974). (In Hebrew).

5. The Arabs believed that the appointment of the Committee meant the suppression of the White Paper of 1939. FO/141/1021/129/143/45. It was suggested that the Arabs should be reminded that the King-Crane Committee of 1919 had been in their favour. Howe to Martin, 28.12.45. Secret. FO/371/45388/E9564.

6. Y. Bauer, *Flight and Rescue: BRICHAH* (New York, 1970), pp. 76 ff. H. S. Truman, *Years of Trial and Hope* (New York, 1956), pp. 141 ff.

7. Minute by Sir Walter Smart, the Oriental Minister in Cairo and the *éminence grise* of the British elite in the Middle East. 6.11.45. FO/141/1021/129/33/45. FO to Washington, 12.10.45. No. 1267. Most Immediate. Top Secret. FO/371/45380. M. J. Cohen, 'The Genesis of the Anglo-American Committee on Palestine, November 1945: A Case Study in the Assertion of American Hegemony', *The Historical Journal*, 22, 1 (1979), pp. 185–207.

8. Extract from the Cabinet Conclusions. 38(45).4.10.45. FO/371/45381/E7956/G.

9. Memorandum by G. H. Hall, the Colonial Secretary, n.d. Top Secret. *Ibid.*

10. *Foreign Relations of the United States* (FRUS), Vol. VII (Washington, 1969), pp. 774 ff. P.(MX45) 2. Meeting Cabinet Palestine Committee Minutes 10.10.45. Report by the Lord President of the Council FO/371/45381/E7637/G. Top Secret. C.M(45) 40th Conclusions. Extract from Cabinet Meeting 11.10.45. FO/733/461/75872. Pt. IV. Note by R. G. Howe, Head of the Foreign Office Middle East Department, to the Colonial Secretary. FO/371/45380/E7479/G. Halifax to FO. 19.10.45. tel. No. 6964. Immediate. Top Secret. *Ibid.* Extract from Cabinet Conclusions. 52(45).13.11.45. FO/FO371/45380/E797.

11. D. Ben-Gurion, *Reply to Bevin* (London, 1945). Report on Weizmann's Talk with the President, 4.12.45. S25/7497. C(entral) Z(ionist) A(rchives).

12. In Whitehall it was felt that by giving their consent to the inclusion of MacDonald, well-known for his pro-Zionist views, they were not paying too high a price. Howe to Martin, 28.12.45. FO/371/45388/E9564.

13. Small Zionist Actions Committee, 11.12.45. S5/363. CZA. Senator was soon to resign. Cf. his letter of resignation in *Commentary* (October, 1946), pp. 384–86.

14. Small Zionist Actions Committee, 12.12.45. *op. cit.*

15. Mapai Archives, Bet-Berl, Israel.

16. C.M. (46) 1st Conclusions. 1.1.46. CAB/128/5. Halifax to FO, 13.1.46 No. 306. FO/371/52504.

17. AZEC. Meeting of the Executive Committee, 14.11, 26.11.30.11, 7.12.45. Z5/1206 CZA.

18. D. Horowitz, *A State in the Making* (New York, 1952), pp. 63 ff. Comay to Gering, 19.2.46. S25/1568. CZA. The Foreign Office feared that the Jewish organizations in America would prejudice the Committee: cf. Minute by Beeley FO/371/45389/E9828, and *ibid.* 9914.

19. All the evidence given to the Committee, including the cross-examination, but only a few memoranda, are conveniently assembled in: A. Carlebach *The Anglo-American Committee of Inquiry on Palestine* (Tel-Aviv, 1946). (In Hebrew). The English originals and other vast material are deposited in the CZA.

20. R. Crossman, *Palestine Mission* (London, 1947), pp. 35–41.

21. Kaplan to the Executive of the Jewish Agency, 10.2.46. Protocol CZA.

22. Epstein to Shertok, 25.1.46. Personal S25/451. CZA Meeting of the Committee of Eight (Jewish Agency Political Committee in America), 21.1.46. S53/2031. *Ibid.*

23. *Ibid.* And Goldmann to Shertok, 20.2.46. Strictly Confidential Z6/Package 18/File 15. CZA. The British were aware of the Zionist shift towards partition e.g. Memorandum on the Present State of Jewish Affairs in the United States by A. H. Tandy, 25.2.46. FO/371/52568/E2198/14/31. Halifax thought the Zionists overplayed their testimony. Halifax to FO, 13.1.46 No. 306. FO/371/52504. Rundall to Tandy, 15.1.46. FO/371/52508/E954.

24. *Baffy: The Diaries of Blanch Dugdale, 1936–1947,* ed. N. A. Rose (Vallentine, Mitchell, London, 1973), pp. 229–30. On the Foreign Office bias cf. Beeley's enthusiasm over Thomas Reid's testimony. FO/371/52507/E771. Manningham-Buller assured Bevin on 22.1.46 that 'so far . . . things have gone pretty well'. *Ibid.* E838. Bevin's remark FO/371/52509/E1413.

25. *Baffy,* op.cit. 27.1.46. Weizmann to Major Hay, 5.2.46 Weizmann Archives. Crossman, pp. 168–69. J. Kimche to E. Braudo, 2.2.46. S25/6450. CZA. Comay to Gering, 19.2.46. *op. cit.*

26. Y. Bauer, pp. 201 ff. Ruffer to Shertok, 24.12.45., 6–15.2.46. S25/3342; S25/7566. Singleton and Manningham-Buller represented official British views. Cf. FO/371/57689/E839. (Minutes of the Refugee Department, 9–15. 1.46.)

27. On Rifkind's views: Jewish Agency Executive Session, 3.3.46. CZA.

28. The Yishuv Elected Assembly (Assefat Hanivcharim) 4th session, 12–13. 2.46. J1/7223. CZA. Bevin to Hall, 12.1.46. Secret. FO/371/52504/E513. Creech Jones to Bevin, 23.1.46. Top Secret. FO/371/5207/E879. Dixon to Attlee, 26.1.46. *Ibid.*

29. Rosenblueth to Shertok, 19.2.46. S25/6490. CZA. Small Zionist Actions Committee, 28.2.46. S25/352. *Ibid.* Bernhard to Shertok, 8.2.46. S25/6463. *Ibid.* Crossman met Yaari, the leader of Hashomer Hatzair, and Georg Landauer of Aliya Hadasha. Crossman, pp. 148–49.

30. Jewish Agency Executive Sessions, 24. 2.46; 27.2.46. CZA.

31. Roberts (Moscow) to FO, 14.1.46. No. 26 FO/371/52506. Same to same, 15.1.46. No. 29. Same to same, 8.2.46. No. 69 (quoting *New Times* attack on the Committee FO/371/52509. Minute by H. T. Morgan, 26.2.46. FO/371/52512/E2085.

32. Boaz to Atara (from Baghdad), 16–31.3.46. S25/6412. CZA. A. Z. Eshkoli to E. Sasson, 13.3.46. S25/6411. *Ibid.* B. Crum, *Behind the Silken Curtain* (New York, 1947), pp. 156–58; 267–70. Stonehewer-Bird to FO, 2.4.46. No. 116. FO/371/25214/E343.

33. Weizmann was assisted by Stein in preparing his speech. Weizmann to Stein 14.2.46. Weizmann Archives. Weizmann to Shertok, 11.3.46. *Ibid.* Jewish Agency Executive Session, 10.3.46. CZA. *The Jewish Case before the Anglo-American Committee of Inquiry on Palestine, Statements and Memoranda* (Jerusalem, 1946), pp. 52, 643. Crossman, *Palestine Mission,* pp. 123 ff. id. *A Nation Reborn* (London, 1960), pp. 23–24. High Commissioner to the Colonial Secretary, 2.4.46. No. 537A. Secret FO/371/52514. Crum, p. 65. The Jewish map left the area of Jenin-Nablus-Hebron-Lydda out of the Jewish State. The area Jerusalem-Bethlehem-Kalia was to be an international zone. S25/7162. CZA.

34. *The Jewish Case, op. cit.* pp. 301–3. Zionism and the Arab World, *Ibid.* p. 349. Note on the Arabs in the War, *Ibid.* pp. 360–71. Memorandum on the position of the Jewish Communities in Oriental Countries. *Ibid.* 372–91. Anti-Jewish Riots in Tripolitania, *Ibid.* pp. 392–406. Paper on the Situation of Iraqi Jewry, *Ibid.* pp. 407–10.

35. The Jewish Resistance Movement. Memorandum submitted to the Anglo-American Committee, 25.3.46, FO/733/463//75872/138/7.

36. *The Jewish Case,* pp. 263–303.

37. Jewish Agency Executive Session, 24.3.46. CZA.

38. Crum, pp. 223–25. Crossman, p. 164.

39. D. Horowitz, *A State in the Making,* pp. 110–11. Talk with Goldmann from London, 31.3.46. Z6/Package 18/File 1. On Hutcheson's role cf. Halifax to FO, 23.4.46. No.

2069. Most Immediate FO/371/52516. Minute by Beeley *Ibid*. 28.4. *Baayot* (Problems), Ichud's organ published by M. Buber (July 1947), pp. 211–12.

40. MacDonald to the President, 5.4.46. (from M. Weisgal) Z6/Package 18/File. Lourie's letters, 11.4.46, *Ibid*. Crum, p. 269.

41. Crossman to McNeil, 22.4.46. FO/371/52524/E4469.

42. B. Joseph in the Jewish Agency Executive Session, 12.5.46; 2.6.46. Horowitz, p. 118. E. Monroe, 'Bevin's "Arab Policy" ', *St. Antony's Papers* (1961), p. 29.

43. Lourie's letters, 11.4.46. Z6/Package 18/Files. CZA. Halifax to FO, 23.4.46. No. 2069. Most Immediate, FO/371/52516.

44. Weizmann to Churchill, 14.4.46. Weizmann Archives. Weizmann to Smuts 14.4.46. *Ibid*. Weizmann to Attlee, 16.4.46. *Ibid*. Weizmann to Locker, 16.4.46. *Ibid*. Weizmann to Bevin, 16.4.46. *Ibid*. Sasson to Joseph, 12.4.46. Z5/1083. CZA.

45. Lourie's letters, 21.4.46. Confidential. Z6/Package 18/File 1. CZA. Crossman confused the Zionists as to his exact views. Shertok to the Executive, 19.6.46. CZA.

46. The Report is included in Cmd. 6808. For refugees statistics see Appendix III. Ch. 2 Paragraph 19. The Agency estimate was higher: 505.450. S25/3342. CZA.

47. The Peel Report and the Woodhead Commission had acknowledged the Zionist contribution for Arab betterment, as did the Survey prepared by the Administration for the Committee's guidance: *A Survey for Palestine, Prepared in December 1945 and January 1946 for the Information of the Anglo-American Committee for Palestine.* (Jerusalem, Government Printing Office, 1946), Ch. 16 p. 23 paragraph 182.

48. Weizmann to Magnes, 8.5.46. Weizmann Archives.

49. Minutes of Meeting held at 77, Gt. Russell St. 29.4.46; 30.4.46 Secret. Z4/10,380. CZA. Jewish Agency Executive Sessions. 30.4.46; 1.5.46; 20.6.46.

50. Jewish Agency Executive Sessions, 5.5.46; 12.5.46; 19.5.46. CZA.

51. Crossman, *Palestine Mission*, 176–87. Weizmann to the Executive, 1.5.46. Eldad, *Maaser Rishon, op. cit.* AZEC (American Zionist Emergency Council). Meeting of the Executive, 3.5.46; 9.5.46. *op. cit.* Z5/1172 CZA. Akzin to Goldmann, 6.5.46. *Ibid*.

52. Weizmann to Magnes, 8.5.46. Weizmann Archives. Weizmann to Attlee, 13.5.46. *Ibid*.

53. Meetings held at 77, Gt. Russell St. 13.5.46; 15–16.5.46; 21.5.46; 23.5.46; 23.5.46; 31.5.46. *op. cit.* CZA. The British press saw the debate over the Report as a new version of the Arab-Jewish conflict. Particularly unfriendly was the Daily Telegraph. R. S. Churchill, *The Sinews of Peace, Post-War Speeches by W. S. Churchill* (London, 1948), p. 125. Gordon to Goldmann, 8.5.46 Z6/Package 2/File 3. CZA.

54. Small Zionist Actions Committee, 23.6.46. S5/355 CZA.

55. *Ibid*. AZEC. Meeting of the Executive, 13.5.46. *op. cit.*

56. Horowitz, pp. 128–29. B. Crum, *op. cit.*

57. C.O.S. (46) 77th Meeting. 15.5.46. Top Secret FO/371/52525/E4774/G. D'Arcy had been misunderstood by the Committee members, and by the Zionists, because he was not permitted to speak about anything beyond the purely military.

58. Beeley to Baxter, 25.3.46. Secret and Personal. FO/371/52514/E3057/G. Memorandum by the Joint Chiefs of Staff to the State-War-Navy Coordinating Committee, 21.6.46. Top Secret. FRUS, 1946. Vol. VII. Record of a Meeting held at the FO, 6.4.46. FO/371/5254/E3057.

59. N. Butler, The United States and the Palestine Report, 26.4.46. FO/371/52520/E4013.

60. Memorandum by Sir D. Harris, 21.3.46. Procedure in Connection with Palestine Policy Top Secret FO/371/52514/E3057/G.

61. Grafftey-Smith to FO, 23.4.46. No. 159. Most Immediate. Top Secret and Personal FO/371/52516. Shone to FO, 23.4.46. No. 365. Top Secret and Personal. *Ibid*. Stonehewer-Bird to FO, 25.4.46. No. 330. Most Immediate. Top Secret. *Ibid*. Same to same, 25.4.46. No. 339. Most Immediate. Top Secret. *Ibid*. Viceroy to the Secretary

of State for India, 23.4.46. Ext. 2880 *Ibid.* Campbell to FO, 25.4.46. No. 734. Important. *Ibid.*

62. The Secretary of State for the Colonies to the High Commissioner, 24.4.46. Most Immediate. Top Secret. Personal. No. 666. *Ibid.*

63. Report of the Anglo-American Committee of Inquiry. Notes for the Secretary of State's discussion with the Defence Committee. Comment. First Impressions by T. Wikeley, 23.4.46. FO/371/52517/E3840/G.

64. Extract from D.O.(46) 14th Meeting, 24.4.46. Palestine (D.O.(46)61). FO/371/E3839/G.

65. C.P. (46) 173. Top Secret. 26.4.46. Palestine. Appointment, Terms of Reference and Constitution of the Committee. Draft of the Ad Hoc Official Committee. FO/371/52517/E3943. Extract from Cabinet Conclusions. 37(46). 24.4.46. *Ibid.* E3838/G.

66. U.K. Delegation to Foreign Ministers' Conference (Paris) to FO, 27.4.46. No. 7. Top Secret. Immediate, *Ibid.* Bevin to Byrnes, 28.4.46. Secret and Personal. *Ibid.* E3815/G. Halifax to FO, 24.4.46. Top Secret and Personal No. 2712. *Ibid.* For details on some division in the State Department of FRUS, Vol. VII. pp. 597–99.

67. C.M. 38(46) 29.4.46. CAB/128/5.

68. P.M.M.(46)8th Meeting of Prime Ministers (U.K., Australia, New Zealand, South Africa), 30.4.46. Top Secret. FO/371/52520/E4061614/G.

69. Halifax to FO, 30.4.46. No. 2742. Most Immediate. FO/371/52519/U.K. Delegation at Paris (Bevin) to FO, 1.5.46. Most Immediate FO/371/52519. Acheson, the Acting Under-Secretary, and Henderson, the Head of the Near East and Africa Division, tried to prevent Truman's statement, but failed because of White House intervention. Halifax to FO, 7.5.46. Immediate and Secret. FO/371/52521.

70. U.K. Delegation to the Conference of Foreign Ministers (Paris) to the FO, 1.5.46. No. 30 Secret. FO/371/52519. Cf. F. Williams, *A Prime Minister Remembers* (London, 1961) pp. 193–95. id. *Nothing So Strange* (London, 1970). p. 249.

71. Cabinet Conclusions. 39(46).1.5.46. Palestine Report. FO/371/52520.

72. Halifax to FO, 4.5.46. No. 2858. Secret. Minutes Beeley, Baxter and Ward. FO/371/52521. FO to Halifax, 18.6.46. No. 825. *Ibid.*

73. FO to U.K. Delegation to the Foreign Ministers Conference (for Bevin), 8.5.46. No. 153. Most Immediate and Top Secret (Truman's message). FO/371/52522/E4305/G. Bevin to Attlee, 9.5.46. *Ibid.* 4318/G.

74. Extract from Cabinet Conclusions 44(46)9.5.46 FO/371/52523/E 4346/G.

75. Extract from Cabinet Conclusions. 50(46)20.5.46. FO/371/52525/E775/G.

76. Stonehewer Bird to FO, 10.5.46. No. 390. FO/371/52523.

77. Crossman to McNeil, 22.4.46. Notes on Palestine Report of the Anglo-American Committee. FO/371/52524/E 4469. Points (by Crossman) for McNeil, n.d. 9.5.46. *Ibid.* Minute by Beeley. Cf. his *Palestine Mission* and *A Nation Reborn* to the P.R.O. contemporary evidence which is more reliable apart from quotations from his diary.

78. Note of a Meeting held at No. 10 Downing St., on 14 May 1946, at which the Prime Minister and the Secretary of State for the Colonies met the Members of the Anglo-American Committee. FO/371/5254/E 4514. A strong plea in favour of abolishing the Agency was made by Crick in a letter to Bevin, 26.4.46. Secret. FO/371/52519/E 3961. It was supported by Sir D. Harris, but doubted by J. M. Martin. *Ibid.* Minutes.

79. Bloudan Resolutions in: *Behind the Curtain* (Tel-Aviv, Maarachot, 1954) pp. 12, 41 (no author).

80. H. Dalton, *High Tide and After, Memoirs 1931–45* (London, 1962), p. 150.

V.

CULTURAL QUESTIONS

28.

The Emergence of a Native Hebrew Culture in Palestine, 1882–1948

Itamar Even-Zohar

During the hundred years of new Jewish settlement in Palestine, whose starting point is conventionally assigned to 1882 (and commonly called "the First Aliyah"),[1] a society was produced whose nature and structure proved to be highly fluid. The periodic influx of relatively large groups of immigrants continually disrupted or disturbed the apparent ad hoc stability of the community insofar as its structure, demographic consistency, and salient characteristics were concerned. Each new wave resulted in a restructuring of the whole system. It is, however, commonly accepted that around the time of the establishment of the State of Israel, in 1948, a relatively crystallized Jewish society existed in Palestine with a specific cultural character and a high level of self-awareness, as well as established social, economic, and political institutions. It differed, culturally and otherwise, from the old Jewish, pre-Zionist Palestinian community, and from that of Jewish communities in other countries. Moreover, this distinctiveness was one of its major goals, involving the replacement of the then-current identifications "Jew" and "Jewish" with "Hebrew."[2] But with the founding of the State of Israel and the massive immigration which followed, what appeared to have been a "final," stabilized system was again subjected to a process of restructuring. The distinction between Jewish and Hebrew cultures has become secondary and eventually obsolete. Hebrew culture in Palestine has become Israeli, and although the latter definitely springs from the previous stage, it seems very different from it. Thus, as a working hypothesis for this

Reprinted by permission of the author and *Studies in Zionism* 4 (autumn 1981): 167–84.

study, it would be convenient to accept 1948 as a more or less imprecise termination of the period which had started in 1882. An adequate description of the development of the thirty years since, that is, subsequent to the establishment of the state, will not be possible without first providing a description of the longer and more complicated period which preceded, and thus laid the foundations for what followed.

The early waves of the new Jewish immigration to Palestine, at least until the early 1930s, seem to be different from other migrations in modern times, including those of later periods. From anthropological and sociological studies on immigration, we know that the cultural behavior of immigrants oscillates between two poles: the preservation of their source culture and the adoption of the culture of the target country. A rather complex mechanism eventually determines, for any specific period in the history of an immigrant group, which option will prevail. The value images of the target country as compared with those of the source country can constitute an important factor in determining the direction of cultural behaviour. Most migrations from England tended to preserve the source culture. European immigrants to the United States at the end of the nineteenth century, on the other hand, left their home countries with the hope of "starting a new life in the new world"—a slogan of highly suggestive potency. Its effect was to encourage the replacement of the "old" by the "new" and often engendered attitudes of contempt towards the "old." Such replacement assumes, of course, the existence of an available cultural repertoire in the target country, and when this is the case the major problem of the immigrants is how to authenticate acquired components so that they will be considered "not foreign" by members of the target community. What actually takes place in the process of acquiring target cultural patterns need not deter us at this point. What is important is only to emphasize the necessity of the existence of an *alternative system,* that is, an aggregate of alternatives, and it is precisely here that the case of immigration to Palestine stands in sharp contradistinction to that of many other migrations. A decision to "abandon" the source culture, partially or completely, could not have led to the adoption of the target culture since the existing culture did not possess the status of an alternative. In order to provide an alternative system to that of the source culture, in this case East-European culture, it was necessary to *invent* one.

The main difference between most other migration movements and that of the Jews to Palestine lies in the deliberate, conscious activity carried out by the immigrants themselves in replacing constituents of the culture they brought with them with those of another. This does not mean that it is possible to establish a full correlation between the principles which apparently underlay the search for alternatives and what ultimately took place in reality; but there is no doubt that these principles were, in fact, decisive—both for the deliberate selection of possible items and the presence, post factum, of those items pressed into the cultural system by the operation of its mechanism. Zionist ideology and its ramifications (or sub-ideologies) provided the major motivation for immigration to Palestine as well as the underlying principles for cultural selection, that is, the principles for the creation of an alternative culture. This does not imply the existence of any kind of bold cultural pattern during this period, nor the acceptance by the immigrants themselves of these principles, either in part or in full, in a conscious fashion. But a schematic examination of the period in retrospect will reveal that the governing principle at work was "the creation of a new Jewish people and a new Jew in the Land of Israel," with emphasis on the concept "new."

At the end of the nineteenth century, there was sharp criticism of many elements in Jewish life in Eastern Europe. Among the secular, or semi-secular Jews, who were the cultural products of sixty years of the Jewish Enlightenment, the *Haskala* movement, Jewish culture was conceived to be in a state of decline, even degenerate. There was a notable tendency to dispense with many of the traditional constituents of Jewish culture. The assimilationists were prepared to give up everything; the Zionists, in the conceptual tradition of the *Haskala*, sought a return to the "purity" and "authenticity" of the existence of the "Hebrew nation in its land," an existence conceived according to the romantic stereotypes of contemporary (including Hebrew) literature, exalting the primordial folk nation. It is interesting to note that both assimilationists and Zionists accepted many of the negative Jewish stereotypes, promulgated by non-Jews, and adapted them to their own purposes. Thus they accepted at face value the ideas that Jews were rootless, physically weak, deviously averse to pleasure, averse to physical labor, alienated from nature, etc., although these ideas had little basis in fact.

Among the numerous ways manifested for counterposing "new Hebrew" to "old Diaspora Jew" were the transition to physical labor (mainly agriculture or "working the land," as it was called); self-defense and the concomitant use of arms; the supplanting of the old, "contemptible" Diaspora language, Yiddish, with a new tongue, colloquial Hebrew (conceived of at one and the same time as being the authentic and the ancient language of the people), adopting the Sephardi rather than the Ashkenazi pronunciation;[3] discarding traditional Jewish dress and adopting other fashions (such as the Bedouin-Circassian, notably among the youth of the First Aliyah and members of *Ha-shomer*, the Watchmen's Association); dropping East-European family names and assuming Hebrew names instead.

The decision to introduce Hebrew as the spoken language of the community was not accepted or agreed upon even by those most active in the creation of modern literary Hebrew. Nor did it immediately appeal to members of the First Aliyah. On the contrary, there were objections to giving Hebrew pride of place in the new colonies, and practical knowledge of the language was quite limited. Furthermore, the adoption of Sephardi pronunciation cannot be explained either by the fact that Sephardi circles in Jerusalem supported the idea of Hebrew as a spoken language or that Eliezer Ben Yehuda was convinced by a Christian priest (while he was lying ill in a French hospital) that Sephardi pronunciation should be preferred. After all, even in Eastern Europe, the Sephardi pronunciation was considered to be the "correct" one, but this did not prevent any Hebrew poet from late nineteenth century until the early 1930s from using the Ashkenazi variant, even in Palestine itself, where it contravened the prevailing Sephardi pronunciation (see below). The most important element in the twin decisions to speak Hebrew and speak Sephardi Hebrew stemmed from their qualities as *cultural oppositions:* Hebrew as against Yiddish, Sephardi as against Ashkenazi; in both cases, new against old. This outweighed any principle or scholarly discussions about "correct" pronunciation (although the latter were often conducted in such terms).

Thus, the establishment of the new Jewish community in Palestine involved a series of decisions in the domain of cultural selection, and the ideology which permeated this project (i.e., Zionism) made explicit decisions compulsory. It was urgent to provide at least a few conspicuous components for an alternative system, for an aggregate of new functions. In some instances it was not even *alternative* extant functions that were needed, but *new* ones, dictated by new conditions of life. A long retrospective view seems to point to the fact that experiments were continuously carried out in Palestine to supply the components necessary for the fulfillment of the basic cultural opposition *new Hebrew–old Jew*. It was not the origin of the components which determined whether or not they would be adopted, but their capacity to fulfill the new functions in accordance with this opposition. Green olives, olive oil and white cheese, Bedouin welcoming ceremonies and *kaffiyehs* all acquired a clear semiotic status. The by-now-classical literary description of the Hebrew worker sitting on a wooden box, eating Arabic bread dipped in olive oil,[4] expresses at once three new phenomena: (a) he is a worker; (b) he is a "true son of the land"; (c) he is not eating in a "Jewish" way (he is not sitting at a table and has obviously not fulfilled the religious commandment to wash his hands). Or we have the typical village elder in Yitzhak Dov Berkovitz's novel *Days of the Messiah* (1938). He builds a house for himself which he considers to be like a *khata* (in Russian—a peasant's hut) "painted white, with small windows, a yard, a gate and a small bench by the gate."[5] His neighbors in the same village, actualizing the same function for themselves, construct houses like those of "Polish noblemen, with high windows." The village elder dreams of Hebrew farmers who will eat "kasha and sugar," and deplores the fact that he cannot obtain "crude galoshes, like those worn by our Ukrainian farmers." The Baron de Rothschild's version of the Jewish farmer in Palestine, on the other hand, was the "authentic" French model: a semi-literate who kept only the Bible on his table. The dominion of such components was short-lived and they gave way in the course of time and in the wake of experimentation to other cultural options. As mentioned before, their survival or disappearance depended on their ability to fulfill a function in accordance with the new ideology of national revival.

Specific materials often mislead those observing them years later. For instance, what precise meaning can be attached to the adoption of items of food and clothing from the culture of the Bedouins and fellahin, first by members of the First Aliyah, and later by those of the Second, most notably among them the tight-knit Watchmen's association, *Ha-shomer?* There can be no doubt that nineteenth-century Romantic norms and "Oriental" stereotypes (including the identification of Bedouin dress with that of our Biblical ancestors, so readily inferred from numerous illustrations of the time) were central factors.[6] They constituted a ready-made model for generating positive attitudes towards these items and, further, for identifying them with the realia of the population and the landscape. All this notwithstanding, this was not a case of non-mediated contacts with a neighboring culture. It was rather a case of reality being filtered through a familiar model. Certain components of that model were fairly well known through the general stereotypes of the "Orient" (through Russian poetry and, subsequently, Hebrew poetry as well). But in fact, one could say that what was taking place was an act of "translating" the new reality back into an old, familiar, traditional cultural model, specifically that which had crystallized in Russia towards the end of the nineteenth century. In this manner, the data of the new reality and the new experience could be understood and absorbed. For neither Bedouin nor fellahin was an unequivocal concept: on the one hand, they were heroes, men of the soil, dedicated to their land; on the other, inferior and almost savage. Again—on the one hand their food, dress, behavior, and music expressed everything alien to the Jew: courage, natural nobility, loyalty, roots; on the other hand these expressed primitiveness and cultural backwardness. This example offers us a simple, uncomplicated "translation" of a familiar East-European model, in which old functions, namely, the Ukrainian peasant and the Cossack, are transferred to new carriers. The "heroic Bedouin robber" replaces the Cossack and the fellah the Ukrainian peasant. The *kaffiyeh* takes the place of crude galoshes and the Palestinian Hebrew song "How Beautiful are the Nights of Canaan" that of a sentimental steppe song of the Don Cossacks.

I said before that the source of the constituents is of secondary importance in the new cultural system-in-the-making. This does not mean that the material aspect of the constituents themselves is neutral. From the point of view of the mechanism which either accepts or rejects them, they may (in principle) be considered neutral. But this is not the case with regard to their availability. The desire to actualize a cultural opposition generates the search for alternative materials able to fulfill the desired functions; but "the-people-in-the-culture" can seek alternatives *only where they are likely to find them,* which means, generally, in nearby or accessible contexts. This is what made the transfers from adjacent systems possible: from the Russian, Yiddish, Arabic, or any construct (imaginary or credible) formulated, at least on an ideological level, as an option within culture. For instance, the desire to discard Yiddish, to give it up as a spoken language, has led to the choice of Hebrew as a replacement. But Hebrew, of course, had been an extant, established phenomenon within Jewish culture during *all* the centuries of dispersion. It was only the option of *speaking* it that had not been actualized and even seemed impossible. Similarly, the desire to discard the most conspicuous features of the European Diaspora led to a decision to drop Ashkenazi pronunciation: it reminded one too much of Eastern Europe and Yiddish. Hence, the popularity of Sephardi pronunciation. But the latter had been an *existing* option even in the repertoire of *Haskala* culture in Eastern Europe, only it had never been actualized in Hebrew *speech*. The desire to dress as a "non-Jew" popularized the *kaffiyeh* and the *rubashka* (a Russian shirt) adorned with a cartridge belt; these were the options that an adjacent, accessible culture provided. Accessibility alone could not have determined the selection. For example, constituents belonging to the English culture were at the time gradually becoming accessible in Palestine, but they were not adopted by the local Hebrew culture because they could not fulfill the functions needed for the cultural opposition.

The deliberate struggle for the massive adoption of new constituents does not, however, ipso facto annihilate all the constituents of the "old" culture. And no system which maintains an uninterrupted existence is able to replace all its constituents. Normally, only the center of the system changes; relations at the periphery change very gradually. From the point of view of the people. who in their behavior and existence actualize what we call, in the abstract, "systemic relations," even a deliberate decision to change behavioral constituents will lead to changes only in the most dominant constituents, i.e., those in which there is a high degree of awareness. But in areas such as proxemic relations, body movement, etc., in which awareness is low and not easily governed by deliberate control, even deliberate decisions will fail to produce change. Nevertheless, since "culture" is not merely the existence of one system attaching to a homogeneous group, but rather a heterogeneous system, one member-group in the culture may be impelled by certain factors, while another is not. Yet both exist simultaneously and are unavoidably correlated with each other within the same polysystem. Thus, only a pseudo-historical idealization would confer on the First Aliyah a homogeneity capable of creating "a new Hebrew people" according to the tenets of a specific ideology. Recent studies and numerous documents from this period clearly demonstrate that there were very few among the first settlers who were even familiar with this ideology and even fewer who identified with it and took it upon themselves to actualize the cultural opposition.

In other words, side by side with the penetration of new constituents, there remained a substantial mass of "old culture." As a result, the cultural opposition to it probably constituted one of the important factors in that system which, in retrospect, must now be recognized as the central, the "official" one. Yet the cultural opposition of the "new Hebrew" was both conditioned by and correlated with other factors operating within the polysystem, some of which supported it, while others neutralized it to a greater or lesser extent. Among other factors which determined (to an extent that still requires further investigation) the penetration of new constituents into the system and its reorganization at each subsequent phase, the following should be considered:

1. The predominance of constituents from one particular source over the entire society. (An example of this—as an illustrative hypothesis only—would be the predominance of the Lithuanian high norm of intonation and vowel quantity over the official norm of Hebrew. For more explanations see below.)
2. The penetration of constituents from other cultural systems as a result of "normal" contacts (such as the continued penetration of Russian models into official, "high" Hebrew culture up to the 1950s, at least).
3. The neutralization of certain features as a result of the impossibility of unilateral domination (for instance, on the phonetic and intonational features of spoken Hebrew).
4. The emergence of local, "native," constituents as a result of the dynamic operation of the repertoire beginning to crystallize, in accordance with the three foregoing principles (e.g., new body movements, neologisms, verbal constituents with pragmatic functions, development of various linguistic registers, such as slang, etc.).

The perseverance of old constituents, both items and functions, is no less important for the dynamics of a system than the penetration of new ones. This principle can be called the "inertia of institutionalization." Established constituents will hold on as long as possible against pressures which try to force them out of the center onto the periphery or out of the system altogether. Many constituents persevered in this way inside the new cultural system in Palestine, either in their original form or by transferring their functions to new forms. For example, with regard to the perseverance of form, Hebrew became institutionalized rather painlessly in the registers of formal, public, and non-intimate communication. But in intimate, familiar, or "popular" language, even among fanatic Hebraists, Yiddish (or rather fragments of Yiddishisms) persevered. Thirty years ago, it was still relatively simple to record macaronic discourse in colloquial Hebrew. Today we are forced to reconstruct it, partly from written testimony, partly from the macaronic speech observable among old-timers still with us.[7] On the other hand, as regards the transfer of functions, this was carried out by domestic carriers. On the linguistic level, to take one instance, this procedure was based on providing loan-translations (calques). Pattern transfer, though, seems to have been possible more in "low profile" areas: in intonation rather than lexicon, gesture rather than morphology and the like.

The inertia of institutionalized constituents can also explain behavioral differences between various sectors of the emerging culture. There were certain areas, for example, where new functions were needed not to replace old ones, but simply to fill slots where there were no old functions to begin with. Here the complex play between selection factors from existing repertoires and the element of creativity was less constrained than in those highly institutionalized areas where quick replacement was impossible because those principles were not valid for them.

We can see this at work in the case of language and literature. The canonized patterns of Hebrew literature and the Hebrew language which had crystallized in Eastern Europe maintained their central positions in these systems throughout the entire period discussed here and even later. The new, "native" constituents, which could have provided alternative options, were forced to remain at the periphery of these systems, penetrating the center only in the late 1950s. Let us look a little closer at these matters.

The process by which Hebrew became a modern language during the nineteenth century and the dominant native tongue later in Palestine illustrates many of the points mentioned above. Hebrew had to mobilize all of its resources to meet the need which arose for writing secular poetry, narrative prose, journalistic non-fiction, and scientific prose. At the same time it had to maintain the existence of the cultural oppositions emerging from the respective ideologies of each phase of development. At the beginning of the *Haskala,* the need to create a language in counterposition to rabbinical vernacular resulted in the rather fanatical reduction of Hebrew exclusively to its Biblical variety. When that need weakened in the face of the greater need to counterpose the accepted form of early *Haskala* prose, many features of rabbinical language were reintroduced, though now with different functions. This process was particularly notable in the language of literature, and was determined by literary requisites. For Mendele Mokher Sfarim (1836?–1917; a founding father of modern Hebrew and Yiddish literatures), for example, the language of the most appreciated writer of the Enlightenment period, Abraham Mapu (1807–1867), was stilted and artificial, especially in dialogue, and totally incompatible with the type of reality he was interested in describing (Mapu's novels described life in ancient Biblical times). Consequently, he introduced various constituents of post-Biblical Hebrew. Moreover, Mendele unhesitatingly turned to Yiddish for further options. It was socially, though not linguistically, the repertoire closest to Hebrew. He borrowed from the Yiddish not words, not even calques, but those linguistic patterns of which there is a very low level of awareness: syntax, sentence rhythm, and intonation. By doing this he achieved an unprecedented effect of naturalness of speech in a language which was confined to writing, thus opening the way for the later development of both literary and spoken language. The effect of natural-ness can be understood only if we keep in mind that Mendele's readers were at home in *both* languages and thus able to appreciate his singular achievement by juxtaposing them.[8] Other writers followed suit.

In observing the history of new *spoken* Hebrew (for which, unfortu-nately, we have only partial documentation),[9] two things become clear: first, an enormous revolution was needed to turn it into a secular tongue for daily use; secondly, the linguistic and paralinguistic phenomena which perforce accompanied its revival had no connection whatsoever with any kind of ancient historical situation. I refer here to those linguis-tic features the conscious control of which is very difficult, even impossi-ble, and whose penetration into the system of spoken language is abso-lutely unavoidable: voice quality, the quantitative and qualitative characteristics of sounds, sentence rhythm and intonation, paralinguistic phenomena accompanying speech (hand and head gestures), onomato-poeic sounds and interjections. In all these areas, Yiddish and Slavic features massively penetrated Hebrew, dominated it for a long time, and can still be observed in part today. Clearly, the so-called Sephardi pronunciation actualized by natives of Eastern Europe was quite differ-ent from that employed in Palestine by non-Europeans. What was actu-alized, in fact, was only the minimum necessary to establish it in opposi-tion to Ashkenazi pronunciation.

Yet one of the most conspicuous phenomena in the area of pronuncia-tion was the gradual rejection of the various foreign linguistic and paralinguistic features and their replacement by a very characteristic and unmistakable native-Hebrew sentence intonation. The most drastic departure from the effects of the interference of other language systems probably took place in the area of voice quality and verbal sounds. Furthermore, contrary to expectations regarding language acquisition, the pronunciation of native Palestinian Hebrew speakers was not in imitation of their parents' pronunciation but appeared rather to follow a neutralization procedure: it sought the common denominator of all pronunciations (of those brought from Eastern Europe, not from Mid-dle-Eastern countries!) and rejected all exceptional features. No existing inventory could have dominated the actual speech of native Hebrew speakers (although it could and did dominate the canonized pronuncia-tion of specific sectors, such as the Hebrew theater, see below). This is a common procedure for a lingua franca. Clearly no new inventory of *sounds* has been created but rather a local *phonological* system. Neutralization on the level of sound *per se* is not a defensible notion. One must say rather, and at a higher level of abstraction, that whatever was *unnecessary* for the phonological system in terms of phonetic oppositions was in fact eliminated.[10]

How did the development of "native Hebrew" influence Hebrew culture in Palestine? It turns out that in spite of the ideology of "the new Hebrew man/woman" and the subsequent adoration of the native-born *sabra*[11] all of whose linguistic "inventions" were zealously collected, neither native phonetic norms nor the majority of other native verbal phenomena were accorded *official* recognition.[12] They did not become central to the cultural system, nor did they constrain the norms of its written texts. Ultimately, they began to penetrate the center through the classical process by which phenomena on the periphery move towards the center, and even then, arduously and without "official" sanction. Thus, when the Palestinian Broadcasting Service was opened to Hebrew broadcasting, no "native" pronunciation was heard there. What one heard was either a "Russian-Yiddish" Hebrew or an attempt at "Oriental" pronunciation, i.e., actualizing some of the guttural consonants as they were *supposed* to be pronounced—in imitation of the equivalent *Arabic* sounds. Both endeavored to maintain the canons of classical Hebrew morphology, that is, in accordance with the canonized "vocalization" system (the so-called Tiberian tradition which crystallized in the city of Tiberias by the Sea of Galilee in the tenth century), as interpreted by later generations.

Similarly, until the 1940s native Hebrew did not have any position in the language of the theater, since the latter was an official cultural institution. The acting and textual models of the Hebrew theater in Palestine were perfectly compatible with the conventions of Russo-Yiddish pronunciation. This included quite a large range of phenomena: phonetic features pertaining to vowels and consonants and voice quality (tone, timbre, stability of voice versus vibration), rhythm, fluency of speech, and intonation. The *Habima* theater, founded in Moscow in 1918 and transferred to Tel Aviv in 1926, perpetuated Russo-Hebrew speech the same way it perpetuated Russian acting conventions and *mise-en-scènes*, at least until the beginning of the 1960s; only with the foundation of the *Cameri Theater* in Tel Aviv in the early 1940s did one get the opportunity to hear a different kind of Hebrew—not exactly native, but relatively liberated from Russo-Yiddish features. Actually, the characteristics of native spoken Hebrew were not only ignored, but even strongly opposed. Native Hebrew was—and still is in certain areas of the establishment—conceived of as an ephemeral phenomenon, which if ignored would gradually go away. This attitude is further reinforced by the school system at all stages by its emphasis on "correct" usage and classical grammar. The various functions required by a colloquial Hebrew and therefore introduced into the language by native speakers, either through transfers or exploitation of indigenous "reserves" of Hebrew, were conceived of as errors.

The official guardians of the language appeared to be impervious to the needs of a living language. To sum up, one may say that native Hebrew assumed in fact the position of a non-canonized, non-official system. Only through a complicated and prolonged process did it begin moving into official culture. Naturally, the generation shift contributed to the acceleration of this process, but the generation shift *per se* is not sufficient to explain this. The acceptance of canonized norms totally opposed to those of common usage is quite common in most cultures. In Palestine, native speakers learned to speak in *Habima* (and the other theaters imitating it) with a Russian accent; on the radio they acquired the habit of pronouncing many features completely absent in their actual speech.[13]

Let us turn now to a consideration of the system of written texts. This is the most highly institutionalized system within culture and as the bearer of official recognition has the central function of generating textual models. Within this system, literature often assumes a central position. In modern Hebrew culture, literature definitely had such a position and such a function, and it makes no difference whether the models adopted by society came directly from Hebrew literature or were mediated by texts such as social, political, and critical writings. The fact that Hebrew developed into a modern language during the nineteenth century in a written form, and further that its long tradition had been primarily literary, enables us to understand why written models had priority over any alternative oral options which might have crystallized during that period. The system of East-European Hebrew literature in Palestine functioned in a manner similar to that of architectural and paralinguistic phenomena by resisting the penetration of native cultural constituents. At least until the end of World War I, the canonized literature produced in Palestine was peripheral to the mainstream of Hebrew literature in other parts of the world; the various types of texts published in Palestine, whether "high" literature or sketches, poems, letters, diaries, etc., disclosed a very strong affinity to earlier stages in the history of Hebrew literature and not to what was the dominant norm at the time in Europe. Therefore, in Palestine not only were new models for Hebrew literature not generated (neither "native" nor any other kinds), with the potential of providing an alternative option; Palestinian Hebrew literature constituted rather a conservative sector within the totality of literary taste and literary activities. On the other hand, when the center of Hebrew literature was transferred to Palestine by means of immigration in the 1920s and early 1930s, it was already an institutionalized system with clear decision-making mechanisms, i.e., clear procedures for employing existing options or finding new ones. The contacts with Russian literature as the available source for alternative options at critical junctures were perpetuated in Palestine at least until the middle of the 1950s.

The gradual rise of Sephardi stress as the metrical norm for Hebrew poetry illustrates the extent to which the institutionalized literary models were closed to the penetration of existing native constituents. For several decades after Sephardi pronunciation dominated spoken Hebrew in Palestine, it still had no impact on the norms of poetic language. Sephardi stress in poetry began to appear in the official sectors only at the beginning of the 1920s; it became the central, dominant norm only at the beginning of the 1930s. This was the case not only with the older generation, but even with poets partly educated in Palestine before World War I, such as Avraham Shlonsky (1900–1977) and his generation. Similarly, when the new "modernist" school of Hebrew poetry emerged in the late 1920s, the models they employed as alternatives to those of the previous generation were based on a massive adoption of Russian constituents, including the rhythm, intonation, word order, rhyming norms, vocabulary, inventory of possible themes, etc., most of which had little connection with local, native constituents. As noted before, the Hebrew poetry created in Palestine before the rise of modernism, as well as the Hebrew prose which had made a certain attempt to deal with the local scene on the thematic level were not considered—nor could they have been—alternative options for introducing change in the literary norms. It was a literature based upon models too old-fashioned for the tastes of the new writers.

Even in the narrative prose written by native Hebrew speakers towards the end of the 1940s, writers who hardly knew any foreign language and who were assuming positions at the center of the literary system, one finds amazingly few constituents of native language. Much of the work of that generation was based on Russian-Hebrew models in accordance with those traditional decision-making procedures which had established themselves in the Hebrew literature of Eastern Europe before the migration to Palestine. Thematic structure, modes of description, narrative composition, segmentation and transition techniques, in short, the entire narrative repertoire of the texts of this generation leaned heavily on both classical Russian and Soviet-Russian models. One may say with justification that in all these areas a vacuum existed in the Hebrew system, and the young writers found the model they needed in the profusion of prose translated from Russian, especially by Shlonsky and his school. Naturally, these texts are not monolithic, and the so-called Russian-Hebrew principles prevailing are not homogeneous; certain local elements are recognizable. But what is decisive here is the fact that the role of native Hebrew was by no means dominant. The conception of what a story would be, the elaboration of narrated reality, the ways of reporting the speech of characters all were linked to a very strong literary tradition, by no means native, the result of the penetration of constituents through contacts with another literature. Only in later texts did native language penetrate narrative prose written by some of the writers belonging to "the generation of the 1940s." Even there it was not quite authentic. Others, who probably had difficulty moving from traditional stylized literary Hebrew, eventually found it easier to write historical novels: in such novels they could employ the "make-believe" literary language with more apparent justification. Furthermore, these phenomena were not exclusively characteristic of the generation in question; they appeared among other groups of writers at the opposite end of the ideological spectrum, the so-called "Canaanites," who favored the total separation of native-born Palestinian Hebrews from the Diaspora Jews. This clearly illustrates the principle that institutionalized options within a cultural system are often stronger than ideologies. True, some of these "Canaanite" writers objected strongly to "non-native" literary Hebrew, and subsequently introduced new language into their journalism. But this was not the case with their literary prose or poetry. Again, we see that new constituents can penetrate the periphery more easily than they can the more official sectors of a system.

Finally, it would be interesting to observe what took place in literature aimed at Hebrew-speaking children. It would be naive to suppose that the situation here would be radically different. Children's literature usually assumes a non-canonized position within the literary polysystem, adopting models that have undergone simplification, or perpetuating models which occupied the center when they were new. Hebrew children were obliged during the period under consideration to read literary translations in an elevated, sometimes pompous literary language, some of which was a stylized Russian-Hebrew, some of which employed the norms of previous stages in the history of literary Hebrew, norms long and far removed from the center of adult literature. These included various components of the literary model such as strophic matrices, composition techniques, thematic and plot models, and so on. The mild attempts of certain writers to alter the language of children's books were considered almost revolutionary, and never became generative for the production of textual models for children. So, the idea of the "new nation" notwithstanding, there was no room for native constituents in the various sub-systems of the culture. Native constituents which could have constituted alternative options found their way only into the periphery. Here, at least, there was not too much opposition. Here conventional constraints which prevailed in canonized literature hardly applied, or did not apply at all. In these texts, often written by amateurs, various native constituents did penetrate, not homogeneously, but as part of a conglomerate of diverse and contradictory features. The texts best known to us of this kind are the short detective novels and the dime novels of the 1930s,[14] but there were other peripheral texts. As for canonized literature, it was only in the mid-1950s that a change took place, and it took place first in poetry where the option of employing the existing and available repertoire of the native system was introduced. The Russian-Hebrew word order, rhythm, and intonation were replaced, in varying degrees, by local Hebrew features. Changes also occurred on more complex levels of the poetic model, such as the phonetic structure, the use of realia materials, and so on. Analogous processes took place in narrative prose too, but these were much more gradual, and have hardly been finalized to date. (For some recent discussions of these problems see Gertz 1983;[15] Shavit 1982.[16])

NOTES

1. "Aliyah" in Hebrew means "ascending." It indicated going to Jerusalem during the high holidays in Biblical times, and in later times going to (the Land of) Israel. In modern Hebrew, it means immigrating to (the Land of) Israel. "The First Aliyah" is the name given to the groups of immigrants who founded the first modern colonies in the 1880s.
2. Thus, during the period under consideration, "Hebrew," as both noun and adjective, had a very precise meaning within the emerging culture, a meaning which no longer

carries much weight in contemporary Israel. It was used in the sense of "a Jew of the Land of Israel," that is, a *non*-Diaspora Jew. One spoke of the "Hebrew (not Jewish) Community [Yishuv]," of the "Hebrew workers," of the "Hebrew army," etc. In Israel's Declaration of Independence, the Arab states are urged to cooperate with the *Hebrew* nation, independent in its land, while the State of Israel appeals to the *Jews* in the Diaspora.

3. "Sephardi" (*sefaradi* in Hebrew, from *Sefarad,* the traditional Hebrew name of Spain) means Hispanic, referring to the large Jewish communities originating in Spain and Portugal (and having spread throughout North Africa, the Balkans, Turkey, Palestine, England, The Netherlands, etc.). The pronunciation current among these communities—and others which have adopted it—differs quite considerably from the pronunciation(s) that have prevailed among the Central and East-European communities, commonly called "Askhenazi" (from *Ashkenaz,* originally referring to medieval Germany), as well as other communities, such as the Yemenite community, which have perpetuated a similar tradition. It has always been considered "superior" by non-Jews, as well as by the Jewish intelligentsia of the Enlightenment movement, though without immediate implications. It was not at all a commonly accepted decision to adopt Sephardi rather than Ashkenazi pronunciation in the 1880s. (The names of Jewish settlements founded in those years, still pronounced with salient Ashkenazi rather than Sephardi features, are relics of this indecisiveness.) The Ashkenazi pronunciation, probably originating in a different geographical part of ancient Palestine, is still current among non-Israeli Jews opposing the State of Israel, or is used in combination with Sephardi features. It is thus identified by Jewish Israelophobes as "Israeli" rather than traditionally "Sephardi."

4. For the Arabs, this was the regular sort of bread produced, consequently called *khubz,* the normal word for "bread" in Arabic. In Hebrew, however, a new word had to be invented. As with many other cases, the Aramaic equivalent—*pita*—was introduced as a new designation. The adoption of this item has been so thorough that the hebraicized Aramaic word has now become known in the West, rather than the originally authentic Arabic one, probably through the propagation of food items by the Israeli emigrants in the United States and Western Europe. (The other popular items, however, such as *humus, tahina* or *falafel,* still bear their Arabic names.)

5. In the opinion of Benjamin Harshav, the notion of the *khata* here stems not from the reality of village life in Russia (or rather the Ukraine), but rather from literary descriptions.

6. On romantic stereotypes of this period, see Gorny, Yosef 1979. "Romantic Elements in the Ideology of the Second Aliyah." *Jerusalem Quarterly* 13: 73–78. (An abridged version of Gorny 1966, in Hebrew).

7. This kind of macaronic language is characterized by the insertion of Yiddishisms when the Hebrew elements are felt by the speaker to be insufficient or inadequate to express emotivity. Thus, even such phrases as "vos iz dos" (literally "what is this"), meaning "what does it mean," "what is the meaning of all this," may be considered more expressive than "ma ze" ("what is it") or "ma perusho shel dabar" ("what is the meaning of this"). Also, established narremes may also under such circumstances be considered more effective than their Hebrew equivalents, conceived of as detached and "high" by the originally Yiddish speaker. Thus "zogt er/zi" ("he/she says") as an interpolated reporting speech device in daily narrative can be heard rather than "hu omer/hi omeret," their established literary equivalents. On top of this, a host of unique Yiddish expressions (such as *nebekh, gevald*) or morphemes (mostly for diminutives: *-le,* plural *-lakh*) penetrated more massively, some to stay, at least in some registers. Such familiar designations as *aba* for *papa* and *ima* for *mama* were introduced from Aramaic, since the Hebrew words *ab* (father) and *em* (mother) belong to

the more official register (i.e., "father" and "mother"). But even these often were felt as stilted, subsequently taking the Yiddish diminutive suffixes, thus generating such forms as *aba-le* and *ima-le*. (The Russian *papochka* and *mamochka*—diminutives of *papa* and *mama*—may also have served as a model in such cases.) It is indeed very unfortunate that the living performers of such a macaronic speech are still not recorded. Although their actual speech today cannot possibly be taken as a fully authentic preservation of macaronic speech in previous decades, the categories of Yiddish insertions must be roughly the same.

8. For a discussion of this issue, see Perry, Menakhem 1984. "Thematic and Structural Consequences of Auto-Translations by Bilingual Yiddish-Hebrew Writers." *Poetics Today* 2, 4:181–92; also Shmeruk, Khone 1978. *Yiddish Literature: Aspects of Its History* (Tel Aviv: Porter Institute); and Even-Zohar, I. and Kh. Shmeruk, 1981. "Authentic Language and Authentic Reported Speech: Hebrew vs. Yiddish." *Ha-Sifrut*, 30/31: 82–87. (Hebrew; English version in Even-Zohar, Itamar 1990. "Polysystem Studies." *Poetics Today* 11, 1:155–63).

9. A rather representative collection of *official* and public documents is available in English (Saulson, Scott B. 1979. *Institutionalized Language Planning: Documents and Analysis of the Revival of Hebrew*. The Hague: Mouton).

10. We must recognize, however, at least as a theoretical option, the possibility that rather than through an internal process of neutralization it was the adoption of a ready-made repertoire that actually took place. Such a repertoire seems indeed to have been there, namely the so-called Lithuanian norm. This norm is markedly different from all the rest of East European norms in its middle-length vowels, which, moreover, are very similar to the Sephardi ones, and its relatively even intonation (in contradistinction, for instance, to the conspicuous "sing-song" of Galician Yiddish or even "rural Lithuanian"). If this is true, the process here termed neutralization did not occur in Palestine, but had been finalized in Lithuania. Unfortunately, there is no research available which would justify our preferring this hypothesis over the neutralization hypothesis. It is, however, clear that the Lithuanian norm, already considered superior prior to the Palestinian development, might have contributed to the preference for the kind of neutralized features which might have developed. One could argue that, had it been the other way round, a non-neutralized, sing-song norm could have been considered "better" or "more beautiful" rather than the "dry" accepted one. (Obviously, the "neutralized" norm is aurally "poorer" than the non-neutralized ones from the point of view of variety of features.)

11. A popular appellation during this period of (Jewish) Palestinian-born people, borrowed from the Arabic word denoting cactus tree. The idea was the image of the *sabra*, who like the cactus, is prickly on the outside but sweet on the inside. The word *sabra* has been replaced with the Hebrew *sabbar* (pronounced "tsabbar"), now almost obsolete.

12. The native-born Hebrew *sabra* evoked—and perhaps still does—an ambiguous response: on the one hand, he is strong, brave, somewhat coarse and outspoken; on the other hand, gentle, childish, and uncultivated. Alter Druyanov collected anecdotes and jokes in *Jokes and Witticisms* (Jerusalem 1945), among which is the following (no. 2636): "Tel Aviv, Herzl Street. A group of children pour out of the Herzlia Gymnasium. Two famous Yiddishists are passing by, having come to visit Palestine [probably just before or after World War I], and the greater Yiddishist says to his junior colleague: 'The Zionists boast that Hebrew is becoming a natural tongue for the children of Palestine. I will now show you that they are lying. I will tweak one of the boys' ears and I promise you that he will not cry out *ima* ["mother" in Hebrew], but *mame* [Yiddish]." So saying, he approached one of the boys and tweaked his ear. The boy turned on him and shouted: 'Idiot!' [*hamor* ("donkey") in Hebrew]. The famous

Yiddishist turned to this friend: 'I am afraid that the Zionists are right.' " The point of this anecdote is not only that the "children of Palestine" were actually speaking Hebrew rather than Yiddish, but that they reacted not at all in the manner supposedly typical of Jewish children. This is, of course, a double disappointment for the famous Yiddishist, as the "new language" also represents a "new (and not familiar) behavior."

13. Some of the most conspicuous features of this kind are still two gutturals (['] and [ḥ]), dental [r] (rather than native velar), shifting stress, and [e] ("schewa mobile"), where speech has a consonant cluster. (For instance, such forms as "kfarim," "pqidim" are thus pronounced "kefarim," "peqidim.")

14. See Shavit, Zohar and Yaacov 1974. "Hebrew Crime Stories During the 1930s in Palestine." *Ha-Sifrut* 18/19:30–73 (English summary: iv).

15. Gertz, Nurit 1983. *Generation Shift in Literary History: Hebrew Narrative Prose in the Sixties.* (Tel Aviv: Porter Institute and Ha-Kibbutz Ha-Meuchad). (Hebrew)

16. Shavit, Zohar 1982. "The Literary Life in Eretz Israel, 1910–1933," *Poetics Today* 11:1 (1990), 175–91. (Hebrew)

29.

The National Idea and the Revival of Hebrew

Chaim Rabin

The revival of Hebrew as a spoken language in the last quarter of the nineteenth century is often called a miracle or a unique event in the world of languages. Yet there is a curious reticence in Israel and elsewhere to subject this event to scientific analysis. I am aware of only one scholarly work devoted exclusively to an analytic account of the process by which the revival was accomplished,[1] though of course the few histories of the Hebrew language devote chapters to it.[2] Neither the centennial of the publication of Eliezer Ben-Yehuda's first article on the subject (1879) nor that of the start of his practical work in Jerusalem (1881), were celebrated by the State of Israel or by the Hebrew Language Academy.[3] Indeed, there are not only Hebrew teachers, writers, and scholars who deny that Ben-Yehuda played a significant role in the language revival; there are quite a few who deny that Hebrew was ever revived, claiming that it never was dead.

It does not seem superfluous, therefore, to define exactly what the revival was, and to look for the factors which produced it precisely at the time it took place. According to some of the Hebrew orthoepists of the present day, Hebrew is not a "revived" language, but "a language in the process of being revived"; in other words, it can not really be considered alive until every Israeli speaks and writes it according to the rules of the Ancient Sources. Without discussing the justification of such a requirement, it will be seen that this concept of revival cannot be subjected to an analysis likely to provide answers to the question we have just asked. But if we do agree to call Hebrew a revived language, this means that the act was completed at some point in the past, and

Reprinted by the permission of the author and *Studies in Zionism* 7 (spring 1983): 31–48.

that the criterion for establishing that point is independent of the linguistic features observable in the active use of Hebrew at the time. It must also be independent of the number of speakers, or the percentage of Jews who spoke it at that moment, since even now not all Israeli citizens of Jewish nationality are fluent in it; and even if all were, they constitute less than 20 percent of the Jewish people—Hebrew speakers and readers outside Israel making up a very small percentage in their communities.

On the other hand, we can hardly claim that a language is "alive" when it is used by just one person, or even by a few people among themselves, or even by hundreds of people only occasionally—as Latin is used by doctors to discuss their patient's state in his presence. A language is alive only if it is used by a community as its means of communication. A community is not defined by criteria of size,[4] but by the existence of a separate network of social interactions, of which language is only one. As is well known, there are well-functioning ethnic communities that use a language which they share with other groups, and other, strongly cohesive nations composed of speakers of different languages in different parts of the territory. We can thus fix the point of revival at that time when Hebrew became the principal vehicle of communication for the communities of Jews in Palestine, or in other words, when there were families who brought up their children with Hebrew as their mother-tongue and, in addition, communicated with other such families in Hebrew on all occasions. This point was reached around 1890, when young people who had been taught in Hebrew-language schools married each other and had children, who could in due course play with each other in Hebrew. This was not true of Ben-Yehuda's first-born son, Itamar Ben-Avi, who by his own testimony could only talk to lizards and birds.

This definition excludes uses of a language as lingua franca for communication between people belonging to different language-communities, as this is used for special purposes and at special times, even if the people who employ it may all belong to a "community" on a higher level. For nearly a century prior to 1879, we have indications that Hebrew, in the Sephardic pronunciation, was used by members of the many separate Jewish communities in the three Holy Cities of Palestine—Jerusalem, Safed, and Tiberias—to communicate with each other in the market or to discuss matters of intercommunal interest. Inside each community and family, the only language spoken was that which they had used in their country of origin, and the Hebrew they used for prayer was pronounced in traditional ways peculiar to each community and quite unlike, in most cases, that Hebrew they used intercommunally. The fact that they were all Jews increased their areas of contact and their need for a common lingua franca, but it did not make Hebrew come "alive" in the sense we have defined. Although it has been claimed that this market talk was really the revival of Hebrew,[5] we have here a phenomenon of an entirely different kind. To my mind, it is most doubtful whether this phenomenon had any part in the process of revival when it came, except for the fact that it enabled Ben-Yehuda to speak only Hebrew from the moment he set foot on the soil of Palestine.

The way in which the traditional Jewish communities of nineteenth century Palestine used a "Jewish language" for oral communication and Hebrew for most written communication (reading and writing books and letters) was typical for Jewish communities in all countries in the nineteenth century, except Western and Central Europe and North America. There Jews conducted both their daily communication and their literary activities in the language of the country and restricted the use of Hebrew to religious purposes. The use of one language for ordinary communication and another for reading and writing is not a phenomenon peculiar to Jews. It was common practice throughout Europe in the Middle Ages, in Greece and China until a short time ago, and in the Arab world, in most of India, in parts of Southeast Asia, and other territories even today. The phenomenon is known to sociolinguistics as "diglossia." The "upper" languages, used for prestigious activities, are in most cases, like Hebrew, ancient languages with impressive literatures, that have changed over the centuries much less than the spoken languages. Because of their often difficult structures, and the need to study their literatures in order to master them, these languages remain the raison d'être of self-perpetuating intellectual élites. Among other parts of the community they are imperfectly known, though they contribute to the vernacular words and phrases necessary for numerous areas of intellectual expression. In many cases, side by side with literary activity in the "upper" language, there also exists a standardized variety of the "lower" language in which religious teaching is available to the less educated, and from which a popular literature, sometimes of great beauty, may evolve. Among the Jews, this happened with Yiddish, Ladino, two forms of Judaeo-Arabic and Kurdish Aramaic, among others.

Here the question arises: in cases where neither the spoken nor the written language fulfills the condition of being the all-purpose means of communication within the community, can either language be called a living language? It becomes obvious here that the metaphor "life" as applied to a language does not mean the same thing as when applied to an organism. A language can, so to speak, lead a partial life, as long as it is regularly employed by a community for some social purpose.[6] The test is whether or not such a language is used not only for reading (e.g., the Hebrew prayer book or the Bible in Westernized Jewish communities), but also for creative expression in writing. The Hebrew language most certainly possessed this feature during the long period from about 200 to 1880, when it was not spoken: it produced an immense and variegated literature and was used for letters, contracts and other private purposes. Care must also be exercised in asking the question with regard not only to the written language, but to the spoken, "lower" language as well: if we deny "life" to Hebrew in eighteenth-century East European Jewish society, we must also deny it to Yiddish, since in a highly literate society a "mere" spoken language cannot be said to be the all-purpose means of communication.

Actually, it appears that the metaphors "live" and "dead" were not applied to languages in the period when diglossia was the normal form of sociolinguistic structure. These terms came into use when the European middle classes developed economic power and demanded political power, within the framework of the nation, itself a new concept in post-medieval Europe. Since Latin, the "upper" language, was common to all West and Central European nations, the national state based itself upon the vernaculars, thus stressing national differences and, incidentally, opening political and administrative office to much broader sections of the population. The vernacular languages gradually usurped the traditional realms of Latin, and in our own century supplanted it even in university theses and Catholic prayer. It took a long time before the national vernaculars were taught in schools on a footing comparable to that of Latin and Greek, and somewhere in the course of that struggle, people came to refer to the vernaculars as "living languages" and to the classical Latin and Greek as "dead languages." It should be noted that in this context "living" does not merely mean "spoken"; it means a language used for all communicative purposes. This type is also referred to as a national language.

National language thus became an ideological necessity for the existence of a nation, European style. England, France, and Spain were states of long standing and could, while developing the national language of the majority, also tolerate the existence of minority languages, on condition that the latter occupy a "lower" diglossic status vis-à-vis the national language. Things changed as the national idea spread eastward.

Germany and Italy achieved unity on linguistic grounds; the Austro-Hungarian Empire was destroyed by the urge of language communities to establish national states of their own; and the Russian Empire began to feel similar pressures until, after 1917, it was reorganized as a union of language-based republics and territories, a device also employed in the creation of Yugoslavia. Today linguistic separatism has once again reared its head in the old Western European states.

The emergence of numerous European nationalities also affected areas which had not, properly speaking, been diglossic, but were rather underdeveloped agricultural countries with a thin layer of literate priests and administrators, where the spoken language had not been standardized and had produced mainly oral folk-literature. In the nineteenth century these countries developed literary forms of their languages and began to produce printed literature, grammars, and dictionaries. This process was termed "revival": the creation of a "living" national language by the addition of a written form to the spoken language and the production of a literature which adopted Western forms and genres.

The movement to standardize and create literary languages did not leave the Jewish languages untouched. Yiddish, Ladino, and North African Judaeo-Arabic created Western-style literatures, with Yiddish attaining the status of a major literary language. It is interesting to note that Shalom Aleichem in a Hebrew article called this process "the revival of the *zhargon*."[7] No doubt the existence of a large Yiddish literature, press, etc., contributed to the recognition of the Jews as a national minority in several East European states after 1918. However, the "upgrading" of Yiddish did not go so far as to rule out diglossia and displace Hebrew from its traditional role. The reason for this is obvious: Jews in different countries spoke different languages; to develop Yiddish to the status of a "complete" national language would have meant breaking up the Jewish people into a number of nations, as the Christian world had been broken up in the preceding centuries.[8] It is significant that the only country where an attempt was made to establish a Yiddish without diglossia was Soviet Russia, where the separation went so far as the phonetic Yiddish spelling of Hebrew words.

But long before the literary modernization of those Jewish languages, which coincides chronologically with the Hebrew revival of the late nineteenth century, a movement had set in for the literary Westernization and modernization of Hebrew. It began modestly in the sixteenth century with a play[9] and a scientific historical work using contemporary methods.[10] In the eighteenth century, modern Hebrew literature was

produced in Holland, Germany, Italy, Bohemia, and Hungary, and crystallized into a literary movement called the *Haskalah* (Enlightenment).
In 1750 Moses Mendelssohn made a short-lived attempt to produce a
Hebrew literary weekly of the type of the London *Tatler,* and in 1784
the literary monthly *Hame'assef* began to appear. Haskalah literature
went through all the stages of European literary fashion: Classicism,
Sturm und Drang, Romanticism, and Realism. In the mid-nineteenth
century there arose a regular press, which in the 1880s spawned two
daily papers, and there were even penny dreadfuls.[11] While there was
jealousy between Hebrew and Yiddish writers, many writers published
in both languages.

From its very beginnings, the Haskalah movement concerned itself
with the problem of improving the political, social, and economic position of East European Jewry. In this respect, it proved itself a national
movement, in keeping with the national character of other language-
revival movements. Until 1881, however, its endeavors and suggestions
were based on the assumption that the Jews would remain in their
countries of residence, and on the hope that the governments of those
countries would improve the status of the Jews and remove the restrictions imposed on them. Although, especially in the first half of the
nineteenth century, biblical themes played a prominent role, no indication was given that the Jews might better their lot by returning to
their ancient land. This was so even though the nineteenth century saw
increased emigration of traditionalist Jewish circles into Palestine, and
some *Maskilim* went there as teachers or as representatives of humanitarian bodies. The books considered to be the forerunners of Zionism,
Moses Hess's *Rome and Jerusalem* (1862) and Leon Pinsker's *Auto-
Emancipation* (1882), were written in German, not in Hebrew.

Nor was any suggestion made to Hebraize Jewish life, beyond the
sphere of the written word. In Haskalah novels and short stories, the
heroes converse on a large number of subjects, all in the pure biblical
Hebrew adopted by the Maskilim. Those writers developed considerable
skill in expressing everything they wanted to say in that Hebrew, and if
those conversations look to us today rather stilted, as our Hebrew is
based on additional sources, it must be admitted that they are effective.
In theory it would have been possible for people to speak like this in real
life. Indeed, one of the last Haskalah personalities, Joseph Halevi, a
Bulgarian Sephardi and later Professor at the Sorbonne, taught in biblical Hebrew and hoped to see it introduced as the language of Jewish
schools.[12] But none of the Haskalah authors in Eastern Europe ever

suggested speaking Hebrew, and when Ben-Yehuda advocated it, some of them opposed the idea.

When we consider these matters in the light of what we have said about the linguistic revival movements of their time—which were of course known to the Jewish intelligentsia—we cannot escape the conclusion that for them the "revival" of the Hebrew language was just that: the acquisition of a modern literature and other written uses, thus giving it the status of a European-style national language.

We have some actual evidence for the application of the term "revival" to written Hebrew literature. A pamphlet, published for the first time in 1891, bears the title *Eine auferstandene Sprache,* "A Resurrected Language."[13] Its author, Fabius Schach, was born in Latvia in 1868, and was an early Zionist, who afterward played a role at the First Zionist Congress in 1897. It seems that he visited Palestine before writing the pamphlet. In the introduction he says

we have become accustomed to look upon Hebrew as a dead language and to place it on the same level as Greek and Latin . . . and yet, this language is even today a living language, the real language of spiritual and cultural life for four million people. Contemporary Hebrew is more alive and more classical than the Hebrew of the Spanish period . . . in our days Hebrew is the national language *(Volkssprache)* of the Jews living in Russia and Galicia.

After describing the literary activity in Eastern Europe and in America (where he mentions Hebrew newspapers in New York and Baltimore), Schach states:

But nowhere is Hebrew to such a degree the sole object of study for Jewish youth as in Palestine. There we find a large number of Hebrew language-associations, two newspapers, *Hahavatzelet* [founded 1864] and *Haor* [of Ben-Yehuda, founded 1890], monthly and annual publications, collections of poems, and other literary products.

Nowhere, however, in the pamphlet does he mention Hebrew as the language of daily speech in Palestine, nor does the name of Ben-Yehuda figure in it. The only reference is:

Many attempts have been made to use Hebrew as language of instruction in schools, and this method has shown tremendous success. Especially in the schools of the Palestinian *colonies* in the last few years, excellent results have been achieved with Hebrew as language of instruction, which was introduced at the request of Baron de Rothschild.[14]

Schach must have heard Hebrew spoken in 1891 in Palestine, and in all probability spoke himself Hebrew—but this did not matter. Literature was all that mattered in the "resurrection" as seen by him, and probably by many of his contemporaries.[15]

To the best of my knowledge, the idea of Hebrew as the language of everyday life, *Umgangssprache* in Schach's terminology, was formulated for the first time by Ben-Yehuda in an article "A Weighty Question," published in the Hebrew monthly *Hashahar*, in Vienna, in March 1878.[16] It cannot be denied, however, that the formulation seems exceedingly weak for a political propaganda article, and especially one written in such a fiery style. In fact, it consists only of a single sentence. After arguing that several nations in the Western world do not have a single language, Ben-Yehuda proceeds (p. 5, H. 42): "We Hebrews, indeed, have an advantage in that we possess a language in which we can even now write anything we care to, *and which it is also in our power to speak if only we wish.*" The article does not return to the issue of Hebrew speaking. Quite the contrary: in the glowing description of life in the future Jewish settlement in Palestine, with which the article concludes, stress is laid on literature and on the way it will flourish (p. 11, H. 48). It seems that even the words—"those who live in the Diaspora will know that 'their people' dwells in its land, that its language and its literature are there. The language too will flourish, and literature will spawn writers in plenty."—do not refer to spoken language, or to the idea that the community in Palestine would be monolingual, and therefore the writers forced to write in Hebrew. The reference is to a renaissance of the written literary language.

This curious disproportion has led George Mandel, in a lecture at the Oxford symposium, to deny that Ben-Yehuda intended, in this first article of his, to advocate the revival of Hebrew speaking.[17] This interesting and detailed article suggests, with due reserve, that Ben-Yehuda might have added the above sentence to an existing text of the article (which had at first been sent to another paper, but without success) as a result of meeting a teacher from Palestine, with whom he had spoken Hebrew for the first time.[18] This would actually make Ben-Yehuda's subsequent efforts for Hebrew as an everyday language for all purposes an offshoot of the use of Hebrew as lingua franca, to which we referred above—for that would have been the source of the teacher's ability to speak it.

Closer inspection of the passage in which this sentence appears proves, however, that it is an integral part of its surroundings and essential for the argument, and thus must have been in the article from the beginning. To prove this, we have not only to reconstruct the argument, but to examine the cause for the inclusion of Hebrew speaking in it.

Ben-Yehuda was born in Luzhki, not far from Kovno, then part of Russia. After a period of Yeshiva study, he attended a Russian secondary school at Dwinsk/Dinaburg, now in Latvia, where he came under the spell of the wave of Slav nationalism generated by the Bulgarian War of Independence against Turkey. His decision to study medicine in Paris seems to have been part of a plan to settle in Palestine. While in Paris, he associated with nationalists, exiles from countries which only after World War I obtained their independence from Russia or from the Hapsburg Empire. He also studied Classical Hebrew and other Semitic languages at the Sorbonne under Prof. Joseph Halevy, who, as we have mentioned before, lectured—sometimes or always—in Hebrew. From his nationalist friends he learnt about the central place language occupied in every national movement, and must have got the message that "national language" meant a written, prestigious literary language. Speaking, apparently, mattered little, being available anyway, though, of course, when necessary, the common spoken idiom could be cited as an argument for the existence and extent of the nationality in question. From Halevy he learnt that Hebrew could be spoken, but of course understood that spoken Hebrew, not being available as were the other national vernaculars, was no suitable argument for the existence of the Jewish people. On the other hand, the Jews possessed what many of the other nations were toiling to acquire: a literary language and a prestigious literature.

This comes out very clearly in his article. The first pages (2–4, H. 37–41) are devoted to a detailed exposition of the concept of nationalism and conclude quoting the assimilationist view that "Hebrew nationality is dead and only the Jewish religion and those who profess it remain on earth." Then, on p. 5 (H. 41–2), in the paragraph from which we have cited the sentence about the possibility of speaking Hebrew, he actually argues that a common language is not "an essential criterion of nationhood," nor is it a necessary condition for the whole nation to dwell in one country, and quotes J. S. Mill, "Considerations on Representative Government," who defines a nationality as "united among themselves by common sympathies . . . But the strongest of all is identity of political antecedents: the possession of a national history, and consequent community of recollections." But on p. 6 (H. 43) Ben-Yehuda passes on to a criterion which the Englishman Mill did not mention at all, namely, literature. He discusses the potential role literature can play in the regeneration of a nation, but bewails the fact that "our literature," i.e., modern Hebrew literature—as is clear from his description—"made no impact on the life of the [Jewish] people either in Russia or in the countries of the West" (p. 7, H. 44). The reason for this, he continues, is that Hebrew literature cannot successfully deal with the problems of the Jewish nation because the Jews, being scattered, have no control over their own fate.

All our efforts will be in vain as long as there is no national center, a center which will attract to it all the elements of the body politic. In vain will be all the effort of our writers to revive the language if the entire people remains scattered in different lands among nations speaking different languages [p. 8, H. 45].

Ben-Yehuda's solution to the problem is to settle part of the people in Palestine, and to develop the country with the help of a society which will collect money and report on its activities to the nation.

And what will be the result of the creation of such a national center?

Only then our literature will renew its vigor, because writers will serve it not for love alone, but also for reward. . . . Jewish scholarship, too, will thrive and blossom and bear fruit, like a healthy plant in its native soil, and it will bring benefit to all the people. Herein lies our people's salvation and our nation's happiness! [p. 11, H. 48].

In other words, literature—and with it the literary language—still remains the greatest achievement of a modern nation. But in order to function, it needs a territory where the population depends on this literature alone, and behind it the national idea, which will provide literature with its purpose.

When Ben-Yehuda published this article, he was twenty years old, and he himself in later years referred to it as an immature work.[19] This should not detract, though, from its innovatory character: it linked the Jewish problem with the national idea in its modern, Western formulation; it linked nationalism with the necessity of some territorial foundation in the land where Jewish history began;[20] and it clearly established the role of language and literature as the foundation and prerequisite for national revival. It is also clear that at that time the spoken language was not for Ben-Yehuda a sine qua non for national existence, though it might be desirable and, at any rate, possible. Its inclusion in his argument was to some extent forced upon him by a chain of circumstances of recent date, which may or may not have been the immediate cause of his decision to write the article, but which were reflected in the crucial paragraph.

On June 12, 1878, the day the International Conference on the Future of the Turkish Empire opened in Berlin, the anti-Semitic delegate, Viktor Istóczy, delivered a speech in the Hungarian parliament, in which he suggested that the parliament urge the Berlin Conference to get the Sultan to place Palestine at the disposal of the Jews, to create a Jewish state, and to transfer the Jews of Hungary there. In 1905 he himself translated the speech into German and published it as a pamphlet called *Die Wiederherstellung des jüdischen Staates in Palästina,* with a preface and a postscript which suggest that he was impressed with the rise of organized Zionism, and saw himself as a precursor of Zionism. In this speech he stressed the link of the Jewish people *(das jüdische Volk)* with Palestine:

Has the Jewish people erased from its heart the attachment to its original homeland? Have the ancient traditions lapsed, which are indissolubly tied to the scenes of past national glory? It is not true that this people clings to its ancient customs, and a large section of it even to its ancient dress, *language,* and script, with a tenacity and attention to detail to which there is no parallel in history?

In Hungary, where the national language had passed through a revival only two generations earlier, the significance of the national language was clear to everyone, and it is certain that Istóczy referred to Hebrew, since at that time Hungarian Jews spoke mostly Hungarian.

In spite of its reference to language, this anti-Semitic proposal (which the speaker withdrew at the end of his oration) would not be worth mentioning in this context, were it not for the fact that Istóczy gave an interview, or sent a German version of the manuscript of his speech, to the prestigious daily *Süddeutsche Presse* in advance, and the paper published an item on it on May 26, 1878. On June 11, 1878, the editor of the *Allgemeine Zeitung des Judenthums* at Leipzig, the Reform Rabbi Ludwig Philippson, reacted to the item in an article headed, like Istóczy's publication, *Die Wiederherstellung des jüdischen Staates.*[21] As the item in the *Presse* was headed *Hierosolyma,* and in Philippson's reply there appear other phrases from Istóczy's 1905 German rendering, it is likely that the newspaper worked from a text resembling, if not identical with, the speech given some weeks later. Philippson does not in this article discuss the general question of whether the Jews are a people or not, apart from mentioning the hope for the coming of the Messiah as something confined to orthodox Jews. Among the "many real factors that reduce the idea of restoring a Jewish national state to the status of a mere fantasy born of love or hatred," he proposes to deal only with one: language.

Real national life includes as an indispensable requirement a common language. The Jews, however, have no such language [a list and details of the languages follow]. Now imagine this many-tongued mass united into one state! One might object that the Jews do have a common language, namely Hebrew. But this is nothing but a chimera. The holy language is restricted to the learned, and most Jewish scholars indeed read and write Hebrew, but, for lack of practice and occasions to use it, they cannot speak it. Add to this the variety of pronunciations of Hebrew. It sounds so different in the mouth of Oriental, Sephardic, German, and Polish Jews, as if they were talking different dialects. Thus the Jews of Jerusalem are divided into communities according to their countries of origin, and these communities have nothing in common, not even synagogues, except for the distribution of alms from Europe. . . . We stress language, because this is the clearest proof that the Jews fully belong to every country and every nation where they have settled for so many centuries. . . . Language is the most permanent link of a nation, and it is just this link which for centuries has connected the Jews with those different nations.

The new element which Philippson's article introduced into the discussion is that of the spoken language. Countries like Germany had given up diglossia centuries before, and could not even imagine what it was like to live with two languages. What Philippson says about the restriction of the knowledge of Hebrew to the learned was just as true of Latin for German-speaking peoples in the Middle Ages, and the fact that the Jews of Jerusalem in his own time could communicate with each other in writing without any difficulty made no impression on him. He may not have known that they had also overcome the obstacle of different reading pronunciations in their Sephardic-based market Hebrew. For a person with a Western European education, "language" was the language he spoke and, as a matter of course, also wrote; all others were foreign languages to be learnt at school, none of which could replace the "mother-tongue." An added factor may have been the peculiarly German ideology, nurtured by W. von Humboldt's book *On the Difference between Human Languages* and by German Romanticism, that language was linked with the national character and largely determined a person's ways of thinking.[22]

Ben-Yehuda mentions "Philippson in his journal" in the paragraph we have been discussing, as one of those who "declare that we are not able to lead a national life because we do not all *speak* one and the same language [my emphasis, C.R.]." To this his reply is twofold: (a) we have a fully developed written language; (b) speaking it is only a matter of wanting to. He also answers the argument that only the learned know Hebrew by saying: "and if many of us spurn Hebrew, if many of our people cannot even read Hebrew, who is to blame? Who has deprived us of a knowledge of the language if not this [assimilationist] philosophy itself?"

It is not our task to examine the objective justification of either Philippson's or Ben-Yehuda's arguments. Of course there are many chinks in the theory that national life is conditioned by a common spoken language. In Philippson's time, even more than in present-day West Germany, the normal spoken language, even of the educated, was dialect, and the dialects were in many cases not mutually intelligible. Standard German, *Hochdeutsch,* was learnt in school, and the ability to express oneself fluently in it orally was limited to a thin layer of intellectuals. Indeed, it may be said, with little exaggeration, that what united European states was precisely the written language. This was coupled with a fairly high rate of literacy which enabled people to read it, and the national consensus that all dialects were part of one and the same language. But then this was still a far cry from a language which nobody spoke. On the other hand, Ben-Yehuda's attempt to explain the widespread ignorance of written Hebrew as a result of assimilationist ideology was not true even for Western Jewry, and certainly did not apply to East European or Oriental Jewry, where the spoken languages were themselves Jewish. But then, language ideologies are not based upon "facts" (which are in any case open to different interpretations), but on attitudes. And it is here that we have to seek an explanation for the peculiar phrasing of that sentence: "and which it is also in our power to speak if only we wish" (p. 7, H. 42).

The phrasing suggests that Ben-Yehuda was somewhat surprised by Philippson's insistence on spoken language and his cavalier treatment of the use of written Hebrew (which Philippson acknowledged as existing among the "learned"). This was not only contrary to all that Ben-Yehuda had learnt about modern nationalism—where all efforts were concentrated upon the written language—but also to ingrained Jewish attitudes, nurtured by millennia of diglossia: one respected written languages and made light of spoken ones. "Zhargon" was suitable for women and manual workers, and vernacular non-Jewish languages of merely practical value, for trade or dealing with officials. If anything, Hebrew was too precious to be spoken—an attitude voiced by some well-known Hebrew writers in the controversies which followed the publication of Ben-Yehuda's first article. Ben-Yehuda could not leave Philippson's argument unanswered, but the reply did not need to be detailed or documented: suffice it to say that we can speak Hebrew if we only wish to, if Philippson thinks this a matter of such importance.

This, however, did not exhaust the matter. The idea that we could speak Hebrew if we wanted to was also literally true. It meant that those who were expert in reading Hebrew and used to writing it had no difficulty in pronouncing it or in forming sentences in it to express what they wanted to say. We have a fair number of anecdotes from the Middle Ages showing that Jews spoke Hebrew to other Jews whose native language was different from their own.[23] We read of sermons and halakhic lectures being delivered in Hebrew by scholars from a foreign country. Some pious Jews spoke Hebrew on Sabbath. Very many Jews, among them quite simple ones, used a form of speech called "Hebrew" as a secret language in the marketplace and on other occasions. The grammatical structure was of their everyday language but the vocabulary consisted mainly of Hebrew words. The Palestinian market Hebrew of the nineteenth century was another example of their skill in turning a passive knowledge of the language into an active one. Jews who prayed regularly and "learnt" aloud the weekly portion of the Pentateuch, Mishnah, or Talmud, had no difficulty in articulating Hebrew words and sentences in a pronunciation compatible with the sound combinations of their local Jewish language. When Ashkenazim changed over to the "Sephardic" pronunciation, they simply omitted from it the difficult sounds which that pronunciation has in common with Arabic, and gave the consonants, the vowels, and the intonation the same forms they had in whatever language they spoke at home. In the various Jewish languages, there were hundreds of Hebrew words and idioms which could be incorporated effortlessly into whole sentences in Hebrew. The Mishnah-based syntax which the traditional Jew used to read and write, and which also largely influenced the language of the Haskalah—in spite of its Biblical vocabulary and grammatical inflections—presented no difficulties for speakers of European languages, including European-Jewish languages. Thus, for an educated Jew, conducting a conversation in Hebrew was not something that had to be learnt or acquired, but simply the realization of an existing potential, triggered by will or by necessity.

Ben-Yehuda's own experience of this has been described dramatically by him in his autobiographical work, "The Dream and Its Interpretation," published almost fifty years later, in 1917/18.[24] At the beginning of 1879, he received confirmation of the acceptance of his article for publication from the editor of Hashahar. Wishing to share his joy, he repaired to the house of an acquaintance and found there, not his host, but another visitor, identified in the passage as Mr. Zundelman.[25] He showed him the letter, and the two went to a large café in Boulevard Montmartre, where

we sat and talked for about two hours about my plans for the future and the work I had been offered in Jerusalem, as well as all the political problems of those days. And this long, enthusiastic, and serious conversation was conducted entirely in Hebrew! This was the first time I spoke Hebrew for so long, on such serious matters, and not just in order to speak Hebrew, but for the sake of the subject at issue. For minutes at a time I almost forgot that I was talking Hebrew.

True, in retrospect Ben-Yehuda states that this conversation convinced him how much the Hebrew language still had to be developed until it could serve all the needs of modern everyday communication. But the fact is that both he and Mr. Zundelman talked for two hours, said what they wanted to say, and did not have to give up, either through exhaustion or through disgust with their inability to express themselves. And Mr. Zundelman was not a Hebrew zealot, as Ben-Yehuda may have been by then; just a Jew with a good Hebrew and Aramaic education. Yet he apparently had as little difficulty in speaking as Ben-Yehuda had. The ability to speak was just beyond the threshold, and only a small push was necessary in order to cross it.

Soon after Ben-Yehuda began his literary career, perhaps even as a result of "A Weighty Question" (Hashahar was widely read in Eastern Europe), hundreds, and soon thousands, of educated Jews in the Pale of Settlement began to speak Hebrew to each other and "language societies" sprang up in many towns, where people met to speak Hebrew and to hear Hebrew lectures. When, after 1881, Russian Jews started to emigrate to the United States, they brought not only Hebrew literature and the Hebrew press with them, but also the habit, in more intellectual circles, of speaking Hebrew, the manifestation of an ability that had lain dormant. In a similar manner, when Ben-Yehuda went to Palestine in 1881 and insisted on speaking nothing but Hebrew, he found friends who were willing and able to discuss his plans and problems with him in that language.

Still, this was not the revival of spoken Hebrew; it was only a kind of trial run, which proved that speaking Hebrew was possible. Those educated enough to use their latent Hebrew were a minority, and they spoke Hebrew only on occasion: they had still to live and communicate through other languages. As Ben-Yehuda himself stated shortly after, reviving Hebrew was a political act. It was accomplished through the creation of a small, but steadily growing body of immigrants into Palestine, the "New Yishuv," who had some concept of political Zionism. It then was accelerated through the establishment of Hebrew-language schools, where everything, including the Hebrew language itself, was taught through the medium of Hebrew. The gradual emergence of a community of monolingual Hebrew speakers, who had to, or were resolved to, conduct their communication on all occasions through the medium of Hebrew, bestowed on it the social status of a national language.

Ben-Yehuda also referred to his first conversation in Hebrew in the Introduction to his *Thesaurus of the Hebrew Language:*[26]

And in one of the streets of Paris, in a café in Bd. Montmartre, I conversed in Hebrew for the first time with one of my acquaintances. We sat at a round table, on which there were two cups of black coffee, and the strange sounds of that ancient, dead Oriental language mingled with the noise of the joyous cadences of the living, beautiful, rich French language.

These words were written around 1920, after Ben-Yehuda had completed several volumes of his great dictionary. He had for this purpose combed the immense Hebrew literature of three thousand years in order to dig up words that could be employed for the thousands of modern concepts that had to be expressed and for the everyday needs not covered by the Bible and by the books normally studied. By then many hundreds of new words had also been created. The two processes—the recovery of words from literature and the creation of new words—have been going on ever since. Such processes take place in every language as a result of the constant changes in the world around us, and are of course more intensive in languages that have entered the orbit of Western civilization only recently, as Hebrew did in the 1880s. The need to supply language material which Hebrew lacked because it had been outside Western life for so long, is expressed in the word "dead." But Hebrew was not a dead language: it merely changed its position from that of the "upper" language in a diglossia to that of a national, Western-style all-purpose language, and it had to fit itself for that new role. The idea that Hebrew was "revived" from the Bible and early Rabbinic literature is wrong. Neither Ben-Yehuda nor his contemporaries had to resort to the Bible, the Mishnah, etc., in order to compose their sentences. They used a language which had been functioning and changing for a long time. It so happened that at the moment when speaking became more common, Hebrew was being written in two forms: that of the modernist Haskalah, trying to preserve Biblical diction; and—more widely among the large traditional majority—that of the Rabbinic language, with little attention being paid to its exact preservation. The revival coincided, whether by accident or through social forces not yet sufficiently investigated, with a reform of modern literary language by Mendele Mokher Sefarim, who reverted to the mixed language of the traditionalists, but treated it stylistically in the Haskalah manner. This confluence of two streams strengthened the language because it considerably enlarged the vocabulary and released the writer and speaker from the nervous anxiety of Haskalah pedantry. But there was no artificiality about the process: modern spoken and written Hebrew is and remains a natural continuation of the language as it was spoken and written for over 1400 years and written for another 1700. Its revival consists in the political act of restoring to it a sphere of usage which it had possessed and temporarily lost. This act was made necessary by another political process, Zionism.

NOTES

1. Jack Fellman, *The Revival of a Classical Tongue,* The Hague, 1973. Reuven Sivan, *The Revival of the Hebrew Language,* Jerusalem, 1980, deals with the linguistic aspects, while Robert St. John, *Tongue of the Prophets,* Garden City, 1952, concentrates on the personality of Ben-Yehuda.

2. William Chomsky, *Hebrew: The Eternal Language,* Philadelphia, 1957, pp. 231–44; Chaim Rabin, *A Short History of the Hebrew Language,* Jerusalem, 1973, pp. 62–73; Reuven Sivan, *History of the Language* (Hebrew), Jerusalem, 1979, pp. 30–31; Eduard Yechezkel Kutscher, *A History of the Hebrew Language,* Jerusalem, 1982, pp. 183–96.

3. The Department for Adult Education of the Ministry for Education and Culture marked the day by a Seminar for Ulpan Teachers at the Habima Theater in Tel Aviv. The English-language *The Jerusalem Post* carried an editorial entitled "Hebrew Centenary," on December 29, 1978.

4. Some ethnic language communities are known to comprise only 150 members.

5. Tudor V. Parfitt, "The Use of Hebrew in Palestine, 1800–1882," *Journal of Semitic Studies* 17 (1972), pp. 237–52.

6. Every language has well-differentiated forms for use in socially recognized circumstances, such as informal and formal, literary, official, and technical. These are often called "registers." Diglossia is an extreme form of this, where a group of prestige registers is based on a different language.

7. In *Hamelitz,* no. 80, 25 Nisan, 5649 (1889), p. 3, col. 3. I use the spelling *zhargon* in order to avoid the negative connotations of the English word "jargon."

8. Similarly the Arab countries have refrained so far from resolving their own diglossia situation by developing the spoken regional dialects; this would turn them linguistically into separate nations. The revival of Arabic in the last century was a modernization of the "upper" language.

9. Judah Sommo, *Elegant Comedy about a Wedding* (Hebrew), ed., Hayyim Schirmann, Jerusalem, 1946.

10. Azariah de' Rossi (Min ha-Adummim), *Light of the Eyes* (Hebrew), Mantua, 1574.

11. David Patterson, *The Hebrew Novel in Czarist Russia,* Edinburgh, 1964.

12. Shlomoh Haramati, *Three Who Preceded Ben-Yehuda* (Hebrew), Jerusalem, 1978, pp. 11–45.

13. Hebrew *tehiyyah* means both "revival" and "resurrection of the dead."

14. I have only seen the undated second edition, pp. 5, 7, 19. Cf. B. Kirschner, *Jüdische Rundschau* (Berlin), January 7, 1938, p. 4.

15. Ben-Yehuda himself uses the term in that way when he says: "In vain will be all the effort of our writers to revive the language." (p. 8, H. 45).

16. Volume 9, pp. 359–66, Adar 5639. All quotations are from the English translation by David Patterson, published in: Eisig Silberschlag, ed., *Eliezer Ben-Yehuda: A Symposium in Oxford,* Oxford Centre for Postgraduate Hebrew Studies, 1981. The page references are followed by "H." with the corresponding page number in Reuven Sivan, ed., *Eliezer Ben-Yehuda, Selected Writings, with an Introduction and Notes* (Hebrew), Jerusalem, 1978.

17. "*She'ela Nikhbada* and the Revival of Hebrew," in Silberschlag, *Oxford Symposium,* pp. 25–39.

18. Ibid., p. 34.

19. Ibid., p. 37.

20. Meir Gertner, "Hebrew—Its Political Life," *Afrasian* (London), 2 (1968) 10, claims that Ben-Yehuda's essential innovation was linking the language to the country.

21. Pages 371–73. Cf. Elyakum Getzel Kressel "The Meaning of *She'ela Nikhbada* by Eliezer Ben-Yehuda" (Hebrew), in Charles Berlin, ed., *Studies. . . in Honor of J. Edward Kiev,* New York, 1971, Hebrew Section, pp. 117–22.

22. The same identification of a "language" with its spoken use is reflected in Herzl's statement in his *Judenstaat* (1896), that the language of the planned Jewish state cannot be Hebrew: "Who among us knows Hebrew sufficiently well to ask for a railway ticket in that language?" These words already occur in this form in his diaries (*Tagebücher,* I. 1922, p. 195). But from the same source (pp. 351–52, February 23, 1896) we learn that in fact Herzl's motives for rejecting Hebrew were more complex. After meeting a Russian Zionist who pressed him to advocate Hebrew as the language for the Jewish state, he notes: "If we create a neo-Hebrew state, it will only become something like the new Greece. But if we avoid enclosing ourselves in a linguistic ghetto, then the whole world will be ours."

23. Cecil Roth, *Personalities and Events in Jewish History,* Philadelphia, 1953, chap. 9; Chomsky, *Eternal Language,* pp. 217–23.

24. Sivan, *Ben-Yehuda, Selected Writings,* p. 47.

25. George Mandel is doing research on the identity of "Zundelman."

26. Sivan, *Ben-Yehuda, Selected Writings,* p. 139; *Thesaurus Totius Hebraitatis,* Prolegomena. Jerusalem, 1948, p. 3.

30.

Shall All Hopes Be Fulfilled? Genre and Anti-Genre in the Hebrew Literature of Palestine

Gershon Shaked

PALESTINE: CONTINUITY OR REVOLUTION?

Did the translocation of the Jewish cultural center from the diaspora to Palestine mark a revolution? A study of the literature produced in Palestine during the First Aliyah and Second Aliyah suggests a negative answer.[1]

In the late nineteenth century and the beginning of the twentieth, Palestine occupied a remote corner on the map of Hebrew and Jewish culture, its eventual preeminence as yet unforeseen. True, Ahad Ha-Am (1856–1927) had hoped the Land of Israel would play a central role in the history of Jewish thought, and serve as a model to communities abroad whose crumbling centers desperately sought new sources of influence.[2] However, even as he began expounding his doctrine, Ahad Ha-Am knew "the truth from Eretz Israel,"[3] too well to entertain any delusions as to a phoenix-like regeneration of Jewish culture.

Recognition that Palestine was not merely a social and economic sanctuary, but a cultural last resort as well, crystallized mainly from World War I onwards. However, signs appeared already at the turn of the century, as members of the Second Aliyah began constructing a new lingual and social culture.

Presaging catastrophe for diaspora Jewry, M. Glickson (1878–1938) writes in *Masuot*, one of the last periodicals published in Odessa:

Translated from the Hebrew and reprinted by permission of the author from *Hasiporet haivrit, 1880–1980*, vol. 2, by Gershon Shaked (Tel Aviv: Hakibbutz Hameuhad, 1982), 17–36.

The diaspora culture, the culture of Romantic sorrow and passive hope, is doomed. What shall we do until our new culture, the culture of venture and construction, shines forth in all its glory? The forces of the Ghetto, the forces of preservation and endurance through contraction, are being destroyed before our very eyes—will we find new strength both for the gigantic creation and for nurturing the national soul throughout the transition? Or are we doomed, God forbid, to the horrible tragedy of "the children are come to the birth, and there is not strength to bring forth"?[4]

Prophetic words indeed. Cultural obliteration preceded the physical. Several years later, Yaakov Rabinowitz (1875–1948) soberly describes the chances and the limitations of the new culture:

Literature here shall be different, not Jewish in the common sense, but human, with multiple concerns and hues. Its Jewishness shall be different as well— adapting to life here and generated by it. There shall be undesirable phenomena, and the occasional reduction and cultural decline. The basis shall expand, the back shall ache a bit. Do not rejoice, do not be bitter. Only watch, and understand.[5]

Figuring prominently on the literary agenda, the mutual relations between Palestine and the diaspora became a major issue of debate during the 1920s and 1930s. Has the change in historical destiny truly occurred, pondered many writers, expressing their lurking incertitudes most often in their correspondence. Indeed, the doubts of writers and consumers of literature are crucial to the understanding of literary phenomena.

What image should the country assume? Will the revolution of immigration yield an existential one as well? Such were the questions running as a *leitmotif* through the authors' minds. Witness the words of Shlomo Zemach (1885–1974), among the first immigrants of the Second Aliyah, who emigrated to study agronomy abroad and return better-equipped for his agricultural mission:

Much suffering have I experienced since the day I left Warsaw. I have lived with the Bolsheviks, been trampled by the Ukrainians, and encountered nothing that is good. Finally I escaped by the skin of my teeth with my wife and my daughter in my arms, and I arrived in Jaffa. I had hoped to rest, regain my strength and work. You undoubtedly know what happened in Jaffa. Riots, dead, wounded, poverty, famine, plunder.

On the third day (May 3rd) I attended the funeral of the thirty-two martyrs, the frigid corpse of Y. H. Brenner heavy on my shoulder. There is no escape, none.[6]

Zemach's words are no exception. He echoes several progenitors of the Second Aliyah, particularly Yosef Hayyim Brenner (1881–1921): a change of place cannot effect a change in Jewish destiny. Thus, the tension between break and transformation on the one hand, and immutable destiny on the other, is never absent from Hebrew literature. Poignantly presented by Brenner during his early days in Palestine, it found reflection in his life and death.[7] The phenomenon evoked diverse literary responses, ranging from a euphoric embracing of the new reality [Wilkanski (1882–1949) and Zemach], to disappointment and despair [Shmuel Joseph Agnon (1888–1970) and A. Reuveni (1886–1951)]. Yet the predominant reaction is akin to Brenner's, conceiving of the new reality as the least evil possible.[8] Implicit in many works, this approach is fully formulated in Yaakov Rabinowitz's letters. In the 1920s he writes as follows to Yizhak Lamdan (1899–1954), then in Germany: "Palestine, my friend, is no paradise, and our people, no people. Nonetheless, if we disparage them, what shall remain for us? We have Palestine, our advantages and disadvantages. What can we do? Such is our lot."[9] And in another letter to Lamdan:

I think it is good to live abroad. Though I have an arrangement enabling me to go there, I will not. For I too am living abroad. I have left *Davar*, and I don't see their people. I wish I weren't writing *Reshimot* either. Gone are the days when the intensiveness of Eretz Israel overshadowed the diaspora. Now Eretz Israel has become inessential . . . The point of Eretz Israel is this: If it is Eretz Israel— it shall live; if it becomes a new diaspora—it shall degenerate . . . And I deem it better to live in a country of orphans than to brood as a worm in horseradish.[10]

Rabinowitz is mindful that the workaday humdrum in Palestine is not far removed from the exilic. The new culture, as its polemics reveal,[11] is merely a carry-over of the cultural atmosphere of Eastern Europe, a petty culture wallowing in its own mire. The literary criticism of the period is riddled with the fear that the new implies no innovation, that Palestine is merely one more diasporic metamorphosis of the Jewish psyche. Indeed, such suspicions figure among the fundamental problems of literature in Palestine from the turn of the century until the 1970s.[12]

THE SOCIAL AND ECONOMIC CONDITIONS FOR THE EMERGENCE OF LITERATURE IN PALESTINE

The development of the Jewish center in Palestine is a demographic fact bearing cultural repercussions. In 1855, there were some 10,500 Jews in Palestine, of whom 5,700 lived in Jerusalem.[13] In 1881 (the year of the pogroms in southern Russia), with the organizing of Hovevei Zion and Bilu, the First Aliyah (1882–1885 and 1890) began, bringing in approximately 1,500 immigrants annually. In 1898, there were already some 50,000 Jews in Palestine, and by the outset of the Second Aliyah in 1907, some 75,000. At the outbreak of World War I, the count reached 85,000,[14] dropping, in its wake, to 65,000. Only in 1922, with the arrival of the Third Aliyah, did the Yishuv resume its expansion. In 1930, Palestine's Jewish population numbered approximately 165,000 people.[15]

These demographic fluctuations may be numerically inconsequential. However, the formation of a cultural center in Palestine coincided with a steady disintegration of the culture of Eastern European Jewry.[16] As mentioned, the change was not abrupt—the Palestine center remained dependent on the diaspora until World War II. Indeed, every periodical in Palestine sought subscribers in Europe and the United States.[17] The editors of *Ketuvim,* Abraham Shlonski (1900–1973) and Eliezer Steinmann (1892–1970), crisscrossed Europe to attract potential subscribers.[18] Editors of various publications appealed to Hebrew writers in the United States to assist them in securing economic support.[19] Many contributors to *Ha-omer, Moledet, Maabarot, Hedim,* and *Gilyonot* were diaspora writers.[20] ["But I need material from Europe," writes Jacob Fichman (1881–1958), the editor of *Moledet,* to Fishel Lachover (1883–1951) in 1912].[21] One should also bear in mind that several leading periodicals of those years were published in Eastern Europe, Germany, and the United States: *Ha-shiloah* (1896–1927), *Ha-tekufah* (1918–1950), *Miklat* (1919–1920), and *Rimon* (1922–1924). Moreover, even Hebrew writers in Palestine writing of local concerns—such as affairs of the Yishuv and the lives of the Arabs—envisaged a Jewish readership in the diaspora. To that audience, such material intimated a distant, exotic world.

The Palestinian author Nehama Pukhachevski (Nehama Bat-Zvi) wrote a sketch of sorts on the trials besetting Jewish Palestinian writers obliged always to bear in mind their readers abroad. Dubbed "Meshorer aluv" (A Wretched Poet), the story was published in 1910 in *Ha-mevaser,* no. 28, Constantinople. Its protagonist writes poems of Palestine which local editors reject. Writing of Palestine in Palestine, they maintain, is redundant. The poet tries his luck among the diaspora Jews, only to be rejected again. "Too much has been written of the lives of our brothers in Palestine," he is told, "the subject is no novelty to the Hebrew reader. However, if you could address your poems to the lives of the Turks or the Arabs, we shall willingly accept them."

Be that as it may, Palestinian journals depended far less on the literary tastes of Jews abroad than on their economic backing. The editors of

Hedim, for example, repeatedly confessed that the periodical survived only by grace of American support.[22] Avraham Joseph Stybel (1884–1946), owner of the Stybel Publishing House and several journals, complained to M. Poznanski of the ingratitude of the members of *Hapoel Hatzair,* whom he had supported during World War I and afterwards:

I cannot suppress the sorrow caused me by the attitude of the members of Hapoel Hatzair towards myself and the Stybel Publishing House. For I have always admired these people and their paper. During the first years of the War, I have sent them [money] the moment I had some. At the end of the War, [I've sent] two hundred and fifty dollars through *Ahiever* or *Ha-toren* [American journals—G.S.]. Immediately after that, at the hands of Mrs. Y. L. Goldberg, [I sent] two thousand or two thousand five hundred dollars, I do not recall the exact sum, although I have the receipts signed by Mrs. Fishman. But at the moment I am too lazy to inquire about it. And presently [I shall provide] another thousand dollars to set the weekly on sound footing.[23]

Yet economic dependence did not alter one basic fact: despite printing problems,[24] the production of books in Palestine proceeded, and in the 1930s even overtook production in the diaspora.

Shmuel Tchernowitz's study of the Hebrew book in Palestine offers several illuminating findings.[25] Tchernowitz traces the decline of Hebrew publishing in Europe: in the span of three years, between 1910–1912, approximately 700 Hebrew books were published in Russia, whereas in 1928, in Poland, only nine appeared. The following lists the numbers of books published in Palestine:

1908—21	1918—23
1910—36	1920—48
1912—60	1922—63
1914—35	1924—151
1916—38	1926—254
	1928—321

A drop in religious literature and an increase in original and translated fiction notably mark the types of books published. Although the "book market" expanded steadily,[26] it had not yet stabilized and bore the brunt of every economic crisis.[27] In a letter to F. Lachover, Y. Rabinowitz analyses the problems of cultural consumption in Palestine during the 1920s:

First of all, the market in Palestine is full of books. The buyer is weary. A new generation of postwar immigrants has not yet graduated from the schools, the workers' farms are doing very badly. After the prices of the German and the Russian books rose, the French were reduced. Most unfortunately for us, we read in seventy tongues, and English—albeit as a foreign language—has been introduced into the primary school as well. Numerous youths are training for government offices, and to this end try to read the English language comics. In a sense, Palestine too is a diaspora. With the rising prices of the Hebrew book, sales have dropped. Moreover: there is no respect in the Land of Israel for Jewish scholarship. I wrote to you once that in the Land of Israel there is a demand for manuals: horticulture, agriculture, sheep and cattle breeding, dairies, epiculture, construction in concrete, road paving, railroad works, post and telegraph, cookbooks, etc. The Jew now holds an essential segment of life which we did not possess in other lands. As a result, the Land of Israel is less abstract. Therefore, books of science and Jewish scholarship are cast aside.[28]

This description would hardly apply to the 1930s and 1940s, let alone the years of statehood. However, it still holds true for certain patterns of local cultural consumption: (a) waves of immigrants who have yet to become consumers of Hebrew books; (b) the issue of the foreign book, and the transition of "continental" consumers to the newly opened worlds of English literature; (c) the intellectual agricultural sector (the *kibbutz*, the cooperative settlement) as a singular consumer elite; (d) an increase in secular-practical literature, and a certain drop in religious literature and its heirs in Jewish scholarship.[29]

MODEST BEGINNINGS: EARLY PERIODICALS IN PALESTINE

As the declining Eastern European periodicals were succeeded by no heirs in Western Europe (Germany) or the United States, Jewish literary life began concentrating in Palestine.

A modest debut was made in the press of the Old Yishuv and the First Aliyah between 1863–1904.[30] Among the first was the monthly *Ha-Levanon,* published in Jerusalem in 1863–1864, edited by Joel Moshe Salomon (1838–1912), Yehiel Bril (1836–1886), and Michl Ha-Cohen (1834–1914). It was the first "secular" paper sponsored by the Ashkenazi-*perushim* leadership. The concurrent monthly *Havatzelet,* edited by Israel Beck (1897–1974), served as an opposition to *Ha-Levanon.* The next round of papers was more intellectual: *Havatzelet* (1870–1874), edited by Israel Dov Frumkin (1850–1914); *Ha-Ariel* (1874–1877, intermittently), edited by Michl Ha-Cohen; *Shaarei Zion* (1876–1885, intermittently), edited by Yizhak Gashzinani and Haim Peres (1843–1894); and *Yehuda vi-Yerushalayim* (1877–1878), edited by J. M. Salomon.

The arrival in Palestine of Eliezer Ben-Yehuda (1858–1922) spelled a hint of innovation. From 1884 to 1914, Ben-Yehuda edited and published newspapers, including the leading *Ha-zvi*. However, his publications served not as a cultural focus, but mainly as a podium for airing the aspirations and notions of the New Yishuv.

Only at the outset of the Second Aliyah did Hebrew writers realize they must create a local spiritual center. This awareness was forged in the periodical *Ha-omer* (1907–1908), edited by David Yelin (1864–1941), Simkha Ben-Zion (1870–1932), and Moshe Smilanski (1874–1953) as secretary of the editorial board. The three represented three camps of the Yishuv: Yelin, born in Jerusalem in 1864—the Old Yishuv; Smilanski, who immigrated in 1891—the First Aliyah; and Ben-Zion, immigrating in 1905—the Second Aliyah.

The three published a manifesto announcing the emergence of a new cultural climate that must be encouraged. Inspired by Ahad Ha-Am, S. Ben-Zion believed that a periodical designed for both local and foreign audiences would further the creation of a center in Palestine.[31] The manifesto proclaims: "The times we live in—a period of revolutionary chaos and of destruction wrought upon the bulk of our nation, our brothers in Russia, and the land we live in—the land of our hopes, which draws the heart of the people seeking a haven—compel us to unite and to begin together the literary work here in Palestine." And further on:

Moreover, whoever resides in our fatherland intuitively sees it is becoming a Jewish center. Here and in the nearby ancient cities of the East there are already important communities, populous and multi-colored. A new community is rising up around us, mostly in cities and partly in colonies . . . No doubt, with the changes we and others shall achieve here, our beautiful country will become a magnet to many Sons of Israel, not only in such dire times as these.

Of fiction it is said:

Of late, this subject has revealed the force and beauty of our tongue in fair original works: brightly shining ideals took spectacular form at the hands of the talented—testimony to the power of the life-seeking ancient people and to the vitality of its language—a treasure which it has cherished throughout the ages, and redeemed. We shall deem it to the credit of our collection when we are able to adorn it with such stories and poems as would resound with our national revival. We would especially like to endow our collection with fine compositions imbued with the spirit of the Land of Israel, namely, vivid, poetic scenes of the country's landscapes and the lives of its inhabitants past and present. (*Ha-omer*, no. 1, 1907, pp. v–vii.)

The editors of *Ha-omer* thus supplemented Ahad Ha-Am's "Manifesto of the *Shiloah*" with a manifesto of their own.[32] Whereas the former required that literature provide a faithful mirror for the problems of Jews and Jewry, the latter added it must also faithfully reflect the setting and the surroundings. Indeed, a bond to the land is the great innovation of this literature. Among the contributors to the first three issues were Ahad Ha-Am, M. Smilanski, Yizhak Shami (1888–1949), Alexander Ziskind Rabinowitz (1854–1945), S. Ben-Zion, Jacob Cahan (1881–1960), Micha Yosef Berdichevski (1865–1921), Yehoshua Eisenstadt-Barzilai (1865–1915), S. J. Agnon, Yizhak Katznelson (1885–1944), Y. Rabinowitz, D. Yelin, and others. Their social origins resemble the three editors': the Old Yishuv (Y. Shami); the First Aliyah (M. Smilanski, Y. Eisenstadt-Barzilai); and above all, the Second Aliyah (S. Y. Agnon, Y. Rabinowitz) and diaspora writers (Ahad Ha-Am, M. Y. Berdichevski, Y. Katznelson).

Literature in Palestine gained new momentum with the establishment of *Hapoel Hatzair*, edited by Yosef Aharonowitz (1877–1937), the leading publication of the Second Aliyah immigrants. The two opening issues were done by hectograph. The message borne by the very first issue is not a literary one. Entitled "Real Work in Palestine" (*Hapoel Hatzair*, no. 1, October–November 1908), the manifesto proclaims: "The time has come to boldly inform all those concerned for our national future in Palestine that without the Hebrew laborer, the Yishuv here is being built on volcanic ground." The first issues featured distinctly local stories by M. Wilkanski, Hawaja Mussa (M. Smilanski), N. Pukhachevski, S. Zemach, and others. In keeping with the spirit of the publication, such stories characteristically reflected the working society of Palestine.

Moledet (Homeland), the third periodical, began publication in April 1911. Conspicuous changes marked its rapid succession of editors. The first volume (1911) was edited by S. Ben-Zion, the second (1911–1912), by Yaakov Fichman. Primarily didactic, the manifesto opening the first volume lays greater stress on the general Jewish trend than on the Palestinian:

To outline for the generation we are educating a path to the eternal truths and to the lofty aspirations of the enlightened world in general, and of the Jewish world in particular. To educate and bolster the spiritual power of the young man approaching life, to awaken and foster the finer emotions, to divulge knowledge through science and to improve the taste with the aid of choice literature—such is our aspiration in *Moledet*.

And in the name of the Hebrew motherland-family and its life, the Hebrew nation and its possessions, the holy motherland and its community—we salute our sons, to fortify their hearts and their hopes. (Vol. 1, 1911)

The editorial policy of S. Ben-Zion and his successor, Mordechai Ben-Hillel Ha-Cohen (1856–1936), draws far more on "local" forces than does that of Fichman. Alongside works by local writers such as Joseph Zevi Rimon (1889–1958), David Shimoni (1886–1956), A. Z. Rabinowitz, and others, Fichman published works by such diaspora writers as Uri Nissan Gnessin (1879–1913), Shaul Tchernichovsky (1875–1943), M. Y. Berdichevsky, Zalman Shneur (1886–1959), Sholem Aleichem, and Yitzhak Leibush Peretz (1852–1915). Moreover, in a letter to F. Lachover, he stresses Palestine's literary dependence on the diaspora ("My first issue will be middling, but I need material from Europe. It would be of great assistance to me if you reminded several of our authors of their promise").[33]

The volumes of *Moledet* are notably flexible in their editorial policy: the best Hebrew literature (both local and Jewish in general), the best translated literature: Selma Lagerlof, Jakob Wasserman, Johan Wolfgang Goethe, Heinrich Heine, Guy de Maupassant, and others. Unlike *Ha-omer* and *Hapoel Hatzair*, *Moledet* had no political orientation. Traveling frequently between Palestine and Europe, perpetually casting his lot with new periodicals and book publications, Fichman was a devotee of Hebrew culture, not necessarily of its underlying ideologies. In any case, *Moledet* became the model for *Hedim*, Palestine's major literary periodical in the 1920s. The latter also tried to recruit writers from the entire Jewish world, addressing a readership abroad no less than a local one. The same is true of *Ketuvim* and *Gilyonot*. Other periodicals were designed for the local audience, such as those affiliated with the workers' movement—*Ha-adamah, Dapim, Al ha-saf, Be-shaah zo,* and *Yizrael,* or the semi-literary periodical *Bustenai,* affiliated with the farmers' organization.

In a spirit of kinship, one periodical published abroad tried to represent Palestine as well as any local journal. This was *Ha-mevaser,* published in Constantinople in 1910–1911 and edited by Nahum Sokolov, with Aharon Avraham Kabak (1883–1944) serving as the literary editor.[34] The journal sought to dedicate itself to Oriental Jewry on the assumption that the Jews of Turkey must contribute to the national blossoming of the Ottoman empire with its 500,000-strong Jewish population:

For the ills of exile have barely tainted our Turkish brothers, the equilibrium of their national soul has not been disturbed . . . The Jews of Turkey have always been sound of spirit, faithful to their land and to their own people. Yet a thorn pricks the heart of every national Jew: the meagre inculcation of our national language among Turkish Jews.

The time has come to reserve, in the center of Oriental regeneration, a small fortress for our spiritual treasures and a Temple-in-miniature to Hebrew regeneration.

In short, *Ha-mevaser* shall be a Hebrew-Oriental weekly bent on disseminating Hebrew wisdom and literature, and broadcasting the spirited activity within the Jewish communities of Turkey and Palestine. (*Ha-mevaser* no. 1, 1910, pp. 2–3)

A. A. Kabak called upon several diaspora authors to send their contributions to the weekly. To Devorah Baron (1887–1956) he writes:

The editorial board of *Ha-mevaser,* of which I am a member, decided to devote considerable space to belletristics and literary criticism. I would be delighted if you too shared your literary work with our journal. As most readers of *Ha-mevaser* are from the "Orient" and far removed from our life in Russia, they should be provided with tales more generally Jewish than Russian-Jewish. For example, I am certain they would not have understood your latest story in *Ha-olam* on the lives of the "external students." I hope you will not refrain from sending us your stories from time to time. When are you going to Palestine?[35]

Despite Kabak's appeals, Hebrew authors of the diaspora rarely participated in this quaint, remote journal. Its noteworthy contributors were, rather, Palestinian authors of the First Aliyah: Y. Eisenstadt-Barzilai, N. Pukhachevski, and M. Smilanski. *Ha-mevaser* often addressed the issues of "The Revival of the Hebrew Language among the Jews of Turkey" (*ibid.,* 1910), and "The Assimilated in Turkey" (*ibid.,* 1910). Here, of all places, one finds an essay by Israel Efrat (1891–1981), a nineteen-year-old Hebrew poet from New York, dubbed "On Our Literature" (*ibid.,* 1910). Hebrew literature, so Efrat's basic argument runs, is not original and lacks inherent quality. Therefore, translations are in order. Mendele, Sholem Aleichem, Bialik, and their like are all exilic in spirit. Only translations can foster a revival of original, non-exilic literature. Efrat thus supported wholeheartedly the publishing houses Yefet and Kohelet in Jaffa, which provided the Hebrew audience mainly with translations.[36]

By the end of World War I, several additional periodicals appeared in on-off publications: *Yizrael,* edited by Alexander Ziskind Rabinowitz, (1913); *Bentayim* (1913), featuring Fichman, Agnon, Shneur, and others; *Revivim,* edited by Brenner (1913–1914); the collection *Be-shaah zo* (1916), featuring Aharon David Gordon (1856–1922), Brenner, Yaakov Steinberg (1887–1947), Asher Barash (1889–1952), and others.[37] Participants in the first two volumes hail both from Palestine and the diaspora. Due to the wartime isolation, the last volume evinces an increase of the former. Other publications of those years include the yearbooks of *Ha-ahdut*—the periodical of Poalei Zion (1910–1915). Immediately after the war came *Al ha-saf* (one-off); *Maabarot,* edited by Fichman (1919–1921); *Shai shel sifrut* (1918–1919), edited by S. Ben-Zion;[38] finally, *Dapim* (1922), edited by Dov Kimche (1889–1961).[39] The last two are Palestinian both in the make-up of their participants and in their editors' ideology.[40] The last periodical edited by Brenner was *Ha-adamah* (1920–1923). Although it spotlighted Yehuda Burla (1886–1970), one of the local naive authors, *Ha-adamah* also presented several of the most important realistic anti-genre works by Second Aliyah writers: Brenner's "Avla"; Reuveni's "Bereshit ha-mevukhah"; Levi Arye Arieli-Orloff's (1886–1943) "Yeshimon"; Zvi Schatz's (1980–1921) "Batya" (posthumously), as well as tales by Menahem Poznanski (1887–1956), and others.

In a preface to *Ha-adamah,* Brenner summed up what he held to be the premises for Hebrew literature in Palestine. A valuable description of the literature of the First Aliyah and Second Aliyah, and highly influential for later generations, two passages of his words merit full citation:

We shall devote a large part of our publication to belletristics both original and translated. However, this part should not follow a formula of florid-professional poesy. Our prose should consist of scenes of life, generated by the tremulous sensibility of a worthy personality. Let us not distinguish between old age and youth, old forms and new; let us not pursue a poetry of "modernism," nor stories with pre-established social tendencies. Hebrew literature, like all others, is first of all a product of society, of the spirit of the people, created by the people for the people. But let us not forget life transcends all formulas, including those with social implications. And let us not forget that true sociability, namely, man's relations with his neighbors and his community, exists in all the works of an involved author, even if he lacks some of the intentions we honor most.[41]

Brenner thus demanded a literature both realistic and relevant, reflecting life as it is without attempting to impose upon reality distorting social trends, no matter how fair and holy. Life and literature, he believed, outweigh all ideological formulas. To reflect life, literature must approximate life rather than the abstractions blurring it. Brenner demanded the same relevance of literary criticism, rejecting that which draws on external doctrines and does not penetrate literary reality from within. He took up arms against what he dubbed "genrism," which painted the world in ideological colors, and against aestheticism, which extolled foreign artistic ideologies.

Both in their editorial policy and in the make-up of their participants, the abovementioned periodicals represent stages in the emergence of literature in Palestine, as it moves to the center of literary life after a protracted spell on the sidelines.

THE FORERUNNERS AS HUMAN BEINGS

Palestinian Hebrew literature was produced by writers representing four generations: the Old Yishuv and the First Aliyah, corresponding to the generation of Mendele (1835–1917) and Frishman (1859–1922) in the diaspora; the Second Aliyah, corresponding to Yizhak Dov Berkowitz's (1885–1967) and Gershom Schofman's (1880–1972) generation; authors of the Third Aliyah; and the "native sons" and the "sons of the State"—those born in Palestine, and later, in Israel.

The majority of the first generation were born in the mid-nineteenth century. Its typical figures include Yoel Moshe Salomon, Suliman Menahem Mani, Eliezer Ben-Yehuda, Yehoshua Eisenstadt-Barzilai, Moshe Smilanski, and Nehama Pukhachevsky.

The second generation consists almost entirely of immigrants, who brought to Palestine the literary traditions of Eastern European countries. Among the founders of local literature were Y. H. Brenner, the standard-setting editor, publisher, and critic;[42] S. Ben-Zion, A. Z. Rabinowitz, and Y. Rabinowitz.[43] Their contemporaries included D. Baron, A. A. Kabak, A. Barash, Y. Steinberg, and Zalman Anochi (1878–1947). Later came Y. D. Berkowitz, G. Schofman, and storytellers of the same literary school, whose work was produced mainly in Palestine: Meir Wilkansky, Aharon Reuveni, L. A. Arieli-Orloff, Yosef Luidor (?–1921), Zvi Schatz, Dov Kimche, and S. J. Agnon. Some of these writers— Kabak, Baron, Zemach, Agnon—arrived with the Second Aliyah, emigrated before or during World War I, and returned to Palestine in the 1920s. On the margins of this group are the native-born authors Yizhak Shami (1888–1949) and Y. Burla. The two had undergone self-education processes akin to those of Eastern European Jewish writers of the Enlightenment.

Two writers straddle the border between old and new: Moshe Stavsky-Stavi (1884–1964), who exchanged his exilic Yiddish for Hebrew in quasi-adult quasi-children's stories; and Yaakov Khurgin (1898–1991), who was Shami's and Burla's junior, but close to them in origins and subject matter. Khurgin served to link Reuveni, Burla and Shami with latecomer Bar-Yosef (1912–1992). In age, Bar-Yosef was the peer of Third Aliyah immigrants. However, in content, his novels lay beyond the world-view of that group.

All too cognizant of their deracination in their new surroundings, this group—especially its second generation members—were often moved by boundless admiration for the land which had bestowed upon them a sense of anchorage and belonging. No outpouring of such emotions is more typical than Wilkanski's, in his preface to the Second Aliyah scenes published in his book *Bimei ha-aliyah* (The Days of Immigration) of 1935:

And the bones arose, and they were alive. Flesh came up upon them and skin. And all had black and curly hair, fire in their eyes and hearts aflame. And they went forth and ascended, and they clung to the summit of the mountain of rock, and dissolved it to dust. And the dust became their living breath and the furrow—their chief goal. And they suddenly saw the heavens and their host— streaks of light and rainbow colors—and felt the tremor of the earth and the murmur of every creature and every [blade of] grass, and they listened and marvelled and broke out in song—and they labored and sang all day and all night. They erected a tabernacle for the homeland and wove its curtains, embroidering upon them the fabric of their dreams. Designing idioms, they used them to adorn their choicest thoughts. And they sang to creation, to truth, purity, beauty—across the vault of heaven, the wheels droned—and the echo never reached their ears. They forsook the charms of the world and its noise, seeing only the great light where they stood. And they heard the divine voice from above: "And I will make of thee a great nation"—and mounted ever higher in their labor. And they would embrace the new universe and all that was in it. (Preface, p. 7)

Wilkanski's experience of redemption evokes prophetic vision, the soil of the land, its skies, and its language. Ascetic, religious, and disregarding the entire world, it takes the form of a most naive pioneering fulfillment. It is not reality that such literature reflects, but rather the youthful enthusiasm of its writers, who, in willing blindness to both their subjective experience and objective reality, chose to live in the world of their dreams. In choosing their fiction's events and characters, they fulfilled the standards of pioneering Zionism. Moreover, to a large extent, they set those standards. Readers both in Palestine and abroad began perceiving reality through the spectacles literature provided. Life was perhaps more affected by texts than the texts were affected by life. However, the encounter with the new land did not always elicit youthful elation in response to the "bond." Many of the writers shared Brenner's experience that the skies do not change the person, that one still lacked a bond to the homeland. Z. Schatz, the young author and pioneer, wrote to his contemporary M. Poznanski: "In body, I have been in Palestine for ten years now, but my soul is still wandering in the diaspora . . . Whenever I attempt to sing, I stammer. I have not yet arrived in Palestine, I am still on my way!" [44]

Writing to critic Shalom Streit (1888–1946) in 1920, Second Aliyah writer Dov Kimche addresses the dilemma using strong language:

We young writers—and even those who are not so young—are presently crossing strange bridges, whose footholds, on the one hand, were uprooted from the Jewish *shtetl,* and, on the other, have yet to stand on another soil—and perhaps never will. Therefore, all is suspended in mid-air: All our individual exilic Judaism is encompassed in Bialik, and what is left to us? As regards the human being, I have grave doubts whether the time has come to sing of him. Whether we can sing of him at all! As I read my pages presently in press, I sometimes experience a peculiar spasm: is this "erlebtes"? Is that the expression? [45]

Brenner described these youths and their relation to literature in his essay "Aliyot vi-yeridot" (Immigrations and Emigrations).[46] Most, he claimed, had come involuntarily, and were "cast up on the shores of Palestine, a minority among the multitude of Jewish youth who left Russia of their own volition or of necessity, and went overseas . . . Few of the young immigrants, members of the broad circles of our people, were laborers since adolescence. Most were intellectuals or mere idlers".[47] Brenner lists the various types of immigrants: the crude laborer, who usually does not stay; the immigrant-cum-tourist; the semi-intelligent son of middle-class parents, who leaves with the first boat out; and the careerist.

As the correspondence of several writers shows (e.g., Fichman, Kimche, Y. Rabinowitz), they were not unlike Brenner's "heroes" by inclination. "In the land desired of our fathers' desire," ran a popular song of the period, "all hopes shall come true." Second Aliyah newcomers arriving on the wings of that belief were soon disappointed. Resuming their wanderings, many returned to Europe (the case of Fichman's wanderings is almost paradigmatic).[48]

Writers following Wilkanski's example produced a literature affirming Zionist values. These were held to be more important than the individual, and he was accordingly portrayed as fulfilling them to the letter. Conversely, those who followed in Brenner's footsteps assumed that Palestine had not changed men. Zionist immigration hinged on normative demands which the psychic reality of the immigrants was unable to accommodate. This disparity yielded a highly complex, fascinating literature.

Brenner may have underrated his contemporaries and done an injustice to those ten percent of the Second Aliyah who did strike roots in the land. However, at the time neither he nor they could grasp the magnitude of the revolution they had generated. In spite of its odd assortment of characters, the group laid the foundations for Jewish life and literature in Palestine. All aspects of active life there, even those that turned out for the worse, became grist for their literary mill. The struggle for the Hebrew press; Jewish labor; settlement in the Galilee, in Segera, in Um-Juni, in Ein-Ganim; the founding of the Hashomer organization for self-defence—all served as inspiration to Brenner, Wilkenski, Kabak Luidor, Y. Rabinowitz, Zemach, Agnon, and others. Occasionally the result was metamorphosis of history into myth.

Another significant feature of the Second Aliyah was its leaders' acknowledgment of the bond between life and literature. Writers and leaders alike often evoked this bond in diverse retrospective descriptions. "Until now," maintained Yitzhak Lofban (1888–1948), one of the editors of *Hapoel Hatzair*, "the realm of literature and culture bore close resemblance to the realm of the Yishuv. It was a culture of 'shnorring', a Levantine culture."[49] S. Zemach, one of the group's literary progenitors, asserted that literature was among the primary causes of immigration.[50] Yizhak Tabenkin (1887–1971), a major leader of the *kibbutz* movement, declared that the Second Aliyah had brought about a renaissance of Hebrew literature: "Disclosure of the revolutionary truth of Jewish reality in all its starkness; the forceful, clear-eyed, analytical approach of Brenner—such were the teachings of Hebrew literature. Together, the ancient Bible and the literature of this era have guided man towards immigration to the Land of Israel."[51]

Hopes for regeneration, a terror of despair—only against this ambiguous background can one interpret such disparate protagonists as Brenner's, Arieli-Orloff's, and Agnon's on the one hand, and Smilanski's, Wilkenski's, and Zemach's on the other. The latter portrayed pioneers and warriors, the former, characters on the brink of madness and suicide—lost, shipwrecked survivors rather than pioneering immigrants bent on new life in a new land. Labour leader Berl Katznelson (1887–1944) gave eloquent expression to this duality, in retrospect: "It [the

Second Aliyah] came under a special star, and the tragedies trailing it have forged it into a power in our nation. For in what state have we arrived? Not in a state of prosperity in Palestine, whether economic, or cultural, or Zionist." Of literature he writes: "The Second Aliyah people came and produced, perhaps not the literature, but the basis upon which future literature will rise, namely, the Hebrew reader."[52]

In other words, literature springs from the social twilight into which the Second Aliyah has stumbled. Zvi Schatz describes the predicament thus: "My body is in Palestine, but my soul is still quivering elsewhere. I have dammed up the source of my previous life in Russia, another source has yet to open to me, and I have been suffocating for the past several years."[53] This group of pioneers created most literary rostrums (Hapoel Hatzair, Kuntres, Ha-ahdut), molded the new consumer of literature, and designated the Hebrew language once and for all as the language of the regenerating Jewish-Israeli society.

MATERIALS, TOPICS, FIGURES

Thus, many Second Aliyah writers dwell in Zion, yet their hearts remain in Eastern Europe. They still describe the shtetl and its problems, and portray uprooted Jews, both pious and heretic. However, they also try their hand at depicting heroes who would strike root and construct a new reality in a new land. Landscapes of pine trees, snows, and wooden houses give way to landscapes between desert and ocean, and scorching winds.[54] Both shtetl and European metropolis are replaced by the colonies, the kevutzah (collective farm) and the "Levantine" village:

The shtetl appears as something remote and bygone. The native of Palestine has never seen one, nor has a city risen here yet. And where there is no tradition—a tradition of life—there can be no tradition of literature. Thus it is understandable that to a man growing up in this life and these surroundings, a large part of the shtetl literature becomes alien and of no essential value.[55]

Concurrently with this sociological change, new groups infiltrate and influence life and literature: Mideastern Jewry, the Old Yishuv of Palestine, Arab society, Jewish farmers and watchmen. In Berdichevsky's works, the Jew as a heroic figure was an inaccessible ideal, a would-be fulfillment of the author's fantasy of "a change of values." Though authors in the new environment craved heroic consummation, their success in molding fictional heroes was patchy. Eisenstadt-Barzilai conjured up the image of Menahem the watchman (Leket), and the heroic figure of Tamar *(Ayelet ha-shahar)*. Smilanski created Hawaja Nazar, Luidor—the orchard keeper Yehuda, and the fearless native son, Yo'ash. Reuveni produced Meir Funk *(Shamot)*, and Arieli-Orloff—Yaakov Perlgold *(Le-or ha-venus)*. Another type of hero, found in Wilkanski's and Zemach's works as well, is the pioneer-laborer marching in the vanguard. A purely indigenous type, it never existed in European Hebrew literature.

Y. Rabinowitz articulated the yearning for a new figure as follows: "Society demands its rights. Simultaneously, the aspiration grows for a complete person, strong and active. The feeble, delicate, refined and conflict-torn person of the novella days—fades away ... A change of life and a change of values. It is hard to hold out against this prose-in-life. Life must effect a change in literature as well." [56] In intention, the Second Aliyah yearned for an ideal figure, but in effect, the characters portrayed were usually children of crisis, feeble and conflict-ridden. Nonetheless, the group never relinquished its dream of a hero whose grandeur matched the prospects and pressures of the new land. [57]

FROM BOOK TO MOUTH

The Second Aliyah produced the Hebrew "reader," as Katznelson significantly remarks. Indeed, local readers spoke and wrote Hebrew. Never during their years in exile had Jews spoken Hebrew. The gap between exilic Jewish letters and oral life produced an over-stylized literature, removed from life and the vernacular alike. "Now," writes Y. Rabinowitz, "we have entered a new era. From the book, we have placed our language in the mouth." [58]

Second Aliyah writers thus met with experiences entirely alien to their fathers. To their own sons, written language became the language of everyday speech. Dov Kimche, for example, writes in this context of "moments of genuine thrill." He relates how his young son came in one afternoon, mirthfully reporting a playmate's error in Hebrew. "Who raised these children," Kimche marvels. Other cases abound, he testifies. [59]

The revival of Hebrew as a spoken language obliged writers to reconsider the future of the language of literature and its link to Scriptures and canonical texts. Arriving in Palestine with only a halting command of Hebrew, Zvi Schatz immediately perceived the stylistic problems of ancient literature in a new land. He spoke out harshly against the exclusive influence of the stylized style and traditional language:

The time has come to understand that there is a limit to the influence of the Bible and the Midrash on our living tongue. For it is ridiculous to adapt all concepts of our times to those of Jews two thousand years ago. One should accept the popular wisdom, the wonderful conciseness, and all that is good—but only the good. In speech, our language has not yet revived. Truly, we have only stammers or rhetoric.[60]

The language of literature had indeed been distorted. Faced, like Brenner before his immigration, with the need to create spoken Hebrew practically *ex nihilo,* writers in Palestine mixed Hebrew with Arabic words, for the same purpose that exilic writers tried to translate Yiddish into Hebrew—namely, in order to evoke a sense of living speech. The narrator-hero of Eisenstadt-Barzilai's *Sultana* speaks Arabic and Spanish with Sultana, a Jewish girl from Damascus. When she speaks Hebrew, he distinctly notes the fact. ("Sultana stood facing me, and pointing to her spouse, said to me in Hebrew: 'This is my husband'.") In 1916, one high-school student, Aharon Feldman (1899–1972) (later, Ever Ha-Dani), used an Arabic term in his story, which eventually took root in both Hebrew vernacular and literary works.[61] The story contains the following dialogue:

— Catch the ball, catch it! That's it, *Jedda!*—the boy said happily.
— No, I have to go—the girl demurred to play ball in public, protesting feebly but throwing the ball nonetheless.[62]

As mentioned, Brenner was among the initiators of the conscious—not to say artificial—transition from literary to spoken language. He imbibed numerous Arabisms and Yiddishisms, merging them into a modern Hebrew of sorts. Indeed, marked changes occurred in the style of Jewish Palestinian literature. Some writers, like Shlonski, experimented with replacing the traditional style with a new one based on wordplay and neologisms. In 1920, Y. Fichman complained in his essay "Signon ha-yahid ve-signon ha-rabim" (The Style of the Individual and the Style of the Many,) that "the entire literature en masse has become devoid of style."[63] Variations of this complaint recurred throughout Hebrew criticism, nostalgic as it was for the brilliant, independent style of the previous generation's writers. Regarding this fond embracing of the traditional style Y. Rabinowitz says:

Whoever fears illegal and barbaric speech is ridiculous. We have resurrected the dead, and now it has risen and grows on its own. The language shall be neither biblical nor mishnaic-midrashic, neither wholly European nor Oriental . . . but something new, unlike any of these, with a little of each . . . If there be many weeds in the language—there is no danger. A field full of weeds evidently has good soil. Some shall be uprooted, others shall become cultivated, tongue-briars dwelling with tongue-flowers.[64]

Such words foreshadow Israeli fiction of later periods. The ongoing change may render the writings more shallow, reduce the innate richness of the language, and diminish the roles of the traditional idiom and the conventional metaphor. The language of literature is no longer self-sustaining. Hereafter, its force and vitality depend on its reciprocal relationship with life. The language of eternity has evolved into the language of mundane experience; Hebrew is to fulfill the functions of Yiddish and Hebrew combined.

Palestine, then, witnessed the abolishment of diglossia.[65] There is no longer a differentiation between the vernacular, the written, and the official tongues. All divergences take place within a single language. Characteristic of all spheres is the steady decline of Yiddish, and the ascent of Hebrew.[66]

However, diglossia lives on in the diaspora. Wallenrod (1899–1966) and Halkin (1898–1987) wrote their literary works in Hebrew, but some of their scholarly works in English. Harry Sackler (1888–1974) wrote his plays in Hebrew, Yiddish, and English.[67] Vogel's Hebrew novels are rife with Germanisms, and he has attempted, not very success-fully, to write in German. Diglossia still plays a prominent role in shaping the language of those Hebrew authors—Y. Shami, Arabic; A. Freeman (1890–1950), Russian; and N. Frankl (1920–), German—who describe Arab, Russian, and German realities totally removed from the Hebrew linguistic material they deploy in their descriptions.

EXTERNAL AND INTERNAL SOURCES

The sources influencing Hebrew literature are copious and diverse. The First Aliyah literature still bears the marks of the Enlightenment litera-ture and of the forthright naturalism of several Hebrew and Yiddish authors of the late nineteenth century. Social realism is conspicuous in the works of the "genrists" of the First Aliyah and Second Aliyah. Several tales of Smilanski and Pukhachevsky are not far removed in this respect from those of the exilic naturalist Avraham Leibl Ben-Avigdor (1866–1921) and his contemporaries.

Preferring the useful to the beautiful, positivist literature of the first two *aliyot,* like its diaspora counterpart of the late nineteenth century, attempts to promote what it holds to be the "advanced" norms of the generation. The same is true of genrist literature produced in the days of the Third Aliyah.

The traditional stylized mode, despite its diminished impact, still resonated forcefully in the language of such authors as Shami or Agnon. However, Brenner's heritage was growing increasingly prominent, setting its stamp on such distinctly different writers as Agnon and Reuveni, Kimche and Arieli-Orloff. All courted Brenner, and created their own image of the writer. Brenner's influence, blending with Berdichevsky's, yielded the sober Romanticism typical of many Second Aliyah writers.

These writers also opened up to new external influences. Russian immigrants introduced Dostoyevsky and Chekhov, Brenner added Gerhard Hauptman in Hebrew translation. Scandinavian neo-Romantics and young German authors wielded powerful influence. In a 1913 letter to S. Streit, Kimche sings the praises of Bjornstjerne Bjornson (1832–1910), Maurice Maeterlinck (1862–1932), and Hermann Hesse (1877–1962). In 1914, he writes he has translated into Hebrew a long story by Bjornson, a pleasant idyll dubbed "Elem Aliz" (Jolly Youth).[68] Kimche alludes again to Knut Hamsun and the Scandinavians on various occasions.[69] At the time, local authors used to exchange Hamsun's works with one another.[70] Many Scandinavian authors were translated into Hebrew.[71] Their impressionist style tells markedly on the early stories of Agnon ("Tishrei," "Leilot," "Be'era shel Miriam"), Kimche ("Sefer ha-kilyonot"), and others. Several features of local literature can be traced to this alien influence: an emotional style, a mysterious atmosphere, a longing for landscapes, admiration for the image of the unusual lover, fantasy suffused with both wistfulness and disappointment. Naturally, imported influences blended with internal ones stemming from the Enlightenment literature and the social realism of several diaspora authors.

TWO TRENDS: NAIVE OR IRONIC LITERATURE

Brenner triggered the pivotal debate—be it overt or covert—over the standards of literature. His point of departure was neither stylistic-structural nor ideological, but, rather, mimetic. The response of readers and critics to his book *Mi-kan u-mi-kan* (From Here and There) prompted Brenner to publish his essay "Ha-genre ha-eretz-israeli va-avizarehu" (The Palestinian Genre and its Vehicles).[72] The ensuing debate was taken up by Rabbi Binyamin (Redler) (1880–1957) and others.[73] Brenner protests against the generistic trend represented by Zeev Yavetz, M. Wilkenski, S. Zemach, and M. Smilanski. The social reality of Palestine, he argues, "still has no constancy and typicality," and the authors simply fake it: "The falsehood dominating the grasp and perception of life here, the ostentation and imposture devastating every lot—potentially good lots as well—infecting like parasites, like a second nature, every movement and every corner one turns—all these are capable of nipping in the bud all flowers of a *real* genre." [74] Brenner's objection to the generistic literature in Palestine is no different from his objection to the works produced by the social realist diaspora authors, who have also distorted reality in their attempts to praise or condemn it excessively.

Generistic writing was in fact pseudo-realistic: the style often lofty, the characterization modes simplistic, and the plot documentary or melodramatic. At heart, it was a naive literature. Its authors usually identified with the values of the "Zionist venture" and with the naive figures bearing its burden. *Zlalim,* the abovementioned collection of the Jaffa Hebrew Gymnasium students, illustrates the nature of this literature. Its participants, aspiring young writers, subsequently became the authors of Eretz Israel. Suffice it to cite the opening story of the collection, Zrubavel Hayutman's "Arbaat ha-halalim" (The Four Who have Fallen). Four brothers—a scholar, a poet, a watchman, and a *yeshivah*-student—come to Palestine to "restore the heritage of our people and rebuild its ruins." All four sacrifice themselves for the land and are mourned by their mother. With stylistic pathos, the story tries to portray the naive "heroes" who have come to Palestine. Though they fail to accomplish their mission, they lose nothing in immortal heroic stature. Indeed, since the very beginnings of Hebrew literature in Palestine, naivete has flourished, prospering through the 1920s and 1930s, well into the 1950s and even later. The innocent belief in the power of the local hero "to build and be built" in his land is deep-seated, and has inspired many authors of the First Aliyah and Second Aliyah—Smilanski, Pukhachevski, Wilkanski, Zemach, Burla, and others. Even the disillusioned secretly clung to it. The naive writers cast reality in the image of their vision, believing it would thus be promoted, and inspire its addressees in exile to grow fonder of the Zionist dream.

True, the ironic writers of the period drew on the same subject matter. However, irony exposed a reality more powerful than the dream. The ironists understood the gap between the ideological norms of the times and the people who were to live up to them. Apparently, the skies have not changed man, nor has the location changed the heroes' luck. Day-by-day they face new challenges, stumbling and falling, astonished and skeptical. The world of Arieli-Orloff, Reuveni, Kimche, and Agnon (and to some extent, of Shami and Khurgin) is complex and ambiguous, as far removed from "genre writing" as irony is from naivete.

Both types are nurtured by the same atmosphere, the one, its captive, the other, disillusioned, breaking loose, and taking its own course. Moreover, both are marked by traces of the so-called realistic school. The naive writers, subscribing to the notion that literature literally reflects reality, are unaware that theirs is no reflection, but rather a selection from reality, guided by ideological assumptions. The ironists, by contrast, are well aware that they cannot depict a comprehensive, clear reality; they are merely people who have strayed into a new environment and seek a foothold in it, as did several pessimistic diaspora authors: U. N. Gnessin (1879–1913), G. Shofman (1880–1972), and Yacob Steinberg (1887–1947). The former type of writing usually features a closed structure and a simple style. The structure of the latter is fractured, its style, fragmented or stylized, designed to overcome the ruptures of the existence it would portray.

Several immigrant authors produced works in Palestine akin to those of the naive, native authors: such works include S. Ben-Zion's *Yekutiel,* A. A. Kabak's *Bein yam u-vein midbar,* Y. D. Berkowitz's *Yemot hamashiah,* and A. Barash's *Gananim.* Brenner, by contrast, was the first ironist and the spiritual progenitor of the trend. Among the Third Aliyah writers, some uphold the naive tradition—Ever Ha-Dani, Yacob Aricha (1906–1971), S. Reichenstein (1902–1942)—others, the ironic tradition—E. Steinman, Y. Horowitz (1901–1975), Hayim Hazaz (1898–1973).

Hebrew fiction in Palestine may be classified as several major types: regional literature dealing mainly with the people's bond with the land (Smilanski, Khurgin, Pukhachevski, Zemach, Reuveni); "pioneering" literature describing the struggle between settler-pioneers and "local" inhabitants (Stavi, Smilanski, Burla); journalistic tales, outlining heroic episodes with documentary precision (Stavi, Wilkanski); tales of immigrants, evoking the estrangement of the newcomers in their new land (Brenner, Y. Rabinowitz, Kimche, Agnon); romantic legendary tales (Arieli-Orloff, Agnon); and exotic tales presenting the readers with an alien reality (Smilanski, Shami, Pukhachevski, Burla, Khurgin).

All these types are marked by the innate tension between generistic and anti-generistic literature, which set its stamp on the period. Such tension was the dialectical transmutation of past archaic principles, and the source of future milestones in Hebrew literature. The bulk of the period's fiction springs from and represents a well-defined reality. Naive literature has recourse to the imaginary in order to flee reality. In the realm of fantasy, its writers conjure up innocent fables (Smilanski), or clandestine amorous melodramas (Khurgin). The ironists too have their fables (Arieli-Orloff's *Hagadat ha-mavet*, Agnon's *Agunot* and *Leilot*) — but these are self-conscious ventures into fantasy, akin to those of the Scandinavian neo-Romantics (Hamsun).

The two trends draw on different sources. Naive writers tend towards local folklore and aetiological fables. The ironists, especially Agnon, find in Jewish sources inspiration for parodic interpretation and symbolic representations of their inner doubts. Clearly, naive literature is "minor," although it has been canonized by many who shared its vision. Conversely, ironic literature has usually won critical approval, but has not yet been presented as canonical.[75]

The two trends represent the two faces of hope and disappointment, dream and reality, in the young immigrants' attitude to the fatherland. Both stem from a profound belief that here, and here alone, all hopes shall be fulfilled.

NOTES

1. "Genre" writing, according to Y. H. Brenner, was that trend of narrative fiction in Palestine, which depicted the new secular Jewish Palestinian community as one with well-established manners, morals, lifestyle, and "local color." Brenner contested this outlook. At the beginning of the twentieth century, he found no authentic "local color" in Jewish Palestinian life. Quite the contrary: the uprooted and and skeptical young pioneers still felt as strangers in the land they would call home. Their lifestyle, Brenner maintained, far from becoming consolidated, was in fact fragmented and disoriented. He therefore denounced the "genre" as a fraud and a distortion of reality. *Anti-genre*—my own term—is the converse literary trend dedicated to portraying precisely the fragmentation and disorientation of the local Jewish community. Brenner himself was the progenitor and most prominent representative of this trend.
2. Ahad Ha-Am, "Hikui ve-hitbolelut," [1893], *Kol kitvei*, 1947, p. 89.
3. Ahad Ha-Am, "Emet me-Eretz Israel," [1891, 1893, 1894], *ibid.*, pp. 23–40.
4. Moshe Glickson, "Hiluf mishmarot," *Masuot*, 1919, no. 10; see also critique of this essay by Shalom Streit, "Masuot," *Ha-adamah* no. 6, 1920, p. 737.
5. Y. Rabinowitz, "Sifrutenu ve-hayenu," *Hedim*, 1924, vol. 3, no. 3, p. 47.
6. Zamach's letter to Lachover, May 10, 1921, published in *Yediot genazim*, no. 86–87, November 1975, p. 261. Compare: Y. H. Brenner, *Mi-kan u-mi-kan, Kol kitvei*, vol. 1, 1955, p. 336: "It thus appears there is no difference . . . the diaspora is everywhere—no difference at all . . . no safety . . . What safety can there be here? Everywhere, the angel of death has eyes."
7. "My soul no longer dreams, my friend Diasporin! There are no Jews in the world! I

myself am no better than other Jews. However, if there *were* Jews in the world, if my voice were heard, I would cry to them: Trust not in this dream, it is a nightmare, a false dream in any case. If there are any remnants of this people, if they can survive wherever they are—let them take heart and do so, and they shall survive somewhere, somehow." Y. H. Brenner, *ibid.*, p. 338.

8. Brenner deals with this them profoundly and comprehensively in his story "Atzabim."

9. Y. Rabinowitz to Lamdan in Germany, *Genazim,* no date, no archival reference. See also Rabinowitz's letter to Barash, 1924 (relating to Lachover's letter to Rabinowitz), *Genazim,* 7364/35.

10. Rabinowitz's letter to Lamdan, January 2, 1928, *Genazim.*

11. U. Z. Greenberg's polemics in *Sadan* and *Davar;* Avigdor Hameiri's biting diatribes in *Ha-mahar;* the atmosphere created with the appearance of Steinman's and Shlonski's *Ketuvim.*

12. Many of the generation's writers betray similar fears in their correspondence: Y. Fichman, Y. Rabinowitz, R. Wallenrod, S. Halkin. The issue is discussed in essays by U. Z. Greenberg: "Ve-elu yesodot la-meshorer kan" (Poetic Principles in Palestine), *"Montenegro eina malkhut"* (Montenegro is no Kingdom), "Klapei tishim ve-tisha" (Towards Ninety-Nine); by A. Barash: "Sifrut shel shevet o sifrut shel am" (The Literature of a Tribe or the Literature of a People); and later by Y. Ratosh: "Sifrut yehudit ba-lashon ha-ivrit" (Hebrew Literature in the Hebrew Language).

13. Dr. A. Ruppin, *Soziologie der Juden* (Berlin, 1931), pp. 145–46.

14. *Ibid.,* pp. 146–47.

15. *Ibid.,* p. 148.

16. The persecutions of the Soviet regime; the assimilation in Poland; the emigration to the United States. See Ruppin, *ibid.,* pp. 173–77.

17. The list of subscribers to *Gilyonot* in the 1930s includes members living in Europe and the United States.

18. Letters from Shlonski and Steinman to Norman and Horowitz, *Genazim.*

19. Rabinowitz asks Lachover, acting manager of the Stybel Publishing House, to assist in distributing *Hedim* in Poland *(Genazim).* In 1924, Halkin and Bavli issue a circular calling upon American authors and Hebrew-lovers to come to the aid of *Hedim.* Rabinowitz admits that without American support, *Hedim* could not hold out (letter of June 30, 1928, *Genazim).* Viewing *Gilyonot* as the legitimate heir to *Hedim,* Lamdan asks Aharoni for help for *Gilyonot,* in 1934 (November 1934, *Genazim).*

20. The Lamdan Archives have a list of *Gilyonot* authors in the United States, Poland, and the Soviet Union.

21. Letter to Lachover, August 18, 1912, *Genazim.*

22. Rabinowitz's letter to Lamdan, April 15, 1928: "The question of *Hedim* is a very difficult one. Asher is exhausted. The funds we raised in America were partly lost in Palestine due to the crisis." *(Genazim).*

23. Stybel's letter to Poznanski, March 12, 1926, sent from Copenhagen *(Genazim).*

24. An issue discussed by "Palestinian" authors and Lachover. On the agenda was the transfer of the Stybel Publishing House to Palestine. See, for example, Rabinowitz's letter to Lachover in the 1920s, *Genazim,* 11194/90.

25. *Moznayim* (Weekly), no. 1, 1929. According to the essay, the following types of books were published at the time in Palestine:

	Orig. Lit.	Trans. Lit	Science	Religion	Textbooks
1908	5	4	5	5	2
1910	8	4	18	1	2
1912	7	3	25	12	7

	Orig. Lit.	Trans. Lit	Science	Religion	Textbooks
1914	14	2	11	—	3
1916	22	4	3	—	7
1918	7	2	1	2	1
1920	6	12	8	7	6
1922	19	10	13	—	7
1924	32	11	27	28	10
1926	61	26	42	63	24
1928	87	65	47	21	16

26. See correspondence between Lachover, Poznanski, Stybel, and Rabinowitz on the publication of Brenner's writings, e.g. Rabinowitz's letters to Lachover: 1920s, *Genazim* 1193/89, and May 12, 1924, *Genazim*.

27. In his letter to Lachover of January 1928 *(Genazim)*, Rabinowitz provides an interesting description of the correlation between the local economic situation and book consumption.

28. Rabinowitz's letter to Lachover of the 1920s, *Genazim* 11195/91. His letters clearly evince a profound comprehension of the socio-literary circumstances in Palestine.

29. Economic troubles were the lot of many writers. See, for example, Kimche's letter to Burla, October 11, 1923, *Genazim*; Arieli-Orloff to Dvorah Baron (in a letter regarding the *Maabarot* journal), *Genazim* 6040/15. There are many such letters. Most writers made a living by teaching or in "literary pursuits" (translation and editing). Very few had means of support other than literature (Smilanski, Streit). On the whole, local writers did not earn a livelihood through their literary work.

30. Galia Yarden, *Ha-itonut ha-ivrit be-Eretz Israel, 1863–1904,* 1969; see also G. Kressel, *Toldot ha-itonut ha-ivrit be-Eretz Israel,* 1964, pp. 100–9.

31. Nurit Govrin, "*Ha-omer* ve-S. Ben-Zion orkho," doctoral dissertation, 1972, p. 106.

32. In his "Manifesto of the *Shiloah*," (1897), Ahad Ha-Am set down the principles and editorial policy for Hebrew literary periodicals in the diaspora.

33. Fichman's letter to Lachover, August 21, 1912, *Genazim*; compare also Fichman's letter to Lachover, May 8, 1813, *Genazim*.

34. See Kabak's letter to D. Baron (from Constantinople), *Genazim* 6184/12.

35. *Ibid.*

36. See Kimche's letter to Streit, May 24, 1920, *Genazim*.

37. A. Barash, "Sifrut shel shevet o sifrut shel am," *Moznayim* (Weekly), vol. 2, no. 38 (88), 1931, pp. 9–13.

38. Nurit Govrin, *Shai shel sifrut,* Prologue, pp. 5–128, 1973.

39. The first collection (June–July 1922) features Y. Fichman, M. Tamkin, M. Siko, D. Simonowitz, D. Baron, S. Ben-Zion, Y. Burla, A. A. Kabak, Y. Karni, M. Smilanski, D. Kimche, Y. Klausner, and others.

40. See the *Dapim* manifesto closing the collection (*Dapim,* Jerusalem 1922, p. 96); compare: D. Kimche (B. Safrir), "Sifrut eretz israelit," *Hapoel Hatzair,* no. 1–2, November 11, 1921, p. 16.

41. Initially published in *Kuntres,* no. 6, July 1, 1919.

42. Brenner's figure played a central role in the literary and social life of Palestine. See: *Igrot S. Y. Agnon le-Brenner,* ed. R. Weiser, 1978; *Igrot Arieli-Orloff le-Brenner,* *Genazim* vol. 4, 1971, B. Karu and A. M. Havermann, eds., pp. 190–200. In his letter to Lachover of May 12, 1924 *(Genazim),* Y. Rabinowitz emphasized that even in death, Brenner was the primary model for Hebrew authors. Not even Bialik, newly arrived in Palestine, could take his place. ("Bialik is here. Apparently, people are

trying to establish a little Odessa. How pitiful. The atmosphere here is different. Literature here takes after Brenner, Berdichevsky, and to a small degree, Frishman.")

43. From the aforesaid regarding Y. Rabinowitz, especially from the letters he wrote and received, it appears he became Brenner's heir as an inspired critic and editor.

44. Schatz's letter to Poznanski, May 16, 1919, "Al gevul ha-demamah," 1929, p. 140.

45. Kimche's letter to Streit, May 24, 1920, *Genazim*.

46. Y. H. Brenner, *Kol kitvei*, vol. 2, 1960, pp. 163–65; compare "Bavuatam shel olei Zion be-sifrutenu," *ibid.*, pp. 366–73.

47. "Aliyot vi-yeridot," *ibid.*, pp. 162–63.

48. See Fichman's letter to Lachover, May 8, 1913, *Genazim;* his postwar letters from Warsaw to D. Baron and Y. Aharonowitz (the 1920s), *Genazim* Archives; letter to Lachover, September 1923, *ibid.* The letters reflect Fichman's vacillations regarding emigration. He left Palestine twice, yearned to return, and after much soul-searching, came to stay, for the second time, in 1925. He was not alone. Some, like Arieli-Orloff, immigrated, then left, never to return. Others, like Halkin and Wallenrod, came for brief periods. Halkin then immigrated, Wallenrod departed.

49. Y. Lofban, "Porzei netivot," [1929], *Sefer ha-aliyah ha-shniyah*, B. Habas, ed., 1947, p. 43.

50. S. Zemach, "Reshit," [1942], *ibid.*, pp. 31–36.

51. Y. Tabenkin, "Ha-mekorot," [1937], *ibid.*, p. 29.

52. B. Katznelson, "Nes ha-aliyah ha-shniyah," [1929], *ibid.*, pp. 11, 13, 14.

53. Z. Schatz. Letter to R. H., 1920, *Al gevul ha-demamah*, p. 164.

54. On man's foreignness in the new surroundings see A. Reuveni, *Shamot*, p. 388, the opening passage: "All is different—the skies are different, the land is different; a hard land, alert and watchful, keeping its thoughts to itself."

55. Y. Rabinowitz, "Sifrutenu ve-hayenu," *Maslulei sifrut*, vol. 2, 1971, pp. 551–52.

56. Y. Rabinowitz, "Megamat harhavah shel ha-sipur ha-ivri," *Ahdut Haavodah*, vol. 2, 1931, p. 316; *Maslulei sifrut*, vol. 1, p. 85.

57. E.g., Arieli-Orloff's 1918 play, *Allah Karim*, especially his presentation of Ali the Arab as a welcome figure (p. 144); also Rabinowitz's ideal of "Jewish Bedouins," *Nedudei Amashai ha-shomer*, vol. 2, 1929, p. 100.

58. Y. Rabinowitz, "Sifrutenu ve-hayenu," *Maslulei sifrut*, vol. 2, p. 554.

59. Kimche's letter to Streit (Jerusalem, 1918) *Genazim* Archives.

60. Schatz's letter to Poznanski, August 1919, *Al gevul ha-demamah*, p. 141–42.

61. Aharon Feldman (Ever Ha-Dani), "Yom Aviv," in: *Zlalim*, collected stories of the seventh department students, Hebrew Gymnasium, Jaffa, 1916, p. 85.

62. *"Jedda"* entry, R. Sapan's *Milon ha-slang be-Israel* (Kiryat Sefer, 1965).

63. Y. Fichman, "Signon ha-yahid ve-signon ha-rabim," *Maabarot* vol. 1, 1920, p. 7.

64. Y. Rabinowitz, "Sifrutenu ve-hayenu," *Maslulei sifrut*, vol. 2, pp. 554–55.

65. The utilization of distinct languages in distinct social contexts within a single community.

66. See the essay by Dr. A. Tartakover, "Mavo la-sociologyah shel leshonot be-Israel" in *Tehumim*, no. 1, Warsaw, 1937, pp. 67, 70, 71–72.

67. See Gershon Shaked, *Ha-mahazeh ha-ivri ha-histori bi-tkufat ha-tehiyah*, 1970, pp. 331, 335–36.

68. Kimche's letter to Streit, July 27, 1914, *Genazim* Archives.

69. Kimche to Streit, July 6, 1927; Kimche to Burla, September 12, 1927, *Genazim* Archives. Rabinowitz to Lachover (1920s) on Nils Lihne, *Genazim* Archives.

70. L. A. Arieli-Orloff to D. Baron, May–June 1937, *Genazim* Archives. Arieli-Orloff's memoirs relate explicitly to the period of the Second Aliyah.

71. Agnon translated Bjornson's "Dust"; Bjornson is also mentioned in Pukhachevski's story "Be-bdidut ba-kfar u-va-avodah," *Hedim* Publications, 1930, p. 179. Besides "Elem Aliz" (1916), Kimche translated Bjornson's "Arne" (1927).

72. Y. H. Brenner, "Ha-genre ha-eretz-israeli va-avizarehu," *Hapoel Hatzair*, no. 4, issue 21, 1911, p. 9.

73. Rabbi Binyamin, "Ha-genre ha-eretz-israeli," *Hapoel Hatzair*, no. 4, issue 22, 1911, p. 9. Binyamin maintains that "The Eretz-Israeli genre did not originate with Zeev Yavetz, rather with one of the great men: Avraham Mapu . . . but there are grounds for assuming that if a decent writer were to find his way into our camp or to emerge among us, he would discover even in this strange world ample material for his tongue. The world of creation is boundless."

74. Y. H. Brenner, "Ha-genre ha-eretz-israeli va-avizarehu," *Kol kitvei*, vol. 2, p. 269.

75. On these twin terms, see I. Even Zohar, "Israeli-Hebrew Literature," *Papers in Historical Poetics* (Tel Aviv, 1978), pp. 11–13; I. Even Zohar, "The Function of the Literary Polysystem in the History of Literature," *ibid.*, pp. 11–13.

31.

Native Sons

Anita Shapira

In 1958, on Israel's tenth anniversary, *Dor ba-aretz* (Native Sons), an anthology of verse and short stories, was published. Its authors described themselves as "Eretz-Israeli writers whose work is grounded in the land, whether they were born here, or have immigrated in their youth." Drawing on local reality, their subject matter savored of youthful and adolescent experiences, and echoed the War of Independence. A manifesto of sorts, the anthology boldly proclaimed: Here we are! Different from our predecessors, unique; though we may not resemble each other, we are nonetheless bound by a sense of existential solidarity, expressed in cultural alliance.[1] *Dor ba-aretz* gave voice to the emergence of the *Sabras* as a social and cultural entity. Issuing forth in the late 1930s, this "generation" of native sons took shape during the turbulent 1940s. Over the years it has come to be dubbed "the Palmach Generation"—a collective name designating an identification group far larger than the 3,000 members of the Haganah's pre-1948 crack unit.

In all social systems, the relationship between "fathers" and "sons" is complex. All the more so in an emerging society shaped by both immigration processes and social revolution. Such was Jewish society in Palestine under the British Mandate.

Dor ba-aretz—the first generation of "native sons"—emerged during the decade preceeding the founding of Israel. Young and old alike expected its members to take the staff of leadership from the tired heroes of the Second Aliyah,[2] and lead the fledgling state. However, the awaited change of guard never occurred. The governments of Israel were headed

Translated from the Hebrew and reprinted by permission of the author and *Alpaim* 2 (1990): 178–203.

by members of the "fathers' " generation—Ben-Gurion, Moshe Sharett, Levy Eshkol, and Golda Meir. Yizhak Rabin was the first *Sabra*—native son—to carve a path to the country's leadership. To this day, he remains the only representative there of the Palmach generation.

To all appearances, we are faced with a group which has developed a self-awareness of generational singularity. Undoubtedly, it strove to express this uniqueness in the spheres of culture, society, and politics. In part, the sons achieved their purpose, first in the cultural sphere, later in the social. However, in the field of politics, the fathers prevailed. Remaining in mentality alone, a form of wishful thinking, the sons' generational rebellion never transcended into practice.

The failure of the Palmach generation to leave its mark on Israel's political system raises basic questions as to the relationship between the generations within a revolutionary society. An animated controversy arose among scholars regarding the causes and implications of this failure. Were the sons castrated by powerful fathers with Bolshevik methods, who blocked their path into the political system? Was the Israeli author Amos Oz right to observe that under massive trees, only mushrooms flourish? Did the fathers' giant shadow prevent their sons from casting off paternal influence, and stamping their own seal on Israeli politics? Or did the sons' inherent weakness, produced by various causes, deny them the skills required for confronting their fathers? One factor cited in this context is education: the fathers, heirs to the cultural pluralism and wealth of Europe, imparted to their sons only a single national culture. The youngsters were thus deprived of an important means of holding their own against their elders.

Another question concerns the specificity of the phenomenon: is it distinctly Israeli, or does it serve as an applicable model for other societies under similar circumstances?

In discussing these questions, we shall have recourse to the generational model set by Karl Mannheim. In his renowned essay, "The Problem of Generations," Mannheim distinguishes between ordinary peer groups, and "generational cohorts." Members of a generational cohort, he claims, display solidarity and a collective self-consciousness. Exposed as they are to the same historical experiences, the members of a cohort tend to share distinctive modes of thought, emotional responses, and behavioral patterns. They are also inclined to contend with their predecessors for a place under the sun, i.e., for independent cultural expression, or political status. Not all generational cohorts realize their inherent potential: the frequency of realization correlates to the pace of social change. A rapid pace, requiring modulation of thought and behavioral patterns, generates a new focus of identification, and heralds a new generational style.[3]

Applying Mannheim's model to the father-son relationship within a revolutionary society, we shall first explore the phenomena suggesting that the generation in question is indeed a distinct generational cohort. Next we shall examine the components of its spiritual world, as compared with its predecessors'. Finally, we shall offer several hypotheses regarding the causes for its failure to realize its political potential.

In immigrant societies, a great gap typically divides the newcomers from their sons. The former grapple with a new land, a new language, unknown codes of behavior and cultural symbols, and unfamiliar systems of social and political relationships. The sons, by contrast, quickly imbibe all these factors, and blend in. In Palestine, the process was essentially different. Guided as it was by ideology, immigration to Palestine from the diaspora did not conform to the usual patterns of immigration. The ideology affected lifestyles, goals, and yearnings. Forged in the diaspora, it was imported to Palestine by the immigrant fathers. It was they who shaped the new reality, set its parameters, and raised their offspring accordingly. Having also shaped a model of "the New Jew," they sought to apply it to their sons. These, they believed, should be wholly different from themselves: they must shake off the dregs of exile, and be natural shoots of their homeland, free of all the diaspora Jews' psychic complexes vis-a-vis their physical and human surroundings. "Earthiness" was to replace "spirituality" as their natural trait: they were to be simple, forthright, loyal, and above all, truly "native," whose claim to the land is intuitive, sensual, requiring no teaching or indoctrination. In vain the fathers labored to acquire this trait for themselves: their Eretz Israel was the fruit of their learning, conscious choices, absorption agonies, and single-mindedness. They made it their own by invoking the Bible, the Jewish traditional sources, and the visions imbibed from contemporary Hebrew literature. Yet the "old country" held magical sway over them. Try as they would, they could not break free of their yearnings for childhood landscapes, winter snows, the beloved and familiar mother-tongue. By contrast, their sons were plagued with no double loyalty: ingrained through experience in earliest childhood, their sense of homeland needed neither proof nor support. The fathers bore allegiance to an abstract ideal of a Jewish homeland, and had no need to acquaint themselves with the land. It was the sons who actually toured and discovered Palestine. For them, the sense of belonging was concrete, experiental. The concept of "love of the land" materialized among them as naturally as the nickname "son of the land."[4]

THE EMERGENCE OF A NATIVE GENERATION

The native sons' divergence from their immigrant fathers had made its debut before World War I, with the emergence of native sons among the settlers of the Jewish colonies in Palestine. The youngsters felt at home with their peers, wore the same clothes, spoke the same language, developed their own accent and slang, laughed at the same jokes, were moved by the same songs, and awestruck by the same landscapes. They even had a particular body language. First and foremost, the native sons shared a unique "life culture," comprised of all those tiny details, which contribute to what may be defined as "style."

Belonging to the elect group of native sons did not pend on one's actual origin. There are no reliable statistics discerning between native and immigrant among the seventeen-year olds in the 1930s. However, it can be safely assumed, that among those who considered themselves native sons (and were perceived as such by society), relatively few were actually native-born.[5]

Although by the early 1920s, several dozen children had already been born in the cooperative settlements, most of the so-called native sons arrived as children during the Fourth Aliyah (1924–1926) and Fifth Aliyah (1929–1936). Some arrived on their own, as refugees, on the eve of World War II; others came during the war, such as the Teheran children—refugees who fled Russia to Palestine via Iran; still others came later, as survivors of the Holocaust, brought in the legal and illegal routes of postwar immigration. "Youth Groups" were established in the 1940s, consisting of youths who have made recent entry to Palestine, and received education and training in the *kibbutzim*. These figured heavily in the Palmach's recruited *hakhsharot* (training groups, singular *hakhsharah*).[6]

Demographic data on the instructors' seminar of the *Hanoar Haoved* (Working Youth) movement, which took place in Haifa in 1946, lists most participants as non-natives.[7] Even in that apparently "native" anthology, *Dor ba-aretz,* proclaiming the specificity of its generation, more than half the authors were newcomers. If one was to become a native son, one had to blend as rapidly as possible into the culture of the local youth. Acceptance hinged on donning the simple clothing of the cooperative settlements and youth movements, throwing foreign manners and caution to the wind, speaking Hebrew with a *Sabra* accent, and displaying a general knack for being "one of the gang"—whether in work on *kibbutz,* Palmach training, or after-hours antics. The adults welcomed this assimilation, which was in line with the youth model they had envisioned. Thus they compounded the pressure exerted on immigrant youngsters by youth societies with that of their own expectations.[8] To become a native son, then, meant to conform to the prevailing model.

Chronologically, the emergence of the *Sabra* generational cohort lasted from the beginning of the twentieth century until the 1940s. However, it was only in the last decade that a generational *awareness* surfaced. Jewish Palestine had had a native-born generation for a good half of the century, before it witnessed the crystallizing of that generation's special public image and its own generational self-awareness. Both of these were brought about by the juxtaposition of several factors: the relatively larger numbers of youths at the time; their cultural singularity; and last but not least, the self-assertion of their generation vis-a-vis their fathers. Sparing no effort to enhance this distinctness, the fathers themselves turned it into the very symbol of the sons' generation, and its self-image.

EDUCATIONAL PATTERNS OF TWO GENERATIONS

One prevalent explanation for the native sons' political inadequacy cites their comparative lack of cultural sophistication. Exposed to an array of European cultures, the argument runs, the fathers were broad-minded and well-educated. As for the sons, their Hebrew language education bred an inferior cultural repertoire. Spiritual provinciality eventually hampered their dealing with the political system's intrinsically complex situations.

All aspects of this notion may be called into question. Were the fathers truly knowledgeable and broad-minded? Were the sons truly narrow-minded and ignorant? What role did Hebrew education actually play in determining their cultural spectrum? Moreover: is cultural excellence necessarily related to qualities ensuring political success?

Several cultural elites existed in the Yishuv, including, for example, the veteran teachers. Its cultural position notwithstanding, this group carried no political clout. Indeed, both the teachers' pay and their social status deteriorated steadily. Writers, poets, and other men of letters all won substantial appreciation and respect, thanks to Hebrew literature's singular role in the Zionist movement; however, they had no corresponding political standing. The elite most versed in European culture hailed from Central Europe, and centered round the Hebrew University. Despite the respect it was accorded, despite the tolerance for its controversial opinions, this elite held no real political sway either. Nor did the intellectual refugees from Nazi Germany, arriving in the Fifth Aliyah of the 1930s, fare any better in the Yishuv's political life.

Are erudition and broad-mindedness truly relevant to political functioning? In the Yishuv, neither trait was required for successful statesmanship. True, the ruling elite, with its manifest political skills, also enjoyed a high intellectual image. However, examination of that elite's composition exposes this image for a myth, albeit containing a grain of truth.

It was Second Aliyah immigrants who formed the backbone of the Yishuv's political elite. Most of these immigrants came from small towns, only few from large cities.[9] Though many had received a Jewish education, most had attended only the *heder*, fewer the *yeshivah* (approximately 16 percent).[10] Less than 10 percent had higher education, 30 percent, high-school education, and the others, informal education, or none at all.[11] We have no detailed statistics regarding the Third Aliyah, and members of the socialist Zionist movement from the Soviet Union, who arrived with the Fourth Aliyah in 1924–1926. However, we do know that these people's coming-of-age spanned two wars—World War I and the post-October Revolution civil war in Russia. Entire Jewish communities and their educational institutions were destroyed at the time. It can therefore be surmised that the contemporaries' Jewish education fell short of their predecessors'. The same is true of general education, for in times of emigration, flight, and constant instability, chances for a systematic education were also slim.

Even without this overall picture at our disposal, its details could have been reconstructed from the personal biographies of members of the uppermost political echelon of the Labor movement. Formal education was not the "forte" of most, including the top triumvirate—Second Aliyah members Berl Katznelson, Yizhak Tabenkin, and David Ben-Gurion. They did enjoy a broad informal education, as did a thin stratum of Third and Fourth Aliyah leaders. But the education of the vast majority of the period's immigrants, including most politicians, was limited and eclectic.

Another debatable point concerns the immigrant elite's "broad-mindedness." Whereas some were truly erudite, others were ignorant and hidebound. In any case, even the broadest intellectual horizons only encompassed the motherland—Eastern Europe. Here lay the source of culture, emulation foci, and cultural and political codes. Acquaintance with the Europe west of the Vistula was superficial, and the attitude towards it, mostly estranged, often hostile. Some, like Chaim Arlosoroff, were versed in German culture; however, these were rare birds indeed among the "graduates" of the Eastern European *shtetl*. Openess towards diverse cultures is as crucial a gauge of "broad-mindedness" as actual knowledge. The fathers' generation can hardly be described as paragons of such tolerance. Their Jewish "legacy," grounded in the mostly traditional heritage of their upbringing, furnished intuitive support for their powerful sense of ethnic identity and hostility towards gentiles. Most viewed Western culture with suspicion, fearing that "excessive" openness towards it could undermine Zionist faith, and bring about an uprooting from the deeply cherished newborn entity in Palestine.

Granted, some members of the fathers' generation were well-read, profound thinkers, who lent a global perspective to all topics on the period's agenda—Jewish destiny, the future of the universal revolution, or developments in capitalism or imperialism. Despite their retrograde, provincial backgrounds and lack of systematic education, they were infected by the current *zeitgeist,* revolutionary literature, and youthful heart-to-heart talks. Thus they took part in the century's great social and political trends. However, such men were rather scarce. As for the leaders among them, whatever administrative or political skills they possessed stemmed neither from education, nor even from political experience acquired in the old country, but rather, from a blend of intuition and practical wisdom revealed in the Palestine environment.

We have established then, that as a whole, the fathers' generation was no better-educated than the sons'. It now remains to be seen, whether Hebrew education truly had an adverse affect on the sons. From time to time, educators and university staff lamented the shortcomings of local education. In the curriculum, they argued, studies of Jewish, especially Hebrew, culture far outweighed general culture, i.e., general literature and history, and, above all, foreign languages.[12] However, a survey of the 1930s curricula of two prominent secondary schools in Tel Aviv— the Herzliyah Gymnasium and *Beit ha-Sefer ha-Tihoni le-Mishar* (The

Secondary School of Trade)—presents a reasonable balance between the components of "national" and general education. For example, in six years of school, studies in the literary trend at Herzliyah comprised thirteen weekly hours of Bible, Talmud, and Hebrew, and ten weekly hours of general ("scientific") studies. Three weekly hours of history have been excluded from this account, as the curriculum does not specify whether it is Jewish or general. On the other hand, the Secondary School of Trade, in a similar four-year curriculum, explicitly allots seventeen yearly hours to general history, and only nine to Jewish history. It stands to reason, then, that Herzliyah's ratio was analogous. Furthermore, according to the testimonies of Herzliyah's students during this period, general history formed the bulk of history studies, as teachers were versed in the subject matter and textbooks were available. By contrast, the teaching of Jewish history was still nascent. Many eras had yet to be studied; material and textbooks accessible to teachers were simply nonexistent. Presumably, then, the teaching of history centered on the annals of Europe and its culture. In both schools, the English language was allocated the largest share of school hours—thirty-eight at Herzliyah, forty-one at the trade school. In the former, the syllabus includes a second foreign language.[13] Thus it seems that the schools furnished students with a sound general education, and with instruments for broadening their minds.

But let us suppose that national content did in fact receive particular emphasis. We should then consider whether this state of affairs intrinsically differed from that of other peoples. Every nation gives priority to its own history and literature. They are a blessed few, whose history coincides with the world's, whose literature comprises Shakespeare and his likes. At the time in question, Eastern European education—Poland serves a valid case in point—most probably provided high-school students with no broader an education than that of their counterparts in Palestine.

Though nationalism may have found favor in Palestine's educational system, politics did not. During the 1930s and 1940s, local schools came under the influence of the European, especially English, liberal tradition, and attempted to adopt its educational tenets. With the exception of the United States, Western tradition hardly subscribed to developing political awareness in the schools or inculcating political activism. Quite the contrary: it was believed that at a tender age, political education (as regards the parties and the power struggles) was corruptive. Local schools accordingly endeavored to close their doors to politics.

On the whole, the educational system represents the prevailing political and social consensus. No such system has ever deliberately bred rebels to rock its foundations. Revolutionaries emerged not by dint of the system's openness, but in defiance of its set of creeds and notions.

Secondary education in Palestine did not differ from other societies', including the most enlightened, either in its conformism or in its stress on national content. Disapproving intellectuals staked their claims not on other national traditions, but on the inclinations of Central and Western European Jews, who sought to become citizens of the world, and to inculcate the youngsters with universalist ideas. However, being cosmopolitan and building a national Jewish society in Palestine were mutually exclusive.

Returning to the language argument: both its aspects are debatable. First of all, contrary to popular convention, not all members of the fathers' generation were versed in European tongues. Indeed, many Second Aliyah and Third Aliyah newcomers were fluent only in Yiddish—hardly a window on European culture. Secondly, a Hebrew education was by no means an obstacle to erudition. Translation projects of remarkable magnitude attended the revival of the Hebrew language, embracing the very best of world literature. Between the two world wars, Stybel, Omanut, Mizpeh, and other publishing houses presented Hebrew readers with the best of Russian, German, Scandinavian, French, and English literature, wherein their fathers' generation felt at home. Turgenev, Tolstoy, Dostoyevsky, Gogol, and Pushkin made popular reading, as did Victor Hugo, Charles Dickens, Knut Hamsun, Romain Roland, Gustave Flaubert, Thomas Mann, Erich Maria Remarque, and Franz Kafka, to name but a few. The Palestine bestsellers' list included Maxim Gorky, Franz Werfel, Howard Fast, Jack London, Arthur Koestler, Ernest Hemingway, Ilya Erenburg, and in the 1940s, Soviet literature—Makarenko, Bek (*The Reserves of General Panfilov*), Vanda Vasilevska, and many others. Nor were the philosophers overlooked; the Hebrew repertoire boasted works by Kropotkin, Herzen, Marx, Engels, Lassalle, Otto Bauer, and the classics from Plato to Spinoza. To all appearances, every work the fathers' generation deemed significant was duly translated for the benefit of the Hebrew public. Philosophical writings may have been in low demand, but foreign literature was welcomed with such relish, as to disconcert devotees of Hebrew literature, who viewed it as unequal competition.[14] Thus there is little to support the notion that the Hebrew language has produced a cultural ghetto and conceptual Zionist isolation, denying the youths acquaintance with the world's complexity, and stunting their socialization process.

At the time, reading was a common, popular behavioral pattern, indeed, one of the only pastimes. The library available to the youthful public played a crucial role in imparting an intrinsically humanistic world view, deeply conscious of the complexities of human nature, and steeped in socialistic pathos, awareness of universal iniquity, and hopes for reforming society. More than all the lectures on the history of the Labor movement—common staple, especially in the 1930s, at youth movement seminars—this library endowed its readers with social sensitivity and a spontaneous leaning to the Left.

Setting down the priorities by determining the material worthy of study and translation, it was the fathers' generation who had outlined the youngsters' education. The world-view projected to the sons, filtered through their elders' spectacles, thus had an element of passive acceptance, with no personal choice or selection. Moreover, for the fathers' generation, literature served as education to political activity. No mere learning for learning's sake, education was rather a tool with which one could change the face of society, and achieve revolutionary ends. The fathers conceived of education in political terms; to them, it was a battle cry, a call to action. The sons, by contrast, took it for granted, as part of their heritage. Although they were as well-learned as their parents, their grasp of the same values and knowledge was conceptually different. It was not education that the young people lacked, but rather the translation of the values they had imbued into an incentive to action. The books they read failed to produce that ideological tension which characterized their parents and prompted them to action.

Despite the similarity between their cultural backgrounds, fathers and sons did diverge in their world-views. Two crucial points of difference, most pertinent to our discussion, are each generation's attitudes to the diaspora, and to socialism.

THE NEGATION OF EXILE: TWO GENERATIONAL APPROACHES

To greater or lesser degrees, the fathers rebelled against Jewish life in the diaspora. For many, immigration was the culminating act in a prolonged process of alienation from their *fons et origo*, stemming as much from total abnegation of the Jewish life pattern "there," as from ardent faith in the future of the Jewish people "here." Other immigrants, in uncertain numbers, arrived in Palestine on the wings of that feeling, which Uri Zvi Greenberg defined so well in his poem "Mukhrahim hayyinu lalekhet"

("We were compelled to leave"): a sense of impending disaster, an urgent need to make good one's escape. These men smothered in their hearts an unrequited love for their fatherland ("We were constrained to hate even that which we loved").[15]

Apprehensive of the old country's secret fascination, they fortified their souls against it by denigrating Jewish life there, and disclaiming all it came to symbolize. Rejection of exile thus became a mirror image of the totality of Zionist faith.

It was Yosef Hayyim Brenner, the Second Aliyah author hailed as the conscience of the Labor movement, who wrote most harshly of his wellspring. Accepting his diagnosis, his contemporaries also perceived the tacit social code: here was shock treatment, aimed to jolt the patient from his apathy into facilitating his own cure. Despite its bitter sarcasm, Brenner's criticism was welcomed, for between the lines his contemporaries discerned great empathy, pity, and compassion. They understood all too well his tumultuous mixed feelings, and shared them. Beyond their proclaimed hostility for their origins, a sense of belonging still glimmered in their souls. Bred by home, family, townlet, and everyday experience, it could not be eradicated by any ideology.

By contrast, Palestine youth took an entirely different view of the diaspora. A case in point is their preference of abstract to concrete nouns when speaking of the diaspora (e.g., the slogan coined in 1942, following reports of the Holocaust, "If I forget thee, O Diaspora!"). In the transition from fathers to sons, the Jewish people in exile seemed to lose its flesh-and-blood concreteness, comprised of specific, familiar people, places, and lifestyles. With its air of an anonymous, faceless mass, it evoked no associations, hence, no empathy. Fathers and sons ostensibly used identical terms, such as "rejection of exile," "degradation of Jewish life in the *shtetl*." However, the attendant mental images were quite dissimilar: whereas the parents envisaged places, situations, experiences, people, the sons formed but a vague idea of something negative, corresponding to no memory or familiar experience.

One of the works especially popular with Hanoar Haoved and Hamahanot Haolim youth movements was Brenner's "Haarakhat azmenu bisheloshet ha-krakhim" (Self-Evaluation in Three Volumes).[16] In this essay, Brenner analyzes the works of Mendele Mokher Seforim, stressing in particular Mendele's increasing sarcasm vis-a-vis Jewish reality. After relentlessly citing a series of ironic passages, Brenner, like Mendele, eventually makes his peace with the wretched people portrayed. Not because this people has changed, but simply because it is their own, and they love and pity it. However, this last stage of Brenner's analysis was most likely overlooked by the youth movements' disciples. Underlined instead were those segments of reality, which stirred repulsion among Palestine's Labor youth: dissociation from menial and agricultural labor, dependence on the strong and "natural" gentile, idleness, wretchedness, cowardice, and resignation. All they had been brought up to reject was embodied in that anonymous, dim entity, "diaspora." In the early 1940s, Brenner's work was conjoined by Hayyim Hazaz's "Ha-deras-hah" (The Sermon),[17] whose hero rails against Jewish history, depicting the eras between the destruction of the Temple and the modern return to Zion as a "black hole." The two pieces served as an ideological foundation for the native sons' natural feeling of dissociation from that entity named "diaspora." Cerebrally, they recognized their link with the Jewish people, even proclaimed identification with its lot. But they bore diaspora Jews no more empathy than that reserved, say, for the hungry children of India, brandished by parents at mealtimes. Indeed, the Russian or Yugoslavian partisans fighting against Nazi Germany could well have commanded more sympathy.

The question arises, why had not the youths' parents, all immigrants from "there," tempered this attitude. In their stories of their fathers' houses, did they not familiarize the foreign, bring the distant near? Moreover, as mentioned above, many of those called native sons were not, in fact, born in Palestine. To be sure, knowing that other reality, they must have been bound to it by profound emotional ties?

Apparently, this was not the case. The past was shrouded in silence. Whether because they nursed the pains of loss, or because they had severed all ties with their past, parents spoke little of their childhood homes. As few families had grandparents in Palestine, there was no one to divulge family tradition to the sons. By no means exceptional, this phenomenon typifies immigrant societies: the first generation strives to leave behind as much of the old country as quickly as possible; only in the second generation does a quest for "roots" emerge. As for those youths who immigrated as children, they quickly forgot their fatherland, identifying wholeheartedly with their new home. The case of older children was more complex: many still bore painfully quivering memories from "there," wounds which had yet to heal. Shutting out the past was the natural way to begin anew. Moreover, they fell under enormous pressures to "fit in," a process which entailed acceptance of local stereotypes. Entire "unacceptable" segments of experience and associations were duly suppressed. Years later many resurged, as the hold of that coveted lifestyle slackened, and with it the social stigma plaguing whoever belonged "there."

TWO ATTITUDES TO SOCIALISM

Socialism was the second major point of disparity between fathers and sons. On the whole, what was true of the diaspora also applied here: to the fathers, socialism was reality, to the sons, an abstract concept. Most Labor movement members among the Yishuv's elite came from lower-middle-class homes. In their social surroundings poverty was a common feature of everyday life. Even if they took no part in the Bund, the Jewish workers' party, its struggle for decent living and working conditions nonetheless informed their adolescence experiences. They also had first-hand knowledge of the privation of tsarist Russia's peasants and workers. To them, class distinctions and social distortions were facts of everyday life.[18] Hope for an impending revolution was real.[19] The period's upheavals played a vital role in their experiential world and socialization processes. For the Second Aliyah, it was revolutionary agitation on the Russian street and the 1905 Revolution; for the Third Aliyah, and for the socialist Zionist youth of the Fourth Aliyah, it was the October Revolution. Although most did not actually participate in the revolutionary movement, they deemed themselves comrades-in-arms, accepting socialism as an almost self-evident practical truth.

For this social stratum, socialism filled a function akin to that of general education for Western Jews: it formed a bridge to the non-Jewish world. Even when acting within distinctly Jewish frameworks, secluded from the "general" revolutionaries, their link to the socialist outlook granted them a sense of sharing in a universal momentum. Through socialism they grew familiar with the world's unfortunates, empathized with their hopes and struggles, envisioned them all marching side by side into a better future. Thus it transpired, paradoxically, that a purely Jewish, zealously national movement, closed by its very nature to non-Jews, took on international aspirations. Viewing itself as part of a trans-national movement, it followed every fluctuation of universal Leftist forces with bated breath, declaring their fate its own. This was by no means a posture; these youths truly believed they belonged to the "Forces of Light" in the imminent apocalyptical upheavals.

In Palestine and abroad, the primary frameworks exposing young Jews to the world of socialism were the youth movements. Zionist youth movements emerged in the diaspora after World War I. Since the late

1920s, they began cropping up in Palestine as well, in ever-increasing numbers and significance (corresponding to the growing numbers of local youth). Although they occupied both sides of the Jewish Yishuv's political spectrum, those with a Leftist bent proved most influential. Rightist movements, such as Betar, or those affiliated with religious Zionism, such as Bnei Akiva, deemed their Leftist counterparts a worthy model.

The largest local youth movement was Hanoar Haoved. Well-acquainted with deprivation, its disciples knew from experience the hardships of the work day. From early childhood they had been subjected to the pressures of the socio-economic reality. Finding socialism's explanations of existing circumstances daily verified, they accepted its tenets quite naturally. Class-awareness was nurtured and heightened by a profusion of "edifying" essays in *Ba-maaleh,* the movement's official journal.

By contrast, local secondary school pupils did not undergo proletarian experiences. The very attendance at school bespoke parental affluence: it was not every family who could afford to pay tuition fees, or to forgo its children's labor wages. No wonder then that when the Hamahanot Haolim youth movement was founded by "the older circle," erstwhile disciples of the Herzliyah Gymnasium, its interest in the history of Zionism far surpassed interest in socialism.[20] The tenets of their world-view—a life of labor, frugality, and equality—were formulated very much as an antithesis to their parents' petit-bourgeois lifestyle, which they loathed and rejected. Deeply idealistic, they wished to sacrifice themselves for the nation, and aspired to lead "proper" lives. Theirs was a predominantly nationalist idealism. The idea of joining a *kibbutz* was generated by desire to establish their own new independent settlement.

During the first decade of Hamahanot Haolim, socialism played a minor role in their curricula and instructional programs. *Bi-vritekh,* the publication summarizing the 1937 Seniors' Seminar in Gevat, overshadowed by controversy regarding the Peel Commission's partition proposal,[21] evinces these trends. Prevalent moods come across vividly. Whereas ardent identification with the land is salient ("We, the people of the land," "native son," "Man is the image of his homeland"), the socialist issue seems practically nonexistent.[22] The links of both these movements to the international workers' movement were insubstantial. True, May 1st was annually celebrated with pomp and circumstance, and constituted a central educational topic. However, national myths outshone it. Members ritually ascended the Masada, and celebrated Tel-Hai Day (commemorating the heroic deaths of Joseph Trumpeldor and his men in 1920, in the Upper Galilee, in a clash with Arab marauders). Essays in *Ba-maaleh* concerning developments in the European workers' movements reflected the educational tendencies of the journal's adult editors, rather than the interest of young readers. The internationalistic trend found no expression among Palestine youth. Whatever socialistic yearnings did exist, they were grounded mainly in local reality. Whatever lay beyond the horizon lacked palpability. Socialism's true content was interpreted as devotion to national missions. Since the workers' movement ascent to power in the 1930s, the equation of socialist trends with national missions was taken for granted. The youth movements were thus dominated by a local-national ideology, coupled with a value system derived from the socialist code.

In the late 1930s, and increasingly in the 1940s, this state of affairs began to change. For example, during the discussions of Hamahanot Haolim's conference in 1945, which culminated in a split, the concrete topic at hand was the attitude towards socialism and the Soviet Union. Comparison of this discussion with the national sentiment and social neutrality of *Bi-vritekh* evinces the enormous distance covered by the movement within but a few years.[23] Hamahanot Haolim's shift in sentiment reflects a trend prevalent among Hanoar Haoved, and, to some extent, among Hazofim (the local Scout federation)—namely, a growing identification with Leftist activism. This trend arose mainly from the juxtaposition of two rising influences among the youth: one, that of Hakibbutz Hameuhad—the largest *kibbutz* movement, and the most radical in both its socialist and nationalist concepts; the other, that of the Soviet Union, following its heroic resistance of Nazi occupation. Russia of World War II furnished activist elements among Palestinian youth with their own window on the world. To a great extent, this Russia was a myth. Local youth spoke no Russian, never encountered Soviet reality, or held a dialogue with anyone who had. Theirs was the Russia of the beloved songs, the translated books, the movies, and, naturally, the heroic tales published in the movements' journals and in the Palmach's pamphlets. Surely, it was not the *kolkhoz* system which fired young imaginations. Russia's fighting power, the Soviet regime's vitality during the crisis of war—these were the factors which impressed them. Queries regarding internal rule, democracy, and dictatorship received little attention. Nor were the theoretical aspects of communism widely debated (as they were in the more intellectual youth movement Hashomer Hatzair [The Young Guard]). Identification with a massive force, marching from strength to strength, granted the youth a profound sense of security and power, a feeling they were taking part in worldwide processes, on the winning side.

Yet this Russia lacked concreteness. The fathers' Russia, on the other hand, was palpable, alive, their links with it grounded in intimate acquaintance with their fatherland, deep emotional involvement with its revolutionary drive, particularly with the great experiment of building a socialist country.

Like the world-view instilled by education, the younger generation's socialist legacy also originated with the fathers. Here too, acceptance was passive. Thus, the world-view and socialist outlook which bred rebelliousness among the fathers, became elements of conservatism among the sons.

COLLECTIVISTIC ETHOS AND GROUP SOLIDARITY

However, neither the passive acceptance of inherited notions, nor the want of socialist drive, can be invoked to explain the native generation's lack of political skills. Other elements in the fathers' life experience, absent from their offsprings', were more significant. One must remember, for example, that the Yishuv's political elite was bred by a merciless double selection: first, willingness to abandon home and family, and sail for the unknown, required unique personal traits; most Jewish youths clung to their homelands, whether hostile or benign. Secondly, even if Ben-Gurion had exaggerated in fixing the Second Aliyah's emigration rate at 90 percent, nonetheless, those who remained were doubtlessly resolute, tough, accustomed to disappointments, and hardened to the turmoils of the time. As for the Third Aliyah and the socialist Zionist men of the Fourth Aliyah, selection was notable at the first stage: they had to struggle for their right to immigrate, steal across borders, experience exile and imprisonment, and risk their lives in the Zionist underground in Russia. Those who eventually made it to Palestine underwent such filteration, that only the strongest survived.[24]

This was not the case with the local second generation: the land was theirs for free. No struggle was necessary to win them a place under the sun, no crucial decisions to be taken at a tender age. No wonder, then, that their political survival skills fell short of their fathers'. This fact, coupled with the fathers' cardinal influence in shaping their image, left the sons inclined toward acquiescence, dependence on authority, and resignation towards the reigning ideology. None of these traits is conducive to leadership. Let us now examine the unique, intrinsic characteristics of local youth movement education, and try to assess its influence on the youths' attitude to politics and their leadership faculties.

Serving as centers for Palestine's activist youth, the youth movements were to be the breeding grounds of the new generation of leaders. Student youth comprised the movements' elite. In time, well-educated members of Hamahanot Haolim and Hashomer Hatzair generated the writers and poets, who granted the "Palmach generation" cultural identity, and hence, self-awareness. However, many youth movement disciples never attended secondary school. Members of the working youth movement, Hanoar Haoved outnumbered both, and constituted the majority of the Palmach's recruited *hakhsharot*.[25] All told, the number of school-age youth movement disciples did not exceed 20 percent of all local youth; of these, only a marginal number remained in the movement until they were eighteen years old—the age for joining a *hakhsharah*. Be that as it may, the movements' influence on local youth was in all probability decisive—whether because they formed a cultural and ideological focus, or because they served as a center of inspiration for the entire Palmach.[26]

Youth-movement education consisted of two major factors: one, ideology, imparted to the disciples through programs differentiated according to age; the other, the movement's ethos. Political parties require fairly limited commitment of their members: voting properly at given times, or, at best, some interim activity—meetings, demonstrations, and other such token and administrative acts. By contrast, the youth movement demands of its disciples total commitment. Merely attending weekly activities does not suffice: one must live daily by the behavioral code promoted by the movement. Inculcated by subtle, indirect means, through collective social experience, the movement's ethos dictates the permitted and forbidden, conventional and unconventional, beautiful and ugly. Such value judgment aims at molding the disciple's personality. In his abovementioned essay, Karl Mannheim observed that the most significant formative concepts and attitudes in a group's life are not transmitted consciously; rather, they seep through, unbeknownst to either giver or receiver. If acquired during adolescence, such attitudes become the adult's natural world-view. Mannheim's analysis corresponds surprisingly well to the role of ethos in the Palestine youth movements, and to its modes of inculcation.

The youth movements' ethos was inherently collectivistic, the individual only figuring as one of a group aspiring to act together. Society, or the team, reigns supreme, the individual must adjust. Group public opinion served to impose the collective's authority on the individual. A cruel, all-pervading measure, public judgment dominated every walk of private life: modes of speech and dress, male-female relationships, ties between group members, manners—realms where no political party would ever dare venture. By submitting to public opinion, the individual expressed total commitment to the group. Group expectations molded his behavior, and, ultimately, a significant part of his character. Members were expected to stand by each other, be honest, forthright, guileless, and modest. The individual was constantly on trial: would he forgo his convenience, his personal gain, and his desires for what the collective defines as "must be done," or "there's no choice"? The public takes a dim view of individualists who defy its will, and frowns upon nonconformists. According to built-in group expectations, the individual must view submission to public authority as a normative procedure, and readily accept it.

Part of the message projected by the youth movements' ethos touched directly upon political life: one must never publicly exhibit aspirations to prominence, or, God forbid, careerism. For this reason, no member volunteers for a role—or, more precisely, a "calling"—but must, rather, be dragged to it kicking and screaming. Rehearsed countless times in the life of the movement, this ritual also became the accepted cultural code in the *kibbutz* movement. According to its underlying message, the collective may compel the individual to perform those tasks it deems significant, whereas the individual must prefer the modesty of the rank-and-file to any distinction. By ultimately accepting, albeit reluctantly, the appointed post, he confirms both the norm of submission to public will, and the norm condemning personal desire for a prominent role.

The central norm of the youth movement ethos demanded living according to one's principles. This was the ethos of *hagshamah*. One cannot preach a life of labor, and live the bourgeois life in the home of one's parents; one cannot preach equality, and keep a private budget. In the final analysis, the worth of group members was determined by their standing on the scale of *hagshamah*.

One group which seemed particularly remote from the ethos of *hags-hamah* were the politicians. Not that other social elements proved more exemplary in this respect; but among the politicians—especially of the lower ranks—the double-standard stood out flagrantly: on the one hand, they sang the praises of living according to one's credo; on the other, their lifestyle did not deviate in any way from that of the rest of the Yishuv. The great majority were not laborers, and to the youngsters' mind, they bore the name of Labor in vain. Perceived as hypocrites, thus especially repulsive to those brought up on the movement's ethos, politicians figured lowest on the scale of commendable lifestyles (by the same measure, *kibbutz* members figured highest). Keeping in mind that the youths' world-view was generated by their elders, it could be said that in the 1940s, a substantial part of those considered "the fathers' generation" did not live up to the image of the desired human type which they themselves had molded.

Moreover, according to the ethos of *hagshamah,* men were judged not by words, but by deeds. In the cramped reality of the youth movement, this matter reflected profoundly on the estimation of each member: public opinion distinguished between true friends in need, and mere smooth talkers. Politicians belonged in the latter group. This human type was in fact fairly common among politicians of the Labor movement of the fathers' generation—verbose men who met with little sympathy from the disciples. The youths reserved their admiration for the antithesis of the politician—men of few words and many actions, who volunteered for a range of national missions, e.g. agricultural and farm work, the Palmach, and the exploits of the illegal immigration. Even for those who did not enlist, these men symbolized the highest-ranking office-holders. Such is the power of norm, that it is accepted even by those who do not abide by it.

A characteristic trend stemmed from this norm: flight from ornate rhetoric. " 'How did I do?'—this is how one of our comrades always mocks himself here after making a highflown speech—which happens quite often." This was the parenthetical remark that Danny Mass—one of the more sensitive and gifted young men, who perished in the War of Independence—saw fit to add to his definition of pioneering: "Relinquishing everything, yourself, your life as an individual, for a sacred cause." Although the letter was a private one, he made a point of mocking his own rhetoric.[27]

The ethos of *hagshamah* functioned as a damper on political ambitions. As social norm dictated, those who chose a route of political advancement met with disparagement and total lack of support. Their choice implied abandonment of the *hagshamah* system, in other words, abandonment of the movement, the *hakhsharah,* the *kibbutz.* At best, this deed was taken as a sign of weakness, of inability to cope with hardships; at worst, it was treated as betrayal. To this day, some senior office-holders in Israel are held in utter contempt by their erstwhile comrades, due to their former standing as "talkers" rather than "doers." To be sure, a handful of individuals broke the normative code of behavior. But were these the group's natural leaders? Or were there perhaps others, of greater gifts and authority, who, guided by the ethos they had imbibed, suppressed these faculties? Both Yigal Allon and Moshe Dayan—the most conspicuous in their political drives among the native generation's leadership—were not, in fact, disciples of youth movements. Was that mere coincidence?

THE COURSE OF ADOLESCENT REBELLION

Another explanation for the second generation's political failings lies, to my mind, in the specific nature of its "adolescent rebellion." I would like to argue, that a Leftist leaning—first to the Le-Ahdut Haavodah party, later, to the Mapam party, was the local version of rebellion against the previous generation, and that in the final analysis, it was a factor which distanced a good deal of the youth from leadership positions.

In the context of Palestine, revolt against the older generation's authority was a complex issue. Zionist socialist ideology was formulated by the fathers, and naturally accepted by the sons as part of their worldview. In the Eretz Israel reality, the Zionist socialist revolution was still underway, seeming daily to be vindicated. Rebellion against its basic tenets was therefore out of the question.

Given the experience of countries that have undergone revolution, this should come as no surprise. The revolutionary generation usually stamps so powerful a seal on its sons that, unable to shrug off their fathers' spiritual authority, they take its hegemony for granted. It is hard to cite a successful revolution, whose sons have again generated one of their own. As a rule, the first generation following a revolution remains obedient and lusterless, loyal to its precepts. With the magic of its success still pervasive, revolt against its ideology or progenitors is unthinkable. In this respect, the processes in Israel must not be compared with change of government in the West, but rather, with that in recently established states, or ones which have undergone revolution. Under such circumstances, it is quite common for the next generation to form no new ideological or political concepts.

Castration of sons by their fathers was a natural outcome of the two generations' relationship in a revolutionary era: having formed no alternative ideology, the sons could not effectively rebel against their elders. Nevertheless, "adolescent rebellion" did occur. This is not the place for a sociological analysis of the concept and its origins. For the purposes of my argument it suffices to define adolescent rebellion as youthful rejection of present society's values, coupled with an aspiration to create "a different society." This uniquely modern social phenomenon facilitates the youngsters' liberation from their fathers' authority. Yet how can "adolescent rebellion" concur with adoption of society's dominant ideology? Palestine youth would have probably applied to this dilemma the model used by religious reformers throughout the ages to attack the Church: the doctrine is as true as ever; it is only its interpreters and ministers who have strayed from the path. Socialist Zionism is right, its ideals ostensibly approved by one and all. But Mapai, the Yishuv's leading socialist party, in charge of implementing this credo, is leading the believers off the straight and narrow, away from the cause. The youths called for a fuller, more complete, and more radical realization of socialist Zionism's basic tenets.

This outlook's relevance lay not in its veracity, but in its acceptance by the youths. Mapai was envisaged as an apparatus party, dishonest and corrupt, devoid of social sensitivity, promoting self-serving yes-men and careerists. Worse yet, it was considered out of touch with the *zeitgeist*, i.e., with the national needs which called for political, even military activism. It was perceived as moderate, in other words, reluctant to confront British imperialism, and willing to give in where Jewish interests were concerned. Local youth were brought up to believe that the White Paper regime (established by the British in 1939, cutting off Jewish immigration to Palestine during and after World War II) could be overcome only by armed struggle. They blamed Mapai and its leadership for the gap between the complacency and inertia of Palestinian Jewry during the war, and their own urgent feeling that something had to be done.[28]

Far from being random, this image of Mapai was nurtured by the propaganda system of Siah Bet (Faction B)—a populist faction of Mapai in Tel Aviv, which emerged in 1937 following an economic crisis. Mapai's heads were persistently reviled as mercenary and oblivious to workers' needs. The pact formed in 1938 between the urban Siah Bet and

Hakibbutz Hameuhad was cemented during the 1940s. Eventually the process culminated in the 1944 split, whereby seceders from Mapai formed a radical Leftist party, Le-Ahdut Haavodah. In youthful public opinion, Hakibbutz Hameuhad was preferred over Mapai, thanks to its activist image, and its nurturing of both the youth movements and the Palmach. Moreover, Hakibbutz Hameuhad declared itself the true heir of the pure ideology of Ahdut Haavodah—Mapai's 1920s predecessor. Mapai, it argued, had since deviated from socialist purism. Prone by nature to black-and-white reasoning, the young people found these radical, indeed, simplistic positions highly attractive. To their minds, these attitudes bespoke all the qualities they admired—honesty, spontaneity, and intractability. Orientation to the Left rose against this background. As previously remarked, the war years witnessed a great wave of sympathy for the Soviet Union. Many were swept along, including some who were not affiliated with the Labor movement. In the Zionist Left, hope resurged for dialogue with that great power, who had so far rebuffed with hostility the love oblations of Palestine's pioneers.[29] Before long, the rival political camps took stands "for" and "against" Soviet Russia: those belonging to the Mapai mainstream doubted its moral supremacy and right to lead "the forces of the morrow." For members of the opposition, the Soviet Union, all goodness and light, embodied everything they held dear. Hence, the Soviet Union became a political code for telling friends from foes. The myth of revolution only enhanced these trends: he who criticizes the Soviet Union obviously seeks to perpetuate the present state of affairs; he who praises it implicitly states his readiness to bring about a revolution in Palestine as well.

In the atmosphere of World War II, the Soviet Union held tremendous appeal for local youth. Stalingrad became a myth; excerpts of Russian war literature were translated and published in Palmach pamphlets prior to the publication of the complete books; war movies projected direct, clear-cut messages. The combined effect was magical.[30] Communist propaganda, and the arguments of Yizhak Tabenkin (the indisputable leader of Hakibbutz Hameuhad), Beni Marshak (the Palmach's beloved "political commissar"), and their friends, projected a Soviet society governed by the same ethos which ruled the local youth movements: simplicity of manner, informality, spontaneity, honest relationships among men, camaraderie, loyalty, and, above all, self-sacrificing devotion to the group. Local youth embraced all these as part of their psyche, something to which they could relate intuitively. The Soviet Union also symbolized activism, willingness to struggle to the end, the advantage of fighters over talkers ("the democracies" ranked among the latter). The guerilla fighter, the partisan, became a model for the members of the Palmach.

The youths' flocking to the Left greatly alarmed the Mapai leadership. We have no research containing statistical data concerning the actual youthful preference for the two distinctly Leftist parties—first Le-Ahdut Haavodah, and later, Mapam (established in 1948 by members of Le-Ahdut Haavodah and Hashomer Hatzair). However, contemporary sources vividly evince strong contemporary feeling that this indeed was the case. The omnipresence of Hakibbutz Hameuhad in the Palmach, especially among its commanders, only confirmed this notion.[31]

The "adolescent rebellion" aspect of the thronging to the Left is perhaps best illustrated by the fact that quite a few sons of Mapai's leaders joined the ranks of Le-Ahdut Haavodah. Keenly apprehensive lest they lose their children to the rival camp, Mapai's leaders spared no efforts to convince them to return.[32] By contrast, no son of a Left-wing leader ever turned Right. During the split in Hakibbutz Hameuhad in the early 1950s, this phenomenon recurred: descendants of many Mapainik families chose to join the Mapam majority, rarely the other way around.

A close analysis of the young generation's "adolescent rebellion" reveals that to a great extent, its ideological outlines were formed by the fathers. The struggle for the soul of the youth between Yizhak Tabenkin, leader of Hakibbutz Hameuhad, and Berl Katznelson and David Ben-Gurion, was basically a struggle between two camps within the fathers' generation. It was the fathers who posed intellectual and ideological challenges for the sons. Youths seeking to shake off paternal authority could channel their frustration into a militancy of thought and deed bred by the latter. Radical Leftism—formulated by a group within the fathers' generation, and legitimized by them as an integral part of the Zionist socialist outlook—became for the youths a symbol of identification. Thus, paradoxically, the fathers simultaneously offered their sons an ideology of rebellion, and channelled them into political frameworks, which they themselves shaped and controlled.

The sons' ability to challenge prevalent ideology, yet remain within the normative bodies, bespoke an element of conformism, a tendency to smooth over conflicts. For the fathers' generation, it served as a safety-valve, which stopped the Palestine "adolescent rebellion" short of becoming a lever for political upheaval.

True, the younger Palestinian generation displayed more awareness, boldness, and independence than the sons of revolutionaries elsewhere.

Furthermore, its members had a prominent sense of their own identity and uniqueness. But the rebellious vigor was channelled into bodies established and guided by the fathers: the youth movements, the Palmach, and Mapam. Although they nurtured a mentality of "adolescent rebellion," the youth movements cast this "rebellion" into frameworks well within the consensus. It was the fathers who directed the movements' disciples towards the national missions highest on the day's agenda—whether to cultivating the land, establishing communal settlements, joining the armed forces, or doing battle. Their spiritual authority was never questioned. This was true even of the Palmach, that alleged quintessence of Palestinian youth. It was, in fact, founded and conducted by the fathers, with Golomb, Tabenkin, and Yizhak Sadeh playing a dominant role in molding its image. Finally, the younger generation's Leftist tendency—its "adolescent rebellion" against "the establishment"—that too was channelled into Mapam, a political framework established and shaped by the fathers. Thus curbed, the youngsters' defiance never materialized into full-fledged rebellion. Only the semblance of rebellion persisted.

It is no accident that the most radical exponents of the ideology regarding the "uniqueness of the native sons" found support in Le-Ahdut Haavodah, and viewed life on *kibbutz* as the quintessential expression of Palestinian culture.[33]

THE SPLIT IN MAPAI: THE CONFORMITY OF REBELS

The fact that a large segment of the active youth, with leadership potential, identified with the opposition within the Labor movement, proved fateful to their integration in the political system. The first years following the establishment of Israel witnessed a fierce struggle between Mapai and the Left; Ben-Gurion never forgave those who joined forces with his friend and rival, Tabenkin. Many young men and women soon found themselves "seeking tomorrow," as a popular song of those days goes. Keenly smarting with a sense that "The Moor has done his work, the Moor may go," they followed Mapam to the "political desert." The stigma entailed in their identification as the opposition clung for years; some never shook free. Suffice it to recall the stymied political career of that "prince" of native sons, Yigal Allon, who never won the leadership he coveted.

Furthermore, for many, the shift from the political center to the sidelines stunted the maturation process, in the course of which a young man struggles free from his "adolescent rebellion," translating his general discontent with his surroundings into concrete terms, or into activity within political frameworks. In more ways than one, identification with Mapam legitimized perpetuation of behavior in accordance with the ethos of youth: as a party where two *kibbutz* movements were predominant, Mapam projected a message of values ostensibly identical with youth movement idealism. With its strong penchant for disengagement from reality, Mapam often mistook *desiderata* for facts. The "eternal youth" which typified these men well past middle age stemmed from preservation of adolescent norms, as though these were also applicable to the adult world. However, the youths who stayed within the framework of Mapai fared no better. Not without reason, the veterans of the Second Aliyah and Third Aliyah interpreted their efforts, to form a distinct, politically discrete group within the party, as an attempt to force a generational putsch on its leadership.

The fathers' castrating power thus found expression both within the establishment and out of it; the sons found both promotion avenues blocked, albeit for different reasons.

Due to the split in Mapai, and the battle waged by its camps over the souls of the youth, many of the *Sabra* generation did not realize whatever leadership potential they may have had. Ousted and neglected, their hostility toward politics and politicians flared into total de-legitimation of all political activity.

Moreover, the split resulted in a schism within this generation's elites, which in turn bred competition. Instead of "generational" solidarity, a tentative political solidarity emerged, based on "historical" party loyalty. Here lay a further reason for the generation's failures.

FACING HISTORICAL CHANGE: A (POLITICALLY) LOST GENERATION

However, all these explanations seem dwarfed by basic historical events: the founding of Israel and the attendant massive immigration. As cited above, Karl Mannheim pins the emergence of generational cohorts on rapid social change, which necessitates re-adjustment of thought and action modes. He then adds an illuminating observation: *if the change is too rapid, it might bring about the destruction of a budding new generational culture.* Frustrated by the destruction of their personal experience, such generations cling to the culture of their predecessors, or to that of the following generation.[34] Let us try to examine the meaning of this observation with respect to the "Palmach generation."

When speaking of a "generational cohort," one must define its period of emergence. True, already in the days of the Second Aliyah, in the Palestine colonies, certain youthful phenomena were typical to a generational cohort. Later, an awareness of generational uniqueness emerged among the younger circles of the local intelligentsia, which centered round the Herzliyah Gymnasium. However, these circles were both numerically and socially restricted.

In any case, during the 1920s, the number of local youth was still too inconsequential to apply the concept. Moreover, apart from their age, nothing distinguished that youth as a group. The 1930s witnessed massive immigration, and an accelerated growth of the Yishuv. A time lapse was required before the young newcomers were "absorbed," incorporating the symbols of the local youth. The years of World War II granted the youth that moratorium necessary to consolidate behavioral patterns, and a set of norms and symbols. The blockade imposed on Palestine and the halt of immigration afforded the maturation of a specific, local youth culture. The youth movements and the Palmach became the key transmitters of this culture, making it a symbol of localism. In 1946, Uri Avneri and his colleagues in the "Young Palestine" Circle of Journalists began the publication of *Ba-maavak,* a periodical presented as "an anthology on policy, security, and youth." A first example of generation-based political-cultural association, the group declared in its manifesto: "The simple basic truth is that native youth constitutes a new, discrete social body in the Yishuv, with its own opinions, attitudes, and style." Its distinction lies in its "being native to the land, raised in it, imbued with its spirit"; indeed, "the land has become an essential component of its soul."[35] Expressing a good deal of aversion for the "ghetto character" of the fathers' generation, they expect the immigrants to "become *Sabra*s." A new local type, they contend, has emerged, typified by style, appearance, dialect, *Sabra* "chuzpah," and "a Palestinian approach to political and spiritual affairs."[36] One salient example of this attitude was the group's position in the Partition controversy: those to whom Palestine is a homeland, they proclaimed, could never consent to its division. Disdaining the "imported" ideologies of their fathers, they pronounced their own one "of deeds."[37] As for their predecessors, their work done, they must clear the way. Now the sons, distinguished as warriors, merit their own right to stamp their seal on the land.

The "Young Palestine" Circle of Journalists may have been a singular phenomenon in the local political fabric, but it was by no means marginal. It merely gave radical expression to the notions of the Palmach youth. The group's appearance enhances the feeling of anyone who reads the period's literature—Palmach pamphlets, memorial volumes, and other journals for the local youth—that here indeed was a true manifestation of generational distinctions. Further evidence is found in the appearance of a group of young writers and poets, who published their works together in *Yalkut ha-reim* (The Friends' Anthology), claiming to bring the scent of open fields to the decadent cafes of Tel Aviv. "We are not merely youth," announced one of the editors, Polish-born Shlomo Tanai, who immigrated at the age of ten, "We are a different *generation,* a Palestinian generation. This fact shall distinguish us from others even as we grow older, when we are no longer, strictly speaking, youth." [38] This generation's self-awareness found its most radical expression in the Kenaanim (Canaanites). Making its first appearance before the foundation of Israel, this political-cultural trend matured during the new state's first decade. Its members—mostly, but not solely, right-wingers—contended that the Hebrew entity in Eretz Israel was an independent national one, tracing its ancestry to the ancient Hebrew nation, or to the geographical region and political traditions of the Middle East. As such, it has nothing to do with the European Jewish people. Thus, the Canaanites sought to expunge all links between the Jewish people and the emerging territorial Hebrew nation.

Initially, the "generational" phenomenon was manifest in social and cultural manners and style. Eventually, it also entailed a common worldview on central issues, e.g. the attitude towards the diaspora, Left and Right, politics. "Generational" ideology was inherent, unarticulated. Attempts to formulate a distinctive ideology began with Uri Avneri and his friends. As usual, the feeling of the group's distinctiveness preceded the quest for ideological expression. Though fumbling and inconsistent, fruit of this quest nonetheless constituted the native generation's budding independent political awareness. On the eve of Israel's War of Independence, the "native generation" had all the promising hallmarks of a fledgling "generational cohort." And then the tidal wave came crashing down, leaving in its wake a changed reality.

The perishing of the finest French and British youth in the trenches of World War I is often cited as the source of those countries' political ills between the wars. Given that the core of youth in Palestine amounted to mere thousands, the trauma of the War of Independence was no less significant. We shall never know how many of that generation's potential leaders were killed. The trauma also had a paralyzing effect on those who survived. The self-confidence, the sweeping optimism so characteristic of these young men and women—both were badly shaken.

At the same time, the *Sabra* generation found itself facing the challenge of massive immigration. There was little chance the few thousand members of the *Palmach* generation could ingest the hundreds of thousands of young newcomers. True, those arriving in the 1950s fervently wished to assimilate as quickly as possible, and many actually did. But numerous as they were, the immigrants could not but stamp their mark on local culture, lifestyle, set of expectations, and accepted norms. Thus, a new Israeli style was generated, discrete both from the indigenous Palestinian, and from those imported by the immigrants.

Bursting forth in 1948, the state transformed overnight the native sons—the Yishuv's heralds of a new era, into an anachronism. As is always the case with historical processes, considerable time elapses between a revolutionary event, and public awareness of it and of its repercussions. In many ways, the 1950s seemed a natural continuation of the Yishuv era: the youth movement frameworks still functioned; the Palmach was replaced by the Nahal—a military unit combining army service with life and work on *kibbutz*. Like its predecessor, the Nahal won immense popularity in the media, public opinion, and new Israeli folklore. *Kibbutz* border settlements were still considered the crowning glory of Zionist *hagshamah,* and the settlers, the nation's pioneers, revered by young and old. Simultaneously, however, immigrant border settlements also appeared; new settlement regions, such as Lachish and the Negev, began vying for both public support and national resources. New human types, apart from the youth clad in *tembel* hat and shorts, began cropping up on Israel's cultural map. *Sabra*-Palestinian distinction was no longer the symbol of the future. The large, relatively open immigrant society could not but perceive it as the snobbism of the Israeli "Mayflower." Its identity symbols became confined to a narrow stratum, which seemed an ancient relic. When speaking of middle-aged people, the *kumzitz* (campfire cookout) ritual, the social get-togethers, the simple dress (shorts were often cherished into ripe old age), the local accent—all appeared slightly odd. The youth movement ethos, as the collectivistic world of values in general, grew irrelevant in a society no longer based on the individual's devotion and the principle of volunteering. Disappointment with the Soviet Union, and the adoption of Western democratic codes, dealt yet another blow to the world view of many native sons.

The young state maintained a semblance of the old values of a revolutionary frontier society, frugal in its needs, dedicated to the collective, bowing individual interests to the public's. However, it steadily edged into the sphere of Western influence, shedding layer by layer its erstwhile revolutionary traits. Imbued as it was with a national ethos of a society under siege, the Palmach generation found itself out of place in this crystallizing society.

Some must have felt disoriented by the new circumstances: this was not the state they had envisioned. But on the personal level, most adapted somehow—whether by accepting the authority of the fathers' generation, and joining their political system, or by turning to studies, or to personal careers. The formation of a governmental bureaucracy afforded an opening for many members of the Palmach generation. Many deemed the newly formed Israeli army a cross between a personal career and the required fulfillment of a national calling. The modernization and accelerated development of the country's economy also provided countless opportunities for energetic young people. Adopting economic affluence as the measure of success, they blended in with the Israeli-born generation. In fact, in all but the political sphere, their influence was profound—a further embodiment of the outlook favoring deeds over words. Nonetheless, the Palmach generation foundered, weakened by its de-legitimation of political activity, castration by the fathers, and immersion in a mounting demographic tide of mass immigration. Within one decade, it found itself crushed between its predecessors and successors. Thus, almost overnight, members of a generational cohort with its own unique stamp were rendered "has-beens" by the pace and power of social change. The buds which blossomed on the eve of the War of Independence wilted before bearing fruit.

CONCLUSION

The distinction of Israeli society at its initial stage lay in the fact that it was simultaneously an immigration and settlement society, and a revolutionary one. *Prima facie,* both these factors are conducive to social and political change. In effect, they exert opposing influences.

In immigration societies, it is customary for the first generation in the new land to carve out a path to economic survival. Never completing their process of adaptation to the new reality, the fathers remain alien in character and mentality. The eventual undermining of their status stems from their limited socialization and adaptation skills. Thus, were Palestine a classical immigration country, we would most likely have witnessed the gradual replacement of the fathers with their well-integrated sons. Here, however, side-by-side with the settlement process, a political, social, and cultural revolution was taking place. No mere immigrants, borne willy-nilly to these shores, the fathers were iron-willed people, who had brought about a sea-change in Jewish self-image, national priorities, lifestyle, and the pictures of the past, the present, and the future. As mentioned above, nothing is more enduring than successful revolutionaries. Of all twentieth-century revolutions, history seems to have smiled particularly upon the Zionist. The solutions offered by the fathers to the Jewish people—founding an independent Jewish entity in Palestine, a Hebrew culture, becoming productive—these were still valid for the native generation; indeed, they seemed only enhanced by local reality and by the historical developments of the first half of the century. Thus, while foreign experience would suggest an overthrowing of the fathers in favor of their native-born sons, the fact that local youth were sons of revolutionaries worked against this trend, leading, instead, to preservation, conformism, and consolidation. The sons' world-view was shaped by their fathers'. In its socialist and Jewish components, it was an unconscious reiteration of truths imparted by their predecessors, and had none of the immediacy and palpability which inspired the latter to rebel against their own fathers. The sons' education, though on a par with that of their fathers, lacked the dynamic, rebellious element typical of the latter. Informal education in the youth movements also fostered social conformism and aversion to political activism. Moreover, even in their "adolescent rebellion," the sons chose a path whose character and frameworks were predetermined by the fathers' generation. These circumstances were later compounded by the extremely rapid mental and demographic change brought about by the establishment of Israel and massive immigration. As a result, the Palmach generation found itself crushed between two other generations. Thus, its inherent weakness cannot be attributed solely to castration by the fathers. Rather, it derived from unique historical circumstances.

In many spheres, including the military, public service, and cultural life, the impact of the Palmach generation was most conspicuous. Not so in the realm of politics. To a large extent, its failure to realize its political potential reflects the failure of its ethos, which it came to perceive as a calling. In the newborn state of Israel, that ethos no longer seemed relevant.

NOTES

1. Azriel Ukhmani, Shlomo Tannai, and Moshe Shamir, eds., *Dor ba-aretz: antologyah shel sifrut israelit* (Tel Aviv, 1958).
2. Immigrants of the Second Aliyah (immigration wave) arrived in Palestine between 1904 and 1918.

3. Karl Mannheim, "The Problem of Generations," *Essays on the Sociology of Knowledge* (Routledge & Kegan Paul, 1952), pp. 276–322. For complexity of generational analysis see also: Paul Ricouer, *Time and Narrative,* trans. Kathleen McLaughlin and David Pellaver (Chicago and London, 1925), vol. II, p. 199, vol. III, pp. 104–12, 183, 229, 234, 293, 301, 326–27; Alfred Schutz, *The Phenomenology of the Social World,* trans. George Walsh and Frederick Lehnert (Evanston, 1967), pp. 139–214; Maurice Mandelbaum, *The Anatomy of Knowledge* (Baltimore and London, 1977), p. 116.

4. See, for example, *Bi-vritekh,* the Hamahanot Haolim publication summarizing the Senior Group camp in Gevat, Summer 1937 (Tel Aviv, 1938).

5. Suffice it to remember the meager numbers (about 2,000) of "survivors" of the Second Aliyah, who greeted the Third Aliyah of 1919–1923.

6. This topic is discussed extensively in Dr. Alon Kadish's (as yet unpublished) research of the recruited training groups. I am indebted to him for enlightening me on the subject. Youth movement disciples enlisted in the Palmach as entire social units. Their service period was designed to prepare them not only for military activity, but for their future life on *kibbutz.* Palmach units were stationed in *kibbutzim,* and paid their keep in labor.

7. A collection of the seminar participants' autobiographies is housed in the Labor Archives (henceforth: L.A.), 213/4, File 279.

8. It was the policy of Beni Marshak, the Palmach's "political commissar," to hasten the transformation of the immigrant youths into native sons. However, by various testimonies, Marshak treated the new boys with remarkable sensitivity.

9. Yosef Gorny, "Ha-shinuyim ba-mivneh ha-hevrati ve-ha-politi shel 'ha-aliyah ha-sheniyah' ba-shanim 1904–1940," *Ha-zionut aleph* (Tel Aviv, 1970), vol. 1, p. 210.

10. *Ibid.,* p. 214.

11. *Ibid.*

12. Hayyim Judah Roth, "Al limud leshonot," in: H. J. Roth, ed., *Al ha-hinukh ha-tihoni ha-ivri be-Eretz Israel* (Jerusalem, 1939), pp. 172–89.

13. Yosef Azaryahu, *Ha-hinukh ha-ivri be-Eretz Israel* (Ramat-Gan, 1954), pp. 191–99.

14. On the subject of translated literature, see Zohar Shavit, *Ha-hayyim ha-sifrutiyim be-Eretz Israel, 1910–1933* (Tel Aviv, 1982). See also the bibliography of "The Seminar Library" of *Hanoar Haoved* at Naan, L.A. 213/4, File 46. The document is undated, but according to its contents, it is obviously from the 1930s. Also "The Recommended Reading List of the Pre-Independence Youth Movements" comprised by Israel Galili, and put at my disposal. The matter is corroborated by the press and material from Hanoar Haoved and Hamahanot Haolim Archives, found in the Labor Archives and in Hakibbutz Hameuhad Archives (henceforth H.H.A., Yad Tabenkin). Fear of competition between original and translated literature is cited in Shavit, above, and also in Berl Katznelson, "Shutfut ha-goral ha-yehudi ke-yesod ba-hinukh: Be-ikvot sihah al ha-golah," Mount Carmel, 6.6.1944, L.A. 14/4, Katznelson, File 16.

15. Uri Zvi Greenberg, "Mukhrakhim hayyinu lalekhet," in *Eimah gedolah ve-yareah,* (1924–1925), published in *Be-emza ha-olam u-ve-emza ha-zemanim* (Israel, 1979), pp. 30–31.

16. Yosef Hayyim Brenner, "Haarakhat azmenu bi-sheloshet ha-krakhim," *Kol kitvei* (Tel Aviv, 1937), vol. 7, pp. 219–67. Brenner's reputation was enhanced following his murder in the 1921 Jaffa riots.

17. Hayyim Hazaz, "Ha-derashah," *Luah ha-aretz,* 1943.

18. See, for example, Berl Katznelson, "Le-loh hitgalut," *Ketavim* (Tel Aviv, 1945), vol. 3, pp. 245–49; also Anita Shapira, *Berl* (Tel Aviv, 1980), pp. 12–38.

19. See Anita Shapira, "Labour Zionism and the October Revolution," *Journal of Contemporary History,* no. 24 (1989), pp. 277–301.

20. Yizhak Cafzafi, ed., *Shenot Hamahanot Haolim* (Tel Aviv, 1975), pp. 61–75.

21. The 1937 plan to divide western Palestine into Jewish and Arab states.
22. *Bi-vritekh.*
23. Hamahanot Haolim Council, Beit ha-Shitah, April 1945, H.H.A. Division 9, Hamahanot Haolim, Container 1, File 4.
24. See, for example, Zalman Aranne, *Autobiografyah* (Tel Aviv, 1971).
25. According to Hahistadrut Hazionit's Youth Center statistics for the summer of 1939, Hanoar Haoved had 7,000 members, Hashomer Hatzair—2,500, and Hamahanot Haolim—2,000. M. Goldstein and E. Sireni to David Ben-Gurion, Tel Aviv, 10.8.1939, Central Zionist Archives (henceforth: C.Z.A.), S32/250. In Dr. Ben-Zion Benshalom's memo to Ben-Gurion from 20.11.1942, other figures are cited: Hanoar Haoved—7,000–8,000; Hashomer Hatzair—no figures provided, but "handsome recent development" noted; Hamahanot Haolim—600–800. Also cited is his assessment that organized youth constitutes 20 percent of all youth. C.Z.A., S32/1055. As for figures pertaining to the Palmach's recruited training groups, see Uri Brenner, *Hahakhsharot ha-meguyasot be-Palmach 1942–1948* (Yad Tabenkin, 1983).
26. For statistical data, see note 22 above, and also Hayyim Adler, *Tenuot ha-noar bahayyim ha-israeliim* (Jerusalem, 1963), pp. 10–21.
27. Danny Mass to his girlfriend; Tel-Yosef, the eve of Tel-Hai Day, 1944, *Bi-nativ ha-Palmach* (Jerusalem, 1958), part 2, p. 18.
28. See, for example, Berl Katznelson's clash with Hamahanot Haolim youth at the Commune Seminar in Gevat, 10.9.1943–10.10.1943, H.H.A., Division 9, Series 7, Container 1, File 21.
29. See Anita Shapira, "Labour Zionism and the October Revolution," *op. cit.;* "The Dynamics of Zionist Leftist Trends," in *Jewish History,* eds. Ada Rapoport-Albert and Steven Zipperstein (London, 1988), pp. 629–82.
30. Bek's *The Reserves of General Panfilov,* for example, was only published in Hebrew in 1946, but excerpts appeared earlier in the Palmach pamphlets. The anthology *Keizad lohamim ha-russim* also appeared at the time. Vasilevska's *The Rainbow* appeared in 1943. Highly popular wartime reading included Makarenko's *The Road to Life: An Epic on Education* (three editions), and Hemingway's *For Whom the Bell Tolls,* which also strengthened the pro-Soviet spirit. More Soviet literature appeared later, e.g. Fadeyev's *The Young Guard* (1947), Simonov's *Days and Nights* (1945), and many others. Youthful readers adored Katayev's *Lonely White Sail* (1942, 1946). Young intellectuals loved *Shirat Rusyah* (Russian Poetry) (1942), compiled by Lea Goldberg and Abraham Shlonsky. I've deliberately left out the philosophical works and Russian classics. Although these were available, it is unclear whether local youth read the former. As for the latter, they cannot be allocated to Soviet Russia alone; however, they too, e.g. Gorky's works, enhanced the prevailing spirit.
31. On the status of Hakibbutz Hameuhad in the Palmach, see Anita Shapira, *The Army Controversy* (Hebrew) (Tel Aviv, 1985), pp. 18–21.
32. Among the children of the movement's prominent men one finds the son and daughter of Shmuel Yavne'eli; Menahem Poznanski, Uri Brenner, Hayyim Guri, Nathan Shaham, and others; in my interview with Golda Meir, she recounted her fear lest her daughter Sarah cross sides. Berl Katznelson also lived haunted by the sense he had been robbed of his youth.
33. See *Bamaavak,* periodicals published by "The Young Palestine Circle of Journalists" in 1946–1947, L.A. 277/4.
34. Karl Mannheim, *op. cit.,* p. 310.
35. "Reshut ha-dibur la-dor ha-eretz-israeli!" *Ba-maavak,* September 1946, L.A. 227/4.
36. "Mihem ha-zabarim halalu," *ibid.*
37. See note 36.
38. Eitan Ram, "Yalkut ha-reim," *ibid.*

Selected Bibliography

A. The National Movement and Its Ideological Origins

Almog, Shmuel. *Zionism and History: The Rise of a New Jewish Consciousness.* New York: St. Martin's Press, 1987.

Halpern, Ben. *The Idea of the Jewish State.* Second ed. Cambridge: Harvard University Press, 1969.

Hertzberg, Arthur, ed. *The Zionist Idea: A Historical Analysis and Reader.* Reprint. New York: Atheneum, 1984.

Katz, Jacob. *Tradition and Crisis: Jewish Society at the End of the Middle Ages.* Translated by B. D. Cooperman. New York: New York University Press, 1993.

———. *Jewish Emancipation and Self-Emancipation.* Philadelphia: Jewish Publication Society, 1986.

Kaufmann, Yehezkel. *Golah ve-nekhar.* 2 Vols. Tel Aviv: Dvir, 1930, 1932.

Luz, Ehud. *Parallels Meet: Religion and Nationalism in the Early Zionist Movement, 1882–1904.* Philadelphia: Jewish Publication Society, 1988.

Mosse, George L. *Confronting the Nation: Jewish and Western Nationalism.* Hanover, N.H.: University Press of New England, 1993.

Vital, David. *The Origins of Zionism,* Vol. 1. Oxford: Clarendon Press, 1975.

———. *Zionism: The Formative Years,* Vol. 2. Oxford: Clarendon Press, 1982.

———. *Zionism: The Crucial Phase,* Vol. 3. Oxford: Clarendon Press, 1987.

B. Diaspora and Zion

Cohen, Stuart A. *English Zionists and British Jews: The Communal Politics of Anglo-Jewry, 1895–1920.* Princeton: Princeton University Press, 1982.

Frankel, Jonathan. *Prophecy and Politics: Socialism, Nationalism, and the Russian Jews, 1862–1917.* Cambridge: Cambridge University Press, 1981.

Gal, Allon. *Brandeis of Boston.* Cambridge: Harvard University Press, 1980.

Halpern, Ben. *A Clash of Heroes: Brandeis, Weizmann, and American Zionism.* New York: Oxford University Press, 1987.

Lavsky, Hagit. *Beterem puranut: darkam veyihudam shel zionei Germanyah 1918–1932.* Jerusalem: Hozaat Sfarim al shem Y. L. Magnes and Hasifriyah Hazionit, 1990.

Mendelsohn, Ezra. *Zionism in Poland: The Formative Years, 1915–1926.* New Haven: Yale University Press, 1990.

Reinharz, Jehuda. *Fatherland or Promised Land: The Dilemma of the German Jew, 1893–1914.* Ann Arbor: University of Michigan Press, 1975.

Shimoni, Gideon. *Jews and Zionism: The South Africa Experience, 1910–1967.* Cape-Town: Oxford University Press, 1980.

C. Zionist Trends—Ideology and Reality

Aaronsohn, Ran. *Habaron vehamoshavot.* Jerusalem: Yad Izhak Ben-Zvi, 1990.

Eisenstadt, S. N. *The Transformation of Israeli Society.* London: George Weidenfeld and Nicolson, 1985.

Gorny, Yosef. *Ahdut Haavodah, 1919–1930: hayesodot haraayoniim vehashitah hamedi-nit.* Tel Aviv: Hakibbutz Hameuchad, 1973.

Heller, Joseph. *Lehi, 1940–1949.* Jerusalem: Merkaz Zalman Shazar, 1989.

Horowitz, Dan, and Moshe Lissak. *Origins of the Israeli Polity: Palestine Under the Mandate.* Chicago: University of Chicago Press, 1978.

Kolatt, Israel. *Avot umeyasdim.* Tel Aviv: Hakibbutz Hameuchad, 1975.

———, ed. *Toldot hayishuv hayehudi be-Eretz Israel meaz haaliyah harishonah.* Jerusa-lem: Mosad Bialik, 1989.

Laskov, Shulamit. *Habiluim.* Jerusalem: Hasifriyah Hazionit, 1979.

Metzer, Jacob. *Hon leumi lebayit leumi.* Jerusalem: Yad Izhak Ben-Zvi, 1979.

Near, Henry. *The Kibbutz Movement: Origins and Growth, 1909–1939.* Oxford: Oxford University Press, 1992.

Penslar, Derek J. *Zionism and Technocracy: The Engineering of Jewish Settlement in Palestine, 1870–1918.* Bloomington: Indiana University Press, 1991.

Ravitzky, Aviezer. *Hakez hameguleh umedinat hayehudim.* Tel Aviv: Am Oved, 1993.

Salmon, Yosef. *Dat vezionut: imutim rishonim.* Jerusalem: Hasifriyah Hazionit, 1990.

Shapira, Anita. *Hamaavak hanikhzav: avodah ivrit, 1929–1939.* Tel Aviv: Hakibbutz Hameuchad, 1977.

———. *Hahalikhah al kav haofek.* Tel Aviv: Am Oved, 1988.

Shavit, Yaacov. *Jabotinsky and the Revisionist Movement, 1929–1948.* London: Frank Cass, 1988.

Tzahor, Ze'ev. *Shorshei hapolitikah haisraelit.* Tel Aviv: Hakibbutz Hameuchad, 1987.

D. The Fateful Triangle: Jews, Arabs and the British

Gorny, Joseph. *Zionism and the Arabs, 1882–1948: A Study of Ideology.* Oxford: Clarendon Press, 1987.

Mandel, Neville J. *The Arabs and Zionism Before World War I.* Berkeley: University of California Press, 1976.

Morris, Benny. *The Birth of the Palestinian Refugee Problem, 1947–1949.* Cambridge: Cambridge University Press, 1987.

Porath, Yehoshua. *The Emergence of the Palestinian-Arab National Movement, 1918–1929.* London: Frank Cass, 1974.

———. *The Palestinian Arab National Movement, 1929–1939.* London: Frank Cass, 1977.

Shapira, Anita. *Land and Power: The Zionist Resort to Force, 1881–1948.* New York: Oxford University Press, 1992.

Stein, Kenneth W. *The Land Question in Palestine, 1917–1939.* Chapel Hill: University of North Carolina Press, 1984.

Teveth, Shabtai. *Ben-Gurion and the Palestinian Arabs: From Peace to War.* Oxford: Oxford University Press, 1985.

Wasserstein, Bernard. *The British in Palestine: The Mandatory Government and the Arab-Jewish Conflict, 1917–1929.* London: Royal Historical Society, 1978.

Zayit, David. *Zionut bedarkei shalom: darko hapolitit shel Hashomer Hatzair, 1927–1947.* Tel Aviv: Sifriat Poalim, 1985.

Zweig, Ronald W. *Britain and Palestine During the Second World War.* Suffolk: The Boydell Press for the Royal Historical Society, 1985.

E. Cultural Questions

Abramson, Glenda, and Tudor Parfitt, eds. *The Great Transition: The Recovery of the Lost Centers of Modern Hebrew Literature.* Totowa, N.J.: Bowman and Allanheld Publishers, 1985.

Halkin, Simon. *Modern Hebrew Literature.* New York: Schocken Books, 1970.

Miron, Dan. *Bodedim bemoadam.* Tel Aviv: Am Oved, 1987.

———. *Mul haah hashotek.* Tel Aviv: Keter, 1992.

Schweid, Eli. *Shalosh ashmorot basafrut haivrit.* Tel Aviv: Am Oved, 1967.

Shaked, Gershon. *Hasiporet haivrit.* 4 Vols. Tel Aviv: Hakibbutz Hameuchad and Keter, 1977–1993.

F. Biography

Pawel, Ernst. *The Labyrinth of Exile: A Life of Theodor Herzl.* New York: Farrar, Straus & Giroux, 1989.

Reinharz, Jehuda. *Chaim Weizmann: The Making of a Zionist Leader.* Vol. 1. New York: Oxford University Press, 1985.

———. *Chaim Weizmann: The Making of a Statesman.* Vol. 2. New York: Oxford University Press, 1993.

Shapira, Anita. *Berl—The Biography of a Socialist Zionist.* Cambridge: Cambridge University Press, 1984.

Teveth, Shabtai. *Ben-Gurion: The Burning Ground, 1886–1948.* Boston: Houghton Mifflin Company, 1987.

Zipperstein, Steven J. *Elusive Prophet: Ahad Ha'am and the Origins of Zionism.* Berkeley: University of California Press, 1993.

Index

Rülf, Issak, *Aruchas Bas-Ammi,* 271
Ruppin, Arthur, 498, 534–35, 622, 624,
    634, 650, 655, 667
  Arab-Jewish relations and, 660, 664
  Revisionism and, 660
Russell, Bertrand, 119, 517–18
Russia. *See also* Hibbat Zion; Soviet Union
  1870s hostility towards Jews in, 75
  1881 pogroms in Ukraine and, 78–81
  government of, and Herzl, 220–29
  Hehalutz in, 242
  kehileh elections and (1917), 176–77
  May Laws of 1882 and, 270
  Pale of Settlement and, 137–38, 147,
    376
  Russians of the Mosaic faith, 79
  Second Aliyah immigration from, 374–
    76
Russian Zionism. *See also* Hibbat Zion
  attitude of Czarist authorities and, 218–
    20
  Balfour Declaration and, 591
  Herzl and, 191–92, 210–37
  Jewish Colonial Trust and, 213–14
  leadership in, 191–209
  negotiations with Russian authorities
    and, 220–29
  Pinsker and, 192
  politics of Second Aliyah and, 423
  Russian Zionist conference, 102, 219
Russischer jüdischer wissenschaftlicher
    Verein, 272–73
Rutenberg, Pinhas, 636

Sabra, 26, 738, 743nn.11, 12, 790, 815.
    See also Native generation
Sacher, Harry, 597–98, 706
Safir, Iluii, 209 n.45
Salmon, Yosef, 94–116
Salomon, Joel Moshe, 768
Samuel, Herbert, 341, 483, 491, 506 n.2,
    601, 606, 638, 696
Samuel, Sir Stuart, 596
San Remo conference, 337
Sandler, A., 305
Sapir, Asher, 630
Sasson, Eliahu, 704
Schach, Fabius, 751–52
Schapira, Hermann, 271, 274
Schatz, Zvi, 774, 776, 778, 779
Schechter, Solomon, 308, 309, 323

Schiff, Jacob H., 310, 330, 333, 334
Schneerson, Rabbi Shalom Dov Ber, 110
Schocken, Salman, 269
Schofman, Gershom, 774
Scholem, Gershom, 2, 3, 13, 296 n.59
Schwartz, Joseph, 695
Schweid, Eliezer, 133–60
Scott, C. P., 588, 594, 610
Scouting societies, 279, 456–57. *See also*
    Wanderbund Blau-Weiss
Second Aliyah. *See also* Second Aliyah pop-
    ulation survey
  Hebrew literature from, 774–78
  Histadrut and, 475–76, 487, 504, 520
  impact on Yishuv, 418
  Jewish population in Palestine and, 766
  leadership during, 480, 520
  literary culture and, 764–65, 770, 782
  national myths in, 422–53
  number of immigrants in, 372
  regional character of, 374–77
  Russian nature of, 509–10, 536, 537–38
  sense of ownership and, 57–58
  split between labor parties in, 475
Second Aliyah population survey
  changes in political alignment, 397–418
  distribution of immigrants by age, 378–
    79
  distribution of immigrants by educa-
    tional background, 381–84
  distribution of immigrants by family sta-
    tus, 379–80
  distribution of immigrants by gender,
    378
  distribution of immigrants by occupa-
    tion in 1930s and 1940s, 392–95
  distribution of immigrants by political
    affiliation in country of origin, 395–
    97
  distribution of immigrants by social
    stratification after *aliyah,* 389–92
  distribution of immigrants by social
    stratification before *aliyah,* 385–89
  distribution of immigrants by type of ini-
    tial reception, 380–81
  distribution of immigrants in Palestine,
    by country of origin, 375
  distribution of immigrants in Palestine,
    by place of residence in Europe, 377
  distribution of immigrants in Palestine,
    by region in Russia, 375–77

About the Editors

Jehuda Reinharz is Richard Koret Professor of Modern Jewish History at Brandeis University. He has coedited and authored numerous volumes including *Fatherland or Promised Land: The Dilemma of the German Jew, 1893–1914* (1975), *Chaim Weizmann: The Making of a Zionist Leader* (1985), and *Chaim Weizmann: The Making of a Statesman* (1993). He currently serves as President of Brandeis University.

Anita Shapira is Professor of Jewish History at Tel Aviv University. She is the coeditor and author of several volumes including *Berl: The Biography of a Socialist Zionist* (1984) and *Land and Power: The Zionist Resort to Force, 1881–1948* (1992). She currently serves as Dean of the Faculty of Humanities at Tel Aviv University.

TECHNIQUES OF CHEMISTRY

ARNOLD WEISSBERGER, *Editor*

VOLUME I

PHYSICAL METHODS OF CHEMISTRY

PART IIA
Electrochemical Methods

TECHNIQUES OF CHEMISTRY

ARNOLD WEISSBERGER, *Editor*

VOLUME I
> PHYSICAL METHODS OF CHEMISTRY, in Five Parts
> Incorporating Fourth Completely Revised and Augmented Edition
> of Physical Methods of Organic Chemistry
> *Edited by Arnold Weissberger and Bryant W. Rossiter*

VOLUME II
> ORGANIC SOLVENTS, Third Edition
> *John A. Riddick and William S. Bunger*

TECHNIQUES OF CHEMISTRY

VOLUME I

PHYSICAL METHODS OF CHEMISTRY

INCORPORATING FOURTH COMPLETELY REVISED AND AUGMENTED
EDITION OF TECHNIQUE OF ORGANIC CHEMISTRY,
VOLUME I, PHYSICAL METHODS OF ORGANIC CHEMISTRY

Edited by
ARNOLD WEISSBERGER
AND
BRYANT W. ROSSITER

Research Laboratories
Eastman Kodak Company
Rochester, New York

PART IIA
Electrochemical Methods

WILEY-INTERSCIENCE

A DIVISION OF JOHN WILEY & SONS, INC.

New York · London · Sydney · Toronto

Library of Congress Catalogue Card Number: 77-114920

ISBN 0 471 92727 9

Printed in the United States of America

10 9 8 7 6 5 4 3 2 1

PLAN FOR
PHYSICAL METHODS OF CHEMISTRY

AUTHORS OF PART II

RALPH N. ADAMS,
Department of Chemistry, University of Kansas, Lawrence, Kansas

BERNARD D. BLAUSTEIN,
Pittsburgh Coal Research Center, Bureau of Mines, U.S. Department of the Interior, Pittsburgh, Pennsylvania

ERIC R. BROWN,
Research Laboratories, Eastman Kodak Company, Rochester, New York

RICHARD P. BUCK,
University of North Carolina, Chapel Hill, North Carolina

JACK CHANG,
Research Laboratories, Eastman Kodak Company, Rochester, New York

JOHN L. EISENMANN,
Ionics, Inc., Watertown, Massachusetts

YUAN C. FU,
Pittsburgh Coal Research Center, Bureau of Mines, U.S. Department of the Interior, Pittsburgh, Pennsylvania

DAVID M. HERCULES,
Department of Chemistry, University of Georgia, Athens, Georgia

SEYMOUR L. KIRSCHNER,
Food and Drug Research Laboratories, Inc., New York, New York

ROBERT F. LARGE,
> Research Laboratories, Eastman Kodak Company, Rochester, New York

FRANK B. LEITZ,
> Ionics, Inc., Watertown, Massachusetts

LOUIS MEITES,
> Department of Chemistry, Clarkson College of Technology, Potsdam, New York

OTTO H. MÜLLER,
> State University of New York, Upstate Medical Center, Syracuse, New York

ROYCE W. MURRAY,
> University of North Carolina, Chapel Hill, North Carolina

RICHARD C. NELSON,
> Department of Physics, The Ohio State University, Columbus, Ohio

STANLEY PIEKARSKI,
> Plastics Department, E. I. du Pont de Nemours & Company, Wilmington, Delaware

GERHARD POPP,
> Research Laboratory, Eastman Kodak Company, Rochester, New York

LEO SHEDLOVSKY,
> Consulting Chemist, New York, New York

THEODORE SHEDLOVSKY,
> The Rockefeller University, New York, New York

MICHAEL SPIRO,
> Imperial College of Science and Technology, London, England

STANLEY WAWZONEK,
> University of Iowa, Iowa City, Iowa

NEW BOOKS AND NEW EDITIONS OF BOOKS OF THE TECHNIQUE OF ORGANIC CHEMISTRY WILL NOW APPEAR IN TECHNIQUES OF CHEMISTRY. A LIST OF PRESENTLY PUBLISHED VOLUMES IS GIVEN BELOW.

TECHNIQUE OF ORGANIC CHEMISTRY

ARNOLD WEISSBERGER, *Editor*

INTRODUCTION TO THE SERIES

Techniques of Chemistry is the successor to the Technique of Organic Chemistry series and its companion—Technique of Inorganic Chemistry. Because many of the methods are employed in all branches of chemical science, the division into techniques for organic and inorganic chemistry has become increasingly artificial. Accordingly, the new series reflects the wider application of techniques, and the component volumes for the most part provide complete treatments of the methods covered. Volumes in which limited areas of application are discussed can be easily recognized by their titles.

Like its predecessors, the series is devoted to a comprehensive presentation of the respective techniques. The authors give the theoretical background for an understanding of the various methods and operations and describe the techniques and tools, their modifications, their merits and limitations, and their handling. It is hoped that the series will contribute to a better understanding and a more rational and effective application of the respective techniques.

Authors and editors hope that readers will find the volumes in this series useful and will communicate to them any criticisms and suggestions for improvements.

Research Laboratories   ARNOLD WEISSBERGER
Eastman Kodak Company
Rochester, New York

PREFACE

Physical Methods of Chemistry succeeds, and incorporates the material of, three editions of *Physical Methods of Organic Chemistry* (1945, 1949, and 1959). It has been broadened in scope to include physical methods important in the study of all varieties of chemical compounds. Accordingly, it is published as Volume I of the new Techniques of Chemistry series.

Some of the methods described in *Physical Methods of Chemistry* are relatively simple laboratory procedures, such as weighing and the measurement of temperature, or refractive index, and determination of melting and boiling points. Other techniques require very sophisticated apparatus and specialists to make the measurements and to interpret the data; x-ray diffraction, mass spectrometry, and nuclear magnetic resonance are examples of this class. Authors of chapters describing the first class of methods aim to provide all information that is necessary for the successful handling of the respective techniques. Alternatively, the aim of authors treating the more sophisticated methods is to provide the reader with a clear understanding of the basic theory and apparatus involved, together with an appreciation for the value, potential, and limitations of the respective techniques. Representative applications are included to illustrate these points, and liberal references to monographs and other scientific literature providing greater detail are given for readers who want to apply the techniques. Still other methods that are successfully used to solve chemical problems range between these examples in complexity and sophistication and are treated accordingly. All chapters are written by specialists. In many cases authors have acquired a profound knowledge of the respective methods by their own pioneering work in the use of these techniques.

In the earlier editions of *Physical Methods* an attempt was made to arrange the chapters in a logical sequence. In order to make the organization of the treatise lucid and helpful to the reader, a further step has been taken in the new edition—the treatise has been subdivided into technical families:

Part I   Components of Scientific Instruments, Automatic Recording and Control, Computers in Chemical Research
Part II   Electrochemical Methods
Part III Optical, Spectroscopic, and Radioactivity Methods

Part IV   Determination of Mass, Transport, and Electrical-Magnetic
           Properties
Part V   Determination of Thermodynamic and Surface Properties

This organization into technical families provides more consistent volumes and should make it easier for the reader to obtain from a library or purchase at minimum cost those parts of the treatise in which he is most interested.

The more systematic organization has caused additional labor for the editors and the publisher. We hope that it is worth the effort. We thank the many authors who made it possible by adhering closely to the agreed dates of delivery of their manuscripts and who promptly returned their proofs. To those authors who were meticulous in meeting deadlines we offer our apologies for delays caused by late arrival of other manuscripts, in some cases necessitating rewriting and additions.

The changes in subject matter from the Third Edition are too numerous to list in detail. We thank previous authors for their continuing cooperation and welcome the new authors to the series. New authors of Part II are Ralph N. Adams, Bernard D. Blaustein, Eric R. Brown, Richard P. Buck, Jack Chang, John L. Eisenmann, Yuan C. Fu, David M. Hercules, Seymour L. Kirschner, Robert F. Large, Frank B. Leitz, Royce W. Murray, Richard C. Nelson, Stanley Piekarski, and Gerhard Popp.

We are also grateful to the many colleagues who advised us in the selection of authors and helped in the evaluation of manuscripts. They are for Part II: Dr. Roger C. Baetzold, Dr. Charles J. Battaglia, Dr. Eric R. Brown, Dr. Jack Chang, Dr. Donald L. Fields, Dr. Robert L. Griffith, Dr. Arthur H. Herz, Mrs. Ardelle Kocher, Dr. Robert F. Large, Dr. Louis Meites, Dr. Louis D. Moore, Jr., Dr. Charles W. Reilley, Mrs. Donna S. Roets, Dr. Willard R. Ruby, Mr. Calvin D. Salzberg, Miss Dianne C. Smith, Dr. Donald E. Smith, Dr. Benjamin B. Snavely, Dr. R. Eliot Stauffer, and Dr. John R. Wilt.

The senior editor expresses his gratitude to Bryant W. Rossiter for joining him in the work and taking on the very heavy burden with exceptional devotion and ability.

ARNOLD WEISSBERGER
BRYANT W. ROSSITER

April 1970
Research Laboratories
Eastman Kodak Company
Rochester, New York

CONTENTS

ELECTROCHEMICAL METHODS

Chapter **I**

POTENTIOMETRY: OXIDATION-REDUCTION POTENTIALS

Stanley Wawzonek

I THEORETICAL INTRODUCTION

Galvanic Cells

An oxidation-reduction reaction is a reaction involving a transfer of electrons from one chemical species (atom, molecule, or ion) to another. In principle, any such reaction can form the basis of a *galvanic cell*. The only requirement is that the site of oxidation (loss of electrons) be physically separated from the site of reduction (gain of electrons) so that the reaction cannot be completed without the passage of an electric current from one site to the other except through the external circuit. The sites of oxidation and reduction are known as *electrodes*. The electrode at which oxidation occurs is called the *anode*. The site of reduction is called the *cathode*. In *potentiometry* no actual reaction is carried out, that is, no appreciable current is passed. Instead, one measures the tendency for the reaction to occur by measuring the difference in electrical potential between the anode and cathode.

The construction of a galvanic cell is conventionally represented by a line formula, beginning with the anode. If it subsequently turns out that the cell actually operates in the opposite direction, then this can be indicated without rewriting the cell formula by a negative sign for the potential, as discussed below. Thus, for example,

$$\text{Zn}; \text{ZnCl}_2(C_1); \text{AgCl}; \text{Ag} \tag{1.I}$$

represents a cell with a zinc anode, a zinc chloride solution at concentration C_1, and a cathode consisting of silver chloride plated on silver. Each semicolon represents a phase boundary. The electrode reactions of this cell, writing the anode reaction first, are

$$\text{Zn} \rightarrow \text{Zn}^{2+} + 2e^-$$
$$2e^- + 2\text{AgCl} \rightarrow 2\text{Ag} + 2\text{Cl}^-$$

and the overall reaction, obtained on adding these, is

$$\text{Zn} + 2\text{AgCl} \rightarrow 2\text{Ag} + \text{Zn}^{2+} + 2\text{Cl}^-$$

It should be noted that the anode and cathode reactions must be written so as to involve the same number of electrons.

A second example is

$$\text{Zn}; \text{ZnSO}_4(C_1); \text{CuSO}_4(C_2); \text{Cu} \tag{1.II}$$

This cell consists of a zinc anode, a ZnSO_4 solution at concentration C_1, a CuSO_4 solution at concentration C_2, and a copper cathode. The ZnSO_4 and CuSO_4 solutions are in contact but are prevented from mixing with one another. This may be achieved, for example, by a porous ceramic plug.

The electrode reactions of cell (1.II) are

$$Zn \rightarrow Zn^{2+} + 2e^-$$

$$2e^- + Cu^{2+} \rightarrow Cu$$

and the overall reaction is

$$Zn + Cu^{2+} \rightarrow Zn^{2+} + Cu$$

An important difference between cells (1.I) and (1.II) is that whereas cell (1.I) contains phase boundaries only at the two electrodes, cell (1.II) contains an additional boundary between the $ZnSO_4$ and $CuSO_4$ solutions. This boundary is known as a *liquid junction*, and it gives rise to a potential difference, known as a *liquid junction potential*. This potential arises from the fact that the rate of diffusion of Zn^{2+} from left to right across the boundary differs from the rate of diffusion of Cu^{2+} from right to left, so that a potential gradient is established. Unless $C_1 = C_2$, an additional contribution to this potential will arise from a difference between the rate of diffusion of sulfate across the boundary and the net rate of cationic diffusion. In any cell containing a liquid junction, therefore, the overall potential difference across the cell is not purely a measure of the tendency for the occurrence of an oxidation-reduction reaction, but also involves a contribution from the liquid junction potential.

The magnitude of the liquid junction potential may be greatly reduced by the introduction of a *salt bridge*. This is a concentrated solution, or often a saturated solution, of a salt whose cation and anion have close to the same mobility. KCl is the preferred salt, but NH_4NO_3 is often used when the adjacent solutions contain Ag^+ or some other ion that forms a precipitate with chloride ion. The salt bridge introduces two liquid junctions instead of one, that is, if a salt bridge were introduced into cell (1.II), there would be a liquid junction between the bridge and the $ZnSO_4$ solution, and another between the bridge and the $CuSO_4$ solution. The ion concentration in the salt bridge, as we have mentioned, is made very high; the concentrations C_1 and C_2 are usually relatively low. Thus the two liquid junction potentials are largely determined by the relative rates of diffusion of K^+ and Cl^- (or NH_4^+ and NO_3^-) into the adjoining solutions. Since these ions have similar mobilities, the two liquid junction potentials remain relatively small. Moreover, the two potentials have about the same value, but in opposing directions, so that the net liquid junction is kept even smaller. It should be emphasized, however, that it can never be completely eliminated.

The use of a salt bridge is indicated in the line formula for a cell by two vertical lines, for example,

$$Zn; ZnSO_4(C_1) \| CuSO_4(C_2); Cu \qquad (1.III)$$

represents the same cell as cell (1.II) with a salt bridge replacing the direct contact between the $ZnSO_4$ and $CuSO_4$ solutions. It might be noted that junction potentials also arise at all connections outside the cell between dissimilar conductors. These are taken into account by a universal agreement that the connection of the cell to the potentiometer is always by means of a copper wire. The symbol e^- in the electrode reactions thus represents an electron in a copper conductor, and all intervening potentials are automatically included in the cell potential.

Electromotive Force and the Thermodynamics of Cell Reactions

The potential difference across a galvanic cell is in general determined by the relative rates of reaction at the anode and the cathode. These rates in turn are determined by thermodynamic factors, by potential energy barriers at the electrode surface, by rates of diffusion, and so on. They may depend strongly on the current flowing and on electrode design. The results of potential measurement in general can be given no simple interpretation. If, however, the transfer of electrons can be made to occur under electrically *reversible* conditions, then the potential difference depends only on the *thermodynamics* of the cell reaction (including the changes resulting from diffusion at liquid junctions). This is a consequence of the fact that the electrical work done by the reversible transfer of electricity is the *maximum* electrical work, and this, at constant temperature and pressure, is a measure of the loss of free energy occurring in the cell reaction. The potential difference of a galvanic cell, measured under reversible conditions, is called the *electromotive force*, or *emf*, of the cell. It is the only kind of potential measurement that can be simply interpreted.

To obtain the quantitative relation between the emf, E and the free energy change a reaction can be considered which, as written, requires for completion the passage of n faradays of electricity, where $F = 1$ faraday $= 1$ mole of electrons $= 96,493$ C. The maximum electrical work that can be done is then given (in joules) by nFE, where E is measured in volts. As has been pointed out, this term represents the decrease in free energy in the over-all cell reaction, that is,

$$\Delta G = -nFE. \tag{1.1}$$

It should be noted that if ΔG is desired in calories, then nFE, in joules, must be divided by 4.1840, which represents the number of joules per defined calorie.

The sign of the free energy change determines the direction in which a reaction proceeds spontaneously. A negative sign means that it proceeds spontaneously in the direction in which it is written; a positive sign means it proceeds in the opposite direction. Equation (1.1) defines the corresponding criterion for galvanic cells. A positive value of E means that the cell operates in the direction in which it is written, with the anode at the left of the linear formula. A negative value of E means that it operates in the opposite direction. Experimentally, the anode and cathode are identified by their relative potential; that at the anode must be more negative.

The free energy change in a chemical reaction depends on the activities of the participating substances. In general, for an overall reaction,

$$aA + bB \rightarrow lL + mM$$

$$\Delta G = \Delta G^0 + RT \ln \frac{\alpha_L^l \alpha_M^m}{a_A^a a_B^b}, \tag{1.2}$$

where a_i is the activity of the chemical species i and ΔG^0 is the *standard free energy change* of the reaction, that is, the free energy change that would be observed if all reactants and products remained at unit activity throughout the reaction. From (1.1) we can write down at once the corresponding expression for the emf of a cell in which the same chemical reaction occurs:

$$E = E^0 - \frac{RT}{nF} \ln \frac{a_L^l a_M^m}{a_A^a a_B^b} = E^0 - \frac{2.303RT}{nF} \log \frac{a_L^l a_M^m}{a_A^a a_B^b}, \tag{1.3}$$

where E^0 is the standard emf of the cell, defined as the emf that would be observed if all reactants and products were at unit activity. Equation (1.3) is the basic equation of the galvanic cell. It should be noted that it does not include any liquid junction potentials which may be present, and it is therefore exact only when applied to cells without liquid junction. A list of values of the constant 2.303 RT/F for various temperatures is given in Table 1.1.

Using (1.3), we can write down, for instance, the emf of cell (1.I) as

$$E = E^0 - \frac{RT}{2F} \ln \frac{a_{Ag}^2 a_{Zn^{2+}} a_{Cl^-}^2}{a_{Zn} a_{AgCl}^2}.$$

Substances present as pure solids have unit activity (by definition) so that this equation reduces to

$$E = E^0 - \frac{RT}{2F} \ln a_{Zn^{2+}} a_{Cl^-}^2. \tag{1.4}$$

Equation (1.4) is exact because cell (1.I) contains no liquid junction. However, the corresponding equation for cell (1.II) or (1.III),

$$E = E^0 - \frac{RT}{2F} \ln \frac{a_{Zn^{2+}}}{a_{Cu^{2+}}}, \tag{1.5}$$

which is only an approximation because it ignores the contribution of the liquid junction potential to E. It is a better approximation for cell (1.III) containing the salt bridge than for cell (1.II), but is nevertheless not exact.

Table 1.1   Values of 2.303 RT/F in Volts for Various Temperatures

Temperature (°C)	2.303 RT/F	Temperature (°C)	2.303 RT/F
0	0.05420	31	0.06035
5	0.05519	32	0.06055
10	0.05618	33	0.06074
12	0.05658	34	0.06094
14	0.05697	35	0.06114
16	0.05737	40	0.06213
18	0.05777	45	0.06312
19	0.05797	50	0.06412
20	0.05816	55	0.06511
21	0.05836	60	0.06610
22	0.05856	65	0.06709
23	0.05876	70	0.06808
24	0.05896	75	0.06908
25	0.05916	80	0.07007
26	0.05935	85	0.07106
27	0.05955	90	0.07205
28	0.05975	95	0.07304
29	0.05995	100	0.07404
30	0.06015		

Single Electrode Potentials

The free energy change for the overall reaction in a galvanic cell can be split into two parts, one for the reaction occurring at the anode and one for the reaction at the cathode. For instance, ΔG for the reaction of cell (1.I) can be written as ΔG for the reaction $Zn \rightarrow Zn^{2+} + 2e^-$ plus ΔG for the reaction $2e^- + 2AgCl \rightarrow 2Ag + 2Cl^-$, that is, as the sum of the free energy change for oxidation at the anode and that for reduction at the cathode. It is more convenient, however, to write all single electrode reactions in the same direction; in America the convention has been to write them in the direction of oxidation, whereas in Europe they are written in the direction of reduction. In 1953 at the 17th IUPAC Conference in Stockholm the Commission on Electrochemistry and the Commission on Physicochemical Symbols and Terminology reached agreement on a "convention concerning the signs of electromotive forces and electrode potentials." This convention essentially conforms to the European system of writing potentials and is used here.

From (1.1) we can write down single electrode potentials corresponding to the free energy changes at each electrode. The total cell potential is the cathode potential minus the anode potential. By using cell (1.I) as an illustration, the anode potential for the reaction $Zn^{2+} + 2e^- \rightarrow Zn$ (written as a reduction according to the IUPAC convention) is

$$E_{Zn^{2+},Zn} = E^0_{Zn^{2+},Zn} - \frac{RT}{2F} \ln \frac{a_{Zn}}{a_{Zn^{2+}}a^2_{e^-}}. \qquad (1.6a)$$

We mentioned earlier that the electrons of the electrode reaction are to reside in a copper wire. Since there are no previous conventions regarding a standard state for free electrons we may arbitrarily call this the standard state, so that $\alpha^{e^-} = 1$. The activity of Zn is also unity, so that (1.6a) becomes

$$E_{Zn^{2+},Zn} = E^0_{Zn^{2+},Zn} - \frac{RT}{2F} \ln \frac{1}{a_{Zn^{2+}}}. \qquad (1.6b)$$

In the same way the potential for the cathode reaction, $2AgCl + 2e^- \rightarrow 2Ag + 2Cl^-$ also written as a reduction is

$$E_{AgCl,Ag,Cl^-} = E^0_{AgCl,Ag,Cl^-} - \frac{RT}{2F} \ln \frac{a^2_{Ag}a^2_{Cl^-}}{a^2_{AgCl}a^2_{e^-}}. \qquad (1.7a)$$

Again solids and electrons are considered to be in standard states at unit activity so (1.7a) simplifies to

$$E_{AgCl,Ag,Cl^-} = E^0_{AgCl,Ag,Cl^-} - \frac{RT}{2F} \ln a^2_{Cl^-}. \qquad (1.7b)$$

The overall cell potential is given by

$$E_{cell} = E_{cathode} - E_{anode}$$

$$E = E^0_{AgCl,Ag,Cl^-} - \frac{RT}{2F} \ln a^2_{Cl^-} - E^0_{Zn^{2+},Zn} + \frac{RT}{2F} \ln \frac{1}{a_{Zn^{2+}}} \qquad (1.8)$$

or

$$E = E^0_{AgCl,Ag,Cl^-} - E^0_{Zn^{2+},Zn} - \frac{RT}{2F} \ln a^2_{Cl^-}a_{Zn^{2+}}.$$

This result is of course identical to that given by (1.4) with the overall $E^0 = E^0_{AgCl,Ag,Cl^-} - E^0_{Zn^{2+},Zn}$.

Single electrode potentials cannot actually be measured so that standard single electrode potentials such as $E^0_{Zn^{2+},Zn}$ and E^0_{AgCl,Ag,Cl^-} cannot be experimentally determined. Accordingly, we arbitrarily assign a value to one particular single electrode potential, and determine all others relative to it. The universal convention is to set

$$E^0_{H^+,H_2} = 0. \qquad (1.9)$$

All other E^0 values for single electrodes can then be determined by measuring E^0 for an overall cell, one electrode of which is either a hydrogen electrode, or another electrode whose E^0 value was previously determined relative to a hydrogen electrode.

In terms of the IUPAC convention, E^0 is negative for electrodes that are better reducing agents than hydrogen and positive for materials that are better oxidizing agents than hydrogen. Other conventions exist but in light of the international agreement they should be abandoned.

Application of Emf Measurements

It can be seen from any of the preceding equations that emf measurements can give us two kinds of results. If we measure the emf of cells with known activities (or concentrations) of the participating substances, then we can determine E^0 for the cell. As we have seen, this is exactly the same as determining the standard free energy of the cell reaction. However, if E^0 is known, then the activities of participating substances can be measured. Only the first application is discussed in the remainder of this chapter.

Activity Coefficients*

The equations for the emf of galvanic cells are expressed in terms of activities and it is often desirable to be able to relate these quantities to concentrations. This presents no problem for gaseous or solid substances. The activity of a gas involved in an electrode reaction may always be replaced by its partial pressure in atmospheres. This assumption becomes inaccurate only at pressures far in excess of 1 atm. The solid substances that participate in electrode reactions are virtually all present as a pure solid phase, and their activity is therefore automatically unity.

The activity of a pure liquid is also unity, and in ordinary dilute solutions, in which the mole fraction of the solvent is, for example, 0.99 or greater, the solvent is so close to being "pure" that its activity can usually be taken as unity without appreciable error. In the case of aqueous solutions a mole fraction of 0.99 corresponds to a concentration of 0.25 M univalent salt. (The water activity is 0.997 in 0.1 M KCl, 0.993 in 0.2 M KCl [2].)

For dissolved ions the activities differ from the concentration and this difference is most important. The relation between these quantities is usually expressed by the equation,

$$a = \gamma C, \tag{1.10}$$

where γ is called the *activity coefficient*. The concentration C may be expressed in terms of *molality*, that is, moles per kilogram of solvent, or in terms of *molarity*, that is, moles per liter of solution. The values of γ depend on the choice of concentration scale. For dilute aqueous solutions, however

---

* For a general discussion see any text on thermodynamics, for example, I. M. Klotz [1].

the difference between molar and molal concentrations is slight, and the activity coefficients on the two scales are almost equal.

In dilute solutions activity coefficients may be estimated by the Debye-Hückel theory, which gives the following relation for the activity coefficient (molar scale) of an ion of charge Z_i

$$-\log \gamma_i = \frac{AZ_i^2\mu^{1/2}}{1 + Ba_i\mu^{1/2}}. \tag{1.11}$$

In this equation A and B are constants depending on the dielectric constant of the solvent and on the temperature:

$$A = \frac{\epsilon^3}{2.303(DkT)^{3/2}} \cdot \frac{(2\pi N)^{1/2}}{(1000)^{3/2}} = \frac{1.8245 \times 10^6}{(DT)^{3/2}} \tag{1.12}$$

$$B = \frac{(8\pi N\epsilon^2)^{1/2}}{(1000DkT)^{1/2}} = \frac{50.290 \times 10^{-8}}{(DT)^{1/2}}, \tag{1.13}$$

where ϵ is the protonic charge, D the dielectric constant, N Avogadro's number, k Boltzmann's constant, and T the absolute temperature. Values of A and B for aqueous solution are listed in Table 1.2.

Table 1.2 The Constants in the Debye-Hückel Equation for Aqueous Solutions

Temperature (°C)	A Concentration (m)	A Concentration (m)	B Concentration (m)	B Concentration (m)
0	0.4883	0.4883	0.3241	0.3241
5	0.4921	0.4921	0.3249	0.3249
10	0.4960	0.4961	0.3258	0.3258
15	0.5000	0.5002	0.3266	0.3267
20	0.5042	0.5046	0.3273	0.3276
25	0.5085	0.5092	0.3281	0.3286
30	0.5130	0.5141	0.3290	0.3297
35	0.5175	0.5190	0.3297	0.3307
40	0.5221	0.5241	0.3305	0.3318
45	0.5270	0.5296	0.3314	0.3330
50	0.5319	0.5351	0.3321	0.3341
60	0.5425	0.5471	0.3338	0.3366
70	0.5537	0.5599	0.3354	0.3392
80	0.5658	0.5739	0.3372	0.3420
90	0.5788	0.5891	0.3390	0.3450
100	0.5929	0.6056	0.3409	0.3482

The factor μ of (1.11) represents the ionic strength,

$$\mu = \tfrac{1}{2} \sum_i C_i Z_i^2,$$

where the summation extends over all ions present in the solution under consideration. The parameter a_i represents the effective distance between centers of neighboring ions at the distance of closest approach, that is, it represents an effective ionic diameter, including the hydration sphere of the ion. Estimated values usually range between 3 and 8 Å. A tabulation of estimates has been made by Kielland [3] and his values may be used as a basis for calculation; for ions not listed by him, one may use an a_i value for another ion that would be expected to have about the same size.

It should be emphasized that the uncertainty in the choice of a_i introduces an uncertainty into the calculated value of γ_i, which becomes increasingly important as the ionic strength increases. Equation (1.11) is in any event not valid beyond an ionic strength of 0.1 to 0.2 for univalent ions, about 0.05 for divalent ions, and about 0.01 for trivalent ions.

Another important aspect of the Debye-Hückel theory is that it relates the activity of ions to their concentration *as ions*. It cannot be used, for instance, to calculate the activity of an ion from the concentration of an added salt, unless it has been established that the salt in question is 100% dissociated into ions, or unless (as in the case of weak acids and bases) a dissociation constant is introduced as well as an activity coefficient. This restriction is not serious in water solution where most salts are completely dissociated, but it is an important limitation in application to nonaqueous solvents.

Activity coefficients may also be computed from experimental data. Experiments always yield values for the product of activity coefficients of all of the ions of a salt, for example, experiments on KCl yield values for $\gamma_{K^+}\gamma_{Cl^-} = \gamma_\pm^2$. To estimate an individual ion activity coefficient, one makes use of one of a number of possible assumptions. The best is probably that of MacInnes, which states that in KCl solutions $\gamma_{K^+} = \gamma_{Cl^-}$ (K$^+$ and Cl$^-$ have about the same hydrated radii in water solution) and that γ_{K^+} and γ_{Cl^-} in other solutions have the same values they would have in KCl at the same ionic strength. The activity coefficients of other ions can then be computed from the mean ion activity coefficients of their chlorides or potassium salts.

Almost as good an assumption is that of Guggenheim, which states that for all univalent electrolytes $\gamma+ = \gamma-$. For extension to higher valence types and for tabulation of experimental values of mean ion activity coefficients of various salts, the reader is referred to standard texts on electrochemistry [4].

To illustrate the magnitude of activity coefficients and the differences involved in the use of the various assumptions listed above, some calculated values are shown in Fig. 1.1. It can be seen that for univalent ions the various estimates differ from one another by less than 0.02 in log γ up to an ionic

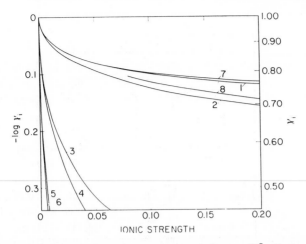

Fig. 1.1 Activity coefficients of ions in aqueous solution at $25°$. Curves 1 to 6 are calculated by equation (11), as follows: 1, univalent ion with $a_i = 6A$; 2, univalent ion with $a_i = 3A$; 3, divalent ion with $a_i = 6A$; 4, divalent ion with $a_i = 3A$; 5, tervalent ion with $a_i = 6A$; 6, tervalent ion with $a_i = 3A$. Curves 7 and 8 are experimental values for Cl^- in HCl, curve 7 being based on the Guggenheim assumption and curve 8 on the MacInnes assumption.

strength of 0.1. For ions of higher valence types, however, the uncertainty is greater.

Activity coefficients of *uncharged solutes* (organic compounds) may be taken as unity at ionic strengths below 0.1, that is, in the region in which the activity coefficients of ionic solutes can be estimated with accuracy.

2 POTENTIOMETERS

It was mentioned earlier that we are interested in the potential of a galvanic cell only when it can be measured under reversible conditions. Therefore, a simple voltmeter cannot be used,* for it draws a small current from the cell, that is, it measures the potential when the cell reaction is proceeding spontaneously at a small rate. The device designed for reversible measurements is known as a potentiometer, and is schematically illustrated by Fig. 1.2. The potential of the cell is opposed by a known variable potential. If this potential is greater than that of the cell to be measured, it will cause current to flow through a galvanometer in one direction; if it is smaller the current will flow in the opposite direction. At a single intermediate point no current flows at all, and at this point the variable potential is equal to the cell potential. Provided that the same balance point is approached from either direction,

* Commercial high input impedance voltmeters based on operational amplifiers draw negligible current from the cell and can measure cell emf accurately.

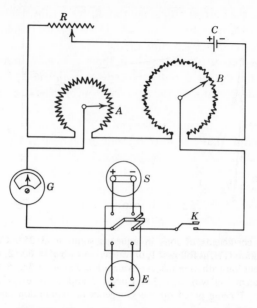

Fig. 1.2   Circuit diagram for a potentiometer.

the measurement is a reversible one, and the measured potential is equal to the emf of the cell.

In Fig. 1.2, C is the battery that is the source of the variable potential. It should be a high-capacity, low-discharge storage cell, which should undergo no appreciable change in voltage during the time of measurement. In series with this battery are a variable resistance R, one or more resistance boxes B, and a slide-wire A. By adjusting the contacts A and B, the resistance between them can be given any desired value. Since the potential between A and B is the product of this resistance and the current flowing through the potentiometer circuit, $E = IR$, the potential can also be given any desired value. In commercial potentiometers the resistance boxes and slide-wire are already calibrated in volts; they therefore require that the current through the potentiometer circuit have always the same fixed value. This value can be obtained by adjustment of the resistance R. To indicate when the adjustment has been correctly made, we use a Weston standard cell. The reaction of this cell is $Cd + Hg_2SO_4 \rightarrow CdSO_4 + Hg$. The operation of the cell is reversible, with an emf of close to 1.0184 V at 25°C, with only a small temperature coefficient. Weston standard cells are commercially available, and, if calibrated against Bureau of Standards' cells, are provided with calibration certificates. They should be checked against a new standard cell about once a year. To make the correct adjustment of R, we set the contacts A and B so that they read the correct emf of the cell. The standard cell S is then put into the galvanometer circuit by means of the double-pole double-throw switch of Fig. 1.2. The key K is depressed. If there is a galvanometer deflection, indicating that the circuit is not balanced, R is adjusted. This procedure is repeated until depression of the key no longer leads to a galvanometer deflection.

In measurement of the unknown emf E, the double-pole double-throw switch is reversed so that E is in the circuit instead of S. The contacts A and B are adjusted until there is no galvanometer deflection on depression of the key. At the end of the measurement the emf of the standard cell is again checked. It should give the correct value without adjustment of R. As mentioned earlier, the measured balance point must be the same when approached from either direction. If it is not, then the cell being measured is not behaving reversibly.

Commercial potentiometers vary in precision. A pH meter may be used as a potentiometer. Most models have a precision of about 1 mV, and this is sufficient for many purposes, such as potentiometric titrations. The most precise pH meters have a precision of about 0.1 mV. The familiar "student potentiometer" has a precision of about 0.01 mV, and the "type K" is readable to 0.001 mV or better. The "type K" potentiometer also has convenient built-in features. A separate slide-wire is provided for the standard cell so that the resistance R may be adjusted frequently without disturbing the settings of contacts A and B. There are also three separate keys with protective resistances. The key with the largest resistance is used when one is far from the balance point and prevents a violent deflection of the galvanometer under these circumstances. The key with the lowest resistance is used only when one is very close to the point of balance. Commercial potentiometers more sensitive than the "type K" are never required for the measurement of the emf of galvanic cells.

The galvanometer required depends on the internal resistance of the cell being used. A more sensitive type is required for solutions of low ion concentration. Enclosed lamp and scale galvanometers suffice for most purposes. Their sensitivity is of the order of 0.04 μA/mm. The galvanometers should always be critically damped so that after the key is released and the circuit opened the pointer swings back to zero without oscillation.

3 OXIDATION-REDUCTION POTENTIALS: THEORY

Introduction

Reversible electrodes formed by immersing an "indifferent" metal such as gold or bright platinum into a solution containing both the oxidized and reduced form of a reversible oxidation-reduction system, for example, Sn^{4+} and Sn^{2+} or quinone and hydroquinone, are known as oxidation-reduction electrodes. The metal in this system acts merely as a conductor for making electrical contact just as in the case of a gas electrode such as a hydrogen or oxygen electrode. There is no fundamental difference between an oxidation-reduction electrode and a system consisting of a metal and its ions. The term "oxidation-reduction" which appears in current usage is treated separately only as a matter of convenience, since it is restricted to systems in which both components are soluble in the solution in contact with the "inert" electrode.

Most oxidations and reductions of organic compounds are irreversible and such reactions cannot be studied by thermodynamic methods. A limited class of organic substances, quinones, hydroquinones, and related compounds, however, undergo reversible oxidations and reductions and their reactions may be followed by potentiometric methods. These compounds may also be studied polarographically and the results obtained in a number of examples are comparable to those obtained potentiometrically but are not as accurate. The rapidity of the polarographic method has made it more popular than the potentiometric method in the past decade. The polarographic results, however, may be complicated by the adsorption of the compound on the mercury electrode (e.g., methylene blue) and by hydration of one of the compounds involved in the electrode reaction (e.g., ascorbic acid).

Oxidation-reduction potentials are of interest in organic chemistry since (1) they provide a method of characterizing the oxidizing power of systems, for example, containing a quinone or, conversely, the reducing strength, for example, of a hydroquinone, (2) they can be used in structure determination, for example, when the quinone can exist in tautomeric forms, and (3) from the changes in potential involved with pH they can be used to study the ionization relations of compounds and to estimate their ionization constants.

Determination of Standard Oxidation-Reduction Potentials

In principle, the determination of the standard potential of an oxidation-reduction system involves setting up electrodes containing the oxidized and reduced state at known activities and measuring the potential E by combination with a suitable reference electrode and inserting this value into the following equation:

$$E = E^0 - \frac{RT}{nF} \ln \frac{a_L{}^l a_M{}^m}{a_A{}^a a_B{}^b},$$ (1.14)

where $aA + bB \rightleftharpoons lL + mM$ represents the cell reaction. For the quinhydrone (an equimolecular compound of quinone and hydroquinone) electrode, which has been studied extensively, the cell is:

$$\text{Au; Hydroquinone, Quinone, HCl}(m)\|\text{HCl}(m); \text{H}_2(\text{Pt})} \qquad (1.\text{IV})$$

and the electrode reaction is:

$$\text{Quinone} + 2\text{H}^+ + 2e^- \rightleftharpoons \text{Hydroquinone}$$

with the potential referred to the normal hydrogen electrode being expressed by the following equation if the change in liquid potential is ignored

$$E = E^0 - \frac{RT}{2F} \ln \frac{\gamma_{QH_2}}{\gamma_Q} + \frac{RT}{F} \ln a_{H^+}. \qquad (1.15)$$

Since Q and QH_2 are uncharged, the ratio of activity coefficients can be assumed to be one. The potential determined in this manner at a given pH is then commonly reported as $E^{0'}$ and is the formal potential of the electrode at a particular pH. This value ($E^{0'}$) is related to E^0, the standard oxidation potential, by the following equation

$$E^{0'} = E^0 - 2.303 \frac{RT}{F} \text{pH}. \qquad (1.16)$$

When the hydrogen and quinhydrone electrodes are immersed in the same solution the cell can be formulated by

$$\text{Au; Quinhydrone, H}^+(a); \text{H}_2(\text{Pt})} \qquad (1.\text{V})[5]$$

with no liquid junction potential being involved, and the expression for the corresponding potential is:

$$E = E_Q - E_H = -\frac{RT}{F} \ln a_{H^+} + E^0 - \frac{RT}{2F} \ln \frac{\gamma_{QH_2}}{\gamma_Q} + \frac{RT}{F} \ln a_{H^+}$$

$$= E^0 - \frac{RT}{2F} \ln \frac{\gamma_{QH_2}}{\gamma_Q}. \qquad (1.17)$$

The use of quinhydrone assures equal concentrations of quinone and hydroquinone, but the activity and activity coefficient ratios are altered by the presence of other dissolved substances. The resulting change in potential often termed the "salt error" can be evaluated by determining the potential for various concentrations of acid or electrolyte. A plot of the potential against the total concentration and an extrapolation to zero concentration gives the standard oxidation potential E^0 of the quinhydrone electrode or of the system quinone-hydroquinone. This value was determined to be $+0.69938 \pm 00003$ V at $25°C$.

Determination of Approximate Standard Potentials

Difficulties involved in obtaining the quinhydrone in other quinone-hydroquinone systems, or in determining the concentrations existing at equilibrium, since the reduced form may be oxidized rather easily by the oxygen of the air before a measurement can be made, and the slowness in establishing the equilibrium with the "inert" metal of the electrode, which is inherent in the method of mixtures, can be avoided by the potentiometric titration method of Clark [6]. This titration can be either oxidative or reductive and is carried out in the absence of oxygen since contact of this gas with the inert electrode develops a potential (gas electrode). The pure oxidized form of the system such as a quinone is dissolved in a buffer, known amounts of a reducing solution are added in the absence of air, and the solution is kept agitated by means of a current of pure nitrogen. The buffer is required since hydrogen ions are involved in most organic systems and the pH must be kept constant. The potential of an inert electrode, for example, platinum or gold, immersed in the reacting solution is measured after each addition of the titrant by combination with a reference electrode. The liquid junction potential involved in such measurements usually is large enough to mask any salt error introduced, that is, the variation in the ln of γ_Q/γ_{QH_2} from 1. For all practical purposes, therefore, the activities may be taken as equal to the molar concentrations.

It might be thought that the presence of the inorganic oxidizing or reducing agent can interfere with the procedure, that is, that the electrode potential might reflect the inorganic redox equilibrium rather than the organic one. It is easily shown, however, that this does not occur. Thus in the oxidation of hydroquinone with ceric ions, the reaction occurs as follows:

$$QH_2 + 2Ce^{4+} \rightleftharpoons Q + 2Ce^{3+} + 2H^+$$

The equilibrium constant for this reaction is

$$K = \frac{a_Q a_{Ce^{3+}}^2 a_{H^+}^2}{a_{QH_2} a_{Ce^{4+}}^2}, \tag{1.18}$$

and since

$$\ln K = \frac{nF}{RT} E^0 \tag{1.19}$$

K for the above reaction can be written as

$$\ln K = \frac{2F}{RT} (E^0_{Ce^{4+}, Ce^{3+}} - E^0_{Q, QH_2}) \tag{1.20}$$

or

$$\ln \frac{a_Q a_{Ce^{+3}}^2 a_{H^+}^2}{a_{QH_2} a_{Ce^{4+}}^2} = \frac{2F}{RT} (E^0_{Ce^{4+}, Ce^{3+}} - E^0_{Q, QH_2}). \tag{1.21}$$

By rearranging this expression,

$$\frac{RT}{2F} \ln \frac{a_Q a_{H^+}^2}{a_{QH_2}} + \frac{RT}{2F} \ln \frac{a_{Ce^{3+}}^2}{a_{Ce^{4+}}^2} = E_{Ce^{4+},Ce^{3+}}^0 - E_{Q,QH_2}^0 \qquad (1.22)$$

$$E_{Q,QH_2}^0 - \frac{RT}{2F} \ln \frac{a_{QH_2}}{a_Q a_{H^+}^2} = E_{Ce^{4+},Ce^{3+}}^0 - \frac{RT}{2F} \ln \frac{a_{Ce^{3+}}^2}{a_{Ce^{4+}}^2}, \qquad (1.23)$$

that is, the potential of the inorganic system is automatically the same as that of the organic system. A platinum electrode inserted into such a solution therefore gives a potential characteristic of the organic system.

In order for the oxidation or reduction of a system to be complete within the limits of accuracy of ordinary volumetric analysis, it is necessary that the concentration of one form at the end point be at least 10^3 times that of the other, or that the oxidation or reduction be complete within 0.1% or better. The equilibrium constant (equation (1.18)) should therefore be smaller than 10^{-6} if n is the same for both systems interacting, or 10^{-9} if n is one for one system and two for the other.

By making use of an equation similar to (1.20), it can be shown that in order to fulfill these conditions the standard potentials should differ by at least 0.34 V if n is 1 for both systems, 0.26 V if n is 1 for one system and 2 for the other, or 0.18 V if n is 2 for both. If the inorganic oxidizing or reducing agent represents an irreversible system, it will have no or little effect upon the potential of the inert electrode.

The results obtained for the titration of a buffered (pH 6.98) solution of 1-naphthol-2-sulfonate indophenol at 30°C are plotted as ordinates against the volumes of added reagent as abscissas (Fig. 1.3). The point at which the

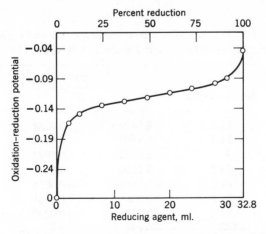

Fig. 1.3 Reduction of 1-naphthol-2-sulfonate indophenol (Clark).

potential undergoes a rapid change is that corresponding to complete reduction, and the quantity of the reducing solution then added is equivalent to the whole of the oxidized organic compound originally present. From the amounts of reducing agent added at various stages, the corresponding ratios of the oxidized [Ox] to the reduced form [Red] may be calculated without any knowledge of the initial amount of the former or of the concentration of the titrating agent. If t_c is the volume of titrant added when the sudden change of potential occurs, that is, when the reduction is complete, and t is the amount of titrant added at any point in the titration, then at any point [Ox] is equivalent to $t_c - t$, and [Red] is equivalent to t, provided the titrant employed is a powerful reducing agent. Accordingly, in the equation

$$E = E^{0'} - \frac{RT}{nF} \ln \frac{a_{Ox}}{a_{Red}} \tag{1.24}$$

Replacing the ratio of the activities by the ratio of concentrations gives the following equation:

$$E = E^{0'} - \frac{RT}{nF} \ln \frac{[Ox]}{[Red]} = E^{0'} - \frac{RT}{nF} \ln \frac{t_c - t}{t}, \tag{1.25}$$

where $E^{0'}$ is the formal potential of the system for the pH employed in the titration. Values of $E^{0'}$ can thus be obtained for a series of points on the titration curve, and if the system is behaving in a satisfactory manner these values should be approximately constant. The results obtained by applying the above equation to the data in Fig. 1.3 are given in Table 1.3.

The experiment described above can also be carried out by starting with the reduced form of the system and titrating it with an oxidizing agent, for example, potassium dichromate. The formal potentials obtained in this

Table 1.3 Evaluation of the Approximate Formal Potential of 1-Naphthol-2-Sulfonate Indophenol at 30°C at pH 6.98 [7]

t	Reduction (%)	E_{obs}	$\frac{RT}{2F} \ln \frac{t_c - t}{t}$	$E^{0'}$
4.0	12.2	−0.1479	−0.0258	−0.1221
8.0	24.4	−0.1368	−0.0148	−0.1220
12.0	36.6	−0.1292	−0.0072	−0.1220
16.0	48.8	−0.1224	−0.0006	−0.1218
20.0	61.0	−0.1159	+0.0058	−0.1217
24.0	73.2	−0.1085	+0.0131	−0.1216
28.0	85.4	−0.0985	+0.0230	−0.1215
32.8 (t_c)	100.	−0.036	—	—

manner agree with those derived from the titration of the oxidized form with a reducing agent and also with the potential measured in mixtures made up from known amounts of oxidized and reduced forms.

These data can be also used to determine n, the number of electrons involved in the oxidation-reduction system. This value can be obtained from the slope of the flat portion of the titration curve shown in Fig. 1.3. The flatter the curve the larger is n. The value of n is obtained more exactly by plotting the measured potential E against log [Ox]/[Red] or its equivalent log $(t_c - t)/t$. This plot, according to the following equation

$$E = E^{0\prime} - \frac{2.303RT}{nF} \log \frac{t_c - t}{t} , \qquad (1.26)$$

should be a straight line of slope $-2.303\, RT/nF$ (cf. Table 1.1). The results derived from Fig. 1.3 are plotted in Fig. 1.4 and give a slope of -0.030 at

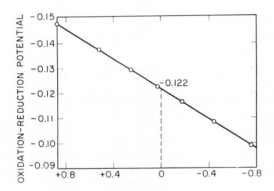

Fig. 1.4 Determination of n and $E^{0\prime}$.

30°C so that n is equal to 2. The formal potential is given by the point at which the ratio [Ox]/[Red] is 1 or log [Ox]/[Red] = 0.

The slope is also often reported as the difference in millivolts between the 50 and 25% points and is known under these circumstances as the index potential E_i. When E_i is 28.6 (± 0.2) mV at 30°C, the redox system is a univalent one. If E_i is 14.3 (± 0.2), the redox system is a bivalent one.

Determination of Acid Dissociation Constants

In the treatment of the quinone-hydroquinone systems thus far the possibility of the hydroquinone ionizing as an acid has not been considered.

Generalization of the equation for the electrode reaction involving a quinone-hydroquinone system can be represented by

$$R + 2H^+ + 2e^- \rightleftarrows H_2R$$

The hydroquinone is a weak dibasic acid for which two ionization equilibria are possible,

$$H_2R \rightleftarrows H^+ + HR^-$$
$$HR^- \rightleftarrows H^+ + R^{2-}$$

for which the ionization constants K_1 and K_2 can be expressed as

$$K_1 = \frac{[H^+][HR^-]}{[H_2R]} \qquad K_2 = \frac{[H^+][R^{2-}]}{[HR^-]}. \qquad (1.27)$$

The potential of the electrode is given by

$$E = E^0 + \frac{RT}{nF} \ln \frac{[R][H^+]^2}{[H_2R]}. \qquad (1.28)$$

Since the reduced substance can be present in three states, H_2R, HR^- and R^{2-}, the total stoichiometric concentration $[H_2R]_s$ is equal to the sum of the concentration of these three species:

$$[H_2R]_s = [H_2R] + [HR^-] + [R^{2-}] \qquad (1.29)$$

Assuming that the activities and the concentrations of these substances are the same and inserting for $[HR^-]$ and $[R^{2-}]$ the values derived from the expressions for K_1 and K_2:

$$[H_2R]_s = [H_2R] + \frac{[H_2R]}{[H^+]} K_1 + \frac{[H_2R]}{[H^+]^2} K_2 K_1 \qquad (1.30)$$

$$[H_2R] = \frac{[H^+]^2[H_2R]_s}{[H^+]^2 + K_1[H^+] + K_2 K_1}, \qquad (1.31)$$

which when substituted in the electrode reaction gives

$$E = E^0 + \frac{RT}{2F} \ln \frac{[R]}{[H_2R]_s} + \frac{RT}{2F} \ln ([H^+]^2 + K_1[H^+] + K_1 K_2). \qquad (1.32)$$

If K_1 and K_2 are very small, as they are for hydroquinone, the above equation becomes,

$$E = E^0 + \frac{RT}{2F} \ln \frac{[R]}{[H_2R]_s} + \frac{RT}{F} \ln [H^+] \qquad (1.33)$$

or the equation used in previous discussions. This equation indicates how the oxidation-reduction potential varies with hydrogen ion concentration in regions where the ionization of the hydroquinone is not important. A change in pH of 1 unit shifts the potential by 2.303 RT Volts/F (cf. Table 1.1). This is the basis for the use of the quinhydrone electrode in determining pH. A critical examination of the kinetics of the quinhydrone electrode is given by Vetter [8].

If the ionization constants are appreciable, the more complicated equation [see (1.32)] must be used, which affords a method in certain examples for estimating K_1 and K_2. Measurements are made with the ratio $[R]/[H_2R]$ equal to unity and the pH of the solution is altered by the addition of acid or alkali. The results for the β-anthraquinone sulfonate system which is stable in alkaline medium, are shown in Fig. 1.5.

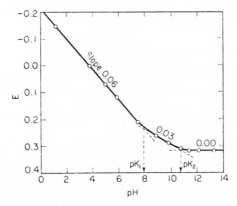

Fig. 1.5 Variation of the potential of β-anthraquinone sulfonate with pH.

It will be seen that the plot consists of three straight lines, one with a slope of 0.06, another with a slope of 0.03, and the third with a slope of zero. At low pH values the term $[H^+]^2$ is large in comparison with $K_1[H^+]$ and K_1K_2. Therefore, as long as K_1 is negligible in comparison with $[H^+]$, the plot of E^0 against pH will be a straight line with a slope of 2.303 RT/F or at 30°C, 0.060. The first line corresponds to the condition $[H^+] \gg K_1$.

If $[H^+]^2$ is negligible in comparison with $K_1[H^+]$ but still larger than K_2, the variation of E^0 with pH should be

$$E = E^0 + \frac{RT}{2F} \ln K_1[H^+] \tag{1.34}$$

or a straight line with a slope of 2.303 $RT/2F$ or 0.030 at 30°C. The second line corresponds to the condition $[H^+] \gg K_2$. Finally, if $K_1K_2 \gg [H^+]$ then,

$$E = E^0 + \frac{RT}{2F} \ln K_1K_2 \tag{1.35}$$

and the slope is not affected by pH and is zero or horizontal. This condition is illustrated in the third line. A rough estimate of pK_1 and pK_2 can be made graphically as shown by extending the straight lines until they cross and reading the corresponding pH values. There is no independent evidence that ionization constants obtained in this way are correct, but they are probably of the right order of magnitude.

The results discussed above are immediately evident if the equation used is differentiated with respect to pH:

$$\frac{dE}{dpH} = -2.303 \frac{RT}{2F} \frac{2[H^+]^2 + K_1[H^+]}{[H^+]^2 + K_1[H^+] + K_1K_2}. \tag{1.36}$$

For $[H^+] \gg K_1 \gg K_2$, $K_1[H^+]$ and K_1K_2 can be neglected and

$$\frac{dE}{dpH} = -2.303 \frac{RT}{F}. \tag{1.37}$$

For $K_1 \gg [H^+] \gg K_2$, $2[H^+]^2$, $[H^+]^2 + K_1K_2$ are insignificant and

$$\frac{dE}{dpH} = -2.303 \frac{RT}{2F}. \tag{1.38}$$

For $K_1 > K_2 \gg [H^+]$, $2[H^+]^2 + K_1[H^+]$ can be neglected and

$$\frac{dE}{dpH} = 0. \tag{1.39}$$

If $K_1 = [H^+]$ and K_1 is much greater than K_2, then

$$\frac{dE}{dpH} = -2.303 \frac{RT}{2F} \frac{3}{2} = -0.045. \tag{1.40}$$

Such a slope is intermediate between 0.060 and 0.030 and corresponds to a point on the first bend of the curve or the point of interaction of the two lines of slope 0.060 and 0.030 as shown in Fig. 1.5. For $[H^+] = K_2$,

$$\frac{dE}{dpH} = -2.303 \frac{RT}{2F} \frac{2[H^+]^2 + K_1[H^+]}{[H^+]^2 + K_1[H^+] + K_1[H^+]}. \tag{1.41}$$

Since $K_1 \gg [H^+]$,

$$\frac{dE}{dpH} = -2.303 \frac{RT}{2F} \frac{K_1[H^+]}{2K_1[H^+]} = -0.015 \text{ at } 30°C. \tag{1.42}$$

This value corresponds to the point of intersection of the two lines of slope 0.030 and zero as shown in Fig. 1.5. The pK values for β-anthrahydroquinone sulfonate are 7.9 and 10.6 and correspond to ionization constants of 1.23×10^{-8} and 2.51×10^{-11}, respectively. The pHs for these values represent the points at which $[RH_2]$ is equal to $[RH^-]$ and $[RH^-]$ is equal to $[R^{2-}]$, respectively.

The results obtained at various pH values for quinone-hydroquinone are given in Fig. 1.6 to illustrate the behavior of a substance (quinone) susceptible to irreversible changes (decomposition). Examination of the upper graph in the figure shows that the change at the pK of the first ionization occurs normally but that at about the point at which the pK of the second ionization should be, the slope reverts to the original 0.058. Furthermore the slope

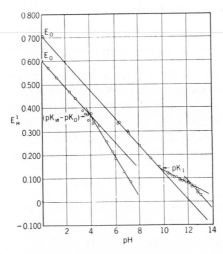

Fig. 1.6 Formal potentials of the hydroquinone system at different pH values.

between pH 9.8 and 12.3 is not the theoretical 0.029 but 0.0261. The irregular slope indicates that in this region the potential is determined by the quinone-hydroquinone and hydroxyquinone-hydroxyhydroquinone systems. The latter is formed by the action of alkali on quinone and gives the behavior indicated by the lower line in Fig. 1.6 [9].

Complex behavior of this type is frequently encountered. The reduced form may have several stages of acidic dissociations; in addition, the oxidized form may exhibit one or more acidic dissociations. Basic dissociation, if it occurs, is treated as an acidic ionization of the conjugate acid. The method of treatment given above can be applied to any case no matter how complex, and the following general rules have been derived which facilitate the analysis of pH-potential curves for oxidation-reduction systems of constant stoichiometric composition [7, 10].

1. Each bend in the curve may be related to an acidic dissociation constant; if the curve becomes steeper with increasing pH, the dissociation has occurred

in the oxidized form (cf. Fig. 1.6), but if it becomes flatter it has occurred in the reduced form (cf. Fig. 1.5).

2. The intersection of the extensions of adjacent linear parts of the curve occurs at the pH equal to pK for the particular dissociation group responsible for the bend.

3. As each dissociation becomes involved the slope of the plot changes by 2.303 RT/nF Volt per pH unit where n is the number of electrons involved in the change between the oxidized and reduced state.

Two-Stage Oxidation-Reductions

The overall reduction of a quinone to a hydroquinone involves two electrons

$$Q + 2e + 2H^+ \rightleftharpoons QH_2$$

The actual mechanism of this change as to whether the electrons are added stepwise or not is important. Potentiometric studies were the first to demonstrate the stepwise addition of electrons in certain examples. More recently the polarographic method has shown that this stepwise addition is general for simple quinones using dimethylformamide or acetonitrile as a solvent.

The addition of one electron to quinone produces an intermediate known as a semiquinone,

$$Q + e^- \rightleftharpoons Q^-$$

This substance is an anion radical which is stabilized by resonance similar to the triarylmethyl free radicals.

The semiquinone upon further reduction gives the hydroquinone dianion

$$Q^- + e^- \rightleftharpoons Q^{2-}$$

Superimposed on these reactions is the reaction of Q^- and Q^{2-} with hydrogen ions in aqueous media to form QH and QH_2. The free radical QH is much less stabilized by resonance and immediately picks up another electron and forms QH^- or QH_2 in the presence of hydrogen ions. The overall reaction for the first stage in the presence of hydrogen ions is then

$$Q + H^+ + e^- \rightleftharpoons QH$$

The intermediate QH, in addition to this reaction, may disproportionate or may dimerize to the meriquinone which is regarded as a molecular compound $(QH_2 \cdot Q)$.

$$2QH \rightleftharpoons Q + QH_2$$

The demonstration that semiquinones are stable in strong alkali or in aprotic solvents (CH_3CN) (polarographic study) is in agreement with the above scheme.

p-Phenylenediamines in strong acid medium form a similarly stabilized radical ion by the loss of an electron,

$$\underset{NR_2}{\overset{NR_2}{C_6H_4}} \rightleftharpoons \underset{NR_2}{\overset{\cdot\overset{+}{N}R_2}{C_6H_4}} + e^-$$

The product is known as a Würster salt and on further oxidation gives the diimine,

$$\underset{NR_2}{\overset{\cdot\overset{+}{N}R_2}{C_6H_4}} \rightleftharpoons \underset{NR_2^+}{\overset{\overset{+}{N}R_2}{C_6H_4}} + e^-$$

which is analogous to a quinone in structure.

The stability of these semiquinone intermediates depends upon the structure of the compounds and the solvent composition involved. Figure 1.7, for example, shows the variation in the shape of the titration curve with change of acidity for the dye hydroxythiazine.

The treatment of these systems in aqueous solution is now discussed.

For meriquinone formation the stages of oxidation-reduction may be written:

$$QH_2 \cdot Q(2QH) + 2H^+ + 2e^- \rightleftharpoons 2QH_2$$
$$2Q + 2H^+ + 2e^- \rightleftharpoons QH_2 \cdot Q$$

so that if E_1' is the formal potential of the first stage at a definite hydrogen ion concentration,

$$E = E_1' + \frac{RT}{2F} \ln \frac{[QH_2 \cdot Q]}{[QH_2]^2}. \tag{1.43}$$

If the original amount of the reduced form $[QH_2]$ in a given solution is a, and x equivalents of a sufficiently strong oxidizing agent are added, x moles of QH are formed and these dimerize to form $\frac{1}{2}x$ moles of meriquinone, $QH_2 \cdot Q$; an amount of $a - x$ moles of QH_2 remains unchanged. It follows that in a solution of volume v

$$E = E_1' + \frac{RT}{2F} \ln \frac{\frac{1}{2}x/v}{(a-x)^2/v^2} = E_1' + \frac{RT}{2F} \ln \frac{x}{(a-x)^2} + \frac{RT}{F} \ln \frac{v}{2} \tag{1.44}$$

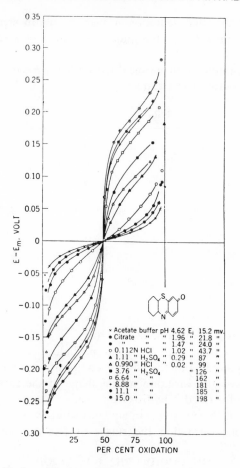

Fig. 1.7   Titration of hydroxythiazine at different pH values (S. Granick, L. Michaelis, and M. P. Schubert, *J. Am. Chem. Soc.*, **62**, 1802 (1940)).

or the potential depends upon the volume of the solution and the position of the potentiometric titration curve since the oxidation of QH_2 varies with the concentration of the solution. At constant volume the above equation becomes

$$E = E_1' + \frac{RT}{2F} \ln x - \frac{RT}{F} \ln (a - x) \qquad (1.45)$$

so that in the earlier stages of oxidation, that is, when x is small, the last term on the right-hand side can be regarded as constant and the slope of the titration curve corresponds to a process in which two electrons are involved, that is, n is 2. In the later stages, however, the change of potential is determined mainly by the last term and the slope of the curve changes to that of a one-electron system, that is, n is effectively unity.

When a true semiquinone is formed, for example, in strong alkali, the two stages of oxidation-reduction are

$$Q^- + e^- \rightleftarrows Q^{2-}$$
$$Q + e^- \rightleftarrows Q^-$$

so that for a definite hydrogen ion concentration,

$$E = E_1' + \frac{RT}{F} \ln \frac{[Q^-]}{[Q^{2-}]} = E_1 + \frac{RT}{F} \ln \frac{(x)}{(a-x)}, \qquad (1.46)$$

where x and a represent similar quantities to those mentioned for the meriquinone. From this expression it is evident that the titration curves are independent of volume and have the same slope, $n = 1$, throughout the curve.

The assumption has been made in the above that the two stages of oxidation are fairly distinct but in most studies in aqueous media in the presence of H$^+$ the two stages usually overlap. The treatment becomes complicated and is only mentioned briefly here. The reactions under these conditions can be represented by

$$QH + H^+ + e^- \rightleftarrows QH_2$$
$$Q + H^+ + e^- \rightleftarrows QH$$

and

$$E = E_1' + \frac{RT}{F} \ln \frac{[QH]}{[QH_2]} \qquad (1.47)$$

$$E = E_2' + \frac{RT}{F} \ln \frac{[Q]}{[QH]} \qquad (1.48)$$

are the potentials for these stages at a definite pH where E_1' and E_2' are the formal potentials for these stages. The potential can also be formulated for the overall reaction,

$$Q + 2H^+ + 2e^- \rightleftarrows QH_2$$

$$E = E_m' + \frac{RT}{2F} \ln \frac{[Q]}{[QH_2]}, \qquad (1.49)$$

where E_m' is the usual formal potential for the overall reaction at a definite hydrogen ion concentration.

$$E_m' + \frac{RT}{2F} \ln \frac{[Q]}{[QH_2]} = E_1' + \frac{RT}{F} \ln \frac{[QH]}{[QH_2]} = E_2' + \frac{RT}{F} \ln \frac{[Q]}{[QH_2]} \qquad (1.50)$$

or

$$2E'_m + \frac{RT}{F} \ln \frac{[Q]}{[QH_2]} = E'_1 + E'_2 + \frac{RT}{F} \ln \frac{[Q]}{[QH_2]} \qquad (1.51)$$

and

$$E'_m = \frac{E'_1 + E'_2}{2}, \qquad (1.52)$$

in which E'_1 and E'_2 are the centers of the first part and second part of the titration curve and E'_m is the potential of the middle of the curve.

An equation for the potential E observed during an oxidation-reduction titration which includes a consideration of the formation of semiquinones can be obtained as follows. Using the relationship

$$Q + QH_2 \rightleftharpoons 2QH$$

an expression using the law of mass action can be obtained in which

$$K = \frac{[QH]^2}{[Q][QH_2]}, \qquad (1.53)$$

where K is the semiquinone formation constant.

If a is the initial amount of QH_2 being titrated and x is the number of moles of oxidant added in a titration, at any point of the titration,

$$[QH] + 2[Q] = x \qquad (1.54)$$

since the formation of Q represents two steps of oxidation and QH only one. By making use of the above relationships and letting $x/a = X$, the following equation can be derived. [11]

$$E = E'_m + \frac{RT}{2F} \ln \frac{X}{2-X} + \frac{RT}{2F} \ln \frac{X - 1 \pm \sqrt{(X-1)^2 + 4X(2-X)K}}{1 - X \pm \sqrt{(X-1)^2 + 4X(2-X)K}}$$

$$(1.55)$$

and gives the variation of $E - E'_m$ with x/a in terms of the semiquinone formation constant.

Some of the results obtained for various K values are shown in Fig 1.8. As long as K is small, the titration curve throughout has the shape of a normal two-electron oxidation-reduction system since the above equation approaches

$$E = E'_m + \frac{RT}{2F} \ln \frac{X}{2-X} \qquad (1.56)$$

and no break occurs at $X = 1$. This equation corresponds to the line labeled $K = 0$ in Fig. 1.8. For K between 4 and 16, the slope corresponds to that of a one-electron process but there is no break at the midpoint. The presence of

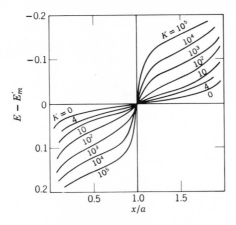

Fig. 1.8 Titration curves for semiquinone formation.

a semiquinone is often indicated in these cases, however, by the appearance of a color that differs from the quinone or hydroquinone. When the semiquinone formation constant exceeds 16, a break appears at the midpoint and the extent of this break becomes larger as K increases since the curve approaches the form

$$E = E'_m + \frac{RT}{F} \ln \frac{[\text{Ox}]}{[\text{Red}]} \qquad (1.57)$$

in two separate steps involving one electron each. The results of such a titration are shown in Fig. 1.9 for the oxidation of reduced α-hydroxyphenazine with benzoquinone.

The values of E'_1, E'_2, and E'_m depend upon the pH of the solution, and since QH_2, QH, and Q may possess acidic or basic functions, the slope of the curves of these formal potentials against pH may change direction at various points and crossings may occur. In Fig. 1.10 such plots for pyocyanine (N-methyl-α-hydroxyphenazine) give a crossing point of the three curves at pH = 5. Here the semiquinone constant K is 1 and $E'_m = E'_1 = E'_2 = 1$, and the maximum ratio of semiquinone to total dye, $(QH/a)_{\text{max}}$ is 0.333. To the left of this crossing point, at higher acidities, the curves diverge, $E'_2 > E'_m > E'$, and the semiquinone formation constant is large. To the right of the crossing point there is the reverse order, $E'_2 < E'_m < E'_1$ and the semiquinone formation is very small. In this region all calculations depend on very slight variations of E_i and have relatively large limits of error which are shown in the graph on the assumption that the index potential may be uncertain to ± 0.2 mV. Such errors in data can be reduced by using an

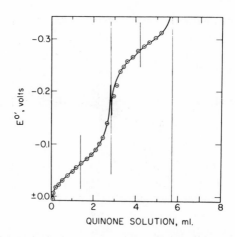

Fig. 1.9 Potentiometric titration of α-hydroxyphenazine with quinone.

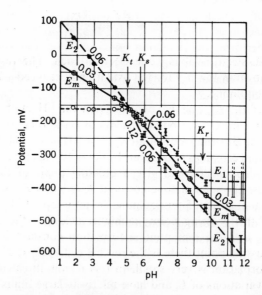

Fig. 1.10 Formal potentials of pyocyanine at different pH values (L. Michaelis, E. S. Hill, and M. P. Schubert, *Biochem. Z.*, **255**, 66 (1932).)

iterative method for analysis of the potentiometric curves employing computers [12]. The bends of the curves correspond to the acidic ionization constants of the reduced, semioxidized, and totally oxidized forms K_{QH_2}, K_{QH}, and K_Q, respectively.

4 OXIDATION-REDUCTION POTENTIALS: EXPERIMENTAL

Reductive Titration: Reducing Agents

Usually the Ox form of a reversible redox system is stable in air, for example, methylene blue. In this case, a solution of Ox is made up in a buffer, the oxygen of the solution is thoroughly removed by bubbling with oxygen-free nitrogen, a reducing agent is added from a buret in successive portions, and at each step the potential is measured. During the titration the solution is guarded against the access of any trace of oxygen.

The buffer should have an ionic strength μ not smaller, or at least not much smaller, than 0.1, and the concentration of the dye should be in the neighborhood of 10^{-3} M. If the concentration is too low ($\ll 10^{-4}$ M), the poise of the system may not be sufficient to establish reproducible potentials. If it is too high (10^{-2} or 10^{-1} M), the capacity of the buffer may not be sufficient to keep the pH constant during the titration if the Ox and Red forms differ with respect to their acidic properties. The reducing agent must be in homogeneous solution and may be the Red form of another reversible redox system of a much more negative normal potential than that of the system to be measured. Or, the reducing agent may be some irreversible system which performs the reduction practically instantaneously, in such a manner that its oxidation product does not interfere with the measurement because of any secondary chemical reaction. The concentration of the reducing agent depends on the purpose of the titration. This may be: (1) the determination of the amount of some oxidizable (or reducible) substance in the solution. Here, the titer of the agent used for titration must be exactly known, and the only aim of the titration is to ascertain the end point. Not all of the reagents mentioned below, especially among the reducing agents, are suitable for making up a standard solution of exactly known titer. In such examples the amount of reagent can be determined by titrating the same volume of agent used with a standard oxidizing agent. Or it may be: (2) the determination of the formal potential and of some other characteristic properties of a redox system. Here, the titer of the oxidizing or reducing agent need be known only approximately. The end point of titration manifests itself by the jump of the potential, and it is the shape of the titration curve from which the wanted data are to be derived. The abscissa, originally plotted in terms of milliliters of the added reagent, is readjusted in terms of percentage of oxidation or reduction.

Out of the multitude of reducing or oxidizing agents, a few are described that have proved to be especially convenient. Some other reagents may be found in the review by Furman [13].

Sodium Dithionite, $Na_2S_2O_4$ (*Sodium Hydrosulfite*). Application of this compound requires detailed directions. The solid substance, when dry, is perfectly stable in air. In solution, however, it is autoxidizable to an extremely high degree. It is not possible to keep a stock solution even approximately at its original titer. The solution must be prepared for immediate use. Even when kept protected from oxygen, it may gradually, sooner or later, undergo an irreversible decomposition, recognizable by turbidity caused by colloidal sulfur. This decomposition does not seem to occur in a slightly alkaline solution.

Dithionite is a very valuable and efficient reducing agent, yet its use is restricted. (1) It can be used only at pH > 4. (2) One must consider that, while acting as a reducing agent, it is oxidized to the bisulfite ion, HSO_3^-. This ion undergoes reactions with many compounds, for example, it combines with quinones, and so on. Furthermore, bisulfite ion, or rather its nonionized form, namely, sulfurous acid, is itself a reducing agent. Although it is much less powerful than dithionite and acts at a much slower rate, it may cause the potentials to drift in time. Dithionite can be used to titrate only dyes of such a potential range that sulfurous acid or bisulfite ion does not reduce them. Dyes with a formal potential decidedly less positive than methylene blue can be titrated, provided they form no addition compounds with bisulfite. Methylene blue itself cannot be titrated with dithionite (unless the titration is carried out within a few minutes) because it is reduced at a slow rate by sulfurous acid. Examples of dyes that can be successfully titrated with dithionite are riboflavin, rosindone sulfonate, and most of the phenazine derivatives, including the safranines.

Since the stability of sodium dithionite is improved by slightly alkaline reaction, its solution may be prepared in about 0.001 M sodium hydroxide. The buffer capacity of such a dilute sodium hydroxide solution is very small. Adding it to a well-buffered solution of great buffer capacity does not change the pH of the buffer to any appreciable extent. The following directions for making up a dithionite solution are therefore derived: A flask containing 20 to 30 ml of water, after adding 1 drop of 0.05 M sodium hydroxide, is closed with a stopper with two holes, one holding a glass tube as an inlet of pure nitrogen, the other as an outlet for the gases. A stream of nitrogen is bubbled for 15 min; then, while the gas flows, the stopper is lifted and a weighed amount of sodium dithionite is added; the stopper is reset, and the bubbling is continued for 5 min more. The glass tube, which has served as a gas outlet, is then pushed farther in so that the lower end is deep below the surface of the solution which, by the application of nitrogen pressure, is pushed into the buret previously washed with nitrogen.

In estimating the amount of solid dithionite, it should be kept in mind that the commercial preparation is about 90% pure, that a small part may be lost by oxidation while the solution is prepared, and that one molecule of dithionite delivers two electrons (or two hydrogen atoms). The titer of the solution is known only to a rough approximation. For most purposes this does not matter, as can be seen later, and one can dispense with a determination of the titer.

Titanous Chloride. The commercially obtainable solution of titanous chloride is made up in 15% hydrochloric acid and is rather stable in this condition. When diluted with water, so as to establish a less acid solution, it is easily oxidized in air. Therefore, any dilute solution must be immediately filled into the buret and protected from oxygen. Titanous chloride is a most useful reagent for reductive titration under the condition that the redox system is dissolved in a very acid solution, for example, $\leqq 0.1$ N hydrochloric or sulfuric acid; and the hydrochloric acid content of the dilute titanous chloride is so low that its addition to the redox solution does not change the pH to any appreciable extent. Because of its potential range, titanous chloride is a useful and convenient reducing agent when applied to acid solutions. If one wishes to carry out a titration in extremely acid solution, for example, 5 M sulfuric acid, the stock solution of titanous chloride may be diluted, not with pure water, but with the same acid in such a concentration that the final concentration of the acid approximately matches that of the redox solution. In such a case, special attention must be paid to establishing constant liquid junction potentials (described under Measurements in Extremely Acid Solutions p. 44).

If one wants to use titanous chloride in less acid or even neutral solutions of the redox system, laborious procedures must be applied. Clark prepared solid titanous chloride, almost free of excessive hydrochloric acid, by evaporating the stock solution *in vacuo* and, protected from air, dissolving it in any desired weakly acid solution, or even in a citrate or tartrate buffer in which complex compounds are formed that are soluble even at rather high pH. The redox system can be dissolved in a similar buffer. In general, one may restrict the use of titanous chloride to very acid solutions, for which it is the most convenient reducing agent for titration.

Chromous Chloride. Chromous chloride is prepared, according to Conant and Cutter [14] by reduction of chromic chloride, using amalgamated zinc and hydrochloric acid. It is either kept over amalgamated zinc or is filtered through glass wool in an atmosphere of carbon dioxide. If the solution is filtered from suspended material and the acidity is not too high, it will keep for months without evolution of hydrogen. If working with a 1 to 10 N sulfuric acid (but not >10 N) solution, chromous sulfate can be prepared by dissolving powdered chromium metal directly in the acid in a stream of hydrogen, with some heating if necessary. This solution can be directly pushed into the buret by nitrogen.

An approximately neutral, very poorly buffered, and, for this reason, convenient solution of a chromous salt can be made as follows. Chromoacetate is prepared according to Clark and Perkins [15] by reducing an aqueous solution of chromic chloride in hydrochloric acid with zinc dust. From the filtrate, crystalline, red chromoacetate is precipitated by addition of sodium acetate. The crystals are washed with water and dissolved in a large volume of air-free water. All manipulations are carried out in a stream of carbon dioxide. The final solution is washed with hydrogen and kept under hydrogen. The titer of such a solution is constant over weeks, for example, 0.0037 N.

Vanadous Chloride and Sulfate.   These compounds have been prepared by Conant and Cutter [14] as follows: Vanadium pentoxide is reduced by amalgamated zinc and acid; although very much zinc is needed, the procedure is convenient and yields a solution containing a large amount of vanadous salt. As regards the range of usefulness of chromous and vanadous salts in their acid solutions, the same considerations hold as for titanous chloride.

Leuco Dyes.   These dyes can be used as reducing agents provided their formal potential is decidedly less positive than that of the redox system to be titrated, so as to ascertain a distinct jump, or least inflection, of the potential curve at the end point of titration. For a number of cases, according to the formal potential of the redox system to be titrated, sodium indigo disulfonate in its leuco form may be used. Rosindone sulfonate (Rosinduline GG) in its leuco form is by far the most convenient "dye" to be used as a titrating agent. It can be used over a wide pH range and is stable even in very alkaline solution, a property shared by few other dyes of sufficiently negative potential and otherwise suitable properties as titrating agents. Rosindone sulfonate is not commercially available. Since it is almost indispensable for systematic redox studies, its preparation is described in the following section.

Preparation of Rosindone Monosulfonate (Rosinduline GG).   A solution of 5 gm of rosindone trisulfonate (rosinduline 2B, National Aniline and Dye Co.) in 60 ml of water is heated in a sealed tube at 180°C for 24 hr. Orange rosettes of free rosindone monosulfonic acid appear on cooling. The solution is acidified with 10 ml of 2 N hydrochloric acid and the precipitate collected on the filter. If the starting material is good, the filtrate is practically colorless.

The yield is 1.9 gm (70%). To convert the acid into the well-crystallized sodium salt it is suspended in 200 ml of water and neutralized with sodium carbonate. Then 2 gm of sodium chloride are added and the solution heated to boiling. After 24 hr at room temperature, the product is filtered and washed with a little 1% sodium chloride solution. The compound should show at pH 4.64 the formal potential of +0.130 V, when the leuco dye is titrated with potassium ferricyanide, and an index potential of 15.1 mV.

The solution of the leuco dyes, either of rosindone sulfonate or of any other suitable dye, is made up as follows: A solution of the dye in adequate concentration (about 10 to 30 times that of the redox solution to be titrated) is made up, either in water or, if solubility properties permit, in the same buffer as is used as solvent for the redox system. However, since the volume change during the titration is small, preferably not more than one-tenth, the pH of the buffered redox system is not changed beyond the limits of error even if the dye is dissolved in pure water. The latter is often preferable because most dyes are more soluble in pure water than in salt solutions. If the concentration of the redox system is $5 \times 10^{-4} M$, the concentration of the titrating leuco dye should be about $10^{-3} M$. The solubility of sodium rosindone sulfonate is about $2 \times 10^{-2} M$, except in very acid solution, in its yellow form, which is much less soluble. Therefore the restrictions imposed on the use of this dye because of its solubility properties are not serious.

A bottle is filled with the dye solution and closed with a two-hole stopper providing an inlet and outlet for gases. Then a small amount of colloidal palladium solution is added and hydrogen is bubbled through the solution until complete reduction of the dye is accomplished. For rosindone sulfonate, the color, originally red, turns on complete reduction to pale yellow or yellowish brown, according to the concentration. The amount of palladium solution depends on the specimen of colloidal palladium used. It is found, for instance by adding one drop of a 1% aqueous solution to each 10 ml of the dye solution. If after 10 min of bubbling the reduction does not proceed visibly, more should be added. The reduction may take, according to the concentration of the dye, from 10 to 30 min. It often starts but does not go to completion, the catalyst becoming inactive. If this happens, another drop should be added. The fact that the catalyst becomes inactive after a while is advantageous because it makes unnecessary the removal of the palladium before using the leuco dye for the titration. In any case the total amount of palladium should be so small that its gray color is not at all, or only slightly, noticeable in the leuco dye solution. When the reduction is complete, the hydrogen is displaced by nitrogen bubbled through the solution for a sufficient time, about 10 min, with 5 bubbles/sec. The tube which served as a gas outlet is pushed deep below the surface of the solution, and the solution is transferred by pressure of nitrogen into the buret previously washed with nitrogen.

A modification of the method, used especially by Clark, is the addition of small pieces of platinum asbestos instead of colloidal palladium solution, and interposing of a glass wool filter between the solution and the buret in order to filter out the platinum asbestos. Even so, microscopic particles of colloidal platinum may be carried over. This is not important because the platinum catalyst also is usually inactivated at the time the solution is used. The only disadvantage in the use of a leuco dye as a reducing agent lies in the fact that the color changes in the redox system during the titration are obscured. The formal potential of rosindone sulfonate is so negative that only rarely are occasions encountered when, in reversible redox systems, no recognizable end point of titration is established.

Ascorbic Acid. Sometimes, at pH < 6, a freshly prepared solution of ascorbic acid may be successfully used as a reducing agent for systems with a fairly positive formal potential.

Sodium Biphenyl. This reagent is used in the aprotic solvents tetrahydrofuran or hexamethylphosphoramide and is prepared by an overnight reaction at room temperature of a 0.1 M solution of biphenyl in the solvent with a sodium mirror [16]. The reaction proceeds to about 16% conversion and at this stage the system seems to reach its equilibrium. The concentration of sodium biphenyl is determined by titrating aliquots of the solution with hydrochloric acid or with methyl iodide.

Oxidative Titration: Oxidizing Agents

A compound in the reduced form can in many cases be titrated with an oxidizing agent. If a compound present in the oxidized form is to be titrated with an oxidizing agent, it is first reduced by a small amount of colloidal palladium and hydrogen gas. The completeness of reduction can be recognized by the change in color. It may be mentioned that when bubbled long enough with hydrogen in the presence of colloidal palladium a bright platinum electrode reaches a constant potential corresponding to that of the hydrogen electrode and that this potential can be used for the measurement of pH at the beginning of the titration. Then the hydrogen is driven out with pure nitrogen as thoroughly as possible. A check as to the completeness of the removal of hydrogen is the following. When the hydrogen potential is established, the bubbling with nitrogen is started, the potential gradually shifts toward the positive direction. The bubbling is kept on until the potential (which is not well reproduced at two bright platinum electrodes) is about 100 mV more negative than the formal potential of the system to be titrated. If the formal potential of the redox system is so positive that this condition cannot be fulfilled, one must use good judgment as to when to start the titration. During the titration, the behavior of the potential rise shows how well the starting time for the titration was chosen, and proper correction for the true zero point may be applied. The following discussion illustrates the manner of handling the situation.

Suppose the removal of hydrogen was practically complete before the first portion of the oxidizing agent was added. Then, even after the addition of the first few drops of the oxidizing agent, a constant and reproducible potential (at least within 1 mV or so) will be established within about half a minute after the addition of the oxidizing agent. Further addition causes the potential to rise and to be firmly established within a very short time, reproducible at different electrodes in the vessel to within 0.1 mV, and further on, even better. Toward the end of the titration, the speed at which the potential is being established, and its reproducibility, may be lessened. This may happen when the oxidation is, for example, 95% complete. In the very neighborhood of the end point, both the stability and the reproducibility of the potential are much less satisfactory. However, on plotting the titration curve, one will see that this uncertainty has no significance as to the determination of the end point.

If the removal of hydrogen was not perfect, however, the potential at the beginning of the titration may not rise sufficiently, or even drift back in time. Then, before proceeding with the titration, the bubbling with nitrogen must be continued to remove the last traces of hydrogen, which may be only slowly released if a somewhat larger amount of colloidal palladium is present. On proceeding with the titration, the potentials behave regularly, and from the plot of the titration curve the true zero point may be extrapolated. Although such an experience is not desirable, the experiment need not be discarded provided the extrapolation is small.

Bromine and Chlorine.   Solutions at any pH can be titrated with bromine and freshly prepared solutions can be easily standardized as to titer, which is maintained over a sufficiently long time. Similarly, a freshly prepared aqueous solution of chlorine may be used.

Potassium Ferricyanide.   A freshly prepared solution of this reagent can be used over a wide pH range, excluding only extremely acid solutions. A similar reagent of still higher potential is $K_3Mo(CN)_8$, potassium molybdicyanide, described by Buchnall and Wardlaw [17].

Potassium Dichromate.   This compound can be used for acid solutions of pH < 4. At higher pH values, the oxidation is sluggish and may cause the potentials to be established with undue slowness.

Ceric Sulfate or Thallic Sulfate.   Ceric sulfate or thallic sulfate dissolved in sulfuric acid of suitable concentration can be used as oxidizing agents if work must be done in strongly acid solutions.

Benzoquinone.   Water is boiled to remove dissolved oxygen and, after cooling down to about 80°C, a proper amount of finely ground quinone is dissolved in it; the solution, still rather warm, is sucked into the buret. It is stable for a sufficiently long time, but gradually decomposes. It is not recommended for the titration of alkaline solutions because quinone is very unstable in alkali and may decompose before the added amount is thoroughly mixed with the solution. For acid solutions it is a fairly convenient oxidizing agent. It has the advantage that no overoxidation takes place in such cases in which the Ox form of the redox system is likely to be irreversibly overoxidized with any appreciable speed. However, the various possible reactions which quinone may undergo make necessary good judgment in the use of this otherwise very useful reagent.

Dyes.   For redox systems of sufficiently positive potential range, the Ox forms of stable dyes of very positive range can be successfully used as oxidizing agents. The use of phenolindophenol is especially recommended and the compound is easily prepared [18] but not commercially available. Other commercially available dyes of the indophenol class should be properly tested on standard substances because the available specimens are rarely pure compounds.

Lead Tetraacetate.   For solutions in water-free glacial acetic acid, a solution of lead tetraacetate in glacial acetic acid can be used as an oxidizing agent [19, 20].

Copper(II) Perchlorate.   The anhydrous salt is prepared by dissolving tetrakis(acetonitrile)copper(II) perchlorate prepared from nitrosyl perchlorate and copper metal in anhydrous acetonitrile [21].

Gold(III) Chloride.   The anhydrous salt is prepared by heating $HAuCl_4 \cdot 4H_2O$ slowly in a stream of chlorine to 200°C, maintaining this temperature for 0.5 hr, cooling under chlorine, and then flushing with nitrogen [22].

Apparatus for Redox Titrations

For the measurement of potentials, a potentiometer or a pH meter can be used.

The electrode is constructed by spot-welding a small piece of platinum foil to a short piece of no. 26 platinum wire, which is then sealed into a narrow soft-glass tube. Pyrex glass cannot be used because its coefficient of thermal expansion is very different from that of platinum, with the result that a perfect seal cannot be obtained.

Whether the electrode should consist of bright platinum or gold has been the subject of much discussion. However, the difference in behavior is slight and there is no reason why the blank platinum electrode should not be used in routine work. It should be frequently cleaned in cleaning solution and in

10% sodium hydroxide, and thoroughly washed in water thereafter. A gold electrode is most easily prepared by coating bright platinum with gold. For this purpose, a platinum electrode is used as cathode, with another platinum electrode as anode, in a solution of 1% gold chloride and excess of potassium cyanide. Current is supplied from a 4-V battery with proper resistance to allow a very slow deposit of gold. The coated electrode is then washed in nitric acid and water. The gold electrode is supposed to establish potential more quickly and more reliably than the platinum electrode in relatively weakly poised redox systems, but sometimes the opposite may be true, and when the system is well poised there should be no difference between the two types. Even mercury can be used as an indifferent electrode when the redox potential of the system is such that all traces of mercury ions, which may be formed at the surface of the mercury electrode [23] on immersing it in the solution, are reduced. This condition is fulfilled for all redox systems with a potential range less positive than that of the indophenol dyes. For phenolindophenol, for instance, mercury cannot be used as an electrode, but it can be used for indigo sulfonates. Since mercury does not absorb any hydrogen gas, the electrode vessel may even be bubbled with hydrogen instead of nitrogen. However, a mercury electrode is much less convenient to handle than a platinum electrode and is therefore not often be used.

It is necessary always to have at least two platinum electrodes in the titration vessel and to read the potentials of each for comparison. When the poise of the system is sufficient, that is, if the redox system is perfectly reversible and the ratio of the oxidized and the reduced forms of the dye is within the range of 10:1 to 1:10, the potentials should agree to at least 0.1 mV; usually, they are better. In the neighborhood of the starting point and of the end point, the agreement may be less perfect. This may also happen in the neighborhood of the 50% point with a bivalent redox system in which the two successive steps are extremely widely separated and, consequently, the titration curve around the 50% point of titration is very steep. However, if the slope of the titration curve is extremely steep an uncertainty of the potential of a few millivolts has in general no bearing on the results obtained from the titration curve.

The electrode vessel, should in general be cylindrical, about 4 to 5 cm in diameter and about 12 cm high (Fig. 1.11). If feasible, 20 to 40 ml of the solution to be titrated should be used, or at least enough to cover the electrode metals entirely. For special cases all dimensions can be increased or decreased. The upper end of the vessel is closed with a well-fitting rubber stopper with a number of holes through which glass tubes are tightly inserted. These tubes provide for two platinum electrodes (or even three), gas inlet, a gas outlet, a potassium chloride–agar bridge, a buret, and a reserve hole which may be closed or used for inserting a thermometer, or for the addition of a reagent, or for the third platinum electrode.

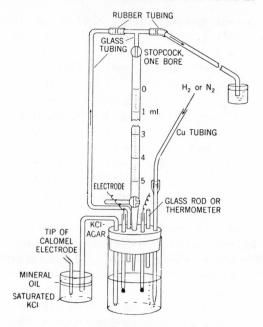

Fig. 1.11 Assembly for oxidimetric titration.

The gases used are pure nitrogen and, alternately, hydrogen. The latter is used when the solution, in the presence of palladium, is being reduced. Nitrogen is used to bubble out the hydrogen, or the oxygen of dissolved air, as the need may be, and is also used throughout the titration. The speed of bubbling nitrogen should be great when oxygen or hydrogen is being removed (about 10 bubbles per second), and slow during the titration proper (about 3 bubbles/sec).

Hydrogen and nitrogen are best supplied from cylinders with reduction valves. The gas train is shown in Fig. 1.12. From the cylinders, heavy-walled vacuum rubber tubes, which have been soaked for a day in about 5% sodium hydroxide solution and thoroughly washed with water, lead the gas to the purifying system in such a way that alternatively the one or the other gas can be used. The gases pass first to a wash bottle with 10% sodium hydroxide, and then to a glass tube filled with copper filings, and are heated in the furnace to about 400 to 450°C. If care is taken that the temperature never exceeds 500°, Pyrex glass can be used. If no temperature control is applied, combustion-tube glass is necessary; however, it is more difficult to build up all glass parts with it. Temperature control can be secured in the use of Pyrex glass with a thermocouple of alumel-chromel, the soldered contact of the two metals being placed right above the Pyrex glass tube and covered by